UNIVERSITY O

EXAMINATION REGULATIONS

2003

[FOR THE ACADEMIC YEAR 2003–4]

OXFORD UNIVERSITY PRESS

OXFORD
UNIVERSITY PRESS
Great Clarendon Street, Oxford OX2 6DP

Oxford University Press is a department of the University of Oxford.
It furthers the University's objective of excellence in research, scholarship,
and education by publishing worldwide in
Oxford New York
Athens Auckland Bangkok Bogotá Buenos Aires Cape Town
Chennai Dar es Salaam Delhi Florence Hong Kong Istanbul Karachi
Kolkata Kuala Lumpur Madrid Melbourne Mexico City Mumbai Nairobi
Paris São Paulo Shanghai Singapore Taipei Tokyo Toronto Warsaw

Oxford is a registered trade mark of Oxford University Press
in the UK and in certain other countries

ISBN 0-19-951895-5

Typeset by Latimer Trend & Company Ltd., Plymouth
Printed in Great Britain
by J. W. Arrowsmith Ltd., Bristol

PREFACE

As in 2002, the 2003 edition of the *Examination Regulations* (formerly *Examination Decrees and Regulations*) is available only in a complete version, rather than separate complete, undergraduate, and postgraduate versions. The complete version contains the regulations of the University in so far as they relate to the various degrees, diplomas, and certificates conferred by the University together with regulations made by boards, and certain other relevant information.

The text of the various regulations incorporates all changes made up to the beginning of Trinity Term 2003. Some alterations are made every year, and candidates for examinations are advised to make sure that they consult the current edition.

The form in which examination regulations are to be published in future is under review. It is expected that publication, in whatever form is decided upon, will next take place during September 2004.

The attention of candidates and other readers is drawn to other publications which summarize much of the information contained here and also give other explanations which may be of interest to those studying or intending to study at the University:

Oxford University Undergraduate Prospectus

Oxford University Graduate Studies Prospectus

These may be obtained without charge from the University Offices, Wellington Square, Oxford OX1 2JD.

DATES OF TERMS 2003–2005

2003	
Michaelmas	Wednesday, 1 October, to Wednesday, 17 December
2004	
Hilary	Wednesday, 7 January, to Thursday, 25 March
Trinity	Tuesday, 20 April, to Tuesday, 6 July
Michaelmas	Friday, 1 October, to Friday, 17 December
2005	
Hilary	Friday, 7 January, to Friday, 25 March
Trinity	Wednesday, 20 April, to Wednesday, 6 July
Michaelmas	Saturday, 1 October, to Saturday, 17 December

DATES OF FULL TERM 2003–2005

2003	
Michaelmas	Sunday, 12 October, to Saturday, 6 December
2004	
Hilary	Sunday, 18 January, to Saturday, 13 March
Trinity	Sunday, 25 April, to Saturday, 19 June
Michaelmas	Sunday, 10 October, to Saturday, 4 December
2005	
Hilary	Sunday, 16 January, to Saturday, 12 March
Trinity	Sunday, 24 April, to Saturday, 18 June
*Michaelmas	Sunday, 9 October, to Saturday, 3 December

DATES OF EXTENDED TERMS 2003–2005

For Part II candidates in Molecular and Cellular Biochemistry

2003	
Michaelmas	Friday, 19 September, to Saturday, 13 December
2004	
Michaelmas	Friday, 17 September, to Saturday, 11 December

For Part II candidates in Chemistry

2003	
Michaelmas	Thursday, 25 September, to Tuesday, 23 December
2004	
Hilary	Tuesday, 6 January, to Wednesday, 7 April
Trinity	Monday, 19 April, to Saturday, 26 June
Michaelmas	Thursday, 23 September, to Tuesday, 21 December
2005	
Hilary	Tuesday, 4 January, to Wednesday, 23 March
Trinity	Monday, 4 April, to Saturday, 25 June

---

* Provisional dates.

For Part II candidates in Materials Science

2003

Michaelmas	Friday, 12 September, to Saturday, 13 December

2004

Hilary	Friday, 9 January, to Saturday, 3 April
Trinity	Friday, 16 April, to Saturday, 26 June
Michaelmas	Friday, 10 September, to Saturday, 11 December

Part II candidates in Engineering (or Metallurgy), Economics, and Management

2003

Michaelmas	Friday, 12 September, to Saturday, 13 December

2004

Michaelmas	Friday, 11 September, to Saturday, 12 December

For Master of Business Administration

2003

Michaelmas	Monday, 6 October, to Friday, 12 December

2004

Hilary	Monday, 12 January, to Friday, 19 March
Trinity	Monday, 19 April, to Friday, 25 June
Long Vacation	Monday, 6 September, to Friday, 17 December
Michaelmas	Monday, 4 October, to Friday, 10 December

2005

Hilary	Monday, 10 January, to Friday, 18 March
Trinity	Monday, 18 April, to Friday, 24 June
Long Vacation	Monday, 12 September, to Friday, 23 September

DATES OF ENCAENIA

2004	Wednesday, 23 June
2005	Wednesday, 22 June

CONTENTS

[*The text is arranged in the order which appears most useful although this is not always the same as the formal legislative order.*]

PROVISIONAL DATES OF EXAMINATIONS

The provisional start dates of examinations and examination entry deadlines which were previously published in this volume are now produced as a separate document. This document is published in mid-September in the *University Gazette* and on the University website (www.ox.ac.uk), and is circulated directly to colleges and departments. The reason for this change is that the publication lead-time for this volume requires the inclusion of dates likely to change before the start of the academic year. The revised publication arrangements will lead to greater reliability of published information on examination dates and entry deadlines, to the benefit of those who make use of it.

NOTE ON CONVENTIONS GOVERNING THE REVISED USE OF HEADINGS IN THIS EDITION

As a result of recent changes in the structure of university legislation, with effect from 1 October 2002, all former decrees concerning examinations have been formally converted into regulations. In order to maintain continuity with earlier editions of this volume, and to assist readers accustomed to the pre-2002 format, the following conventions have been observed as far as is practicable:

1. All former decrees governing the award of a degree, diploma, or certificate in general terms (as opposed to those decrees dealing with examinations in particular subjects leading to the award of such a qualification) are now headed GENERAL REGULATIONS.

2. All former decrees relating to a particular subject course are now headed SPECIAL REGULATIONS.

3. All elements of examination legislation which were regulations under the previous dispensation, and remain so under the new structure, are also now to be found under the heading SPECIAL REGULATIONS.

4. In order to distinguish between the two types of Special Regulation described above, those which were formerly decrees are to be found, printed in larger type, under a sub-heading 'A', while those which were formerly regulations are printed in smaller type (as in previous editions) under a sub-heading 'B'.

REGULATIONS ON THE NUMBER AND LENGTH OF TERMS

Made by Council on 8 May 2002

1. The academic year shall be divided into three terms and three vacations.

2. (1) The first, or Michaelmas, Term shall begin on and include 1 October and end on and include 17 December.

(2) The second, or Hilary, Term shall begin on and include 7 January and end on and include 25 March or the Saturday before Palm Sunday, whichever is the earlier.

(3) The third, or Trinity, Term shall begin on and include 20 April or the Wednesday after Easter, whichever is the later, and end on and include 6 July.

3. (1) In each term there shall be prescribed by Council a period of eight weeks to be known as Full Term, beginning on a Sunday, within which lectures and other instruction prescribed by statute or regulation shall be given.

(2) The dates on which each Full Term will begin and end in the next academic year but one shall be published by the Registrar in the *University Gazette* during Hilary Term.

REGULATIONS FOR MATRICULATION OF STUDENT MEMBERS

Made by Council on 8 May 2002

1. In these regulations, unless the context requires otherwise, 'college' means any college, society, or Permanent Private Hall or any other institution designated by Council by regulation as being permitted to present candidates for matriculation.

Academic qualifications

2. (1) In order to be matriculated as student members candidates must show evidence of an appropriate educational background and good standards of literacy and numeracy.[1]

(2) The University sets no formal 'Course Requirements' other than for the First Examination for the Degree of Bachelor of Medicine; candidates must, however, show that they are qualified to study the particular course they which to take at Oxford.

(3) Acceptance by a college for presentation for matriculation will be deemed to be adequate evidence of an appropriate educational background, of good standards of literacy and numeracy, and of qualifications to study the course.

3. All candidates for matriculation shall supply to the Registrar such particulars as Council may from time to time determine, and may be required to produce to the Registrar (through the authorities of their colleges) evidence of their qualification to be matriculated.

4. Certificates in a language other than English must be accompanied by an English translation certified as correct by a duly authorized official of the country to which the candidate belongs.

Presentation for matriculation

5. Unless regulation 6 below applies, every head of a college or in their absence their deputies shall present to the Vice-Chancellor for matriculation all members of their college who are prospective

---

[1] GCSE passes at grade C and above in English Language, in a Mathematics or Science Subject, and in a language other than English and at least two A-level passes (or the equivalent in AS levels or a mixture of A and AS levels) would normally satisfy these requirements, as would an appropriate level of attainment in other qualifications such as Scottish Highers, the Irish Leaving Certificate, BTEC National Certificate, an Open University Foundation Course Credit, the European and International Baccalaureates, and degrees of other universities.

student members of the University within a fortnight from the date of their admission to the college.

6. A person who wishes to become a Senior Student under the provisions of the Regulations for Senior Student Status, or a graduate of another university who is applying for admission as a Probationer Research Student or as a student for any of the Degrees of Master of Fine Art, Master of Letters, Master of Philosophy, Master of Science, Master of Studies, Magister Juris, Bachelor of Philosophy, Bachelor of Civil Law, or Bachelor of Divinity must be presented to the Vice-Chancellor for matriculation by the head of his or her college or deputy within one month from the date of his or her admission to membership of his or her college.

7. A candidate who is matriculated during vacation shall be deemed to have been matriculated on the first day of the term following the vacation.

8. A person who becomes a student member by incorporation under regulations 1.7–1.18 of the Regulations for Degrees, Diplomas, and Certificates shall be deemed to have been matriculated on the first day of the term in which he or she was incorporated (or, in the case of a person incorporated during vacation, on the first day of the term following the vacation).

9. The procedure at the matriculation ceremony shall be in accordance with the arrangements laid down in the Regulations of Congregation for the Conduct of Ceremonies in Congregation.

Provisional matriculation

10. (1) Any person who is eligible to be matriculated may, if in the opinion of the head of his or her college there is good reason for that person not to be presented for matriculation under regulation 5 above, and on payment of the matriculation fee (if payable), be 'provisionally matriculated' (in absence) in accordance with arrangements made by Council and shall then be treated for all purposes as a member of the University until the end of the term in which he or she is provisionally matriculated.

(2) The duty under regulation 5 above of a head of a college to present any person for matriculation within a specified period from the date of his or her admission to the college shall be deemed to have been satisfied by that provisional matriculation, subject to the following conditions:

(*a*) any person who is matriculated not later than the term following the date of his or her provisional matriculation shall be deemed for all purposes to have been matriculated on the date of his or her provisional matriculation;

(*b*) if any person has not been matriculated in or before the term following his or her provisional matriculation, his or her provisional matriculation shall, unless Council determines otherwise, be cancelled but the fee shall not be returned.

11. Notwithstanding the provisions of regulation 10 above, any person who has been provisionally matriculated and who, in accordance with arrangements approved by Council, spends the first two terms of his or her studies at any of the universities approved by Council under the ERASMUS postgraduate exchange scheme for Law and Economics may be matriculated up to the end of the third term after the term in which he or she was provisionally matriculated, and the duty under regulation 5 above of a head of a college to present any person for matriculation within a specified period from the date of his or her admission to the college shall be deemed to have been satisfied by that provisional matriculation, subject to the following conditions:

(1) any person who is matriculated not later than the third term after the term in which he or she was provisionally matriculated shall be deemed for all purposes to have been matriculated on the date of his or her provisional matriculation;

(2) if any person has not been matriculated in or before the third term after the term in which he or she was provisionally matriculated, his or her provisional matriculation shall, unless Council determines otherwise, be cancelled but the fee shall not be returned.

12. The matriculation fee (if payable), the particulars which the candidate is required to supply under the provisions of regulation 3 above, and (if requested) evidence of his or her qualification to be matriculated shall be sent by the authorities of the candidate's college to the Registrar with a request that the candidate be provisionally matriculated.

St Catherine's Society

13. All persons who were matriculated through St Catherine's Society shall be deemed to have been matriculated through St Catherine's College, except that those who were matriculated in Michaelmas Term 1961 or later and who were not reading for the

Degree of Bachelor of Arts shall be deemed to have been matriculated through Linacre College.

Matriculation for Theological Courses of members of certain institutions in Oxford

14. In each academic year up to and including 2005–6, St Stephen's House, and Ripon College, Cuddesdon, shall be permitted between them, subject to the conditions laid down in regulations 15–17 below, to present for matriculation by the University:

(1) not more than thirty-six full-time-equivalent qualified candidates offering themselves for the qualifications listed in regulation 17 below other than the M.Th. in Applied Theology or the Diploma in Applied Theology; and

(2) not more than twenty-four qualified candidates offering themselves for the M.Th. in Applied Theology or the Diploma in Applied Theology.

15. No person may be matriculated under the authority of these regulations unless the institution presenting that person for matriculation can certify that he or she is a minister of religion or a genuine candidate for the ministry.

16. Before presenting any candidate for matriculation under the authority of these regulations, the institution presenting him or her shall consult the Board of the Faculty of Theology or such nominee or nominees as the board may appoint to act for it.

17. Persons matriculated under the authority of regulations 14–16 above shall have in relation to the University the same privileges and obligations as if they had been matriculated through a college, except that they may not (unless they migrate to a college listed in Statute V) offer themselves for any degree, diploma, or certificate examinations of the University other than those for:

(1) the Honour School of Theology or any joint Honour School which includes Theology;

(2) the Diploma in Theology or a Certificate in Theology or the Degree of Bachelor of Theology;

(3) the Degree of Master of Studies or Master of Philosophy in Theology, or Master of Studies or Master of Philosophy in Philosophical Theology, or Master of Theology in Applied Theology, or the Diploma in Applied Theology;

(4) the Degree of Bachelor of Divinity or Doctor of Divinity.

REGULATIONS FOR RESIDENCE IN THE UNIVERSITY

Made by Council on 8 May 2002

1. Where under any statute or regulation a student member is required, in order to be admitted to any examination or degree or obtain any other qualification of the University, to keep a number of terms or any other period of residence in the University these regulations shall apply for the purpose of:

(1) defining the place or places of residence; and

(2) calculating any period of residence necessary to satisfy that requirement.

2. Residence as defined by those regulations is called 'statutory residence'.

3. In these regulations, unless the context otherwise requires, 'college' means any college, society, or Permanent Private Hall or any other institution designated by Council by regulation as being permitted to present candidates for matriculation as student members of the University.

Place of residence

4. (1) Unless relations 4(2), 6, or 7 below apply, student members who are reading for a degree awarded on passing the Second Public Examination must reside, for the period prescribed for that degree, within six miles from Carfax.

(2) A student member to whom paragraph (1) above applies may reside within twenty-five miles from Carfax if he or she:

(*a*) holds the status of Senior Student or has already satisfied the examiners in a Second Public Examination; or

(*b*) is married; or

(*c*) resides in the home of his or her parent or guardian.

5. Unless regulations 6 or 7 below apply, student members who are reading for any other degree of the University shall reside, for the period prescribed for that degree, within twenty-five miles from Carfax.

6. The Proctors may, upon the application in writing of the head or another officer of the applicant's college, authorize a student member to reside and keep terms in a house or flat situated more than the number of miles from Carfax prescribed in his or her case

if there are special circumstances which appear to the Proctors to justify such authorization.

7. All student members who are engaged on part-time courses, or who are exceptionally permitted to undertake their research in a well-found laboratory outside Oxford under the provisions of the Regulations for the Degree of Doctor of Philosophy, shall be exempt from the residence limit.

8. If any student member (other than one engaged on a part-time course, or one exceptionally permitted to undertake his or her research in a well-founded laboratory outside Oxford under the provisions of the Regulations for the Degree of Doctor of Philosophy) shall reside more than the number of miles from Carfax prescribed in his or her case without the permission of the Proctors, he or she shall not be permitted to count such residence towards any period or periods during which he or she is required to reside to obtain a degree or other qualification from the University.

9. (1) If any student member is dissatisfied with a decision by the Proctors under regulation 6 above or regulation 14 below, he or she, or his or her college, may within fourteen days of the date of the decision appeal in writing to the Chairman of the Educational Policy and Standards Committee of Council.

(2) The appeal shall be adjudged expeditiously by the Chairman or another member of that committee, other than one of the Proctors, nominated by the Chairman.

Calculating periods of residence

10. Whenever the required time for any degree or other qualification is reckoned in terms, 'term' shall mean a term as prescribed in regulation 2 of the Regulations on the Number and Length of Terms.

11. A person on whom any degree has not yet been conferred shall not be reckoned as having completed a term of residence for his or her degree unless he or she has resided within the University for six weeks of each such term.

12. Whenever the required time for any degree or other qualification is reckoned in years, a year shall be deemed to be the equivalent of three terms. (For example, if three years are required, nine terms shall be understood, if four years, twelve terms, and so on.)

13. If a student member is presented for matriculation during the course of a term he or she shall be entitled to count the whole of that term as one term's residence if he or she has been residing

at a place of residence authorized under these regulations for the whole of that term.

14. A person who wishes to become a Senior Student under the provisions of the Regulations for Senior Student Status, or a graduate of another university who is applying for admission as a Probationer Research Student or as a student for any of the Degrees of Master of Fine Art, Master of Letters, Master of Philosophy, Master of Science, Master of Studies, Magister Juris, Bachelor of Philosophy, Bachelor of Civil Law, or Bachelor of Divinity, may be given permission by the Proctors to count towards his or her statutory residence any period not exceeding one calendar month during which he or she has resided, before his or her matriculation, under conditions approved by his or her college, within the relevant distance from Carfax as specified in these regulations.

15. Any person who has been given dispensation from the requirements of regulation 11 (1) of the Regulations for Matriculation of Student Members only after he or she has come into residence shall be permitted to reckon as part of his or her statutory residence under these regulations any period, not exceeding one term, during which he or she has resided before his or her matriculation, under conditions approved by his or her college, within the appropriate distance from Carfax as specified in these regulations.

16. If a student member is suspended from access to the premises and facilities of the University, the period of suspension shall not count towards the fulfilment of that student's statutory residence requirements.

Dispensations

17. Council may by regulation provide for student members to be excused from any required period of statutory residence up to a specified limit.

REGULATIONS FOR SENIOR STUDENT STATUS

Made by Council on 8 May 2002

1. The following may be admitted to the status and privileges of a Senior Student, subject to the decision of the Educational Policy and Standards Committee of Council in any case of doubt or difficulty:

(1) persons who have obtained a degree at another university after having pursued a course of study extending over three years of full-time study, or its equivalent on a part-time basis;

(2) persons who, having been a student at a university in a European country, have successfully completed a course of study on a full-time, or equivalent part-time, basis deemed to be equivalent to that of an undergraduate degree qualification;

(3) persons who have obtained a degree at another university and have also been selected to come to Oxford by some body recognized for the purposes of this regulation by the University;

(4) persons who, though not eligible under paragraphs (1) or (2) or (3) above, have satisfied the Educational Policy and Standards Committee of Council that they are well qualified to be admitted as Senior Students.

2. The status and privileges of Senior Students shall be as follows:

(1) The term in which they are matriculated shall be reckoned, for the purposes of any provisions respecting the standing of members of the University, as the fourth term from their matriculation.

(2) They shall not be required to pass the First Public Examination as a condition for the Degree of Bachelor of Arts or of Master of Biochemistry or Chemistry or Earth Sciences or Engineering or Mathematics or Physics, or the Preliminary Examination in Fine Art as a condition for the Degree of Bachelor of Fine Art, as the case may be.

(3) They shall be entitled to supplicate for the Degree of Bachelor of Arts, or of Bachelor of Fine Art, or of Master of Biochemistry or Chemistry or Earth Sciences or Engineering or Mathematics or Physics, as the case may be, if they have kept statutory residence, as defined in the relevant regulations, for

six terms in the case of courses of study lasting three years, or nine terms in the case of courses of study lasting four years, and:

(*a*) have obtained a place, or have been declared to have deserved Honours under the Regulations for the Conduct of Examinations, in the class list of an Honour school of the Second Public Examination or the Final Examination in Fine Art, or they are entitled under the relevant regulations to supplicate for one of those degrees as if they had obtained Honours in such an examination; or

(*b*) have passed the Pass School of the Second Public Examination under the relevant regulations.

3. Any persons who desire to become Senior Students under the provisions of these regulations shall send their applications, through an officer of a college, society, or Permanent Private Hall or another institution designated by Council by regulation as being permitted to present candidates for matriculation, to the Registrar and shall at the same time produce all necessary certificates and information in support of their applications.

REGULATIONS FOR READMISSION AND MIGRATION

Made by Council on 8 May 2002

1. In these regulations, unless the context requires otherwise, 'college' means any college, society, or Permanent Private Hall or any other institution designated by Council by regulation as being permitted to present candidates for matriculation.

2. If any person has been expelled by any college, that person shall not be readmitted to the college without the written permission of the Proctors if:

(1) his or her expulsion has taken place while he or she was still subject to any penalty imposed by the Proctors or by the Court of Summary Jurisdiction or the Disciplinary Court or the Appeal Court; or

(2) the Proctors have given specific notice in writing to the college that the consent of the Proctors will be required.

3. A student member of the University may migrate from any college to any other, and a graduate of the University who is a minister of religion or a candidate for the ministry may migrate to St Stephen's House or Ripon College, Cuddesdon, in order to read for the Honour School of Theology, for any joint Honour School which includes Theology, for the Diploma in Theology, for the Certificate in Theology, or for the Degree of Bachelor of Theology, if in each case he or she has first obtained:

(1) written permission for his or her migration from the college to which he or she belongs; and

(2) a certificate signed by the two Proctors that they have seen that permission and do not oppose his or her migration.

4. If the Proctors decline to give their consent under regulation 2 above, or to sign the certificate specified in regulation 3 (2) above, the person concerned may dispute the Proctors' decision in accordance with Statute XVII.

5. No person who has previously been admitted as a member by any college within the University shall be admitted as a member by any other without the production of the proper certificates.

6. In granting a certificate of migration, the Proctors, with the consent of the Vice-Chancellor, may append such conditions as to

residence during the next three terms as may appear to them desirable.

7. If any permission or testimonial required under the provisions of regulations 2 and 3 above is refused, the Vice-Chancellor may nevertheless, if he or she thinks fit, grant consent in writing for the migration.

8. If any student member of the University has been expelled by the authorities of any college, that person shall not be readmitted to membership of the University unless the Vice-Chancellor has heard the case and has given consent in writing for the readmission of that person; and it shall be the duty of the authorities of colleges to satisfy themselves that any person applying to them for admission has not previously been so expelled.

9. Any student member of the University migrating or having been readmitted to membership of the University except under the conditions laid down above shall forfeit all the privileges of the University from the date of his or her migration or readmission; except that the two Proctors, if they are satisfied that there was no reason why that person should not have been allowed to migrate or to be readmitted, may exempt him or her from the penalties imposed by this regulation, and any person so exempted shall pay to the University through the Registrar a further sum equivalent to one-half of the matriculation fee payable at the date of the exemption.

10. (1) Nothing in regulations 2–9 above shall be taken to apply to any person:

(*a*) who becomes a member of another college by virtue of his or her election to any office or emolument;

(*b*) who, being a graduate of the University, becomes a member of another college in order to pursue a further course of study (other than one which continues the academic programme for which he or she has been already been admitted as a Probationer Research Student).

(2) It shall be the responsibility of the head or bursar of the college of which a person becomes a member under paragraph (1) (*a*) or (*b*) above to include the name of that a person in the termly schedule of the names of the members of the college who are liable to pay composition fees to the University, unless that person's name is included in the schedule prepared by the head or bursar of any other college of which the person is already a member.

GENERAL REGULATIONS FOR ADMISSION TO DEGREES AWARDED ON PASSING THE SECOND PUBLIC EXAMINATION

Made by Council on 8 May 2002

Part 1

General

1.1. These regulations apply to the following degrees of the University:

Bachelor of Arts
Bachelor of Fine Art
Master of Biochemistry
Master of Chemistry
Master of Earth Sciences
Master of Engineering
Master of Mathematics
Master of Physics

1.2. In these regulations where the context admits:

(1) the expression 'statutory residence' means residence at any place authorized by the Regulations for Residence in the University ('the Residence Regulations');

(2) references to divisions and faculty boards shall include a reference to the Committee for the Ruskin School of Drawing and Fine Art; and

(3) 'college' means any college, society, or Permanent Private Hall or any other institution designated by Council by regulation as being permitted to present candidates for matriculation.

1.3. Any member of the University may be admitted to a degree to which these regulations apply if he or she:

(1) has kept statutory residence for the period prescribed in these regulations for the degree in question; and

(2) has employed himself or herself in study and hearing lectures and has (unless exempt) passed the First and Second Public Examinations in accordance with the requirements laid down by regulation.

Part 2

Residence

2.1. A member reading for the Degree of Bachelor of Arts or of Fine Art must unless regulation 2.2 below applies keep nine terms of statutory residence.

2.2. A member who has taken Honour Moderations in Classics or Classics and English (Course II) as the First Public Examination or who intends to apply for Honours in the Second Public Examination in Mathematics and Philosophy (Part II) or Physics and Philosophy (Part C) must keep twelve terms of statutory residence.

2.3. A member reading for any of the Master's degrees referred to in regulation 1.1 above must keep twelve terms of statutory residence.

2.4. The Proctors may, for any reason judged by them to be sufficient and on such conditions as they think fit, excuse a member reading for a degree to which these regulations apply from up to three terms of statutory residence.

2.5. (1) If any member is dissatisfied with a decision by the Proctors under regulation 2.4 above, he or she, or his or her college, may within fourteen days of the date of the decision appeal in writing to the Chairman of the Educational Policy and Standards Committee of Council.

(2) The appeal shall be adjudged expeditiously by the Chairman or another member of that committee, other than one of the Proctors, nominated by the Chairman.

2.6. Applications for dispensation under regulation 2.4 above must be made through the applicant's college.

2.7. A member who is granted dispensation from statutory residence under regulation 2.4 above must nevertheless, unless expressly exempted, pay in respect of any term for which he or she is excused residence any university fee which would have been payable if he or she had actually resided.

2.8. Council may permit time spent outside Oxford, as part of an academic programme approved by it, to be counted towards residence for the purposes of these regulations.

Part 3

First Public Examination

3.1. The First Public Examination shall include Honour Moderations, Moderations, and Preliminary Examinations in the subjects respectively listed in Tables 1, 2, and 3 below.

3.2. The examinations shall be conducted by Moderators under the supervision of the divisional and faculty boards assigned to each subject respectively in Tables 1, 2, and 3 below.

TABLE 1: HONOUR MODERATIONS

Subject	*Board(s)*
Archaeology and Anthropology	Life and Environmental Sciences Division
Biological Sciences	Life and Environmental Sciences Division
Classical Archaeology and Ancient History	Life and Environmental Sciences Division and Faculty of Classics
Classics	Faculty of Classics
Classics and English	Faculties of Classics and English Language and Literature
Computer Science	Mathematical and Physical Sciences Division
Geography	Life and Environmental Sciences Division
Mathematics	Mathematical and Physical Sciences Division
Mathematics and Computer Science	Mathematical and Physical Sciences Division
Mathematics and Philosophy	Mathematical and Physical Sciences Division and Faculty of Philosophy
Music	Faculty of Music

TABLE 2: MODERATIONS

Subject	*Board(s)*
English Language and Literature	Faculty of English Language and Literature
Law	Faculty of Law
Oriental Studies	Faculty of Oriental Studies
Physics and Philosophy	Mathematical and Physical Sciences Division and Faculty of Philosophy

TABLE 3: PRELIMINARY EXAMINATIONS

(For the explanation of the asterisks see regulation 3.12 below.)

Subject	*Board(s)*
Ancient and Modern History	Faculties of Classics and Modern History

* Archaeology and Anthropology	Life and Environmental Sciences Division
* Biological Sciences	Life and Environmental Sciences Division
Chemistry	Mathematical and Physical Sciences Division
* Classical Archaeology and Ancient History	Life and Environmental Sciences Division and Faculty of Classics
Classics	Faculty of Classics
* Classics and English	Faculties of Classics and English Language and Literature
* Computer Science	Mathematical and Physical Sciences Division
Economics and Management	Social Sciences Division
Engineering Science	Mathematical and Physical Sciences Division
English and Modern Languages	Faculties of English Language and Literature and Medieval and Modern Languages
* English Language and Literature	Faculty of English Language and Literature
European and Middle Eastern Languages	Faculties of Medieval and Modern Languages and Oriental Studies
Fine Art	Committee for Ruskin School of Drawing and Fine Art
* Geography	Life and Environment Sciences Division
Human Sciences	Life and Environmental Sciences Division
* Mathematics	Mathematical and Physical Sciences Division
* Mathematics and Computer Science	Mathematical and Physical Sciences Division
* Mathematics and Philosophy	Mathematical and Physical Sciences Division and Faculty of Philosophy
Modern History	Faculty of Modern History
Modern History and Economics	Faculty of Modern History and Social Sciences Division
Modern History and English	Faculties of Modern History and English Language and Literature

Modern History and Modern Languages	Faculties of Modern History and Medieval and Modern Languages
Modern History and Politics	Faculty of Modern History and Social Sciences Division
Modern Languages	Faculty of Medieval and Modern Languages
Molecular and Cellular Biochemistry	Life and Environmental Sciences Division
* Music	Faculty of Music
* Oriental Studies	Faculty of Oriental Studies
Philosophy and Modern Languages	Faculties of Philosophy and Medieval and Modern Languages
Philosophy, Politics, and Economics	Faculty of Philosophy and Social Sciences Division
Physical Sciences: Earth Sciences, Materials Science	Mathematical and Physical Sciences Division
Physics	Mathematical and Physical Sciences Division
* Physics and Philosophy	Mathematical and Physical Sciences Division and Faculty of Philosophy
Physiological Sciences	Medical Sciences Division
Psychology, Philosophy, and Physiology	Medical Sciences Division and Faculty of Philosophy
Theology	Faculty of Theology

3.3. The boards shall from time to time make and publish Special Regulations respecting the examinations under their supervision and shall publish lists of subjects and (where appropriate) of books which may be offered for examination, maintaining as far as possible a distinction between the subjects and any books prescribed in the First and Second Public Examinations respectively.

3.4. Special Regulations made and lists drawn up by boards under regulation 3.3 above shall not have effect until:

(1) they have been approved by the Educational Policy and Standards Committee of Council;

(2) in the case of regulations made and lists drawn up by faculty boards or other bodies within the Humanities and Social Sciences Divisions, they have also first been approved by the Humanities Board or the Social Sciences Board as appropriate;

(3) they have then been duly published, and if necessary approved by Congregation, in accordance with the procedure laid down in sections 13–18 of Statute VI.

Method of examining

3.5. Subject to regulation 3.6 below the examinations shall be conducted in writing.

3.6. A board may specify by Special Regulation that an examination shall be partly aural, oral, practical, or visual.

Admission to the First Public Examination

3.7. No person who is not a student member of the University may be admitted to the First Public Examination.

3.8. Candidates may be admitted to Honour Moderations at any time not earlier than the third term from matriculation, but no candidate who has exceeded the sixth term from matriculation inclusively, or the eighth term in the case of candidates for Honour Moderations in Classics, shall be capable of obtaining Honours.

3.9. Candidates may be admitted to each of the Moderations listed in Table 4 below not earlier than the term from matriculation specified in each case.

TABLE 4: ADMISSION TO MODERATIONS

Moderations	*Earliest term from matriculation*
English Language and Literature	3rd
Law	2nd
Oriental Studies:	
Chinese	5th, subject to regulation 3.10 below
Egyptology and Ancient Near Eastern Studies	3rd
Japanese	3rd, subject to regulation 3.11 below
Physics and Philosophy	3rd

3.10. A candidate may be admitted to Moderations in Oriental Studies (Chinese) only if he or she has:

(1) passed an examination in Chinese under the auspices of the Board of the Faculty of Oriental Studies: or

(2) otherwise satisfied the faculty board as to his or her competence in Chinese.

3.11. A candidate may be admitted to Moderations in Oriental Studies (Japanese) only if he or she has:

(1) during his or her first year of study passed an examination in Japanese under the auspices of the Board of the Faculty of Oriental Studies and spent a period of not less than ten weeks on an approved course of language study in Japanese; or

(2) otherwise satisfied the faculty board as to his or her competence in Japanese.

3.12. (1) Candidates shall not be admitted to any of the Preliminary Examinations which has the same title as any Honour Moderations or Moderations, and which is one of those marked with an asterisk in Table 3 above, unless they have either failed the examination for the Honour Moderations or Moderations with the same title or, subject to the consent of the Proctors, have been prevented by illness or other urgent and reasonable cause from taking that examination.

(2) If any member of the University is dissatisfied with a decision by the Proctors under paragraph (1) above, he or she, or his or her college, may within fourteen days of the date of the decision appeal in writing to the Chairman of the Educational Policy and Standards Committee of Council.

(3) The appeal shall be adjudged expeditiously by the Chairman or another member of the committee, other than one of the Proctors, nominated by the Chairman.

3.13. Candidates may be admitted to each of the Preliminary Examinations listed in Table 5 below not earlier than the term from matriculation specified in each case.

TABLE 5: ADMISSION TO PRELIMINARY EXAMINATIONS

Preliminary Examination	*Earliest term from matriculation*
Ancient and Modern History	3rd
Biological Sciences	3rd
Chemistry	2nd
Classics	2nd
Computer Science	3rd
Earth Sciences	2nd

English and Modern Languages:	
English	3rd
Modern Language	2nd
Fine Art	3rd
Mathematics	3rd
Mathematics and Computer Science	3rd
Mathematics and Philosophy	3rd
Modern History	3rd
Modern History and Economics	3rd
Modern History and English	3rd
Modern History and Modern Lanaguages	3rd
Modern History and Politics	3rd
Modern Languages	2nd
Molecular and Cellular Biochemistry	2nd
Oriental Studies:	
Arabic, Arabic with Turkish, Japanese	3rd
Other languages	2nd
Philosophy and Modern Languages	2nd
Philosophy, Politics, and Economics	2nd
Physics and Philosophy	3rd
Physiological Sciences	3rd
Psychology, Philosophy, and Physiology	2nd
Theology	2nd

3.14. No person whose name has been placed in any Class List issued by Moderators shall be admitted again as a candidate in the same Honours Examination.

Passing the First Public Examination

3.15. A candidate shall be deemed to have passed the First Public Examination if he or she has satisfied the Moderators in any one of the parts of the examination as set out in Tables 1, 2, and 3 above.

3.16. Any person who has sastified the Moderators in Part I of the First Examination for the Degree of Bachelor of Medicine shall be deemed to have passed the First Public Examination.

Part 4

Second Public Examination

4.1. The Second Public Examination shall, except in the case of the Degree of Bachelor of Fine Art, consist of a Final Examination in the Honour Schools or Pass Schools in each of the subjects listed in Tables 6 and 8 below.

4.2. The Second Public Examination for the Pass Schools shall be for those candidates who do not seek or are not eligible to obtain Honours.

4.3. The examinations shall be conducted by the Public Examiners under the supervision of the divisional or faculty boards assigned to each school in Tables 6 and 8 below.

TABLE 5: HONOUR SCHOOLS AND PASS SCHOOLS

Subject	*Board(s)*
Ancient and Modern History	Faculties of Classics and Modern History
Archaeology and Anthropology	Life and Environmental Sciences Division
Classical Archaeology and Ancient History	Life and Environmental Sciences Division and Faculty of Classics
Classics and English	Faculties of Classics and English Language and Literature
Classics and Modern Languages	Faculties of Classics and Medieval and Modern Languages
Computer Science	Mathematical and Physical Sciences Division
Economics and Management	Social Sciences Division
Engineering and Computing Science	Mathematical and Physical Sciences Division
Engineering, Economics, and Management	Mathematical and Physical Sciences and Social Sciences Divisions
Engineering and Materials	Mathematical and Physical Sciences Division
Engineering Science	Mathematical and Physical Sciences Division
English Language and Literature	Faculty of English Language and Literature
English and Modern Languages	Faculties of English Language and Literature and Medieval and Modern Languages
European and Middle Eastern Languages	Faculties of Medieval and Modern Languages and Oriental Studies
Experimental Psychology	Medical Sciences Division
Geography	Life and Environmental Sciences Division

Human Sciences	Life and Environmental Sciences Division
Jurisprudence	Faculty of Law
Literae Humaniores	Faculties of Classics and Philosophy
Materials, Economics, and Management	Mathematical and Physical Sciences and Social Sciences Divisions
[**Until 1 October 2004:** Mathematical Sciences	Mathematical and Physical Sciences Division]
[**Until 1 October 2004:** Mathematical and Statistical Sciences	Mathematical and Physical Sciences Division]
Mathematics (3-year and 4-year)	Mathematical and Physical Sciences Division
Mathematics and Computer Science	Mathematical and Physical Sciences Division
Mathematics and Philosophy	Mathematical and Physical Sciences Division and Faculty of Philosophy
[**From 1 October 2005:** Mathematics and Statistics (3-year and 4-year)	Mathematical and Physical Sciences Division]
Modern History	Faculty of Modern History
Modern History and Economics	Faculty of Modern History and Social Sciences Division
Modern History and English	Faculties of Modern History and English Language and Literature
Modern History and Modern Languages	Faculties of Modern History and Medieval and Modern Languages
Modern History and Politics	Faculty of Modern History and Social Sciences Division
Modern Languages	Faculty of Medieval and Modern Languages
Music	Faculty of Music
Natural Science	*See Table 6*
Oriental Studies	Faculty of Oriental Studies
Philosophy and Modern Languages	Faculties of Philosophy and Medieval and Modern Languages
Philosophy, Politics, and Economics	Faculty of Philosophy and Social Sciences Division
Philosophy and Theology	Faculties of Philosophy and Theology

Physics (3-year and 4-year)	Mathematical and Physical Sciences Division
Physics and Philosophy	Mathematical and Physical Sciences Division and Faculty of Philosophy
Psychology, Philosophy, and Physiology	Medical Sciences Division and Faculty of Philosophy
Theology	Faculty of Theology

TABLE 8: NATURAL SCIENCE: HONOUR SCHOOLS AND PASS SCHOOLS

Subject	*Board(s)*
Biological Sciences	Life and Environmental Sciences Division
Chemistry	Mathematical and Physical Sciences Division
Earth Sciences (4-year)	Mathematical and Physical Sciences Division
Geology (3-year)	Mathematical and Physical Sciences Division
Materials Science	Mathematical and Physical Sciences Division
Molecular and Cellular Biochemistry	Life and Environmental Sciences Division
Physiological Sciences	Medical Sciences Division

4.4 The Second Public Examination for the Degree of Bachelor of Fine Art shall consist of a Final Honour School under the supervision of the Committee for the Ruskin School of Drawing and Fine Art.

4.5. The boards shall from time to time make and publish Special Regulations respecting the examinations under their supervision and shall publish lists of subjects and (where appropriate) of books which may be offered for examination.

4.6. Special Regulations made and lists drawn up by boards under regulation 4.5 above shall not have effect until:

(1) they have been approved by the Educational Policy and Standards Committee of Council;

(2) in the case of regulations made and lists drawn up by faculty boards or other bodies within the Humanities and Social Sciences Divisions, they have also first been approved by the Humanities Board or the Social Sciences Board as appropriate.

(3) they have then been duly published, and if necessary approved by Congregation, in accordance with the procedure laid down in sections 13–18 of Statute VI.

Method of examining

4.7. Every candidate in a Second Public Examination shall be examined in writing; and any candidate who seeks Honours may be examined viva voce where Special Regulations made by the divisional board, board of a faculty, or other body responsible for an examination (or jointly by the relevant bodies where an examination is a joint responsibility) expressly provide.

4.8. A board may specify by Special Regulation that an examination shall be partly aural, oral, practical, or visual.

Admission to the Second Public Examination

4.9. No person who is not a student member of the University may be admitted to the Second Public Examination.

4.10. No person may be admitted to the Second Public Examination unless he or she has passed or been exempted from the First Public Examination.

4.11. No person may be admitted as a candidate in any Final Honour School or Pass School unless he or she:

(1) has satisfied the conditions, if any, which are required by regulations (including Special Regulations) relating to the School in which he or she is a candidate; and

(2) will by the end of the term in which the examination is taken have kept statutory residence for the number of terms which, under Part 2 or 5 of these regulations or the Regulations for Senior Student Status, is appropriate to his or her status and to the School in which he or she is a candidate.

Maximum time allowed for Honours

4.12. No person may be admitted as a candidate in any Final Honour School after the lapse of twelve terms from the term of matriculation inclusively, except in the following cases:

(1) A candidate who has obtained Honours in some other Final Honour School may be admitted not more than six terms after the date on which he or she first obtained Honours in a Final Honour School.

(2) A candidate who has obtained Honours (or has satisfied the Moderators under the Regulations for the Conduct of

Examinations) in Honour Moderations may be admitted as a candidate in Part II of the examination in Chemistry or in Molecular and Cellular Biochemistry or in Materials Science in the Honour School of Natural Science up to the end of the eighteenth term.

(3) A candidate in any of the following Final Honour School examinations may be admitted up to the end of the fifteenth term:

(*a*) any Final Honour School, if the candidate has obtained Honours (or has satisfied the Moderators under the Regulations for the Conduct of Examinations) in Honour Moderations in either the fifth or sixth term, or the eighth term in the case of Honour Moderations in Classics, from matriculation;

(*b*) the second part of any Final Honour School which is divided into two parts, except the Honour School of Physics (three-year course);

(*c*) the third part of any Final Honour School which is divided into three parts;

(*d*) the Honour School of Classics and Modern Languages, English and Modern Languages, European and Middle Eastern Languages, Jurisprudence, Modern Languages, Modern History and Modern Languages, or Philosophy and Modern Languages, if the candidate is certified by his or her college to have spent an academic year of approved residence in appropriate country or appropriate countries;

(*e*) the examination in Chinese or Japanese, or, if the candidate is certified to have spent an academic year abroad on a course approved by the Board of the Faculty of Oriental Studies, the examination in Arabic, or Hebrew, or Persian, or Turkish, in the Honour School of Oriental Studies.

(4) A person whose position is not covered by any of paragraphs (1)–(3) above may be admitted as a candidate in a Final Honour School for which there is at least one candidate other than those offering themselves for examination under the provisions of this paragraph (4), but he or she shall not be capable of obtaining Honours.

4.13. The candidate's college shall be required to certify on the entry form, by the time determined for entry, whether or not the candidate will have met the requirement for statutory residence by the end of the term in which the examination is held, and to notify the University of any change in the candidate's status in this respect between entry and the date of the examination.

4.14. No person whose name has been placed in any class list by the Public Examiners (other than a candidate who has been declared to have deserved Honours under the Regulations for the Conduct of Examinations) shall be admitted again as a candidate in the same Final Honour School, but this regulation shall not affect the regulations concerning the Final Honour Schools of Modern Languages, Natural Science, and Oriental Studies which enable candidates under certain conditions to offer themselves again in the same School.

4.15. (1) No person whose name has been placed in any class list by the Public Examiners (with the exceptions in regulations 4.13 and 4.14 above) shall be admitted as a candidate in a second Final Honour School having papers in common with the first, except with the permission of the Proctors.

(2) If any member of the University is dissatisfied with a decision by the Proctors under paragraph (1) above, he or she, or his or her college, may within fourteen days of the date of the decision appeal in writing to the Chairman of the Educational Policy and Standards Committee of Council.

(3) The appeal shall be adjudged expeditiously by the Chairman or another member of the committee, other than one of the Proctors, nominated by the Chairman.

Pass Schools

4.16. No candidate shall be admitted to examination in a Pass School without the approval of his or her college.

Passing the Second Public Examination

4.17. Candidates shall be deemed to have passed the Second Public Examination if they either have obtained Honours, or satisfied the examiners, in any one of the Honour Schools listed in Tables 5 and 6 above or in the Honour School of Fine Art, or have satisfied the examiners in any one of the Pass Schools listed in those tables.

Part 5

Foundation Courses at the Department for Continuing Education

5.1. Any member of the University who has successfully completed the course for a Foundation Certificate at the Department for Continuing Education (whether or not he or she was a member when he or she did so) may apply for admission to the Degree of Bachelor of Arts if he or she has:

(1) kept statutory residence in accordance with regulations 5.2 and 5.3 below; and

(2) passed the Second Public Examination.

5.2. A person who has successfully completed the course for the Foundation Certificate in English Language and Literature may be admitted as a candidate in the Final Honour School of English Language and Literature if by the end of the term in which the examination is held he or she has kept statutory residence for six terms.

5.3. A person who has successfully completed the course for any Foundation Certificate may not be admitted as a candidate in any Final Honour School more than nine terms inclusively from the term of matriculation.

Part 6

Degrees awarded on passing the Second Public Examination

6.1. The Degree of Bachelor of Arts shall be awarded to members of the University who have obtained Honours, or have satisfied the examiners but have not obtained Honours, in any Final Honour School other than the School of Fine Art or the Schools listed in Table 7 below, or have satisfied the examiners in any Pass School, subject to these regulations and to the Special Regulations for the Second Public Examination concerned.

6.2. The Degree of Bachelor of Fine Art shall be awarded to members of the University who have obtained Honours, or who have satisfied the examiners, in the Final Honour School for that degree, subject to these regulations and to the Special Regulations for that School.

6.3. The Master's Degrees to which these regulations apply shall be awarded to members of the University who have obtained Honours in the Second Public Examination in the relevant Final Honour Schools, as set out in Table 7 below, subject also the conditions laid down in the Special Regulations for each School.

TABLE 7: MASTER'S DEGREES

Degree	*Final Honour School*
Master of Biochemistry	Natural Science (Molecular and Cellular Biochemistry)
Master of Chemistry	Natural Science (Chemistry)
Master of Earth Sciences	Natural Science (Earth Sciences)
Master of Engineering	Engineering Science
	Engineering and Computing Science
	Engineering, Economics, and Management
	Engineering and Materials
	Materials, Economics, and Management
	Natural Science (Materials Science)
Master of Mathematics	Mathematics (four-year course)
	Mathematics and Statistics (four-year course)
Master of Physics	Physics (four-year course)
	Physics and Philosophy (for those following option 1: Physics in Part C)

Special Regulations for the Honour Moderations in Archaeology and Anthropology

A

Honour Moderations in Archaeology and Anthropology shall be under the supervision of the Life and Environmental Sciences Board and shall consist of such subjects as it shall by regulation prescribe.

B

1. Every candidate shall offer four papers of three hours each, as follows:
Paper (1) Introduction to world archaeology.
Paper (2) Introduction to anthropological theory.
Paper (3) Perspectives on human evolution.
Paper (4) The nature of archaeological enquiry.

2. All candidates will be required to undertake a course of practical work, including laboratory work.

All candidates will be assessed on their practical ability under the following provisions:

(*a*) Class co-ordinators shall make available to the chairman of the examiners records showing the extent to which each candidate has pursued an adequate course of practical work.

(*b*) Candidates shall submit notebooks containing reports on the practical work completed during the first three terms of study signed by their practical class supervisor to the Clerk of Schools, High Street, Oxford, not later than noon on Friday of the eighth week of Trinity Term of the year in which they sit the examination. Upon receipt of the notebook and a signed declaration that the work is the candidate's own, the Clerk of Schools will issue a formal receipt.

These notebooks must bear the candidate's examination number but not the candidate's name, which must be concealed.

(*c*) Failure to submit reports or to reach an adequate standard will be communicated to the Examiners who may deduct up to 10 per cent in penalty from Paper (4).

Special Regulations for the Honour Moderations in Biological Sciences

A

The subjects of the examination, the syllabus, and the number of papers shall be as prescribed by regulation from time to time by the Life and Environmental Sciences Board.

B

1. Each candidate shall offer three papers (each of three hours' duration) corresponding to the first three sections (1–3) of the schedule below.

2. The Chairman of the Steering Committee, or a deputy, shall make available to the moderators, by the end of the seventh week of the term in which the examinations are first held, records showing the extent to which each candidate has completed the prescribed class work and laboratory work to a satisfactory standard in each of the four sections (1–4) of the schedule below. The moderators may request coursework from any candidate; such candidates will be named in a list posted by the day of the first written paper. Each notebook submitted shall be accompanied by a certificate signed by the candidate indicating that the notebook is the candidate's own work. Failure to complete the coursework to the satisfaction of the moderators, in the absence of appropriate documentary evidence, will normally constitute failure of the examination.

3. The moderators will not provide calculators, but will permit the use of any hand-held pocket calculator subject to the conditions set out under the heading 'Use of calculators in examinations' in the *Special Regulations concerning Examinations*.

4. Candidates are required to carry out fieldwork, as specified by the Biological Sciences Steering Committee, as an integral part of this course.

Schedule

1. *Organisms*

History and present day diversity of organisms. Origin of life, evolution and diversity of procaryotes; algae; aquatic animal groups, both invertebrate and vertebrate. The origin and terrestrial radiation of fungi, green plants, insects and tetrapod animals. The biology and diversity of birds and mammals. The evolution of humans and their impact on the environment.

2. *Cells and Genes*

Machinery of the cell: structural features of the building blocks of life; enzymes and metabolism; structure and function of membranes; mitochondria, chloroplasts and energy transduction; the cytoskeleton; the extracellular matrix; interactions between cells; cell division and growth.

Genetics: Mendelian and population genetics; genetics of multicellular and unicellular organisms; molecular genetics; recombinant DNA; the gene at work.

3. *Populations*

Interrelationships of organisms and their interactions with the physical environment. Competition, co-operation, predator-prey and host-parasite interactions.

The nature and origin of species and their interactions as communities. Energy flow, bio-geochemical cycles and biotic structure of ecosystems.

4. *Computing and data handling*

Hands-on introduction to computers; use of files, printers, word-processing and spreadsheets. Introduction to the importance of quantitative methods in biology. Descriptive statistics and graphical representations of data. Frequency distributions. Populations and samples. Sampling distribution of the mean, standard errors, confidence intervals. Estimation and hypothesis testing. The Central Limit theorem. The Binomial, Poisson and Normal Distributions.

Special Regulations for the Honour Moderations in Classical Archaeology and Ancient History

A

The subjects of the examination shall be under the joint supervision of the Board of the Faculty of Classics and the Life and Environmental Sciences Board.

B

Every candidate shall offer four papers [of three hours each] as follows:

I. *Aristocracy and democracy in the Greek world, 550–450* BC

The paper studies the history and archaeology of the changing culture of the Greek *polis* states between the aristocracies in the later sixth century and the emergence of the new *demos* culture in the first half of the fifth century. Areas of emphasis will include: aristocracy, tyranny, and the history of the interacting archaic states; Achaemenids and the Greek collision with Persia; competing models of social and political culture after the Persian invasion; the archaeology of sanctuaries and cities; and the visual revolution in art and representation.

II. *Republic to Empire: Rome, 50 BC to AD 50*

The paper studies the impact of the first emperors on the history and archaeology of Rome and its subject states in the period from Late Republic to Early Empire. Areas of emphasis will include: Roman political culture from the Republican war-lords to Augustan *princeps*; emperor, senate, and the evolving administration; the Julio–Claudian dynasty and court culture: wallpainting, marbles, gardens and suburban parks; municipal culture: houses, tombs, and freedman art; land and countryside: estates, *vici*, and centuriated settlement; manufacture, trade, and natural resources; the archaeology of the frontier armies; traditional religion and emperor cult.

III, IV. Two papers from the following groups, provided that not more than one paper may be chosen from any one group:

A. Special subjects in archaeology:

1. *Homeric archaeology and early Greece, 1550–700 BC*

Evidence on the composition and history of the poems provided by extant archaeological remains, with special emphasis on burial practices, architecture, metals, and the world outside the Aegean. An overall knowledge will be required of the archaeological evidence for the Late Bronze Age and Early Iron Age of the Aegean from 1550 BC to 700 BC.

2. *Greek vases*

The study of the general history of Greek decorated pottery from *c.*800 BC to *c.*300 BC, including study of the Attic black-figure and red-figure styles and of South

Italian Greek vase painting. Knowledge will be required of the techniques used in making Greek pottery and in drawing on vases, also of the ancient names for vases and the shapes to which they refer. Candidates should in addition study the subjects of the paintings and their treatment by painters as compared with their treatment by writers and should be familiar with actual vases, for example those in the Ashmolean Museum.

3. *Greek sculpture,* c.*600–300* BC

The major monuments of archaic and classical Greek sculpture—their context and purpose as well as their subjects, styles, and techniques. Candidates will be expected to show some knowledge of the external documentary evidence, such as literary and epigraphic texts, on which the framework of the subject depends, and to be acquainted with the major sculptures of the period represented in the Ashmolean Cast Gallery. The examination will consist of one picture question and three essay questions.

4. *Roman architecture*

The subject comprises the study of Roman architecture from the Republic to the Tetrarchy in Italy and in the provinces, looking at public buildings, private housing, and imperial palaces. Particular attention is paid to developments in building materials and techniques, the evolution of architectural styles and ideas, and the ways in which different provinces show variations on a common theme as Roman influences interacted with local culture.

B. Special subjects in Ancient History:

Note: All texts are studied in translation. Except as otherwise indicated, passages for comment will be set from the most recent Penguin Classics edition: see Course Handbook for details.

1. *Thucydides and the west*

The prescribed text is Thucydides VI and VII. Compulsory passages for comment will be set from these books. Candidates will also be expected to be familiar with Plutarch, *Nicias*.

2. *Aristophanes' political comedy*

The prescribed plays are *Acharnians* and *Lysistrata*. Compulsory passages for comment will be set from these. Candidates will also be expected to be familiar with *Frogs*.

3. *Cicero and Catiline*

The prescribed texts are Sallust, *Catiline*: Cicero, *Against Catiline* I–IV; Asconius, *In orationem in toga candida* (in Asconius, *Commentaries on Five Speeches of Cicero*, ed. S. Squires, Bristol Classical Press, 1990). Compulsory passages for comment will be set from these.

4. *Tacitus and Tiberius*

The prescribed text is Tacitus, *Annals* I and III. Compulsory passages for comment will be set from these books. Candidates will also be expected to be familiar with *Annals* II and IV–VI.

5. *The ancient city*

The prescribed texts are Aristotle, *Politics* I and III.1–13; Polybius VI. Candidates will be expected to show knowledge of ancient and modern views of relevant aspects of both Greek and Roman civic life.

C. Ancient languages:

1. *Beginning ancient Greek*

(This subject is not available to candidates with A-level, or an equivalent qualification, in ancient Greek).

Candidates will be required to show knowledge of the main grammatical structures of ancient Greek and of basic vocabulary. The paper will consist of a test involving knowledge of Greek accidence, a passage for comprehension, and two further passages for translation from ancient Greek into English.

2. *Beginning Latin*

(This subject is not available to candidates with A-level, or an equivalent qualification, in Latin).

Candidates will be required to show knowledge of the main grammatical structures of Latin and of basic vocabulary. The paper will consist of a test involving knowledge of Latin accidence, a passage for comprehension, and two further passages for translation from Latin into English.

Special Regulations for the Honour Moderations in Classics

A

The subjects of the examination shall be as prescribed by regulation from time to time by the Board of the Faculty of Classics and the Board of the Faculty of Philosophy.

B

Candidates shall take one of the following courses IA, IB, IC, IIA, IIB.

Course IA

The examination will consist of the following papers. In the assignment of honours, particular account will be taken of a candidate's performance in Papers I (Homer, *Iliad*), II (Virgil, *Aeneid*) and V, VI (Special Subjects).

I. HOMER, *ILIAD*

One paper (3 hours) of translation and questions. A passage for translation will be set from each of:

(i) *Iliad* I–XII and

(ii) *Iliad* XIII–XXIV.

Candidates will be required to translate *both* passages and to answer *three* questions. They will also be required to scan a short passage.

II. VIRGIL, *AENEID*

One paper (3 hours) of translation and questions. A passage for translation will be set from each of:

(i) *Aeneid* I–IV,

(ii) *Aeneid* V–VIII,

(iii) *Aeneid* IX–XII.

Candidates will be required to translate *two* passages and to answer *three* questions. They will be expected to show knowledge of the whole poem. They will also be required to scan a short passage.

III. GREEK AUTHORS

One paper (3 hours) of translation. One passage will be set from each of the books prescribed, and candidates will be required to translate *four* passages, including at least *one* prose passage and at least *two* verse passages.

1. Hesiod, *Works and Days* (including the bracketed portions)
2. Aeschylus, *Prometheus Bound*
3. Sophocles, *Antigone*
4. Euripides, *Bacchae*
*5. Aristophanes, *Frogs* 1–268, 674–1533
6. Theocritus 1, 2, 5, 6, 11, 14
7. Herodotus I. 1–119
*8. Thucydides VII, 27–end
*9. Plato, *Symposium* 189c–end
10. Lysias 1, 10, 16, 24, and Demosthenes 54.

IV. Latin Authors

One paper (3 hours) of translation. One passage will be set from each of the books prescribed, and candidates will be required to translate *four* passages, including at least *one* prose passage and at least *two* verse passages.

1. Terence, *Adelphoe*
2. Catullus 1–17, 21–60, 69–70, 72–3, 75–9, 83–8, 92–6, 100, 101, 109, 115–16
3. Lucretius V. 1–234, 772–1457
4. Propertius I
5. Horace, *Odes* III
6. Ovid, *Metamorphoses* VIII
7. Cicero, *Pro Murena*
*8. Livy, *Preface*, I. 1–41
9. Seneca, *Epistles* 28, 47, 53, 56, 57, 63, 77, 108, 114, 122
10. Tacitus, *Annals* IV.

V, VI. Special Subjects

All candidates must offer *two* Special Subjects, one of which must be from Group A or B in the following list and the other from one of Groups C to F. Candidates who offer *only* two special subjects may not combine a subject from Group B with a subject from Group E. Candidates may offer a *third* Special Subject in lieu of either Paper X (Greek Language) or Paper XI (Latin Language), provided that it is chosen from a different Group from their other subjects. One three-hour paper will be set in each subject.

A.

1. *Early Greek Philosophy*, to be studied in Diels, *Die Fragmente der Vorsokratiker*, sixth or any later edition, edited by Kranz (Berlin, 1951 and later).

The texts prescribed are:

(*a*) Heraclitus (Diels–Kranz 22), B 1, 2, 10, 12, 17, 18, 21, 26, 28–32, 40, 41, 45, 50–62, 64, 67, 78–80, 88, 90, 93, 94, 101, 101*a*, 102, 103, 107, 108, 111, 113–15, 117–19, 123–6, and the first part of A 22 (Aristotle *Eudemian Ethics* $1235^{a}25$–7); Parmenides (Diels–Kranz 28), B 1–9, 19; Empedocles (Diels–Kranz 31), B 6, 8, 11–13, 17, 28–30, 35, 112, 115, 117, 134, 146; Anaxagoras (Diels–Kranz 59), B 1–17, 21, 21*a*;

(*b*) (i) early Ionian natural philosophy: Anaximander (Diels-Kranz 12) A 9 and B 1; Anaximenes (Diels–Kranz 13) B 2; Aristotle *Metaphysics* A $3.983^{a}24$–$984^{a}18$, *Physics* III $4.203^{a}16$–18 and $203^{b}3$–15;

* For the purposes of the General Paper (VII), candidates who offer these options will be expected to have knowledge of the whole of these books, not merely the prescribed portions.

(ii) Xenophanes: Xenophanes (Diels–Kranz 21), B 1, 7, 10–12, 14–16, 18, 23–9, 32, 34–6, 38; Aristotle *Metaphysics* A 5.986^{b}10–27;

(iii) Zeno: Zeno (Diels–Kranz 29) B 1–4; Plato *Parmenides* 127a7–128e4; Aristotle *Physics* VI 2.233^{a}21–31 and 9.239^{b}5–240^{a}18;

(iv) early atomists: Leucippus (Diels–Kranz 67) B 2; Democritus (Diels–Kranz 68) B 4, 6–8, 9, 10, 11, 117, 118, 125, 156, 164, 167; Aristotle *De Generatione et Corruptione* I 8.324^{b}35–325^{a}36, *Metaphysics* A 4.985^{b}3–22.

Where Diels–Kranz B-texts are prescribed, the prescription includes only what Diels–Kranz print in spaced type.

Candidates will be expected to show a general knowledge of the pre-Socratic philosophers, and to make a special study of the philosophers in (*a*) and in at least one of the four groups in (*b*). There will be a compulsory question containing passages for translation and comment from the texts prescribed in (*a*), and a compulsory question containing passages only for comment from the texts prescribed in (*a*) and from the texts in each of the groups prescribed in (*b*).

2. Plato, *Euthyphro and Meno*

The paper will include questions on the philosophical topics discussed in the dialogues. There will be a compulsory question containing passages for translation and comment.

B.

1. *Introduction to Logic*

As specified for section III of *Introduction to Philosophy* in the Preliminary Examination for Philosophy, Politics and Economics.

2. *Philosophical Problems*

Either Moral Philosophy, to be studied in connection with Mill's *Utilitarianism, or* General Philosophy, to be studied in connection with Descartes' *Meditations on First Philosophy* (trans. Cottingham, Cambridge University Press). Candidates will not be permitted to answer questions on both Moral Philosophy and General Philosophy. (Questions will not be confined to the detailed views of the authors of the set texts, and there will be no compulsory questions containing passages for comment. But the paper will be satisfactorily answerable by a candidate who has made a critical study of either of the set texts.)

C.

1. *Sophocles*

The prescribed plays are *Oedipus Tyrannus* and *Philoctetes.* Compulsory passages for translation and comment will be set from these. Candidates will also be expected to be familiar with *Antigone.* They will be required to scan a short passage of iambic trimeters taken from the prescribed plays.

2. *Thucydides and the West*

The prescribed text is Thucydides VI. Compulsory passages for translation and comment will be set from this book. Candidates will also be expected to be familiar with Thucydides VII and Plutarch, *Nicias.*

3. *Aristophanes' Political Comedy*

The prescribed plays are *Acharnians* and *Lysistrata.* Compulsory passages for translation and comment will be set from these. Candidates will also be expected to be familiar with *Frogs*. They will be required to scan a short passage of iambic trimeters taken from the prescribed plays.

D.

1. *Latin Elegy*

The prescribed texts are:

Propertius II. 1, 5, 7, 10, 13, 15, 16, 19, 28, 31–2, 34
Propertius III. 1–6, 8–12, 16–18, 20–5
Tibullus I. 1, 7–10
Ovid, *Amores* I. 1–7, 9–10, 13–15.

Compulsory passages for translation and comment, and a compulsory short passage for scansion, will be set from these. Candidates will also be expected to be familiar with Propertius I, with Callimachus, *Aetia* fr. 1, 2, 67–75 in the Loeb edition by C. A. Trypanis, and with Gallus fr. 2 in E. Courtney's *The Fragmentary Latin Poets* (Oxford).

2. *Cicero and Catiline*

The prescribed texts are: Sallust, *Catiline*; Cicero, *In Catilinam* I–IV, *Pro Sulla*; Asconius, *In orationem in toga candida.* Compulsory passages for translation and comment will be set from these.

3. *Tacitus and Tiberius*

The prescribed text is Tacitus, *Annals* I and III. Compulsory passages for translation and comment will be set from these books. Candidates will also be expected to be familiar with *Annals* II and IV–VI.

E.

1. *Homeric Archaeology and Early Greece from 1550 BC to 700 BC*

Evidence on the composition and history of the poems provided by extant archaeological remains, with special emphasis on burial practices, architecture, metals, and the world outside the Aegean. An overall knowledge will be required of the archaeological evidence for the Late Bronze Age and Early Iron Age of the Aegean from 1550 BC to 700 BC.

2. *Greek Vases*

The study of the general history of Greek decorated pottery from *c.*800 BC to *c.*300 BC, including study of the Attic black-figure and red-figure styles and of South Italian Greek vase painting. Knowledge will be required of the techniques used in making Greek pottery and in drawing on vases, also of the ancient names for vases and the shapes to which they refer. Candidates should in addition study the subjects of the paintings and their treatment by painters as compared with their treatment by writers and should be familiar with actual vases, for example those in the Ashmolean Museum.

3. *Greek Sculpture, c.600–300 BC.* The major monuments of archaic and classical Greek sculpture—their context and purpose as well as their subjects, styles, and techniques. Candidates will be expected to show some knowledge of the external documentary evidence, such as literary and epigraphic texts, on which the framework of the subject depends, and to be acquainted with the major sculptures of the period represented in the Ashmolean Cast Gallery. The examination will consist of one picture question and three essay questions.

4. *Roman Architecture*

The subject comprises the study of Roman Architecture from the Republic to the Tetrarchy in Italy and in the provinces, with particular reference to form, materials, technology, and function, and the movement of both materials and ideas.

F.

1. *Historical Linguistics and Comparative Philology*

The subject includes an introduction to the methods and aims of historical and comparative linguistics, the reconstruction of the Indo-European protolanguage and its development into Latin and Greek. The questions set will require specific competence in *one* of the two classical languages but not necessarily in both. An opportunity will be given for (optional) commentary on Greek or Latin texts.

VII. General Paper

One paper (3 hours). Candidates will be required to answer four questions. Questions will be set on each of the texts prescribed under III and IV above, and candidates must attempt at least two of these questions. A small number of more general questions will also be set, including one on metre.

VIII. Unprepared Translation from Greek

One paper (3 hours).

IX. Unprepared Translation from Latin

One paper (3 hours).

X. Greek Language

(See also the introductory note to paper V, VI)

One paper (three hours). The paper will be divided into two main sections:

(*a*) part (i) exercises designed to test Greek accidence and syntax;
part (ii) questions on selected passages from D. A. Russell, *An Anthology of Greek Prose* (OUP 1991), nos. 17, 18, 23, 24, 33, 40, 44, 66, 78;

(*b*) a passage for translation into Greek prose.

Candidates will be required to offer *either* both parts of (*a*) *or* (*b*).

XI. Latin Language

(See also the introductory note to paper V, VI)

One paper (three hours). The paper will be divided into two main sections:

(*a*) part (i) exercises designed to test Latin accidence and syntax;
part (ii) questions on selected passages from D. A. Russell, *An Anthology of Latin Prose* (OUP 1991), nos. 7, 12, 22, 23, 34, 52, 63;

(*b*) a passage for translation into Latin prose.

Candidates will be required to offer *either* both parts of (*a*) *or* (*b*).

XII. (Optional paper) Verse Composition or Additional Translation

This paper (3 hours) will consist of:

(*a*) passages for translation into Greek iambics and Latin elegiacs and hexameters, candidates being required to translate *one* passage;

(*b*) passages for translation into English from each of the following eight books, candidates being required to attempt passages from any *three* of them:

1. Pindar, *Olympian* 13, *Pythian* 4, *Nemean* 8, *Isthmian* 8; Bacchylides 3; D. A. Campbell, *Greek Lyric Poetry* (2nd edn, Bristol Classical Press, 1982) Archilochus 7, 196A; Mimnermus 1 and 2; Solon 1; Sappho 1, 16 and 31; Alcaeus 42, 129, 130; Ibycus 286 and 287; Anacreon 357, 358, 395 and 417; Theognis lines 237–54; Simonides 531 and 543
2. Callimachus, *Hymns* 3, 4; Theocritus 18, 22, 24; Bion 1
3. *Acts of the Apostles*; St. Paul, *First Epistle to the Corinthians*
4. Plutarch, *Antony*

5. Plautus, *Rudens*
6. Petronius, *Cena Trimalchionis*
7. Statius, *Thebaid* IX, X
8. St. Augustine, *Confessions* I–IV.

Candidates will be required to offer *either* (*a*) *or* (*b*).

Course IB

The Examination will consist of the following papers. In the assignment of honours, particular account will be taken of a candidate's performance in Papers I (Homer, *Iliad*), II (Virgil, *Aeneid*) and V, VI (Special Subjects).

I. HOMER, *ILIAD*

One paper (3 hours) of translation and questions. Passages for translation will be set from *Iliad* I, IX, XXII, XXIV. Candidates will be expected to show knowledge of the whole of the *Iliad*. They will also be required to scan a short passage.

II. VIRGIL, *AENEID* [Course IA paper II]

III. GREEK AUTHORS

One paper (3 hours) of translation from the following works: Euripides, *Bacchae*; Plato, *Meno*; Herodotus I. 1–94.

IV. LATIN AUTHORS [Course IA, paper IV]

V, VI. SPECIAL SUBJECTS

All candidates must offer *two* special subjects, one of which must be from Group A or B in the following list and the other from one of Groups C to F. Candidates who offer *only* two special subjects may not combine a subject from Group B with a subject from Group E. Candidates may offer a third special subject in lieu of Paper XI (Latin Language), provided that it is chosen from a different Group from their other two subjects. One three-hour paper will be set in each subject.

A.

1. Plato, *Euthyphro* and *Meno*

The paper will include questions on the philosophical topics discussed in the dialogues. Candidates will be expected to have read *Meno* in Greek and *Euthyphro* in English. There will be a compulsory question containing passages for translation and comment from *Meno*; any passages for comment from *Euthyphro* will be accompanied by a translation (to be taken from *The Last Days of Socrates*, tr. Tredennick & Tarrant (Penguin, revised 1993)).

2. Lucretius, *De Rerum Natura* IV

There will be a compulsory question containing passages for translation and comment from the prescribed book.

The paper will also include questions on the philosophical topics examined in that book, together with some questions of a more general character on Epicurean philosophy as expressed in *De Rerum Natura* as a whole.

B.

1. *Introduction to Logic* [Course IA, paper V, VI, B(1)]

2. *Philosophical Problems* [Course IA, paper V, VI, B(2)]

C.

1. *Sophocles*

The prescribed plays are *Oedipus Tyrannus* and *Philoctetes*. Compulsory passages for translation will be set only from *Oedipus Tyrannus*. Compulsory passages for comment will be set from both plays; passages set from *Philoctetes* will be accompanied by the English translation of H. Lloyd-Jones (Loeb). Candidates will also be expected to be familiar with *Antigone*. They will be required to scan a short passage of iambic trimeters taken from *Oedipus Tyrannus*.

2. *Thucydides and the West*

The prescribed text is Thucydides VI. Compulsory passages for translation will be set only from chapters 1–61. Compulsory passages for comment will be set from the whole book; passages set from 62–105 will be accompanied by the English translation of Crawley (reissued, Everyman 1993). Candidates will also be expected to be familiar with Thucydides VII and Plutarch, *Nicias*.

3. *Aristophanes' Political Comedy*

The prescribed plays are *Acharnians* and *Lysistrata*. Compulsory passages for translation will be set only from *Acharnians*. Compulsory passages for comment will be set from both plays; passages set from *Lysistrata* will be accompanied by the English translation of A. H. Sommerstein (Aris & Phillips 1990). Candidates will also be expected to be familiar with *Frogs*. They will be required to scan a short passage of iambic trimeters taken from *Acharnians*.

D.

1. *Latin Elegy* [Course IA, paper V, VI D(1)]
2. *Cicero and Catiline* [Course IA, paper V, VI D(2)]
3. *Tacitus and Tiberius* [Course IA, paper V, VI D(3)]

E.

1. *Homeric Archaeology and Early Greece from 1550 BC to 700 BC* [Course IA, paper V, VI E(1)]
2. *Greek Vases* [Course IA, paper V, VI E(2)]
3. *Greek Sculpture* [Course IA, paper V, VI E(3)]
4. *Roman Architecture* [Course IA, paper V, VI E(4)]

F.

1. *Historical Linguistics and Comparative Philology* [Course IA, paper V, VI F(1)]

VII. General Paper

One paper (3 hours). Candidates will be required to answer four questions. Questions will be set on each of the texts prescribed under III and IV above, and candidates must attempt at least two of these questions. The paper will also include a small number of more general questions, including one on metre.

VIII. Unprepared Translation from Greek

One paper (3 hours).

IX. Unprepared Translation from Latin [Course IA, paper IX]

X. Greek Language

One paper (three hours). The paper will consist of two main sections:

(*a*) part (i) exercises designed to test Greek accidence and syntax;
part (ii) translation into Greek of a short passage of English;

(*b*) translation into Greek of a longer passage of English.

Candidates are required to offer *either* both parts of (*a*) *or* (*b*). The passages set will be related, in their demands of vocabulary and syntax, to the Greek prose literature used in the elementary Greek instruction provided for the course.

XI. LATIN LANGUAGE [Course IA, paper XI].

(See also the introductory note to paper V, VI.)

XII. (OPTIONAL PAPER) VERSE COMPOSITION OR ADDITIONAL TRANSLATION (Course IA, Paper XII).

Course IC

The examination will consist of the following papers. In the assignment of honours, particular account will be taken of a candidate's performance in Papers I (Homer, *Iliad*), II (Virgil, *Aeneid*), and V, VI (Special Subjects).

I. HOMER, *ILIAD* [Course IA, Paper I].

II. VIRGIL, *AENEID*

One paper (3 hours) of translation and questions. Passages for translation will be set from *Aeneid* I, IV, VI. Candidates will be expected to show knowledge of the whole of the *Aeneid*. They will also be required to scan a short passage.

III. GREEK AUTHORS [Course IA, Paper III]

IV. LATIN AUTHORS

One paper (3 hours) of translation from the following works:
either Lucretius IV *or* Ovid, *Metamorphoses* VIII;
Cicero, *In Catilinam* I, *Pro Archia*
Catullus 1–17, 21–60, 69–70, 72–3, 75–9, 83–8, 92–6, 100, 101, 109, 115–16.

V, VI. SPECIAL SUBJECTS

All candidates must offer *two* special subjects, one of which must be from Group A or B in the following list and the other from one of Groups C to F. Candidates who offer *only* two special subjects may not combine a subject from Group B with a subject from Group E. Candidates may offer a third special subject in lieu of Paper X (Greek Language), provided that it is chosen from a different Group from their other two subjects. One three-hour paper will be set in each subject.

A.

1. *Early Greek Philosophy* [Course IA, paper V, VI A(1)]
2. Plato, *Euthyphro* and *Meno* [Course IA, paper V, VI A(2)]
3. Lucretius, *De Rerum Natura* IV [Course IB, paper V, VI A(2)]

B.

1. *Introduction to Logic* [Course IA, paper V, VI B(1)]
2. *Philosophical Problems* [Course IA, paper V, VI B(2)]

C.

1. *Sophocles* [Course IA, paper V, VI C(1)]
2. *Thucydides and the West* [Course IA, paper V, VI C(2)]
3. *Aristophanes' Political Comedy* [Course IA, paper V, VI C(3)]

D.

1. *Latin Elegy* [Course IIA, paper V, VI D(1)]

2. *Cicero and Catiline* [Course IIA, paper V, VI D(2)]
3. *Tacitus and Tiberius* [Course IIA, paper V, VI D(3)]

E.

1. *Homeric Archaeology and Early Greece from 1550 BC to 700 BC* [Course IA, paper V, VI E(1)]
2. *Greek Vases* [Course IA, paper V, VI E(2)]
3. *Greek Sculpture* [Course IA, paper V, VI E(3)]
4. *Roman Architecture* [Course IA, paper V, VI E(4)]

F.

1. *Historical Linguistics and Comparative Philology* [Course IA, paper V, VI F(1)]

VII. General Paper

One paper (3 hours). Candidates will be required to answer four questions. Questions will be set on each of the texts prescribed under III and IV above, and candidates must attempt at least two of these questions. The paper will also include a small number of more general questions, including one on metre.

VIII. Unprepared Translation from Greek [Course IA, paper VIII]

IX. Unprepared translation from Latin [Course IIA, paper VIII]

X. Greek language [Course IA, paper X]

(see also the introductory note to paper V, VI.)

XI. Latin Language [Course IIA, paper IX]

XII. (Optional Paper) Verse Composition or Additional Translation [Course IA, paper XII]

Course IIA

The examination will consist of the following papers. In the assignment of honours, particular account will be taken of a candidate's performance in papers I (Virgil, *Aeneid*) and V, VI (Special Subjects).

I. Virgil, *Aeneid*

One paper (3 hours) of translation and questions.

Passages for translation will be set from *Aeneid* I, II, IV, VI, and XII. Candidates will be required to translate *two* passages and to answer *three* questions. They will be expected to show knowledge of the whole poem. They will also be required to scan a short passage.

II, III. Latin Authors

Two papers (3 hours each). In each paper one passage will be set for translation from each prescribed text. Candidates will be required to translate *three* of the four passages set in paper II, and *all three* of the passages set in paper III. They will also be required to write a literary commentary on any one passage in each paper.

II
1. Lucretius IV
2. Catullus 1–17, 21–60, 69–70, 72–3, 75–9, 83–8, 92–6, 100, 101, 109, 115–16
3. Horace, *Odes* III
4. Ovid, *Metamorphoses* VIII.

III
1. Cicero, *In Catilinam* I, *Pro Archia*
2. Seneca, *Epistles* 28, 47, 53, 56, 57, 63, 77, 108, 114, 122
*3. Tacitus, *Annals* IV. 1–12, 28–43, 52–75.

---

* For the purposes of the General Paper (VII), candidates will be expected to have knowledge of the whole book, not merely the prescribed chapters.

IV. The Ancient City

The texts for study in translation will be Aristotle *Politics* I and III. 1–13 (Penguin Classics ed. T. J. Saunders); Polybius VI (in *Polybius: The Rise of the Roman Empire*, Penguin Classics ed. F. W. Walbank). Candidates will be expected to show knowledge of ancient and modern views of relevant aspects of both Greek and Roman civic life.

V, VI. Special Subjects

All candidates must offer *two* Special Subjects, one of which must be from Group A or B in the following list and the other from Groups D to F. One three-hour paper will be set in each subject.

A.

1. Lucretius, *De Rerum Natura* IV [Course IB paper V, VI A(2)]

B.

1. Plato, *Euthyphro* and *Meno*

To be studied in *The Last Days of Socrates*, tr. Tredennick & Tarrant (Penguin, revised 1993) and *Meno*, tr. Sharples (Aris & Phillips). The paper will include questions on the philosophical topics discussed in the dialogues. There will be a compulsory question containing passages for comment.

2. *Introduction to Logic* [Course IA, paper V, VI B(1)]

3. *Philosophical Problems* [Course IA, paper V, VI B(2)]

D.

1. *Latin Elegy*

The prescribed texts, from which compulsory passages for comment will be set, are:

Propertius II. 1, 5, 7, 10, 13, 15, 16, 19, 28, 31–2, 34
Propertius III. 1–6, 8–12, 16–18, 20–5
Tibullus I. 1, 7–10
Ovid, *Amores* I. 1–7, 9–10, 13–15.

Compulsory passages for translation will be set only from Propertius II. 1, 10; III. 1–6; Tibullus I. 1, 7–10; Ovid, *Amores* I. 1–7, 9–10. Passages for comment from Propertius II. 5, 7, 13, 15, 16, 19, 28, 31–2 and 34 and III. 8–12, 16–18 and 20–5 will be accompanied by the English translation of G. P. Goold (Loeb, 1990); those from Ovid, *Amores* I. 13–15 by the English translation of J. Barsby (Oxford, 1973; reprinted Bristol, 1979). Candidates will also be expected to be familiar with Propertius I. They will be required to scan a short passage taken from the texts prescribed for translation.

2. *Cicero and Catiline*

The prescribed texts, from which compulsory passages for comment will be set, are Sallust, *Catiline*; Cicero, *In Catilinam* I–IV, *Pro Sulla*; Asconius, *In orationem in toga candida*. Compulsory passages for translation will be set only from Sallust, *Catiline* and Cicero, *In Catilinam* IV. Passages for comment from Cicero, *In Catilinam* I–III and *Pro Sulla* will be accompanied by the English translation of C. Macdonald (Loeb, 1977) and from Asconius, *In orationem in toga candida* by the English translation of S. Squires (Bristol, 1990).

3. *Tacitus and Tiberius*

The prescribed text is Tacitus, *Annals* I and III. Compulsory passages for translation will be set only from *Annals* I. Compulsory passages for comment will be set from

Annals I and III; passages set from *Annals* III will be accompanied by the English translation of M. Grant (Penguin, revised ed. 1989). Candidates will also be expected to be familiar with *Annals* II and IV–VI.

E.

1. *Homeric Archaeology and Early Greece from 1550 BC to 700 BC* [Course IA, paper V, VI E(1)]
2. *Greek Vases* [Course IA, paper V, VI E(2)]
3. *Greek Sculpture* [Course IA, paper V, VI E(3)]
4. *Roman Architecture* [Course IA, paper V, VI E(4)]

F.

1. *Historical Linguistics and Comparative Philology* [Course IA, paper V, VI F(1)]

VII. GENERAL PAPER

One paper (3 hours). Candidates will be required to answer four questions. Questions will be set on all the texts prescribed under II, III above, and candidates must attempt at least two of these. The paper will also include a small number of more general questions, including one on metre.

VIII. UNPREPARED TRANSLATION FROM LATIN

One paper (3 hours).

IX. LATIN LANGUAGE

One paper (three hours). The paper will consist of two main sections:

(*a*) part (i) exercises designed to test Latin accidence and syntax;
part (ii) translation into Latin of a short passage of English;

(*b*) translation into Latin of a longer passage of English.

Candidates are required to offer *either* both parts of (*a*) *or* (*b*). The passages set will be related, in their demands of vocabulary and syntax, to the Latin prose literature used in the elementary Latin instruction provided for the course.

XII. (OPTIONAL PAPER) VERSE COMPOSITION OR ADDITIONAL TRANSLATION [Course IA, paper XII]

Course IIB

The examination will consist of the following papers. In the assignment of honours, particular account will be taken of a candidate's performance in Papers I (Homer, *Iliad*) and V, VI (Special Subjects).

I. HOMER, *ILIAD*

One paper (3 hours) of translation and questions. Passages for translation will be set from *Iliad* I, VI, IX, XVI, XXII, XXIV. Candidates will be expected to show knowledge of the whole of the *Iliad*. They will also be required to scan a short passage.

II, III. GREEK AUTHORS

Two papers (3 hours each). In each paper three passages will be set for translation, one from each prescribed text; candidates will also be required to write a literary commentary on any one passage.

II *1. Sophocles, *Antigone* 163–928, 1023–1114, 1155–1260
2. Euripides, *Bacchae*
*3. Aristophanes, *Frogs* 1–268, 674–1533.

III 1. Herodotus I. 1–94
2. Lysias 1, 16, 24
3. Plato, *Meno*.

IV. THE ANCIENT CITY [Course IIA, paper IV]

V, VI. SPECIAL SUBJECTS

All candidates must offer *two* Special Subjects, one of which must be from Group A or B in the following list and the other from Group C, E, or F. One three-hour paper will be set in each subject.

A.

1. Plato, *Euthyphro* and *Meno* [Course IB, paper V, VI A(1)]

B.

1. *The Introduction to Logic* [Cousrse IA, paper V, VI B(1)]
2. *Philosophical Problems* [Course IA, paper V, VI B(2)]

C.

1. *Sophocles* [Course IB, paper V, VI C(1)]
2. *Thucydides and the West* [Course IB, paper V, VI C(2)]
3. *Aristophanes' Political Comedy* [Course IB, paper V, VI C(3)]

E.

1. *Homeric Archaeology and Early Greece from 1550 BC* to 700 *BC* [Course IA, paper V, VI E(1)]
2. *Greek Vases* [Course IA, paper V, VI E(2)]
3. *Greek Sculpture* [Course IA, paper V, VI E(3)]
4. *Roman Architecture* [Course IA, paper V, VI E(4)]

F.

1. *Historical Linguistics and Comparative Philology* [Course IA, paper V, VI F(1)]

VII. GENERAL PAPER

One three-hour paper. Candidates will be required to answer four questions. Questions will be set on all the texts prescribed under II, III above, and candidates must attempt at least two of these. The paper will also include a small number of more general questions, including one on metre.

VIII. UNPREPARED TRANSLATION FROM GREEK [Course IB, paper VIII]

IX. GREEK LANGUAGE [Course IB, paper X]

XII. (OPTIONAL PAPER) VERSE COMPOSITION OR ADDITIONAL TRANSLATION (Course IA, paper XII)

Prescribed texts

In addition to editions specified in the above regulations, the following editions will be used in the examination; if more than one impression has appeared, the latest

---

* For the purposes of the General Paper (VII), candidates will be expected to have knowledge of the whole of these plays, not merely the prescribed portions.

will be used. Where no publisher's name is given, the book is published by the Clarendon Press.

Aeschylus: *Prometheus Bound*, Griffith (Cambridge University Press).
Aristophanes: *Acharnians*, Sommerstein (Aris and Phillips); *Frogs*, Dover; *Lysistrata*, Henderson.
Aristotle: *De Generatione et Corruptione*, Mugler (Budé); *Metaphysics*, *Jaeger; *Physics*, *Ross.
Asconius: *Clark.
Augustine: *Confessions* I–IV, Clark (Cambridge University Press).
Bacchylides: Snell and Maehler (Teubner).
Bion: *Gow (*Bucolici Graeci*).
Callimachus: Pfeiffer.
Catullus: *Mynors.
Cicero: *Clark.
Demosthenes; *Selected Private Speeches*, Carey and Reid (Cambridge University Press).
Euripides: *Bacchae*, Dodds.
Herodotus: *Hude.
Hesiod: *Solmsen.
Homer (including the Homeric Hymns): *Monro and Allen.
Horace: *Wickham and Garrod.
Livy: *Ogilvie.
Lucretius: Rouse-Smith (Loeb, 1975 edn. or later.
Lysias: *Hude.
New Testament: United Bible Societies, edn 3.
Ovid: *Amores*, *Kenney; *Metamorphoses* VIII, Hollis.
Petronius: *Cena Trimalchionis*, Smith.
Pindar: *Bowra.
Plato: *Symposium*, Dover (Cambridge University Press); *Euthyphro*, *Duke *et al.*; *Meno*, *Burnet.
Plautus: *Lindsay.
Plutarch: *Antony*, Pelling (Cambridge University Press).
Pre-Socratic Philosophers: Diels–Kranz, edn. 6 or later.
Propertius: Goold (Loeb).
Sallust: *Reynolds.
Seneca: *Select Letters*, Summers (Macmillan, repr. Bristol Classical Press).
Sophocles: *Lloyd-Jones and Wilson.
Statius: Mozley (Loeb).
Tacitus: *Annals* IV, Martin and Woodman (Cambridge University Press); other books, *Fisher.
Terence: *Adelphoe*, Martin (Cambridge University Press).
Theocritus: Dover (Macmillan, repr. Bristol Classical Press).
Thucydides: *Stuart Jones.
Tibullus: *Postgate.
Virgil: *Mynors.

Special Regulations for the Honour Moderations in Classics and English

A

1. Honour Moderations in Classics and English shall be under the joint supervision of the Boards of the Faculties of Classics and

* Oxford Classical Texts.

English Language and Literature and shall consist of such subjects as they shall jointly by regulation prescribe.

2. The Chairman of the Moderators in English Language and Literature shall designate such of the number of moderators as may be required for the English subjects of the examination for Honour Moderations in Classics and English, and the nominating committee for examiners appointed by the Board of the Faculty of Classics shall nominate such of the number of moderators as may be required for the Classics subjects of the examination. When these appointments shall have been made the number of moderators shall be deemed to be complete.

B

The committee appointed by the Boards of the Faculties of English Language and Literature and Classics to advise on the examination for the Honour School of Classics and English shall make proposals to the two boards for regulations for this examination.

Candidates shall take one of the following courses

1. Course I

Each candidate shall offer six papers, each of three hours' duration, as follows:

1. English Literature 1509–1600 (excluding the plays of Shakespeare).

2. *Either* English Literature 1600–1660 (excluding the plays of Shakespeare) *or* Old English translation and literature as specified for the Preliminary Examination in English and Modern Languages.

3. Critical commentary: passages for comment for the period 1509–1660 (a preliminary 15 minutes' reading time will be allowed for this paper).

4. Unseen translation from Greek and Latin. Candidates may offer either Latin or Greek or both. Two passages must be offered and in each language one prose passage and one verse passage will be set.

5, 6. Greek and Latin Literature. Candidates must offer two of the following. They must offer either (*a*) or (*b*), but may not offer both.

(*a*) Homer, *Iliad* I, VI, IX, XVI–XIX, XXI–XXIV.

(*b*) Virgil, *Aeneid* I–VI.

(*c*) Sophocles, *Antigone*; Euripides, *Bacchae*; Plato, *Symposium* 189 c–end.

(*d*) Catullus 1–17, 21–60, 69–70, 72–3, 75–9, 83–8, 92–6, 100–1, 109, 115–16; Ovid, *Metamorphoses 8*; Tacitus, *Annals* 4.

Both papers will relate to all the texts. Paper 5 will consist of essay questions and paper 6 will comprise passages for translation and comment.

The Moderators shall publish the names of candidates who have satisfied them in all six papers or all of papers 1, 2, and 3 or all of papers 4, 5, and 6.

In addition to editions specially prescribed in the above regulations, the following editions of Greek and Latin texts will be used in the examination. Where no publisher's name is given, the book is published by the Clarendon Press. An asterisk (*) indicates texts in the Oxford Classical Texts series; where more than one edition has appeared, the latest will be used.

Catullus. *Mynors.
Euripides, *Bacchae.* Dodds.
Homer. *Monro and Allen.
Ovid, *Metamorphoses* VIII, Hollis.

Plato, *Symposium*, Dover (Cambridge University Press).
Sophocles. *Lloyd-Jones and Wilson.
Tacitus, *Annals IV*, Martin and Woodman (Cambridge University Press).
Virgil. *Mynors.

2. *Course II*

Candidates for Course II shall be required:

(*a*) during their first year of study to have passed an examination under the auspices of the Board of the Faculty of Literae Humaniores during the Trinity Term. Candidates who fail to satisfy the examiners shall be permitted to offer themselves for re-examination during the following September. Each candidates shall offer two papers, each of three hours' duration, as follows:

(1) Greek or Latin texts. Candidates must offer either (*a*) or (*b*):

(*a*) Homer, *Iliad* I. 1–336; Sophocles, *Antigone* 1023–1114, 1155–1260; Lysias I.

(*b*) Virgil, *Aeneid* I. 1–367; Horace, *Odes* III.5, 7, 9, 13, 14, 18, 21, 26, 30; Seneca, *Epistles* 47, 77.

The paper will comprise passages from these texts for translation and comment.

2. Greek or Latin Language. The paper will consist of passages for unseen translation out of Greek or Latin and sentences for translation from English into Latin or Greek.

(*b*) during their second year of study, to offer papers as for Course I.

Special Regulations for the Honour Moderations in Computer Science

A

The subject of the examination shall be Computer Science. The syllabus and the number of papers shall be as prescribed by regulation from time to time by the Mathematical and Physical Sciences Board.

B

1. Each candidate shall offer four papers as follows:

CS1 Functional Programming, Data Structures, and Algorithms
CS2 Procedural Programming, and Digital Hardware
CS3 Mathematics for Computer Science
M1 (CS) Mathematics I.

Each paper will be of three hours' duration.

2. The syllabus for each paper will be published by the Computing Laboratory in a handbook for candidates by the end of Trinity Full Term in the academic year of the examination, after consultation with the Subfaculty of Computation (for papers CS1, CS2, and CS3) and the Subfaculty of Mathematics (for paper M1 (CS)). Each paper will contain questions of a straightforward character.

3. All candidates will be assessed as to their practical ability under the following provisions:

(*a*) The Director of the Computing Laboratory, or a deputy, shall make available to the examiners evidence showing the extent to which each candidate has pursued an adequate course of practical work.

(*b*) Candidates shall submit to the Chairman of the Moderators, Honour School of Computer Science, Examination Schools, Oxford, by noon on Monday of the fifth week of the Trinity Term in which the examination is being held, their reports of practical exercises completed during their course of study. For a report on a practical exercise to be considered by the moderators, it must have been marked by a demonstrator and must be accompanied by a statement that it is the candidate's own work except where otherwise indicated.

(*c*) The moderators shall take the evidence (*a*) and the reports (*b*) into account in assessing a candidate's performance.

4. The use of calculators is generally not permitted but certain kinds may be allowed for certain papers. Specifications of which papers and which types of calculators are permitted for those exceptional papers will be announced by the examiners in the Hilary Term preceding the examination.

Special Regulations for the Honour Moderations in Geography

A

The subjects of the examination, the syllabus and the number of papers shall be as prescribed by regulation from time to time by the Life and Environmental Sciences Board.

B

Each candidate shall offer five papers corresponding to the five sections of the schedule below.

Candidates shall submit to the examiners not later than noon on the Monday of the sixth week of Trinity Full Term their folders containing accounts of field work completed during their course of study (Section 4(*b*)). The fieldwork must be the equivalent of three days' field activity approved by the Head of the School of Geography and the Environment.

1. *Physical Geography* (3 hours)

The paper will examine the following topics, on the global scale and with regional examples: meteorology and climatology; geomorphology; drainage basin hydrology; ecosystems. Candidates will be expected to display a knowledge of the techniques required to study these topics and to incorporate the results of their own field work.

2. *Human Geography* (3 hours)

The paper will examine the following themes and the relationships between them at the global scale and with regional examples: the growth and distribution of world population; the origin, evolution, and distribution of human settlements; natural resource use and technological innovation; forms of territorial organization. Candidates will be expected to display a knowledge of the techniques required to study these themes and to incorporate the results of their own field work.

3. *Ideas in Geography* (2 hours)

The paper will require an examination of selected writings of individual authors working in the nineteenth and twentieth centuries who have importance to Geography. The authors and works will be those on a list prescribed by the Geography Undergraduate Teaching and Examining Committee which shall be obtainable from the School of Geography and the Environment on request from Monday of eighth week of Trinity Term in the year preceding that in which candidates will be examined.

4. *Geographical Techniques*

The subject will comprise theoretical and practical aspects of geographical techniques. Candidates will be expected to be conversant with problem-solving in both physical and human branches of the discipline. Details of the areas to be covered will be published in the School of Geography and the Environment during Michaelmas Full Term. The subject will be examined in two parts, the paper accounting for 75 per cent of the marks and the practical the remaining 25 per cent.

(*a*) *An examination paper of 3 hours*

The examination will include both practical and theoretical aspects of the subject. The examiners will not provide calculators, but will permit the use of any hand-held pocket calculators subject to the conditions set out under the heading 'Use of calculators in examinations' in the *Special Regulations concerning Examinations*.

(*b*) *Practical work*

A field-work folder comprising the equivalent of three days' field activity approved by the Head of the School of Geography and the Environment.

5. One subject chosen from the following list:

(*a*) *Social and Cultural Anthropology*

The comparative study of the world's civilizations and peoples, including cross-cultural, power-based and gender perspectives upon social practice and theories of human life. Specific topics will include production and consumption; transactions and modes of exchange; elementary aspects of kinship and marriage; belief systems and social control; political and social organization; classification; technology and social change; material culture and ethnographic resources; the impact of colonialism; space, place, and culture; environment and cultural landscapes in transition; land and property rights. Candidates will be expected to be familiar with appropriate ethnographic monographs.

(*b*) *Political History from 1919 to 1945*

The main developments in political history with special reference to the international relations of the principal states.

(*c*) *Plant Ecology*

The elements of ecology, including the concept of the eco-system. Communities, successions, and populations (their characteristics, interactions, and control). The physical and biotic environment. The management and mismanagement of natural systems, including the ecology of crop plants.

(*d*) *Introduction to Sociology*

Sociology and its relation to other disciplines. The logic and method of sociological inquiry. The social structure of contemporary societies; social relations and social institutions; the family, education, work and leisure; deviance. Social stratification; class, status, and party. Urbanization. Social order and social change.

(*e*) *Geomorphology of Britain*

Stratigraphic and tectonic background; denudation chronology; the Quaternary impact; regional geomorphology case studies; contemporary processes. The study of geomorphology in the field.

(*f*) *Modern Language*

Communication in French about topics in human and physical geography.

There will be a qualifying test in Michaelmas Term of each year (only undergraduates with A level or AS Level French may apply). Fifteen candidates will be selected; the course will not run with fewer than ten. The oral examination will be held at the end of the Hilary Term in which the course is taught by the Language

Centre. The written examination will be held with the remainder of Moderations in Trinity Term. The course will have thirty-two hours of instruction.

Special Regulations for the Honour Moderations in Mathematics

A

The subjects of examination shall be Mathematics and its applications. The syllabus and the number of papers shall be as prescribed by regulation from time to time by the Mathematical and Physical Sciences Board.

B

1. Each candidate shall offer four papers as follows:

A. Pure Mathematics I
B. Pure Mathematics II
C. Applied Mathematics I
D. Applied Mathematics II

2. The syllabus for each paper will be published by the Mathematical Institute in a handbook for candidates by the end of Trinity Full Term in the year preceding the examination, after consultation with the Subfaculty of Mathematics. Each paper will contain questions of a straightforward character.

3. The Chairman of Mathematics, or a deputy, shall make available to the moderators evidence showing the extent to which each candidate has pursued an adequate course of practical work. In assessing a candidate's performance in the examination, the moderators shall take this evidence into account.

4. No candidate shall be declared worthy of Honours who is not deemed worthy of Honours on the basis of papers A–D and no candidate shall be awarded a Pass who has not shown competence on these papers.

5. The use of calculators is generally not permitted but certain kinds may be allowed for certain papers. Specifications of which papers and which types of calculators are permitted for those exceptional papers will be announced by the examiners in the Hilary Term preceding the examination.

Special Regulations for the Honour Moderations in Mathematics and Computer Science

A

The subjects of the examination shall be Mathematics and Computer Science. The syllabus and the number of papers shall be as prescribed by regulation from time to time by the Mathematical and Physical Sciences Board.

B

1. Each candidate shall offer four papers as follows:

CS1 Functional Programming, Data Structures, and Algorithms
CS2 Procedural Programming, and Digital Hardware
M1 Mathematics I
M2 Mathematics II

Each paper will be of three hours' duration.

2. The syllabus for each paper will be published by the Computing Laboratory in a handbook for candidates by the beginning of Michaelmas Full Term in the academic year of the examination, after consultation with the Subfaculty of Computation (for papers CS1 and CS2) and the Subfaculty of Mathematics (for papers M1 and M2). Each paper will contain questions of a straightforward character.

3. All candidates will be assessed as to their practical ability in the subjects of papers CS1 and CS2 under the following provisions:

(*a*) The Director of the Computing Laboratory, or a deputy, shall make available to the examiners evidence showing the extent to which each candidate has pursued an adequate course of practical work.

(*b*) Candidates shall submit to the Chairman of the Moderators, Honour School of Computer Science, Examination Schools, Oxford, by noon on Monday of the fifth week of the Trinity Term in which the examination is being held, their reports of practical exercises completed during their course of study. For a report on a practical exercise to be considered by the moderators, it must have been marked by a demonstrator and must be accompanied by a statement that it is the candidate's own work except where otherwise indicated.

(*c*) The moderators shall take the evidence (*a*) and the reports (*b*) into account in assessing a candidate's performance.

4. The use of calculators is generally not permitted but certain kinds may be allowed for certain papers. Specifications of which papers and which types of calculators are permitted for those exceptional papers will be announced by the examiners in the Hilary Term preceding the examination.

Special Regulations for Honour Moderations in Mathematics and Philosophy

A

1. The subjects of Honour Moderations in Mathematics and Philosophy shall be (*a*) Mathematics, (*b*) Philosophy.

2. All candidates must offer both (*a*) and (*b*).

3. The Moderators shall indicate on the pass list each candidate who has not passed this examination, but has passed in one subject, and shall indicate in which subject the candidate has passed.

4. The examination shall be under the joint supervision of the Divisional Board of Mathematical and Physical Sciences and the Board of the Faculty of Philosophy, which shall appoint a standing joint committee to make regulations concerning it, subject always to the preceding clauses of this subsection.

5. (i) The Honour Moderators for Mathematics shall be such of the Moderators for Honour Moderations in Mathematics as may be required, not being less than three; those for Philosophy shall be nominated by a committee of which the three elected members shall be appointed by the Board of the Faculty of Philosophy.

(ii) It shall be the duty of the chairman of the Honour Moderators in Mathematics to designate such of their number as shall be required for Mathematics in Honour Moderations in Mathematics and Philosophy, and when this has been done and the Honour Moderators for Philosophy have been nominated, the number of the Honour Moderators in Mathematics and Philosophy shall be deemed to be complete.

B

The highest honours can be obtained by excellence either in Mathematics or in Philosophy provided that adequate knowledge is shown in the other subject of the examination.

1. Four papers shall be set in the examination. Each candidate shall take all four papers.

2. The papers will each be devoted to the appropriate sections of the schedule.

3. The use of calculators is generally not permitted but certain kinds may be allowed for certain papers. Specifications of which papers and which types of calculators are permitted for those exceptional papers will be announced by the examiners in the Hilary Term preceding the examination.

Schedule

Section 1. Pure Mathematics I
Section 2. Pure Mathematics II } as specified for Honour Moderations in Mathematics

Section 3. Elements of Deductive Logic.

Subjects to be studied include: propositional and predicate languages; truth tables; tableaux; relations; the critical application of formal logic to the analysis of English sentences and inferences (problems of symbolization; scope, truth-functionality, quantification, identity, descriptions); elementary metatherorems about propositional calculus (including the following topics: expressive adequacy, duality, substitution, interpolation, compactness, consistency, soundness and completeness). Some questions of a mathematical nature will be set.

The logical symbols and tableaux rules to be used are those found in Wilfrid Hodges, *Logic*, 2nd edition (Penguin Books). Philosophical questions about logic may be studied by reading Mark Sainsbury, *Logical Forms*, 1st or 2nd edition (Blackwell), Chapters 1–2.

Section 4. Introduction to Philosophy.

The paper will be studied in connection with Descartes' *Meditations on First Philosophy,* trans. Cottingham, Cambridge University Press; Frege, *Foundations of Arithmetic*, trans. J. L. Austin, Blackwell, 1980; and *The Leibniz–Clarke Correspondence,* ed. H. G. Alexander, Manchester University Press, 1956.

This paper, while not being confined to the detailed views of the authors of the set texts, will be satisfactorily answerable by a candidate who has made a critical study of these texts. There will be no compulsory question containing passages for comment. Candidates will be required to show adequate knowledge of both Descartes and Frege.

Special Regulations for the Honour Moderations and the Preliminary Examination in Music

A

1. The subjects of the examinations and the number of papers shall be as prescribed by regulation from time to time by the Board of the Faculty of Music.

2. In the case of candidates in the Preliminary Examination who have satisfied the Moderators in all the written and practical subjects the Moderators may award a distinction to those of special merit.

B

The regulations are the same both for Honour Moderations and the Preliminary Examination.

Each candidate will be required to offer papers 1–4 and one of the options in paper five.

1. *Techniques of Composition*

Candidates will be tested on basic compositional techniques in the context of eighteenth-century idioms. The examination paper will be available for collection in the Music Faculty Library from noon on Friday of the sixth week in the Trinity Term in which candidates are presenting themselves for examination. Completed papers must be submitted to the Chairman of Moderators in Music, Examination Schools, High Street, Oxford, not later than noon on Friday of the seventh week of the same term.

2. *Analysis*

A three-hour paper which will test the ability to produce analyses of the formal, structural, and motivic aspects of two pieces. Candidates will be required to write two essays: one on a piece from the early eighteenth century and one on a piece from the later eighteenth century. The essays will allow candidates to display their own interests in analytical method.

3. *History of Music*

A three-hour paper on general issues relating to the study of music history and on topics specified by the Board of the Faculty of Music. Candidates will be required to answer four questions.

The Board of the Faculty of Music shall approve, and publish each year by notice in the Faculty of Music not later than the end of the Trinity Term a list of the topics to be examined in the following academic year.

4. *Keyboard skills*

A practical examination in score reading and playing from a figured bass.

5. *Options*

Candidates must choose one from the following:

(*a*) *A portfolio of compositions*

Candidates will be required to submit two compositions, totalling between 10–12 minutes in performance, as follows:

(i) a work for *either* solo voice and piano *or* for four unaccompanied voices (SATB);

(ii) a work for one of the following:
string quartet (two violins, viola, and cello);
wind quintet (flute, oboe, clarinet, horn, and bassoon);
mixed ensemble, with or without piano but without percussion.

(*b*) *Performance*

A solo performance of some 10–12 minutes in length.

(*c*) *Extended essay*

An essay of 4,000–5,000 words on a subject to be chosen in consultation with the candidate's tutor.

The Board of the Faculty of Music will approve and publish by notice in the Faculty of Music not later than the end of the Trinity Term in the academic year preceding that in which the material is to be examined, an indicative list of possible titles for extended essays. This list is intended as guidance for tutors and candidates, not as an exhaustive list of acceptable titles.

Each portfolio submitted for the subjects of a portfolio of compositions and Extended essay must be accompanied by a declaration placed in a sealed envelope bearing the candidate's examination number and in the following prescribed form.

Form of Declaration

I, ..., hereby declare that this submission is my own work, except where otherwise stated, and that it has not previously been submitted, either wholly or in part, for any other examination.

Signed..

.... *College*

Date ....

Special Regulations for the Moderations in English Language and Literature

A

1. The subjects of the examination, the syllabus, and the number of papers shall be as prescribed by regulation from time to time by the Board of the Faculty of English Language and Literature.

2. A candidate shall be deemed to have passed the examination when he or she shall have satisfied the Moderators in all the papers specified in the regulations.

3. Candidates must offer all the papers at a single examination, except that a candidate must resit at the same time as the Preliminary Examination in English Language and Literature any paper or papers in which he or she has previously failed to satisfy the Moderators.

4. The Moderators may award a distinction to any candidate of special merit who has satisfied the Moderators in all the papers at a single examination.

B

Each candidate shall offer four papers, as set out below. The papers will be of three hours, with the exception of paper 1, which will be a two-hour paper.

1. *Text, Context, Intertext: An Introduction to Literary Studies*

Candidates will be expected to answer two questions, one on a topic connected with such technical and conceptual issues as genre, metre, rhetoric, narrative, realism, inter-textuality, and interpretation, the other on an issue connected with the variety of alternative critical approaches to literary texts.

2. One of the following:

(*a*) *Victorian Literature* (*1832–1900*)

(*b*) *Modern Literature* (*1900 to the present day*)

3. One of the following:

(*a*) *Introduction to Medieval Studies: Old English Literature*

The paper will contain a compulsory element involving a prose translation or commentary as specified in the English Undergraduate Handbook, Mods edition.

(*b*) *Introduction to Medieval Studies: Middle English Literature*

The paper will contain a compulsory commentary element as specified in the English Undergraduate Handbook, Mods edition.

4. One of the following: options (*a*), (*b*), (*c*), (*d*), (*h*), (*i*), (*j*), (*k*), and (*l*) will each contain a compulsory commentary element as specified in the English Undergraduate Handbook, Mods edition.

(*a*) *Victorian Literature (1832–1900)* (if not taken for paper 2).

(*b*) *Modern Literature (1900 to the present day)* (if not taken for paper 2).

(*c*) *Beowulf and its cultural background*

(*d*) *Middle English Dream Poetry*

(e) *Classical Literature*

Texts will be studied in translation. Candidates must show knowledge of at least *three* from the following list:

Homer, *Iliad*; Virgil, *Aeneid*; Ovid, *Metamorphoses*; Juvenal, *Satires*; Seneca, *Thyestes*; Sophocles, *Oedipus the King*; Aristophanes, *The Frogs*; Plautus, *Menaechmi*; Apuleius, *The Golden Ass*; Longus, *Daphnis and Chloe*.

(*f*) *Introduction to the Study of Language and Linguistics*

The paper will contain a passage for phonetic transcription and commentary. Candidates will be expected to show knowledge of such topics as modern linguistic theory, phonetics and phonology, the structure of words and sentences, meaning, regional and social variation in language, and principles and mechanisms of language change.

(*g*) *Introduction to Critical Theory*

Candidates will be expected to answer questions on such topics as the nature of literary language, the formation of English literature as a discipline, the canon, literary form, textuality and intertextuality, theories of narrative, interpretation, the production and reception of literary texts, the relation of literature to gender, sexuality, history, ideology, philosophy and psychoanalysis, and theories of culture, cultural difference, ethnicity, and the post-colonial.

(*h*) *Special author: Christina G. Rossetti*

(*i*) *Special author: Thomas Hardy*

The paper will be concerned with Thomas Hardy's prose writings and poetry.

(*j*) *Special author: Virginia Woolf*

(*k*) *Special author: Samuel Beckett*

(*l*) *Special author: Seamus Heaney*

Special Regulations for Law Moderations

A

1. The subjects of Law Moderations shall be:

(1) Roman Law.

(2) Introduction to Law.

(3) Criminal Law.

(4) Constitutional Law.

2. Every candidate who has passed in three subjects shall be deemed to have satisfied the Moderators, provided that

(*a*) he shall have passed in not less than two subjects at one and the same time, and

(*b*) he shall not be permitted to count any pass obtained in any subject before he satisfied the provision in (*a*).

3. Any candidate may offer himself for examination in one, two, or three subjects.

4. The Moderators may award a Distinction to any candidate of special merit who passes in three subjects at any one examination.

B

Every candidate who wishes to pass Law Moderations must offer Criminal Law and Constitutional Law and *either* Roman Law *or* Introduction to Law.

The individual specifications for Law Moderations subjects will be published in the Law Faculty Student Handbook for the academic year ahead by Monday of Noughth Week of Michaelmas Term each year.

Statutes and other source material

Details of the statutes and other sources of material which will be available to candidates in the examination room will be given in the teaching conventions. Any changes after the beginning of the academic year will be notified in a moderators' edict.

Special Regulations for the Moderations in Oriental Studies (Chinese)

A

1. The subjects and papers in the examination shall be as prescribed by regulation from time to time by the Board of the Faculty of Oriental Studies.

2. A candidate shall be deemed to have passed the examination when he or she shall have satisfied the Moderators in all the papers specified in the regulations.

3. Candidates must offer all the papers at the same time, except that a candidate may offer in the Preliminary Examination in Oriental Studies (Chinese) any paper in which he or she has previously failed to satisfy the Moderators.

4. In the case of candidates who have satisfied the Moderators in all the papers at a single examination, the Moderators may award a distinction to those of special merit.

B

Candidates offering Chinese are required

Either (*a*) during their first year of study to have passed an examination under the auspices of the Board of the Faculty of Oriental Studies during the eighth week of Trinity Term or in a resit during the following September

or (*b*) otherwise to have satisfied the faculty board as to their competence in Chinese.

Candidates will be required to offer three three-hour papers and to take an oral examination:

1. Modern Chinese prose composition and unprepared translation from Modern Chinese.
2. Spoken Chinese.*
3. Classical texts.
Translation from and comment on:
Mengzi 6a and *6b*, 1–5;
Shi ji (ed. Beijing: Zhonghua shuju 1959) 76.2365–70, col. 6, and 77.
4. History and civilization of China.

Special Regulations for the Moderations in Oriental Studies (Egyptology and Ancient Near Eastern Studies)

A

1. The subjects and papers in the examination shall be as prescribed by regulation from time to time by the Board of the Faculty of Oriental Studies.

2. A candidate shall be deemed to have passed the examination when he or she shall have satisfied the Moderators in all the papers specified in the regulations.

3. Candidates must offer all the papers at the same time, except that a candidate may offer in the Preliminary Examination in Oriental Studies (Egyptology and Ancient Near Eastern Studies) any paper or papers in which he or she has previously failed to satisfy the Moderators.

4. In the case of candidates who have satisfied the Moderators in all the papers at a single examination, the Moderators may award a distinction to those of special merit.

B

Candidates offering Egyptology and Ancient Near Eastern Studies are required to offer four three-hour papers:

1, 2

Either

Akkadian texts. (Lists are available from the Oriental Institute)

and

Akkadian grammar and unprepared translation.

Or

---

* The oral examination will be conducted in two parts: a comprehension test conducted in groups (for which up to 20 minutes will be allowed), and an individual test (up to 20–5 minutes).

In the comprehension test candidates will hear a passage or passages lasting up to five minutes and read twice by a native speaker or speakers. They will be allowed 15 minutes to give written evidence in English that they have understood the material.

Candidates will be required to read aloud a short passage in Chinese selected from texts that they have prepared during their course of study.

Candidates will be required to conduct a short conversation in Chinese with the Moderators in an imagined situation.

Egyptian texts: *Middle Egyptian texts*, ed. Baines and Smith. (Copies are available from the Oriental Institute)
and
Middle Egyptian grammar and unprepared translation.

3. Civilizations of the Ancient Near East.
4. History of the Ancient Near East to 30 BCE.

Special Regulations for the Moderations in Oriental Studies (Japanese)

A

1. The subjects and papers in the examination shall be as prescribed by regulation from time to time by the Board of the Faculty of Oriental Studies.

2. A candidate shall be deemed to have passed the examination when he or she shall have satisfied the Moderators in all the papers specified in the regulations.

3. Candidates must offer all the papers at the same time, except that a candidate may offer in the Preliminary Examination in Oriental Studies (Japanese) any paper or papers in which he or she has previously failed to satisfy the Moderators.

4. In the case of candidates who have satisfied the Moderators in all the papers at a single examination, the Moderators may award a distinction to those of special merit.

B

Candidates offering Japanese are required
Either (*a*) during their first year of study to have passed an examination under the auspices of the Board of the Faculty of Oriental Studies during the ninth week of Hilary Term or in a resit during the following September and to have spent a period of not less than ten weeks on an approved course of language study in Japan.
or (*b*) otherwise to have satisfied the Faculty Board as to their competence in Japanese.

Candidates will be required to offer four three-hour papers:

1. *Classical and modern texts*
   Hōjōki and *Tsurezuregusa*, section 137, in *Nihon koten bungaku zenshū*, vol. 27 (Tokyo: Shōgakkan, 1971), pp. 27–49 and 200–4, and Selected texts in modern Japanese (lists of texts are available from the Oriental Institute).
2. *Unprepared translation (Japanese to English) and grammar*
3. *Prose composition (English to Japanese) and the Japanese language*
4. *The history and culture of Japan.*

Special Regulations for the Moderations in Physics and Philosophy

A

1. The subjects of Moderations in Physics and Philosophy shall be (*a*) Physics and Mathematics, (*b*) Philosophy.

2. All candidates must offer both (*a*) and (*b*).

3. The Moderators shall indicate on the pass list each candidate who has not passed the examination, but who has passed in one subject, and shall indicate in which subject the candidate has passed.

4. The examination shall be under the joint supervision of the Board of the Faculty of Philosophy and the Mathematical and Physical Sciences Board, which shall appoint a standing joint committee to make regulations concerning it, subject always to the preceding clauses of this sub-section.

5. (i) The Moderators for Physics and Mathematics shall be such of the Moderators in the Preliminary Examination in Physics as may be required; those for Philosophy shall be nominated by a committee of which the three elected members shall be appointed by the Board of the Faculty of Philosophy.

(ii) It shall be the duty of the chairman of the Moderators in the Preliminary Examination in Physics to designate such of their number as shall be required for Mathematics and Physics in Moderations in Physics and Philosophy, and when this has been done and the Moderators for Philosophy have been nominated, the number of the Moderators in Physics and Philosophy shall be deemed to be complete.

B

Distinction can be obtained by excellence either in Physics and Mathematics or in Philosophy provided that adequate knowledge is shown in the other subject of the examination.

Candidates will be required to take five papers, as follows:

(*a*) three papers in Physics and Mathematics;

(*b*) two papers in Philosophy.

(*a*) *Physics and Mathematics*

Candidates will be required to take the following three papers:

CP1: *Mechanics & Special Relativity*

CP3: *Mathematical Methods*

CP4P: *Differential Equations & Waves.*

Their syllabuses shall be approved by the Sub-Faculty of Physics and published in the Physics Course Handbook not later than the beginning of Michaelmas Full Term for examination three terms thence. Except for papers for which their use is forbidden, the Moderators will permit the use of any hand-held calculator subject to the conditions set out under the heading 'Use of calculators in examinations' in the *Special Regulations Concerning Examinations* and further elaborated in the Physics Course Handbook.

(*b*) *Philosophy*

Candidates will be required to take two papers:

(1) Elements of Deductive Logic.

(2) Introduction to Philosophy.

(1) *Elements of Deductive Logic*

As specified for Honour Moderations in Mathematics and Philosophy.

(2) *Introduction to Philosophy*

This paper will be studied in connection with Descartes' *Meditations on First Philosophy,* trans. Cottingham, Cambridge University Press; *The Leibniz–Clarke Correspondence,* ed. H. G. Alexander, Manchester University Press, 1956 (to be studied principally as an introduction to the philosophy of space and time); and Frege, *Foundations of Arithmetic*, trans. J. L. Austin, Blackwell, 1980.

This paper, while not being confined to the detailed views of the authors of the set texts, will be satisfactorily answerable by a candidate who has made a critical study of these texts. There will be no compulsory question containing passages for comment. Candidates will be required to show knowledge of both Descartes and the Leibniz–Clarke correspondence.

Special Regulations for the Preliminary Examination in Ancient and Modern History

A

The Preliminary Examination in Ancient and Modern History shall be under the joint supervision of the Boards of the Faculties of Classics and Modern History and shall consist of such subjects as they shall jointly by regulation prescribe.

B

Every candidate shall offer four papers, as follows:

1. General History: any one of the following period papers I: 370–900 (*The Transformation of the Ancient World*), II: 1000–1300 (*Medieval Christendom and its neighbours*); III: 1400–1650 (*Renaissance, Recovery, and Reform*), and IV: 1815–1914 (*Society, Nation, and Empire*).

2. *Either* Greek History *c.*650–479 BC *or* Roman History 200–80 BC.

3. *Either The World of Homer and Hesiod* (Homer, *Iliad, Odyssey* (tr. Lattimore); Hesiod, *Works and Days* (tr. Wender, Penguin)); *or Augustan Rome* (as specified in the Handbook for the Preliminary Examination in Modern History); *or* any other Optional Subject specified for the Preliminary Examination in Modern History.

4. *Either* Approaches to History, as specified for the Preliminary Examination in Modern History; *or* Historiography: Tacitus to Weber, as specified for the Preliminary Examination in Modern History; *or* Herodotus, V. 26–VI. 131, to be read in Greek, ed. C. Hude (Oxford Classical Texts, 3rd edn., 1927); *or* Sallust, *Jugurtha,* to be read in Latin, ed. L. Reynolds (OCT, 1991).

For Herodotus and Sallust, candidates will be required to illustrate their answers by reference to the specified texts.

The individual specifications and prescribed texts for Optional Subjects, Approaches to History, and Historiography: Tacitus to Weber as specified for the Preliminary Examination in Modern History will be published for candidates in the Handbook for the Preliminary Examination in Modern History by Monday of Week 0 of Michaelmas Term each year for the academic year ahead. The individual specifications and prescribed texts for the Optional Subject *Augustan Rome* will be published for candidates in the Handbook for the Preliminary Examination in Modern History by Monday of Week 0 of Michaelmas Term each year for the academic year ahead. Depending on the availability of teaching resources, with the exception of Optional Subject 1, not all the Optional Subjects listed in the Handbook will be available to candidates in any given year. Candidates may obtain details of the choice for that year by consulting the Definitive List of Optional Subjects posted at the beginning of the first week of Michaelmas Full Term in the Modern History Faculty and circulated to Ancient and Modern History Tutors.

Candidates who fail one or more of papers 1, 2, 3, or 4 above may resit that subject or subjects at a subsequent examination.

Special Regulations for the Preliminary Examination in Archaeology and Anthropology

A

1. The Preliminary Examination in Archaeology and Anthropology shall be under the supervision of the Life and Environmental Sciences Board, and shall consist of such subjects as it shall by regulation prescribe.

2. The Chairman of the Moderators for the Honour Moderations in Archaeology and Anthropology shall designate such of their number as may be required for the Preliminary Examination in Archaeology and Anthropology.

B

1. Two papers shall be set in the examination, Paper 1 Introduction to World Archaeology and Paper 2 Introduction to Anthropological Theory.

2. All questions set shall be of an elementary and straightforward nature.

3. Paper 1 will be on the topics in Paper (1) and Paper (4) of the Schedule for Honour Moderations in Archaeology and Anthropology.

4. Paper 2 will be on the topics in Paper (2) and Paper (3) of the Schedule for Honour Moderations in Archaeology and Anthropology.

Special Regulations for the Preliminary Examination in Biological Sciences

A

1. The subjects of the examination, the syllabus, and the number of papers shall be as prescribed by regulation from time to time by the Life and Environmental Sciences Board.

2. The Chairman of the Moderators for Honour Moderations in Biological Sciences shall designate such of their number as may be required for the Preliminary Examination in Biological Sciences.

B

1. Three written papers shall be set in the examination, corresponding to the first three sections of the Schedule for Honour Moderations in Biological Sciences.

2. Paper 1 will be on topics specified in Section 1: *Organisms* of the Schedule for Honour Moderations in Biological Sciences.

Paper 2 will be on topics specified in Section 2: *Cells and Genes* of the Schedule for Honour Moderations in Biological Sciences.

Paper 3 will be on topics specified in Section 3: *Populations* of the Schedule for Honour Moderations in Biological Sciences.

3. The questions set may be of an elementary and straightfoward nature.

4. A practical examination and/or a computer/data handling exercise may be set in the case of candidates deemed to have an inadequate record of practical or class work.

Special Regulations for the Preliminary Examination in Chemistry

A

1. The subjects of the Preliminary Examination in Chemistry shall be Chemistry (comprising Inorganic, Organic, and Physical Chemistry) and Mathematics for Chemistry.

2. The number of papers and other general requirements of the Preliminary Examination in Chemistry shall be prescribed by regulation from time to time by the Mathematical and Physical Sciences Board.

B

1. Candidates in the Preliminary Examination in Chemistry must offer four subjects at one examination, provided that a candidate who has failed in one or two subjects may offer that number of subjects at a subsequent examination.

2. The subjects for the Preliminary Examination in Chemistry shall be taken from the annexed schedule. The syllabuses for Papers (1) to (4) shall be approved by the Subfaculty of Chemistry and published in the Chemistry course handbook and on the Chemistry www pages not later than the beginning of the Michaelmas Full Term for examination three terms thence. The syllabuses for Paper (5) shall be as for papers CP3 and CP4P in Moderations in Physics and Philosophy and published in the Physics course handbook not later than the beginning of the Michaelmas Full Term for examination three terms thence.

3. The four examinations will comprise Inorganic, Organic, and Physical Chemistry and either Mathematics for Chemistry, Mathematics 1 and Mathematics 2. Those students taking Mathematics 1 and Mathematics 2 will carry the average mark for the two papers towards the overall total.

4. Candidates shall be deemed to have passed the examination if they have satisfied the Moderators in four different subjects *either* at a single examination *or* at two examinations in accordance with the proviso to clause 1, and provided further that the same number of subjects as were failed at the first sitting have been passed at the same attempt at a subsequent examination.

5. In the case of candidates who offer all four subjects, the Moderators shall publish the names only of those who have satisfied them in two or more subjects. Candidates whose names do not appear on the pass list must offer four subjects at a subsequent examination. In the case of candidates who, in accordance with the proviso in clause 1, offer one or two subjects, the Moderators shall publish the names only of those who have satisfied them in each of the subjects offered.

6. The Moderators may award a distinction to candidates of special merit who have satisfied them in all four subjects at a single examination.

7. The Moderators will not provide calculators but unless otherwise specified will permit the use of any hand-held pocket calculator subject to the conditions set out under the heading 'Use of calculators in examinations' in the *Special Regulations Concerning Examinations* and further elaborated in the Course Handbook. Candidates taking subject 4 are restricted to models of calculators included in a list provided by the Chairman of the Moderators not later than the Wednesday of the fourth week of the Michaelmas Full Term preceding the examination.

8. Heads of laboratories, or their deputies, and the IT Training Officer, shall if requested make available to the Moderators records showing the extent to which each candidate has pursued an adequate course of laboratory work. A practical examination may be set for candidates whose record of practical work is not satisfactory. Notwithstanding the above, the moderators may set a practical examination for all candidates.

Schedule

The subjects shall be as follows:

(1) Chemistry 1: Inorganic Chemistry
(2) Chemistry 2: Organic Chemistry, including Biological Chemistry
(3) Chemistry 3: Physical Chemistry, including Physics
(4) Mathematics for Chemistry or
(5) Mathematics 1 and Mathematics 2

One $2\frac{1}{2}$ hour paper will be set for subects (1), (3), (4), one 3 hour paper for subject (2).

Special Regulations for the Preliminary Examination in Classical Archaeology and Ancient History

A

1. The Preliminary Examination in Classical Archaeology and Ancient History shall be under the joint supervision of the Life and Environmental Sciences Board and the Board of the Faculty of Classics, and shall consist of such subjects as they shall jointly by regulation prescribe.

2. The Chairman of the Moderators for Honour Moderations in Ancient History and Classical Archaeology shall designate such of their number as may be required for the Preliminary Examination in Ancient History and Classical Archaeology.

B

Every candidate shall offer three of the papers specified in the Regulations for Honour Moderations in Classical Archaeology and Ancient History, namely

1. *Aristocracy and democracy in the Greek world, 550–450 BC*, and
2. *Republic to Empire: Rome 50 BC to AD 50*, and
3. A special subject chosen from the topics specified *either* under III–IV A *or* under III–IV B of those Regulations.

Special Regulations for the Preliminary Examination in Classics

A

1. The subjects of the examination shall be:

(1) Unseen translation from one or both of the Greek and Latin languages.
(2) Translation from such Greek and Latin authors as the Board of the Faculty of Classics may from time to time by regulation require.
(3) Questions on the texts prescribed for Subject (2).

(4) Such Special Subjects as the Board of the Faculty of Classics may from time to time by regulation require.

2. A candidate shall be deemed to have passed the examination if he shall have satisfied the Moderators in all four subjects:

Provided that he shall have passed in not less than three of his four subjects at one and the same examination.

3. A candidate shall be allowed to offer himself for examination in one or four subjects:

Provided that no candidate may offer a single subject unless he has already satisfied the Moderators in three subjects.

4. The Moderators shall not publish the name of any candidate as having satisfied them in only one subject, unless that subject shall have been offered by the candidate as a single subject.

5. In the case of candidates who have satisfied the Moderators in all four subjects at a single examination, the Moderators may award a Distinction to those of special merit.

B

Candidates shall take one of the following courses IA, IB, IC, IIA, IIB.

Course IA

Candidates will be required to offer:

1. Greek and Latin Unprepared Translation.
2. Translation from the following books:
   (*a*) Homer, *Iliad* I, XXII
   (*b*) Euripides, *Bacchae*
   (*c*) Herodotus I. 1–119
   (*d*) Lysias 1, 10, 16, 24 and Demosthenes 54
   (*e*) Virgil, *Aeneid* VI
   (*f*) Horace, *Odes* III
   (*g*) Cicero, *Pro Murena*
   (*h*) Tacitus, *Annals* IV.

One passage will be set from each of (*a*) to (*h*), and candidates will be required to translate any *four* passages.

3. General Paper: questions on the texts prescribed for paper 2.
4. *Either*: any one of the Special Subjects listed under Honour Moderations in Classics Course IA, paper V, VI

Or: either Xenophon, *Anabasis*, Books I–IV or Caesar, *De Bello Gallico*, Books I, II, V, and VIII. Candidates will be required not only to translate passages but also to answer questions on the background, subject-matter, and interpretation of the books.

Course IB

Candidates will be required to offer:

1. Latin Translation, with simpler Greek Translation.
2. Translation from the following books:
   (*a*) Homer, *Iliad* I, XXII
   (*b*) Euripides, *Bacchae*
   (*c*) Herodotus I. 1–94

(*d*) Plato, *Meno*
(*e*) Virgil, *Aeneid* VI
(*f*) Horace, *Odes* III
(*g*) Cicero, *Pro Murena*
(*h*) Tacitus, *Annals* IV.

One passage will be set from each of (*a*) to (*h*), and candidates will be required to translate any *four* passages.

3. General Paper: questions on the texts prescribed for paper 2.

4. *Either*: any one of the Special Subjects listed under Honour Moderations in Classics Course IB, paper V, VI

Or: either Xenophon, *Anabasis*, Books I–IV or Caesar, *De Bello Gallico*, Books I, II, V, and VIII. Candidates will be required not only to translate passages but also to answer questions on the background, subject-matter, and interpretation of the books.

Course IC

Candidates will be required to offer:

1. Greek Translation, with simpler Latin Translation.
2. Translation from the following books:
   (*a*) Homer, *Iliad* I, XXII
   (*b*) Euripides, *Bacchae*
   (*c*) Herodotus I. 1–119
   (*d*) Lysias 1, 10, 16, 24 and Demosthenes 54
   (*e*) Virgil, *Aeneid* VI
   (*f*) Catullus 1–17, 21–60, 69–70, 72–3, 75–9, 83–8, 92–6, 100, 101, 109, 115–16
   (*g*) Ovid, *Metamorphoses* VIII
   (*h*) Cicero, *In Catilinam* I, *Pro Archia*

One passage will be set from each of (*a*) to (*h*), and candidates will be required to translate any *four* passages.

3. General Paper: questions on the texts prescribed for paper 2.

4. *Either*: any one of the Special Subjects listed under Honour Moderations in Classics Course IC, paper V, VI

Or: either Xenophon, *Anabasis*, Books I–IV or Caesar, *De Bello Gallico*, Books I, II, V and VIII. Candidates will be required not only to translate passages but also to answer questions on the background, subject-matter, and interpretation of the books.

Course IIA

Candidates will be required to offer:

1. Latin Translation: as specified for Honour Moderations in Classics Course IIA, paper VIII.
2. Translation from the following books:
   (*a*) Virgil, *Aeneid* VI
   (*b*) Catullus 1–17, 21–60, 69–70, 72–3, 75–9, 83–8, 92–6, 100, 101, 109, 115–16
   (*c*) Horace, *Odes* III
   (*d*) Ovid, *Metamorphoses* VIII
   (*e*) Cicero, *In Catilinam* I, *Pro Archia*
   (*f*) Seneca, *Epistles* 28, 47, 53, 56, 57, 63, 77, 108, 114, 122
   (*g*) *Tacitus, *Annals* IV. 1–12, 28–43, 52–75.

---

* For the purposes of the General Paper (3), candidates who offer this option will be expected to have knowledge of the whole book, not merely the prescribed chapters.

One passage will be set from each of (*a*) to (*g*), and candidates will be required to translate any *four* passages.

3. General Paper: questions on the texts prescribed for paper 2.

4. *Either: The Ancient City*, as specified for Honour Moderations in Classics Course IIA, paper IV

Or: any one of the Special Subjects listed under Honour Moderations in Classics Course IIA, paper V, VI

Or: Caesar, *De Bello Gallico*, Books I, II, V, and VIII. Candidates will be required not only to translate passages but also to answer questions on the background, subject-matter, and interpretation of the books.

Course IIB

Candidates will be required to offer:

1. Greek Translation: as specified for Honour Moderations in Classics Course IB, paper VIII.

2. Translation from the following books:

(*a*) Homer, *Iliad* I, XXII
(*b*) *Sophocles, *Antigone* 163–928, 1023–1114, 1155–1260
(*c*) Euripides, *Bacchae*
(*d*) *Aristophanes, *Frogs* 1–268, 674–1533
(*e*) Herodotus I. 1–94
(*f*) Plato, *Meno*.

One passage will be set from each of (*a*) to (*f*), and candidates will be required to translate any *four* passages.

3. General Paper: questions on the texts prescribed for paper 2.

4. *Either*: *The Ancient City*, as specified for Honour Moderations in Classics Course IIA, paper IV

Or: any one of the Special Subjects listed under Honour Moderations in Classics Course IIB, paper V, VI

Or: Xenophon, *Anabasis*, Books I–IV. Candidates will be required not only to translate passages but also to answer questions on the background, subject-matter, and interpretation of the books.

Special Regulations for the Preliminary Examination in Classics and English

A

1. The Preliminary Examination in Classics and English shall be under the joint supervision of the Boards of the Faculties of Classics and English Language and Literature and shall consist of such subjects as they shall jointly by regulation prescribe.

2. The Chairman of the Moderators for Honour Moderations in Classics and English shall designate such of their number as may be required for the Preliminary Examination in Classics and English.

---

* For the purposes of the General Paper (3), candidates who offer these options will be expected to have knowledge of the whole of these plays, not merely the prescribed portions.

B

The committee appointed by the Boards of the Faculties of English Language and Literature and Classics to advise on the Honour School of Classics and English shall make proposals to the two boards for regulations for this examination.

Candidates must offer *six* papers as specified for Honour Moderations in Classics and English provided that

(i) a candidate who has satisfied the Moderators in papers 4, 5, and 6 in Honour Moderations in Classics and English will be required to offer only papers 1, 2, and 3;

(ii) a candidate who has satisfied the Moderators in papers 1, 2, and 3 in Honour Moderations in Classics and English will be required to offer only papers 4, 5, and 6;

(iii) a candidate who has been prevented by illness or other urgent and reasonable cause from taking Honour Moderations in Classics and English and has been permitted by the Vice-Chancellor and Proctors to enter for the Preliminary Examination will be required to offer only papers 1, 2, 4, and 5 and 6, subject (*a*) or subject (*b*).

Papers will be of three hours' duration except that papers 5 and 6 set for candidates falling under proviso (iii) above may consist of two papers each of one-and-a-half hours' duration.

Special Regulations for the Preliminary Examination in Computer Science

A

The subject of the examination shall be Computer Science.

The syllabus and the number of papers shall be as prescribed by regulation from time to time by the Mathematical and Physical Sciences Board.

B

1. Two papers shall be set in the examination.
2. Paper 1 shall be on the topics prescribed for papers CS1 and CS2 of the regulations for Honour Moderations in Computer Science.
3. Paper 2 shall be on the topics prescribed for papers CS3 and M1 (CS) of the regulations for Honour Moderations in Computer Science.
4. Each paper will contain ten questions.
5. Each paper will be of three hours' duration.
6. All questions set shall be of an elementary and straightforward nature.

Preliminary Examination in Earth Sciences

A

1. The subject of the Preliminary Examination in Earth Sciences shall be Earth Sciences, including basic practical and mathematical techniques.

2. The number of papers and other general requirements of the Preliminary Examination in Earth Sciences shall be prescribed by regulation from time to time by the Mathematical and Physical Sciences Board.

B

1. The Preliminary Examination in Earth Sciences shall consist of 4 compulsory papers taken at one examination, subject to the conditions of cl. 5 below:

(*a*) Earth Sciences 1: Physics and Chemistry of the Earth
(*b*) Earth Sciences 2: Earth Materials
(*c*) Earth Sciences 3: Earth Surface Processes
(*d*) An approved paper in Mathematics

The syllabus for these papers shall be published annually in the course handbook, not later than the beginning of Michaelmas Full Term for examination three terms thence.

2. In addition to the above four papers a candidate in Earth Sciences shall be required:

(*a*) to submit to the Examiners such evidence as they require of the successful completion of practical and field work normally pursued during the three terms preceding the examination, and
(*b*) to submit to the Examiners such evidence as they require of the successful completion of work carried out in crystallography classes normally pursued prior to the examination.

3. Candidates shall be deemed to have passed the examination if they have:

(*a*) satisfied the Examiners in the four papers in clause 1 either at a single examination or at two examinations in accordance with clause 5, and provided further that the same number of papers as were failed at the first sitting have been passed at the same attempt at a subsequent examination, and
(*b*) satisfied the additional requirements in clause 2.

4. The Examiners may award a distinction to candidates of special merit who have satisfied them in all four papers in clause 1 in one examination and in the requirements of clause 2.

5. Candidates who fail in one or two papers listed in clause 1 may offer that number of papers at a subsequent examination. Candidates who fail more than two papers in clause 1 must resit all four papers at a subsequent examination.

6. Candidates who fail either (*a*) or (*b*) in clause 2 may be required to sit either a practical examination or a written examination in crystallography respectively.

7. In the case of candidates who offer all four papers of clause 1, the Examiners shall publish the names only of those who have satisfied them in two or more papers. Candidates whose names do not appear on the pass list must offer four papers at a subsequent examination. In the case of candidates who, in accordance with clause 5, offer one or two papers, the Examiners shall publish the names of only those who have satisfied them in each of the papers offered.

8. The examination conventions of each examination paper listed in clause 1 will be published annually in the course handbook.

Special Regulations for the Preliminary Examination in Economics and Management

A

1. The subjects of the Preliminary Examination in Economics and Management shall be:

(1) Introductory Economics

(2) Mathematics and Statistics for Economics and Management

(3) Introduction to Management.

2. A candidate shall be allowed to offer himself or herself for examination in one, two, or three subjects.

3. A candidate shall be deemed to have passed the examination if he or she shall have satisfied the Moderators in three subjects.

4. The Moderators may award a distinction to candidates of special merit who have passed all three subjects at a single examination.

B

Three three-hour papers will be set as follows:

Introductory Economics

As specified in the first paragraph of the regulation relating to the Introductory Economics paper of the Philosophy, Politics, and Economics Preliminary Examination.

Mathematics and Statistics for Economics and Management

Applications of mathematics and statistics in economics and management, including the following topics:

Mathematics: multivariate calculus (total and partial differentiation and integration of functions of one or more variables), constrained and unconstrained optimization, linear algebra (basic vector and matrix operations), applications to economics (including utility and profit maximization), applications to management (including planning, scheduling, and production).

Statistics: descriptive statistics (presentation of data, measures of central tendency and dispersion), statistical inference (elementary probability theory and probability distributions, sampling estimation and hypothesis testing), correlation and regression (correlation coefficients, correlation and causality, ordinary least squares regressions, statistical inference of simple regression equations), applications of the above topics in economics or management, further applications in statistics for management (including methods for categorical variables and analysis of variance).

Candidates will be required to answer questions from both sections of this paper.

Calculators may be used in the examination room subject to the conditions set out under the heading 'Use of calculators in examinations' in the *Special Regulations concerning Examinations.*

Introduction to Management

Historical context; organisational behaviour; strategic management; technology and operations management; accounting; finance; marketing, information management. Candidates may be charged for the provision of study packs.

Special Regulations for the Preliminary Examination in Engineering Science

A

The subjects of the examination, the syllabus, and the number of papers shall be as prescribed by regulation from time to time by the Divisional Board of Mathematical and Physical Sciences.

B

1. Candidates shall take four written papers of three hours each:

Paper P1 Mathematical and Computational Methods
Paper P2 Electrical and Digital Systems
Paper P3 Engineering Materials and Thermodynamics
Paper P4 Structures and Mechanics.

In addition Engineering Coursework (P5) shall be considered by the Moderators as equivalent to a written paper.

2. Candidates must offer all subjects at one examination provided that a candidate who fails in one, two, three or four written subjects may offer those written subjects at a subsequent examination.

3. Candidates shall be deemed to have passed the examination if they shall have satisfied the Moderators in all four written papers and in the engineering coursework *either* at a single examination *or* at two examinations in accordance with the proviso to clause 2. Any written subjects failed at the first sitting must be passed at the same attempt at a subsequent examination.

4. All candidates shall be assessed as to their practical ability in engineering coursework under the following provisions:

(*a*) The coursework shall be considered by the Moderators as equivalent to a written paper.

(*b*) The Chairman of the Sub-faculty, or a deputy, shall make available to the Moderators, by the date of the first written paper, evidence showing the extent to which each candidate has completed coursework.

(*c*) Candidates will not normally be required to submit their coursework. The Moderators may request coursework from some candidates. Such candidates will be named in a list posted by the day of the last written examination.

(*d*) Engineering coursework cannot be retaken. Failure of coursework will normally constitute failure of the examination.

5. In the case of candidates who offer all four written papers, the Moderators shall publish the name of candidates who have satisfied them either in the whole examination or in any written paper. In the case of candidates who, in accordance with the proviso of clause 2, offer one, two, three, or four written papers the Moderators shall publish the names only of those candidates who have satisfied them in each of the papers offered.

6. The Moderators may award a distinction to candidates of special merit who have passed all four written subjects and the engineering coursework at a single examination.

7. The Moderators will not provide calculators, but will permit the use of one hand-held pocket calculator from a list of permitted calculators published by the Chairman of the Sub-faculty not later than the end of the fourth week of the Trinity Full Term in the academic year preceding the examination.

Schedule

Paper P1: Mathematical and Computational Methods

Differential and integral calculus, Taylor's theorem: concept of linearization; simple expansions in power series: limits. partial differentiation, simple transformations of first-order partial differential coefficients. Multiple integrals and their evaluation by change of variables; Cartesian, cylindrical polar and spherical polar co-ordinates; Jacobians.

Complex algebra: the Argand diagram and de Moivre's theorem; phasors.

Solution of linear differential equations with constant coefficients; initial and boundary conditions; the use of the Laplace Transform; frequency response; poles and zeros.

Probability; conditional probability; expectation; Bayes' theorem; binomial, Poisson and normal distributions. Introduction to reliability and control charts.

Vectors and matrices; rotation and translation of axes, linear transformations; eigenvalues and eigenvectors of real symmetric matrices; application to coupled systems, normal modes.

Introduction to engineering computation. Algorithms and rounding error. Introduction to numerical integration and solution of ordinary differential equations. Sorting and searching. Fourier Series.

Paper P2: Electrical and Digital Systems

Charge, capacitance, magnetic flux, electromagnetic induction, inductance. Linear circuits operating under direct current, alternating current and transient conditions. Diodes and single bipolar transistors; incremental models and equivalent circuits; input and output impedances. Ideal operational amplifiers. Combinational and sequential logic.

Paper P3: Engineering Materials and Thermodynamics

A. Engineering Materials

Introduction to the classes of engineering materials. Elementary electron theory and the origin of interatomic forces. Metals, semiconductors, and insulators. The structure of crystalline and non-crystalline solids. The PN junction and simple solid state devices. Materials selection on the basis of electrical properties. Elastic properties of materials, materials selection for deflection-limited design. Yield of materials, plastic behaviour and tensile strength. Ductile and brittle fracture. Materials selection for load-limited design. Polymers and composites.

B. Thermodynamics

Basic concepts of fluid mechanics. Hydrostatics. Conservation of mass, momentum and energy. Bernoulli's Equation. Simple incompressible viscous flows. Turbulent flow in pipes and pipe circuits.

Thermodynamic concepts and definitions. First Law for closed and open systems. Internal energy and enthalpy; specific heats. Steady flow. Ideal and real gases; liquids and vapours. Thermodynamic processes for closed and open systems. Linked processes, simple cycles, cycle efficiencies. An introduction to combustion. Conduction, use of heat transfer coefficients.

Paper P4: Structures and Mechanics

Equilibrium: forces on a particle, rigid body and assemblies of rigid bodies in a plane. Loads, reactions and interactions. Statical determinacy. Forces in plane, pin-jointed statically determinate frames.

Definitions of stress and strain at a point. Hooke's law. Thermal strain. Plasticity of one-dimensional systems.

Shear force and bending moment in beams. Bending moment – stress – curvature relationships for homogeneous symmetrical beams. Displacements of beams by Macaulay's method and superposition methods. Elastic torsion of circular sections.

Kinematics: compatibility in simple static problems. Displacement diagrams for assemblies of rigid bodies and simple extensible bar frameworks. Kinematics of a particle under constant acceleration.

Dynamics of particles and non-rotating rigid bodies including systems with variable mass; rotation of bodies about fixed axes. Concepts of energy, work, power, momentum, and impulse.

Paper P5: Engineering Coursework

Practical exercises including: engineering science; computing; drawing and design communication; workshop practice and fabrication. Design, build, and test projects: structural/mechanical engineering; electrical engineering; computing.

Special Regulations for the Preliminary Examination in English and Modern Languages

A

1. Candidates in this Preliminary Examination shall be examined in English and one Modern Language. The modern languages that may be offered shall be those which may be offered in the Honour School of Modern Languages.

2. The subjects of the examination, the syllabus, and the number of papers shall be as prescribed by regulation from time to time by the Boards of the Faculties of English Language and Literature and Medieval and Modern Languages.

3. It shall be the duty (*a*) of the chairman of the Moderators for Moderations in English Language and Literature to designate such of their number as may be required for English in the Preliminary Examination in English and Modern Languages, and when this has been done the number of examiners in English shall be deemed to be complete; and (*b*) of the chairman of the Moderators for the Preliminary Examination for Modern Languages to designate such of their number as may be required for Modern Languages in the Preliminary Examination in English and Modern Languages, and when this has been done, the number of examiners in Modern Languages shall be deemed to be complete.

B

The Boards of the Faculties of English Language and Literature and of Medieval and Modern Languages shall appoint a standing joint committee to make, and to submit to the two faculty boards, proposals for regulations for this examination.

A candidate shall be deemed to have passed the examination if he shall have satisfied the Moderators in part 1 (a Modern Language) and part 2 (English).

The examiners may award distinctions in part 1 or in part 2 or in both to candidates who have done work of special merit in the part or parts concerned.

A candidate who has failed a subject or both the subjects in part 1 will be allowed to resit the subject or subjects in which he has failed at a subsequent examination in accordance with the regulations for the Preliminary Examination for Modern Languages. A candidate who has failed one or both of the papers in part 2 will be allowed to resit the paper or papers in accordance with Ch. VI, Sect. i. B, **§ 3, cl. 2.**

Part 1

Each candidate shall offer the following two subjects in the modern language:

(1) *Language papers* (one paper of three hours and two papers each of one-and-a-half hours).

As specified for papers I, IIA, and IIB in the regulations for the Preliminary Examination for Modern Languages.

(2) *Literature papers* (two papers, each of three hours).

As specified for papers III and IV in the regulations for the Preliminary Examination for Modern Languages.

Part 2

Each candidate shall offer the following papers, as specified in the regulations for Paper 1 to 3, of Moderations in English Language and Literature:

(1) Text, Context, Intertext: An Introduction to Literary Studies
(2) *Either* (*a*) Victorian Literature (1832–1900)
or (*b*) Modern Literature (1900 to the present day)
or (*c*) Introduction to Medieval Studies: Old English Literature
or (*d*) Introduction to Medieval Studies: Middle English Literature.

Special Regulations for the Preliminary Examination in English Language and Literature

A

1. The Preliminary Examination in English Language and Literature shall be under the supervision of the Board of the Faculty of English Language and Literature and shall consist of such subjects as it shall prescribe by regulation.

2. The Chairman of the Moderators for Moderations in English Language and Literature shall designate such of their number as may be required for the Preliminary Examination in English Language and Literature and the Moderators so designated shall set these and such other papers as may be required.

B

Each candidate must offer two papers as follows.

1. *Either* Victorian Literature (1832–1900) (as specified for paper 2 in Moderations in English Language and Literature).

Or Modern Literature (1900 to the present day) (as specified for paper 2 in Moderations in English Language and Literature).

2. *Either* Introduction to Medieval Studies: Old English Literature (as specified for paper 3 in Moderations in English Language and Literature).

Or Introduction to Medieval Studies: Middle English Literature (as specified for paper 3 in Moderations in English Language and Literature).

Candidates may not offer any paper in which they have already satisfied the Moderators in Moderations in English Language and Literature.

Special Regulations for the Preliminary Examination in European and Middle Eastern Languages

A

1. The Preliminary Examination in European and Middle Eastern Languages shall be under the joint supervision of the Boards of the Faculties of Medieval and Modern Languages and Oriental Studies and shall consist of such subjects as they shall jointly by regulation prescribe.

2. Candidates in this Preliminary Examination shall be examined (*a*) in one language from among those which may be offered in the Honour School of Modern Languages, and (*b*) in Arabic or in Hebrew or in Persian or in Turkish.

3. It shall be the duty (*a*) of the Chairman of the Moderators for the Preliminary Examination for Modern Languages to designate such of their number as may be required for European Languages in the Preliminary Examination in European and Middle Eastern Languages, and when this has been done the number of examiners in European Languages shall be deemed to be complete; and (*b*) of the Chairman of the Moderators for the Preliminary Examination in Oriental Studies to designate such of their number as may be required for Arabic, Hebrew, Persian, and Turkish in the Preliminary Examination in European and Middle Eastern Languages, and when this has been done the number of examiners in Middle Eastern Languages shall be deemed to be complete.

B

There shall be two subjects in the examination.

(1) *The European Language*

Candidates will be required to offer:

(i) Language papers in the European Language (one paper of three hours and two papers each of one-and-a-half hours).

As specified for Papers I, IIA, and IIB in the regulations for the Preliminary Examination for Modern Languages.

(ii) Literature paper in the European Language (one paper of three hours).

As specified *either* for Paper III *or* for Paper IV in the regulations for the Preliminary Examination in Modern Languages (Candidates offering French *must* offer Paper IV).

(2) *Language papers in the Middle Eastern Language*

Candidates will be required to offer two three-hour papers and, in the case of Arabic, an oral/aural examination.

Arabic

(i) Translation and precis into English.
(ii) Comprehension, composition, and grammar.
(iii) Oral/aural examination.

Hebrew

(i) Biblical and Modern Texts (1 Kings 17–2 Kings 2; S.Y. Agnon *Ha-mitpahat* in *Sippurim ve-aggadot* (Schocken).
(ii) Grammar and translation into Hebrew (Biblical and Modern).

Persian

(i) Texts:
Selected Persian Texts, ed. Gurney and Meisami (copies are available from the Oriental Institute).
(ii) Grammar and translation into Persian.

Turkish

(i) Prepared texts and unseen translation from Turkish. (This paper will be divided into two separate parts (each of $1\frac{1}{2}$ hours), one for translation of passages from *Selected Elementary Turkish Texts*, ed. Kerslake (copies available from the Oriental Institute), and the other for unseen translation from Turkish. The use of dictionaries will be permitted for the part of unseen translation).

(ii) Turkish grammar and translation into Turkish.

Candidates shall be deemed to have passed the examination if they shall have satisfied the examiners in subject (1) (The European Language) and subject (2) (Language papers in the Middle Eastern Language).

The examiners may award distinctions in either or both subjects to candidates who have done work of special merit in the subject or subjects concerned.

A candidate who has failed (i) or (ii) of subject (1) may resit the paper or papers at a subsequent examination in accordance with the regulations for the Preliminary Examination in Modern Languages. A candidate who has failed a paper or papers in subject (2) may resit that paper or papers at a subsequent examination.

§2. Special Regulations for the Preliminary Examination in Fine Art

A

1. No person who is not a member of the University may be admitted to the Preliminary Examination in Fine Art.

2. A candidate may enter his or her name for the examination not earlier than the third term from his matriculation.

3. The subjects of the examination shall be

(1) Drawing;
(2) Painting, Printmaking, and Sculpture;
(3) History and Theory of Visual Culture;
(4) Human Anatomy.

4. Candidates must offer all four subjects of the examination at the same time, provided that a candidate who has passed in at least two of the subjects but failed in the other subjects (or subject) of the examination may offer at a subsequent examination the subjects (or subject) in which he or she has failed.

5. The examination shall be under the supervision of the Committee for the Ruskin School of Drawing and Fine Art, which shall make regulations for the examination.

6. The examiners may award a distinction in the examination to any candidate.

B

I. Preliminary Examination in Fine Art

1. The examination shall include both practical and written work.

2. Every candidate will be required in respect of

(1) *Drawing*
to submit a portfolio of not less than twelve drawings in any medium;

(2) *Painting, Printmaking, and Sculpture*
(*a*) to submit evidence of study in each of these three areas which should comprise at least one painting, print, and sculpture (photographic evidence is acceptable); and
(*b*) *either* to choose one discipline (i.e. painting, printmaking, or sculpture) as his or her major course option and to submit at least three works in that

discipline, *or* to choose two disciplines as his or her course options and to submit at least two works in each;

(3) *History and Theory of Visual Culture*

(*a*) to submit three essays of about 2,000 words each on aspects of the history and theory of visual culture in accordance with the provisions of clause 3 of these regulations;

(*b*) to offer a paper on history and theory of visual culture;

(4) *Human Anatomy*

(*a*) to offer a paper on form and function in human anatomy.

(*b*) to submit notebooks and a portfolio of not less than six examples of supporting visual material on the candidate's work in human anatomy.

The work required by (1), (2), and (4) (*b*) above must be submitted to the Chairman of Examiners, Preliminary Examination in Fine Art, Ruskin School of Drawing and Fine Art, 74 High Street, in the case of the examination held in Trinity Term not later than noon on Monday in the seventh week of that term, and in the case of the examination held in the vacation preceding Michaelmas Term not later than noon on Wednesday in the week before Michaelmas Full Term.

3. Of the essays required by the provisions of clause (3) (*a*) of these regulations, one must be submitted not later than noon on the Friday of the ninth week of the Michaelmas Full Term preceding the examination, one must be submitted not later than noon on the Monday of the first week of Hilary Full Term preceding the examination and one must be submitted not later than noon on the Friday of the ninth week of the Hilary Full Term preceding the examination. One copy of these essays, which may be either typed or in manuscript, must be delivered to the Chairman of Examiners, Preliminary Examination in Fine Art, Examination Schools. Each essay must be accompanied by a certificate signed by the candidate that the essay has not been submitted for any previous examination, and that the essay is the candidate's own unaided work save for advice on the choice and scope of the subject, the provision of a reading list, and guidance on matters of presentation. This certificate must be submitted separately in a sealed envelope addressed to the chairman of examiners. The chairman of the examiners will announce the list of subjects on which the essays may be submitted by the end of the first week of the Michaelmas Full Term preceding the examination.

Special Regulations for the Preliminary Examination in Geography

A

1. The Preliminary Examination in Geography shall be under the supervision of the Divisional Board of Life and Environmental Sciences and shall consist of such subjects as it shall prescribe by regulation.

2. The Chairman of the Moderators for Honour Moderations in Geography shall designate such of their number as may be required for the Preliminary Examination in Geography.

B

1. Two papers shall be set in the examination, Paper 1 on Human Geography and Paper 2 on Physical Geography.

2. All questions set shall be of an elementary and straightforward nature.

3. Paper 1 will be on the topics in Section 2 of the Schedule for Honour Moderations in Geography.

Paper 2 will be on the topics in Section 1 of the Schedule for Honour Moderations in Geography.

4. Both papers will contain material relating to the written component of the Honour Moderations paper on 'Geographical Techniques'.

Special Regulations for the Preliminary Examination in Human Sciences

A

The examination shall be under the supervision of the Life and Environmental Sciences Board in accordance with the same arrangements as those established under clause 3 of the decree concerning the Honour School of Human Sciences.

B

1. The subjects of the examination shall be the five subjects listed below.

2. All candidates must offer all five subjects at one examination:
Provided that a candidate who has passed in two (or more) subjects but failed in the other subject (or subjects) may offer at a subsequent examination the subjects (or subject) in which he has failed.

3. A candidate shall be deemed to have passed the examination if he or she shall have satisfied the Moderators in all five subjects *either* at one and the same examination *or* at two examinations in accordance with the proviso to cl. 2.

4. In the case of candidates who have satisfied the Moderators in all five subjects in a single examination, the Moderators may award a distinction to those of special merit.

5. The examiners will permit the use of any hand-held pocket calculator subject to the conditions set out under the heading 'Use of calculators in examinations' in the *Special Regulations concerning Examinations*.

Subject 1. The Biology of Organisms including Humans

An introduction to the evidence for mammalian, primate, and human evolution.

Principles of mammalian physiology: the cell, body fluids, the cardiovascular and respiratory systems, reproduction, hunger and thirst, movement, the senses, and the integrative organization of the central nervous system.

Principles of ecology: ecosystems, plant and animal communities and numbers, biotic interaction, the impact of man on the environment.

One three-hour paper will be set.

Subject 2. Genetics and Evolution

Principles of genetics and evolution illustrated by examples from human and other organisms.

Mechanisms of evolutionary change: selection and adaptation, evolution of sex, altruism, kin selection and co-operation. Alternative models of evolution.

The genetic material—its nature, mode of action, and manipulation: the chromosomal basis of heredity; molecular genetics; mapping the human genome; sex determination; mutation at the level of the gene and the chromosome.

Mendelian inheritance; genetic variation in populations and its maintenance; quantitative variation and its genetic basis.

One three-hour paper will be set. The paper will be divided into two sections: (A) Genetics and (B) Evolution. Candidates will be required to answer four questions with at least one question from each section. Candidates shall submit notebooks containing reports, initialled by the demonstrators, of practical work completed during their course of study. These notebooks shall be available to the examiners at any time after the end of the first week of the term in which the examination is held, and shall be taken into consideration by the examiners. A practical examination may be set for candidates whose record of practical work is not satisfactory.

Subject 3. Society, Culture, and Environment

Social and Cultural Anthropology: the comparative study of the world's civilizations and peoples, including cross-cultural, power-based and gender perspectives upon social practice and theories of human life. Specific topics will include production and consumption; transactions and modes of exchange; elementary aspects of kinship and marriage; belief systems and social control; political and social organization; classification; technology and social change; material culture and ethnographic resources; the impact of colonialism; space, place and culture; environment and cultural landscapes in transition; land and property rights. Candidates will be expected to be familiar with appropriate ethnographic monographs.

Human Geography: Physical and human factors affecting the growth and distribution of world population; international migration and its consequences for ethnic diversity; historical and contemporary patterns of urbanization; urban spatial segregation on social, cultural and ethnic criteria; the behavioural consequences of urban social segregation.

One three-hour paper will be set, on which candidates will be required to answer four questions. The paper will be divided into two sections: (A) Social and Cultural Anthropology, and (B) Human Geography. Candidates will be required to display knowledge of both sections, and will be required to answer at least two questions from section (A) and at least one question from section (B).

Subject 4. Sociology and Demography

Sociology: Current and classic discussions of explanatory strategies and social mechanisms, models of individual action and the consequences of aggregation. Empirical research involving these approaches in areas of substantive sociological interest such as social class, ethnicity, religion, the family, politics.

Demography: Elementary aspects of population analysis. Comparative study of fertility, mortality and family systems in selected human societies. The long-term development of human population and its relation to habitat and resources. The demographic transition.

One three hour paper will be set. The paper will be divided into two sections: (A) Sociology and (B) Demography. Candidates will be required to display knowledge of both sections.

Subject 5. Quantitative Methods for the Human Sciences

The use and importance of statistics and quantitative methods in the human sciences. Graphs, scales, indices, and transformations. Frequency distributions and their parameters, including the binomial, normal, and Poisson distributions. Notions of probability and risk. Problems of sampling. Tests of statistical significance including t-tests, χ^2, and confidence intervals. Elementary analysis of variance, correlation, and regression.

One three-hour paper will be set, consisting mostly of examples taken from the human sciences. Graded questions will be set, not all of which will require numerical answers.

Preliminary Examination in Materials Science

A

1. The subject of the Preliminary Examination in Materials

Science shall be Materials Science, including basic practical and mathematical techniques.

2. The number of papers and other general requirements of the examination shall be as prescribed by regulation from time to time by the Mathematical and Physical Sciences Board.

B

1. The Preliminary Examination in Materials Science shall comprise four compulsory papers:

(*a*) Materials Science 1: Structure of Materials
(*b*) Materials Science 2: Properties of Materials
(*c*) Materials Science 3: Transforming Materials
(*d*) Mathematics for Materials and Earth Sciences

The syllabus for these papers shall be published annually in the course handbook, not later than the beginning of Michaelmas Full Term for examination three terms thence. In addition, Materials Science Coursework shall be considered by the Moderators as equivalent to a written paper.

2. Materials Science Coursework shall comprise practical work and work carried out in crystallography classes, and it shall be assessed under the following provisions:

(*a*) The coursework shall be considered by the Moderators as equivalent to a written paper.

(*b*) The Chairman of Subfaculty, or deputy, shall make available to the Moderators, by the date of the first written paper, evidence showing the extent to which each candidate has completed coursework normally pursued during the three terms preceding the examination.

(*c*) Candidates will not normally be required to submit their coursework. The Moderators may request coursework from some candidates. Such candidates will be named in a list posted by the day of the last written examination.

(*d*) If a candidate fails the coursework then the Moderators may require the candidate to present such evidence as they require that the candidate has successfully completed, before the date of the second written examination, coursework prescribed by the Moderators. The Moderators may require the candidate to undertake a practical examination or a written examination on crystallography.

3. Candidates shall be deemed to have passed the examination if they have:

(*a*) satisfied the Moderators in the four papers in clause 1 either at a single examination or at two examinations in accordance with clause 5, and provided further that the same number of papers as were failed at the first sitting have been passed at the same attempt at a subsequent examination, and

(*b*) satisfied the additional requirements in clause 2.

4. The Moderators may award a distinction to candidates of special merit who have satisfied them in all four papers in clause 1 in one examination and in the requirements of clause 2.

5. Candidates who fail one or two written papers listed in clause 1 may offer that number of written papers at a subsequent examination. Candidates who fail more than two written papers in clause 1 must resit all four written papers at a subsequent examination.

6. In the case of candidates who offer all four written papers of clause 1, the Moderators shall publish the names only of those who have satisfied them in two

or more papers. Candidates whose names do not appear on the pass list must offer four papers at a subsequent examination. In the case of candidates who, in accordance with clause 5, offer one or two papers, the Moderators shall publish the names of only those who have satisfied them in each of the papers offered.

7. The use of calculators in the papers listed in clause 1 is restricted to those models published annually in the course handbook.

8. The examination conventions of each examination paper listed in clause 1 shall be published annually in the course handbook.

Special Regulations for the Preliminary Examination in Mathematics

A

The subjects of the examination, the syllabus, and the number of papers shall be as prescribed by regulation from time to time by the Divisional Board of Mathematical and Physical Sciences.

B

1. Two papers shall be set in the examination.
2. Paper 1 will be on the topics in Papers A and B of Honour Moderations in Mathematics.
3. Paper 2 will be on the topics in Papers C and D of Honour Moderations in Mathematics.
4. Each paper will contain ten questions.
5. Each paper will be of three hours' duration.
6. All questions set shall be of an elementary and straightforward nature.

Special Regulations for the Preliminary Examination in Mathematics and Computer Science

A

1. The subjects of the examination shall be Mathematics and Computer Science. The syllabus and the number of papers shall be as prescribed by regulation from time to time by the Mathematical and Physical Sciences Board.

2. The Chairmen of the Moderators for the Preliminary Examination in Mathematics and for the Preliminary Examination in Computer Science shall respectively designate such of their number as may be required for Mathematics and for Computer Science in this examination.

B

1. Two papers shall be set in the examination.
2. Paper 1 shall be on the topics prescribed for papers CS1 and CS2 of the regulations for Honour Moderations in Mathematics and Computer Science.
3. Paper 2 shall be on the topics prescribed for papers M1 and M2 of the regulations for Honour Moderations in Mathematics and Computer Science.
4. Each paper will contain ten questions.

5. Each paper will be of three hours' duration.

6. All questions set shall be of an elementary and straightforward nature.

Special Regulations for the Preliminary Examination in Mathematics and Philosophy

A

1. The subjects of the examination, the syllabus, and the number of papers shall be as prescribed by regulations from time to time by the Divisional Board of Mathematical and Physical Sciences and the Board of the Faculty of Philosophy.

2. (i) The Moderators for Mathematics shall be such of the Moderators in the Preliminary Examination in Mathematics as may be required, not being less than two; those for Philosophy shall be nominated by a committee of which the three elected members shall be appointed by the Board of the Faculty of Philosophy.

(ii) It shall be the duty of the Chairman of the Moderators for the Preliminary Examination in Mathematics to designate such of their number as shall be required for Mathematics in the Preliminary Examination in Mathematics and Philosophy, and when this has been done and the Moderators for Philosophy have been nominated, the number of the Moderators for the Preliminary Examination in Mathematics and Philosophy shall be deemed to be complete.

B

1. Two papers shall be set in the examination, one on each of the subjects: (*a*) Mathematics, (*b*) Philosophy. Each candidate shall take both papers, provided that no candidate may take a paper on a subject previously passed in Honour Moderations in Mathematics and Philosophy or in the Preliminary Examination in Mathematics and Philosophy.

2. All questions set shall be of an elementary and straightforward nature.

3. *Paper (a): Mathematics*

As specified for Paper 1 of the Preliminary Examination in Mathematics.

4. *Paper (b): Philosophy*

As specified in Sections 3 and 4 of The Schedule for Honour Moderations in Mathematics and Philosophy, except that no question will be set on the Leibniz–Clarke Correspondence. Candidates will be required to answer two questions on the Elements of Deductive Logic, one question on Descartes, and one question on Frege.

Special Regulations for the Preliminary Examination in Modern History

A

The subjects of the examination, the syllabus, and the number of papers shall be as prescribed by regulation from time to time by the Board of the Faculty of Modern History.

B

Each candidate shall offer four papers, as follows:

1. History of the British Isles: any one of the following periods:.

(I) *c.*300–1087; (II) 1042–1330; (III) 1330–1550; (IV) 1500–1700; (V) 1685–1830; (VI) 1815–1924; (VII) since 1900.

2. General History: any one of the period papers I: 370–900 (*The Transformation of the Ancient World*), II: 1000–1300 (*Medieval Christendom and its neighbours*); III: 1400–1650 (*Renaissance, Recovery, and Reform*), and IV: 1815–1914 (*Society, Nation, and Empire*). Candidates will be given a wide choice of questions relating to themes in the history of the period and they are advised not to concentrate narrowly on a particular period or topic.

3. Optional Subject: any one of an approved list of subjects, examples of which are given below. A detailed list of Optional Subjects, including the prescribed texts, will be published in the Handbook for Preliminary Examination in Modern History by the Board of the Faculty of Modern History by Monday of noughth Week of Michaelmas Term each year for the academic year ahead. Depending on the availability of teaching resources, with the exception of Optional Subject 1, not all the Optional Subjects listed in the Handbook will be available to all candidates in any given year. Candidates may obtain details of the choice of options for that year by consulting the Definitive List of Optional Subjects posted at the beginning of the first week of Michaelmas Full Term in the Modern History Faculty and circulated to Modern History Tutors.

1. Theories of the State (Aristotle, Hobbes, Rousseau, Marx).
2. The Age of Bede *c.*660–*c.*740.
3. Early Gothic France *c.*1100–*c.*1150.
4. The English and Celtic Peoples, 1154–1216.
5. English Chivalry and the French War *c.*1330–*c.*1400.
6. Gunpowder, Compass, and Printing Press: Technology and Society in Renaissance and Early Modern Europe.
7. Witch-craft and witch-hunting in early modern Europe.
8. Nobility and Gentry in England 1560–1660.
9. Conquest and Colonization: Spain and America in the Sixteenth Century.
10. Culture, Society, and Politics in England 1700–1795.
11. Revolution and Empire in France 1789–1815.
12. Theories of War and Peace in Europe 1890–1914.
13. Industrial Work and Working-Class Life in Britain 1870–1914.
14. The World of Homer and Hesiod, as specified for Preliminary Examination in Ancient and Modern History.
15. Augustan Rome, as specified for Preliminary Examination in Ancient and Modern History.

4. *Either* (*a*) Approaches to History *or* (*b*) Historiography: Tacitus to Weber *or* (*c*) Foreign Texts *or* (*d*) Quantification in History, as specified in the Handbook for Preliminary Examination in Modern History.

Candidates who fail one or more of papers 1, 2, 3, or 4 above may resit that subject or subjects at a subsequent examination.

Special Regulations for the Preliminary Examination in Modern History and Economics

A

The Preliminary Examination in Modern History and Economics shall be under the joint supervision of the Divisional Board of

Social Studies, and the Board of the Faculty of Modern History and shall consist of such subjects as they shall jointly by regulation prescribe.

B

Every candidate shall offer four papers, as follows:

1. Introductory Economics, as specified for the Preliminary Examination in Philosophy, Politics, and Economics.

2. General History: any one of the periods specified for the Preliminary Examination in Modern History.

3. Optional Subject: any one of the following, as specified for the Preliminary Examination in Modern History:

Nobility and Gentry in England 1560–1680.

Industrial Work and Working-Class Life in Britain 1870–1914.

or Industrialization in Britain and France 1750–1870, which is available only for candidates for this examination.

4. *Either* (*a*) Approaches to History *or* (*b*) Historiography: Tacitus to Weber *or* (*c*) Foreign Texts *or* (*d*) Quantification in History, as specified for the Preliminary Examination in Modern History.

The individual specifications and prescribed texts for papers 3 and 4 above will be published in the Handbook for Preliminary Examination in Modern History by Monday of noughth Week of Michaelmas Term each year for the academic year ahead. Depending on the availability of teaching resources, with the exception of Optional Subject 1, not all the Optional Subjects listed in the Handbook will be available to candidates in any given year. Candidates may obtain details of the choice of options for that year by consulting the Definitive List of Optional Subjects posted at the beginning of the first week of Michaelmas Full Term in the Modern History Faculty and circulated to tutors.

Schedule

Note. The letter C against a text indicates that it is available as a photocopy from the History Faculty Library. The letter T against a text indicates that it is to be read in specially prepared translation.

INDUSTRIALIZATION IN BRITAIN AND FRANCE 1750–1870

This is a paper in comparative economic history and is concerned with the main relationships involved in the industrialization of these two countries.

The texts have been selected to exemplify British commentaries on economic developments in France and French perceptions of Britain's economic progress from 1750 to 1870.

A. Texts by British Authors:

A. Young, *Travels in France During the Years 1787, 1788 and 1789*, ed. Constantia Maxwell (Cambridge, 1950), pp. 279–300, 312–13. (Available in the History Faculty Library.)

C M. Birkbeck, *Notes on a Journey Through France in 1814*, 3rd edn. (London, 1815), pp. 99–115. (Bodleian reference 8θ R 88 BS.)

E. Baines, *History of the Cotton Manufacture in Great Britain* (London, 1835), pp. 512–26. (Bodleian reference 35. 734.)

C H. Colman, *The Agricultural and Rural Economy of France, Belgium, Holland and Switzerland* (London, 1848), pp. 20–40. (Bodleian reference 48. 105.)

C Great Exhibition, *The Industry of Nations as Exemplified in the Great Exhibition of 1851* (London, 1852), pp. 223–7. (Bodleian reference 177e. 15.)

c A. B. Reach, *Claret and Olives* (London, 1852), pp. 256–63. (Bodleian reference 203. b. 301.)

c F. Marshall, *Population and Trade in France in 1861–2* (London, 1862), pp. 156–207. (Bodleian reference 232. b. 61.)

T. E. Cliffe Leslie, 'The Land System in France', in *Systems of Land Tenure in Various Countries* (London, 1881), ed. J. W. Probyn, pp. 291–312. (Bodleian reference 24754. e. 174.)

B. Texts by French Authors (translated into English):

Leon Faucher, *Manchester in 1844: Its Present Condition and Future Prospects* (London, 1844), pp. 1–20 and 85–152. (Bodleian reference Gough Adds. Lancs., 8θ17.)

c A. P. A. Ledru-Rollin, *The Decline of England* (London, 1850), pp. 19–27, 27–32, 189–225, 249–62, 282–91, 328–47. (Bodleian reference 24712 f.43 [R].)

c H. A. Taine, *Notes on England* (London, 1872), pp. 153–75 and 272–99. (Bodleian reference 226. j. 172.)

c La Rochefoucauld, F. de, *A Frenchman in England* (Cambridge, 1933), pp. 157–242.

c Nickolls, Sir J., pseud. (i.e. R. B. Plumard de Danguel), *Remarks on the advantages and disadvantages of France and of Great Britain* (London, 1754), pp. 1–48.

c t F. Chaumont, *Mémoire sur la France et l'Angleterre* (1769).

D'Eichthal, G., *A French sociologist looks at Britain,* tr. and ed. B. M. Ratcliffe and W. H. Chaloner (Manchester, 1977), pp. 13–108.

Candidates who fail one or more of papers 1, 2, 3, or 4 above may resit that subject or subjects at a subsequent examination.

Special Regulations for the Preliminary Examination in Modern History and English

A

1. The Preliminary Examination in Modern History and English shall be under the joint supervision of the Boards of the Faculties of Modern History and English Language and Literature and shall consist of such subjects as they shall jointly by regulation prescribe.

2. The Chairmen of the Examiners for the Preliminary Examination in Modern History and of the Moderators for Moderations in English Language and Literature shall consult together and designate such of their number as may be required for the examination for the Preliminary Examination in Modern History and English, whereupon the number of examiners shall be deemed to be complete.

B

Each candidate shall offer four papers as set out below. The papers will be of three hours' duration except where otherwise specified. The Moderators shall publish the names of candidates who have satisfied them in the whole of the examination, or in papers 1 and 2 only, or in papers 3 and 4 only.

1. *The History of the British Isles* (any one of the periods specified for the Preliminary Examination in Modern History).

2. *One* of the following:

(*a*) One of the *Optional Subjects* specified for the Preliminary Examination in Modern History.

(*b*) *Approaches to History* (as specified for the Preliminary Examination in Modern History).

(*c*) *Historiography*: Tacitus to Weber (as specified for the Preliminary Examination in Modern History).

(*d*) *Quantification in History* (as specified for the Preliminary Examination in Modern History).

(*e*) *Foreign texts* (as specified for the Preliminary Examination in Modern History).

The individual specifications and prescribed texts for these papers will be published in the Handbook for the Preliminary Examination in Modern History by Monday of noughth Week of Michaelmas Term each year for the academic year ahead. Depending on the availability of teaching resources, with the exception of Optional Subject 1, not all the Optional Subjects listed in the Handbook will be available to candidates in any given year. Candidates may obtain details of the choice of options for that year by consulting the Definitive List of Optional Subjects posted at the beginning of the first week of Michaelmas Full Term in the Modern History Faculty and circulated to tutors.

3. *Text, Context, Intertext: An Introduction to Literary Studies* (two hours) (as specified for Moderations in English Language and Literature).

4. *One of the following:*

(*a*) *Victorian Literature (1832–1900)* (as specified for Paper 2, Moderations in English Language and Literature).

(*b*) *Modern Literature (1900 to the present day)* (as specified for Paper 2, Moderations in English Language and Literature).

(*c*) *Introduction to Medieval Studies: Old English Literature* (as specified for Moderations in English Language and Literature).

(*d*) *Introduction to Medieval Studies: Middle English Literature* (as specified for Moderations in English Language and Literature).

Candidates who fail one or more of papers 1, 2, 3, or 4 above may resit that subject or subjects at a subsequent examination.

Special Regulations for the Preliminary Examination in Modern History and Modern Languages

A

1. The Preliminary Examination in Modern History and Modern Languages shall be under the joint supervision of the Boards of the Faculties of Modern History and Medieval and Modern Languages and shall consist of such subjects as they shall jointly by regulation prescribe.

2. The chairmen of the examiners for the Preliminary Examination in Modern History and for the Preliminary Examination in Modern Languages shall respectively designate such of their number as may be required for Modern History and for Modern Languages in this examination.

B

Candidates are required to offer Modern History and any one of the languages that may be offered in the Honour School of Modern Languages. The examination shall be in two parts, as follows:

Part 1

Each candidate shall offer the following two subjects in the language:

1. *Language papers* (one paper of three hours and two papers each of one and a half hours).

As specified for papers I, IIA, and IIB in the regulations for the Preliminary Examination for Modern Languages.

2. *Literature papers* (two papers, each of three hours).

As specified for papers III and IV in the regulations for the Preliminary Examination in Modern Languages.

Part 2

Each candidate shall offer subject 3 and any one of the subdivisions of subject 4.

3. General History: any one of the periods specified for the Preliminary Examination in Modern History.

4. (*a*) A period of The History of the British Isles as specified for the Preliminary Examination in Modern History;
   (*b*) An Optional Subject as specified for the Preliminary Examination in Modern History;
   (*c*) Approaches to History *or* Historiography: Tacitus to Weber *or* Foreign Texts as specified for the Preliminary Examination in Modern History.

The individual specifications and prescribed texts for (*b*) and (*c*) above will be published in the Handbook for the Preliminary Examination in Modern History by Monday of noughth Week of Michaelmas Term each year for the academic year ahead. Depending on the availability of teaching resources, with the exception of Optional Subject 1, not all the Optional Subjects listed in the Handbook will be available to candidates in any given year. Candidates may obtain details of the choice of options for that year by consulting the Definitive List of Optional Subjects posted at the beginning of the first week of Michaelmas Full Term in the Modern History Faculty and circulated to tutors.

Candidates who have satisfied the Moderators in both parts shall be deemed to have passed the examination. The Moderators may award distinctions in either or both parts to candidates who have done work of special merit in the part or parts concerned.

Candidates who fail one or both subjects of part 1 may resit that subject or those subjects at a subsequent examination. Candidates who fail one or two subjects of part 2 may resit that subject or subjects at a subsequent examination.

Special Regulations for the Preliminary Examination in Modern History and Politics

A

1. The Preliminary Examination in Modern History and Politics shall be under the joint supervision of the Board of the Faculty of Modern History and the Social Sciences Board and shall consist of such subjects as they shall jointly prescribe.

2. The Chair of the Examiners for the Preliminary Examination in Modern History and the Chair of the Examiners for the Preliminary Examination in Philosophy, Politics, and Economics shall consult together and designate such of their number as may be required for the examination for the Preliminary Examination in Modern History

and Politics, whereupon the number of examiners shall be deemed to be complete.

B

Every candidate shall offer four papers as follows:

1. *Either* (*a*) any one of the periods in the History of the British Isles specified for the Preliminary Examination in Modern History *or* (*b*) any one of the four periods in General History specified for the Preliminary Examination in Modern History. For the First or Second Public Examination candidates are required to choose *at least one* paper—whether in General History or the History of the British Isles—covering a period before the nineteenth century. The list of papers satisfying this provision is given in the Handbook for Modern History and Politics. They are also required to choose *at least one* of the periods in The History of the British Isles at some point in their course, for either the First or the Second Public Examination. Candidates who take British History paper VII for the Preliminary Examination or the Final Honour School may not also take Politics core paper 202 for the Final Honour School.

2. Optional subject 1, 'Theories of the State (Aristotle, Hobbes, Rousseau, Marx)' as specified for the Preliminary Examination in Modern History.

3. Any *one* of the following, as specified for the Preliminary Examination in Modern History: (*a*) Quantification in History *or* (*b*) any of the Optional Subjects except No. 1 (Theories of the State), *or* (*c*) Approaches to History, *or* (d) Historiography: Tacitus to Weber, *or* (*e*) any one of the seven Foreign Texts.

4. *Introduction to Political Institutions*

Candidates will be required to answer *three* questions drawn from section (*b*) of the paper Introduction to Politics: The Theory and Practice of Democracy as specified for the Preliminary Examination in Philosophy, Politics, and Economics. Candidates must show knowledge of at least three of the following political systems: the United States of America; the United Kingdom; France; Germany.

In addition, candidates must also pursue a course of study in Information Technology, and are required to submit an information technology-based project by the first day of the Trinity Full Term in which the examination is taken. Details of the course are to be found in the First Year Handbook for Modern History and Politics.

A candidate shall be deemed not to have passed the examination unless he or she has submitted a satisfactory project for the Information Technology course (as described above). Any candidate who fails to submit a project for the Information Technology course by deadline, or whose project is deemed to be unsatisfactory, will be allowed to resubmit the project once by the Monday of the week falling three weeks before First Week of the following Michaelmas Full Term.

The individual specifications and prescribed texts for papers 2 and 3 above will be published in the Handbook for the Preliminary Examination in Modern History by Monday of noughth Week of Michaelmas Term each year for the academic year ahead. Depending on the availability of teaching resources, with the exception of the Optional Subject 1, not all the Optional Subjects listed in the Handbook will be available to candidates in any given year. Candidates may obtain details of the choice of options for that year by consulting the Definitive List of Optional Subjects posted at the beginning of the first week of Michaelmas Full Term in the Modern History Faculty and circulated to tutors.

Candidates who fail one or more of papers 1, 2, 3, or 4 above may resit that subject or subjects at a subsequent examination.

Special Regulations for the Preliminary Examination for Modern Languages

A

The languages, subjects, and papers in the examination shall be as prescribed by regulation from time to time by the Board of the Faculty of Medieval and Modern Languages.

B

Not more than two languages may be offered.

1. The languages which may be offered shall be Latin and Greek and those languages which may be offered in the Final Honour School of Modern Languages.* Candidates who offer both Latin and Ancient Greek shall be deemed to be offering one ancient language.

2. The subjects of the examination shall be:

(*a*) Language papers;
(*b*) Literature papers;
(*c*) Linguistics.
(*d*) Further Topics (for candidates taking French sole or German sole only).
(*e*) Russian Course B (for candidates who entered Oxford without A-level or equivalent knowledge of Russian).

3. A candidate shall be deemed to have passed the examination if he or she shall have satisfied the Moderators

either (i) in both subjects (*a*) and (*b*) in each of two languages, at least one of the languages being modern;

or (ii) in both subjects (*a*) and (*b*) in one modern language (other than Czech (with Slovak) or Celtic) and in subject (*c*);

or (iii) in both subjects (*a*) and (*b*) in *either* French or German and in subject (*d*) in the same language;

or (iv) in subject (*e*).

Provided that

(1) candidates must offer all the papers at one examination, provided that a candidate may at a subsequent examination offer any paper or papers in which he or she has previously failed to satisfy the Moderators; and
(2) a candidate shall not be required to resit a paper or papers in which he or she has satisfied the Moderators.

4. To a candidate who has done work of special merit in the papers concerned, the Moderators may award a mark of distinction in a language, and in Linguistics. A candidate may be awarded either one or two distinctions except that candidates taking the French-only or German-only examination may be awarded one distinction.

5. Candidates must offer:

Either: I, IIA, IIB, III, IV in two modern languages:
Or: I, IIA, IIB, III, IV in a modern language together with V, VI, and VII in Latin and/or Ancient Greek;
Or: I, IIA, IIB, III, IV in a modern language together with VIII, IX, and X in Linguistics.

---

* Czech (with Slovak) and Celtic may not be available in given years. Notice that these subjects will not be available will be given in the *Gazette* in the Trinity Term but one before the examination concerned.

Or: BI, BIIA, BIIB, BIII, and an oral test (for candidates admitted to Russian Course B). These papers may not be offered with papers V, VI, VII, VIII, IX, X.

6. *a. Language papers*

Modern Languages

I. Language I. 3 hours.

French: The paper will consist of: (*a*) monolingual exercises, instructions for which will be written in French; and (*b*) comprehension of a passage of modern prose with questions to be answered in French (one question will require candidates to write a short piece of continuous prose).

German: 'Deutsche Gesellschaft und Kultur seit 1890.' Reading comprehension (in German) on a passage which relates to the theme of the paper. One essay in German on a topic relating to the theme of the paper.

Italian: The paper will consist of: (*a*) audio or video listening comprehension exercises; (*b*) reading comprehension exercises; (*c*) one guided essay in Italian.

Spanish: The paper will consist of: (*a*) translation into Spanish: (*b*) an essay of approximately 500 words. $1\frac{1}{2}$ hours will be allowed for each part.

Portuguese: The paper will consist of: (*a*) audio or visual listening comprehension exercises; (*b*) translation into Portuguese; (*c*) monolingual exercises.

Russian: Translation into Russian and/or exercises in Russian.

Modern Greek: Translation into Modern Greek and exercises in Modern Greek.

Czech (with Slovak): (*a*) a modern English prose passage; and (*b*) English sentences testing basic grammar, both to be translated into *either* Czech *or* Slovak.

Celtic: (*a*) a modern English prose passage; and (*b*) English sentences testing basic grammar, both to be translated into Welsh.

II. Language II. The paper will be in two parts of $1\frac{1}{2}$ hours each.

French:
IIA. Translation from French of a prose passage.
IIB. Translation into French of a prose passage.

German:
IIA. Translation into German of a prose passage.
IIB. Translation from German of a prose passage in a modern literary register.

Italian:
IIA. Translation into Italian of a prose passage *or* sentences.
IIB. Translation from Italian. A passage of modern prose will be set.

Spanish:
IIA. Translation from Spanish.
IIB. An exercise in which candidates will make a schematic analysis of the discursive structure of a Spanish prose passage of approximately 700 words, and write a summary of its content in approximately 150 words, both in English.

Portuguese:
IIA. Translation from Portuguese of a prose passage in a modern literary register.

IIB. Translation from Portuguese of a prose passage in an informal register such as journalism, and an exercise or exercises in reading comprehension.

Russian: IIA. Translation from Russian. A passage of modern prose will be set.

IIB. Comprehension exercise. A modern passage in the language will be set to test comprehension. All answers in this paper will be in English.

Modern Greek: IIA. Translation from Modern Greek. A passage of modern prose will be set.

IIB. Comprehension exercises. A modern passage or passages in the language will be set to test comprehension. All answers in this paper will be in English.

Czech (with Slovak): IIA and IIB. One passage of modern prose in each paper for translation from Czech into English.

Celtic: IIA. A passage of Middle Welsh prose to be translated into English.

IIB. A passage of Old Irish prose *or* a passage of Modern Welsh prose to be translated into English.

Latin and Ancient Greek

V. Unseen translation. 3 hours.

Candidates may offer either Latin or Ancient Greek or both. Two passages must be offered, and in each language one prose passage and one verse passage will be set.

b. Literature papers

Modern Languages

III. Literature I. 3 hours.

French: Short texts. Candidates will be required to study six brief but self-contained works arranged in three contrasting pairs:

A Montaigne, 'Des coches' from the *Essais*
Graffigny, *Lettres d'une Péruvienne.*

B Baudelaire, *'Spleen et Idéal'* from *Les Fleurs du Mal*, with 30 poems to be identified for detailed study
Aimé Césaire, *Cahier d'un retour au pays natal*

C Racine, *Phèdre*
Beckett, *En attendant Godot*

The paper will be examined by commentary only, with all texts set, and candidates required to offer three passages, one from each of sections A, B and C.

German: Commentary. Two commentaries on a choice of poems taken from an anthology, which will include some medieval poems. One commentary on an extract from one of the set texts listed under paper IV. Each year two such texts will be designated as the ones from which an extract for commentary may be taken. Texts to be studied for commentary in any given year will be published in the *University Gazette* during noughth week of Michaelmas Term each year.

Italian: Aspects of Italian lyric poetry. Compulsory passages for explanation and detailed comment will be set.

The sonnet from the Middle Ages to the present. (Copies of the list of sonnets for the examinations in the academic year concerned will be available in the Modern Languages Faculty Office,

41 Wellington Square, from the beginning of the Michaelmas Full Term of the year).

Ungaretti, Selections from *L'Allegria* and *Sentimento del tempo* (in Giuseppe Ungaretti, *Vita d'un uomo, 106 poesie 1914–1960,* Mondadori Oscar).

Spanish: Prescribed texts to be studied in relation to various possible approaches to literature. One compulsory passage will be set for translation into English and one for commentary. Candidates will also be required to undertake two essays, to be written on texts other than the one from which the passage chosen for commentary was taken.

M. Vargas Llosa, *La fiesta del chiro.*

Antonio Machado, *Campos de Castilla* (excluding 'La tierra de Alvargonzález', but including 'Elogios': in *Poesías completas*, Selecciones Austral).

Calderón de la Barca, *El médico du su honra* (ed. D. W. Cruickshank, Clásicos Castalia).

Cervantes, 'Rinconete y Cortadillo', from vol. 1 of *Novelas ejemplares*, ed. H. Sieber, 2 vols. (Madrid: Cátedra, 1989).

Portuguese: Prescribed texts to be studied in relation to various possible approaches to literature. Compulsory passages for explanation and detailed comment will be set. There will be a compulsory essay or commentary question on each of the set texts.

Mário de Sá-Carneiro, *A confissão de Lúcio*

Graciliano Ramos, *São Bernardo*

Clarice Lispector, *Laços de família.*

Russian: Poetry. The examination will consist of three commentaries, each on a different author, on the set works by five authors detailed below. One commentary passage will be compulsory.

Derzhavin, *Felitsa*

Pushkin, *Mednyi vsadnik*

Lermontov, *Mtsyri*

Blok, *Na pole Kulikovom* and *Dvenadtsat'*

Akhmatova, *Rekviem*

Examiners may give some guidance to candidates about how to approach the passages set for commentary; they may also require candidates to translate some portion of the passages set for commentary into English.

Modern Greek: *War, society and culture in twentieth-century Greece.* Candidates will be examined on their knowledge of two topics. For each topic there is also one prescribed novel that deals with the topic. The topics and prescribed texts are: (1) The Asia Minor Disaster: its political and cultural background and its repercussions (text: Dido Sotiriou, *Matomena chomata*); and (2) Dictatorship and War: Greek history, society and culture 1936–49 (text: Kostas Tachtisis, *To trito stefani*).

The paper will consist of a choice of questions on topics 1 and 2. Candidates must answer three questions. Each candidate must answer *either* one question relating to each of the historical topics and one to a literary text, *or* one question on history and one on each of the two literary texts.

Czech (with Slovak): Prescribed texts to be studied as literature. Three compulsory passages for commentary will be set.

Short stories:

Milan Kundera, *Falešný autostop*

Bohumil Hrabal, *Pábitelé*

Ota Pavel, *Zlatí úhoři*

Jan Neruda, *Doktor Kazisvět*

Celtic: Prescribed texts to be studied as literature. Commentary. One commentary on a poem taken from an anthology. Poems will be set from:

Oxford Book of Welsh Verse, ed. T. Parry (Oxford: Oxford University Press, 1962), nos. 31, 40, 78, 298, 318.

Early Irish Lyrics, ed. G. Murphy (Oxford: Oxford University Press, 1956; repr. Dublin: Four Courts Press, 1998), nos. 5, 7, 11, 35, 36.

and Two commentaries on extracts from the texts listed under paper IV.

IV. Literature II: Prescribed texts. 3 hours.

French: French narrative fiction:

La Chastelaine de Vergi

Laclos, *Los Liaisons dangereuses*

Balzac, *La Peau de chagrin*

Proust, *Combray*

The paper will be examined entirely by essay, with candidates required to answer on *three* texts. There will be a choice of questions on each text, and candidates will be encouraged to make connections and comparisons between texts where appropriate.

German: Three essays from a choice of questions on the set texts covering genre, themes and period:

Prose:

Fontane, *Die Poggenpuhls*

Kafka, *Die Verwandlung*

Thomas Mann, *Mario und der Zauberer*

Remarque, *Im westen nichts Neues*

Drama:

Wedekind, *Frühlings Erwachen*

Schnitzler, *Liebelei*

Kaiser, *Von morgens bis mitternachts*

Brecht, *Die Dreigroschenoper*

Italian: Candidates will be expected to show knowledge of four of the six set texts listed below. Candidates will be expected to have such knowledge of the literary, intellectual, and historical background as is necessary for the understanding of these texts. Compulsory passages for commentary will not be set in the examination.

Modern Italian Narrative

Primo Levi, *Se questo è un uomo*

Cesare Pavese, *La luna e i falò*

Leonardo Sciascia, *A ciascuno il suo*

Natalia Ginzburg, *Lessico famigliare*

Italo Calvino, *Palomar*

Antonio Tabucchi, *Sostiene Pereira*

Spanish: Prescribed texts to be studied in relation to general trends in literature or thought or to historical background. Compulsory passages for explanation and detailed comment will *not* be set.

The Spanish Ballad Tradition:

Traditional romances:

El romancero viejo (ed. M. Díaz Roig, Cátedra, Madrid, 1979), poems Nos. 1–3, 5–6, 8–9, 11, 13–14, 23–4, 29–32, 38–59, 63–6, 68, 71–3, 76, 78, 83, 85–6, 88, 91, 94, 96–9, 101, 104, 111, 115–9, 121, 125–8.

Golden Age:

Lope de Vega, *Lírica* (ed. J. M. Blecua, Clásicos Castalia), poems Nos. 1–2, 6–10, 125, and 126.

Góngora, *Romances* (ed. Antonio Carreño, Cátedra, Madrid, 1982), poems Nos. 3, 10–11, 15–16, 18, 23, 27, 48, 52, 58, and 79.

Francisco de Quevedo, *Poemas escogidos* (ed. J. M. Blecua, Clásicos Castallia, Madrid), poems Nos. 155, 160, 165, 167, and 172.

Nineteenth and Twentieth Centuries:

Duque de Rivas, *El conde de Villamediana; El Alcázar de Sevilla; El fratricidio; Bailén* (from *Romances históricos,* ed. S. García, Cátedra).

Antonio Machado, 'La tierra de Alvargonzález' (from *Poesías completas,* Selecciones Austral).

F. García Lorca, *Romancero gitano* (ed. Mario Hernández, Alianza).

Portuguese: The examination will consist of:

(*a*) a commentary on passsages chosen from two of the set texts given below; (*b*) an essay, on one of the remaining three texts; (*c*) an essay on the historical development of the *auto*. Candidates will be expected to show knowledge of at least one text from each of groups A, B, and C below.

A	Gil Vicente	*Auto da Barca do Inferno* *Auto da India*
B	Almeida Garrett	*Um auto de Gil Vicente*
C	Suassuna	*Auto da Compadecida*
	Cabral de Melo Neto	*Vida e Morte Severina*

Russian: The paper will consist of: (*a*) one compulsory commentary; and (*b*) two essays each from a choice of two covering the other two set authors. Examiners may give some guidance to candidates about how to approach the passage set for commentary; they may also require candidates to translate some portion of the passage set for commentary into English.

Pushkin, *Pikovaya dama*

Chekhov, *Sluchai iz praktiki; Anna na shee; Dom s mezoninom*

Zoshchenko, *Ispoved', Agitator, Banya, Obez'yany yazyk, Rezhim ekonomii, Monter, Prelesti kul'tury, Koshka i lyudi, Zakoryuchka, Trezvye mysli, Vrachevanie i psikhika, Anna na shee, V Pushkinskie dni, Kocherga.*

Modern Greek: Twentieth-century Greek poetry and prose. The syllabus will consist of a selection of poems and short stories by a variety of authors. (A list of the selection for the examinations in the academic year concerned will be available in the Modern Languages Faculty

Office, 41 Wellington Square, from the beginning of the Michaelmas Full Term of that year). (Specific sections of the prescribed texts may be designated as including the passages which will be set for commentary.)

The examination paper will be divided into two sections. Section A will consist of two compulsory commentary passages from prescribed texts (one poetry passage and one prose passage). Section B will consist of a choice of essay questions, from which each candidate must choose one.

Czech (with Slovak): Prescribed texts to be studied as literature. Essay-type questions will be set on the plays, and a compulsory passage for commentary from the poem. Candidates will be required to answer on all three texts.

Čapek, *R.U.R.*
Havel, *Vyrozumění*
Mácha, *Máj*

Celtic: Prescribed texts. Three essays from a choice of questions on the following set texts:
Pwyll Pendefig Dyfed, ed. R. L. Thomson (Dublin, 1957);
Branwen ferch Lyr, ed. D. Thomson (Dublin, 1961);
Saunders Lewis, *Brandwen*, in Saunders Lewis, *Dramâu'r Parlwr: Branwen a Dwy Briodas Ann* (Llandybïe: Christopher Davies, 1975);
Poems of the Cywyddwyr, ed. E. I. Rowlands (Dublin, 1976);
Scéla Muicce Meic Dathó, ed. R. Thurneysen (Dublin, 1976), pp. 33–41;
Longes Mac n-Uislenn, ed. V. Hull (New York: Modern Language Association of America, 1949).

Latin and Ancient Greek

VI. Prescribed books. 3 hours.

The paper will consist of passages for translation and comment.

VII. Prescribed books. 3 hours.

The paper will consist of essay questions.

Papers VI and VII

Candidates must choose two of the following four groups of texts, and state on their examination entry form which two groups they propose to offer. They must offer the same two groups for both papers.

(*a*) Aristophanes, *Frogs* 1–268, 674–1533[1]; Euripides, *Bacchae*; Plato, *Symposium* 189c–end[1];

(*b*) Aeschylus, *Prometheus Bound*; Sophocles, *Antigone*; Herodotus 1.1–119;

(*c*) Cicero, *pro Murena*; Sallust, *Catiline*; Tacitus, *Annals* 4;

(*d*) Terence, *Adelphoe*; Catullus 1–17, 21–60, 69–70, 72–3, 75–9, 83–8, 92–6, 100–1, 109, 115–16; Ovid, *Metamorphoses* 8.

The following editions of Greek and Latin texts will be used in the examination. Where no publisher's name is given, the book is published by the Clarendon Press. An asterisk (*) indicates texts in the Oxford Classical Texts series; where more than one edition has appeared, the latest will be used.

[1] For the purposes of the essay paper (VII), candidates who offer these texts will be expected to have knowledge of the whole work and not merely the prescribed portions.

Aeschylus, *Prometheus Bound*: Griffith (Cambridge University Press).
Aristophanes, *Frogs*: Dover.
Catullus: *Mynors.
Cicero: *Clark.
Euripides, *Bacchae*: Dodds.
Herodotus: *Hude.
Ovid, *Metamorphoses* 8: Hollis.
Plato, *Symposium*: Dover (Cambridge University Press).
Sallust: *Reynolds.
Sophocles: *Lloyd-Jones and Wilson.
Tacitus, *Annals* 4: Martin and Woodman (Cambridge University Press).
Terence, *Adelphoe*: Martin (Cambridge University Press).

c. Linguistics

VIII. General Linguistics. 3 hours.

Candidates will be expected to be familiar with the development of contemporary linguistic theory, both synchronic and historical, and be able to discuss problems and issues in areas including semantics, pragmatics, sociolinguistics, psycholinguistics, language acquistion and language change.

IX. Phonetics and Phonology. 3 hours.

Candidates will be expected to be familiar with principles and practice in the analysis, classification, and transcription of speech, as applied to languages in general, but with an emphasis on European languages.

X. Grammatical Analysis. 3 hours.

Candidates will be expected to be familiar with modern grammatical theory, in particular as applied to the analysis of European languages.

d. Further Topics

XI.

French: Introduction to French Film Studies:

Four films as prescribed from time to time by the sub-faculty of French. Films chosen will be publicized in the *University Gazette* in Week Nought of Michaelmas Term immediately preceding the examination.

German: Introduction to German Film Studies:

The paper will consist of one commentary and two essays from a choice of questions. The commentary will be on a set of stills from one of the films.

Siegfrieds Tod (Dir. Fritz Lang, 1924)
Menschen am Sonntag (Dir. Robert Siodmak, Billy Wilder, Edgar G. Ulmer, 1929)
Mädchen in Uniform (Dir. Leontine Sagan, 1931)
Kuhle Wampe oder Wem gehört die Welt (Dir. Slatan Dudow, 1932)

XII.

French: Introduction to French Literary Theory:

Four texts as prescribed from time to time by the sub-faculty of French. Texts chosen will be publicized in the *University Gazette* in Week Noughth of Michaelmas Term immediately preceding the examination.

German: Introduction to German Medieval Studies:

The paper will consist of one commentary and two essays from a choice of questions.

Close study of a single text: Hartmann von Aue, *Gregorius* (Reclam edition Middle High German text with a facing page translation in modern German).

XIII.

French: Key Texts in French Thought:

Four texts as prescribed from time to time by the sub-faculty of French. Texts chosen will be publicized in the *University Gazette* in Week Nought of Michaelmas Term immediately preceding the examination.

German: Key Texts in German Thought:

Kant, *Idee zu einer allgemeinen Geschichte in weltbürgerlicher Absicht*
Marx und Engels, *Das kommunistische Manifest*
Nietzsche, 'Zur Naturgeschichte der Moral' in *Jenseits vom Gut und Böse*
Freud, *Warum Krieg?*

Candidates will be permitted to use translations alongside, but not instead of, the original texts.

e. Russian Course B: for students who enter Oxford without A level or equivalent level knowledge of Russian

BI Translation from English into Russian and Russian grammar exercises.
BIIA Translation from Russian into English.
BIIB Comprehension of a passage of written Russian.
BIII Dictation and Aural Comprehension.
Oral Test.

Special Regulations for the Preliminary Examination in Molecular and Cellular Biochemistry

A

1. The subjects of the Preliminary Examination in Molecular and Cellular Biochemistry shall be:

(1) Molecular Cell Biology
(2) Biological Chemistry
(3) Biophysical Chemistry
(4) Organic Chemistry
(5) Elementary Mathematics and Statistics.

2. The syllabus and number of papers shall be as prescribed by regulation from time to time by the Life and Environmental Sciences Board.

3. Candidates must offer all five subjects at one examination; provided that a candidate who has failed in one, two, or three subjects may offer that number of subjects at a subsequent examination.

4. A candidate shall have passed the examination if he or she has satisfied the Moderators in all five subjects either at a single examination or at two examinations in accordance with the proviso to clause 3 above.

5. In the case of candidates who offer all five subjects, the Moderators shall publish only the names of those who have satisfied them in two or more subjects; in the case of candidates who, in accordance with the proviso to clause 3 above, offer one, two, or three subjects, the Moderators shall publish only the names of those who have satisfied them in each of the subjects offered.

6. The Moderators may award a distinction to candidates of special merit who have satisfied them in all five subjects at a single examination.

B

One written paper will be set in each subject. The duration of the written papers will be three hours for subjects 1, 2, and 3, and two hours for subjects 4 and 5. The syllabus for each subject will be that set out in the schedule below.

The Moderators will permit the use of hand-held pocket calculators subject to the conditions set out under the heading 'Use of Calculators in examinations' in the *Special Regulations concerning Examinations*. A list of recommended calculators will be provided by the Chairman of the Moderators not later than the Wednesday of the fourth week of the Michaelmas Full Term preceding the examination. The use of calculators may not be permitted in certain papers.

All candidates shall be assessed as to their practical ability in coursework under the following provisions:

(*a*) The Chairman of the Teaching Committee, or a deputy, shall make available to the Moderators, at the end of the fifth week of the term in which the examinations are first held, evidence showing the extent to which each candidate has completed the prescribed coursework.

(*b*) The Moderators may request coursework from any candidate. Such candidates will be named in a list posted by the day of the first written paper.

(*c*) Coursework cannot normally be retaken. Failure to complete the coursework to the satisfaction of the Moderators, in the absence of appropriate documentary evidence (e.g. a signed medical certificate), will normally constitute failure of the examination.

SCHEDULE

(1) *Molecular Cell Biology*

Classification, evolution and structure of bacterial, archeal, and eukaryotic cells; structure of subcellular organelles and the cytoskeleton of eukaryotes. Multicellularity and cell specialization. Differences between plant and animal cells. Nuclear and cell division in plants, animals, and bacteria. Introduction to the properties of cells; nutrition, growth, transport, contractility, and co-ordinated functioning. Intra- and intercellular signalling.

Chromosomes and genes. Transmission of information between generations. Mitosis and meiosis. Evidence for DNA as the genetic material. The nature of the gene; transformation, transduction, and conjugation. Organization and expression of genetic information: mechanism of DNA replication; mechanism and control of transcription; mechanisms and structures involved in protein synthesis; the genetic code; phages, plasmids, and hosts.

Major metabolic pathways – chemical and thermodynamic principles. ATP. Oxidation of fuels: glucose, glycogen, proteins, amino acids, fats. The TCA cycle. Synthesis of carbohydrates and fats. The glyoxylate cycle. Photosynthesis. Urea cycle.

Structure and properties of lipids and biological membranes. Membrane potentials and ion channels. Membrane transport; biological pumps. Bioenergetics; electron transfer, oxidative and photophosphorylation.

(2) *Biological Chemistry*

Chemical constraints on biology. Energy transformations. Biological polymers. Polysaccharides: amylose and cellulose. Membranes. Lipid and protein components of membranes.

Structure and properties of proteins: amino acids, peptide bonds, conformational preferences, α-helices, β-sheets, stabilization by non-covalent interactions; protein sequences and amino acid modification; glycoproteins.

Tertiary structure and protein folding. Structural proteins. Myoglobin and haemoglobin.

Membrane proteins, lipids, and carbohydrates.

Principles of enzyme catalysis – acid–base and nucleophilic catalysis. Proteases and other enzymes.

Organic chemistry of enzyme reactions, particularly those in glycolysis.

Biological aspects of sulphur and phosphorus chemistry.

Organic chemistry of sugars and other heterocyclic compounds.

Structure and properties of nucleic acids; ribose and deoxyribose, keto-enol tautomerism and H-bonding in purines and pyrimidines, phosphate as linking group; nucleotides; polymeric chains of nucleotides; differences in stability between RNA and DNA; the double helix.

Techniques in Molecular Biology: purification of DNA and proteins. Electrophoresis. DNA sequencing, cloning, blotting.

(3) *Biophysical Chemistry*

Principles of Newtonian mechanics and electrostatics. Quantum theory: concepts of quantum mechanics in terms of energy levels. Boltzmann distribution. Atomic and molecular structure, atomic orbitals: crystal field theory; LCAO approach to molecular orbitals.

Electromagnetic radiation and its interaction with matter. Light absorption. Spectroscopy, Beer's Law. Diffraction; Bragg's Law. X-ray diffraction by crystals. Modern optical microscopy. Electron microscopy. Introduction to vision.

Thermodynamics of solutions: introduction to First and Second Laws. Gibbs function, chemical potential and electrochemical potential. Osmotic equilibria; chemical equilibria; redox equilibria. Buffer solutions and pH. Non-ideal solutions: activity co-efficients. Debye-Huckel theory. Solubility of proteins and other compounds.

Kinetics: order and molecularity; first, second, and pseudo-first order kinetics, steady state. Half lives. Theories of reaction rates; collision theory, transition state theory. Activation energy and the Arrhenius equation. Isotope effects, acid–base catalysis. Radioactive decay as a first order process. Biological effects of radiation.

Enzyme kinetics, Michaelis-Menten equation and the steady state derivation. Irreversible and reversible inhibitors of enzymes. Classification of reversible inhibitors. Allostery.

Non-covalent interactions. Electrostatic forces and dipoles. Electronegativity. Lennard-Jones potential and van der Waal's radii. Hydrogen bonding in proteins, DNA and oligosaccharides. The hydrophobic effect; role of entropy. Accessible surface area and solubility. Protein folding—thermodynamic and kinetic aspects. Co-operativity of folding. Protein denaturation and misfolding.

(4) *Organic Chemistry*

Structure: Elementary atomic and molecular orbital theory. Bonding and molecular geometry. Methods for structure determination (e.g. spectroscopy, mass spectrometry, nmr). Stereochemistry: Absolute configuration. Cis-trans and other isomerisations.

Reactivity: Electronegativity; inductive, mesomeric and stereoelectronic effects. Lowry-Bronsted acidity and basicity of organic compounds. Nucleophilicity and electrophilicity. Simple molecular orbital theory as unifying concept.

Mechanism: Classification of reactions proceeding via intermediates and transition states. Substitution, elimination and addition processes. Rate determining steps; kinetic and thermodynamic control. Carbocation, carbanion, carbene and radical intermediates.

Functional group chemistry: Characteristic chemistry of carbonyl groups. Structure, properties and reactions of carbonyls.

(5) *Elementary Mathematics and Statistics*

An elementary treatment of the following topics will be expected:

Elementary Mathematics

Indices, logarithms and exponential functions. Graphs and graphical representation of simple equations, slopes, inflexion points. Partial fractions. Basic trigonometric functions: sine and cosine functions, representation of waves. Differentiation: maxima and minima; rates of progress, use of Product and Chain rules. Partial differentiation. Integration: of powers of x including x^{-1}; by substitution, by parts and using partial fractions. Introduction to Complex numbers, simple separable diferential equations and their solution. Zeroth, first and second order processes. Permutations and combinations. Factorials and the Binomial Theorem. Binomial and Poisson distributions.

Statistics

Mean, median and mode – measures of central tendency. Normal, unimodal and bimodal distributions. Standard deviation, standard error and coefficient of variance. Confidence limits. Experimental errors and biological variation. Relationships between variables—line fitting. Accuracy and precision. Experimental design. Significance testing; t-tests and non-parametric tests.

Special Regulations for the Preliminary Examination in Oriental Studies

A

1. The languages, subjects, and papers in the examination shall be as prescribed by regulation from time to time by the Board of the Faculty of Oriental Studies.

2. A candidate shall be deemed to have passed the examination when he or she shall have satisfied the Moderators in all the papers associated with one of the languages specified in the regulations.

3. Candidates must offer all the papers at the same time, except that a candidate may at a subsequent examination offer any paper or papers in which he or she has previously failed to satisfy the Moderators.

4. In the case of candidates who have satisfied the Moderators in all the papers at a single examination, the Moderators may award a distinction to those of special merit.

B

The languages which may be offered shall be Arabic, *Chinese, *Egyptology and Ancient Near Eastern Studies, Hebrew, *Japanese, Persian, Sanskrit, and Turkish.

---

* Candidates may only offer in Chinese or Egyptology and Ancient Near Eastern Studies or Japanese a paper or papers which they have previously failed in Moderations.

Arabic

Candidates will be required to offer three three-hour papers (papers (i), (ii), and (iv) below, plus an oral/aural examination as specified under (iii) below.

(i) Translation and precis into English.
(ii) Comprehension, composition, and grammar.
(iii) Oral/aural examination (to be done at the Oriental Institute)*.
(iv) Islamic history and culture.

Chinese

Each candidate shall offer the papers specified for Moderations save that candidates who have passed any paper or papers in Moderations need not offer those papers again.

Egyptology and Ancient Near Eastern Studies

Each candidate shall offer the papers specified for Moderations save that candidates who have passed any paper or papers in Moderations need not offer those papers again.

Hebrew

Candidates will be required to offer three three-hour papers.

(i) Biblical and Modern Texts (1 Kings 17–2 Kings 2; Ora Band, *Reader: Modern Hebrew Prose and Poetry.* New Jersey: Behrman House, 1990: pp. 17–18; 44; 63–67; 94–5; 102–3; 121–2).
(ii) Grammar and translation into Hebrew (Biblical and Modern).
(iii) General Paper.

Japanese

Each candidate shall offer the papers specified for Moderations save that candidates who have passed any paper or papers in Moderations need not offer those papers again.

Persian

Candidates will be required to offer three three-hour papers.

(i) Prepared and unprepared texts for translation from Persian.
Texts: *Selected Modern Texts*, ed. Gurney.
(Copies are available from the Oriental Institute).
(ii) Grammar and translation into Persian.
(iii) General Paper: Islam; Early Islamic History; Medieval Persian Literature and Culture.

Sanskrit

Candidates will be required to offer three three-hour papers.

(i) Texts: C. R. Lanman, *Sanskrit Reader,* pp. 1–34, l. 11. *Bhagavad-Gītā* (ed. Belvalkar), Books II, IV, VI, and XI.
(ii) Grammar: the subject will be studied from M. A. Coulson, *Teach Yourself Sanskrit*; A. A. Macdonell, *Sanskrit Grammar for Students.*
(iii) General paper.

Turkish

Candidates will be required to offer three three-hour papers.

(i) Prepared texts and unseen translation from Turkish. (This paper will be divided into two separate parts (each $1\frac{1}{2}$ hours), one for translation of passages from *Selected Elementary Turkish Texts*, ed. Kerslake (copies available from the Oriental Institute), and the other for unseen translation from Turkish,

---

* Details of the areas in which candidates will be expected to show competence are provided in the examination conventions and in the handbook.

and the use of dictionaries will be permitted for the part consisting of unseen translation).

(ii) Turkish grammar and translation into Turkish.

(iii) Islamic history and culture.

Special Regulations for the Preliminary Examination in Philosophy and Modern Languages

A

1. Candidates in this Preliminary Examination shall be examined in Philosophy and one Modern Language. The languages that may be offered shall be those languages which may be offered in the Final Honour School of Modern Languages.

2. The subjects of the examination shall be:

In Philosophy,

(1) Introduction to Philosophy

and, in the Modern Language offered

(2) Language papers

(3) Literature papers.

3. Candidates must offer all three subjects at one examination provided that

(*a*) a candidate who fails in either two subjects or one subject may in a subsequent examination offer the two subjects or the one subject only;

(*b*) a candidate who has offered two subjects at a subsequent examination under (*a*) above and has failed in one subject may offer in a subsequent examination that subject only.

Provided that a candidate who fails one only of the papers in 2(1) above may offer, in a subsequent examination or subsequent examinations, the paper in which he or she has failed.

4. A candidate shall be deemed to have passed the examination if he shall have satisfied the Moderators in all three subjects.

5. In the case of candidates who have satisfied the Moderators in three subjects at a single examination the Moderators may award a distinction either in Philosophy or in the Modern Language or in both to those who have done work of special merit.

6. This Preliminary Examination shall be under the joint supervision of the Boards of the Faculties of Philosophy and of Medieval and Modern European Languages and Literature, which shall appoint a standing joint committee to make regulations concerning it, subject always to the preceding clauses of this subsection.

7. It shall be the duty of the chairman of the Moderators for the Preliminary Examination for Modern Languages to designate such

of their number as may be required for Modern Languages in the Preliminary Examination in Philosophy and Modern Languages, and when this has been done and the Moderator for Philosophy has been nominated, the number of the examiners in Philosophy and Modern Languages shall be deemed to be complete.

B

There shall be three subjects in the examination.

(1) *Introduction to Philosophy* (two papers of three hours each).

I. *General Philosophy*

This shall be studied in connection with Descartes' *Meditations on First Philosophy*, trans. Cottingham, Cambridge University Press. This paper, while not being confined to the detailed views of Descartes, will be satisfactorily answerable by a candidate who has made a critical study of the text. There will be no compulsory question containing passages for comment.

II. (*a*) *Moral Philosophy* and (*b*) *Logic*

Candidates will be required to answer four questions, which may be taken from section (*a*), section (*b*), or both. (*a*) Moral Philosophy shall be studied in connection with Mill, *Utilitarianism*. This section of the paper, while not being confined to the detailed views of Mill, will be satisfactorily answerable by a candidate who has made a critical study of the text. There will be no compulsory question containing passages for comment. (*b*) Logic: As specified for the regulations for the Preliminary Examination for Philosophy, Politics, and Economics.

(2) *Language papers* (one paper of three hours and two papers each of one and a half hours).

As specified for Papers I, IIA, and IIB in the regulations for the Preliminary Examination for Modern Languages.

(3) *Literature papers* (two papers, each of three hours).

As specified for Papers III and IV in the regulations for the Preliminary Examination for Modern Languages.

Special Regulations for the Preliminary Examination for Philosophy, Politics, and Economics

A

1. The subjects of the Preliminary Examination for Philosophy, Politics, and Economics shall be:

(1) Introductory Economics

(2) Introduction to Philosophy

(3) Introduction to Politics: The Theory and Practice of Democracy.

2. A candidate shall be allowed to offer himself for examination in one, two, or three subjects. Candidates must also pursue a course of study in Information Technology, and are required to submit an information technology-based project by the first day of the Trinity Full Term in which the examination is taken. Details of the course

are to be found in the Student Handbook for Philosophy, Politics, and Economics.

3. A candidate shall be deemed to have passed the examination if he shall have satisfied the Moderators in three subjects, and has submitted a satisfactory project for the Information Technology course (as described above). Any candidate who fails to submit a project for the Information Technology course by the deadline, or whose project is deemed to be unsatisfactory, will be allowed to resubmit the project by the Monday of the week falling three weeks before First Week of the following Michaelmas Full Term.

4. The Moderators may award a distinction to candidates of special merit who have passed all three subjects at a single examination.

B

Three three-hour papers will be set as follows.

Introductory Economics

Elementary economics: including demand theory, production theory, perfect competition, monopoly, monopolistic competition, oligopoly, factor markets, general equilibrium and welfare, the theory of international trade, national income accounting, the determination of national income and employment, monetary institutions and the money supply, inflation, balance of payments, and exchange rates.

Elementary mathematical economics: applications of functions and graphs, differentiation, partial differentiation, maxima and minima, maximization subject to constraints.

Economic statistics: presentation of statistics, descriptive statistics, index numbers, elementary sampling and significance, simple correlation and regression.

Calculators may be used in the examination room subject to the conditions set out under the heading 'Use of calculators in examinations' in the *Special Regulations concerning Examinations.*

Introduction to Philosophy

The paper shall consist of three sections: (I) General Philosophy, (II) Moral Philosophy, (III) Logic. Each candidate shall be required to show adequate knowledge in at least two sections.

I. *General Philosophy* and II. *Moral Philosophy*

These sections shall be studied in connection with respectively: Descartes' *Meditations on First Philosophy,* trans. Cottingham, Cambridge University Press, and Mill, *Utilitarianism.* These sections while not being confined to the detailed views of the authors of the set texts, will be satisfactorily answerable by a candidate who has made a critical study of these texts. In neither section will there be a compulsory question containing passages for comment.

III. *Logic*

Subjects to be studied include: propositional and predicate languages; truth tables; tableaux; relations; the critical application of formal logic to the analysis of English sentences and inferences (problems of symbolization; scope; truth-functionality; quantification, identity, descriptions).

These topics may be studied in Wilfrid Hodges, *Logic*, 2nd edition (Penguin Books), sections 1–11 and 16–40, omitting theorem XII of section 24. The logical symbols and tableaux rules to be used are those found in that book. Some philosophical questions about logic may be studied by reading Mark Sainsbury, *Logical Forms*, 1st or 2nd edition (Blackwell), chapters 1–2.

Introduction to Politics: the Theory and Practice of Democracy

The paper will contain two sections. Candidates are required to answer four questions, of which at least one must be from section (*a*) and two from section (*b*). Candidates choosing to answer two questions from section (*b*) must show knowledge of at least two of the following political systems: the United States of America; the United Kingdom; France; Germany. Candidates choosing to answer three questions from section (*b*) must show knowledge of at least three of the following political systems: the United States of America; the United Kingdom; France; Germany.

(*a*) *Theorizing the Democratic State*

Questions will be set on the following topics: the nature and grounds of democracy; power and influence in the democratic state; ideology; civil society; public choice approaches to democracy; the nature and limits of liberty. Questions will also be set on the following texts: J. J. Rousseau, *The Social Contract*; J. S. Mill, *On Liberty*; Alexis de Toqueville, *Democracy in America*; Karl Marx and Freidrich Engels, *The Communist Manifesto, Eighteenth Brumaire of Louis Napoleon, Preface to a Critique of Political Economy, Critique of the Gotha Programme*, plus readings 14, 37, 39 in David McLellan, ed., *Karl Marx: Selected Writings*, Second Edition (Oxford, Oxford University Press, 2000).

(*b*) *Analysis of Democratic Institutions*

Questions will be set on the following topics: the state and its institutions (executives, legislatures, parties and party systems, courts, constitutions and centre-periphery relations); political representation; the politics of instability; policy continuity and policy change; democratic transitions and consolidation. Questions will also be set on these topics, with reference to the following political systems: the United States of America; the United Kindgom; France; Germany.

Special Regulations for the Preliminary Examination in Physics

A

1. The subject of the Preliminary Examination in Physics shall be Physics, including basic practical and mathematical techniques.

2. The number of papers and other general requirements of the Preliminary Examination in Physics shall be as prescribed by regulation from time to time by the Mathematical and Physical Sciences Board.

B

1. Candidates in Physics must offer four Compulsory Papers at one examination, provided that a candidate who has failed in one or two papers may offer that number of papers at a subsequent examination. The titles of the papers shall be:

CP1: Mechanics & Special Relativity

CP2: Introductory Electromagnetism & Circuits

CP3: Mathematical Methods

CP4: Differential Equations, Waves & Optics.

Their syllabuses shall be approved by the sub-faculty of physics and shall be published in the physics Course Handbook by the sub-faculty of Physics not later than tbe beginning of Michaelmas Full Term for examination three terms thence.

2. In addition to the four papers of cl. 1, a candidate in physics shall be required
   (i) to submit to the Moderators such evidence as they require of the successful completion of practical work normally pursued during the three terms preceding the examination, *and*
   (ii) to offer a written paper on one Short Option.

3. Candidates shall be deemed to have passed the examination if they have satisfied the Moderators in the four Compulsory Papers either at a single examination or at two examinations in accordance with the proviso to cl. 1, and provided further that the same number of papers as were failed at the first sitting have been passed at the same attempt at a subsequent examination.

4. In the case of candidates who offer all four papers of cl. 1, the Moderators shall publish the names only of those who have satisfied them in two or more papers. Candidates whose names do not appear on the pass list must offer four papers at a subsequent examination. In the case of candidates who, in accordance with the proviso to cl. 1, offer one or two papers, the Moderators shall publish the names only to those who have satisfied them in each of the papers offered.

5. The Moderators may award a distinction to candidates of special merit who have satisfied them in all four papers of cl. 1 at the single examination and in the requirements of cl. 2.

6. If the evidence of practical work submitted under cl. 2(i) is deemed insufficient, the Moderators may require the candidate to undertake a further practical test.

7. The list of Short Option subjects in cl. 2(ii) and their syllabuses shall be approved by the sub-faculty of physics and shall be published in the physics Course Handbook by the sub-faculty of Physics not later than the beginning of Michaelmas Full Term for examination three terms thence.

8. With respect to subjects under cl. 2(ii) a candidate may propose to the Chairman of the sub-faculty of Physics or deputy, not later than the last week of Michaelmas Full Term preceding the examination, another subject paper. Candidates shall be advised of the decision by the end of the first week of the subsequent Hilary Full Term.

9. Except for papers for which their use is forbidden, the Moderators will permit the use of any hand-held calculator subject to the conditions set out under the heading 'Use of calculators in examinations' in the *Special Regulations concerning Examinations* and further elaborated in the Course Handbook.

Special Regulations for the Preliminary Examination in Physics and Philosophy

A

1. The subjects of the examination, the syllabus, and the number of papers shall be as prescribed by regulation from time to time by the Board of the Faculty of Philosophy and the Mathematical and Physical Sciences Board.

2. (1) The Moderators for Physics shall be such of the Moderators in the Preliminary Examination in Physics as may be required; those for Philosophy shall be nominated by a committee of which three elected members shall be appointed by the Board of the Faculty of Philosophy.

(2) It shall be the duty of the Chairman of the Moderators in the Preliminary Examination in Physics to designate such of their number as shall be required in the Preliminary Examination in Physics and Philosophy, and when this has been done and the Moderators for Philosophy have been nominated, the number of Moderators for the Preliminary Examination in Physics and Philosophy shall be deemed to be complete.

B

1. For candidates who have previously been examined in Moderations in Physics and Philosophy, only those who failed in the Physics and Mathematics subject of the examination are required to take papers in that subject (1–3 in the Schedule below) which correspond to the papers they have failed in Moderations. Only those candidates who fail in the Philosophy subject in Moderations shall take paper 4 below.

2. Candidates who have not previously been examined in Moderations in Physics and Philosophy shall take papers 1–4.

3. Except for papers for which their use is forbidden, the Moderators will permit the use of any hand-held calculator subject to the conditions set out under the heading 'Use of calculators in examinations' in the *Special Regulations concerning Examinations* and further elaborated in the Physics Course Handbook.

Schedule

1–3. Three papers in *Physics and Mathematics*, which shall be the three papers referred to in section (*a*) *Physics and Mathematics* of the Regulations for Moderations in Physics and Philosophy.

4. *Philosophy.* As specified in both papers (b) (1) and (b) (2) for Moderations in Physics and Philosophy, except that no question on Frege will be available. Candidates will be required to answer two questions on the Elements of Deductive Logic, one question on Descartes, and one question on the Leibniz-Clarke Correspondence.

Special Regulations for the Preliminary Examination in Physiological Sciences

A

1. The subjects of the Preliminary Examination in Physiological Sciences shall be:

I. Physiology and Pharmacology of the Systems of the Body
II. Neuroscience
III. Biochemistry and Cell Biology.

2. The syllabus, number of papers, and their format shall be as prescribed from time to time by regulations made by the Medical Sciences Board.

3. A candidate shall be deemed to have passed the examination if he has satisfied the Moderators in all three subjects.

4. Candidates may offer one or more subjects at any examination and the Moderators may publish the name of a candidate as having satisfied them in that examination in one or more subjects.

5. The Moderators may award a distinction to candidates of special merit who have passed all three subjects at a single attempt.

B

One three-hour paper will be set in each of subjects of the examination as specified in the above decree. The syllabus for each will be published by the Medical Sciences Board annually in Michaelmas Term. Candidates shall submit notebooks, initialled as satisfactory by the demonstrators, or other certified records of practical work, including work in statistics, carried out during their course of study.

Each notebook shall be accompanied by a certificate signed by the candidate indicating that the notebook submitted is the candidate's own work. These notebooks or records shall be available to the examiners at a time before the written examination prescribed by the examiners, and shall be taken into consideration by the examiners. Candidates whose practical notebooks or other records are unsatisfactory may be required by the examiners to submit to further examination. Failure to submit an initialled notebook or certified evidence shall result in the candidate being failed in the relevant subject of the examination, unless the candidate has an adequate attendance record at the relevant practical classes and provided that the examiners are satisfied, after taking account of the candidate's examination script and any further examination they shall deem necessary, that the candidate has a satisfactory knowledge and understanding of the practical course.

Candidates may be required to undergo oral examination in the subjects (including practical work) covered by the papers they offer.

Special Regulations for the Preliminary Examination for Psychology, Philosophy, and Physiology

A

1. The subjects of the examination shall be:

(1) Physiology
(2) Neurophysiology
(3) Introduction to Philosophy
(4) Introduction to Probability Theory and Statistics
(5) Introduction to Psychology.

2. A candidate shall be allowed to offer himself for examination in one, two, or three subjects.

3. A candidate shall be deemed to have passed the examination if he shall have satisfied the Moderators in three subjects.

4. In the case of candidates who have satisfied the Moderators in three subjects in a single examination or in two subjects in Hilary Term and in Physiology in Trinity Term the Moderators may award a Distinction to those of special merit.

B

(1) *Physiology*

The paper is as specified for Subject I* Physiology and Pharmacology of the Systems of the Body for the Preliminary Examination in Physiological Sciences. In addition, questions on Excitable Tissues as specified for paper (2) Neurophysiology will be available only to those candidates who do not offer paper (2) Neurophysiology.

Candidates will be required to submit notebooks or other records of practical work, in General Physiology only, as specified for the Preliminary Examination in Physiological Sciences.

(2) *Neurophysiology*

Excitable Tissues. Membrane potential, ion pumps. Action potential, refractory period. Receptor potentials. Neuromuscular transmission. Synaptic mechanisms.

Chemical Transmitters. Storage and release of transmitter. Removal and synthesis of transmitter. Selected drugs acting on the nervous system.

Efferent Mechanisms. Muscle contraction. Muscle receptors. Spinal reflexes. Higher motor centres. Autonomic nervous system.

Afferent Mechanisms. Hearing. Vision. Somaesthetic system, including pain.

One three-hour paper will be set.

(3) *Introduction to Philosophy*

As specified for the Preliminary Examination for Philosophy, Politics, and Economics.

(4) *Introduction to Probability Theory and Statistics*

This examination is intended to test the candidate's understanding of the elements of probability theory and of the principles of statistics as applied to the design and analysis of surveys and experiments and to the interpretation of the results of such investigations. The topics below are more fully detailed in *Definitions and Formulae with Statistical Tables for Elementary Statistics and Quantitative Methods Courses*, which is prepared by the Department of Statistics. Copies of this will be available at the examination.

Descriptive statistics and statistical presentation using graphs and simple measures of central tendency and dispersion. Frequency distributions. Samples and populations. The addition and multiplication laws of probability; conditional probability and Bayes' Rule. The binomial, Poisson and normal distributions: their properties and uses and the relationships between them. Statistical inference using sampling distributions, standard errors and confidence limits. Common uses of z, t, chi-square and F tests and nonparametric tests including tests of hypothesis for the mean, median or proportion of a single population or for the difference between two or more populations, goodness-of-fit tests and tests of difference between two population distributions.

Factorial designs involving one, two, or three factors; repeated measures designs. The analysis of variance for these designs including the interpretation of interactions where appropriate. Nonparametric analysis of variance: Kruskal-Wallis and Friedman tests.

The analysis of 2-way contingency tables using chi-square tests. Linear regression and correlation.

A comprehensive list of formulae together with statistical tables will be available at the examination.

One three-hour paper will be set.

---

* Until further notice, the Physiology paper will not be available in Hilary Term.

(5) *Introduction to Psychology*

Methods and topics in: development; individual differences; social behaviour; animal behaviour; the neural basis of behaviour; perception; learning; memory; language; cognition; skills; abnormal behaviour.

One three-hour paper will be set.

For papers (4) and (5) only examiners will permit the use of any hand-held pocket calculator subject to the following conditions set out under the heading 'Use of calculators in examinations' in the *Special Regulations concerning Examinations*.

Special Regulations for the Preliminary Examination for Theology

A

1. The subjects of the Preliminary Examination for Theology shall be:

(1) The Christian Doctrine of Creation.
(2) The Study of Old Testament set texts
(3) The Study of a New Testament set text
(4) The History of the Church from Nero to Constantine
(5) Introduction to Philosophy
(6) New Testament Greek
(7) Biblical Hebrew.

2. Candidates must offer at least one from amongst papers (5), (6), and (7).

3. A candidate shall be deemed to have passed the examination if he shall have satisfied the Moderators in three of the subjects from the Preliminary Examination:

Provided that he shall have passed in not less than two subjects at one and the same examination and in the third subject at that or a subsequent examination.

4. Candidates may offer an additional subject if they so wish.

5. All candidates must offer at least three subjects in one examination:

Provided that a candidate who has failed in one subject (or in two subjects if he has offered four) but has passed in the other subjects offered may offer at a subsequent examination the subject or subjects in which he failed.

6. In the case of candidates who have satisfied the Moderators in at least three subjects in a single examination, the Moderators may award a mark of distinction to those of special merit.

B

Candidates must offer at least one from amongst papers 5, 6, or 7.

1. *The Christian Doctrine of Creation*

This paper will serve as an introduction to Systematic Theology through the critical examination of different aspects of one basic Christian doctrine, the doctrine of Creation.

2. *The Study of Old Testament set texts: Genesis 1–11 and Amos*

Candidates will be expected to comment on passages from the set texts and will be expected to show a general knowledge of their historical, literary, and theological background.*

3. *The Study of a New Testament set text: Mark*

Candidates will be expected to show a general knowledge of the text and to answer questions on theological and historical issues which are raised by the Gospel according to Mark.*

4. *The History of the Church from Nero to Constantine*

Candidates will be expected to show a general knowledge of the history of the Church, and its relations to the Roman empire, from the late first century to the death of Constantine in 337 AD. Questions will be set on some but not necessarily all of the following topics: the growth of the church and the meaning of conversion; the causes, scope, and effects of persecution; patterns of ministry and the threefold hierarchy; ecclesiastical discipline and the beginnings of monasticism; schisms caused by Judaizers, Gnostics, Montanists, Novatianists, and Donatists; the development of orthodoxy and synodical government; the evolution of the Biblical canon; the role of Christianity in the Constantinian Empire.

5. *Introduction to Philosophy*

As specified for the Preliminary Examination for Philosophy, Politics, and Economics.

6. *New Testament Greek*†

Candidates will be expected to show a knowledge of Greek grammar, syntax, and vocabulary (as set out in J. W. Wenham, *The Elements of New Testament Greek*) and its importance for the exegesis of the New Testament, with particular reference to Mark 1–6, from which passages will be chosen for translation and grammatical comment.

7. *Biblical Hebrew*‡

The paper will include questions on elementary Hebrew grammar (to include only the topics covered in J. Weingreen, *Practical Grammar of Classical Hebrew*, 2nd edn., pp. 1–123), and short passages will be set for translation and grammatical comment from Jonah 1:1–2:2, 2:11–3:10, and 4:1–11.

---

* The texts will be studied in English in the New Revised Standard Version.

† The Greek text will be the text of the United Bible Societies, 4th edition.

‡ The Hebrew text will be the *Biblia Hebraica Stuttgartensia* (Stuttgart, 1977).

SPECIAL REGULATIONS FOR THE HONOUR SCHOOL OF ANCIENT AND MODERN HISTORY

A

1. The examination in the Honour School of Ancient and Modern History shall consist of such subjects in Ancient and Modern History as the Boards of the Faculties of Classics and Modern History from time to time shall in consultation prescribe by regulation.

2. No candidate shall be admitted to the examination in this school unless he has either passed or been exempted from the First Public Examination.

3. The examination shall be under the joint supervision of the Boards of the Faculties of Classics and Modern History. They shall appoint a standing joint committee to consider any matters concerning the examination which cannot expeditiously be settled by direct consultation between them. Whenever any matter cannot otherwise be resolved they shall themselves hold a joint meeting and resolve it by majority vote.

B

Each candidate shall offer the following subjects:

[Until 1 October 2004: 1. One of the following (one paper):

(*a*) Greek History 478–323 BC;
(*b*) Greek History 404–200 BC;
(*c*) Roman History 80 BC–AD 138;
(*d*) Roman History AD 14–284.

2. Any one of the periods of General History specified for the Honour School of Modern History.

3. Any one of the periods of the History of the British Isles specified for that school except any such period that has already been offered on passing the First Public Examination (one paper).

The individual specifications for the Further and Special Subjects in Ancient History are set out below.]

[From 1 October 2004: I. A period of Ancient History (one paper).

One of the following:

(*a*) Greek History 478–323 BC;
(*b*) Greek History 404–200 BC;
(*c*) Roman History 80 BC–AD 138;
(*d*) Roman History AD 14–284.

II. A period of Modern History (one paper).

Either

(*a*) Any one of the periods of General History specified for the Honour School of Modern History;

or:

(*b*) Any one of the periods of the History of the British Isles specified for the Honour School of Modern History except any such period that has already been offered on passing the First Public Examination.]

[Until 1 October 2004: 4.] **[From 1 October 2004:** III] FURTHER SUBJECTS

Either, (*a*) (i) any one of the Further Subjects as specified for the Honour School of Modern History (one paper) **[Until 1 October 2004:** or (ii) a thesis on a subject within the scope of that school (one paper)];

or, (*b*) any one of the following Further Subjects in Ancient History (one paper) provided that any candidate who offers alternative **[Until 1 October 2004:** 5] **[From 1 October 2004:** IV] (*a*) below may only offer alternative **[Until 1 October 2004:** 4] **[From 1 October 2004:** III] (*b*):

(i) *Athenian democracy in the Classical Age*

[Until 1 October 2004: Candidates will be required to study the social, administrative, and constitutional developments in Athens from 462 to 321 BC, and will only be required to show such knowledge of external affairs as is necessary for an understanding of the working of Athenian democracy. The following texts are prescribed for special study: although compulsory passages will not be set, candidates will be expected to show knowledge of these texts in their answers.

Aristotle, *Constitution of Athens* (tr. P. J. Rhodes, Penguin Classics).

Herodotus III. 80–2 (Loeb).

Thucydides I. 31–44, 66–79, 140–5; II. 35–65; III. 35–50, 82–3; V. 43–6; VI. 8–29; VIII. 47–97 (tr. Crawley, *Everyman*).

Xenophon, *Hellenica* I. 6 and 7; II. 3 and 4 (Loeb).
Memorabilia I. 1 and 2; III. 6 (Loeb).
Revenues (tr. P. J. Rhodes, Loeb).

[Xenophon], *Constitution of Athens* (Loeb).

Andocides I (Loeb, *Minor Attic Orators* I).

Lysias XXII, XXV (Loeb).

Aeschines II (Loeb).

Demosthenes VI, XIX, LIX (Loeb).

Aristophanes, *Wasps, Clouds, Ecclesiazusae, Acharnians* 1–173, *Thesmophoriazusae* 295–530 (Penguin Classics).

Plato, *Apology, Gorgias, Protagoras* 309–28 (Penguin Classics).

Aeschylus, *Eumenides* (tr. ed. Grene & Lattimore).

Sophocles, *Antigone* (tr. ed. Grene & Lattimore).

Euripides, *Supplices* (tr. ed. Grene & Lattimore).

C. W. Fornara, *Translated Documents of Greece and Rome,* I, nos. 15, 68, 75, 97, 100, 103, 106, 114, 119, 120, 128, 134, 140, 147, 155, 160, 166.

P. Harding, *Translated Documents of Greece and Rome,* II, nos. 3, 5, 9, 45, 47, 54, 55, 56, 66, 78, 82, 101, 108, 111, 121.

Opportunity will be given to show knowledge of the archaeology of Classical Athens.]

(ii) *Civic Life of the Roman Empire from the Flavian to the Severan Period.*

[Until 1 October 2004: Candidates will be required to study the economic, social, and cultural history of the cities of the Roman empire in the prescribed period, and to show an adequate knowledge of the general history of the period. The following texts are prescribed for special study; although compulsory passages for comment will not be set, candidates will be expected to show knowledge of these texts in their answers.

Pliny, *Letters* I. 8, 10; III. 9, 13; V. 7, 11, 20; VI. 5, 13; VIII. 24; IX. 5; X. 8, 15–121 (tr. Loeb or Penguin),

Dio Chrysostom, *Orations* (or *Discourses*) 38, 40, 43–9 (tr. Loeb),

Apuleius, *Apology* (tr. H. E. Butler), *The Apologia and Florida of Apuleius of Madaura* (1909),

Apuleius, *Florida* 16, 20 (tr. H. E. Butler), *The Apologia and Florida of Apuleius of Madaura* (1909),

Fronto, *Ad Pium* I. 8 (Loeb I. 236–9); *Ad M. Caesarem* III. 2–5 (Loeb I. 58–69); *Ad Amicos* I. 1 (Loeb I. 282–7); II. 7 (Loeb II. 176–87), II (Loeb I. 292–5),

Aelius Aristides, *Oration* 26 (*To Rome*) 1–14, 28–39, 58–100 (tr. with notes by C. A. Behr, *The Complete Works* (1981–6)), II. 73–97 (tr. with commentary by J. H. Oliver, *The Ruling Power* (1953)),

Aelius Aristides, *Oration* 30 (=*Sacred Tales* 4), 68–108 (tr. with notes by C. A. Behr, *The Complete Works* (1981–6)), II. 318–39 (also in C. A. Behr, *Aelius Aristides and the Sacred Tales* (1968), 253–77)),

Lucian, *Alexander, or the False Prophet*; *Peregrinos* (both tr. Loeb),

Epictetus, *Discourses* III. 7, 13; VI. 7 (tr. Loeb),

Philostratus, *Lives of the Sophists*, preface; I. introduction; I. 8 (Favorinus), 21 (Scopelian, 25 (Polemo); II. 1 (Herodes), 2 (Theodotus), 9 (Aristeides), 23 (Damianus), 24 (Antipater) (tr. Loeb),

Plutarch, *Precepts of Statecraft* 17–20, 25–32 (tr. Loeb *Plutarch, Moralia* X. 234–53, 262–99),

P. A. Brunt, *Select Texts from the Digest* (copies are available from the Classics Office),

H. A. Musurillo, *Acts of the Christian Martyrs* (1972) nos. 1, 6, 8,

Eusebius, *Ecclesiastical History* IV. 8–9, 26; V. 1 (tr. Loeb or Penguin),

Tertullian, *Apologeticum*, 1–2, 37–50 (tr. Loeb),

J. Stevenson (ed.), *A New Eusebius* (revised by W. H. C. Frend, 1987), nos. 31–2, 34–6, 39, 41, 92, 110, 111, 112–16, 117, 136.

Inscriptions and other documentary material:

N. Lewis and M. Reinhold, *Roman Civilization* (3rd edn., 1990), II. 186–9, 231–337,

J. H. Oliver, *The Ruling Power* (1953), 958–63 (oil law of Hadrian),

Hesperia 24 (1955), 340–3 (s.c. on reduction of costs of gladiators),

J. H. Oliver, *Marcus Aurelius: Aspects of Civic and Cultural Policy in the East* (*Hesperia* Supp. 13, 1970), 1–33 (with emendations by C. P. Jones, *ZPE* 8 (1971), 161–83) (Herodes Atticus and his enemies),

Journal of Roman Studies 63 (1973), 86–7 (tr. in Lewis and Reinhold II. 56–8) (tabula Banasitana),

Journal of Roman Studies 74 (1984), 173–80 (Palmyra tax law),

Journal of Roman Studies 76 (1986), 182–99 (lex Irnitana) (selection available from the Classics Office),

Journal of Roman Studies 80 (1990), 183–7 (Demostheneia at Oenoanda),

G. M. Rogers, *Sacred Identity of Ephesos: Foundation Myths of a Roman City* (1991), 152–85 (Vibius Salutaris).

Special attention will be given to the following archaeological sites:

Ostia, Carthage, Leptis Magna, Trier, Silchester, Athens, Ephesus, Palmyra.]

(iii) *The Greeks and the Mediterranean World 950–500* BC, as specified for the Honour School of Literae Humaniores.

[Until 1 October 2004: (iv) *The Archaeology and Art of Roman Italy in the Late Republic and Early Empire*, as specified for the Honour School of Literae Humaniores.**]**
[From 1 October 2004: (iv) *Art under the Roman Empire,* AD *14–337*, as specified for the Honour School of Literae Humaniores.**]**

[Until 1 October 2004: 5.**] [From 1 October 2004:** IV**]** SPECIAL SUBJECTS

Either, (*a*) any one of the Special Subjects as specified for the Honour School of Modern History **[Until 1 October 2004:** (two papers)**] [From 1 October 2004:** (one paper and one extended essay)**]**;

or, (*b*) any one of the following Special Subjects in Ancient History (two papers), provided that any candidate who offers alternative **[Until 1 October 2004:** 4**]** **[From 1 October 2004:** III**]** (*a*) above may only offer alternative **[Until 1 October 2004:** 5**]** **[From 1 October 2004:** IV**]** (*b*)

(i) *Alexander the Great and his Early Successors (336–302* BC*).* **[Until 1 October 2004:** The following texts are prescribed for study in translation; compulsory passages for comment will be set:

Arrian, *Anabasis* (Loeb, Brunt), [Demosthenes] XVII (Loeb), Diodorus Siculus, XVI.89, 91–5; XVII.5–7, 16–21, 32, 47–8, 62–3, 69–73, 76–7, 93–5, 100–1, 108–11, 113–15, 117–18; XVIII, the whole; XIX.12–64, 66–8, 77–100, 105; XX.19–21, 27–8, 37, 45–53, 81–99, 100–3, 106–13 (Loeb), Plutarch, *Lives of Alexander, Eumenes and Demetrios* 1–27 (Loeb), the inscriptions translated in a dossier available from the Classics Office, 37 Wellington Square and the texts in P. Harding, *Translated Documents of Greece and Rome 2: From the End of the Peloponnesian War to the Battle of Ipsus* (Cambridge, 1989) Nos. 123, 125, 126, 128, 129, 132, 133, 136, 138.

Optional passages in Greek for comment will be set from: Arrian, *Anabasis VII* (Loeb, Brunt).**]**

(ii) *Cicero: Politics and Thought in the Late Republic*] **[From 1 October 2004:** The individual specifications for the Further and Special Subjects in Ancient History will be given in the Handbook for the Joint Honour School of Ancient and Modern History and on the Modern History Faculty Website. This will be published by the Modern History Board by Monday of Week 1 of the first Michaelmas Full Term of candidates' work for the Honour School.**]**

[Until 1 October 2004: The following texts are prescribed for study in translation; compulsory passages for comment will be set:

Sallust, *Catilina* (Loeb)
Cicero, *In Verrem* (Actio I) (Loeb)
De Imperio Cn. Pompei (Loeb)
Pro Sestio 97–137 (Loeb)
In. M. Antonium Philippica XI (Loeb)
Pro Murena (Loeb)
In Catilinam IV (Loeb)
Epistulae ad Atticum I.1, 2, 13, 14, 16, 17, 19; II.1, 3, 16, 18; IV.1, 3, 5; V.16 and 21; VI.1 and 2; VII.7, 9, 11; VIII.3 and 11; IX.6A, 10, 11A, 18; X.8 (incl. A and B); XI.6; XII.21 and 40; XIII.19 and 52; XIV.1, 12, 13, 13A and B; XV.1A and 11; XVI.7, 8 and 11 (Loeb)
Epistulae ad Familiares I.1, 8, 9; II.12; III.6 and 7; IV.4, 5; V.1, 2, 7, 12; VI.6; VII.3, 5, 30; VIII.1, 5, 6, 8, 13, 14, 16; IX.16 and 17; X.24 and 28; XI.3, 20, 27, 28; XII.3 and 5; XIII.1 and 9; XIV.4; XV.1, 4, 5, 6, 16, 19; XVI.12 (Loeb)
Epistulae ad Quintum fratrem II.3, 15; III.5 and 6 (Loeb)
Epistulae ad M. Brutum 17, 25 (Loeb)
Brutus 301–33 (Loeb)
De Oratore I.137–59, 185–203; II.30–8 (Loeb)
Orator 113–20, 140–6 (Loeb)
De Re Publica I.1–18, 58–71 (Loeb)
De Legibus II.1–33; III.1–49 (Loeb)
Tusculanae Disputationes I.1–8 (Loeb)
De Divinatione II.1–24; 136–50 (Loeb)
De Natura Deorum I.1–13; III.1–10 (Loeb)
De Officiis I.1–60; II.1–29, 44–60, 73–89 trans. Griffin and Atkins (Cambridge),
Cornelius Nepos, *Atticus* (Loeb).

Optional passages in Latin for comment will be set from:

In Catilinam I (Loeb), *De Finibus* I 1–12 (Loeb, pending Reynolds OCT).]

The individual detailed specifications and prescribed texts for the Further and Special subjects as specified for the Honour School of Modern History will be given in the Handbook for the Honour School of Modern History. This will be published by the Modern History Board by Monday of Week 1 of the first Michaelmas Full Term of candidates' work for the Honour School.

Depending on the availability of teaching resources, not all Further and Special Subjects will be available to all candidates in every year. Candidates and Ancient and Modern History tutors will be circulated by the beginning of the fourth week of the first Hilary Full Term of their work for the Honour School with (i) details of any Further and Special Subjects which will not be available for the following year, (ii) the supplement to the Handbook for the Honour School of Modern History. This book will contain full specifications and prescribed texts for any Further or Special Subjects specified for Modern History introduced for the following year, and any amendments to the specifications and prescribed texts for existing Further and Special Subjects approved by the Modern History Board by its first meeting of the preceding Hilary Term.

[**Until 1 October 2004:** 6. Comparative History and Historiography (extended essay). Each candidate shall be examined in Comparative History and Historiography in accordance with regulation VI of the Honour School of Modern History.]

[**From 1 October 2004:** V. DISCIPLINES OF HISTORY

Each candidate shall be examined in the *Disciplines of History* in accordance with regulation V of the Honour School of Modern History.]

[**Until 1 October 2004:** Each candidate who so desires may also offer a thesis in accordance with the regulations for theses in regulation VII of the Honour School of Modern History as modified below. This optional extra is not to be confused with the thesis which may be offered in lieu of the Further Subject paper in Modern History or the second paper of every Modern History Special Subject (both in that school and this). Each candidate will also be examined viva voce unless excused by the examiners.

Modifications to regulation VII of the Honour School of Modern History

Cl. 2. Delete 'a paper in the History of British Isles. General History'. and delete 'If a thesis is offered in place of a paper in the History of the British Isles or General History, a candidate must also offer three papers in those subjects in Honour Moderations and the Honour School of which one shall be included in each of the three groups listed above under II;

Cl. 3. (For the avoidance of doubt) the Arnold Ancient History Prize and the Barclay Head Prize in Numismatics are to be read with the schedule.

Cl. 4. For 'Honour School of Modern History' read 'Honour School of Ancient and Modern History'.

Cl. 5. For theses concerning the years before A.D. 285 read 'Chairman of the Board of the Faculty of Classics' for 'Chairman of the Examiners, Honour School of Modern History'.

Cl. 6. For 'Chairman of Examiners, Honour School of Modern History' read 'Chairman of Examiners, Honour School of Ancient and Modern History'.]

[**From 1 October 2004:** VI. A THESIS FROM ORIGINAL RESEARCH

Regulation VI of the Honour School of Modern History applies with the following modifications:

Cl. 3.(a) (For the avoidance of doubt) the Arnold Ancient History Prize and the Barclay Head Prize in Numismatics are to be read with the schedule.

Cl. 5. For 'Honour School of Modern History' read 'Honour School of Ancient and Modern History'. For theses concerning the years before AD 285 read 'Chairman of the Board of the Faculty of Classics' for 'Chairman of the Examiners, Honour School of Modern History'.

Cl. 8. For 'Chairman of Examiners, Honour School of Modern History' read 'Chairman of Examiners, Honour School of Ancient and Modern History'.

VII. AN OPTIONAL ADDITIONAL THESIS

Regulation VII *An Optional Additional Thesis* of the Honour School of Modern History shall apply with the following modifications:

Cl. 4. For dissertations concerning the years before AD 285 read 'Chairman of the Board of the Faculty of Classics' for 'Chairman of the Examiners, Honour School of Modern History'.

Cl. 7. For 'Chairman of Examiners, Honour School of Modern History' read 'Chairman of Examiners, Honours School of Ancient and Modern History'.]

PASS SCHOOL OF ANCIENT AND MODERN HISTORY

Each candidate shall offer the following four subjects:

(i) a period of Ancient History (as prescribed for the Honour School of Ancient and Modern History, paper 1) (one paper)

(ii) a period of the History of the British Isles (as prescribed for the Honour School of Modern History, except any such period as has already been offered in passing the First Public Examination) (one paper)

(iii) a period of General History (as prescribed for the Honour School of Modern History, except any such period as has already been offered in passing the First Public Examination) (one paper)

(iv) one of the Further Subjects in Ancient or Modern History (as prescribed for the Honour School of Ancient and Modern History,) (one paper).

Thesis

In place of a Further Subject paper in Modern History under (iv) above candidates may offer a thesis. The regulations governing theses shall be those prescribed **[From 1 October 2004:** under Regulation VII *An Optional Additional Thesis***]** for the Honour School of Ancient and Modern History.

SPECIAL REGULATIONS FOR THE HONOUR SCHOOL OF ARCHAEOLOGY AND ANTHROPOLOGY

A

1. The examination in the Honour School of Archaeology and Anthropology shall consist of such subjects in Archaeology and Anthropology as the Life and Environmental Sciences Board shall prescribe by regulation from time to time.

2. No candidate shall be admitted to the examination in this school unless he or she has either passed or been exempted from the First Public Examination.

3. The examination shall be under the supervision of the Life and Environmental Sciences Board. Under the overall direction of the board, the examination shall be administered by the School of Archaeology and the School of Anthropology, which shall jointly appoint a standing committee to advise the board as necessary in respect of this examination, and of Honour Moderations and the Preliminary Examination in Archaeology and Anthropology.

4. Candidates will be required to take part in approved fieldwork as an integral part of their course. The fieldwork requirement will normally have been discharged before the Long Vacation of the second year of the course.

B

Candidates are required to offer the following subjects:

1. Social analysis and interpretation.

2. Cultural representations, beliefs, and practices.

[Until 1 October 2005: 3. Approaches to material evidence.**]**

[Until 1 October 2005: 4. Human evolution and ecology.**] [From 1 October 2005:** 3. Ecology and landscape.**]**

5. **[4]** Urbanization and change in complex societies: comparative approaches.

[5, 6, and 7] An approved combination of **[Until 1 October 2005:** two**] [From 1 October 2005:** three**]** optional subjects, from Schedule A (Anthropology) and Schedule B (Archaeology) [see below] or any other optional subject approved by the Committee for the School of Archaeology or the Committee for the School of Anthropology. To encourage a wide-ranging understanding of archaeology and anthropology, options shall be chosen in such a way that they constitute **[Until 1 October 2005:** two**] [From 1 October 2005:** three**]** independent, non-overlapping subjects.

8. A thesis, of not more than 15,000 words, which may be based on research in either archaeology or anthropology or on an interdisciplinary topic.

Candidates may be examined *viva voce*.

9. All candidates will be required to undertake a course of practical work, including laboratory work and the use of computers.

All candidates will be assessed on their practical ability under the following provisions:

(*a*) Class co-ordinators shall make available to the chairman of the examiners records showing the extent to which each candidate has pursued an adequate course of practical work.

(*b*) Candidates shall submit notebooks containing reports on the practical work completed during their final two years of study signed by their practical class supervisor to the Clerk of Schools, High Street, Oxford, not later than noon on Friday of the Fourth week of Trinity Term of the year in which they sit the examination. Upon receipt of the notebook and a signed declaration that the work is the candidate's own, the Clerk of Schools will issue a formal receipt. These notebooks must bear the candidate's examination number but not the candidate's name, which must be concealed.

(*c*) Notebooks which do not achieve a satisfactory standard should be revised and resubmitted.

Schedule A (Anthropology)

6. (*a*) Peoples of North East Africa
(*b*) South Asia (caste and Hinduism)
(*c*) Lowland South America (the political organization and world view of shifting agriculturists)
(*d*) Maritime South East Asia (comparative approach to social organization, religion and art)
(*e*) Gender in cross cultural perspective
(*f*) Human genetical variation
(*g*) Primates in anthropology
(*h*) Material culture and the anthropology of things
(*i*) Visual anthropology and the anthropology of art
(*j*) Japanese society
(*k*) China and the overseas Chinese

Schedule B (Archaeology)

7. (*a*) The origins of modern humans
(*b*) Prehistoric hunter-gatherers in Africa
(*c*) Farming and early states in Sub-Saharan Africa
(*d*) Mesopotamia and Egypt from the emergence of complex society to *c.*2000 BC
(*e*) Mesopotamia and Egypt 1000–500 BC
(*f*) The Late Bronze Age and Early Iron Age Aegean
(*g*) The Greeks and the Mediterranean World *c.* 950–500 BC
(*h*) Greek archaeology and art *c.* 500–323 BC
(*i*) The transformation of the Celtic World, 500 BC–AD 100
(*j*) Neolithic and Bronze Age Europe
(*k*) Roman Archaeology: Cities and settlement under the Empire
(*l*) Art under the Roman Empire, AD 14–336
(*m*) The emergence of Medieval Europe AD 400–900
(*n*) Byzantium: the transition from Antiquity to the Middle Ages, AD 500–1100
(*o*) The formation of the Islamic World, AD 550–950
(*p*) Advanced topics in Archaeological Science
(*q*) The Palaeolithic Period
(*r*) The Archaeology of Minoan Crete: 7000–700 BC.
(*s*) The Archaeology of Anglo-Saxon England in the early Christian Period *c.* 600–750
(*t*) Archaeology and Geographical Information Systems
(*u*) Landscape Archaeology

Because of the potential overlap in subject matter, approval will not be given to candidates who wish to select either two of papers 7(*f*), 7(*g*) or 7(*j*), or both papers 7(*k*) and 7(*l*).

Some options may not be available in every year. Candidates may obtain information about which options may be offered for examination in the following year by consulting lists posted by the Friday of Noughth week of the Hilary Full Term on notice-boards in the Institute of Archaeology, the Institute of Social and Cultural Anthropology, the Research Laboratory for Archaeology and the History of Art and the Balfour Library.

Notice of the options to be offered by candidates must be given to the Registrar not later than the Friday in the fourth week of the Michaelmas Full Term immediately preceding the examination.

8. *Thesis*

1. (*a*) The subject of every thesis shall to the satisfaction of the regulating authority concerned fall within the field of Archaeology or Anthropology or both.

(*b*) The subject of the thesis may, but need not, overlap a subject or period on which the candidate offers papers. Candidates are warned, however, that they must avoid repetition in the papers of material used in their thesis, and that they will not be given credit for material extensively repeated.

(*c*) Candidates must submit through their college, to the Chairman of the Standing Committee for the Undergraduate Degree in Archaeology and Anthropology (c/o the Secretary of the Standing Committee, Institute of Archaeology, Beaumont Street), the title of the proposed thesis, together with (*a*) a synopsis of the subject in about 100 words; and (*b*) a letter of support from the tutor who will supervise the thesis, not later than Monday of the Noughth week of the Trinity Full Term preceding that in which the examination is held.

(*d*) The Standing Committee for the Undergraduate Degree in Archaeology and Anthropology will decide as soon as possible, and in every case by the end of the Fifth week of the Michaelmas Full Term preceding the examination, whether or not to approve the title, and will advise candidates of its decision forthwith.

2. Every thesis must be the candidate's own work, although it is expected that tutors will discuss with candidates the proposed field of study, the sources available, and the method of presentation. Tutors may also read and comment on a first draft.

Candidates must sign a certificate stating that the thesis is their own work, and their tutors shall countersign the certificate affirming that they have assisted the candidate no more than these regulations allow. This certificate must be presented at the same time that the thesis is submitted, but in a separate sealed envelope addressed to the chairman of the examiners.

3. Theses previously submitted for the Honour School of Archaeology and Anthropology may be resubmitted. No thesis will be accepted if it has already been submitted, wholly or substantially, for another final honour school or degree of this University or a degree of any other institution. The certificate must also contain confirmation that the thesis has not already been so submitted.

4. No thesis shall be ineligible because it has been submitted, in whole or in part, for any scholarship or prize of this University advertised in the *Oxford University Gazette*.

5. No thesis shall exceed 15,000 words in length, that limit to include all notes and bibliographies, but not catalogues of material evidence, gazetteers or technical appendices.

All theses must be typed in double-spacing on one side of A4 paper, and must be bound or held firmly in a stiff cover. Two copies must be submitted to the chairman of the examiners, and a third copy must be retained by the candidate. All copies must bear the candidate's examination number but not his or her name.

6. The thesis must be sent, not later than noon on Friday of the Ninth week of Hilary Full Term preceding the examination, to the Chairman of the Examiners, Honour School of Archaeology and Anthropology, Examination Schools, High Street, Oxford.

Candidates may be examined viva voce.

PASS SCHOOL OF ARCHAEOLOGY AND ANTHROPOLOGY

1. The Pass School of Archaeology and Anthropology shall be under the supervision of the Life and Environmental Sciences Board and shall consist of such subjects as it shall by regulation prescribe.

2. No candidate shall be admitted to examination in this school without either having passed, or having been exempted from, the First Public Examination.

1. All candidates will be required to offer *either* four of the following five subjects, as prescribed for the Honour School of Archaeology and Anthropology and a dissertation, in accordance with the detailed regulations for the Honour School of Archaeology and Anthropology, *or* the following five subjects:

(i) Social analysis and interpretation (1 paper)

(ii) Cultural representations, beliefs, and practices (1 paper)

(iii) **[Until 1 October 2005:** Approaches to material evidence**] [From 1 October 2005:** Ecology and landscape**]** (1 paper)

[Until 1 October 2005: (iv) Human evolution and ecology (1 paper)**]**

(v) **[**(iv)**]** Urbanization and change in complex societies: comparative approaches (1 paper)

[From 1 October 2005:

(v) An optional subject from either Schedule A (Anthropology) or Schedule B (Archaeology) (1 paper)**]**.

SPECIAL REGULATIONS FOR THE HONOUR SCHOOL OF CLASSICAL ARCHAEOLOGY AND ANCIENT HISTORY

A

1. The Honour School of Classical Archaeology and Ancient History shall consist of such subjects as the Life and Environmental Sciences Board and the Board of the Faculty of Classics shall jointly prescribe by regulation from time to time.

2. No candidate shall be admitted to the examination in this school without either having passed, or having been exempted from, the First Public Examination.

3. The examination shall be under the joint supervision of the Board of the Faculty of Classics and the Committee for the School of Archaeology, and they shall appoint a joint standing committee, consisting of three representatives of each body, to consider matters relating to the examination and to Honour Moderations and the Preliminary Examination in Classical Archaeology and Ancient History. Whenever any matter cannot be resolved, the Committee for the School of Archaeology and the Board of the Faculty of Classics shall themselves hold a joint meeting and resolve it by majority vote.

4. Candidates shall be required to take part in approved fieldwork as an integral part of the course. The fieldwork requirement shall normally have been discharged before the Long Vacation following the second year of the course.

B

1. Each candidate shall offer the following elements:

I–IV Four period papers chosen from the following group:

A. *Early Greece and the Mediterranean, c.800–500 BC: archaeology and history*

Candidates will be expected to show knowledge of the material and written evidence for the Greek world and the areas of contact between Greek and other Mediterranean peoples. Areas of emphasis will include: the development of Athens and Attica; the non-Greek states bordering the Mediterranean; the relationships between them and the Greeks; Greek settlement overseas; trade and coinage; problems of method in history and archaeology; and problems of chronology.

B. *Greek history, 478–323 BC*

As specified for the Honours School in Ancient and Modern History Paper 1 (*a*).

C. *Greek art and archaeology c.500–300 BC*

As specified for the Honours School in Literae Humaniores Paper IV.2.

D. *Rome, Italy, and the Hellenistic East, c.300–30 BC: archaeology and history*

The course studies the political and cultural interaction and conflict between the Hellenistic East and Roman Italy. Candidates will be expected to show knowledge of the material, visual, and written evidence of the period and to show ability in interpreting it in its archaeological and historical contexts. Candidates should be familiar with the relevant archaeology of the following cities and sites: Pella, Alexandria, Pergamon, Ai Khanoum, Athens, Priene, Delos, Praeneste, Pompeii, Rome.

E. *Roman history AD 14–284*

As specified for the Honours School in Ancient and Modern History Paper 1(*d*).

F. *Roman Archaeology: Cities and Settlement under the Empire*

The subject comprises the study of the Roman city from Augustus to the Tetrarchy placed in the broader context of patterns of rural settlement, agricultural production, transport, and trade. Areas of emphasis include selected key sites (Corinth, Caesarea Maritima, Palmyra, Lepcis Magna, Verulamium [St Albans], and Silchester) and major landscape studies in Italy, Greece, and North Africa. Particular attention is paid to problems and biases in assessing the character of the surviving evidence and in testing theoretical models against physical data. Candidates will be expected to show knowledge of written evidence where relevant as well as of the main categories of surviving ancient material evidence. The subject may not be combined with subject V–VI.B.5, 'Civic Life of the Roman Empire from the Flavian to the Severan Period'.

V, VI Two papers chosen from the following groups, provided that not more than one paper may be chosen from any one group. One subject chosen from Group A or B may be examined not by a paper, but by a thesis covering a topic within that subject, prepared in accordance with Regulation 3 below. Not all the subjects listed below will necessarily be available in any given year.

A. Special subjects in archaeology:

1. *The archaeology of Minoan Crete, 7000–700 BC*

As specified for the Honour School in Archaeology and Anthropology Paper 7(*r*).

2. *The Late Bronze Age in the Aegean*

(This option is not available to those who offered Paper III–IV.A.1 in Honour Moderations in Ancient History and Classical Archaeology).

As specified for the Honour School in Archaeology and Anthropology Paper 7(*f*).

3. *The archaeology of Greek cities*

Candidates will be expected to show knowledge of the material evidence relating to Greek cities from *c.*750 to 50 BC. Areas of emphasis will include physical provision for political institutions, the development of sanctuaries, the choice and use of imagery for public display, domestic architecture and domestic life, and the defence of city and territory.

4. *Art under the Roman Empire, AD 14–337*

The art and visual culture of the Roman empire is studied in its physical, social, and historical contexts. Candidates will be expected to be familiar with major monuments in Rome and Italy and other leading centres of the empire (such as Aphrodisias, Athens, Ephesus, and Lepcis Magna) and with the main strands and contexts of representation in the eastern and western provinces. They will be expected to show knowledge of written evidence where relevant as well as of the main media and categories of surviving images—statues, portrait busts, historical reliefs, funerary monuments, cameos, wallpaintings, mosaics, silverware, and coins.

5. *Greek and Roman wallpainting*

Candidates will be expected to show knowledge of surviving Greek and Roman wallpainting from the archaic period to the imperial period, of its various archaeological and architectural settings, and of the literary and other relevant visual evidence (painted pottery and mosaics) that bears on the study of the evolution and iconography of ancient pictorial representation. In the examination candidates will be required to answer one picture question and three others.

6. *Epigraphy of the Greek and Roman world, c.700 BC–AD 300*

The course focuses on the inscribed text, mainly on stone and bronze, as monument, physical object and medium of information in the classical community, and it explores the evidence of particular inscriptions, or groups of inscriptions, for the political, social and economic history of communities in classical Greece, the Hellenistic world, and the Roman Republic and Empire. Candidates will be expected to show knowledge of epigraphic texts, either in the original languages or in translation, available in standard collections.

R. Sherk, *Roman Documents from the Greek East*,

R. Sherk, E. Badian (series editors), *Translated Documents of Greece and Rome*, Vols. 1–6,

B. Levick, *The Government of the Roman Empire*,

D. Braund, *Augustus to Nero, a sourcebook on Roman history*,

V. Ehrenberg and A. H. M. Jones, *Documents Illustrating the Reigns of Augustus and Tiberius* (2nd edn. reprint),

E. M. Smallwood, *Documents Illustrating the Principates of Gaius, Claudius, and Nero*; *Documents Illustrating the Principates of Nerva, Trajan, and Hadrian*,

M. McCrum, A. G. Woodhead, *Documents of the Principates of the Flavian Emperors*,

M. H. Crawford, *Roman Statutes* I–II,

R. Meiggs, D. M. Lewis, *Greek Historical Inscriptions*,

M. M. Austin, *The Hellenistic World*,

J.-A. Shelton, *As the Romans Did. A Sourcebook in Roman Social History*, (2nd edn.).

7. *Greek and Roman coins*

Candidates will be expected to show knowledge of the principal developments in coinage from its beginnings *c.*600 BC until the reign of Diocletian (AD 284–305). Emphasis will be placed on the ways in which numismatic evidence may be used to address questions of historical and archaeological interest.

8. *The transformation of the Celtic world, 500 BC–AD 100*

As specified for the Honour School in Archaeology and Anthropology Paper 7(*i*).

9. *The emergence of Medieval Europe, AD 400–900*

As specified for the Honour School in Archaeology and Anthropology Paper 7(*m*).

10. *The Late Roman Empire, AD 284–565*

The paper studies the archaeology and art of the Roman Empire from Diocletian through the death of Justinian. Subjects include: urban change; development of the countryside in the east; industry; patterns of trade; persistence of pagan art; and the impact of Christianity (church building, pilgrimage, monasticism) on architecture and art. The main sites to be studied are: Rome, Constantinople, Trier, Verulamium,

Ravenna, Justiniana Prima, Caesarea Maritima, Scythopolis, Jerusalem, and sites in the Roman provinces of Syria and Palestine.

11. *Byzantium: the transition from Antiquity to the Middle Ages,* AD *500–1000*
As specified for the Honour School in Archaeology and Anthropology Paper 7(*n*).

12. *The formation of the Islamic world,* AD *550–950*
As specified for the Honour School in Archaeology and Anthropology Paper 7(*o*).

13. *Approaches to material evidence*
As specified for the Honour School in Archaeology and Anthropology Paper 3.

B. Special subjects in history:

1. *Athenian democracy in the Classical age*
As specified for the Honour School in Literae Humanoires Paper I.8.

2. *Alexander the Great and his early successors, 336–302* BC
As specified for the Honour School in Literae Humaniores Paper I.9.

3. *Cicero: politics and thought in the Late Republic*
As specified for the Honour School in Literae Humaniores Paper I.10.

4. *Civic life of the Roman Empire from the Flavian to the Severan period*
(This option may not be combined with either Paper I–IV.F. or Paper V–VI.A.7.)
As specified for the Honour School in Literae Humaniores Paper I.11.

5. *Religions in the Greek and Roman world, c.30* BC–AD *312*
As specified for the Honour School in Literae Humaniores Paper I.12.

6. *Sexuality and gender in Greece and Rome*
As specified for the Honour School in Literae Humaniores Paper I.13.

7. *From Julian the Apostate to St Augustine,* AD *350–95*
As specified for the Honour School in Modern History Paper IV.1.

8. *Francia in the age of Clovis and Gregory of Tours*
As specified for the Honour School in Modern History Paper IV.2.

C. Ancient languages:

1. *Further ancient Greek*
(This option is available to those who offered Paper III–IV.C.1 in Honour Moderations in Classical Archaeology and Ancient History and to any other candidate whose knowledge of ancient Greek is deemed by the Standing Committee to be appropriate to the course.)

Candidates will be required to show more advanced knowledge of ancient Greek grammar and vocabulary. The set texts for the course are Xenophon, *Hellenica*, 1–2.3.10 and Pausanias, *Description of Greece*, 1.1–24.7. The paper will consist of a passage of unseen translation, and two further passages for translation, one from each set text.

2. *Further Latin*
(This option is available to those who offered Paper III–IV.C.2 in Honour Moderations in Classical Archaeology and Ancient History, and to any other candidate whose knowledge of Latin is deemed by the Standing Committee to be appropriate to the course).

Candidates will be required to show more advanced knowledge of Latin grammar and vocabulary. The set texts for the course are Livy, Book 21 and Pliny the Elder, *Natural History* 35.1–40 (148). The paper will consist of a passage of unseen translation, and two further passages for translation, one from each set text.

3. *Beginning ancient Greek*

(This option is not available to those who offered Paper III–IV.C.1 in Honour Moderations in Classical Archaeology and Ancient History).

As specified for Honour Moderations in Classical Archaeology and Ancient History Paper III–IV.C.1.

4. *Beginning Latin*

(This option is not available to those who offered Paper III–IV.C.2 in Honour Moderations in Classical Archaeology and Ancient History).

As specified for Honour Moderations in Classical Archaeology and Ancient History Paper II–IV.C.2.

VII *A Site or Museum report*, prepared in accordance with Regulation 3 below. The report must be on

Either (i) an excavation or archaeological site, based on participation or autopsy and on a consideration of all relevant historical and archaeological sources;

Or (ii) a coherent body of finds from one site or of one category, based as far as possible on autopsy and on a consideration of all relevant historical and archaeological sources.

VIII An optional *Additional Thesis*, prepared in accordance with Regulation 3 below. This Additional Thesis is not to be confused with the thesis which may be offered in place of Paper V or VI.

2. Candidates may also be examined viva voce.

3. *Theses.*

(*a*) This regulation governs theses submitted under Regulation 1.V–VI and VIII, and the Site or Museum report submitted under VII.

(*b*) The subjects for all theses and for the Site or Museum report must, to the satisfaction of the Standing Committee, fall within the scope of the Honour School of Classical Archaeology and Ancient History. The subject may, but need not, overlap any subject on which the candidate offers papers. Candidates are warned that they should avoid repetition in papers of materials used in their theses, and that substantial repetition may be penalized. Candidates who offer an optional Additional Thesis under Regulation 1.VIII and another thesis must avoid all overlap between them.

(*c*) Candidates proposing to offer a thesis must submit, through their college, to the Chairman of the Standing Committee not later than the Wednesday of the first week of the Michaelmas Full Term preceding the examination the following: (i) the title of the proposed thesis or report, together with (ii) a synopsis of the subject in about 100 words, (iii) a statement whether the thesis is to be submitted under Regulation 1.VI–VI.A or B, or under Regulation 1.VIII, and (iv) a letter of approval from their tutor. The Standing Committee shall decide as soon as possible whether or not to approve the title and shall advise the candidate immediately. No decision shall be deferred beyond the end of the third week of Michaelmas Full Term.

(*d*) Every thesis or report shall be the candidate's own work. Tutors may, however, discuss with candidates the field of study, the sources available, and the method of presentation, and may also read and comment on a first draft. The amount of assistance a candidate may receive shall not exceed an amount equivalent to the teaching of a normal paper. Candidates shall make a declaration that the thesis or report is their own work, and their tutors shall countersign the declaration confirming that, to the best of their knowledge and belief, this is so. This declaration must be placed in a sealed envelope bearing the candidate's examination number and presented together with the thesis or report.

(*e*) Theses and reports previously submitted for the Honour School of Classical Archaeology and Ancient History may be resubmitted. No thesis or report shall be accepted which has already been submitted, wholly or substantially, for another Honour School or degree of this or any other institution, and the certificate shall also state that the thesis or report has not been so submitted. No thesis or report shall, however, be ineligible because it has been or is being submitted for any prize of this university.

(*f*) Candidates should aim at a length of 10,000 words but must not exceed 15,000 words (both figures inclusive of notes and appendices but excluding bibliography). No person or body shall have authority to permit the limit of 15,000 words to be exceeded. Where appropriate, there shall be a select bibliography and a list of sources.

(*g*) All theses and reports must be typed in double spacing on one side only of quarto or A4 paper with any notes and references at the foot of each page, and must be bound or held firmly in a stiff cover and identified by the candidate's examination number only. Two copies of each thesis or report shall be submitted to the examiners. Any candidate wishing to have one copy of his or her thesis or report returned must enclose with it, in an envelope bearing only his or her candidate number, a self-addressed sticky label.

(*h*) Candidates wishing to change the title of a thesis or report after it has been approved may apply for permission for the change to be granted by the Chairman of the Standing Committee (if the application is made before the first day of Hilary Full Term preceding the examination) or (if later) the Chairman of the Examiners, Honour School of Classical Archaeology and Ancient History.

(*i*) Candidates shall submit any thesis or report, identified by the candidates' examination number only, not later than noon on Friday of the week before the Trinity Full Term of the examination to the Examination Schools, High Street, Oxford, addressed to the Chairman of the Examiners, Honour School of Classical Archaeology and Ancient History.

PASS SCHOOL OF CLASSICAL ARCHAEOLOGY AND ANCIENT HISTORY

A

1. The Pass School of Classical Archaeology and Ancient History shall consist of such subjects as the Committee for Archaeology and the Board of the Faculty of Classics shall jointly prescribe by regulation from time to time.

2. No candidate shall be admitted to the examination in this school without either having passed, or having been exempted from, the First Public Examination.

B

1. Candidates must satisfy the examiners in the following four papers:

I–II. Two papers selected from the options specified under I–IV.A–F of the Regulations for the Honour School of Classical Archaeology and Ancient History.

III. A paper selected from the options specified under V–VI.A of the Regulations for the Honour School of Classical Archaeology and Ancient History.

IV. A paper selected from the options specified under V–VI.B of the Regulations for the Honour School of Classical Archaeology and Ancient History.

2. A thesis on a subject approved by the Standing Committee may be offered in place of *either* Paper III or Paper IV, prepared in accordance with Regulation 3 of the Honour School of Classical Archaeology and Ancient History.

NOTES

SPECIAL REGULATIONS FOR THE HONOUR SCHOOL OF CLASSICS AND ENGLISH

A

1. The Honour School of Classics and English shall be under the joint supervision of the Boards of the Faculties of Classics and English Language and Literature and shall consist of such subjects as they shall jointly by regulation prescribe. The boards shall establish a joint committee consisting of three representatives of each faculty, of whom at least one on each side shall be a member of the respective faculty board, to advise them as necessary in respect of the examination and of Honour Moderations and of the Preliminary Examination in Classics and English.

2. No candidate shall be admitted to the examination in this school unless he has either passed or been exempted from the First Public Examination.

3. Candidates who have been adjudged worthy of Honours or who have satisfied the moderators in Honour Moderations in Classics will not be permitted to enter their names for the examination.

4. The Chairman of the Examiners for the Honour School of English Language and Literature shall designate such of the number of the examiners as may be required for the English subjects of the examination for the Honour School of Classics and English, and the nominating committee for examiners appointed by the Board of the Faculty of Classics shall nominate such of the number of examiners as may be required for the Classics subjects of the examination. When these appointments shall have been made the number of examiners shall be deemed to be complete.

B

Candidates who have been adjudged worthy of Honours or have satisfied the examiners in Honour Moderations in Classics will *not* be permitted to offer the course.

All candidates must offer seven papers: A, two in English; B, two in Classics; and C, three linking both sides of the school. They may offer in addition *either* an eighth paper selected from papers 2 and 4, *or* a thesis, provided that a candidate may not offer more than one option from either 2(*d*) or 2 (*e*). Each paper will be of three hours' duration except where otherwise indicated.

[Until 1 October 2004: Any candidate may be examined viva voce.**]**

A. English

1. One of the following periods of English literature as specified for the Honour School of English Language and Literature: 1100–1509 (one paper of three hours

and one paper of two hours), 1509–1642, 1642–1740, 1740–1832, 1832–1900, 1900–present day, provided that candidates who have passed Honour Moderations in Classics and English may not offer the period 1509–1642, and candidates who have passed the First Public Examination in English Language and Literature, or any subject and English, may not offer whichever of the periods 1832–1900 or 1900–present day they have already offered in that examination. Candidates will be given an opportunity to show their knowledge of classical influence.

2. One of the following as specified for the Honour School of English Language and Literature:

(*a*) a second of the periods specified in 1 above;
(*b*) Shakespeare (Course I, Subject 2);
(*c*) the History, Use, and Theory of the English Language (Course I, Subject 1);
(*d*) any of the Special Authors from the list for the year concerned which will be published in the *University Gazette* by the beginning of the fifth week of the Trinity Term two years before the examination (Course I, Subject 7) (extended essay);
(*e*) Special topics subjects (*a*), (*b*), (*c*), (*e*), (*f*), (*g*), (*h*), (*i*) (Course I, Subject 8) (extended essay);
(*f*) The Development of Standard Literary English to *c.*1750 (Course II, A.5);
(*g*) English Literature, 600–1100 (Course II, A1);
(*h*) Old English Philology (Course II, B1);
(*i*) Middle English Dialectology (Course II, B2);
(*j*) Modern English Philology (Course II, B3);
(*k*) Linguistic Theory (Course II, B4);
(*l*) The Archaeology of Anglo-Saxon England, seventh to ninth centuries AD (Course II, B10);
(*m*) Gothic (Course II, B11);
(*n*) Old Saxon (Course II, B12);
(*o*) Old High German (Course II, B13);
(*p*) Middle High German (Course II, B14);
(*q*) Old Norse (Course II, B15);
(*r*) Old Norse Texts (Course II, B16);
(*s*) Old French Language 1150–1250 (Course II, B18);
(*t*) Medieval French Literature 1100–1300 (Course II, B19) *or* Medieval French Literature 1300–1500 (Course II, B20);
(*u*) Medieval Welsh Language and Literature I (Course II, B21) *or* Medieval Welsh Language and Literature II (Course II, B22);
(*v*) Old and Early Middle Irish Language and Literature (Course II, B23)
(*w*) The Latin Literature of the British Isles before the Norman conquest of England (Course II, B25);
(*x*) Medieval and Renaissance Romance (Course II, B7(*a*));
(*y*) Scottish Literature pre-1600 (Course II, B7(*b*))

provided that candidates who offer Shakespeare or Special Authors will not be permitted to answer in other papers questions on the authors chosen.

B. CLASSICS

3. *Either* (*a*) Greek Literature of the Fifth Century BC (one paper of three hours (commentary and essay) with an additional paper (one-and-a-half hours) of translation) [Honour School of Literae Humaniores, subject III.1].

or (*b*) Latin Literature of the First Century BC (one paper of three hours (commentary and essay) with an additional paper (one-and-a-half hours) of translation) [Honour School of Literae Humaniores, subject III.5].

4. One of the following. (It cannot be guaranteed that university lectures or classes or college teaching will be available on all subjects in every academic year. Candidates are advised to consult their tutors about the availability of teaching when selecting their subjects.)

(i) *Either* (*a*) Greek Literature of the Fifth Century BC
or (*b*) Latin Literature of the First Century BC
(whichever is not offered under 3 above).

(ii) *Either* (*a*) Greek Lyric and Elegiac Poetry [Honour School of Literae Humaniores, subject III.2(*b*)]
or (*b*) Pindar and Bacchylides [Honour School of Literae Humaniores, subject III.2(*c*)].

(iii) [Honour School of Literae Humaniores, subject III.3; not to be offered in combination with the Link paper *Tragedy* at C.6, 7 (*a*)]
Either (*a*) Aeschylus
or (*b*) Euripides.

(iv) [Honour School of Literae Humaniores, subject III.4]
Either (*a*) *Plato*
or (*b*) Hellenistic Poetry.

(v) [Honour School of Literae Humaniores, subject III.6]
Either (*a*) Latin Didactic Poetry
or (*b*) Latin Satire (not to be offered in combination with the Link paper *Satire* at C.6, 7 (*c*))

(vi) *Either* (*a*) Cicero the Orator [Honour School of Literae Humaniores, subject III.7 (*a*)]
or (*b*) Horace [Honour School of Literae Humaniores, subject III.7 (*b*)]
or (*c*) Ovid [Honour School of Literae Humaniores, subject III.7 (*c*)].

(vii) [Honour School of Literae Humaniores, subject III.8; in each case candidates may offer whichever version they choose]
Either (*a*) Greek and Roman Comedy (not to be offered in combination with the Link Paper *Comedy* at C.6, 7 (*b*))
or (*b*) Ancient Literary Criticism (not to be offered in combination with the Link paper *Rhetoric and literary theory in ancient and modern times* at C.6, 7 (*f*))
or (*c*) The Ancient Novel.

(viii) Greek Textual Criticism [Honour School of Literae Humaniores, subject III.9].

(ix) Latin Textual Criticism [Honour School of Literae Humaniores, subject III.10].

(x) Greek Historical Linguistics [Honour School of Literae Humaniores, subject V.1].

(xi) Latin Historical Linguistics [Honour School of Literae Humaniores, subject V.2].

(xii) Historical Linguistics and Comparative Philology [Honour Moderations in Classics Course IA, paper V, VI F(1)].

(xiii) General Linguistics and Comparative Philology [Honour School of Literae Humaniores, subject V.3]. (Candidates offering section (*a*), General Linguistics, may not also offer the English subject *Linguistic Theory* and may not answer a question from *Section A* of the English subject *The History, Use, and Theory of the English Language*.)

(xiv) *Either* (*a*) Plato, *Republic* (subject 130(*a*)) *or* (*b*) Aristotle, *Nicomachean Ethics* (Subject 131 (*a*)), as specified in 'Regulations for Philosophy in some of the Honour Schools'.

(xv) *Either* (*a*) The Early Greek World and Herodotus' Histories: [Honour School of Literae Humaniores, subject I. 1].
or (*b*) Thucydides and the Greek World: [Honour School of Literae Humaniores, subject I. 2].
or (*c*) The End of the Peloponnesian War to the Death of Phillip II of Macedon: [Honour School of Literae Humaniores, subject I. 3].
or (*d*) Rome and the Mediterranean and the Histories of Polybius: [Honour School of Literae Humaniores, subject I. 4].
or (*e*) The End of the Roman Republic: Cicero and Sallust: [Honour School of Literae Humaniores, subject I. 5].
or (*f*) Rome, Italy and Empire under Caesar, the Triumvirate and early Principate: [Honour School of Literae Humaniores, subject I. 6].
or (*g*) The World of Tacitus and Pliny: Politics and Culture: [Honour School of Literae Humaniores, subject I. 7].

Note: Candidates offering any of subjects (xv) (*a*)–(*g*) must also offer the associated translation paper set in the Honour School of Literae Humaniores.

C. LINK PAPERS

For Paper 5 *Epic* and Papers 6, 7 (*a*), (*b*), (*c*), and (*d*) *Tragedy, Comedy, Satire,* and *Pastoral*: Candidates will be expected to be familiar with the texts specified. Opportunities will, however, be given to show knowledge of authors and texts beyond those prescribed. Candidates must answer at least one question that relates Classical and English Literature.

5. *Epic*

With special reference to Homer, Virgil, Lucan, Milton, Dryden, Pope.

There will be a compulsory question requiring candidates to comment on and bring out points of comparison between *either* (*a*) a passage of Homer and one or more English translations *or* (*b*) a passage of Virgil and one or more English translations. The passages will be drawn from (*a*) *Odyssey*, Books 6 and 9–12, (*b*) *Aeneid*, Books 7, 8 and 12. There will also be a passage for compulsory comment from Milton, *Paradise Lost.*

6, 7. Two of the following papers of which at least one must be from (*a*), (*b*), (*c*), and (*d*). Course II candidates may not offer a paper which they have previously offered in their first year of study.

(*a*) *Tragedy* [Candidates who offer paper B.4(iii) (*Aeschylus* or *Euripides*) may not also offer this paper]

With special reference to:
Aeschylus, *Agamemnon.*
Sophocles, *Oedipus the King.*
Euripides, *Medea, Hecuba.*
Seneca, *Medea, Thyestes.*
Kyd, *The Spanish Tragedy.*
Marlowe, *Tamburlaine the Great* (Parts I and II), *Edward II, Dr Faustus, Dido Queen of Carthage.*
Shakespeare.
Jonson, *Sejanus, Catiline.*
Webster, *The White Devil, The Duchess of Malfi.*
Middleton, *The Changeling, Women Beware Women.*
Ford, *'Tis Pity She's a Whore.*
Milton, *Samson Agonistes.*

There will be an optional commentary question with passages drawn from Aeschylus, *Agamemnon,* and Seneca, *Thyestes.*

(*b*) *Comedy* [Candidates who offer *Greek and Roman Comedy* under B.4 may not also offer this paper]

With special reference to:

Aristophanes, *Birds*.
Menander, *Dyscolus*.
Plautus, *Amphitryo* and *Menaechmi*.
Terence, *Adelphoe*.
Gascoigne, *Supposes*.
Lyly, *Campaspe, Mother Bombie*.
Shakespeare.
Jonson, *Every Man in his Humour, Volpone, Epicoene, The Alchemist, Bartholomew Fair*.
Wycherley, *The Country Wife*.
Vanbrugh, *The Relapse*.
Congreve, *The Double Dealer, The Way of the World*.
Sheridan, *The Rivals, The School for Scandal, The Critic*.

There will be an optional commentary question with passages drawn from Aristophanes, *Birds*, and Terence, *Adelphoe*.

(*c*) *Satire* [Candidates who offer paper B.4 (v)(*b*) *Latin Satire* may not also offer this paper]

With special reference to Horace, *Satires,* Book I, 1, 4–6, 9–10, and Book II, 1, 6; Persius 1 and 5; Juvenal 1, 3, 6, and 10; and the satires of Wyatt, Donne, Marston, Dryden, Johnson, Pope.

There will be an optional commentary question with passages drawn from Juvenal, *Satires*, 1, 3, 6, 10.

(*d*) *Pastoral*

With special reference to Theocritus, *Idylls*, 1, 3, 4, 6, 7, 10, 11; Bion, *Adonidis Epitaphium*; [Moschus], *Epitaphium Bionis*; Virgil, *Eclogues*; Mantuan 1; Tasso, *Aminta*; Guarini, *Il Pastor Fido*; Spenser, *Astrophel* and *The Shepheardes Calendar, Faerie Queen* VI ix–xii; Fletcher, *The Faithful Shepherdess*; Milton, *Lycidas* and *Epitaphium Damonis*; Pope, *Windsor Forest, Pastorals*; Shelley, *Adonais*; Arnold, *Thyrsis*.

There will be an optional commentary question with passages drawn from Theocritus, *Idylls* 1, 3, 4, 6, 7, 10, 11, and Virgil, *Eclogues*.

(*e*) *Medieval Latin*

As specified for the Honour School of Literae Humaniores.

(*f*) *Rhetoric and literary theory in ancient and modern times*

[Candidates who offer *Ancient Literary Criticism* under B.4 may not also offer this paper]

(*g*) *The Reception of Greece and/or Rome in British Literature, 1830–1900*

There will be four topics:

1. The Reception of Homer.
2. The Reception of Greek Drama (Aeschylus, Sophocles, Euripides, Aristophanes).
3. The Reception of Virgil and Horace.
4. Roman Historical Fictions, with special reference to Lytton, *The Last Days of Pompeii*, Macaulay, *Lays of Ancient Rome*, and Pater, *Marius the Epicurean*.

The examination paper will contain questions on all four topics in Section A, and a broad range of more general questions in Section B. Candidates will be required to answer four questions, including at least one from Section B; they will be required to show knowledge of the reception of either Greece (topics 1 and 2) or Rome (topics 3 and 4), but will have the opportunity to show knowledge of both. English authors whose works may be considered include Arnold, the Brownings, Pater, Ruskin, and Tennyson.

Thesis

1. Any candidate who does not offer an eighth paper may offer a thesis, subject to the following provisions:

(i) The subject of an optional thesis must be substantially connected with any subject area currently available in those parts of the Honour School of Literae Humaniores and Course I or Course II of the Honour School of English Language and Literature which are available to candidates for the Honour School.

(ii) The subject of the thesis may, but need not, overlap any subject or period on which the candidates offer papers. But candidates are warned that they must avoid repetition in their papers of material used in their theses, and that they will not be given credit for material extensively repeated.

(iii) Candidates proposing to offer a thesis must submit, through their college, to the Chairman of the Board of the Faculty of Classics or the Deputy Chairman of the Board of the Faculty of English Language and Literature as appropriate, the title of the proposed thesis, together with (*a*) a synopsis of the subject in about 100 words; and (*b*) a letter of support from a tutor, not later than Wednesday of the second week of the Michaelmas Full Term preceding the examination.

(iv) The faculty board will decide as soon as possible, and in every case by the end of the fifth week of the Michaelmas Full Term preceding the examination, whether or not to approve the title, and will advise candidates of its decision forthwith.

(v) Candidates must give notice of withdrawal of submission of a thesis to the chairman of examiners not later than the end of the eighth week of the Hilary Full Term preceding the examination.

2. Every thesis must be the candidate's own work. Tutors may, however, advise on the choice and scope of the subject, provide a reading list, and read and comment on a first draft.

Candidates must sign a certificate stating that the thesis is their own work, and their tutors shall countersign the certificate affirming that they have assisted the candidates no more than these regulations allow. This certificate must be placed in a sealed envelope bearing the candidate's examination number and presented together with the thesis.

3. No thesis will be accepted if it has already been submitted, wholly or substantially, for a degree of this or any other university; and the certificate must also contain confirmation that the thesis has not already been so submitted.

4. No thesis shall be ineligible because it has been submitted, in whole or in part, for any scholarship or prize of this University advertised in the *Oxford University Gazette*.

5. The thesis shall not exceed 6,000 words in length. In the case of a commentary on a text, and at the discretion of the chairman of the examiners, any substantial quoting of that text need not be included in the word limit. Where appropriate, there must be a select bibliography and a list of sources.

All theses must be typed in double-spacing on one side only of quarto or A4 paper, and must be bound or held firmly in a stiff cover. The top copy must be submitted to the chairman of the examiners, and a second copy must be retained by the candidate.

6. Any candidate proposing to submit a thesis shall give notice of this to the Registrar on the examination entry form not later than Friday of the fourth week of the Michaelmas Full Term preceding the examination (this in addition to seeking approval for the thesis as stipulated in clause 1(iii) above). The thesis itself, identified by the candidate's examination number only, must be sent, not later than noon on the first Monday of the Trinity Full Term in which the examination will be held, to the Chairman of the Examiners, Honour School of Classics and English, Examination Schools, High Street, Oxford.

Texts of Greek and Latin authors

Passages from Aristophanes, *Birds* will be set from the edition of N. Dunbar (Oxford, Student Edition). Passages from Terence, *Adelphoe* will be set from the edition of R. H. Martin (Cambridge University Press). The texts of other Greek and Latin authors used in the examination will be as prescribed by the regulations for the Honour School of Literae Humaniores.

PASS SCHOOL OF CLASSICS AND ENGLISH

Candidates must offer five papers, except that any candidate may submit a thesis in place of one of the papers subject to the provisions below. The papers shall be: A, two in English; B, two in Classics; and C, one linking both sides of the school. The papers in English must be chosen from List A (English) as prescribed for the Honour School of Classics and English; the papers in Classics must be chosen from List B (Classics) as prescribed for the same Honour School; the linking paper must be chosen from List C (Linking Papers) as prescribed for the same Honour School. The regulations of the Honour School of Classics and English shall apply to these papers, including any regulations concerning the combination of options.

Thesis

In place of any paper candidates may offer a thesis, provided that no candidate may substitute a thesis for more than one paper altogether. The subject of the thesis must fall within the scope of the paper for which it is substituted; the remaining regulations concerning the thesis are those prescribed for the Honour School of Classics and English.

NOTES

SPECIAL REGULATIONS FOR THE HONOUR SCHOOL OF CLASSICS AND MODERN LANGUAGES

A

1. The subjects of the examination in the Honour School of Classics and Modern Languages shall be (*a*) the Greek and Latin languages and literatures and the thought and civilization of the Ancient World and (*b*) those modern European languages and literatures studied in the Honour School of Modern Languages.

2. No candidate shall be admitted to the examination in this School unless he or she has either passed or been exempted from the First Public Examination.

3. The examiners shall indicate in the lists issued by them the language offered by each candidate obtaining honours or satisfying the examiners under Ch. VI, Sect. II. C, §1, cl. 21 (iv) and (v).

4. The examination in the Honour School shall be under the joint supervision of the Boards of the Faculties of Classics and of Modern Languages, which shall appoint a standing joint committee to make, and to submit to the two boards, proposals for regulations concerning the examination.

5. (i) The Public Examiners for Classics in this school shall be such of the Public Examiners in the Honour School of Literae Humaniores as may be required, together with one or two additional examiners, if required, who shall be nominated by the committee for the nomination of Public Examiners in the Honour School of Literae Humaniores; those for Modern Languages shall be such of the Public Examiners in the Honour School of Modern Languages as shall be required.

(ii) It shall be the duty of the chairman of the Public Examiners in the Honour School of Modern Languages to designate such of their number as may be required for Modern Languages in the Honour School of Classics and Modern Languages, and when this has been done, and the examiners for Classics have been nominated, the number of the examiners in Classics and Modern Languages shall be deemed to be complete.

B

Candidates will be examined in accordance with the examination regulations set out below.

They will also be required to spend, after their matriculation, a year of residence in an appropriate country or countries, and to provide on their entry form for the examination a certificate that they have done this, signed by the Head or by a tutor of their society. Candidates wishing to be dispensed from the requirement to undertake a year of residence abroad must apply in writing to the Chairman of the Medieval and Modern Languages Board, 41 Wellington Square, Oxford, OX1 2JF, stating their reasons for requesting dispensation and enclosing a letter of support from their society.

Candidates will be expected to carry out during this year abroad such work as their society may require. It is strongly recommended that candidates should apply through the Central Bureau for Educational Visits and Exchanges for an Assistantship, where these are available, and should accept one if offered. Candidates who are not able to obtain an Assistantship should during their year abroad follow a course or courses in an institution or institutions approved by their society, or should spend their time in such other circumstances as are acceptable to their society. Candidates will agree with their College Tutor in advance of their year abroad an independent course of study to be followed during that period.

Except in a Special Subject or an alternative to a Special Subject, a candidate shall offer one modern language and its literature only except that candidates offering Ancient Greek may offer the subject Modern Greek Poetry, **[From 1 October 2004:** and all candidates may offer the subject Byzantine Literature**]** as specified in the regulations below, if and only if they are not offering Medieval and Modern Greek as their modern language.

Any candidate may be examined viva voce.

Oral Examination: as specified for the Honour School of Modern Languages.

In every case where, under the regulations for the school, candidates have any choice between one or more papers or subjects, every candidate shall give notice to the Registrar not later than the Friday in the fourth week of Michaelmas Full Term preceding the examination of all the papers and subjects being so offered.

Candidates offering two papers both of which involve the study of the same author or authors, may not make the same text or texts the principal subject of an answer in both the papers.

All candidates must offer eight subjects as specified below and may also offer an Additional Subject as specified at no.9.

[Until 1 October 2005: 1. Unprepared translation into the modern language [Honour School of Modern Languages, paper I].

2. Unprepared translation from the modern language [Honour School of Modern Languages, paper II A (*i*) and paper II B (*i*)] (two papers of one and a half hours each).

3. A period of the literature of the modern language [Honour School of Modern Languages, paper VI, VII, or VIII].

4. One of the following:

(i) Linguistic Studies I [Honour School of Modern Languages, paper IV].

(ii) Linguistic Studies II [Honour School of Modern Languages, paper V].

(iii) Early texts prescribed for study as examples of literature [Honour School of Modern Languages, paper IX].

(iv) Modern Prescribed Authors (i) [Honour School of Modern Languages, paper X].

(v) Modern Prescribed Authors (ii) [Honour School of Modern Languages, paper XI].

(vi) Special Subject [Honour School of Modern Languages, paper XIII]] **[From 1 October 2005:**

1. Honour School of Modern Languages, Paper I.
2. Honour School of Modern Languages, Papers IIA(i) and IIB(i).
3. Honour School of Modern Languages, *one* paper chosen from Papers VI, VII or VIII.
4. Honour School of Modern Languages, *one* paper chosen from Papers IV, V, IX, X, XI or XII.**]**

5. *Either* (*a*) Greek Literature of the fifth century BC (one paper of three hours (commentary and essay) with an additional paper (one-and-a-half hours) of translation) [Honour School of Literae Humaniores, subject III.1].

or (*b*) Latin Literature of the first century BC (one paper of three hours (commentary and essay) with an additional paper (one-and-a-half hours) of translation) [Honour School of Literae Humaniores, subject III.5].

6, 7. Two of the following subjects (i) to (xxiii). Candidates not offering (xxii), Second Classical Language must include at least one of subjects (i)–(xiv).

Note: (*a*) Subject (xxii), (xxiii), Second Classical Language counts as *two* subjects. It may not be offered by candidates who have satisfied the Moderators in Course IA, IB, or IC of Honour Moderations in Classics or of the Preliminary Examination in Classics, or who offered both Ancient Greek and Latin in the Preliminary Examination for Modern Languages. Candidates offering it must also offer at least one of subjects (i)–(xix) under 8 or 9 below.

Note: (*b*) It cannot be guaranteed that university lectures or classes or college teaching will be available on all subjects in every academic year. Candidates are advised to consult their tutors about the availability of teaching when selecting their subjects.

(i) *Either* (*a*) Greek Literature of the fifth century BC
or (*b*) Latin Literature of the first century BC
(whichever is not offered under 5 above).

(ii) [Honour School of Literae Humaniores, subject III.2].
Either (*a*) Early Greek Hexameter Poetry
or (*b*) Greek Lyric and Elegiac Poetry
or (*c*) Pindar and Bacchylides.

(iii) [Honour School of Literae Humaniores, subject III.3] (not to be offered in combination with subject 8 (iii), Ancient and French Classical Tragedy).
Either (*a*) Aeschylus
or (*b*) Euripides.

(iv) [Honour School of Literae Humaniores, subject III.4].
Either (*a*) Plato
or (*b*) Hellenistic Poetry.

(v) [Honour School of Literae Humaniores, subject III.6].
Either (*a*) Latin Didactic Poetry
or (*b*) Latin Satire

(vi) [Honour School of Literae Humaniores, subject III.7].
Either (*a*) Cicero the Orator
or (*b*) Horace
or (*c*) Ovid

or (*d*) Seneca and Lucan (not to be offered in combination with (v)(*d*) Silver Latin Epic or subject 8 (iii), Ancient and French Classical Tragedy).

(vii) [Honour School of Literae Humaniores, subject III.8; **in each case version (i) is the only version available to candidates who have satisfied the Moderators in Course IA, IB, or IC of Honour Moderations in Classics or of the Preliminary Examination in Classics, or who offered both Ancient Greek and Latin in the Preliminary Examination for Modern Languages]**

Either (*a*) Greek and Roman Comedy

or (*b*) Ancient Literary Criticism

or (*c*) The Ancient Novel.

(viii) Greek Textual Criticism [Honour School of Literae Humaniores, subject III.9].

(ix) Latin Textual Criticism [Honour School of Literae Humaniores, subject III.10].

(x) Homer, *Iliad* [Honour Moderations in Classics Course IA, paper I]. (This subject may not be offered by candidates who have satisfied the Moderators in Course IA, IB, IC, or IIB of Honour Moderations in Classics and may not be offered in combination with subject (ii)(*a*), Early Greek Hexameter Poetry.)

(xi) Virgil, *Aeneid*. Translation and essay questions will be required; commentary questions will be optional. Candidates will be required to scan a short passage. (This subject may not be offered by candidates who have satisfied the Moderators in Course IA, IB, IC, or IIA of Honour Moderations in Classics.)

(xii) *Either* (*a*) The Conversion of Augustine [Honour School of Literae Humaniores, subject III.11(*a*)].

or (*b*) Medieval Latin [Honour School of Literae Humaniores, subject III.11(*b*)].

or (*c*) The Latin Works of Petrarch, with special study of *Africa* (ed. N. Festa, Florence, 1926), Books I, II, V, VII, IX. Candidates will also be expected to have read *Vita Scipionis* (in *La vita di Scipione l'Africano*, ed. G. Martillotti, Milano-Napoli, 1954), and to show acquaintance with Petrarch's major Latin works (e.g. *Rerum memorandarum libri* (ed. G. Billanovich, Florence, 1945), *De secreto conflictu curarum mearum*, *De vita solitaria*, *Epistolae familiares* (in F. Petrarca, *Prose*, ed. G. Martillotti, P. G. Ricci, E. Carrara, E. Bianchi, Milano-Napoli, 1955)).

[Until 1 October 2004: *or* *(*d*) Procopius, with special study of *Bellum Persicum* 1.24, 2.22–3; *Bellum Gothicum* 4.20, 4.29–35; *Historia Arcana* 6–12 (all in Dewing's Loeb edition).**] [From 1 October 2004:**

or **(*d*) Byzantine Literature [Honour School of Literae Humaniores, subject III.11(*c*)]. (This subject is not available to candidates offering Medieval and Modern Greek as their modern language.)**]**

(xiii) Greek Historical Linguistics [Honour School of Literae Humaniores, subject V.1]. (This subject may be combined with one but not more than one of (xiv), (xv), and (xvi).)

(xiv) Latin Historical Linguistics [Honour School of Literae Humaniores, subject V.2]. (This subject may be combined with one but not more than one of (xiii), (xv), and (xvi).)

---

* Paper (xii) (*d*) on Procopius may not be offered after October 2003 by candidates following Course I.

[From 1 October 2004:

** Paper (xii) (*d*) on Byzantine Literature may not be offered before October 2005 by candidates following Course II.**]**

(xv) Historical Linguistics and Comparative Philology [Honour Moderations in Classics Course IA, paper V, VI F(1)]. (This subject may not be offered by candidates who offered it in Honour Moderations in Classics or in the Preliminary Examination in Classics. It may be combined with one but not more than one of (xiii), (xiv), and (xvi).)

(xvi) General Linguistics and Comparative Philology [Honour School of Literae Humaniores, subject V.3]. (This subject may be combined with one but not more than one of (xiii), (xiv), and (xv). Candidates offering section (*a*), General Linguistics, may not also offer the Modern Languages Special Subject General Linguistics under 4 above.

(xvii) *Either* (*a*) The Early Greek World and Herodotus' Histories: [Honour School of Literae Humaniores, subject I.1].
or (*b*) Thucydides and the Greek World: [Honour School of Literae Humaniores, subject I.2].
or (*c*) The End of the Peloponnesian War to the Death of Phillip II of Macedon: [Honour School of Literae Humaniores, subject I.3].
or (*d*) Rome and the Mediterranean and the Histories of Polybius: [Honour School of Literae Humaniores, subject I.4].
or (*e*) The End of the Roman Republic: Cicero and Sallust: [Honour School of Literae Humaniores, subject I.5].
or (*f*) Rome, Italy and Empire under Caesar, the Triumvirate and Early Principate: [Honour School of Literae Humaniores, subject I.6].
or (*g*) The World of Tacitus and Pliny: Politics and Culture: [Honour School of Literae Humaniores, subject I.7].
or (*h*) Athenian Democracy in the Classical Age [Honour School of Literae Humaniores, subject I.8].
or (*i*) Alexander the Great and his Early Successors (336 BC–302 BC) [Honour School of Literae Humaniores, subject I.9].
or (*j*) Cicero: Politics and Thought in the Late Republic [Honour School of Literae Humaniores, subject I.10].
or (*k*) Civic Life of the Roman Empire from the Flavian to the Severan Period [Honour School of Literae Humaniores, subject I.11].
or (*l*) Religions in the Greek and Roman World (*c*.30 BC–AD 312) [Honour School of Literae Humaniores, subject I.12].
or (*m*) Sexuality and Gender in Greece and Rome [Honour School of Literae Humaniores, subject I.13].

Note: Candidates offering any of subjects (xvii) (*a*)–(*g*) must also offer the associated translation paper set in the Honour School of Literae Humaniores.

(xviii) *Either* (*a*) Art and Archaeology *c*.500 BC–300 BC [Honour School of Literae Humaniores, subject IV.2].
or (*b*) Art under the Roman Empire, AD 14–337 [Honour School of Literae Humaniores, subject IV.3].

(xix) *Either* (*a*) Plato, *Republic* (subject 130 (*a*)) *or* (*b*) Aristotle, *Nicomachean Ethics* (subject 131 (*a*)), as specified in **Regulations for Philosophy in all Honour Schools including Philosophy**.

(xx) Modern Greek Poetry [Honour School of Literae Humaniores, subject **[Until 1 October 2004:** III.11(*c*)**] [From 1 October 2004:** III.11 (*d*)**]**]. (This subject is available only to candidates offering Greek Literature of the Fifth Century BC under 5 above who are neither offering Medieval and Modern Greek as their modern language nor offering (xii)(*d*), **[Until 1 October 2004:** Procopius**] [From 1 October 2004:** Byzantine Literature**]** or (xxii), (xxiii), Second Classical Language.)

(xxi) Thesis. Any candidate may offer a thesis in Classics, or in a subject linking Classics and Modern Languages, in accordance with the Regulation on Theses in the regulations for the Honour School of Literae Humaniores, save that references there to the Honour School of Literae Humaniores shall be deemed to be references to the Honour School of Classics and Modern Languages. Candidates who offer two of subjects (xiii)–(xvi) may not also offer a thesis in Philology or Linguistics.

(xxii), (xxiii) (**see introductory note 6, 7 (*a*)**) Second Classical Language [Honour School of Literae Humaniores, subject VI.1 and VI.2]. (Candidates who offer Second Classical Language must offer *either both* subjects in Greek *or both* subjects in Latin, and may not offer either subject in the same language as they offered in Course IIA or IIB of Honour Moderations or the Preliminary Examination in Classics or in the Preliminary Examination for Modern Languages.)

8. One of the following:

(i) A second subject chosen from those listed under 4 above.

(ii) A third subject chosen from those listed under 6, 7 above, subject to the groupings there set out and the restrictions there placed upon choice of subjects.

(iii) Ancient and French Classical Tragedy (not to be offered in combination with any of the following: Aeschylus or Euripides (subject 6, 7 (iii)); Seneca and Lucan (subject 6, 7 (vi)(*d*)); Racine [Honour School of Modern Languages, paper X(5)]; Dramatic Theory and Practice in France 1605–60 with special reference to Corneille [Honour School of Modern Languages, paper XII Special Subject)]).

Candidates must make a special study of either of the following pairs of texts, on which a compulsory comparative commentary question will be set: *either* (*a*) Seneca, *Phaedra* and Racine, *Phèdre*, *or* (*b*) Euripides, *Medea* and Corneille, *Médée*. In addition, essay questions will be set with special reference to the following texts:

Aeschylus, *Agamemnon*
Sophocles, *Oedipus the King*
Euripides, *Hippolytus, Andromache, The Phoenician Women, Iphigenia at Aulis*
Seneca, *Medea*
Corneille, *Discours, Horace, Oedipe, Suréna*
Racine, *La Thébaïde, Andromaque, Iphigénie.*

Candidates will be required to answer two essay questions, one from a choice of questions specifically on the authors and texts prescribed above, the other from a choice of questions requiring a comparative or generic approach. The following editions will be used in the case of the texts prescribed for commentary: Euripides, J. Diggle (Oxford Classical Text); Seneca, *Phaedra*, M. Coffey and R. Mayer (Cambridge University Press); Corneille, A. Stegmann (L'Intégrale); Racine, J. Morela and A. Viala (Classiques Garnier).

(iv) The Creative Reception of Greek Tragedy in German.

Candidates must make a special study of Sophocles, *Antigone* and Hölderlin, *Antigone*, on each of which a compulsory commentary question will be set. In addition, they will be required to answer two essay questions, one from a choice of questions specifically on the authors and texts listed below, the other from a choice of questions requiring a comparative or generic approach.

Sophocles, *Oedipus Tyrannus*
Euripides, *Medea, Iphigenia in Tauris*
Plato, *Republic* II, III, X
Aristotle, *Poetics*
Goethe, *Iphigenie auf Tauris*
Kleist, *Penthesilea*

Nietzsche, *Die Geburt der Tragödie*
Brecht, *Antigone*
Christa Wolf, *Medea: Stimmen*

The following editions will be used in the case of the texts prescribed for commentary: Sophocles, Lloyd-Jones and Wilson (Oxford Classical Text); Hölderlin, Frankfurt edition.

9. Additional Subject.

Good performance in such subjects will be taken in account in allocating all classes. Candidates wishing to offer an Additional Subject may offer one of the following.

(i) A further subject chosen from the list prescribed under 4 above.

(ii) A further subject chosen from the list prescribed under 6, 7 (i)–(xx) above, subject to the groupings there set out and the restrictions there placed upon choice of subjects.

(iii) **[From 1 October 2005:** Except in French, an essay**]** in the modern language, on one of a choice of literary and other subjects [Honour School of Modern Languages, paper III] **[From 1 October 2005:** all languages except French*].**]**

* *The changes at 9 (iii) come into effect from 1 October 2004 for candidates offering Course I.*

(iv) Greek Prose Composition. (This subject may not be offered by candidates who have satisfied the Moderators in Course IA or IC of Honour Moderations in Classics.)

(v) Latin Prose Composition. (This subject may not be offered by candidates who have satisfied the Moderators in Course IA or IB of Honour Moderations in Classics.)

(vi) An extended Essay on a topic in the modern language or combining the modern language and Classics (to be examined under the regulations for the Honour School of Modern Languages).

(vii) A Special Thesis on a topic in Classics (to be examined under the regulations for the Honour School of Literae Humaniores).

PASS SCHOOL OF CLASSICS AND MODERN LANGUAGES

Candidates shall offer papers in Classics, and in any single modern language; they may choose any of the modern languages which may be offered for the Honour School of Classics and Modern Languages.

Candidates shall take the following papers:

In Classics

Candidates are required to offer **two** of the following:

(*a*) Greek Literature of the Fifth Century BC (one paper of three hours (commentary and essay) with an additional paper (one-and-a-half hours) of translation) [Honour School of Literae Humaniores, subject III.1].

(*b*) Latin Literature of the First Century BC (one paper of three hours (commentary and essay) with an additional paper (one-and-a-half hours) of translation) [Honour School of Literae Humaniores, subject III.5].

(*c*) *Either* Any one of the remaining subjects prescribed for the Honour School of Classics and Modern Languages, 6, 7 (ii)–(xxi), subject to the restrictions there placed upon choice of subjects *or* Ancient and French Classical Tragedy [Honour School of Classics and Modern Languages, subject (8) (iii) *or* The Creative Reception of Greek Tragedy in German [Honour School of Classics and Modern Languages, subject 8 (iv)].

In a Modern Language

(The numbering used is that in the Honour School of Modern Languages).

I
IIA (i)
IIB (i)
One of VI, VII, VIII.
The oral examination in the language.

SPECIAL REGULATIONS FOR THE HONOUR SCHOOL OF COMPUTER SCIENCE

[for candidates embarking on the Honour School in or after October 2003]

A

1. (1) The subject of the Honour School of Computer Science shall be the theory and practice of Computer Science.

(2) The examination in Computer Science shall consist of two parts (A, B) as prescribed by the Board of the Division of Mathematical and Physical Sciences.

2. (1) The name of a candidate shall not be published in a class list until he or she has completed both parts of the examination.

(2) The Examiners in Computer Science shall be entitled to award a pass or classified Honours to candidates in the Second Public Examination who have reached the appropriate standard; the Examiners will give due consideration to the performance of candidates in both parts of the examination.

(3) A candidate who obtains only a pass or fails to satisfy the Examiners may enter again for Part B of the examination on one, but not more than one, subsequent occasion.

3. All candidates will be assessed as to their practical ability under the following provisions:

(1) The Director of the Computing Laboratory, or a deputy, shall make available to the examiners evidence showing the extent to which each candidate has pursued an adequate course of practical work.

(2) Candidates for each part of the examination shall submit to the Chairman of the Examiners, Honour School of Computer Science, c/o the Clerk of the Schools, Examination Schools, Oxford, by noon on Monday of the fifth week of the Trinity Term in which the examination is being held, their reports of practical exercises completed during their course of study. For a report on a practical exercise to be considered by the examiners, it must have been marked by a demonstrator and must be accompanied by a statement that it is the candidate's own work except where otherwise indicated.

(3) The examiners shall take the evidence (1) and the report (2) into account in assessing a candidate's performance.

4. No candidate shall be admitted to examination in this school unless he or she has either passed or been exempted from the First Public Examination.

5. In order to proceed to Part B, candidates must pass Part A. The examiners will publish a pass list for Part A.

6. (1) The Examination in Computer Science shall be under the supervision of the Board of the Division of Mathematical and Physical Sciences.
   (2) The Board shall have power, subject to this decree, from time to time to frame and vary regulations for the different parts and subjects of the examination.

B

The syllabus for each paper will be published by the Computing Laboratory in a handbook for candidates by the beginning of Michaelmas Full Term in the academic year of the examination for Part A, after consultation with the Subfaculty of Computation. This handbook shall apply to both Part A and Part B of the examination.

The use of calculators is generally not permitted but certain kinds may be allowed for certain papers. Specifications of which papers and which types of calculators are permitted for those exceptional papers will be announced by the examiners in the Hilary Term preceding the examination.

1. The examination shall be in two parts, A and B, taken at times not less than three and six terms, respectively, after passing or being exempted from the First Public Examination.

2. In Part A of the examination, candidates shall be required to offer two papers as follows, each of three hours' duration.

CS4 Object-oriented programming,
CS5 Concurrency, networks and operating systems.

In addition, each candidate shall be required to offer four optional subjects from Schedule A in the Course Handbook, each to be examined by a paper of one and a half hours' duration.

3. In Part B of the examination, each candidate shall be required to offer six optional subjects from Schedules B1 and B2 in the Course Handbook, subject to the conditions that

(*a*) no candidate shall offer any subject from Schedule B1 that he or she has already offered in Part A of the examination.
(*b*) each candidate shall offer no more than two subjects from Schedule B1.

Each optional subject shall be examined by a paper of one and a half hours' duration. In addition, each candidate in Part B of the examination shall submit a project report.

4. The schedules of optional subjects for Parts A and B of the examination shall be approved by the Sub-faculty of Computation, and shall be published in the Course Handbook.

5. The examiners shall have power to combine two papers on related optional subjects into a single paper of three hours' duration for those candidates who offer both the optional subjects concerned.

6. Each candidate shall carry out a project on a topic in Computer Science approved by the Teaching Committee of the Computing Laboratory. Each project will be supervised by a member of the Sub-faculty of Computation, the Sub-faculty of Mathematics or the Sub-faculty of Engineering Science, or by some other person of equivalent seniority approved by the Teaching Committee. Two copies of a report of the project shall be submitted to the Chairman of Examiners, Honour School of Computer Science, c/o the Clerk of the Schools, Examination Schools, Oxford by noon on Monday of the fifth week of the Trinity Term in which Part B of the examination is held. The report must not exceed 6,000 words plus twenty-five pages of additional material (e.g., diagrams, program text).

Projects previously submitted for the Honour School of Computer Science, or (where applicable) the Honour School of Computation or the Honour School of Mathematics and Computation, may be resubmitted. No project may be resubmitted if it has already been submitted, wholly or substantially, for another honour school or degree of the University, or of any other institution.

PASS SCHOOL OF COMPUTER SCIENCE

1. Candidates shall be required to offer the following parts of the examination for the Honour School of Computer Science:

For Part A,

(*a*) Papers CS4 and CS5.
(*b*) Two optional subjects chosen from Schedule A in the Course Handbook.

For Part B,

(*c*) Two optional subjects chosen from Schedules B1 and B2 in the Course Handbook.
(*d*) A project, governed by the regulations prescribed for the Honour School of Computer Science.

2. Candidates shall be assessed as to their practical ability under the regulations set out for the Honour School of Computer Science.

NOTES

[Until 1 October 2004: [*for candidates embarking on the Honour School in or before October 2002*]

SPECIAL REGULATIONS FOR THE HONOUR SCHOOL OF COMPUTER SCIENCE

A

1. The subjects of the Honour School of Computer Science shall be the theory and practice of Computation, and other cognate disciplines, including Mathematics.

2. No candidate shall be admitted to examination in this school unless he or she has either passed or been exempted from the First Public Examination.

3. The examination in this school shall be under the supervision of the Divisional Board of Mathematical and Physical Sciences.

4. The Board shall have power to issue a syllabus of the subjects in which candidates shall be examined, and to vary the same from time to time.

B

1. The examination will consist of Sections I, II and E. Six papers will be set in Section I, on the subjects set out in the Schedule. The subjects of papers in Section II will be those approved in Trinity Term, two years in advance of the relevant examination. The subjects of papers in Section E will be those of Papers a1–a6, and b1 from the Honour School of Mathematical Sciences, together with any additional papers approved in the Michaelmas Term of the year preceding the academic year in which the relevant examination is held.

The subjects of Sections II and E, together with the information relating to practicals and lengths of papers required under paragraphs 6 and 7 below, shall be published in the *University Gazette*.

2. (*a*) Every candidate shall take seven papers and undertake a project.

(*b*) Every candidate shall take at least three, but no more than five papers from Section I.

(*c*) Every candidate shall take two papers from Section II.

(*d*) Each candidate may take up to two papers from Section E.

3. No paper from Section II shall require knowledge of the subject of any other Section II paper.

4. Each of the papers, inclusive of practicals where relevant, will be given equal weight by the examiners. The project will be given the weight of one paper.

5. Each candidate shall carry out a project on a topic in computation approved by the Teaching Committee of the Computing Laboratory. Each project will be supervised by a member of the Sub-faculty of Computation, the Sub-faculty of Mathematics or the Sub-faculty of Engineering Science, or by some other person of equivalent seniority approved by the Teaching Committee. Two copies of a report of the project shall be submitted to the Chairman of Examiners, Honour School of Computer Science, Examination Schools, Oxford, by noon on Monday of the fifth

week of the Trinity Term in which the examination is held. The report must not exceed 6,000 words plus twenty-five pages of additional text (e.g. diagrams, program text).

Projects previously submitted for the Honour School of Computer Science or the Honour School of Mathematics and Computer Science may be resubmitted. No project may be resubmitted if it has already been submitted, wholly or substantially, for another honour school or degree of the University, or for a degree of any other institution.

6. Candidates who offer the respective papers will be assessed as to their practical ability in the subjects of those Section I papers so indicated in the Schedule and such of the subjects of Section II as shall be determined when the subjects of this section are approved each Trinity Term, under the following provisions.

(*a*) The Director of the Computing Laboratory, or a deputy, shall make available to the examiners evidence showing the extent to which each candidate has pursued an adequate course of practical work.

(*b*) Candidates shall submit to the Chairman of the Examiners, Honour School of Computer Science, Examination Schools, Oxford, by noon on Monday of the fifth week of the Trinity Term in which the examination is held, their reports of practical exercises completed during their course of study. For a report to be considered by the examiners, it must be signed by a demonstrator and must be accompanied by a statement that it is the candidate's own work except where otherwise indicated.

(*c*) The examiners shall take the evidence (*a*) and the reports (*b*) into account in assessing the candidate's performance on the papers to which the work relates. The extent to which practical marks will be counted towards the total for each paper in Section I is specified in the Schedule as a proportion of the total. Proportions for subjects in Section II will be published with the list of these subjects.

7. Each written paper will be of three hours' duration except, for Section I, where otherwise specified in the Schedule or, in Sections II and E, where specified when the list of these subjects is determined.

8. The use of calculators is generally not permitted but certain kinds may be allowed for certain papers. Specifications of which papers and which types of calculators are permitted for those exceptional papers will be announced by the examiners in the Hilary Term preceding the examination.

Schedule

Paper I.1: Formal Program Design

No practicals. Paper of 3 hours.

Predicate notation for program specification: connectives and quantifiers. Example calculations in the predicate calculus. The language of guarded commands for expressing programs. Assertions, invariants, and variant functions. Strategies for finding invariants; head and tail invariants. General programming techniques for developing efficient programs. Examples from sorting and searching problems.

Procedures and parameter passing. Recursion in procedural programs. Modules and encapsulation. Data refinement. Example refinements, including use of hashing and tree structures. Pointer algorithms and their development. Specification using modules, abstract data types and their operations.

Paper I.2: Compilers and Programming Languages

Practical weight one-sixth. Paper of 2 hours 30 minutes.

Programming language representation: concrete and abstract syntax, context free grammars. Use of lexer and parser generators. Description of language semantics by definitional source-level interpreters. Implementation of expressions and statements in a simple language by post-fix code and by simple machine code; simple optimizations. Language paradigms: imperative programming, functional programming, logic programming, object-oriented programming. Applicative and normal order evaluation. Procedures: value, name and reference parameters, local and non-local variables, static and dynamic binding. abstract machines and storage management: activation records, static and dynamic chains, stacks and heaps. Type systems: static, dynamic and polymorphic typing.

Paper I.3: Concurrency and Distributed Systems

Practical weight: one-sixth. Paper of 2 hours and 30 minutes

Concurrency: Deterministic processes: traces; prefixing, choice, concurrency, and communication. Nondeterminism: failures and divergences; nondeterministic choice, hiding and interleaving. Further operators: sequential composition, subordination, pipes, iterative arrays. Refinement, specification and proof. Process algebra: equational and inequational reasoning.

Distributed Systems: Forms of distributed system: loosely and tightly coupled. Networks and protocols. Distributed file systems: file and directory services, concurrency control, replicated files. Case study.

Paper I.4: Computer Architecture and Operating Systems

Practical weight one-sixth. Paper of 2 hours and 30 minutes.

Computer Architecture: Register Transfer model of processors. Datapaths and control structures. Comparison of architectural styles for general purpose computers, including RISC/CISC. Pipelining; pipeline hazards and their resolution by stalling and forwarding. The hierarchy of storage in a computer; caches and virtual memory.

Operating systems: The functions and structure of an operating system. Processes, synchronization and simple scheduling. Input/output: examples of hardware and software. Memory management, segmentation, and virtual memory. File systems, and file system management.

Paper I.5: Algorithms and Data Structures

Practical weight one-sixth. Paper of 2 hours 30 minutes.

Graph algorithms: spanning trees, shortest paths, maximum flow. Amortized analysis. Data structures: hashing, B-trees, efficient heaps, union-find. Sorting and searching. Pattern matching in strings. Randomized algorithms. Number-theoretic algorithms and cryptography.

Paper I.6: Numerical Analysis

No practicals. Paper of 3 hours.

Interpolation and approximation of functions: Lagrange and Hermite interpolation, applications to quadrature, error analysis. Global polynominal approximation in the L^{∞} and L^{2} norms: inner product spaces; orthogonal polynomials, Gauss quadrature, trapezoidal rule for periodic functions. Piecewise polynominal approximation: linear and Hermite cubic splines, B-splines. Aitken and Richardson extrapolation, Romberg integration.

Numerical linear algebra: Gaussian elimination, pivoting, and $PA = LU$ decomposition; Cholesky factorization. Householder reflectors, QR factorization, least-squares problems. Eigenvalue decomposition, Gershgorin's theorem. Eigenvalue algorithms for symmetric matrices: tridiagonalization, QR algorithm.

Introduction to nonlinear systems and optimization: Newton's method for systems of equations; Newton's method for multivariate minimization; numerical approximation of Jacobian matrices; BFGS quasi-Newton iteration.

PASS SCHOOL OF COMPUTER SCIENCE

1. Candidates shall be required to offer the following parts of the examination for the Honour School of Computer Science:

(*a*) Either five papers from Section I, or four papers from Section I and one from Section E.

(*b*) A project, the regulations governing which shall be those prescribed for the Honour School of Computer Science.

2. Candidates shall be assessed as to their practical ability in the subjects of each paper offered from Section I where so indicated in the Schedule under the regulations set out for the Honour School of Computer Science. 1

3. The use of calculators is generally not permitted but certain kinds may be allowed for certain papers. Specifications of which papers and which types of calculators are permitted for those exceptional papers will be announced by the examiners in the Hilary Term preceding the examination.]

SPECIAL REGULATIONS FOR THE HONOUR SCHOOL OF ECONOMICS AND MANAGEMENT

A

1. The examination in the Honour School of Economics and Management shall include, as stated subjects to be offered by all candidates:

(i) Macroeconomics

(ii) Microeconomics

2. Candidates shall be required to offer, in addition to the above subjects, at least two subjects from Schedule A and a further four subjects from Schedules A and B.

3. No candidate shall be admitted to examination in this school unless he or she has either passed or been exempted from the First Public Examination.

4. The examination in this school shall be under the supervision of the Social Sciences Board, which shall appoint a standing committee to make regulations concerning it, subject always to the preceding clauses of this sub-section.

B

All candidates will be required to take *eight* subjects in all.

On entering his or her name for the examination by the date prescribed, each candidate must give notice to the Registrar of the papers being offered.

Any candidate may be examined viva voce.

Calculators may be used in the examination room for all subjects set out under the heading 'Use of calculators in examinations' in the *Special Regulations concerning Examinations*.

All candidates will be required to offer the following subjects:

(i) *Macroeconomics*

As specified for the Honour School of Philosophy, Politics, and Economics.

(ii) *Microeconomics*

As specified for the Honour School of Philosophy, Politics, and Economics.

(iii) *Two* subjects selected from Schedule A. Candidates may be charged for the provision of study packs for these compulsory subjects.

(iv) *Four* optional subjects selected from Schedule A, except that a candidate cannot offer a subject selected from Schedule A offered under (iii), and Schedule B.

Depending on the availability of teaching resources, not all Management Options will be available to all candidates in every year. Candidates and Management tutors will be circulated in Trinity Term with details of all Options which will be available for the following year. The list, from which papers in Schedule A may be selected, and the syllabus for each, shall be approved by the Faculty of Management Studies and published in the *Gazette* by the Chairman of the Standing Committee not later than the end of the Trinity Full Term of the academic year preceding the year of the examination.

Schedule A

(1) *Accounting*

Nature and regulation of financial reporting, analysis of company accounts. Nature of management accounting, including: cost behaviour, budgetary planning and control, capital budgeting, divisional performance.

(2) *Either* (*a*) *Organizational Behaviour and Analysis*

The individual in the organization; motivation and job satisfaction; groups at work; decision making; gender; organizational strategy and structure; the organizational environment; managerial work and behaviour; leadership; culture; power, conflict and change; contemporary and comparative approaches.

Or (*b*) *Employment Relations*

The structure and management of the employment relationship, including its environment, and economic and social consequences; human resource strategy and style; systems of collective representation; trade union objectives and organization; pay systems and performance appraisal; explicit and psychological contracts; the management of co-operation and conflict; employee involvement, participation and team working; technology, work design and work organization; job regulation; the utilization of human resources; training and performance; contemporary and comparative approaches to the management of employees.

(3) *Finance*

Investment appraisal under conditions of certainty/uncertainty. Portfolio theory and capital asset pricing model. Sources of finance, debt capacity, dividends, and cost of capital. Financial market efficiency. Emerging issues in finance. Takeovers and mergers.

(4) *Strategic Management*

Theoretical foundations of strategic management. Structural analysis of industries and industry dynamics. The resource and capability based view of the firm. Strategy and Organization. Nature and sources of competitive advantage and patterns of competition. Competitive and co-operative strategies. Corporate strategy and competitive advantage. International strategy. Strategic management in the public sector and not-for-profit organizations. Current issues in strategic management.

(5) *Marketing*

Exchange in a modern economy. The marketing concept; the marketing mix, its formulation and common components; the product life-cycle and new product development; segmentation and positioning. Buyer behaviour. Marketing information and the analysis of markets and competitors. Marketing planning and marketing strategies. Models for evaluating strategic marketing opportunities.

(6) *Technology and Operations Management*

Goods and service operations. Vertical integration, facilities location and capacity, volume/mix and process relationships, scale economies, automation. Goods/service design, facilities, process planning, aggregate capacity decisions, resource scheduling. Product/service quality assurance, facilities maintenance.

Schedule B

Subjects (1) to (13) are as specified in the Honour School of Philosophy, Politics, and Economics. Not all of these subjects may be offered in any particular year. There may also be restrictions on numbers permitted to offer some of these subjects in any particular year.

(1) *Economic Theory*
(2) *Money and Banking*
(3) *Public Economics*
(4) *International Economics*
(5) *Command and Transitional Economies*
(6) *Economics of Developing Countries*
(7) *Classical Economic Thought: Smith, Ricardo, and Marx*
(8) *British Economic History since 1870*
(9) *Economics of OECD Countries*
(10) *Economics of Industry*
(11) *Statistical Methods in Social Science*
(12) *Econometrics*
(13) *Labour Economics and Industrial Relations*
(14) *Economic Decisions within the Firm*

As specified in Paper E3, *Economic Decisions within the Firm*, in the Honour Schools of Engineering, Economics, and Management and Materials, Economics, and Management.

(*v*) *Thesis*

Any candidate may offer a thesis instead of a subject from Schedule A or Schedule B under (*iv*) above, subject to the following provisions:

(*a*) *Subject*

The subject of every thesis should fall within the scope of the honour school. The subject may, but need not, overlap any subject on which the candidate offers papers. Candidates are warned that they should avoid repetition in papers of materials used in their theses and that substantial repetition may be penalised.

Every candidate shall submit through his or her college for approval to the Chairman of the Standing Committee for Economics and Management the title he or she proposes together with

(i) an indication as to the branch of the school in which the subject falls, i.e. Economics or Management;
(ii) an explanation of the subject in about 100 words;
(iii) a letter of approval from his or her tutor,

not earlier than the first day of the Trinity Full Term of the year before that in which he or she is to be examined and not later than the date prescribed for entry to the examination. The standing committee shall decide as soon as possible whether or not to approve the title and shall advise the candidate immediately. No decision shall be deferred beyond the end of the fifth week of Michaelmas Full Term.

(*b*) *Authorship and origin*

Every thesis shall be the candidate's own work. His or her tutor may, however, discuss with him or her the field of study, the sources available, and the method of presentation; the tutor may also read and comment on a first draft. Theses previously submitted for the Honour School of Economics and Management may be resubmitted. No thesis will be accepted if it has already been submitted, wholly or substantially, for another Honour School or degree of this University, or for a degree of any other institution. Every candidate shall sign a certificate to the effect that the thesis is his or her own work and that it has not already been submitted for a degree of this or any other unversity and his or her tutor shall countersign the certificate confirming that, to the best of his or her knowledge and belief, these statements are true. This certificate shall be submitted separately in a sealed envelope addressed to the chairman of examiners. No thesis shall, however, be ineligible because it has been or is being submitted for any prize of this University.

(*c*) *Length and format*

No thesis shall exceed 15,000 words, the limit to include all notes, appendices, but not bibliographies; no person or body shall have authority to permit any excess. There shall be a select bibliography or a list of sources. All theses must be typed in double spacing on one side of quarto or A4 paper. Any notes and references may be placed *either* at the bottom of the relevant pages *or* all together at the end of the thesis, but in the latter case two loose copies of the notes and references must be supplied. The thesis must be bound or held firmly in a stiff cover. *Two* copies shall be submitted to the examiners; they shall be returned to the Saïd Business School library after the examination.

(*d*) *Notice to Registrar and submission of thesis*

Every candidate who wishes to submit a thesis shall give notice of his or her intention to do so to the Registrar on his or her examination entry form (in addition to seeking approval of the subject from the Chairman of the Standing Committee for Economics and Management under (*a*) above); and shall submit his or her thesis not later than noon on Monday of the first week of the Trinity Full Term of the examination to the Chairman of the Examiners, Honour School of Economics and Management, Examination Schools, Oxford.

PASS SCHOOL OF ECONOMICS AND MANAGEMENT

Candidates for the Pass School in Management and Economics shall be required to offer five subjects selected from those offered for the Honour School of Economics and Management. These subjects shall always include Macroeconomics, Microeconomics, together with two subjects chosen from Schedule A, and one further subject chosen from Schedule A and B as set out in the regulations for the Honour School.

SPECIAL REGULATIONS FOR THE HONOUR SCHOOL OF ENGINEERING SCIENCE

A

1. No candidate shall be admitted to the examination in this school unless he or she has either passed or been exempted from the First Public Examination.

2. The subject of the examination shall be Engineering Science.

3. The examination in this school shall be under the supervision of the Divisional Board of Mathematical and Physical Sciences, which shall make regulations concerning it, subject always to the provisions of this subsection.

4. The examination shall consist of two parts and shall be partly of a practical nature.

5. No candidate may present himself or herself for examination in Part II unless previously adjudged worthy of Honours by the examiners in Part I. The name of a candidate shall not be published in a Class List unless he or she has been adjudged worthy of Honours by the examiners in Part I and in Part II of the examination in consecutive years, save where approval has been given by the Board for an intercalated year of study or industrial attachment between Parts I and II.

6. A candidate adjudged worthy of Honours in Part I and Part II in Engineering Science may supplicate for the Degree of Master of Engineering provided that he or she has fulfilled all the conditions for admission to a degree of the University as specified in Ch. I, Sect. 1, § 1, cl. 1.

B

Part I

Candidates will be required to take seven written papers, each of three hours, as follows: the five papers A1 to A5 in group A together with two papers taken from B1 to B5 in group B. In addition, they will be required to take three coursework subjects A6 to A8, each to be considered by the examiners as equivalent to one written paper.

Group A: Core course

Paper A1. Mathematical Methods.
Paper A2: **[Until 1 October 2004:** Electricity and Electronics.**]**
[From 1 October 2004: Electrical Systems.**]**
Paper A3: **[Until 1 October 2004:** Control, Dynamics and Computers.**] [From 1 October 2004:** Modelling, Dynamics and Control.**]**
Paper A4: Structures and Materials.
Paper A5: Fluid Mechanics and Thermodynamics.

Paper A6: Engineering Practical Work.
Paper A7: Engineering and Society Coursework.
Paper A8: Part I Design Project.

Group B: Basic options

Paper B1: Mechanical Engineering.
Paper B2: Civil Engineering.
Paper B3: **[Until 1 October 2004:** Electrical] **[From 1 October 2004:** Electronic] Engineering.
Paper B4: Information Engineering.
Paper B5: Chemical Engineering.

The examiners will not provide calculators, but will permit the use of one hand-held pocket calculator from a list of permitted calculators published by the Chairman of the Sub-faculty not later than the end of the fourth week of the Trinity Full Term in the academic year preceding the examination.

Candidates shall be required to submit a portfolio for Engineering and Society coursework (A7) comprising:

(*a*) an essay on a management case study, AND (*b*) an essay or a report on an assessment of safety, environmental impact, or sustainability, AND (*c*) EITHER an essay on an approved topic OR evidence of completion of an approved course in a foreign language

as specified in a list published by the Chairman of the Sub-faculty of Engineering Science not later than Friday of the fourth week of Hilary Full Term in the academic year preceding that in which the written examination is to be taken. A candidate may if he or she wishes submit to the Chairman of the Sub-faculty one alternative essay topic to replace one of the approved topics in the published list. Such submission must take place before noon on Friday of the seventh week of Hilary Full Term and the alternative topic shall be adjudged acceptable or otherwise by noon on Friday of the eighth week. Written work shall be typed and each essay or report shall have not more than 3,000 words, except where specified in the published list. **[Until 1 October 2004:** The] **[From 1 October 2004:** Two copies of the] portfolio of work shall be submitted to the Chairman of Examiners, Honour School of Engineering Science, c/o Clerk of the Schools, Examination Schools, High Street, Oxford, not later than noon on Friday of the ninth week of the Trinity Term of the year preceding the written examinations. The material must be the candidate's own work and the candidate shall sign and present with the portfolio a detachable certificate to this effect. Essays or reports previously submitted for the Honour School of Engineering Science may be resubmitted. No essay or report will be accepted if it has already been submitted wholly or substantially for another honour school or degree of this University, or for a degree at any other institution. Resubmitted work must be physically presented at the time and in the manner prescribed for submission.

Candidates shall submit to the examiners reports and supporting material on the Part I Design Project (A8) completed as a part of their course of study. The subject of the project shall be approved by the Projects Committee of the Sub-faculty of Engineering Science and two copies of the report and one copy of supporting material shall be submitted to the Chairman of the Examiners, Honour School of Engineering Science, c/o Clerk of the Schools, Examination Schools, High Street, Oxford, by noon on Friday of the fourth week of Trinity Term in the year of the Part I examination. The examiners shall consider the project report as the equivalent of a written paper. The project report must not exceed 6,000 words plus 25 pages of diagrams, photographs etc. The report must be the candidate's own work and should include a signed statement to this effect. Project reports previously submitted for the Honour School of Engineering Science may be resubmitted. No project report will be accepted if it has already been submitted wholly or substantially for another honour school or degree of this University, or for a degree at any other institution. Resubmitted work must be physically presented at the time and in the manner prescribed for submission.

In the assessment of Paper A6 the examiners shall take into consideration failure of a candidate to complete the practical work to a level prescribed from time to time by the Sub-faculty. Failure to complete coursework modules to a satisfactory standard will also be taken into account by the examiners, except that exemption from the requirement to complete coursework modules shall be granted to any candidate who, in Trinity term of the second year, participates in an exchange scheme approved by the Sub-faculty. The Chairman of the Sub-faculty of Engineering Science shall provide a list, by the end of the sixth week of the Trinity term in the year of the Part I examination, showing the extent to which each candidate has satisfied these requirements.

Candidates may be examined viva voce at the examiners' discretion.

Part II

In Part II a candidate shall be required to offer three written papers from Group C or an equivalent approved collection of course options if taking part in an exchange scheme. The detailed requirements and arrangements for written papers to be taken by students in Oxford, and the list of subjects and the syllabuses from which the papers in Group C may be selected shall be approved by the Sub-faculty of Engineering Science and published in the *Gazette* by the Chairman of the Sub-faculty of Engineering Science not later than the end of the Trinity full term of the academic year preceding the year of the examination of Part II. The Sub-faculty will divide the papers into Lists; candidates not on an exchange scheme will be required to take two papers from one of the Lists having an associated B paper. The third paper must be from one of the other Lists. Candidates taking part in an exchange scheme shall have the proposed set of papers to be taken in the host institution approved by the Sub-faculty by the end of Trinity full term before going on the exchange.

The examiners will not provide calculators, but will permit the use of one hand-held pocket calculator from a list of permitted calculators published by the Chairman of the Sub-faculty not later than the end of the fourth week of the Trinity Full Term in the academic year preceding the examination.

Each individual candidate taking part in a full year exchange at a host institution approved by the University will provide a collated set of coursework to the Exchange Co-ordinator of the Sub-faculty of Engineering Science. Each individual candidate will ensure that the host institution forwards a full transcript of the courses taken certified by the host institution. Each individual candidate will ensure that the host institution retains the examination papers for the approved courses undertaken and that these are submitted under seal, together with the collated coursework and transcript of courses taken, to the Chairman of Examiners, Honour School of Engineering Science, c/o Clerk of the Schools, Examination Schools, High Street, Oxford by noon on Friday of the sixth week of Trinity Term.

Each individual candidate shall submit three copies of his or her own report on the Part II Design Project completed as part of the course of study. The subject of the project shall be approved by the Projects Committee of the Sub-faculty of Engineering Science and the report on the project shall be submitted to the Chairman of the Examiners, Honour School of Engineering Science, c/o Clerk of the Schools, Examination Schools, High Street, Oxford, by noon on Friday of the fourth week of Trinity Term. The project and report together shall be considered by the examiners in deciding the class of a candidate as equivalent to three written papers. The report must not exceed 10,000 words plus 40 pages of diagrams, photographs, etc. The report must be the candidate's own work and should include a signed statement to this effect. Reports previously submitted for Part II for the Honour School of Engineering Science may be resubmitted. No work will be accepted if it has already been submitted, wholly or substantially, for Part I or for another honour school or degree of this University, or for a degree of any other institution. Resubmitted work must be physically presented at the time and in the manner prescribed for submission.

Exceptionally, and with the approval of the Chairman of the Sub-faculty of Engineering Science, candidates may undertake their Design Project during a twenty-four-week placement overseas and take a specified equivalent of three Group C papers. The placement shall always include the period from the fifth Friday before to the first Saturday after the end of Michaelmas Full Term.

Candidates may be examined viva voce at the examiners' discretion.

Schedule

Group A: Core course

Paper A1: *Mathematical Methods*

Convolution; Fourier transforms; spectra; sampling and reconstruction; random processes.

Vector algebra; vector calculus; Gauss' and Stokes' theorems; derivation of vector equations; describing properties of continuous media such as continuity and Laplace's equation.

Solution of partial differential equations in two independent variables; boundary conditions; application to engineering problems; the wave equation; wave propagation and dispersion.

Linear transformations and equations; matrix rank and diagonalisation; computation of solutions of simultaneous linear equations, iterative algorithms; eigenvalue computation; curve fitting and algorithms for data approximation; computational solution of differential equations.

[**Until 1 October 2004:** *Paper* A2: *Electricity and Electronics*

Field effect and bipolar transistors; switching circuits. Differential amplifiers and feedback. Electronic instrumentation and signal conditioning. Interface to computer systems.

Steady electric and magnetic fields. Slowly varying fields; Faraday's law, generation of e.m.f. Rapidly varying fields; Maxwell's equations. Electromagnetic waves and the wave equation. RF to optical examples.

The transmission line; wave propagation and impedance matching. Analogue and digital communication systems. Noise. Introduction to typical systems, including optical fibres.

Introduction to electrical power systems. Magnetic circuits; BH loops, reluctance and inductance. Transformers. Electromechanical energy conversion; d.c. and a.c. machines; design constraints and construction.

Paper A3: *Control, Dynamics and Computers*

Introduction to Control, system modelling; steady state and transient behaviour. Stability. Analysis and design of simple control systems, both continuous and discrete time.

Introduction to practical systems including computer implementation.

Dynamics; motion with rotation and translation. Kinematics; motion in rotating frames of reference. Mechanism analysis. Gear trains.

Mechanical vibrations; system modelling, applications.

Elements of computer architecture; separation of data and control; hardware description languages; input/output; data buses.]

[**From 1 October 2004:**

Paper A2: Electrical Systems

Applied Electromagnetism. Integral form of Maxwell's equations, origin of ρ, ε, and μ, capacitance and inductance for simple geometries, slow moving fields. Single phase transformer, electro-mechanical conversion, separately excited DC motor. Balanced three-phase circuits, induction motor.

Digital Logic and Computer Architecture. Finite State Machines, RTL, hardware implementation. The CPU, ALU, instructions and hardware support. Memory devices and organization. Process scheduling, processor performance, interfacing.

Communications. Modulation schemes, Carson's rule. Fibre transmission systems. Fixed networks, protocols and routing, Ethernet, simple traffic model. Mobile communications, cellular concept, GSM, CDMA.

Paper A3: Modelling, Dynamics and Control

Modelling of dynamic systems in terms of ordinary differential equations. Steady state and transient behaviour.

Mechanical vibrations; system modelling, applications.

Dynamics; motion with rotation and translation. Kinematics; motion in rotating frames of reference. Mechanism analysis. Gear trains.

Introduction to Control. Stability. Analysis and design of simple control systems.

Electronic instrumentation and signal conditioning. Interface to computer systems; computer implementation of control.]

Paper A4: *Structures and Materials*

[Until 1 October 2004: Elastic analysis of statically determinate and indeterminate frames; the stiffness matrix method. Shear stresses due to torsion.

Elastic continuum problems in two and three dimensions; equilibrium, compatibility, stress–strain relationships and boundary conditions. The finite element method in two dimensions.

Elastic instability of struts; plastic collapse of beams and frames.

Alloys and strengthening mechanisms; equilibrium diagrams, diffusion, heat treatment.

Plasticity; microscopic and macroscopic behaviour, Von Mises' yield criterion. Creep. Fracture and fatigue.]

[From 1 October 2004:

Elastic continuum problems in two and three dimensions; equilibrium, compatibility, stress-strain relationships and boundary conditions. Stress distributions in structural members.

Elastic analysis of structures using matrix methods; the stiffness matrix method, the finite element method in one and two dimensions.

Elastic instability of struts; plasticity in bending; plastic collapse of beams and frames.

Alloys and strengthening mechanisms; equilibrium diagrams, diffusion, heat treatment.

Plasticity; microscopic and macroscopic behaviour, Von Mises' yield criterion. Creep. Fracture and fatigue.]

Paper A5: *Fluid Mechanics and Thermodynamics*

[Until 1 October 2005: Basic concepts of fluid mechanics. Hydrostatics. Conservation of mass, momentum and energy. Stream function. Potential theory. Examples of potential flows. Lift and drag coefficients. Vorticity, circulation. Magnus effect, Kutta-Joukowsky theorem.

Applied fluid mechanics. Dimensional analysis, similarity and model testing. Turbomachinery. Boundary layer theory. Friction drag. Simple incompressible viscous flows. Turbulent flow in pipes and pipe circuits. Steady flow in open channels.

Thermodynamic Machines. Refrigeration systems, steam cycles, internal combustion engines, gas turbines, compressors.

Heat and Mass Transfer. Conduction, radiation, convection, heat exchangers, heat transfer coefficients. Mass transfer by convection and diffusion. An introduction to combustion.]

[**From 1 October 2005:**
Stream function. Potential theory. Examples of potential flows. Lift and drag coefficients. Vorticity, circulation. Magnus effect, Kutta-Joukowsky theorem.

Applied fluid mechanics. Dimensional analysis, similarity and model testing. Turbomachinery. Boundary layer theory. Friction drag. Steady flow in open channels.

Second Law, reversibility, Carnot cycle, thermodynamic temperature, Carnot theorem, entropy, process efficiencies.

Thermodynamics Machines. Refrigeration systems, steam cycles, internal combustion engines, gas turbines, compressors.

Heat and Mass Transfer. Radiation, convection, determination of heat transfer coefficients, heat exchangers. Mass transfer by convection and diffusion.]

Paper A6: *Engineering Practical Work*

Practical exercises including: engineering computation, electricity, electronics, control, computer architecture, structures, mechanics, materials, thermodynamics, fluid mechanics.

Paper A7: *Engineering and Society*

Paper A8: *Design Project.*

Group B: Basic Options

Paper B1: *Mechanical Engineering*

Applications of elasticity and plasticity, mechanics of non-metallic materials, power transmission, dynamics of machines, gas dynamics and hygrometry.

Paper B2: *Civil Engineering*

Structural analysis and design, soil mechanics, water engineering.

[**Until 1 October 2004:** *Paper* B3: *Electrical Engineering*

Communications systems, electrical properties of materials, signal processing, semiconductor devices and integrated circuits.]

[**From 1 October 2004:**
Paper B3: Electronic Engineering

Semiconductor devices, analogue and digital circuits, communication systems.]

Paper B4: *Information Engineering*

State-space systems, feedback control, computer-controlled systems, applied estimation, two-dimensional signal analysis, computational geometry.

Paper B5: *Chemical Engineering*

Chemical thermodynamics, mass transfer processes, chemical reactors, process design.

Group C: Advanced Options

These papers will contain questions on the subjects for each paper as published in the *Gazette* by the Chairman of the Sub-faculty of Engineering Science.

PASS SCHOOL OF ENGINEERING SCIENCE

[**Until 1 October 2004:** Candidates will be required to take the equivalent of six papers chosen from (i)–(x) below as specified for Part I in the Honour School of Engineering Science.

(i)–(viii) Papers A1, A2, A3, A4, A5, A6, A7, A8 in Group A;
(ix)–(x) two of the papers B1, B2, B3, B4, B5, in Group B;]

[From 1 October 2004:

Candidates will be required to satisfy the examiners in six papers as specified for Part I in the Honour School of Engineering Science, comprising:

(i) *EITHER* three papers from A1–A5 and one paper from B1–B5
OR four papers from A1–A5

(ii) A6

(iii) either A7 or A8.]

The examiners will not provide calculators, but will permit the use of one hand-held pocket calculator from a list of permitted calculators published by the Chairman of the Sub-faculty not later than the end of the fourth week of the Trinity Full Term in the academic year preceding the examination.

Candidates shall submit to the examiners reports and supporting material on the coursework modules undertaken as part of their course of study. Failure to complete coursework to a satisfactory standard will also be taken into account by the examiners, except that exemption from the requirements to complete coursework modules shall be granted to any candidate who, in Trinity Term of the second year, participates in an exchange scheme approved by the Sub-faculty.

NOTES

SPECIAL REGULATIONS FOR THE HONOUR SCHOOL OF ENGINEERING AND COMPUTING SCIENCE

A

1. No candidate shall be admitted to the examination in this school unless he or she has either passed or been exempted from the First Public Examination.

2. The examination in this school shall be under the supervision of the committee set up in accordance with the provisions of cl. 3 below, which shall have power to make regulations concerning it, subject always to the other clauses of this subsection and to the concurrence of the Divisional Board of Mathematical and Physical Sciences.

3. There shall be a standing committee to supervise the arrangements for this school, whose composition and terms of reference shall be as specified in Regulations 8–13 below.

4. The examination shall consist of two parts. In both parts candidates shall be examined in the subjects prescribed by the committee set up in accordance with the provisions of cl. 3 above.

5. No candidate may present himself or herself for examination in Part II unless previously adjudged worthy of Honours by the examiners in Part I. The name of a candidate shall not be published in a Class List unless he or she has been adjudged worthy of Honours by the examiners in Part I and in Part II of the examination in consecutive years, save where approval has been given by the Committee for an intercalated year of study or industrial attachment between Parts I and II.

6. A candidate adjudged worthy of Honours in Part I and Part II may supplicate for the Degree of Master of Engineering provided that he or she has fulfilled all the conditions for admission to a degree of the University as specified in Ch. I, Sect. 1, §1, cl. 1.

7. The examiners for Engineering Science shall be appointed by the committee for the nomination of examiners in Engineering Science; those for Computing Science shall be appointed by the committee for the nomination of examiners in Computation.

8. The standing committee for the Honour School of Engineering and Computing Science shall comprise:

Four persons appointed by the Divisional Board of Mathematical and Physical Sciences, two on the recommendation of the Sub-faculty of Engineering Science, and two on the recommendation of the Sub-faculty of Computation.

The committee shall have power to co-opt not more than six additional members and to elect its own chairman. All members shall serve for three-year periods but shall be re-eligible.

9. The committee shall keep under review the syllabuses for the honour school and the arrangements for lectures and practical course work, and where necessary ask the Divisional Board to make suitable arrangements either in connection with the timing of existing courses or the provision of special ones. The committee shall prepare each term a list of lectures and practical classes to be published in the Lecture Lists.

10. The committee shall be recognized as having an interest in the appointments to university lecturerships specifically concerned with the honour school. The Divisional Board shall ensure that the selection committees shall include two members of the standing committee.

11. The committee shall maintain a list of persons willing to give tuition in the subjects of the courses and shall collaborate with any college which requests assistance in this connection. The committee may from time to time issue advisory lists of books recommended for study.

12. The committee shall assist in the operation of any arrangement necessary to keep within any limits set by the Divisional Board on the number of candidates admitted to read for the Honour School of Engineering and Computing Science, provided always that the committee shall report forthwith to the Divisional Board in the event of any difficulty arising or anticipated in connection with numbers admitted for the honour school.

13. The minutes of the committee or a summary of them shall be forwarded to the Sub-faculty of Engineering Science and to the Sub-faculty of Computation.

B

Part I

Candidates will be required to take the equivalent of seven three-hour written papers as follows:

Papers A1 and A2 in the Honour School of Engineering Science.
Papers ECS1, ECS2 and ECS3, as specified in the appended schedule.
Two papers chosen from the following:
Papers B3 or B4 in the Honour School of Engineering Science, or, Paper ECS4, or ECS5, as specified in the appended schedule.

The examiners will not provide calculators but will permit the use of one hand-held pocket calculator as specified in the Honour School of Engineering Science.

In addition the following, as specified in the appended schedule, shall each be considered by the Examiners as equivalent to one written paper:

ECS7 Practical work,

ECS8 Engineering and Society coursework,

ECS9 Project report.

In the assessment of Paper ECS7 the examiners shall take into consideration failure of a candidate to complete practical work associated with the Engineering papers to a level prescribed from time to time by the Sub-faculty of Engineering Science. Failure to complete coursework modules to a satisfactory standard will also be taken into account, except that exemption from the requirement to complete coursework modules shall be granted to a candidate who, in Trinity Term of the second year, completes an approved exchange scheme. The Chairman of the Sub-faculty of Engineering Science shall provide a list, by the end of the sixth week of the Trinity Term in the year of the Part I examination, showing the extent to which each candidate has satisfied these requirements.

By noon on Friday of the ninth week of Trinity Term in the year preceding the Part I examination, each candidate shall submit **[From 1 October 2004:** two copies of] a portfolio for Engineering and Society coursework (ECS8) containing one essay or report on each of three approved topics as specified in the regulations of the Honour School of Engineering Science.

By noon on Friday of the fourth week of Trinity Term in the year of the Part I examination, candidates shall submit the following:

Two copies of the project report ECS9.

Work submitted for ECS8 and ECS9 shall be addressed to the Chairman of Examiners, Honour School of Engineering and Computing Science, c/o Clerk of the Examination Schools, Examination Schools, High Street, Oxford.

Reports of practical exercises associated with papers ECS2, ECS3, ECS4, ECS5 shall be submitted as specified in the regulations for the examination from which they are drawn.

Candidates may resubmit practical work and work previously submitted for ECS7, ECS8, ECS9. It must be physically presented at the time and in the manner prescribed for current submission. No such work will be accepted if it has already been submitted, wholly or substantially, for another honour school or degree of this University, or for a degree of any other institution.

Candidates may be examined viva voce at the examiner's discretion.

Schedule

ECS1 Control, Computing and Numerical Computing
ECS2 Functional Programming, Data Structures and Algorithms
ECS3 Procedural Programming and Discrete Mathematics
ECS4 Object Oriented Programming
ECS5 Concurrency, Networks and Operating Systems

The syllabus for Papers ECS1, ECS2, ECS3, ECS4, and ECS5 will be published by the Standing Committee for Engineering and Computing Science in a Course Handbook for candidates by the end of Trinity Full Term two years preceding the examination, after consultation with the Sub-faculties of Computation and Engineering Science.

ECS7 Practical work associated with papers A1, A2 and ECS1, together with coursework modules as specified from time to time by the Standing Committee for Engineering and Computing Science

ECS8 Engineering and Society coursework (Honour School of Engineering Science Part I, Paper A7)

ECS9 Project Report A report on a project carried out under supervision as approved by the Standing Committee for the Honour School of Engineering and Computing Science. The report must not exceed 6,000 words plus 25 pages of diagrams, listings, photographs, etc. The report must be the candidate's own work and should include a signed statement to this effect.

PART II

[Until 1 October 2004: Candidates will be required to take a total of three papers as follows:

One or two papers chosen from a selection of the Group C papers offered for the Honour School of Engineering Science.

One or two papers chosen from a selection of those available for Section I and Section II of the Honour School of Computer Science.

Specification of which Group C papers may be taken will be published in the *University Gazette* by the Standing Committee for Engineering and Computing Science not later than the end of the Trinity Full Term of the academic year preceding the year of the examination of Part II.

Specification of which Section I and Section II papers may be taken will be published in the *University Gazette* by the Standing Committee for Engineering and Computing Science in Trinity Term two years in advance of the relevant examination.**]**

[From 1 October 2004: Candidates will be required to take the equivalent of three three-hour papers from:

A selection of the Group C papers offered for the Honour School of Engineering Science.

A selection of those papers available for the Honour School of Computer Science.

One of ECS4, ECS5, B3, B4 not offered for the Part I examination.

Specification of which papers may be selected will be published in the *University Gazette* by the Standing Committee for Engineering and Computing Science not later than the end of Trinity Term of the academic year preceding the Part II examination.**]**

Performance in papers from **[Until 1 October 2004:** Section II of**]** the Honour School of Computer Science will be taken to include performance both in the written paper and any practical work associated with the papers. The examiners will consider all **[From 1 October 2004:** three-hour**]** papers as having equal weight. Any practical work associated with papers from **[Until 1 October 2004:** Section II of**]** the Honour School of Computer Science must be submitted to the Chairman of Examiners of the Honour School of Engineering and Computer Science, c/o Clerk of Schools, Examination Schools, High Street, Oxford by noon of the Friday of the fourth week of Trinity Term.

The examiners will not provide calculators, but will permit the use of one hand-held pocket calculator as specified in the Honour School of Engineering Science.

Candidates shall submit three copies of a report on a project carried out under supervision as approved by the Standing Committee of the Honour School of Engineering and Computing Science. Project reports must be submitted to the Chairman of Examiners of the Honour School of Engineering and Computing Science, c/o Clerk of the Schools, Examination Schools, High Street, Oxford by noon of the Friday of the fourth week of Trinity Term. The project report shall be considered by the examiners in deciding the class of a candidate as equivalent to three written papers. The project report must not exceed 10,000 words plus 40 pages of diagrams, listings, photographs, etc. The report must be the candidate's own work and should include a signed statement to this effect. Project reports previously submitted for Part II of the Honour School of Engineering and Computing Science may be resubmitted. No project report will be accepted if it has already been submitted, wholly or substantially, for another honour school or degree of this University, or for a degree of any other institution. Resubmitted reports must be physically presented at the time and in the manner prescribed for current submission.

Candidates may be examined viva voce at the examiners' discretion.

PASS SCHOOL OF ENGINEERING AND COMPUTING SCIENCE

[**Until 1 October 2004:** Candidates for the Pass Degree in Engineering and Computing Science will be required to take the equivalent of six papers chosen from (i)–(vii) below as specified for Part I in the Honour School of Engineering and Computing Science.

(i)–(v) Papers A1, A2, ECS1, ECS2, ECS3;
(vi) one of the papers B3, B4, ECS4, ECS5;
(vii) Paper ECS9, the Project report.

The examiners will not provide calculators, but will permit the use of one hand-held pocket calculator as specified in the Pass School of Engineering Science.

Candidates shall submit to the examiners reports and supporting material on the coursework (Papers ECS7 and ECS8) undertaken as part of their course of study. These will be taken into consideration in the assignment of the degree.]

[**From 1 October 2004:**

Candidates for the Pass Degree in Engineering and Computing Science will be required to satisfy the examiners in six papers chosen from those listed below as specified for Part I in the Honour School of Engineering and Computing Science:

(i) three papers from Papers A1, A2, ECS1, ECS2, ECS3;
(ii) one of the papers B3, B4, ECS4, ECS5;
(iii) Paper ECS7 (Engineering Practical Work);
(iv) *EITHER* Paper ECS8 (Engineering and Society) *OR* Paper ECS9 (the Project report).

The examiners will not provide calculators, but will permit the use of one hand-held pocket calculator as specified in the Final Honour School of Engineering Science.

Candidates shall submit to the examiners reports and supporting material for the papers offered as specified in the regulations for the Honour School of Engineering and Computing Science.]

NOTES

SPECIAL REGULATIONS FOR THE HONOUR SCHOOL OF ENGINEERING, ECONOMICS, AND MANAGEMENT

A

1. No candidate shall be admitted to examination in this school unless he or she has either passed or been exempted from the First Public Examination.

2. The examination in this school shall be under the joint supervision of the Mathematical and Physical Sciences Board and the Social Sciences Board, which shall appoint a standing joint committee to make regulations concerning it, subject always to the preceding clauses of this sub-section.

3. The examination shall consist of two parts. In both parts candidates shall be examined in the subjects prescribed by the committee set up in accordance with the provisions of cl. 3 above. In Part II candidates shall also present, as part of the examination, a report on a project carried out during a period of attachment to an industrial firm or an industrially-related internal university project.

4. No candidate may present himself or herself for examination in Part II unless previously adjudged worthy of Honours by the examiners in Part I. The name of a candidate shall not be published in a Class List unless he or she has been adjudged worthy of Honours by the examiners in Part I and in Part II of the examination in consecutive years, save where approval has been given by the committee for an intercalated year of study or industrial attachment between Parts I and II.

5. A candidate adjudged worthy of Honours in Part I and Part II may supplicate for the Degree of Master of Engineering provided that he or she has fulfilled all the conditions for admission to a degree of the University as specified in Ch. I, Sect, 1, § 1, cl. 1.

6. The examiners for Engineering Science shall be appointed by the committee for the nomination of examiners in Engineering Science; those for Economics shall be appointed by the committee for the nomination of examiners in Economics in the Honour School of Philosophy, Politics, and Economics; those for Management shall be appointed by the committee for the nomination of examiners in Management Studies.

B

The following is a list of the written papers which may be offered. Papers in Groups A, B, and C are identical with those coded in the same way and specified in the Honour School of Engineering Science. Papers in Group E are those which will be set in Economics, and those in Group M are those which will be set in Management. The syllabuses for papers in Groups E and Paper M1 are set out in the appended schedule.

Engineering

Group A

A1 Mathematical Methods
A2 **[Until 1 October 2004:** Electricity and Electronics**] [From 1 October 2004:** Electrical Systems**]**
A3 **[Until 1 October 2004:** Control, Dynamics and Computers**] [From 1 October 2004:** Modelling, Dynamics and Control**]**
A4 Structures and Materials
A5 Fluid Mechanics and Thermodynamics
A6 Engineering Practical Work

Group B

B1 Mechanical Engineering
B2 Civil Engineering
B3 **[Until 1 October 2004:** Electrical**] [From 1 October 2004:** Electronic**]** Engineering
B4 Information Engineering
B5 Chemical Engineering

Group C

The list of subjects and the syllabuses from which the papers in Group C may be selected shall be approved by the Sub-faculty of Engineering Science and published in the *Gazette* by the Chairman of the Standing Committee for EEM and Related Schools not later than the end of the Trinity Full Term of the academic year preceding the year of the examination of Part II. The chairman also will specify the examination requirements for each C paper.

Economics

Group E

E1 The Organization of Production
E2 The National Economy
E3 Economic Decisions within the Firm
E4 Statistical Methods in Social Science (this paper may not be available in any particular year)
E5 Econometrics (This paper may not be available in any particular year. Notice of the availability of this course will be given by Monday of fourth week in the Hilary Term of the second year for those with examinations in the fourth year).

Management

Group M

M1 Introduction to Management
Candidates may be charged for the provision of study packs.

Optional papers

The list, from which papers in Group M may be selected, and the syllabus or each, shall be approved by the Faculty of Management Studies and published in the *Gazette* by the Chairman of the Standing Committee not later than the end of the

Trinity Full Term of the academic year preceding the year of the examination of Part II.

In Economics papers candidates will be expected to show a knowledge of economic principles, of statistics, of institutions, and of mathematical techniques, so far as they are relevant to each subject paper.

PART I

1. *Written papers*

Candidates will be required to take nine papers, consisting of all papers in Group A, any one from Group B, together with paper E1 and paper M1.

In the case of written papers in Engineering Science, candidates are restricted to the use of one hand-held pocket calculator as specified in the Honour School of Engineering Science. For all other written papers, the examiners will permit the use of any hand-held calculator subject to the conditions set out under the heading 'Use of calculators in examinations' in the *Special Regulations concerning Examinations.*

2. *Coursework*

In the assignment of honours the examiners shall take into consideration performance in coursework modules and failure by a candidate to complete the coursework to the level prescribed from time to time by the Sub-faculty of Engineering Science. The chairman of that sub-faculty shall provide a list, by the end of the sixth week of Trinity Term of the year in which the Part I examination is taken, showing the extent to which each candidate has satisfied the requirements.

3. *Viva Voce*

Each candidate may be examined viva voce.

PART II

1. *Written papers*

Candidates will be required to take three papers, consisting of paper E2 and any two papers from E3, E4, E5, from the list of optional M papers published annually and from Group C (from which the equivalent of only one paper may be offered).

In the case of written papers in Engineering Science, candidates are restricted to the use of one hand-held pocket calculator as specified in the Honour School of Engineering Science. For all other written papers, the examiners will permit the use of any hand-held calculator subject to the conditions set out under the heading 'Use of calculators in examinations' in the *Special Regulations concerning Examinations.*

2. *Industrial placements and projects*

Candidates will be required to undertake a twenty-four-week period of attachment to an industrial firm, or an industrially-related internal university project, between the end of Trinity Full Term in the year in which the Part I examination is held and the beginning of Hilary Full Term in the year in which the Part II examination is held. This twenty-four-week project shall always include the period from the fifth Friday before to the first Saturday following Michaelmas Full Term. Candidates will be required to present, as part of the Part II examination, a report on the project carried out during this period. The report shall not exceed 20,000 words. The project report shall be considered by the examiners in deciding the class of a candidate as equivalent to two written papers. The project will be carried out under the supervision of a person or persons approved by the standing committee for the school.

The industrial attachment, or industrially related project, will normally be arranged by, and must be approved by, the project co-ordinators in Management and/or Engineering. The report shall be on a topic, approved by the standing committee, normally in Management or Engineering. Topics in Economics may be approved, but the project co-ordinators cannot undertake to arrange projects in the field of Economics.

3. *Submission of project reports*

All reports on projects must be submitted by noon on Friday of the week before the start of Hilary Full Term in the year following the year in which the Part I examination is held. They must be addressed to 'The Clerk of the Schools, High Street, Oxford OX1 4BG, for the Chairman of Examiners in Part II of the examination for the the Honour School of Engineering, Economics, and Management'. Reports must be accompanied by a signed statement by the candidate that it is his or her own work. Candidates must submit two copies of each project report. Successful candidates will be required to deposit one of these copies in the library of the Department of Engineering Science and the other in the library of the School of Management.

4. *Viva Voce*

Candidates may be examined viva voce on any part of their course of study, including their industrial project.

Schedule

E1 *The Organization of Production*

The price mechanisms, resource allocation, and their welfare aspects. Market structures, costs, and scale economics, oligopoly and the theory of games, entry, empirical studies of pricing and profitability, advertising, product differentiation, innovation, theories of the firm, mergers and vertical integration, investment, finance and the capital market, the labour market, public polity towards industry in the U.K., public enterprise.

E2 *The National Economy*

The formation and distribution of the national income. Social accounts. Consumption and investment. Foreign trade and the balance of payments. Price and wage levels.

Control of the level of economic activity. Budgetary policy. Monetary policy and institutions. National planning.

E3 *Economic Decisions within the Firm*

Linear economic models, simplex method for linear programming, duality and sensitivity analysis. Network models, including the transportation and assignment problems, shortest path problems, project scheduling. Dynamic and integer programming.

Expected utility theory and decision trees. Markov chain models. Queuing systems. Stochastic dynamic programming. Inventory control. Monte Carlo methods and simulation. Two-person, zero-sum games.

E4 *Statistical Methods in Social Science*

The paper shall be as specified for Economics paper 313 of the Honour School of Philosophy, Politics, and Economics.

E5 *Econometrics*

The paper shall be as specified for Economics paper 314 of the Honour School of Philosophy, Politics, and Economics.

M1 *An Introduction to Management*

Historical context; organizational behaviour; strategic management; technology and operations management; accounting; finance; marketing.

PASS SCHOOL OF ENGINEERING, ECONOMICS, AND MANAGEMENT

Candidates for the Pass School of Engineering, Economics, and Management will be required to take six papers, which should consist of: papers E1 (The Organization of Production) and M1 (Introduction to Management) as specified in the Honour School of Engineering, Economics, and Management and any four papers chosen from papers A1, A2, A3, A4, A5, A6 in Group A, and B1, B2, B3, B4, B5, in Group B as specified in the Honour School of Engineering Science, but subject to the restriction that not more than one paper may be taken from Group B.

In the case of written papers in Engineering Science, candidates are restricted to the use of one hand-held pocket calculator as specified in the Pass School of Engineering Science. For all other written papers, the examiners will permit the use of any hand-held calculator subject to the conditions set out under the heading 'Use of calculators in examinations' in the *Special Regulations concerning Examinations.*

Candidates shall submit to the examiners reports and supporting material on the coursework undertaken as part of their course of study. These will be taken into consideration in the assessment of the candidates.

NOTES

SPECIAL REGULATIONS FOR THE HONOUR SCHOOL OF ENGINEERING AND MATERIALS

A

1. No candidate shall be admitted to examination in this school unless he or she has either passed or been exempted from the First Public Examination.

2. The examination in this school shall be under the supervision of the committee set up in accordance with the provisions of cl. 3 below, which shall have power to make regulations concerning it, subject always to the other clauses of this subsection and to the concurrence of the Divisional Board of Mathematical and Physical Sciences.

3. There shall be a standing committee to supervise the arrangements for this school, whose composition and terms of reference shall be as specified in Regulations 8–13 below.

4. The examination shall consist of two parts. In both parts candidates shall be examined in the subjects prescribed by the committee set up in accordance with the provisions of cl. 3 above.

5. No candidate may present himself or herself for examination in Part II unless previously adjudged worthy of Honours by the examiners in Part I. The name of a candidate shall not be published in a Class List unless he or she has been adjudged worthy of Honours by the examiners in Part I and in Part II of the examination in consecutive years, save where approval has been given by the Committee for an intercalated year of study or industrial attachment between Parts I and II.

6. A candidate adjudged worthy of Honours in Part I and Part II may supplicate for the Degree of Master of Engineering provided that he or she has fulfilled all the conditions for admission to a degree of the University as specified in Ch. I, Sect. 1, §1, cl. 1.

7. The examiners shall be appointed by the committees for the nomination of Public Examiners in Engineering Science, and in Metallurgy and the Science of Materials in the Honour School of Natural Science.

8. The standing committee for the Honour School of Engineering and Materials shall comprise:

Four persons appointed by the Divisional Board of Mathematical and Physical Sciences, two on the recommendation of the Sub-faculty of Engineering Science, and two on the recommendation of the Sub-faculty of Materials.

The committee shall have power to co-opt not more than six additional members and to elect its own chairman. All members shall serve for three-year periods but shall be re-eligible.

9. The committee shall keep under review the syllabuses for the honour school and the arrangement for lectures, practical classes, vacation courses, projects, and required periods of industrial attachment, and where necessary ask the Divisional Boards to make suitable arrangements either in connection with the timing of existing courses or the provision of special ones. The committee shall prepare each term a list of lectures and practical classes to be published in the Lecture Lists.

10. The committee shall be recognized as having an interest in the appointments to university lecturerships specifically concerned with the honour school. The Divisional Boards responsible for such appointments shall ensure that the selection committees include two members of the standing committee.

11. The committee shall maintain a list of persons willing to give tuition in the subjects of the courses and shall collaborate with any college which requests its assistance in this connection. The committee may from time to time issue advisory lists of books recommended for study.

12. The committee shall assist in the operation of any arrangement necessary to keep within any limits set by the Divisional Board on the number of candidates admitted to read for the Honour School of Engineering and Materials provided always that the committee shall report forthwith to the Divisional Board in the event of any difficulty arising or anticipated in connection with numbers admitted for the honour school.

13. The minutes of the committee or a summary of them shall be forwarded to the Sub-faculties of Engineering Science and Materials.

B

PART I

Candidates will be required to take six papers, as follows:

Papers A1, A2, A5 as set for the Honour School of Engineering Science, and:

ME1. Microstructure and Transformations.

ME2. Electronic Properties and Structure.

ME3. Mechanical Properties.

In addition candidates will sit shortened versions of the Honour School of Engineering Science papers A3 and A4. The results of the two papers (A3s and A4s) in combination will be treated by the examiners as the equivalent of one paper.

The subjects of the papers are specified in the appended schedule. They will be required to take two further subjects, as follows:

ME4, a subset of the Engineering Practical Work (A6), the Materials Practical Work, and the Part I Design Project.

A7, Engineering and Society Coursework.

ME4 will be considered by the examiners as equivalent to two written papers, and A7 will be considered equivalent to one paper.

The examiners will not provide calculators, but will permit the use of one hand-held pocket calculator as specified in the Honour School of Engineering Science.

Candidates shall be required to submit a portfolio for Engineering and Society coursework (A7) as specified in the regulations for the Honour School of Engineering Science. **[Until 1 October 2004:** The**] [From 1 October 2004:** Two copies of the**]** portfolio of work shall be submitted to the Chairman of the Examiners, Honour School of Engineering and Materials, Examination Schools, Oxford, by noon on Friday of the eighth week of the Michaelmas Full Term preceding the examination. Candidates may seek advice on the selection of a title and the scope of the subject, and may be given reading lists, but otherwise each essay must be the candidate's own work and the candidate shall sign and present with the portfolio a detachable certificate to this effect. Essays or reports previously submitted for the Honour School of Engineering and Materials may be resubmitted. No essay or report will be accepted if it has already been submitted, wholly or substantially, for another honour school or degree of this University, or for a degree of any other institution. Resubmitted work must be physically presented at the time and in the manner prescribed for submission.

In the assessment of paper ME4 the examiners shall take into consideration failure of a candidate to complete the Engineering Practical Work to a level prescribed from time to time by the Sub-faculty of Engineering Science.

The examiners shall also require evidence of satisfactory Materials Practical Work (including a team design project). The details of the team design project will be specified in the Course Handbook.

Candidates shall submit detailed reports of Materials Practical Work (not including the team design project) to the Chairman of Examiners in the Honour School of Engineering and Materials, c/o Clerk of the Schools, Examination Schools, High Street, Oxford by 5 p.m. on the Friday of the seventh week of the Trinity full Term in which the Part I examination takes place. The Chairman of the Sub-faculty of Engineering Science and the Head of the Department of Materials, or their deputies, shall make available to the examiners evidence showing the extent to which each candidate has pursued an adequate course of practical work. Practical work previously submitted for the Honour School of Engineering and Materials may be resubmitted. No Practical work will be accepted if it has already been submitted, wholly or substantially, for another honour school or degree of this University, or for a degree of any other institution. Resubmitted work must be physically presented at the time and in the manner prescribed for submission.

Each candidate may be examined viva voce.

Schedule

A1, A2, A5 and A7: as specified in the Honour School of Engineering Science

A3s: a shortened version of A3 as specified in the Honour School of Engineering Science

This paper will contain questions on dynamics, kinematics and vibrations.

A4s: a shortened version of A4 as specified in the Honour School of Engineering Science

This paper will contain questions on structural forms and analysis: analysis of elastic continua; structural failure.

ME1. Microstructure and Transformations
Thermodynamics and kinetics, phase transformations, microstructure, diffusion, surfaces, and interfaces. Engineering alloys.

ME2. Electronic Properties and Structure
Crystallography; quantum and statistical mechanics, bonding, electronic structure of materials, electrical, optical, and magnetic properties of materials; physics of semiconductors.

ME3. Mechanical Properties
Crystal defects; hardness, toughness, and strength; plasticity; fracture. Mechanical properties of polymers and composites. Ceramics, polymers, and composites.

ME4.
A shortened version of A6 as specified in the Honour School of Engineering Science omitting control, computer architecture and materials, a selection of Materials Practical Work as specified by the Sub-faculty of Materials, and a Part I Design Project.

Part II

Candidates will be required to take three written papers from a selection of Engineering and Materials papers.

The subjects of these papers shall be published in the *University Gazette* by the Standing Committee for Engineering and Materials not later than the end of the Trinity full term of the academic year preceding the year of the examination of Part II.

The examiners will not provide calculators, but will permit the use of one hand-held pocket calculator as specified in the Honour School of Engineering Science.

Candidates shall also undertake an eight week minimum period of attachment to an industrial firm before the beginning of the Michaelmas Full Term preceding the Part II examination. Candidates shall submit a report on this industrial attachment, which must be delivered to the Chairman of Examiners in the Honour School of Engineering and Materials, c/o Clerk of the Schools, Examination Schools, High Street, Oxford by noon on Friday of the first week of the Hilary Full Term preceding the Part II examination. The report on the industrial attachment previously submitted for the Honour School of Engineering and Materials may be resubmitted. No report will be accepted if it has already been submitted, wholly or substantially, for another honour school or degree of this University, or for a degree of any other institution. The report shall not exceed 2,000 words.

Each individual candidate shall submit three copies of his or her own report on a project carried out under the supervision of a person approved by the Standing Committee for the Honour School of Engineering and Materials. The project report must not exceed 10,000 words plus 40 pages of diagrams, photographs, etc. and must be submitted to the Chairman of Examiners of the Honour School of Engineering and Materials, c/o Clerk of the Schools, Examination Schools, High Street, Oxford by noon on the Friday of the fourth week of the Trinity Full Term in which the Part II examination takes place, and should be accompanied by a signed statement by the candidate that it is his or her own work. The project report shall be considered by the examiners as equivalent to three written papers. Project reports previously submitted for the Honour School of Engineering and Materials may be resubmitted. No project report will be accepted if it has already been submitted, wholly or substantially, for another honour school or degree of this University, or for a degree of any other institution.

Each candidate may be examined viva voce.

PASS SCHOOL OF ENGINEERING AND MATERIALS

[**Until 1 October 2004:** Candidates for the Pass Degree in Engineering and Materials will be required to take the equivalent of six papers chosen from (i)–(viii) below specified for Part I of the Honour School of Engineering and Materials.
(i)–(vi) Papers A1, A2, A5, ME1, ME2, ME3, provided that at least two of papers ME1, ME2, ME3 are included;
(vii) Papers A3s and A4s. The results of the two papers (A3s and A4s) in combination will be treated as the equivalent of one paper.
(viii) Paper A7, Engineering and Society.

The examiners will not provide calculators, but will permit the use of one hand-held pocket calculator as specified in the Honour School of Engineering Science.

Candidates shall submit to the examiners reports and supporting material on the course work undertaken as part of their course of study (Paper ME4). These will be taken into consideration in the assignment of the degree.]

[**From 1 October 2004:**

Candidates for the Pass Degree in Engineering and Materials will be required to satisfy the examiners in the equivalent of six papers as specified for Part I of the Honour School of Engineering and Materials, comprising:

(i) Two of papers ME1, ME2, ME3;
(ii) Two papers from:
- Papers A1, A2, A5;
- Papers A3s and A4s (the result of which, in combination, will be treated as the equivalent of one paper);
- Paper A7 (Engineering and Society)

(iii) Paper ME4 (which will be treated as the equivalent of two papers)

The examiners will not provide calculators, but will permit the use of one hand-held pocket calculator as specified in the Honour School of Engineering Science.

Candidates shall submit to the examiners reports and supporting material on the course work undertaken as part of their course of study (Paper ME4).]

NOTES

SPECIAL REGULATIONS FOR THE HONOUR SCHOOL OF ENGLISH AND MODERN LANGUAGES

A

1. The subjects of the examination in the Honour School of English and Modern Languages shall be (*a*) English Language and Literature and (*b*) those modern languages and literatures studied in the Honour School of Modern Languages.

2. All candidates must offer both (*a*) and one of the languages in (*b*) with its literature.

3. No candidate shall be admitted to the examination in this school unless he or she has either passed or been exempted from the First Public Examination.

4. The examiners shall indicate in the lists issued by them the language offered by each candidate obtaining honours or satisfying the examiners under Ch. VI, Sect. II. C, §1, cl. 22 (iv) and (v).

5. The examination in this school shall be under the joint supervision of the Boards of the Faculties of English Language and Literature and of Medieval and Modern Languages, which shall appoint a standing joint committee to make, and to submit to the two faculty boards, proposals for regulations for this examination and for the Preliminary Examination in English and Modern Languages.

6. (i) The examiners in the honour school shall be such of the Public Examiners in the Honour Schools of English and Modern Languages as shall be required.

(ii) It shall be the duty of the chairmen of examiners in the Honour School of English and in the Honour School of Modern Languages to consult together and designate such examiners as shall be required for the honour school, whereupon the number of the examiners shall be deemed to be complete.

B

Candidates will be examined in accordance with the examination regulations set out below.

They will also be required to spend, after their matriculation, a year of residence in an appropriate country or countries, and to provide on their entry form for the examination a certificate that they have done this, signed by the Head or by a tutor of their society. Candidates wishing to be dispensed from the requirement to undertake a year of residence abroad must apply in writing to the Chairman of the Medieval and Modern Languages Board, 41 Wellington Square, Oxford, OX1 2JF, stating their reasons for requesting dispensation and enclosing a letter of support from their society.

Candidates will be expected to carry out during this year abroad such work as their society may require. It is strongly recommended that candidates should apply through the Central Bureau for Educational Visits and Exchanges for an Assistantship, where these are available, and should accept one if offered. Candidates who are not able to obtain an Assistantship should during their year abroad follow a course or courses in an institution or institutions approved by their society, or should spend their time in such other circumstances as are acceptable to their society. Candidates will agree with their College Tutor in advance of their year abroad an independent course of study to be followed during that period.

The papers and choices of options available to candidates for each of the two courses will be the same.

Each candidate shall offer Part I and either Part II or Part III as prescribed below.

Except in a Special Subject or an alternative to a Special Subject, a candidate shall offer (in addition to English) one modern language and its literature only.

Any candidate may be examined viva voce.

In every case where, under the regulations for the school, candidates have a choice between one or more papers or subjects, every candidate shall give notice to the Registrar not later than Friday in the fourth week of the Michaelmas Full Term preceding the examination of all the papers and subjects being so offered.

Candidates are warned that they must avoid duplicating in their answers to one part of the examination material that they have used in another part of the examination.

New optional subjects may be added to those parts of the syllabus for both Part II and Part III where options are already provided by regulation published in the *Gazette* by the beginning of the fifth week of Trinity Full Term of the year before the year of the examination in which the subjects will first be available.

Oral examination

As specified for the Honour School of Modern Languages.

Part I

[Until 1 October 2005: 1. Unprepared translation into the modern language (one paper of three hours) [Honour School of Modern Languages, Paper I].

2. Unprepared translation from the modern language (two papers of one-and-a-half hours each) [Honour School of Modern Languages, Paper IIA(*i*) and Paper IIB(*i*)].

3. A period of the literature of the modern language (one paper of three hours) [Honour School of Modern Languages, Paper VI or VII or VIII].

4. *One* of the following papers in the modern language:

(i) Linguistic Studies I (one paper) [Honour School of Modern Languages, Paper IV].

(ii) Linguistic Studies II (one paper) [Honour School of Modern Languages, Paper V].

(iii) Early texts prescribed for study as examples of literature (one paper) [Honour School of Modern Languages, Paper IX].

(iv) Modern Prescribed Authors (*i*) (one paper) [Honour School of Modern Languages, Paper X].

(v) Modern Prescribed Authors (*ii*) (one paper) [Honour School of Modern Languages, Paper XI].

(vi) Special subject [Honour School of Modern Languages, Paper XII].]

[From 1 October 2005:

1. Honour School of Modern Languages, Paper I.
2. Honour School of Modern Languages, Papers IIA(i) and IIB(i).
3. Honour School of Modern Languages, *one* paper chosen from Papers VI, VII, or VIII.
4. Honour School of Modern Languages, *one* paper chosen from Papers IV, V, IX, X, XI, or XII.]

Either

Part II

5. Shakespeare (one paper) [Honour School of English Language and Literature, Course I, Subject 2].

6, 7. *Two* of the following periods of English Literature:

(i) English Literature from 1100 to 1509 (two papers) [Honour School of English Language and Literature, Course I, Subject 3 (*a*) and (*b*)].

(ii) English Literature from 1509 to 1642 (one paper) [Honour School of English Language and Literature, Course I, Subject 4].

Candidates who have satisfied the Moderators in Honour Moderations in Classics and English may not offer this paper.

(iii) English Literature from 1642 to 1740 (one paper) [Honour School of English Language and Literature, Course I, Subject 5].

(iv) English Literature from 1740 to 1832 (one paper) [Honour School of English Language and Literature, Course I, Subject 6].

(v) Introduction to Medieval Studies: Old English Literature (one paper) [Honour School of English Language and Literature, Course I, Subject 9]. Candidates who have satisfied the Examiners in this paper in a First Public Examination may not offer this paper.

(vi) Victorian Literature (1832–1900) (one paper) [Honour School of English Language and Literature, Course I, Subject 10]. Candidates who have satisfied the Examiners in this paper in a First Public Examination may not offer this paper.

(vii) Modern Literature (1900 to the present day) (one paper) [Honour School of English Language and Literature, Course I, Subject 11]. Candidates who have satisfied the Examiners in this paper in a First Public Examination may not offer this paper.

8. *One* of the following:

(i) The History, Use, and Theory of the English Language (one paper) [Honour School of English Language and Literature, Course I, Subject 1].

(ii) Special Authors (an extended essay of not fewer than 5,000 nor more than 6,000 words) [Honour School of English Language and Literature, Course I, Subject 7].

Each candidate must inform the Head Clerk, University Offices, through the Senior Tutor of his college or society by the Friday of the second week of Michaelmas Full Term preceding the examination, of the author on which he or she proposes to offer the essay.

(iii) Special topics [Honour School of English Language and Literature, Course I, Subject 8] (*a*), (*b*), (*c*), (*d*), (*e*), (*f*), (*g*), (*h*) *i.* (may not be taken by candidates offering linguistics options under Part I. 4), *ii.*, *iii.*, *iv.* (may not be taken by candidates offering 'Old Norse' under Part I. 4, (vi)), *vi.* (may not be taken by candidates offering Welsh options under Part I. 4(vi)), *vii., viii.*, (i)].

(iv) One subject, not already selected, from among those listed under 4, 6, 7.

9. In addition a candidate may offer one of the following:

either

(i) One subject not already selected from amongst those listed under 4, 6, 7, 8.*

or

(ii) An Extended Essay on a topic in the modern language or combining the modern language and English (to be examined under the regulations for the Honour School of Modern Languages).

or

(iii) An optional thesis on a topic in English (to be examined under the regulations for the Honour School of English Language and Literature).

or

Part III

5. English Literature 1100–1530 (one paper) [Honour School of English Language and Literature, Course II, Subject A2]

6, 7. *Two* papers chosen from the Honour School of English Language and Literature Course II, Subjects A: 1, 3–5, B: 1–4, 7, provided that a candidate who has not taken paper 3(*c*) in part 2 of the Preliminary Examination must offer Subject A1. Subject B7 will be examined by extended essay. This is with the exception of Course II papers available under B7 (*h*) for which the Course II regulations specify that these shall be assessed by written examination.

8. *Either*

(*a*) One subject, not already selected, from among those listed under 4, 6, 7 of this course.

or

(*b*) One subject chosen from English Course II Subjects B6, 8–9, 15, 21 *or* 2, 23–5, provided that no candidate may offer (i) both B15 and Modern Languages paper XII Special Subject 'Old Norse', or (ii) both B21 or 22 and Modern Languages paper XII Special Subject 'Medieval Welsh Tales and Romances, the Poets of the Welsh Princes and the Poetry of Dafydd ap Gwilym'. Subject B6 will be examined by extended essay (as specified in the regulations for the Honour School of English Language and Literature).

9. In addition a candidate may offer one of the following:

either

(i) One subject not already selected from among those listed under 4, 6, 7, 8 of this course subject to the restrictions listed under 8 above.

or

(ii) English Course II Subject B16, provided this paper may only be offered by a candidate who also offers English Course II Subject B15.

or

(iii) An Extended Essay on a topic in the modern language or combining the modern language and English (to be examined under the regulations for the Honour School of Modern Languages).

---

* No candidate may offer an extended essay for both 8(ii) and 8(iii) in his selection of options for the honour school.

or

(iv) An optional thesis on a topic in English (to be examined under the regulations for the Honour School of English Language and Literature).

PASS SCHOOL OF ENGLISH AND MODERN LANGUAGES

Candidates shall offer papers in English, and one of the languages and its literature from those studied in the Honour School of Modern Languages.

Candidates shall take the following papers:

In English

Three papers from papers 5, 6, 7 and 8, as specified for the Joint School of English and Modern Languages, provided that not more than one option may be chosen from paper 8.

In the Modern Language

(The numbering used is that in the Honour School of Modern Languages.)

I

IIA (i)

IIB (i)

One of VI, VII, VIII.

The oral examination in the language.

NOTES

SPECIAL REGULATIONS FOR THE HONOUR SCHOOL OF ENGLISH LANGUAGE AND LITERATURE

A

1. The subjects of examination in the School of English Language and Literature shall be the history of the English Language and of English Literature, together with such texts or authors as may from time to time be prescribed by the Board of the Faculty of English Language and Literature for special study.

Candidates shall be permitted to offer, in addition, Special Subjects forming a part of or connected with the study of English Language and Literature.

2. No candidate shall be admitted to examination in this school unless he or she either (*a*) has passed or been exempted from the First Public Examination or (*b*) has successfully completed the Foundation Course in English Language and Literature at the Department for Continuing Education.

3. The board of the faculty shall by notice from time to time make regulations respecting the examination, and shall have power:

(1) To prescribe authors or portions of authors.

(2) To specify one or more related languages or dialects to be offered either as a necessary or as an optional part of the examination.

(3) To name periods of the history of English Literature and to fix their limits.

(4) To issue lists of Special Subjects in connection either with English Language or with English Literature, or with both; and to prescribe authors and texts.

B

Candidates shall offer either Course I (a general course in English Language and Literature) or Course II (a special course in English Language and early English Literature). Each course shall consist of eight subjects, as prescribed below.

In addition to these eight subjects, any candidates may offer as a thesis an essay, **[From 1 October 2004:** of 4,000 to 6,000 words in length (including footnotes but excluding bibliography)**]** the subject of which must be substantially connected with any subject area currently available in Course I or Course II of the FHS in English, including any of the syndicated options under 8(i) in the year in question. Candidates should submit to the Deputy Chairman of the Faculty Board by Wednesday of the second week of Michaelmas Full Term preceding the examination, the title of the proposed thesis, together with a synopsis of the subject in about 100 words. Alternatively candidates may offer as a thesis any essay or part of an essay which he or she has already sent in, or proposes to send in, for any University essay prize, **[Until 1 October 2004:** the whole not exceeding about 6,000 words], provided that its subject is, in the opinion of the Deputy Chairman of the Board, relevant to the study of the English language or of English literature **[From 1 October 2004:** and that the submitted thesis is between 4,000 and 6,000 words in length (including footnotes but excluding bibliography).] Every thesis must be the candidate's own work. Tutors may, however, advise on the choice and scope of the subject, provide a reading list, and read and comment on a first draft. Two typed copies of the thesis must be delivered to the Chairman of Examiners, Honour School of English, Examination Schools, Oxford, not later than noon on the Friday of the week before the Hilary Full Term preceding the examination. A certificate signed by the candidate to the effect that the thesis is the candidate's own work, and that the candidate has read the faculty guidelines on plagiarism, placed in a sealed envelope bearing the candidate's examination number and addressed to the Chairman of Examiners, must be presented together with the thesis. The examiners, in deciding the class of a candidate who offers a thesis, shall consider the thesis as if it were a single additional paper.

Candidates who offer a thesis must not use this material in any other part of the examination.

Theses previously submitted for Honour School of English Language and Literature may be resubmitted. No thesis will be accepted if it has already been submitted, wholly or substantially, for another Honour School or degree of this University, or for a degree of any other institution.

Every candidate shall, not later than the Friday in the second week of the Michaelmas Full Term preceding the examination, send to the Head Clerk, University Offices, through the Senior Tutor of his or her college or society, a statement to say:

(i) whether he or she offers Course I or Course II;

(ii) if he or she offers Course I, which subjects he or she offers under the options provided for Subject 7 (Special Authors) and Subject 8 (Special Topics)

(iii) if he or she offers Course II, which subjects he or she offers from List B, and, in the case of B1, B2, and B3, whether he or she intends to offer (an) extended essay(s) or sit (the) three-hour paper(s);

(iv) whether he or she is offering a thesis *in addition to* the eight subjects of the examination and has obtained or is seeking the Deputy Chairman's approval of its subject.

New optional subjects may be added to those parts of the syllabus for both Course I and Course II where options are already provided, by regulation published in the *Gazette* by the beginning of the fifth week of Trinity Term of the year before the year of the examination in which the subjects will first be available.

Any candidate may be examined viva voce in the subjects of the school; the examiners will dispense from the viva voce examination any candidate concerning whom they shall be satisfied that his or her performance in the viva voce examination could not properly be allowed to affect his or her class.

Course I: General Course in English Language and Literature

Each candidate for Course I shall offer, from the list below, subjects 1 to 6, and two further subjects chosen from subjects 7 to 11. Candidates may not offer any period of English literature in which they have already satisfied Examiners in a First Public Examination in English.

Extended essays

(*a*) Subjects 7 and 8 shall be examined by extended essay except in the case of specified Course II options on Subject 8.

(*b*) An extended essay shall contain no fewer than 5,000 nor more than 6,000 words and shall be on a theme chosen from a list circulated by the examiners.

(*c*) The list of themes for the extended essay for Subject 7 shall be circulated on Thursday of the fifth week of Michaelmas Term next before the examination. The list of themes for the extended essay for Subject 8 shall be circulated on Thursday of the sixth week of Hilary Term next before the examination. The appropriate lists, addressed at his or her college, shall be sent, for both Subject 7 and Subject 8, to all candidates, and it shall be the responsibility of the candidate to collect the list in college. A copy of each list shall be posted at the same time in the Examination Schools.

(*d*) Two typed copies of each essay for Subject 7 must be delivered to the Chairman of Examiners, Honour School of English Language and Literature, Examination Schools, Oxford, by noon on Thursday of the eighth week of Michaelmas Term; and each essay for Subject 8 by noon on Tuesday of the ninth week after the commencement of Hilary Full Term. A certificate signed by the candidate to the effect that each essay is the candidate's own work, and that the candidate has read the Faculty guidelines on plagiarism, placed in a sealed envelope bearing the candidate's examination number and addressed to the Chairman of Examiners, must be presented together with each essay (see (*e*) below).

(*e*) Every extended essay must be the work of the candidate alone, and he or she must not discuss with any tutor either his or her choice of theme or the method of handling it.

(*f*) No essay will be accepted if it has already been submitted, wholly or substantially, for a final honour school or other degree of this University, or degree of any other institution.

(*g*) Essays deemed to be either too short or of excessive length may be penalized.

Candidates are warned (i) that in the papers for Subjects 3–6 they must not answer questions on individual authors of whom they offer a special study for Subject 7, (ii) that they must avoid duplicating, in their answers to one paper, material that they have already used in answering another paper or in the extended essay under Subject 7 or Subject 8 and must show knowledge, in each of the papers for Subjects 3–6, of other literary genres than that of which they offer a special study for Subject 8.

1. *The History, Use, and Theory of the English Language* (one paper of 3 hours).

The paper will cover the history, use, and theory of the English language, with special reference to literary language. The periods covered are those from Chaucer to the present day, but candidates may include material from earlier periods if it is of particular relevance to their answers. It will consist of three sections, candidates being required to answer three questions, selected from more than one section. Questions will be set on all topics listed under sections A and B, but questions will not be set on topics which do not fall within these lists.

Section A: Linguistic History and Theory—diachronic and synchronic approaches to the following topics:

vocabulary (lexis, word-formation, and meaning);
syntax and morphology;
standards of grammaticality and correctness;
history of language study, including writing of grammars and dictionaries;
register and codes;
social and geographical aspects of the use of English.

Section B: History and Theories of Literary Language

Questions will be set on the following topics:

concepts of literary language;
poetic diction;

figurative language;
rhyme and metre;
relations between written and oral discourse;
ideas of linguistic decorum and genre;
literary language as persuasion and social action;
social and institutional contexts of literary discourse.

Section C: Passages for comment

The section will consist of one question containing ten passages, eight of which will be from prescribed authors. All passages will be ascribed and dated. Candidates will be invited to write on one or two passages, and will be required to comment on the ways in which authors exemplify the characteristics and exploit the resources of the language of their periods.

The prescribed authors will be Chaucer, Spenser, Shakespeare, Milton, Clare, Austen, Dickens, and Joyce.

2. *Shakespeare* (one paper).

The paper will include questions on Shakespeare's relation to contemporary dramatists. Candidates must address more than one work by Shakespeare in at least two of their answers.

3. *English Literature from 1100 to 1509* (two papers).

(*a*) A three-hour paper of questions on Medieval English Literature;

[Until 1 October 2004: (*b*) A two-hour paper consisting of two parts (both compulsory):

(i) Passages for translation, to be set from *A Book of Middle English* eds. J. A. Burrow and T. Turville-Petre:

(*a*) no. 2 *The Owl and the Nightingale*
(*b*) no. 3 Layamon's *Brut*
(*c*) no. 4 *Ancrene Wisse* **and** no. 6 *The Cloud of Unknowing*
(*d*) no. 7 *Piers Plowman* (extracts a and b)
(*e*) no. 8 *Patience* **or** no. 9 *Sir Gawain and the Green Knight*
(*f*) no. 14 *The York Play of the Crucifixion*

The paper will contain passages from **five** of (*a*) to (*f*) and candidates will be required to translate **three**. Under (*c*) there will be a passage from **either** no. 4 or no. 6; under (*e*) there will be a passage from both texts and candidates may translate **either** of them (but **not** both).

(ii) Passages for critical comment, to be set from the following texts:**]**

[From 1 October 2004:

(*b*) A two-hour paper consisting of passages for critical comment, to be set from the following texts:**]**

(*a*) Chaucer, *Troilus and Criseyde* (ed. L. D. Benson)

[From 1 October 2004:

(*b*) *Ancrere Wisse*, Books 6 and 7 (ed. Shepherd)**]**
(*b*)**[**(*c*)**]** Langland, *Piers Plowman,* B Text, Passus XVI–XX (ed. A. V. C. Schmidt)
(*c*)**[**(*d*)**]** *Pearl* (ed. E. V. Gordon)
(*d*)**[**(*e*)**]** Malory, *Morte Darthur,* Books XVIII–XXI (ed. E. Vinaver)
(*e*)**[**(*f*)**]** Henryson, *Fables* (ed. D. Fox)

(A passage or passages will be set from each of the **[Until 1 October 2004:** texts in part (ii)**]** **[From 1 October 2004:** specific texts**]**. Candidates will be required to write on two passages, one from *Troilus and Criseyde,* and one from one of the other texts.)

4. *English Literature from 1509 to 1642* (one paper).

Candidates who have satisfied the Moderators in Honour Moderations in Classics and English may not offer this paper. They may offer instead one of the following:

(*a*) English Literature from 1832–1900;
(*b*) English Literature from 1900 to the present day.

5. *English Literature from 1642 to 1740* (one paper).

6. *English Literature from 1740 to 1832* (one paper).

7. *Special Authors* (an extended essay of not fewer than 5,000 nor more than 6,000 words) (see introduction to regulations for Course I).

Candidates may offer any *one* of the following, provided that they may not offer in the Final Honour School any author they offered in Paper 3 of Moderations in English Language and Literature.

(*a*) (i) The *Beowulf* Poet, or (ii) Alfred, or (iii) Ælfric
(*b*) (i) Chaucer, or (ii) Julian of Norwich or (iii) the York Cycle.
(*c*) (i) Donne, or (ii) Milton, or (iii) Marlowe.
(*d*) (i) Marvell or (ii) Swift, or (iii) Lady Mary Wortley Montagu.
(*e*) (i) Wordsworth, or (ii) Fielding, or (iii) Hazlitt
[Until 1 October 2004: (*f*) (i) R. Browning, or (ii) G. Eliot, or (iii) Wilde.**]**
[From 1 October 2004:
(*f*) (i) Tennyson, or (ii) Dickens, or (iii) Wilde**]**
(*g*) (i) Joyce, or (ii) T. S. Eliot, or (iii) Woolf.
(*h*) (i) Bishop, or (ii) Coetzee, or (iii) Stoppard

Named authors will be replaced in order, in rotation, in three groups (first: *a, d, g*; second: *b, e, h*; third: *c, f*) in cycles of three years, the first replacement to occur in 2002, for first examination in 2003. Notice of new named authors will be published in the *University Gazette* by the beginning of the fifth week of Trinity Term two years before first examination.

8. *Special Topics* (an extended essay of not fewer than 5,000 nor more than 6,000 words with the exception of option (*h*) *i, iv, v, vi*, and *vii*; which must be offerd as written papers) (see introduction to regulations for Course I).

In all Special Topics, candidates will be expected to show such historical and/or contextual knowledge as is necessary for the profitable study of the periods, genres, authors, or topics concerned. Candidates should show knowledge of more than one author.

Candidates may offer *one* of the following:

(*a*) Fiction in English
(*b*) The Drama in English
(*c*) Prose in English
(*d*) Poetry in English
(*e*) American Literature from 1800 to the present day
(*f*) Women's Writing
(*g*) The History and Theory of Criticism
(*h*) Any one of the following Course II options;

i. Linguistic Theory (one paper; as specified for Course II paper B4)
ii. Medieval and Renaissance Romance (extended essay; as specified for Course II paper B7*a*)
iii. Scottish Literature pre-1600 (extended essay; as specified for Course II paper B7*b*)
iv. Old Norse (one paper, as specified in Course II paper B15)

v. Medieval French Literature 1100–1300 *or* Medieval French Literature 1300–1500 (one paper, as specified for Course II papers B19 and B20)

vi. Medieval Welsh Language and Literature I *or* Medieval Welsh Language and Literature II (one paper, as specified for Course II papers B21 and B22)

vii. Medieval Latin (one paper, as specified for Course II paper B24)

viii. Classical Literature (extended essay, as specified for Course II paper B26).

(*i*) Any one of the syndicated Special Topics from the list for the year concerned, which will be published in the *University Gazette* by the beginning of the fifth week of the Trinity Term one year before the examination.

9. *Introduction to Medieval Studies: Old English Literature* (one paper)

10. *Victorian Literature (1832–1900)* (one paper)

11. *Modern Literature (1900 to the present day)* (one paper).

COURSE II: SPECIAL COURSE IN ENGLISH LANGUAGE AND EARLY ENGLISH LITERATURE

Each candidate shall offer the five subjects of List A below, and three subjects chosen from List B, subject to the restrictions set out below. Candidates may not offer more than two papers as extended essays.

Extended essays

(*a*) The following subjects will be assessed by extended essay only: B5 *Old English Special Authors*, B6 *Medieval and Renaissance Special Authors*, B7 *Special Topics* (except any Course II papers available under B7(*h*), for which the Course II regulations specify that these shall be assessed by written examination), B17 *Old Norse–Icelandic Literature*, and B26 *Classical Literature*.

(*b*) The following subjects will be assessed by extended essay or examination: B1 *Old English Philology*, B2 *Middle English Dialectology*, B3 *Modern English Philology*. Candidates will be required to specify their chosen mode of examination for these papers on their registration form and may not revert from this choice.

(*c*) An extended essay for subjects B5, B6, B7, B17, and B26 shall contain no fewer than 5,000 nor more than 6,000 words and shall be on a theme chosen from a list circulated by the examiners. Subjects B1, B2, and B3 will require two essays, each not exceeding 3,000 words, and shall be on a theme chosen from a list circulated by the examiners.

(*d*) The list of themes for B1, B3, B5, and B6 shall be circulated on Thursday of the Fifth Week of Michaelmas Term next before the examination. The list of themes for B2, B7, B17, and B26 shall be circulated on Thursday of the Sixth Week of Hilary Term next before the examination. The appropriate lists, addressed at his or her college, shall be sent to each candidate who on entering for the examination has stated that he or she wishes to submit an extended essay, and it shall be the responsibility of the candidate to collect the list in college. A copy of each list shall be posted at the same time in the Examination Schools.

(*e*) Two typed copies of each essay for B1, B3, B5, and B6 must be delivered to the Chairman of Examiners, Honour School of English Language and Literature (Course II), Examination Schools, Oxford, by noon on Thursday of the eighth week of Michaelmas Term; and those for B2, B7, B17 and B26 by noon on Tuesday of the ninth week after the commencement of Hilary Full Term. A certificate signed by the candidate to the effect that each essay is the candidate's own work, and that the candidate has read the Faculty guidelines on plagiarism, placed in a sealed envelope bearing the candidate's examination number and addressed to the Chair of Examiners, must be presented together with each essay (see (*f*) below).

(*f*) Every extended essay shall be the candidate's own work. Every extended essay must be the work of the candidate alone, and he or she must not discuss with any tutor either his or her choice of theme or the method of handling it.

(*g*) No essay will be accepted if it has already been submitted, wholly or substantially, for a final honour school or other degree of this University, or degree of any other institution.

(*h*) Essays deemed to be either too short or of excessive length may be penalized.

List A: English Language and Literature (compulsory subjects).

1. *English Literature 600–1100* (one paper)

Candidates will be expected to show knowledge of a wide range of Old English literature and should show an awareness of the historical and cultural contexts of the period.

2. *English Literature 1100–1530* (one paper)

Candidates will be expected to show knowledge of a wide range of Middle English literature, and should show an awareness of the historical and cultural contexts of the literature of the period. Candidates should not answer on this paper on works by Chaucer on which they intend to answer on paper A3(*a*); candidates should not write on this paper on Langland and/or Gower if they are answering on those authors on paper A3(*b*).

3. *Chaucer, Langland, and Gower* (two papers)

Candidates will be required to take *two* papers as follows:

(*a*) A three-hour paper of questions on Chaucer.

Questions will be set that require a wide knowledge of Chaucer's writings. Candidates will be required to answer two questions.

(*b*) A two-hour paper of questions on Langland and Gower and on comparative studies of the three authors. Candidates will be required to write one essay.

4. *Old and Middle English Texts* (one paper)

Candidates will be expected to have made a detailed study of *Exodus* (rev. edn. ed. P. Lucas, 1994), *Aelfric, Homilies 14, 20, and 21,* ll. 1–291, 494–676 (ed. J. C. Pope, 1968), *Ancrene Wisse*, and *Sir Gawain and the Green Knight* (ed. J. R. R. Tolkien, E. V. Gordon, rev. N. Davis, 1967). Question 1, which will be compulsory, will consist of passages for translation and commentary from three of the set texts; passages from *Ancrene Wisse* will be taken from the edition of books 6 and 7, ed. G. Shepherd (1985). Candidates must answer two further essay questions. Essay questions will require answers on issues of genre, sources, textual history, interpretative difficulties, manuscript dissemination.

5. *The Development of Standard Literary English to c.1750* (one paper)

Candidates will be expected to show an understanding of the development of the written language from the earliest records to *c.*1750, with particular attention to the emergence of a standard form. Candidates will be required to answer question 1 and two other questions, and to demonstrate a knowledge of Old, Middle and early Modern English in their answers. Question 1 will require comment on the language of *either* (*a*) passages of biblical translation *or* (*b*) other representative texts (four passages of each will be set of which candidates must comment on two). Questions on lexicography will include Johnson's *Dictionary.*

List B: English Language and Literature and Subsidiary Languages (optional subjects)

Candidates are required to note that the availability of options is subject to the provision of teaching in the year in question.

1. *Old English Philology* (extended essay or one paper)

Candidates should have made a study of the Old English language in its various dialects up to *c.*1100, paying particular attention to the evidence available from primary materials; they will be expected to have such awareness of Germanic philology as is necessary for an understanding of the background to Old English.

All aspects of the language are included: its orthography, phonology, morphology, syntax, lexis. No texts are prescribed, but those in Sweet's *Anglo-Saxon Reader* (rev. Whitelock, 1967), nos ii, vi–viii, xiv, xvi, xxxii–xxxviii, indicate the range of dialects to be covered. In the three-hour paper the first question (which will be compulsory) will require comment on passages set from texts in these dialects.

Candidates taking the paper by extended essay will be required to write two extended essays, each a maximum of 3,000 and a minimum of 2,500 words in length, on topics from a list to be circulated by the examiners in the fifth week of Michaelmas Term next preceding the examination.

2. *Middle English Dialectology* (extended essay or one paper)

Candidates will be expected to have made a study of a wide range of Middle English and Middle Scots dialects from *c.*1100 to *c.*1500, paying particular attention to the evidence available from primary materials. All aspects of the language are included: its orthography, phonology, morphology, syntax, lexis. No texts are prescribed, but those in Burrow and Turville-Petre (eds), *A Book of Middle English*, nos 2–4, 8–9, 11, 14, and Sisam (ed.), *Fourteenth-Century Verse and Prose* no. 10, indicate the range of dialects to be covered. In the three-hour paper the first question, which will be compulsory, will require comment on passages set from texts in these dialects.

Candidates taking the paper by extended essay will be required to write two extended essays, each a maximum of 3,000 and a minimum of 2,500 words in length, on topics from a list to be circulated by the examiners in sixth week of Hilary Term preceding the examination.

3. *Modern English Philology* (extended essay or one paper)

Candidates will be expected to show an understanding of developments in the written and spoken language with reference to the period from *c.*1500 to the present day, paying particular attention to the evidence available from primary materials. The paper involves the consideration of all aspects of the language, including orthography, phonology, morphology, syntax, and lexis. There are no prescribed texts, but candidates are expected to read a range of writings in the language in this period. Candidates must answer questions from both Section A, texts for comment and transcription, and Section B, questions on the history and development of the language in the period in question.

Candidates taking the paper by extended essay will be required to write two extended essays, each a maximum of 3,000 and a minimum of 2,500 words in length, on topics from a list to be circulated by the examiners in the fifth week of Michaelmas Term preceding the examination.

4. *Linguistic Theory* (one paper).

Candidates will be expected to show a general knowledge of theoretical linguistics with special reference to phonology, phonetics, grammar, lexis, semantics, and discourse structure and pragmatics. Opportunities will be given to answer questions on major developments in linguistic theory since 1800.

5. *Old English Special Authors* (extended essay)

Candidates must answer on any one of the *Beowulf* poet, Alfred, or Aelfric. Candidates answering substantially on any of these writers in paper A1, *English Literature 600–1100* may not offer the same writer in this paper. Candidates answering on Aelfric on paper A4 should not discuss the same texts in detail in this paper.

6. *Medieval and Renaissance Special Authors* (extended essay)

As defined in Course I Subject 7 (*b*) and (*c*) for the year concerned, except that candidates may not answer on any author made the focus of an answer eleswhere in the examination.

7. *Special Topics* (extended essay)*

In all special topics, candidates will be expected to show such historical and/or contextual knowledge as is necessary for the profitable study of the periods, genres, or authors concerned. Candidates should show knowledge of more than one writer except where otherwise specified. The list of themes for subjects (*c*) to (*h*) will be the same as those set for Course I Subjects 8 (*b*) to (*d*), (*f*), (*g*) and (*i*).

(*a*) *Medieval and Renaissance Romance*
(*b*) *Scottish Literature pre-1600*
(*c*) *Drama in English*
(*d*) *Prose in English*
(*e*) *Poetry in English*
(*f*) *Women's Writing*
(*g*) *The History and Theory of Criticism*
(*h*) Any one of the Special Topics for the year concerned, as published in the *University Gazette* by the beginning of the fifth week of the Trinity Term one year before the examination.

8. *English Literature from 1509 to 1642* (one paper).

The paper will be the same as that set for Course I (Subject 4), but candidates who offer Course II must not answer questions on authors on whom they have answered questions in paper A2, or on whom they offer an optional subject.

Candidates who have satisfied the Moderators in Honour Moderations in Classics and English may not offer this option.

9. *Shakespeare* (one paper).

The paper will be the same as that set for Course I.

10. *The Archaeology of Anglo-Saxon England, seventh to ninth centuries AD* (one paper).

Questions will be set on such topics as the archaeology of kingship; Celtic influence on Anglo-Saxon material culture; rural settlement and landscape; the archaeology of the Conversion; the emergence of towns; and the 'Golden Age' of Northumbria. The identification, description and discussion of artefacts will be compulsory.

11. *Gothic* (one paper)

Candidates will be expected to show a knowledge of the elements of Gothic phonology, morphology, syntax, and lexicology, and to show special knowledge of the Gospels in Gothic. Three questions must be answered, including a compulsory translation set from passages from the surviving parts of the translation of St Mark's gospel and of II Timothy, as printed in J. Wright, *Grammar of the Gothic Language* (2nd edn. rev. O. L. Sayce, 1954); linguistic commentary may be required.

12. *Old Saxon* (one paper)

Candidates will be expected to show a knowledge of the elements of Old Saxon phonology, morphology, syntax, and lexicology. They will be expected to have made special study of the language of the *Heliand*, and to show detailed knowledge of its text from l. 3516 to the end (l. 5983) as edited by O. Behagel (9th edn. rev. B. Taeger, 1984), and of the *Genesis* fragments, as edited by A. N. Doane (1991). Three questions must be answered, including a compulsory translation and comment question.

13. *Old High German* (one paper)

Candidates will be expcted to show a detailed knowledge of the elements of Old High German phonology, morphology, syntax, and lexicology, and to have made a

* This is with the exception of Course II papers available under B7(*h*) for which the Course II regulations specify that these shall be assessed by written examination.

special study of the texts set for Paper V (I): German in the Honour School of Modern Languages.

Passages for translation and linguistic commentary, general linguistic questions, and literary questions on these texts will be set. Three questions must be answered, including a compulsory translation and commentary question.

14. *Middle High German* (one paper)

Candidates will be expected to study the texts prescribed for Paper IX: German, of the Honour School of Modern Languages, and to show detailed knowledge of three of them.

Passages for translation and literary commentary, and general literary questions on these texts will be set. Three questions must be answered, including a compulsory translation and commentary question.

15. *Old Norse* (one paper)

Three questions must be answered, including one compulsory translation and commentary question from passages from *Íslendingabók; Hrafnkels saga Freysgoða; Skírnismál; Hamðismál;* Snorri's *Edda* (ed. Faulkes, Oxford, 1982): *Gylfaginning*, ch. 43 to end. Literary questions on these texts will be set and candidates will also be given an opportunity to show a knowledge of the elements of Old Norse phonology, morphology, syntax, and lexicology.

16. *Old Norse Texts* (one paper)

Candidates will be expected to have made a spcial study of the following: *Auðunar þáttr; Víga Glúms saga; Völundarkviða; Atlakviða*. They will be expected to have read but not to have studied in detail, *Fóstbræðra saga; Gísla saga Súrssonar; Hervarar saga; Gylfaginning; Völuspá; Hávamál*. Three questions must be answered, including one compulsory translation and commentary question from passages from the texts set for special study. Literary questions will be set on all the set texts.

This subject may be offered only by candidates who also offer Subject B15.

17. *Old Norse–Icelandic Literature* (extended essay)

Candidates will be expected to have read widely, especially in Old Icelandic prose. This subject may be offered only by candidates who also offer either Subject B15 or Subjects B15 and B16.

18. *Old French Language 1150–1250* (one paper)

Candidates will be expected to show a knowledge of the elements of Old French (including Anglo-Norman) orthography, morphology, phonology, syntax, and lexicology, paying particular attention to the evidence available from primary materials. Three questions must be answered, including one compulsory translation and commentary question on passages set from *La Vie de S. Alexis*, ed. C. Storey; *La Chanson de Roland*, ll. 1–660, ed. F. Whitehead; *Piramus et Tisbé*, ed. C. de Boer; *La folie Tristan d'Oxford*, ed. E. Hoepffner (2nd edn.), *Aucassin et Nicolette*, ed. M. Roques; *La Seinte Resureccion* (ANTS 4).

19. *Medieval French Literature 1100–1300* (one paper)

Candidates will be expected to have made a special study of at least two of the following: *La Chanson de Roland*, Chrétien de Troyes, *Yvain; La Mort le roi Artu; Le Roman de la Rose*, ll. 1–4058. Candidates will also be expected to have read, but not to have studied in detail, *either Le Roman de La Rose*, ll. 4059–21780 *or* at least three of the following: Béroul, *Tristan*; Marie de France, *Lais*; *Charroi de Nîmes*; *Aucassin et Nicolette*; Jean Renart, *La Lai de l'ombre*; Wace, *Roman de Brut*, 9005–13298; Jean Bodel, *Le Jeu de Saint Nicolas*, and Villehardouin, *La Conquête de Constantinople, Le Roman de Renart*, ed. M. Roques, ll. 3733–4796. Three questions must be answered, including one requiring literary and linguistic commentary on passages from the set texts, of which candidates must answer **one**. Translation will not be required.

20. *Medieval French Literature 1300–1500* (one paper)

Candidates will be expected to have made a special study of the following: Guillaume de Machaut, *Le Jugement du roy de Behaigne*; Christine de Pisan, *Epistre au dieu d'amours*; François Villon, *Le Testament*. Candidates will also be expected to have read, but not to have studied in detail at least three of the following: Machaut, *La Fonteine amoureuse*, Machaut, *Le Livre du Voir-Dit*; Alain Chartier, *La Belle Dame sans Mercy*; Alain Chartier, *La Quadrilogue invectif*, Charles d'Orléans, *Ballades et rondeaux*; *Les Quinze Joies de mariage*. Three questions must be answered, including one requiring literary and linguistic commentary on passages from the set texts, of which candidates must answer **one**. Translation will not be required.

21. *Medieval Welsh Language and Literature I* (one paper)

Candidates will be expected to show a knowledge of the elements of Medieval Welsh phonology, morphology, syntax, and lexicology. Opportunities will be provided to discuss the literary qualities of texts. Three questions must be answered, including one compulsory translation and commentary question from passages from *Pwyll Pendeuic Dyuet*, ed. R. L. Thomson (1957, repr. 1972), *Branwen Uerch Lyr*, ed. D. S. Thomson (1961, repr. 1968), *Poems of the Cywyddwyr*, ed. E. I. Rowlands (1976) nos 1, 2, 4, 7, 13, 19, 21–4, *Gwaith Dafydd ap Gwilym*, ed. T. Parry (1979), nos 2, 23, 26, 27, 42, 48, 84, 87, 114, 117, 122, 124. This paper may not be taken by candidates offering B22 *Medieval Welsh Language and Literature II*.

22. *Medieval Welsh Language and Literature II* (one paper)

Candidates will be expected to show a knowledge of the elements of Old and Middle Welsh phonology, morphology, syntax, and lexicology. Opportunities will be provided to discuss the literary qualities of the prescribed texts. Three questions must be answered, including one compulsory translation and commentary question from passages from *Pedeir Keinc y Mabinogi*, ed. I. Williams (1930), *Culhwch and Olwen*, ed. R. Bromwich and D. S. Evans (1992), 'The Juvencus Poems', ed. I. Williams, *The Beginnings of Welsh Poetry* (1980, 1990) *Gwaith Llywelyn Fardd I ac Eraill o Feirdd y Ddeuddegfed Ganrif*, ed. M. E. Owen *et al.* (1994), nos 6–15, 18–21, *Poems of the Cywyddwyr*, ed. E. I. Rowlands (1976), nos 1, 2, 4, 7, 13, 19, 21–4, *Gwaith Dafydd ap Gwilym*, ed. T. Parry (1979), nos 2, 13, 23, 26, 27, 28, 42, 48, 84, 87, 114, 117, 122, 124. They will be expected to have read but not to have studied in detail *Breudwyt Ronabwy*, ed. M. Richards (1984), *Peredur*, ed. G. Goetinck (1976), *Gwaith Iolo Goch*, ed. D. R. Johnston (1988). This paper may not be taken by candidates offering B21 *Medieval Welsh Language and Literature I*.

23. *Old and Early Middle Irish Language and Literature* (one paper)

Candidates will be expected to show a knowledge of the elements of Old Irish phonology, morphology, syntax, and lexicology. They will be given an opportunity to comment on the literary qualities of the prescribed texts. Three questions must be answered, including one compulsory translation and commentary question from passages from *Stories from the Táin*, ed. J. Strachan and O. Bergin (1944), *Scéla Mucce Meic Dathó*, ed. R. Thurneysen (1951), *Longes mac nUislenn*, ed. V. Hull (1949), *Early Irish Lyrics*, ed. G. Murphy (1956), nos 1–3, 5.

24. *Medieval Latin Language and Literature* (one paper) [as specified for the Honour School of Literae Humaniores Subject III 11(*b*)].

25. *The Latin Literature of the British Isles before the Norman Conquest of England (one paper).*

The following texts are prescribed: Gildas, De Excidio, pref. chaps. 1–10, ed. M. Winterbottom, Arthurian Period Sources 7 (London/Chichester, 1978). Aldhelm, *De*

Virginitate, prose, chaps. 1–5; verse, ll. 1–105, 2861–904, ed. R. Ehwald, *M.G.H.*; *Auctores Antiquissimi,* xv (Berlin, 1919). Bede, *Vita S. Cuthberti,* prose, *pref.*; chaps. 1–5, ed. B. Colgrave *Two 'Lives' of Saint Cuthbert* (repr. New York, 1969); metrical *Life pref.*; chaps. 1–5, ed. W. Jaager, *Palaestra,* 198. Alcuin, *Two Alcuin Letter-Books,* 1, nos. 1–14, ed. C. Chase, Toronto Medieval Latin Texts (Toronto, 1975). *Oxford Book of Mediaeval Latin Verse,* rev. edn. F. J. E. Raby (Oxford, 1970), no. 80. *Versus de . . . Sanctis Euboricensis Ecclesiae,* ll. 1–130, 1596–1657, ed. E. Dümmler, *M.G.H. Poetae,* 1 (Berlin, 1881). Asser, *Vita Alfredi* chaps. 1–15, ed. Stevenson, rev. D. Whitelock (Oxford, 1959). Æthelweard, *Chronicle,* Book IV, ed. A. Campbell (London, 1962). Ælfric, *Life of St. Ethelwold,* ed. M. Winterbottom, *Three Lives of English Saints,* Toronto Medieval Latin Texts (Toronto, 1972). Columbanus, *Epistle* 1, ed. G. Walker, Scriptores Latini Hiberniae II (Dublin, 1970). *Hisperica Famina,* vv. 571–612, ed. M. Herren (Toronto, 1974).

26. *Classical Literature* (extended essay)

Candidates will be expected to have studied one of the forms specified below in Greek and/or Latin Literature (and should specify their choice on their entry form).

(i) Epic
(ii) Tragedy

[From 1 October 2004:

27. *Introduction to Medieval Studies: Old English Literature*

Three questions must be answered, including one compulsory question of either translation or commentary. Commentary passages will be taken from *The Dream of the Rood, The Wanderer, The Battle of Maldon,* Aelfric's life of St Edmund, Bede's account of the poet Caedmon and from *Beowulf,* the *'Lament of the last survivor'* (ll. 2247–66) and *Beowulf's funeral* (ll. 3156–82). Literary questions will cover these texts, but candidates will also be given an opportunity to show a knowledge of a wider range of Old English literature, and of aspects of Old English history, culture, and language. Candidates may not offer this paper if it is one in which they have previously satisfied Examiners in any First Public Examination in English.**]**

PASS SCHOOL OF ENGLISH LANGUAGE AND LITERATURE

Candidates for the Pass Degree in English Language and Literature must satisfy the examiners in five papers chosen from (i)–(vii) below:

(i) Shakespeare (as prescribed for the Honour School of English Language and Literature);
(ii) English Literature from 1509 to 1642 (as prescribed for the Honour School of English Language and Literature);
(iii) English Literature from 1642 to 1740 (as prescribed for the Honour School of English Language and Literature);
(iv) English Literature from 1740 to 1832 (as prescribed for the Honour School of English Language and Literature);
(v) English Literature from 1832 to 1900 (as prescribed for Moderations in English Language and Literature);
(vi) English Literature from 1900 to the present (as prescribed for Moderations in English Language and Literature);
(vii) Special authors (as prescribed for the Honour School of English Language and Literature).

Candidates who have satisfied the Moderators in Honour Moderations in Classics and English may not offer paper (ii).

Candidates who have satisfied the Moderators in Moderations in English Language and Literature may not offer papers (v) and (vi) nor any author from paper (vii) whom they have offered in paper 3 (*a*) in that examination.

Candidates for option (vii) shall offer an extended essay. The regulations for extended essays shall be as prescribed for the Honour School of English Language and Literature.

NOTES

SPECIAL REGULATIONS FOR THE HONOUR SCHOOL OF EUROPEAN AND MIDDLE EASTERN LANGUAGES

A

1. The subjects of the examination in the Honour School of European and Middle Eastern Languages shall be (*a*) those modern languages and literatures studied in the Honour School of Modern Languages, and (*b*) Arabic, Hebrew, Persian, and Turkish.

2. All candidates must offer (*a*) one of the languages which may be studied in the Honour School of Modern Languages, with its literature, and (*b*) one of the languages specified in clause 1 (*b*) above.

3. No candidate shall be admitted to the examination in this school unless he or she has either passed or been exempted from the first Public Examination.

4. The examiners shall indicate in the lists issued by them the languages offered by each candidate obtaining Honours or satisfying the examiners under Ch. VI, Sect. II. c, § 1, cll. 22 (v) and (vi).

5. The examination in this school shall be under the joint supervision of the Boards of the Faculties of Medieval and Modern Languages and Oriental Studies, which shall appoint a standing joint committee to make, and to submit to the two faculty boards, proposals for regulations for this examination and for the Preliminary Examination in European and Middle Eastern Languages.

6. (i) The examiners in the Honour School shall be such of the Public Examiners in the Honour Schools of Modern Languages and Oriental Studies as shall be required.

(ii) It shall be the duty of the Chairman of Examiners in the Honour School of Modern Languages and in the Honour School of Oriental Studies to consult together and designate such examiners as shall be required for the Honour School, whereupon the number of the examiners shall be deemed to be complete.

B

Candidates will be examined in accordance with the examination regulations set out below.

They will also be required to spend, after their matriculation, a year of residence in an appropriate country or countries, and to provide on their entry form for the examination a certificate that they have done this, signed by the Head or by a tutor of their society. Candidates wishing to be dispensed from the requirement to undertake a year of residence abroad must apply in writing to the Chairman of the Medieval and Modern Languages Board, 41 Wellington Square, Oxford, OX1 2JF, stating their reasons for requesting dispensation and enclosing a letter of support from their society.

Candidates will be expected to carry out during this year abroad such work as their society may require. Candidates will agree with their College Tutor in advance of their year abroad an independent course of study to be followed during that period.

Each candidate shall offer the prescribed papers from *either* List A *or* List B as provided below. Each candidate shall also offer the oral examination in the European language.

Except in a Special Subject or an alternative to a Special Subject, a candidate shall offer one European language and its literature only.

Any candidate may be examined viva voce.

In every case where, under the regulations for the school, candidates have a choice between one or more papers or subjects, every candidate shall give notice to the Registrar not later than Friday in the fourth week of the Michaelmas Full Term preceding the examination of all the papers and subjects being so offered.

Candidates are warned that they must avoid duplicating in their answers to one part of the examination material that they have used in another part of the examination.

[From 1 October 2004:

For those papers in the Middle Eastern language where a selection of unspecified texts is to be examined, the selection of texts will be determined by the Oriental Studies Board in Hilary Term for the examination in the next academic year, and copies of the list of selected texts will be available for candidates no later than Friday of the third week of the same term.**]**

Oral examination in the European language

As specified for the Honour School of Modern Languages.

[Until 1 October 2005: *List A: With the European Language as the first subject*

1. Unprepared translation into the European language (one paper of three hours) [Honour School of Modern Languages, Paper I].

2. Unprepared translation from the European language (two papers of one-and-a-half hours each) [Honour School of Modern Languages, Paper IIA (i) and Paper IIB (i)].

3. An essay in the European language, on one of a choice of literary and other subjects (one paper of three hours) [Honour School of Modern Languages, Paper III].

4. A period of literature of the European language (one paper of three hours) [Honour School of Modern Languages, Paper VI or VII or VIII].**]**

[From 1 October 2005:

1. Honour School of Modern Languages, Paper I.
2. Honour School of Modern Languages, Papers IIA(i) and IIB(i).
3. Honour School of Modern Languages, Paper III.
4. Honour School of Modern Languages, *one* paper chosen from Papers VI, VII or VIII.**]**

[Until 1 October 2004: 5, 6. Honour School of Modern Languages, *two* papers chosen from IV, V, IX, X, XI, or XII.**]** **[From 1 October 2004:** 5. Honour School of Modern Languages, *one* paper chosen from IV, V, IX, X, XI, or XII.**]**

[Until 1 October 2004: 5, 6. *Two*] **[From 1 October 2004:** 5. *One*] of the following papers in the European language:

(i) Linguistic Studies I (one paper) [Honour School of Modern Languages, Paper IV].

(ii) Linguistic Studies II (one paper) [Honour School of Modern Languages, Paper V].

(iii) Early texts prescribed for study as examples of literature (one paper) [Honour School of Modern Languages, Paper IX].

(iv) Modern Prescribed Authors (*i*) (one paper) [Honour School of Modern Languages, Paper X].

(v) Modern Prescribed Authors (*ii*) (one paper) [Honour School of Modern Languages, Paper XI].

(vi) Special Subject (one paper) [Honour School of Modern Languages, Paper XII].

[Until 1 October 2004: (vii) *Either* an Extended Essay on a topic in the European language or combining the European language and Middle Eastern language (to be examined under the regulations for the Honour School of Modern Languages) *or* a special subject (to be examined under the regulations in the Honour School of Oriental Studies for the Middle Eastern language being offered in 7, 8, 9, 10).]

[From 1 October 2004:

6. An extended essay on a topic bridging the European and the Middle Eastern language.]

Arabic

7. Composition in Arabic.

8. Arabic unprepared translation into English and comprehension.

9. Classical texts:
the texts will be those specified for Arabic with Modern Middle Eastern Studies, Paper 4.

10. Modern texts:
the texts will be those specified for Arabic with Modern Middle Eastern Studies, Paper 5.

11. Oral examination (as specified for the Honour School of Oriental Studies).

Hebrew

7. Hebrew composition and unprepared translation.

8 and 9. Two papers from the following:

(i) Prepared texts I: Biblical texts:
the texts will be those specified for Hebrew only, paper 2.

(ii) Prepared texts II: Mishnaic and Medieval Hebrew Texts:
the texts will be those specified for Hebrew only, paper 3.

(iii) Prepared texts III: Modern Hebrew literature:
the texts will be those specified for Hebrew only, paper 4.

10. General paper: language, history, religion, and culture.

Persian

7. Persian prose composition and unprepared translation.

8 and 9. Two papers as prescribed for subsidiary Persian, papers 2 and 3.

10. General questions on one of the following periods of history:

(*a*) The transition from Sasanian to Islamic Persia (up to the tenth century AD).

(*b*) The Safavids from 1501 to 1722.

(*c*) The rise of the Qajars to the end of the Constitutional Revolution.

(*d*) The Pahlavis from 1926 to 1979.

11. Oral examination (as specified for the Honour School of Oriental Studies).

Turkish

7. Unprepared translation from modern Turkish.

8. Translation into Turkish and essay in Turkish.

9. Turkish history and thought in the nineteenth and twentieth centuries. The following texts are prescribed for study:

Either Mode A:

M. Cavid Baysun, ed., *Tarihî Eserlerden Seçilmiş Eski Metinler* (Istanbul, 1964), pp. 9–18, 36–60, 118–24.

Selected late Ottoman and modern Turkish political documents.*

Selected late Ottoman writings on political and cultural issues.*

Selected modern Turkish writings on political and cultural issues.*

Or Mode B, in which all the texts are presented in Latin script:

Selected late Ottoman and modern Turkish political documents.*

Selected late Ottoman writings on political and cultural issues.*

Selected modern Turkish writings on political and cultural issues.*

The volume of texts set for Mode B will be about 25 per cent greater than that set for Mode A.

Candidates will be required to translate and/or comment on passages from the prescribed texts, and to write essays on questions relating either to the texts themselves and their background, or to more general historical topics.

10. Modern Turkish literary texts.

The following texts are prescribed for study:

Either Mode A:

Selected late Ottoman literary texts (post-1860).*

Selected modern Turkish short stories.*

Selected modern Turkish poetry.*

or Mode B, in which all the texts are presented in Latin script:

Selected late Ottoman literary texts (post-1860).*

Selected modern Turkish short stories.*

Selected modern Turkish poetry.*

The volume of texts set for Mode B will be about 25 per cent greater than that set for Mode A.

The questions set in the examination will require translation, commentary and essays.

11. Oral examination (as specified for the Honour School of Oriental Studies).

List B: With the Middle Eastern Language as the first subject

1. Unprepared translation into the European language (one paper of three hours) [Honour School of Modern Languages, Paper I].

2. Unprepared translation from the European language (two papers of one-and-a-half hours each) [Honour School of Modern Languages, Paper IIA (i) and Paper IIB (i)].

3. A period of literature of the European language (one paper of three hours) [Honour School of Modern Languages, Paper VI or VII or VIII].

4. *One* of the following papers in the European language:

(i) Linguistic Studies I (one paper) [Honour School of Modern Languages, Paper IV].

(ii) Linguistic Studies II (one paper) [Honour School of Modern Languages, Paper V].

---

* Lists of texts are available from the Oriental Institute.

(iii) Early texts prescribed for study as examples of literature (one paper) [Honour School of Modern Languages, Paper IX].
(iv) Modern Prescribed Authors (*i*) (one paper) [Honour School of Modern Languages, Paper X].
(v) Modern Prescribed Authors (*ii*) (one paper) [Honour School of Modern Languages, Paper XI].
(vi) Special subject (one paper) [Honour School of Modern Languages, Paper XII].

[Until 1 October 2004:
5. An extended essay on a topic bridging the European and the Middle Eastern language.**]**

with Arabic

5 **[**6**]**. Composition in Arabic.

6 **[**7**]**. Arabic unprepared translation into English and comprehension.

7 **[**8**]**. Qur'ān and Ḥadīth:
the texts will be those specified for Arabic only, paper 4.

8 **[**9**]**. Classical texts:
the texts will be those specified for Arabic only, paper 5(*a*): classical texts.

9 **[**10**]**. Modern texts:
the texts will be those specified for Arabic only, paper 5(*b*): modern texts.

[From 1 October 2004: 10. A special subject, to be approved by the Board of the Faculty of Oriental Studies.**]**

11. Oral examination (as specified for the Honour School of Oriental Studies).

with Hebrew

5 **[**6**]**. Hebrew composition and unprepared translation.

6 **[**7**]**. Prepared texts I: Biblical texts:
the texts will be those specified for Hebrew only, paper 2.

7 **[**8**]**. Prepared texts II: Mishnaic and Medieval Hebrew texts:
the texts will be those specified for Hebrew only, paper 3.

8 **[**9**]**. Prepared texts III: Modern Hebrew literature:
the texts will be those specified for Hebrew only, paper 4.

9 **[**10**]**. General paper: language, history, religion, and culture.

[Until 1 October 2004: 10. *Either* a special subject *or* an extended essay, the subject of which must be approved by the Board of the Faculty of Oriental Studies.**]**

with Persian

5 **[**6**]**. Persian prose composition and unprepared translation.

6, 7, and 8 **[**7, 8, and 9**]**. Three papers from those listed under main Persian, papers 3, 4, and 5.

9 **[**10**]**. General questions on one of the following periods of history:
(*a*) The transition from Sasanian to Islamic Persia (up to the tenth century AD).
(*b*) The Safavids from 1501 to 1722.
(*c*) The rise of the Qajars to the end of the Constitutional Revolution.
(*d*) The Pahlavis from 1926 to 1979.

[Until 1 October 2004: 10. *Either* a special subject *or* an extended essay, the subject of which must be approved by the Board of the Faculty of Oriental Studies.**]**

11. Oral examination (as specified for the Honour School of Oriental Studies).

with Turkish

5 **[**6**]**. Unprepared translation from Ottoman and modern Turkish.

6 **[**7**]**. Translation into Turkish and essay in Turkish.

[From 1 October 2004: 8, 9. *Two* of the following papers**]**

[Until 1 October 2004: 8**] [From 1 October 2004:** (*a*)**]**. Ottoman history and historical texts, 1300–1700.
The following texts are prescribed for study:
Selected Ottoman documents.*
Naima, *Tarih* (Istanbul, AH 1281–3), vol. ii, pp. 207–64.
M. Cavid Baysun, ed., *Tarihî Eserlerden Seçilmiş Eski Metinler* (Istanbul, 1964), pp. 29–35, 125–29.
Candidates will be required to translate and/or comment on passages from the prescribed texts, and to write essays on questions relating either to the texts themselves and their background, or to more general historical topics.

(*b*) Turkish and Ottoman literary texts, 1300–1900. The following texts* are prescribed for study:

Selected Turkish/Ottoman poetry, thirteenth to eighteenth centuries.

Selected late Ottoman literary texts (post-1860).

[Until 1 October 2004: 8.**] [From 1 October 2004:** (*c*)**]** Turkish history and thought in the nineteenth and twentieth centuries.
The following texts are prescribed for study:
M. Cavid Baysun, ed., *Tarihî Eserlerden Seçilmiş Eski Metinler* (Istanbul, 1964), pp. 9–18, 36–60, 118–24.
Selected late Ottoman and modern Turkish political documents.*
Selected late Ottoman writings on political and cultural issues.*
Selected modern Turkish writings on political and cultural issues.*
Candidates will be required to translate and/or comment on passages from the prescribed texts, and to write essays on questions relating either to the texts themselves and their background, or to more general historical topics.

[Until 1 October 2004: 9. Turkish literary texts: translation and commentary.
Selected Turkish/Ottoman poetry, thirteenth to eighteenth centuries.*
Selected late Ottoman literary texts (post-1860).*
Selected modern Turkish short stories.*
Selected modern Turkish poetry.*

10. *Either*

(*a*) Turkish literature: essay questions.

Some of the questions set will relate to the texts prescribed for paper 9, but others will be of wider scope. Candidates will be expected to demonstrate knowledge of the general historical development and characteristics of Ottoman and modern Turkish literature.

or

(*b*) a special subject, to be approved by the Board of the Faculty of Oriental Studies.

or

(*c*) an extended essay, on a topic to be approved by the Board of the Faculty of Oriental Studies.**]**

[From 1 October 2004:

10. Twentieth-century Turkish literary texts.*

11. Oral examination (as specified for the Honour School of Oriental Studies).

---

* Lists of texts are available from the Oriental Institute.

Extended Essay

1. The Extended Essay shall be subject to the following provisions:

(i) The subject of every essay shall, to the satisfaction of the boards of the faculties, fall within the scope of the Honour Schools of Modern Languages and of Oriental Studies.

(ii) Candidates proposing to offer an essay must submit, through their college, to the Chairman of the Board of the Faculty of Medieval and Modern Languages (on a form obtainable from the Modern Languages Faculty Office, 41 Wellington Square) a statement of their name, college, the academic year in which they intend to take the examination, and the title of the proposed essay together with (*a*) a statement in about fifty words of how the subject is to be treated, (*b*) a statement signed by a supervisor or tutor, that he or she considers the subject suitable, and suggesting a person or persons who might be invited to be an examiner or assessor (the boards will not approve the title unless they are satisfied that a suitably qualified examiner or assessor based in Oxford will be available), and (*c*) a statement by a college tutor that he or she approves the candidate's application, not later than the Wednesday of the second week of the Michaelmas Full Term preceding the examination.

(iii) The faculty boards will decide by the end of the third week of the Michaelmas Full Term preceding the examination whether the proposed essay title is approved. Approval may be granted on condition that the candidate agrees to amend details of the title to the satisfaction of the boards and submits the required amendments to the Modern Languages Faculty Office by the Friday of sixth week of the Michaelmas Full Term preceding the examination.

(iv) A candidate may seek approval after Friday of sixth week of the Michaelmas Full Term preceding the examination for an amendment of detail in an approved title, by application to the Modern Languages Faculty Office. The Chairman of Examiners and the chairmen of the boards, acting together, will decide whether or not a proposed amendment shall be approved.

1. While the topic of the essay may be taught by a series of tutorials, candidates will be solely responsible for the final draft, which will not be read by the supervisor or tutor. Candidates must sign a certificate stating that the essay is their own work and that it has not already been submitted, wholly or substantially, for any honour school or degree of this university or a degree of any other institution. This certificate must be sent at the same time as the essay, but under separate cover, addressed to the chairman of examiners.

2. No essay shall exceed 10,000 words, exclusive of notes, appendices, and bibliographies. The examiners will not take account of such parts of the essay as are beyond this limit. When appropriate, there must be a select bibliography and a list of sources.

Essays must be typed in double-spacing on one side only of quarto or A4 paper, and must be firmly held in a stiff cover. Two copies must be submitted to the chairman of examiners, and a third copy should be kept by the candidate.

3. The two copies of the essay must be sent, not later than noon on the second Friday after the Hilary Full Term of the year in which the examination will be held, to the Chairman of Examiners, Honour School of European and Middle Eastern Languages, Examination Schools, High Street, Oxford.]

PASS SCHOOL OF EUROPEAN AND MIDDLE EASTERN LANGUAGES

Candidates shall offer one of the languages and its literature from those studied in the Honour School of Modern Languages and papers in *either* Arabic *or* Hebrew *or* Persian *or* Turkish.

Candidates shall take the following papers:

In the Modern Language

(The numbering used is that in the Honour School of Modern Languages.)

I
IIA(i)
IIB(i)
One of VI, VII, VIII.
The oral examination in the language.

In Arabic or Hebrew or Persian or Turkish

Candidates must offer three papers. The papers to be offered must be taken from those for the syllabus for the final Honour School in the language concerned, the actual selection being subject to the approval of the faculty board.

All applications for approval by the board must be sent to the Secretary of the Board of the Faculty of Oriental Studies, Oriental Institute, on or before the Monday in the second week of the Michaelmas Full Term preceding the examination.

All candidates must give notice, on their examination entry forms, of their choice of papers, to the Registrar on or before the Friday in the fourth week of the Michaelmas Full Term preceding the examination.

SPECIAL REGULATIONS FOR THE HONOUR SCHOOL OF EXPERIMENTAL PSYCHOLOGY

A

1. The subject of the Honour School of Experimental Psychology shall be the study of psychology as an experimental science.

2. The examination in Experimental Psychology shall consist of two parts. In Part I candidates shall be examined in the subjects prescribed by the Medical Sciences Board. In Part II candidates shall be examined in the subjects prescribed by the Medical Sciences Board and shall also present, as part of the examination, a project report based on work carried out under supervision prescribed by the Board.

3. No candidate shall be admitted for the Part I examination in this school unless he or she has either passed or been exempted from the First Public Examination.

4. No candidate shall be admitted for the Part II examination in this school unless

(*a*) he or she has passed the Part I examination for Experimental Psychology; and

(*b*) he or she has satisfied the Moderators for the Preliminary Examination for Psychology, Philosophy, and Physiology in the subject *Introduction to Probability Theory and Statistics* or has passed the Qualifying Examination in Statistics as prescribed for candidates offering Psychology in the Honour School of Psychology, Philosophy, and Physiology.

The Head of the Department of Experimental Psychology may dispense a candidate from the Qualifying Examination in Statistics in cases where it is clear that the candidate has reached an adequate standard in Statistics by virtue of previous study and qualification.

5. The examinations in the school shall be under the supervision of the Medical Sciences Board, which shall make regulations concerning them, subject always to the preceding clauses of this subsection.

B

1. General

Decree (7) of 3 June 1947 permits the number of candidates offering Psychology to be limited, if necessary.

2. The subjects of the examination shall be those prescribed in Parts I and II below.

3. The examination for Part I shall be taken during week 0 and 1 of Trinity Term of the candidate's second year. The examination for Part II shall be taken during Trinity Term of the candidate's third year. The dates of submission for the Part I practical work and Part II project work and library dissertation are those prescribed in Parts I and II below.

4. No candidate shall be admitted for Part II examination in this school unless (*a*) he or she has passed the Part I examination for Experimental Psychology, and (*b*) he or she has satisfied the Moderators for the Preliminary Examination for Psychology, Philosophy, and Physiology in the subject *Introduction to Probability Theory and Statistics* or he or she has passed the Qualifying Examination in Statistics as prescribed for candidates offering Psychology in the Honour School of Psychology, Philosophy, and Physiology.

The Head of the Department of Experimental Psychology may dispense a candidate from the Qualifying Examination in Statistics in cases where it is clear that the candidate has reached an adequate standard in Statistics by virtue of previous study and qualification.

5. Candidates may also be examined viva voce in Part II; except that the examiners may dispense from the viva voce examination any candidate concerning whom they shall have decided that his or her performance in the viva voce examination could not affect his or her class. The topics of the viva voce examination may include the subject of any of the written papers and the research project or the practical work done during the course.

6. Every candidate shall give notice to the Registrar of all papers being offered not later than Friday in the eighth week of Michaelmas Full Term preceding the examination.

PART I

1. Four written papers, each of three hours, will be set:

Paper I Biological Bases of Behaviour
Components: (i) Brain and Behaviour, (ii) Biology of Learning and Memory, (iii) Psychological Disorders.

Paper II. Human Experimental Psychology.
Components: (i) Perception, (ii) Memory, Attention, and Information Processing, (iii) Language and Cognition.

Paper III. Social Psychology, Developmental Psychology, and Individual Differences.
Components: (i) Social Psychology, (ii) Developmental Psychology, (iii) Individual Differences.

Paper IV. Experimental Design and Statistics.
In papers I–III candidates will be required to answer at least one question from each of the components.

2. Candidates will be required to undertake practical work, as specified by the Head of Department of Experimental Psychology, and this will constitute a part of the examination. In exceptional circumstances, the Proctors may dispense a candidate from the specified requirements on the recommendation of the head of department, or deputy.

3. Candidates shall submit to the Head of Department of Experimental Psychology or deputy, not later than tenth week in Hilary Term preceding the term in which the Part I examination is to be held, portfolios containing reports of practical work completed during their course of study for Part I. These portfolios shall be available to the examiners as a part of the examination. Each portfolio shall be accompanied by a certificate signed by the candidate indicating that the portfolio submitted is the candidate's own work. This certificate must be submitted separately in a sealed envelope addressed to the chairman of examiners. Where the work submitted has been produced in collaboration the candidates shall indicate the extent of their own contributions. Reports of practical work previously submitted for the Honour School of Experimental Psychology may be resubmitted, but reports will not be accepted if they have already been submitted, wholly or substantially, for another Honour School or degree of this University, or for a degree of any other institution. The head of department, or deputy, shall inform the examiners by the end of the noughth week of the Trinity Term in which the Part I examination is to be held (*a*) as to which candidates have failed to satisfy the requirement to undertake practical work, and (*b*) as to which candidates have failed to satisfy the requirement to submit portfolios. Failure to satisfy either requirement will result in a candidate's being deemed to have withdrawn from the examination under the Regulations of the Proctors concerning Conduct at Examinations (see Special Regulations concerning Examinations). The head of department or deputy shall also make available to the examiners records showing the extent to which each candidate has adequately pursued a course of practical work. The examiners shall take this evidence into consideration along with evidence of unsatisfactory or distinguished performance in each portfolio of practical work.

For all papers in Psychology and for the Qualifying Examination in Statistics but not for papers taken from the Honour School of Physiological Sciences, the examiners will permit the use of any hand-held pocket calculators subject to the conditions set out under the heading 'Use of calculators in examinations' in the *Special Regulations concerning Examinations*.

4. A candidate who fails the Part I examination may retake the examination once only, in Michaelmas Term of the following academic year.

PART II

Part II will consist of a research project and *either* three written papers each of 3 hours duration, *or* two written papers, each of 3 hours duration, and a Library Dissertation.

1. *Research Project*

The research project will normally be carried out in the Trinity Term and the following Michaelmas Term in the year preceding the Part II examinations.

Candidates will be required to do project work under the supervision of one of the following:

(i) any member of the sub-faculty of Psychological Studies.

(ii) any other person approved by the Divisional Board provided that such approval shall be applied for not later than Friday of fourth week of Michaelmas Full Term in the year preceding the Part II examinations.

2. Candidates will be required to undertake practical work, as specified by the Head of Department of Experimental Psychology, and this will constitute a part of the examination. In exceptional circumstances the Proctors may exempt a candidate from the specified requirements on the recommendation of the Head of Department or deputy.

3. Candidates shall submit to the chairman of examiners not later than tenth week in Hilary Term preceding the term in which the Part I examination is to be held, portfolios containing reports of practical work completed during their course of study for Part I. These portfolios shall be available to the examiners as a part of the examination. Each portfolio shall be accompanied by a certificate signed by the candidate indicating that the portfolio submitted is the candidate's own work.

The certificate must be submitted separately in a sealed envelope addressed to the chairman of examiners. Where the work submitted has been produced in collaboration, the candidates shall indicate the extent of their own contributions. Reports of practical work previously submitted for the Honour School of Experimental Psychology may be resubmitted but reports will not be accepted if they have been submitted, wholly or substantially, for another Honour School or degree of this University, or for a degree of any other institution. The Head of Department or deputy shall inform the examiners by the end of noughth week of the Trinity Term in which the Part I examintion is to be held as to which candidates have failed to satisfy the requirement to undertake practical work. Failure to satisfy the requirement to undertake practical work or to submit a portfolio will result in a candidate having been deemed to have withdrawn from the examination under the Regulations of the Proctors concerning Conduct at Examinations (see Special Regulations concerning Examinations). The Head of Department, or deputy, shall make available to the examiners records showing the extent to which candidates have adequately pursued a course of practical work. The examiners shall take this evidence into consideration along with evidence of unsatisfactory or distinguished performance in each portfolio of practical work.

The subject of the research project must not overlap with the subject of the library dissertation, if chosen, but either may (but need not), overlap any subject in which the candidate offers Part II examination papers. Candidates are warned that they should avoid repetition in examination papers of material used in the research project or library dissertation and that substantial repetition may be penalised.

All proposed research projects or library dissertations must be approved in advance by the Head of the Department of Experimental Psychology. The procedures for obtaining this approval will be notified to students by the Head of Department of Experimental Psychology.

Two copies of completed projects and library dissertations must be submitted to the Chairman of Examiners, Honour School of Experimental Psychology, Examination Schools, Oxford, not later than noon on Friday of the eighth week of Hilary Term, in the year of the examination. A certificate signed by the candidate indicating that the work submitted is the candidate's own work, and a statement of the number of words in the project or dissertation, must be submitted separately in respect of each research project and library dissertation in a sealed envelope addressed to the chairman of examiners. Research projects and library dissertations previously submitted for the Honour School of Experimental Psychology may be resubmitted. No project or dissertation will be accepted if it has already been submitted wholly or substantially, for another Honour School or degree of this University, or for a degree of any other institution.

4. Candidates will be required to undertake practical work, as specified by the Head of Department of Experimental Psychology, and this will constitute a part of the examination. In exceptional circumstances the Proctors may exempt a candidate from the specified requirements on the recommendation of the Head of Department or deputy.

5. Candidates shall submit to the chairman of examiners not later than tenth week in Hilary Term preceding the term in which the Part II examination is to be held, portfolios containing reports of practical work completed during their course

of study for Part II. These portfolios shall be available to the examiners as a part of the examination. Each portfolio shall be accompanied by a certificate signed by the candidate indicating that the portfolio submitted is the candidate's own work.

The certificate must be submitted separately in a sealed envelope addressed to the chairman of examiners. Where the work submitted has been produced in collaboration, the candidates shall indicate the extent of their own contributions. Reports of practical work previously submitted for the Honour School of Experimental Psychology may be resubmitted but reports will not be accepted it they have been submitted, wholly or substantially, for another Honour School or degree of this University, or for a degree of any other institution. The Head of Department or deputy shall inform the examiners by the end of noughth week of the Trinity Term in which the Part II examination is to be held as to which candidates have failed to satisfy the requirement to undertake practical work. Failure to satisfy the requirement to undertake practical work or to submit a portfolio will result in a candidate having been deemed to have withdrawn from the examination under the Regulations of the Proctors concerning Conduct at Examinations (see Special Regulations concerning Examinations). The head of department, or deputy, shall make available to the examiners records showing the extent to which candidates have adequately pursued a course of practical work. The examiners shall take this evidence into consideration along with evidence of unsatisfactory or distinguished performance in each portfolio of practical work.

PASS SCHOOL OF EXPERIMENTAL PSYCHOLOGY

1. No candidate shall be admitted to the Pass School of Experimental Psychology unless he or she has satisfied the Moderators for the Preliminary Examination in Psychology, Philosophy, and Physiology in the subject *Introduction to Probability Theory and Statistics* or has passed the Qualifying Examination in Statistics as prescribed for candidates offering Psychology in the Honour School of Psychology, Philosophy, and Physiology.

2. The candidates shall offer the four papers for Part I as prescribed for the Honour School of Experimental Psychology. They shall be required to pass Part I before sitting the examination for Part II. Candidates shall offer for Part II *either* two papers, *or* one paper and a library dissertation, chosen from amongst those prescribed for the Honour School of Experimental Psychology.

NOTES

§3. SPECIAL REGULATIONS FOR THE FINAL EXAMINATION IN FINE ART

A

1. No person who is not a member of the University may be admitted to the Final Examination in Fine Art.

2. No member of the University shall be admitted to the Final Examination in Fine Art unless he has either passed or been exempted from the Preliminary Examination in Fine Art.

3. (*a*) No one shall be admitted as a candidate for the examination unless by the end of the term in which the examination is held he shall have kept statutable residence for nine terms, except that a candidate who is a Senior Student may be admitted as a candidate if by the end of the term in which the examination is held he shall have kept statutable residence for six terms.

(*b*) Time spent outside Oxford as part of an academic programme approved by Council shall count towards residence for the purposes of this clause.

(*c*) The Proctors shall have power to excuse from one term of statutable residence any member of the University who shall have been duly certified by them to have been prevented by illness or other reasonable cause from keeping such residence for one or more terms, subject to the conditions set out in Ch. VI, Sect. I. A, cl. 2. Application shall be made through the college or other society or approved institution to which the member belongs. The student, or his or her society, may within fourteen days of the date of the Proctors' decision appeal in writing to the Chairman of the Educational Policy and Standards Committee (who may nominate another member of the committee, other than one of the Proctors, to adjudicate the appeal).

(*d*) The Proctors shall have power to dispense, subject to such conditions as it may from time to time determine, from up to three terms of statutable residence any member of the University who has not completed such residence for any reason which the Proctors shall judge to be sufficient. Application shall be made through the college or other society or approved institution to which the member belongs. The student, or his or her society, may within fourteen days of the date of the Proctors' decision appeal in writing to the Chairman of the Educational Policy and Standards Committee (who may nominate another member of the committee, other than one of the Proctors, to adjudicate the appeal).

(*e*) The candidate's college or other society or approved institution shall be required to certify on the entry form, by the time determined for entry, whether or not the candidate will have met the requirement for statutable residence by the end of the term in which the examination is held, and to notify the University of any change in the candidate's status in this respect between entry and the date of the examination.

(*f*) Nothing in this clause shall affect the conditions required for admission to degrees set out in Ch. I, Sect. I, §1.

4. No one shall be admitted as a candidate for the examination after the lapse of twelve terms from the term of his matriculation inclusively, except that a candidate who has been prevented by urgent cause from offering himself for examination may offer himself as a candidate at the next ensuing examination provided that he has satisfied the conditions of Sect. II. C, §4, cll. 1, 2, and 3.

5. The examination shall be under the supervision of the Committee for the Ruskin School of Drawing and Fine Art, which shall make regulations for the examination.

B

1. The examination shall include both practical and written work. Candidates will also be examined viva voce, except that the examiners may dispense from the viva voce examination any candidate concerning whom they shall have decided that performance in the viva voce examination could not properly be allowed to affect the result.

2. Every candidate will be required

(1) To produce a selection of work completed throughout the course preceding the examination in each of the categories scheduled below:

(*a*) *Drawing*
A portfolio of drawings in any medium;

(*b*) One *or* two of *Painting*; *Printmaking*; *Sculpture*; *Mixed Media*; *Photography*; *Video/film*; *Performance*.

(i) if one discipline is chosen, at least twelve original works in that discipline;
(ii) if two disciplines are chosen, at least six original works in each discipline.

Work which in the judgement of the candidate's tutor cannot for practical reasons be submitted for examination may be represented by documentation.

(*c*) *Supporting Work*
A body of supporting work in at least one medium not offered under (*a*) and (*b*) of this sub-clause.

The work required by the provisions of (*a*), (*b*), and (*c*) of this sub-clause must be submitted by noon on Tuesday in the eighth week of the Trinity Full Term in which the examination is taken to the Chairman of Examiners, Final Examination in Fine Art, Ruskin School of Drawing and Fine Art, 74 High Street, Oxford.

(2) To submit an essay of about 6,000 words which should normally be on some aspect of visual culture since 1900 in accordance with the provisions of clause 6 of these regulations.

(3) To satisfy the examiners in a paper on the history and theory of visual culture since 1900.

3. A candidate submitting an essay in accordance with the provisions of clause 5 (2) of these regulations must apply for the approval of the Ruskin Master not later than Friday in the second week of the Michaelmas Full Term preceding the examination. Such application shall include the title of the proposed essay and a synopsis of not more than 350 words setting out the manner in which it is proposed to treat the subject. Candidates must give notice to the Registrar of the title of the essay they intend to offer not later than Friday in the fourth week of the Michaelmas Full Term preceding the examination. One typed copy of the essay must be delivered to the Chairman of Examiners, Final Examination in Fine Art, Examination Schools not later than noon on the Monday of the eighth week of the Hilary Full Term preceding the examination. Each essay must be accompanied by a certificate signed by the candidate that the essay has not been submitted for any previous examination, and that the essay is his or her own unaided work. Tutors may provide advice on the choice and scope of the subject, the sources available, and the method of presentation. They may also read and comment on a first draft of the essay. This certificate must be submitted separately in a sealed envelope addressed to the chairman of examiners.

NOTES

SPECIAL REGULATIONS FOR THE HONOUR SCHOOL OF GEOGRAPHY

A

1. The examination in the Honour School of Geography shall always include, as stated subjects to be offered by all candidates:

(1) The Geographical Environment;

(2) The Philosophy, Nature, and Practice of Geography.

2. Candidates shall be required to offer, in addition to the above subjects, and after giving due notice of the subjects they select, two Special Subjects chosen under arrangements determined by the board by regulation.

3. The examination shall be partly practical.

4. No candidate shall be admitted to the examination in the Honour School unless *either*

(*a*) he or she is a Senior Student, *or*

(*b*) he or she has passed or been exempted from the First Public Examination.

5. The examination in the Honour School shall be under the supervision of the Life and Environmental Sciences Board.

B

1. All candidates will be required to offer the following subjects:

(i) The Geographical Environment: Physical (1 paper).

(ii) The Geographical Environment: Human (1 paper).

(iii) The Philosophy, Nature and Practice of Geography (1 paper).

(iv) **[Until 1 October 2004:** Four**]** **[From 1 October 2004:** Two**]** Special Subjects to be chosen from a list published by the department (**[Until 1 October 2004:** 4 papers).**]** **[From 1 October 2004:** 2 papers.**]** Submitted work will also be required in two subjects, and the combined submitted work will be treated as the equivalent of one further paper.

(v) A Geographical Dissertation in accordance with the detailed regulations given below. The Dissertation will be treated as the equivalent of two papers.

2. Candidates are required to have undertaken field-work as an integral part of their course.

Candidates may be examined viva voce.

Theses, practical notebooks or extended essays previously submitted for the Honour School of Geography may be resubmitted. No thesis, practical notebook or extended essay will be accepted if it has already been submitted, wholly or substantially, for another final honour school or degree of this University, or a degree of any other institution.

3. The requirements for each subject are as follows:

I. *The Geographical Environment: Physical*

The nature of the major world physical environments; their internal inter-relationships and their significance to humans, plants, and animals; processes of environmental change with particular reference to those that directly affect humans; humans as agents of change in the physical environment.

II. *The Geographical Environment: Human*

The philosophical, technical, and social basis of approaches to and use of the environment; the history, economics, and politics of environmental exploitation and conservation in the major physical regions of the world; the definition of space and territories and the principles of spatial organization in different societies; geographical variations in patterns of resource use, human activity, population growth, and well-being, and their expression in the cultural landscape; the processes of international interdependence.

Candidates will be expected to show knowledge of specific examples at a variety of scales.

III. *Philosophy, Nature, and Practice of Geography*

The development of theory and practice in physical and human geography from the start of the twentieth century; the ideas and methods associated with the major schools of thought.

IV. Candidates must offer **[Until 1 October 2004:** four**] [From 1 October 2004:** two**]** Special Subjects to be chosen from a list to be published by the Head of the School not later than the end of the Trinity Full Term preceding the candidate's admission to the Final Honour School. One paper of three hours will be set on each subject.

Each candidate must also submit an individual piece of work (as specified on the rubrics for each special subject) for **[Until 1 October 2004:** two out of the four**] [From 1 October 2004:** both**]** Special Subjects to the Chairman of Examiners in the Final Honour School of Geography, c/o the Examination Schools, High Street not later than 12 noon on the Friday of the first week of the Trinity Term in which they present themselves for examination. The submitted work, which will be combined and treated as equivalent to one paper, should not duplicate material in the candidate's dissertation.

Instructions for the submitted work will be published by the Head of the School not later than the end of the Trinity Full Term preceding the candidate's admission to the Final Honour School. The specified word limit is exclusive of tables, diagrams, and appendices. Information about the Special Subjects and submitted work will be published on the departmental website under "Information for Undergraduates" by early October.

Each candidate will submit

A Geographical Dissertation on a Selected Topic.

The Dissertation, exclusive of bibliography, maps and statistical appendices, must not be more than 12,000 words. The attention of candidates is drawn to the fact that limited rather than large areas are more likely to allow for adequate depth of study. The Dissertation should embody original practical work based on primary data (e.g. data collected in the field, archival materials, census data, etc.), and not be based on secondary material (e.g. text books, published local histories, published papers in learned journals, government or local government reports).

Candidates having first secured the approval of their tutors are required to submit to the Head of the School for approval, not later than noon on Friday at the end of the fourth week of the Trinity Full Term in the year preceding that in which they propose to take the examination, an outline of approximately 500 words of the proposed Dissertation. Special permission must also be sought from the Head of the School for any substantive change in the original proposal.

Candidates must give notice to the Registrar of the subject on which they propose to submit a Dissertation not later than the Friday in the fourth week of the Michaelmas Full Term preceding the examination. Such notice to the Registrar must be accompanied by a statement from the candidate's tutor that permission to offer the intended Dissertation has been granted by the Head of the School.

The Dissertation must be typed in double-spacing and bound simply or filed securely. It must be the work of the author alone and aid from others must be limited to prior discussion as to the subject and sources and advice on presentation. Every candidate shall sign a certificate to the effect that the Dissertation is his or her own work, and this certificate shall be presented with the Dissertation.

Candidates must submit two copies of their Dissertation not later than 12 noon on the Friday in the first week of the following Hilary Term, to the Chairman of Examiners in the Final Honour School of Geography c/o the Examination Schools, High Street.

PASS SCHOOL OF GEOGRAPHY

1. All candidates will be required to offer the following subjects, as prescribed for the Honour School of Geography:

(i) The Geographical Environment: Physical (1 paper)
(ii) The Geographical Environment: Human (1 paper)
(iii) The Philosophy, Nature and Practice of Geography (1 paper)
(iv) *Either*: One Special Subject to be chosen from those specified for the Honour School of Geography, *or* a Geographical Dissertation in accordance with the detailed regulations for the Honour School of Geography.

NOTES

SPECIAL REGULATIONS FOR THE HONOUR SCHOOL OF HUMAN SCIENCES

A

1. The subject of the Honour School of Human Sciences shall be the biological and social aspects of the study of human beings.

2. No candidate shall be admitted for examination in this school unless he or she has either passed or been exempted from the First Public Examination.

3. The examination shall be under the supervision of the Life and Environmental Sciences Board, which shall appoint a Teaching Committee for Human Sciences to supervise the arrangements for this examination, the Preliminary Examination in Human Sciences, and the Pass School of Human Sciences; to consult as necessary with contributing teachers and others; and to carry out such other functions as may be laid down by the Divisional Board by standing order. The committee shall be recognized as having an interest in appointments specifically concerned with the Honour School, and the bodies responsible for such appointments shall ensure that the selection committees for such posts include at least one member appointed in consultation with the committee. It shall be responsible for such funds as the Divisional Board may place at its disposal for general purposes connected with Human Sciences.

B

The Honour School is divided into two sections. All candidates will be required to offer the following six compulsory subjects:

(1) Behaviour and its Evolution: Animal and Human

(2) Human Genetics and Evolution

(3) Human Ecology

(4) Demography and Population

Within paper 4, there will be an examination in Demographic Techniques and Analysis, in which candidates will be required to demonstrate their ability to interpret demographic measures and to apply quantitative skills to demographic problems. All candidates must pass this examination before being admitted for examination in the remainder of the Honour School.

(5*a*) Anthropological analysis and Interpretation *or* (5*b*) Sociological Theory

Candidates may answer questions from either (5*a*) or (5*b*), but not from both.

(6) Dissertation

Candidates will also be required to offer any two optional subjects from a list posted in the Human Sciences Centre at the beginning of the first week of Hilary Full Term in the year preceding the final examination. These lists will also be circulated to College Tutors. The date by which students must make their choice will be stated in the course handbook.

Candidates may be examined viva voce.

SCHEDULE OF SUBJECTS

1. *Behaviour and its Evolution: Animal and Human*

Introduction to the study of behaviour including the evolution of behavioural interactions within groups. Behavioural strategies that have evolved in humans and other animals. The use of models to understand complex behaviour. Advanced ethology and cognition, including learning. Perception and decision-making. Primate behaviour and evolutionary ecology, including the development of primate social systems and the evolution of cognition. Evolution of human behaviour and culture, including an evaluation of the relative roles 'nature' and 'nurture'.

2. *Human Genetics and Evolution*

The nature and structure of the human genome, including single gene traits, gene function, and assessment of social implications. Population genetics of humans and primates. Quantitative genetics and complex trait analysis in humans. Genomic complexity as illustrated by the genetic basis for immune response. Molecular evolution, human genetic diversity and the genetic basis of human evolution. Genetic basis of common complex diseases.

3. *Human Ecology*

Evolutionary ecology of humans, including palaeoecology and the adaptive significance of human specializations during the past five million years. Human ecology of infectious disease, emphasizing diseases that significantly contribute to the global burden of mortality. Human ecology of non-infectious disease, with an emphasis on diseases associated with cultural change. Adaptation, nutrition, and growth in human societies. Socio-cultural systems in their environmental context, including philosiphical and religious values, differences in ecological perception, and the development of viable conservation strategies. Ecology of human reproduction, including cultural differences in reproductive strategies and an overview of human palaeodemography.

4. *Demography and Population*

Past, present, and future growth and distribution of human populations; geography of population distribution, including international and rural–urban migration; biological, psychological, and social factors affecting fertility and mortality; family planning and contraceptive technology; the age and sex structures of populations; the stable population and other quantitative population models; population theories; historical demography and demographic transition; circumstances and consequences of population change in developed and developing countries; population policies.

5(*a*). *Anthropological analysis and interpretation*

The comparative study of social and cultural forms in the global context: to include economics and exchange, domestic structures and their reproduction, personal and collective identity, language and religion, states and conflict, understanding of biology and environment, historical perspectives on the social world and upon practice in anthropology.

5(*b*). *Sociological Theory*

The critical study of the major theoretical approaches to the study of social order and integration; social structure and action; social change; social norms and roles; class and stratification; deviance; the link between micro- and macro-sociology; the scientific status of sociological theory. Candidates will be expected to show knowledge of the application of theoretical approaches to the explanation and understanding of empirical social phenomena.

6. *Dissertation*

(*a*) *Subject*

In the dissertation the candidate will be required to focus on material from within the Honour School, and must show knowledge of more than one of the basic approaches to the study of Human Sciences. The subject may, but need not, overlap any subject on which the candidate offers papers. Candidates are warned that they should avoid repetition in papers of material used in their dissertation and that substantial repetition may be penalized.

Every candidate shall submit through his or her college for approval to the Chairman of the Human Sciences Teaching Committee the title he or she proposes together with

(i) an explanation of the subject in about 100 words explicitly mentioning the two or more basic approaches to the study of Human Sciences that will be incorporated in the dissertation.

(ii) a letter of approval from his or her tutor **and** the name(s) of the advisor(s) who will supervise the dissertation.

This should not be earlier than the first day of and not later than the end of the seventh week of Trinity Full Term of the year before that in which the candidate is to be examined.

The Chairman of the Teaching Committee, in consultation with the Chairman of Examiners and other Senior Members if necessary, shall as soon as possible decide whether or not to approve the title and shall advise the candidate through his or her college. No decision shall normally be deferred beyond the end of the eighth week of the relevant Trinity Term.

Proposals to change the title of the dissertation may be made in exceptional circumstances and will be considered by the Chairman of the Teaching Committee until the first day of Hilary Full Term of the year in which the student is to be examined, or only by the Chairman of Examiners thereafter. Proposals should be made through the candidate's college via the Course Administrator, Institute of Human Sciences, The Pauling Centre, 58 Banbury Road.

(*b*) *Authorship and origin*

The dissertation must be the candidates' own work. Tutors may, however, discuss with candidates the proposed field of study, the sources available and the method of presentation. They may also read and comment on a first draft. Every candidate shall sign a certificate to the effect that the thesis is his or her own work and that it has not already been submitted, wholly or substantially, for another Honour School or degree of this University, or for a degree of any other institution. This certificate shall be submitted separately in a sealed envelope addressed to the chairman of examiners. No dissertation shall, however, be ineligible because it has been or is being submitted for any prize of this University.

(*c*) *Length and format*

No dissertation shall be less than 5,000 words nor exceed 10,000 words; no person or body shall have authority to permit any excess. Candidates may include appendices which will not count towards the word limit. However the examiners are not bound to read the appendices and they shall not be taken into consideration when marking the dissertation. There shall be a select bibliography or a list of sources; this shall not be included in the word count. All dissertations must be typed on A4 paper and be held firmly in a cover. Two copies of the dissertation shall be submitted to the examiners; they shall be returned to the candidate's college after the examination.

(*d*) *Submissions of dissertation*

Every candidate shall deliver two copies of the dissertation to the Chairman of Examiners, Honour School of Human Sciences, Examination Schools, Oxford, not later than noon on Friday of the week preceding Trinity Full Term in the year of the examination.

(*e*) *Resubmission of dissertation*

Dissertation previously submitted for the Honour School of Human Sciences may be resubmitted. No dissertation will be accepted if it has already been submitted, wholly or substantially, for another Honour School or degree of this University, or for a degree of any other institution.

PASS SCHOOL OF HUMAN SCIENCES

Each candidate will be required to offer the six subjects in the list below.

Papers (1), (2), (3), (4), (5), and (6) as specified for the Honour School of Human Sciences.

SPECIAL REGULATIONS FOR THE HONOUR SCHOOL OF JURISPRUDENCE

A

1. Candidates in the School of Jurisprudence shall be examined in subjects from such branches of the law and of philosophy as may be prescribed by regulation.

2. No candidate shall be admitted to examination in this school unless he has either passed or been exempted from the First Public Examination.

3. The examination in this school shall be under the supervision of the Board of the Faculty of Law, which shall make regulations concerning it, subject always to the preceding clauses of this subsection and to the concurrence of the Divisional Board of Humanities in respect of regulations concerning philosophy.

Candidates shall take one of the following courses.

Course 1. Candidates shall be examined in **[Until 1 October 2005:** eight standard subjects and one special subject**]** **[From 1 October 2005:** *either* nine standard subjects *or* eight standard subjects and two special subjects.**]**. Candidates will be examined in accordance with the Examination Regulations set out below.

Course 2. Candidates shall be examined **[Until 1 October 2005:** in eight standard subjects and one special subject**]** **[From 1 October 2005:** *either* nine standard subjects *or* eight standard subjects and two special subjects.**]**. Candidates will be examined in accordance with the Examination Regulations set out below. They will also be required to spend, after their matriculation, an academic year of residence in a European university approved in accordance with these regulations, and to have attended such courses at the approved university as are approved in accordance with these regulations, and to provide on their entry form a statement that they have done this, signed by the head or by a tutor of their society. Candidates will also be required to have successfully completed such examinations at the approved university as the faculty board may specify.

B

Regulations applying to Course 2

1. The Law Board will approve courses at Certain European universities. The list of approved courses will be available at the Institute of European and Comparative Law, St Cross Building, Manor Road.

2. Candidates may proceed to an academic year of residence at an approved university only if so permitted by the Board of the Faculty of Law. The board shall

not give such permission unless the candidate presents (*a*) a certificate of linguistic competence relevant to the proposed year of residence and (*b*) a certificate from his or her society stating that he or she will have resided in Oxford for six terms (or three terms in the case of an applicant with senior status) since matriculation before proceeding to such residence, and (*c*) a statement in support from the head or a tutor of the candidate's society.

3. The certificate of linguistic competence may be provided only by a member of the University approved by the board.

4. Candidates will be required to take certain examinations at the approved universities. Details will be available from the Institute of European and Comparative Law.

5. Certification of successful completion of the examinations referred to in the previous regulation must be submitted with the entry form for the Final Examination.

6. The board may amend or add to any provision in Regulations 1, 4, and 5 by regulation published in the *Gazette* at any time before the commencement of the academic year to which such addition or amendment applies.

Regulations applying to both Course 1 and Course 2:

[Until 1 October 2006: Course 1. Candidates shall be examined in **[Until 1 October 2005:** eight standard subjects, viz. 1, 2, 3, and either 4 or 13 and four from 5–22 (excluding 13 if substituted for 4); and one special subject**]** **[From 1 October 2005:** standard subjects 1, 2, 3, 4, 10, 13 and 14, and *either* in two further standard subjects from 5–9, 11, 12, and 15–22 *or* in one further standard subject from 5–9, 11, 12 and 15–22, and in two special subjects**]**, and must have satisfactorily completed the Research Skills Programme.

Course 2. Candidates shall be examined in **[Until 1 October 2005:** eight standard subjects, viz. 1, 2, 3, and either 4 or 13 and four from 5–22 (excluding 13 if substituted for 4); and one special subject**]** **[From 1 October 2005:** standard subjects 1, 2, 3, 4, 10, 13, and 14, and *either* in two further standard subjects from 5–9, 11, 12, and 15–22 *or* in one further standard subject from 5–9, 11, 12, and 15–22, and in two special subjects.**]** **[From 1 October 2004:** , and must have satisfactorily completed the Research Skills Programme.**]**

Candidates who have been awarded the Diploma in Legal Studies shall be examined in the same number of subjects as other candidates but shall not be required to repeat in the Final Honour School papers taken for the Diploma which would otherwise be compulsory.

STANDARD SUBJECTS

Papers will be set on the following subjects, viz.:

1. Jurisprudence;
2. Contract;
3. Tort;
4. Land Law;
5. Roman Law (Delict);
6. Comparative Law of Contract;
7. Criminal Justice and Penology;
8. Public International Law;
9. History of English Law;
10. European Community Law;
11. Ethics, as specified for Philosophy in all Honour Schools*;

---

* This paper shall not be offered by any candidate who offered it when he passed in any other Honour School.

12. International Trade;
13. Trusts;
14. Administrative Law;
15. Family Law;
16. Company Law;
17. Labour Law;
18. Criminal Law;*
19. Principles of Commercial Law;
20. Constitutional Law;*

[From 1 October 2004:

21. Taxation Law]
22. Any other subject that may be approved from time to time by regulation published in the *Gazette* by the end of Trinity Full Term of the year three years before the year of the examination in which the option will first be available.

SPECIAL SUBJECTS

A list of special subjects approved by the Board of the Faculty of Law from time to time by regulation published in the *Gazette* shall be posted in the Law Faculty and sent to college tutors, together with individual specifications and examination methods, not later than the beginning of the eighth term before that in which the Honour School examination will be held. Depending on the availability of teaching resources, not all special subjects will be available to all candidates in every given year. A list of possible special subjects is given below.

1. *European Community Social, Environmental and Consumer Law* (Special Subject)

(*a*) The growth of EC competence in environment law; the principle of subsidiarity; the relationship between trade and environment in EC law; general issues relating to the implementation and enforcement of EC environmental law.

(*b*) The growth of EC competence in consumer law.

(*c*) *Locus standi* and the legal remedies available to the individual to enforce EC law; the role of the citizen in the enforcement of EC environmental and consumer law.

The subject will be examined by means of a two-hour written examination in which candidates will be required to answer two questions.

2. *European Community Competition Law* (Special Subject)

(*a*) The law relating to cartels and Article 81 of the EC Treaty.

(*b*) The law concerning abuse of a dominant position dealt with in Article 82 of the EC Treaty.

(*c*) Enforcement of competition law by the Commission and in national courts.

(*d*) The law relating to merger control covered by Reg. 4064/89 EC (as amended).

The subject will be examined by means of a two-hour written examination in which candidates will be required to answer two questions.

3. *Introduction to the Law of Copyright and Moral Rights* (Special Subject)

(*a*) The justification and development of copyright and moral rights.

(*b*) The UK law of copyright and moral rights.

(*c*) Issues in the harmonization of European copyright and moral rights.

(*d*) Issues in the protection of computer software.

The subject will be examined by means of a two-hour written examination in which candidates will be required to answer two questions.

---

* This paper shall not be offered by any candidate who has passed Law Moderations.

4. *Lawyers' Ethics* (Special Subject) comprises four topics as follows:

A. Ethics, Applied Ethics, and Professional Ethics; together with

B. Two or one of the following substantive topics:

(1) Confidentiality.

(2) Conflict of interest.

(3) Costs and charging practices.

(4) Citizenship.

(5) Competence.

(6) Commitment (e.g. Christianity, Marxism, Feminism, Liberalism); together with:

C. One or two of the following areas of legal endeavour:

(1) Criminal justice.

(2) Family lawyering.

(3) Commercial practice.

(4) Constitutional law and civil liberties.

(5) Environmental regulation.

The subject will be examined by means of a two-hour written examination in which candidates will be required to answer two questions.

5. *Personal Property* (Special Subject)

(1) The taxonomy of personal property.

(2) Original and derivative acquisition of title to personalty at law and in equity.

(3) The principle *Nemo dat quod non habet* and the exceptions to that principle.

(4) The protection of property in personalty, with comparative reference to civilian jurisdictions.

This subject will be examined by means of a two-hour examination in which candidates will be required to answer two questions. It shall not be offered by any candidate who is also offering the standard subject Principles of Commercial Law.

6. *Commercial leases* (special subject)

(1) The nature of leases of commercial property and regulation of business tenancies.

(2) The law relating to management issues within commercial leases, with particular reference to rent review, repairing obligations, and user covenants.

(3) Alienation of commercial leases and the impact on enforcement of leasehold covenants.

(4) Termination of commercial leases, forfeiture, and rights of renewal.

The subject will be examined by means of a two-hour written examination in which candidates will be required to answer two questions.

The following further regulations shall apply to the undermentioned:]

[From 1 October 2006:

Candidates shall be examined in the following seven standard subjects

1. Jurisprudence
2. Contract
3. Tort
4. Land Law
5. European Community Law
6. Trusts
7. Administrative Law

and *either* in two further standard optional subjects, *or* in one further standard optional subject and in two special subjects, and must have satisfactorily completed the Research Skills Programme. A list of standard optional subjects and a list of special subjects approved by the Board of the Faculty of Law for the following academic year shall be posted in the Law Faculty Office and sent to college tutors, together with individual specifications and examination methods, not later than the beginning of the fifth week of the Hilary Term in the year before the Honour School examination will be held. Depending on the availability of teaching resources, not all standard optional subjects and special subjects will be available to all candidates in every given year. If any such subject has to be withdrawn after it has appeared on the lists approved by the Board of the Faculty of Law, notice will be given in the Law Faculty Student Handbook for the relevant academic year, which will be published by Monday of Noughth Week of Michaelmas Term that year.

Candidates who have been awarded the Diploma in Legal Studies shall be examined in the same number of subjects as other candidates but shall not be required to repeat in the Final Honour School papers taken for the Diploma which would otherwise be compulsory.

The following further regulations shall apply to the undermentioned Standard Subjects:]

2. CONTRACT

Candidates will be required to show a knowledge of such parts of the law of restitution as are directly relevant to the law of contract.

Questions may be set in this paper requiring knowledge of the law of tort.

3. TORT

Questions may be set in this paper requiring knowledge of the law of contract.

4. LAND LAW comprises

(*a*) The nature of ownership in land; estates, interests, and equities.

[From 1 October 2004:

(*b*) Formalities required for transactions relating to land: estoppel]

(*b*)[(*c*)] Successive and concurrent interests.

(*c*)[(*d*)] Leases **[Until 1 October 2004**: creation; the running of covenants.]

(*d*)[(*e*)] Easements: covenants: licences.

(*e*)[(*f*)] Mortgages **[Until 1 October 2004**: interests of mortgagors and mortgagees; remedies of mortgagees.]

(*f*)[(*g*)] Protection of title to and of rights in and over land by registration.

(*g*) **[Until 1 October 2004:** [(*h*)] Limitation.]

[Until 1 October 2006: 5. ROMAN LAW (Delict) comprises

(*a*) The Roman law of delict and quasi-delict, studied in connection with the following texts: Gaius, *Inst.* III. 182–225; IV. 75–9; Justinian, *Inst.* IV. 1–5; 8–9.

(*b*) The Roman law of damage to property, studied in connection with Digest IX. 2. Candidates will be required to compare the Roman Law with the relevant portions of the English law of torts.

6. COMPARATIVE LAW OF CONTRACT comprises

(*a*) Sources and methods of French law: the structure of the legislature and the style of legislation; the significance of the Codes and of their reform; the structure of the courts and the significance of case law in the development of the law; academic legal research and writing and its influence on the development of the law.

(*b*) The French law of contract: formation of contracts and conditions for their validity; rights arising from contracts and their enforcement. Questions will not be set on the law of agency. Candidates will be required to compare the French law with the relevant portions of English law.

Candidates will be required to have an adequate knowledge of the original source material in French.

7. CRIMINAL JUSTICE AND PENOLOGY comprises

(*a*) The dimensions and patterns of crime and criminal behaviour; the interpretation of official and other statistics.

(*b*) The exercise of discretion in the criminal process by police, prosecutors, and courts prior to sentencing.

(*c*) The law and practice of sentencing.

(*d*) The development of English penal policy and practices.

(*e*) The contemporary forms of penal and other sanctions and the assessment of their efficacy.

Notes:

(1) Theories of punishment are included in the syllabus in so far as they are relevant to any of the above headings.

(2) The above headings include children and young persons and offences committed by them.

(3) Headings (*d*) and (*e*) will comprise about half of the course.

8. PUBLIC INTERNATIONAL LAW comprises

(*a*) The law of peace.

(*b*) The law governing the use of force and the settlement of international disputes.

(*c*) The general structure, powers, and principles of the United Nations Organization.

9. HISTORY OF ENGLISH LAW comprises

The history of the land law, contract, and tort, and the sources of English legal history.

Candidates will be required to show a sufficient knowledge of the history and structure of the judicial system.]

10[5]. EUROPEAN COMMUNITY LAW comprises

A. The basic structure and functions of the three communities; the aims of EC; law-making; the composition and jurisdiction of the Court of Justice; directly effective Community norms.

B. Free movement of persons and services.

C. Free movement of goods.

Questions will not be asked specifically on the market in coal and steel; the substantive law of the EC other than B and C above; Euratom; the relation between Community law and the national laws of other Member States.

[Until 1 October 2006: 12. INTERNATIONAL TRADE comprises

(*a*) Sale of goods, with special reference to export and import sales.

(*b*) Carriage of goods by sea.

(*c*) Bankers' commercial credits.**]**

13[6]. TRUSTS comprises

(*a*) The nature and classification of trusts.

(*b*) Express private trusts: purpose trusts.

(*c*) The creation **[Until 1 October 2004:** and variation**]** of private trusts: secret trusts.

(*d*) Resulting and constructive trusts.

(*e*) Charitable trusts: the cy-pres doctrine.

(*f*) Liability of trustees for breaches of trust: remedies.

[Until 1 October 2004: (*g*) Retention of title.**]**

14[7]. ADMINISTRATIVE LAW

Questions will not be set on the law of local government or of public corporations except as illustrating general principles of administrative law.

Candidates will be required to show a sufficient knowledge of such parts of the general law of the constitution as are necessary for a proper understanding of this subject.

[Until 1 October 2006: 15. FAMILY LAW comprises

(*a*) The formation, validity, and dissolution of a marriage, including the process according to which marriages are dissolved.

(*b*) The mutual rights and obligations of husband and wife, including the effect of marriage on the property rights of the spouse; the relevant principles of intestate succession and family provision; the legal position of unmarried persons who live together in a domestic arrangement.

(*c*) Parental responsibility and children's rights; child support; adoption; the powers and duties of courts and local authorities with respect to children (excluding juvenile delinquents).

16. COMPANY LAW comprises

(*a*) Incorporation and its consequences.
(*b*) The company's constitution and its alteration.
(*c*) Corporate management.
(*d*) Publicity and meetings.
(*e*) Shares and shareholders.
(*f*) Capital.
(*g*) Organic changes.

17. LABOUR LAW comprises

(*a*) The law relating to collective bargaining.
(*b*) The law relating to industrial disputes.
(*c*) Trade Union law.
(*d*) Individual employment law.

18. CRIMINAL LAW

(*a*) General principles of criminal liability—actus reus and mens rea, omissions, causation, negligence, strict liability, complicity, and inchoate offences.
(*b*) General defences.
(*c*) The law relating to offences against the person (including sexual offences) and offences against property and other economic interests.

19. PRINCIPLES OF COMMERCIAL LAW comprises

(*a*) The structure and organization of commercial contracts, and the impact of market mechanisms, rules, and usages.
(*b*) The discharge of delivery and payment obligations arising from dealings on a market.
(*c*) Concepts of ownership and possession, with particular reference to commercial assets.
(*d*) The property aspects of the contract of sale.
(*e*) Dealings in pure and documentary intangibles, both absolute and by way of security.
(*f*) The resolution of priority conflicts arising from commercial dealings in personal property.
(*g*) The role of good faith and equity in commercial law.
(*h*) The future development of commercial law.

The above subject shall not be offered by any candidate who is also offering the special subject Personal Property.

20. CONSTITUTIONAL LAW comprises

The law of the constitution, excluding administrative, local government, and nationality law; and the organization of the judicial system in England together with such parts of history of the judicial system as are essential to an understanding of its present organization. Questions will not be set specifically upon the following topics: sources of law, the organization of the legal profession, and legal aid.**]**

[From 1 October 2004:

21. TAXATION LAW

(*a*) Definition of tax, the objectives and functions of a tax system: types of tax, theories of the tax base; definition of income and alternative tax bases; outline structure of the UK tax system, sources of tax law and interpretation.

(*b*) Taxation of employment income and business profits.

(*c*) Capital gains tax and inheritance tax.

(*d*) Taxation of private trusts.

(*e*) Tax avoidance.**]**

Statutes and other source material

Details of the statutes and other sources of material which will be available to candidates in the examination room for certain papers will be given in the teaching conventions and in examiners' edicts circulated to candidates.

Notice of options

Notice of the options to be offered by candidates must be given to the Registrar not later than the Friday in the fourth week of the Michaelmas Full Term immediately preceding the examination.

For course 1 students **[From 1 October 2004:** for course 2 students**]**

Research Skills Programme

The Law Board will approve and offer a Research Skills Programme, which will provide training in the use of legal information resources (both paper and electronic), legal research, and team-working. The programme will also check students' competence in the use of Information Technology. Students are required to undertake this programme and to complete the assessments which form part of it, to the satisfaction of the Programme Co-ordinator appointed by the Law Board. The Programme Co-ordinator will certify to the Clerk of the Schools the names of those students who have done so.

PASS SCHOOL OF JURISPRUDENCE

Candidates for the Pass School in Jurisprudence shall satisfy the examiners in five standard subjects, from among those prescribed by regulation for the Honour School of Jurisprudence, including not less than three from among Papers 1–4. A candidate shall not take more than one of the subjects in a branch of philosophy specified for the Honour School.

SPECIAL REGULATIONS FOR THE HONOUR SCHOOL OF LITERAE HUMANIORES

A

1. The Subjects of the Honour School of Literae Humaniores shall be (I) Greek and Roman History, (II) Philosophy, (III) Greek and Latin Literature, (IV) Greek and Roman Archaeology, (V) Philology and Linguistics, (VI) Second Classical Language.

2. Each candidate must offer at least two of Subjects (I)–(V).

3. No candidate shall be admitted to the examination in this school unless he or she has either passed or been exempted from the First Public Examination.

4. The examination in this school shall be under the joint supervision of the Boards of the Faculties of Classics and Philosophy, which shall appoint a joint standing committee to make regulations concerning it, subject always to the preceding clauses of this subsection.

B

1. Candidates shall take either Course I or Course II. Persons who have satisfied the Moderators in Course IA, IB, or IC of Honour Moderations in Classics or of the Preliminary Examination in Classics may not enter for the Honour School of Literae Humaniores Course II without permission from the Board of the Faculty of Classics after consultation where appropriate with the Board of the Faculty of Philosophy. Such permission, which will be given only for special reasons, must be sought as early as possible, and in no case later than noon on the Friday of the First Week of Michaelmas Term before the examination, by writing to the Chairman of the Board of the Faculty of Classics, c/o 34, St Giles'. Applications must be accompanied by a letter of support from the applicant's society.

2. Candidates must offer eight subjects (and any associated papers of translation), which may include: between two and five subjects in Greek and Roman History; up to five subjects in Philosophy; up to five subjects in Greek and Latin Literature; up to two subjects in Greek and Roman Archaeology; up to two subjects in Philology and Linguistics, two subjects in Second Classical Language; except that (i) candidates in Course I may not offer Second Classical Language and (ii) candidates in Course II who offer Second Classical Language may not offer more than four subjects in any one of Greek and Roman History, Philosophy, and Greek and Latin Literature. The combinations of subjects permitted are set out in I–VI below. No candidate may offer more than one thesis, except that a Special Thesis may be offered in addition to one other thesis.

3. All candidates must offer at least four text-based subjects, except that candidates in Course II who offer Second Classical Language must offer at least three text-based subjects. All candidates in Course I must offer at least one text-based subject in each of (1) classical Greek and (2) classical Latin. The text-based subjects are as follows:

(1) in classical Greek
- I.1: *Greek History* 1
- I.2: *Greek History* 2
- I.3: *Greek History* 3
- I.4: *Roman History* 4
- II.130: *Plato*
- II.131: *Aristotle*
- II.132: *Sextus Empiricus*
- III.1: *Greek Literature of the 5th Century BC*
- III.2(*a*): *Early Greek Hexameter Poetry*
- III.2(*b*): *Greek Lyric and Elegiac Poetry*
- III.2(*c*): *Pindar and Bacchylides*
- III.3(*a*): *Aeschylus*
- III.3(*b*): *Euripides*
- III.4(*a*): *Plato*
- III.4(*b*): *Hellenistic Poetry*
- III.8(*b*)(i): *Ancient Literary Criticism* (for candidates offering Aristotle and Longinus)
- III.9: *Greek Textual Criticism*
- V.1: *Greek Historical Linguistics*

(2) in classical Latin
- I.5: *Roman History* 5
- I.6: *Roman History* 6
- I.7: *Roman History* 7
- II.133: *Cicero and Seneca*
- III.5: *Latin Literature of the 1st Century BC*
- III.6(*a*): *Latin Didactic Poetry*
- III.6(*b*): *Latin Satire*
- III.7(*a*): *Cicero the Orator*
- III.7(*b*): *Horace*
- III.7(*c*): *Ovid*
- III.7(*d*): *Seneca and Lucan*
- III.8(*b*)(i): *Ancient Literary Criticism* (for candidates offering Horace and Tacitus)
- III.10: *Latin Textual Criticism*
- III.11(*a*): *The Conversion of Augustine*
- III.11(*b*): *Medieval Latin*
- V.2: *Latin Historical Linguistics*

(3) other
- III.8(*a*): *Greek and Roman Comedy*
- III.8(*b*)(ii) and (iii): *Ancient Literary Criticism* (for Course II candidates only)
- III.8(*c*): *The Ancient Novel*

4. In the assignment of honours all eight subjects offered by a candidate shall count equally. In assessing a candidate's performance in a subject, the examiners shall have regard to performance in any associated translation papers.

5. In addition to their eight subjects candidates may also offer, but are not required to offer, a Special Thesis in accordance with VII below.

I. *Greek and Roman History*

Candidates will be expected to show such knowledge of Classical Geography and Antiquities, and of the general History of Greece and Rome, as shall be necessary for the profitable study of the authors or periods which they offer.

Candidates may offer up to five subjects (or up to four if they are offering Second Classical Language in Course II), which must include at least two subjects from A below, together with associated translation papers from D below.

A. Greek and Roman History Periods

Candidates are required to offer not fewer than two and not more than four period subjects from the following schedule; each subject will be examined in one paper (3 hours). If they offer two subjects, these must be a chronologically consecutive pair in either Greek or Roman History; if they offer four subjects, they must offer chronologically consecutive pairs in both Greek and Roman History. If they offer three subjects, both Greek and Roman History must be offered, and two subjects must be a chronologically consecutive pair.

In Course I all period subjects must be offered as text-based. In Course II one consecutive pair of period subjects in either Greek or Roman History must be offered as text-based, but other period subjects may be offered not as text-based.

I.1 *The Early Greek World and Herodotus' Histories: 776 BC to 479 BC*

For those offering this period as a text-based subject, passages for compulsory comment and translation will be set from

Herodotus I.1–91 and 141–77, III.39–end, IV.144–VI.end,
and from Aristotle, Athenaion Politeia i-xxii.

The following texts are prescribed for study in translation apart from those sections listed above), and candidates will be expected to show knowledge of these texts in their answers:

Herodotus I–IX,
Aristotle, *Athenaion Politeia* i–xxii
and R. Meiggs and D. M. Lewis edd., *A Selection of Greek Historical Inscriptions to the end of the fifth-century BC* (revised edition, Oxford 1988) nos. 1–29 (translated in C. W. Fornara, *Translated Documents of Greece and Rome 1: Archaic Times to the End of the Peloponnesian War* (Cambridge, 1983) nos. 11, 14, 18, 19, 21, 23–5, 29, 33, 35, 37, 38, 41D, 42, 43, 44B, 47, 49, 50, 51, 54, 55, 59, 64 and in a dossier obtainable from the Classics Office, 65–7 St Giles').

This subject may not be combined with IV.1, *The Greeks and the Mediterranean World* c. *950 BC–500 BC*.

I.2 *Thucydides and the Greek World: 479 BC to 403 BC.*

For those offering this period as a text-based subject, passages for compulsory comment and translation will be set from

Thucydides I–IV.41, and VIII,
and from Xenophon, *Hellenica* I.5–end, II.2 and 3.

The following texts are prescribed for study in translation (apart from those sections listed above), and candidates will be expected to show knowledge of these texts in their answers:

Thucydides I–VIII,
Xenophon, *Hellenica* I and II
and R. Meiggs and D. Lewis (eds.), *A Selection of Greek Historical Inscriptions to the End of the Fifth Century BC* (revised edition, 1988) nos. 28–95 and 67 bis at p. 312 of 1988 reprint, *Supplementum Epigraphicum Graecum* XXXI 985, *Inscriptiones Graecae* I (ed. 3) 1454, *Historia Einzelschrift* 74 (1992), *Hesperia* 22 (1953), extracts from pp. 252, 254, 263, 271, 288.

Translated in C. W. Fornara, *Translated Documents of Greece and Rome 1: Archiac Times to the End of the Peloponnesian War* (Cambridge, 1983) nos. 15B, 54, 63, 64, 66, 68, 70, 77, 78, 80, 81, 89, 90B, 91, 93, 97–101, 103, 112–15, 118B, 119–21, 124–6,

128, 129, 132–6, 138–40, 142–4, 146, 147D, 149–50, 152–5, 160–3, 165, 166 and in a dossier obtainable from the Classics Office, 65–7 St Giles'.

I.3 *The End of the Peloponnesian War to the Death of Philip II of Macedon: 403 BC to 336 BC.*

For those offering this period as a text-based subject, passages for compulsory comment and translation will be set from:

Xenophon, *Hellenica* III, V and VII,
Xenophon, *Anabasis* VII,
Xenophon, *Constitution of the Spartans,*
Hellenica Oxyrhynchia,
Plutarch, *Pelopidas*,
and Demosthenes, *Philippics* i and iii.

The following texts are prescribed for study in translation (apart from those sections listed above), and candidates will be expected to show knowledge of these texts in their answers:

Xenophon, *Hellenica III-end, Anabasis* VII, *Constitution of the Spartans,*
Hellenica Oxyrhynchia,
Aeneas Tacticus, *Poliorcemata*,
Isocrates, *Evagoras*,
Plutarch, *Pelopidas* and *Timoleon*,
Demosthenes, *Philippics* i and iii,

and M. N. Tod, *A Selection of Greek Historical Inscriptions*, vol. 2 (Oxford, 1948) nos. 97, 101–3, 106–9, 111–8, 120–4, 126–7, 129–33, 136–9, 141–7, 150–8, 160–5, 167–72, 174–9, *Supplementum Epigraphicum* XII 87, XXVII 942, XXIX 86, XXXIV 155, XXXV 480, *Sylloge Inscriptionum Graecarum* ed. 3 (ed. W. Dittenberger) nos. 963, 986, 1004, *Inscriptiones Graecae* XII 8.4 and *Hesperia* 43 (1974) 155 ff.

Translated in P. Harding, *Translated Documents of Greece and Rome 2: From the End of the Peloponnesian War to the Battle of Ipsus* (Cambridge, 1985) nos. 2, 5, 12D, 14A, 16, 17, 20, 21, 24, 26, 27, 29, 31, 33, 34, 35, 37, 38, 40–3, 45, 46, 51–9, 63–6, 68–70, 74, 79, 81–4, 88, 94, 97, 99A, 100, 101, and in a dossier obtainable from the Classics Office, 65–7 St Giles'.

I.4 *Rome and the Mediterranean and the Histories of Polybius: 240 BC to 134 BC.*

For those offering this period as a text-based subject, passages for compulsory comment and translation will be set from Polybius, the following selections:

I.1–4, 62–5, 88.5–12; II.21–4; III.1–34, 40, 56, 77–8, 106–7, 118; V.101–10; VI.3–18; VII.9; IX.3–9, 11a; XI.4–6; XV.1–2, 9–24; XVI.24–35; XVIII.1–12, 34–52; XXI.11–24, 29–32, 41–6; XXII.3–15, 18; XXIII.1–5, 9, 17; XXIV.6–13; XXV.3–5; XXVII.8–10; XXVIII.6–7, 12–13, 16–17; XXIX.23–7; XXX.1–5, 11–13, 25–32; XXXI.1–2, 21–30; XXXVI.1–6; XXXVIII.1–18; XXXIX.1–8.

The following texts are prescribed for study in translation (apart from those sections listed above), and candidates will be expected to show knowledge of these texts in their answers:

Polybius (Penguin Classics selection, ed. F. W. Walbank), together with those passages listed above.
Livy XXXVI – IX, *Periochae* of Books XLVI–LVIII,

and *Inscriptiones Creticae* III 4; *IG* (= *Inscriptiones Graecae*) IX^2 2.241; Justin 30.2.8, 31.1.2, Valerius Maximus 6.6.1, M. H. Crawford, *Roman Republican Coinage* I (1974), no. 419/2; R. K. Sherk, *Roman Documents from the Greek East* (= *RDGE*) 33; *Die Inschriften von Lampsakos* (ed. P. Frisch) 4; *IG* XII 9.931, *SEG* (*Supplementum Epigraphicum Graecum*) XXII 214, *SIG*^{3} (= *Sylloge Inscriptionum Graecarum*^{3} (ed. W. Dittenberger) 592, *IG* XII 9.233 (cf. Addenda, p. 177), *SIG*^{3} 616, *SEG* XXIII

412, *SEG* XXII 266.13–14; *SIG*[3] 595 A–B; *RDGE* 34; *IG* XI 4.712; *IG* XI 4.756; *SEG* XV 254; *RDGE* 37; *SIG*[3] 606; *RDGE* 35; *RDGE* 1; *RDGE* 38; *SEG* XXV 445; *SEG* XVIII 570.62–79; *Fouilles de Delphes* III 4.75; *RDGE* 3; *RDGE* 2; *SEG* XVI 255; *SEG* XXV 118; *Inscriptiones Latinae Liberae Rei Publicae* (ed. A. Degrassi) 323; *Orientis Graecae Inscriptiones Selectae* (ed. W. Dittenberger) 762; *SIG*[3] 656; P. Fraser, *Samothrace* 29a, 30, 32; *RDGE* 5; C. B. Welles, *Royal Correspondence in the Hellenistic Period,* no. 61; *Inscriptiones Antiquae Orae Septentrionalis Ponti Euxini Graecae et Latinae* (ed. B. Latyschev) I[2] 402; *SEG* IX 7; *RDGE* 6B; *SIG*[3] 693; *RDGE* 7; Pausanias 7.16.7–10; *Bulletin de correspondence hellénique* 98 (1974), 814; *RDGE* 44; *RDGE* 9.

Translated in R. K. Sherk, *Rome and the Greek East to the Death of Augustus* (*Translated Documents of Greece and Rome* 4), nos. 1–38.

I.5 *The End of the Roman Republic: Cicero and Sallust: 133* BC *to 50* BC.

For those offering this period as a text-based subject, passages for compulsory comment and translation will be set from:

Sallust, *Histories* the following fragments:
1.55 = 1.48 McG (Speech of Lepidus)
1.77 = 1.67 McG (Speech of Philippus)
2.47 = 2.44 McG (Speech of Cotta)
2.98 = 2.82 McG (Letter of Pompey)
3.48 = 3.34 McG (Speech of Macer)
4.69 = 4.67 McG (Letter of Mithridates)
(the first number is that in the OCT, the second is that in the translation and commentary of P. McGushin (Oxford, 1992 and 1994))
Cicero, *Verrines* I, *De imperio Cn. Pompei, De lege agraria* II, *Pro Balbo*
Caesar, *De bello Gallico* I,

Cicero, *Letters: Ad fam.* I.1, 2, 9; II.13; V.7, 12; VII.5; VIII.1, 4, 6, 8, 14; XIII.9; XV.2, 5, 6. *Ad Att.* I.1, 2, 13, 14, 16, 19; II.1, 16, 18, 19, 24; III.23; IV.1, 3, 5, 15; V.11, 16, 21; VI.2; VII.7, 9. *Ad Qu. f.* I.2; II.3, 4; III.8.

The following texts are prescribed for study in translation (apart from those sections listed above), and candidates will be expected to show knowledge of these texts in their answers:

Appian, *Civil Wars* I,
Sallust, *Jugurtha*,
Cicero, *Verrines* I, *De imperio Cn. Pompei, De lege agraria* II, *Pro Balbo*,
Caesar, *De bello Gallico* I, IV–VII,

and M. H. Crawford (ed.), *Roman Statutes* (London 1996) I, nos. 1, 2, 7, 12, 13, 15, 19; *Journal of Roman Studies* 73 (1983), 33, which contain texts and translations.

I.6 *Rome, Italy and Empire under Caesar, the Triumvirate and early Principate: 46* BC *to* AD *54*.

For those offering this period as a text-based subject, passages for compulsory comment and translation will be set from:

Suetonius, *Life of Augustus*,
Res Gestae divi Augusti, ed. Brunt & Moore (Oxford, 1967),
Tacitus, *Annals* I, XI–XII.

The following texts are prescribed for study in translation (apart from those sections listed above), and candidates will be expected to show knowledge of these texts in their answers:

Cicero, *Letters: Ad Atticum* XI.6; XII.2, 21; XIII.52; XIV.I, 12, 13B, 21; XV.II; XVI.7, 8, 11; *Ad fam.* IV.4, 5, 12; V.10A; VI.6, 15; VII.3, 30; IX.14, 15, 17, 18; X.II,

23, 24, 28, 30, 35; XI.1, 10, 27, 28; XII.4, 5, 12, 18; XIII.4, 11, 16, XVI.27.

Caesar, *Civil Wars* I, III,
Suetonius, *Life of Tiberius, Life of Claudius*,
Seneca, *Apocolocyntosis*

and V. Ehrenberg and A. H. M. Jones (eds.), *Documents illustrating the Reigns of* Augustus and Tiberius, 2nd ed. 1976 (=*EJ*^{2}) 300; 301; 10; 329; 365; 21; 197; 355; 224; 366; 98; 357; 311; 312; 315; 69; 231; 379, part 1; 102; 379, part 2; *L'Année Epigraphique* (=*AE*) 1978, 145, *Zeitschrift für Papyrologie und epigraphik* (=*ZPE*) 55, (1984), 55–110, with *EJ*^{2} 94a; W. Eck *et al.* (eds.), *Vestigia* 48 (1996); *Journal of Roman Studies* (=*JRS*) 66 (1976), 107–9; *EJ*^{2} 53; 158; E. M. Smallwood (ed.) *Documents illustrating the Principates of Gaius, Claudius and Nero* (1967), 254, 367, 368, 370, 365, 369, 380, 407, 44, 295, 197.

Translated in R. K. Sherk (ed.), *Translated Documents of Greece and Rome vol. 4 = Rome and the Greek East to the Death of Augustus*, (1984), =*TDGR* 4), 85; 86; D. C. Braund, *Augustus to Nero: A Source Book on Roman History 31 BC–AD 68* (1985, =Braund), 645; *TDGR* 4, 95; Braund 423; 360; 669; 438; R. K. Sherk (ed.) *Translated Documents of Greece and Rome* vol. 6=*The Roman Empire: Augustus to Hadrian*, (1988, =*TDGR* 6), 12; *TDGR* 4, 101; Braund 720; *TDGR* 4, 102; 103; 105; *TDGR* 6, 19; 22; *TDGR* 4, 11; Braund 127; *TDGR* 6, 34A; 35; 36A and B; 40A; 178D; Braund 458; 568; *TDGR* 6; 53; 44; Braund 711; *TDGR* 6, 55; Braund 586; *TDGR* 6, 50; Braund 214; *TDGR* 6, 58; Braund 627; for *EJ*^{2} 10 and the *SC de Cn. Pisone patre* a dossier is available from the Classics Office, 65–7 St Giles'.

I.7 *The World of Tacitus and Pliny: politics and culture:* AD *54 to* AD *138.*

For those offering this period as a text-based subject, passages for compulsory comment and translation will be set from:

Tacitus, *Annals* XIII–XVI;

Pliny, *Letters* I.1, 5, 10, 12, 14, 17, 19, 23, 24; II.1, 6, 7, 11, 12, 13, 14, 16; III.1, 2, 4, 5, 7, 8, 9, 11, 14, 16, 18, 19, 20, 21; IV.1, 8, 9, 11, 13, 15, 17, 22, 25; V.4, 7, 8, 9, 13, 14, 19, 20; VI.2, 4, 5, 6, 10, 13, 15, 16, 19, 25, 27, 29, 31, 33; VII.5, 6, 10, 11, 18, 19, 20, 24, 29, 31, 32, 33; VIII.2, 6, 10, 12, 14, 16, 23, 24; IX.5, 11, 13, 19, 23, 37, 39; X (Pliny and Trajan), the whole.

The following texts are prescribed for study in translation (apart from those sections listed above), and candidates will be expected to show knowledge of these texts in their answers:

Seneca, *On Clemency*,
Tacitus, *Histories; Agricola*,
Suetonius, *Life of Vespasian, Life of Titus, Life of Domitian*,
Historia Augusta: Life of Hadrian,

and E. M. Smallwood (ed.), *Documents illustrating the Principates of Gaius, Claudius and Nero*, (1967, Sm.) 297; 386; 261; 259; 391; 392; M. H. Crawford (ed.), *Roman Statutes* vol. 1 (1996), no. 39; M. McCrum and A. G. Woodhead (eds.), *Select Documents of the Principates of the Flavian Emperors*, (1961, =MW), 61; 128; 461; *Madrider Mitteilungen* 1, (1960), 148–9; R. G. Collingwood and R. P. Wright (eds.), *Roman Inscriptions of Britain* 1, 662–3; *Journal of Roman Studies* (=*JRS*) 76, (1986), 147–243; MW 462; 58; 466; 61; 464; 458; 369; 66; E. M. Smallwood (ed.) *Documents illustrating the Principates of Nerva, Trajan and Hadrian*, (1966, =Sm. *NTH*), 30; *Corpus Inscriptionum Latinarum* (=*CIL*) 16, 42; Sm. *NTH* 435; *JRS* 60, (1970), 142–53; Sm. *NTH* 479; 230; 109; 268; MW 320; *JRS* 63, (1973), 80 f. Sm. *NTH* 47; 378a, b; 463; 464; 281; 462; 423; *JRS* 74, (1948), 157–80.

Translated in D. C. Braund, *Augustus to Nero, a Source Book on Roman History 31 BC–AD 68*, (1985, =Braund) 533, 595, 465, 461, 600, 601, M. H. Crawford (ed.) *Roman Statutes* Vol. 1, (1996), 39; Braund 401; B. Levick, *The Government of the*

Roman Empire, (1985), 122; R. K. Sherk (ed.), *Translated Documents of Greece and Rome,* vol. 6 = *The Roman Empire: Augustus to Hadrian*, (1988), 86; 92; S. Ireland, *Roman Britain, a sourcebook*, (1986), 108; *JRS* 76, (1986), 147–243; *TDGR* 6, 96; *TDGR* 6, 95; 107; 84 and 108; 85; 110B; *TDGR* 6, 111; N. Lewis and M. Reinhold, *Roman Civilization, Sourcebook* 2, *The Empire*, ed. 2, (1966), pp. 346–7; *TDGR* 6, 117; 122; 200; 125; 116; 112C; A. E. Gordon, *Illustrated Introduction to Latin Epigraphy*, (1983), 57; D. Kehoe, *The Economics of Agricluture on Roman Imperial Estates in North Africa*, (1988), 33–7; 58 f; *TDGR* 6, 156; 157; *JRS* 74, (1984), 157–80; for MW 58; 61; Sm. *NTH* 30; MW 320; Sm. *NTH* 47; 281, a dossier is available from the Classics Office, 65–7 St Giles'.

B. Ancient History Topics

Candidates who offer two or more Greek or Roman History period papers (i.e. two or more papers under A) may also offer *one* of the following (one three-hour paper).

Note: It cannot be guaranteed that university lectures or classes or college teaching will be available in all subjects in this section in every academic year. Candidates are advised to consult their tutors about the availability of teaching when selecting their subjects.

I.8 *Athenian Democracy in the Classical Age*

Candidates will be required to study the social, administrative, and constitutional developments in Athens from 462 BC to 321 BC, and will only be required to show such knowledge of external affairs as is necessary for an understanding of Athenian democracy. The following texts are prescribed for study in translation; although compulsory passages will not be set, candidates will be expected to show knowledge of these texts in their answers.

Aristotle, *Constitution of Athens* (tr. P. J. Rhodes, Penguin Classics),

Herodotus III.80.2 (Loeb),

Thucydides I.31–44, 66–79, 140–5; II.35–65; III.35–50, 82–3; V.43–6; VI.8–29; VIII.47–97 (tr. Crawley, Everyman),

Xenophon, *Hellenica* I.6 and 7; II.3 and 4 (Loeb),

Memorabilia I.1 and 2; III.6 (Loeb),

Revenues (Loeb),

[Xenophon], *Constitution of Athens* (Loeb),

Andocides I (Loeb, *Attic Minor Orators* I),

Lysias XXII, XXV (Loeb),

Aeschines II (Loeb),

Demosthenes VI, XIX, LIX (Loeb),

Aristophanes, *Wasps, Clouds, Ecclesiazusae, Acharnians* 1–173, *Thesmophoriazusae* 295–530 (Penguin Classics),

Plato, *Apology, Gorgias, Protagoras* 309–28 (Penguin Classics),

Aeschylus, *Eumenides*; Sophocles, *Antigone*; Euripides, *Supplices* (*The Complete Greek Tragedies*, ed. R. Lattimore, D. Grene, Chicago 1958–9),

C. W. Fornara, *Translated Documents of Greece and Rome 1: Archaic Times to the End of the Peloponnesian War* (Cambridge, 1983) nos. 15, 68, 75, 97, 100, 103, 106, 114, 119, 120, 128, 134, 140, 147, 155, 160, 166,

P. Harding, *Translated Documents of Greece and Rome 2: From the End of the Peloponnesian War to the Battle of Ipsus* (Cambridge, 1985) nos. 3, 5, 9, 45, 47, 54, 55, 56, 66, 78, 82, 101, 108, 111, 121.

Opportunity will be given to show knowledge of the archaeology of Classical Athens.

I.9 *Alexander the Great and his Early Successors* (*336 BC–302 BC*)

The following texts are prescribed for study in translation; although compulsory passages for comment will not be set, candidates will be expected to show knowledge of these texts in their answers.

Arrian, *Anabasis* (Loeb, Brunt),
[Demosthenes] XVII (Loeb),
Diodorus Siculus, XVI.89, 91–5; XVII.5–7, 16–21, 32, 47–8, 62–3, 69–73, 76–7, 93–5, 100–1, 108–11, 113–15, 117–18; XVIII, the whole; XIX.12–64, 66–8, 77–100, 105; XX.19–21, 27–8, 37, 45–53, 81–99, 100–3, 106–13 (Loeb), Plutarch, *Lives of Alexander, Eumenes and Demetrios* 1–27 (Loeb), the inscriptions translated in a dossier available from the Classics Office, 65–7 St Giles' and the texts in P. Harding, *Translated Documents of Greece and Rome 2: From the End of the Peloponnesian War to the Battle of Ipsus* (Cambridge, 1989) Nos. 123, 125, 126, 128, 129, 132, 133, 136, 138.

Optional passages for comment will be set from these texts in translation and from Arrian, *Anabasis* VII (Loeb, Brunt) in Greek only.

I.10 *Cicero: Politics and Thought in the Late Republic*

The following texts are prescribed for study in translation; although compulsory passages for comment will not be set, candidates will be expected to show knowledge of these texts in their answers.

Sallust, *Catilina* (Loeb),
Cicero, *In Verrem* (Actio I) (Loeb),
De Imperio Cn. Pompei (Loeb),
Pro Sestio 97–137 (Loeb),
In M. Antonium Philippica XI (Loeb),
Pro Murena (Loeb),
In Catilinam IV (Loeb),
Epistulae ad Atticum I.1, 2, 13, 14, 16, 17, 19; II.1, 3, 16, 18; IV.1, 3, 5; V.16 and 21; VI.1 and 2; VII.7, 9, 11; VIII.3 and 11; IX. 6A, 10, 11A, 18; X.8 (incl. A and B); XI.6; XII.21 and 40; XIII.19 and 52; XIV.1, 12, 13, 13A and B; XV.1A and 11; XVI.7, 8 and 11 (Loeb),
Epistulae ad Familiares I.1, 8, 9; II.12; III.6 and 7; IV.4, 5; V.1, 2, 7, 12; VI.6; VII.3, 5, 30; VIII.1, 5, 6, 8, 13, 14, 16; IX.16 and 17; X.24 and 28; XI.3, 20, 27, 28; XII.3 and 5; XIII.1, and 9; XIV.4; XV.1, 4, 5, 6, 16, 19; XVI.12 (Loeb),
Epistulae ad Quintum fratrem II.3, 15; III.5 and 6 (Loeb),
Epistulae ad M. Brutum 17, 25 (Loeb),
Brutus 301–33 (Loeb),
De Oratore I.137–59, 185–203; II.30–8 (Loeb),
Orator 113–20, 140–6 (Loeb),
De Re Publica I.1–18, 58–71 (Loeb),
De Legibus II.1–33; III. 1–49 (Loeb),
Tusculanae Disputationes I.1–8 (Loeb),
De Divinatione II.1–24; 136–50 (Loeb),
De Natura Deorum I.1–13; III.1–10 (Loeb),
De Officiis I.1–60; II.1–29, 44–60, 73–89 trans. Griffin and Atkins (Cambridge),
Cornelius Nepos, *Atticus* (Loeb).

Optional passage and comment will be set from these texts in translation, and from *In Catilinam I* (Loeb) and *De Finibus I.1–12* (OCT) in Latin only.

This subject may not be combined with III.7(*a*), *Cicero the Orator*.

I.11 *Civic Life of the Roman Empire from the Flavian to the Severan Period*

Candidates will be required to study the economic, social, and cultural history of the cities of the Roman empire in the prescribed period, and to show an adequate knowledge of the general history of the period. The following texts are prescribed for study in translation; although compulsory passages for comment will not be set, candidates will be expected to show knowledge of these texts in their answers.

Pliny, *Letters* I. 8, 10; III. 9, 13; V. 7, 11, 20; VI. 5, 13; VIII. 24; IX. 5; X. 8, 15–121 (tr. Loeb or Penguin),

Dio Chrysostom, *Orations* (or *Discourses*) 38, 40, 43–9 (tr. Loeb),

Apuleius, *Apology* (tr. H. E. Butler), *The Apologia and Florida of Apuleius of Madaura* (1909),

Apuleius, *Florida* 16, 20 (tr. H. E. Butler), *The Apologia and Florida of Apuleius of Madaura* (1909),

Fronto, *Ad Pium* I. 8 (Loeb I. 236–9); *ad M. Caesarem* III. 2–5 (Loeb I. 58–69); *Ad Amicos* I. 1 (Loeb I. 282–7); II. 7 (Loeb II. 176–87), II (Loeb I. 292–5),

Aelius Aristides, *Orations* 26 (*To Rome*) 1–14, 28–39, 58–100 (tr. with notes by C. A. Behr, *The Complete Works* (1981–86), II. 73–97 (tr. with commentary by J. H. Oliver, *The Ruling Power* (1953)),

Aelius Aristides, *Oration* 30 (=*Sacred Tales* 4), 68–108 (tr. with notes by C. A. Behr, *The Complete Works* (1981–6)), II. 318–39 (also in C. A. Behr, *Aelius Aristides and the Sacred Tales* (1968), 253–77)),

Lucian, *Alexander, or the False Prophet*; *Peregrinos* (both tr. Loeb),

Epictetus, *Discourses* III. 7, 13; VI. 7 (tr. Loeb),

Philostratus, *Lives of the Sophists*, preface; I. introduction; I. 8 (Favorinus), 21 (Scopelian, 25 (Polemo); II. 1 (Herodes), 2 (Theodotus), 9 (Aristeides), 23 (Damianus), 24 (Antipater) (tr. Loeb),

Plutarch, *Precepts of Statecraft* 17–20, 25–32 (tr. Loeb *Plutarch, Moralia* X. 234–53, 262–99),

P. A. Brunt, *Select Texts from the Digest* (copies are available from the Classics Office),

H. A. Musurillo, *Acts of the Christian Martyrs* (1972) nos. 1, 6, 8,

Eusebius, *Ecclesiastical History* IV. 8–9, 26; V. 1 (tr. Loeb or Penguin),

Tertullian, *Apologeticum*, 1–2, 37–50 (tr. Loeb),

J. Stevenson (ed.), *A New Eusebius* (revised by W. H. C. Frend, 1987), nos. 31–2, 34–6, 39, 41, 92, 110, 111, 112–16, 117, 136.

Inscriptions and other documentary material:

N. Lewis and M. Reinhold, *Roman Civilization* (3rd edn., 1990), II. 186–9, 231–337,

J. H. Oliver, *The Ruling Power* (1953), 958–63 (oil law of Hadrian),

Hesperia 24 (1955), 340–3 (s.c. on reduction of costs of gladiators),

J. H. Oliver, *Marcus Aurelius: Aspects of Civic and Cultural Policy in the East* (*Hesperia* Supp. 13, 1970), 1–33 (with emendations by C. P. Jones, *ZPE* 8 (1971), 161–83) (Herodes Atticus and his enemies),

Journal of Roman Studies 63 (1973), 86–7 (tr. in Lewis and Reinhold II. 56–8) (tabula Banasitana),

Journal of Roman Studies 74 (1984), 173–80 (Palmyra tax law),

Journal of Roman Studies 76 (1986), 182–99 (lex Irnitana) (selection available from the Classics Office),

Journal of Roman Studies 80 (1990), 183–7 (Demostheneia at Oenoanda),

G. M. Rogers, *Sacred Identity of Ephesos: Foundation Myths of a Roman City* (1991), 152–85 (Vibius Salutaris).

Special attention will be given to the following archaeological sites: Ostia, Carthage, Leptis Magna, Trier, Silchester, Athens, Ephesus, Palmyra.

This subject may not be combined with IV.4, *Cities and Settlement in the Roman Empire*.

I.12 *Religions in the Greek and Roman World* (c. *30 BC–AD 312*)

Candidates will be required to study the workings of Greek and Roman religions, including relevant aspects of Judaism and Christianity and other elective cults, between around 30 BC and AD 312. They will be encouraged to display an understanding of relevant modern theories of religious practice, and to be familiar with the relevant literary, epigraphic and archaeological evidence contained in the following texts prescribed for study in translation; although compulsory passages for comment will not be set, candidates will be expected to show knowledge of these texts in their answers.

Ovid, *Fasti* IV (Loeb),
Acts of the Apostles (New English Bible),
Josephus, *Against Apion* II (Loeb),
Plutarch, *Decline of Oracles* (Loeb),
Lucian, *Alexander; Peregrinus* (Loeb),
Aelius Aristides, *Oration* XLVIII (=*Sacred Tales* II) (tr. C. A. Behr),
Pausanias I.1–38 (Loeb),
Apuleius, *Metamorphoses* XI (Hanson, Loeb),
Minucius Felix, *Octavius* (Loeb, with Tertullian),
H. A. Musurillo, *Acts of the Christian Martyrs* (1972) nos. 1, 6, 8, 10,
Eusebius, *Ecclesiastical History* VIII–X (Penguin),
M. Beard, J. A. North & S. R. F. Price, *Religions of Rome* vol. 2 (Cambridge 1998).

I.13 *Sexuality and Gender in Greece and Rome*

The following texts are prescribed for study in translation; although compulsory passages for comment will not be set, candidates will be expected to show knowledge of these texts in their answers.

M. R. Lefkowitz and M. B. Fant, *Women's Life in Greece and Rome* (2nd edn, London, 1992),
Semonides and Theognis II (Campbell, Loeb),
Sophocles, *Antigone*, Euripides, *Medea* (in D. Grene and R. Lattimore (eds.) *The Complete Greek Tragedy in Translation* II–III (Chicago 1958–9)),
Aristophanes, *Thesmophoriazusae* (Penguin),
Lysias I and III (Loeb),
[Demosthenes] (*In Neaeram*) (Loeb),
Xenophon, *Symposium, Oeconomicus* (Loeb),
Livy I (Loeb),
Senatusconsultum de Bacchanalibus in N. Lewis and M. Reinhold, *Roman Civilization I: The Republic* (3rd edn, New York 1990) no. 176,
Laudatio Turiae (Lefkowitz and Fant no. 168),
Pliny, *Letters* I.12, 14, 16; III.1, 11, 16, 19; IV.10, 19; V.16; VI.24, 33; VII.19, 24; VIII.5, 18, 23; IX.13; X.120 (Penguin),
Apuleius, *Apology* (tr. Butler),
H. Musurillo, *The Acts of the Christian Martyrs* (Oxford 1972) nos. 5, 6, 8, 9, 22, 24,
Ambrose, *De Virginibus* trans. in P. Schaff and H. Wace, *A Select Library of Nicene and Post-Nicene Fathers of the Christian Church* second series X (Edinburgh, reprint Grand Rapids 1989) 361ff.

Opportunity will also be given to show knowledge of the artistic evidence.

C.

I.14 Thesis in Ancient History

Candidates who offer four subjects under A and B may also offer a thesis in Ancient History as a fifth subject, in accordance with the Regulation on Theses below. This subject may not be combined with any of II.199, III.12, IV.5 or V.5.

D. TRANSLATION

Two papers will be set. Candidates are required to offer translation (one or two papers as appropriate) from the texts prescribed for all the period subjects which they offer under A as text-based.

II. *Philosophy*

Candidates may offer any subjects in Philosophy in accordance with the Schedules below, up to the number of five (or four if they are offering Second Classical Language in Course II), provided that (i) candidates offering more than one subject in Philosophy must select at least one from Schedule A, (ii) candidates offering more than two subjects in Philosophy must also select at least one from Schedule B, and (iii) candidates offering subject 199 must offer at least three other subjects in Philosophy. The syllabus of each subject (including thesis regulations) is specified in **Regulations for Philosophy in all Honour Schools including Philosophy.** In the list below, numbers in parenthesis after a subject's title indicate other subjects with which it may not be combined by any candidate. One 3-hour paper will be set on each subject except 199.

SCHEDULE A

130 Plato, *either* (*a*) *Republic or* (*b*) *Theaetetus, Sophist* (115)
131 Aristotle, *either* (*a*) *Nicomachean Ethics or* (*b*) *Physics* (116)
132 Sextus Empiricus, *Outlines of Pyrrhonism*
133 Cicero, *De Finibus* III; *De Officiis* I in translation; Seneca, *Epistulae Morales* 92, 95, 121, *De Constantia, De Vita Beata* (Course II only)
115 Plato, *Republic*, in translation (Course II only) (130)
116 Aristotle, *Nicomachean Ethics*, in translation (Course II only) (131)

SCHEDULE B

101 *History of Philosophy from Descartes to Kant*
102 *Knowledge and Reality*
103 *Ethics*
104 *Philosophy of Mind*
108 *The Philosophy of Logic and Language*

SCHEDULE C

105 *Philosophy of Science and Philosophy of Psychology and Neuroscience* (106)
106 *Philosophy of Science and Social Science* (105)
107 *Philosophy of Religion*
109 *Aesthetics and the Philosophy of Criticism*
110 *Medieval Philosophy*
111 *Continental Philosophy from Descartes to Leibniz*
112 *The Philosophy of Kant*
113 *Post-Kantian Philosophy*
114 *Theory of Politics*
115 Plato, *Republic*, in translation (Course I only) (130)
116 Aristotle, *Nicomachean Ethics*, in translation (Course I only) (131)
117 *Frege, Russell, and Wittgenstein* (118)
118 *The Later Philosophy of Wittgenstein* (117)
119 *Formal Logic*
120 *Intermediate Philosophy of Physics*
122 *Philosophy of Mathematics*
133 Cicero, *De Finibus* III; *De Officiis* I in translation; Seneca, *Epistulae Morales* 92, 95, 121, *De Constantia, De Vita Beata* (Course I only)
199 *Thesis in Philosophy* (I.14, III.12, IV.5, V.5)

III. *Greek and Latin Literature*

Course I: Candidates may offer up to a maximum of five subjects from 1–12 below. Candidates offering more than three subjects must offer both III.1 and III.5; candidates offering more than one must offer III.1 or III.5 (and may offer both).

Course II: Candidates may offer up to a maximum of five subjects from 1–15 below, or four if they take VI, Second Classical Language. Candidates offering more than one subject must offer III.1 or III.5 (and may offer both).

One paper (3 hours) will be set on each subject except 12, and additional translation papers (one-and-a-half hours each) will be set on subjects III.1 and III.5.

Note: It cannot be guaranteed that university lectures or classes or college teaching will be available in all subjects in every academic year. Candidates are advised to consult their tutors about the availability of teaching when selecting their subjects.

III.1 *Greek Literature of the 5th Century* BC

One paper of three hours (commentary and essay) with an additional paper (one-and-a-half hours) of translation. With special reference to the following texts, from which the passages for translation and comment will be set:

Pindar, *Olympians* 1, 7; *Pythians* 1, 8, 9
Euripides, *Hippolytus*
Sophocles, *Ajax*
Aristophanes, *Clouds*
Herodotus III. 1–88, 118–60
Thucydides III.1–85.

III.2 One of the following:

(*a*) *Early Greek Hexameter Poetry* with special reference to the following texts. Compulsory passages for translation and comment will be set from those in list α.

α *Odyssey* I–XIII.92
Hesiod, *Works and Days* (including the bracketed portions)
Homeric Hymns 2 (*Demeter*), 5 (*Aphrodite*).

β *Odyssey* XIII.93–XXIV.548
Hesiod, *Theogony*
Homeric Hymns 3 (*Apollo*), 4 (*Hermes*), 7 (*Dionysus*)
Fragments of the Epic Cycle (in H. G. Evelyn-White, *Hesiod, The Homeric Hymns and Homerica* (Loeb), pp. 480–533).

Candidates will also be expected to be familiar with the *Iliad*.

(*b*) *Greek Lyric and Elegiac Poetry* with special reference to the following text. Compulsory passages for translation and comment will be set from: D. A. Campbell, *Greek Lyric Poetry* (Macmillan, repr. Bristol Classical Press) pp. 1–97 (omitting Archilochus 112, 118, Semonides 29, Ibycus 282a); M. L. West, *Delectus ex Iambis et Elegis Graecis* (Oxford Classical Text) Archilochus 23, 188–92, 196 and 196A; M. Davies, *Poetarum Melicorum Graecorum Fragmenta* (Oxford), Stesichorus pp. 154–75 (*Geryoneis*), Fr. 193, 209, 217, 222(b), Ibycus S151; M. L. West, *Iambi et Elegi Graeci*, 2nd edition, vol. 2 (Oxford, 1992), Simonides Fr. eleg. 11 and 19–20.

(*c*) *Pindar and Bacchylides* with special reference to the following texts. Compulsory passages for translation and comment will be set from those in list α.

α Bacchylides 3, 5, 17, 18
Pindar, *Olympians* 2, 3, 6, 12, 14; *Pythians* 3, 4, 5, 6, 10; *Nemeans* 1, 5, 7, 9, 10; *Isthmians* 1, 2, 5.

β Bacchylides 9, 10, 11, 13
Pindar, *Olympians* 1, 7; *Pythians* 1, 8, 9; frr. 40 (*Paean* 6), 109, 114, 116, 127 Bowra.

III.3 One of the following:

(*a*) *Aeschylus* with special reference to the following texts. Compulsory passages for translation and comment will be set from those in list α.

α *Seven against Thebes, Agamemnon, Choephori, Eumenides.*
β *Persae, Supplices.*

(*b*) *Euripides* with special reference to the following texts. Compulsory passages for translation and comment will be set from those in list α.
α *Medea, Electra, Heracles, Ion, Orestes.*
β *Alcestis, Hippolytus, Hecuba, Trojan Women, Helen.*

III.4 One of the following:

(*a*) *Plato* with special reference to the following texts. Compulsory passages for translation and comment will be set from those in list α.
α Plato, *Phaedrus; Gorgias*, opening–462e4, 470c9–505c6, 521a2–end.
β Plato, *Gorgias* 462e5–470c8, 505c7–521a1, *Ion, Republic* X; Gorgias, *Helen.*

Candidates should be familiar with some of the surviving material relating to sophistic rhetoric, particularly Protagoras, Gorgias and the *Dissoi Logoi*, and consultation of these in Diels–Kranz, *Die Fragmente der Vorsokratiker* (Berlin, 6th edition 1951 or later edition) ii, nos. 80, 82, and 90, with the translation ed. by R. K. Sprague, *The Older Sophists* (Univ. of S. Carolina 1972) 3–28, 30–67, 279–93 is expected.

(*b*) *Hellenistic Poetry* with special reference to the following texts. Compulsory passages for translation and comment will be set from those in list α.
α Theocritus 1, 3, 7, 10, 13, 15, 16, 28
Callimachus, *Hymns* 1, 5, 6; frr. 1, 67–75, 110, 178, 191, 194, 260 (this last fr. to be read in Callimachus, *Hecale* (ed. A. S. Hollis) frr. 69–74); epigrams 2, 4, 8, 13, 16, 19, 21, 25, 27, 28, 29, 30, 41, 43, 46, 50 Pf.
Herodas 4
Apollonius, *Argonautica* III.439–1162
Asclepiades 1, 2, 3, 10, 11, 12, 16, 18, 25, 26, 28, 32 Page.
β Apollonius, *Argonautica* III.1–438, 1163–IV.481
Moschus, *Europa*
Herodas 2, 6
Callimachus, *Hymn* 2.

III.5 *Latin Literature of the 1st Century* BC

One paper of three hours (commentary and essay) with an additional paper (one-and-a-half hours) of translation. With special reference to the following texts, from which the passages for translation and comment will be set:
Lucretius I
Catullus 61–4, 68
Cicero, *Pro Caelio*
Virgil, *Eclogues*
Horace, *Odes* I
Propertius IV.

III.6 One of the following:

(*a*) *Latin Didactic Poetry* with special reference to the following texts. Compulsory passages for translation and comment will be set from those in list α.
α Lucretius **[Until 1 October 2004:** IV, VI**] [From 1 October 2004:** III, IV**]**
Virgil, *Georgics*
Ovid, *Ars Amatoria* I.
β Hesiod, *Works and Days*
Aratus, *Phaenomena* 1–136, 733–1154
Lucretius I.

(*b*) *Latin Satire* with special reference to the following texts. Compulsory passages for translation and comment will be set from those in list α.

α Horace, *Satires* I, II 1, 2, 4, 5, 6, 8
Persius, *Prologus*, 1, 5, 6
Juvenal 1, 3–6, 8–11, 14.
β Horace, *Satires* II 3, 7
β Persius 2, 3, 4
Juvenal 2, 7, 12, 13, 15, 16
Lucilius 35, 46, 84–93, 102–5, 109–10, 172–81, 186–93, 200–7, 252–3, 267–8, 368–72, 384–7, 401–10, 567–73, 632–5, 650–1, 713–14, 1145–51, 1196–1208 in E. H. Warmington, *Remains of Old Latin* (Loeb, Vol. III).

III.7 One of the following:
(*a*) *Cicero the Orator* with special reference to the following texts. Compulsory passages for translation and comment will be set from those in list α.
α *Pro Sexto Roscio Amerino*
Pro Archia
Pro Milone
Pro Marcello
Philippics I, II.
β *Auctor ad Herennium* I; II.1–12, 47–50; IV.11–16
De Imperio Cn. Pompei
Pro C. Rabirio perduellionis reo
Pro Caelio
De Oratore II.71–216, 290–349.
This subject may not be combined with I.11, *Cicero: Politics and Thought in the Late Republic.*

(*b*) *Horace* with special reference to the following texts. Compulsory passages for translation and comment will be set from those in list α.
α *Epodes*
Odes II, IV
Carmen Saeculare
Epistles I, II.
β *Satires* I
Odes I.

(*c*) *Ovid* with special reference to the following texts. Compulsory passages for translation and comment will be set from those in list α.
α *Heroides* 18–21
Metamorphoses I–IV
Fasti IV
Tristia I.
β *Amores* I
Metamorphoses XIII–XV.

(*d*) *Seneca and Lucan* with special reference to the following texts. Compulsory passages for translation and comment will be set from those in list α.
α Seneca, *Phaedra, Thyestes*
Lucan I.1–182, VII, VIII, IX.
β Lucan I.183–695, X.

III.8 One of the following (in each case (*i*) is the only version available to Course I candidates):
(*a*) *Either*
(i) *Greek and Roman Comedy* with special reference to the following texts. Compulsory passages for translation and comment will be set from those in list α.
α Aristophanes, *Wasps, Ekklesiazousai*
Menander, *Dyskolos*

Plautus, *Pseudolus*
Terence, *Eunuchus*
β Aristophanes, *Birds, Thesmophoriazousai*
Menander, *Aspis, Dis Exapaton, Epitrepontes, Misoumenos, Perikeiromene, Samia, Sikyonios*
Plautus, *Bacchides*
Terence, *Heauton Timorumenos*
or (for Course II candidates only)

(ii) *Greek and Roman Comedy* (Greek version) with special reference to the following texts. Compulsory passages for translation and comment will be set from those in list α.

α Aristophanes, *Wasps, Thesmophorizousai, Ekklesiazousai*
Menander, *Dyskolos, Samia*
β Aristophanes, *Birds*
Meander, *Aspis, Dis Exapaton, Epitrepontes, Misoumenos, Perikeiromene, Sikyonios*
Plautus, *Bacchides, Pseudolus*
Terence, *Heauton Timorumenos, Eunuchus*
or (for Course II candidates only)

(iii) *Greek and Roman Comedy* (Latin version) with special reference to the following texts. Compulsory passages for translation and comment will be set from those in list α.

α Plautus, *Bacchides, Pseudolus*
Terence, *Heauton Timorumenos, Eunuchus*
β Aristophanes, *Wasps, Birds, Thesmophoriazousai, Ekklesiazousai*
Menander, *Aspis, Dis Exapaton, Dyskolos, Epitrepontes, Misoumenos, Perikeiromene, Samia, Sikyonios.*

(*b*) *Either*

(i) *Ancient Literary Criticism*

(α) with special reference to *three* of the following, from which texts alone compulsory passages for translation and comment will be set. Candidates will be required to state on their examination entry form which texts they propose to offer. Those who offer Aristotle and Longinus as two of their three texts may count this as a text-based subject in Greek; those who offer Horace and Tacitus may count it as a text-based subject in Latin.

(i) Aristotle, *Poetics*
(ii) Longinus, *On the Sublime* 1–17, 33–44
(iii) Horace, *Satires* 1.4 and 10, *Epistles* II.1 and *Ars Poetica*
(iv) Tacitus, *Dialogus.*

(β) Candidates will also be expected to be familiar with all the texts in (α); and in addition Plato, *Republic* X. 595–607; Demetrius, *On Style* 36–113; Cicero, *Orator* 75–121; Quintilian X.1; Longinus, *On the Sublime* 18–32; and Plutarch, *On the Study of Poetry* 1–9. These additional texts are available in translation in *Ancient Literary Criticism*, ed. D. A. Russell and M. Winterbottom (Oxford, 1972).

or (for Course II candidates only)

(ii) *Ancient Literary Criticism* (Greek version) with special reference to Aristotle, *Poetics* and Longinus, *On the Sublime* 1–17 and 33–44 (from which texts alone compulsory passages for translation and comment will be set); and Tacitus, *Dialogus* (to be offered in the translation by M. Winterbottom in *Ancient Literary Criticism*, ed. D. A. Russell and M. Winterbottom (Oxford, 1972), from which a compulsory passage for comment will be set).

Candidates will also be expected to be familiar with Plato, *Republic* X. 595–607; Demetrius, *On Style* 36–113; Cicero, *Orator* 75–121; Horace, *Satires* I.4 and 10, *Epistles* II.1 and *Ars Poetica*; Quintilian X.1; Longinus, *On the Sublime* 18–32; and

Plutarch, *On the Study of Poetry* 1–9. These additional texts are available in translation in *Ancient Literary Criticism*, ed. Russell and Winterbottom.

or (for Course II candidates only)

(iii) *Ancient Literary Criticism* (Latin version) with special reference to Horace, *Satires* I.4 and 10, *Epistles* II.1 and *Ars Poetica*, and Tacitus, *Dialogus* (from which texts alone compulsory passages for translation and comment will be set); and Aristotle, *Poetics* (to be offered in the translation by M. E. Hubbard in *Ancient Literary Criticism*, ed. D. A. Russell and M. Winterbottom (Oxford, 1972), from which a compulsory passage for comment will be set).

Candidates will also be expected to be familiar with Plato, *Republic* X. 595–607; Demetrius, *On Style* 36–113; Cicero, *Orator* 75–121; Quintilian X.1; Longinus, *On the Sublime*; and Plutarch, *On the Study of Poetry* 1–9. These additional texts are available in translation in *Ancient Literary Criticism*, ed. Russell and Winterbottom.

(*c*) *Either*

(i) *The Ancient Novel* with special reference to the following texts. Compulsory passages for translation and comment will be set from those in list α.

α Apuleius, *Metamorphoses* I, IV.28–VI.24, IX, XI
Longus, *Daphnis and Chloe*
Heliodorus, *Aethiopica* X.

β Apuleius, *Metamorphoses* II, III, IV.1–27, VI.25–32, VII, VIII, X
[Lucian], *Onos*
Petronius, *Satyrica*
Heliodorus, *Aethiopica* I–IX
Chariton, *Callirhoe.*

or (for Course II candidates only)

(ii) *The Ancient Novel* (Greek version) with special reference to the following texts. Compulsory passages for translation and comment will be set from those in list α.

α Longus, *Daphnis and Chloe*
Heliodorus, *Aethiopica* I–III, IX–X
Chariton, *Chaereas and Callirhoe* I.

β Apuleius, *Metamorphoses*
[Lucian], *Onos*
Petronius, *Satyrica*
Heliodorus, *Aethiopica* IV–VIII
Chariton, *Callirhoe* II–VIII.

or (for Course II candidates only)

(iii) *The Ancient Novel* (Latin version) with special reference to the following texts. Compulsory passages for translation and comment will be set from those in list α.

α Apuleius, *Metamorphoses* I, IV.28–VI.24, VIII–XI
Petronius, *Satyrica* 26.7–78 [*Cena Trimalchionis*].

β Apuleius, *Metamorphoses* II, III, IV.1–27, VI.25–32, VII
[Lucian], *Onos*
Petronius, *Satyrica* 1–26.6, 79–117
Longus, *Daphnis and Chloe*
Heliodorus, *Aethiopica*
Chariton, *Callirhoe.*

III.9 *Greek Textual Criticism* Sophocles, *Ajax* 1–1184
The paper will consist of passages for comment.

III.10 *Latin Textual Criticism*: Ovid, *Heroides* 3, 5, 8, 9, 16, 17
The paper will consist of passages for comment.

III.11 One of the following:

(*a*) *The Conversion of Augustine*. Compulsory passages for translation and comment will be set from Augustine, *Confessions* V – IX. Candidates will also be expected to show knowledge of Symmachus, *Relationes* III; Ambrose, *Epist.* 17–18; Jerome, *Epist.* 22, 38, 45, 107, 127.

(*b*) *Medieval Latin.* Passages for translation and comment will be set from: *Abelard, *Historia Calamitatum* ed. J. Monfrin (Paris, 1967). *Abelard, *Planctus*, sections 'Ad festas choreas caelibes' (Lament for Jephtha's daughter), 'Abissus vere multa' (Lament for Samson), 'Dolorum solatium' (David's Lament for Saul and Jonathan), in the edition of P. Zumthor (Paris, 1992). Geoffrey of Monmouth, *Historia Regum Britanniae*, Bern MS 568, preface and Book 9 (=sections 1–4 and 143–62), ed. N. Wright (Cambridge, 1985). The Archpoet, *Poems*, ed. H. Watenphul/ H. Krefeld (Heidelberg, 1958). *Walter of Châtillon, *Moralisch-satirische Gedichte* 2, 6, 17, 18 ed. K. Strecker (Heidelberg, 1929). *Walter of Châtillon, *Alexandreis* Book II, ed. M. L. Colker (Padua, 1978). *Nivard of Ghent, *Ysengrimus* Book I, ed. J. Mann (Leiden, 1987). *Carmina Burana* 3, 6, 24, 62, 77, 126, 193, 196, 219 ed. A. Hilka and O. Schumann (Heidelberg, 1930–1970).

Candidates will also be expected to show knowledge of: *Fulbert of Chartres, Ep. 29 to Adalbero of Laon, in *The Letters and Poems of Fulbert of Chartres*, ed. F. Behrends (Oxford, 1976). *Peter the Venerable, Ep. 115 to Heloise, in *Selected Letters of Peter the Venerable* ed. J. Martin (Toronto, 1974). *John of Salisbury, Ep. 172 to his brother Richard, in *The Letters of John of Salisbury*, vol. II ed. W. J. Millor and C. N. L. Brooke (Oxford, 1979). Anselm, *Proslogion*, preface and sections 1–10, in *Anselm: Proslogion*, ed. M. J. Charlesworth (Oxford, 1965). St. Bernard of Clairvaux, *Life of St. Malachy*, preface and part I, in *Vita sancti Malachiae*, ed. P.–Y. Émery (Paris, 1990). *Adam of St. Victor, sequences, 'Ave virgo singularis/Mater nostri salutaris' and 'Gaude Sion et laetare', from *Sämtliche Sequenzen*, ed. F. Wellner (2nd edn, Munich, 1955).

[From 1 October 2004:

(*c*) *Byzantine Literature.* Compulsory passages for translation and comment will be set; candidates will be required to take all the passages they offer either from (i) below or from (ii). In their essays, candidates will be expected to show knowledge of both (i) and (ii). Texts will be available in a leaflet from the Classics Office, Classics Centre, 65–67 St Giles'.

(i) [sixth century AD]. Romanos the Melodist, Kontakia 1, 17, and 54, from *Sancti Romani Melodi Cantica: Cantica Genuina*, ed. C. A. Trypanis and P. Maas (Oxford, 1963); Procopius, *Persian Wars* 1.24, 2.22–23, *Gothic Wars* 4.20, *Secret History* 6–12, from *Opera omnia*, ed. J. Haury, rev. P. Wirth (Leipzig, 1962–4); Agathias, Book 1, from *Historiarum libri quinque*, ed. R. Keydell (Berlin, 1967); Agathias, Epigrams 1–24, 66–75, from G. Viansino, *Epigrammi* (Milan, 1967).

(ii) [twelfth century AD]. Anna Komnene, *Alexias*, Book 1, ed. D.-R. Reinsch (Berlin, 2001); Niketas Choniates, *Historia*, Book 4, ed. J.-L. van Dieten (Berlin, 1975); *Digenis Akritis*, Grottaferrata version Book 4, from *Digenis Akritis*, ed. E. M. Jeffreys (Cambridge, 1998); Theodore Prodromos, Poems 3, 4, and 6, from *Historische Gedichte*, ed. W. Hörandner (Vienna, 1974).**]**

(*c*)**[**(*d*)**]** *Modern Greek Poetry.* Candidates will be expected to have read Kavafis, *Poiemata*, and G. Seferis, *Mythistorema, Gymnopaidia, Hemerologio Katastromatos* I–III and *Kichle*. Compulsory passages for translation and comment will be set.

(*d*)**[**(*e*)**]** *The Reception of Greece and/or Rome in British Literature, 1830–1900*

There will be four topics:

1. The Reception of Homer.
2. The Reception of Greek Drama (Aeschylus, Sophocles, Euripides, Aristophanes).
3. The Reception of Virgil and Horace.

---

* Available in a dossier from the Classics Office, 37 Wellington Square.

4. Roman Historical Fictions, with special reference to Lytton, *The Last Days of Pompeii*, Macaulay, *Lays of Ancient Rome*, and Pater, *Marius the Epicurean*.

The examination paper will contain questions on all four topics in Section A, and a broad range of more general questions in Section B. Candidates will be required to answer four questions, including at least one from Section B; they will be required to show knowledge of the reception of either Greece (topics 1 and 2) or Rome (topics 3 and 4), but will have the opportunity to show knowledge of both. English authors whose works may be considered include Arnold, the Brownings, Pater, Ruskin, and Tennyson.

III.12 *Thesis in Literature*

Any candidate may offer a thesis in classical Greek and Latin Literature (excluding the subjects in III.11) in accordance with the Regulation on Theses below. This subject may not be combined with any of I.14, II.199, IV.5 or V.5.

IV. *Greek and Roman Archaeology*

Course I and *Course II*: Candidates may offer *one* or *two* of the following subjects 1–5. Each of subjects 1–4 will be examined in one paper (3 hours).

IV.1 *The Greeks and the Mediterranean World* c.*950* BC–*500* BC

Candidates will be expected to show knowledge of the material evidence from the Greek world and the areas of contact between Greek and other Mediterranean peoples. Areas of emphasis will include Athens and Attica; the non-Greek states bordering the Mediterranean and their reciprocal relationships with the Greeks; Greek colonial settlements; trade and coinage; problems of method and chronology. Knowledge of the principal series of artefacts of the period, their development and problems of method and chronology will be examined.

This subject may not be combined with I.1, *Greek History from 776* BC *to 479* BC.

IV.2 *Greek art and archaeology,* c.*500–300*BC

Candidates will be expected to show knowledge of the architecture, sculpture, and other representational arts of the classical Greek city. Areas of emphasis will include the city of Athens and the historical context and significance of the art and monuments of the period. In the examination candidates will be required to answer one picture question and three others, one each from the following sections: (*a*) architecture, buildings, and urbanism, (*b*) statues, reliefs, temple sculptures, (*c*) painting, painted pottery, and other figured artefacts. Credit will be given for knowledge of relevant material in the Ashmolean Museum and Cast Gallery.

IV.3 *Art under the Roman Empire,* AD *14–337*

The art and visual culture of the Roman empire is studied in its physical, social, and historical contexts. Candidates will be expected to be familiar with major monuments in Rome and Italy and other leading centres of the empire (such as Aphrodisias, Athens, Ephesus, and Lepcis Magna) and with the main strands and contexts of representation in the eastern and western provinces. They will be expected to show knowledge of written evidence where relevant as well as of the main media and categories of surviving images—statues, portrait busts, historical reliefs, funerary monuments, cameos, wallpaintings, mosaics, silverware, and coins.

IV.4 *Roman Archaeology: Cities and Settlement under the Empire*

The subject comprises the study of the Roman city from Augustus to the Tetrarchy placed in the broader context of patterns of rural settlement, agricultural production, transport, and trade. Areas of emphasis include selected key sites (Corinth, Caesarea Maritima, Palmyra, Lepcis Magna, Verulamium [St Albans], and Silchester) and major landscape studies in Italy, Greece, and North Africa. Particular attention is paid to problems and biases in assessing the character of the surviving evidence and in testing theoretical models against physical data. Candidates will be expected to show knowledge of written evidence where relevant as well as of the main categories of surviving ancient material evidence. The subject may not be combined with subject I.12, 'Civic Life of the Roman Empire from the Flavian to the Severan Period'.

IV.5 *Thesis in Greek and Roman Archaeology*

Any candidate may offer a thesis in Greek or Roman Archaeology in accordance with the Regulation on Theses below. This subject may not be combined with any of I.14, II.199, III.12 or V.5.

V. *Philology and Linguistics*

Course I and *Course II*: Candidates may offer *one* or *two* of the following subjects 1–5. Each of subjects 1–4 will be examined in one paper (3 hours).

V.1 *Greek Historical Linguistics*

The paper will consist of two sections: (*a*) the dialects of Greek poetry; Greek dialect inscriptions; Linear B; (*b*) the history of the Greek language with special reference to the development of the literary languages. Candidates must answer questions from both sections. In (*a*) compulsory passages will be set for translation and linguistic commentary.

V.2 *Latin Historical Linguistics*

The paper will consist of two sections: (*a*) Oscan and Umbrian; Archaic Latin; the language of Plautus; Imperial Latin; Late Latin; (*b*) the history of the Latin language; with special reference to the development of the literary language. Candidates must answer questions from both sections. In (*a*) compulsory passages will be set for translation and linguistic commentary. All candidates must answer from *two* of the five parts of (*a*). Lists and/or reproductions of the texts prescribed for section (*a*) are available from the Classics Office, 65–7 St Giles'.

V.3 *General Linguistics and Comparative Philology*

This paper will be divided into three sections: (*a*) General Linguistics; (*b*) synchronic/descriptive analysis of *either* the Greek language *or* the Latin language; (*c*) the reconstruction of Indo-European. Candidates must answer questions from two sections.

V.4 *Comparative Philology: Indo–European, Greek and Latin*

The paper will consist of two sections: (*a*) the methods and aims of historical and comparative linguistics, the reconstruction of the Indo-European protolanguage and its development into Latin and Greek (the questions set will require specific competence in one of the two classical languages, but not necessarily both); (*b*) linguistic commentary on passages of Greek or Latin. Candidates must answer questions from both sections.

This subject may not be offered by any candidate who offered the Special Subject *Historical Linguistics* and *Comparative Philology* in Honour Moderations in Classics or in the Preliminary Examination in Classics.

V.5 *Thesis in Philology and Linguistics*

Any candidate may offer a thesis in Philology and Linguistics in accordance with the Regulation on Theses below. This subject may not be combined with any of I.14, II.199, III.12 or IV.5.

VI. *Second Classical Language*

Second Classical Language is available only in Course II. It comprises two subjects, VI.1 and VI.2, each examined in one 3-hour paper. Candidates who offer Second Classical Language must offer *either both* subjects in Greek *or both* subjects in Latin, and may not offer either subject in the same language as that in which they satisfied the Moderators in Course IIA or IIB of Honour Moderations in Classics or the Preliminary Examination in Classics. In each paper candidates will be required (i) to translate and comment on two passages, one from each of the prescribed texts in the language they offer, and (ii) to translate into English one unseen passage from the language they offer.

VI.1 *Verse*

Either (*a*) Homer, *Iliad* XXIV
Euripides, *Bacchae*.
or (*b*) Virgil, *Aeneid* VI
Ovid, *Metamorphoses* VIII.

VI.2 *Prose*

Either (*a*) Plato, *Symposium* 189c-end
Herodotus I.1–94.
or (*b*) Cicero, *In Catilinam I, Pro Archia*
Seneca, *Epistles* 28, 47, 53, 56, 57, 63, 77, 108, 114, 122.

VII. *Special Theses*

Candidates may offer, but are not required to offer, a Special Thesis in addition to the eight subjects required above, in accordance with the Regulation on Theses below.

Regulation on Theses

1. This regulation governs theses in Ancient History (subject I.14), Literature (III.12), Archaeology (IV.5), Philology and Linguistics (V.5) and Special Thesis (VII). For theses in Philosophy (II.199) see **Regulations for Philosophy in all Honour Schools including Philosophy.**

2. The subject of every thesis shall, to the satisfaction of the board of the faculty, fall within the scope of the Honour School of Literae Humaniores. The subject may but need not overlap any subject or period on which the candidate offers papers. Candidates are warned that they should avoid repetition in papers of material used in their theses and that substantial repetition may be penalized. Candidates who offer a Special Thesis and another thesis must avoid all overlap between them.

3. Candidates proposing to offer a thesis must submit, through their college, to the Chairman of the Board of the Faculty of Classics the title of the proposed thesis, together with (*a*) a synopsis of the subject in about 100 words, (*b*) a statement whether the thesis is to be submitted in Ancient History, or Literature, or Philology and Linguistics, or Archaeology, or as a Special Thesis, and (*c*) a letter of approval from their tutor, not later than the Wednesday of the first week of the Michaelmas Full Term preceding the examination. The faculty board shall decide as soon as possible whether or not to approve the title and shall advise the candidate immediately. No decision shall be deferred beyond the end of the third week of Michaelmas Full Term.

4. Every thesis shall be the candidate's own work. Tutors may, however, assist candidates by discussing with them, for example, the field of study, the sources available, bibliography and the method of presentation, and may also read and comment on drafts. The amount of assistance a candidate may receive shall not exceed an amount equivalent to the teaching of a normal paper. Candidates shall make a declaration that the thesis is their own work, and their tutors shall countersign the declaration confirming that, to the best of their knowledge and belief, this is so. This declaration must be placed in a sealed envelope bearing the candidate's examination number and presented together with the thesis.

5. Theses previously submitted for the Honour School of Literae Humaniores may be resubmitted. No thesis shall be accepted which has already been submitted, wholly or substantially, for another Honour School or degree of this or any other institution, and the certificate shall also state that the thesis has not been so submitted. No thesis shall, however, be ineligible because it has been or is being submitted for any prize of this university.

6. No thesis shall exceed 10,000 words (the limit to include all notes and appendices but not including the bibliography). No person or body shall have authority to permit the limit of 10,000 words to be exceeded, except that, in the case of a commentary on a text and at the discretion of the chairman of examiners, any substantial quoting of that text need not be included in the word limit. Where appropriate, there shall be a select bibliography and a list of sources.

7. All theses must be typed in double spacing on one side only of quarto or A4 paper with any notes and references at the foot of each page, and must be firmly bound and identified by the candidate's examination number only. *Two* copies of the thesis shall be submitted to the examiners.

8. Candidates wishing to change the title of their thesis after it has been approved may apply for permission for the change to be granted by the Chairman of the Board of the Faculty of Classics (if the application is made before the first day of Hilary Full Term preceding the examination) or (if later) the Chairman of the Examiners, Honour School of Literae Humaniores.

9. Candidates shall submit their thesis, identified by the candidate's examination number only, not later than noon on Friday of the week before the Trinity Full Term of the examination to the Examination Schools, High Street, Oxford, addressed to the Chairman of the Examiners, Honour School of Literae Humaniores.

Texts

In addition to editions specified in the above regulations, the following editions will be used in the examination; if more than one impression has appeared, the latest will be used. Where no publisher's name is given, the book is published by the Clarendon Press.

Aeschylus: *Page.
Ambrose: *Epistles*, in Lavarenne, *Prudence*, vol. iii (Budé).
Antiphon: Maidment (Loeb).
Apollonius: Hunter (Cambridge University Press).
Apuleius: Hanson (Loeb).
Aristophanes: *Clouds*, Dover; *Wasps*, MacDowell; *Thesmophoriazousai*, Sommerstein (Aris and Phillips); *Ekklesiazousai*, Usher (Oxford, repr. Bristol Classical Press).
Aristotle: *Nicomachean Ethics*, *Bywater; *Physics*, *Ross; *Poetics*, *Kassel; *Ath.Pol.*, *Kenyon.
Asclepiades: *Page (*Epigrammata Graeca*).
Augustine: *Confessions*, Gibb and Montgomery (Cambridge University Press).
Bacchylides: Snell and Maehler (Teubner).
Callimachus: Pfeiffer.
Catullus: *Mynors.
Caesar: *du Pontet.
Chariton: Goold (Loeb).
Cicero: *De Finibus,* *Reynolds; *De Officiis*, in translation, Griffin and Atkins (*Cicero, On Duties*, Cambridge); *Speeches*, *Clark and Peterson; *Letters*, *Shackleton Bailey and Watt.
Demosthenes: *Butcher and Rennie.
Euripides: *Bacchae*, Dodds; other plays, *Diggle.
Gorgias: *Helen*, MacDowell (Bristol Classical Press).
Heliodorus: Rattenbury and Lumb (Budé).
Hellenica Oxyrhynchia: McKechnie and Kern (Aris and Phillips).
Herodas: Cunningham (Loeb).
Herodotus: *Hude.
Hesiod: *Solmsen.

---

*Oxford Classical Texts.

Homer (including the Homeric Hymns): *Monro and Allen.
Horace: *Wickham and Garrod.
Jerome: Wright (Loeb).
Juvenal: *Clausen.
Kavafis: *Poiemata*, Savidis (Athens, 1975; two volumes).
Livy: *Preface* and Book I, *Ogilvie; XXI, Walsh (University Tutorial Press, repr. Bristol Classical Press).
Longinus: Russell.
Longus: Reeve (Teubner).
Lucan: Housman (Blackwell).
Lucretius: Rouse-Smith (Loeb, 1975 edn. or later).
Menander: *Sandbach.
Ovid: *Heroides*, 18–21, Kenney (Cambridge University Press), others, Showerman rev. by Goold (Loeb); *Ars Amatoria*, Hollis; *Metamorphoses* I–VI Hill (Aris and Phillips), VIII, Hollis; *Fasti*, IV, Fantham (CUP); *Tristia* I, *Owen.
Persius: *Clausen.
Petronius: *Cena Trimalchionis*, Smith.
Pindar: *Bowra.
Plato: *Gorgias*, Dodds; *Symposium*, Dover (Cambridge University Press); *Theaetetus, Sophist*, *Duke et al.; other dialogues, *Burnet.
Plautus: *Bacchides*, Barsby (Aris and Phillips); *Pseudolus*, Willcock (Bristol Classical Press).
Pliny: *Letters*, *Mynors.
Plutarch: *Pelopidas*, Perrin (Loeb).
Polybius: Buttner-Wobst (Teubner).
Propertius: Goold (Loeb).
Sallust: *Reynolds.
Seferis: *Poiemata* (Athens, 1972).
Seneca: *Epistulae Morales* (in Philosophy), *Reynolds; *Epistles* (in Second Classical Language), Summers (*Select Letters*, Macmillan, repr. Bristol Classical Press); *De Constantia*, *De Vita Beata*, *Reynolds; *Apocolocyntosis*, Eden (Cambridge University Press); *Phaedra*, Coffey and Mayer (Cambridge University Press); *Thyestes*, Tarrant (American Philological Association).
Sextus Empiricus: Bury (Loeb).
Sophocles: *Lloyd-Jones and Wilson.
Statius, *Thebaid* 9: Dewar; *Achilleid*: *Garrod.
Suetonius; Ihm (Teubner, *ed. min.*).
Symmachus; *Relationes*, in Lavarenne, *Prudence*, vol. iii (Budé).
Tacitus: *Dialogus*, *Winterbottom; *Annals* and *Histories*, *Fisher; *Agricola,* *Ogilvie.
Terence: *Eunuchus*, Barsby (CUP); *Heauton Timorumenos*, Brothers (Aris and Phillips).
Theocritus: Dover (Macmillan, repr. Bristol Classical Press).
Thucydides: *Stuart Jones.
Virgil: *Mynors.
Xenophon: *Marchant.

PASS SCHOOL OF LITERAE HUMANIORES

Candidates for the Pass Degree in Literae Humaniores must satisfy the examiners in any five subjects listed in the Regulations for the Honour School of Literae Humaniores. Their selection of subjects must meet *either* the conditions which apply to Course I *or* the conditions which apply to Course II of the Honour School; except that (i) not more than *three* subjects may be offered from any one of the branches I–III, (ii) at least *two* of the subjects offered must be text-based, (iii) persons who have satisfied the Moderators in Course IA, IB or IC of Honour Moderations in Classics or of the Preliminary Examination in Classics may not offer either of the subjects in (VI) Second Classical Language, and (iv) no candidate may offer a Special Thesis.

---

*Oxford Classical Texts.

SPECIAL REGULATIONS FOR THE HONOUR SCHOOL OF MATERIALS ECONOMICS, AND MANAGEMENT

A

1. The subjects of the honour school shall be (*a*) Materials, (*b*) Economics, and (*c*) Management.

2. All candidates must offer (*a*), (*b*), and (*c*). The examination in all three subjects may be partly practical.

3. No candidate shall be admitted to examination in this school unless he or she has either passed or been exempted from the First Public Examination.

4. The examination in this school shall be under the joint supervision of the Mathematical and Physical Sciences Board and the Social Sciences Board. The standing joint committee set up in accordance with the sub-section relating to the Honour School of Engineering, Economics, and Management shall have power to make regulations concerning this school, subject always to the preceding clauses of this sub-section.

5. The examination shall consist of two parts. In both parts candidates shall be examined in the subjects prescribed by the committee set up in accordance with the provisions of clause 4 above. In Part II candidates shall also present, as part of the examination, a report on a project carried out during a period of attachment to an industrial firm, or an industrially-related internal university project.

6. The name of a candidate in this school shall not be published in a class list unless he or she has been adjudged worthy of Honours by the examiners in Part I and in Part II of the respective examinations in consecutive years, and no candidate may present himself or herself for examination in Part II unless he or she has been adjudged worthy of Honours by the examiners in Part I.

7. A candidate adjudged worthy of Honours in Part I and Part II may supplicate for the Degree of Master of Engineering provided that he or she has fulfilled all the conditions for admission to a degree of the University as specified in Ch. I, Sect. 1 §1, cl.1.

8. The examiners for Materials shall be appointed by the committee for the nomination of Public Examiners in Materials Science in the Honour School of Natural Science; those for economics shall be appointed by the committee for the nomination of examiners in

Economics in the Honour School of Philosophy, Politics, and Economics; those for Management shall be appointed by the committee for the nomination of examiners in Management Studies for the Degree of Master of Philosophy.

B

Part I

Candidates will be required to take six papers as follows:

(*a*) *Materials Science*

The four general papers of three hours each on the fundamental principles and engineering applications of the subject as specified for Part I of the Honour School of Natural Science: Materials Science.

(*b*) *Economics*

One paper, E1, *The Organization of Production* as specified for Part I of the Honour School of Engineering, Economics, and Management.

(*c*) *Management*

One paper, M1, *Introduction to Management*, as specified for Part I of the Honour School of Engineering, Economics, and Management. Candidates may be charged for the provision of study packs.

In the case of written papers in Materials Science, candidates are restricted to models of hand-held calculators approved by the Sub-faculty of Materials. For all other written papers, the examiners will permit the use of any hand-held calculator subject to the conditions set out under the heading 'Use of calculators in examinations' in the *Special Regulations concerning Examinations*.

In addition to the written papers, candidates shall submit detailed reports of the practical work in Materials completed during their course of study. Such reports should be handed into the Chairman of the Examiners in the Honour School of Materials, Economics, and Management, c/o Clerk of the Schools, Examination Schools, High Street, Oxford not later than 5 p.m. on the Friday of the seventh week of Trinity Full Term. The Head of the Department of Materials or his deputy, shall make available to the examiners evidence showing the extent to which each candidate has pursued an adequate course of practical work.

[Until 1 October 2004: (*for candidates embarking on the Honour School in or before October 2002*) The examiners shall require evidence of satisfactory practical work (including a team design project) in Materials over a period of five terms subsequent to the sitting of the first public examination. The details of the team design project will be specified in the Course Handbook.**]**

[From 1 October 2004: (*for candidates embarking on the Honour School in or after October 2003*) The examiners shall require evidence of satisfactory practical work (including a team design project and reports on a number of industrial visits) in Materials over a period of five terms subsequent to the sitting of the first public examination. The details of both the team design project, and the number and definition of industrial visits and the nature of the subsequent reports, will be specified in the Course Handbook.**]** The examiners shall take this evidence and the reports of the candidates into consideration as part of the Part I examination and they shall have power to require a practical examination of any candidate.

Each candidate may be examined viva voce.

Candidates will be required to keep statutory residence for an additional week immediately after the end of Hilary Full Term in the year in which the Part I examination is taken in order to prepare for the projects to be carried out as part of the Part II examination.

[Until 1 October 2004: (*for candidates embarking on the Honour School in or before October 2002*) Candidates will be required to undertake a period of attachment to an industrial firm of not less than six weeks in the Long Vacation of the academic year after that in which the First Public Examination is taken. The work carried out during this attachment shall be on a topic with substantial materials science or materials engineeering content.

The industrial attachment must be approved by the Materials Project Co-ordinator. Candidates will be required to present a report, not exceeding 2,000 words in length, on their work carried out during this period of attachment. Such reports shall be delivered to the Chairman of the Examiners in Materials, c/o Clerk of the Schools, Examination School, High Street, Oxford, not later than noon on Monday of the first week of the Hilary Full Term preceding the Part I examination.]

Schedule

PART II

Candidates will be required to present a report on a project carried out during a twenty-four week period of attachment to an industrial firm, or an industrially related internal university project, and to take three papers. In addition they may take a fourth paper, though those choosing not to do so will not thereby be precluded from the award of Honours at the highest level.

The three required papers are as follows:

(*a*) *Materials*

One option paper of three hours, which will contain a wide choice of questions. The subject for this paper will be published annually by the Chairman of the Sub-faculty of Materials who will put up a notice in the Department of Materials not later than Monday of the last week of the Trinity Term preceding the academic year in which the options are given. The Chairman will also indicate suitable courses of lectures.

(*b*) *Economics* (*c*) *Management*

Two papers, E2 *The National Economy*, and either E3, E4, E5, or one of the M papers, as specified for Part II of the Honour School of Engineering, Economics, and Management, other than M1.

The regulations on the use of calculators in Part I also apply in Part II.

Candidates will be required to undertake a twenty-four week period of attachment to an industrial firm, or an internal university project, between the end of the Trinity Full Term in the year in which the Part I examination is held and the beginning of Hilary Full Term in the year in which the Part II examination is held. This twenty-four week project shall always include the period from the fifth Friday before to the first Saturday following Michaelmas Full Term. Candidates will be required to present, as part of the Part II examination, a report on a project carried out during this period under the supervision of a person approved by the standing committee for the school.

The industrial or industrially related attachment and project required for the course will normally be arranged by, and must be approved by, the Management Project Co-ordinator.

The report shall not exceed 20,000 words.

Two copies of the report on the project must be submitted by noon on the Friday of the week before the start of Hilary Full Term in the year in which the Part II examination is held, addressed 'The Clerk of the Schools, High Street, Oxford, OX1 4BG, for the Chairman of the Examiners in the Honour School of Materials, Economics, and Management', and should be accompanied by a signed statement by the candidate that it is his or her own work. Successful candidates will be required to deposit one copy of the report in the library of the Department of Materials and the other in the library of the Business School. Project reports previously submitted for the Honour School of Materials, Economics, and Management may be re-submitted. No project report will be accepted if it has already been submitted, wholly or substantially, for another Honour School or degree of this University, or for a degree of any other institution.

Candidates may be examined viva voce on any part of their course of study, including their project.

PASS SCHOOL OF MATERIALS, ECONOMICS, AND MANAGEMENT

Candidates for the Pass School of Materials, Economics, and Management shall satisfy the examiners in (i)–(v) below:

(i)–(iii) any three of the four papers in Materials Science as specified for the Honour School of Materials, Economics, and Management, Part I;

(iv) Economics paper E1 and Management paper M1, as specified for the Honour School of Engineering, Economics, and Management, Part I;

(v) the detailed reports of practical work in Materials completed during their course of study as specified for the Honour School of Materials, Economics, and Management, Part I.

The examiners will permit the use of any hand-held calculator subject to the conditions set out under the heading 'Use of calculators in examinations' in the *Special Regulations concerning Examinations*.

[Until 1 October 2004: [*for candidates embarking on the Honour School in or before October 2002*]

SPECIAL REGULATIONS FOR THE HONOUR SCHOOL OF MATHEMATICAL SCIENCES

A

1. The subjects of examination in the Honour School of Mathematical Sciences shall be Mathematics and its applications, including Statistics, together with certain other cognate disciplines.

2. No candidate shall be admitted to examination in this school without having first either passed or been exempted from the First Public Examination.

3. The examination in this school shall be under the supervision of the Divisional Board of Mathematical and Physical Sciences.

4. The Board shall have power to issue a syllabus of the subjects in which candidates shall be examined, and to vary the same from time to time.

B

1. The examination will consist of Sections a, b, and o. Seven papers will be set in Section a and ten in Section b. The subjects available in Section o will be those listed in the Schedule below, together with those published by the Department of Mathematics in a supplement to the handbook for candidates not later than the Michaelmas Term of the year preceding the academic year in which the relevant examination is held. Any extended essay, dissertation or practical work which may be required for a Section o subject, unless subject to other regulations, shall be submitted to the Chairman of Examiners, FHS of Mathematical Sciences and Mathematics Part I, Examination Schools. The deadline for such submissions, and other details, will be published at the same time as the list of subjects available.

2. (*a*) Every candidate shall either take eight papers or take seven papers and submit an extended essay.

   (*b*) Every candidate shall take Paper a1 and Paper a2 and at least two of Papers a3–a7.

   (*c*) Every candidate shall take at least one but not more than three papers from Section b.

   (*d*) Every candidate shall take at least one but not more than two papers from Section o.

3. (*a*) Each of papers a1–a6 and each paper from Section b, except Papers b1, b8, b9 and b10, will contain eight questions.

   (*b*) Paper b1 will contain nine questions of which eight questions will be set on the material not drawn from the last paragraph of the schedule for that Paper.

   (*c*) Paper b8 will contain seven questions

   (*d*) Paper b10 will contain four questions on each of an approved list of subjects, which will be revised each year by the Board in Trinity Term, two years in advance of the examination.

(*e*) Approval of Section o subjects, other than for the extended essay, will be given by the Teaching Committee of the Department of Mathematics by not later than the Michaelmas Term of the year preceding the academic year in which the relevant examination is held. Candidates are not permitted to offer a paper they have previously offered for another examination in the University, other than for the Honour School of Mathematical Sciences.

4. (*a*) None of the Papers a3, a4, a5, a6 shall require knowledge of the subjects of any of the other three.

(*b*) Each paper from b1–b8, shall not require knowledge from any other Section b paper.

5. Each of papers a1–a6, b1–b7, b10 will be of three hours' duration; Paper b8 will be of two and a half hours' duration.

6. Candidates offering Paper b8 shall be assessed as to their practical ability under the following provisions.

(*a*) The Head of the Department of Statistics, or a deputy, shall make available to the examiners evidence showing the extent to which each candidate has pursued an adequate course of practical work.

(*c*) Candidates shall submit to the Chairman of the Examiners, Honour School of Mathematical Sciences, Examination Schools, Oxford, by noon on Monday of the fifth week of the Trinity Term in which the examination is held, their reports on practical exercises completed during their course of study. For a report on an exercise to be considered by the examiners, it must be signed by a demonstrator and must be accompanied by a statement that it is the candidate's own work except where otherwise indicated.

(*d*) The examiners shall take the evidence (*a*) and reports, (*b*) into account in assessing the candidate's performance.

7. *Extended essay* (subject o2)

(*a*) *Subject, authorship, and format* The subject of the extended essay shall be a topic either in mathematics or in the applications of mathematics in another field. Every essay shall be the candidate's own work. The candidate's tutor, or a person of equivalent seniority approved by the Chairman of the Projects Committee of the Teaching Committee of the Department of Mathematics, may discuss with the candidate the field of study, recommend references, discuss presentation and read and comment on a first draft. Candidates shall sign a certificate to the effect that the essay is their own work, except as permitted by this regulation or where acknowledgement is made, and this certificate shall be placed in a sealed envelope bearing the candidate's examination number and presented together with the essay. Essays should be typed and must be held firmly in a stiff cover. Its length should not exceed the equivalent of 7,500 words (excluding diagrams, tables, references, and texts of computer programs).

(*b*) *Approval of topic* Candidates intending to offer an extended essay shall, after consultation with their tutors, submit through their colleges to the Chairman of the Projects Committee of the Teaching Committee of the Department of Mathematics in the Mathematical Institute the title that they propose together with

— an explanation (of at least 100 words) of the subject of the essay. This should be sufficient for the members of the committee to judge whether the project is of appropriate depth and whether it is possible to find a suitable assessor in the University. If possible, candidates should include details of the *main* references – books, papers, etc.

— a letter of approval from the candidate's tutor or other person approved under (*a*) above.

No essay will be accepted if it has already been submitted, wholly or substantially, for a final honour school other than Mathematical Sciences under subject 02 or for another degree of this University, or for a degree of any other institution.

The application shall be made not earlier than the first day of Trinity Full Term in the year preceding the examination and not later than Friday of third week of the Michaelmas Full Term preceding the examination. The Teaching Committee of the Department of Mathematics will decide as soon as possible, and in any case not later than Monday of the seventh week of Michaelmas Full Term preceding the examination, whether or not to approve the proposal, and will advise the candidate forthwith. Details of approved subjects shall be forwarded by the chairman of the committee to the Chairman of Examiners not later than the first day of the following Hilary Full Term.

(*c*) *Submission* Essays (two copies), identified by the candidate's examination number only, must be sent to the Chairman of Examiners, Honour School of Mathematical Sciences, Examination Schools, Oxford, to arrive not later than noon on the Friday of the first week following the end of the Hilary Full Term preceding the examination. At the same time, the tutor or other person approved under (*a*) above shall submit to the Chairman of Examiners a confidential report the purpose of which is to assist the examiners to determine how much assistance the candidate has received in the preparation of the essay; this report will be on a form supplied for the purpose by the Chairman of Examiners. A candidate may withdraw notice of submission of an essay at any time and shall be deemed to have done so if the essay is not submitted by the time and date specified unless a special dispensation is received from the Proctors.

The examiners will give an essay the weight of one paper.

8. The use of calculators is generally not permitted but certain kinds may be allowed for certain papers. Specifications of which papers and which types of calculators are permitted for those exceptional papers will be announced by the examiners in the Hilary Term preceding the examination.

Schedule

Paper a1: Linear Algebra and Differential Equations

Linear Algebra

Vector spaces, subspaces, direct sums; projection operators. Dual spaces of finite-dimensional spaces [the natural isomorphism between a space and its second dual is excluded]; dual transformations, and their matrix representation with respect to dual bases; triangular form. The theory of a single linear transformation on a finite-dimensional space: characteristic polynomial, minimal polynomial, the Cayley–Hamilton theorem; minimal polynomial and diagonalisability [the Primary Decomposition Theorem is excluded].

Real and complex inner product spaces: examples of finite- and infinite-dimensional spaces, including function spaces and their inner products [excluding completeness]; orthonormal bases in finite-dimensional inner product spaces; Bessel's inequality and the Cauchy–Schwarz inequality; orthogonal complements; the Gram–Schmidt process. The dual space of a finite-dimensional inner product space. The adjoint of a linear transformation; eigenvectors, eigenvalues and diagonalisability of a self-adjoint linear transformation on a finite-dimensional inner product space; spectral theorem (self-adjoint case only).

Differential equations

Reformulation of first- and second-order ordinary differential equations as integral equations. Picard's method, with application to the iterative solutions of Fredholm and Volterra integral equations and existence and uniqueness of solutions of first-order ordinary differential equations. Picard's theorem for a system of first-order ordinary differential equations [proof excluded], with application to the second-order linear equation.

The second-order linear homogeneous equation, Wronskians. The second-order non-homogeneous linear equation: variation of parameters, Green's function for equations with homogeneous boundary conditions.

First-order quasi-linear partial differential equations: characteristics, informal discussion of existence and uniqueness of solutions with given Cauchy data, domains of definition.

Solutions in series to second-order ordinary differential equations, including elementary discussion of ordinary and regular singular points, and the possibility that the roots of the indicial equation differ by an integer. Bessel functions and Legendre polynomials.

Paper a2: Complex Analysis and Geometry

Geometry and topology of the complex plane; equivalence of connectedness and path connectedness of open subsets [without proof]; the Riemann sphere. Holomorphic functions of one complex variable; Cauchy–Riemann equations. Power series; differentiation of power series. Uniform convergence, continuity of limit, Weierstrass' M-test. Integrals along paths; interchange of limit and integral. Cauchy's Theorem [no proof]. Cauchy's formulae, Liouville's Theorem. Taylor's Theorem (including multiplication of power series). Morera's Theorem. Zeros of holomorphic functions; Identity Theorem. Laurent series, classification of singularities, residues. Cauchy's Residue Theorem, simple examples. Informal treatment of branches of the logarithm. [The following are not included: Maximum Modulus Theorem, 'Principle of the Argument', Rouché's Theorem.]

Transforms: basic properties of the Laplace transform and the discrete and continuous Fourier transforms; inversion and convolution theorems [no proofs in continuous case]. Application to solution of second order ordinary differential equations and of the diffusion equation. Techniques of contour integration, including use of Jordan's Lemma and indentations; applications to the inversion of Fourier and Laplace transforms and summation of series.

Conformal mapping. Möbius transformations; powers and exponentials [Joukowski transformation excluded]. Mappings of regions bounded by circlines.

Curves: arc length, curvature, torsion, Serret–Frenet formulae. Parameterised surfaces: examples, including surfaces of revolution; first fundamental form, isometries, areas; second fundamental form, principal curvatures and directions, geodesic and normal curvatures of curves on a surface; geodesics.

Paper a3: Algebra

The action of a group on a set. Orbits, transitivity, coset spaces. Examples, including groups acting on themselves by translation and conjugation, the standard actions of the linear and orthogonal groups. Symmetric and alternating groups; the action of the symmetry groups of the Platonic solids. Formula for counting orbits, combinatorial applications.

Rings, commutative rings with unity, integral domains. Subrings, homomorphism, ideals. The rings $\mathbf{Z}$ and $K[X]$ as Euclidean domains, and the principal ideal property. Definition of a field; vector spaces over arbitrary fields.

Quotient groups, rings, and vector spaces, and the associated homomorphism theorems. Primary decomposition theorem. Maximal ideals and the associated quotients. The construction, given the natural number system, of the integers, rational numbers, real numbers and complex numbers (construction of the real numbers from the rational numbers via Cauchy sequences). Unique factorisation in the ring of integers and in the ring of polynomials in a single indeterminate. Factorisation in $\mathbf{Z}[X]$: Gauss' Lemma and Eisenstein's criterion.

Field extensions. Finite extensions, algebraic elements, algebraic extensions, transitivity of algebraicity. Construction of simple algebraic extensions. Existence of splitting fields, uniqueness [without proof]; examples. Application to ruler and compass constructions. Finite fields.

Paper a4: Analysis and Topology

Analysis

The Lebesgue integral on the real line, null sets [technical results on the construction of the integral not examinable.] Properties of the integral. Simple examples of non-integrable functions.

The Monotone Convergence Theorem [proof not examinable] and deduction of the Dominated Convergence Theorem; applications. Examples of integrable functions and of improper integrals. Integrals of complex-valued functions. Measurable functions [proof of equivalence of alternative definitions excluded]; comparison theorem for integrability. The Dominated Convergence Theorem with a continuous parameter; examples of continuity and differential of functions defined by integrals. The Lebesgue integral in two dimensions; the theorems of Fubini and Tonelli; simple form of change of variables theorem [no proof]; examples. Fourier series: Riemann–Lebesgue lemma; Dirichlet kernel, Riemann localization theorem, Dini's test, pointwise convergence of the Fourier series of a piecewise smooth function; Fejér's theorem, Weierstrass' approximation theorem.

Topology

Definition of a topological space in terms of the family of open sets. Subspaces. Closed sets, closure, limit points. Continuous mappings, homeomorphisms. Hausdorff spaces.

Compact subsets. Heine–Borel Theorem. Connected subsets. The characterisation of connected subsets of the real line. Pathwise connected subsets, the equivalence of connexion and pathwise connexion of open subsets of the real plane.

The product of two topological spaces, projection mappings. The theorem that the product of two compact spaces is compact; the theorem that the product of two connected spaces is connected. Quotient spaces.

Sequential compactness, completeness and total boundedness in metric spaces. The set of continuous functions on a compact interval with the sup metric. Uniform continuity in metric spaces.

Paper a5: Non-Physical Applied Mathematics

Probability

Random variables and their distribution; joint distribution, conditional distribution; functions of one or more random variables. Generating functions and applications. Characteristic functions, definition only. Statements of the continuity and uniqueness theorems for moment generating functions. Chebychev and Markov inequalities. The weak law of large numbers and central limit theorem for independent identically distributed variables with a second moment.

Discrete-time Markov chains: definition, transition matrix, n-step transition probabilities, communicating classes, absorption, irreducibility, calculation of hitting probabilities and mean hitting times, recurrence and transience. Invariant distributions, mean return time, positive recurrence, convergence to equilibrium, time reversal. Examples of applications in areas such as: genetics, branching processes, Markov chain Monte Carlo.

Poisson processes in one dimension: exponential spacings, Poisson counts, thinning and superposition.

Statistics

Data summaries. Method of moments, maximum likelihood estimation for multi-parameter models, distributions of maximum and minimum order statistics, iterative calculation of maximum likelihood estimates, information inequality, statement of asymptotic distribution of maximum likelihood estimator in single parameter case. Joint distribution of sample mean and variance of a normal random sample. Exact confidence intervals, approximate confidence intervals.

Hypothesis tests, simple and composite hypotheses, p-value, type I and II errors, Neyman-Pearson lemma, likelihood ratio and composite hypotheses. Likelihood ratio statistic, statement of its asymptotic null distribution, z-test, t-test, chi-squared test (normal variance), F-test (ratio of normal variances). Relationship between tests and confidence intervals.

Goodness of fit: examining modeling assumptions, probability plotting, intuitive approach using $F(X) \sim U(0, 1)$, chi-squared goodness of fit test. Transformations using ladder of powers, informal approach to robustness and outliers.

Scatterplots, correlation. Linear regression, least squares and maximum likelihood estimation, use of matrices, generalization to multiple regression. Distributions of estimators of regression coefficients and residual sum of squares under normal assumptions, derivation of variance estimator, hypothesis tests for coefficients, associated confidence intervals, and prediction intervals. Examining assumptions, analysis of residuals, and informal treatment of leverage, outliers. One-way analysis of variance.

Paper a6: Physical Applied Mathematics

Classical Mechanics

Lagrange's equations for conservative systems subject to holonomic constraints. Applications to particle motion. Rigid bodies; degrees of freedom, Euler angles, inertia tensor, principal moments, angular momentum and kinetic energy. Application of Lagrange's equations to tops and other simple systems [excluding use of vector equations of motion]. Normal modes and normal frequencies for small oscillations near equilibrium. Hamilton's equations, Hamiltonian for conservative systems and as constant of motion. Hamilton's Principle. Poisson brackets. Limitations of classical mechanics.

Fluid Dynamics

Mass conservation for a compressible fluid. Convective derivative, streamlines, particle paths. Euler's equation. Vorticity, circulation and Kelvin's theorem. Irrotational flow. Velocity potential, Bernoulli's equation. Two-dimensional flow, stream function, complex potential. Line sources and vortices. Images, circle theorem. Blasius' theorem. Conformal mappings—development of examples from Paper a2. Joukowski transformation for flat plate [excluding lenses and general aerofoil]. Flow past a flat plate at incidence. Lift and circulation.

Stokes waves on uniform stream of constant depth. Dispersion [questions on group velocity excluded]. Linearised theory of sound waves in one dimension and with spherical symmetry.

Paper a7: Numerical Analysis

(as specified for paper 1.6 of the FHS of Computer Science)

Paper b1: Foundations

Set Theory and Computability

Naïve axiomatic set theory; cartesian products, relations and functions. Axiom of Infinity and the construction of the natural numbers; induction and the recursion theorem. Cardinality; finite, countable and uncountable sets; Cantor's Theorem; the Schröder–Bernstein Theorem. Linear orders and well-orders: order-isomorphism, dense linear order. Transfinite induction and recursion. Comparability of well-orders. Equivalence of the Axiom of Choice, Zorn's Lemma and the Well-Ordering Principle; comparability of cardinals. Ordinals. Arithmetic of cardinals and ordinals.

The register machine model of computability; Church's Thesis. Decision problems; the *s-m-n* Theorem. Undecidability of the halting problem and other problems.

Logic

The notation, meaning and use of propositional and predicate calculus. The formal language of propositional calculus: truth functions; conjunctive and disjunctive normal form; tautologies and logical consequence. The formal language of predicate calculus: satisfaction, truth, validity, logical consequence. Deductive system for propositional calculus: proofs and theorems; Soundness and Completeness Theorems. Statement of Soundness and Completeness Theorems for a deductive system for predicate calculus; derivation of the Compactness Theorem; simple applications of the Compactness Theorem.

Analysis of a deductive system for predicate calculus: proofs and theorems; proof of Completeness Theorem; existence of countable models.

Paper b2: Algebra

Commutative rings with identity: integral domains and their fields of fractions, Euclidean domains, principal ideal domains and unique factorisation domains. Quadratic extensions of the rational number field: rings of integers, norms, factorisations and elementary applications to number theory.

Finitely generated modules over a euclidean domain, with particular reference to abelian groups and to finite-dimensional vector spaces and their endomorphisms. Cyclic modules, annihilators, primary decompositions, existence and uniqueness of cyclic decompositions. Elementary divisors of a matrix and the computation of Smith normal form. Applications: Jordan and rational canonical forms for a linear transformation; finitely generated abelian groups.

Cauchy's theorem for finite groups. Dihedral groups and their subgroups; the symmetric group S_4 and its subgroups. Jordan–Hölder theorem for finite groups. Soluble groups and the characterisation of finite soluble groups by composition factors. The simplicity of the alternating groups and insolubility of the symmetric groups of degree $\geqslant 5$.

Finite algebraic extensions of fields in characteristic zero; theorem of the primitive element, normal extensions, splitting fields, Galois groups and the fundamental theorem of Galois theory. Computation of Galois groups in simple cases. Solution of equations by radicals. Finite fields; their subfields and automorphisms.

Paper b3: Geometry

Geometry of Surfaces

The concept of a 2-manifold; examples, including polygons with pairs of sides identified and Riemann surfaces. Orientation and the Euler characteristic. Classification theorem for closed surfaces (the proof will not be examined).

Surfaces in $\mathbf{R}^3$ (including statement of the Implicit Function Theorem). The Gauss map. The concept of a Riemannian 2-manifold. Gaussian curvature and mean curvature. Theorema Egregium. Geodesics. The Gauss–Bonnet Theorem. The hyperbolic plane, its isometries and geodesics. Compact surfaces of constant negative curvature.

Projective Geometry

Projective spaces and their duals, homogeneous and non-homogeneous coordinates. Projective transformations, the cross-ratio.

Conics and quadrics and their parameterisations. Simultaneous diagonalisation of quadratic forms. The projective model of the hyperbolic plane. Exterior algebra, subspaces and decomposable vectors. The geometry of the Klein quadric.

Paper b4: Analysis

Real and complex normed vector spaces, their geometry and topology. Finite-dimensional normed spaces. Completeness; Banach spaces, in particular l^1, l^∞, L^1, $C(K)$. Separable spaces. Continuous linear functionals; dual spaces. Hahn–Banach Theorem [proof for real separable spaces only] and applications. Hilbert spaces; completeness of l^2, L^2. Orthogonality, orthogonal complement. Projection theorem. The Riesz Representation Theorem.

Orthonomal sets, Pythagoras' Theorem, Bessel's inequality. Complete orthonormal sets, Parseval's formula. Convergence in L^2 norm. Completeness of trigonometric systems. Orthogonal expansions; examples. The L^2-theory of the Fourier transform. Plancherel Theorem. Hermite functions as eigenfunctions. Inversion theorem for the L^2 Fourier transform. Bounded linear operators, examples. Adjoint operators. Spectrum and resolvent. Spectral mapping theorem for polynomials. Operators on Hilbert space, adjoint operators. Self-adjoint operators, orthogonal projections. Unitary operators; the Fourier transform as a unitary operator.

Paper b5: Applied Analysis

Integral and Differential Equations

Fredholm alternative for degenerate kernels. Hilbert–Schmidt theory for equations with symmetric kernels: orthonormal families, Bessel's inequality and eigenvalues, the expansion theorem [proof of the existence of an eigenvalue and of the expansion theorem excluded]. Iterative methods and Neumann series applied to Fredholm integral equations.

Calculus of variations: Euler's equation as a necessary condition. Extension to a finite number of dependent functions and their derivatives, a finite number of independent variables, integral and non-integral constraints and varying boundary conditions. Applications to geometry and mechanics.

Sturm–Liouville theorem, with application to eigenfunction expansions. Bessel functions and Legendre, Hermite and Laguerre polynomials as examples of singular systems of solutions. Sturm–Liouville equation derived from a variational principle.

Plane autonomous systems of ordinary differential equations: phase-plane and critical points, linear systems, elementary non-linear systems and linearisation. Bendixson-Dulac criterion.

Partial Differential Equations

Nonlinear first-order equations. Charpit's method. Classification of second-order quasilinear partial differential equations and transformation to canonical form.

Hyperbolic equations in two variables, Cauchy data, characteristic domains and uniqueness, Riemann function. Applications to wave equation, telegraph equation. Extension to hyperbolic systems. Discontinuities. Weak solutions.

Elliptic equations (applications to potential theory, Poisson's equation, Helmholtz equation). Maximum principles and uniqueness. Green's functions in two dimensions for circle and half-plane.

Parabolic equations, the diffusion equation for heat and chemical reactions. Maximum principles, uniqueness, similarity solutions.

Paper b6: Theoretical Mechanics

Viscous Flow

Derivation of Navier–Stokes equations for an incompressible Newtonian fluid. Exact solutions for unidirectional flows; shear flow, Poiseuille flow, Rayleigh flow. Couette flow between rotating cylinders. Vorticity. Energy equation and dissipation. Simple examples. Jeffrey–Hamel flow. Dimensional analysis, Reynolds number. Derivation of equations for high and low Reynolds number flows.

Slow flow past a circular cylinder, nonuniformity of the approximation, Oseen's equation. Lubrication theory for a slider bearing and squeeze film.

Derivation of Prandtl's boundary layer equations. Similarity solution for flow past a semi-infinite flat plate. Discussion of separation and application to the theory of flight.

Waves and Compressible Flow

Euler equations referred to rotating axes. Rossby number. Rossby waves, Taylor–Proudman theorem. Applications to atmospheric and oceanic flows (descriptive). Dispersion in gravity waves, group velocity.

Equations of inviscid compressible gas, elementary thermodynamics. One-dimensional steady flow in a slowly varying nozzle. One-dimensional unsteady flow. Nonlinear wave propagation, method of characteristics, simple wave flows. Shock waves, Rankine–Hugoniot equations. Oblique shocks, description of subsonic and supersonic flow past a thin two-dimensional wing.

Paper b7: Mathematical Physics

Quantum Theory

The Schrödinger equation; interpretation of the wave function; probability density and current. States and observables; expectation values of observables. Potential wells and barriers, tunnelling, parity.

The one-dimensional harmonic oscillator. Oscillators in two and three dimensions. Degeneracy of energy levels. The hydrogen atom with fixed nucleus.

Commutation relations. Poisson brackets and Dirac's quantisation scheme. Heisenberg's uncertainty principle for position and momentum.

Creation and annihilation operators for the harmonic oscillator. Measurements and the interpretation of quantum mechanics, Bell's inequalities and simple 'paradoxes'.

Relativity and Electromagnetism

Lorentz transformations and the invariance of the wave operator; time dilatation, length contraction and the relativistic Doppler effect.

Four-vectors; four-velocity and four-momentum; equivalence of mass and energy. Particle collisions and four-momentum conservation. Four-acceleration and four-force.

Maxwell's equations *in vacuo* (with sources); the Lorentz force law. Scalar and vector potentials; the four-potential. Gauge invariance; Maxwell's equations in Lorentz gauge. Plane waves and their polarization. Energy density and the Poynting vector.

The electromagnetic field tensor. The transformation law for the electric and magnetic field. The Lorentz four-force law.

Paper b8: Statistics

Simulation: pseudo-random numbers, inversion, rejection, composition, ratio-of-uniforms and alias methods, computational efficiency.

Practical aspects of linear models: review of multiple regression, model selection, fit criteria, use of residuals, outliers, leverage, Box–Cox transformation, added-variable plots, model interpretation.

Logistic regression. Linear exponential families and generalized linear models, scale parameter, link functions, canonical link. Maximum likelihood fitting and iterated weighted least squares. Asymptotic theory: statement and applications to interference, analysis of deviance, model checking, and residuals. Examples: binomial, Poisson and gamma models.

Robust statistics. Univariate methods, robust regression (M-estimation), resistant regression.

Computer-intensive statistics. Smoothing methods (kernels, splines, local polynomials). Boot-strapping. Monte Carlo tests.

Paper b9: Numerical Solution of Differential Equations (as specified for paper b9 in FHS of Mathematics and Computer Science).

Paper o2: Extended essay

Paper o6: History of Philosophy from Descartes to Kant (as specified for subject 101 in Philosophy in all Honour Schools)

Paper o7: Knowledge and Reality (as specified for subject 102 in Philosophy in all Honour Schools)

Paper o8: Philosophy of Mathematics (as specified for subject 122 in Philosophy in all Honour Schools). No candidate will be permitted this option who is not offering paper b1.

PASS SCHOOL OF MATHEMATICAL SCIENCES

1. Candidates will be required to offer the following elements of the examination for the Honour School of Mathematical Sciences:

Papers a1, a2 and a further four papers/subjects taken from Sections a, b and o, provided that not more than one subject may be taken from Section o.

2. The use of calculators is generally not permitted but certain kinds may be allowed for certain papers. Specifications of which papers and which types of calculators are permitted for those exceptional papers will be announced by the examiners in the Hilary Term preceding the examination.

NOTES

NOTES

NOTES

NOTES

SPECIAL REGULATIONS FOR THE HONOUR SCHOOL OF MATHEMATICS

A

In the following 'the Course Handbook' refers to the Mathematics Undergraduate Handbook and supplements to this published by the Mathematics Teaching Committee and also posted on the website at http://www.maths.ox.ac.uk/current-students/undergraduates/handbooks-synopses.

1. The subject of the Honour School of Mathematics shall be Mathematics and its applications.

2. No candidate shall be admitted to examination in this School unless he or she has either passed or been exempted from the First Public Examination.

3. The Examination in Mathematics shall be under the supervision of the Mathematical and Physical Sciences Board. The Board shall have the power, subject to this decree, from time to time to frame and vary regulations for the different parts and subjects of the examination.

4. (*a*) The examination in Mathematics shall consist of three parts (A, B, C) for the four-year course, and of two parts (A, B) for the three-year course.
   (*b*) Parts A, B, and C shall be taken at times not less than three, six, and nine terms, respectively, after passing or being exempted from the First Public Examination.

5. The name of a candidate on either the three-year course or the four-year course shall not be published in a Class List until he or she has completed all parts of the respective examination.

6. (*a*) In order to proceed to Part B, candidates must pass Part A. The examiners will publish a pass list for Part A.
   (*b*) In order to proceed to Part C, a candidate must achieve Honours standard in Part A and Part B together. A list of candidates satisfying this requirement shall be published by the Examiners.
   (*c*) A candidate on the three-year course who obtains only a Pass or fails to satisfy the Examiners in Part B may retake Part B on at most one subsequent occasion; a candidate on the four-year course who obtains only a Pass or fails to satisfy the Examiners in Part C may retake Part C on at most one subsequent occasion.

7. A candidate adjudged worthy of Honours on both Parts A and B together, and on Part C may supplicate for the degree of Master of Mathematics if he or she has fulfilled all the conditions in the General Regulations for Admission to Degrees Awarded on Passing the Second Public Examination.

B

1. In Part A each candidate shall be required to offer the four written papers from the schedule of papers for Part A (see 'Schedule' below).

2. In Part B each candidate shall offer a total of four units from the schedule of units and half units for Parts B and C (see 'Schedule' below).
   (*a*) A total of at least three units offered should be from the schedule of 'Approved units and half units' (i.e. those units and half units which have been approved by the Teaching Committee of the Department of Mathematics).
   (*b*) At most one unit may be offered from those designated as M level.

3. In Part C each candidate shall offer a total of three units from the schedule of units and half units for Parts B and C (see below).
   (*a*) All three units offered should be from those designated as M level.
   (*b*) A total of at least two of the units offered should be from the schedule of 'Approved units and half units' (i.e. those units and half units which have been approved by the Teaching Committee of the Department of Mathematics).

4. Each unit of half unit on the schedule of Approved units and half units, other than an extended essay or dissertation, will be examined by an examination paper or mini-project.

5. Each candidate on the four-year course shall offer at least one half unit on the schedules of Approved units for Part B and Part C which is an extended essay, dissertation or assessed by a mini-project.

6. The use of calculators is generally not permitted for written papers. However, their use may be permitted for certain exceptional examinations. The specification of calculators permitted for these exceptional examinations will be announced by the Examiners in the Hilary Term preceding the examination.

Schedule

Papers in Part A

AC1 Algebra, Analysis and Differential Equations
AC2 Algebra, Analysis and Differential Equations
AO1 Options
AO2 Options

Syllabus details will be published in the Course Handbook by the beginning of the Michaelmas Full Term in the academic year of the examination for Part A.

Units and half units for Part B [from October 2004] and Part C [from October 2005]

Provisional lists of 'Approved' (i.e. approved by the Teaching Committee of the Department of Mathematics), Other Mathematics, and Other Non-Mathematical units and half units will be published in the *Examination Regulations*. Not all listed units and half units will be available each year and some extra units and half units may be added. The final list of units and half units will be published in the Course Handbook by the beginning of the Michaelmas Full Term in the academic year of the examination concerned, together with the following details.

1. Designation as either 'H' level or 'M' level.

2. 'Weight' as either a whole unit or half-unit.

3. Method of assessment (as either extended essay, dissertation, mini-project or examination paper). Details of methods of assessment for Other Mathematics or Other Non-Mathematical units or half units delivered by other faculties or departments will be given elsewhere. The Course handbook will indicate where such details will be specified.

4. Rules governing submission of any extended essay, dissertation or mini-project, including deadlines, provided that these shall always be submitted to the Chairman of Examiners, Honour School of Mathematics, c/o the Clerk of the Schools, Examination Schools, High Street, Oxford.

5. Syllabus content.

6. Whether there is a requirement to register or apply for a place to take a unit or half unit, and details of any registration or application procedure.

PASS SCHOOL OF MATHEMATICS

1. Candidates will be required to offer the following elements of the examination for the Honour School of Mathematics: Paper AC1 Algebra, Analysis and Differential Equations; Paper AC2 Algebra, Analysis and Differential Equations; Paper AO1 Options; Paper AO2 Options; and 2 units from the schedule for Part B, of which at least one and a half units must be 'Approved' units.

2. The use of calculators is generally not permitted for written papers. However, their use may be permitted for certain exceptional examinations. The specification of calculators permitted for these exceptional examinations will be announced by the Examiners in the Hilary Term preceding the examination.]

NOTES

[Until 1 October 2005: [*for candidates embarking on the Honour School in or before October 2002*]

SPECIAL REGULATIONS FOR THE HONOUR SCHOOL OF MATHEMATICS

A

1. The subjects of examination in the Honour School of Mathematics shall be Mathematics and its applications, including Statistics.

2. No candidate shall be admitted to examination without having first either passed or been exempted from the First Public Examination.

3. The name of a candidate in the Honour School of Mathematics shall not be published in a Class List unless that candidate has been adjudged worthy of Honours by the examiners in Part I and Part II of the respective examinations in consecutive years, and no candidate may enter the Part II examination unless previously adjudged worthy of Honours by the examiners in Part I.

4. A candidate adjudged worthy of Honours in Part I and Part II may supplicate for the Degree of Master of Mathematics provided that he or she has fulfilled all the conditions for admission to a degree of the Univesity as spcified in Ch. I, Sect. I, § 1, cl. 1.

5. The examination shall be under the supervision of the Divisional Board of Mathematical and Physical Sciences.

6. The Board shall have power to issue a syllabus of the subjects in which candidates shall be examined, and to vary the same from time to time.

B

1. The examination will be in two parts. The papers in Part I will be those prescribed for Sections a and b in the Honour School of Mathematical Sciences; and certain of the Section o subjects approved for this Honour School. Section o subjects which are available to candidates will be identified when the Section o subjects for the Honour School of Mathematical Sciences are approved (and published as a supplement to the handbook for candidates) in the Michaelmas Term preceding the academic year in which the examination is held. Part II will consist of four papers set in Section c.

2. (*a*) Every candidate shall take eight papers in Part I.
 (*b*) Every candidate shall take Paper a1 and paper a2 and shall also take two, three, or four papers from papers a3–a7.
 (*c*) Every candidate shall take two, three, or four papers from Section b and Section o of which a maximum of one may be from Section o.

3. (*a*) Each paper from Section a, and each paper from Section b, except Papers b1, b8, b9 and b10, will contain eight questions.

(*b*) Paper b1 will contain nine questions (as specified for the Honour School of Mathematical Sciences).

(*c*) Paper b8 will each contain seven questions.

(*d*) Paper b10 will contain four questions on each of an approved list of subjects, which will be revised each year by the Board in Trinity Term, two years in advance of the examination.

4. (*a*) None of the Papers a3, a4, a5, a6 shall require knowledge of the subjects of any of the other three.

(*b*) Each paper from b1–b8, shall not require knowledge from any other Section b paper.

5. Candidates offering Paper b8, and such of the subjects of Section c as are designated to contain a practical element, shall be assessed as to their practical ability under the following provisions.

(*a*) Concerning Paper b8 and Section c subjects in Statistics, the Head of the Department of Statistics, or a deputy, shall make available to the examiners evidence showing the extent to which each candidate has pursued an adequate course of practical work.

(*b*) Candidates shall submit to the Chairman of the Examiners, Honour School of Mathematics, Examination Schools, Oxford, by noon on Monday of the fifth week of the Trinity Term in which the examination is held, their reports of practical exercises completed during their course of study. For a report on an exercise to be considered by the examiners, it must be signed by a demonstrator and must be accompanied by a statement that it is the candidate's own work except where otherwise indicated.

(*c*) The examiners shall take the evidence (*a*) and reports (*b*), into account in assessing the candidate's performance.

6. In Section c, candidates are required to offer one of the following:

(1) Four papers: c1, c2, c3 and c4. The subjects of the papers will be

(*a*) the subjects of an approved list of lecture courses, which will be revised each year by the Teaching Committee of the Department of Mathematics and be published in a supplement to the handbook for candidates in Trinity Term for the following academic year, and

(*b*) additional subjects proposed by candidates and approved by the Teaching Committee of the Department of Mathematics not later than its second meeting of Michaelmas Term (a candidate who wishes to propose an additional subject must make the proposal through his or her college to the Chairman of the Mathematics Teaching Committee, Mathematical Institute, not later than the Friday of the fifth week of the Michaelmas Full Term preceding the examination). These must be either the subjects of other lecture courses or subjects specified by detailed syllabuses submitted by the candidate. Candidates will be promptly advised of the Teaching Committee's decision. Details of the specially approved subjects shall be forwarded by the Chairman of the Teaching Committee to senior mathematics tutors and the Chairman of the Examiners not later than the first day of Hilary Full Term.

(*c*) Papers c1 and c2 will each contain two questions on each of the subjects of approved lecture courses given in Michaelmas Term. Papers c3 and c4 will each contain two questions on each of the subjects of approved lectures courses given in Hilary Term and of additional subjects approved under (*b*) above.

(2) Subject to the approval of the Teaching Committee of the Department of Mathematics, three papers: c1, c2 and c5, and a dissertation

(*a*) The subjects of Paper c5 will be taken from those specified above for Papers c3 and c4. Candidates shall choose not more than two approved subjects and on entering for the examination by the date prescribed must give notice of their choice to the Registrar. The paper will contain four questions on each subject for which such notice is given.

(*b*) *Dissertation*

(i) *Subject, authorship, and format*

The subject of the dissertation shall be a project which shall be supervised by a member of the Faculty of Mathematical Sciences or, in exceptional circumstances, by some other person of equivalent seniority approved by the Chairman of the Projects Committee of the Teaching Committee. Every dissertation shall be the candidate's own work; it may, for example, be a computation based on known results or a critical review of published mathematics. The supervisor may discuss with the candidate the field of study, recommend references, and discuss what methods are appropriate: the supervisor may also read and comment on a first draft. Candidates shall sign a certificate to the effect that the dissertation is their own work, except as permitted by this regulation or where acknowledgement is made, and this certificate shall be placed in a sealed envelope bearing the candidate's examination number and presented together with the dissertation. Dissertations should be typed. and must be held firmly in a stiff cover. Its length should not exceed the equivalent of 10,000 words (excluding diagrams, tables, references, and texts of computer programs).

(ii) *Approval of topic*

Candidates intending to offer a dissertation shall, after consultation with their tutors, submit through their colleges to the Chairman of the Projects Committee of the Teaching Committee of the Department of Mathematics in the Mathematical Institute the title that they propose together with

— a brief description (of at least 100 words) of the project which will be the subject of the dissertation. This should be sufficient for the members of the committee to judge whether the project is of appropriate depth and whether it is possible to find a suitable assessor in the University. If possible, candidates should include details of the *main* references – books, papers, etc.;

— a letter of approval from the person who has agreed to act as supervisor (a potential supervisor may be approached either by the candidate or through the candidate's tutor: alternatively advice may be sought at an earlier stage from the Projects Committee).

No dissertation will be accepted if it has already been submitted, wholly or substantially, for a final honour school, other than Mathematics or Mathematics and Philosophy as specified under Option (i), or for another degree of this University, or for a degree of any other institution.

The application shall be made not earlier than the first day of Trinity Full Term in the year preceding the examination and not later than Friday of the third week of the Michaelmas Full Term preceding the examination. The Teaching Committee of the Department of Mathematics will decide as soon as possible, and in any case not later than Monday of the seventh week of the Michaelmas Full Term preceding the examination, whether or not to approve the proposal, and will advise the candidate forthwith. Details of approved projects shall be forwarded by the chairman of the committee to the Chairman of the Examiners not later than the first day of the following Hilary Full Term.

(iii) *Submission*

Dissertations (two copies), identified by the candidate's examination number only, must be sent to the Chairman of the Examiners, Honour School of Mathematics, Examination Schools, Oxford, to arrive not later than noon on the Friday of the first week following the end of the Hilary Full Term preceding the examination. At the same time, the supervisor shall submit to the Chairman of the Examiners a confidential report the purpose of which is to assist the examiners to determine how much assistance the candidate has received in the preparation of the dissertation; this report will be on a form supplied for the purpose by the Chairman of the Examiners. A candidate may withdraw notice of submission of a dissertation at any time and shall be deemed to have done so if the dissertation is not submitted by the time and date specified unless a special dispensation is received from the Proctors.

7. Candidates offering Papers c1, c2, c3, and c4 can gain the highest honours by preparing no more than six Section c subjects. The examiners will give a dissertation the weight of two Section c subjects.

8. The duration of papers in sections a, b, o shall be as prescribed for the FHS of Mathematical Sciences; each of papers c1–c4 will be of three hours' duration; Paper c5 will be of two hours' duration.

9. The use of calculators is generally not permitted but certain kinds may be allowed for certain papers. Specifications of which papers and which types of calculators are permitted for those exceptional papers will be announced by the examiners in the Hilary Term preceding the examination.

PASS SCHOOL OF MATHEMATICS

1. Candidates will be required to offer the following elements of the examination for the Honour School of Mathematics: Papers a1, a2, and a further four papers-/subjects taken from Sections a, b and approved subjects in Section o of which a maximum of one may be from Section o in Part I, together with four subjects from Section c in Part II. A candidate may offer a dissertation in place of two of the four Section c subjects, in accordance with the regulations for a dissertation in the Honour School of Mathematics.

2. The use of calculators is generally not permitted but certain kinds may be allowed for certain papers. Specifications of which papers and which types of calculators are permitted for those exceptional papers will be announced by the examiners in the Hilary Term preceding the examination.]

SPECIAL REGULATIONS FOR THE HONOUR SCHOOL OF MATHEMATICS AND COMPUTER SCIENCE

[*for candidates embarking on the Honour School in or after October 2003*]

A

1. (1) The subject of the Honour School of Computer Science shall be Mathematics and the theory and practice of Computer Science.

   (2) The examination in Mathematics and Computer Science shall consist of two parts (A, B) as prescribed by the Board of the Division of Mathematical and Physical Sciences.

2. (1) The name of a candidate shall not be published in a class list until he or she has completed both parts of the examination.

   (2) The Examiners in Mathematics and Computer Science shall be entitled to award a pass or classified Honours to candidates in the Second Public Examination who have reached the appropriate standard; the Examiners will give due consideration to the performance of candidates in both parts of the examination.

   (3) A candidate who obtains only a pass or fails to satisfy the Examiners may enter again for Part B of the examination on one, but not more than one, subsequent occasion.

3. All candidates will be assessed as to their practical ability under the following provisions:

   (1) The Director of the Computing Laboratory, or a deputy, shall make available to the examiners evidence showing the extent to which each candidate has pursued an adequate course of practical work.

   (2) Candidates for each part of the examination shall submit to the Chairman of the Examiners, Honour School of Mathematics and Computer Science, c/o the Clerk of the Schools, Examination Schools, Oxford, by noon on Monday of the fifth week of the Trinity Term in which the examination is being held, their reports of practical exercises completed during their course of study. For a report on a practical exercise to be considered by the examiners, it must have been marked by a demonstrator and must be accompanied by a statement that it is the candidate's own work except where otherwise indicated.

(3) The examiners shall take the evidence (*a*) and (*b*) into account in assessing a candidate's performance.

4. No candidate shall be admitted to examination in this school unless he or she has either passed or been exempted from the First Public Examination.

5. In order to proceed to Part B, candidates must pass Part A. The examiners will publish a pass list for Part A.

6. (1) The Examination in Mathematics and Computer Science shall be under the supervision of the Board of the Division of Mathematics and Physical Sciences.

(2) The Board shall have power, subject to this decree, from time to time to frame and vary regulations for the different parts and subjects of the examination.

B

The syllabus for each paper will be published by the Computing Laboratory in a handbook for candidates by the beginning of Michaelmas Full Term in the academic year of the examination for Part A, after consultation with the Subfaculty of Mathematics and the Subfaculty of Computation. This handbook shall apply to both Part A and Part B of the examination.

The use of calculators is generally not permitted but certain kinds may be allowed for certain papers. Specifications of which papers and which types of calculators are permitted for those exceptional papers will be announced by the examiners in the Hilary Term preceding the examination.

1. The examination shall be in two parts, A and B, taken at times not less than three and six terms, respectively, after passing or being exempted from the First Public Examination.

2. In Part A of the examination, candidates shall be required to offer four papers as follows.

AC1(MC) Algebra and analysis ($2\frac{1}{4}$ hours)

AC2(MC) Algebra and analysis ($2\frac{1}{4}$ hours)

AO1(MC) Mathematics options ($1\frac{1}{2}$ hours)

AO2(MC) Mathematics options ($1\frac{1}{2}$ hours)

Candidates shall also be required to offer one of the following two papers.

CS4 Object-oriented programming (3 hours),

CS5 Concurrency, networks and operating systems (3 hours).

In addition, each candidate shall be required to offer two optional subjects in Computer Science from Schedule A in the Course Handbook, each to be examined by a paper of one and a half hours' duration.

3. In Part B of the examination, each candidate shall be required to offer eight optional subjects, chosen from Schedules B1, B2, and B3 in the course handbook. The choice of optional subjects shall be subject to the following conditions.

(*a*) no more than two subjects shall be chosen from Schedule B1.

(*b*) no candidate shall offer any subject from Schedule B1 that he or she has already offered in Part A of the examination.

(*c*) at least two subjects shall be chosen from Schedules B1 and B2.
(*d*) at least two subjects shall be chosen from Schedule B3.

Each optional subject in Schedules B1 and B2 shall be examined by a paper of one and a half hours' duration. The manner of examining each subject in Schedule B3 shall be the same as that prescribed for the same subject in the Honour School of Mathematics.

4. The schedules of optional subjects for Parts A and B of the examination shall be approved by the Subfaculty of Mathematics and the Subfaculty of Computation, and shall be published in the Course Handbook.

5. The examiners shall have power to combine two papers on related optional subjects in Computer Science into a single paper of three hours' duration for those candidates who offer both the optional subjects concerned.

PASS SCHOOL OF MATHEMATICS AND COMPUTER SCIENCE

1. Candidates shall be required to offer the following parts of the examination for the Honour School of Mathematics and Computer Science:

For Part A,

(*a*) Papers AC1(MC) and AC2(MC).
(*b*) Either Paper CS4 or Paper CS5.
(*c*) Either Papers AO1(MC) and AO2(MC) or two optional subjects chosen from Schedule A in the course handbook.

For Part B,

(*d*) Two optional subjects chosen from Schedules B1 and B2 in the course handbook, with the restriction that no subject from Schedule B1 shall be offered by any candidate who has offered the same subject in Part A of the examination.
(*e*) Two optional subjects chosen from Schedule B3 in the course handbook.

2. Candidates shall be assessed as to their practical ability under the regulations set out for the Honour School of Mathematics and Computer Science.

NOTES

[Until 1 October 2004: [*for candidates embarking on the Honour School in or after October 2002*]

SPECIAL REGULATIONS FOR THE HONOUR SCHOOL OF MATHEMATICS AND COMPUTER SCIENCE

A

1. The subjects of the examination shall be Mathematics and Computation.

2. No candidate shall be admitted to the examination in this school unless he or she has either passed or been exempted from the First Public Examination.

3. The examination in this school shall be under the supervision of the Divisional Board of Mathematical and Physical Sciences.

4. The Board shall have power to issue a syllabus of the subjects in which candidates shall be examined, and to vary the same from time to time.

5. (i) The examiners for Mathematics in this school shall be one to be nominated by the nominators in Mathematics and such of the examiners in the Honour School of Mathematics as may be required being not less than four; those for Computation shall be appointed by the committee for the nomination of examiners in Computation.

(ii) It shall be the duty of the chairman of the examiners in the Honour School of Mathematics to designate such of their number as may be required for Mathematics in the Honour School of Mathematics and Computer Science. When this has been done, and the other examiner for Mathematics and the examiners for Computation have been nominated, the number of examiners in Mathematics and Computer Science shall be deemed to be complete.

B

1. The examination will consist Sections a(MC), b(MC), I and II(MC). The papers of Sections a(MC) will be Papers a1–a6 of the Final Honour School of Mathematical Sciences. The papers of Section b(MC) will be Papers b1–b8 and b10 of the Final Honour School of Mathematical Sciences, together with those set out in the Schedule. The papers of Section I will be the papers of Section I of the Final Honour School of Computer Science. The subjects of papers in Section II(MC) will be those approved in Trinity Term two years in advance of the examination.

The subjects of Section II(MC), together with the information relating to practicals and lengths of papers required under paragraphs 6 and 7 below, shall be published in the *University Gazette*.

2. (*a*) Every candidate shall take eight papers, or shall take seven papers and undertake a project.

(*b*) Every candidate shall take at least two, but not more than four, papers from Section a(MC).

(*c*) Every candidate shall take one or two papers from Section b(MC).

(*d*) Every candidate shall take at least two, but no more than four, papers from Section I.

(*e*) Every candidate shall take one or two papers from Section II(MC).

3. No paper from Section II(MC) shall require knowledge of the subject of any other Section II(MC) paper.

4. Each of the papers, inclusive of practicals where relevant, will be given equal weight by the examiners. The project will be given the weight of one paper.

5. Each project must be on a topic in computation approved by the Teaching Committee of the Computing Laboratory. Each project will be supervised by a member of the Sub-faculty of Computation, the Sub-faculty of Mathematics or the Sub-faculty of Engineering Science, or by some other person of equivalent seniority approved by the Teaching Committee. Two copies of a report of the project shall be submitted to the Chairman of Examiners, Honour School of Mathematics and Computer Science, Examination Schools, Oxford, by noon on Monday of the fifth week of the Trinity Term in which the examination is held. The report must not exceed 6,000 words plus twenty-five pages of additional text (e.g. diagrams, program text).

Projects previously submitted for the Honour School of Computer Science or the Honour School of Mathematics and Computer Science may be resubmitted. No project may be resubmitted if it has already been submitted, wholly or substantially, for another honour school or degree of the University, or for a degree of any other institution.

6. Candidates who offer the respective papers will be assessed as to their practical ability in the subjects of Paper b8, the subjects of those papers so indicated in the Schedule, and such of the subjects of Section II(MC) as shall be determined when the subjects of this section are approved each Trinity Term, under the following provisions.

(*a*) Concerning Paper b8, the Head of the Department of Statistics, or a deputy, shall make available to the examiners evidence showing the extent to which each candidate has pursued an adequate course of practical work.

(*b*) The Director of the Computing Laboratory, or a deputy, shall make available to the examiners evidence showing the extent to which each candidate has pursued an adequate course of practical work in each of those practical subjects offered from Section I and Section II (MC).

(*c*) Candidates shall submit to the Chairman of the Examiners, Honour School of Mathematics and Computer Science, Examination Schools, Oxford, by noon on Monday of the fifth week of the Trinity Term in which the examination is held, their reports of practical exercises completed during their course of study. For a report to be considered by the examiners, it must be signed by a demonstrator and must be accompanied by a statement that it is the candidates own work except where otherwise indicated.

(*d*) The examiners shall take the evidence (*a*) and (*b*) and the reports (*c*) into account in assessing the candidate's performance on the papers to which the work relates. The extent to which practical marks will be counted towards the total for each paper in Section I is specified in the regulations for the Honour School of Computation as a proportion of the total. Proportions for subjects in Section II(MC) will be published with the list of these subjects.

7. Each written paper will be of three hours' duration except for Sections a(MC) and b(MC), where otherwise specified in the regulations for the Honour School of

Mathematical Sciences, or, for Section I, where otherwise specified in the regulations for the Honour School of Computer Science or, in Section II(MC), where specified when the list of these subjects is determined.

8. The use of calculators is generally not permitted but certain kinds may be allowed for certain papers. Specifications of which papers and which types of calculators are permitted for those exceptional papers will be announced by the examiners in the Hilary Term preceding the examination.

Schedule

Paper b9: Numerical solution of differential equations

No practicals. Paper of 3 hours.

Initial value problems for ordinary differential equations: Euler, multistep and Runge—Kutta methods; stiffness; error control and adaptive algorithms.

Boundary value problems for ordinary differential equations: shooting, finite differences.

Boundary value problems for partial differential equations: finite difference discretisations; Poisson equation. Associated methods of sparse numerical linear algebra: sparse Gaussian elimination, classical and conjugate gradient iterations, multigrid iterations.

Initial value problems for partial differential equations: parabolic equations, hyperbolic equations; explicit and implicit methods; accuracy, stability and convergence, Fourier analysis, CFL condition.

PASS SCHOOL OF MATHEMATICS AND COMPUTER SCIENCE

1. Candidates shall be required to offer the following parts of the examination for the Honour School of Mathematics and Computer Science:

Three papers from Section a(MC), and either any three papers from Section I or any two papers from Section I and a project. The regulations governing projects shall be those prescribed for the Honour School of Mathematics and Computer Science.

2. Candidates shall be assessed as to their practical ability in the subjects of each paper offered from Section I where so indicated in the Schedule, under the regulations set out for the Honour School of Mathematics and Computer Science.

3. The use of calculators is generally not permitted but certain kinds may be allowed for certain papers. Specifications of which papers and which types of calculators are permitted for those exceptional papers will be announced by the examiners in the Hilary Term preceding the examination.]

NOTES

SPECIAL REGULATIONS FOR THE HONOUR SCHOOL OF MATHEMATICS AND PHILOSOPHY

[for candidates embarking on the Honour School in or after October 2003]

A

In the following 'the Mathematics Course Handbook' refers to the Mathematics Undergraduate Handbook and supplements to this published by the Teaching Committee of the Department of Mathematics and also posted on the website at http://www.maths.ox.ac.uk/current-students/undergraduates/handbooks-synopses/.

1. All candidates shall be examined in Mathematics and in Philosophy.

2. No candidate shall be admitted to the examination in this School unless he or she has either passed or been exempted from the First Public Examination.

3. (*a*) The examination in Mathematics and Philosophy shall consist of three parts:
Part A, Part B and Part C.

(*b*) Parts A, B and C shall be taken at times not less than three, six, and nine terms, respectively, after passing or being exempted from the First Public Examination.

4. (*a*) The name of a candidate in this school shall not be published in a Class List until he or she has completed all parts of the examination.

(*b*) In order to proceed to Part C, a candidate must achieve Honours standard in Part A and Part B together. A list of candidates satisfying this requirement shall be published by the Examiners.

(*c*) A candidate who obtains only a Pass or fails to satisfy the Examiners in Part C may enter again for Part C on at most one subsequent occasion.

5. The examinations in this school shall be under the joint supervision of the Divisional Board of Mathematical and Physical Sciences and the Board of the Faculty of Philosophy, which shall appoint a standing joint committee to make regulations concerning it, subject in all cases to clauses 1–4 above.

6. (*a*) The Public Examiners for Mathematics in this school shall be such of the Public Examiners in the Honour School of Mathematics as may be required, not being less than three; those for Philosophy shall be appointed by a committee

whose three elected members shall be appointed by the Board of the Faculty of Philosophy.

(*b*) It shall be the duty of the chairmen of the Public Examiners in Parts A, B and C of the Honour School of Mathematics to designate such of their number as may be required for Mathematics in the Honour School of Mathematics and Philosophy, and when this has been done and the examiners for Philosophy have been nominated, the number of the examiners in Mathematics and Philosophy shall be deemed to be complete.

B

1. In **Part A** each candidate shall be required to offer the three written papers in *Mathematics* from the schedule of papers for Part A (see 'Schedule' below). Each paper will be of $2\frac{1}{4}$ hours' duration.

2. In **Part B** each candidate shall offer

(i) a total of at least two units in *Mathematics* from the schedule of 'Approved units and half units' (i.e. those units and half units which have been approved by the Teaching Committee of the Department of Mathematics) for Part B and Part C for the Honour School of Mathematics (see 'Schedule' below), of which one must be *Foundations* as specified for the Honour School of Mathematics, and

(ii) at least three subjects in *Philosophy* from subjects 101–18, 120–2 as prescribed in the Regulations for Philosophy in all Honour Schools including Philosophy, of which two must be subjects 102 and 122, such that

(iii) the total number of units and subjects together is six.

At most one unit in *Mathematics* at level M is permitted in Part B.
Each subject in *Philosophy* shall be examined in one 3-hour paper.

3. In **Part C**, each candidate shall offer one of the following options:

Option (*i*) *Mathematics*
Option (*ii*) *Mathematics and Philosophy*
Option (*iii*) *Philosophy*

No unit or half unit in *Mathematics* may be offered in both Part B and Part C. Each subject in *Philosophy* except subject 199 *Thesis* will be examined in one 3-hour paper. No subject in Philosophy may be offered in both Part B and Part C, and subjects must be selected in conformity with the Regulations for Philosophy in all Honour School including Philosophy.

Option (*i*) *Mathematics*

Candidates must offer a total of three units in *Mathematics* at level M from the schedule of units and half units for Parts B and C (see 'Schedule' below).

Option (*ii*) *Mathematics and Philosophy*

Candidates must offer

— a total of one and a half units in *Mathematics* at level M from the schedule of units and half units for Parts B and C (see 'Schedule' below), and

— two subjects in *Philosophy* chosen from subjects 101, 103–18, 120, 121, and 199 in the Regulations for Philosophy in all Honour Schools including Philosophy. Each subject in *Philosophy* shall be examined in one 3-hour paper, except 199. The examiners shall give the same weight to the one and a half units in *Mathematics* taken together as to the two subjects in *Philosophy* taken together.

Option (iii) Philosophy

Candidates must offer four subjects in *Philosophy* chosen from subjects 101, 103–18, 120, 121, and 199 in the Regulations for Philosophy in all Honour Schools including Philosophy. Each subject in *Philosophy* shall be examined in one 3-hour paper, except 199.

4. For the award of the highest honours it is not necessary to perform with excellence in each of *Mathematics* and *Philosophy* separately.

5. The use of calculators is generally not permitted for written papers. However, their use may be permitted for certain exceptional examinations. The specification of calculators permitted for these exceptional examinations will be announced by the Examiners in the Hilary Term preceding the examination.

Schedule

Papers in Part A

AC1(P) Algebra and Analysis
AC2(P) Algebra and Analysis
AO3(P) Options

Syllabus details will be published in the Mathematics Course Handbook by the beginning of the Michaelmas Full Term in the academic year of the examination for Part A.

Units and half units in Mathematics for Part B [from October 2004] and Part C [from October 2005]

See the Special Regulations for Honour School of Mathematics for a provisional list of 'approved units and half-units' (i.e. those units and half units which have been approved by the Teaching Committee of the Department of Mathematics).

Provisional lists of 'approved' units and half units in *Mathematics* will be published in the *Examination Regulations*. Not all listed 'approved' units and half units will be available each year and some extra units and half units may be added. The list of units and half units for level M shall include units in Mathematical Logic as specified by the Joint Committee for Mathematics and Philosophy. The final list of 'approved' units and half units will be published in the Mathematics Course Handbook by the beginning of the Michaelmas Full Term in the academic year of the examination concerned.

PASS SCHOOL OF MATHEMATICS AND PHILOSOPHY

1. Candidates will be required to offer the following elements of the examination for the Honour School of Mathematics and Philosophy:
   (i) Paper AC1(P) Algebra and Analysis, Paper AC2(P) Algebra and Analysis, Paper AO3(P) Options, and *Foundations* in *Mathematics*, and
   (ii) three subjects in *Philosophy* from subjects 101–18, 120–2, and 199 as prescribed in the Regulations for Philosophy in all Honour Schools including Philosophy, of which two must be subjects 102 and 122.

2. The use of calculators is generally not permitted for written papers. However, their use may be permitted for certain exceptional examinations. The specification of calculators permitted for these exceptional examinations will be announced by the Examiners in the Hilary Term preceding the examination.

NOTES

[Until 1 October 2005: [*for candidates embarking on the Honour School in or before October 2002*]

SPECIAL REGULATIONS FOR THE HONOUR SCHOOL OF MATHEMATICS AND PHILOSOPHY

A

1. All candidates shall be examined in Mathematics and in Philosophy.

2. No candidate shall be admitted to examination in this school unless he or she has either passed or been exempted from the First Public Examination.

3. The name of a candidate for the Honour School of Mathematics and Philosophy shall not be published in a Class List unless that candidate has been adjudged worthy of Honours by the examiners in Part I and Part II of the respective examinations in consecutive years, and no candidate may enter the Part II examination unless previously adjudged worthy of Honours in Part I.

4. The examination in this school shall be under the joint supervision of the Divisional Board of Mathematical and Physical Sciences and the Faculty Board of Philosophy, which shall appoint a standing joint committee to make regulations concerning it, subject always to the preceding clauses of this subsection.

5. (i) The Public Examiners for Mathematics in this school shall be such of the Public Examiners in the Honour School of Mathematics as may be required, not being less than three; those for Philosophy shall be appointed by a committee whose three elected members shall be appointed by the Board of the Faculty of Philosophy.

(ii) It shall be the duty of the chairman of the Public Examiners in the Honour School of Mathematics to designate such of their number as may be required for Mathematics in the Honour School of Mathematics and Philosophy, and when this has been done and the examiners for Philosophy have been nominated, the number of the examiners in Mathematics and Philosophy shall be deemed to be complete.

B

1. The examination will be in two parts, Part I and Part II. Each of Parts I and II will consist of two subject areas, *Mathematics* (which shall include Mathematical Logic) and *Philosophy*.

2. Part I will contain the following subjects:

Mathematics

Seventeen subjects a1–a7 and b1–b10 as prescribed for papers a1–a7 and b1–b10 in the Honour School of Mathematical Sciences.

Philosophy

Subjects 101–18, 120–2 as prescribed in the Regulations for Philosophy in all Honour Schools including Philosophy.

3. Each candidate is required to offer eight subjects in Part I, which must include:
—at least three subjects in *Mathematics*, of which one must be subject b1 and two must be chosen from subjects a1–a7, and
—at least three subjects in *Philosophy*, of which two must be subjects 102 and 122.

4. In Part II each candidate is required to offer one of the *Options* specified in the Schedule. *Option* (*i*) counts as four subjects in *Mathematics, Option* (*ii*) counts as two subjects in *Mathematics* and two subjects in *Philosophy*, and *Option* (*iii*) counts as four subjects in *Philosophy*.

5. No subject may be offered in both Part I and Part II. Subjects must be selected in such a way that in Parts I and II taken together at least four subjects are in *Mathematics* and at least three subjects are in *Philosophy*. Subjects in *Philosophy* must be selected in conformity with the Regulations for Philosophy in all Honour Schools including Philosophy.

6. Candidates must give notice to the Registrar of their choice of subjects in Part I of the examinations not later than Friday of the eighth week of the Michaelmas Full Term preceding that part of the examination.

Candidates for Part II must give notice to the Registrar of their choice of *Option* not later than Friday of the eighth week of the Michaelmas Full Term preceding that part of the examination, and those offering *Option* (*ii*) or *Option* (*iii*) must at the same time specifiy their choice of subjects in *Philosophy*.

7. For the award of the highest honours it is not necessary to perform with excellence in each of *Mathematics* and *Philosophy* separately.

8. The use of calculators is generally not permitted but certain kinds may be allowed for certain papers. Specifications of which papers and which types of calculators are permitted for those exceptional papers will be announced by the examiners in the Hilary Term preceding the examination.

Schedule of Subjects

Part I

Mathematics

The syllabuses for each of the sixteen subjects a1–a7 and b2–b10 in the Honour School of Mathematical Sciences and each subject shall be examined in the manner prescribed for these papers. The syllabus for subject b1 will be as specified for Paper b1 of the Honour School of Mathematical Sciences. It will be examined in a 3-hour paper containing eight questions.

Philosophy

The syllabuses for subjects 101–118, 120–122 will be as specified in the Regulations for Philosophy in all Honour Schools including Philosophy. Each subject will be examined in one 3-hour paper.

Part II

Each candidate shall be required to offer one of the following options.

Option (i) Mathematics
Option (ii) Mathematics and Philosophy
Option (iii) Philosophy

Option (i) Mathematics

Candidates must offer

either Papers C1, C2, C3 and C4,
or Papers C1, C2, C5 and a dissertation.

Papers C1–C5 will be those specified for Section C in the Honour School of Mathematics. The list of approved subjects for Section C shall include subjects in Mathematical Logic as specified by the Joint Committee for Mathematics and Philosophy during Trinity Term for the following academic year. Each paper will be of 3 hours' duration except Paper C5 which will be of 2 hours' duration.

Dissertation

(*a*) *Subject, authorship, and format*

The subject of the dissertation shall be a project which shall be supervised by a member of the Faculty of the Mathematical Sciences or, in exceptional circumstances, by some other person of equivalent seniority approved by the Chairman of the Projects Committee of the Teaching Committee of the Department of Mathematics. Every dissertation shall be the candidate's own work; it may, for example, be a computation based on known results or a critical review of published mathematics. The supervisor may discuss with the candidate the field of study, recommend references, and discuss what methods are appropriate: the supervisor may also read and comment on a first draft. Candidates shall sign a certificate to the effect that the dissertation is their own work, except as permitted by this regulation or where acknowledgement is made, and this certificate shall be placed in a sealed envelope bearing the candidate's examination number and presented together with the dissertation. A dissertation may be typed or written by hand (subject to the special regulation concerning the typing of illegible scripts) and must be held firmly in a stiff cover. Its length should not exceed the equivalent of 10,000 words (excluding diagrams, tables, references, and texts of computer programs).

(*b*) *Approval of topic*

Candidates intending to offer a dissertation shall, after consultation with their tutors, submit through their colleges to the Chairman of the Projects Committee of the Teaching Committee of the Department of Mathematics in the Mathematical Institute the title that they propose together with

—a brief description (of at least 100 words) of the project which will be the subject of the dissertation. This should be sufficient for the members of the committee to judge whether the project is of appropriate depth and whether it is possible to find a suitable assessor in the University. If possible, candidates should include details of the *main* references – books, papers, etc.;

—a letter of approval from the person who has agreed to act as supervisor (a potential supervisor may be approached either by the candidate or through the candidate's tutor; alternatively advice may be sought at an earlier stage from the Projects Committee);

No dissertation will be accepted if it has already been submitted, wholly or substantially, for a final honour school, other than Mathematics and Philosophy as specified under option (i) or Mathematics, or for another degree of this University, or for a degree of any other institution.

The application shall be made not earlier than the first day of Trinity Full Term in the year preceding the examination and not later than Friday of the third week of the Michaelmas Full Term preceding the examination. The Teaching Committee of the Department of Mathematics will decide as soon as possible, and in any case not later than Monday of the seventh week of the Michaelmas Full Term preceding the examination, whether or not to approve the proposal, and will advise the candidate forthwith. Details of approved projects shall be forwarded by the chairman of the committee to the Chairman of the Examiners not later than the first day of the following Hilary Full Term.

(*c*) *Submission*

Dissertations (two copies), identified by the candidate's examination number only, must be sent to the Chairman of the Examiners, Honour School of Mathematics and Philosophy, Examination Schools, Oxford, to arrive not later than noon on the Friday of the first week following the end of the Hilary Full Term preceding the examination. At the same time, the supervisor shall submit to the Chairman of the Examiners a confidential report whose purpose is to assist the examiners to determine how much assistance the candidate has received in the preparation of the dissertation; this report will be on a form supplied for the purpose by the Chairman of the Examiners. A candidate may withdraw notice of submission of a dissertation at any time and shall be deemed to have done so if the dissertation is not submitted by the time and date specified unless a special dispensation is received from the Proctors.

Candidates offering Papers c1, c2, c3 and c4 can gain the highest honours by preparing no more than six Section c subjects. The examiners will give a dissertation the weight of two approved Section c subjects.

Option (*ii*) *Mathematics* and *Philosophy*

Candidates must offer Papers c1(P) and c2(P) and two subjects in *Philosophy* chosen from subjects 101, 103–118, 120, 121 and 199 in the Regulations for Philosophy in all Honour Schools including Philosophy. Each of Papers c1(P) and c2(P) shall be of 3 hours' duration. Each subject in *Philosophy* except subject 199 *Thesis* shall be examined in one 3-hour paper.

The subjects of the Papers c1(P) and c2(P) will be

(*a*) the subjects approved by the Mathematics Teaching Committee for the Papers c1 and c2 of the Honour School of Mathematics, which shall include subjects in Mathematical Logic, and are the subjects of lecture courses given in Michaelmas Term, and

(*b*) with the approval of the Joint Committee for Mathematics and Philosophy, subjects in Mathematical Logic approved for Papers c3 and c4 in the Honour School of Mathematics, which are subjects of lecture courses given in Hilary Term.

Applications for the approval of one or two subjects under (*b*) above must be made through the candidate's college and received by the Secretary of the Joint Committee for Mathematics and Philosophy, Mathematical Institute, St. Giles', not later than the Friday of the second week of the Michaelmas Full Term preceding the examination, and candidates will be promptly advised of the Committee's decision.

Papers c1(P) and c2(P) will each contain two questions on each of the subjects of lecture courses approved for these papers. Candidates can gain the highest honours by preparing no more than three of these subjects.

The examiners shall give the same weight to Papers c1(P) and c2(P) taken together as to the subjects in *Philosophy*.

Option (iii) Philosophy

Candidates must offer four subjects in *Philosophy* chosen from subjects 101, 103–118, 120, 121 and 199 in the Regulations for Philosophy in all Honour Schools including Philosophy. Each subject except subject 199 *Thesis* will be examined in one 3-hour paper.

PASS SCHOOL OF MATHEMATICS AND PHILOSOPHY

1. Candidates shall be required to offer the following elements of the examination for the Honour School of Mathematics and Philosophy:

(i) subject b1 and three of subjects a1–a7 in *Mathematics*, and

(ii) two of subjects 101, 102, 122, and 199 in *Philosophy*, as prescribed in the Regulations for Philosophy in all Honour Schools including Philosophy.

2. The use of calculators is generally not permitted but certain kinds may be allowed for certain papers. Specifications of which papers and which types of calculators are permitted for those exceptional papers will be announced by the examiners in the Hilary Term preceding the examination.]

NOTES

SPECIAL REGULATIONS FOR THE HONOUR SCHOOL OF MATHEMATICS AND STATISTICS

A

In the following 'the Course Handbook' refers to the Mathematics and Statistics Undergraduate Handbook and supplements to this published by the Statistics Academic Committee.

1. The subjects of the Honour School of Mathematics and Statistics shall be Mathematics and its applications, and Statistics.

2. No candidate shall be admitted to examination in this School unless he or she has either passed or been exempted from the First Public Examination.

3. The Examinations in Mathematics and Statistics shall be under the supervision of the Mathematical and Physical Sciences Board. The Board shall have the power, subject to this decree, from time to time to frame and vary regulations for the different parts and subjects of the examination.

4. (*a*) The examination in Mathematics and Statistics shall consist of three parts (A, B, C) for the four-year course, and of two parts (A, B) for the three-year course.
   (*b*) Parts A, B, and C shall be taken at times not less than three, six, and nine terms, respectively, after passing or being exempted from the First Public Examination.

5. The name of a candidate on either the three-year course or the four-year course shall not be published in a Class List until he or she has completed all parts of the respective examination.

6. (*a*) In order to proceed to Part B, candidates must pass Part B. The examiners will publish a pass list for Part A.
   (*b*) In order to proceed to Part C, a candidate must achieve Honours standard in Part A and Part B together. A list of candidates satisfying this requirement shall be published by the Examiners.
   (*c*) A candidate on the three-year course who obtained only a Pass or fails to satisfy the Examiners in Part B may retake Part B on at most one subsequent occasion; a candidate on the four-year course who obtains only a Pass or fails to satisfy the Examiners in Part C may retake Part C on at most one subsequent occasion.

7. A candidate adjudged worthy of Honours on both Parts A and B together, and on Part C may supplicate for the degree of Master of Mathematics if he or she has fulfilled all the conditions in the General Regulations for Admission to Degrees Awarded on Passing the Second Public Examination.

B

1. **In Part A** each candidate shall be required to offer the four written papers from the schedule of papers for Part A (see 'Schedule' below).

2. **In Part B** each candidate shall offer a total of four units from the schedule of units and half units for Parts B and C (see 'Schedule' below).

(*a*) Each candidate shall offer the unit *Applied Statistics*.
(*b*) Each candidate shall offer at least one of the following units:
(i) *Statistical Inference*
(ii) *Applied Probability and Stochastic Processes*
(*c*) Each candidate may offer up to one unit from those designated as M level.

3. **In Part C** each candidate shall offer a total of two units from the schedule of units and half units for Parts B and C (see 'Schedule' below), and each candidate shall also offer a dissertation on a statistics project.

(*a*) The two units offered should be from those designated as M level.
(*b*) At least half a unit should be offered from the schedule of 'Statistics' units.

4. Each unit or half unit on the schedule, other than extended essay or a dissertation, will be assessed by an examination paper, or by an examination paper plus evidence of practical work, or by a mini-project.

5. The use of calculators is generally not permitted for written papers. However, their use may be permitted for certain exceptional examinations. The specification of calculators permitted for these exceptional examinations will be announced by the Examiners in the Hilary Term preceding the examination.

Schedule

Papers in Part A
AC1 Algebra, Analysis and Differential Equations
AC2 Algebra, Analysis and Differential Equations
AS1 Probability, Statistics and Options
AS2 Probability, Statistics and Options

Syllabus details will be published in the Course Handbook by the beginning of the Michaelmas Full Term in the academic year of the examination for Part A.

Units and half units for Part B [from October 2004] and Part C [from October 2005]

Provisional lists of 'Mathematics' and of 'Statistics' units and half units will be published in the *Examination Regulations*. Not all listed units and half units will be available each year and some extra units and half units may be added. The list will include:

Statistics units, H level
Applied Statistics (*whole unit*)
Statistical Inference (*whole unit*)
Applied Probability and Stochastic Processes (*whole unit*)
Acturial Science (*whole unit*)

The final list of units and half units will be published in the Course Handbook by the beginning of the Michaelmas Full Term in the academic year of the examination concerned, together with the following details.

1. Designation as either 'H' level or 'M' level.

2. 'Weight' as either a whole unit or half-unit.

3. Method of assessment (as either extended essay, dissertation, mini-project, examination paper plus evidence of practical work, or examination paper). Details of methods of assessment for units or half units delivered by other departments will be given elsewhere. The Course handbook will indicate where such details will be specified.

4. Rules governing submission of any extended essay, dissertation or mini-project, including deadlines, provided that these shall always be submitted to the Chairman of Examiners, Honour School of Mathematics and Statistics, c/o the Clerk of the Schools, Examination Schools, High Street, Oxford.

5. Syllabus content.

6. Whether there is a requirement to register or apply for a place to take a unit or half unit, and details of any registration or application procedure.

PASS SCHOOL OF MATHEMATICS AND STATISTICS

1. Candidates will be required to offer the following elements of the examination for the Honour School of Mathematics: Paper AC1 Algebra, Analysis and Differential Equations; Paper AC2 Algebra, Analysis and Differential Equations; Paper AO1 Probability, Statistics and Options; Paper AO2 Probability, Statistics and Options; and 2 units from the schedule for Part B, of which at least one must be a 'Statistics' unit.

2. The use of calculators is generally not permitted for written papers. However, their use may be permitted for certain exceptional examinations. The specification of calculators permitted for these exceptional examinations will be announced by the Examiners in the Hilary Term preceding the examination.

NOTES

NOTES

NOTES

NOTES

NOTES

SPECIAL REGULATIONS FOR THE HONOUR SCHOOL OF MODERN HISTORY

A

1. The examination in the School of Modern History shall be under the supervision of the Board of the Faculty of Modern History, and shall always include:

(1) The History of the British Isles (including the History of Scotland, Ireland, and Wales; and of British India and of British Colonies and Dependencies as far as they are connected with the History of the British Isles);

(2) General History during some period, selected by the candidate from periods to be named from time to time by the Board of the Faculty;

(3) A Special Historical subject, studied with reference to original authorities.

2. No candidate shall be admitted to examination in this school unless he or she has *either* passed or been exempted from the First Public Examination *or* has successfully completed the Foundation Course in Modern History at the Department for Continuing Education.

3. The Board of the Faculty of Modern History shall, by notice from time to time, make regulations respecting the above-named branches of examination, and shall have power

(1) To name certain periods of General History, and to fix their limits;

(2) To issue lists of Special Historical subjects, prescribing particular authorities where they think it desirable.

4. The examination in the Special Historical subject may be omitted by candidates, but such candidates shall not be placed in the Class List.

5. The Board of the Faculty may include in the examination, either as necessary or as optional, other subjects which they may deem suitable to be studied in connection with Modern History, including translation from foreign languages of passages not specially prepared, and may prescribe books or portions of books in any language.

B

The Modern History Board shall issue annually the Handbook for the Honour

School of Modern History by Monday of Week 1 of the first Michaelmas Full Term of candidates' work for the Honour School. A supplement to the handbook shall be issued to candidates at the beginning of Week 4 of the first Hilary Full Term of their work for the Honour School, and posted in the Modern History Faculty Building and circulated to tutors.

All candidates are required to offer Subjects I, II, III, **[Until 1 October 2004:** IV, and VI**]** **[From 1 October 2004:** V and VI**]**, below. No candidate may be placed in the Class List unless he or she also offers Special Subject **[Until 1 October 2004:** (V below).**]** **[From 1 October 2004:** IV, below**]**.

Candidates who have taken the Foundation Course in Modern History rather than Honour Moderations are required to offer at least one paper which relates to a period between 285 and **[Until 1 October 2004:** 1409**]** **[From 1 October 2004:** 1550**]** (this may be taken to include Periods **[Until 1 October 2004:** (I) or (II)**]** **[From 1 October 2004:** Periods (I), (II), or (III)**]** of the History of the British Isles).

I. History of the British Isles: any one of the following periods:

(I) *c.*300–1087;
(II) 1042–1330;
(III) 1330–1550;
(IV) 1500–1700;
(V) 1685–1830;
(VI) **[Until 1 October 2004:** since 1830**]** **[From 1 October 2004:** 1815–1924;**]**;
[From 1 October 2004: (VII) since 1900**]**.

No candidate may offer a period offered when passing the First Public Examination.

The History of the British Isles is taken to include the history of the Irish Republic in the twentieth century, and of British India and British Colonies and Dependencies as far as they are connected with the History of Britain. **[Until 1 October 2004:** Candidates who offer British History papers (I) and (II), or (III) and (IV), or (IV) and (V), for the Final Honour School, must not substantially duplicate material in those two papers.**]**

[Until 1 October 2004: II. General History: any one of the listed periods in the following three groups.

Group A: (i) 285–476; (iii) 700–900; (v) 1122–1273; (vii) 1409–1525; (ix) 1618–1715; (xi) 1799–1856; (xv) The History of the United States 1600–1830.

Group B: (ii) 476–750; (iv) 900–1122; (viii) 1517–1618; (x) 1715–1799; (xii) 1856–1914; (xiv) 1941–1973; (xvi) The History of the United States since 1815.

Group C: (vi) 1273–1409; (xiii) 1914–1945; (xvii) Europe and the Wider World 1815–1914.**]**

[From 1 October 2004: II. General History: any one of the listed periods:

(i) 285–476; (ii) 476–750; (iii) 700–900; (iv) 900–1122; (v) 1122–1273; (vi) 1273–1409; (vii) 1409–1525; (viii) 1517–1618; (ix) 1618–1715; (x) 1715–1799; (xi) 1799–1856; (xii) 1856–1914; (xiii) 1914–1945; (xiv) 1941–1973; (xv) The History of the United States 1600–1830; (xvi) The History of the United States since 1815; (xvii) Europe and the Wider World 1815–1914.**]**

[Until 1 October 2004: III. *EITHER* a second period of British History OR a second period of General History OR a thesis, in accordance with the detailed regulation stated below under VII Theses.**]**

[Until 1 October 2004: The five periods of British and General History offered by a candidate in Honour Moderations and the Honour School or four periods if a thesis is offered to satisfy requirement III (above) or requirements IV or V (*b*) (below) must include at least one from each of the following period groups:**]**

[From 1 October 2004:
The four periods of British and General History offered by a candidate in the First Public Examination and the Honour School must include at least one from the following groups:**]**

1. Medieval History

(I) *c*.300–1087; (II) 1042–1330; General History (taken in **[Until 1 October 2004:** Honour Moderations**] [From 1 October 2004:** the First Public Examination**]**): I: 370–900, II: 1000–1300; (taken in the Final Honour School); (i) 285–476, (ii) 476–750, (iii) 700–900, (iv) 900–1122, (v) 1122–1273, (vi) 1273–1409.

2. Early Modern History

(III) 1330–1550, (IV) 1500–1700; General History (taken in **[Until 1 October 2004:** Honour Moderations**] [From 1 October 2004:** the First Public Examination**]**): III: 1400–1650; (taken in the Final Honour School): (vii) 1409–1525; (viii) 1517–1618, (ix) 1618–1715.

3. Modern History

(V) British History 1685–1830; **[Until 1 October 2004:** (VI) since 1830**] [From 1 October 2004:** (VI) 1815–1924; (VII) since 1900**]**, General History (taken in **[Until 1 October 2004:** Honour Moderations**] [From 1 October 2004:** the First Public Examination**]**): VI: 1815–1914; (taken in the Final Honour School): (x) 1715–1799; (xi) 1799–1856, (xii) 1856–1914; (xiii) 1914–1945; (xiv) 1941–1973; (xv) History of the United States 1600–1830, (xvi) History of the United States since 1815, (xvii) Europe and the Wider World 1815–1914.

Candidates with Senior Student status, and candidates who have passed the First Public Examination in a course other than Modern History are required to offer **[Until 1 October 2004:** at least**]** one paper in British History and one in General History, to be taken from two out of the three period groups (1. Medieval History, 2. Early Modern History, 3. Modern History).

Candidates who have taken the Foundation Course in Modern History **[Until 1 October 2004:** rather than Honour Moderations**]** are required to offer at least one paper which relates to a period between 285 and **[Until 1 October 2004:** 1409**] [From 1 October 2004:** 1550**]** (this may be taken to **[Until 1 October 2004:** include Periods (I) or (II)**] [From 1 October 2004:** Periods (I), (II), or (III)**]** of the History of the British Isles).

[Until 1 October 2004: If two periods of General History are offered by any student, they must be taken from two of the three different groups (Group A, Group B, Croup C) listed above under II.**]**

IV**[**III**]**. Further Subject: any one of the Further Subjects specified below.

1. Anglo-Saxon Archaeology of the Early Christian Period
2. The Near East in the Age of Justinian and Muhammad 527–*c*.700
3. The Carolingian Renaissance
4. The Crusades
5. Culture and Society in Early Renaissance Italy 1290–1348
6. Flanders and Italy in the Quattrocento 1420–1480
7. Literature and Politics in Early Modern England
8. English Society in the Seventeenth Century
9. Society and Government in France 1610–1715
10. Court Culture and Art in Early Modern Europe
11. British Economic and Social History 1700–1870
12. The American Revolution and Constitution
13. Culture and Society in France from Voltaire to Balzac
14. Intellect and Culture in Victorian Britain
15. Imperialism and Nationalism 1830–1980

16. Modern Japan 1868–1972
17. British Economic History since 1870 (as prescribed for the Honour School of Philosophy, Politics, and Economics
18. British Society in the Twentieth Century (as prescribed for the Honour School of Philosophy, Politics, and Economics)
19. Revolutionary Mexico 1910–40
20. Nationalism, Politics and Culture in Ireland *c.*1870–1921
21. A Comparative History of the First World War, 1914–20
22. China in War and Revolution, 1890–1949
23. The Soviet Union, 1924–41
24. Scholasticism and Humanism
25. The Science of Society 1650–1800
26. Political Theory and Social Science.

[From 1 October 2004:

27. Medicine, Empire, and Improvement, 1720 to 1820]

V[IV]. Special Subject, consisting of

(*a*) a paper including compulsory passages for comment;

[Until 1 October 2004: (*b*) a second paper.**]** **[From 1 October 2004:** an extended essay]

1. From Julian the Apostate to St Augustine 350–396
2. Francia in the Age of Clovis and Gregory of Tours
3. Byzantium in the Age of Constantine Porphyrogenitus 913–959
4. The Norman Conquest of England
5. Saint Francis and Saint Clare
6. Crisis and Conflict in France: King, Pope, Cathars and Templars, 1294–1314
7. Lancaster and York 1444–1461
8. The High Renaissance in Rome and Florence 1478–1513
9. Government, Politics, and Society in England, 1547–1558
10. The Scientific Movement in the Seventeenth Century
11. Commonwealth and Protectorate 1647–1658
12. English Architecture 1660–1720
13. Politics, Reform, and Imperial Crisis 1774–1784
14. Church, State, and English Society 1829–1854
15. Slavery, Emancipation, and the Crisis of the Union 1857–1875
16. Political Pressures and Social Policy, 1899–1914
17. [*suspended*]
18. The Russian Revolution of 1917
19. India, 1916–1934: Indigenous Politics and Imperial Control
20. The Great Society Era, 1960–70
21. Nazi Germany, a racial order, 1933–45
22. France from the Popular Front to the Liberation 1936–1944
23. War and reconstruction: ideas, politics and social change 1939–1945
24. The Northern Ireland Troubles, 1965–1985

[Until 1 October 2004: A thesis may be offered in place of IV or V (*b*) provided that a thesis has not been offered to satisfy requirement III, in accordance with the detailed regulations stated below under VII THESES**]**.

[From 1 October 2004:

Candidates will be examined by means of a timed paper including compulsory passages for comment, and by means of an extended essay, which shall not exceed 6,000 words (including footnotes but excluding bibliography), and shall be on a topic or theme selected by the candidate from a question paper published by the examiners on the Friday of the fourth week of Michaelmas Term in the year of examination.

Essays should be typed or word-processed in double spacing and should conform to the standards of academic presentation prescribed in the course handbook.

Essays (two copies) shall normally be written during the Michaelmas Term in the year of examination and must be delivered by hand to the Examination Schools (addressed to the Chairman of Examiners, Honour School of Modern History, Examination Schools, Oxford) not later than 12 noon on the Friday before the beginning of Hilary Full Term of the year of examination. Candidates delivering essays will be required to complete a receipt form, which will only be accepted as proof of receipt if it is counter-signed by a member of the Examination Schools staff. Each essay must be accompanied by a sealed envelope (bearing only the candidate's examination number) containing a formal declaration signed by the candidate that the essay is his or her own work. The University's regulations on *Late Entries* will apply. Any candidate may be examined viva voce.]

Depending on the availability of teaching resources, not all Further and Special Subjects will be available to all candidates in every year. Candidates may obtain details of the choice of options for the following year by consulting lists posted at the beginning of the week four of Hilary Full Term in the **[Until 1 October 2004:** Modern History Faculty] **[From 1 October 2004:** Modern History Faculty, on the Modern History Faculty website] and circulated to Modern History Tutors.

[Until 1 October 2004: VI. Comparative History and Historiography: an extended essay.

Candidates shall be examined in Comparative History and Historiography by means of an extended essay, which shall not exceed 7,500 words (excluding footnotes, references, and bibliography) and shall be on a topic or theme chosen from a list circulated by the examiners by the end of Fifth Week of the Trinity Term of the year prior to the examination. The examiners' list shall be drawn from a syllabus approved by the Modern History Faculty Board, details of which shall be circulated to candidates at the beginning of the first Michaelmas Term of their work for the Honour School in the course handbook.

Candidates will be expected to demonstrate a detailed knowledge of *either* at least two societies or historical periods or a representative number of relevant historians.

Essays should be typed and should conform to the standards of academic presentation prescribed in the course handbook.

Essays (two copies) must be delivered by hand to the Examination Schools by 12 noon on the Friday of the Eighth Week of the Hilary Term immediately preceding the examination; candidates delivering essays will be required to complete a receipt form, which will only be accepted as proof of receipt if it is countersigned by a member of the Examination Schools staff. Each essay must be accompanied by a sealed envelope (bearing only the candidate's examination number) containing a formal declaration signed by the candidate that the essay is his or her own work. The University's regulations on *Late Entries* will apply.

Any candidate may be examined viva voce.]

[From 1 October 2004:

V. *Disciplines of History*

Candidates will be expected to answer three examination questions selected from a paper divided into three sections. No more than two questions may be answered from one section. The sections are:

1. Comparative History (Candidates will be expected to demonstrate knowledge of at least two societies or historical periods):
2. Sources of History;
3. Varieties of History.]

[Until 1 October 2004: VII. THESES

1. Any candidate may offer an Optional Thesis.

2. Any candidate may offer a thesis EITHER in fulfilment of clause III above, OR in place of a Further Subject (IV above) or the essay paper of the Special Subject (V(b) above).

3. A candidate may submit

(*a*) any essay or part of any essay which the candidate has submitted or intends to submit for any university essay prize; *or*

(*b*) any other work provided in either case that (i) no thesis will be accepted if it has already been submitted, wholly or substantially, for a final honour school other than one involving Modern History, or another degree of this University, or a degree of any other university and (ii) the candidate submits a statement to that effect and (iii) the subject is approved by the Chairman of the Examiners for the Honour School of Modern History.

The provisos in cl. 3 above shall not debar any candidate from submitting work *based* on a previous submission towards the requirements for a degree of any other university provided that

(i) the work is substantially new;

(ii) the candidate also submits both the original work itself and a statement specifying the extent of what is new.

The examiners shall have sole authority to decide in every case whether proviso (i) to this clause has been met.

4. Every candidate intending to offer a thesis except as defined in cl. 3 (*a*) must submit the title proposed together with the written approval of a supervisor or tutor to the Chairman of the Examiners for the Honour School of Modern History, The History Faculty, Broad Street, Oxford not earlier than the beginning of Trinity Full Term in the year preceding that in which the candidate takes the examination and not later than Friday of the first week of the following Hilary Full Term. The chairman shall decide whether or not to approve the title, consulting the faculty board if so desired, and shall advise the candidate as soon as possible. Candidates who have given notice that they propose to offer a thesis instead of a Further Subect or paper (*b*) of a Special Subject may withdraw that notice not later than Friday of the eighth week of Hilary Full Term in the year of examination.

5. Theses should normally include an investigation of relevant printed or unprinted primary sources, and must include proper references and a select bibliography. They must be the work of the author alone. In all cases, the candidate's tutor or supervisor shall discuss with the candidate the field of study, the sources available, and the methods of presentation. In the case of an optional thesis, the tutor or supervisor may read and comment on a first draft. In the case of thesis submitted in lieu of a paper, the tutor or supervisor shall set essential background and further reading, and shall read not more than two draft parts or chapters of the thesis and comment upon them.

6. No thesis offered above shall exceed 15,000 words in length (including footnotes, appendices, and bibliographies). Any such theses may be shorter. All such theses must be typed in double spacing on one side of quarto or A4 paper with the notes and references at the foot of each page, and must be bound or held firmly in a stiff cover.

7. All candidates must submit two copies of their theses, addressed to the Chairman of the Examiners, Honour School of Modern History, Examination Schools, Oxford, not later than noon on Monday of the first week of Trinity Full Term in which they are presenting themselves for examination. Every candidate shall present a certificate, signed by him or herself and by a college tutor, in a separate envelope bearing the candidate's examination number, addressed to the Chairman of the Examiners. The certificate (forms are available from the Faculty Office) should declare that (*a*) the

thesis is the candidate's own work, (*b*) that no substantial portion of it has been presented for any other degree course or examination, (*c*) that it does not exceed 15,000 words in length.

8. Every thesis shall be the candidate's own work. Every candidate shall sign a certificate to the effect that the thesis is his or her own work, and his or her tutor or supervisor shall countersign the certificate confirming that, to the best of his or her knowledge and belief, this statement is true. This certificate shall be presented together with the thesis, in a separate sealed envelope addressed to the Chairman of Examiners.

9. Candidates shall not answer in any other paper, with the exception of Comparative History and Historiography (VI), questions which fall very largely within the scope of their thesis. No candidate may present a thesis in replacement of a period of General or of British History, the subject matter of which falls within the parameters of a Further or Special Subject paper which the candidate proposes to offer.

10. The above regulations shall apply *mutatis mutandis* to all theses submitted under IV (Further Subjects) and V (Special Subjects).]

[From 1 October 2004:

VI. *A thesis from original research*

1. Candidates must submit a thesis as part of the fulfilment of their Final Examination.

2. Theses shall normally be written during the Hilary Term of the Final Year. All theses must be submitted not later than noon on Friday of Eighth Week of the Hilary Term of the Final Year.

3. A candidate may submit

(*a*) any essay or part of any essay which the candidate has submitted or intends to submit for any university essay prize; or

(*b*) any other work

provided in either case that (i) no thesis will be accepted if it has already been submitted, wholly or substantially, for a final honour school other than one involving Modern History, or another degree of this University, or a degree of any other university, and (ii) the candidate submits a statement to that effect, and (iii) the subject is approved by the Chairman of the Examiners for the Honour School of Modern History.

4. The provisos in cl. 3 above shall not debar any candidate from submitting work based on a previous submission towards the requirements for a degree of any other university provided that

(i) the work is substantially new;

(ii) the candidate also submits both the original work itself and a statement specifying the extent of what is new. The examiners shall have sole authority to decide in every case whether proviso (i) to this clause has been met.

5. Every candidate except when offering a thesis as defined in cl. 3(*a*) must submit the title proposed together with the written approval of their College History Tutor to the Chairman of the Examiners for the Honour School of Modern History, the History Faculty, Broad Street, Oxford, not earlier than the beginning of Trinity Full Term in the year preceding that in which the candidate takes the examination and not later than the Friday of Eighth Week of Michaelmas Term in the Final Year. If no notification is received from the Chairman of Examiners by the first Monday of Hilary Full Term of the Final Year, the title shall be deemed to be approved. Any subsequent changes to title require formal application to and approval by the Chairman of Examiners.

6. Theses should normally include an investigation of relevant printed or unprinted primary historical sources, and must include proper footnotes and a bibliography. They must be the work of the author alone. In all cases, the candidate's tutor or thesis adviser shall discuss with the candidate the field of study, the sources available, and the methods of presentation. Candidates shall be expected to have had a formal meeting with their College History Tutor, and, if necessary, an additional meeting with a specialized thesis adviser in the Trinity Term of their Second Year, as well as a second formal meeting with their thesis adviser in the Michaelmas Term of their Final Year prior to submitting the title of their thesis. In addition candidates are permitted to have no more than three one-hour advisory sessions at which bibliographical, structural, and other problems can be discussed. A first draft of the thesis may be commented on by the thesis adviser.

7. No thesis shall exceed 12,000 words in length (including footnotes, but excluding bibliography and, in cases for which specific permission has been obtained from the Chairman of Examiners, appendices). All theses must be typed or word-processed in double spacing on one side of A4 paper with the notes and references at the foot of each page, with a left-hand margin of one-and-a-half inches and all other margins of at least one inch. The thesis should conform to the standards of academic presentation prescribed in the course handbook. Failure to conform to such standards may incur penalties as outlined in the course handbook.

8. All candidates must submit two copies of their thesis, addressed to the Chairman of Examiners, Honour School of Modern History, Examination Schools, Oxford, not later than noon on Friday of Eighth Week of the Hilary Term of the year in which they are presenting themselves for examination. The University's regulations on *Late Entries* will apply. Every candidate shall present a certificate, signed by him or herself and by his or her College History Tutor, in a separate envelope bearing the candidate's examination number, addressed to the Chairman of Examiners. The certificate (forms are available from the Modern History Faculty Office) should declare that (*a*) the thesis is the candidate's own work, (*b*) that no substantial portion of it has been presented for any other degree course or examination, (*c*) that is does not exceed 12,000 words in length, (*d*) that no more than five advisory meetings have taken place between the candidate and his or her College History Tutor or thesis adviser, and (*e*) that only the first draft of the thesis has been seen by the thesis adviser. Candidates delivering theses will be required to complete a receipt form, which will only be accepted as proof of receipt if it is countersigned by a member of the Examination Schools staff.

9. Candidates shall not answer in any other paper, with the exception of Disciplines of History (V), questions which fall very largely within the scope of their thesis. Candidates should not choose a thesis that substantially reworks material studied in the Further or Special Subjects, and should demonstrate familiarity with and use of substantially different and additional primary sources.

VII. *An optional additional thesis*

1. Any candidate may offer an optional additional thesis.

2. Regulation VI 3. above applies.

3. Regulation VI 4. above applies.

4. Every candidate intending to offer an optional thesis except as defined in VI 3(*a*) above must submit the title proposed together with the written approval of a thesis adviser or College History Tutor to the Chairman of the Examiners for the Honour School of Modern History, the History Faculty, Broad Street, Oxford, not earlier than the beginning of Trinity Full Term in the year preceding that in which the candidate takes the examination and not later than Friday of the first week of

the following Hilary Full Term. The Chairman shall decide whether or not to approve the title, consulting the faculty board if so desired, and shall advise the candidate as soon as possible.

5. Optional additional theses should normally include an investigation of relevant printed or unprinted historical sources, and must include proper footnotes and a bibliography. They must be the work of the author alone. In all cases, the candidate's College History Tutor or thesis adviser shall discuss with the candidate the field of study, the sources available, and the methods of presentation (which should conform to the standards of academic presentation described in the course handbook). The College History Tutor or thesis adviser may comment on the first draft.

6. No optional additional thesis shall exceed 12,000 words in length (including footnotes but excluding bibliographies). All theses must be typed or word-processed in double spacing on one side of A4 paper wih the notes and references at the foot of each page, with a left-hand margin of one-and-a-half inches and all other margins of at least one inch.

7. Candidates must submit two copies of their theses, addressed to the Chairman of Examiners, Honour School of Modern History, Examination Schools, Oxford, not later than noon on Monday of the first week of Trinity Full Term in which they are presenting themselves for examination. Every candidate shall present a certificate signed by him or herself and by a College History Tutor or thesis adviser, in a separate envelope bearing the candidate's examination number, addressed to the Chairman of Examiners. The certificate (forms are available from the Faculty Office) should declare that (*a*) the thesis is the candidate's own work, (*b*) that no substantial portion of it has been presented for any other degree course or examination, (*c*) that is does not exceed 12,000 words in length.

8. Candidates shall not answer in any other paper, with the exception of Disciplines of History (V), questions which fall very largely within the scope of their optional additional thesis.]

PASS SCHOOL OF MODERN HISTORY

Candidates must satisfy the examiners in the following four papers:

(i) Any one or two papers in the History of the British Isles as specified for the Honour School of Modern History;
provided that no candidate may offer a period offered when passing the First Public Examination. A candidate who offers two papers must offer one period of General History; a candidate who offers one paper in British History must offer two periods of General History.

(ii) Any one or two periods of General History as specified for the Honour School of Modern History;
provided that no candidate may offer a period offered when passing the First Public Examination. A candidate who offers two periods must offer one paper in the History of the British Isles (see above); a candidate who offers one period must offer two papers in the History of the British Isles.

(iii) *either* a Further Subject as specified for the Honour School of Modern History *or* a thesis in lieu of the Further Subject. The regulations for theses shall be as prescribed for the Honour School of Modern History **[From 1 October 2004:** , according to Regulation VII. An Optional Additional Thesis**]**.

NOTES

SPECIAL REGULATIONS FOR THE HONOUR SCHOOL OF MODERN HISTORY AND ECONOMICS

A

1. The examination in the Honour School of Modern History and Economics shall consist of such subjects in Modern History and Economics as the Board of the Faculty of Modern History and Division of Social Sciences from time to time shall in consultation prescribe by regulation.

2. No candidate shall be admitted to examination in this School unless he has either passed or been exempted from the First Public Examination.

3. The examination in the Honour School shall be under the joint supervision of the Board of the Faculty of Modern History and the Social Sciences Divisional Board, which shall appoint a standing joint committee to make proposals for regulations concerning the examination. Such proposals shall be submitted to the boards of the two faculties which shall make regulations concerning the examination and which, in the case of difference of opinion, shall hold a joint meeting at which the matter in dispute shall be resolved by the vote of the majority.

4. The Chairmen of Examiners for the Honour School of Modern History and for the Honour School of Philosophy, Politics, and Economics shall consult together and designate such of their number as may be required for the examination for the Honour School of Modern History and Economics, whereupon the number of examiners shall be deemed to be complete.

B

Each candidate shall offer:

1. *Macroeconomics.*
2. *Microeconomics.*
3. *British Economic History since 1870.*
4. *Either* one period of General History *or* one period of The History of the British Isles, except any such period offered as a successful candidate in the First Public Examination.
5. One of the following:

(*a*) *English Society in the Seventeenth Century.* (As prescribed in the Honour School of Modern History)

(*b*) *British Economic History 1700–1870.* (As prescribed in the Honour School of Modern History) (*c*) *British Social History since 1870.* (As prescribed in the Honour School of Philosophy, Politics, and Economics)

6. *Either* (*a*) one Special Subject in Modern History;

or (*b*) two Further Subjects in Modern History;

or (*c*) two Further Subjects in Economics;

or (*d*) (i) one Further Subject in Modern History and (ii) one Further Subject in Economics.

Either of subjects 5(*a*) and (*b*) not offered under that section may be offered under section 6(*b*) or (*d*). The same subject may not be offered under both section 5 and section 6.

[Until 1 October 2004: A**] [From 1 October 2004:** An optional substitute**]** thesis may be offered *either* instead of one paper in the History of the British Isles, General History, a Further Subject in Modern History or a Special Subject **[Until 1 October 2004:** paper (*b*)**] [From 1 October 2004:** extended essay**]** in Modern History *or* instead of one Further Subject in Economics, under the regulations of the respective parent school.

[From 1 October 2004: For optional substitute theses in Modern History, Regulation VII. *An Optional Additional Thesis* applies with the following additions:

Cl. VII. 4. Add: In the case of an optional substitute thesis, where a thesis is offered in lieu of a paper, the College History Tutor or thesis advisor shall set essential background and further reading, and shall read not more than two draft parts or chapters of the thesis and comment upon them.

Cl. VII. 5. The last sentence ("The College History Tutor or thesis advisor may comment on the first draft.") does not apply.

Cl. VII. 8. Add: No candidate may present a thesis in replacement of a period of General or of British History, the subject matter of which falls within the parameters of a Further or Special Subject paper which the candidate proposes to offer.**]**

A second thesis, in addition to the papers listed under sections 1 to 6 may be offered in accordance with the Regulation **[Until 1 October 2004:** VII. THESES**] [From 1 October 2004:** VII. *An Optional Additional Thesis*] of the Honour School of Modern History **[Until 1 October 2004:** modified as follows:**] [From 1 October 2004:** (see below)**]**

The syllabus for sections 1–3, 5(*c*), and 6(*c*) and (*d*) (ii) is as specified in the Honour School of Philosophy, Politics, and Economics and for sections 4, 5(*a*)–(*b*), and 6(*a*), (*b*), and (*d*) (i) as specified for the Honour School of Modern History.

The individual detailed specifications and prescribed texts for the Further and Special Subjects as specified for the Honour School of Modern History will be given in the Handbook for the Honour School of Modern History. This will be published by the Modern History Board by Monday of Week 1 of the first Michaelmas Full Term of candidates' work for the Honour School.

Depending on the availability of teaching resources, not all Further and Special Subjects will be available to all candidates in every year. Candidates may obtain details of the choice of Further and Special Subjects in Modern History available for the following year by consulting the supplement to the Handbook for the Honour School of Modern History and the Economics Supplement to the PPE Handbook for details of the choice of Further Subjects in Economics. This will be issued by the beginning of the fourth week of the first Hilary Full Term of candidates' work for the Honour School and will contain full specifications and prescribed texts for any Further or Special Subjects specified for Modern History introduced for the following year, and any amendments to the specifications and prescribed texts of existing Further and Special Subjects approved by the Modern History Board by its first meeting of the preceding Hilary Term.

No candidate may offer the same subject twice.

Any candidate may be examined viva voce.

Calculators may be used in the examination room for all Economics papers (which shall be taken to include *British Economic History since 1870* but not other papers in Economic History) subject to the conditions set out under the heading 'Use of calculators in examinations' in the *Special Regulations concerning Examinations.*

In every case where, under the regulations for this honour school, candidates have any choice between one or more papers or subjects, every candidate shall give notice to the Registrar not later than Friday in the fourth week of Michaelmas Full Term preceding the examination of all the papers and subjects being so offered.

In addition to the compulsory papers listed above, candidates who so desire may offer a thesis in accordance with Regulation **[Until 1 October 2004:** VII. THESES**]** **[From 1 October 2004:** VII. *An Optional Additional Thesis***]** of the Honour School of Modern History, *q.v.* modified as follows:

(*a*) the subject shall, to the satisfaction of the examiners, fall within the scope of the Honour School of Modern History and Economics; or

(*b*) the prizes listed in that regulation with the addition of the Webb Medley Essay Prize and the Sir John Rhys Prize;

(*c*) theses must be submitted to the Chairman of the Examiners, Honour School of Modern History and Economics, Examination Schools, Oxford. In the assignment of honours, attention will be paid to the merits of any such thesis;

(*d*) not more than two theses may be offered.

PASS SCHOOL OF MODERN HISTORY AND ECONOMICS

Candidates must satisfy the examiners in the following four papers as specified for the Honour School of Modern History and Economics.

(i) Macroeconomics.

(ii) British Economic History since 1870.

(iii) *Either* one period of General History *or* one period of the History of the British Isles, except any such period as has already been offered in passing the First Public Examination.

(iv) *either* one of the following *or* a thesis within the scope of one of these subjects. The regulations for the thesis shall be as prescribed for the Honour School of Modern History **[From 1 October 2004:** (Regulation VII. *An Optional Additional Thesis* modified as for the Honour School of Modern History and Economics)**]** for subjects (*a*) and (*b*) and as for the Honour School of Philosophy, Politics and Economics for subject (*c*).

(*a*) English Society in the Seventeenth century.

(*b*) British Economic History 1700–1870.

(*c*) British Social History since 1870.

NOTES

SPECIAL REGULATIONS FOR THE HONOUR SCHOOL OF MODERN HISTORY AND ENGLISH

A

1. The Honour School of Modern History and English shall be under the joint supervision of the Boards of the Faculties of Modern History and English Language and Literature and shall consist of such subjects as they shall jointly by regulation prescribe. The boards shall establish a joint committee consisting of three representatives of each faculty, of whom at least one of each side shall be a member of the respective faculty board, to advise them as necessary in respect of the Honour School of, and Honour Moderations in, and of the Preliminary Examination in Modern History and English.

2. No candidate shall be admitted to the examination in this school unless he has either passed or been exempted from the First Public Examination.

3. The Chairmen of Examiners for the Honour School of Modern History and for the Honour School of English Language and Literature shall consult together and designate such of their number as may be required for the examination for the Honour School of Modern History and English, whereupon the number of examiners shall be deemed to be complete.

B

Each candidate shall offer seven papers as set out below. Papers will be of three hours' duration, except where otherwise indicated.

The subjects of the examination in the Honour School shall be:

(i) and (ii) Two compulsory interdisciplinary papers, **[From 1 October 2004:** one of which is to be examined by extended essay,] chosen from the list below (candidates should note that this list will vary from time to time, according to the availability of teaching resources, but will always cover a range of periods):

(*a*) Literature and the Public in England, *c.*1350–1430

(*b*) Mapping New Territories, *c.*1770–1830

(*c*) Literature and Religion in Early Modern England.

[From 1 October 2004:

(*d*) Postcolonial historiography: Writing the (Indian) Nation.]

Further details of the inderdisciplinary papers will be available from the English Faculty Office and Modern History Faculty Office **[From 1 October 2004:**

Candidates may choose to submit an extended essay in lieu of a timed paper for both interdisciplinary papers provided that no more than *two* out of the total of *seven* Final Honour School papers are extended essays. Candidates should note that some English and Modern History papers are examined *only* by extended essay and should bear this restriction in mind when making their choices].

(iii) A period of British History not taken in **[Until 1 October 2004:** Honour Moderations**] [From 1 October 2004:** the First Public Examination**]**.

(iv) and (v) Two subjects from Course One or Course Two of the Honour School of English Language and Literature [the English Board may wish to specify at least one compulsory paper]. Candidates may offer papers 9, Introduction to Medieval Studies: Old English Literature, 10, Victorian Literature (1832–1900), and 11, Modern Literature (1900 to the present day), so long as they have not offered equivalent papers in a First Public Examination in English or its joint schools.

[Until 1 October 2004: (vi) and (vii) *Either* two papers from the Honour School of Modern History, which shall consist of a Special Subject, or some combination of a Further Subject, General History Period, or additional British History period (though with only one Further Subject allowed)**] [From 1 October 2004:**

(vi) and (vii) *Either* two papers from the Honour School of Modern History, consisting of

either (*a*) Special Subject (which comprises a three hour paper and an extended essay),

or (*b*) Two of the following:

1. a Further Subject,
2. a General History Period.
3. an additional British History period not taken in the First Public Examination.**]**

or one additional subject from the Honour School of English Language and Literature, plus one subject from the Honour School of Modern History which shall be either a Further Subject, a General History period or an additional British History period.

The individual detailed specifications and prescribed texts for the Further and Special Subjects as specified for the Honour School of Modern History will be given in the Handbook for the Honour School of Modern History. This will be published by the Modern History Board by Monday of Week 1 of the first Michaelmas Full Term of candidates' work for the Honour School.

Depending on the availability of teaching resources, not all Further and Special Subjects will be available to all candidates in every year. Candidates may obtain details of the choice of Further and Special Subjects available for the following year by consulting the supplement to the Handbook for the Honour School of Modern History. This will be issued by the beginning of the fourth week of the first Hilary Full Term of candidates' work for the Honour School and will contain full specifications and prescribed texts for any Further or Special Subjects specified for Modern History introduced for the following year, and any amendments to the specifications and prescribed texts of existing Further and Special Subjects approved by the Modern History Board by its first meeting of the preceding Hilary Term.

Candidates may offer up to two extended essays, provided that, if they offer two, at least one of these shall be a substitute for one of the two interdisciplinary papers. **[From 1 October 2004:** Candidates offering a Modern History Special Subject must do an extended essay for the Special Subject second paper, and therefore can only do one other extended essay for the Final Honour School examination.**]** An extended essay shall not exceed 6,000 words including **[From 1 October 2004:** footnotes and**]** notes but *excluding* bibliography **[From 1 October 2004:** and should conform to the standards of academic presentation prescribed in the course handbook**]**. When an extended essay is to be substituted for an interdisciplinary paper, the candidate should write, through the Senior Tutor of his or her college or society, to request the approval of the Chairman of the Examiners for the Joint School of Modern History and English for the proposed essay title, not later than Friday of the second week of the Michaelmas Full Term immediately preceding the examination. Notification of whether or not approval is forthcoming will be given by the Friday of Week Four of that term. Essays on approved interdisciplinary titles, should be submitted to the Chairman of the Examiners for the Joint School of Modern History and English at the Examination Schools, Oxford, by the Friday of Eighth Week of the Hilary Full Term preceding the examination.

[Until 1 October 2004: A thesis may be offered as under the existing regulations of the Modern History syllabus in lieu of any one of the following papers: a paper on the History of the Brtish Isles, *or* a paper on a period of General History; *or* a Further Subject paper; *or* a Special Subject paper (*b*). In addition, an optional thesis**]** **[From 1 October 2004:** An optional additional thesis**]** may also be offered providing that no more than one thesis can be submitted if extended essays are offered. Any candidate may be examined viva voce. **[Until 1 October 2004:** The optional thesis shall be as under the regulations of the Modern History syllabus *except that* it shall be 10,000 words, including notes, but excluding the bibliography, and shall be on an interdisciplinary theme.**]** **[From 1 October 2004:**

The optional additional thesis shall be as under the regulations of the Modern History syllabus *except that* it shall not be less than 8,000 words and shall not exceed 10,000 words, including footnotes and notes, but excluding the bibliography, and shall be on an interdisciplinary theme. For regulations VII 4 and 7 of the Modern History syllabus regulations read 'Honour School of Modern History and English' instead of 'Modern History'.**]**

PASS SCHOOL OF MODERN HISTORY AND ENGLISH

Candidates must offer *five* papers as follows:

(*a*) *One* of the interdisciplinary papers as prescribed for the Honour School of Modern History and English (candidates should note that this list will vary from time to time, according to the availability of teaching resources; details of the interdisciplinary papers available in any given year may be obtained from the English Faculty Office and Modern History Faculty Office);

(*b*) *Two* papers as prescribed for the Honour School of Modern History: (i) *one* period paper on the History of the British Isles not taken in the First Public Examination; and (ii) *one* paper taken from the list of Further Subjects (candidates should note that all Further Subjects may not be available to all candidates in every year). **[Until 1 October 2004:** A thesis may be offered in accordance with the detailed regulations for the Honour School of Modern History in lieu of *either* (i) *or* (ii);**]**

(*c*) *Two* papers as prescribed for the Honour School of English Language and Literature.

NOTES

SPECIAL REGULATIONS FOR THE HONOUR SCHOOL OF MODERN HISTORY AND MODERN LANGUAGES

A

1. The subjects of the examination in the Honour School of Modern History and Modern Languages shall be (*a*) Modern History, and (*b*) those modern European languages and literatures studied in the Honour School of Modern Languages.

2. All candidates must offer both (*a*) and one of the languages in (*b*) with its literature.

3. No candidate shall be admitted to examination in the School unless he has either passed or been exempted from the First Public Examination.

4. The examination shall always include a period of General History selected by the candidate from periods to be named from time to time in the Regulations of the Honour School.

5. The examiners shall indicate in the lists issued by them the language offered by each candidate obtaining Honours or satisfying the examiners under Ch. VI, Sect. II. C, §1, cll. 21 (iv) and (v).

6. The examiners in the Honour School shall be under the joint supervision of the Boards of the Faculties of Modern History and Modern Languages, which shall appoint a standing joint committee to make proposals for regulations concerning the examination. Such proposals shall be submitted to the boards of the two faculties which shall make regulations concerning the examination and which, in case of difference of opinion, shall hold a joint meeting at which the matter in dispute shall be resolved by the vote of the majority.

7. (i) The examiners in the Honour School shall be such of the Public Examiners in the Honour Schools of Modern History and Modern Languages as shall be required.

(ii) It shall be the duty of the Chairman of Examiners in the Honour Schools of Modern History and Modern Languages to consult together and designate such examiners as shall be required for the Honour School, whereupon the number of examiners shall be deemed to be complete.

B

Candidates will be examined in accordance with the examination regulations set out below.

They will also be required to spend, after their matriculation, a year of residence in an appropriate country or countries, and to provide on their entry form for the examination a certificate that they have done this, signed by the Head or by a tutor of their society. Candidates wishing to be dispensed from the requirement to undertake a year of residence abroad must apply in writing to the Chairman of the Medieval and Modern Languages Board, 41 Wellington Square, Oxford, OX1 2JF, stating their reasons for requesting dispensation and enclosing a letter of support from their society.

Candidates will be expected to carry out during this year abroad such work as their society may require. It is strongly recommended that candidates should apply through the Central Bureau for Educational Visits and Exchanges for an Assistantship, where these are available, and should accept one if offered. Candidates who are not able to obtain an Assistantship should during their year abroad follow a course or courses in an institution or institutions approved by their society, or should spend their time in such other circumstances as are acceptable to their society. Candidates will agree with their College Tutor in advance of their year abroad an independent course of study to be followed during that period.

The papers and choices of options available to candidates for each of the two courses will be the same.

Save in a Special Subject **[Until 1 October 2005:** or an alternative to a Special Subject**]**, each candidate shall offer in his language and literature papers one language and literature only.

Oral Examination: as specified for the Honour School of Modern Languages.

Candidates are advised, where possible, to ensure that their choice of options provides some chronological overlap between their history and literature papers.

Any candidate may be examined viva voce.

In addition to the compulsory papers listed below, candidates who so desire may offer **[Until 1 October 2004:** a thesis in accordance with Regulation VII, THESES**]** **[From 1 October 2004:** an optional additional thesis in accordance with Regulation VII. *An Optional Additional Thesis***]** of the Honour School of Modern History *q.v.*, modified as follows:

(*a*) the subject shall, to the satisfaction of the examiners, fall within the scope of the Honour School of Modern History and Modern Languages; or

(*b*) the prizes listed in that regulation with the addition of the Sir John Rhys Prize;

(*c*) theses must be submitted to the Chairman of the Examiners, Honour School of Modern History and Modern Languages, Examination Schools, Oxford. In the assignment of Honours attention will be paid to the merits of any such thesis.

[Until 1 October 2005: (*d*) A thesis may also be offered in place of General History in Regulation 1. below, *or* in place of paper (*b*) of a Special Subject or the History of the British Isles or the Further Subject in Regulations 7, 8, and 9 below. If an extended essay is offered under Regulations 7, 8, and 9, (*b*) (iii) below only one thesis may be offered.**]**

Further and Special Subjects, additional to those listed in the regulations for the Honour School of Modern History, may be approved from time to time by regulation published in the *Gazette* by the beginning of the fifth week of Trinity Full Term of the year before the year of the examination in which the subjects will first be available.

Every candidate shall offer:

1. One period of General History as specified for the Honour School of Modern History.

2. A bridge essay of 7,500 words on an interdisciplinary topic, designed to draw together interests and develop skills from both sides of the course.

The candidate will submit a title and short statement of up to fifty words on the manner in which he/she proposes to treat the topic, together with a note from his/her tutor approving the topic, addressed to the convener of the Joint School of Modern History and Modern Languages, c/o the Modern History Faculty, no later than Monday of sixth week of Trinity Term of his/her second year. Titles will be approved by the convener and one other member of the Standing Committee of the Joint School of Modern History and Modern Languages. Notification of whether or not approval is forthcoming will be given by eighth week of Trinity Term.

Changes to the title must be submitted to the convener of the joint school at the latest by the Friday of second week of the Michaelmas Term of the candidate's final year. Notification of whether or not approval is forthcoming will be given no later than fourth week of the Michaelmas Term of the candidate's final year. Bridge essays on approved titles should be submitted to the Chairman of the Examiners for the Joint School of Modern History and Modern Languages at the Examination Schools, High Street, Oxford, by the Monday of eighth week in the Michaelmas Term preceding the examination.

Candidates will be entitled to two tutorial hours with a supervisor to define a topic and establish a bibliography.

[Until 1 October 2005: 3. A period of literature as specified for the Honour School of Modern Languages, Papers VI, VII, or VIII.

4. One of the Honour School of Modern Languages, Papers IV, V, IX, X, XI, XII.

5. Unprepared translation into the language (one three hour paper—the Honour School of Modern Languages, Paper I).*

6. Unprepared translation from the language (two one and a half hour papers—the Honour School of Modern Languages, Papers II A (*i*) and II B (*i*)).***] [From 1 October 2005:**

3. Honour School of Modern Languages, Paper I.*

4. Honour School of Modern Languages, Papers IIA(i) and IIB(i).

5. Honour School of Modern Languages, *one* paper chosen from Papers VI, VII, or VIII.

6. Honour School of Modern Languages, *one* paper chosen from Papers IV, V, IX, X, XI, or XII.**]**

[Until 1 October 2005: 7, 8, 9. *Either (a)* a Special Subject as specified for the Honour School of Modern History **[Until 1 October 2004:** (two papers)**] [From 1 October 2004:** , except that assessment of the Special Subject paper (*b*) shall be by timed paper rather than by extended essay,**]** and one of the items (*b*) (i), (ii) or (iii) below.

or (*b*) the following three items:

(i) A period of The History of the British Isles as specified for the Honour School of Modern History **[Until 1 October 2004:** ;**] [From 1 October 2004:** , except that British History Paper VI covers the period since 1830, and British History Paper VII is not available for this Joint School.**]**

(ii) A Further Subject *or* thesis in lieu thereof as specified for the Honour School of Modern History **[From 1 October 2004:** under Regulation VII *An Optional Additional Thesis, except* Cl. 4 of that regulation should read 'beginning of

---

* Except that candidates offering Polish with Russian take unprepared translation from modern Polish in place of unprepared translations from Russian (Earlier).

Trinity Full Term of the academic year preceding that in which the students spend a year abroad**]**;

(iii) An Extended Essay *or* any one of Papers IV, V, IX, X, XI, XII not already offered [Honour School of Modern Languages].**] [From 1 October 2005:**

7, 8, 9. *Either* (*a*) a Special Subject as specified for the Honour School of Modern History (two papers, paper (*b*) of which shall be by extended essay) and one of the items (*b*), (i), (ii), (iii), or (iv) below.

or (*b*) any three of the following four items:

(i) Any period of The History of the British Isles as specified for the Honour School of Modern History;

(ii) A Further Subject as specified for the Honour School of Modern History;

(iii) Any one of the Papers IV, V, IX, X, XI, XII not already offered, as specified for the Honour School of Modern Languages;

(iv) An Extended Essay as specified for the Honour School of Modern Languages *or* a thesis based on original research as specified in Regulation VI for the Honour School of Modern History, *except* Cl. 4. of that regulation should read 'beginning of Trinity Full Term of the academic year preceding that in which the candidate spends a year abroad.**]**

The individual detailed specifications and prescribed texts for the Further and Special Subjects as specified for the Honour School of Modern History will be given in the Handbook for the Honour School of Modern History. This will be published by the Modern History Board by Monday of Week 1 of the first Michaelmas Full Term of candidates' work for the Honour School.

Depending on the availability of teaching resources, not all Further and Special Subjects will be available to all candidates in every year. Candidates may obtain details of the choice of Further and Special Subjects available for the following year by consulting the supplement to the Handbook for the Honour School of Modern History. This will be issued by the beginning of the fourth week of the first Hilary Full Term of candidates' work for the Honour School and will contain full specifications and prescribed texts for any Further or Special Subjects specified for Modern History introduced for the following year, and any amendments to the specifications and prescribed texts of existing Further and Special Subjects approved by the Modern History Board by its first meeting of the preceding Hilary Term.

Mutual exclusions and other restrictions

No candidate may offer a period of British History which he or she has offered as a successful candidate in the First Public Examination.

No candidate may offer both the Modern History Further Subject *Culture and Society in Early Renaissance Italy 1290–1348* and the Modern Languages Early Texts paper in Italian.

Candidates offering a paper from the Honour School of Modern Languages and a paper from the Honour School of Modern History, both of which involve the study of the same author or authors, may not make the same text or texts the principal subject of an answer in both the papers. **[From 1 October 2004:** The same regulation applies to the use of material in the Bridge essay and any other papers.**]**

PASS SCHOOL OF MODERN HISTORY AND MODERN LANGUAGES

Candidates shall offer papers in Modern History, and one of the languages and its literature from those studied in the Honour School of Modern Languages.

Candidates shall take the following papers:

In Modern History

(i) one period of General History (as prescribed for the Honour School of Modern History) **[Until 1 October 2004:**, except any such period as has already been offered in passing the First Public Examination;**]**

(ii) *either* one period of the History of the British Isles, except any such period as has already been offered in passing the First Public Examination; *or* a Further Subject as specified for the Honour School of Modern History *or* a thesis in lieu of the Further Subject.

In the Modern Language

(The numbering used is that in the Honour School of Modern Languages).

I

IIA (i)

IIB (i)

One of VI, VII, VIII.

The oral examination in the language.

NOTES

SPECIAL REGULATIONS FOR THE HONOUR SCHOOL OF MODERN HISTORY AND POLITICS

A

1. The examination in the Honour School of Modern History and Politics shall consist of such subjects in Modern History and Politics as the Board of the Faculty of Modern History and the Social Sciences Board shall from time to time in consultation prescribe by regulation.

2. No candidate shall be admitted to examination in this School unless he or she has either passed or been exempted from the First Public Examination.

3. The examination in the Honour School shall be under the joint supervision of the Board of the Faculty of Modern History and the Social Sciences Board, which shall appoint a standing joint committee to make proposals for regulations concerning the examination. Such proposals shall be submitted to the boards which shall make regulations concerning the examination and which, in the case of difference of opinion, shall hold a joint meeting at which the matter in dispute shall be resolved by the vote of the majority.

4. The Chairs of Examiners for the Honour School of Modern History and for the Honour School of Philosophy, Politics, and Economics shall consult together and designate such of their number as may be required for the examination for the Honour School of Modern History and Politics, whereupon the number of examiners shall be deemed to be complete.

B

[From 1 October 2004:

1. Except where indicated that a paper cannot be substituted, students are required to substitute one paper of those specified below for a compulsory substitute thesis based on original research, as specified under Regulation 6 below.]

1.[2] Each candidate shall offer any *two* periods of General History and the History of the British Isles, as specified for the Honour School of Modern History, provided that:

(*a*) Any candidate who has successfully taken the First Public Examination in Modern History and Politics, or Modern History, or any other joint school with Modern History, may not offer any period in the History of the British Isles that he or she has already offered in that examination.

(*b*) Any candidate who has not offered in the First Public Examination in Modern History and Politics, or Modern History, or any other joint school with

Modern History, a paper—whether in General History or the History of the British Isles—covering a period before the nineteenth century is required to choose at least one such paper. The list of papers satisfying this provision is given in the Handbook for Modern History and Politics.

(*c*) Any candidate who has not offered in the First Public Examination in Modern History and Politics, or Modern History, or any other joint school with Modern History, one of the periods in the History of the British Isles is required to choose at least one such period.

(*d*) Any candidate who has passed a First Public Examination in a subject other than Modern History and Politics, Modern History, or any other joint school with Modern History, or who has been recognized as a Senior Student as defined by decree of Council, must offer:

(i) at least one paper—whether in General History or the History of the British Isles—covering a period before the nineteenth century. The list of papers satisfying this provision is given in the Handbook for Modern History and Politics.

(ii) At least one paper in the History of the British Isles.

(*e*) **[Until 1 October 2004:** Any candidate who in the Second Public Examination offers two General History papers must offer one from any two of Groups A, B, and C, as specified for the Honour School of Modern History.**]** Candidates taking Politics paper 212 (International Relations in the Era of Two World Wars) cannot also take General History (xiii); candidates taking Politics paper 213 (International Relations in the Era of the Cold War) cannot also take General History (xiv); candidates who have taken **[Until 1 October 2004:** British History VI in the First Public Examination **[From 1 October 2004:** British History VII**]** or who are taking **[Until 1 October 2004:** it**] [From 1 October 2004:** British History VII (since 1900)**]** for the Final Honour School cannot also take Politics paper 202 (British Politics and Government in the Twentieth Century). **[From 1 October 2004:** Candidates who are taking British History VI (1815–1924) for the Final Honour School, and who are also taking Politics paper 202 must not substantially duplicate material in those two papers.**]**

2.**[3]** Each candidate shall offer any *two* of the five 'core subjects' in Politics, as specified for the Honour School of Philosophy, Politics, and Economics (i.e. 201, 202, 203, 214, and 220). **[From 1 October 2004:** A thesis in Politics as specified in Regulation 6 below may not be substituted for a Politics core subject.**]**

3**[4]**. Each candidate shall offer any *one* of the following combinations:

(*a*) one Special Subject (consisting of two papers **[From 1 October 2004:** only paper (*b*) may be substituted by a compulsory substitute thesis as specified in Regulation 6 below**]**) as specified for the Honour School of Modern History and one of subjects 201–27 in Politics as specified for the Honour School of Philosophy, Politics and Economics which is not offered under Regulation **[Until 1 October 2004:** 2**] [From 1 October 2004:** 3**]** above.

(*b*) Two Further Subjects in Modern History as specified for the Honour School of Modern History and one of subjects 201–27 in Politics as specified for the Honour School of Philosophy, Politics and Economics which is not offered under Regulation **[Until 1 October 2004:** 2**] [From 1 October 2004:** 3**]** above.

(*c*) One Further Subject as specified for the Honour School of Modern History and two of subjects 201–27 in Politics as specified for the Honour School of Philosophy, Politics and Economics which are not offered under Regulation **[Until 1 October 2004:** 2**] [From 1 October 2004:** 3**]** above.

Provided that:
Candidates who choose Politics Further Subject 215 (Classical Political Thought) cannot also take Modern History Further Subject 23 and 24 (Scholasticism and Humanism and The Science of Society). Candidates who choose Politics Further Subject 216 (Foundations of Modern Social and Political Thought) cannot also take Modern History Further Subject 25 (Political Theory and Social Science).

4.[5] Any candidate may offer an optional thesis in Modern History in addition to all other papers. Such a thesis must be submitted in accordance with the Regulation **[Until 1 October 2004:** VII, 'Theses'**] [From 1 October 2004:** VII, *An Optional Additional Thesis*], for the Final Honour School of Modern History. No candidate may offer more than one optional thesis.

[Until 1 October 2004: 5.[6] Any candidate may offer a substitute thesis in Modern History in place of a paper in Modern History or a substitute thesis or supervised dissertation in Politics in place of a paper in Politics:
[From 1 October 2004:
6. All candidates must offer *either* a substitute thesis based on original research in place of a paper in Modern History *or* a thesis in place of an optional paper in Politics, which shall be *either* a substitute thesis *or* a supervised dissertation submitted in accordance with the regulations prescribed for Politics in the Honour School of Philosophy, Politics, and Economics.**]**

(*a*) a thesis in Modern History submitted in accordance with the **[Until 1 October 2004:** Regulation VII, 'Theses',**] [From 1 October 2004:** Regulation VI, *A thesis based on original research*, for the Final Honour School**]** for the Final Honour School of Modern History may be offered in place of any paper in Modern History except for Special Subject paper (*a*). If a thesis is offered in place of a paper in the History of the British Isles or General History the candidate (unless he or she is a Senior Student, as defined by decree of Council, or has passed the First Public Examination in a course other than Modern History and Politics, Modern History, or any other joint school with Modern History) must also offer a paper satisfying those requirements specified in Regulations 1(*b*) and 1(*c*) above which have not been satisfied in the First Public Examination.

(*b*) A thesis **[From 1 October 2004:** , Special Subject in Politics**]** or supervised dissertation in Politics submitted in accordance with the regulations prescribed for Politics in the Honour School of Philosophy, Politics, and Economics may be offered in place of any one of subjects 201–27 in Politics (as specified for the Honour School of Philosophy, Politics, and Economics) which is not offered under Regulation **[Until 1 October 2004:** 2**] [From 1 October 2004:** 3**]** above.

[Until 1 October 2004: No candidate may offer more than one substitute thesis **[From 1 October 2004:** , Special Subject in Politics**]** or supervised dissertation.**]**
[From 1 October 2004:
All candidates must offer a substitute thesis or supervised dissertation, but may not offer more than one substitute thesis or supervised dissertation in place of a paper.**]**

6.[7] Any candidate may be examined viva voce.

7.[8] In every case where, under the regulations for this honour school, candidates have any choice between one or more papers or subjects, every candidate shall give notice to the Registrar not later than Friday in the fourth week of Michaelmas Full Term preceding the examination of all the papers and subjects being offered.

PASS SCHOOL OF MODERN HISTORY AND POLITICS

Each candidate must satisfy the examiners in the following four papers as specified for the Honour School of Modern History and Politics.

1. Each candidate shall offer any *two* periods of General History and the History of the British Isles, as specified for the Honour School of Modern History, provided that:

(*a*) any candidate who has successfully taken the First Public Examination in Modern History and Politics, or Modern History, or any other joint school with Modern History, may not offer any period in the History of the British Isles that he or she has already offered in that examination.

(*b*) Any candidate who has not offered in the First Public Examination in Modern History and Politics, or Modern History, or any other joint school with Modern History, a paper—whether in General History or the History of the British Isles—covering a period before the nineteenth century is required to choose at least one such paper. The list of papers satisfying this provision is given in the Handbook for Modern History and Politics.

(*c*) Any candidate who has not offered in the First Public Examination in Modern History and Politics, or Modern History, or any other joint school with Modern History, one of the periods in the History of the British Isles is required to choose at least one such period.

(*d*) Any candidate who has passed a First Public Examination in a subject other than Modern History and Politics, Modern History, or any other joint school with Modern History, or who has been recognized as a Senior Student as defined by decree of Council, must offer:

(i) at least one paper—whether in General History or the History of the British Isles—covering a period before the nineteenth century. The list of papers satisfying this provision is given in the Handbook for Modern History and Politics.

(ii) At least one paper in the History of the British Isles.

(*e*) **[Until 1 October 2004:** Any candidate who**]** specified for the Honour School of Modern History**]** in the Second Public Examination offers two General History papers must offer one from any two of Groups A, B, and C, as specified for the Honour School of Modern History.**]** Candidates taking Politics paper 212 (International Relations in the Era of Two World Wars) cannot also take General History (xiii); candidates taking Politics paper 213 (International Relations in the Era of the Cold War) cannot also take General History (xiv); candidates who have taken **[Until 1 October 2004:** British History VI in the First Public Examination**] [From 1 October 2004:** British History VIII**]** or who are taking **[Until 1 October 2004:** it**] [From 1 October 2004:** British History VII (since 1900)**]** for the Pass School cannot also take Politics paper 202 (British Politics and Government in the Twentieth Century).

[From 1 October 2004:

Candidates who are taking British History VI (1815–1924) for the Pass School and who are also taking Politics paper 202 must not substantially duplicate material in those two papers.**]**

2. Any *one* of the five 'core subjects' in Politics, as specified for the Honour School of Philosophy, Politics, and Economics (i.e. 201, 202, 203, 214, and 220).

3. *One* of the following:

(i) any one of subjects 201–27 in Politics as specified for the Honour School of Philosophy, Politics, and Economics which is not offered under Regulation 2 above.

(ii) a thesis in Modern History submitted in accordance with **[Until 1 October 2004:** Regulation VII, 'Theses',**]** **[From 1 October 2004:** Regulation VI, *A thesis based on original research*,**]** for the Final Honour School of Modern History.

(iii) a thesis or supervised dissertation in Politics submitted in accordance with the regulations prescribed for Politics in the Honour School of Philosophy, Politics, and Economics.

NOTES

SPECIAL REGULATIONS FOR THE HONOUR SCHOOL OF MODERN LANGUAGES

A

1. The subjects of examination in the Honour School of Modern Languages shall be the French, German, Italian, Spanish, Portuguese, Russian, Medieval and Modern Greek, Czech (with Slovak),* and Celtic* languages and the literatures associated with them, and Linguistics. Save in the case of the subjects Czech (with Slovak) and Celtic, which may be offered only with another of the languages, a candidate may offer one or two languages, or one language and Linguistics. The standard of competence required of a candidate shall be the same in any language which he or she offers whether it be his or her sole language or one of two languages.

2. Every candidate shall be required to show, in the case of any language which he or she offers, a competent knowledge

(1) of the language as it is spoken and written at the present day, such knowledge to be tested by oral and written examination;
(2) of at least one specified period in its literature;
(3) of the history, thought, and civilization of the country necessary for the understanding of the language and literature.

3. A candidate offering one language shall be required to show a competent philological knowledge of the language he or she is offering. A candidate offering two languages shall be permitted to offer a paper or papers on philological topics.

4. Candidates offering the subject Linguistics shall be required to show a competent knowledge of analytical techniques and problems in descriptive and theoretical linguistics and the application of these to the language they are offering.

5. No candidate shall be admitted to examination in this School unless he or she has either passed or been exempted from the First Public Examination.

6. The examiners shall indicate in the lists issued by them the subject or subjects offered by each candidate obtaining honours or satisfying the examiners under Ch. VI, Sect. II. C, §1, cll. 21 (iv) and

---

* Czech (with Slovak) and Celtic may not be available in every year. Notice that these subjects, or a particular paper or particular papers, will not be available in a given year will be published in the *University Gazette* in the Trinity Term three years before the examination concerned.

(v). In drawing up the Class List the examiners shall satisfy themselves that each candidate has shown an appropriate level of competence both in literature (and linguistic studies where this applies) and in language.

7. The board of the faculty shall by notice from time to time make regulations concerning the examination; and shall have power in respect of each subject included in the examination

(1) to determine, within the limits of this decree, the form and content of the individual papers of the examination, and

(2) to issue a list of Special Subjects, prescribing books or authorities where they think it desirable. Such books or authorities may be in other languages than that to which the Special Subject is related. A Special Subject may be concerned with a language or literature not specified in clause 1 of this Decree.

8. A candidate whose name has been placed in the Class List upon the result of the examination in any one or more of the subjects included in the examination shall be permitted to offer himself or herself for examination in any of the other subjects so included at the examination in either the next year or the next year but one, provided that no such candidate shall offer any of the languages or subjects already offered by him or her in the Honour School of Modern Languages or in the Honour Schools of Modern History and Modern Languages, Philosophy and Modern Languages, Classics and Modern Languages, or English and Modern Languages, and provided always that he or she has not exceeded six terms from the date on which he or she first obtained Honours in a Final Honour School.

B

Candidates will be examined in accordance with the examination regulations set out below.

They will also be required to spend, after their matriculation, a year of residence in an appropriate country or countries, and to provide on their entry form for the examination a certificate that they have done this, signed by the Head or by a tutor of their society. Candidates wishing to be dispensed from the requirement to undertake a year of residence abroad must apply in writing to the Chairman of the Medieval and Modern Languages Board, 41 Wellington Square, Oxford OX1 2JF, stating their reasons for requesting dispensation and enclosing a letter of support from their society.

Candidates will be expected to carry out during this year abroad such work as their society may require. It is strongly recommended that candidates should apply through the Central Bureau for Educational Visits and Exchanges for an Assistantship, where these are available, and should accept one if offered. Candidates who are not able to obtain an Assistantship should during their year abroad follow a course or courses in an institution or institutions approved by their society, or should spend their time in such other circumstances as are acceptable to their society. Candidates will agree with their College Tutor in advance of their year abroad an independent course of study to be followed during that period.

It is strongly recommended that candidates offering two languages who spend their year abroad in a country or countries of one of the languages only should in addition spend between their matriculation and examination at least four weeks in a country of the other language.

Candidates may offer either one or two languages. The standard of competence shall be as high for candidates who offer two languages as for those who offer only one. A candidate offering one language may also offer Linguistics. The papers and choices of options available to candidates for each of the two courses will be the same.

Candidates may additionally offer an Extended Essay, good performance in which will be taken into account in allocating all classes.

The following is the scheme of papers for each language:

I. Unprepared translation into the language. **[From 1 October 2005:** (except that candidates for French are required to offer an essay in French**]**

IIA. Unprepared translation from the language ((i) Modern, *and* (ii) †Earlier). **[From 1 October 2005:** (except for candidates for IIA(i) in French are required to offer Literary translation into French)**]**

IIB. Unprepared translation from the language ((i) Modern, *and* (ii) †Earlier). **[From 1 October 2005:** (except that candidates for IIB(i) in French are required to offer Literary translation from French)**]**

III. An Essay in the language, on one of a choice of literary and other subjects. **[From 1 October 2005:** (except that candidates for French are required to offer Non-literary translation from and into French)**]**

IV. Linguistic Studies I.

V. Linguistic Studies II.

VI. Period of literature **[Until 1 October 2005:** or Period Topics (*French only*)**]** **[From 1 October 2005:** (except that candidates for French are required to offer Period Topics)**]** (i).

VII. Period of literature **[Until 1 October 2005:** or Period Topics (*French only*)**]** **[From 1 October 2005:** (except that candidates for French are required to offer Period Topics)**]** (ii).

VIII. Period of literature **[Until 1 October 2005:** or Period Topics (*French only*)**]** **[From 1 October 2005:** (except that candidates for French are required to offer Period Topics)**]** (iii).

IX. Early texts prescribed for study as examples of literature.

X. Modern Prescribed Authors (i).

XI. Early Modern Literary Texts (*German only*) or Modern Prescribed Authors (ii).

XII. Special Subject

XIII. General Linguistics

A candidate who offers *one* language only must take Papers

I

IIA. (i) *and* (ii)

IIB. (i) *and* (ii).

III

IX

Two of VI, VII, VIII, XIII

---

† Except that candidates offering Polish with Russian take unprepared translation from modern Polish in place of unprepared translations from Russian (Earlier).

Three of IV, V, X, XI, XII, Special Subject (Paper XII) Modern Catalan (for candidates offering *Spanish*), Special Subject (Paper XII) Modern Galician (for candidates offering *Spanish*), of which at least *one* must be IV *or* V **[From 1 October 2004:** *for first examination in Trinity Term 2005, but with effect from 1 October 2003 for first examination in 2004 for candidates on course I*: unless the sole language is French, in which case the candidate must take Papers:

I

IIA(i) *and* (ii)

IIB(i) *and* (ii)

III

One of VI, VII, VIII

Five of IV, V, VI, VII, VIII, IX, X, XI, XII, XIII]

Optionally Extended Essay

A candidate who offers *one* language and *Linguistics* must take:

In the language:

I

IIA. (i) ($1\frac{1}{2}$ hours)

IIB. (i) ($1\frac{1}{2}$ hours)

III

One of VI, VII, VIII

One or two of IX, X, XI

In Linguistics:

IV (in the language)

V (in the language)

XII (provided that the Special Subject chosen bears the Linguistics identifier as stated on the published list)

XIII

Also:

XII (unless two of IX, X, XI are offered in the language)

Also Optionally, Extended Essay.

Candidates must avoid substantial overlap between subjects offered as Special Subjects, and other Linguistics papers.

A candidate who offers *two* languages must take:

In one language:

I

IIA. (i) ($1\frac{1}{2}$ hours)

IIB. (i) ($1\frac{1}{2}$ hours).

III (unless offered in the other language)

One of VI, VII, VIII

Two of IV, V, IX, X, XI, XII Special Subject (Paper XII) Modern Catalan (for candidates offering *Spanish*), Special Subject (Paper XII) Modern Galician (for candidates offering *Spanish*).

In the other language:

I

IIA. (i) ($1\frac{1}{2}$ hours)

IIB. (i) ($1\frac{1}{2}$ hours).

III (unless offered in the other language)

One of VI, VII, VIII

One of IV, V, IX, X, XI, XII (provided that the Special Subject chosen bears the appropriate language identifier as stated on the published list).

Also, Optionally, Extended Essay.

Provided that:

(i) all candidates offering Italian must offer at least *one* of IV, V, IX;

(ii) **[Until 1 October 2005:** for candidates offering two languages, at least *one* of IV, V, IX is offered in *one* language;**]**

(iii)**[**(ii)**]** only *one* paper XII may be offered, except that candidates offering Spanish may offer *two* Special Subjects (Paper XII) provided *one* is *either* Modern Catalan *or* Modern Galician, and that candidates offering Linguistics may offer *two* Special Subjects (Paper XII) provided that at least *one* bears the appropriate Linguistics identifier as stated on the published list;

(iv)**[**(iii)**]** Paper XIII is not available to candidates offering two languages in the Honour School or to candidates for any joint school involving Modern Languages, nor may it be offered with the Special Subject (paper XII) General Linguistics.

[From 1 October 2005: (iv) a candidate offering two languages is required to offer *either* one of papers IV or V in one language, *or* at least one Pre-modern paper in one language, as designated below:

French: VI, VII, IX, X
German: VI, VII, IX, XI
Italian: IX
Spanish: VI, IX
Portuguese: VI, VII, IX, X
Russian: VI, VII, IX
Medieval and Modern Greek: VI, VII, IX, X
Celtic: VI, IX, X
Czech: IX;

And designated Paper XIIs in each language.

Details of Paper XII subjects which have been designated as Pre-modern will be provided in the list of Special Subjects published in the *University Gazette* by the beginning of the fifth week of the Trinity Term two years before the examination.**]**

Candidates who offer Russian as their sole language may offer 'Russian with Polish' by substituting Papers II A (ii) *and* II B (ii). Unprepared translation from Polish (Modern) in place of the same numbered papers in Russian. They may also substitute one or both of the Polish papers V and VII specified below in place of the same numbered papers in Russian. The Polish options are not available to candidates offering two languages in the Honour School or to candidates for any joint school involving Modern Languages.

V. The history of the Polish language.

VII. Polish literature: 1750–1916.

Candidates who offer Celtic may offer *either* Paper IIA(i) *and* Paper IIB(i) unprepared Translation from the language (Modern) *or* Paper IIA(ii) and Paper IIB(ii) unprepared Translation from the language (Earlier), *or* they may offer Paper IIA(ii) (Earlier) in place of Paper IIA(i) (Modern), *and* may also offer IIB(ii) (Earlier) in place of IIB(i) (Modern).

Answers must be written in English except when directions are given to the contrary.

Candidates will be required to attend for an oral examination in each language they offer. A candidate failing to appear for the oral examination, without good cause shown, will be deemed to have withdrawn from the whole examination.

In the oral examination a candidate will be required to show in each language he offers competence in the following:

(i) Comprehension of a passage or passages of text;

(ii) A short discourse;

(iii) Conversation. Reading aloud may be required of candidates as a further test of their pronunciation.

The following are the details for papers II A (ii), II B (ii), and IV to XII:

II A (ii). Unprepared translation from the language (Earlier).

II B (ii). Unprepared translation from the language (Earlier).

French:

Candidates will be required in each case to translate *either* a passage from the period up to 1530 *or* a passage from the period 1530–1715.

German:

Candidates will be required in each case to translate *either* a passage from the period 1150–1450 *or* a passage from the period 1450–1730.

Italian:

Candidates will be required in each case to translate a passage from the period up to 1750.

Spanish:

Candidates will be required in each case to translate *either* a passage from the period up to 1500 *or* a passage from the period 1543–1695.

Portuguese:

Candidates will be required in each case to translate *either* a passage from the period up to 1500 *or* a passage from the period 1500–1697.

Russian:

Candidates will be required in each case to translate *either* a passage from the period up to 1500 *or* a passage from the period 1500–1800.

Medieval and Modern Greek:

Candidates will be required in each case to translate *either* a passage of Byzantine Greek from the period up to 1453 *or* a passage of Medieval Greek from the period up to 1600.

Celtic: Candidates will be required in each case to translate *either* an Irish passage from the period up to 1200 *or* a Welsh passage from the period up to 1400.

IV. Linguistic Studies I.

French:

The History of the French language up to the mid-twentieth century.

The paper will consist of two sections as follows. Candidates must answer questions from both sections.

(1) The history of the language (phonetics, phonology, grammar, vocabulary, semantics, sociolinguistics, external history).

(2) The description of the language of literary and non-literary texts from past periods. Candidates may confine their answer(s) to *one* of the following sub-sections:

(*a*) From Latin to Early Old French: Before 1150;

(*b*) Old and Middle French: 1100–1530;

(*c*) Renaissance and Classical French: 1530–1715;

(*d*) Into Modern French: 1715–1940.

Optional passages from texts for linguistic and stylistic commentary will be set for each period. The following are suggested as illustrative texts:

(*a*) Studer and Waters, *Historical French Reader,* 1, 6, 7, 10, 11, 13.

(*b*) Studer and Waters, *Historical French Reader,* 20, 26, 34, 40, 41, 45, 46, 47, 65.

Passages for commentary will be selected from the texts listed above.

In (*c*) and (*d*) the texts will be selected from appropriate literary and non-literary works.

German:

The development of the German language from 1170 to the present, with a special study of:

Werner der Gärtner, *Helmbrecht* (Reclam edn.).

Martin Luther, *Sendbrief vom Dolmetschen,* ed. K. Bischoff, pp. 6/7–28, l. 21/29, l. 22, and pp. 36–57.

Andreas Gryphius, *Verliebtes Gespenst—Die geliebte Dornrose,* ed. E. Mannack (Reclam, 1958).

Italian:

The history of the Italian language from the earliest times to the twentieth century.

Spanish:

The history of the Spanish language to 1700. The paper will be divided into three sections, and candidates must answer from two: (*a*) to 1250; (*b*) 1250–1500; (*c*) 1500–1700.

Portuguese:

The history of the Portuguese language.

Russian:

The history of the Russian language with the following texts prescribed:

(1) for linguistic comment:

(*a*) Marginalia to Novgorod service books (V. V. Ivanov *et al.*, *Khrestomatiya po istorii russkogo yazyka*, Moscow, 1990, pp. 26–7).

Novgorod birchbark texts nos. 247, 644, 605, 424, 724, 717, 731, 531, 705, 142, 370, 363, 361, 125, 43, 49, 154, (A. A. Zaliznyak, *Drevnenovgorodskii dialekt*, Moscow, 1995, pp. 223–4, 244–5, 246–8, 295–300, 325–9, 344–7, 349–51, 440–1, 494–5, 508–9, 514, 536, 542–3, 562–4).

Vkladnaya Varlaama (Zaliznyak, pp. 374–7).

Treaty of Alexander Nevsky and Novgorod with the Germans, 1262–3 (S. P. Obnorsky and S. G. Barkhudarov, *Khrestomatiya po istorii russkogo yazyka*, part 1, 2nd edn., Moscow, 1952, pp. 51–2).

Novgorod First Chronicle, *s.a.* 6738–9 (ed. A. N. Nasonov, *Novgorodskaya Pervaya letopis' starshego i mladshego izvoda*, Moscow–Leningrad, 1950, pp. 69–71).

(*b*) Afanasy Nikitin, *Khozhenie za tri morya* (Ivanov *et al.*, pp. 322–5).

Dukhovnaya gramota I. Yu. Gryaznogo (Ivanov *et al.*, pp. 279–80).

Letter of T. I. Golitsyna to V. V. Golitsyn (S. I. Kotkov *et al.*, *Moskovskaya delovaya i bytovaya pis'mennost' XVII veka*, Moscow, 1968, p. 20).

Letters of D. V. Mikhalkov to M. I. Mikhalkova and P. D. Mikhalkov (Kotkov *et al.*, pp. 39–40 (17b-v), 41 (18b)).

Letters of U. S. Pazukhina to S. I. Pazukhin and E. Klement'ev to F. M. Chelishchev (S. I. Kotkov and N. P. Pankratova, *istochniki po istorii narodno-razgovornogo yazyka XVII-nachala XVIII veka*, Moscow, 1964, pp. 169–70, 233).

Letters of Peter I to Tsaritsa Natal'ya Kirillovna, to F. M. Apraksin, to B. P. Sheremetev (S. P. Obnorsky and S. G. Barkhudarov, *Khrestomatiya po istorii russkogo yazyka*, part 2:1, Moscow, 1949, pp. 83, 96–7, 99–100).

Evidence of A. Turcheninov on fire of 29 May 1737 (A. I. Sumkina and S. I. Kotkov, *Pamyatniki moskovskoi delovoi pis'mennosti XVIII veka*, Moscow, 1981, pp. 159–60).

Letters of V. B. Golitsyn to Vl. B. Golitsyn, M. D. Kurakina to B. I. Kurakin, M. M. Shcherbatov to D. M. Shcherbatov (Sumkina and Kotkov, pp. 24–6, 49–50 (50), 73–4).

(2) for translation and linguistic comment:

(*a*) Colophon to Ostromir Codex (Ivanov *et al.*, pp. 15–16).

Mstislavova gramota (Ivanov *et al.*, pp. 39–41).

Colophon to Mstislav's Gospel Book (Ivanov *et al.*, pp. 49–50).

Treaty of Novgorod with Grand Prince Yaroslav Yaroslavich, 1264 or 1265 (Obnorsky and Barkhudarov, part 1, pp. 52–4).

Russkaya Pravda (Ivanov, *et al.*, pp. 67–73).

Novgorod First Chronicle, *s.a.* 6633–8, 6675–7, 6700, 6712, 6777–80 (Nasonov, pp. 21–2, 32–3, 40, 46–9, 87–90).

(*b*) *Sudebnik* of 1497 (Ivanov *et al.*, 169–72).

Domostroi (Ivanov *et al.*, 255–60).

Ulozhenie Alekseya Mikhailovicha, Chapter 10 (Ivanov *et al.*, pp. 380–1).

G. Kotoshikhin, O Rossii v tsarstvovanie Alekseya Mikhailovicha, Chapter 4, Section 24, Chapter 13, Sections 1–4 (ed. A. E. Pennington, Oxford, 1980, pp. 65–7, 159–63).

Stateinyi spisok P. A. Tolstogo (Obnorsky and Barkhudarov, part 2:1, 1949, pp. 72–5).

Candidates will be required to show knowledge *either* of the texts listed under (1) (*a*)–(*b*), *of* those listed under (1) (*a*) and (2) (*a*), *or* of those listed under (1) (*b*) and (2) (*b*).

Medieval and Modern Greek:

Either

(1) Early history of the language: Medieval Greek to AD 959 with the following texts prescribed for linguistic study:

Romanos, *Cantica* (ed. Maas-Trypanis, nos. 1, 17–19, 33, 34, 41, 54, 55).

Moschos, selected excerpts from the *Leimonarion* (ed. Hesseling).

G. Soyter, *Byzantinische Geschichtsschreiber und Chronisten,* nos. 1–10.

Or

(2) The literary vernacular of the twelfth to fifteenth centuries, with the following texts prescribed for linguistic study:

Ptochoprodromos (ed. H. Eideneier), III and IV (pp. 117–75).

L'Achilléide Byzantine (ed. Hesseling), ll. 706–837 (pp. 61–4) and ll. 486–570 (pp. 103–5).

Le Roman de Callimaque et de Chrysorrhoé (ed. Pichard).

Or

(3) The dialects of Modern Greece.

Czech (with Slovak):

The history of Czech and Slovak.

Passages for commentary and translation will be taken from Porák, *Chrestomatie k vývoji českého jazyka* (1979), pp. 31–131.

Candidates will be required to write one translation, one commentary, and two essay-type questions.

Celtic: Comparative and Historic Celtic Linguistics. Passages will be set for linguistic commentary on *one* of (*a*) The history of Welsh *or* of Irish and Scottish Gaelic *or* (*b*) Comparative Celtic Linguistics*

V. Linguistic Studies II.

French:

Modern French. Candidates will be required to show knowledge of the descriptive analysis of the contemporary language, and will have the opportunity of discussing the historical development of the language where this illuminates present-day usage. The paper will contain optional questions on the principles of descriptive linguistics to be answered with particular reference to French.

---

* It is possible to do this paper with a knowledge of either Irish (with Scottish Gaelic) or Welsh, together with some Continental Celtic, or with a knowledge of both Irish and Welsh. Details of the passages for translation and comment are available from the Modern Languages Faculty Office.

German:

Either

(1) Old High German, with the following texts prescribed for study: W. Braune, *Althochdeutsches Lesebuch* (17th edn., by E. A. Ebbinghaus): V *Gespräche*; VIII Isidor, cap. iii; XX Tatian, subsections 2, 4, and 7; XXIII Notker, subsections 1 and 13; XXVIII *Hildebrandslied*; XXIX *Wessobrunner Gebet*; XXX *Muspilli*; XXXII Otfrid, subsections 7 (*Missus est Gabrihel angelus*) and 21 (*De die judicii*); XXXVI *Ludwigslied*; XLIII *Ezzos Gesang*, Strasbourg version only.

Or

(2) Descriptive analysis of German as spoken and written at the present day (phonetics, phonology, grammar, vocabulary, semantics, style). The paper will contain optional questions on the principles of descriptive linguistics to be answered with particular reference to German.

Italian:

Modern Italian. Candidates will be required to show knowledge of the descriptive analysis of the contemporary language, and will have the opportunity of discussing the historical development of the language where this illuminates present-day usage. The paper will contain optional questions on the principles of descriptive linguistics to be answered with particular reference to Italian.

Spanish:

Modern Spanish. Candidates will be required to show knowledge of the descriptive analysis of the structure of the contemporary language, as used in Spain and in the Americas.

Portuguese:

Modern Portuguese. Candidates will be required to show knowledge of the descriptive analysis of the contemporary language, as used in Portugal and in Brazil, and will have the opportunity of discussing the historical development of the language where this illuminates present-day usage. The paper will contain optional questions on the principles of descriptive linguistics to be answered with particular reference to Portuguese.

Russian:

Either

(1) The development of the Church Slavonic language, with the following texts prescribed:

(*a*) for linguistic comment:

Kiev Missal and *Euchologium Sinaticum* (R. Auty, *Handbook of Old Church Slavonic*, London, 1968 and subsequent reprints, Pt. ii, Texts and Glossary, passages IV, pp. 52–7, and VI, pp. 64–9).

Luke x: 25–37 (Auty, passage XIV, pp. 97–106: ed. L. P. Zhukovskaya *et al.*, *Aprakos Mstislava Velikogo*, Moscow, 1983, p. 131).

Psalm liv (ed. S. Sever'yanov, *Sinaiskaya Psaltyr'*, Petrograd, 1922, pp. 67–9; ed. E. V. Cheshko *et al.*, *Norovskaya psaltyr'. Srednebolgarskaya rukopis' XIV veka*, Sofia, 1989, Pt. ii, pp. 387–91; *Psaltir s posljedovanjem Đurđa Crnojevića 1494*, reprinted Cetinje, 1986; the Synodal Bible of 1751 and subsequent editions, e.g. Moscow, 1815, St Petersburg, 1820).

(*b*) for translation and linguistic comment:

Vita Constantini, xiv–xv, xvii–xviii, *Vita Methodii*, v–xvii, the Treatise on Letters, the Acrostich Prayer (A. Vaillant, *Textes vieux-slaves*, Paris, 1968, Pt. i, Textes et glossaire, passages I, pp. 30–3, 37–40, II, pp. 46–55, III, pp. 57–61, IV C. pp. 68–70).

Kniga Konstantina filosofa i grammatika o pismenex, sections 4–9 (V. Jagić, *Codex slovenicus rerum grammaticarum*, Berlin, 1896, reprinted Munich, 1968, V, pp. 108–13).

Zhitie sv. Stefana episkopa Permskogo (ed. V. Druzhinin, St Petersburg, 1897, reprinted The Hague, 1959, pp. 69–74).

V. F. Burstov's *Bukvar'* (V. V. Ivanov *et al.*, *Khrestomatiya po istorii russkogo yazyka*, Moscow, 1990, pp. 369–74).

Candidates will be required to show knowledge of the texts listed under (1) (*a*) and (1) (*b*).

Or

(2) Descriptive analysis of Russian as spoken and written at the present day (phonetics, phonology, grammar, vocabulary, semantics, style). The paper will contain optional questions on the principles of descriptive linguistics to be answered with particular reference to Russian.

Medieval and Modern Greek:

Either

(1) The structure of the standard language as spoken and written at the present day (phonetics, phonology, grammar, vocabulary, semantics, style). The paper will contain optional questions on the principles of descriptive linguistics to be answered with particular reference to Modern Greek.

Or

(2) The Language Controversy.

VI. Topics in the period of literature (*French only*) *or* Period of literature (i):
French: to 1530.
German: Medieval German Culture (to 1450): Texts, Contexts, and Issues.
Italian: 1220–1430.
Spanish: to 1499.
Portuguese: to 1540.*
Russian: to 1660.
Medieval and Modern Greek: Byzantine Greek to 1453.
Celtic: Medieval Irish up to 1600 and Medieval Welsh up to 1500. [Candidates will be able to confine their answers to questions on *either* Irish *or* Welsh topics.

VII. Topics in the period of literature (*French only*) *or* Period of literature (ii):
French: 1530–1800.†
German: Early Modern German Culture (1450–1730): Texts, Contexts, and Issues.
Italian: 1430–1635.
Spanish: 1543–1695
Portuguese: 1500–1697‡

---

* Candidates offering both Portuguese paper VI and Portuguese paper VII may answer questions on the period 1500–40 in one of the two papers only. In papers VI and VII the questions affected by this provision will be indicated by an asterisk.

† (*a*) Candidates offering both French paper VII and French paper VIII may answer questions on the period 1715–1800 in *one* of the two papers only. In both papers, the questions most obviously affected by this provision will be indicated by an asterisk.

(*b*) Candidates offering subject 8(iii), Ancient and French Classical Tragedy, in the Honour School of Classics and Modern Languages or the Pass School of Classics and Modern Languages will not be permitted to discuss the work of Corneille and Racine in French paper VII.

‡ Candidates offering both Portuguese paper VI and Portuguese paper VII may answer questions on the period 1500–40 in one of the two papers only. In papers VI and VII the questions affected by this provision will be indicated by an asterisk.

Russian: 1660–1820.
Medieval and Modern Greek: Medieval Greek to 1669.

VIII. Topics in the period of literature (*French only*) *or* Period of literature (iii):
French: 1715 to the present.†
German: Modern German Literature (1730 to the present): Texts, Contexts, and Issues.
Italian: 1750 to the present.
Spanish: The literature of Spain and of Spanish America: 1811 to the present.

Candidates may offer themselves for examination *either* in the literature of both Spain and Spanish America, *or* in the literature of Spain only, *or* in the literature of Spanish America only.

Portuguese: The literature of Portugal and Brazil: 1761 to the present.

Candidates may offer themselves for examination *either* in the literature of both Portugal and Brazil, *or* in the literature of Portugal only, *or* in the literature of Brazil only.

Russian: 1820–1917.
Medieval and Modern Greek: Modern Greek, 1821 to the present.
Czech (with Slovak): Czech and Slovak literature, 1774 to the present.

Candidates will be required to answer three questions.

*IX. Early texts prescribed for study as examples of literature:

French:

In French paper IX, the commentary section of the paper will include compulsory passages for translation.

La Chanson de Roland, ed. Whitehead (Blackwell).
Béroul, *The Romance of Tristran,* ed. Ewert (Blackwell).
Villon, *Œuvres,* ed. Longnon-Foulet, 4th edn., with a special study of *Le Testament,* 1–909, 1660–end, and *Poésies Diverses* IX–XVI.
Candidates will be required to translate from one or more passages set for comment.

German:

Das Nibelungenlied, ed. K. Bartsch *et al.* (Reclam 1997), avent. 1, 14–17, 23–30, 36–9.
Wolfram von Eschenbach, *Parzival*, books 3, 5, and 9.
Frauenlieder des Mittelalters, ed. I. Kasten (Reclam 1990), nos. 1–47.
Der Stricker, *Erzählungen, Fabeln, Raden*, ed. O. Ehrismann (Reclam 1992).

Italian:

Dante, *La divina commedia*, with a special study of two of the three *Cantiche*.

Spanish:

Poema de mio Cid, ed. Michael (Clásicos Castalia).
Juan Ruiz, *Libro de Buen Amor*, ed. Gybbon-Monypenny (Clásicos Castalia).
Comedia o tragicomedia de Calisto y Melibea, ed. P. E. Russell (Clásicos Castalia).

Portuguese:

E. Gonçalves and M. A. Ramos, *A Lírica Galego–Portuguesa* (Comunicação).
Alfonso X of Castile, *Cantigas de Santa Maria*, ed. W. Mettmann (Clásicos Castalia, vol. I, 1986).

---

* Each paper will be divided into two sections, one containing questions on the general aspects of the books and authors, and the other containing passages for explanation and comment. Both sections will be compulsory.

Fernão Lopes, *Crónica de D. João* I (textos escolhidos), ed. T. Amado (Comunicação).

Zurara, *Crónica dos feitos de Guiné* (chs. 1–25). (Candidates are advised also to read Zurara, *Chronique de Guinée*, ed. L. Bourdon (Ifan–Dakar, 1960)).

Russian:

Chtenie Borisa i Gleba.

Slovo o polku Igoreve.

Slovo o zakone i blagodati Ilationa.

Povest' o Petre i Fevronii.

Slovo o zhitii i o prestavlenii velikago knyazya Dmitriya Ivanovicha, tsarya Ruskago (Fennell and Obolensky, pp. 86–98).

Kurbsky's Correspondence with Ivan IV (Fennell and Obolensky, pp. 136–46).

Avvakum, *Zhitie.*

Petrine Povest

1. Istoriya o rossiiskom dvoryanine Frole Skobeeve
2. Povest' zelo prechudna i udivleniya dostoina nekogo kuptsa Fomy Grudtsyna o syne eg Saave
3. Povest' o Bove Koroleviche.

Medieval and Modern Greek:

Candidates may choose one of either A or B:*

The commentary section of the paper will include compulsory passages for translation.

A: Byzantine texts:

Paul the Silentiary, *Ekphrasis* of Haghia Sophia (ed. Friedlander).

Christ and Paranikas, *Anthologia graeca carminum Christianorum*, pp. 147–236 and 247–52.

The Life of St Andreas Salos (ed. L. Ryden).

Michael Psellos, *Chronographia,* bk. VI (ed. S. Impellizzeri, vol. 1, pp. 246–320, and vol. 2, pp. 8–152).

B: Medieval vernacular texts:

Digenis Akritis: the Grottaferrata and Escorial Versions (ed. E. M. Jeffreys).

Livistros kai Rodamni (ed. P. A. Agapitos).

Ptochoprodromos (ed. H. Eideneier).

Passages will *not* be set from:

Digenis Akritis, Grottaferrata version, book V.

Ptochoprodromus, poem IV.

Czech (with Slovak):

Dalimilova kronika, chs. 1–32, 41, 66–70, 102–6.

Život svaté Kateřiny.

Tkadleček.

Candidates will be required to answer one question on each of the three texts, including one commentary. They will also be required to translate a passage.

Celtic:

Any four of the following: Early Texts (commentary section of the paper will include compulsory passages for translation).

Togail Bruidne Da Derga, ed. E. Knott (Dublin, 1936)

Fingal Rónáin and Other Stories, ed. D. Greene (Dublin, 1955).

Scéla Cano meic Gartnáin, ed. D. A. Binchy (Dublin, 1963).

Serglige Con Culainn, ed. M. Dillon (Dublin, 1953).

Cath Almaine, ed. P. O. Riain (Dublin, 1978).

---

* Those who offer B may not offer options (1) and (2) in Paper X.

The Irish Adam and Eve Story from Saltair na Rann, ed. D. Greene and F. Kelly (Dublin, 1976).

Canu Aneirin, ed. I. Williams (Cardiff, 1938).

Canu Llywarch Hen, ed. I. Williams (Cardiff, 1935).

Armes Prydein, ed. I. Williams (Cardiff, 1955; or Dublin, 1972).

M. Haycock, *Blodeugerdd Barddas o Ganu Crefyddol Cynnar* (Y Bala: Barddas, 1994).

Culhwch ac Olwen, ed. R. Bromwich and D. Simon Evans (Cardiff, 1992).

Selection from the series: R. Geraint Gruffydd (gen. ed.), Cyfres Beirdd y Tywysogion vols. I, II, V–VII (Cardiff, 1991–6).

*X. Modern Prescribed Authors (i): †Passages for explanation and comment will be taken from the works prescribed for special study. Candidates will be expected to have read works by their chosen authors other than those prescribed for special study.

French:

Any two of the following:

(1) Rabelais, with a special study of *Gargantua* and *Le Quart Livre.*

(2) Montaigne, with a special study of *Essais,* I. 20 (Que philosopher, c'est apprendre à mourir), I. 23 (De la coutume et de ne changer aisément une loi reçue), I. 26 (De l'institution des enfants), II. 17 (De la praesumption), II. 6 (De l'exercitation), III. 2 (Du repentir), III. 5 (Sur des vers de Virgile), III. 13 (De l'expérience).

(3) Pascal, *Œuvres,* in *Collection l'Intégrale, Éds. du Seuil,* with a special study of: *Pensées,* Section I, Section II (omitting Series VI–VIII, X, XII–XX), Section III, Section IV (913–48, 978); *De l'esprit géométrique et de l'art de persuader.*

(4) Molière, with a special study of *L'École des femmes, Les Fourberies de Scapin, Le Tartuffe, Dom Juan, Le Misanthrope, Le Malade Imaginaire.*

(5) Racine, with a special study of: *Andromaque, Britannicus, Bérénice, Bajazet, Iphigénie, Athalie.*

(6) Voltaire, with a special study of *Romans et contes,* ed. E. Guitton (Pochothèque, Livre de Poche, 1994): the following works: *Zadig, Paméla* (pp. 138–96), *Candide, Contes de Guillaume Vadé* (pp. 339–453), *La Princess de Babylone, Les Lettres d'Amabed, Le Taureau blanc., Lettres philosophiques,* ed. F. Deloffre, Folio.

(7) Diderot, with a special study of *'Le Rêve de d'Alembert*, ed. Chouillet, Livre de Poche, *Jacques le fataliste*, ed. Belaval, Folio *Le Neveu de Rameau*, ed. Varloot, Folio, *Le Salon de 1765*, ed. Bukdahl and Lorenceau, Hermann.

German:

Any two of the following:

(1) Luther, with a special study of *Von der Freyheyt eyniß Christenmenschen* in Martin Luther: Selections, ed. Lewis Jillings and Brian Murdoch, New German Studies Monographs, Hull.

(2) Gryphius, with a special study of Gedichte, ed. Elschenbroich (Reclam). Candidates will further be expected to have studied a representative selection of Gryphius's drama.

---

* Each paper will be divided into two sections, one containing questions on the general aspects of the books and authors, and the other containing passages for explanation and comment. Both sections will be compulsory.

† Except in the case of Medieval and Modern Greek.

(3) Grimmelshausen, with a special study of *Simplicissimus* (*Teutsch*). Candidates will further be expected to have studied other of the 'Simplizianische Schriften'.

(4) Goethe as dramatist, with a special study of *Faust*, part I. Candidates will further be expected to have studied at least three other dramatic works by Goethe.

(5) Goethe as poet and novelist, with a special study of *Selected Verse*, ed. Luke (Penguin), excepting the extracts from *Faust*. Candidates will further be expected to have studied at least two novels by Goethe.

(6) Schiller, with a special study of *Wallenstein*. Candidates will further be expected to have studied other works representative of Schiller's development as a dramatist.

(7) Hölderlin, with a special study of Friedrich Hölderlin, *Gedichte*, ed. Nussbächer, Stuttgart 1963 (Reclam Universalbibliothek No. 6266 [3]).

(8) Kleist, with a special study of *Amphitryon*. Candidates will further be expected to have studied a representative selection of Kleist's plays and prose works.

(9) Hoffmann, with a special study of *Der Sandmann* and *Der goldne Topf*. Candidates will further be expected to have studied at least one of the novels and a representative selection of the shorter fiction.

(10) Heine, with a special study of *Atta Troll* and *Deutschland, ein Wintermärchen*. Candidates will further be expected to have studied a representative selection of Heine's poetry and prose, the latter to include the *Reisebilder*.

(11) Rilke, with a special study of *Der neuen Gedichte anderer Teil*. Candidates will further be expected to have studied a representative selection of Rilke's other writings.

(12) Thomas Mann, with a special study of *Der Tod in Venedig*. Candidates will further be expected to have studied at least one of the novels and a representative selection of the shorter fiction.

(13) Kafka, with a special study of *Der proceß: Roman in der Fassung der Hanschrift*, ed. Malcolm Pasley (Fischer Taschenbuch Verlag, No. 114123). Candidates will further be expected to have studied a representative selection of Kafka's other fiction.

(14) Brecht, with a special study of *Der gute Mensch von Sezuan*. Candidates will further be expected to have studied other works representative of Brecht's development as dramatist and poet.

(15) Grass, with a special study of *Die Blechtrommel*. Candidates will further be expected to have studied a representative selection of Grass's prose fiction.

(16) Christa Wolf, with a special study of *Nachdenken über Christa T.* Candidates will further be expected to have studied a representative selection of Christa Wolf's prose works.

Note. The paper will contain questions of a general nature, and questions on specific texts. Candidates will not be allowed to make any one text the principal subject of more than one answer.

Italian:

Any two of the following:

(1) Petrarch, with a special study of the *Canzoniere,* Nos. 1–12; 16–24; 30; 34–7; 50–4; 60–2; 70; 72; 77; 80–1; 90–2; 102; 119; 125–6; 128–9; 132–4; 136; 142; 145; 148; 159–60; 164; 197; 211; 219; 263–4; 268; 272; 279–80;

287–92; 302–4; 310–11; 315; 327; 353; 359–60; 364–6. Candidates will further be expected to have studied a representative selection of Petrarch's other Italian poems and of works originally written in Latin.

(2) Boccaccio, with a special study of the *Decameron,* I. 1–3; II, 2, 5, 10; III, 2; IV, 1, 2, 5, 7, 9; V, 6, 8, 9; VI, 1, 9, 10; VII, 4, 9; VIII, 3, 8; IX, 1, 2; X, 2, 9, 10. Candidates will further be expected to have studied a representative selection of other parts of the *Decameron* and of other works by Boccaccio.

(3) Machiavelli, with a special study of *Il Principe*. Candidates will further be expected to have studied a representative selection of Machiavelli's other works, including *I discorsi* and *La mandragola.*

(4) Ariosto, with a special study of *Orlando Furioso,* cantos I–XIII.45; XVIII.146–XXIV; XXVIII–XXX; XXXIV; XLV–XLVI. Candidates will further be expected to have studied other parts of the *Orlando Furioso* and a selection of the *Satire*.

(5) Tasso, with a special study of *Gerusalemme Liberata,* cantos I–VII, XI–XVI; XIX–XX, and *Aminta*. Candidates will further be expected to have studied other parts of the *Gerusalemme Liberata.*

Spanish:

Any two of the following:

(1) Garcilaso de la Vega, *Poesías castellanas completas* (ed. E. L. Rivers, Clásicos Castalia, 3rd edn. 1996).

(2) Cervantes, with a special study of *El ingenioso hidalgo don Quijote de la Mancha.* (Passages for commentary will be set from the Second Part only.)

(3) Góngora, with a special study of *Soledad primera* (from *Soledades*, ed. R. Jammes, Castalia). *Fábula de Polifemo y Galatea* (ed. A. A. Parker, Cátedra), *Sonnets* (*Poems of Góngora,* ed. R. O. Jones, pp. 87–92). Candidates will be expected to have read *Soledad segunda.*

(4) Quevedo, with a special study of 'Infierno', 'El mundo por de dentro', 'Sueño de la muerte', in *Sueños y discursos* (ed. J. O. Crosby, Castalia); *La cuna y la sepultura*, and *España defendida* (Preliminaries and Chapter 5 only), in *Obras completas, I: Prosa* (ed. F. Buendía, Aguilar); *Poesía varia* (ed. J. O. Crosby, Cátedra), nos. 16–30, 35–53, 71–83, 987–106, 127–33, 160–1; *El buscón* (ed. D. Ynduráin, Cátedra).]

(5) Calderón, with a special study of *La vida es sueño* (ed. A. E. Sloman, Manchester University Press) (candidates will be expected to have read the *auto* of the same name), *El pintor de su deshonra* (ed. Ruiz Lagos, Colección Aula Magna), *El mágico prodigioso,* and *El Alcalde de Zalamea* (both Clásicos castellanos), *El gran teatro del mundo.*

Portuguese:

Any two of the following:

(1) Gil Vicente, with a special study of *Auto da Alma, Auto da Feira, Farsa de Inês Pereira, Farsa dos Almocreves, O Triunfo do Inverno, Dom Duardos.*

(2) João de Barros, with a special study of *Rópica Pnefma* (ed. I. S. Révah, Lisbon, 1955) and *Décadas,* vol. I (ed. A. Baião, Sá da Costa, Lisbon, 1945).

(3) Camões, with a special study of *Os Lusíadas* (ed. F. Pierce) and *Líricas* (ed. Rodrigues Lapa, 1970 or later).

(4) Francisco Manuel de Melo, with a special study of *Epanáfora política, Relógios falantes, Hospital das Letras, Carta de Guía de Casados, O Fidalgo Aprendiz.*

(5) António Ferreira, *Bristo, Cioso, Poemas Lusitanos* (including *A Castro*).

Russian:

Any two of the following:

(1) Pushkin, with a special study of *Tsygany, Evgeny Onegin*, *Povesti Belkina,*

Selected lyrics (copies of the list of prescribed poems are available from the Slavonic Library, 47 Wellington Square).

[**Until 1 October 2004:** (2) Gogol, with a special study of *Mirgorod, Shinel', Zapiski Sumasshedshego, Nevsky Prospekt, Portret, Nos, Mertvye dushi.*]

[**From 1 October 2004:** (2) Gogol, with a special study of *Mirgorod,* (excluding *Taras Bul'ba*) *Shinel', Zapiski sumasshedshego, Nevsky Prospekt, Portret, Nos, Mertvye dushi* Part I, *Revizor.*]

(3) Mandel'shtam. Selected lyrics (copies of the prescribed poems are available from the Slavonic Library, 47 Wellington Square). Candidates will also be expected to have read a representative selection of Mandel'shtam's artistic prose and articles on literary topics.

(4) Mayakovsky, with a special study of *Oblako v shtanakh, Pro eto, Lyublyu, Klop*, and selected lyrics (copies of the prescribed poems are available from the Slavonic Library, 47 Wellington Square). Candidates will also be expected to have read *Kak delat' stikhi* and a representative selection of Mayakovsky's other works.

(5) Bulgakov, with a special study of *Belaya gvardiya, Sobach'e serdtse, Beg, Master i Margarita.*

Medieval and Modern Greek:

Any two of the following:

(1) *Digenis Akritis: the Grottaferrata and Escorial Versions* (ed. E. M. Jeffreys).

(2) The vernacular verse romances.

(3) Cretan drama, with a special study of Chortatsis' *Erophile, Katzourbos,* and *Panoria* (ed. R. Bancroft-Marcus).

(4) *Erotokritos.*

(5) Greek oral poetry.

Czech (with Slovak):

Any three of the following:

(1) Comenius, with a special study of *Labyrint světa a ráj srdce.*

(2) Hrabal, with a special study of *Obsluhoval jsem anglického krále.*

(3) Hodrová, with a special study of *Podobojí.*

(4) Holan, with a special study of *Terezka Planetová.*

(5) Johnides, with a special study of *Marek koniar a uhorský pápež.*

(6) Mitana, with a special study of the volume *Prievan.*

Candidates will be required to answer questions on each of their three authors, including one commentary.

Celtic:

Any two of the following:

(1) *Gwaith Guto'r Glyn*, ed. I. Williams and J. Llywelyn Williams (Cardiff, 1939).

(2) *Gwaith Tudur Aled*, ed. T. Gwynn Jones (Cardiff, 1926).

(3) *Gwaith Iorwerth Fynglwyd*, ed. H. Ll. Jones and E. I. Rowlands (Cardiff, 1973).

(4) *Gramadegau'r Penceirddiaid*, ed. G. J. Williams and E. J. Jones (Cardiff, 1934), Texts A and C (pp. 1–18, 39–58).

(5) *Acallam na Senórach* (in the selection ed. M. Dillon, *Stories from the Acallam* [Dublin, 1970]).

(6) *Caithréim Cellaig*, ed. K. Mulchrone, 2nd edn. (Dublin, 1971).

(7) *Buile Shuibne*, ed. J. G. O'Keefe (Dublin, 1931).

(8) *Tóruigheacht Dhiarmada agus Ghráinne*, ed. N. Ní Sheaghdha, Irish Texts Society 48 (Dublin, 1967).

(9) *Dánta Grádha*, ed. T. F. O'Rahilly, 2nd edn. (Cork: Cork University Press, 1926).

*XI. Early Modern Literary Texts (*German only*) or
*Modern Prescribed Authors (ii):

Passages for explanation and comment will be taken from the works prescribed for special study. Candidates will be expected to have read works by their chosen authors other than those prescribed for special study.

French:

Any two of the following:

(1) Stendhal, with a special study of *Le Rouge et le Noir* and *La Chartreuse de Parme.*

(2) Baudelaire, with a special study of *Les Fleurs du Mal* and the *Petits Poèmes en prose.*

(3) Flaubert, with a special study of *Madame Bovary, Trois Contes* and *L'Éducation sentimentale.*

(4) Mallarmé, with a special study of *Poésies*, ed. L. J. Austin (GF-Flammarion) (omitting Sections III (*Poèmes de jeunesse*) and IV (*Poèmes d'enfance et d'adolescence*)) and *Igitur,* ed. Gallimard, 'Collection Poésie' (omitting *Igitur, Quelques médaillons et portraits en pied* and *Pages diverses).*

(5) Gide, with a special study of *L'Immoraliste, La Porte étroite, Si le grain ne meurt* and *Les Faux-Monnayeurs.*

(6) Sartre, with a special study of *La Nausée, Les Mouches, Les Séquestrés d'Altona* and *Les Mots.*

[From 1 October 2004:

(7) Duras, with a special study of *Un barrage contre le Pacifique, Le Ravissement de Lol V. Stein, L'Amant,* and *Hiroshima, mon amour* (film script).**]**

German:

Any four out of the following five topics:

(1) Luther: *Von der Freyheyt eyniß Christenmenschen* and *Ein Sendbrieff vom Dolmetzschenn.*

(2) 16th century fiction: Wickram, *Von guten und bösen Nachbarn* and *Historia von D. Johann Fausten* (Reclam edition).

(3) Baroque drama: Gryphius, *Catharina von Georgien* and Lohenstein, *Cleopatra* (both in Reclam editions).

(4) Grimmelshausen: *Courasche* (Reclam edition).

(5) Baroque Poetry: Fleming, *Deutsche Gedichte* and Günther, *Gedichte* (both Reclam editions).

Note. This paper will require candidates to attempt a commentary and two essay questions.

Italian:

Any two of the following:

(1) Manzoni, with a special study of *I promessi sposi.* Candidates will further be expected to have studied Manzoni's tragedies and a selection of his other works.

(2) Leopardi, with a special study of *I Canti.* Candidates will further be expected to have studied the *Operette morali* and a selection of Leopardi's other writings.

---

* Each paper will be divided into two sections, one containing questions on the general aspects of the books and authors, and the other containing passages for explanation and comment. Both sections will be compulsory.

(3) D'Annunzio, with a special study of *Alcyone*. Candidates will further be expected to have studied a selection of D'Annunzio's other works in verse and prose.

(4) Verga, with a special study of *I Malavoglia* and *Mastro-don Gesualdo*. Candidates will further be expected to have studied a selection of Verga's other fiction.

(5) Pirandello, with a special study of *Il fu Mattia Pascal, Sei personaggi in cerca d'autore* and *I giganti della montagna*. Candidates will further be expected to have studied a representative selection of Pirandello's drama and prose work.

(6) Montale, with a special study of 'Ossi di seppia' in *Ossi di seppia,* Section IV of *Le occasioni,* 'Finisterre' in *La bufera e altro* and 'Xenia I' in *Satura*. Candidates will further be expected to have studied a representative selection of Montale's other poems.

(7) Calvino, with a special study of *Il cavaliere inesistente* and *Se una notte d'inverno un viaggiatore.* Candidates will further be expected to have studied other works representative of Calvino's development as a writer.

Spanish:

Any two of the following:

(1) Pérez Galdós, with a special study of *Juan Martín el Empecinado, El amigo Manso, Miau, Nazarín.*

(2) Leopoldo Alas, with a special study of *La Regenta* (ed. Gonzalo Sobejano, Clásicos Castalia), and *Cuentos escogidos* (ed. G. G. Brown, Oxford, 1964).

(3) Valle-Inclán, with a special study of *Sonatas*; *Águila de blasón*; *Romance de lobos*; *Divinas palabras*; *Luces de Bohemia* (ed. A. Zamora Vicente, Clásicos castellanos); *Martes de carnaval*; *Tirano Banderas* (ed. A. Zamora Vicente, Clásicos castellanos). Candidates will also be expected to have read *La lámpara maravillosa* and *La corte de los milagros.*

(4) Federico García Lorca, with a special study of *Amor de Don Perlimplín con Belisa en su jardín, Así que pasen cinco años, Bodas de sangre, Canciones, Diván del Tamarit, Llanto por Ignacio Sánchez Mejías, Mariana Pineda, Poeta en Nueva York* (ed. Millán), *El público, La zapatera prodigiosa.*

(5) Neruda, with a special study of *Veinte poemas de amor y una canción desesperada* (ed. Montes, Clásicos Castalia, Madrid, 1987); *Canto general* (I, II, XIV, XV); *Memorial de Isla Negra* (I, IV) (Seix Barral, Barcelona, 1976); *Pablo Neruda: A Basic Anthology* (ed. Pring-Mill, Dolphin, Oxford, 1975), pp. 8–42 and 80–109, and those poems included in the *Basic Anthology* from the following collections: *Estravagario, Plenos poderes, Jardín de invierno*, and *El mar y las campanas.*

(6) Borges, with a special study of *Ficciones* (ed. either Emecé or Alianza-Emecé); *El aleph*; *El informe de Brodie*; *Obra poética 1923–1976* (ed. Alianza-Emecé, sections entitled *El hacedor* and *El otro, el mismo*).

Portuguese:

Any two of the following:

(1) Almeida Garrett, with a special study of *Portugal na balança da Europa, Frei Luís de Sousa, O Arco de Sant' Ana, Viagens na Minha Terra, Folhas Caídas.*

(2) Eça de Queirós, with a special study of *O Crime do Padre Amaro, Os Maias,* and *A ilustre casa de Ramires.*

(3) Machado de Assis, with a special study of *Memórias póstumas de Brás Cubas, Dom Casmurro,* and *Quincas Borba.*

(4) Fernando Pessoa, with a special study of *Obras completas,* vol. I (Ática).

(5) Graciliano Ramos, with a special study of *Caetés, São Bernardo, Angústia, Vidas Secas, Infância.*

(6) Clarice Lispector, with a special study of *Perto do Coração Selvagem, A Paixão segundo G. H., A Hora da Estrela.*

Russian:

Any two of the following:

(1) Dostoevsky, with a special study of *Prestuplenie i nakazanie, Brat'ya Karamazovy, Zapiski iz podpol'ya.*

(2) Tolstoy, with a special study of *Anna Karenina, Voyna i mir.*

(3) Chekhov, with a special study of *Palata No. 6, Poprygun'ya, Moya zhizn, Muzhiki, Dama s sobachkoy, V ovrage, Dushechka, Arkkhierey,* and *Nevesta,* as well as *Chayka, Dyadya Vanya, Tri sestry, Vishnevi sad.*

(4) Solzhenitsyn, with a special study of *Odin den' Ivana Denisovicha, V kruge pervom* (candidates are expected to be familiar with the 96-chapter version of the novel first published in 1978), *Rakovy korpus.*

Medieval and Modern Greek:

Any two of the following:

(1) Solomos, with a special study of the poems composed between 1825 and 1849 (*Apanta,* ed. L. Politis (Athens, 1961), pp. 139–255), the *Dialogos,* and the *Gynaika tes Zakythos.*

(2) Palamas, with a special study of *O dodekalogos tou Gyftou, Oi khairetismoi tes Eliogennetes* and the following sections of *E asalefte zoe*: *Patrides, Foinikia, Askraios, Alysides.*

(3) Kavafis, with a special study of *Poiemata,* vols. i and ii, ed. G. P. Savidis (Ikaros, Athens, 1963, or later).

(4) Seferis, with a special study of *Poiemata* (Athens, 1972, or later).

(5) Tsirkas, with a special study of the trilogy *Akyvernetes politeies (E leskhe, Ariagne,* and *E nykhterida)*

(6) The novels of Kazantzakis, with a special study of *Vios kai politeia tou Alexe Zorba* and *O Khristos xanastavronetai.*

XII. Special Subjects.

1. A candidate may offer one of the Special Subjects from the list below. Fuller details, including the method of examination for each Special Subject, will be published in the *University Gazette* by the beginning of the fifth week of the Trinity Term two years before the examination.

Depending on the availability of teaching resources, not all Special Subjects will be available to all candidates in every year.

Modern literary theory.
European cinema.

Syntax.
Semantics.
Phonetics and Phonology.
Sociolinguistics.
Translation Theory.

Romance philology and linguistics.
Anglo-Norman language and literature.
Old Provençal.
The Old French epic.
The twelfth- and thirteenth-century Grail Romances.
French historical writing to 1515.
French poetry of the mid-sixteenth century.
Dramatic theory and practice in France 1605–60.
Jean-Jacques Rousseau.

French satire from Rabelais to Beaumarchais.
Honoré de Balzac.
French poetry 1870–1918.
French literature and the First World War.
Marcel Proust.
Surrealism.
The 'Nouveau Roman'.
Literature and the visual arts from Diderot to Zola.
French women writers.
Advanced French translation: theory and practice.

Old Norse.
Old High German, with *either* Gothic *or* Old Saxon *or* Old English.
The German Minnesang.
Wolfram von Eschenbach.
Mechthild von Magdeburg and women's writing in German 1150–1300.
German poetry and drama of the seventeenth century.
Eighteenth-century German aesthetics from Baumgarten to Schiller.
Friedrich Nietzsche.
Weimar Classicism 1794–1805.
The *Bildungsroman*.
German Political Writing.
Nineteenth-Century German Drama.
Expressionism and Dada in literature and the visual arts.
Shorter modernist prose fiction 1901–27.
The poetry of Hugo von Hofmannsthal, Stefan George, and Rainer Maria Rilke.
German poetry from 1945.
The German novel from 1945.
Literature in the GDR.
Advanced German translation.

Italian lyric poetry of the thirteenth century.
Dante's minor works.
'Questione della lingua'.
Women writers of the Italian Renaissance.
The aesthetics and literary criticism of Croce.
The works of Carlo Emilio Gadda.
Sicilian literature 1945 to the present day.
Italian women writers 1945 to the present day.

The civilisation of Muslim Spain.
Spanish drama before Lope de Vega.
The Spanish Erasmians.
The discovery and conquest of Mexico and the Antilles.
Spanish devotional and mystical writing 1577–88.
Federico García Lorca.
Modern Catalan literature.
Modern Galician literature.
Modern Catalan.
Modern Galician.
Bilingualism: Spanish and English.

The work of Alfonso the Wise as author and patron of literature and learning.
Spanish and Portuguese prose romances of the fifteenth and sixteenth centuries.
Latin American fiction from 1940.

The Galician-Portuguese *Cancioneiros.*
The chronicles of the Portuguese expansion in Asia.
The Brazilian novel of the North-East 1880–1960.
Twentieth-century Portuguese and Brazilian women writers.
The literature of Portuguese-speaking Africa.

Old Church Slavonic in relation to Common Slavonic and Russian.
Comparative Slavonic Philology.
The structure and history of *one* of the following languages: Bulgarian, Czech, Macedonian, Polish, Serbo-Croat, Slovak, Slovene, Sorbian, Ukrainian, White Russian.
The Russian Literary Language, 1648–1917.
Russian Literature of the twentieth century (1890 to the present day).
Russian Religious Philosophy in the late nineteenth and early twentieth centuries, with special reference to the works of Fedorov, Solov'ev, Berdyaev, Florensky, and S. Bulgakov.
Russian Drama of the nineteenth and twentieth centuries.
Russian women's writing.

The School of the Ionian Islands 1797–1912, with special reference to the works of Solomos, Kalvos, Laskaratos, Matesis, Valaoritis, and Mavilis.
The New Athenian School of Poetry 1880–1912, with special reference to the works of Palamas, Drosinis, Gryparis, Krystallis, Malakasis, and Hadzopoulos.
The Greek novel 1918–40, with special reference to the works of K. Theotokis, G. Theotokas, Karagatsis, Myrivilis, Venezis, K. Politis, and G. N. Abbot.
Greek women writers.

Medieval Welsh Arthurian literature.
The poetry of Cynddelw.
The poetry of Dafydd ap Gwilym.
The Ulster Cycle of tales.
The classical Irish bardic tradition.
Keating.
Iolo Morgannwg.
Saunders Lewis.
Twenteith-century Scottish Gaelic poetry.

Hebrew poetry and prose of medieval Spain and Provence.
Early twentieth-century Hebrew literature.
The literature of the State of Israel.
Yiddish linguistics.
Modern Yiddish literature.
Postwar Polish literature.

Any other subject approved by the Modern Language Board.

2. Candidates may not be permitted to offer certain Special Subjects in combination with certain other papers. Candidates offering a Special Subject and another paper both of which involve the study of the same author or authors, may not make the same texts the principal subject of an answer in both the papers.

3. Instead of a Special Subject from the list for the year concerned, a candidate may offer:

Either

(i) (if offering Spanish as their sole language or as one of two languages) Paper X or XI or a half (i.e. of the period covered) of Paper VII or VIII in Portuguese, provided that, in the case of candidates offering two languages, Portuguese is not one of those languages.

Or

(ii) (if offering Portuguese as their sole language or as one of two languages) Paper X or XI or a half (i.e. of the period covered) of Paper VII or VIII in Spanish, provided that, in the case of candidates offering two languages, Spanish is not one of those languages.

Or

(iii) any one of the Special Topics (*a*) to (*g*) inclusive or (*h*) ii, iii, or vii from Course I for the Honour School of English Language and Literature or any one of the following from Course II: B10(*f*), B10(*g*), C12 (as specified for the Honour School of Literae Humaniores, Subject III 14 (*b*)). This option is not available to candidates for any joint school involving Modern Languages.

Extended Essay

1. Candidates may offer an Extended Essay, subject to the following provisions:

(i) The subject of every essay shall, to the satisfaction of the board of the faculty, fall within the scope of the Honour School of Modern Languages.

(ii) The subject of an essay may, but need not, overlap any subject or period on which the candidate offers a paper, but candidates should avoid repetition of material presented in the extended essay in other parts of the examination. Candidates should not offer a title involving the reading of works only or mainly in translation from the original.

(iii) Candidates are prohibited from making the same *text or texts* the principal subject of their Special Subject or Extended Essay and of an answer or essay in papers VI–XI but they are *not* prohibited from making an *author* the focus of their Special Subject or Extended Essay on whom they also intend to write in another part of the examination, as long as they make use of different texts and have due regard to the need to avoid repetition of the same material.

(iv) Candidates proposing to offer an essay must submit, through their college, to the Chairman of the Board of the Faculty of Medieval and Modern Languages (on a form obtainable from the Modern Languages Administration and Faculty Office, 41 Wellington Square,) a statement of their name, college, the honour school they intend to offer, the academic year in which they intend to take the examination, and the title of the proposed essay together with (*a*) a statement in about fifty words of how the subject is to be treated, (*b*) a statement signed by a supervisor or tutor, preferably in the language or in one of the languages or in the field of study with which the extended essay is concerned, that he or she considers the subject suitable, and suggesting a person or persons who might be invited to be an examiner or an assessor (the board will not approve a title unless it is satisfied that a suitably qualified examiner or assessor based in Oxford will be available), and (*c*) a statement by a college tutor that he or she approves the candidate's application, not later than the Wednesday of the second week of the Michaelmas Full Term preceding the examination.

(v) Subject to the agreement of the faculty board, candidates may offer an essay written in the language or one of the languages they are offering in the Honour School; application, with a letter of support from a college tutor, should be made at the same time as the proposed title of the essay is submitted for approval. (*This provision is not available in the case of Russian*).

(vi) The faculty board will decide by the end of the third week of the Michaelmas Full Term preceding the examination whether the candidate has permission to offer an essay. Permission may be granted on the condition that the candidate agrees to amend details of the title to the satisfaction of the board, and submits the required amendments to the Administration and Faculty

Office for the board's approval by Friday of the sixth week of the Michaelmas Full Term preceding the examination. If the proposed title is approved, this will be notified by the Administration and Faculty Office, together with any conditions attached to the approval, to the candidate and to the Chairman of the Examiners for the Honour School.

(vii) A candidate may seek approval after Friday of the sixth week of the Michaelmas Full Term preceding the examination for an amendment of detail in an approved title, by application to the Administration and Faculty Office. The Chairman of the Examiners and the Chairman of the Board, acting together, will decide whether or not a proposed amendment shall be approved.

2. Every essay must be the candidate's own work. Tutors may, however, discuss with candidates the proposed field of study, the sources available, and the method of presentation. Tutors may also read and comment on a first draft.

All quotations, whether direct or indirect, from primary or secondary sources must be explicitly acknowledged. The use of unacknowledged quotations will be penalized.

Candidates must sign a certificate stating that the essay is their own work and this certificate must be sent at the same time as the essay, but under separate cover, addressed to: The Chairman of the Examiners, Honour School of Modern Languages, Examination Schools, High Street, Oxford.

3. Essays previously submitted for the Honour School of Modern Languages may be resubmitted. No essay will be accepted if it has already been submitted, wholly or substantially, for another Honour School or degree of this University or a degree of any other institute. The certificate must contain a confirmation that the essay has not already been so submitted.

4. No essay shall be ineligible because it has been submitted, in whole or in part, for any scholarship or prize in this university.

5. Candidates shall present a one-page summary of the arguments in English at the beginning of their essay and are advised to aim at producing an essay of about 8,000 words; no essay shall exceed 10,000 words (in each case exclusive of the summary, all notes, appendices, and bibliographies). No person or body shall have authority to permit the limit of 10,000 words to be exceeded, except that, in the case of a commentary on a text, and at the discretion of the chairman of the examiners, any substantial quoting of that text need not be included in the word limit. The examiners will not take account of such parts of an essay as are beyond these limits. There must be a select bibliography, listing all primary and secondary sources consulted when writing the essay, and full details must be given of all citations (either in the text, or in footnotes).

All essays must be typed in double-spacing on one side only of quarto or A4 paper, and must be bound or held firmly in a stiff cover. Two copies must be submitted to the chairman of the examiners, and a third copy must be retained by the candidate.

6. The two copies of the essay must be sent, not later than noon on the first Friday after the Hilary Full Term of the year in which the examination will be held, to: The Chairman of the Examiners, Honour School of Modern Languages, Examination Schools, High Street, Oxford.

XIII. General Linguistics.

Candidates will be required to show knowledge of analytic techniques and problems in contemporary syntax and semantic theory, phonetics, and phonology, and their relation to issues of linguistic variation, language acquisition, and language change.

PASS SCHOOL OF MODERN LANGUAGES

A candidate who offers *one* language only must take the following papers, as prescribed for the Honour School of Modern Languages:

I
IIA (i)
IIB (i)
III
One of VI, VII, VIII
One of X, XI
One other paper from IV–XI inclusive.
The oral examination in the language.

Candidates may offer an extended essay instead of Papers X or XI.

A candidate who offers *two* languages must take the following papers, as prescribed for the Honour School of Modern Languages, *in each language*:

I
IIA (i)
IIB (i)
One of VI, VII, VIII.
The oral examination in each of the two languages.

SPECIAL REGULATIONS FOR THE HONOUR SCHOOL OF MUSIC

A

1. The subject of the Honour School of Music shall be the study of the history, criticism, theory, composition, performance, and practice of music.

2. No candidate shall be admitted to examination in this school, unless he has either passed or been exempted from the First Public Examination.

3. The examination in this faculty shall be under the supervision of the Board of the Faculty of Music which shall make regulations concerning it subject always to the preceding clauses of this sub-section.

B

Each candidate will be required to offer papers (1) and (2) from List A, any two of papers (3), (4), and (5) in that list, and four other papers, always provided that of these four at least one **[Until 1 October 2004:** be chosen from each of Lists B and C**] [From 1 October 2004:** but not more than three to be chosen from List B**]**. Candidates may always offer both List A (3) and B (1); but certain other combinations of papers may from time to time be disallowed, always provided that notice of such disallowance be communicated to candidates not later than the third week of Michaelmas Full Term in the academic year preceding that of examination.

Candidates must inform the Registrar, not later than Friday of the fourth week of Michaelmas Full Term in the academic year of examination, of the eight papers they propose to offer.

Candidates may also be examined viva voce.

List A (core subjects)

(1) *History of Western Music I*: *c.*800–*c.*1630 (one three-hour paper)

(2) *History of Western Music II*: *c.*1600 to the present day (one three-hour paper)

The Board of the Faculty of Music shall approve, and publish each year by notice in the Faculty of Music, not later than the eighth week of Trinity Full Term, a list of specified areas of study in (1) and (2) above for the examination six terms thence.

(3) Either *Techniques of Composition I* (one three-hour paper)

Candidates will be required to complete or continue in the appropriate style a piece of music from which at least one part will be given. One question must be answered from four set as follows:

(*a*) later sixteenth-century continental vocal polyphony in four parts;

(*b*) aria in three parts (voice, obbligato instrument, and basso continuo) from the period *c.*1700–*c.*1760;

(*c*) four-part texture, of the period *c.*1760–*c.*1830;

(*d*) nineteenth-century song accompaniment for piano, in the Austro–Germanic tradition.

or *Techniques of Composition II* (portfolio submission): see under List B (1)

(4) *Musical Analysis and Criticism* (one three-hour paper)

Analytical and critical comment on one musical work (or movement of a work), normally from the late eighteenth or nineteenth century. The score will be provided but the music will not be heard in performance.

(5) *Musical Thought and Scholarship* (one three-hour paper)

A paper on the history, criticism, and philosophy of music. Candidates may choose to answer either one or two questions.

Lists B **[Until 1 October 2004:** *and C***]** **[From 1 October 2004:** *, C, and D***]** (optional subjects)

List B (Portfolio **[Until 1 October 2004:** submissions; practical tests **[From 1 October 2004:** and performance options**])**

(1) *Techniques of Composition II* (portfolio submission)

Candidates will be required to write, at their choice and on material set by the examiners in the eighth week of Hilary Full Term in the academic year of examination, one of the following:

(*a*) a fugue;
(*b*) a sixteenth-century motet or Mass movement in five parts;
(*c*) an eighteenth-century (Baroque style) aria or other ritornello-based movement;
(*d*) A sonata movement (not necessarily the first) from the period from Haydn to Brahms;
(*e*) a movement in a twentieth-century idiom (questions requiring familiarity with indeterminate or electronic techniques will not be set);
(*f*) such other form of music as the examiners may offer,

provided that the examiners shall always offer material on each of (*a*)–(*e*).

Papers will be available for collection in the Music Faculty Library from 12 noon on Friday in the eighth week of Hilary Full Term in the academic year of examination. The portfolio, accompanied by a declaration in the form prescribed in the schedule annexed to these regulations, must be submitted by candidates not later than noon on Friday of the first week of Trinity Full Term in the academic year of examination, to the Chairman of the Examiners, Honour School of Music, Examination Schools, Oxford.

This option may not be selected under List B(1) if it has already been selected under list A(3).

(2) *Orchestration* (portfolio submission)

Candidates will be required to submit one piece of orchestration, the style and technique of the orchestration being appropriate to the material set. A choice of pieces, taken from the period 1750 to the present day, will be set. Papers will be available for collection in the Music Faculty Library from 12 noon on Friday in the eighth week of Hilary Full Term in the academic year of examination. The portfolio, accompanied by a declaration in the form prescribed in the schedule annexed to these regulations, must be submitted by candidates not later than noon on Friday of the fourth week of Trinity Full Term in the academic year of examination, to the Chairman of the Examiners, Honour School of Music, Examination Schools, Oxford.

(3) *Solo Performance, instrumental or vocal* (practical test)

Candidates shall prepare a programme of works in varying styles and submit it for the approval of the examiners, not later than Friday in the fourth week of Hilary Full Term in the academic year of examination, addressed to the Chairman of the Examiners, Honour School of Music, Examination Schools, Oxford. They may indicate a single work or a complete movement which they would like to play in full. The time each piece takes to play must be stated. The programme shall be timed to last between 35–40 minutes, including breaks and pauses. If the programme significantly exceeds 40 minutes the examiners are entitled to curtail or interrupt the performance. Candidates must provide for accompaniment, where required.

Candidates may offer self-accompanied vocal performance, which will be judged on both the singing and playing elements. They may not, however, propose a programme on more than one instrument in turn (such as violin and cello), other than such as might occur in the context of normal recital convention. Any candidate contemplating such a proposal should seek early advice from the Chairman of the Faculty Board, whose decision on behalf of the Board will be final.

Candidates are required to provide for the examiners one copy of each piece to be performed, in the edition used. The copies shall be presented to the examiners at the beginning of the examination and collected from them at the end.

(4) *Composition* (portfolio submission)

Candidates will be required to submit a portfolio of four original compositions as follows:

(*a*) a work of approximately five minutes' duration for solo instrument and piano;

(*b*) three of the following:

(i) a work of 8–10 minutes' duration for mixed choir (SATB) in up to eight parts;

(ii) a work for mixed ensemble (with or without vocal soloist) of 8–10 minutes' duration and scored for up to fourteen players (including one percussionist playing several instruments);

(iii) a work of 8–10 minutes' duration for one 'live' performer and electronic resources, demonstrating both technical skill in the use of studio techniques and compositional imagination in dealing with the transformation of live and computer-generated sound;

(iv) a work (which may be of a partly or wholly electro–acoustic nature) at the candidate's pleasure.

Candidates intending to use the electronic studio in connection with this option are required to have attended the preliminary courses offered to undergraduates in their first year.

(5) *Dissertation* (portfolio submission)

Candidates must submit a dissertation of between 8,000 and 10,000 words (exclusive of bibliography) which has not been previously submitted for a degree of another university. The subject and title must be approved by the Board of the Faculty of Music. Details relating to approval and submission are given in the general note below.

(6) *Edition with commentary* (portfolio submission)

Candidates must submit an edition with commentary. Editions previously submitted for the Honour School of Music may be resubmitted. No edition will be accepted if it has already been submitted, wholly or substantially, for another Honour School or degree of this University, or a degree of any other institution. The work or works to be edited must be approved by the Board of the Faculty of Music. Details relating to approval and submission are given in the general note below.

(7) *Analysis* (portfolio submission)

Candidates must submit an analytical study of not more than 10,000 words which has not been previously submitted for a degree of another university. The subject and title must be approved by the Board of the Faculty of Music. Details relating to approval and submission are given in the general note below.

List C (**[Until 1 October 2004:** written papers; further practical tests**] [From 1 October 2004:** (three-hour paper options) and *List D* (practical options)**]**)

The Board of the Faculty of Music shall approve, and publish each year by notice in the Faculty of Music, not later than the eight week of Trinity Full Term, a list of subjects for the examination six terms hence.

General Note on approval of subjects for List B (5), (6), and (7); and the submission of written work for List B (4)–(7).

(*a*) *Approval of subjects*

Candidates intending to submit any of B(5), (6), or (7) must obtain prior approval of the subject and title from the Board of the Faculty of Music. They are urged to seek early guidance from their college tutor on whether the subject is likely to be acceptable and must submit the proposed subject and title, together with the signed approval of the tutor, to the Chairman of the Board of the Faculty of Music, Faculty of Music, St Aldates, not earlier than the beginning of Trinity Full Term in the academic year preceding that of examination, and not later than noon on Friday of the first week of Michaelmas Full Term in the academic year of examination. The faculty board shall decide whether or not to approve the subject and title and shall advise the candidate as soon as possible.

(*b*) *Submission of written work*

Candidates must also submit one copy of the written work related to the examination of subjects B(4)–(7) by noon on Friday of the second week of Trinity Full Term in the academic year of examination. It must be addressed to the Chairman of the Examiners, Honour School of Music, Examination Schools, Oxford. Each submission must be accompanied by a declaration in the form prescribed in the schedule annexed to these regulations. In the case of B(5–7) the text of the work must be presented in typescript.

Each portfolio submitted for the subjects of Techniques of Composition II and Orchestration must be accompanied by a declaration placed in a sealed envelope bearing the candidate's examination number and in the following prescribed form.

Form of Declaration

I,..hereby declare that the contents of this portfolio are entirely my own unaided work, that they have not been submitted to any other person for advice, assistance, or revision, or for a degree of another university.

Signed ....

....College

Date ....

Each portfolio submitted for the subject Composition must be accompanied by a declaration placed in a sealed envelope bearing the candidate's examination number and in the following prescribed form.

Form of Declaration

I,..hereby declare that these are my own original compositions and that they have not been submitted for the degree of another university.

Signed ....

....College

Date ....

Each portfolio submission of Dissertation, Edition with Commentary, and Analysis, the written submission related to the subject of Performance, and the submission related to the subject of Performance, and the submissions related to Electro-acoustic and computer music must be accompanied by a declaration placed in a sealed envelope bearing the candidate's examination number and in the following prescribed form.

Form of Declaration

I,..hereby declare that this submission is my own work, except where otherwise stated, and that it has not been submitted for the degree of another university.

Signed ....

......................................College

Date ....

The candidate's examination number, and the subject of the examination, should be clearly shown on the outside cover of the portfolio, which should be addressed to the Chairman of the Examiners, Honour School of Music, Examination Schools, Oxford.

PASS SCHOOL OF MUSIC

Each candidate will be required to offer the six subjects in the list below.

(1) *Either* Techniques of Composition I *or* Techniques of Composition II (as specified in List A of the Honour School of Music).

(2) *Either* History of Western Music I *or* History of Western Music II (as specified in List A of the Honour School of Music).

(3) Musical Thought and Scholarship (as specified in List A of the Honour School of Music).

(4) Critical Comment (as specified in List A of the Honour School of Music).

(5), (6) Two subjects chosen by the candidate from Lists B, C, and D of the Honour School of Music.

NOTES

SPECIAL REGULATIONS FOR THE HONOUR SCHOOL OF NATURAL SCIENCE

[*Note:* **For candidates embarking on the Honour School of Natural Science (Physics) in or before October 2001, see Addendum I at the back of the book.]**

A

1. (*a*) The examination shall include:

Biological Sciences;
Chemistry;
Earth Sciences (four-year course);
Geology (three-year course);
Materials Science;
Molecular and Cellular Biochemistry;
Physiological Sciences.

The examination shall in each subject be partly practical.

Provided that this requirement may be satisfied, in the case of a subject for which the board concerned has so prescribed by regulation made under cl. 10 below, by the assessment by the examiners of the practical work done by candidates during their course of study.

No candidate shall be required to offer more than one of these subjects.

(*b*) The examination in *Chemistry* shall consist of three Parts. In Parts IA and IB candidates shall be examined in the subjects prescribed by the Mathematical and Physical Sciences Board.

[Until 1 October 2005: (*b*)**]** The examination in **[Until 1 October 2005:** *Chemistry* and in**]** *Materials Science* shall consist of two Parts. In Part I candidates shall be examined in the subjects prescribed by the Mathematical and Physical Sciences Board.

For Part II in Chemistry and in Materials Science each candidate must present, at a time to be fixed by the board, a record of investigations carried out under supervision as prescribed by the Board.

(*c*) The examination in *Molecular and Cellular Biochemistry* shall consist of two parts. In Part I candidates shall be examined in the subjects prescribed by the Life and Environmental Sciences Board.

In Part II candidates shall be examined in the subjects prescribed by the Life and Environmental Sciences Board, and shall also present, as part of the examination, a dissertation based on work carried out under supervision as prescribed by the board.

2. The name of a candidate offering *Chemistry,* or *Biochemistry,* or *Materials Science,* shall not be published in a Class List unless he has been adjudged worthy of Honours by the examiners in all Parts of the respective examinations in consecutive years, and no candidate may present himself for examination in Part II unless he has been adjudged worthy of Honours by the examiners in Part I.

3. A candidate adjudged worthy of Honours in Parts IA and IB **[Until 1 October 2004:** Part I**]** and Part II in Chemistry may supplicate for the Degree of Master of Chemistry provided that he or she has fulfilled all the conditions for admission to a degree of the University.

4. A candidate adjudged worthy of Honours in Part I and Part II in Molecular and Cellular Biochemistry may supplicate for the Degree of Master of Biochemistry provided that he or she has fulfilled all the conditions for admission to a degree of the University as specified in Ch. I, sect. I, § I, cl. I.

5. (*a*) Save as provided in cl. 5 (*c*) below, the name of a candidate offering Earth Sciences in the four-year course shall not be published in a Class List until he or she has completed Parts A and B of the examination.

(*b*) A student who has been admitted to the status of Senior Student may be admitted to either the final examination for the three-year course or Part A of the examination for the four-year course in the term in which he or she has completed not fewer than five terms of residence.

(*c*) In such cases as shall be approved by the Divisional Board of Mathematical and Physical Sciences a Senior Student may be deemed to have satisfied the examiners in Part A of the examination for the four-year course in Earth Sciences and may be admitted to Part B of the examination in the term in which the student has completed at least six terms of residence.

(*d*) The Examiners in Earth Sciences for the four-year course shall be entitled to award a pass or classified honours to candidates in the Second Public Examination who have reached a standard considered adequate. The Examiners shall give due consideration to the performance in both parts of the examination. A candidate who obtains only a pass or fails to satisfy the Examiners may enter again for Part B of the examination on one, but not more than one, subsequent occasion.

(*e*) A candidate adjudged worthy of honours in the Second Public Examination for the four-year course in Earth Sciences may supplicate for the Degree of Master of Earth Sciences provided that he or she has fulfilled all the conditions for admission to a degree of the University as specified in Ch. I, Sect. 1, § 1, cl. 1.

6. A candidate adjudged worthy of Honours in Part I and Part II in Materials Science may supplicate for the Degree of Master of Engineering provided that he or she has fulfilled all the conditions for admission to a degree of the University as specified in Ch. I, sect. 1, § 1, cl. 1.

7. Any candidate in this school shall be permitted to offer, with the approval of the board or of the person or persons authorized by the board to give approval on its behalf, in addition to one of the subjects enumerated in clause 1, a Special Subject connected therewith.

8. No candidate shall be admitted to examination in this school unless he has either passed or been exempted from the First Public Examination.

9. Candidates may, in addition to any one or more of the above-mentioned subjects, offer themselves for examination in one or more *Supplementary Subjects.*

Candidates for Supplementary Subjects may offer themselves for examination in the academic year preceding that in which they take the Final Honour School; they may also offer themselves for examination in the year in which they take the Final Honour School. In the case of candidates offering *Chemistry* in the Final Honour School, Supplementary Subjects may be offered in any of the years in which they take any Part of the Second Public Examination.

The Supplementary Subjects available in any year will be published, together with the term in which each subject will be examined, in the *University Gazette* not later than the end of the Trinity Term of the academic year prior to delivery of the courses.

10. After each examination in any Supplementary Subject a list, to be signed by the chairman of the examiners (or in the case of a subject consisting of two or three Parts, the chairman of the examiners for Part I of the examination) in the appropriate subject of the Honour School, shall be published showing the candidates who have satisfied the examiners or have distinguished themselves in the examination, and in the Class List issued by the examiners letters or signs shall be affixed to the names of those candidates

who may either have satisfied the examiners or have distinguished themselves in the examination in any Supplementary Subject or Subjects.

11. In determining the place in the Class List of candidates in any of the subjects mentioned in clause 1 the examiners shall take account of success in any Supplementary Subjects which have been offered.

12. A candidate whose name has been placed in the Class List upon the result of the examination in any one of the subjects mentioned in clause 1 or who has obtained Honours in Part I of the Subjects *Chemistry* or *Molecular and Cellular Biochemistry* or *Materials Science*, shall be permitted to offer himself for examination in any other of the subjects mentioned in the same clause at the examination in either the next year or the next year but one, provided always that he has not exceeded six terms from the date on which he first obtained Honours in a Final Honour School.

13. The examinations in General Subjects: Chemistry, Geology, and Materials Science shall be under the supervision of the Divisional Board of Mathematical and Physical Sciences Board. The examinations in General Subjects: Molecular and Cellular Biochemistry, and Biological Sciences, shall be under the supervision of the Life and Environmental Sciences Board. The examinations in General Subject: Physiological Sciences shall be under the supervision of the Board of the Faculty of Physiological Sciences. The respective boards shall have power, subject to the provisions of these decrees, from time to time to frame and to vary regulations for the different subjects of examination, and in particular to prescribe the conditions under which a candidate shall be permitted to offer a Special Subject.

B

The examination comprises the undermentioned General Subjects:

Biological Sciences;
Chemistry;
Geology;
Materials Science;
Molecular and Cellular Biochemistry;
Physiological Sciences:

and any subjects taken as supplementary to one or more of the General Subjects:

Anthropology;
Chemical Pharmacology;
History and Philosophy of Science;
Materials Chemistry of Polymers and Ceramics;
Quantum Chemistry.

In all the subjects of the school candidates will be expected to show knowledge based on practical work.

The several sections which follow give the detailed regulations for the different subjects of the school and the conditions under which Special Subjects may be offered. It is not necessary for the attainment of the highest honours that any Special Subject should be offered, but weight will be attached in the assignment of honours to excellence in a Special Subject. Candidates offering a Special Subject must give notice of their intention to the Registrar, and specify the subject, not later than the Friday in the fourth week of the Michaelmas Full Term preceding the examination.

For the General Subjects Materials Science, and Molecular and Cellular Biochemistry, candidates are restricted to models of calculators included in a list provided by the Chairmen of the Examiners not later than Wednesday of the fourth week of the Michaelmas Full Term preceding the examination.

For the following General Subjects:

Biological Sciences;
Chemistry;
Geology;
Earth Sciences;

the examiners will permit the use of any hand-held pocket calculator subject to the conditions set out under the heading 'Use of calculators in examinations' in the *Special Regulations concerning Examinations* and further elaborated in the Course Handbook.

Regulations governing the use of calculators in individual Supplementary Subjects will be notified when the availability of these subjects is published in the *Gazette* in accordance with Cl. 10 of the decree.

BIOLOGICAL SCIENCES (BIOLOGY, PLANT SCIENCE, ZOOLOGY)

1. Candidates will be required to offer themselves for examination in five subjects chosen from the following

   1. Evolution and Systematics
   2. Quantitative Methods
   3. Animal Biology
   4. Plant and Microbial Biology
   5. Environmental Biology
   6. Cell and Developmental Biology
   7. The Biology of Animal and Plant Disease

All candidates will be required to offer subjects 1 and 2 and three out of subjects 3–7. In all subjects knowledge of first year coursework will be assumed.

2. The examination shall be conducted as follows.

(a) **Part A**

Each candidate will be required to offer

(i) Subject 1: One three-hour written paper, to be taken on a date to be specified in the ninth week of Trinity Term of the academic year preceding the examination.

(ii) Subjects 3–7: One three-hour written paper in one of the five subjects, to be taken on a date to be specified in the ninth week of Trinity Term of the academic year preceding the examination. Candidates may not offer themselves for examination in Part A in a subject which they also intend to offer in Parts B and C.

After completion of these two papers, the examiners will issue a list of candidates deemed to have completed Part A of the examination.

(b) **Part B**

Each candidate must complete a course assignment on each of the two major subjects, from within 3–7, which they intend to offer in Part C. The assignment will be in a format specified by the course convener on a topic proposed by the student and approved by the Chairman of the Biological Sciences Steering Committee. The approval of assignments shall be given not later than Friday of the eighth week of the Michaelmas Full Term of the academic year in which the examination is taken.

Course assignments in Part B must be the candidate's own work. Candidates may discuss the proposed topic, the sources available, and the method of presentation with an adviser. This adviser must also read and comment on a first draft.

Assignments shall be of not more than 3,000 words, excluding any tables, figures, or references, and must be prefaced by an Abstract of not more than 250 words, to be included within the word limit.

Assignments (two copies) must be legibly typed or wordprocessed on one side only of A4 paper, held firmly in a stiff cover, and submitted by noon on Friday of the noughth week of the Trinity Term of the academic year in which the examination is taken, addressed to The Clerk of the Schools, Examination Schools, High Street, Oxford for the Chairman of the Examiners in the Final Honour School of Natural Science (Biological Sciences).

Candidates shall not deal with substantially the same material in their Part B assignments as is covered in their project report. Candidates must sign a certificate stating that the assignment is their own work. This certificate must be submitted at the same time as the assignment in a sealed envelope addressd to the Chairman of Examiners. Each assignment, and the envelope containing the certificate, must be clearly labelled with the candidate's number. The name and college of the candidate must not appear on the assignment or on the envelope. Assignments previously submitted for the Honour School of Natural Science (Biological Sciences) may be resubmitted. No assignment will be accepted if it has already been submitted, wholly or substantially, for another degree in the University or elsewhere; and the certificate must also contain a confirmation that the assignment has not already been so submitted. No assignment shall be ineligible because it has been submitted, in whole or in part, for any scholarship or prize in this University. All sources used in the assignments must be fully documented. Each assignment shall clearly indicate on the first page the part of the examination and the subject under which the assignment is submitted.

(c) **Part C**

Each candidate will be required to offer written papers in three subjects, as follows.

(i) One paper in subject 2.

(ii) Two papers in each of two subjects chosen from subjects 3–7.

Each written paper shall be of three hours duration. For subjects 3–7, one paper shall consist of short answer questions, problems and questions based on the interpretation of observations, and data analysis; the other will consist of essay questions.

No candidate may take the written papers in the same subject offered in Part A.

(d) **Part D**

(i) Candidates will be required to offer a written report on a project in any area of biology. The project report shall be of not more than 7,000 words, excluding any tables, figures, or references, and must be prefaced by an Abstract of not more than 250 words, to be included within the word limit. The project report (two copies) must be legibly typed or wordprocessed on one side only of A4 paper, held firmly in a stiff cover, and submitted on or before 12 noon on the Friday of week 6 of Hilary Full Term of the academic year in which Part C of the examination is taken. It must be addressed to The Clerk of the Schools, Examination Schools, High Street, Oxford, for the Chairman of Examiners for the Honour School of Natural Science (Biological Sciences). Each project report shall be accompanied by a certificate signed by the candidate indicating that the project report is the candidate's own work. This certificate shall be submitted separately in a sealed envelope addressed to the Chairman of Examiners. No report will be accepted if it has already been submitted, wholly or substantially, for another Honour School or degree of this University, or for a degree of any other institution.

(ii) All candidates shall be assessed as to their practical ability in coursework under the following provisions:

(*a*) The Chairman of the Steering Committee, or a deputy, shall make available to the examiners, at the end of the first week of the term in which the examinations in Part C are held, records showing the extent to which each candidate has completed the prescribed practical work and exercises in Quantitative Methods to a satisfactory standard.

(*b*) The examiners may request coursework from any candidate. Such candidates will be named in a list posted by the day of the first written paper in Part C of the examination. Each notebook submitted shall be accompanied by a certificate signed by the candidate indicating that the notebook is the candidate's own work.

(*c*) In assessing the record of practical work and exercises in Quantitative Methods, the examiners shall have regard to the attendance record of the candidates at the classes provided, and to the marks awarded for the classes provided. Candidates whose overall performance in practical work and Quantitative Methods is judged by the examiners to be insufficient to warrant the award of Honours may either be deemed to have failed the examination, or may, at the discretion of the examiners, be awarded a Pass degree.

4. *Field Work*

Candidates shall be required to carry out field work and attend such vacation courses as are approved from time to time by the Biological Sciences Steering Committee.

5. *Viva voce Examinations*

All candidates will be examined on their project *viva voce*.

6. *Use of Calculators*

The examiners will not provide calculators, but will permit the use of any hand-held pocket calculator subject to the conditions set out under the heading 'Use of calculators in examinations' in the *Special Regulations concerning Examinations.*

Schedule of Subjects

1. *Evolution and Systematics*

Evolution as the central theme of biology. Methods and data of phylogeny reconstruction. Biogeography. Macro-evolutionary change; origin of the major groups, extinction, punctuated equilibrium. Adaptation. Comparative Method. Natural selection. Units of selection. Molecular evolution. Evolution of sex. The modern synthesis.

2. *Quantitative Methods*

Principles and practice of the application to biology of statistics.

3. *Animal Biology*

The structure, function, evolution and behaviour of animals. Control and information systems, homeostasis and biomechanics of movement. Life history strategies and evolution of mammals. Evolutionary, causal and developmental aspects of animal behaviour. The biology of social behaviour including the evolution of aggression, co-operation and communication. Mate choice and kin selection. Behavioural ecology. Perception, learning and decision-making in animals. The genetics of behaviour. Neuro-biological bases of behaviour.

4. *Plant and Microbial Biology*

The biological diversity of plants and micro-organisms, including aspects of their ecology and evolution, structural and functional characteristics, life histories, reproduction, taxonomy and systematics, physiology and biochemistry, genetics and molecular biology, biotechnology, and also the importance of interactions between plants and micro-organisms.

5. *Environmental Biology*

Methods in ecology including the description and analysis of plant and animal communities. Ecology and conservation biology examining the genetic and population consequences and possible remedies for biodiversity loss. The ecology of forest and agricultural systems. Studies of major causes and biological consequences of global environmental change. The theory and practice of wild-life resource management.

6. *Cell and Developmental Biology*

Mechanisms operating to co-ordinate cellular changes in the development of tissues and organs and complete animal and plant forms. Regulation of cell division and differentiation. Environmental signals coordinating and modulating development. Regulation of gene expression. Techniques of genetic modification used in the study of cellular and developmental processes.

7. *Biology of Animal and Plant Disease*

The biology, epidemiology and control of animal and plant disease. The biology of macro- and micro-parasites, host genetics and disease resistance. Molecular genetics of plant and animal parasites, epidemiology and control of disease. Modelling disease and vector-borne disease.

CHEMISTRY

[Until 1 October 2004: *(for candidates embarking on the Honour School in or before October 2002)*

PART I

In Part I of the examination two written General Papers will be set in each of the three divisions, Inorganic, Organic, and Physical Chemistry, together with written Advanced Papers as provided below. The General Papers will be designed to test knowledge of the fundamental principles of all important aspects of the subject. The questions set will be such that candidates may reasonably be expected to answer a high proportion of them.

In the Inorganic division one General Paper will be concerned with more descriptive aspects of the subject, and the other General Paper will include problems, exercises and questions involving the interpretation of experimental data.

In the Organic division both General Papers will include a balance of questions on problems in synthesis and mechanisms, questions involving interpretation of experimental data, and the more descriptive aspects of the subject.

In the Physical division both General Papers will be concerned with the more descriptive aspects of the subject, and also the more quantitative aspects, including problems, exercises and questions involving the interpretation of experimental data.

One written Advanced Paper will be set in each of the three divisions, Inorganic, Organic, and Physical Chemistry, and candidates will be required to offer two of these Advanced Papers. In the Advanced Papers the choice of questions will be sufficiently wide to avoid the need for an excessive burden of factual knowledge. Ten minutes' reading time will be allowed for the Advanced Papers.

Heads of laboratories, or their deputies and the I.T. training officer, shall make available to the examiners records showing the extent to which each candidate has pursued an adequate course in laboratory work and information technology. Only that work completed and marked by five o'clock of the Friday of the fourth week of the Trinity Term in which the candidate takes Part I will be included in these records. The examiners will require evidence of satisfactory work during the course over a period of three years in respect of two of the three divisions, Inorganic,

Organic, and Physical Chemistry, and in Information Technology and over a period of two years in respect of the remaining division, with the following exceptions:

(i) in the case of candidates who have passed the examination in a Supplementary Subject before the year in which they take Part I of the Final Honour School, evidence of satisfactory work during the course over a period of three years will be required in respect of one division and over a period of two years in respect of the remaining two divisions;]

(For candidates embarking on the Honour School in or after October 2003)

PARTS IA AND IB

In the Part IA examination one three hour General Paper 1 will be set in each of the three divisions, Inorganic, Organic, and Physical Chemistry. These papers will be designed principally to cover the fundamental aspects of the material covered in Year 2, although some knowledge of material of Year 1 may also be required. Each paper will offer a choice of five from eight questions.

In the Part IB examinations there will be one three hour General Paper 2 in each of the three divisions. Inorganic, Organic, and Physical Chemistry. These papers will cover material in first, second and third year core courses. Each paper will offer a choice of 5 from at least 8 questions. In addition there will be three two hour examinations, one on each of the three Options chosen by the student. These will primarily examine the content of the Option courses but will also require knowledge of core course material. These papers will offer a choice of three questions from at least five.

Heads of Laboratories, or their deputies, and the IT Training Officer, will make available to the Examiners records which show the extent to which the candidate has achieved a satisfactory performance in the practical classes run in inorganic, organic and physical chemistry and in information technology. Only that work that has been designated as completed by five o'clock on the Friday of the Fourth week of the Trinity term in which the candidates take Part IA and IB will be included in these records.

In assignment of Honours the examiners will take into consideration failure of the candidate to complete the practical course as specified in Evaluation Regulations published on the Chemistry www pages. Any candidate who has not thus completed the practicals may be required to sit a practical examination in one or more of Inorganic, Organic, or Physical Chemistry.

Those candidates who have passed an examination in a Supplementary Subject before the year in which they take Part IB will have a lower overall requirement of satisfactory practical work as defined in the Examination Regulations published on the Chemistry www pages.

[Until 1 October 2004: (ii) in**]** In the case of candidates who are Senior Students, evidence of satisfactory work during one year and a half will be required in respect of each of the three divisions, whether or not they have passed the examination in a Supplementary Subject.

[Until 1 October 2004: In the assignment of Honours the examiners shall take into consideration failure by a candidate to complete the practical course as set out above, and they may require any such candidate to sit a practical examination in one or more of the three divisions.**]**

No candidate shall be adjudged worthy of Honours unless he has completed satisfactory work during one year and a half in respect of each of the three divisions, or has satisfied the examiners in a practical examination (see above), but performance in such an examination shall not be taken into account in determining eligibility for Honours unless the candidate was prevented by illness from completing the course of laboratory work.

Candidates may be examined viva voce at the examiners' discretion.

Candidates are not permitted to enter their names for examination in **[Until 1 October 2004:** Part I**]** Part IA until they have entered upon the fifth term from their matriculation, and in Part IB. until they have entered upon the eighth term from their matriculation, except by special leave of the board. No candidate may enter for Part IB before sitting all the papers set for Part IA in a previous year. All applications for leave to take Part **[Until 1 October 2004:** I**]** IB at the end of a candidate's second year must be made to the board not later than the Friday of the eighth week of the Michaelmas Full Term preceding the examination.

PART II

Each candidate must present a record of investigations carried out under the supervision of one of the following:

(i) any professor, reader, university lecturer, departmental demonstrator, or senior research officer who is also an official member of the Sub-faculty of Chemistry;

(ii) any other person nominated by the Head of the Sub-department and approved by the Chemistry Academic Committee. A second co-supervisor defined under (i) above must also be nominated and approved. Applications for project approval, including the names of a supervisor and a co-supervisor and a short project summary (not more than 250 words), should be sent by the student to the Chemistry Graduate Studies Committee, c/o Chemistry Sub-faculty Office, New Chemistry Laboratory, South Parks Road, by Friday of the first week of Hilary Full Term preceding the Part II examination. Candidates who are uncertain whether their intended Part II supervision is in category (ii) above should consult their Chemistry Tutor or the Chemistry Sub-faculty Office.

Each candidate shall be examined viva voce, and, if the examiners think fit, in writing, on the subject of his work and on matters relevant thereto. The examiners may obtain a report on the work of each candidate from the supervisor concerned.

A candidate intending to offer Part II shall give notice to the Registrar not later than Friday in the second week of the Hilary Full Term in the calendar year after that in which he satisfied the examiners in Part I. He shall at the same time give notice of the subject of his investigations together with evidence (*a*) that it has been approved by his supervisor and (*b*), if it is to be carried out in a laboratory, that the person in charge of the laboratory considers that it is suitable for investigation in that laboratory.

Every candidate for Part II is required to send in not later than noon on the Friday of the seventh week of Trinity Full Term a record of the investigations which he has carried out under the direction of his supervisor. Such record should be addressed 'The Clerk of the Schools, Oxford, for the Chairman of the Examiners in the Final Honour School of Natural Science (Chemistry)' and should be accompanied by a signed statement by the candidate that it is his or her own work.

Candidates for Part II will be required to keep statutory residence and pursue their investigations at Oxford during a period of thirty-eight weeks between the dates specified below, except that the Mathematical and Physical Sciences Board shall have power to permit candidates to vary the dates of their residence so long as the over-all requirement is met.

Periods of residence required

From the third Thursday before to the third Tuesday following Michaelmas Full Term

From the second Tuesday before Hilary Full Term to the Wednesday following Palm Sunday

From the Monday following Easter Monday to the first Saturday following Trinity Full Term.

SPECIAL SUBJECTS

In addition to the Stated Subjects of examination candidates are permitted to offer a Special Subject connected with the study of Chemistry, to be selected by the candidate subject to the approval of the board of the faculty.

GEOLOGY (THREE-YEAR COURSE)

A candidate shall be required to offer:

(i) two practical papers on observational and interpretational techniques, to be taken in week 8 of Trinity Term of the second year; and

(ii) a report on an individual mapping or practical project, the report to be submitted by Monday of week 1 of Hilary Term of the third year; and

(iii) an extended essay, the work to be undertaken in Hilary Term of the third year and the essay to be submitted by the Monday of week 1 of Trinity Term of the third year. The subject of the essay must have been approved by the Chairman of the Sub-faculty of Earth Sciences or deputy no later than the end of Michaelmas Full Term of the third year; and

(iv) six papers on the fundamental principles of Geology, to be taken in week 5 of Trinity Term of the third year.

The Head of Department of Earth Sciences or deputy shall provide the examiners with information showing the extent to which each candidate has satisfactorily completed the practicals and field courses. In addition, practical notebooks containing records of both field and laboratory courses must also be made available to the examiners. Such evidence will be taken into consideration by the examiners in awarding classes.

Candidates may be examined viva voce at the examiners' discretion.

EARTH SCIENCES (FOUR-YEAR COURSE)

1. The examination shall be in two parts.

2. Part A of the examination shall be the same as the requirements for the three-year course in Geology, and the same conditions, arrangements and examination timings shall apply.

3. Part B of the examination shall be taken at a time not less than three terms after Part A. In Part B a candidate shall be required to offer:

(i) written papers on four subjects chosen from a list published by the Sub-faculty of Earth Sciences for examination in Trinity Term of the fourth year of study, and (ii) *either* an extended essay, *or* a report on an advanced practical project or other advanced work, the work to be undertaken in Michaelmas, Hilary, and Trinity Terms of the fourth year, and the essay or report to be submitted by Friday of week 4 of Trinity Term of the fourth year. The proposed nature and duration of the practical or other advanced work shall be submitted for approval to the Chairman of the Sub-faculty of Earth Sciences or deputy with the agreement of the Head of the Department of Earth Sciences or deputy not later than the end of Trinity Full Term of the third year.

4. The list of subjects and syllabuses for the written papers in 3(i) will be published in the *Gazette* by the Sub-faculty of Earth Sciences not later than the end of Michaelmas Full Term for examination five terms thence. The subjects and syllabuses shall be approved by the Sub-faculty of Earth Sciences with the agreement of the Head of the Department of Earth Sciences or deputy.

5. Candidates may be examined viva voce at the examiners' discretion.

MATERIALS SCIENCE

Part I (MATERIALS SCIENCE)

The examination will consist of:

1. Four general papers of three hours each on the fundamental principles and engineering applications of the subject in accordance with the subjoined schedule. The questions set in these papers will normally be such that candidates may reasonably be expected to answer a high proportion of them.

2. Two option papers, each of three hours, containing a wide choice of questions in accordance with the subjoined schedule.

3. In addition to the written papers, candidates shall submit detailed reports of the practical work completed during their course of study and carried out before the beginning of Trinity Full Term in which the Part I examination is held. Such reports should be handed in to the Chairman of the Examiners in the Honour School of Natural Science (Materials Science, Part I), c/o Clerk of the Schools, Examination Schools, High Street, Oxford, not later than 5 p.m. in the Friday of the seventh week of Trinity Full Term. The Head of the Department of Materials, or deputy, shall make available to the examiners evidence showing the extent to which each candidate has pursued an adequate course of practical work.

[Until 1 October 2004: (*For candidates embarking on the Honour School in or before October 2002*) The examiners shall require evidence of satisfactory practical work (including a team design project) in Materials over a period of five terms subsequent to the sitting of the first public examination. The details of the team design project will be specified in the Course Handbook. The examiners shall take this evidence and the reports of the candidates into consideration as part of the Part I examination and they shall have the power to require a practical examination of any candidate.**]**
[From 1 October 2004: (*For candidates embarking on the Honour School in or after October 2003*) The examiners shall require evidence of satisfactory practical work (including a team design project and reports on a number of industrial visits) in Materials over a period of five terms subsequent to the sitting of the first public examination. The details of both the team design project, and the number and definition of industrial visits and the nature of the subsequent reports, will be specified in the Course Handbook. The examiners shall take this evidence and the reports of the candidates into consideration as part of the Part I examination and they shall have the power to require a practical examination of any candidate.**]**

[Until 1 October 2004: (*for candidates embarking on the Honour School in or before October 2002*) Candidates shall submit a detailed report on *either* an industrial attachment *or* an industrially relevant laboratory-based project carried out before the end of the Michaelmas Term preceding the Part I examination. The work carried out during the industrial attachment or the laboratory-based project shall be on a topic with substantial materials science or materials engineering content, which must be approved by the Materials Project Co-ordinator. Such reports shall be handed in to the Chairman of the Examiners in Materials, c/o Clerk of the Schools, Examination Schools, High Street, Oxford, by noon on the Friday of the week before the start of Hilary Full Term preceding the Part I examination.**]**

[Until 1 October 2004: (*for candidates embarking on the Honour School in or before October 2002*) 4. Candidates shall be required to submit a portfolio of Engineering and Society coursework containing one piece of work on each of two topics, as follows: (*a*) Entrepreneurship and new ventures, and (*b*) Safety, risk, and the environment; except that candidates who have completed an approved course of instruction in a foreign language, or who offer, or have offered successfully, one or more Supplementary Subjects, shall be required to submit one piece of work on one of the two approved topics (*a*) and (*b*) above. For (*a*) above, candidates must submit a business plan of no more than 3,000 words. For (*b*) above, candidates must submit an essay or a report on an assessment of safety, environmental impact, or sustainability of not more than 3,000 words. Written work shall be typed. The portfolio of work shall be submitted to the Chairman of the Examiners in Materials, c/o Clerk of the Schools, Examination Schools, High Street, Oxford, not later than noon on Monday of the first week of the Hilary Full Term preceding the Part I examination. The material must be the candidate's own work and the candidate shall sign and present with the portfolio a detachable certificate to this effect.]

[**From 1 October 2004:** (*For candidates embarking on the Honour School in or after October 2003*) 4. Candidates shall be required to submit one piece of Engineering and Society Coursework, the details of which shall be stated in the Course Handbook. The coursework shall be submitted to the Chairman of Examiners in Materials, c/o Clerk of the Schools, Examination Schools, High Street, Oxford, not later than noon on the Monday following the end of Hilary Full Term in the year preceding the Part I examination. The work must be the candidate's own and the candidate shall sign and present with the work a detachable certificate to this effect.]

Essays or reports previously submitted for the Honour School of Natural Science (Materials Science) may be resubmitted. No essay or report will be accepted if it has already been submitted wholly or substantially for another honour school or degree of this University, or for a degree at any other institution. Resubmitted work must be physically presented at the time and in the manner prescribed for submission.

Candidates may be examined viva voce at the examiners' discretion.

[**Until 1 October 2004:** (*For candidates embarking on the Honour School in or before October 2002*) 5. A candidate may, as an alternative to offering one or more Supplementary Subjects, take a course of instruction in a foreign language. A candidate proposing to be assessed on competence in a foreign language must have the proposal approved by the Chairman of the Sub-faculty of Materials or deputy, and by the Director of the Language Centre or deputy.]

[**From 1 October 2004:** (*For candidates embarking on the Honour School in or after October 2003*) 5. A candidate may, as an alternative to offering Engineering and Society Coursework, offer either a Supplementary Subject or the completion of an approved course of instruction in a foreign language. A candidate proposing to be assessed on competence in a foreign language must have the proposal approved by the Chairman of the Sub-faculty of Materials or deputy, and by the Director of the Language Centre or deputy.]

Schedule

(*a*) *General papers*

All candidates will be expected to have such knowledge of mathematics as is required for the study of the subjects of the examination.

Structure and Transformations: Ternary phase diagrams. Diffusion laws and mechanisms. Surfaces and interfaces. Phase transformations; nucleation, solidification, diffusion, martensite and growth mechanisms. Reaction kinetics. Extraction. Powder processing. Corrosion. Polymer synthesis.

Electronic Properties of Materials: Quantum Mechanics and Statistical Mechanics. Free electron theory. Band theory in both nearly-free electron and tight binding approximations. Physics of Semiconductors. Electrical, optical, and magnetic properties. Tensor properties of materials.

Mechanical Properties: Elasticity. Macroplasticity. Microplasticity; principles of deformation mechanisms. Creep and Superplasticity. Strengthening mechanisms. Fracture. Mechanical properties of polymers and of composites.

Engineering Applications of Materials: Engineering alloys; plain carbon-, stainless- and alloy-steels. Cast irons. Aluminium-, copper-, titanium-, and nickel-based alloys.

Ceramics and Glasses; manufacture, thermal and mechanical properties, dielectric properties, Polymers. Semiconductor materials. Design and fabrication routes for different materials classes. Characterisation techniques.

(*b*) *Option papers*

The subjects for these papers will be published annually by the Chairman of the sub-faculty of Materials, who will put up a notice in the Department of Materials not later than Monday of the last week of Trinity Term in the year preceding the examination. The Chairman will also indicate suitable courses of lectures.

PART II

Candidates offering Part II of the examination will be expected to carry out investigations in Materials Science or in related subjects under the supervision of one of the following:

(i) any professor who is a member of the Faculty of Physical Sciences;
(ii) a reader or university lecturer or senior research officer who is a member of the Faculty of Physical Sciences;
(iii) a tutor or lecturer in any Society who is a member of the Faculty of Physical Sciences;
(iv) any other person listed in a Register of Part II Supervisors to be maintained by the Sub-faculty of Materials.

Each candidate shall be examined viva voce, and, if the examiners think fit, in writing, on the subject of his work and on matters relevant thereto. The examiners may obtain a report on the work of each candidate from the supervisor concerned.

A candidate intending to offer Part II shall give notice to the Registrar not later than Friday in the fourth week of Michaelmas Full Term in the year in which he satisfied the examiners in Part I. Such notice must be given on a form to be obtained from the Head Clerk, University Offices.

Every candidate for Part II is required to submit three copies of a record of investigations which he has carried out under the direction of his supervisor. The record of investigation shall include a literature survey, a brief account of the project management aspects of the investigation, and a description of the engineering context of the investigation and should be accompanied by a signed statement by the candidate that it is his or her own work. The copies should be handed in to the Chairman of the Examiners in the Honour School of Natural Science (Materials Science, Part II), c/o Clerk of the Schools, Examination Schools, High Street, Oxford, not later than noon on the Friday of the seventh week of Trinity Full Term. This record shall be typewritten on one side of A4 paper and presented in a loose-leaf binder. The text should not normally exceed **15,000 words** (A4 size, double-spaced type), *including* written appendices, but there is no limit on graphs, diagrams, photographs, tables, references, computer programs, etc. Candidates seeking exemption from this rule (e.g. for non-experimental projects) should apply to the chairman of examiners at an early stage.

Candidates for Part II will be required to keep statutory residence and pursue their investigations at Oxford during a period of thirty-six weeks between the dates specified below, except that the Divisional Board of Mathematical and Physical Sciences shall have power to permit candidates to vary the dates of their residence so long as the over-all requirement is met. The faculty board may, on the recommendation of the Department of Materials, permit candidates to carry out their investigations for the required period at an approved institution outside Oxford; the board shall determine the conditions upon which applications for such permission may be approved and will require to be satisfied in each case (*a*) that adequate arrangements are made for the candidate's supervision and (*b*) that the proposals for the investigations are agreed in advance between the Department of Materials and the host institution.

Periods of required residence

From the fifth Friday before to the first Saturday following Michaelmas Full Term.

From the second Friday before Hilary Full Term to the Saturday before Palm Sunday.

From the Friday following Easter to the first Saturday following Trinity Full Term.

MOLECULAR AND CELLULAR BIOCHEMISTRY

PART I

Six written papers will be set:

Paper I Structure and Function of Macromolecules;
Paper II Energetics and Metabolic Processes;
Paper III Genetics and Molecular Biology;
Paper IV Cell Biology and the Integration of Function;
Paper V General Paper.
Paper VI Data Analysis and Interpretation

Candidates will be required to show knowledge of the fundamental biochemistry of animals, plants, and micro-organisms. This will include the chemical and physical basis of the subject, its relevance to living systems; structure, function, and metabolism of viruses, cells and subcellular components, organs and organisms; biochemical aspects of nutrition, differentiation, genetics, absorption, secretion, biosynthesis, and maintenance of a dynamic state. In the general paper, candidates will be expected to bring together a knowledge of these disparate areas of Biochemistry. The data analysis and interpretation paper will consist of questions designed to examine candidates' skills in data handling and the interpretation of experimental data; relevant tables and formulae will be supplied.

Except with the express permission of the Head of the Department of Biochemistry, no one shall be admitted to the Final Honour School of Molecular and Cellular Biochemistry course of practical work and exercises in biochemical reasoning who has not passed, or been exempted from, the First Public Examination.

Candidates shall submit notebooks containing reports, initialled by the demonstrators, of practical work and exercises in biochemical reasoning completed during their course of study for Part I. These notebooks shall be available to the examiners at any time after the end of the first week of the term in which the examination is held. Each notebook shall be accompanied by a certificate signed by the candidate indicating that the notebook submitted is the candidate's own work. This certificate must be placed in a sealed envelope addressed to the Chairman of Examiners and submitted with the notebooks. Each notebook, and the envelope containing the certificate, must be clearly labelled with the candidate's number. The name and college of the candidate should not appear on any of the notebooks or on the envelope. Heads of laboratories, or their deputies, shall make available to the examiners records showing the extent to which each candidate has adequately pursued a course of laboratory work and exercises in biochemical reasoning.

In assessing the record of practical work and exercises in data handling, the examiners shall have regard to the attendance record of the candidates at each and every class provided, and to the marks recorded for each and every class provided. Candidates whose overall performance in either the written papers or in practical work and data handling is judged by the examiners to be insufficient to warrant the award of Honours may either be deemed to have failed the examination, or may, at the discretion of the examiners, be awarded a Pass degree. Candidates in either category will not be allowed to proceed to Part II.

Candidates may be examined viva voce.

PART II

Part II will consist of project work, an extended essay, and two written papers, each of three hours' duration.

Candidates will be required to keep statutory residence and pursue their investigations at Oxford during a period of twenty-eight weeks including an extended Michaelmas Term which will begin on the fourth Friday before the stated Full Term and extend until the first Saturday following it, provided that the divisional board shall have power to permit candidates to vary the dates of their residence so long as the overall requirement is met.

Project work: The project will normally be carried out in the extended Michaelmas Term.

Candidates will be required to do project work under the supervision of one of the following:

(i) any member of the Faculty of Biological Sciences;

(ii) any other person approved by the Biochemistry Steering Committee provided that such approval shall be applied for not later than Friday in the second week of Trinity Full Term in the year preceding the Part II examination.

Candidates will be required to present an account of such work in the form of a dissertation (not more than 5,000 words excluding tables, figures, references, and summary). Dissertations (two copies) must be legibly typed on one side only of A4 paper and must be held firmly in a stiff cover. Each dissertation must begin with an abstract of not more than 300 words, which should include a brief statement of the aims of the project and a summary of its important findings. The two copies of the dissertation must be submitted by noon on Friday of the week immediately following the Hilary Full Term preceding the examination, addressed to The Clerk of the Schools, Examination Schools, High Street, Oxford, for the Chairman of the Examiners in the Final Honour School of Natural Science (Molecular and Cellular Biochemistry, Part II). Each candidate must submit, together with his project, a statement to the effect that the project is the candidate's own work or indicating where the work of others has been used, save that supervisors should give advice on the choice and scope of the project, provide a reading list, and comment on the first draft. This statement must be submitted at the same time as the project in a sealed envelope addressed to the Chairman of Examiners. Each project, and the envelope containing the statement, must be clearly labelled with the candidate's number. The name and college of the candidate must not appear on the project or on the envelope. The examiners may obtain a written report on the work of each candidate from the supervisor concerned.

Dissertations previously submitted for the Honour School of Natural Science (Molecular and Cellular Biochemistry) may be resubmitted. No dissertation will be accepted if it has already been submitted, wholly or substantially, for another Honour School other than Natural Science, or for another degree of this University, or for a degree of any other institution.

Extended essay and written papers: Each candidate will be examined on three areas of Biochemistry by means of (1) an extended essay and (2) and (3) two written papers. At least two of these will be on topics studied by candidates within options selected from a list of eight options approved by the Biochemistry Steering Committee and published by the Department of Biochemistry. The list of options will be posted in the Department of Biochemistry and sent to Senior Tutors of all colleges not later than noon on Friday of the seventh week of Trinity Term in the year preceding that in which the examination is taken. Studies will be guided by an adviser who will be a member of the Faculty of Biological Sciences or a person approved by the Biochemistry Steering Committee as under (ii) above.

(1) *Extended Essay*

Candidates will be required to write an essay of not more than 3,000 words excluding any tables, figures, or references. The extended essay should be a critical review based on independent reading. It should attempt to evaluate the primary literature, making a critical appraisal. Except as provided below, the essay shall be on a subject that falls within a topic selected from a list of three topics for each of the eight options, which will be published by the Examiners in the Final Honour School of Natural Science (Biochemistry, Part II) not later than 12 noon on Friday of the eighth week of Michaelmas Term in the academic year in which the examination is to be taken.

Candidates are free to choose their own title provided that it falls clearly under the topics published by the Examiners. A candidate wishing to offer an essay on a topic other than one of those published by the Examiners must, not later than noon on Friday of the first week of Hilary Term in the academic year in which the examination is to be taken, give notice to the Secretary of the Biochemistry Steering Committee, on a form to be obtained from the teaching office in the Department of Biochemistry, of the proposed title of the essay and a brief outline of the subject matter. It shall be the duty of the Secretary of the Steering Committee to submit this proposal to the Chairman of the Steering Committee and the Chairman of the Examiners for approval. The Chairman of the Steering Committee and the Chairman of the Examiners shall determine the option (if any) in which the proposed essay falls. In the event of the two Chairmen not giving their joint approval, the candidate shall write the essay on a topic from the list published by the Examiners. It shall be the duty of the Secretary of the Steering Committee to communicate the outcome of the submission to the candidate, stating the option in which the essay is to be written, not later than 12 noon on Friday of the third week of Hilary Term in the academic year in which the examination is to be taken.

No candidate may take the written examination in the option in which his or her essay has been written.

The essay must be the candidate's own work. Tutors and advisers may, however, discuss with candidates the proposed field of study, the sources available, and the method of presentation. They may also read and comment on a first draft.

The essay (two copies) must be legibly typed on one side only of A4 paper, held firmly in a stiff cover, and submitted by 12 noon on Friday of the fourth week of the Full Term in which the examination is held, addressed The Clerk of the Schools, Examination Schools, Oxford, for the Chairman of the Examiners in the Final Honour School of Natural Science (Molecular and Cellular Biochemistry Part II).

Candidates shall not deal with substantially the same material in their essay as was covered in their dissertation. Candidates must sign a certificate stating that the essay is their own work and their advisers shall countersign the certificate confirming that, to the best of their knowledge and belief, this is so. This certificate must be submitted at the same time as the essay in a sealed envelope addressed to the Chairman of Examiners. Each essay, and the envelope containing the certificate, must be clearly labelled with the candidate's number. The name and college of the candidate must not appear on the essay or on the envelope. No essay will be accepted if it has already been submitted, wholly or substantially, for a degree in this University or elsewhere; and the certificate must also contain a confirmation that the essay has not already been so submitted. No essay shall be ineligible because it has been submitted, in whole or in part, for any scholarship or prize in this University. All sources used in the essay must be fully documented. Each essay shall clearly indicate on the first page the option or the approved subject under which the essay is submitted.

Candidates shall notify the Registrar, not later than Friday of the first week of the Trinity Term in which the examination is taken, on a form to be obtained from the Head Clerk, University Offices, which options they intend to offer in the examinations and, if approval has not already been obtained, the option in which they offer their essay.

(2) *and* (3) *Written Papers*

One paper of three hours' duration will be set for each option and candidates will be required to take two papers.

Each candidate may be examined viva voce.

[*Note:* For candidates embarking on the Honour School of Natural Science (Physics) in or before October 2001, see Addendum I at the back of the book]

PHYSIOLOGICAL SCIENCES

Thirteen papers will be set in the written part of the examination:

(1) Biochemistry: Molecular Mechanisms of Disease
(2) Neurosciences I.
(3) Neurosciences II.
(4) Circulation.
(5) Respiration.
(6) Physiology of Epithelia.
(7) Endocrinology.
(8) Cell biology.
(9) Immunology.
(10) Pharmacology.
(11) Developmental Biology.
(12) Cellular Physiology.
(13) Physiological Sciences.

Candidates whose names have not been entered on the Register of Medical Students must offer six papers. They may include one or two papers chosen from amongst the advanced options available for the Honour School of Experimental Psychology, subject to any restrictions set out in the list of available options published in the first week of Hilary Full Term in the year preceding the examination.

Candidates whose names have not been entered on the Register of Medical Students shall offer a dissertation on a special topic *in addition* to the six written papers. Candidates who take two of the papers from the Honour School of Experimental Psychology may not offer a dissertation involving work in a psychological topic.

Candidates on the Register of Medical Students

Candidates whose names have been entered on the Register of Medical Students must offer five papers, which shall include the general paper, Physiological Sciences (13). At the start of Trinity Term in the year before that in which such candidates intend to sit the examination, they will be advised of the limits to the numbers of places available in each of the courses examined in papers (1)–(12). By no later than the sixth week of that term, places on those courses will be allocated to candidates, account having been taken of their preferences. Subsequently, candidates may migrate between courses only with the written agreement of the Director of Pre-clinical Studies in consultation with the relevant course organizers. Candidates may enter for examination papers only in courses for which they hold allocated places. Candidates whose names have been entered on the Register of Medical Students may include as *one* of their papers a paper chosen from amongst the advanced options available for the Honour School of Experimental Psychology, subject to any restrictions set out in the list of available options published in the first week of Hilary Full Term in the year preceding the examination.

Candidates on the Register of Medical Students *may* offer a dissertation in place of one of the five written papers.

Dissertations

The subject of a special topic (which shall be supervised by a member of the Faculty of Physiological Sciences or any other person approved by the Medical Sciences Board) may be experimental work performed by the candidate himself or a report based on a temporary association with an established worker or research group (as when the necessary practical skills cannot be mastered in the time available), or a critical review based on individual reading. The dissertation shall be typed but need not be bound provided it is held firmly in a stiff cover. A dissertation shall not exceed 10,000 words (excluding figures, diagrams, and references), but a dissertation of 4,000–5,000 words will be considered ample when the candidate has performed an appreciable quantity of personal experimental work. Lists of topics for dissertations approved by the Medical Sciences Board shall be circulated to the appropriate college tutors by the beginning of each Trinity Full Term. These topics shall be (unless otherwise indicated in the case of any particular topic on the list) available both to candidates on the Register of Medical Students who may wish to offer a dissertation in the honour school examination in the Trinity Term of the following academic year and also to candidates not on the Register of Medical Students for offering in the honour school examination in the Trinity Term of the next but one academic year.

Timetable for notification by candidates of dissertation topics selected from the approved list

(*a*) *Candidates not on the Register of Medical Students* (compulsory dissertation)

They shall inform the Administrative Officer, Physiological Sciences Faculty Office (with the written consent of their tutors) which topic they propose to offer not earlier than the end of the Trinity Full Term six terms before that in which they intend to take the examination and not later than the Friday of the eighth week of Michaelmas Full Term in the academic year in which they intend to take the examination.

(*b*) *Candidates on the Register of Medical Students* (optional dissertation)

They shall inform the Administrative Office as above (with the written consent of their tutors) which topic they propose to offer not earlier than the first day of Trinity Full Term in the academic year preceding that in which they intend to take the examination and not later than the Friday of the eighth week of Michaelmas Term in the academic year in which they intend to take the examination.

Approval and notification of dissertation topics not on the approved list

A candidate may, with the written consent of his tutor, seek the approval of the Medical Sciences Board, c/o the Administrative Officer, Physiological Sciences Faculty Office to offer a dissertation on a topic not on the approved list provided that such requests (including the name of the potential supervisor) are made to the committee in accordance with the following timetable.

(*a*) *Candidates not on the Register of Medical Students* (compulsory dissertation): not earlier than the Wednesday of the sixth week of Trinity Full Term six terms before that in which they intend to take the examination and not later than the Friday of the fifth week of Michaelmas Full Term in the academic year in which they intend to take the examination.

(*b*) *Candidates on the Register of Medical Students* (optional dissertation): not earlier than the first day of Trinity Full Term in the academic year preceding that in which they intend to take the examination and not later than the Friday of the fifth week of Michaelmas Full Term in the academic year in which they intend to take the examination.

The decision of the Medical Sciences Board whether to approve topics shall be communicated to candidates as soon as possible and in any case not later than Monday in the eighth week of Michaelmas Full Term in the academic year in which they intend to take the examination.

Dissertations (two copies) must be sent to the Chairman of the Examiners in Physiological Sciences, Honour School of Natural Science, c/o the Clerk of the Schools, Examination Schools, High Street, Oxford, not later than noon on the Friday of the first week of the Trinity Term in which the examination is to be held. The copies shall be accompanied (in a separate sealed envelope) by a certificate signed by each candidate indicating that the dissertation is the candidate's own work. Where the work submitted has been produced in collaboration the candidate shall indicate the extent of the candidate's own contribution. The examiners may obtain a written report on the work of each candidate from the supervisor concerned.

Theses previously submitted for the Honour School of Natural Science (Physiological Science) may be resubmitted. No dissertation will be accepted if it has already been submitted, wholly or substantially, for another Honour School or degree of this University, or a degree of any other institution.

Candidates whose names have not been entered on the Register of Medical Students shall submit signed notebooks providing evidence of attendance at at least two practical classes during their course of study, and candidates whose names have been entered on the Register of Medical Students shall submit signed notebooks providing evidence of attendance at at least one practical class during their course of study provided that candidates offering a dissertation involving substantial laboratory work may apply to the Medical Sciences Board for exemption from one practical class. Each notebook shall be accompanied by a certificate signed by the candidate indicating that the notebook submitted is the candidate's own work. Any practical class which does not constitute a regular departmental practical shall be subject to the approval of the Medical Sciences Board.

The signed notebooks shall be available to the examiners at any time before the written examination prescribed by the examiners and shall be taken into consideration by them. The examiners may also require further examination of the candidate on practical work.

The signed notebooks will constitute part of the examination. Any candidate who fails to submit a signed notebook will be deemed to have withdrawn from the examination.

Candidates may be examined viva voce; the topics may include the subject of any of the written papers and the practical work done during their course of study.

PASS SCHOOL OF NATURAL SCIENCE

Pass School of Natural Science (Molecular and Cellular Biochemistry)

The candidate will be required:

(i) to satisfy the examiners in four written papers of his or her choice from among Papers I–VI for Part I of the Honour School of Natural Science (Molecular and Cellular Biochemistry);

(ii) to pursue a course of laboratory work as specified in Part I of the Honour School of Natural Science (Molecular and Cellular Biochemistry) and to satisfy the examiners therein.

No candidate for the Pass School will be eligible to continue to Part II.

Pass School of Natural Science (Biological Sciences)

The candidate will be required to satisfy the examiners in

(i) Parts A and B of the examination for the Honour School of Natural Science (Biological Sciences);

(ii) Subject 2 of the Honour School of Natural Science (Biological Sciences); and

(iii) One subject (two papers) chosen from subjects 3–7 of the Honour School of Natural Science (Biological Sciences).

All candidates must pursue a course of practical work and exercises in Quantitative Methods as specified for the Honour School of Natural Science (Biological Sciences) and must satisfy the examiners therein. They will also be required to carry out field work and attend such vacation courses as are approved from time to time by the Biological Sciences Teaching Committee.

Pass School of Natural Science (Chemistry)

Candidates shall:

(i) satisfy the examiners in the six General Papers specified for Part I of the Honour School of Natural Science in Chemistry;

(ii) pursue a course of laboratory work as specified in Part I of the Honour School of Natural Science in Chemistry.

Pass School of Natural Science

Three-year course (Geology)

1. Candidates shall be required to satisfy the examiners in six papers on the fundamentals of Geology as specified in the requirements for the three-year course for the Honour School of Natural Science (Geology) and also in practical examinations at the discretion of the examiners.

2. Candidates are required to attend such field courses during each year of study as are approved annually by the Sub-faculty of Earth Sciences.

3. Practical notebooks containing records of both field and laboratory courses must also be made available to the examiners.

Four-year course (Earth Sciences)

Candidates shall be required to satisfy the examiners:

(*a*) as prescribed in sections (1), (2), and (3) of the Pass School of Natural Sciences (*Geology: Three-Year Course*);

(*b*) in two of the written papers prescribed under section (3)(i) of Part B of the four-year course for the Honour School of Natural Science (Earth Sciences);

(*c*) in an extended essay *or* report on practical work *or* project as prescribed in section (3)(ii) of Part B of the four-year course for the Honour School of Natural Science (Earth Sciences).

Pass School of Natural Science (*Materials Science*)

Candidates shall satisfy the examiners in five out of (i) to (vi) below:

(i)–(iv) the four general papers as specified in Part I (1) of the Honour School of Materials Science;

(v) the Engineering and Society specified in Part I of the Honour School of Materials Science;

(vi) the detailed reports of practical work as specified in Part I of the Honour School of Materials Science.

Pass School of Natural Science (*Physiological Sciences*)

Candidates whose names have been entered on the Register of Medical Students must offer three papers of those set for Physiology in the Honour School of Natural Science, which may include the general paper (13) Physiological Sciences. Candidates whose names have not been entered on the Register of Medical Students must offer five papers from the same list. All candidates, whether or not on the Register, may include as one of their papers a paper chosen from those set in the written part of the examination for the Honour School of Experimental Psychology. Normally this should be one of the following but exceptionally a candidate may substitute another paper from the Honour School of Experimental Psychology with the prior approval of the Physiological Sciences Board:

(1) Brain and Behaviour;
(2) Biology of Learning and Memory;
(3) Perception.

Applications for approval of other papers should be submitted by not later than the Friday of the fourth week of Trinity Term in the year preceding the examination.

All candidates may offer a dissertation on a special topic in place of one of the written papers in accordance with the regulations for the Honour School of Natural Science (Physiological Sciences).

Candidates shall submit notebooks providing evidence of attendance at least one practical class during the course of study.

SPECIAL REGULATIONS FOR THE HONOUR SCHOOL OF ORIENTAL STUDIES

A

1. The main subjects of the examination in the Honour School of Oriental Studies shall be Arabic, Chinese, Classics, Egyptology and Ancient Near Eastern Studies, Hebrew, Japanese, Jewish Studies, Persian, Sanskrit, and Turkish, together with such other subjects as may be determined by the Board of the Faculty of Oriental Studies.

2. Every candidate in the examination shall be required to offer one of the main subjects listed above: candidates offering one of the above languages shall also be required to show an adequate knowledge of the literature and history of the civilization concerned, and candidates offering a history subject listed above shall also be required to show an adequate knowledge of the language concerned.

3. No candidate shall be admitted to examination in this school unless he or she has either passed or been exempted from the First Public Examination.

4. In the Class List issued by the examiners in the Honour School of Oriental Studies the main subject and (where appropriate) additional language offered by each candidate who obtains Honours shall be indicated.

5. Any candidate whose name has been placed in the Class List, upon the result of the examination in any one of the subjects mentioned in clause 1, shall be permitted to offer himself or herself for examination in any other of the subjects mentioned in the same clause at the examination in either the next year or the next year but one, provided always that he or she has not exceeded six terms from the date on which he or she first obtained Honours in a Final Honour School, and provided that no such candidate shall offer any of the main subjects already offered by him or her in the School of Oriental Studies.

6. The examination in this school shall be under the supervision of the Board of the Faculty of Oriental Studies, which shall make regulations concerning it subject always to the preceding clauses of this sub-section and subject also to the agreement of the Board of the Faculty of Classics to any regulations concerning Classics.

B

Candidates proposing to offer a Special Subject not included in the lists below must obtain the approval of the board both for their subject and for the treatises or documents (if any) which they propose to offer with it.

Except in the case of Chinese and Japanese, if the candidate so desires and the board thinks it appropriate, such a Special Subject may be examined in the form of a dissertation, to be sent to the Chairman of Examiners, Honour School of Oriental Studies, c/o Clerk of the Schools, Examination Schools, High Street, Oxford, not later than 12 noon on Friday of the tenth week of the Hilary Term preceding the examination. A signed statement that the dissertation is the candidate's own work should be submitted separately in a sealed envelope, to the Chairman of Examiners (forms are available from the Faculty Office, Oriental Institute). Theses previously submitted for the Honour School of Oriental Studies may be resubmitted. No thesis will be accepted if it has already been submitted, wholly or substantially, for another Honour School or degree of this University, or for a degree of any other insitution. It is recommended that the dissertation shall not exceed 15,000 words.

All applications for approval by the board must be sent to the Secretary of the Board of the Faculty of Oriental Studies, Oriental Institute, on or before the Monday in the second week of the Michaelmas Full Term preceding the examination, and must be accompanied by two copies of a list of the treatises or documents (if any) offered.

The general regulations concerning optional dissertations also apply to the compulsory dissertation in Chinese, Egyptology and Ancient Near Eastern Studies, and Japanese.

All candidates must give notice, on their examination entry forms, of their Special Subjects and choice of books or subjects, where alternatives exist, to the Registrar on or before the Friday in the fourth week of the Michaelmas Full Term preceding the examination. The notice must specify the subject so offered, and, if a subject specially approved by the board, also the treatises or original documents (if any) which it has approved.

Any candidate may be examined viva voce.

The editions of texts specified in the Regulations are the ones which will be used for the reproduction of material for examination purposes, not necessarily the ones which provide the most useful material for the study of the texts concerned.

For those papers where a selection of unspecified texts is to be examined, the selection of texts will be determined by the Undergraduate Studies Committee of the board at its first meeting in Hilary Term for the examination in the next academic year, and copies of the lists of selected texts will be available for candidates not later than Friday of the third week of the same term.

Oral examinations for Arabic, Chinese, Japanese, Persian, and Turkish will be held in the week before Trinity Full Term in the year in which the Honour School examination is taken.

Regulations Concerning Individual Subjects

The subjects of the school are arranged below in two sections: (i) main subjects; (ii) additional languages. Within each section subjects are listed in alphabetical order as follows:

Main Subjects	*Additional Languages*	
Arabic	Akkadian	Hebrew
Chinese	Arabic	Hittite
Classics	Aramaic and Syriac	**[From 1 October 2005:**
Egyptology and Ancient Near Eastern Studies	Armenian	Japanese**]**
Hebrew	**[From 1 October 2005:**	Korean
Japanese	Chinese**]**	Old Iranian
	Classics	Pali
	Coptic	Persian
	Egyptology	Prakrit

Main Subjects (contd)	*Additional Languages (contd)*	
Jewish Studies	Sanskrit	Turkish
Persian	Spanish	
Sanskrit	Sumerian	
Turkish	Tibetan	

Candidates offering Arabic, Chinese, Hebrew, Persian or Turkish *may* offer an additional language as specified below **[Until 1 October 2004:** , and candidates offering Classics, Egyptology and Ancient Near Eastern Studies, or Sanskrit *must* offer an additional language as specified below.**]** **[From 1 October 2004:** ; candidates offering Classics or Sanskrit *must* offer an additional language as specified below; and candidates offering Egyptology and Ancient Near Eastern Studies *must* offer either an additional language or Archaeology and Anthropology as specified below.**]**

Candidates offering Arabic or Turkish or Persian as their main subject will be required to spend a period of at least one academic year on an approved course of language study in the Middle East.

Candidates offering Chinese are required to spend a period of at least four months on an approved course of language study in East Asia.

Candidates offering Hebrew shall take one of the following courses:

Course I: Candidates will be examined in accordance with the regulations set out below.

Course II: Candidates will be examined in accordance with the regulations set out below. Candidates offering Hebrew **Course II** as their main subject will be required to spend a period of at least one academic year on an approved course of language study in Israel.

Candidates taking Arabic or Turkish or Persian with Islamic Art and Archaeology will also be required to participate in one or more approved projects of fieldwork or museum-based study normally to be completed in year 2 in a country within the historic *Dār al-Islām*.

Main Subjects

Arabic

Candidates for entry to the Final Honour School offering Arabic as their main subject will be required

either (*a*) to have passed an examination in Arabic at the end of their approved course abroad, the examination being under the auspices of the Board of the Faculty of Oriental Studies,

or (*b*) otherwise to have satisfied the faculty board as to their competence in Arabic.

Candidates for entry to the Final Honour School of Arabic with Islamic Art and Archaeology will also be required to have satisfied the faculty board, by means of written testimonials and a written report upon the project(s) completed in Year 2, as to their active and useful participation in the approved project(s).

Candidates will be required to offer ten papers.

Either, for Arabic only,

1. Arabic unprepared translation into English and comprehension.
2. Composition in Arabic.
3. Spoken Arabic*
4. Qur'ān and Ḥadīth:
   The Qur'ān, *Sūras* 5, 12, 19, 37, 62, 63, 80, 81, 91–6.
   'Al-Nawawī, *Arbaʿūna hadīthan*

---

* See footnote on page 397.

5. and 6. Two of the following:

(*a*) Classical Texts:

Selected Classical Arabic literary prose and poetry (list and copies are available from the Oriental Institute).

(*b*) Modern Texts:

Ṭāhā Ḥusayn: *al-Ayyām,* vol. I. Maḥmūd Ṭāhir Lāshīn, *Ḥadīth al-qarya.* Yūsuf Idrīs, *Arkhaṣ layālī, Bayt min laḥm.* Idwār al-Kharrāt: *Turābuhā za'farān* (Dār al-Ādab 1991, pp. 23–40). Emile Ḥabībī: *al-Kharaza al-zarqā' wa'-awdat jubaynā.* al-Ṭayyib Ṣāliḥ: *Dūmat wād ḥāmid.* Tawfīq al-Ḥakīm, *Ughniyat al-mawt.* Maḥfūẓ, *al-Liṣṣ wa'l-kilāb.* M. M. Badawi, *An Anthology of Modern Arabic Verse,* Poems by al-Bārūdī, Shawqī, Ḥāfiẓ Ibrāhīm, Zahāwī, Ruṣāfī, Muṭrān, Shukrī, Nājī, Ṭāhā, al-Shābbī, Nu'ayma, Abū Rīsha, Abū Shabaka, al-Bayyātī, al-Sayyāb, 'Abd al-Ṣabūr, Adūnīs.

(*c*) Historical Texts:

Arabic Historical Texts (copies are available from the Oriental Institute).

7. The Formative Period: Islamic History and Thought until the Mid-Twelfth Century.

8. A special subject, to be approved by the Board of the Faculty of Oriental Studies.

9. and 10.

Either

(*a*) *Classical* (Two papers, each of which will consist of passages for translation and comment, and essay questions.)

9(*a*) Prose: Selected Classical Arabic prose (list and copies are available from the Oriental Institute).

10(*a*) Poetry:

Selected Classical Arabic poetry (list and copies are available from the Oriental Institute).

or

(*b*) *Modern Arabic Literature*

9(*b*) Essay questions on modern set texts and the history and development of Modern Arabic literature.

and 10(*b*) Tawfīq al-Ḥakīm, *Yawmiyyāt nā'ib fī 'l-aryāf.* Yaḥyā Ḥaqqī, *Qindīl Umm Hāshim.* Ghassān Kanafānī, *Rijāl fi'l-shams.* Salwā Bakr, *Maqām 'Atiyya.*

or, for Arabic with Islamic Studies/History, Papers 1–8 above **and**

11. and 12. Two papers chosen from the following:

(i) Early Islamic History I: from the time of the Prophet to the early 'Abbasids, 570–809 AD.

(ii) Early Islamic History II: from the early 'Abbasids to the Saljuqs, 809–1055 AD.

(iii) The Saljuq period.

(iv) Egypt and Syria under the Ayyubids and Mamluks.

(v) The Ottoman Empire 1300–1566.

(vi) The Ottoman Empire 1566–1807.

(vii) Modern Iranian history.

(viii) The Arab world 1798–1914.

(ix) The Arab world 1914–1960.

(x) Medieval religious and political thought.

(xi) The life and times of a major medieval thinker.

(xii) Intellectual history of the Middle East in the nineteenth and twentieth centuries.

(xiii) Another subject in Islamic studies or history, to be approved by the Board of the Faculty of Oriental Studies.

or, for Arabic with a subsidiary language, Papers 1–7 above, **and**

13, 14, and 15 Three papers from one of the following:

Akkadian.
Aramaic and Syriac.
Armenian.
Classics.
Hebrew.
Persian.
Spanish.
Turkish.

16. An *optional* special subject to be approved by the Board.

Applications for the approval of options in papers 8, 11, 12, and 16 must be submitted not later than Monday of the second week of the Michaelmas Term preceding the examination.

or, for Arabic with Modern Middle Eastern Studies, each candidate shall offer the ten papers listed below.

1. Arabic unprepared translation into English and comprehension.
2. Composition in Arabic.
3. Spoken Arabic.*
4. Classical texts:
   Selected Classical Arabic literary prose and poetry (list and copies are available from the Oriental Institute).
5. Modern Arabic Texts I:
   Ṭāhā Ḥusayn: *al-Ayyām,* vol. I. Maḥmūd Ṭāhir Lāshīn, *Ḥadīth al-qarya.* Yūsuf Idrīs, *Arkhaṣ layālī, Bayt min laḥm.* Idwār al-Kharrāt: *Turābuhā za'farān* (Dār al-Ādab 1991, pp. 23–40). Emile Ḥabībī: *al-Kharaza al-zurqā' wa'-awdat jubaynā.* al-Ṭayyib Ṣāliḥ: *Dūmat wād ḥāmid.* Tawfīq al-Ḥakīm, *Ughniyat al-mawt.* Maḥfūẓ, *al-Liṣṣ wa'l-kilāb.* M. M. Badawi, *An Anthology of Modern Arabic Verse,* poems by al-Bārūdī, Shawqī, Ḥāfiẓ Ibrāhīm, Zahāwī, Ruṣāfī, Muṭrān, Shukrī, Nājī, Ṭāhā, al-Shābbī, Nu'ayma, Abū Rīsha, Abū Shabaka, al-Bayyātī, al-Sayyāb, 'Abd al-Ṣabūr, Adūnīs.
6. Modern Arabic Texts II:
   Tawfīq al-Ḥakīm, *Yawmiyyāt nā'ib fī 'l-aryāf.* Yaḥyā Ḥaqqī, *Qindīl Umm Hāshim.* Ghassan Kanafānī, *Rijāl fi'l-shams.* Salwā Bakr, *Maqām 'Aṭiyya.*
7. The Formative Period: Islamic History and Thought until the Mid-Twelfth Century.

8 and 9. Two papers chosen from the following:

(i) Modern Middle Eastern culture and society.
(ii) State and politics in the contemporary Middle East.
(iii) Problems of modern Middle Eastern history.
(iv) Modern Arab thought.
(v) Geography of the Middle East.

10. A special subject, to be approved by the Board of the Faculty of Oriental Studies.

Applications for the approval of options in papers 8 and 9 must be submitted to the Oriental Studies board by Monday of the third week of Michaelmas Term in the academic year preceding that in which the examination is to be taken. Applications for the approval of the special subject in paper 10 should be submitted to the Oriental

---

* Details of the oral examination and of the areas in which candidates will be expected to show competence are provided in the examination conventions and in the handbook.

Studies Board by Monday of the second week of Michaelmas Term preceding the examination.

or, for Arabic with Islamic Art and Archaeology, candidates shall offer ten papers listed below.

1. Arabic unprepared translation into English and comprehension.
2. Composition in Arabic.
3. Spoken Arabic*.
4. Qur'ān and Hadīth.
5. Selected Arabic texts.
6. From Late Antiquity to Islam. The archaeology of the Near East during the transition from Late Antiquity and the formation of Islam, 550–900.
7. The breakdown of the caliphate. The art and archaeology of the Islamic world 900–1250.
8. The great empires. The art and archaeology of the Islamic world 1250–1600.
9. One paper in history chosen from the following:

(*a*) Early Islamic History I: from the time of the Prophet to the early ʻAbbasids, 570–809 AD.
(*b*) Early Islamic History II: from the early ʻAbbasids to the Saljuqs, 809–1055 AD.
(*c*) Arab and Norman Sicily 827–1250.
(*d*) The Crusades.
(*e*) The Saljuq period.
(*f*) Egypt and Syria under the Ayyubids and Mamluks.
(*g*) The Ottoman Empire 1300–1566.
(*h*) Another historical subject, to be approved by the Board of the Faculty of Oriental Studies.

10. One special subject to be chosen from the following:

(*a*) Human settlement in Greater Syria, 600–1250.
(*b*) Islamic ceramics: the China question.
(*c*) Material culture, ceremonial, and power in the Fatimid Mediterranean.
(*d*) Metalwork, technology, and patronage, 1100–1300.
(*e*) Patrons and artisans in the Ottoman ceramic industry.
(*f*) Inscriptions and images: problems of iconography.
(*g*) Islamic Numismatics.
(*h*) Another special subject, which may be a language subject, to be approved by the Board of the Faculty of Oriental Studies.

Some options and special subjects may not be available in every year. Candidates may obtain from the Oriental Institute information about which options may be offered for examination the following year at the beginning of Trinity Term of the preceding year.

Applications for the approval of options in paper 9 and of the special subjects in paper 10 must be submitted to the Oriental Studies Board by Monday of the second week of Michaelmas Term preceding the examination.

Chinese

Either, for Chinese only.

The following papers will be set:

1. Modern Chinese prose composition.
2. Spoken Chinese*.
3. Unprepared translation from Modern Chinese.

---

* See footnote on page 397.

4. Classical Chinese I.
Translation from and comment on:
Zhuangzi 17 (ed. Guo Qingfan, repr. Beijing: Zhonghua shuju 1961); *Selected Chinese Poems*, ed. Liu (copies are available from the Institute for Chinese Studies).

5. Classical Chinese II: Narrative Prose.
Candidates will be required to translate unprepared passages and passages drawn from:
Yangzhou shi ri ji (ed. *Yangzhou congke*, Yangzhou 1934); Hong Taeyong, *Tamhon yon'gi* (repr. in *Yonhaengnok sonjip*, Seoul 1960).

6. Special texts I.
Translation from and comment on:
Either (*a*) early historical texts;
Or (*b*) traditional literary texts;
Or (*c*) modern literary texts;
Or (*d*) Korean historical texts in Chinese;
Or (*e*) texts on the modern politics and society of China.
Lists of texts are available from the Institute for Chinese Studies at the beginning of the academic year before that in which the examination is taken.

7. Special texts II.
Candidates will be required to answer questions on the texts offered in paper 6, their subject-matter and background.

8. History of China in the nineteenth and twentieth centuries.

9. A dissertation on a subject approved by the Board of the Faculty.

10. Special language paper.
Either Japanese;
Or Korean;
Or Unprepared translation in the field chosen for Paper 6;
Or General Linguistics for students of Chinese;
***Or* Chinese with a subsidiary language** papers 1–5, 8, and 9 above and 11, 12, and 13. **[Until 1 October 2005:** Three papers in Tibetan and Korean.**] [From 1 October 2005:** Three papers in Japanese, Tibetan or Korean.**]**

Classics

Candidates will be required to offer five of the following subjects (i)–(xxiv), and also three papers on one of the additional languages Akkadian, Arabic, Aramaic and Syriac, Armenian, Coptic, Egyptology, Hebrew, Old Iranian, Pali, Persian or Sanskrit.

Candidates who have satisfied the Moderators in Course IA, IB, or IC of Honour Moderations in Classics or of the Preliminary Examination in Classics must offer (i) and (v) as two of their five subjects; they may not offer (xxiii), (xxiv), Second Classical Language.

Other candidates not offering (xxiii), (xxiv), Second Classical Language must include at least two of subjects (i)–(xv), of which one must be either (i) or (v); they may offer both (i) and (v) if they wish.

Subject (xxiii), (xxiv), Second Classical Language counts as two subjects. Candidates offering it must also offer either (i) or (v), and may offer both.

Note: It cannot be guaranteed that university lectures or classes or college teaching will be available on all subjects in every academic year. Candidates are advised to consult their tutors about the availability of teaching when selecting their subjects.

(i) Greek Literature of the Fifth Century BC (one paper of three hours (commentary and essay) with an additional paper (one-and-a-half hours) of translation) [Honour School of Literae Humaniores, subject III.1].

(ii) [Honour School of Literae Humaniores, subject III.2]

Either (a) Early Greek Hexameter Poetry

Or (b) Greek Lyric and Elegiac Poetry

Or (c) Pindar and Bacchylides.

(iii) [Honour School of Literae Humaniores, subject III.3]

Either (a) Aeschylus

Or (b) Euripides.

(iv) [Honour School of Literae Humaniores, subject III.4]

Either (a) Plato

Or (b) Hellenistic Poetry.

(v) Latin Literature of the First Century BC (one paper of three hours (commentary and essay) with an additional paper (one-and-a-half hours) of translation) [Honour School of Literae Humaniores, subject III.5].

(vi) [Honour School of Literae Humaniores, subject III.6]

Either (a) Latin Didactic Poetry

Or (b) Latin Satire

(vii) [Honour School of Literae Humaniores, subject III.7]

Either (a) Cicero the Orator

Or (b) Horace

Or (c) Ovid

Or (d) Seneca and Lucan.

(viii) [Honour School of Literae Humaniores, subject III.8; in each case version (i) is the only version available to candidates who have satisfied the Moderators in Course IA, IB, or IC of Honour Moderations in Classics or of the Preliminary Examination in Classics]

(a) Greek and Roman Comedy

Either (b) Ancient Literary Criticism

Or (c) The Ancient Novel.

(ix) Greek Textual Criticism [Honour School of Literae Humaniores, subject III.9].

(x) Latin Textual Criticism [Honour School of Literae Humaniores, subject III.10].

(xi) Homer, *Iliad* [Honour Moderations in Classics Course IA, paper I]. (This subject may not be offered by candidates who have satisfied the Moderators in Course IA, IB, IC, or IIB of Honour Moderations in Classics and may not be offered in combination with subject (ii)*(a)*, Early Greek Hexameter Poetry.)

(xii) Virgil, *Aeneid*. Translation and essay questions will be required; commentary questions will be optional. (This subject may not be offered by candidates who have satisfied the Moderators in Course IA, IB, IC, or IIA of Honour Moderations in Classics.)

(xiii) *Either (a)* The Conversion of Augustine [Honour School of Literae Humaniores, subject III.11*(a)*].

Or (c) Medieval Latin [Honour School of Literae Humaniores, subject III.11*(b)*].

Or (c) The Latin Works of Petrarch, with special study of *Africa* (ed. N. Festa, Florence, 1926). Books I, II, V, VII, IX. Candidates will also be expected to have read *Vita Scipionis* (in *La Vita di Scipione l' Africano*, ed. G. Martillotti, Milano-Napoli, 1954), and to show acquaintance with Petrarch's major Latin works (e.g. *Rerum memorandarum libri* (ed. G. Billanovich, Florence, 1945), *De secreto conflictu curarum mearum, De vita solitaria, Epistolae familiares* (in F. Petrarca, *Prose*, ed. G. Martillotti, P. G. Ricci, E. Carrara, E. Bianchi, Milano-Napoli, 1955)).

[From 1 October 2004:

Or (d) Byzantine Literature [Honour School of Literae Humaniores, subject III.11*(c)*].]

(xiv) Greek Historical Linguistics [Honour School of Literae Humaniores, subject V.1]. (This subject may be combined with one but not more than one of (xv), (xvi), and (xvii).)

(xv) Latin Historical Linguistics [Honour School of Literae Humaniores, subject V.2]. (This subject may be combined with one but not more than one of (xiv), (xvi), and (xvii).)

(xvi) Historical Linguistics and Comparative Philology [Honour Moderations in Classics Course IA, paper V, VI F(1)]. (This subject may not be offered by candidates who offered it in Honour Moderations in Classics or in the Preliminary Examination in Classics. It may be combined with one but not more than one of (xiv), (xv), and (xvii).)

(xvii) General Linguistics and Comparative Philology [Honour School of Literae Humaniores, subject V.3]. (This subject may be combined with one but not more than one of (xiv), (xv), and (xvi).)

(xviii) *Either* (*a*) Greek History from 776 BC to 479 BC [Honour School of Literae Humaniores, subject I.1; not to be offered in combination with subject (xix)(*a*), The Greeks and the Mediterranean World *c*.950 BC–500 BC].

Or (*b*) Greek History from 479 BC to 403 BC [Honour School of Literae Humaniores, subject I.2].

Or (*c*) Greek History from 403 BC to 336 BC [Honour School of Literae Humaniores, subject I.3].

Or (*d*) Roman History from 240 BC to 133 BC [Honour School of Literae Humaniores, subject I.4].

Or (*e*) Roman History from 133 BC to 50 BC [Honour School of Literae Humaniores, subject I.5].

Or (*f*) Roman History from 49 BC to AD 54 [Honour School of Literae Humaniores, subject I.6].

Or (*g*) Roman History from AD 54 to AD 138 [Honour School of Literae Humaniores, subject I.7].

Note: Candidates offering any of subjects (xviii)(*a*)–(*g*) must also offer the associated translation paper set in the Honour School of Literae Humaniores.

(xix) *Either* (*a*) The Greeks and the Mediterranean World *c*.950 BC–500 BC [Honour School of Literae Humaniores, subject IV.1; not to be offered in combination with subject (xviii)(*a*), Greek History from 776 BC to 479 BC].

Or (*b*) Greek Art and Archaeology, *c*.500–300 BC [Honour School of Literae Humaniores, subject IV.2].

Or (*c*) Art under the Roman Empire, AD 14–337 [Honour School of Literae Humaniores, subject IV.3].

Or (*d*) Cities and Settlement in the Roman Empire [Honour School of Literae Humaniores, subect IV.4].

(xx) *Either* subject 130 *or* subject 131 *or* subject 132, as specified in Regulations for Philosophy in all Honour Schools including Philosophy.

(xxi) Modern Greek Poetry [Honour School of Literae Humaniores, subject **[Until 1 October 2004:** III.11(*c*)**]** **[From 1 October 2004:** III.11(*d*)**]**
(This subject is available only to candidates offering subject (i), Greek Literature of the Fifth Century BC who are offering neither (xiii)(*d*), **[Until 1 October 2004:** Procopius**]** **[From 1 October 2004:** Byzantine Literature**]** nor (xxiii), (xxiv), Second Classical Language.)

(xxii) Thesis. Any candidate may offer a thesis in Classics, or in a subject linking Classics and their Additional Language, in accordance with the Regulation on Theses in the regulations for the Honour School of Literae Humaniores, save that references there to the Honour School of Literae Humaniores shall be deemed to be references to the Honour School of Oriental Studies (with Classics as Main Subject) and that the Board of the Faculty of Literae Humaniores shall consult the Board of the Faculty of Oriental Studies as appropriate. Candidates who offer two of subjects (xiv)–(xvii) may not also offer a thesis in Philology or Linguistics.

(xxiii), (xxiv) (see introductory notes) Second Classical Language [Honour School of Literae Humaniores, subject VI.1 and VI.2]. (Candidates who offer Second Classical Language must offer *either both* subjects in Greek *or both* subjects in Latin, and may not offer either subject in the same language as they offered in Course IIA or IIB of Honour Moderations or the Preliminary Examination in Classics.)

Egyptology and Ancient Near Eastern Studies
[From 1 October 2004:
Either, for Egyptology and Ancient Near Eastern Studies with a subsidiary language,]

The languages which may be offered shall be:
As first language: Akkadian or Egyptian
As second language (which must be different from the first language):
Akkadian
Egyptian
Arabic
Aramaic and Syriac
Classics
Coptic
Hebrew (Biblical and Mishnaic)
Hittite (may not be available every year)
Old Iranian
Sumerian

[Until 1 October 2004: The following papers will be set:**] [From 1 October 2004:** Candidates will be required to offer the following papers:**]**

1. Translation paper (first language).
2. Translation paper (second language).

3, 4. Literary and historical topics including prepared translation from first language.

5, 6. Literary and historical topics including prepared translation from second language.

For papers 4 and 6, in each case four passages from a list of prescribed texts will be set for examination by essay. For each paper, candidates must present a translation of and essay on one passage. Papers should be typed and provided with proper scholarly apparatus. The passages for paper 4 will be assigned in the Oriental Institute at 10 a.m. on Monday of First Week in Full Term in the term in which the final examination is to be offered, and must be handed in to the Clerk of the Examination Schools no later than 12 noon on Monday of Second Week. A signed statement that the essay is the candidate's own work should be submitted separately in a sealed envelope bearing his or her candidate number, to the Chairman of examiners (forms are available from the Faculty Office, Oriental Institute). The passages for paper 6 will be assigned in the Oriental Institute at 10 a.m. on Monday of Third Week in Full Term in the term in which the final examination is to be offered, and must be handed in to the Clerk of the Examination Schools no later than 12 noon on Monday of Fourth Week. Essays should not exceed 3,500 words. A signed statement that the essay is the candidate's own work should be submitted separately in a sealed envelope bearing his or her candidate number, to the Chairman of examiners (forms are available from the Faculty Office, Oriental Institute).

Lists of prescribed texts for papers 3–6 are available from the Oriental Institute. As papers 2, 5, and 6 in Arabic, Aramaic and Syriac, Coptic, Hebrew (Biblical and Mishnaic), and Old Iranian, candidates may offer the papers prescribed for Arabic, Aramaic and Syriac, Coptic, Hebrew (Biblical and Mishnaic), and Old Iranian as additional languages in the Honour School of Oriental Studies. In the case of candidates offering Classics, they must offer for papers 2, 5 and 6 three of subjects (i)–(xxiv) listed under Classics as an additional language in Oriental Studies, according to the conditions specified there (pp. 460–3).

7. A field of concentration to be chosen from a list of topics published at the beginning of Michaelmas Term each year by the Oriental Studies Faculty Board for examination in the following academic year. Candidates may propose their own field of concentration. The choice must be approved by the Board in each case.

8. Selected Egyptian and/or Ancient Near Eastern artefacts (one and a half hours, to be examined in the Ashmolean Museum and to have half the weight of the other papers).

9. General paper, including questions on Egyptology and Ancient Near Eastern Studies today.

10. A dissertation on a topic to be approved by the Faculty Board, of a different character from that chosen for paper 7.

11. An optional special subject to be approved by the Board of the Faculty of Oriental Studies, including topics such as have been approved under the present FHS syllabuses in Hebrew, and the additional language syllabus in Classics.

[From 1 October 2004:

***Or*, for Egyptology and Ancient Near Eastern Studies with Archaeology and Anthropology,** candidates will be required to offer papers 1, 3–4, and 7–11 above, **and** the following papers:

12. Anthropological theory and archaeological enquiry.
13. Urbanization and change in complex societies: comparative approaches.
14. Social analysis and interpretation **or** Cultural representations, beliefs and practices.

All candidates will be required to undertake a course of practical work, including laboratory work.

Candidates will be assessed, at the end of the sixth term from matriculation, on their practical ability, under the provisions for Honour Moderations in Archaeology and Anthropology.

Candidates will be required to take part in approved fieldwork as an integral part of their course. The fieldwork requirement will normally have been discharged before the Long Vacation of six terms from matriculation.**]**

Hebrew

Either, for Hebrew only,

candidates for **Course I** will be required to offer nine papers. Candidates for **Course II** will be required to offer nine papers, a compulsory Special Subject, and an oral examination. They will be expected to carry out during their year abroad such work as the Board of the Faculty of Oriental Studies may require. This will include substantial essays *or* a dissertation not exceeding 15,000 words, in addition to such programmes of reading and written work in preparation for the examination as their tutors/the Oriental Studies Board may prescribe.

1. (for **Course I**): Hebrew composition and unprepared translation.
   (for **Course II**): Essay in modern Hebrew and unprepared translation.
2. Prepared texts I: Biblical texts (lists of texts are available from the Oriental Institute).
3. Prepared texts II: **[Until 1 October 2004:** Mishnaic**] [From 1 October 2004:** Rabbinic**]** and Medieval Hebrew texts (lists of texts are available from the Oriental Institute).
4. Prepared texts III: Modern Hebrew literature (lists of texts are available from the Oriental Institute).
5. General paper; language, history, religion, and culture.
6. Prepared texts IV:

(*a*) Jewish Aramaic and *either* (*b*) Biblical Hebrew *or* (*c*) Mishnaic and Medieval Hebrew *or* (*d*) Modern Hebrew (lists of texts are available from the Oriental Institute).

7, 8, and 9. Three papers chosen from the following:

Any of the papers in Jewish Studies paper *c*.

10. (for **Course I**): Candidates who so desire may offer any special subject as may be approved by the Board of the Faculty of Oriental Studies. Applications for the approval of options must be submitted to the Board not later than Monday of the second week of the Michaelmas Term preceding the examination.

(for **Course II**): Candidates shall offer a special subject, to be approved by the Board of the Faculty of Oriental Studies. Applications for the approval of options must be submitted to the Board not later than Monday of the second week of the Michaelmas Term preceding the examination.

11. (for **Course II**) Spoken Hebrew.*

***Or*, for Hebrew with a subsidiary language,**

papers 1–5 above, *one* paper from 6–9 (in the case of Paper 6, candidates may offer *any two* sections, except that candidates taking Aramaic and Syriac may not offer section (*a*)), and three papers from one of the following additional subjects: Akkadian, Arabic, Aramaic and Syriac, Classics, Egyptology. Candidates who so desire may offer a special subject as specified in 10.

Japanese

The following papers will be set:

Either, for Japanese only,

1. Japanese prose composition.
2. Japanese unprepared translation I: classical and modern literature (there will be one compulsory classical question).
3. Japanese unprepared translation II: modern non-fiction.
4. Spoken Japanese.†

---

* The oral examination will be held in the week before Trinity Full Term.

The oral examination will be conducted in two parts, namely a comprehension test conducted in a group and an individual test involving a prepared discourse, conversation, and reading aloud. In the oral examination a candidate will be required to show competence in the following:

1. Comprehension of a passage of text. Candidates will hear a passage lasting about five minutes read twice at normal speed and they will be required to write brief answers in Hebrew to questions, relating to the text, supplied on a question sheet. Candidates will be allowed fifteen minutes to complete their answers.
2. A short prepared discourse. Candidates will be required to discourse on a subject chosen by them from three alternative subjects supplied to them one hour before commencement of the oral examination (fifteen minutes).
3. Conversation of not more than five minutes.
4. Reading aloud of a passage of text.

† The oral examination will be held in the week before Trinity Full Term in the year in which the honour school examination is taken. In the oral examination a candidate will normally be required to show that he or she offers competence in the following:

(i) Comprehension of a passage or passages of text (this part of the examination to be conducted in a group; up to one hour will be allowed). In the comprehension test, candidates will hear either one passage lasting up to five minutes or two passages each lasting up to three minutes, the passage or passages being read twice at normal speed by a native speaker or speakers. After the two readings of each passage, candidates will be required to give written evidence in English that they have understood it. (Candidates will be allowed fifteen minutes after the two readings

5. Special Texts 1. Translation from texts in *any one* of the following sections:
(*a*) Classical literature
(*b*) Theatre
(*c*) Modern literature
(*d*) Politics
(*e*) Society and social history
(*f*) Economics
(*g*) Linguistics

Lists of the texts specified will be available from the Oriental Institute by the end of the Trinity Term of the year in which a candidate sits Moderations.

6. Special texts II. Essay questions on the background to the texts studied under 5 above.

7. General questions.

8. A special subject from among the following, or such other special subject as may be approved by the Board of the Faculty:

(*a*) Japanese art.
(*b*) Japanese history I: to 1185.
(*c*) Japanese history II: feudal Japan.
(*d*) Japanese history III: the emergence of modern Japan, 1868–1972.
(*e*) The government and politics of Japan.
(*f*) The intellectual history of the Tokugawa period.
(*g*) The history of Japanese literature to the end of the Tokugawa period.
(*h*) The history of modern Japanese literature (from the beginning of the Meiji period).
(*i*) Modern Japanese economic history.
(*j*) The modern Japanese economy.
(*k*) Japanese theatre.
(*l*) Classical Chinese.
(*m*) Modern Chinese.
(*n*) Japanese Linguistics.
(*o*) Korean Lanaguage.
(*p*) Korean History I: to 1392.
(*q*) Korean History II: 1392 to 1876.
(*r*) Korean History III: 1876 to the present.

Note: Options in the history of Japanese–Korean relations may be available, by arrangement with the Korea Foundation Lecturer in Korean Studies.

9. A dissertation on a subject approved by the Board of the Faculty.

[Until 1 October 2005: *Or*, Japanese with a subsidiary language, papers 1, 4–6, and 9 above **and** 10, 11, 12. One paper in Japanese:

(i) Unprepared translation.

Three papers in Korean.

(i) Prescribed Texts. (Lists of texts will be available from the Oriental Institute).

---

of a single passage, or ten minutes after the two readings of each of two passages, to provide this written evidence.)

(ii) A short discourse (up to five minutes, based on illustrations submitted to the candidates).

(iii) Reading aloud of a passage or passages of text.

(iv) Conversation (not more than ten minutes, on any subject previously introduced under (i), (ii), or (iii) above).

(ii) Korean History and Culture. Essay questions on the background to the texts studied under (i) above.

(iii) Unprepared translation, Prose Composition, and Grammatical Questions.]

[From 1 October 2005:

***Or*, for Japanese with a subsidiary language,** papers 1, 4–6, and 9 above; **and**

10. One paper in Japanese: Unprepared translation; **and**

11, 12, and 13. Three papers in Chinese, Korean or Tibetan.]

Jewish Studies

The following papers will be set.

a. Jewish History, Religion and Culture

b. Hebrew prepared texts (lists of texts are available from the Oriental Institute).

c. Eight of the following, of which at least one must be chosen from each of sections I, II, and III. At least two must be chosen from papers which require study of set texts.

Section I
- (*a*) Biblical History[1]
- (*b*) Biblical Religion
- (*c*) Biblical Archaeology
- (*d*) Biblical Narrative[1]
- (*e*) The Prophets and Prophecy[1]

Section II
- (*f*) Second Temple Judaism[1]
- (*g*) Second Temple History
- (*h*) History of the Talmudic Period
- (*i*) Medieval Jewish History[1]
- (*j*) Medieval Jewish Thought[1]
- (*k*) Jewish Aramaic Literature[1,2]
- (*l*) The Formation and Historical Context of the Talmuds[1]

Section III
- (*m*) Haskalah[1]
- (*n*) Jewish History 1750–1948
- (*o*) Modern Jewish Society
- (*p*) State of Israel
- (*q*) Modern Hebrew Literature[1]
- (*r*) Yiddish Literature[1,2]
- (*s*) Modern Jewish Thought[1]

Section IV
- (*t*) History of Jewish-Christian Relations
- (*u*) History of Jewish-Muslim Relations
- (*v*) History of Jewish Bible Interpretation[1]
- (*w*) History of Hebrew Literature

Special subjects may be offered subject to the approval of the Oriental Studies Board.

Some options may not be available in every year.

Candidates may obtain from the Oriental Institute information about which options may be offered for examination the first Monday of Michaelmas Full Term of the academic year preceding that in which the papers will be set.

Applications for the approval of options must be submitted not later than Monday of the second week of the Michaelmas Term preceding the examination.

---

[1] List of texts (some of which will be in the original language) available in Oriental Institute.

[2] These courses are available only to students with adequate knowledge of the relevant language.

Korean (for candidates offering Japanese as main subject)

The following papers will be set:

1. Prescribed Texts. (List of texts will be available from the Oriental Institute).
2. Korean History and Culture. Essay questions on the background to the texts studied under (1) above.
3. Prose Composition, Unprepared translation, and Grammatical Questions.

Persian

Candidates for entry to the Final Honour School will be required

either to have passed an examination in Persian at the end of their approved course abroad, the examination being under the auspices of the Board of the Faculty of Oriental Studies,

or otherwise to have satisfied the faculty board as to their competence in Persian, *and* to have spent one academic year on an approved course of language study in the Middle East.

Candidates taking Persian with Islamic Art and Archaeology will also be required to have satisfied the faculty board, by means of written testimonials and a written report upon the project(s) completed in Year 2, as to their active and useful participation in the approved project(s).

The following papers will be set. Candidates will be required to offer nine papers.

Either, for Persian with a subsidiary language,

1. Persian prose composition and unprepared translation.
2. Spoken Persian*

3, 4, and 5. Three papers from the following:

(*a*) Classical Poetry: Lyric Genres. *Qaṣīdeh*: selected texts from ʿUnṣurī, Farrukhī, Manūchihrī, Nāṣir-i Khusrau, Sanāʾī, Ḥasan-i Ghaznavī, Anvarī, Khāqānī, ʿAṭṭār. *Ghazal*: selected texts from Sanāʾī, Ḥasan-i Ghaznavī, Anvarī, ʿAṭṭār, Rūmī, Saʿdī, Auḥadī Marāghī, Khvājū, Salmān Sāvajī, Ḥāfiẓ. (Copies are available from the Oriental Institute.)

(*b*) Classical Poetry: Narrative Genres. Selected *masnavī* texts: epic (Firdausī: *Shāh-nāmeh*); didactic (Sanāʾī: *Ḥadīqat al-Ḥaqīqeh*; ʿAṭṭār: *Ilāhī-nāmeh*; Rūmī: *Masnavi-yi Maʿnavī*); romance (Gurgānī: *Vīs u Rāmīn*; Niẓāmī Ganjavī: *Khusrau u Shīrīn, Lailī u Majnūn, Haft Paikar*; Jāmī: *Lailī u Majnūn*). (Copies are available from the Oriental Institute.)

---

* The oral examination will be held in the week before Trinity Full Term in the year in which the Honour School examination is taken. It must be taken in the same year as the written examination. The oral examination will consist of the following parts:

(i) *Comprehension of passages of text*
In this comprehension test, candidates will listen once to the passage read at normal speed, then be given a list of specific questions, listen again to the passage read in short sections, write answers to the questions, and finally listen to the passage again.

(ii) *Conversation*
Each candidate will be required to discuss with the examiner a topic chosen by the candidate from a list of three announced one hour before the commencement of the oral examination (approximate duration 10–15 minutes).

(iii) *Interpreting*
Each candidate will be required to interpret, in a non-technical subject area, between a person speaking Persian and a person speaking English (approximate duration 10 minutes).

(*c*) Classical Prose. Selected texts: historical (*Tārīkh-i Baihaqī, Rāḥat al-Ṣudūr, Tārīkh-i Jahān-Gushā*); ethical (*Qābūs-nāmeh*; *Siyāsat-nāmeh*); religious and mystical (*ʿAbhar al-ʿĀshiqīn, Fīhi mā Fīhi*); biographical (*Taẕkirat al-Auliyā*); literary (*Javāmiʿ al-Ḥikāyāt*; *Marzbān-nāmeh*; *Maqāmāt-i Ḥamīdī*; *Gulistān*). (Copies are available from the Oriental Institute.)

(*d*) Modern Literature. Prose: selected texts from Jamālzādeh, Hidāyat, Buzurg ʿAlavī, Chūbak, Āl-i Aḥmad, Bihrangī, Sāʿidī, Gulshīrī. Poetry: selected texts from Nīmā, Shāmlū, Akhavān-i S̱ālis̱, Furūgh Farrukhzād, Nādir Nādirpūr, Sipihrī. (Copies are available from the Oriental Institute.)

(*e*) Modern social and political writing. Selected texts. (Copies are available from the Oriental Institute.)

6. General questions: the transition from Sasanian to Islamic Persia (up to the tenth century AD); or one of the options (i), (ii) or (iii) in papers 11 and 12 below.

7. A special subject, to be approved by the Board of the Faulty of Oriental Studies.

8, 9, and 10. Subsidiary language. Three papers on one of the following languages: Arabic, Armenian, Old Iranian, Classics and Turkish.

or, for Persian with Islamic Studies/History,

Papers 1–7 above *and*

11 and 12. Two papers from the following:

(i) Iranian history from 1501 to 1722.

(ii) Iranian history from the rise of the Qajars to the end of the Constitutional Revolution.

(iii) Iranian history from 1921 to 1979.

(iv) The development of Shiʿism up to the late nineteenth century.

(v) Modern Shiʿism.

(vi) Any paper under 11 and 12 of the Arabic syllabus except option (vii), Modern Iranian history.

13. A further special subject, to be approved by the Board of the Faculty of Oriental Studies.

Applications for the approval of options in papers, 6, 10, 11, and 12 must be submitted not later than Monday of the second week of the Michaelmas Term preceding the examination.

or, for Persian with Islamic Art and Archaeology, candidates shall be required to offer nine papers.

1. Persian prose composition and unprepared translation.

2. Spoken Persian.

3 and 4. Two papers from the following:

(*a*) Classical poetry.

(*b*) Classical prose.

(*c*) Selected modern texts.

5. From Late Antiquity to Islam. The archaeology of the Near East during the transition from Late Antiquity and the formation of Islam, 550–900.

6. The breakdown of the caliphate. The art and archaeology of the Islamic world from 900 to 1250.

7. The great empires. The art and archaeology of the Islamic world from 1250 to 1600.

8. One paper in history chosen from the following:

(*a*) Early Islamic history I: from the time of the Prophet to the early ʿAbbasids, AD 570–809.

(*b*) Early Islamic History II: from the early ʿAbbasids to the Saljuqs, AD 809–1055.
(*c*) Arab and Norman Sicily 827–1250.
(*d*) The Crusades.
(*e*) The Saljuq period.
(*f*) Egypt and Syria under the Ayyubids and Mamluks.
(*g*) The Ottoman Empire 1300–1566.
(*h*) Safavid Persia 1501–1722.
(*i*) Another historical subject, to be approved by the Board of the Faculty of Oriental Studies.

9. One special subject to be chosen from the following:

(*a*) Human settlement in Greater Syria, 600–1250.
(*b*) Islamic ceramics: the China question.
(*c*) Material culture, ceremonial, and power in the Fatimid Mediterranean.
(*d*) Metalwork, technology, and patronage, 1100–1300.
(*e*) Patrons and artisans in the Ottoman ceramic industry.
(*f*) Inscriptions and images: problems of iconography.
(*g*) Islamic numismatics.
(*h*) Another special subject, which may be a language subject, to be approved by the Board of the Faculty of Oriental Studies.

Some options and special subjects may not be available in every year. Candidates may obtain from the Oriental Institute information about which options may be offered for examination the following year at the beginning of Trinity Term of the preceding year.

Applications for the approval of options in paper 8 and of the special subjects in paper 9 must be submitted to the Oriental Studies Board by Monday of the second week of Michaelmas Term preceding the examination.

Sanskrit

The following papers will be set:

1. Sanskrit unprepared translation.
2. Essay questions on the history of classical Indian literature and civilization. This paper may include questions on the visual arts in ancient India.
3. Indian linguistics. Candidates will be examined on their general knowledge and understanding of *vyākaraṇa śāstra,* with particular reference to Pāṇini, *Aṣṭādhyāyī* (ed. Böhtlingk, 1,1,1–1,3,16; 1,4–2,2 (inclusive); and 3,1,91–132).
4. For candidates offering Old Iranian, Pali, or Prakrit as additional language) The historical philology of Old and Middle Indo-Aryan, with particular reference to:
   (*a*) Selected *sūktas* from the *Ṛg Veda* (ed. Müller). A list of *sūktas* is available from the Oriental Institute.
   (*b*) the Major Rock Edicts and Pillar Edicts of Asoka (ed. Bloch).

5 and 6. Two papers in a chosen area of Sanskrit studies approved by the Board of the Faculty. Applications for approval must be submitted by the Monday of the sixth week of the Trinity Term of the academic year preceding the examination. (*Note*: These papers are intended to allow candidates to specialize in a particular area of Sanskrit studies such as *kāvya, dharmaśāstra,* philosophy, grammar, or religion.)

5. Unprepared translation from Sanskrit texts.
6. Essay questions on the chosen area.
7. A special subject from among the following, or such other special subjects as may be approved by the board of the faculty:
   (*a*) Comparative grammar of Sanskrit and Old Iranian.

(*b*) Indian art and archaeology.

(*c*) Composition in Sanskrit prose and/or verse.

(*d*) Practical criticism and appreciation, including translation from the Sanskrit.

The use of Monier-Williams's *Sanskrit–English Dictionary* will be permitted in papers 5 and 7 (*c*) and (*d*).

Either

8 and 9. Two papers on one of the following additional languages: Old Iranian, Pali, Prakrit, Tibetan.

Or 8, 9, 10. Three papers on Classics as an additional language.

Turkish

Candidates for entry to the Final Honour School offering Turkish as their main subject will be required

either (*a*) to have passed their examination in Turkish at the end of an approved course abroad, the examination being under the auspices of the Board of The Faculty of Oriental Studies,

or (*b*) otherwise to have satisfied the faculty board as to their competence in Turkish.

Candidates for entry to the Final Honour School of Turkish with Islamic Art and Archaeology will also be required to have satisfied the faculty board, by means of written testimonials and a written report on the project(s) completed in Year 2, as to their active and useful participation in the approved project(s).

The following papers will be set:

Either, **for Turkish only**,

1. Unprepared translation from Ottoman and modern Turkish.
2. Translation into Turkish and essay in Turkish.
3. Spoken Turkish*.

---

* The oral examination will be held in the week before Trinity Full Term in the year in which the Honour School examination is taken. It must be taken in the same year as the written examination. The oral examination will consist of the following parts:

(i) *Listening comprehension*

Candidates will be presented with a list of factual questions, in Turkish, relating to the content of the text which they are about to hear. They will be allowed ten minutes to study these questions. A recorded Turkish text, lasting about five minutes, will then be played to them twice, with a pause of five minutes between the two playings. Candidates will be required to write brief answers to each question, in Turkish, in the spaces provided on the question sheet. A further five minutes after the end of the second playing of the recorded text will be allowed for candidates to complete their answers.

(ii) *Conversation*

(*a*) Candidates will be presented with a brief written description, in English, of a situation from everyday life in which they are required to imagine themselves. The description will include instructions as to what they are to try to achieve by verbal communication in that situation. Each candidate will be given five to ten minutes' preparation time, and will then be asked to conduct a dialogue with the examiner, in Turkish, appropriate to the situation and goal specified. (Approximate duration, excluding preparation time, five to ten minutes.)

(*b*) Each candidate will be required to discuss with the examiner a topic chosen by the candidate from a list of three announced one hour before the commencement of the oral examination. (Approximate duration ten to fifteen minutes.)

4. Ottoman history and historical texts, 1300–1700.

The following texts are prescribed for study:
Selected Ottoman documents.§
Naima, *Tarih* (Istanbul, AH 1281–3), vol. ii, pp. 207–64.
M. Cavid Baysun, *Tarihî Eserlerden Seçilmiş Eski Metinler* (Istanbul, 1964), pp. 29–35, 125–9.

Candidates will be required to translate and/or comment on passages from the prescribed texts, and to write essays on questions relating either to the texts themselves and their background, or to more general historical topics.

5. Turkish history and thought in the nineteenth and twentieth centuries.

The following texts are prescribed for study:
M. Cavid Baysun, *Tarihî Eserlerden Seçilmiş Eski Metinler* (Istanbul, 1964), pp. 9–18, 36–60, 118–24.
Selected late Ottoman and modern Turkish political documents.†
Selected late Ottoman writings on political and cultural issues.†
Selected modern Turkish writings on political and cultural issues.†

Candidates will be required to translate and/or comment on passages from the prescribed texts, and to write essays on questions relating either to the texts themselves and their background, or to more general historical topics.

6. Turkish and Ottoman literary texts, 1300–1900.

The following texts are prescribed for study:
Selected Turkish/Ottoman poetry, thirteenth to eighteenth centuries.†
Selected late Ottoman literary texts (post-1860).†

7. Twentieth-century Turkish literary texts.

The following texts are prescribed for study:
Selected modern Turkish short stories.†
Selected modern Turkish poetry.†

8. Turkish literature: general questions.

Questions will be asked about the general historical development and characteristics of Turkish and Ottoman literature from 1300 to the present day.

9. Turkish language reform and language politics from 1850 to the present day.

10. A special subject, to be approved by the Board of the Faculty of Oriental Studies.

or, **for Turkish with a subsidiary language**, Papers 1–5 above **and**

6. Twentieth-century Turkish literary texts.

The following texts are prescribed for study:
Selected modern Turkish short stories.‡
Selected modern Turkish poetry.‡

7. *Either*

(*a*) Turkish and Ottoman literary texts, 1300–1900.

(iii) *Interpreting*

Each candidate will be required to interpret, in a non-technical subject area, between a person speaking Turkish and a person speaking English. (Approximate duration ten minutes.)

§ Lists of texts are available from the Oriental Institute.

* See footnote on page 410. † See footnote* on page 412.

‡ List of texts are available from the Oriental Institute.

The following texts are prescribed for study:
Selected Turkish/Ottoman poetry, thirteenth to eighteenth centuries.*
Selected late Ottoman literary texts (post-1860).*

or

(*b*) a special subject, to be approved by the Board of the Faculty of Oriental Studies.

8, 9, 10. Three papers on one of the following languages: Arabic, Armenian, Persian.

Applications for the approval of subjects in paper 7(*b*) must be submitted not later than Monday of the second week of the Michaelmas Term preceding the examination.

or, **for Turkish with Ottoman History**, Papers 1–3 above **and**

4. Ottoman historical texts.*

5. Turkish political and cultural texts, 1860–2000.*

6. Twentieth-century Turkish literary texts.

The following texts are prescribed for study:
Selected modern Turkish short stories.*
Selected modern Turkish poetry.*

7, 8, 9. Three papers chosen from the following:

(*a*) The Formative Period: Islamic History and Thought until the Mid-Twelfth Century.
(*b*) The Ottoman Empire 1300–1566.
(*c*) The Ottoman Empire 1566–1807.
(*d*) The Ottoman Empire and the Republic of Turkey, 1807–1980.
(*e*) Any other option listed under Arabic with Islamic Studies/History, Papers 11 and 12.

10. A special subject, to be approved by the Board of the Faculty of Oriental Studies.

or, **for Turkish with Islamic Art and Archaeology**, candidates will be required to offer nine papers.

urkish prose composition and unprepared translation.

poken Turkish†.

ttoman texts.*

4. Modern Turkish texts.*

5. From Late Antiquity to Islam. The archaeology of the Near East during the transition from Late Antiquity and the formation of Islam, 550–900.

6. The breakdown of the caliphate. The art and archaeology of the Islamic world from 900 to 1250.

7. The great empires. The art and archaeology of the Islamic world 1250–1600.

8. One paper in history chosen from the following:

(*a*) Early Islamic History I: from the time of the Prophet to the early ʿAbbasids, 570–809 AD.
(*b*) Early Islamic History II: from the early ʿAbbasids to the Saljuqs, 809–1055 AD.
(*c*) Arab and Norman Sicily 827–1250.
(*d*) The Crusades.
(*e*) The Saljuq period.
(*f*) Egypt and Syria under the Ayyubids and Mamluks.
(*g*) The Ottoman Empire 1300–1566.

---

* Lists of texts are available from the Oriental Institute.

† See footnote * on page 410.

(*h*) The Ottoman Empire 1566–1807.
(*i*) Another historical subject, to be approved by the Board of the Faculty of Oriental Studies.

9. One special subject to be chosen from the following:
(*a*) Human settlement in Greater Syria, 600–1250.
(*b*) Islamic ceramics: the China question.
(*c*) Material culture, ceremonial, and power in the Fatimid Mediterranean.
(*d*) Metalwork, technology, and patronage, 1100–1300.
(*e*) Patrons and artisans in the Ottoman ceramic industry.
(*f*) Inscriptions and images: problems of iconography.
(*g*) Islamic numismatics.
(*h*) Another special subject, which may be a language subject, to be approved by the Board of the Faculty of Oriental Studies.

Additional Languages

Akkadian (for candidates offering Arabic, Classics or Hebrew as main subject).

The following papers will be set:

1, 2, 3 = Papers 2, 5, and 6 as specified for Akkadian in the Honour School of Oriental Studies (Egyptology and Ancient Near Eastern Studies). (Instead of either paper 5 or paper 6, candidates may offer one of papers 7, 9 or 10 as specified for the Honour School of Oriental Studies (Egyptology and Ancient Near Eastern Studies).

Arabic (for candidates offering Classics, Egyptology and Ancient Near Eastern Studies, Hebrew, Persian, or Turkish as main subject).

The following papers will be set:

1. Arabic prose composition and unprepared translation.

2. Classical Arabic prepared texts:
The Qur'ān, *Sūras* 12, 19, 37, 62, 63, 80, 81, 91–6;
Selected Classical prose texts (copies available from the Oriental Institute).

3. Modern Arabic prepared texts:
Selected modern prose texts (copies available from the Oriental Institute).

Papers 2 and 3 *may* contain general and linguistic questions.

Aramaic and Syriac (for candidates offering Arabic, Classics, Egyptology and Ancient Near Eastern Studies, or Hebrew as main subject).

The following papers will be set:

1. Syriac prose composition and Aramaic and Syriac unprepared translation.

2. Aramaic prepared texts:
Ezra v–vi: 18, Daniel iv, vii.
Aramaic inscriptions (ed. S. P. Brock, available from the Oriental Institute).
Targum Neofiti to Genesis (ed. A. Diez Macho), chs. iv, xxii (with reference also to Targum Onkelos and to Peshitta).
Fragment Targum (ed. M. L. Klein), acrostic poem at Exodus xiv. 29.
Targum to Isaiah (ed. A. Sperber), lii–liii, lx–lxi.
F. Schulthess, *Grammatik des Christlich-palästinischen Aramäisch* (1924), texts 14–15.

3. Syriac prepared texts:
Odes of Solomon (ed. J. H. Charlesworth, 1973), nos. 6–8, 11, 19, 24, 26, 31, 35, 40, 42.
Acts of Thomas (ed. W. Wright, *Apocryphal Acts of the Apostles,* 1871), vol. ii, pp. 274* (l. 7)–279* (l. 12).

Ephrem, *Comm. in Genesim* (ed. R. M. Tonneau), III. 1–8, VI. 1–8, XX

Aphrahat, *Demonstration* IV. 1–4, 9.

Martyrdom of Narsai (ed. P. Bedjan, *Acta Martyrum et Sanctorum,* vol. IV, pp. 170–80).

Simeon of Beth Arsham, *Letter* I on the Najran Martyrs (ed. Guidi), pp. 1–7 (l.21).

Anonymous Chronicle (ed. S. P. Brock, available from the Oriental Institute), sections 8–10, 14–16, 48–54.

C. Brockelmann, *Syrische Grammatik* (1925, or later editions), texts II, XI–XIII.

Memra II on Genesis 22 (ed. S. P. Brock, *Le Muséon*, 1986).

Selections from early Syriac poetry (ed. S. P. Brock) (available from the Oriental Institute).

Papers 2 and 3 may contain general and grammatical questions.

Armenian (for candidates offering Arabic, Classics, Persian, or Turkish as main subject).

The following papers will be set:

1. Classical Armenian prose composition and unprepared translation.
2. Prepared texts I:

Aristakes of Lastivert, *History of Armenia* (ed. Erevan, 1963), chs. 13–25 (for candidates offering Turkish as main subject).

Moses of Khoren, *History of Armenia* (ed. Tiflis, 1913), Bk. III (for candidates offering Classics or Persian as main subject).

Sebēos, *History of Heraclius* (ed. Erevan, 1979), chs. 38–52 (for candidates offering Arabic or Persian as main language).

Thomas Artsruni, *History of the Artsrunis* (ed. St. Petersburg, 1887), Bk. III, chs. 1–17 (for candidates offering Arabic or Turkish as main subject).

3. Prepared texts II:

Eznik of Kolb, *Against the Sects* (ed. *Patrologia Orientalis,* t. xviii, Paris, 1959), Bk. II, chs. 1–28.

Papers 2 and 3 will include questions on the subject-matter and grammar of the texts offered, and Paper 3 will also include questions on Armenian language, literature, and history.

[From 1 October 2005:

Chinese (for candidates offering Japanese as main subject)

The following papers will be set:

1. Chinese Prescribed Texts. (Lists of texts will be available from the Oriental Institute.)
2. Unprepared translation, Prose Composition, and Grammatical Questions.
3. Modern China.]

Classics (for candidates offering Arabic, Egyptology and Ancient Near Eastern Studies, Hebrew, Persian or Sanskrit as main subject).*

---

* Persons who have satisfied the Moderators in Honour Moderations or the Preliminary Examination in Classics may not offer Classics as an additional language without permission from the Board of the Faculty of Oriental Studies in consultation with the Board of the Faculty of Classics. Such permission, which will be given only for special reasons, must be sought as early as possible, and in no case later than noon on the Friday of the First Week of Michaelmas Term before the examination, by writing to the Chairman of the Board of the Faculty of Oriental Studies, c/o University Offices, Wellington Square. Applications must be accompanied by a letter of support from the applicant's society.

Applicants for such permission must state which Course they offered in the First Public Examination. Those who satisfied the Moderators in Course IA, IB, or IC

Candidates will be required to offer three of the following subjects (i)–(xxiv).

Candidates not offering (xxiii), (xxiv), Greek or Latin for Beginners must include at least two of subjects (i)–(xv), of which one must be either (i) or (v); they may offer both (i) and (v) if they wish.

Candidates may offer, but are not required to offer, a Special Thesis in Classics, or in a subject linking Classics and their Additional Language, in accordance with the Regulations on Theses in the regulations for the Honour School of Literae Humaniores, save that reference there to the Honour School of Literae Humaniores shall be deemed to be reference to the Honour School of Oriental Studies (with Classics as a main subject) and that the Board of the Faculty of Literae Humaniores shall consult the Board of the Faculty of Oriental Studies as appropriate. Such a thesis is in addition to the eight subjects required. **Candidates whose eight subjects already include a thesis under the terms of (xxii) below are not permitted to offer a Special Thesis in addition.**

Subject (xxiii), (xxiv), Greek or Latin for Beginners counts as two subjects. Candidates offering this must offer as their third subject one of (i), (ii), (iii), (iv), (xi), (xiv), (xviii)(*a*)–(*d*) and (xx) if offering Greek, or one of subjects (v), (vi), (vii), (xii), (xv) and (xviii)(*e*)–(*g*) if offering Latin.

Note: It cannot be guaranteed that university lectures or classes or college teaching will be available on all subjects in every academic year. Candidates are advised to consult their tutors about the availability of teaching when selecting their subjects.

(i) Greek Literature of the Fifth Century BC (one paper of three hours (commentary and essay) with an additional paper (one-and-a-half hours) of translation) [Honour School of Literae Humaniores, subject III.1].

(ii) [Honour School of Literae Humaniores, subject III.2].

Either (*a*) Early Greek Hexameter Poetry (not to be offered in combination with subject (xi), Homer, *Iliad*)

Or (*b*) Greek Lyric and Elegiac Poetry

Or (*c*) Pindar and Bacchylides.

(iii) [Honour School of Literae Humaniores, subject III.3]

Either (*a*) Aeschylus

Or (*b*) Euripides.

(iv) [Honour School of Literae Humaniores, subject III.4]

Either (*a*) Plato

Or (*b*) Hellenistic Poetry.

(v) Latin Literature of the First Century BC (one paper of three hours (commentary and essay) with an additional paper (one-and-a-half hours) of translation) [Honour School of Literae Humaniores, subject III.5].

(vi) [Honour School of Literae Humaniores, subject III.6]

Either (*a*) Latin Didactic Poetry

Or (*b*) Latin Satire

(vii) [Honour School of Literae Humaniores, subject III.7]

Either (*a*) Cicero the Orator

Or (*b*) Horace

---

will not be allowed to offer subject (xi), Homer, *Iliad,* (xii), Virgil, *Aeneid,* or (xxiii), (xxiv), Greek or Latin for Beginners, and may offer only version (i) of subject (viii)(*a*), (*b*), or (*c*). Those who satisfied the Moderators in Course IIA will not be allowed to offer subject (xii), Virgil, *Aeneid* or to offer subject (xxiii), (xxiv) in Latin. Those who satisfied the Moderators in Course IIB will not be allowed to offer subject (xi), Homer, *Iliad* or to offer subject (xxiii), (xxiv) in Greek. Subject (xvi), Historical Linguistics and Comparative Philology may not be offered by candidates who offered it in the First Public Examination.

Or (*c*) Ovid

Or (*d*) Seneca and Lucan.

(viii) [Honour School of Literae Humaniores, subject III.8]

Either (*a*) Greek and Roman Comedy (not to be offered in combination with *Or* (*b*) Ancient Literary Criticism

Or (*b*) The Ancient Novel.

(ix) Greek Textual Criticism [Honour School of Literae Humaniores, subject III.9].

(x) Latin Textual Critisicm [Honour School of Literae Humaniores, subject III.10].

(xi) Homer, *Iliad* [Honour Moderations in Classics Course IA, paper I; not to be offered in combination with subject (ii)(*a*), Early Greek Hexameter Poetry].

(xii) Virgil, *Aeneid.* Translation and essay questions will be required; commentary questions will be optional.

(xiii) *Either* (*a*) The Conversion of Augustine [Honour School of Literae Humaniores, subject III.11(*a*)]

Or (*b*) Medieval Latin [Honour School of Literae Humaniores, subject III.11(*b*)]

Or (*c*) The Latin Works of Petrarch, with special study of *Africa* (ed. N. Festa, Florence, 1926), Books I, II, V, VII, IX. Candidates will also be expected to have read *Vita Scipionis* (in *La vita di Scipione l'Africano,* ed. G. Martillotti, Milano-Napoli, 1954), and to show acquaintance with Petrarch's major Latin works (e.g. *Rerum memorandarum libri* (ed. G. Billanovich, Florence, 1945), *De secreto conflictu curarum mearum, De vita solitaria, Epistolae familiares* (in F. Petrarca, *Prose*, ed. G. Martillotti, P. G. Ricci, E. Carrara, E. Bianchi, Milano-Napoli, 1955)).

[From 1 October 2004:

Or (*d*) Byzantine Literature [Honour School of Literae Humaniores, subject III.11(*c*)].**]**

(xiv) Greek Historical Linguistics [Honour School of Literae Humaniores, subject V.1].

(xv) Latin Historical Linguistics [Honour School of Literae Humaniores, subject V.2].

(xvi) Historical Linguistics and Comparative Philology [Honour Moderations in Classics Course IA, paper V, VI F(1)].

(xvii) General Linguistics and Comparative Philology [Honour School of Literae Humaniores, subject V.3].

(xviii) *Either* (*a*) Greek History from 776 BC to 479 BC [Honour School of Literae Humaniores, subject I.1].

Or (*b*) Greek History from 479 BC to 403 BC [Honour School of Literae Humaniores, subject I.2].

Or (*c*) Greek History from 403 BC to 336 BC [Honour School of Literare Humaniores, subject I.3].

Or (*d*) Roman History from 240 BC to 133 BC [Honour School of Literae Humaniores, subject I.4].

Or (*e*) Roman History from 133 BC to 50 BC [Honour School of Literae Humaniores, subject I.5].

Or (*f*) Roman History from 49 BC to AD 54 [Honour School of Literae Humaniores, subject I.6].

Or (*g*) Roman History from AD 54 to AD 138 [Honour School of Literae Humaniores, subject I.7].

Note: Candidates offering any of subjects (xviii)(*a*)–(*g*) must also offer the associated translation paper set in the Honour School of Literae Humaniores.

(xix) *Either* (*a*) The Greeks and the Mediterranean World *c*.950 BC–500 BC [Honour School of Literae Humaniores, subject IV.1].

Or (*b*) Greek Archaeology and Art *c*.500 BC–323 BC [Honour School of Literae Humaniores, subject IV.2].

Or (*c*) The Archaeology and Art of Roman Italy in the Late Republic and Early Empire [Honour School of Literae Humaniores, subject IV.3].

Or (*d*) Cities and Settlement in the Roman Empire [Honour School of Literae Humaniores, subject IV.4].

(xx) *Either* subject 130 *or* subject 131 *or* subject 132, as specified in Regulations for Philosophy in all Honour Schools including Philosophy.

(xxi) Modern Greek Poetry [Honour School of Literae Humaniores, subject **[Until 1 October 2004:** III.11(*c*)**]** **[From 1 October 2004:** III.11(*d*)**]**. (This subject is available only to candidates offering subject (i), Greek Literature of the Fifth Century BC who are offering neither (xiii)(*d*), **[Until 1 October 2004:** Procopius**]** **[From 1 October 2004:** Byzantine Literature**]** nor (xxiii), (xxiv), Greek or Latin for Beginners.)

(xxii) Thesis. Any candidate may offer a thesis in Classics, or in a subject linking Classics and their Main Subject, in accordance with the Regulations on Theses in the regulations for the Honour School of Literae Humaniores, save that references there to the Honour School of Literae Humaniores shall be deemeed to be references to the Honour School of Oriental Studies (with Classics as an Additional Language) and that the Board of the Faculty of Classics shall consult the Board of the Faculty of Oriental Studies as appropriate.

(xxiii), (xxiv) (see introductory notes) Greek or Latin for Beginners [Honour School of Literae Humaniores, subject VI.1 and VI.2, Second Classical Language]. (Candidates who offer Greek or Latin for Beginners must offer *either both* subjects in Greek *or both* subjects in Latin).

Coptic (for candidates offering Classics or Egyptology as main subject).

The following papers will be set:

1. Coptic unprepared translation and grammar.
2. Prepared texts I:
   (Lists of texts are available from the Oriental Institute.)
3. Prepared texts II, with general questions:
   (Lists of texts are available from the Oriental Institute.)

Egyptology (for candidates offering Classics or Hebrew as main subject).

The following papers will be set:

1, 2, 3 = Papers 2, 5, and 6 as specified for Egyptian in the Honour School of Oriental Studies (Egyptology and Ancient Near Eastern Studies). (Instead of either paper 5 or paper 6, candidates may offer one of papers 7, 9 or 10 as specified for the Honour School of Oriental Studies (Egyptology and Ancient Near Eastern Studies).

Hebrew (for candidates offering Arabic, Classics or Egyptology and Ancient Near Eastern Studies as main subject).

Candidates taking Arabic may offer *either* (*a*) Biblical and Mishnaic *or* (*b*) Medieval *or* (*c*) Modern Hebrew. Candidates taking Classics may offer *either* (*a*) Biblical and Mishnaic or (*b*) Medieval Hebrew. Candidates taking Egyptology may offer only Biblical and Mishnaic Hebrew. Biblical texts will be set from *Biblia Hebraica Stuttgartensia* (ed. Elliger and Rudolph).

The following papers will be set:

(*a*) Biblical and Mishnaic Hebrew:

1. Prose composition and unprepared translation.
2. Prepared texts I:
   Biblical texts (lists of texts are available from the Oriental Institute)

3. Prepared texts II:
   Biblical and Mishnaic texts (list of texts are available from the Oriental Institute)

Papers 2 and 3 may contain general and grammatical questions.

(*b*) Medieval Hebrew:

1. Unprepared translation.
2. Prepared texts I:
   (lists of texts are available from the Oriental Institute).
3. Prepared texts II:
   (lists of texts are available from the Oriental Institute).

Papers 2 and 3 may contain general and grammatical questions.

(*c*) Modern Hebrew:

1. Prose composition and unprepared translation.
2. Prepared texts I:
   (lists of texts are available from the Oriental Institute).
3. Prepared texts II:
   (lists of texts are available from the Oriental Institute).

Papers 2 and 3 may contain general and grammatical questions.

[From 1 October 2005:

Japanese (for candidates offering Chinese as main subject)

The following papers will be set:

1. Japanese Prescribed Texts. (Lists of texts will be available from the Oriental Institute).
2, Unprepared translation, Prose Composition, and Grammatical Questions.
3. Modern Japan.]

Korean (for candidates offering Chinese as main subject)

The following papers will be set:

1. Prescribed Texts. (List of texts will be available from the Oriental Institute).
2. Korean History and Culture.
3. Prose Composition and Unprepared translation.

[From 1 October 2005:

Korean (for candidates offering Japanese as main subject)

The following papers will be set:

1. Prescribed Texts. (Lists of texts will be available from the Oriental Institute.)
2. Korean History and Culture. Essay questions on the background to the texts studies under 1. above.
3. Unprepared translation, Prose Composition, and Grammatical Questions.]

Old Iranian (for candidates offering Classics, Egyptology and Ancient Near Eastern Studies or Persian as main subject).

The following papers will be set:

1. Avestan Texts (lists of texts are available from the Oriental Institute).
2. (i) Old Persian texts (lists of texts are available from the Oriental Institute)
   (ii) *either* (*a*) Questions on the content of the Old Persian texts and their historical background *or* (*b*) Questions on the history of the Persian language.
3. Questions on Avestan and Old Persian language, and on pre-Islamic Iranian history, religion, and literature.

Old Iranian (for candidates offering Sanskrit as main subject).

The following papers will be set:

1. Old Persian and Avestan Texts (lists of texts are available from the Oriental Institute).
2. Questions on Old Persian and Avestan language and literature, and on the religious and historical background to the texts studied for Paper 1.

Pali (for candidates offering Classics or Sanskrit as main subject).

The following papers will be set:

1. Pali unprepared translation.
2. Questions on Pali language and literature, on Theravāda Buddhist doctrine, and on the early history of Buddhism in South Asia.

For candidates offering Classics as main subject:

3. Prepared texts, with questions on contents.

Persian (for candidates offering Arabic, Classics or Turkish as main subject).

The following papers will be set:

1. Persian prose composition and unprepared translation.

2 and 3. Two papers from the following:

(*a*) Classical Poetry: selections from lyric texts (Farrukhī, Sanā'ī, Rūmī, Saʿdī, Ḥāfiẓ) and selections from narrative texts (Firdausī, Niẓāmī, Rūmī). (Copies are available from the Oriental Institute.)

(*b*) Classical Prose: selected texts from Tārīkh-i Baihaqī, Qābūsnāmeh, Siyāsat-nāmeh, Fīhi mā Fīhi, Taẕkirat al-Auliyā, Javāmiʿ al-Ḥikāyat, Marzbān-nāmeh, Gulistān. (Copies are available from the Oriental Institute.)

(*c*) Modern Literature. Prose: selected texts from Jamālzādeh, Hidāyat, Buzurg ʿAlavī, Āl-i Aḥmad, Bihrangī, Sāʿidī.
Poetry: selected texts from Nīmā, Shāmlū, Akhavān-i S̲ālis̲, Furūgh Farrukhzād, Nādir Nādirpūr, Sipihrī. (Copies are available from the Oriental Institute.)

(*d*) Modern social and political writing. Selected texts. (Copies are available from the Oriental Institute.)

Prakrit (for candidates offering Sanskrit as main subject).

The following papers will be set:

1. Prakrit unprepared translation.
2. Questions on Prakrit language and literature and on the doctrine and early history of the Jains.

Sanskrit (for candidates offering Classics as main subject.)

The following papers will be set:

1. Sanskrit unprepared translation.
2. Questions on Sanskrit language and literature.
3. Prepared texts, with general questions.
(Lists of texts available from the Oriental Institute).

Spanish (for candidates offering Arabic as main subject).

The following papers will be set:

1. Unprepared translation from Old Spanish.
2. Spanish literature to 1499.
3. Early texts prescribed for study as examples of literature:
The prescribed texts will be those prescribed for Spanish in Paper IX of the Honour School of Modern Languages.

4. The history of the Spanish Language to 1500.

Candidates must offer papers 1 and 2 and *either* 3 *or* 4.

Tibetan (for candidates offering Chinese **[From 1 October 2005:** or Japanese] as main subject)

1. Tibetan prose composition and unprepared translation.
2. Prepared texts, with questions. (Lists of texts are available from the Oriental Institute.)
3. Questions on Tibetan culture and history.

Tibetan (for candidates offering Sanskrit as main subject).

The following papers will be set:

1. Tibetan prose composition and unprepared translation.
2. Prepared texts, with questions on Tibetan culture and history.

Turkish (for candidates offering Arabic or Persian as main subject).

The following papers will be set:

1. Turkish prose composition and unprepared translation.
2. *Either* (*a*) Late Ottoman and modern Turkish literary texts:

Selected post-Tanzimat literary and political texts.*
Selected modern Turkish short stories.*
Selected modern Turkish poetry.*

Or (*b*) Modern Turkish literary texts:

Selected modern Turkish short stories.*
Selected modern Turkish poetry.*

3. *Either* (*a*) Nineteenth and twentieth-century Turkish history and thought.

Candidates will be required to answer questions on Ottoman/Turkish history from 1826 to 1960, and to translate and/or comment on passages from, and/or to write essays on, the following texts:

M. Cavid Baysun, ed., *Tarihî Eserlerden Seçilmiş Eski Metinler* (Istanbul, 1964), pp. 9–18, 36–60.

Selected nineteenth- and twentieth-century Turkish writings on political and cultural issues.*

Selected nineteenth- and twentieth-century Ottoman/Turkish political documents.*

Or (*b*) Modern Turkish history and thought.

Candidates will be required to answer questions on Ottoman/Turkish history from 1826 to 1960, and to translate and/or comment on passages from, and/or to write essays on, the following texts:

Selected modern Turkish writings on political, historical, and cultural issues.*

PASS SCHOOL OF ORIENTAL STUDIES

(*a*) Candidates not offering Classics as their main subject must offer six papers in one of the other main subjects in the Final Honour School of Oriental Studies, i.e. Arabic, Chinese, Egyptology and Ancient Near Eastern Studies, Hebrew, Japanese, Jewish Studies, Persian, Sanskrit, and Turkish, together with such other subjects as may be determined by the Board of the Faculty of Oriental Studies. The papers to be offered must be taken from those in the syllabus for that Final Honour School, the actual selection being subject to the approval of the faculty board. Candidates

* Lists of texts are available from the Oriental Institute.

offering one of the above languages shall also be required to show an adequate knowledge of the literature and history of the civilization concerned.

In place of one of the six papers, an essay of not more than 10,000 words, on a topic approved by the Board of the Faculty of Oriental Studies, may be offered. This must be sent to the Chairman of Examiners not later than 12 noon on Monday of the ninth week of the Hilary Term preceding the examination, together with a signed statement that it is the candidate's own work (forms are available from the Faculty Office, Oriental Institute).

(*b*) Candidates offering Classics as their main subject must offer either two or three of the subjects prescribed for Classics as a main subject in the Honour School of Oriental Studies (including at least one of (i) and (v)), subject to the restrictions there placed upon choice of subjects; and in addition either all three or two (as the case may be) of the papers prescribed for one of the additional languages that may be offered with Classics in the Honour School, subject in the latter case to the approval of the Board of the Faculty of Oriental Studies.

(*c*) All applications for approval by the board must be sent to the Secretary of the Board of the Faculty of Oriental Studies, Oriental Institute, on or before the Monday in the second week of the Michaelmas Full Term preceding the examination.

(*d*) All candidates must give notice, on their examination entry forms, of their choice of papers, to the Registrar on or before the Friday in the fourth week of the Michaelmas Full Term preceding the examination.

NOTES

SPECIAL REGULATIONS FOR PHILOSOPHY IN ALL HONOUR SCHOOLS INCLUDING PHILOSOPHY

Candidates offering Philosophy papers* in any honour school must conform to the General Regulations below, and to those for their particular school, as specified elsewhere.

Subjects in Philosophy

The syllabuses of the subjects in Philosophy are specified below. A three hour written examination paper will be set in each subject except 121 and 199.

101. *History of Philosophy from Descartes to Kant*

Candidates will be expected to show critical appreciation of the main philosophical ideas of the period. The subject will be studied in connection with the following texts: Descartes, *Meditations, Objections and Replies;* Spinoza, *Ethics*; Leibniz, *Monadology, Discourse on Metaphysics*; Locke, *Essay Concerning Human Understanding*; Berkeley, *Principles of Human Knowledge, Three Dialogues Between Hylas and Philonous*; Hume, *Treatise of Human Nature*; Kant, *Critique of Pure Reason.* Candidates will not be required to show knowledge of all the texts, but will be required to show adequate knowledge of at least two authors. Some questions will be set to allow detailed discussion of the interpretation and historical significance of the texts.

102. *Knowledge and Reality*

Candidates will be expected to show knowledge in some of the following areas: knowledge and justification; perception; memory; induction; other minds; *a priori* knowledge; necessity and possibility; reference; truth; facts and propositions; definition; existence; identity, including personal identity; substances, change, events; properties; causation; space; time; essence; natural kinds; realism and idealism; primary and secondary qualities. There will also be a section on Philosophy of Science. Candidates' answers must not be confined to questions from the section on Philosophy of Science.

Candidates who also offer paper 108, *The Philosophy of Logic and Language*, may not answer certain questions which will be starred.

103. *Ethics*

Candidates will be given an opportunity to show some first-hand knowledge of some principal historical writings on this subject, but will not be required to do so. Questions will normally be set on the following topics: 1. Ethical concepts: obligation, goodness, virtue. 2. Objectivity and the explanation of value beliefs. 3. Moral Psychology: akrasia, conscience, guilt and shame. 4. Freedom and responsibility. 5. Consequentialism and deontology. 6. Self-interest, prudence and amoralism. 7. Rights, justice and equality. 8. Kant: The Groundwork. 9. Happiness, welfare and a life worth living.

104. *Philosophy of Mind*

Topics to be studied include the nature of persons, the relation of mind and body, self-knowledge, knowledge of other persons, consciousness, perception, memory,

* The paper 'History and Philosophy of Science', which is set as a supplementary subject in the Honour School of Natural Science, is not here counted as a Philosophy paper, since it is a joint paper in both History and Philosophy.

imagination, thinking, belief, feeling and emotion, desire, action, the explanation of action, subconscious and unconscious mental processes.

105. *Philosophy of Science and Philosophy of Psychology and Neuroscience*

This paper will include such topics as:

Part A: The nature of theories; scientific observation and method; scientific explanation; the interpretation of laws and probability; rationality and scientific change; major schools of philosophy of science.

Part B: philosophical issues arising from the history and practice of psychology and neuroscience.

Candidates will be required to answer at least one question from each part of the paper.

106. *Philosophy of Science and Social Science*

The paper will include such topics as:

Part A: the nature of theories; scientific observation and method; scientific explanation; the interpretation of laws and probability; rationality and scientific change; major schools of philosophy of science.

Part B: social meaning; individualism; rationality; rational choice theory; prediction and explanation in economics; the explanation of social action; historical explanation, ideology.

Candidates will be required to answer at least one question from each part of the paper.

107. *Philosophy of Religion*

The subject will include an examination of claims about the existence of God, and God's relation to the world; their meaning, the possibility of their truth, and the kind of justification which can or needs to be provided for them; and the philosophical problems raised by the existence of different religions. One or two questions may also be set on central claims peculiar to Christianity, such as the doctrines of the Trinity, Incarnation, and Atonement.

108. *The Philosophy of Logic and Language*

The subject will include questions on such topics as: meaning, truth, logical form, necessity, existence, entailment, proper and general names, pronouns, definite descriptions, intensional contexts, adjectives and nominalization, adverbs, metaphor, and pragmatics. Some questions will be set which allow candidates to make use of knowledge of linguistics.

109. *Aesthetics and the Philosophy of Criticism*

Candidates will have the opportunity to show first-hand knowledge of some principal authorities on the subject, including Plato, *Ion* and *Republic*; Aristotle, *Poetics*; Hume, *Of the Standard of Taste*; Kant, *Critique of Aesthetic Judgment*. Questions will normally be set on the following topics: the nature of aesthetic value; the definition of art; art, society, and morality; criticism and interpretation; metaphor; expression; pictorial representation.

110. *Medieval Philosophy*

The subject will be studied in the following texts.

Either

Aquinas, *Summa Theologiae*, Ia, 2–11, 75–89; *or* Ia IIae 1–21. (Blackfriars edition, vol. 2, 11–12, 16–18.)

Or

Duns Scotus, *Philosophical Writings*, tr. Wolter (Nelson Philosophical Texts).
Ockham, *Philosophical Writings*, tr. Boehner (Nelson Philosophical Texts).

111. *Continental Philosophy from Descartes to Leibniz*

The following works are recommended for particular study (they may be studied in translation): Descartes, *Discourse on The Method, Meditations, Objections and Replies I–VI* (translated by J. Cottingham, R. Stoothoff, and D. Murdoch); *The Selected Works of Pierre Gassendi*, edited and translated by C. B. Brush; Spinoza, *Ethics* (either in the translation in *Collected Works of Spinoza*, Vol. 1, ed. E. Curley (Princeton University Press), or in the translation by S. Shirley in *Baruch Spinoza: The Ethics and Selected Letters*, ed. S. Feldman (Hackett)); Malebranche, *Nicolas Malebranche: Philosophical Selections*, ed. S. Nadler (Hackett); Leibniz, *Discourse on Metaphysics* (translated by P. G. Lucas and L. Grint), *The Leibniz–Arnauld Correspondence*, edited and translated by H. T. Mason, *The Leibniz–Clarke Correspondence*, edited and translated by H. G. Alexander.

Candidates will be expected to show adequate knowledge of at least three philosophers.

112. *The Philosophy of Kant*

Critique of Pure Reason, Groundwork of the Metaphysic of Morals. The editions to be used are N. Kemp Smith, *Immanuel Kant's Critique of Pure Reason* (Macmillan 1929), and H. J. Paton's translation of the *Groundwork of the Metaphysic of Morals* (Hutchinson, 1948).

Candidates may answer no more than one question on Kant's moral philosophy.

113. *Post-Kantian Philosophy*

The main developments of philosophy in Continental Europe after Kant, excluding Marxism and analytical philosophy. Questions on the following authors will regularly be set: Hegel, Schopenhauer, Nietzsche, Husserl, Heidegger, Sartre, Merleau-Ponty. There will be some general and/or comparative questions, and questions on other authors may be set from time to time. Candidates will be required to show adequate first-hand knowledge of works of at least two authors (who may be studied in translation).

114. *Theory of Politics*

The critical study of political values and of the concepts used in political analysis: the concept of the political; power, authority, and related concepts; the state; law; liberty and rights; justice and equality; public interest and common good; democracy and representation; political obligation and civil disobedience; ideology; liberalism, socialism, and conservatism.

115. Plato: *Republic*, tr. Grube, revised Reeve (Hackett).

There will be a compulsory question containing passages for comment. This subject may not be combined with either part of subject 130.

116. Aristotle: *Nicomachean Ethics*, tr. Irwin (Hackett, second edition).

There will be a compulsory question containing passages for comment. This subject may not be combined with either part of subject 131.

117. *Frege, Russell, and Wittgenstein*

Works principally to be studied are:

Frege, *Foundations of Arithmetic*, trans. Austin; *Begriffsschrift* ch. 1, 'Function and Concept', 'Sense and Meaning', 'Concept and Object', and 'Frege on Russell's Paradox', in Geach and Black, eds. *Translations from the Philosophical Writings of Gottlob Frege*;

Russell, 'On Denoting', 'Mathematical Logic as Based on the theory of Types', and 'On the Nature of Acquaintance', in Marsh, ed., *Logic and Knowledge*; 'The Ultimate Constituents of Matter', 'The Relation of Sense-Data to Physics', and 'Knowledge by Acquaintance and Knowledge by Description', in *Mysticism and Logic; Our Knowledge of the External World*, chs. I–IV; **either** *Introduction to Mathematical Philosophy*, chs. 1–3 and 12–18, **or** 'The Philosophy of Logical Atomism', in Marsh, ed., *Logic and Knowledge*;

Wittgenstein, *Tractatus Logico-Philosophicus*.

Candidates will be required to show adequate knowledge of at least two authors.

118. *The Later Philosophy of Wittgenstein*

Works principally to be studied are *Philosophical Investigations* and *The Blue and Brown Books*.

119. *Formal Logic*

The paper will consist of three sections:

(i) Propositional and Predicate Logic

Formal languages of propositional logic, adequate sets of connectives, conjunctive and disjunctive normal form, tautologies, logical consequence; formal languages of predicate logic, satisfaction, truth, validity, logical consequence. Deductive systems of propositional and predicate calculus; proofs and theorems; prenex normal forms; the soundness and completeness theorems. Derivation of the compactness theorem, simple applications of the compactness theorem. Predicate calculus with identity, normal models. Elementariness. The Löwenheim–Skolem theorems. First-order theories and their properties: completeness, categoricity. Differences between first-order and second-order logic.

(ii) Set Theory.

Basic axioms of set theory. Cartesian products, relations and functions. Axiom of infinity and the construction of the natural numbers; induction and the recursion theorem. Cardinality: finite, countable and uncountable sets; Cantor's theorem; the Schröder–Bernstein theorem. Linear orders and well-orders; order isomorphism, dense linear order. Transfinite induction and recursion. Comparability of well-orders. Ordinals, and their arithmetic. Equivalence of the axiom of choice, Zorn's lemma, the well-ordering principle, and cardinal comparability. Cardinals, and their arithmetic.

(iii) Metamathematics.

Primitive recursion and general recursion. Total and partial functions. Computability: Turing machines or register machines; existence of a universal machine; the s-m-n theorem. Decision problems; undecidability of the halting problem. Church's thesis. Formal systems of arithmetic; representability of sets and functions. Undefinability of truth. Gödel's first incompleteness theorem; Rosser's theorem; Löb's theorem; the Hilbert–Bernays adequacy conditions on a provability predicate; Gödel's second incompleteness theorem. No decision procedure for first-order logical validity; no complete proof procedure for second-order logical validity.

[Until 1 October 2004: In addition to questions requiring precise knowledge of topics of the syllabus and some problem solving ability, there will also be questions which give candidates an opportunity to discuss philosophical implications of some of the topics.

Candidates will be required to attempt at least one question from section (i) and at least one from section (ii) or section (iii).**]**

120. *Intermediate Philosophy of Physics*

The paper will consist of two sections. Section A will include philosophical problems associated with classical physics and some basic philosophical issues raised by the Special Theory of Relativity. Section B will be concerned with introductory philosophical problems related to the interpretation of quantum mechanics. Candidates will be required to answer at least one question from each section.

121. *Advanced Philosophy of Physics I** (two-hour paper)

The subject will include advanced topics in the philosophy of space, time, and relativity and in the philosophical foundations of quantum mechanics. It will also include some philosophical issues raised by thermodynamics and statistical mechanics.

---

* Only available as part of the four-year course in Physics and Philosophy.

122. *Philosophy of Mathematics*

Questions may be set which relate to the following issues: Incommensurables in the development of Greek geometry. Comparisons between geometry and other branches of mathematics. The significance of non-Euclidean geometry. The problem of mathematical rigour in the development of the calculus. The place of intuition in mathematics (Kant, Poincaré). The idea that mathematics needs foundations. The role of logic and set theory (Dedekind, Cantor, Frege, Russell). The claim that mathematics must be constructive (Brouwer). The finitary study of formal systems as a means of justifying infinitary mathematics (Hilbert). Limits to the formalization of mathematics (Gödel). Anti-foundational views of mathematics. Mathematical objects and structures. The nature of infinity. The applicability of mathematics.

123. *Advanced Philosophy of Physics II** (three-hour paper)

The subject will include advanced topics in the philosophy of space, time, and relativity and in the philosophical foundations of quantum mechanics. It will also include some philosophical issues raised by thermodynamics and statistical mechanics.

130. *Either* (*a*) Plato, *Republic.*

Candidates will be expected to have read books I, IV–VII, X in Greek (Burnet, Oxford Classical Text), and books II–III, VIII–IX in translation (Grube, revised Reeve, Hackett). There will be a compulsory question containing passages for translation and comment from the books read in Greek; any passages for comment from the remaining books will be accompanied by a translation.

Or (*b*) Plato, *Theaetetus* and *Sophist.*

Candidates will be expected to have read both dialogues in Greek (Duke *et al.*, Oxford Classical Text). There will be a compulsory question containing passages for translation and comment.

131. *Either* (*a*) Aristotle, *Nicomachean Ethics.*

Candidates will be expected to have read books I–III, VI–VII, X in Greek (Bywater, Oxford Classical Text), and books IV–V, VIII–IX in translation (Irwin, Hackett second edition). There will be a compulsory question containing passages for translation and comment from the books read in Greek; any passages for comment from the remaining books will be accompanied by a translation.

Or (*b*) Aristotle, *Physics*

[Until 1 October 2004: Candidates will be expected to have read the work in Greek (Ross, Oxford Classical Text). There will be a compulsory question containing passages for translation and comment.**]**

[From 1 October 2004:

Candidates will be expected to have read books I–IV and VIII in Greek (Ross, Oxford Classical Texts), and books V–VII in translation (in Barnes, ed., *The Complete Works of Aristotle: The Revised Oxford Translation* (Princeton), vol. 1). There will be a compulsory question containing passages for translation and comment from the books read in Greek; any passages for comment from the remaining books will be accompanied by a translation.**]**

132. Sextus Empiricus: *Outlines of Pyrrhonism* (Bury, Loeb).

There will be a compulsory question containing passages for translation and comment.

133. Cicero: *De Finibus* III (Reynolds, Oxford Classical Text), *De Officiis* I in translation (Griffin and Atkins, *Cicero, On Duties*, Cambridge); Seneca, *Epistulae Morales* 92, 95, 121, *De Constantia, De Vita Beata* (Reynolds, Oxford Classical Text).

---

* Only available as part of the four-year course in Physics and Philosophy.

There will be a compulsory question containing passages for translation and comment from the texts read in Latin; any passages for comment from Cicero, *De Officiis* I will be accompanied by a translation.

198. *Special Subjects*

From time to time special subjects may be approved by the Faculty of Philosophy by regulations published in the *University Gazette* and communicated to college tutors by the end of the fifth week of Trinity Term two years before examination. Candidates may not be permitted to offer certain special subjects in combination with certain other subjects, or may be permitted to do so only on condition that in the papers on the other subjects they will not be permitted to answer certain questions. No candidate may offer more than one special subject. Subject to these qualifications, any candidate may offer any special subject.

199. *Thesis*:

1. *Subject*

The subject of every thesis should fall within the scope of philosophy. The subject may but need not overlap any subject on which the candidate offers papers. Candidates are warned that they should avoid repetition in papers of material used in their theses and that substantial repetition may be penalized. Every candidate shall submit through his or her college for approval by the body responsible for his or her honour school, the title he or she proposes, together with (*a*) an explanation of the subject in about 100 words; and (*b*) a letter of approval from his or her tutor, not earlier than the first day of the Trinity Full Term of the year before that in which he or she is to be examined and not later than Friday of the fourth week of the Michaelmas Full Term preceding his or her examination (except in the case of the Honour School of Psychology, Philosophy, and Physiology, for which submission must be made not later than Wednesday of the first week of the Michaelmas Full Term preceding his or her examination). (The date before which a proposal cannot be submitted is different in certain circumstances in the case of the Honour School of Philosophy and Modern Languages. See the regulations below for that honour school.) Applications must be directed to the office-holder specified for the particular honour school. The body responsible shall decide as soon as possible whether or not to approve the title and shall advise the candidate immediately. No decision shall be deferred beyond the end of the fifth week of Michaelmas Full Term. If a candidate wishes to change the title of his or her thesis after a title has already been approved by the body responsible, he or she may apply for such permission to be granted by the body responsible: applications should be directed to the office-holder specified for the honour school in question (if the application is made before the first day of Hilary Full Term preceding the examination) or (if later) the appropriate chairman of examiners.)

2. *Authorship and origin*

Every thesis shall be the candidate's own work. A candidate's tutor may, however, discuss with the candidate the field of study, the sources available, and the method of presentation; the tutor may also read and comment on drafts. The amount of assistance the tutor may give is equivalent to the teaching of a normal paper. Every candidate shall sign a certificate to the effect that the thesis is his or her own work and the tutor shall countersign the certificate confirming, to the best of his or her knowledge and belief, that this is so. This certificate shall be placed in a sealed envelope bearing the candidate's examination number presented together with the thesis. No thesis shall be accepted which has already been submitted for a degree of this or any other university, and the certificate shall also state that the thesis has not been so submitted. No thesis shall, however, be ineligible because it has been or is being submitted for any prize of this university.

3. *Length and format*

No thesis shall exceed 15,000 words, the limit to include all notes and appendices but not including the bibliography; no person or body shall have authority to permit any excess, except that in Literae Humaniores, in a thesis consisting in commentary on a text, quotation from the text will not be counted towards the word limit. The word count should be indicated at the front of the thesis. There shall be a select bibliography or a list of sources. All theses must be typed in double spacing on one side of quarto or A4 paper with any notes and references at the foot of each page. *Two* copies of the thesis shall be submitted to the examiners.

4. *Submission of thesis*

Every candidate shall submit the thesis, identified by the candidate's examination number only, not later than noon on Friday of the week before the Trinity Full Term of the examination to the Examination Schools, Oxford, addressed to the Chairman of the Examiners in the candidate's honour school.

General Regulations

The following restrictions on combinations apply to candidates whatever their honour school:

(i) A candidate may not take both of subjects 105 and 106.

(ii) Both of subjects 117 and 118 may be offered *only* by candidates in *Mathematics and Philosophy.*

(iii) A candidate may not take subject 199 unless he or she also takes three other philosophy subjects.

(iv) In the paper on subject 101, questions exclusively on Descartes, Spinoza, and Leibniz will not be answerable by candidates taking subject 111 in the same year, and questions exclusively on Kant will not be answerable by candidates taking subject 112 in the same year.

(v) In the paper on subject 102, questions in the Philosophy of Science section will not be answerable by any candidate who is taking either subject 105 or subject 106 in the same year.

(vi) Notwithstanding any contrary indication in these regulations, subjects 130, 131, and 132 and 133 may be offered *only* by candidates in *Classics and Modern Languages* (130 (a) and 131 (a) only), *Literae Humaniores*, and *Oriental Studies* (not 133).

Whichever a candidate's honour school, where it is prescribed that he or she must take one or other of certain specified subjects and must take in addition some further subjects, a subject that is not chosen from among the specified ones may be chosen as a further subject.

Regulations for Particular Honour Schools

Literae Humaniores

The Honour School is divided into two Courses; for restrictions on entry to Course II, see the regulations under *Honour School of Literae Humaniores*. Candidates in either Course may offer any number of subjects in Philosophy up to five, or up to four if they are offering Second Classical Language in Course II. Any selection is permitted which conforms to the General Regulations above and also to (i)–(v) following:

(i) candidates offering more than one subject in Philosophy must select at least one from Schedule A below;

(ii) candidates offering more than two subjects in Philosophy must also select at least one from Schedule B below;

(iii) candidates offering subject 199, Thesis in Philosophy, may not offer any other thesis except a Special Thesis;

(iv) all candidates must offer at least four text-based subjects, not necessarily in Philosophy (or three if offering Second Classical Language in Course II);

(v) all candidates in Course I must offer at least one text-based subject in each of classical Greek texts and classical Latin texts, not necessarily in Philosophy.

The text-based subjects in Philosophy are 130 (Greek), 131 (Greek), 132 (Greek), 133 (Latin).

COURSE I

Schedule A Greek Philosophy: 130, 131, 132.
Schedule B Main Subjects in Modern Philosophy: 101, 102, 103, 104, 108.
Schedule C Further Subjects in Philosophy: all other subjects except 121 and 123.

COURSE II

Schedule A Ancient Philosophy: 115, 116, 130, 131, 132, 133.
Schedule B Main Subjects in Modern Philosophy: 101, 102, 103, 104, 108.
Schedule C Further Subjects in Philosophy: all other subjects except 121 and 123.

The body responsible for approving applications to offer subject 199 is the Board of the Faculty of Philosophy. Applications should be directed to the Chairman of the Board, c/o the Administrator, Philosophy Centre, 10 Merton Street.

Candidates may also offer a Special Thesis, which may be in Philosophy, in accordance with the regulations under *Honour School of Literae Humaniores.*

Mathematics and Philosophy

[For candidates embarking on the Honour School in or after October 2003:

In Part B candidates are required to take subjects 102 and 122, and in addition are required to take at least one and not more than two subjects chosen from among subjects 101, 103–118, 120.

In Part C, candidates who offer Option (ii) Mathematics and Philosophy are required to take two subjects, and candidates who offer Option (iii) Philosophy are required to offer four subjects from among subjects 101, 103–118, 198, 199, in conformity with the condition that no subject may be offered in both Part B and Part C.**]**

[For candidates who embarked on the Honour School in or before October 2002:

In Part I, candidates are required to take subjects 102 and 122, and in addition are required to take at least one and not more than three subjects chosen from among subjects 101, 103–18, 120. A candidate who takes five subjects in Philosophy in Part I cannot offer Option (iii) Philosophy in Part II.

In Part II, candidates who offer Option (ii) Mathematics and Philosophy are required to take two subjects, and candidates who offer Option (iii) Philosophy are required to offer four subjects, from among subjects 101, 103–18, 120, 198, 199, in conformity with the condition that no subject may be offered in both Part I and Part II.**]**

Where subject 199 is taken the body responsible for approving applications is the Board of the Faculty of Philosophy. Applications for approval of subject should be directed to the Chairman of the Board, c/o The Administrator, Philosophy Centre, 10 Merton Street.

Philosophy and Modern Languages

Candidates are required to take either subject 101 *or* subject 102. In addition to this subject, they must take two or three or four further subjects in Philosophy, depending upon whether the number of subjects they take in part II in Modern Languages is three or two or one. Further subjects in Philosophy must be chosen in conformity with the General Regulations.

Where subject 199 is taken, every candidate shall submit his or her application for approval of the subject to the Chairman of the Board of the Faculty of Philosophy, c/o The Administrator, Philosophy Centre, 10 Merton Street, Oxford OX1 4JJ, not earlier than the first day of Trinity Full Term two years before the term of the written examination in the case of candidates planning to spend a year abroad.

Philosophy, Politics and Economics

Any candidate in this school offers *either* Philosophy Politics and Economics *or* Philosophy and Politics *or* Philosophy and Economics *or* Politics and Economics; and takes eight subjects in all. Subjects in Philosophy must be chosen in conformity with the regulations for the honour school and with the General Regulations above; and subject 114 may not be offered by any candidate who takes subject 203 in Politics.

Candidates offering Philosophy Politics and Economics are required to take (i) *either* subject 101 *or* subject 102, and (ii) subject 103. In addition to these subjects, they may take one or two further subjects in Philosophy.

Candidates offering Philosophy and Politics are required to take (i) *either* subject 101 *or* subject 102, and (ii) subject 103. In addition to these two, they must take one, and they may take two or three, further subjects in Philosophy.

Candidates offering Philosophy and Economics are required to take (i) *either* subject 101 *or* subject 102, and (ii) subject 103. In addition to these two, they must take one, and they may take two or three, further subjects in Philosophy.

Candidates offering Politics and Economics may take any one subject in Philosophy.

Where subject 199 is taken, the body responsible for approving applications is the Board of the Faculty of Philosophy. Applications for approval of subject should make it clear that Philosophy is the branch of the School for which the application is made, and should be directed to the Chairman of the Board, c/o the Administrator, Philosophy Centre, 10 Merton Street.

Philosophy and Theology

Candidates are required to take subject 101 and subject 107 and *either* subject 102 *or* subject 103. In addition to these three, they may take one or two further subjects in Philosophy, depending upon whether they take five or four or three subjects in all in Theology. Further subjects in Philosophy must be chosen in conformity with the General Regulations.

Where subject 199 is taken, the body responsible for approving applications is the Standing Joint Committee for Philosophy and Theology. Applications for approval of subject should be directed to the Chairman of the Board of the Faculty of Theology, c/o Secretary of the Theology Board, Humanities Division, 34 St Giles', Oxford. Candidates who wish to write their thesis during the Long Vacation may submit titles for approval before noon on Friday of the fourth week of the Trinity Term in the year preceding the examination, and approval will be notified before the end of the term.

[For candidates embarking on the Honour School in or after October 2002 (for candidates embarking on the Honour School in or before October 2001, see Addendum II at the back of the book)

Physics and Philosophy

Part B: candidates are required to take subject 102, subject 120, and one further subject selected from the list of subjects 101–23 above, except that neither subject 105 nor subject 106 nor subject 121 nor subject 123 may be taken. In this school, candidates must answer at least one question from the section on Philosophy of Science in subject 102.

Part C: those candidates offering one or more further Philosophy subjects (under *Option 2* or *Option 3* or *Option 4*) must choose them from the subjects 101–4, 107–99 above, except that (*a*) subject 121 may only be taken under *Option 3*, and (*b*) subject 123 may not be taken under *Option 3*.

Where subject 199 is taken, the body responsible for approving applications is the Board of the Faculty of Philosophy. Applications for approval of subject should be directed to the Chairman of the board, c/o The Administrator, Philosophy Centre, 10 Merton Street.

The same Philosophy subject may not be taken in more than one part of the final examination.]

Psychology, Philosophy, Physiology

Candidates may take at most five subjects in Philosophy. Candidates who take at least one subject in Philosophy and no more than two subjects in Physiology must take eight subjects in total. Candidates who take at least one subject in Philosophy and at least three subjects in Physiology must take seven subjects in total. Candidates may only take subjects in Psychology if they offer *Psychology Parts I and II*.

Candidates who take one or two subjects in Philosophy must take at least one of 101, 102, 104, or 105. Those offering three or more Philosophy subjects must choose at least two from the above list. Their further subjects taken in Philosophy must be chosen in conformity with the General Regulations.

Where subject 199 is taken, the body responsible for approving applications is the Board of the Faculty of Philosophy, and applications should be directed to the Chairman of the Board, c/o The Administrator, Philosophy Centre, 10 Merton Street. Applications must be made not later than Wednesday of the first week of the Michaelmas Full Term preceding the examination.

SPECIAL REGULATIONS FOR THE HONOUR SCHOOL OF PHILOSOPHY AND MODERN LANGUAGES

A

1. The subjects of the examination in the Honour School of Philosophy and Modern Languages shall be (*a*) Philosophy and (*b*) those modern European languages and literatures studied in the Honour School of Modern Languages.

2. All candidates must offer both (*a*) and one of the languages in (*b*) with its literature.

3. No candidate shall be admitted to examination in this school unless he or she has either passed or been exempted from the First Public Examination.

4. The examiners shall indicate in the lists issued by them the language offered by each candidate obtaining honours or satisfying the examiners under Ch. VI, Sect. II. C, §I, cl. 21 (iv) and (v).

5. The examination in this school shall be under the joint supervision of the Boards of the Faculties of Philosophy and of Medieval and Modern European Languages and Literature, which shall appoint a standing joint committee to make regulations concerning it, subject always to the preceding clauses of this subsection.

6. The examiners for Philosophy shall be nominated by a committee of which the three elected members shall be appointed by the Board of the Faculty of Philosophy. It shall be the duty of the chairman of the examiners for the Honour School of Modern Languages to designate such of their number as may be required for Modern Languages in the Honour School of Philosophy and Modern Languages, and when this has been done and the examiners for Philosophy have been nominated, the number of examiners in Philosophy and Modern Languages shall be deemed to be complete.

B

Candidates will be examined in accordance with the examination regulations set out below.

They will also be required to spend, after their matriculation, an academic year of approved residence in an appropriate country or appropiate countries, and to provide on their entry form for the exmination a certificate that they have done this, signed by the Head or by a tutor of their society. Candidates wishing to be dispensed from the requirement to undertake a year of residence abroad must apply in writing to the Chairman of the Medieval and Modern Languages Board, 41 Wellington

Square, Oxford, OX1 2JF, stating their reasons for requesting dispensation and enclosing a letter of support from their society.

Candidates will be expected to carry out during this year abroad such work as their society may require. It is strongly recommended that candidates should apply through the Central Bureau for Educational Visits and Exchanges for an Assistantship, where these are available, and should accept one if offered. Candidates who are not able to obtain an Assistantship should during their year abroad follow a course or courses in an institution or institutions approved by their society, or should spend their time in such other circumstances as are acceptable to their society. Candidates will agree with their College Tutor in advance of their year abroad an independent course of study to be followed during that period.

A candidate shall offer in his or her language and literature papers one modern language and its literature only, except in a Special Subject or an alternative to a Special Subject (Honour School of Modern Languages, paper XII).

No candidate will be examined viva voce unless the examiners elect to do so and have been given leave by the Proctors to take into account illness or other urgent and reasonable cause that may have affected the candidate's performance in any part of the examination.

Oral Examination: as specified for the Honour School of Modern Languages.

In the assignment of honours, in the case of a candidate who offers four Philosophy subjects, Philosophy shall count for the same as the Modern Language and, in the case of a candidate who offers three or five Philosophy subjects, it shall count for correspondingly less or more, provided in each case that the highest honours can be obtained by marked excellence in either Philosophy or the Modern Language subject to an adequate standard being shown in the other branch.

In every case where, under the regulations for the school, candidates have any choice between one or more papers or subjects, every candidate shall give notice to the Registrar not later than the Friday in the fourth week of Michaelmas Full Term preceding the examination of all the papers and subjects being so offered.

Candidates must take eight subjects in all. They must take three subjects in Philosophy of which one shall be either 101 or 102, and they must take three subjects in Modern Languages of which two must be 1. and 2. prescribed in part I of Modern Languages. Candidates take *either* one subject in part II of Modern Languages and five subjects in all in Philosophy *or* two subjects in part II of Modern Languages and four subjects in all in Philosophy *or* three subjects in part II of Modern Languages and three subjects in all in Philosophy.

Candidates offering a paper from the Honour School of Modern Languages and a paper in Philosophy, both of which involve the study of the same author or authors, may not make the same text or texts the principal subject of an answer in both the papers.

Philosophy

Subjects as specified in **Regulations for Philosophy in all Honour Schools including Philosophy.**

Modern Languages

There are nine subjects in Modern Languages, specified below. They are divided between Part I and Part II. The language papers (*a*) and (*b*) in 1 in Part I constitute one subject. Subject 9 (an extended essay) may not be offered as an additional optional subject.

PART I

[Until 1 October 2005: 1. Three papers as follows:

(*a*) Unprepared translation into the modern language (one paper of three hours) (Honour School of Modern Languages, Paper I).

(*b*) Unprepared translation from the modern language (two papers of one and a half hours each) (Honour School of Modern Languages, Paper II A (*i*) and Paper II B (*i*))

2. *A period of the literature of the modern language.*

One paper of three hours will be set (Honour School of Modern Languages, Paper VI or VII or VIII).]

[From 1 October 2005:

1. Three papers as follows:

(*a*) Honour School of Modern Languages Paper I.

(*b*) Honour School of Modern Languages, Papers IIA(i) and IIB(i).

2. Honour School of Modern Languages, *one* paper chosen from VI, VII or VIII]

PART II

[Until 1 October 2005: 3. *Linguistic Studies I* (Honour School of Modern Languages, Paper IV).

4. *Linguistic Studies II* (Honour School of Modern Languages, Paper V).

5. *Early texts prescribed for literary study* (Honour School of Modern Languages, Paper IX).

6. *Modern Prescribed Authors* (*i*). (Honour School of Modern Languages, Paper X).

7. *Modern Prescribed Authors* (*ii*). (Honour School of Modern Languages, Paper XI).

8. *Special Subject* (Honour School of Modern Languages, Paper XII).]

[From 1 October 2005:

3. Honour School of Modern Languages Paper IV.

4. Honour School of Modern Languages Paper V.

5. Honour School of Modern Languages Paper IX.

6. Honour School of Modern Languages Paper X.

7. Honour School of Modern Languages Paper XI.

8. Honour School of Modern Languages Paper XII.]

9. An extended essay as specified for the Honour School of Modern Languages. Candidates may not offer a Special Topic from Course I for the Honour School of English Language and Literature. They also may not offer an extended essay as well as subject 199 in Philosophy.

Candidates who are offering one subject only from Part II may not offer subject 9 as that subject.

PASS SCHOOL OF PHILOSOPHY AND MODERN LANGUAGES

Candidates shall offer papers in Philosophy, and in any single modern language; they may choose any of the modern languages which may be offered for the Honour School of Philosophy and Modern Languages.

Candidates shall take the following papers:

1. *In Philosophy*

Candidates must offer two subjects from Philosophy as prescribed for the Honour School of Philosophy and Modern Languages.

2. *In the Modern Language*

(The numbering used is that in the Honour School of Modern Languages).

I

IIA (i)

IIB (i)
One of VI, VII, VIII.
The oral examination in the language.

3. *All candidates must also* offer one further paper, or alternatively a thesis in Philosophy. The regulations for the thesis are those prescribed for the Honour School of Philosophy and Modern Languages. The paper may be either in Philosophy, in which case it must be one of the papers prescribed for Philosophy in the regulations for the Honour School of Philosophy and Modern Languages; or in Modern Languages, in which case it must be one of the papers prescribed in Modern Languages Part II of the regulations of the Honour School of Philosophy and Modern Languages.

SPECIAL REGULATIONS FOR THE HONOUR SCHOOL OF PHILOSOPHY, POLITICS, AND ECONOMICS

A

1. The subject of the Honour School of Philosophy, Politics, and Economics shall be the study of modern philosophy, and of the political and economic principles and structure of modern society.

2. Candidates must offer Philosophy, Politics, and Economics or such combination of these subjects as may be determined by the Division of Social Sciences.

3. No candidate shall be admitted to examination in this school unless he or she either (*a*) has passed or been exempted from the first Public Examination or (*b*) has successfully completed the Foundation Course in Social and Political Science at the Department for Continuing Education.

4. The examination for this school shall be under the joint supervision of the Social Sciences Board and the Humanities Board which shall appoint a standing joint committee to make regulations concerning it subject always to the preceding clauses of this sub-section.

B

Candidates may offer *either* Philosophy, Politics, and Economics *or* Philosophy and Politics *or* Politics and Economics *or* Philosophy and Economics.

The highest Honours can be obtained by excellence in a minority of subjects offered provided that adequate knowledge is shown throughout the examination.

[Until 1 October 2004: The heads of the departments of Economics and Politics shall make available to the examiners records showing whether candidates have pursued a course in information technology to an adequate standard. The examiners shall deduct one per cent of the aggregate mark of those candidates who have failed to reach an adequate standard.**]**

Candidates must take *eight* subjects in all **[Until 1 October 2004:** (excluding the course in information technology referred to above)**]**, and must satisfy requirements of particular branches of the school, including, in Philosophy, those set out in the *Regulations for Philosophy in all Honour Schools including Philosophy*, and, in Politics and Economics, requirements to take core subjects. In Politics, the core subjects are any two of 201, 202, 203, 214 and 220; in Economics, the core subjects are 301 and 302. In Politics, any of 201, 202, 203, 214 and 220 which are not offered as core subjects may be offered as further subjects.

On entering his or her name for the examination by the date prescribed, each candidate must give notice to the Registrar of the papers being offered.

Calculators may be used in the examination room for all Economics subjects, subject to the conditions set out under the heading 'Use of calculators in examinations' in the *Special Regulations concerning Examinations*.

A. *Philosophy, Politics, and Economics.*

Candidates must take subjects (i) *either* subject 101 *or* 102, and (ii) subject 103, 301 and 302 and any two of 201, 202, 203, 214 and 220.

Their other two subjects may be chosen freely from those listed under Philosophy and under Politics and under Economics, except that certain combinations of subjects may **not** be offered (see List of Subjects below), and except that not all Economics subjects may be offered in any particular year (see below for details). There may also be restrictions on numbers permitted to offer some Economics subjects in any particular year.

B. *Philosophy and Politics.*

Candidates must take (i) *either* subject 101 *or* subject 102, and (ii) subject 103 and any two of 201, 202, 203, 214 and 220.

Their other four subjects may be chosen freely from those listed under Philosophy and under Politics, except that (i) at least one must be a subject in Philosophy and the *Regulations for Philosophy in all Honour Schools including Philosophy* must be adhered to; (ii) at least one must be a further subject in Politics (other than the thesis (or the supervised dissertation) if offered); (iii) certain combinations of subjects may **not** be offered (see List of Subjects below).

C. *Politics and Economics.*

Candidates must take subjects 301 and 302 and any two of 201, 202, 203, 214 and 220.

Their other four subjects may be chosen freely from those listed under Politics and under Economics except that (i) at least one must be a further subject in Politics (other than the thesis (or the supervised dissertation) if offered); (ii) at least one must be a further subject in Economics (other than the thesis if offered); (iii) one but only one may be a subject in Philosophy; (iv) certain combinations of subjects may **not** be offered (see List of Subjects below); (v) not all Economics subjects may be offered in any particular year (see below for details). There may also be restrictions on numbers permitted to offer some Economics subjects in any particular year.

D. *Philosophy and Economics.*

Candidates must take (i) *either* subject 101 *or* subject 102, and (ii) subjects 103, 301 and 302.

Their other four subjects may be chosen freely from those listed under Philosophy and under Economics, except that (i) at least one must be a subject in Philosophy and the *Regulations for Philosophy in all Honour Schools including Philosophy* must be adhered to; (ii) at least one must be a further subject in Economics (other than the thesis if offered); (iii) certain combinations of subjects may **not** be offered (see List of Subjects below); (iv) not all Economics subjects may be offered in any particular year (see below for details). There may also be restrictions on numbers permitted to offer some Economics subjects in any particular year.

List of Subjects

Certain combinations of further subjects may not be offered: in parentheses after the title of each further subject is the number of any other subject or subjects with which it may *not* be combined. The syllabuses for the subjects in this List are given in *Regulations for Philosophy in all Honour Schools including Philosophy* or in the schedule below.

Philosophy

101. History of Philosophy from Descartes to Kant
102. Knowledge and Reality
103. Ethics

104. Philosophy of Mind
105. Philosophy of Science and Philosophy of Psychology and Neuroscience (106)
106. Philosophy of Science and Social Science (105)
107. Philosophy of Religion
108. The Philosophy of Logic and Language
109. Aesthetics and the Philosophy of Criticism
110. Medieval Philosophy
111. Continental Philosophy
112. The Philosophy of Kant
113. Post-Kantian Philosophy
114. Theory of Politics (203)
115. Plato *Republic*
116. Aristotle *Nicomachean Ethics*
117. Frege, Russell, and Wittgenstein (118)
118. The Later Philosophy of Wittgenstein (117)
119. Formal Logic
120. Intermediate Philosophy of Physics
122. Philosophy of Mathematics
198. Special Subjects
199. Thesis (298, 299, 399)

Politics (including Sociology)

201. Comparative Government
202. British Politics and Government in the Twentieth Century
203. Theory of Politics (114)
204. Modern British Government and Politics
205. Government and Politics of the United States
206. Government and Politics in Western Europe
207. Russian Government and Politics
208. Politics in Sub-Saharan Africa
209. Politics in Latin America
210. Politics in South Asia
211. Politics in the Middle East
212. International Relations in the Era of Two World Wars
213. International Relations in the Era of the Cold War
214. International Relations
215. Classical Political Thought up to 1800
216. Foundations of Modern Social and Political Thought
217. Marxism
218. Sociological Theory
219. The Sociology of Industrial Societies
220. Political Sociology
221. British Society in the Twentieth Century
222. Labour Economics and Industrial Relations (307)
223. The Government and Politics of Japan
224. Social Policy
225. Comparative Demographic Systems (315)

[Until 1 October 2004: 226. Statistical Methods in Social Science (313)] **[From 1 October 2004:**

226. Quantitative Methods in Politics and Sociology (313)]
227. Politics in China

[From 1 October 2004: 297. Special subject in Politics (199, 298, 299, 399)]

298. Supervised dissertation (199, 297, 299, 399)
299. Thesis (199, 298, 399)

Economics

Not all Economics subjects may be offered in any particular year. There may also be restrictions on numbers permitted to offer some Economics subjects in any particular year.

Economics subjects available to candidates in any particular year will depend on the availability of teaching resources. Candidates may obtain details of the choice available for the following year by consulting the Economics Supplement to the handbook of the Honour School of Philosophy, Politics, and Economics. This will be issued by the beginning of the fourth week of the first Hilary Full Term of candidates' work for the Honour School.

301. Macroeconomics
302. Microeconomics
303. Economic Theory
304. Money and Banking
305. Public Economics
306. Economics of Industry
307. Labour Economics and Industrial Relations (222)
308. International Economics
309. Command and Transitional Economies
310. Economics of Developing Countries
311. British Economic History since 1870
312. Classical Economic Thought: Smith, Ricardo, and Marx
313. Statistical Methods in Social Science (226)
314. Econometrics
315. Comparative Demographic Systems (225)
316. Economics of OECD Countries
399. Thesis (199, 298, 299)

SCHEDULE

The schedule of subjects in Philosophy is given in the *Regulations for Philosophy in all Honour Schools including Philosophy*

201. *Comparative Government*

Candidates will be expected to show knowledge of the following topics: party systems; electoral systems; political parties as organizations; forms of government and the constitutional allocation of power between institutions; the political executive and sources of political leadership; the roles of legislatures; the structure and political power of bureaucracy; public policy-making; judicial review, and judicial influence on politics; the territorial decentralization of power; regime transformation, civil-military relations, and democratization. Candidates will be required to answer all questions comparatively.

202. *British Politics and Government in the Twentieth Century*

British politics (including the major domestic political crises, ideologies and political issues) and the evolution of the British political and constitutional system (including elections and the electoral system, political parties, parliament, the cabinet system, and machinery of government). 'Political issues' will be taken to include the political implications of social and economic development and the domestic implications of foreign and imperial policy. Candidates will be expected to show knowledge of developments both before and since 1945.

203. *Theory of Politics**

The critical study of political values and of the concepts used in political analysis: the concept of the political; power, authority, and related concepts; the state; law; liberty and rights; justice and equality; public interest and common good; democracy and representation; political obligation and civil disobedience; ideology; liberalism, socialism, and conservatism.

204. *Modern British Government and Politics*

A study of the structure, powers, and operations of modern British Goverment, including its interaction with the European Community: the Crown, Ministers, Parliament, elections, parties and pressure groups, the legislative process; Government departments, agencies, and regulatory bodies; local authorities; administrative jurisdiction and the Courts. Candidates will be expected to show familiarity with certain prescribed documents, a schedule of which may be revised annually. All of these documents will be displayed on the open shelves of the PPE Reading Room in the Bodleian Library. Any revisions to the schedule shall apply only to candidates taking the Final Honour School five terms hence, and if no proposals for revising the schedule have been received by noon on Friday of week one of Hilary Term, the previous year's list shall stand. The revised schedule will be displayed on the PPE syllabus notice-board at the Department of Politics and International Relations, George Street.

205. *Government and Politics of the United States*

The constitution; federalism and separation of powers; the presidency; congress; the federal courts; the federal bureaucracy; parties and the party system; electoral politics; mass media; interest groups; state and local politics; processes of policy-formation and implementation; political culture.

206. *Government and Politics in Western Europe*

The emphasis of the paper will be upon the three major countries (France, the Federal Republic of Germany, and Italy) but candidates will have the opportunity of showing knowledge of other Western European countries and of the European Union. They will be required to show knowledge of at least two major countries and of one further country or the European Union: knowledge of the United Kingdom will not count towards the satisfaction of this requirement. Nor should questions be answered *solely* with reference to the United Kingdom, though comparisons of the United Kingdom with other Western European countries may be appropriate.

207. *Russian Government and Politics*

Candidates will be required to show knowledge of government and politics both in the Soviet Union (with particular reference to the period from the end of the Stalin era in 1953 to the end of the USSR in 1991) and in post-Soviet Russia. Major objects of study are the power structure and the changing relationships between political institutions under Communism and post-Communism, the process of political transformation of the Soviet system, and the post-Soviet transition. Specific attention is devoted to political leadership, the development of representative institutions, the national question and federalism, the relationship between economic and political power, political parties and interests, ideology, and political culture.

208. *Politics in Sub-Saharan Africa*

Candidates will be required to show knowledge of the politics of the countries of sub-Saharan Africa with respect to their political institutions, political sociology, and political economy. The following topics may be considered: nationalism; forms of government, civilian and military; parties and elections; conditions for democracy;

---

* May be offered alternatively as a further subject in Philosophy as 114.

class, ethnicity, religion, and gender; business, labour, and peasantries; structural adjustment and agricultural policies; the influence of external agencies.

209. *Politics in Latin America*

Candidates will be required to show knowledge of politics in Latin America; of the structure of government of the major states of the area; and of their political sociology and political economy. The following topics may be considered: presidential systems; the role of congress; public administration; party and electoral systems; the politics of major groups such as the military, trade unions and business groups, and the churches; political ideologies; political movements; the politics of economic stabilization; the politics of gender; theories of regime breakdown, and of democratic transition and consolidation; the influence of external factors.

210. *Politics in South Asia*

Candidates will be expected to show knowledge of political developments in South Asian countries since their independence, with regard to their political institutions, political sociology, and political economy. The following topics may be considered: the nature of the state; government and political institutions; party and electoral systems; politics in the provinces or states of a federation; the evolution of political ideologies; the politics of gender, caste, religion, language, ethnic regionalism, and national integration; the political economy of development, social change, and class relations; 'New' social movements and Left politics; regional conflicts in South Asia and the influence of external factors on South Asian politics. South Asia is taken to include India, Pakistan, Sri Lanka, and Bangladesh.

211. *Politics in the Middle East*

Candidates will be expected to show knowledge of the politics of the Middle East with regard to their political institutions, political sociology, and political economy. The following topics may be considered: the emergence of the state system in the modern Middle East; the influence of colonialism and nationalism in its development; the military in state and politics; party systems and the growth of democratic politics; the politics of religion; women in the political sphere; the influence of major inter-state conflicts and external factors on internal politics. The Middle East is taken to comprise Iran, Israel, Turkey, and the Arab States.

212. *International Relations in the Era of Two World Wars*

The relations between the major powers; the twentieth-century origins of the First World War and the origins of the Second World War; war aims, strategies, and peace-making; the disintegration of war-time alliances; the League of Nations and the establishment of the United Nations; the impact of major political movements (Communism, Fascism, nationalism) on international society; monetary and economic developments as they affected international politics.

Knowledge of events before 1900 and after 1947 will not be demanded, nor will questions be set on extra-European developments before 1914.

213. *International Relations in the Era of the Cold War*

The relations among the major powers 1945–85, including domestic and external factors shaping foreign policy: the origins and course of the Cold War, detente, and subsequent developments; East–West relations in Europe, with particular reference to the foreign policies of France and the Federal Republic of Germany; the movement towards European unity; the external relations of China and Japan, particularly with the Soviet Union and the United States; the Soviet Union's relations with eastern Europe and the USA's relations with its allies; decolonization; conflict in the developing world, including regional and global dimensions.

214. *International Relations*

The principal theories, concepts, and institutions of international relations. Topics include: law and norms, order, self-determination, security, war and conflict resolution, foreign-policy analysis, international political economy, dominance and dependence, regional integration, and international institutions. Candidates will be required to show knowledge (in at least two answers) of developments in international affairs since 1985. Questions requiring specific knowledge of earlier events will not be set, but opportunities will be given to display it.

215. *Classical Political Thought*

The critical study of political theorists whose ideas are still influential. Candidates will be expected to show knowledge of at least three of the following authors, with a primary though not necessarily exclusive focus on the following texts: Plato, *The Republic*; Aristotle, *Politics*; Aquinas, *Selected Political Writings* ed. D'Entreves; Machiavelli, *The Prince, The Discourses* ed. Plamenatz; Hobbes, *Leviathan*, Parts I and II; Locke, *Second Treatise of Civil Government*; Montesquieu, *The Spirit of the Laws*, Books I–VIII, XI, XII, XIX; Rousseau's *Discourse on the Origin of Inequality, The Social Contract*; Hume, *Moral and Political Writings* ed. Aiken. Questions may also be set on the following topics: theories of political stability and civic virtue; the relationship between the personal and the political; utopian political thought; theories of natural law. In answering examination questions candidates are expected to discuss the primary texts identified in this rubric, but may also draw on their knowledge of a range of other primary texts from the canon of classical political thought, as indicated in the bibliography issued by the Department of Politics and International Relations.

216. *Foundations of Modern Social and Political Thought*

The critical study of modern social and political theorists. Candidates will be expected to show knowledge of at least three of the following authors, with a primary though not necessarily exclusive focus on the following texts: Bentham, *Political Thought* ed. Parekh; J. S. Mill, *On Liberty*, essays 'The Spirit of the Age', 'Civilization', 'Bentham', 'Coleridge'; Hegel, *The Philosophy of Right, Lectures on the Philosophy of World History* (Introduction) (CUP edn.); Saint-Simon, *Selected Writings 1760–1825*, ed. Taylor; Tocqueville, *Democracy in America* (Vol. I: Introduction, chapters 2–6, the last section of chapter 8, chapters 11, 12, the first section of chapter 13, chapters 14–17; Vol II: Book II, chapters 1–8, 16–20, Book III, chapters 1, 2, 13–21, Book IV, chapters 1–8); Marx, *Selected Writings*, ed. McLellan, nos. 6–8, 13, 14, 18, 19, 22, 23, 25, 30, 32, 37–40; Weber, *From Max Weber*, eds. Gerth and Mills; Durkheim, *The Division of Labour in Society* (Prefaces, Introduction, Book I, chapters 1–3, 7; Book 2, chapters 1, 3; Book 3, chapters 1, 2; Conclusion), *Professional Ethics and Civic Morals*, chapters 4–9. Questions may also be set on the following topics: state, society, and the family; individual and community; history and social change; science and religion. In answering examination questions candidates are expected to discuss the primary texts identified in this rubric, but may also draw on their knowledge of other primary texts from the canon of modern social and political thought, as indicated in the bibliography issued by the Department of Politics and International Relations.

217. *Marxism*

The study of the ideas of Marx and Engels, of later Marxists and critics of Marxism. Candidates will be expected to study Marxism as an explanatory theory, and also to examine its political consequences. They will be required to show first-hand knowledge of the principal writings of Marx and Engels and of some later Marxists.

218. *Sociological Theory*

The critical study of the major theoretical approaches to social order and integration; social structure and action; social norms and roles; social change; class and stratification; deviance; the link between micro- and macro-sociology; the scientific status of sociological theory. Candidates will be expected to show knowledge of the application of theoretical approaches to the explanation and understanding of empirical social phenomena.

219. *The Sociology of Industrial Societies*

Candidates will be expected to show knowledge of the following aspects of the social structure of urban-industrial societies: occupation and economic structure; social stratification and mobility; education; the social significance of gender and ethnicity; demography and the family; the social structure of religion; and the impact on society of the state and politics. They must show knowledge of modern Britain and at least one other industrial society, and of the main general theories of industrial society.

220. *Political Sociology*

The critical study of the major sociological approaches to politics and their application to the following topics: the social bases of political identities: forms of state and organization of interests; the sources and distribution of political power; political transformations. Candidates must show knowledge of more than one major industrial country.

221. *British Society in the Twentieth Century*

This further subject offers an opportunity to study in depth the profound changes that affected British society and popular culture in the past century. The focus is on the history of society rather than on social policy and the paper extends to the present day. Themes explored within the Further Subject are: population, sexuality, and the family; class, gender, and stratification; immigration and ethnicity; health and living standards; urban life; the experience of work and of unemployment; religion; education; crime; leisure and the influence of the mass media; and methods of social research. There is an extensive, lively, and often topical secondary literature and primary source material includes oral history and memoirs as well as social surveys and commentaries, official reports and quantitative data. There are opportunities, too, for using film.

The paper will include questions that require familiarity with primary sources, notably Statistical material in A. H. Halsey and J. Webb (eds.), *Twentieth-Century British Social Trends* (2000, Parts I–III and VI); Royal Commission on Alien Immigration Report (Parliamentary Papers, 1903 ix, Part I, Results, Recommendations); Royal Commission on Population Report (P.P. 1948–9 xix chs. 2–15, 20, and pp. 218–37); Royal Commission in the Press Report (1949, Cmnd. 7700, including Appendices III, IV, and VII); Wolfenden Report on Homosexual Offences and Prostitution (1957); Report of the Committee on Broadcasting (Pilkington report, 1962, Cmnd 1753); The Brixton Disorders April 10 to 12, 1981; Report of an Inquiry (the Scarman Report, 1981, Cmnd. 8427); B. S. Rowntree, Poverty, a study of townlife (1901, chs. 4, 5, 9), and Poverty and Progress (1941, pp. 28–33, 96–126, 150–71, 276–7, 286–98, 450–77); Lady Bell, *At the Works* (1907); George Sturt, Change in the Village (1912; repr 1955, 1984); Pilgrim Trust, *Men without Work* (1938); J. B. Priestley, *English Journey* (1934; latest repr. 1997); Terence Young, *Becontree and Dagenham* (1934); George Orwell, *The Road to Wigan Pier* (1937; latest repr. 1998); Richard Hoggart, *The Uses of Literacy* (1958; latest repr. 1992); R. Roberts, *The Classic Slum* (1971); Marie Stopes, *Married Love* (1918); M. Spring-Rice, *Working-Class Wives* (1939); N. Last, *Nella Last's War. A Mother's Diary 1939–45* (ed. R. Broad and S. Fleming, 1983); E. Roberts, *Women and Families; an oral history 1940–70* (1995); J. Sarsby, *Missuses and Mouldrunners. An oral history of women pottery workers at home and at work* (1988); N. Dennis, F. Henriques and C. Slaughter, *Coal Is Our Life* (1951; repr. 1969); J. B. Mays, *Growing Up in the City. A study of juvenile delinquency in an urban neighbourhood* (1954); J. White, *The Worst Street in North London* (1986); *Faith in the City. A Call for Action by Church and Nation* (The Report of the Archbishop of Canterbury's Commission on Urban Priority Areas, 1985); ed. S. MacLure, *Educational Documents. England and Wales* (3rd edn., 1985); B. S. Rowntree and G. R. Lavers, *English Life and Leisure* (1951); M. Young and P. Willmott, *Family and Kinship in East London* (1957, repr. 1984); and *Family and Class in a London Suburb* (1967); J. H. Goldthorpe *et al.*, *The Affluent Worker in the Class Structure* (1969); Q. D. Leavis, *Fiction and the Reading Public* (1932, repr. 1968, Part I chs. 1–3, Part II ch. 4, Part III chs. 1–3); H. T. Himmelweit, *Television and the Child* (1958); Joseph Rowntree Foundation, *Inquiry into Income and Wealth* (1995).

222. *Labour Economics and Industrial Relations*
As specified for 307 below.

223. *The Government and Politics of Japan*
The constitutional framework and structure of government; parliamentary and local politics; the electoral and party systems; the role of corporate interests and pressure groups; the bureaucracy; foreign policy. Candidates will be expected to show knowledge of Japanese political history since 1945 and of the social context of Japanese political institutions and policy-making.

224. *Social Policy*
The nature and development of social policy and welfare states. Public, private and informal systems of welfare. Alternative definitions and explanations of poverty and deprivation. The sources, growth, organization and outcomes of British social policy with special reference to health, housing, social security, and education.

225. *Comparative Demographic Systems*
As specified for 315 below.

[**Until 1 October 2004:** 226. *Statistical Methods in Social Science*
As specified for 313 below.]
[**From 1 October 2004:**
226. *Quantitative Methods in Politics and Sociology*
Candidates will be expected to show an understanding of applications of quantitative methods in politics and sociology including the following: the principles of research design in social science: data collection, the logic of casual inference, and comparative method; major statistical methods and concepts: types of random variables, independence, correlation and association, sampling theory, hypothesis testing, linear and non-linear regression models, event-history analysis, and time-series. Candidates will also be expected to interpret information and show familiarity with major methodological debates in politics and sociology.]

227. *Politics in China*
Candidates will be required to show knowledge of the government and politics of China since 1949, and with particular reference to the period since 1978, with respect to its political institutions, political sociology, and political economy. The following topics may be considered: the Communist party and its structure, urban and rural reform since 1978, foreign relations, nationalism, elite politics, gender, legal culture, and the politics of Hong Kong and Taiwan.

[**From 1 October 2004:** 297. Special Subject in Politics (199, 298, 299, 399)
Special Subjects will be examined by examination paper. No candidate may offer more than one Special Subject. A Special Subject may not be offered by candidates also offering a thesis (199, 299, 399) or Supervised dissertation (298). Depending on the availability of teaching resources, not all Special Subjects will be available to all candidates in every year. Candidates may obtain details of the choice of Special Subjects for the following year by consulting lists posted at the beginning of the

Fourth Week of Hilary Term in the Department of Politics and International Relations and circulated to Politics tutors at colleges admitting undergraduates.]

298. *Supervised dissertation**

With the approval of the Politics sub-faculty, members of staff willing to supervise a research topic shall through the Administrator of the Department of Politics and International Relations place on the noticeboard of that Department not later than Friday of Fourth Week of Hilary Term a short description of an area of politics (including international relations and sociology) in which they have a special interest, a list of possible dissertation topics lying within that area, an introductory reading list, and a time and place at which they will meet those interested in writing a dissertation under their supervision for assessment in the following year's examination. Members of staff agreeing to supervise an undergraduate shall provide him or her with tutorials or intercollegiate classes equivalent to a term's teaching for a normal paper, the cost of such tutorials or classes to be met by the college. They shall notify the colleges of the undergraduates involved and the Administrator of the Department of Politics and International Relations. Candidates offering a thesis (199, 299, or 399) **[From 1 October 2004:** or a Special Subject in Politics (297)] may not also offer a supervised dissertation. The regulations governing the length, the format, and the time, date and place of submission of a supervised dissertation shall be the same as those for the thesis. Every candidate who wishes to submit a supervised dissertation shall give notice of his or her intention to do so to the Registrar on his or her examination entry form. Every candidate shall sign a certificate to the effect that the supervised dissertation is his or her own work and that it has not already been submitted, wholly or substantially, for another Honour School of this University or for a degree of any other institution. The supervisor(s) shall countersign the certificate confirming that to the best of his, her or their knowledge and belief these statements are true, and shall also submit a short statement of the supervision provided, together with the original specification of the research topic and any other course material provided. The candidate's certificate and the supervisor's or supervisors' statements shall be presented together with the supervised dissertation. Candidates are warned that they should avoid repetition in papers of material in their supervised dissertation and that substantial repetition may be penalized. Every candidate who wishes to have his or her supervised dissertation returned is required to enclose with the thesis, in an envelope bearing only his or her candidate number, a self-addressed sticky label.

299. *Thesis*

As specified for 399 below.

301. *Macroeconomics*

Alternative macroeconomic theories and policy implications; aggregate consumption; aggregate investment; demand for money; growth and fluctuations; productivity and the determinants of competitiveness; unemployment and inflation; balance of payments adjustment and exchange rates; supply-side policies; monetary and fiscal policy; international aspects of macroeconomic policy.

Applied issues are to be studied mainly in relation to the UK and its membership of the European Community, but the opportunity will be given to candidates to show knowledge of other OECD countries.

The paper will contain both theoretical and applied questions, and candidates will be required to answer two questions of each type.

302. *Microeconomics*

Risk, uncertainty and information; the firm and market structures; welfare economics, externalities, public goods and the sources of market failure; the distribution

* This option may not be available every year.

of income; trade and protection; applications of microeconomics to public policy issues.

The paper will contain both theoretical and applied questions, and candidates will be required to answer two questions of each type. The topics to be examined under the rubric of applications of microeconomics to public policy issues will be announced by the chairman of the Sub-faculty of Economics not later than Trinity Term each year for the examination two years later.

303. *Economic Theory*

The paper will be set in two parts. Candidates will be required to answer at least one question from Part A. They will not be *required* to answer questions from Part B.

Part A. Questions on the following topics: consumers, producers, and general equilibrium; uncertainty and contracts; game theory; macroeconomic equilibrium and disequilibrium; welfare and social choice; distribution, growth, and capital.

Part B. Questions on the use of mathematical methods in economic theory.

Questions may be set on theoretical topics in areas covered by other economic papers.

304. *Money and Banking*

The nature and definition of money; the demand for money and other assets; the role and behaviour of banks and other financial intermediaries; the supplies of money and credit; the aggregate and sectoral effects of changes in money and credit on expenditure and prices; the interest rate structure and equity prices; the aims, instruments, and practice of monetary policy; the regulation of banks and other financial intermediaries; foreign exchange markets and monetary policy in an open economy; debt management and the relations between monetary and fiscal policy.

Candidates will be given the opportunity to show knowledge of relevant experience in the UK and other countries.

305. *Public Economics*

Welfare-economic foundations; the measurement of well-being; taxation and incentives; taxation, debt and behaviour over time; commodity taxation; taxation of persons; taxation of companies; cost-benefit analysis; health; education; social security; jurisdictional issues; public goods, externalities and market failure; policy towards natural resources and the environment.

306. *Economics of Industry*

Market structures, costs and scale economies, oligopoly and the theory of games, entry, empirical studies of pricing and profitability, advertising, product differentiation, managerial theories of the firm, investment and finance, mergers and vertical integration, innovation, public policy towards market structure and conduct, public enterprises.

Candidates will be expected to show knowledge of empirical studies relating to one or more of the advanced industrial economies, but questions relating to specific industrial economies will not be set.

307. *Labour Economics and Industrial Relations**

The organization and policies of trade unions and employers' associations; problems of employee involvement and attachment; employer–employee relations, with special reference to industrial co-operation and conflict; the theory and practice of collective bargaining, including the role of government and the impact of work groups on the bargaining process. The application of economic analysis to labour markets; economic aspects of trade unions; the economics of labour policy, including incomes policies; factors affecting the distribution of income.

* May be offered alternatively as a subject in Politics as 222.

308. *International Economics*

Theories of international trade and factor movements, positive and normative, and their application to economic policy and current problems. Theory and practice of economic integration. Current problems of the international trading system. Methods of balance of payments adjustment and financing; policies for attaining internal and external balance. Behaviour of floating exchange rates: theory and evidence. Optimum Currency Areas and Exchange Rate Regimes. International Policy Co-ordination and the International Monetary System.

309. *Command and Transitional Economies*

This paper covers the traditional command economy, attempts to reform it in the direction of market socialism, and transition to a market economy. Candidates will be expected first to be familiar with the evolution of the command economy in the pre-war USSR (War Communism, New Economic Policy, Stalinist central planning) and in the post-war period in the USSR, Eastern Europe and China. But emphasis is placed on knowledge of the features and policies of the main variants of the command system (e.g. central planning, performance of state enterprises, fiscal and monetary policies, foreign trade), rather than of the details of economic history or experiences of countries. The second area includes the 1965 reform and perestroika in the USSR, the New Economic Mechanism in Hungary, self-management in Yugoslavia, and post-1978 reforms in China. The third area comprises the theory of the transition from command to market systems, as well as policies and economic developments in the major countries after 1989. Although most questions will deal with the Soviet Union and Eastern Europe, at least two will relate fully or partially to the economy of China.

310. *Economics of Developing Countries*

Theories of growth and development. Poverty and income distribution. Human resources. Labour markets and employment. Industrialisation and technology. Agriculture and rural development. Monetary and fiscal issues; inflation. Foreign trade and payments. Foreign and domestic capital; economic aid. The role of government in development; the operation of markets.

Where appropriate, candidates will be expected to illustrate their answers with knowledge of actual situations.

311. *British Economic History since 1870*

Trends and cycles in national income, factor supplies, and productivity; changes in the structure of output, employment, and capital; management and entrepreneurship; the location of industries, industrial concentration, and the growth of large firms; prices, interest rates, money, and public finance; wages, unemployment, trade unions, and the working of the labour market; the distribution of incomes, poverty, and living standards; foreign trade, tariffs, international capital movements, and sterling; Government economic policy in peace and war.

Questions concerned *exclusively* with the periods before 1900 or after 1973 will not be set.

312. *Classical Economic Thought: Smith, Ricardo, and Marx*

The theories of value, distribution, money, international trade and growth of Smith, Ricardo, and Marx.

The principal works to be studied are:

(*a*) Smith, *The Wealth of Nations*, Books I–IV.

(*b*) Ricardo (ed. Sraffa): Vol. I (Principles of Political Economy); Vol. II (Notes on Malthus, ch. 7, pp. 300–452); Vol. IV (Pamphlets, Proposals for an Economical and Secure Currency, pp. 43–141; Absolute Value and Exchangeable Value, pp. 357–412).

(*c*) Marx (ed. Lawrence and Wishart): Vol. I, chs. 1–9, 12, 15–19, 23–5; Vol. II, chs. 20–1; Vol. III, chs. 8, 9, 13, 14, 15.

313. *Statistical Methods in Social Science* **[Until 1 October 2004: *]**

Candidates will be required to answer four questions. Each candidate must offer at least one question from Part A and at least one question from either Part B (if offering it as an Economics option) or Part C (if offering it as a Politics option).

Candidates will be expected to show knowledge of the following topics:

Part A (Statistical Theory). Probability (concepts of probability, probability laws, Bayes' theorem); random variables (moments, sums and differences of random variables, frequency and cumulative distributions, joint random variables, conditional and marginal distributions); distribution theory (standard distributions including the binomial, Poisson, and normal distributions); measures of association (correlation, rank correlation, and multiple correlation); hypothesis testing (concepts of hypothesis testing, size and power, use of normal, t, χ^2 and F distributions); sampling theory (including properties of estimators); linear models (including regression, analysis of variance, logistic and loglinear models).

Part B (Economic Statistics) (questions may be asked which involve simple calculations). Applications of the theory defined by Part A to economic topics which may be drawn from areas related to the scope of the Microeconomics and Macroeconomics papers; the preparation and presentation of economic statistics (histograms, seasonal adjustment, issues relating to data quality); index numbers (including Paasche, Laspeyres and Divisia indices); size distributions (including measures of concentration, inequality and poverty).

[Until 1 October 2004: *Part C* (Politics and Sociology). Application of the theory defined in Part A to social and political research, with reference to the problem of collection, analysis, and interpretation of data arising in the fields of electoral behaviour, social stratification, and comparative social policy.**]**

314. *Econometrics*

Candidates will be required to answer four questions.

I Regression and correlation; interpretation, estimation, and prediction in single equation two- and three-variable linear models, including tests of significance and goodness of fit, problems of bias, multi-collinearity, and autocorrelation. Simultaneous equations problems: reduced form, identification.

II Application of econometric methods including the estimation of consumption functions, demand analysis, production functions, macroeconomic policy models.

Candidates will be required to show knowledge on both parts of the paper.

315. *Comparative Demographic Systems*†

Candidates will be expected to show knowledge of controversies in demographic theory (Malthus and his critics, Easterlin, Caldwell, the New Home Economics school and others) and to illustrate their answers with varied and specific examples. The paper will contain essay questions and questions involving computation. Candidates will be required to answer three questions, two of the former and one of the latter.

I Demographic analysis and techniques: data sources, adequacy and remedies. Statistical analysis of fertility, mortality, and other demographic phenomena.

[Until 1 October 2004: * May be offered alternatively as a subject in Politics as 226.**]**

† May be offered alternatively as a subject in Politics as 225.

The life table, stable population, and other models of population structure and growth. Population dynamics, projections and simulations.

II Limits to fertility and the lifespan. Contrasts between stable and transitional population systems in historical European and current non-European societies: the decline of mortality, fertility patterns in relation to systems of household formation, kin organization and risk environments, marital fertility decline and the current status of transition theory. Social, economic, and political consequences of rapid population growth at the national level and the local level.

Demographic systems in post-transitional societies (modern Europe and other industrial areas): low fertility, trends in health and survival, and age structure change; their economic and social causes and consequences. New patterns of marriage and family, women in the workforce, labour migration and the demography of ethnic minorities, population policies.

316. *Economics of OECD Countries*

Main phases of development since 1945. Institutional framework of policy formation; conduct of demand management policies; the welfare state and public expenditure; experience of policies and strategies. The behaviour of major macroeconomic aggregates; the labour market and industrial relations. Development of external trade and financial relations; competitiveness and exchange rates; economic integration and the international coordination of economic policies.

Questions will be set requiring knowledge of one or more of the following countries: France, Germany, Italy, Japan, UK, and US. Candidates will be expected to answer at least one question (out of three) from Part A.

Part A. Comparative analysis of the OECD countries
Part B. The Major Areas
Section 1: Western Europe
Section 2: the United States
Section 3: Japan.

399. *Thesis*

(*a*) *Subject*

The subject of every thesis should fall within the scope of the honour school. The subject may but need not overlap any subject on which the candidate offers papers. Candidates are warned that they should avoid repetition in papers of material used in their theses and that substantial repetition may be penalized.

Every candidate shall submit through his or her college for approval to the head of the Department of Politics and International Relations, or the head of the Department of Economics the title he or she proposes together with

(i) an indication as to the branch of the school in which the subject falls, e.g. Economics;
(ii) an explanation of the subject in about 100 words;
(iii) a letter of approval from his or her tutor;

not earlier than the first day of the Trinity Full Term of the year before that in which he or she is to be examined and not later than the date prescribed for entry to the examination. The relevant chair or head of department shall decide as soon as possible whether or not to approve the title and shall advise the candidate immediately. No decision shall be deferred beyond the end of the fifth week of Michaelmas Full Term.

Proposals to change the title of the thesis may be made through the college and will be considered by the chair of the relevant sub-faculty until the first day of the Hilary Full Term of the year in which the student is to be examined, and by the chair of the examiners thereafter.

(*b*) *Authorship and origin*

Every thesis shall be the candidate's own work. His or her tutor may, however, discuss with him or her the field of study, the sources available, and the method of presentation; the tutor may also read and comment on a first draft. The amount of assistance that may be given is equivalent to the teaching of a normal paper. Theses previously submitted for the Honour School of Philosophy, Politics, and Economics may be resubmitted. No thesis will be accepted if it has already been submitted, wholly or substantially, for another Honour School or degree of this University, or for a degree of any other institution. Every candidate shall sign a certificate to the effect that the thesis is his or her own work and that it has not already been submitted, wholly or substantially, for another Honour School or degree of this University, or for a degree of any other institution and his or her tutor shall countersign the certificate confirming that, to the best of his or her knowledge and belief, these statements are true. This certificate shall be presented together with the thesis. No thesis shall, however, be ineligible because it has been or is being submitted for any prize of this University.

(*c*) *Length and format*

No thesis shall exceed 15,000 words, the limit to include all notes and appendices, but not bibliographies; no person or body shall have authority to permit any excess. There shall be a select bibliography or a list of sources. All theses must be typed in double spacing on one side of quarto or A4 paper. Any notes and references may be placed *either* at the bottom of the relevant pages *or* all together at the end of the thesis, but in the latter case two loose copies of the notes and references must be supplied. The thesis must be bound or held firmly in a stiff cover. *Two* copies shall be submitted to the examiners; they shall be returned to the candidate's college after the examination.

(*d*) *Notice to Registrar and submission of thesis*

Every candidate who wishes to submit a thesis shall give notice of his or her intention to do so to the Registrar on his or her examination entry form (in addition to seeking approval of the subject from the relevant Chair of the sub-faculty or head of department under (*a*) above); and shall submit his or her thesis not later than noon on Friday of the week before the Trinity Full Term of the examination to the Chair of the Examiners, Honour School of Philosophy, Politics, and Economics, Examination Schools, Oxford. Every candidate who wishes to have his or her thesis returned is required to enclose with the thesis, in an envelope bearing only his or her candidate number, a self-addressed sticky label.

PASS SCHOOL OF PHILOSOPHY, POLITICS, AND ECONOMICS

The subjects of the Pass School of Philosophy, Politics, and Economics shall be the study of modern philosophy, and of the political and economic principles and structures of modern society. Candidates must offer Philosophy, Politics, and Economics or such combination of these subjects as may be determined jointly by the Social Sciences Board and the Humanities Board. Candidates must offer five papers in all, selected from those offered for the Honour School of Philosophy, Politics, and Economics, including two core subjects in each branch of the school offered, unless offering three branches of the school, when two core papers must be offered in two branches, and one in the third. Candidates who are not offering three branches of the school may offer a thesis instead of one *non*-core subject. The regulations for the thesis shall be as prescribed for the Honour School of Philosophy, Politics, and Economics.

NOTES

SPECIAL REGULATIONS FOR THE HONOUR SCHOOL OF PHILOSOPHY AND THEOLOGY

A

1. The subjects of the Honour School of Philosophy and Theology shall be (*a*) Philosophy and (*b*) Theology.

2. All candidates must offer both (*a*) and (*b*).

3. No candidate shall be admitted to examination in this school unless he or she has either passed or been exempted from the First Public Examination.

4. The examination in this school shall be under the joint supervision of the Boards of the Faculties of Philosophy and Theology, which shall appoint a standing joint committee to make regulations concerning it, subject always to the preceding clauses of this sub-section.

5. (i) The examiners for Philosophy in this school shall be such of the Public Examiners in Philosophy in the Honour School of Psychology, Philosophy, and Physiology, and those for Theology shall be such of the Public Examiners in the Honour School of Theology, as may in each case be required.

(ii) It shall be the duty of the chairman of the Public Examiners in Psychology, Philosophy, and Physiology to designate such of the examiners in Philosophy as may be required for Philosophy in the Honour School of Philosophy and Theology, and the duty of the chairman of the Public Examiners in the Honour School of Theology to designate such of their number as may be required for Theology in the Honour School of Philosophy and Theology, and when this has been done the number of the examiners in Philosophy and Theology shall be deemed to be complete.

B

The highest honours can be obtained by excellence either in Philosophy or in Theology provided that adequate knowledge is shown in the other subject of the examination.

Candidates are required to take *either* four subjects in Philosophy and four in Theology, *or* five in Philosophy and three in Theology, *or* three in Philosophy and five in Theology. No candidate may offer more than one thesis.

(a) Philosophy Subjects as specified in **Regulations for Philosophy in all Honour Schools including Philosophy**

(b) Theology

All candidates must take papers (i) (unless they intend to offer both papers 3 and 7 as prescribed for the Honour School of Theology) and (ii) below. In addition they must take either (iii) or (iv) below. Candidates may select their remaining papers from the paper not selected from (iii) and (iv), paper (v) below, and any other papers prescribed for the Honour School of Theology.

(i) The Theology and Ethics of the New Testament (with special reference to the gospels of Matthew and John, Romans, and I Corinthians).

Questions will be set on the theology of the individual gospels (not just those specified), Pauline theology, the historical Jesus, the ethics of the New Testament, and the different methods of New Testament interpretation. There will be a compulsory question containing passages for comment from Matthew, John, Romans, and I Corinthians, printed in both Greek and English. Comment on passages in Greek will be optional.

(ii) *God, Christ, and Salvation* (Paper (6) in the Honour School of Theology).

(iii) *The Development of Doctrine in the Early Church to* AD *451* (Paper (5) in the Honour School of Theology).

(iv) *Christian Moral Reasoning*

Candidates will be expected to elucidate and assess themes in the Christian tradition of ethical teaching and their contribution to contemporary moral and social debates.

The paper will consist of four sections: (1) Christian Moral Concepts; (2) Government and its tasks; (3) Medical Ethics; (4) Sexual Ethics. Candidates will be required to answer three or four questions, of which at least one question must be answered from section (1), and at least one from another section.

(1) *Christian Moral Concepts*

The major moral concepts in Christian thought, such as: love, natural and revealed law, the supreme good, conscience, virtues, sin, justification, and grace; and their contribution to contemporary discussions. Candidates may treat questions on these subjects *primarily* with reference to their sources in the Bible, if they so wish.

(2) *Government and its tasks*

Theological interpretations of: justice, law and authority; forms of government, local, national and international; government, society and the church; the coercive use of force in punishment and war, responsibilities for education, employment, economy, and environment.

(3) *Medical Ethics*

Such topics as: the doctor–patient relationship and its social context; planned parenthood, contraception, and abortion in both personal and social contexts; artificial reproduction; genetic manipulation; eugenics; experimentation on humans; organ transplantation; priorities in treatment and research; the prolongation of life, terminal care, and the ending of life.

(4) *Sexual Ethics*

Such topics as: celibacy, the goods of marriage, the sacramentality of marriage, divorce, polygamy, homosexuality, the sexual sins, the social differentiation of the sexes, the connection of body and soul in sexual contexts, erotic affection.

(v) Thesis. **[Until 1 October 2004:** The subject of every thesis should fall within the scope of theology.**] [From 1 October 2004:** A thesis may be offered either in Theology or in Philosophy or in both Philosophy and Theology jointly. A candidate who offers a thesis in Philosophy and Theology cannot also offer any other thesis.**]** The provisions governing theses are the same as those given for theses in Philosophy in this school, as specified in *Regulations for Philosophy in some of the Honour Schools*, except that the provisions in the Regulations for Philosophy for subject 199 that 'The subject of every thesis should fall within the scope of philosophy' does not apply to theses in theology.

Optional translation papers (2 hours each).

The translation components of papers (25), *The Hebrew of the Old Testament*, and (29), *The New Testament in Greek*, of the Honour School of Theology may be offered individually as optional extra papers by candidates for the Honour School of Philosophy and Theology.

No candidate may offer both the Aquinas part of philosophy paper 110: *Medieval Philosophy*, and Aquinas for study as a major theologian for paper 11: *Further Studies in History and Doctrine* as prescribed for the Honour School of Theology.

PASS SCHOOL OF PHILOSOPHY AND THEOLOGY

1. Candidates will be required to offer five papers from the syllabus for the Honour School of Philosophy and Theology, at least one of which must be from section (*a*) *Philosophy*, and at least one from section (*b*) *Theology*. In paper (b)(i) the question containing passages for comment will not be compulsory for candidates in the Pass School of Philosophy and Theology.

2. Candidates may offer an extended essay in place of one three-hour examination paper, provided that the minimum requirement of at least one paper from each of sections (*a*) and (*b*) of the syllabus is fulfilled in the form of three-hour examinations. The regulations concerning essays shall be as for the Honour School of Philosophy and Theology.

NOTES

SPECIAL REGULATIONS FOR THE HONOUR SCHOOL OF PHYSICS

[For candidates embarking on the Honour School in or after October 2002. (For candidates embarking on the Honour School of Natural Science (Physics) in or before October 2001, see Addendum I at the back of the book)

A

1. (1) The subject of the Honour School in Physics shall be the study of Physics as an experimental science.

(2) The examination in Physics shall consist respectively of three parts for the four-year course (A, B, C) and of two parts for the three-year course (A, B) as prescribed by regulation by the Mathematical and Physical Sciences Board.

2. (1) The name of a candidate in either the three-year course or the four-year course shall not be published in a Class List until he or she has completed all parts of the respective examinations.

(2) The Examiners in Physics for the three-year course or the four-year course shall be entitled to award a pass or classified Honours to candidates in the Second Public Examination who have reached a standard considered adequate; the Examiners shall give due consideration to the performance in all parts of the respective examinations.

(3) (*a*) A candidate who obtains only a pass or fails to satisfy the Examiners may enter again for Part B (three-year course) or Part C (four-year course) of the examination on one, but not more than one, subsequent occasion.

(*b*) Part A (three-year and four-year courses) and Part B (four-year course) shall be entered on one occasion only.

(4) A candidate adjudged worthy of Honours in the Second Public Examination for the four-year course in Physics may supplicate for the Degree of Master of Physics if he or she has fulfilled all the conditions in Ch. I, Sect. 1, § 1, cl. 1.

3. The examination shall be partly practical: this requirement shall normally be satisfied by the Examiners' assessment of the practical work done by candidates during their course of study; exceptionally, the Examiners may require a candidate to take a practical examination.

4. No candidate shall be admitted to examination in this school unless he or she has either passed or been exempted from the First Public Examination.

5. (1) The Examination in Physics shall be under the supervision of the Mathematical and Physical Sciences Board.

(2) The board shall have power, subject to this decree, from time to time to frame and to vary regulations for the different parts and subjects of the examination.

B

In the following 'the Course Handbook' refers to the Physics Undergraduate Course Handbook, published annually at the start of Michaelmas Term by the sub-faculty of Physics.

Candidates will be expected to show knowledge based on practical work.

The Examiners will permit the use of any hand-held calculator subject to the conditions set out under the heading 'Use of calculators in examinations' in the *Special Regulations concerning Examinations* and further elaborated in the Course Handbook.

The various parts of the examinations for the three and four year courses shall take place in Trinity Term of the year in question and, unless otherwise stated, deadlines shall apply to the year in which that part is taken.

Physics (four year course)

1. The examination shall be in three parts, A, B, C, taken at times not less than three, six and nine terms, respectively after passing the First Public Examination.

2. In order to proceed to Parts B and C of the four-year course in physics a minimum standard of achievement in Part A may be required, as determined by the sub-faculty of Physics from time to time. Any such requirement shall be published in the Course Handbook not later than the beginning of Michaelmas Full Term of the academic year preceding the year of the Part A examination. Names of those satisfying the requirement shall be published by the Examiners.

3. **In Part A**

(*a*) the candidate shall be required

(i) to offer three written papers on the Fundamental Principles of Physics, *and*

(ii) to submit to the Examiners such evidence as they require of the successful completion of practical work normally pursued during the three terms preceding the examination, *and*

(iii) to offer a written paper on one Short Option.

(*b*) A candidate may also offer a written paper on a second Short Option, in which case the candidate need only submit evidence of the successful completion of practical work normally pursued during one and a half terms of the three terms specified in cl. 3(*a*)(ii).

4. **In Part B**

(*a*) the candidate shall be required

(i) to offer three written papers on Physics, *and*

(ii) to submit to the Examiners such evidence as they require of the successful completion of practical work normally pursued during the three terms preceding the examination, *and*

(iii) to offer a written paper on one Short Option.

(*b*) A candidate may also offer a written paper on a second Short Option, in which case the candidate need only submit evidence of the successful completion of practical work normally pursued during one and a half terms of the three terms specified in cl. 4(*a*)(ii).

5. The titles of the written papers of cl. 3(*a*)(i) & cl. 4(*a*)(i) are given in the Schedule below. Their syllabuses shall be approved by the sub-faculty of physics and shall be published in the Course Handbook not later than the beginning of Michaelmas Full Term for the examination three terms thence.

6. The list of Short Option subjects in cls 3(*a*)(iii), 3(*b*), 4(*a*)(iii), 4(*b*) and their syllabuses shall be approved by the sub-faculty of physics and shall be published in the Course Handbook not later than the beginning of Michaelmas Full Term for the examination three terms thence.

7. In cl. 4(*a*)(ii), practical work may be replaced by project work, if an appropriate supervisor is available. The subject, duration, and replacement value shall be approved by the Chairman of the sub-faculty of Physics or deputy, by the end of Michaelmas Full Term.

8. With respect to cl. 3(*a*)(iii) or cl. 4(*a*)(iii) a candidate may take, as alternative to the written examination, an assessed course of instruction in a foreign language. A candidate proposing to take this alternative must have the proposal approved by the Chairman of the sub-faculty of Physics or deputy and by the Director of the Language Teaching Centre or deputy, by the end of the first week of Hilary Full Term preceding the examination.

9. With respect to subjects under cl. 3(*a*)(iii) or cl. 4(*a*)(iii) a candidate may propose to the Chairman of the sub-faculty of Physics or deputy, not later than the fourth week of Michaelmas Full Term preceding the examination, either to offer another subject paper, *or* to offer instead a written account of extended practical work, in addition to that specified in cl. 3(*a*)(ii) or cl. 4(*a*)(ii). Candidates will be advised of the decision by the end of eighth week of that term.

10. **In Part C** the candidate shall be required to offer

(*a*) written papers on each of two Major Options, *and*

(*b*) a project report on *either* advanced practical work, *or* other advanced work.

11. In cl. 10(*a*), the Major Options and their syllabuses shall be approved by the sub-faculty of Physics and the Physics Academic Committee. The titles of the Major Options are given in the Schedule below and the syllabuses shall be published in the Course Handbook not later than the beginning of Michaelmas Full Term for the examination three terms thence.

12. With respect to subjects under cl. 10(*a*) a candidate may propose to the Chairman of the sub-faculty of Physics or deputy, not later than the fourth week of Trinity Full Term in the academic year preceding the examination, another subject paper or papers. Candidates will be advised of the decision by the end of eighth week of that term.

13. In cl. 10(*b*), the proposed nature of the practical or other advanced work and its duration shall be submitted for approval to the Chairman of the sub-faculty of Physics or deputy with the agreement of the Physics Academic Committee.

Schedule

Fundamental Principles (Part A)

A1: *Thermal Physics*

A2: *Electromagnetism and Optics*

A3: *Quantum Physics*

Physics (Part B)

B1: *Atomic Structure, Special Relativity, and sub-Atomic Physics*
B2: *Condensed Matter Physics and Photonics*
B3: *Astrophysics and Atmospheric Physics*

Major Options (Part C)

C1: *Astrophysics*
C2: *Atoms, Lasers and Optics*
C3: *Condensed Matter Physics*
C4: *Particle Physics*
C5: *Physics of Atmospheres and Oceans*
C6: *Theoretical Physics*

Physics (three year course)

1. The examination shall be in two parts, A and B, taken at times not less than three and six terms, respectively, after passing the First Public Examination.

2. **Part A** of the examination shall be the same as the Part A of the examination of the four-year course in Physics and the same conditions, arrangements and examination timings shall apply.

3. **In Part B**

(*a*) the candidate shall be required

(i) to offer two written papers on Physics, *and*

(ii) to submit to the Examiners such evidence as they require of the successful completion of practical work normally pursued during one and a half terms in the academic year of the examination, *and*

(iii) to offer a written paper on one Short Option.

(*b*) to offer a project report in the form of *either* an extended essay on a subject approved by the Chairman of the sub-faculty of Physics or deputy (by the end of sixth week of Hilary Full Term), *or* an account of extended practical work undertaken in the academic year in which the examination takes place.

4. With respect to the two papers under cl. 3(*a*)(i), they shall be chosen from the list of Physics subjects specified in the Schedule of the four-year course (Part B).

5. With respect to cl. 3(*a*)(ii) a candidate may offer instead a written paper on a second Short Option.

6. The Short Options of cl. 3(*a*)(iii) and cl. 5 are those specified in cl. 6 of the four-year course.

7. In cl. 3(*a*)(ii), practical work may be replaced by project work, if an appropriate supervisor is available. The subject, duration, and replacement value shall be approved by the Chairman of the sub-faculty of Physics or deputy, by the end of Michaelmas Full Term.

8. With respect to cl. 3(*a*)(iii) a candidate may take, as alternative to the written examination, an assessed course of instruction in a foreign language. A candidate proposing to take this alternative must have the proposal approved by the Chairman of the sub-faculty of Physics or deputy and by the Director of the Language Teaching Centre or deputy, by the end of the first week of Hilary Full Term.

9. With respect to subjects under cl. 3(*a*)(iii) a candidate may propose to the Chairman of the sub-faculty of Physics or deputy, not later than the fourth week of Michaelmas Full Term preceding the examination, another subject paper. Candidates shall be advised of the decision by the end of eighth week of that term.

PASS SCHOOL OF PHYSICS

In the following 'the Course Handbook' refers to the Physics Undergraduate Course Handbook, published annually at the start of Michaelmas Term by the sub-faculty of Physics.

Candidates will be expected to show knowledge based on practical work.

The Examiners will permit the use of any hand-held calculator subject to the conditions set out under the heading 'Use of calculators in examinations' in the *Special Regulations concerning Examinations* and further elaborated in the Course Handbook.

Pass School of Physics (three year course)

1. Candidates shall be required to

(*a*) to satisfy the examiners in three papers on Fundamental Principles of Physics as specified for Part A of the Honour School of Physics (four-year course) (cl. 3(*a*)(i)), *and*

(*b*) to submit to the Examiners such evidence as they require of the successful completion of practical work normally pursued during the three terms preceding the examination, *and*

(*c*) to satisfy the examiners in one paper on Physics as specified for Part B of the three-year course of the Honour School of Physics (cl. 3(*a*)(i)), *and*

(*d*) to satisfy the examiners in one Short Option as specified for Part B of the three-year course of the Honour School of Physics (cl. 3(*a*)(iii)).

Pass School of Physics (four year course)

1. Candidates shall be required to

(*a*) to satisfy the examiners as prescribed for Parts A and B of the four-year course of the Honour School of Physics, *and*

(*b*) to satisfy the examiners in one Major Option paper as specified for Part C of the four-year course of the Honour School of Physics.]

NOTES

SPECIAL REGULATIONS FOR THE HONOUR SCHOOL OF PHYSICS AND PHILOSOPHY

[For candidates embarking on the Honour School in or after October 2002. (For candidates embarking on the Honour School in or before October 2001, see Addendum II at the back of the book).

A

1. The subject areas of the Honour School of Physics and Philosophy shall be (*a*) Physics and (*b*) Philosophy.

2. (1) All candidates must offer both (*a*) and (*b*).
   (2) The examination shall consist of three parts: Part A, Part B, and Part C.

3. (1) The name of a candidate in this school shall not be published in a Class List until he or she has completed all parts of the examination.
   (2) The Examiners shall be entitled to award a pass or classified Honours to candidates in this school who have reached a standard considered adequate; the Examiners shall give due consideration to the performance in all three parts of the examination.
   (3) A candidate who obtains only a pass or fails to satisfy the Examiners may enter again for Part C on one, but not more than one, subsequent occasion; Parts A and B shall be entered on one occasion only.
   (4) A candidate adjudged worthy of Honours in the Second Public Examination for the Honour School of Physics and Philosophy may supplicate for the Degree of Master of Physics if he or she has *both* taken Option 1 (Physics) under Part C of the Schedule *and* fulfilled all the conditions in Ch. I, Sect. 1, § 1, cl. 1.

4. No candidate may be admitted to the examination in this school unless he or she has either passed or been exempted from the First Public Examination.

5. The examination in this school shall be under the joint supervision of the Board of the Faculty of Philosophy and the Mathematical and Physical Sciences Board, which shall appoint a standing joint committee to make regulations concerning it, subject in all cases to clauses 1–4 above.

6. (1) The examiners for Physics shall be such of the Public Examiners in Physics in the Honour School of Physics as may be required; those for Philosophy shall be nominated by a committee of which three elected members shall be appointed by the Board of the Faculty of Philosophy.

(2) It shall be the duty of the Chairman of the Public Examiners in Physics in the Honour School of Physics to designate such of their number as may be required for Physics and Philosophy, and when this has been done and the Examiners for Philosophy have been nominated, the number of the Examiners in Physics and Philosophy shall be deemed to be complete.

1. The examination consists of Part A, Part B, and Part C, taken at times of not less than six, nine, and twelve terms from matriculation.

2. In Part A, candidates will take three papers in Physics and complete practical work in Physics, as specified in the *Schedule* below. In Part B, candidates will take three papers in Physics, as specified in the *Schedule* below, and will be examined on three subjects in Philosophy, one of these subjects being open to choice. In Part C, candidates will be required to offer one of four Options, as specified in the *Schedule* below.

3. The highest honours can be obtained by excellence either in Physics or Philosophy, provided that adequate knowledge is shown in the other subject areas. An honours classification will be awarded only if performance in both Physics and Philosophy is of honours standard either in Parts A and B taken together, or in Part C.

4. Candidates for Part B must give to the Registrar notice of their choice of the optional Philosophy subject not later than Friday in the eighth of the Michaelmas Full Term preceding that part of the examination. Candidates for Part C must give to the registrar notice of their choice of written papers not later than Friday in the eighth week of the Michaelmas Full Term preceding that part of the examination.

5. For the Physics papers, the Examiners will permit the use of any hand-held calculator subject to the conditions set out under the heading 'Use of calculators in examinations' in the *Special Regulations concerning Examinations* and further elaborated in the Physics Course Handbook.

Schedule

B

Part A

Physics

Candidates are required to

(i) offer three written papers on Fundamental Principles of Physics, *and*

(ii) submit to the Examiners such evidence as they require of the successful completion of practical work normally pursued during the three terms preceding the examination.

The titles of the written papers under (i) are given below. Their syllabuses shall be approved by the sub-faculty of physics and shall be published in the Physics Course Handbook not later than the beginning of Michaelmas Full Term for the examination three terms thence.

Fundamental Principles of Physics:

A1: *Thermal Physics*
A2P: *Electromagnetism*
A3: *Quantum Physics*

Part B

Physics

Candidates are required to offer

(i) two papers in Theoretical Physics, *and*
(ii) one paper in Physics.

The titles of the written papers under (i) and (ii) are given below. Their syllabuses shall be approved by the sub-faculty of physics and shall be published in the Physics Course Handbook not later than the beginning of Michaelmas Full Term for the examination three terms thence.

Theoretical Physics:

BT1: *Classical Mechanics*
BT2: *Electromagnetic Theory*

Physics (one of)

B1: *Atomic Physics, Special Relativity, and Sub-Atomic Physics*
B2: *Condensed Matter Physics and Photonics*
B3: *Astrophysics and Atmospheric Physics*

Philosophy

Candidates are required to take three subjects as specified in the provisions for Physics and Philosophy in the regulations for Philosophy in all Honour Schools including Philosophy.

Part C

Candidates are required to offer one of the following options

Option 1: Physics
Option 2: Physics with Philosophy
Option 3: Philosophy with Physics
Option 4: Philosophy

Option 1: Physics

Candidates are required to offer

(*a*) written papers in each of two major physics options, *and*
(*b*) a project report on *either* advanced practical work in physics *or* other advanced work in physics.

The options under (*a*) and the project under (*b*) shall be those specified in the published requirements and arrangements for Part C of the Honour School of Physics.

Option 2: Physics with Philosophy

Candidates are required to offer

(*a*) *either* written papers in each of two major physics options *or* one written paper in one major physics option together with a project report on either advanced practical work in physics or other advanced work in physics, *and*
(*b*) one subject in Philosophy as specified in the provisions for Physics and Philosophy in the regulations for Philosophy in all Honour Schools including Philosophy.

The options and project under (*a*) shall be those specified in the published requirements and arrangements for Part C of the Honour School of Physics.

Option 3: Philosophy with Physics

Candidates are required to offer

(*a*) two subjects in Philosophy as specified in the provisions for Physics and Philosophy in the regulations for Philosophy in all Honour Schools including Philosophy, *and*

(*b*) *Advanced Philosophy of Physics I*, the syllabus for which is as specified in the provisions for Physics and Philosophy in the Regulations for Philosophy in all Honour Schools including Philosophy, *and*

(*c*) *either* one written paper in one major physics option *or* a project report on either advanced practical work in physics or other advanced work in physics.

The option and project under (*c*) shall be those specified in the published requirements and arrangements for Part C of the Honour School of Physics.

Option 4: Philosophy

Candidates are required to offer four subjects in Philosophy, as specified in the provisions for Physics and Philosophy in the regulations for Philosophy in all Honour Schools including Philosophy.

PASS SCHOOL OF PHYSICS AND PHILOSOPHY

The examination consists of Part A, Part B, and Part C.

A candidate may be admitted to Part A of the examination no earlier than the sixth term from matriculation, to Part B of the examination no earlier than the ninth term after matriculation and to Part C of the examination no earlier than the twelfth term from matriculation.

In Part A, a candidate must offer two papers on the Fundamental Principles of Physics from those specified for Part A of the Honour School of Physics and Philosophy.

In Part B, a candidate must offer two subjects in Philosophy, which are 102 (*Knowledge and Reality*) and 120 (*Intermediate Philosophy of Physics*) as specified in the provisions for Physics and Philosophy in the Regulations for Philosophy in all Honour Schools involving Philosophy.

In Part C, a candidate must offer one paper in Physics and one subject in Philosophy. The physics paper shall be chosen from the list of Physics papers specified for Part B of the Honour School of Physics and Philosophy. The philosophy subject will be chosen from the subjects specified in the Regulations for Philosophy in all Honour Schools including Philosophy, except subjects 102, 105, 106, and 120; the arrangements for subject 199 are as specified in the provisions for Physics and Philosophy in those Regulations.]

SPECIAL REGULATIONS FOR THE HONOUR SCHOOL OF PSYCHOLOGY, PHILOSOPHY, AND PHYSIOLOGY

A

1. The branches of the Honour School of Psychology, Philosophy, and Physiology shall be Psychology, Philosophy, and Physiology. Candidates must offer two or three branches.

2. The examiners shall indicate in the class list issued by them the name(s) of the branch(es) in which each candidate has taken papers.

3. No candidate shall be admitted to the examination in this school unless he or she has either passed or been exempted from the First Public Examination.

4. For candidates offering Psychology, the examination shall consist of two parts. Part I shall consist of the one subject area, Psychology. Part II shall consist of two or three subject areas: Psychology, and one or both of Philosophy and Physiology. For candidates not taking Psychology Parts I and II, the examination shall consist only of papers in Physiology and Philosophy.

5. No candidate who offers Psychology shall be admitted for the Part II examination in this school unless

(*a*) he or she has passed the Part I examination specified for this school; and

(*b*) he or she has satisfied the Moderators for the Preliminary Examination for Psychology, Philosophy, and Physiology in the subject *Introduction to Probability Theory and Statistics* or has passed the Qualifying Examination in Statistics for this school.

The Head of the Department of Experimental Psychology may dispense a candidate from the Qualifying Examination in Statistics in cases where it is clear that the candidate has reached an adequate standard in Statistics by virtue of previous study and qualification.

6. Candidates offering Psychology shall be examined by such of the Public Examiners in the Honour School of Experimental Psychology as may be required; candidates offering Physiology shall be examined by such of the Public Examiners in Physiological Sciences in the Honour School of Natural Science as may be required; and candidates offering Philosophy shall be examined by

such examiners as are nominated by a committee of which the three elected members shall be appointed by the Board of the Faculty of Philosophy.

7. The examinations in this school shall be under the supervision of the Medical Sciences Board which shall make regulations concerning them subject always to the preceding clauses of this subsection.'

B

1. Decree (7) of 3 June 1947 permits the number of candidates offering Psychology to be limited, if necessary.

For candidates offering Psychology, the examination shall consist of two parts. Part I will consist of one subject area, Psychology. Part II will consist of two or three subject areas Psychology, and one or both of Philosophy and Physiology. For other candidates, the examination shall consist only of papers in Philosophy and Physiology.

Candidates taking papers in Psychology must take four papers for Part I and six papers for Part II. The four papers for Psychology Part I shall count as two papers for the Final Honour School. Other candidates must take eight subjects in all, except that where three or more subjects are taken in Physiological Sciences the total number of subjects required is seven. Candidates taking only seven subjects will be required to attend at least one practical class in Physiology. Not more than four subjects in Physiology may be taken.

No candidate who offers Psychology shall be admitted for the Part II examination in this school unless

(*a*) he or she has passed the Part I examination specified for this school, and

(*b*) he or she has satisfied the Moderators for the Preliminary Examination for Psychology, Philosophy, and Physiology in the subject *Introduction to Probability Theory and Statistics* or passed the Qualifying Examination in Statistics for this school. The Head of Department of Experimental Psychology may dispense a candidate from the Qualifying Examination in Statistics in cases where it is clear that the candidate has reached an adequate standard in Statistics by virtue of previous study and qualification.

The examination for Psychology Part I shall be taken during weeks 0 and 1 of Trinity Term of the candidate's second year. The examination for Psychology Part II and for Philosophy and Physiology shall be held during Trinity Term of the candidate's third year. The dates of submission for assessed work are those prescribed in sections 2–4 below.

The subjects in Psychology shall be those specified in 2. *Psychology* below; in Philosophy those listed in the *Regulations for Philosophy in all Honour Schools including Philosophy*, and in Physiology *the papers and the Dissertation listed under Physiological Sciences* in the *Honour School of Natural Science*.

Candidates may offer *either* a research project *or* a library dissertation in Psychology, *or* a thesis in Philosophy, *or* a dissertation in Physiology.

There are further restrictions on the choice of subjects and requirements to be satisfied within each branch, which are set out below.

The highest honours can be obtained by excellence in any of the branches offered, provided that the candidate has taken sufficient subjects in the branch and that adequate knowledge is shown in the other branch(es) of examination.

Every candidate shall give notice to the Registrar of all papers being offered not later than Friday in the eighth week of Michaelmas Full Term preceding the examination.

2. PSYCHOLOGY

PART I

1. The four written papers as specified for Part I of the Honour School of Experimental Psychology will be set:

Paper I Biological Bases of Behaviour.
Component parts: (i) Brain and Behaviour, (ii) Biology of Learning and Memory, (iii) Psychological Disorders.

Paper II Human Experimental Psychology
Component parts: (i) Perception, (ii) Memory, Attention, and Information Processing, (iii) Language and Cognition.

Paper III Social and Developmental Psychology, and Individual Differences.
Component parts: (i) Social Psychology, (ii) Developmental Psychology, (iii) Individual Differences.

Paper IV Experimental Design and Statistics.
Candidates will be required to show knowledge of *five* of the nine components of Papers I–III.

They may do so by offering *either* two papers of two hours and one paper of one hour *or* one paper of three hours and two papers of one hour. All candidates are required to offer Paper IV (one and a half hours).

In order to be deemed eligible for Graduate Membership of the British Psychological Society (BPS), candidates should ensure that the papers they take provide coverage of at least five of the six areas defined in the BPS Qualifying Examination syllabus. To do this, for paper I they must select at least one of components (i) and (ii); for paper II they must select at least one component, but *not both* components (ii) and (iii); and for paper III they must select at least two components. The other requirements for BPS Graduate Membership are set out in Part II below.

Candidates will be required to undertake practical work, as specified by the Head of Department of Experimental Psychology, and this will constitute a part of the examination. In exceptional circumstances the Proctors may dispense a candidate from the specified requirements on the recommendation of the Head of Department or deputy. Candidates shall submit to the chairman of examiners not later than tenth week in Hilary Term preceding the term in which the Part II examination is to be held, portfolios containing reports of their practical work. These portfolios shall be available to the examiners as a part of the examination. Each portfolio shall be accompanied by a certificate signed by the candidate indicating that the portfolio submitted is the candidate's own work. This certificate must be submitted separately in a sealed envelope addressed to the chairman of examiners. Where the work submitted has been produced in collaboration, the candidates shall indicate the extent of their own contributions. Reports of practical work previously submitted for the Honour School of Psychology, Philosophy, and Physiology may be resubmitted but reports will not be accepted if they have already been submitted, wholly or substantially, for another Honour School or degree of this University, or for a degree of any other institution. The Head of Department or deputy shall inform the examiners by the end of noughth week of the Trinity Term in which the Part II examination is to be held as to which candidates have failed to satisfy the requirement to undertake practical work or to submit a portfolio will result in a candidate's being deemed to have withdrawn from the examination under the Regulations of the

Proctors concerning Conduct at Examinations (see Special Regulations concerning Examinations). The Head of Department or deputy shall also make available records showing the extent to which candidates have adequately pursued a course of practical work. The examiners shall take this evidence into consideration along with evidence of unsatisfactory or distinguished performance in each portfolio of practical work.

A candidate who fails the Part I examination may retake the examination once only, in Michaelmas Term of the following academic year.

Qualifying Examination in Statistics

Any candidate offering Psychology who has not satisfied the Moderators for the Preliminary Examination for Psychology, Philosophy, and Physiology in the subject *Introduction to Probability Theory and Statistics* must pass a Qualifying Examination in Statistics before being admitted for examination in the Honour School. The Head of Department of Experimental Psychology shall have the capacity to dispense a candidate from the examination in cases where it is clear that an individual has reached an adequate standard by virtue of previous study and qualification.

The syllabus and paper set for the examination shall be that for the subject *Introduction to Probability Theory and Statistics* in the *Preliminary Examination for Psychology, Philosophy, and Physiology.*

For all papers in Psychology and for the Qualifying Examination in Statistics, the examiners will permit the use of any hand-held pocket calculator subject to the conditions set out under the heading 'Use of calculators in examinations' in the *Special Regulations concerning Examinations.*

PART II

(*a*) Candidates taking papers in Psychology

Candidates must offer six papers for Part II unless they are taking three or more subjects in Physiological Sciences in which case the total number of papers is five. At least one and at most three of the papers must be in Psychology, the others to be chosen from those available in Philosophy and/or Physiology below. Candidates taking three papers in Psychology may offer a research project or a Library Dissertation in place of one of the three Psychology papers. Candidates taking two papers in Psychology and three papers in Physiology may offer a Research Project in place of one of the two Psychology papers.

(*b*) Candidates not taking papers in Psychology

Candidates must offer eight papers for Part II unless they are taking three or more subjects in Physiological Sciences in which case the total number of papers is seven.

In order to be deemed eligible for Graduate Membership of the BPS, candidates must take at least two subjects in Psychology.

Written papers, research project, and Library Dissertation:

Each candidate will be examined in either one, two or three areas of Psychology by means of one, two or three written papers, each of three hours *or* two written papers, each of three hours, and *either* a research project *or* a Library Dissertation. The written papers will be selected from the list of at least 12 options approved by the Medical Sciences Division and published at the Department of Experimental Psychology, as specified for the Honour School of Experimental Psychology. A list of options will be posted in the Department of Experimental Psychology and sent to Senior Tutors of all colleges not later than noon on Monday of the first week of Hilary Term in the year preceding that in which the examination is taken.

Research Project

As specified for the Honour School of Experimental Psychology.

Library Dissertation
As specified for the Honour School of Experimental Psychology.

Candidates will be required to undertake practical work, as specified by the Head of Department of Experimental Psychology, and this will constitute a part of the examination. In exceptional circumstances the Proctors may dispense a candidate from the specified requirements on the recommendation of the Head of Department or deputy. Candidates shall submit to the chairman of examiners not later than tenth week in Hilary Term preceding the term in which the Part II examination is to be held, portfolios containing reports of their practical work. These portfolios shall be available to the examiners as a part of the examination. Each portfolio shall be accompanied by a certificate signed by the candidate indicating that the portfolio submitted is the candidate's own work. This certificate must be submitted separately in a sealed envelope addressed to the chairman of examiners. Where the work submitted has been produced in collaboration, the candidates shall indicate the extent of their own contributions. Reports of practical work previously submitted for the Honour School of Psychology, Philosophy, and Physiology may be resubmitted but reports will not be accepted if they have already been submitted, wholly or substantially, for another Honour School or degree of this University, or for a degree of any other institution. The Head of Department or deputy shall inform the examiners by the end of noughth week of the Trinity Term in which the Part II examination is to be held as to which candidates have failed to satisfy the requirement to undertake practical work. Failure to satisfy the requirement to undertake practical work or to submit a portfolio will result in a candidate's being deemed to have withdrawn from the examination under the Regulations of the Proctors concerning Conduct at Examinations (see Special Regulations concerning Examinations). The Head of Department or deputy shall also make available records showing the extent to which candidates have adequately pursued a course of practical work. The examiners shall take this evidence into consideration along with evidence of unsatisfactory or distinguished performance in each portfolio of practical work.

3. PHILOSOPHY

Candidates must satisfy both the General Regulations, and those relating specifically to Psychology, Philosophy, and Physiology, in the *Regulations for Philosophy in all Honour Schools including Philosophy.*

4. PHYSIOLOGY

Candidates may take any of the subjects (1) to (12) and the dissertation specified under Physiological Sciences in the Honour School of Natural Science. A dissertation may only be offered if at least three other papers in Physiology are taken and should be on a topic related to the physiological sciences as approved by or on behalf of the Medical Sciences Board.

The subject of a dissertation may be experimental work performed by the candidates themselves, or a report based on a temporary association with an extablished worker or research group (as when the necessary practical skills cannot be mastered in the time available), or a critical review based on individual reading. The dissertation shall be typed but need not be bound provided it is held firmly in a stiff cover. The dissertation shall not exceed 10,000 words (excluding figures, diagrams, and references), but a dissertation of 4,000–5,000 words will be considered ample when the candidate has performed an appreciable quantity of personal experimental work. Topics for dissertations shall be included on the list circulated by the Medical Sciences Board for candidates in the Honour School of Physiological Sciences and candidates may also propose topics not on that list in accordance with the same regulations.

The timetable for giving notice of an intention to offer a dissertation or for seeking approval for a dissertation not on the approved list shall be the same as those set out in the same regulations for candidates *not* on the Register of Medical Students.

Dissertations (two copies) must be sent to the Chairman of the Examiners of the Honour School of Psychology, Philosophy, and Physiology, Examination Schools, Oxford, not later than noon on the Friday of the second week of Trinity Term in which the examination is to be held. A certificate signed by the candidate indicating that the dissertation is the candidate's own work must be submitted in respect of each dissertation in a sealed envelope addressed to the chairman of examiners. Where the work submitted has been produced in collaboration the candidates shall indicate the extent of their own contributions.

Dissertations previously submitted for the Honour School of Psychology, Philosophy, and Physiology may be resubmitted. No dissertation will be accepted if it has already been submitted, wholly or substantially, for another Honour School or degree of this university, or for a degree of any other institution.

Candidates offering three or more papers in Physiology shall submit signed notebooks providing evidence of attendance at one practical class during their course of study provided that candidates offering a dissertation involving substantial laboratory work and also offering at least three papers in Psychology may apply to the Medical Sciences Board for exemption from one such practical class. Each notebook shall be accompanied by a certificate signed by the candidate indicating that the notebook submitted is the candidate's own work. This certificate must be submitted separately in a sealed envelope addressed to the chairman of examiners. Where the work submitted has been produced in collaboration the candidates shall indicate the extent of their own contributions. Any practical class which does not constitute a regular departmental practical shall be subject to approval by or on behalf of the Medical Sciences Board.

The signed notebooks shall be available to the examiners at any time prescribed by them before the written examination and shall be taken into consideration by them. The examiners may also require further examination of the candidate on practical work.

PASS SCHOOL OF PSYCHOLOGY, PHILOSOPHY, AND PHYSIOLOGY

1. Candidates may offer *either* Psychology and Philosophy *or* Philosophy and Physiology *or* Physiology and Psychology. Candidates must take six papers in all. These shall consist of three papers from one subject and three papers from the other, as prescribed for the Honour School of Psychology, Philosophy and Physiology, provided that candidates may offer a thesis in place of one paper in Philosophy or one paper in Physiology. The regulations governing the thesis shall be as prescribed for the Honour School of Psychology, Philosophy, and Physiology.

2. Candidates offering Psychology shall take the four papers for Part I as prescribed for the Honour School of Psychology, Philosophy and Physiology (these four papers count as two for the Final Honour School). They shall be required either to pass Part I before sitting the examinations for Part II. They are also required to have passed the Qualifying Examination in Statistics as prescribed for the Honour School of Psychology, Philosophy, and Physiology, or to have satisfied the Moderators for the Preliminary Examination in Psychology, Philosophy, and Physiology in the subject *Introduction to Probability Theory and Statistics* before sitting for the Pass School. Candidates offering Psychology shall offer for Part II one paper chosen from those prescribed for Psychology, and three papers from those prescribed for either Philosophy or Physiology for the Honour School of Psychology, Philosophy and Physiology.

SPECIAL REGULATIONS FOR THE HONOUR SCHOOL OF THEOLOGY

A

1. The examination in the Honour School of Theology shall include:

(1) Biblical Studies including such sections of the New Testament in Greek as the Board of the Faculty of Theology shall from time to time prescribe by regulation.

(2) Christian Doctrine and its Historical Context.

(3) The study of non-Christian religions.

(4) Such other subjects as the Board of the Faculty of Theology shall from time to time prescribe by regulation.

2. No candidate shall be admitted to examination in this school unless he or she has either passed or been exempted from the First Public Examination.

3. The examination in this school shall be under the supervision of the Board of the Faculty of Theology, which shall prescribe the necessary regulations.

B

1. All candidates will be required to offer eight papers, as specified below, from the Schedule of Papers. There shall be four compulsory papers, taken by all candidates, covering the Old and New Testaments and the development of Christian Doctrine in its historical context. In addition to these compulsory papers, candidates will be required to offer four further papers chosen according to the schedules in either Track I, Track II, or Track III.

Examination regulations applying to all Tracks

2. With the permission of the Board of the Faculty of Theology, any candidate may offer an essay *either* in place of one of the eight papers, *or* in addition to the eight required papers. The regulations governing essays are set out below.

3. Candidates not offering either paper (25) or (29) as optional papers may, in addition to their eight papers, also offer the *Optional Translation papers* in Old Testament Hebrew and/or New Testament Greek.

4. In papers (8) to (39), teaching may not be available every year on every subject.

5. Any candidate may be examined *viva voce*.

6. In the following regulations, the English version of the Bible used will be the New Revised Standard Version. The Greek text used will be the text of the United Bible Societies, 4th edn., but in paper (3), *The Synoptic Gospels*, parallel texts will be taken from K. Aland, *Synopsis Quattuor Evangeliorum* (15th edn., Stuttgart, Deutsche Bibel Gesellschaft, 1997). The Hebrew text used will be the *Biblia Hebraïca Stuttgartensia* (Stuttgart, 1977).

All candidates must offer eight subjects, as specified below, from the Schedule of Papers.

TRACK I

(i) Paper (1) *or* Paper (2)
(ii) Paper (3)
(iii) Paper (5)
(iv) Paper (6)
(v) Paper (7)
(vi) EITHER Paper (1) or Paper (2) (whichever paper is not offered under (i) above) OR one paper chosen from Papers (23), (24), (25), (26), (27) or (30)
(vii) One further paper.
(viii) One further paper.

Candidates may not offer Paper (4).

TRACK II

(i) Paper (1) *or* Paper (2)
(ii) Paper (3) *or* Paper (4) (candidates choosing Paper (3) must choose Paper (7) under (viii) below)
(iii) Paper (5)
(iv) Paper (6)
(v) One paper chosen from Papers (8), (9) or (10)
(vi) Paper (11)
(vii) EITHER Paper (12) or Paper (13)
OR a further option from Paper (11)
(viii) One further paper.

Candidates may not offer the following combination of options: Paper (3) and Paper (4), Paper (4) and Paper (7).

TRACK III

(i) Paper (1) *or* Paper (2)
(ii) Paper (3) *or* Paper (4) (candidates choosing Paper (3) must choose Paper (7) under (viii) below)
(iii) Paper (5)
(iv) Paper (6)
(v) Paper (14)
(vi) &
(vii) EITHER Papers (15) and (16) OR Papers (17) and (18) OR Papers (19) and (20) OR Papers (21) and (22)
(viii) One further paper.

Candidates may not offer the following combination of options: Paper (3) and Paper (4), Paper (4) and Paper (7).

Regulations concerning essays

1. Candidates may offer an extended essay *either* in place of the paper to be chosen under clause (viii) of Tracks I–III, *or* in addition to the eight required papers. Candidates should in general aim at a length of 10,000 words, but must not exceed 15,000 words (both figures inclusive of notes and appendices, but excluding bibliography).

2. Prior approval of the subject of the essay must be obtained from the Board of the Faculty of Theology. Such approval must be sought not later than Friday in the fourth week of Trinity Full Term in the year preceding the examination. The request for approval should be addressed to the Secretary of the Board of the Faculty of Theology, Humanities and Social Sciences Divisional Offices, 34 St Giles', Oxford OX1 3LH. The request must be accompanied by a letter from the tutor stating that

this subject has his or her approval. The application should include, in about 100 words, an explanation as to how the topic will be treated, and a brief bibliography.

3. The candidate's application for approval of title should be submitted through and with the support of his or her college tutor or the tutor with overall responsibility for his or her studies, from whom he or she should seek guidance on whether the subject is likely to be acceptable to the Board.

4. The candidate is advised to have an initial discussion with his or her supervisor regarding the proposed field of study, the sources available, and the method of presentation. He or she should have further discussions with his or her supervisor during the preparation of the essay. His or her supervisor may read and comment on drafts of the essay.

5. The subject of the essay need not fall within the areas covered by the papers listed in the Honour School of Theology. It may overlap any subject or period on which the candidate offers papers, but the candidate is warned against reproducing the content of his or her essay in any answer to a question in the examination. Subject to the provisions of cl. 4 above, every candidate shall sign a certificate to the effect that the essay is his or her own work and that it has not already been submitted (wholly or substantially) for a final honour school other than one involving Theology, or another degree of this University, or a degree of any other institution. This certificate shall be presented together with the essay. No essay shall, however, be ineligible because it has been or is being submitted for any prize of this University.

6. The candidate must submit two typed copies of the essay (bound or held firmly in a stiff cover), addressed to the Chairman of the Examiners, Honour School of Theology, Examination Schools, Oxford not later than noon on the Friday of the eighth week of Hilary Term in the academic year in which he or she is presenting himself or herself for examination. The certificate signed by the candidate in accordance with cl. 5 above must be submitted separately in a sealed envelope addressed to the Chairman of the Examiners at the above address at the same time as the copies are submitted.

7. The provisions of clauses 2–4 and clause 6 of these regulations will also apply to candidates submitting an extended essay as part of paper (39).

Schedule of papers

(1) *Israel to the end of the Exile*

The paper will include historical, literary, and theological questions, and candidates will be required to comment on passages from the following texts in English, showing knowledge of at least three of the five groups of texts:

(*a*) Exodus 1–3; 6; 12–15; 19; 20; 24.
(*b*) Isaiah 1–12; 28–32.
(*c*) Psalms 2; 18; 45–8; 72; 74; 77; 89; 93; 110; 132; 137.
(*d*) 2 Kings 18–25.
(*e*) Ezekiel 1–18.

There will be an opportunity to comment on passages in Hebrew from:
Exodus 20; 24.
Psalms 45–48.

Credit will be given to candidates demonstrating competence in Biblical Hebrew.

2. *Israel from the beginning of the Exile to 4* BC

The paper will include historical, literary, and theological questions, and candidates will be required to comment on passages from the following texts in English, showing knowledge of at least three of the five groups of texts:

(*a*) Job 1–14; 38–42.
(*b*) Nehemiah 1:1–11:2; 13.
(*c*) Jonah; Ruth.
(*d*) Daniel.
(*e*) Isaiah 40–55.

There will be an opportunity to comment on passages in Hebrew from:
Nehemiah 4–5.
Isaiah 40–1.

Credit will be given to candidates demonstrating competence in Biblical Hebrew.

(3) *The Synoptic Gospels*

Candidates will be expected to show a general knowledge of the Synoptic Gospels, their theology and ethics, literary and historical problems, and historical research concerning Jesus, and to comment on a passage in Greek from Matthew, and on a passage in Greek with English supplied from Matthew 3–13 inclusive with parallels in Mark and/or Luke. Candidates may restrict their comment to English texts if their other papers include translation and/or comment on at least two passages of Hebrew.

(4) *The Theology and Ethics of the New Testament* (with special reference to the gospels of Matthew and John, Romans, and I Corinthians)

Questions will be set on the theology of the individual gospels (not just those specified), Pauline theology, the historical Jesus, the ethics of the New Testament, and the different methods of New Testament interpretation.

There will be a compulsory question containing passages for comment from Matthew, John, Romans and 1 Corinthians, printed in both Greek and English. Candidates will be required to comment on four passages from at least three of the set texts. Candidates who have not passed either paper 6 (*New Testament Greek*) or paper 7 (*Biblical Hebrew*) in the Preliminary Examination for Theology will have to translate and comment on passages from Matthew 5–7, 26–8 and John 1–6 which will be printed only in Greek, unless their other papers include translation and/or comment on at least two passages of Hebrew.

The passages printed only in Greek will be optional for all other candidates.

(5) *The Development of Doctrine in the Early Church to AD 451*

Candidates will be expected to explain how early Christian thinkers undertook to clarify the teachings of the primitive Church and formulate a coherent system of thought in their cultural context. The paper will not only concern itself with formal pronouncements on the doctrines of the Trinity and Incarnation, but also with other controversies and the contributions of particular theologians.

Questions relevant to the Gnostic, Arian, Nestorian and Pelagian controversies will always be set; other questions may relate, wholly or partly, to such topics as anthropology, soteriology, hermeneutics, ecclesiology, political theology, and the doctrine of creation and the fall. Candidates will be required to comment on a passage from one of the following texts or group of texts:

The Nicene Definition, Arius' Letter to Eusebius, Arius' Letter to Alexander (from E. R. Hardy, *Christology of the Later Fathers*, Library of Christian Classics).

Gregory of Nyssa, *That there are not Three Gods* (in Hardy, *op. cit.*).

Cyril's Second Letter to Nestorius (in R. A. Norris, *The Christological Controversy*, Philadelphia: Fortress Press).

The tome of Leo and the Chalcedonian Definition (in Norris *op. cit.*).

Credit will be given to candidates who show knowledge (where appropriate) of the other texts contained in Norris.

(6) *God, Christ, and Salvation*

Questions will be set on the Christian doctrine of God, the person and work of Christ, and the nature of sin and salvation. Candidates will be expected to show critical understanding of the sources, content, and interrelation of these doctrines, and of some of the twentieth-century discussions of the material.

(7) *Paul and John*

Candidates will be expected to show a knowledge of the theological, ethical, literary and historical issues posed by (*a*) the Gospel of John, (*b*) Romans and (*c*) I Corinthians. They will be required to comment on passages from these texts in English, and will have the opportunity to translate and comment on John 1–10; Romans 3–8; and 1 Corinthians 1–7; 15 in Greek.

(8) *The History and Theology of Western Christianity, 1050–1350*

The paper will consist of questions on the thought of the leading theologians (especially Anselm, Peter Abelard, Aquinas, Duns Scotus, and William of Ockham), and of questions on the main developments in the western church. It will be so set that any period of 150 years, with its theological writers, will provide sufficient coverage.

(9) *The History and Theology of Western Christianity, 1500–1619*

The subject includes the work and thought of the leading reformers, especially Luther, Zwingli, and Calvin, together with the radicals, and the development of the Reformation in European society. Questions will be set both on renewal in the Roman Catholic Church, and on religious change in England from the Henrician reforms to the reign of James I.

(10) EITHER

A. *Christian Life and Thought in Europe, 1789–1914*

Candidates will be expected to show knowledge of the life and thought of the Christian Church (with special reference to Britain) and the development of Christian theology in its historical context. Candidates will be given opportunity to demonstrate knowledge of the following texts:

J. H. Newman, *The Via Media of the Anglican Church*, ed. with introduction and notes by H. D. Weidner (Clarendon Press, 1990).

S. Kierkegaard, *Philosophical Fragments*—Johannes Climacus, ed. and trans. by H. V. Hong and E. H. Hong (Princeton University Press, 1987).

L. Feuerbach, *The Essence of Christianity*, trans. G. Eliot (Harper/Prometheus Books, New York 1989).

A. Ritschl, *Justification and Reconciliation*, vol. 3 (T. & T. Clark, 1990 reprint 1996).

F. D. E. Schleiermacher, *On Religion. Speeches to its Cultured Despisers*, trans. by R. Crouter (Cambridge Universiy Press 1996).

OR

B. *Christology from Kant to Troeltsch, 1789–1914*

Candidates will be expected to show knowledge of the impact of modern philosophy and of cultural and historical criticism on Christology, as reflected in some of the following writers: Kant, Schleiermacher, Hegel, Strauss, Baur, Kierkegaard, Thomasius, Ritschl, Kähler, Nietzsche, Harnack, Wrede, Schweitzer, Kautsky and Troeltsch. Candidates will be required to comment on a selection of the following texts:

I. Kant, *Religion within the Limits of Reason Alone* (Harper Torchbooks, 1960), pp. 85–138.

F. D. E. Schleiermacher, *The Christian Faith* (T. & T. Clark, 1956), pp. 374–475.

G. W. F. Hegel, *Lectures on the Philosophy of Religion*, ed. P. C. Hodgson (University of California Press, 1985), vol. III, pp. 310–47.

D. F. Strauss, *The Life of Jesus Crtically Examined*, ed. P. C. Hodgson (Fortress, 1972), pp. 40–63 and 757–84; *The Christ of Faith and the Jesus of History*, ed. L. E. Keck (Fortress, 1977), pp. 19–37 and 159–69.

C. Thomasius, *Christ's Person and Work*, Part 2: The Person of the Mediator, in *God and Incarnation in Mid-Nineteenth Century German Theology*, ed. C. Welch (Oxford University Press, 1965), pp. 31–88.

A. Ritschl, *Justification and Reconciliation* (T. & T. Clark, 1900, reprint 1966), vol. III, pp. 385–484.

M. Kähler, *The So-Called Historical Jesus and the Historic Biblical Christ*, ed. C. E. Braaten (Fortress, 1964), pp. 46–97.

E. Troeltsch, 'The Significance of the Historical Existence of Jesus for Faith' in *Ernst Troeltsch: Writings on Theology and Religion*, ed. R. Morgan and M. Pye (Duckworth, 1977), pp. 182–207.

(11) *Further Studies in History and Doctrine*

Candidates will be expected to study one major theologian in relation to the situation and problems of the time, with special attention to certain texts. In the Trinity Term of each year the Board of the Faculty of Theology will publish a list of theologians (with texts) on which teaching will be provided in the following academic year and on which the examination will be based. In the event of a candidate's opting to take a year out after having studied a chosen theologian, the examiners will set questions on that theologian in the year of that candidate's examination, even if that theologian is not available for study that year. Texts will be studied in English. One or two optional questions may be set which will require knowledge of the texts in original languages when these are other than English.

A candidate may offer a second major theologian from amongst those available in the year of his or her examination. In the event that a candidate does choose to offer a second major theologian, that candidate will offer paper 11 as two papers. To facilitate this, separate papers (11(*a*), 11(*b*) etc.) will be set for each major theologian.

(12) *Philosophy of Religion*

The subject will include an examination of claims about the existence of God, and God's relation to the world: their meaning, the possibility of their truth, and the kind of justification which can or needs to be provided for them, and the philosophical problems raised by the existence of different religions. One or two questions may also be set on central claims peculiar to Christianity, such as the doctrines of the Trinity, Incarnation, and Atonement.

(13) *Christian Moral Reasoning*

Candidates will be expected to elucidate and assess themes in the Christian tradition of ethical teaching and their contribution to contemporary moral and social debates. The paper will consist of four sections (*a*) Christian Moral Concepts; (*b*) Government and its tasks; (*c*) Medical Ethics; (*d*) Sexual Ethics. Candidates will be required to answer three or four questions, of which at least one question must be answered from section (*a*), and at least one from another section.

(*a*) *Christian Moral Concepts*

The major moral concepts in Christian thought, such as: love, natural and revealed law, the supreme good, conscience, virtues, sin, justification, and grace; and contribution to contemporary discussions. Candidates may treat questions on these subjects *primarily* with reference to their sources in the Bible, if they so wish.

(*b*) *Government and its Tasks*

Theological interpretations of: justice, law and authority; forms of government, local national and international; government, society and the church; the coercive use of force in punishment and war, responsibilities for education, employment, economy, and environment.

(*c*) *Medical Ethics*

Such topics as: the doctor–patient relationship and its social context; planned parenthood, contraception, and abortion in both personal and social context; artificial reproduction, genetic manipulation; experimentation on humans; organ transplantation; priorities in treatment and research; the prolongation of life, terminal care, and the ending of life.

(*d*) *Sexual Ethics*

Such topics as celibacy, the goods of marriage, the sacramentality of marriage, divorce, polygamy, homosexuality, the sexual sins, the social differentiation of the sexes, the connection of body and soul in sexual contexts, erotic affection.

(14) *The Nature of Religion*

The paper will consist of questions on the main classical and contemporary approaches to the study of religions; the main attempts to define religion; differing approaches to the study of religion and anthropology, sociology, philosophy and theology; and the major explanations that have been offered for religious belief. Candidates should be aware of issues involved in claims for religious truth and rationality, and of twentieth century discussions of religious conflict and diversity.

(15) *Judaism I: The Formation of Rabbinic Judaism*

This paper examines the history of rabbinic Judaism from the first century CE to the Renaissance against the background of the societies in which it flourished.

(16) *Judaism II: Judaism in History and Society*

This paper examines the nature of modern Judaism against the background of recent history, including such topics as: the impact on Jewish thought and society of the Enlightenment and the Emancipation; the growth of Hasidism in the eighteenth and Reform in the nineteenth century; responses to the Holocaust, to the establishment of the State of Israel, and to the women's movement. *This paper may only be offered by candidates also offering paper 15.*

(17) *Islam I: the Classical Period of Islam*

This paper examines the historical development of theological thought in Islam, from the Prophet Muhammad to the end of the classical period (seventh to the fifteenth century CE). Particular attention is paid to (i) the interaction between the theology of *Kalâm* and the other major religious disciplines—exegesis (*tafsîr*) Tradition (*hadîth*), Law (*Fiqh*), sects (*firaq*), mysticism (*tasawwuf*), and philosophy (*falsafa*); (ii) the structuring of the doctrinal debate in respect of theodicy, prophetology, and humanism. Candidates will be expected to show knowledge of such texts (in English translation) as are prescribed by the Board of the Faculty of Theology in the Michaelmas Term of the academic year preceding the examination.

(18) *Islam II: Islam in the Modern World*

This paper examines the development of Islam as a world religion since 1500, paying special attention to Islamic religious thought in the nineteenth and twentieth centuries. Topics include: the historical, political, and ideological contexts; new interpretations of traditional sources; Islamic movements; Islamic modernism. Candidates will be expected to show knowledge of such primary texts and secondary sources (in English translation) as are prescribed by the Board of the Faculty of Theology in the Michaelmas Term of the academic year preceding the examination. *This paper may only be offered by candidates also offering paper (17).*

(19) *Buddhism I: Early Buddhist Doctrine and Practice*

The earliest Buddhist doctrine is studied against the background of the early Upanishads and other religious movements in north-east India about the fifth century BC. Practice includes both meditation and monastic life. The primary source is the Pali Canon supplemented by the commentarial literature of the Theravadin tradition.

(20) *Buddhism II: Buddhism in History and Society*

The paper falls into two main parts. The first part covers the history of Buddhism's diffusion through Asia, beginning with the emperor Asoka (third century BC); what forms of Buddhism have dominated which states and societies (and when), and their main similarities and differences; the development of Buddhist institutions. The second part deals with Buddhism in modern Asia. *This paper may only be offered by candidates also offering paper 19.*

(21) *Hinduism I*

Vedism, monism, traditional (*smărta*) ritual. This paper will be concerned with the main components of brahminical tradition; they are of ancient origin but still relevant today. The subject will be mainly studied with reference to the following concepts: *brahman, karman, mokṣa, saṃskāra, saṃnyāsa, yajña, śruti, smṛti, dharma, varṇa, āśrama, āśauca* (impurity), *dāna, tapas* (austerity), *bhakti, yoga, mantra, adhikāra, dīkṣā* (initiation).

(22) *Hinduism II*

Hindu theism. The principal sects/denominations. Theistic ritual and theology, including, in addition to the contents mentioned under Hinduism I, the concepts of *pūjā, prapatti, prasāda, sevā, nyāsa, śakti*. The main teachings of Rāmmohan Roy and Dayānanda Sarasvatī.

(23) *Selected topics (Old Testament) I*

Candidates will be required to show detailed knowledge of one of the following topics. They will be required to comment on passages from the prescribed texts in English (New Revised Standard Version), and will be given an opportunity to comment upon the Hebrew text of certain specified chapters and sections.

(i) *Prophecy*
1 Samuel 9; 10
2 Samuel 7
1 Kings 13; 18; 22
Isaiah 1; 5–8; 10; 40; 42–4; 49; 51–3; 55
Jeremiah 1–5; 7–9; 11; 12; 26–8; 31
Ezekiel 1–4; 8–11; 14; 18; 20; 23; 36; 37
Amos 1–5; 6–9
Zechariah 1–8; 13

Among these the following may be offered in Hebrew:
1 Kings 13; 18; 22
Isaiah 42–4
Amos 1–5

(ii) *Apocalyptic*
Isaiah 24–7
Daniel
Zechariah
1 Enoch 1–16 (ed. H. F. D. Sparks, *The Apocryphal Old Testament*, OUP, 1984)
2 Esdras 3–14
Revelation

Among these the following may be offered in Hebrew:
Isaiah 24–7
Zechariah 9–14

(24) *Selected topics (Old Testament) II*

Candidates will be required to show detailed knowledge of one of the following topics. They will be required to comment on passages from the prescribed texts in English (Revised Standard Version), and will be given an opportunity to comment upon the Hebrew text of certain selected chapters and sections.

(i) *Wisdom*
Proverbs 1–9; 22:17–31:31
Job 1–19; 38–42
Ecclesiastes
Wisdom of Solomon 1–9
Ecclesiasticus (Sirach) Prologue; 1:1–25:12; 36:18–43:33; 51

Among these the following may be offered in Hebrew:
Proverbs 1–9

(ii) *Worship and Liturgy*
Exodus 12–15; 19; 20; 24
Leviticus 1–7; 16
Deuteronomy 12–18
1 Kings 5–8
1 Chronicles 16
Psalms 2; 18; 24; 27; 47–51; 68; 72; 78; 89; 95–100; 110; 113–18; 122; 124; 126; 128; 130–2
A. E. Cowley, *Aramaic Papyri of the Fifth Century* BC (OUP, 1923), nos. 21; 30–4

Among these the following may be offered in Hebrew:
Exodus 19; 20; 24
Leviticus 16
Psalms 24; 95–100

(25) *The Hebrew of the Old Testament*

Candidates will be required to show a general knowledge of the language, with a special study of the following prose texts from which passages will be set for translation and comment:
Genesis 6–9
Exodus 20; 24
1 Kings 17–2 Kings 2
Nehemiah 4–6

Candidates will also be given an opportunity to show knowledge of Hebrew verse, and especially of the following texts, from which passages will be set for translation and comment:
Joel
Psalms 1; 23; 24; 45–8; 96
Isaiah 40–5

Candidates who do not offer Hebrew verse will not thereby be penalized.

(26) *Archaeology in relation to the Old Testament*

The subject includes the geography of Palestine and of the neighbouring lands; the history of the development of Canaanite, Hebrew and Jewish social life and culture; the history of places of worship and their furniture; and the general results of recent archaeological research in the Ancient Near East, insofar as they throw light on these subjects.

(27) *Religions and Mythology of the Ancient Near East*

The paper will include a wide range of questions. The following texts are prescribed for special study:

(*a*) Akkadian Myths and Epics: The Epic of Gilgamesh (standard version) and the Creation Epic, in S. Dalley, *Myths from Mesopotamia* (OUP, 1989), pp. 50–125, 233–74.

(*b*) Hittite Myths: The disappearance of Telepinu (version 1), The Song of Kumarbi, in H. A. Hoffner, *Hittite Myths* (Scholars Press, 1990), pp. 14–17, 40–3.

(*c*) Egyptian Myths, Hymns and Prayers: in M. Lichtheim, *Ancient Egyptian Literature* (Berkeley, University of California Press, 1975–1980), vol. I, pp. 51–7, 131–3; vol. II, pp. 81–132, 197–9, 203–23.

(*d*) Ugaritic Myths: Baal and Yam, The Palace of Baal, Baal and Mot, in J. C. L. Gibson, *Canaanite Myths and Legends* (2nd ed., T. & T. Clark, 1978).

(*e*) The Sefire Inscriptions, in J. C. L. Gibson, *Textbook of Syrian Semitic Inscriptions*, vol. II (OUP, 1975), pp. 18–56.

(*f*) Philo of Byblos' Phoenician History, in H. W. Attridge and R. A. Oden, *Philo of Byblos, The Phoenician History* (Catholic Biblical Association of America, 1981).

(28) *Luke–Acts, Epistles and Apocalypse*

Candidates will be expected to answer questions on *two* out of the following three sections, including comment questions on the English passages selected, where the text will be that of the New Revised Standard Version. The Greek texts also set for translation and comment (from United Bible Societies, 4th edn.) are optional.

(*a*) Luke–Acts, with Luke 19–24 and Acts 1–15 set in English for comment, and Luke 19–24 set in Greek for optional translation and comment.

(*b*) The Pauline corpus (13 epistles), with Galatians, Philippians and Ephesians set in English for comment; and Galatians set in Greek for optional comment.

(*c*) Hebrews to the Apocalypse, with Hebrews and 1 John set in English for comment and Hebrews 1–2 and 1 John set in Greek for optional comment.

(29) *The New Testament in Greek*

Candidates will choose passages for translation from amongst a number taken from the Greek New Testament and will be required to show a knowledge of the critical and theological issues involved in some of the passages they translate. The text used will be that of the United Bible Societies, 4th edn. The selection of passages set will allow this detailed knowledge to be limited to the following texts and chapters: Acts 20–6, Colossians, 1 and 2 Thessalonians, Hebrews 7–10, James, 1 and 2 Peter, Revelation 1–12. But there will also be opportunity to show such detailed knowledge outside these specified chapters.

(30) *Varieties of Judaism 100 BC–AD 100*

The paper will include a number of general questions and the following texts are prescribed for special study:

Set texts in English:

Qumran Community Rule, MMT (*Miqsat Ma'ase Ha-Torah*) (*Some Observances of the Law*) and *Commentary on Habakkuk*, in G. Vermes, *The Complete Dead Sea Scrolls in English* (Allen Lane/Penguin, 1997).

Josephus, *Jewish War* II (Loeb, 1956); *Antiquities* XVIII, 1–119 (Loeb, 1965); *Against Apion* II, 145–296 (Loeb, 1956).

IV Ezra, ed. B. M. Metzger, in J. H. Charlesworth, ed., *The Old Testament Pesudepigrapha* (2 vols., DLT, 1983–5).

Wisdom of Solomon (New Revised Standard Version).

Philo, *Migration of Abraham; Life of Moses* I, 1–84 (Loeb, 1958).

Mishnah, Berakoth, Bikkurim, and Aboth, chapter 1 (translated Danby, OUP, 1933).

Psalms of Solomon XVII, tr. S. P. Brock, in H. F. D. Sparks, ed., *The Apocryphal Old Testament* (OUP, 1984).

I Enoch 92–105, tr. M. A. Knibb, in Sparks, *op. cit.*

Any or all of the following texts may be offered in the original languages. Such questions will only be set when a candidate or candidates have given notice on the entry form of an intention to comment on texts in Hebrew and/or Greek.

Qumran Community Rule 1–4, in E. Lohse (ed.), *Die Texte aus Qumran, Hebräisch und Deutsch* (2nd end., Darmstadt, Wissenschaftliche Buchgesellschaft, 1971).

Qumran Commentary on Habakkuk, ed. E. Lohse, *op. cit.*

Josephus, *Antiquities* XVIII, 1–28, 63–4, 109–19 (Loeb, 1965).

Philo, *Life of Moses* I, 1–44 (Loeb, 1958).

(31) *The Beginnings of the Church and its Institutions to AD 170*

Candidates will be expected to show a knowledge of the history, worship, and institutions of the church in this period, including baptism, eucharist, forms of ministry, models of the church, house-churches, heresy and orthodoxy, apostolic tradition, appeals to scripture, relations with the synagogue, marriage, communications, diet. They will be required to comment on passages from the following texts in English translation:

Set Texts:

Ephesians, 1 & 2 Timothy, Titus, Jude, 1 Clement (Loeb Apostolic Fathers I, 1912) Chs. 1–6, 36–65.

Epistles of Ignatius (Loeb Apostolic Fathers I, 1912) to The Ephesians, Smyrneans, Philadelphians.

The Didache (Loeb Apostolic Fathers I, 1912).

The Epistle of Barnabas (Loeb Apostolic Fathers I, 1912).

Ptolemy's Letter to Flora. *New Eusebius* ed. J. Stevenson (revised edn., 1983).

Shepherd of Hermas, Vision 3 (Loeb Apostolic Fathers II, 1913).

Justin First Apology 31–41, 61–7 (1997) L. W. Barnard in Ancient Christian Writers Vol. 56 (Paulist NY, 1997).

Justin Dialogue with Trypho 47, 90–111 (Ante-Nicene Fathers, reprinted 1989).

The following may also be offered in Greek:

1 Timothy, 2 Timothy, Titus, Ignatius to the Ephesians (Loeb): Didache 7–16 (Loeb); Justin First, Apology 61, 65–7 (ed. M. Marcovich, 1994).

(32) *Early Liturgy*

Candidates will be expected to study the rites of initiation and the eucharist with the development of the Christian liturgical year up to AD 451 and the theology of liturgical worship in the light of anthropological, sociological, artistic and linguistic considerations.

The following texts are set for special study:

E. C. Whitaker, *Documents of the Baptismal Liturgy* (2nd edn., SPCK, 1970), pp. 1–19, 30–41, 44–50, 83–5, 127–33.

R. C. D. Jasper and G. J. Cuming, *Prayers of the Eucharist: Early and Reformed* (3rd edn., Pueblo, 1987), pp. 7–12, 20–44, 52–81, 88–113, 129–37, 143–67.

E. J. Yarnold, *The Awe-Inspiring Rites of Initiation* (2nd edn., T. & T. Clark, 1994) pp. 70–97.

J. Wilkinson, tr. and ed., *Egeria's Travels* (SPCK, 1971), pp. 123–47 (section 24 to the end).

(33) *Early Syriac Christianity*

Candidates will be expected to show a general knowledge of symbolism in the theology of the early Syriac Church.

The following texts are prescribed for special study:

Odes of Solomon 6, 11, 17, 19, 21, 24, 30, 36, 42, tr. J. A. Emerton in H. F. D. Sparks. *The Apocryphal Old Testament* (OUP, 1984).

Acts of Thomas, secs. 1–29, 108–14, tr. A. F. J. Klijn (E. J. Brill, 1962).

Aphrahat, *Demonstrations* 1, 4, 6, 12 (*Dem.* 1 and 6 tr. in J. Gwynn, ed. *Select Library of Nicene and Post-Nicene Fathers* II.13 [1898, repr. W. B. Eerdmans, 1956], Dem. 4, tr. S. P. Brock, *The Syriac Fathers on Prayer and the Spiritual Life* [1987], ch. 1; *Dem.* 12, tr. in J. Neusner, *Aphrahat and Judaism* [E. J. Brill, 1971]).

Ephrem, *Sermon on Our Lord*, tr. in E. Mathews and J. Amar, St Ephrem the Syrian.

Selected Prose Works (1994);

Hymns on the Nativity, nos. 1 and 2, tr. K. McVey, St Ephrem the Syrian. Hymns (*Classics of Western Spirituality*, 1989);

Hymns on Faith, no. 10, *Hymns on the Church*, no. 36; *Hymns on Epiphany*, nos. 1 and 6; tr. S. P. Brock in T. Finn, *Early Christian Baptism and the Catechumenate* (1992).

The Hymns, tr. S. P. Rock, *The Harp of the Spirit: Eighteen Poems of St Ephrem* (Fellowship of St Alban and St Sergius, 2nd edn. 1983).

Letter to Publius, tr. S. P. Brock, *Le Muséon* (1976)

Book of Steps, Homily 12, tr. R. Murray, *Symbols of Church and Kingdom* (CUP, 1975).

(34) *History and Theology of the Church in the Byzantine Empire from AD 1000 to AD 1453*

Candidates will be expected to show knowledge of the constitution and worship of the Church; monasticism; the development of mystical theology; the relations between Church and state and with the Western Church.

(35) *English Church and Mission 597–754*

Candidates will be expected to study the main lines of the history of the English Church in this period, and some aspects of its theology. There will also be an opportunity to study works of art. Candidates will be expected to have studied the texts in Group I, on which alone gobbets will be set, and in at least one of sections (*a*), (*b*), (*c*) in Group II.

Group I

(*a*) Bede, *Ecclesiastical History of the English People*, Preface, Bks I, 23–24; II; III; IV; V, 9–10, 19. (trans. L. Sherley-Price, revised R. E. Latham, with introduction and notes by D. H. Farmer, Penguin Classics, 1990) pp. 41–4, 72–265, 278–82, 300–6.

(*b*) *Bede's Letter to Egbert*, trans. D. H. Farmer, ibid., pp. 337–51.

(*c*) Bede, *On the Temple*, trans. S. Connolly, in J. O'Reilly (Liverpool University Press: Translated Texts for Historians 21, 1995), Prologue and Book I to I, 8.4, pp. 1–33; Book II, 18.8 to 20.9, pp. 76–100.

(*d*) *Eddius Stephanus, Life of Wilfrid* in *The Age of Bede* (ed. D. H. Farmer, trans. J. Webb, Penguin Classics, 1988) pp. 105–82.

(*e*) 'The Dream of the Rood', in *A Choice of Anglo-Saxon Verse*, ed. and trans. R. Hamer (Faber, 1970), pp. 161–71.

Group II

(*a*) *Adomnan of Iona, Life of St Columba*, ed. and trans. R. Sharpe, (Penguin Classics, 1995).

(*b*) Bede, *Life of Cuthbert*, in *The Age of Bede* (Penguin Classics, 1988), pp. 41–102.
Bede, *Lives of the Abbots of Wearmouth and Jarrow*, ibid., pp. 185–208.
Bede's Homily on the Gospel for the Feast of St Benedict Biscop, in *Bede, Homilies on the Gospels*, trans. L. T. Martin and D. Hurst, Preface by B. Ward (Cistercian Studies Series, 110, 1991), pp. 125–32.
Letters of Aldhelm, in *Aldhelm, The Prose Works*, trans. M. Lapidge and M. Herren (Boydell and Brewer, 1979), pp. 152–70.

(*c*) *Willibald's Life of St Boniface* and *The Correspondence of St Boniface*, in C. H. Talbot, *The Anglo-Saxon Missionaries in Germany* (Stead and Ward, 1954), pp. 25–62, 65–149.

(36) *Christian Spirituality*

Candidates will be expected to discuss Christian prayer in its theological, psychological and historical aspects, paying particular attention to contemplation and mystical prayer. There will be *four* groups of texts, and candidates will be expected to have studied *two* of them.

(*a*) *Patristics*
Gregory of Nyssa, *The Life of Moses*, Book 2, tr. A. J. Malherbe and E. Ferguson, *The Classics of Western Spirituality* (SPCK/Paulist Press, 1978) pp. 55–137.
Ps.-Macarius, *Homilies* 1, 5, 15, tr. G. A. Maloney, *The Classics of Western Spirituality* (SPCK/Paulist Press, 1992).
Evagrius Ponticus, *The Praktikos* and *Chapters on Prayer*. (Translations available in Faculty Library).
Ps.-Dionysius the Areopagite, *The Mystical Theology*. (Translations available in Faculty Library).

(*b*) *English Fourteenth-century Mysticism*
The Cloud of Unknowing, tr. J. Walsh, *The Classics of Western Spirituality* (PSPCK/Paulist Press, 1981).
Julian of Norwich: *Revelations of Divine Love*, tr. E. Colledge and J. Walsh, *The Classics of Western Spirituality* (SPCK/Paulist Press, 1978).

(*c*) *Spanish Mysticism*
Teresa of Avila, *The Interior Castle*, tr. Allison Peers in *Complete Works*, vol. II (Sheed and Ward, 1946), pp. 199–351.
John of the Cross, *Living Flame of Love*, 2nd redaction, tr. Allison Peers in *Complete Works*, vol. III (3 vols in one, Anthony Clarke, 1978) pp. 103–95.

(*d*) *The Wesleys and William Law*
Texts in A. C. Outler, ed., *John Wesley*, Library of Protestant Theology (OUP, 1964), pp. 197–231, 251–98 (i.e. Sermons on *Justification by Faith* and on *The Witness of the Spirit*; Discourse II on *The Law Established by Faith*; Sermon on *Christian Perfection; The Scripture Way of Salvation; Thoughts on Christian Perfection*.)
E. H. Sugden, ed., *The Standard Sermons of John Wesley*, vol. II (7th edn. Epworth Press, 1968). Sermons 32 (*The Nature of Enthusiasm*), 34 (*Catholic Spirit*), 39 (*New Birth*), 40 (*Wilderness State*).
H. A. Hodges and A. M. Allchin, *A Rapture of Praise: Hymns of John and Charles Wesley* (Hodder and Stoughton, 1966). The following hymns: 3. 9. 22. 27. 38. 54. 55. 81. 84. 90. 105, 118, 124, 126, 131.
William Law: *The Spirit of Prayer*: Part 1, ed. S. Spencer (James Clarke, 1969).

(37) *The Sociology of Religion*

The paper will consist of two parts. Candidates will be expected to answer at least one question from each part.

(*a*) *Texts*

Candidates will be expected to know at least **[Until 1 October 2004:** two**]** **[From 1 October 2004:** one**]** of the following in detail:

(i) **[Until 1 October 2004:** K. Marx, *Theses on Feuerbach* and *The German Ideology* ch. 1, ed. C. Arthur (Lawrence and Wishart, 1985),**]** **[From 1 October 2004:** Karl Marx, *Marx on Religion*, ed. John Raines, Temple University Press, 2002**]** together with *Capital*, chapters 1 and 13 (Penguin Books, 1990).

(ii) E. Durkheim, *The Elementary Forms of the Religious Life* (Allen and Unwin, 1976).

(iii) M. Weber, *The Protestant Ethic and the Spirit of Capitalism* (Harper Collins, 1991).

(iv) E. Troeltsch, *The Social Teaching of the Christian Churches* (2 vols., J. Knox, 1992).

[Until 1 October 2004: (v) *Religion and History*, ed. Adams (T. & T. Clark, 1991).**]**

(vi)**[**(v)**]** Talcott Parsons, *Action Theory and the Human Condition* (New York, 1978).

(*b*) *Themes*

Candidates will be expected **[Until 1 October 2004:** to be able to discuss the following issues in their relation to religious formations: class, gender, race, legitimation, power structures, violence, sects and cuts. Questions will be set on**]** **[From 1 October 2004:** to show an understanding of some of the following issues in sociology of religion: secularization, fundamentalism, church and sect, new religious movements, civil religion, fundamentalism. Questions will also be set on issues relating to class, race, legitimation, power and violence in religion and religious organization; and**]** sociological readings of other parts of the Theology syllabus, including Biblical studies, doctrine and Church history. Familiarity with contemporary sociological discussion will be assumed.

(38) *Psychology of Religion*

The paper will cover theories about aspects of behaviour or experiences relevant to religion and the empirical evidence on these theories. Psychological research methods and their applicability to different aspects of religion such as conversion, prayer, worship. Cognitive and non-cognitive (i.e. psychoanalytic and affective) accounts of religion. Normal and abnormal religious behaviour. Origin and development of religious concepts. Moral development. Constructs of theological psychology (e.g. soul; conscience, sin and guilt; repentance; forgiveness; mercy) and their status in contemporary psychology. Psychology applied to pastoral concerns: religious education; marriage; health; death and bereavement; substance abuse.

(39) *The Bible: Its Use and Influence*

Candidates for this paper will be expected to have an understanding of the authority and role of the Bible in theological and ethical discussion and in Christian practice and liturgy. There will also be an opportunity to consider theories of interpretation, the use of the Bible in non-academic as well as academic as well as academic contexts, and visual, dramatic and musical, as well as literary explorations of the Bible. A wide range of questions will be set, allowing candidates to concentrate on particular periods and issues. The Board (through the Handbook for Students in the Final Honour School of Theology) may prescribe for more detailed study the interpretation of one or more biblical texts. The paper will be examined by three hour written examination and short essay of not more than 3,000 words.

The provisions of cll. 2–4 and clause 6 of the regulations concerning essays will apply to the submission of the short essay, save that in cl. 2, approval must be sought not later than Friday in the fourth week of Michaelmas Term in the year of the examination.

(40) Any other subject that may be approved by the Board of the Faculty of Theology from time to time by regulation published in the *Gazette* and communicated to college tutors by the end of the first week of the Trinity Full Term in the academic year preceding the examination in which the option will be available.

Optional translation papers (2 hours each)

The translation components of papers (25), *The Hebrew of the Old Testament*, and (29), *The New Testament in Greek*, may be offered individually as optional extra papers by candidates who are not taking one or both of the full papers.

PASS SCHOOL OF THEOLOGY

1. Candidates will be required to offer six papers from the syllabus for the Honour School of Theology.

2. Amongst these six papers candidates will be required to offer at least one from amongst papers 1 (*Israel to the end of the Exile*), 2 (*Israel from the beginning of the Exile to 4 BC*), 3 (*The Synoptic Gospels*), and 4 (*The Theology and Ethics of the New Testament*); and at least one from amongst papers 5 (*The Development of Doctrine in the Early Church to AD 452*), 6 (Christian Doctrine and Interpretation), 8 (*The History and Theology of Western Christianity 1050–1350*), 9 (*The History and Theology of Western Christianity 1500–1619*) and 10 EITHER (*Christian Life and Thought in Europe 1789–1914*) OR (*Christology from Kant to Troeltsch 1789–1914*) of the syllabus for the Honour School of Theology. Candidates may not offer both paper 3 and paper 4. In paper 4 the question containing passages for comment will not be compulsory for candidates for the Pass School.

3. Candidates may offer extended essays in place of not more than two three-hour examination papers (excluding the two papers they are required to offer under cl. 2 above). The regulations concerning essays shall be as for the Honour School of Theology, save that essay subjects must fall within the area covered by the paper being replaced.

NOTES

REGULATIONS FOR THE DEGREE OF BACHELOR OF THEOLOGY

Ch. VI, Sect. XXXIV]

(i) General Regulations

1. The examination for the Degree of Bachelor of Theology shall be under the supervision of the Board of Faculty of Theology which shall have power to make regulations governing the examination.

2. Any person who has been admitted under the provisions of this section as a Student for the Degree of Bachelor of Theology, who has satisfied the conditions prescribed in this section, and who has satisfied the examiners for the degree may supplicate for the Degree of Bachelor of Theology.

3. No full-time student for the Degree of Bachelor of Theology shall be granted leave to supplicate unless, after admission, he or she has kept statutory residence and pursued his or her course of study at Oxford for at least nine terms. Time spent outside Oxford as part of an academic programme approved by the faculty board shall count towards residence for the purposes of this clause.

4. No full-time student for the Degree of Bachelor of Theology shall retain that status for more than twelve terms in all.

5. Part-time students for the Degree of Bachelor of Theology shall in each case be required to pursue their course of study for twice the number of terms required of an equivalent full-time student. Students taking the course wholly part-time may hold the status of Student for the Degree of Bachelor of Theology for up to twenty-one terms. Students may also pursue their course of study for two years full-time followed by part-time study, and in this case may hold the status of Student for the Degree of Bachelor of Theology for up to fifteen terms.

6. Part-time students shall not be required to keep statutory residence, but must attend for such instruction at their college for such times during full term as shall be required by the faculty board concerned, and must also attend at least one week's residential course each year, the total hours of attendance in each year of the course being as prescribed by the faculty board concerned.

7. Students for the Degree of Bachelor of Theology may supplicate for the Certificate in Theology after two years, provided

they have satisfied the course requirements as specified for the two-year Certificate in Theology.

Examination for the course of instruction at Blackfriars; Campion Hall; Greyfriars; Harris Manchester College; Mansfield College; Regent's Park College; Ripon College, Cuddesdon; St Benet's Hall; St Stephen's House; and Wycliffe Hall

8. There shall be a committee for the supervision of arrangements for the Degree of Bachelor of Theology called the Supervisory Committee for the Degree of Bachelor of Theology and the Theology Certificates. This committee shall consist of two representatives of the Board of the Faculty of Theology and one representative of each of the participating institutions, namely, Blackfriars; Campion Hall; Greyfriars; Harris Manchester College; Mansfield College; Regent's Park College; Ripon College, Cuddesdon; St Benet's Hall; St Stephen's House; and Wycliffe Hall. The committee shall have such powers and duties in respect of the Degree of Bachelor of Theology as may from time to time be prescribed by the Board of the Faculty of Theology.

9. Candidates for this degree may be admitted by Blackfriars; Campion Hall; Greyfriars; Harris Manchester College; Mansfield College; Regent's Park College; Ripon College, Cuddesdon; St Benet's Hall; St Stephen's House; and Wycliffe Hall.

10. The Registrar shall keep a register of all candidates so admitted.

(ii) Special Regulations

A. REGULATIONS FOR THE COURSE OF INSTRUCTION AT BLACKFRIARS; CAMPION HALL; GREYFRIARS; HARRIS MANCHESTER COLLEGE; MANSFIELD COLLEGE; REGENT'S PARK COLLEGE; RIPON COLLEGE, CUDDESDON; ST BENET'S HALL; ST STEPHEN'S HOUSE; AND WYCLIFFE HALL.

A. 1. *Course requirements*

(For those candidates admitted after 1 October 2000). Candidates must take at least *twelve* papers. In Part 1 candidates must take all four papers. In Part 2 they must take: two papers from section B; paper C1; and two papers out of D1, D2, and D3. The Supervisory Committee may dispense a candidate from individual compulsory papers on the basis of previous academic work, but not from the total number of papers required.

Details of which subjects may be taken by 5,000 or 7,000 word long essays in place of written examination papers are given in the syllabus in section B below.

A.2 *Examinations*

Candidates will be examined at the end of each academic year of their course of study. Examination will be held in April or May, beginning on the Monday of the second week of Trinity Term, and in September or October, at the end of the second week before Michaelmas Full Term.

Every candidate shall send through his or her college an entry form, showing the subject he or she intends to take in that year, to the Head Clerk, University Offices, Wellington Square, Oxford OX1 2JD, by noon on Friday of the fourth week of Hilary Term for the May examination, and by noon on Friday of the seventh week of Trinity Term for the Autumn examination. All entries shall be accompanied by certification of college approval and by the examination fee prescribed in Ch. VII, Sect. I, § 2 (see Appendix I).

The examiners may examine the candidate viva voce, no candidate who has passed in a subject may sit that examination again.

A candidate who has failed in more than two subjects in an examination shall be deemed to have failed in all the subjects offered at that examination. A candidate may offer at a subsequent examination a subject or subjects in which he or she has failed. Normally only one resit will be allowed in each subject, provided that the B.Th. Supervisory Committee shall have power in exceptional circumstances and on submission of a case by a candidate's college to approve a second resit.

A.3 *Long Essays*

Approval for the subjects proposed for 5,000 and 7,000 word long essays must be obtained from the B.Th. Supervisory Committee. Applications will be considered by the committee at three times during the year. The deadlines for submitting titles to these meetings are respectively: not later than noon on Friday in week four of Michaelmas Term, in week four of Hilary Term, or in week seven of Trinity Term. Candidates are advised to seek approval for titles as early as practicable in advance of the examination. Dated certification of the committee's approval must be retained for submission with the completed work.

A proposed long essay title must cover a theme within the rubric of the paper, and the application must include a list of four college-assessed pieces of work which adequately cover the syllabus. Certification from the college confirming that this other work has been satisfactorily completed must accompany the long essay when it is submitted.

Long essays must be the candidate's own work and accompanied by a statement from him or her to that effect, and must be typed on one side of the paper. Long essays must include a bibliography and, where appropriate, footnotes (only the latter being included in the word count). Candidates may receive tutorial guidance in the preliminary stages of composition, and tutors may also read or comment on a first draft.

Long essays must be submitted to the Chairman of the Examiners, Bachelor of Theology, c/o the Clerk of the Schools, High Street, Oxford OX1 4BG, not later than noon on the Friday before Trinity Full Term for work submitted as part of the May examination, and not later than noon on the second Monday before Michaelmas Full Term for work submitted as part of the Autumn examination.

The dated certification of the committee's approval of long essay titles, the certification from the college confirming that the other work in a subject area has been satisfactorily completed, and the signed statement from the candidate that the long essays are his/her own work must accompany the long essays when submitted for examination. For each paper, two copies of the essay or field study (marked A and B) must be submitted along with the accompanying certification which must be put in a sealed envelope marked with the paper number and the candidate's examination number. These items together must be submitted or sent to the Chairman of Examiners for the Bachelor of Theology, at the above address.

Note. All communications for the Supervisory Committee for the Degree of Bachelor of Theology should be addressed to the Secretary of the B.Th. Supervisory Committee, whose address may be obtained from each college's B.Th. course director or from the Theology Faculty Centre, 41 St Giles', Oxford OX1 3LW.

B. THE SYLLABUS

† assessed by three-hour written examination

‡ assessed by long essay of 5,000 words in Part 1 or 7,000 words in Part 2, along with four college-assessed pieces of work. Candidates must submit the titles of each long essay and the attendant college-assessed work to the Supervisory Committee for approval. Together these must adequately cover the syllabus of the paper or of the option(s) selected.

§ assessed by other means, as noted in the rubric.

Note that most papers may be examined by more than one means.

Full-time candidates must attempt all Part 1 papers in their first year. They may attempt Part 2 papers at any examination session following the first Trinity Term. Part-time candidates must attempt all Part 1 papers in their first two years. They may attempt Part 2 papers at any examination session after their first year, provided they have completed Part 1 or are completing it in the same session.

Part 1 papers will be assessed at first year level, and will be given reduced weighting in considering a candidate's degree classification or certificate award.

In all written examinations candidates will be provided with a copy of the New Revised Standard Version with the Apocrypha (Anglicized Edition), except when they are answering questions on Hebrew or Greek texts. Those who wish to answer questions on Hebrew or Greek texts must specify this on their entry forms. The texts used in these cases will be: *The Greek New Testament* (United Bible Societies, 4th edn. 1993); *Biblia Hebraica Stuttgartensia* (Stuttgart, 1977).

PART 1

This part addresses fundamental issues of Biblical Study, Christian Thought and Christian Ministry, laying a foundation for further study.

SECTION A. Foundation Studies

† A.1—Old Testament A

Candidates will study the Historical Books (from 1 Samuel to Nehemiah), the Prophets and the Psalms, including issues raised in their study and interpretation. They will also study in detail at least one of the following texts in English: 2 Samuel 1–12, Isaiah 1–12, Psalms 73–89.

† A.2—New Testament A

Candidates will study Matthew and 1 Corinthians, addressing such issues as methodology in New Testament study, the person and ministry of Jesus, the context and theology of the authors, and ecclesiological issues. They will also study in detail *either* Matthew 5–7, 26–8 and 1 Corinthians 11–15 in English, *or* Matthew 5–7 in Greek, *or* 1 Corinthians 11–12 in Greek.

†‡ A.3—Christian Life and Thought

Foundation studies in this discipline can take different routes:

Either **†‡ A.3.A—Foundations of Christian Thought**

Candidates will study some of the foundational issues involved in the study of Christian theology including faith, revelation, Scripture, authority, tradition, development, religious language, and the relationship of Christian theology to other disciplines.

Or **†‡ A.3.B—Development of Christian Life and Thought**

Candidates will study the development of Christian life and thought in its cultural and historical context, including issues of authority, spirituality and ministry within Christian communities; and sources and forms of theological reflection and conflict. They should demonstrate some awareness of primary sources (in translation).

Candidates will study the following foundational period:

(*a*) First to fifth centuries.

They may also study one of the following periods:

(*b*) Sixth to eleventh centuries;
(*c*) Eleventh to fourteenth centuries;
(*d*) Fifteenth and sixteenth centuries.

Candidates must specify the periods studied on their examination entrance forms; they cannot subsequently be assessed on these periods in Paper C.2.

†‡ A.4—Christian Witness and the Contemporary World

Candidates will study the relationship between Christian faith and contemporary culture, including religious and secular understandings of society, environment, personhood, and faith. Candidates will be expected to reflect on the practice of mission and pastoral care.

PART 2

SECTION B. BIBLICAL STUDIES

†‡ B.1—Old Testament B

Candidates will study the Pentateuch, Joshua, Judges, and the Writings (other than the Psalms), including issues raised in their study and interpretation. They will also study in detail *either* two of the following books in English: Genesis; Job; Daniel; *or* Genesis 1–4 and 12–15 in Hebrew. Candidates who wish to be assessed on texts in Hebrew must take this paper by written exam.

†‡ B.2—New Testament B

Candidates will study at least two of the following books: John, Romans, Hebrews; and broader issues of New Testament theology, ethics, and interpretation. They will study in detail texts from John, Romans, Hebrews in English; and they may study John 1–3, 6, 17, and/or Romans 5–8 in Greek. They may also study Mark, Luke, Acts, the Pastoral Epistles, and Revelation. Candidates who wish to be assessed on texts in Greek must take this paper by written exam.

†‡ B.3—Biblical Interpretation

Candidates will study Part A or Part B or both.

Part A: Candidates will study: central themes in both testaments such as God, creation, the people of God, redemption, messiah, community, worship, hope; and the methodological issues of constructing biblical theology.

Part B: Candidates will study the history and practice of biblical interpretation, including major contemporary trends.

SECTION C. DOCTRINE AND HISTORY

†‡ C.1—Christian Doctrine

Candidates will study the central doctrines of the Christian church, as set out in the historic creeds and formulae, including critical reflection on traditional and recent expositions of these doctrines and engagement with contemporary theological discussion.

†‡ C.2—Church History

Candidates will study the development of Christian life and thought in its cultural and historical context, including issues of authority, spirituality, and ministry within Christian communities; and sources and forms of theological reflection and conflict. They should demonstrate some awareness of primary sources (in translation).

Candidates must specify one period for assessment by written exam or long essay, which must not be one on which they were assessed in Paper A.3.B:

(*a*) First to fifth centuries;
(*b*) Sixth to eleventh centuries;
(*c*) Eleventh to fourteenth centuries;
(*d*) Fifteenth and sixteenth centuries;
(*e*) Seventeenth and eighteenth centuries;

(*f*) Nineteenth and twentieth centuries.

†‡ C.3—Ecclesiology

Candidates will study the theology of the church, including ministry and the sacraments, in its historical development annd contemporary practice.

†‡ C.4—Study of Theology

(Candidates who have taken A.3.A may not take this paper.)

Candidates will study some of the major issues involved in the study of Christian theology, including faith, revelation, reason, Scripture, authority, tradition, development, religious language, and the relationship of Christian thought to other disciplines and other religions.

SECTION D. PRACTICAL THEOLOGY

‡ D.1—Mission and Ministry

Candidates will study and reflect on issues of mission and ministry. College assessed essays should demonstrate knowledge of contributory disciplines. The long essay must be based on a supervised placement of at least twenty-one days in a church or secular setting in which the candidate shares in the experiences of those involved, and should contain theological reflection on the situation.

§ D.2—Christian Ethics

This paper will be assessed by two written papers:

(*a*) Ethics and Faith (three hour examination)
Candidates will study the foundations of Christian moral thought and practice; contemporary moral and social problems; and the relation of Christian moral life to faith, witness, and worship.

(*b*) Ethics and Ministry (two hour examination)
Candidates should demonstrate ethical and pastoral competence in analysis of, reflection on, and response to a particular situation. This will be a situation relating to sexuality, marriage, and the family, unless the Supervisory Committee gives notice otherwise.

†‡ D.3—Christian Worship

Candidates will study the history and theology of Christian initiation, the Eucharist, the daily worship; the place of prayer in worship; non-verbal aspects of liturgy and their cultural factors; relevant insights from the human sciences; word and sacrament, liturgical symbolism, and the place of preaching; worship and the Church's mission; other forms of corporate worship.

†‡ D.4—Christian Spirituality

Candidates will study the history and theology of Christian spirituality including major traditions and figures; and the relationship of spirituality to: scripture, liturgy, hymnody, doctrine, and current trends.

SECTION E. OTHER SUBJECTS

†‡ E.1—Christian Mission

Candidates will study the following: the biblical and theological foundations of mission; the relationshiip of the Church to the *missio Dei*; factors in the contemporary world affecting mission, such as industrialisation, urbanisation, secularism, pluralism, and new forms of imperialism. These subjects may be focused through the study of: the history of Christian mission; the distinction between mission and evangelism; the encounter with other faiths; issues of contextualization; apologetics; liberation movements; and the work of significant missiologists.

†‡ E.2—Christian Faith and Other Religions

Candidates will study methodology in the study of religion; Christian approaches to other religions; and one religion other than Christianity, chosen from (and to be specified on the entry form): Hinduism, Buddhism, post-Biblical Judaism, Islam, or a religion proposed by the candidate and approved by the Supervisory Committee.

†‡ E.3—Christian Faith and Philosophy

Candidates will study the relationship between Christianity and the Western philosophical tradition. They will also study relevant issues including: the relation between reason and revelation; the existence of God; the problem of evil; non-objective theism; religious language; religious experience; resurrection and the immortality of the soul.

†‡ E.4—Christian Faith and Science

Candidates will study the relationship between Christian theology and the development of modern science, including: methodology and epistemology in science and theology; the origin of the universe and humanity; the quantum world; the biosphere and ecosystems; and ethical issues of scientific research and development.

†‡ E.5—Christian Faith and Social Sciences

Candidates will study the relationship between Christian theology and the social sciences, including such areas as methodology in both disciplines; sociological and anthropological interpretations of religion; theological and sociological understandings of social phenomena; sociological understandings of religious organisation; and theological critiques of social sciences.

†‡ E.6—Christian Faith and Psychology

Candidates will study the contribution of psychological theory to pastoral theology and pastoral care, in areas such as: developmental theory and the life cycle; human sexuality; love and attachment; and mental health. They will also study: major psychological theories and their critique of religious systems; the counselling movement; the role of the pastor; the nature of pastoral ministry in relation to birth, marriage, and death.

†‡ E.7—Canon Law

Candidates will study the sources, history, and theology of Western canon law or the Eastern canonical tradition or both (to be specified on the entry form); and current systems of canons, e.g. the Roman Catholic *Code of Canon Law* and the *Canons of the Church of England*, including an introduction to comparative issues.

‡ E.8—Confessional Study

Candidates will study the tradition of a Christian denomination as expressed in its formularies, liturgy, spirituality, and ethics.

†‡ E.9—Special Subject

Candidates may propose a Special Study and assessment method for approval by the Supervisory Committee. This should include the title, a brief description of the subject and/or the proposed approach, and a preliminary bibliography.

NOTES

4

REGULATIONS FOR THE DEGREE OF MASTER OF ARTS

Ch. VI, Sect. III]

1. A Bachelor of Arts (other than one covered by the provisions of clause 2 below) or a Bachelor of Fine Art may, with the approval of his or her society, supplicate for the Degree of Master of Arts in or after the twenty-first term from his or her matriculation.

2. A Bachelor of Arts whose qualification for admission to a Final Honour School was the successful completion of a Foundation Course at the Department for Continuing Education may, with the approval of his or her society, supplicate for the Degree of Master of Arts in or after the eighteenth term from his or her matriculation.

3. A Bachelor of Arts or a Bachelor of Fine Art who has been admitted to the Degree of Doctor of Philosophy may supplicate for admission to the Degree of Master of Arts, provided that he has satisfied all other necessary conditions, at any time after his admission to the Degree of Doctor of Philosophy.

4. If a Bachelor of Civil Law or a Bachelor of Medicine shall first have been admitted to the Degree of Bachelor of Arts, he may supplicate for the Degree of Master of Arts with the approval of his society in or after the nineteenth term from his matriculation, and may retain the Degree of Bachelor of Civil Law or of Medicine, as the case may be.

NOTES

5

REGULATIONS FOR DEGREES IN MUSIC

Ch. VI, Sect. IV]

(i) General Regulations

§1. Qualifications of Candidates for the Degree of Bachelor of Music

Any persons who have been admitted to the Degree of Bachelor of Arts and have been placed in the First or Second Class (Division 1) in the Final Honour School of Music may apply to the Board of the Faculty of Music for the appointment of examiners and for leave to supplicate for the Degree of Bachelor of Music.

§2. Musical Exercise for the Degree of Bachelor of Music

1. Candidates shall submit to the Board of the Faculty of Music through the Secretary of Faculties a Musical Exercise of their own unaided composition. The board shall make and publish regulations concerning the type and content of the Exercise.

2. The Exercise shall be accompanied by:

(1) a statement signed by the candidate that the whole of the Exercise is his or her own unaided work and has not been submitted to any other person for advice, assistance, or revision or presented for examination in whole or in part in the Final Honour School of Music;

(2) a certificate signed by an officer of, or person deputed by, the society to which the candidate belongs, showing that the entry is made with the approval of such society and that he or she has paid the fee prescribed in Ch. VIII, Sect. 1, § 2 (see Appendix I).

3. The Musical Exercise shall be examined by at least two examiners appointed by the Board of the Faculty of Music. The examiners shall report to the board, and it shall be the duty of the board to decide whether leave to supplicate for the degree should be granted to the candidate, provided that such leave shall in no

case be granted unless the examiners have reported that the Exercise submitted by the candidate is of a high standard of merit such as to entitle him or her to supplicate for the Degree of Bachelor of Music.

4. Candidates shall not be permitted to submit their Exercise for approval earlier than the third term after that in which they have passed the examination in the Final Honour School of Music.

5. No candidate shall be permitted to supplicate for the Degree of Bachelor of Music who has not delivered his or her Exercise in a form approved by the examiners to the Secretary of Faculties, who shall deposit it in the Bodleian Library.

§3. Degree of Doctor of Music

1. Any person belonging to one of the following classes may apply to the Board of the Faculty of Music for leave to supplicate for the Degree of Doctor of Music:

(*a*) Persons who have been admitted to the Degree of Bachelor of Music at this University; provided that no Bachelor of Music may submit evidence for approval until he has entered upon the ninth term after that in which he was admitted to the Degree of Bachelor of Music;

(*b*) Masters of Arts who have incepted in this University and have entered upon the thirtieth term from their matriculation;

(*c*) Masters of Arts of the University of Cambridge or Dublin who have been incorporated in this University and have entered upon the thirtieth term from their matriculation at Cambridge or Dublin;

(*d*) Undergraduates or Bachelors of Arts of the University of Cambridge or Dublin who have been incorporated and have incepted in the Faculty of Arts in this University and have entered upon the thirtieth term from their matriculation at Cambridge or Dublin;

(*e*) Persons on whom the Degree of Master of Arts has been conferred by decree or special resolution, other than a degree *honoris causa,* and who have entered upon the ninth term from their admission to that degree.

2. A candidate for the Degree of Doctor of Music shall be required to submit through the Secretary of Faculties a major musical work or works of his own composition and of outstanding merit for approval by the Board of the Faculty of Music. The application shall be accompanied by:

(1) evidence that the candidates application has the approval of his society;

(2) the fee prescribed in Ch. VIII, Sect. 1, §2 (see Appendix I).

3. On receipt of an application under clause 2 above, the Secretary of Faculties shall submit it to the Board of the Faculty of Music as soon as may be, for approval. The board shall appoint judges to consider the works submitted by the candidate and to report thereon to the board. The board shall decide whether the evidence submitted by the candidate is of sufficient merit to entitle him to supplicate for the Degree of Doctor of Music.

4. If the board approves the evidence as of sufficient merit it shall give leave to the candidate to supplicate for the degree, and shall notify its decision in the *University Gazette.* One copy of each musical work so approved shall remain in the possession of the University for deposit in the Bodleian Library.

(ii) Special Regulations

DEGREE OF BACHELOR OF MUSIC

1. *The Exercise for the Degree of Bachelor of Music*

(*a*) The Exercise shall consist of a portfolio of three or more original musical compositions of varied character, lasting in total at least thirty minutes. Music for any combination of three or more of the categories specified below will be acceptable, provided that the portfolio includes some purely instrumental music and some vocal music with words. Candidates may also submit recordings of any of their works, and shall submit recordings of electro-acoustic compositions and of any pieces whose ordering or content is not fixed by the notation. The categories are (i) music for one or two instruments, or instrument and voice; (ii) music for choral or solo vocal ensemble, accompanied or unaccompanied; (iii) music for chamber ensemble, with or without voice or voices; (iv) music for larger forces than the above; (v) music involving electro-acoustic composition, accompanied by a commentary describing the technical procedures.

(*b*) A viva-voce examination may be held unless candidates are individually dispensed by the examiners.

2. *General Regulations about the Exercise*

(*a*) The score of each work must be written out so as to accord with the standards and methods that a professional performer, copyist, or publisher would expect, with rehearsal letters and/or regular bar-numbering. The pages should be numbered consecutively throughout the portfolio.

(*b*) **The Exercise must be accompanied by a declaration on a prescribed form, which must be obtained beforehand by application to the Clerk of the Examination Schools, High Street, Oxford. It must be sent in by the Friday in Trinity Term in the fifth week.**

FORM OF DECLARATION

I, ...
hereby declare that these compositions are entirely my own unaided work and that no part of them has been presented for examination on any previous occasion.

Signed ....

....College,
in the presence of

....

Witnesses' names and addresses in full.

....

....

....

Date ....

The Exercise must show the private address as well as the name and college of the composer.

It must be strongly bound and paged, and lettered (with clearly stamped lettering) up the spine with title and composer's name, and also on the outside cover with title, name, and college, and the words 'B.Mus. Exercise'.

Any electronic tape submitted in addition to the Exercise must be in a box on which the title, the composer's name and college, and the words 'B.Mus. Exercise' are again clearly shown.

DEGREE OF DOCTOR OF MUSIC

A candidate is required to submit for approval by the board of the faculty a major musical work or works of his own composition and of outstanding merit. Two copies of each work must be submitted

Evidence submitted for the Degree of Doctor of Music

The work or works submitted must show the private address as well as the name and college of the composer. The work or works must be strongly bound and paged, and lettered (with clearly stamped lettering) up the spine with title and composer's name, and also on the outside cover with title, name, and college, and the degree for which it was composed.

6

REGULATIONS FOR THE DEGREE OF BACHELOR OF PHILOSOPHY OR MASTER OF PHILOSOPHY

Ch. VI, Sect. VI]

General Regulations

§1. Degrees of Bachelor and Master of Philosophy

1. Any person who has kept six terms of statutory residence after admission as a student for the Degree of Bachelor or Master of Philosophy (or, in the case of a Student for the Degree of Doctor of Philosophy or Student for the Degree of Master of Letters or Student for the Degree of Master of Studies who has transferred to the Degree of Bachelor or Master of Philosophy, after his or her admission as a Student for the Degree of Doctor of Philosophy or Student for the Degree of Master of Letters or Student for the Degree of Master of Studies, as the case may be), and who has satisfied the examiners in one of the examinations hereinafter provided may supplicate for the Degree of Bachelor or Master of Philosophy as appropriate; provided that the board or other authority specified in cl. 3 of §2 below may dispense a student on application through his or her college and with the support of his or her supervisor from not more than two terms of such statutory residence if he or she has been granted leave to pursue his or her course of study at some other place than Oxford for those terms under the provisions of cl. 2(*c*) of §3 hereof.

2. A Student for the Degree of Bachelor or Master of Philosophy who is not a graduate of the University may wear the same gown as that worn by Students for the Degree of Doctor of Philosophy.

§2. Examinations for the Degrees of Bachelor and Master of Philosophy

1. For the Degree of Bachelor of Philosophy there shall be an examination in Philosophy.

For the Degree of Master of Philosophy there shall be examinations in Byzantine Studies, Celtic Studies, Classical Archaeology, Comparative Social Research, Development Studies, Eastern Christian Studies, Economic and Social History, Economics, English

Studies, Ethnology and Museum Ethnography, European Archaeology, European Literature, General Linguistics and Comparative Philology, Greek and Latin Languages and Literature, Greek and/or Roman History, History of Science, Medicine, and Technology, International Relations, Judaism and Christianity in the Graeco-Roman World, Latin American Studies, Mathematics for Industry, Modern European History, Music, Oriental Studies, Philosophical Theology, Politics (Comparative Government, Political Theory, European Politics and Society), Russian and East European Studies, Slavonic Studies, Social Anthropology, Sociology, Theology, World Archaeology, and such other subjects as the University may hereafter determine.

2. There shall be a Register of students who are studying for the Degrees of Bachelor and Master of Philosophy which shall be entitled the Register of Bachelor and Master of Philosophy Students and the University may from time to time determine by decree the conditions of admission to the Register.

3. Subject to such regulations as the University may make under the provisions of cl. 2, any person who has obtained permission from the board concerned (or other authority as hereinafter specified) may enter for the examinations as follows. The bodies specified below shall be responsible for the examinations as listed.

Byzantine Studies—Classics and Modern History
Celtic Studies—Modern Languages
Classical Archaeology—Life and Environmental Sciences
Comparative Social Policy—Social Sciences
Development Studies—Inter-faculty Committee for Queen Elizabeth House
Eastern Christian Studies—Oriental Studies and Theology
Economic and Social History—Modern History
Economics—Social Sciences
English Studies—English Language and Literature
European Archaeology—Life and Environmental Sciences
European Literature—Modern Languages
General Linguistics and Comparative Philology—Committee for Comparative Philology and General Linguistics
Greek and/or Latin Languages and Literature } Classics
Greek and/or Roman History } Classics
History of Science, Medicine, and Technology—Modern History
International Relations—Social Sciences
Judaism and Christianity in the Graeco-Roman World—Oriental Studies and Theology

Latin American Studies—Area and Development Studies Committee
Law—Law (see Ch. VI, Sect. X*)
Material Anthropology and Museum Ethnography—Life and Environmental Sciences
Mathematics for Industry—Mathematical and Physical Sciences
Medical Anthropology and Museum Anthropology—Life and Environmental Sciences
Modern European History—Modern History
Music—Music
Oriental Studies—Oriental Studies
Philosophical Theology—Theology
Philosophy (Bachelor of Philosophy)—Philosophy
Politics (Comparative Government, Political Theory, European Politics and Society)—Social Sciences
Russian and East European Studies—Area and Development Studies Committee
Slavonic Studies—Modern Languages
Social Anthropology—Life and Environmental Sciences
Sociology—Social Sciences
Theology—Theology
World Archaeology—Life and Environmental Sciences

The subjects of each examination shall be determined by regulation of the board or other authority concerned, which shall have power to include therein a thesis written by the candidate on a subject approved by the board or other authority or by a person or persons to whom the board or other authority may delegate the function of giving such approval. The thesis submitted shall be wholly or substantially the result of work undertaken while a candidate is studying for the Degree of Bachelor or Master of Philosophy, except that a candidate may make application for dispensation from this requirement to the Educational Policy and Standards Committee not later than the fourth term after his or her admission to the Register of Bachelor and Master of Philosophy Students.

4. A candidate who has failed to satisfy the examiners in any one of the examinations for the Degrees of Bachelor or Master of Philosophy may enter again for that examination on one (but not more than one) subsequent occasion.

§3. Register of Students for the Degree

1. The Secretary of Faculties shall keep a Register of students who are studying for the Degrees of Bachelor or Master of

* See p. 887.

Philosophy. The Register shall be entitled the Register of Bachelor and Master of Philosophy Students.

2. No candidate for the Degree of Bachelor or Master of Philosophy shall be admitted to the examination for the degree unless

(*a*) he or she has applied through the Head or a tutor of his or her college to the Secretary of Faculties to have his or her name entered by the appropriate board or other authority on the Register of Bachelor and Master of Philosophy Students;

(*b*) his or her name shall have been kept on the Register for at least six terms inclusive of the term in which it was placed on the Register;

(*c*) he or she shall have pursued his or her course of study at Oxford for not less than six terms, except that the board or other authority concerned may grant him or her leave of absence for up to two of these terms if it is desirable in the interests of his or her work that he or she should be allowed to pursue his or her studies at some other place; time spent outside Oxford during term as part of an academic programme approved by Council shall count towards residence for the purpose of this clause:

Provided that

(i) a graduate may be admitted to the examination after his or her name has been on the Register and he or she has pursued his or her course of study at Oxford for only four or five terms if he or she has been given leave by the appropriate board or other authority to enter for the examination;

(ii) a Student for the Degree of Doctor of Philosophy or Student for the Degree of Master of Letters or Student for the Degree of Master of Studies or a Diploma Student may apply through his or her college to the appropriate board or other authority for the transference of his or her name to the Register of Students for the Degrees of Bachelor and Master of Philosophy and, if it is transferred, the number of terms he or she held the status of Student for the Degree of Doctor of Philosophy or Student for the Degree of Master of Letters or Student for the Degree of Master of Studies or Diploma Student shall be reckoned for the purpose of this clause;

3. No person shall attend seminars or advanced classes for Bachelor or Master of Philosophy Students unless his or her name

is on the Register of Bachelor and Master of Philosophy Students: Provided that the holder of a seminar or advanced class may give leave to a person who is not studying for the Degree of Bachelor or Master of Philosophy to attend his or her seminar or advanced class.

4. Any person shall be entitled to have his name entered on the Register of Bachelor and Master of Philosophy Students if he has obtained permission from the appropriate faculty board or other authority under the provisions of Ch. VI, Sect. VI, §2, cl. 3, provided he or she has matriculated as a member of the University.
5. The name of any Bachelor and Master of Philosophy Student may be removed from the Register by the body which entered it.
6. No name shall remain on the Register for more than twelve terms in all.
7. A Student for the Degree of Master of Philosophy shall cease to hold that status if:
   (i) he or she shall have been refused permission to supplicate for the Degree of Master of Philosophy;
   (ii) the board concerned shall, in accordance with provisions set down by regulation by the Educational Policy and Standards Committee, and after consultation with the student's society and supervisor, have deprived the student of such status;
   (iii) he or she shall have been transferred under the relevant provisions to another status;
   (iv) he or she shall not have entered for the relevant examination within the time specified under this subsection.

§4. Supervision of Students for the Degrees

1. Any board or other authority having power to make regulations for the subjects for the Degrees of Bachelor and Master of Philosophy may place a student for those degrees under the supervision of a graduate member of the University or other competent person selected by it, and it shall have power, for sufficient reason, to change the supervisor of any student. If a student requires special supervision in some branch of his or her studies, the supervisor may give this himself or herself or, with the approval of the board or other authority concerned, arrange for it to be given by some other person or persons.

2. A supervisor shall send a report on the progress of a student to the board at the end of each term (excepting the term in which the student is admitted to the examination) and at any other time

when the board so requires or he or she deems it expedient. The supervisor shall communicate the contents of the report to the student on each occasion that a report is made, so that the student is aware of the supervisor's assessment of his or her work during the period in question. In addition he or she shall inform the board if he or she is of the opinion that a student is unlikely to reach the standard required for the Degree of Bachelor or Master of Philosophy.*

§5. Examination Regulations

1. *Notice of Options*

In the Michaelmas Full Term preceding the examination, candidates must give notice to the Secretary of Faculties of all the subjects and options which they intend to offer, together with the subject of their thesis (if offered) by the following weeks:

B.Phil. in Philosophy	By Friday in the second week†
M.Phil. in Classical Archaeology and in European Archaeology and in World Archaeology and M.Phil. in Comparative Social Policy	By Friday in the eighth week†
All other M.Phil. courses	By Friday in the second week†

2. *Preparation and dispatch of B.Phil. and M.Phil. theses*

The theses (**two copies**) must be typewritten and sent to the Chairman of the Examiners for the Degree of B.Phil. [or M.Phil.], c/o the Clerk of the Schools, High Street, Oxford, at least fourteen days before the first day of the examination, **except where stated otherwise in the particular regulations for individual courses in the following pages.**

The parcel should bear the words 'B.PHIL. [or M.PHIL.] THESIS IN [here insert subject]' in **BLOCK CAPITALS** in the bottom left-hand corner. The thesis must be printed or typed on one side of the paper only, with a margin of 3 to 3.5 cms on the left-hand edge of each page, and must be securely and firmly bound in either hard or soft covers. Loose-leaf binding is not acceptable.

* Notification to the examiners of factors which may affect a candidate's performance in the examination. It should be noted that Ch. VI, Sect. II. c, §4, cl. 8 applies to examinations for the Degree of B.Phil. or M.Phil. This provision prescribes the procedure which should be followed if it is considered that the performance of a candidate in any part of the examination may be affected by factors of which the examiners have no knowledge.

† The attention of candidates is drawn to pp. 1058–9 concerning late entry and failure to give notice of options by the due date.

3. *Deposit of theses or dissertations in a university library*

If the examiners are satisfied that the candidate's thesis or dissertation, as submitted, is of sufficient merit but they consider, nevertheless, that before the thesis is deposited in a university library the candidate should make minor corrections, they may require the candidate to correct the thesis to their satisfaction. The library copy of the thesis must be hard bound.

4. ***Submission of theses, dissertations and other material***

Except where otherwise indicated, all material submitted for examination (dissertations, extended essays, etc) shall be accompanied by a statement signed by the candidate indicating that it is the candidate's own work, except where otherwise specified. This statement must be submitted separately in a sealed envelope addressed to the chairman of examiners of the degree course in question.

SPECIAL REGULATIONS

Bachelor of Philosophy

Philosophy

The regulations made by the Board of the Faculty of Philosophy are as follows:

Each candidate will be admitted to take the examination in a specific year, which will normally be the academical year after that in which his or her name was first entered on the Register of B.Phil. and M.Phil. students. Any candidate who wishes to take an examination later than the one to which he or she has been admitted must apply to the Graduate Studies Committee in Philosophy for permission to do so not later than Friday of the second week of the Michaelmas Full Term of the year in which he or she was to have taken the examination.

Every candidate must offer:

(1). Three subjects from the following list, of which at least one must be from Part A and at least one from Part B. Candidates must inform the Graduate Studies Committee in Philosophy of the subjects they intend to offer as soon as they have made their decision and in any case not later than Friday of the second week of Michaelmas Full Term of the year of the examination. Candidates may, if special permission is given by the Graduate Studies Committee in Philosophy, offer subjects not included in this list. The candidate should seek the approval of the Graduate Studies Committee in Philosophy, with his or her supervisor's support, for a subject not on the approved list *as soon as the candidate decides that he or she would like to offer it*, and in any case by the Friday of the fifth week of the Hilary Full Term of the year preceding the year of the examination so that, if it is *not* approved, the candidate has as much time as possible to work on an alternative.

Part A

Chosen Philosophical Authorities, i.e. the cardinal doctrines of some major philosopher or group of philosophers, and Chosen Periods of Scientific Thought.

(*a*) Plato
(*b*) Aristotle
(*c*) Medieval Philosophers
(*d*) Early Modern Philosophy from Descartes to Reid. Candidates will be required to show detailed knowledge of the philosophical ideas of at least two of the following: Descartes, Spinoza, Malebranche, Locke, Leibniz, Berkeley, Hume, and Reid
(*e*) Kant
(*f*) *Either* Hegel *or* Political Theories of Hegel and Marx
(*g*) Frege
(*h*) Wittgenstein
(*i*) The original authorities for the Rise of Modern Logic. The period of scientific thought to be covered is from 1879 to 1931 and includes principally the logical and foundational works of Frege, Russell, Hilbert, Brouwer, and Godel that fall within this period. Questions may also be asked concerning Cantor, Dedekind, Poincaré, Zermelo, Skolem, Wittgenstein (*Tractatus* only), and Ramsey
(*j*) The historical and critical study of ideas on scientific explanation and method in relation to certain fundamental scientific problems and theories in *one* of the following periods: seventeenth-century physics; nineteenth-century biology.

Part B

(*k*) Moral Philosophy
(*l*) Philosophy of Religion
(*m*) Political Philosophy and Philosophy of Law
(*n*) Metaphysics and the Theory of Knowledge. At least two essay topics will be set in each part of the subject
(*o*) Philosophical Logic and Philosophy of Language
(*p*) Formal Logic
(*q*) Philosophy of Science
(*r*) Philosophy of Art
(*s*) Philosophy of Mind and Action.

Candidates will be examined by submitting two essays on each subject they offer. Topics for essays will be prescribed by the examiners on every subject offered by any candidate and will be published on the notice board of the Examination Schools, High Street, Oxford, OX1 4BG, on the morning of the Wednesday of the sixth week of Michaelmas Full Term in the year in which the examination is to be taken. The examiners shall (i) offer a choice of topics in each subject, (ii) for each subject set an upper limit, which shall in no case exceed 10,000 words, to the total extent of the two essays together. A penalty may be imposed on any work that exceeds this limit. Two copies of each essay submitted must be delivered to the Clerk of the Schools at the above address by 10 a.m. on the Wednesday of the sixth week of Hilary Full Term in the year in which the examination is to be taken. Essays must be typed or printed. Candidates who on any of their subjects have not delivered essays as prescribed by the due date shall, unless they show exceptional cause to the examiners, be deemed to have withdrawn from the examination.

Candidates are not permitted to seek or accept any help, even bibliographical, from supervisors or anybody else, with the preparation of essays.

(2)* A thesis of not more than 30,000 words, exclusive of bibliographical references, on a subject proposed by the candidate in consultation with his or her supervisor, and approved by the Graduate Studies Committee in Philosophy. A subject and thesis title must be submitted to the Committee not later than the Friday of the fifth week of the Trinity Term preceding the year in which the examination is to be taken. Requests for permission to make later changes to the thesis title should be submitted, with the support of the candidate's supervisor, to the Director of the Graduate Studies in Philosophy *as soon as the candidate has decided to seek such permission.* The thesis is to be delivered to the Clerk of the Schools, High Street, Oxford OX1 4BG, by 10 a.m. on Wednesday of the eighth week of Trinity Full Term in the year in which the examination is taken. The thesis shall be accompanied by a brief abstract and a statement of the number of words it contains (exclusive of bibliographical references). A penalty may be imposed on any thesis that exceeds the word limit. Successful candidates will be required to deposit one copy of the thesis in the Bodleian Library.†

Every candidate will be examined viva voce unless individually dispensed by the examiners.

The examiners may award a distinction for excellence in the whole examination.

If it is the opinion of the examiners that the work done by a candidate, while not of sufficient merit to qualify for the Degree of B.Phil., is nevertheless of sufficient merit to qualify for the Degree of Master of Studies in Philosophy, the candidate shall be given the option of resitting the B.Phil. (as provided by Ch. VI, Sect. VI, §2, paragraph 4, and in accordance with this regulation) or of being granted leave to supplicate for the Degree of Master of Studies. A candidate who retakes the examination in the year immediately following the failed examination need not resubmit a thesis that was judged satisfactory in the first examination, while such a candidate whose submitted essays in all three subjects offered under (1) above, were judged satisfactory in the first examination will not be required to retake that part of the examination, but need only submit an amended or different thesis.

A candidate whose thesis is judged satisfactory, but who fails to satisfy the examiners in just one essay subject under (1), may choose to be re-examined in that subject alone in the September immediately following the examination, provided that application is made to the Graduate Studies committee in Philosophy by the fourth Friday after the end of Trinity Full Term, or to be re-examined in all three subjects under (1) according to the time table for the examination in the following year.

Candidates who choose to be re-examined in September and fail to satisfy the examiners a second time may not retake the examination on any subsequent occasion.

Master of Philosophy

Byzantine Studies

(*See also the general notice at the commencement of these regulations.*)

1. Each candidate shall be required

(*a*) to present himself/herself for a written examination as defined in 2, below;

(*b*) to present a dissertation of not more than 30,000 words on a subject approved by his/her supervisor; the dissertation (*two copies*) must be typewritten and

---

* See the regulation on p. 508 concerning the preparation and dispatch of theses. Candidates are reminded that work submitted for the Degree of B.Phil. or M.Phil. may be subsequently incorporated in a thesis submitted for the Degree of D.Phil.

† Candidates will also be required to sign a form stating that they give permission for the thesis to be consulted.

delivered to the Clerk of the Schools, High Street, Oxford, at least fourteen days before the first day of the examination.

(*c*) to present himself/herself for a viva voce examination when required to do so by the examiners.

2. The written examination shall consist of five papers. Each candidate may, with the agreement of his/her supervisor, submit two extended essays, each not more than 5,000 words in length, on topics approved by the Committee for Byzantine Studies, in lieu of any *one* of papers I, III, IV, or V.

I. All candidates will be required to demonstrate knowledge of two auxiliary disciplines by offering a paper on either Byzantine Papyrology or any two of the following:

(1) Greek Palaeography.
(2) Byzantine Epigraphy.
(3) Byzantine Numismatics.
(4) Byzantine Sigillography.

II. All candidates will be required to offer an unseen translation paper in any one of the following languages:

(1) Byzantine Greek
(2) Classical Armenian
(3) Syriac
(4) Classical Arabic
(5) Church Slavonic
(6) Medieval Latin

III, IV, and V. Candidates will be required to offer three options which they must take from three different sections in the schedule A–G below, *except* that candidates may take two options from *either* Section D *or* Section E.

A. General Byzantine History

Candidates will be required to offer a paper which focuses on *either* early Byzantine history (to 717) *or* later Byzantine history (to 1453). Candidates will be given a wide choice of questions on the history of Byzantium and its neighbours.

B. History Special Subjects

(1) *The Eastern Roman Empire in the reign of Justinian, 527–65.*

(i) Procopius, *History of the Wars,* trans. H. B. Dewing (Loeb Classics, 1914–28), Bks. i, ii; Bk. iii, 9–20; Bk. v. 5–11, 14; Bk. vi, 11–13, 16–30; Bk. vii, 14, 38, 40; Bk. viii, 1–17, 25.

(ii) Procopius, *Buildings,* trans. H. B. Dewing (Loeb Classics, 1940).

(iii) Procopius, *Secret History,* trans. H. B. Dewing (Loeb Classics, 1935).

(iv) *The History of Menander the Guardsman,* trans. R. C. Blockley (Liverpool, 1985), fragments 1–6, pp. 41–91.

(v) *The Chronicle of John Malalas,* trans. E. Jeffreys, M. Jeffreys, and R. Scott (Melbourne, 1986), Bk. xviii, pp. 245–307.

(vi) Justinian, *Novellae,* 7–8, 13, 15, 17, 32–4, 38, 43, 45, 80, 85–6, 106, 110, 120, 128, 130, 136, 146, 161, trans. S. P. Scott, *The Civil Law* (Cincinnati, 1932), vols. xvi–xvii.

(vii) *The Syriac Chronicle known as that of Zachariah of Mitylene,* trans. F. J. Hamilton and E. W. Brooks (London, 1899), ix, 15–16, 19–26.

(viii) John of Ephesus, *Lives of the Eastern Saints,* trans. E. W. Brooks, *Patrologia Orientalis,* xviii, pp. 513–26 (John of Tella), 526–40 (John of Hephaestopolis), 690–70 (James Baradai): xix, pp. 153–8 (James Baradai and Theodore).

(2) *Byzantium in the Age of Constantine Porphyrogenitus, 913–959.*

(i) *The Book of the Eparch,* trans. E. H. Freshfield in *Roman Law in the Later Roman Empire* (Cambridge, 1938).

(ii) Philotheus, *Cletorologium,* trans. N. Oikonomidès in *Les Listes de préséance byzantines des IX et X siècles* (Paris, 1972), pp. 100/1–24/12.

(iii) Nicholas I, Patriarch of Constantinople, *Letters,* 5, 8, 9, 16, 25, 27, trans. R. J. H. Jenkins and L. G. Westerink (Washington D.C., 1973).

(iv) Constantine Porphyrogenitus, *De Administrando Imperio,* chapters 1–13, 29–46, trans. R. J. H. Jenkins (Washington D.C., 1967).

(v) Constantine Porphyrogenitus, *De Cerimoniis,* ed. J. J. Reiske (Bonn, 1829), Bk. ii, chapters 44 (pp. 660/13–664/2), 45 (pp. 664/3–669/14), 47–8 (pp. 680/1–692/2) (in translation).

(vi) Georgius Monachus Continuatus, *Vitae Imperatorum Recentiorum,* ed. I. Bekker (Bonn, 1838), pp. 874/5–924 (in translation).

(vii) Theophanes Continuatus, *Chronographia,* Bk. vi: *De Constantino Porphyrogenneto,* ed. I. Bekker (Bonn, 1838), pp. 426/3–430/21, 436/1–469/4 (in translation).

(viii) Georgius Cedrenus, *Historiarum Compendium,* ed. I. Bekker, vol. ii (Bonn, 1839), pp. 320/17–338/13 (in translation).

(ix) Cosmas, *Le Traité contre les Bogomiles,* trans. A. Vaillant (Paris, 1945), Part 1, pp. 53–92.

(x) *The Russian Primary Chronicle,* trans. S. H. Cross and O. P. Sherbowitz-Wetzor (Cambridge, Mass., 1953), ad. an. 904–955, pp. 64–84.

(xi) Yahya ibn Said, Ibn al-Atir, Kamal al-Din, trans. M. Canard in A. A. Vasiliev, *Byzance et les Arabes,* vol. ii (2) (Brussels, 1950), pp. 91–8, 145–62, 180–4.

(xii) Ibn Miskawaih, trans. D. S. Margoliouth in H. F. Amedroz and D. S. Margoliouth, *The Eclipse of the Abbasid Caliphate,* iv (Oxford, 1921), pp. 163–213 (A.H. 313–16).

(xiii) *Vie de saint Luc de Stylite* (879–979), trans. F. Vanderstuyf, in *Patrologia Orientalis,* vol. xi (1915), chapters 10–32 (pp. 199–225), 43–7 (pp. 237–43).

(xiv) Nicephorus Phocas, *Skirmishing,* trans. G. T. Dennis, *Three Byzantine Military Treatises* (Washington D.C., 1985), preface, chapters 1–9, 19–20 (pp. 147–73, 215–23).

(xv) Nicholas I, Patriarch of Constantinople, *Miscellaneous Writings,* trans. L. G. Westerink (Washington D.C., 1981), no. 200 B.

(xvi) J. Zepos and P. Zepos, *Jus Graecoromanum,* i (Athens, 1931), Collatio Tertia, *Novellae* 5, 6, 8, pp. 205–17, 222–26 (in translation).

C. Theology and Church History

The Iconoclast Controversy and the Missions to the Slavs, 717–886.

(i) Theophanes, *Chronicle,* Annus mundi 6209 to the end, trans. H. Turtledove (Philadelphia, 1982), pp. 85–182.

(ii) Extracts from the Acts of the Council of Constantinople (754) and the Council of Nicaea (787) as given in D. J. Sahas, *Icon and Logos: Sources in Eighth-Century Iconoclasm* (Toronto, 1986), pp. 47–185.

(iii) Germanus of Constantinople, *On the Divine Liturgy,* trans. P. Meyendorff (Crestwood, 1984).

(iv) John of Damascus, *On the Divine Images,* trans. D. Anderson (Crestwood, 1980).

(v) Theodore the Studite, *On the Holy Icons,* trans. C. P. Roth (Crestwood, 1981).

(vi) Photius, *Homilies,* 3, 4, 10, 17, trans. C. Mango (Cambridge, Mass., 1958).

(vii) *Epanagoge,* extracts as given in E. Barker, *Social and Political Thought in Byzantium* (Oxford, 1957), pp. 89–96.

(viii) The Life of Peter of Atroa, trans. V. Laurent (*Subsidia Hagiographica* 29: Brussels, 1956).

(ix) The Lives of Constantine/Cyril and Methodius, trans F. Dvornik, *Les Légendes de Constantin et de Méthode vues de Byzance* (Prague, 1933), pp. 349–93.

D. ART AND ARCHAEOLOGY

(1) *City, country, and economy in the Byzantine Empire*, AD *284–700.*
Constantinople; a selection of major provincial cities; the development of the Holy Land; land tenure and farming; manufacture and trade.

(2) *City, country, and economy in the Byzantine Empire*, AD *630–1453*
Urban decline from 600; urban revival in the middle Byzantine period; land tenure and farming; manufacture and trade; the role of the monastery.

(3) *Byzantine art and archtecture,* AD *284–700.*
Church buildings; the cult of martyrs; Christian iconography; secular buildings; secular and pagan iconography; mosaics and wallpaintings; illuminated MSS; luxury objects; objects of daily use.

(4) *Byzantine art and architecture,* AD *630–1453.*
Architectural development; architectural decoration; impact of Iconoclasm on art; mosaics and wallpainting; illuminated MSS; luxury objects; objects of daily use (metal, ceramic, glass); influence of Byzantine art on other cultures.

(5) *Byzantium: the transition from Antiquity to the Middle Ages,* AD *500–1100.*
Study of material evidence illuminating the transformation of Byzantium from an antique to a medieval society. Coverage extends from its period of greatest territorial expansion through to its economic and political recovery after the 'Dark Age'. Subjects include changes in urban life, in land tenure and use, in the role of the monastery, in church architecture, in manufacture and trade, and the Byzantine impact on foreign prestige monuments.

(6) *Byzantine Constantinople.*
Utilitarian infrastructure, ceremonial architecture, cult building, and general topography will be studied, combining surviving structures, excavated sites, and key written texts. The social and economic character of the city will be assessed during periods of initial expansion, recession, economic recovery until its conquest by the Fourth Crusade and the final centuries before its fall to the Ottoman Turks.

E. LITERATURE

(1) *Byzantine hagiography.*
Texts; Life of Anthony; Theodoret of Cyrrhus, selections; Theodore of Sykeon; Miracles of Demetrios; Andreas Salos, Luke the Stylite.

(2) *Byzantine historiography.*
Texts; selections from: Zosimus; Procopius; Theophanes; Psellos; Choniates; Anna Comnena; Sphrantzes.

(3) *Byzantine vernacular literature* (in Greek).
Texts: selections from: Malalas, *Chronicle*; John Moschos, *Pratum Spirituale*; Leontios of Neapolis, Symeon the Fool; Prodromic Poems; one example of Chivalry Romance; Digenis Akrites.

(4) *Byzantine scholarship.*
Selected texts will be prescribed.

F. EASTERN AREAS AND NEIGHBOURS

(1) *Armenian History, c.450–800.*
Selected texts will be prescribed.

(2) *Armenian History, c.800–1100*
Selected texts will be prescribed.

(3) *Armenian Literature.*
Selected texts will be prescribed.

(4) *Syria before and after the Arab conquest, c.450–860.*
Selected texts will be prescribed.
(5) *Syriac literature.*
Selected texts will be prescribed.
(6) *Byzantium and Islam, c.630–900*
Selected texts will be prescribed.
(7) *Byzantium and Islam, c.800–1100*
Selected texts will be prescribed.
(8) *The formation of Islamic Art.*
(9) *Early Arabic thought and its classical heritage.*
Selected texts will be prescribed.

G. BYZANTIUM AND ITS NORTHERN NEIGHBOURS
(1) 370–800.
Selected texts will be prescribed.
(2) 800–1204.
Selected texts will be prescribed.

3. *Teaching in all the options may not be available each year, and applicants for admission will be advised whether teaching will be available in the options of their choice.*

4. The examiners may award a distinction for excellence in the whole examination.

5. If it is the opinion of the examiners that the work done by a candidate, while not of sufficient merit to qualify for the degree of M.Phil., is nevertheless of sufficient merit to qualify for the degree of Master of Studies in Byzantine Studies, the candidate shall be given the option of resitting the M.Phil. (as provided by Ch. VI. Sect. VI, §2, paragraph 4) or of being granted leave to supplicate for the degree of Master of Studies.

Celtic Studies

(*See also the general notice at the commencement of these regulations.*)

The regulations made by the Board of the Faculty of Medieval and Modern Languages are as follows:

1. All candidates shall be required at the time of admission to satisfy the Board of Faculty of Medieval and Modern Languages (if necessary, by written test) that they possess the appropriate qualifications for the proposed course, including suitable proficiency in relevant languages. Normally the course will be restricted to candidates who have taken a first degree in a relevant subject area.*

2. All candidates shall be required

(*a*) To offer themselves for written examination as defined in section 5 below.

(*b*) To present themselves for viva voce examination at the time appointed by the examiners.

3. The subjects and papers of the examination shall be as follows:

(*a*) Historical and comparative Celtic linguistics.

(*b*) Irish literature up to the Cromwellian wars. Compulsory passages for translation and commentary will be set from the prescribed texts, but there will also be more general questions on the history of Irish literature in the period. The following are the prescribed texts:

---

* Even though their first degree is considered to have fitted them to pursue a course of study for an M.Phil. in Celtic Studies candidates may be required to take an intensive course in a Modern Celtic language *either* in the long vacation prior to their admission *or* in the long vacation following the third term of their course of instruction.

Old Irish:

Scéla mucce Meic Dathó, ed. R. Thurneysen (Dublin, 1951).
Togail bruidne Dá Derga, ed. E. Knott (Dublin, 1936).
Longes mac n-Uislenn, ed. V. Hull (New York, 1949).

Middle Irish:

Stories from the Acallam, ed. M. Dillon (Dublin, 1970).
Aislinge meic Conglinne, ed. K. H. Jackson (Dublin, 1990).
Caithreim Cellaig, ed. K. Mulchrone (Dublin, 1933).

Early Modern Irish:

An introduction to Irish syllabic poetry of the period 1200–1600, ed. E. Knott (2nd edn., Dublin, 1957).
Tóruigheacht Dhiarmada agus Ghráinne, ed. Nessa Ni Shéaghdha (Dublin, 1967)
The Bardic poems of Tadhg Dall O Huiginn, ed. E. Knott (2 vols., London, 1922–6).

(*c*) Welsh literature up to the Reformation. Compulsory passages for translation and commentary will be set from the prescribed texts, but there will also be more general questions on the history of Welsh literature in the period. The following are prescribed texts:

Old Welsh:

Canu Taliesin, ed. I. Williams (Cardiff, 1960).
Canu Aneirin, ed. I. Williams (Cardiff, 1938).
Canu Llywarch Hen, ed. I. Williams (Cardiff, 1953).

Middle Welsh:

Pedeir Keinc y Mabinogi, ed. I. Williams (Cardiff, 1951).
Culhwch and Olwen, ed. R. Bromwich and D. Simon Evans (Cardiff, 1992).
A selection of the poetry of the *Gogynfeirdd*.

Early Modern Welsh:

Gwaith Dafydd ap Gwilym, ed. T. Parry (3rd edn., Cardiff, 1979).
Poems of the Cywyddwyr, ed. E. I. Rowlands (Dublin, 1976).
Rhagymadroddion 1547–1659, ed. Garfield H. Hughes (Cardiff, 1951).

(*d*) Special Subjects

(1) The archaeology of Celtic Society in pre-Christian Europe.
(2) Pre-Christian art and iconography.
(3) The records of Continental Celtic.
(4) Irish and Welsh origin legends.
(5) The Celtic context of Old and Middle English literature.
(6) The history of Ireland up to 1216.
(7) The history of Scotland up to 1153.
(8) The history of Wales *either* from *c.*550 to 1063 *or* from 1063 to 1415.
(9) The history of the Celtic peoples from *c.*400 to *c.*900.
(10) The Normans and the Celtic peoples 1066–1216.
(11) Celtic law texts.
(12) The Ulster Cycle of tales.
(13) The Classical Irish bardic tradition.
(14) Irish 'vision' and 'voyage' literature.
(15) The medieval Welsh Arthurian romances.
(16) Middle Cornish language and literature *or* Middle Breton language and literature.
(17) Twentieth-century Scottish Gaelic literature.
(18) Literature of the modern revival in Irish.

(19) The Welsh literary renaissance of the twentieth century.
(20) Language and Society in *either* modern Ireland *or* Modern Scotland.
(21) Language and Society in modern Wales.
(22) The comparative syntax of modern Celtic languages.
(23) The history of *either* early modern Ireland (1540–1691) *or* late modern Ireland (*either* 1782–1850 *or* 1850–1922).
(24) The history of early modern Scotland (1400–1707).

The Special Subjects listed above are not prescriptive: candidates are allowed to offer a Special Subject or Special Subjects of their own devising, provided that these are similar in character and scope to those listed and that they are approved under the arrangements set out in section 6 below.

(*e*) A thesis of approximately 20,000 words and not more than 25,000 words on a subject approved by the board or by a person or persons to whom the board may delegate this function. When seeking approval for the subject of the thesis, every candidate shall submit with the proposed title a written statement of not more than 500 words explaining the scope of the topic and the manner in which it is proposed to treat it.

4. Candidates shall be required to offer three papers and a thesis, as follows:

(*a*) *Either*

(i) Two papers, one on each of two subjects selected from those described in section 3 (*a*), (*b*), and (*c*) above.
(ii) One paper on a Special Subject as described in Section 3 (*d*) above.

Or

(i) One paper on a subject selected from those described in section 3 (*a*), (*b*), and (*c*) above.
(ii) Two papers, one on each of two Special Subjects as described in section 3 (*d*) above.

(*b*) A thesis as described in section 3 (*e*) above.

5. Candidates shall seek approval (by application to the Modern Languages Graduate Office, 41 Wellington Square, Oxford) for the proposed subject of their thesis by the end of the fourth week of the second term after that in which their names have been placed on the register of M.Phil. Students, i.e. normally by the end of the fourth week of Trinity Term in their first year.

The thesis (*two copies*) must be typewritten and must be delivered to the Clerk of the Schools, High Street, Oxford, not later than Friday of the first week of the Trinity Full Term in which the examination is to be taken.*

Successful candidates will be required to deposit one copy of their thesis in the Bodleian Library.†

6. Each candidate's choice of papers shall be subject to the approval of the Board of the Faculty of Medieval and Modern Languages or of a person or persons to whom the board may delegate the function of giving such approval. Approval shall be given only if the choice of papers proposed, and any titles of Special Subjects of the candidate's own devising, have the written support of the candidate's supervisor. Approval of the choice of papers proposed will be dependent on the availability of teaching and examining resources at the relevant times. Candidates shall seek approval (by application to the Modern Languages Graduate Office, 41 Wellington Square, Oxford) by the end of the first term after that in which their names have

---

* See the regulation on p. 508 concerning the preparation and dispatch of theses. Candidates are reminded that work submitted for the Degree of M.Phil. may subsequently be incorporated in a thesis submitted for the Degree of D.Phil.

† Such candidates will also be required to sign a form stating whether they give permission for their theses to be consulted.

been placed on the register of M.Phil. students, i.e. normally by the end of Hilary Term in their first year.

A proposal for a Special Subject or Special Subjects of the candidate's own devising shall be accompanied by a *brief* statement of the candidate's view of the character and scope of the Special Subject or Special Subjects proposed.

7. If it is the opinion of the examiners that the work done by a candidate while not of sufficient merit to qualify for the degree of M.Phil. is nevertheless of sufficient merit to qualify for the degree of Master of Studies in Celtic Studies, the candidate shall be given the option of resitting the M.Phil. examination under Ch. VI., Sect. VI, §2, cl. 4 or of being granted permission to supplicate for the Degree of Master of Studies.

8. The examiners may award a distinction for excellence in the whole examination.

Classical Archaeology

Within the Division of Life and Environmental Sciences, the course shall be administered by the Committee for the School of Archaeology. The regulations made are as follows:

1. Candidates for admission must apply to the Committee for the School of Archaeology. They will be required to produce evidence of their appropriate qualifications for the proposed course, including their suitable proficiency in relevant ancient or modern languages.

2. Candidates must follow for six terms a course of instruction in Classical Archaeology.

3. The registration of candidates shall lapse from the Register of M.Phil. Students on the last day of Trinity Term in the academic year after that in which their name is first entered in it, unless the committee decides otherwise.

4. All candidates are required:

(*a*) to satisfy the examiners in a Qualifying Examination identical with that for the degree of Master of Studies in Classical Archaeology and governed by regulations 4–8 for that degree, in the Trinity Full Term of the academic year in which their name is first entered on the Register of M.Phil. students except that under regulation 4(*b*) of that degree a 10,000 word dissertation may not normally be offered in place of one of the subject options (examined by two pre-set essays or by three-hour written paper). Candidates whose work in the Qualifying Examination is judged by the examiners to be of the standard required for the degree of M.St. in Classical Archaeology but not of the standard required to proceed to the second year of the M.Phil. in Classical Archaeology, may be offered the option of resitting the Qualifying Examination under Ch. VI, Sect. VI, § 2, cl. 4, or of being granted permission to supplicate for the degree of Master of Studies in Classical Archaeology;

(*b*) to deliver to the Clerk of the Schools, High Street, Oxford, not later than noon on the Friday of the sixth week of Trinity Full Term in the academic year after that in which their name is first entered on the Register for M.Phil. Students, a thesis* of not more than 25,000 words (excluding bibliography and any descriptive catalogue or other factual matter, but including notes and

* See the regulation following Ch. VI, sect. VI, §4, concerning the preparation and dispatch of theses. Candidates are reminded (i) that two copies are required but that one of these may be a reproduction or carbon copy of the other, provided that any maps, diagrams, or other illustrations in the second copy are adequately reproduced, (ii) that the copy of the thesis deposited in the Ashmolean Library shall be the one containing the original illustrations, and (iii) that work submitted for the Degree of M.Phil. may be subsequently incorporated in a thesis submitted for the Degree of D.Phil.

appendices) on the subject approved in accordance with regulations 7 and 10 below; the thesis should bear the candidate's examination number but not his or her name.

(*c*) to present themselves for written examination in accordance with regulation 5 below in the Trinity Full Term of the academic year after that in which their name is first entered on the Register for M.Phil. Students;

(*d*) to present themselves for an oral examination as required by the examiners.

5. The written examination shall comprise one subject chosen from Schedules A–C for the Master of Studies in Classical Archaeology. [Candidates who offered a subject from Schedule C in the qualifying examination may not normally offer another subject from Schedule C.] The subject may be examined, at the candidate's choice, either by two pre-set essays of 5,000 words each, or by a written paper.

6. The choice of subjects for thesis and examination must be approved by the candidate's supervisor and by the committee, having regard to the candidate's previous experience and to the availability of teaching. The subject for the thesis will normally be related to the period or subject chosen under regulation 5 above.

7. Candidates will be expected to show sufficient general knowledge of Ancient History and Geography for a proper understanding of their periods and subjects.

8. The period or subject for examination and the chosen method of examination must be submitted for approval by the committee in time for its meeting in the eighth week of the Trinity Full Term of the academic year in which the candidate's name is first entered on the Register for M.Phil. Students. Notice of the period or subject to be offered by each candidate must be given to the Registrar not later than Friday of the eighth week of the Michaelmas Term preceding the examination.

9. Candidates intending to offer pairs of pre-set essays in place of the written examination (as specified in 5 above) will select essay topics from a list offered by their supervisors. The proposed essay titles, countersigned by the supervisor, must be submitted for approval to the Chairman of Examiners by noon on Friday of the seventh week of the term in which the instruction for that subject is given. Candidates must submit two copies of their essays by not later than noon on the Monday of the second week of the term following that in which the instruction for that subject was given to the Examination Schools. Essays must be typed or printed and should bear the candidate's examination number but not his or her name.

10. The proposed thesis title must be submitted for approval by the committee in time for its meeting in the eighth week of the Trinity Term of the year in which the candidate's name is first entered on the Register for M.Phil. Students.

11. Candidates will normally be expected to undertake a programme of relevant practical work (e.g. excavation, travel, or museum study), to be approved by their supervisors beforehand.

12. Candidates are advised that adequate reading knowledge of an appropriate language or languages (other than English) may be necessary to reach the standard required by the examiners.

13. Candidates will be required to deposit one copy of the thesis with the Clerk of the Schools. Successful candidates will be required to deposit one copy of the thesis in the Ashmolean Library. Such candidates will be required to complete a form stating whether they give permission for their thesis to be consulted.

14. Candidates whose work in the Final Examination is judged by the examiners not to be of the standard required for the degree of M.Phil. in Classical Archaeology but whose work in the Qualifying Examination nevertheless reached the standard required for the degree of M.St. in Classical Archaeology, may be offered the option of resitting the M.Phil. Final Examination under Ch. VI, Sect. VI, § 2, cl. 4, or of

being granted permission to supplicate for the degree of Master of Studies in Classical Archaeology.

15. The examiners may award a distinction for excellence in the whole examination.

Comparative Social Policy

(*See also the general notice at the commencement of these regulations.*)

The regulations made by the Board of the Divisional Board of Social Sciences are as follows:

Qualifying Test

Every candidate must pass a qualifying test at the end of the third term from the beginning of the course in the *two* compulsory papers, *Methods of Social Research*, and *Comparative Social Policy/Welfare States* and *one Optional Paper* from the list of optional papers, specified by the Department of Social Policy and Social Work. This will be from a list published annually by Friday of the third week of Michaelmas Full Term in the Department of Social Policy and Social Work. Candidates may, after special permission of the Director of Studies for Social Policy, offer subjects outside this list. This may include subjects from the list published in conjunction with the M.Phil. or M.Sc. in Sociology with the permission of the Director of Graduate Studies for Sociology. This may also include papers offered in any other relevant master's degree in the University subject to the permission of the relevant Graduate Studies Committee as appropriate. The examiners may examine candidates viva voce. Candidates who fail the qualifying test may, in exceptional circumstances, at the discretion of the Sociology and Social Policy Graduate Studies Committee, be allowed to retake the test before the beginning of the first week of the next academic year. The Sociology and Social Policy Graduate Studies Committee can decide that the retake shall consist of the whole test or parts thereof.

Final Examination

Every candidate must offer:

1. One further optional paper. This will be from a list published annually by Friday of the third week of Michaelmas Full Term in the Department of Social Policy and Social Work. Candidates may, after special permission of the Director of Studies for Social Policy, offer subjects outside this list. This may include subjects from the list published in conjunction with the M.Phil. or M.Sc. in Sociology with the permission of the Director of Graduate Studies for Sociology. This may also include papers offered in any other relevant master's degree in the University subject to the permission of the relevant Graduate Studies Committee as appropriate.

2. A thesis* of not more than 30,000 words to be delivered to the Clerk of the Schools, High Street, Oxford, by noon on Friday of the sixth week of Trinity Full Term in which the examination is to be taken. Successful candidates will be required to deposit a copy of their thesis in the library of the Department of Social Policy and Social Work.

The examiners may examine any candidate viva voce.

The examiners may award a Distinction for excellence in the whole examination on the basis of the material submitted to them in both the qualifying and the final examination.

Compulsory Papers

Methods of Social Research. As specified for the M.Phil in Sociology.

Comparative Social Policy/Welfare States. Concepts and typologies of social policies and welfare states. Approaches to the study of social policy. Theories of the origin

---

* See the regulation on p. 508 concerning the preparation and dispatch of theses.

and growth of the welfare state. Goals and means in social policy. Effectiveness and efficiency in social policy: unintended side effects. Methodological issues in comparative social research.

Optional Papers

These will be from a list published annually by Friday of the third week of Michaelmas Full Term in the Department of Social Policy and Social Work. Candidates may, after special permission of the Director of Studies for Social Policy, offer subjects outside this list. This may include subjects from the list published in conjunction with the M.Phil. or M.Sc. in Sociology with the permission of the Director of Graduate Studies for Sociology. This may also include papers offered in any other relevant master's degree in the University subject to the permission of the relevant Graduate Studies Committee as appropriate.

Development Studies

(*See also the general notice at the commencement of these regulations.*)

The regulations made by the Area and Development Studies Committee are as follows:

1. Candidates for admission must apply to the Area and Development Studies Committee. They will be required to produce evidence of their appropriate qualifications for the proposed course.

2. Candidates must follow for six terms courses of instruction as laid down for the M.Phil. in Development Studies by the Area and Development Studies Committee.

3. Candidates will be admitted to take the examination as defined below in a specific year. In exceptional circumstances candidates may be allowed to take an examination later than the one to which they were admitted. Permission for this must be sought from the Area and Development Studies Committee not later than the Monday of the week before the first week of the Trinity Term in which the examination was to have been taken. The application must have the support of the candidate's college and be accompanied by a statement from the supervisor.

4. The registration of candidates shall lapse from the Register of M.Phil. Students on the last day of Trinity Term in the academic year after that in which their name is first entered in it, unless the Area and Development Studies Committee decides otherwise.

5. *Qualifying Test*

5.1 Every candidate must pass a qualifying test in two foundation papers to be taken at the start of the Trinity Term of the first year of study.

5.2. The qualifying test will be set and administered by the examiners appointed to examine for the M.Phil. in Development Studies. Candidates must notify their entry on the appropriate form, obtainable from the University Offices, by Friday of eighth week of Michaelmas Term of the first year of study.

5.3. Candidates may select the two foundation papers which they offer from the list set out below except that candidates with a non-economics background are required to include Economics as one of the two papers and candidates are not permitted, except with the permission of the committee, to offer a paper in the subject of their bachelor's degree.

(i) *History and Politics*

Questions will be set on the themes of state formation and development; colonialism, collaboration, and resistance; nationalism, decolonisation; class formation, gender relations, and the formation of political identities; politics and policy. Students will be expected to show knowledge of developments in countries from more than one of the following regions: Africa, South Asia, and Latin America.

(ii) *Economics*

Questions will be set on the basic elements of macro- and micro-analysis for open, less developed, economies. Topics may include national income accounting and analysis; macro-economic policy, theories of inflation and growth; supply and demand; theories of the firm; the functioning of markets, externalities and other market failures; theories of international trade; trade policy, exchange rates, and balance of payments management; the operation of the international monetary system. The emphasis will be on concepts and their application in the context of development.

(iii) *Social Anthropology*

Questions will be set on the perspectives of anthropology upon social change; personhood and well-being; social and personal agency, authority and responsibility in the field of productive activity; marriage, kinship, family and gender in theory and practice; agencies of managed change and their interaction with local communities.

5.4. A candidate who fails to pass the qualifying test may, at the discretion of the Area and Development Studies Committee, be permitted to retake the test before the beginning of the first week of the next academic year. The inter-faculty committee can decide whether the retake shall consist of the whole test or part thereof.

5.5. Only candidates who have passed the qualifying test may proceed to the second year of the course.

6. *Core Course in Development Studies*

Candidates must pursue a core course in development studies which runs throughout the two years of the degree. The core course covers the following three aspects: (i) social theory and development theory, (ii) analysis of major interdisciplinary issues, and (iii) international dimensions of development. Issues which may be included are, under (i) the intellectual origins and legacies of development; under (ii) the agrarian question; industrialization; urbanization; gender, ethnicity, culture and development and environmental aspects of development; and under (iii) finance, trade, aid, information technology, the United Nations and global governance.

7. *Final Examination*

7.1. The final examination shall consist of the following:

(*a*) One written paper on *Research Techniques* which is taken at the end of the Trinity Term of the first year of study. Questions will be set on: Epistemology of social science, social science paradigms; ethics and values; quantitative methods; the presentation of stastitical information, hypothesis testing; research design; sampling theory; questionnaire design; the critical reading of documents; participant observation; action research; rapid research; evaluation research. A candidate who fails to pass the paper in Research Techniques may, at the discretion of the Area and Development Studies Committee, be permitted to retake the paper before the beginning of the first week of the next academic year. Only candidates who have passed the paper in Research Techniques may proceed to the second year of the course.

(*b*) The successful completion of three essays assessed by the examiners appointed to examine for the M.Phil. in Development Studies. Candidates are required to submit these essays at specified intervals over the two years of the course. The topics to be covered in these essays must fall within the three themes (one per essay) included in the core course in development studies: social theory and development; major interdisciplinary issues; and the international dimension of development. Candidates must pass all three essays. In the event of a candidate's failing either or both essays submitted in the first year of the course, either or both must be rewritten, resubmitted and a pass mark awarded before the candidate may proceed to the second year of the course.

(*c*) The assessment of a thesis of not more than 30,000 words (excluding bibliography but including footnotes and appendices) on a topic approved by the Area and Development Studies Committee or by a person or persons to whom the Committee may delegate this function.

The thesis must be on a topic in the general field of development studies and must include as one of the appendices an analytical discussion of the research technique or techniques appropriate to the topic chosen. This appendix should be 3,000–5,000 words in length, and the appendix and the written paper in (*a*) above shall each constitute 50% of the marks available for the examination of the candidate's knowledge of research techniques. The topic of the thesis must be chosen in consultation with and approval of the candidate's supervisor. If a separate thesis supervisor is required, he or she must have agreed to undertake the supervision prior to the approval of the topic as specified above.

(*d*) Two written papers selected from a range of options as specified below.

The examiners may at their discretion require any candidate to attend for a viva voce examination.

7.2. Theses must be delivered to the Clerk of the Schools, High Street, Oxford not later than the Friday of the first week of the Trinity Full Term in which the examination is to be taken. At the discretion of the examiners, successful candidates may be required to deposit one copy of the thesis in the International Development Studies Library.

7.3. The range of options from which candidates must select the two papers which they offer are as follows:

(*a*) **Rural Development and Social Change**

Candidates selecting this option may offer one or two of the following three papers:

(i) *Rural Development and Natural Resources*

Agricultural land and other natural resources in economic development; production economics; land, water, labour, inputs, product and credit markets; contractual arrangements and social institutions; sources of dynamism and crisis; market failures and resource use; soil degradation and the depletion of natural resources; tragedy of the commons and its critique; resource use conflicts, competing demands and environmental inequality, local development, national and international resource policy.

(ii) *Rural Societies and Politics*

Major theoretical approaches to the analysis of rural societies including the formalist-substantivist debate in anthropology; peasant differentiation; economic mobility and relations with capitalism; peasant rationality; theories of peasant politics and peasant rebellions; theories regarding gender and generation; agrarian capitalism, dominant and subaltern classes; analyses of relations between the state, peasants, and pastoralists.

(*b*) **Forced Migration**

Candidates selecting this option may offer one or two of the following papers:

(i) *International Legal and Normative Framework*

The international legal and normative framework in relation to refugees and displaced persons. International and domestic application of individual and group rights to displaced persons and refugees. Implications of displaced populations for international order and for the security and stability of states. Activities and involvement of the relevant international organs, governments, and intergovernmental and non-governmental organizations regarding forced migration. The creation and dissolution of states. Concepts of intervention and their justifications. The evolution of humanitarian responses to forced migration. The organizational culture of assistance.

(ii) *Causes and consequences of forced migration*

Theories of the causes of forced migration and humanitarian crises. Historical dimensions and social dynamics of forced migration. Coercion and conflict. Poverty and vulnerability. The impact of forced migrants on host populations and governments. Coping mechanisms, survival strategies and psychological adaptation of affected populations. Nationalism, ethnicity and group identity. Integration in rural and urban settings. The impact of resettlement programmes on the livelihood and economic autonomy of affected populations. Repatriation and social reconstruction.

(*c*) **Theory and Practice of Economic Development**

This option is only available to those with substantial previous training in economics. Candidates must offer two papers from the M.Sc. in Economics for Development, including *Economic Theory* and either *Quantitative Methods* or *Development Economics.*

(*d*) **Latin American Development Issues**

This paper will cover the main trends in the evolution of the Latin American economies in the twentieth century. Themes will include export economies, import substituting industrialization, the impact of external shocks, integration movements, the role of international agencies, trends in poverty and income distribution.

(*e*) **African Studies**

Candidates selecting this option may offer one or two papers from the following four.

(i) *North East Africa*

The peoples of North-east Africa (Sudan, Ethiopia, Somalia, Uganda, and Kenya); social and cultural history; the classical anthropological literature and modern evaluations; colonialism and after; Imperial and post-imperial Ethiopian society; development issues.

(ii) *The History and Politics of West Africa*

The political history, political sociology, political institutions and political economy of West Africa since 1939: nationalism and transfers of power; forms of government, civilian and military; parties and elections; conditions for democracy; class, ethnicity, religion, and gender; business, labour, and peasantries; agricultural policies and economic reforms; West African regional politics and institutions and the influence of external agencies. Candidates will be required to show knowledge of Nigeria and of at least one Francophone country.

(iii) *The History and Politics of East/Central Africa*

The political history, political sociology, political institutions, and political economy of East Africa since 1939: nationalism and transfers of power; forms of government, civilian and military; parties and elections; conditions for democracy; class, ethnicity, religion, and gender; business, labour, and peasantries; agricultural policies and economic reforms; East African regional politics and institutions and the influence of external agencies. East/Central Africa is taken to include Zimbabwe, Zambia, Malawa, Mozambique, Angola, Congo (Kinshasa), Rwanda, Burundi, Uganda, Tanzania, Kenya.

(iv) *The History and Politics of Southern Africa*

The political history, political sociology, political institutions and political economy of South Africa since 1902: the formation of the South African state; liberalism; Afrikaner and African nationalisms; segregation, apartheid, and capitalism; the transformation of the agrarian economy; parties and elections; class, race, ethnicity, and gender; business and labour; the politics of Botswana, Lesotho, Swaziland, and Namibia; Southern African regional politics and institutions and the influence of external agencies.

(*f*) **South Asian Studies**

Candidates selecting this option may offer one or both the following papers:

(i) *The History and Politics of South Asia*

The political history, political sociology, political institutions, and political economy of South Asia (India, Pakistan, Sri Lanka, and Bangladesh) since 1947; the state, political institutions, party politics, and 'movement' politics; conditions for democracy; the politics of gender, class, caste, religion, and ethnicity; the evolution of political idologies; social organization, culture, and identities as they bear on politics; the politics of development.

(ii) *The Indian Political Economy*

Population and human resources; the economics of the sex ratio; the work force; the Indian agrarian question and the technical transformation of agriculture; industrialization – the evolution of corporate capital, petty production and industrial districts; trade, markets, and the informal economy; poverty and anti-poverty policy; the Indian state and the limits to planned development; liberalization and globalization and their impact on the Indian economy.

(*g*) **The International Relations of the Developing World**

The International relations of developing countries from 1945 to the present day, focusing on the characteristics of developing states and their interaction with the international system at the political, economic, and military levels. Topics include: decolonization and the emergence of the Third World; the nature of the state, self-determination and the problems of state building; the political and economic forces shaping international arrangements for trade, investment, and finance; the political and economic constraints on growth in the world economy; international financial institutions and their political impact; the politics of global investment; security, conflict, and intervention; the politics of alliance formation including Third World coalitions and their impact on international order; regionalism and 'regimes'.

(*h*) **Transitional Economies of the Former Soviet Union, Eastern Europe, and China**

The theory and reality of the complex process of transition to a market economy; similarities and differences between economies in transition and conventionally-defined developing countries. The development of market socialism in the context of its inheritance from the command economy. Strategies of transition; macroeconomic stabilization; liberalization of price and markets; privatization; creation of social safety nets; developments in foreign economic relations. The main countries studied are Russia, China, those in the Caucasus and Central Asia.

(*i*) **Economic Development Problems and Policies**

Questions will be set on development topics from a series of taught modules. The modules offered may vary from year to year, but will normally include such topics as: human development, poverty and income distribution; rural development; environment; industry and technology; fiscal policy; project evaluation; macro-economic policy and adjustment; aspects of the international economy.

(*j*) **Environment and Development in Twentieth-Century Southern and Central Africa: an historical approach**

The links between environment and development in twentieth-century southern and central Africa. Social, economic and environmental consequences of settler colonialism, imperial rule, the commercialization of agriculture and the growth of industry. Historical conservation strategies. Relationships with contemporary environmental problems.

Major topics include: hunting and game conservation; disease, ecology, and the state; the impact of settler and peasant agriculture; political conflicts over state regulations of natural resources and their role in rural and nationalist movements; drought, famine, and poverty; deforestation and fuel resources; property regimes and the environment; urbanization, industry, and their environmental impact.

(*k*) **Gender and Development**

Key concepts in Gender and Development relating to: Population; Land-use and the environment; Employment, assets, markets and credit; social issues; Civil society; violence and conflict; Political organization and theories of power.

7.4. Not all the above options will necessarily be available in any year.

7.5 Candidates may, after special permission from the Area and Development Studies Committee, offer subjects from outside this list. Candidates may include papers offered in other relevant masters degrees in the University, subject to permission from the relevant graduate studies committee. Applications to do this must normally be made by the first Friday of Trinity Term in the student's first year.

7.6 The examiners may award a Distinction for excellence in the whole examination.

Eastern Christian Studies

(*See also the general notice at the commencement of these regulations.*)

The regulations made by the Boards of the Faculties of Oriental Studies and Theology are as follows:

Candidates will be admitted to take the examination as defined below in a specific year. In exceptional circumstances candidates may be allowed to take an examination later than one to which they were admitted. Permission for this must be sought from the faculty board not later than Monday of the week before the first week of the Trinity Term in which the examination was to have been taken. The application must have the support of the candidate's college and be accompanied by a statement from the supervisor.

I. Every candidate shall be required

(*a*) to present himself or herself for a written examination, as prescribed below;

(*b*) to present a thesis* of not more than 30,000 words on a subject approved by the faculty boards. Theses should be presented not later than noon on the Friday of the second week of the Trinity Term in which the examination is taken. Successful candidates may be required to deposit one copy of the thesis in the Bodleian;†

(*c*) to present himself or herself for a viva voce examination, unless individually dispensed by the examiners.

II. The written examination shall consist of four papers:

(1) A general paper on the development of doctrine and the history of the Church in the Christian East to AD 717.

(2), (3), (4) Three papers on one of the following options.

A. *Greek*

(i) The philosophical background of the Greek Fathers, with special study of the following texts:

Albinus, *Epitome* viii–xi (Budé)
Plotinus, *Enneads,* i. 6, v. 1 (Loeb or *Oxford Classical Texts*)
Origen, *Contra Celsum* vii (*Sources Chrétiennes*)
Gregory of Nyssa, *De Hominis Opificio* 1–16 (Migne, P.G. 44)
Dionysius the Areopagite, *De Mystica Theologica* (P.G. 3)

(ii) The history of the Church in the Byzantine Empire, AD 717–886, with special study of the following texts:

---

* See the regulation on p. 508 concerning the preparation and dispatch of theses.

† Candidates will also be required to sign a form stating whether they give permission for the thesis to be consulted.

St John of Damascus, *On the Holy Icons,* i. 1–27 and iii. 27–40 (ed. Kotter)
St Theodore the Studite, *Ep. ad Platonem*; Epp. ii. 85–6, 129; *Testamentum* (P.G. 99)
Extracts from *The Life of St. Stephen the Younger* (P.G. 100, 1084B–1089D, 1109C–1148A, 1156D–1160B)
Epanagoge, Tituli ii, iii, viii, ix, xi (ed. K. E. Zacharias von Lingenthal, *Jus Graeco-Romanum,* iv. 181 ff.)
Extracts from Theophanes, *Chronographia,* from the acts of the Iconoclast Councils of 754 and 815, and related texts (as given in H. Hennephof, *Textus Byzantinos ad Iconomachian pertinentes,* Leiden, 1969, pp. 1–24, 61–82)
Photius, *Homilies* 10 and 17 (ed. B. Laourdas, Thessalonika, 1959); and *Encyclical Letter* (P.G. 102, 721–41)

(iii) Byzantine ecclesiastical texts:

St Symeon the New Theologian, *Epistle on Confession* (ed. K. Holl, *Enthusiasmus und Bussgewalt,* pp. 110–27)
———*Catecheses* 18, 20, 22, 26, *Second Thanksgiving* (ed. Krivocheine, *Sources chrétiennes,* vols. 104 and 113)
———*Hymns,* 1, 15, 28 (ed. Koder, *Sources chrétiennes,* 156 and 174)
St. Gregory Palamas, *Triads in Defence of the Holy Hesychasts,* I 2–3 (ed. Meyendorff)
Nicolas Cabasilas, *Explanation of the Divine Liturgy,* 27–32 (eds. Salaville and Perichon, *Sources chrétiennes* 4 *bis*)

The three papers will include passages for comment as well as general questions relating to the set texts.

B. *Armenian with Greek*

(i) Armenian historical texts:

Moses of Khoren, *History of Armenia,* i. 1–6; ii. 10, 28–36, 86 (ed. Erevan 1991)
Eliseus Vardapet, *History of St Vardan and the Armenian War,* Books I–IV (ed. Erevan 1957, pp. 3–97)

(ii) Armenian theological and ecclesiastical texts:

Eznik of Kolb, *Refutation of the Sects*
either Book II (ed. Paris 1959, P.O. 28, pp. 460–96)
or Books III and IV (ibid., pp. 496–537)
Yovhannēs Mandakuni, *Homilies,* ed. Venice 1860, nos. 1, 2, 5, 17, 20, 21, 23, 24, 26.

(iii) A translation paper from Greek ecclesiastical texts. Passages for translation will be set from unspecified texts, and also from the following set texts:

3 (1) Kings 8–12; 4 (2) Kings 18–25 (LXX)
Psalms 117 (118), 119 (120)–138 (139) (LXX)
Isaiah 40–55 (LXX)
Wisdom 1: 1–11: 1 (LXX)
The Gospels of St Mark and St John
The Epistle to the Romans
St Cyril of Jerusalem, *Procatechesis* and *Catecheses* 19–23 (*Mystagogicae Catecheses* 1–5) (ed. F. L. Cross, SPCK 1951)
The Liturgy of St John Chrysostom (ed. F. E. Brightman, *Liturgies Eastern and Western,* pp. 353–99)

Papers (i) and (ii) will include passages for translation and comment as well as general questions relating to the set texts.

C. *Syriac with Greek*

(i) Syriac historical texts:

John of Ephesus, *Lives of the Eastern Saints* (ed. E. W. Brooks), nos. 10, 13, 47–9 (*Patrologia Orientalis,* vol. 17, pp. 137–58, 187–213; vol. 18, pp. 676–97)

Chronicon Anonymum (ed. I. Guidi), in *Chronica Minora* I, CSCO, Scriptores Syri, vol. 1, pp. 15–39.

(ii) Syriac theological texts:

Afrahat, *Demonstration* 4 (ed. R. Graffin, *Patrologia Syriaca,* vol. 1)

Ephrem, *Hymni de Fide,* nos. 10, 13, 31, 40, 83 (ed. E. Beck, CSCO, Scriptores Syri, vol. 73)

Narsai, *Homily* 17 (ed. A. Mingana, *Narsai Homiliae et Carmina,* vol. 1)

Philoxenus, *Letter to Patricius,* §§1–46 (ed. R. Lavenant, *Patrologia Orientalis,* vol. 30, pp. 744–92).

(iii) as Paper B (iii) above.

Papers (i) and (ii) will include passages for translation and comment as well as general questions relating to the set texts.

Teaching in all three options (Greek, Armenian with Greek, Syriac with Greek) may not be available every year, and applicants for admission will be advised whether teaching will be available in the option of their choice.

Note. Candidates with sufficient knowledge of Greek may offer Paper A (i) in place of Paper B (iii)/C (iii). Except in the case of Papers A (i) and B (iii)/C (iii), and subject to the approval of the faculty boards, a candidate may offer texts—or, in the case of Paper A (ii), a period of Greek church history—other than those specified in the regulations.

III. The examiners may award a Distinction for excellence in the whole examination.

Economic and Social History

(*See also the general notice at the commencement of these regulations.*)

The regulations of the Board of the Faculty of Modern History are as follows:

1. Every candidate must follow for at least six terms a course of instruction in Economic and Social History and must upon entering for the examination produce from his or her society a certificate to that effect.

2. The examination will consist of the following parts:

Qualifying test

Every candidate must pass a qualifying test. The test shall consist of the satisfactory completion of two courses on

(1) Methodological introduction to research in the social sciences and history.

(2) *Either* Quantitative methods and computer applications for historians

or A paper from another established course within the University where this would provide a more appropriate training for the candidate's dissertation focus. Such a choice will need formal approval from both the Course Director and the Chairman of the Graduate Studies Committee of the Board of the Faculty of Modern History.

The organizers of each course shall not later than the Friday of the sixth week of the Trinity Term preceding the examination submit to the examiners a list of candidates who have satisfactorily completed a qualifying course. No candidate who has failed the qualifying test of two courses will be permitted to supplicate for the degree. Candidates who fail a qualifying course once will be permitted to take it again, not later than one year after the initial attempt.

Final examination

The examination shall consist of four papers and a dissertation.

I. Three advanced papers at least two of which must be selected from Schedule I below (Advanced Papers for the M.Phil. and M.Sc. in Economic and Social History), and not more than one from any other M.Phil. the choice of which must be approved by the chairman of the Graduate Studies Committee of the Modern History Board not later than Monday of the fourth week of the second Michaelmas Term of the course.

Candidates must take at least two of their advanced papers as three-hour written examinations. For each of their remaining advanced papers candidates must choose to be assessed either by written examination or by two 5,000 word essays. Essays may be only submitted in lieu of written papers for subjects in Schedule I or for papers from other M.Phil.s where similar provision exists in the regulations for those examinations. The essays must be the work of the candidates alone and they must not consult any other person including their supervisors in any way concerning the method of handling the themes chosen. The themes chosen by the candidate must be submitted for approval by the chairman of examiners, c/o the Clerk of the Schools, High Street, Oxford, not later than the Monday of the fifth week of Hilary Term. Candidates will be informed within two weeks, by means of a letter directed to their colleges, whether the topics they have submitted have been approved. The finished essays must be delivered by the candidate to the Clerk of the Schools, Examination Schools, High Street, Oxford, by noon on Monday of the third week of Trinity Full Term. The essays must be presented in proper scholarly form, and two typed copies of each must be submitted. Candidates may be examined viva voce on the subjects on which they submit essays. Candidates who have not delivered essays as prescribed by the due date on any of their subjects must sit the written examination in those subjects.

II. *Either* (i) one paper in a discipline or skill or sources or methods selected from Schedule II below.

or (ii) A fourth advanced paper selected from Schedule I or from any additional list of papers for the M.Phil. and M.Sc. in Economic and Social History approved by the Graduate Studies Committee of the Board of the Faculty of Modern History and published in the definitive list of Advanced Papers as set out in Schedule I.

III. A dissertation of not more than 30,000 words, including appendices but excluding bibliography on a topic approved by the candidate's supervisor. The dissertation must be delivered not later than noon on the Monday of the first week of the Trinity Full Term in which the examination is to be taken to the Clerk of the Schools, High Street, Oxford. Dissertations submitted must not exceed the permitted length. If they do the examiners will reduce the marks awarded. The presentation and footnotes should comply with the requirements specified in the Regulations of the Educational Policy and Standards Committee for the degree of M.Litt. and D.Phil. and follow the *Conventions for the presentation of dissertations and theses* of the Board of the Faculty of Modern History.

Each dissertation must include a short abstract which concisely summarizes its scope and principal arguments, in about 300 words.

Candidates must submit by the specified date two copies of their dissertations. These must be securely and firmly bound in either hard or soft covers. One copy of an M.Phil. dissertation which is approved by the examiners must be deposited in the Bodleian Library. This finalized copy should incorporate any corrections or amendments which the examiners may have requested. It must be in a permanently fixed binding, drilled and sewn, in a stiff board case in library buckram, in a dark colour, and lettered on the spine with the candidate's name and initials, the degree, and the year of submission.

3. Candidates may, if they so wish, be examined in up to two of their four papers (or submit essays in lieu of these papers as provided for above) at the end of their first year.

4. The examiners will permit the use of any hand-held pocket calculator subject to the conditions set out below under the heading 'Use of calculators in examinations' in the *Special Regulations concerning Examinations.*

5. Each candidate must attend an oral examination when required to do so by the examiners.

6. The examiners may award a distinction for excellence in the whole examination.

7. If it is the opinion of the examiners that the work done by a candidate, while not of sufficient merit to qualify for the degree of M.Phil., is nevertheless of sufficient merit to qualify for the degree of Master of Science in Economic and Social History, the candidate shall be given the option of re-sitting the M.Phil. (as provided by Ch. VI Sect. VI, §2, para 4) or of being granted leave to supplicate for the degree of Master of Science.

8. A candidate who fails the examination will be permitted to re-take it on one further occasion only, not later than one year after the initial attempt.

Such a candidate whose dissertation has been of a satisfactory standard may re-submit the same piece of work, while a candidate who has reached a satisfactory standard on the written papers will not be required to re-take that part of the examination.

Schedule I

Advanced Papers for the M.Phil. and M.Sc. in Economic and Social History

A broad range of the course resources are shared with the corresponding courses in History of Science, Medicine, and Technology, and Advanced Papers are therefore available in the subject areas listed here.

1. Economic and business history
2. History of science and technology
3. Social history
4. Historical demography
5. History of medicine

A descriptive list of Advanced Papers will be published by the Board of the Faculty of Modern History in September for the academic year ahead (not all options may be available in every year). The definitive list of the titles of Advanced Papers for any one year will be circulated to candidates and their supervisors and posted on the Faculty notice board not later than Friday of Third Week of Michaelmas Term of the academic year in which the paper is to be taken.

Schedule II

The paper in a relevant discipline or skill may be:

1. One of the papers from the M.Phil. in Economics.
2. One of the papers from the M.Phil. in Sociology or in Comparative Social Policy.
3. One of the papers from the M.Phil. in Russian and East European Studies.
4. One suitable paper from another Master's degree under the auspices of the Faculty of Modern History approved from time to time by the Graduate Studies Committee of the Board of Modern History.
5. One suitable paper from another Master's degree on the recommendation of the candidate's supervisor and endorsed by the Course Director.

Choices under Schedule II have to be approved by the chairman of the Graduate Studies Committee of the Board of the Faculty of Modern History not later than Monday of the fourth week of the second Michaelmas Term of the course. Candidates wishing to take a paper under 1, 2, 3, or 5 will also need the approval of the appropriate course convenor and the Graduate Studies Committee of the relevant faculty board or inter-faculty committee who need to be satisfied that each candidate has an adequate background in the subject. Not all options may be available in any one year.

Economics

(*See also the general notice at the commencement of these regulations.*)

The regulations made by the Divisional Board of Social Sciences are as follows:

The examiners will not provide calculators, but will permit the use of any hand-held pocket calculator in the examination room, both for the first year examinations and for the final examination, subject to the conditions set out under the heading 'Use of calculators in examinations' in the *Special Regulations concerning Examinations*.

First-year examinations

There will be three compulsory papers to be taken at the end of the first year of the course.

(*a*) *Macroeconomics*

Investment, consumption, and the demand for money and other assets. The IS-LM and fixed-price models. Inflation and unemployment. Rational expectations. Open economy models. Overlapping generations models. Price formation, price stickiness, and the effects of imperfect information. Monetary and fiscal policy. Business cycles and economic growth.

(*b*) *Microeconomics*

Consumer and producer theory. Uncertainty. Game theory. Bargaining and contracts. Auctions. Industrial organization. Markets and equilibrium. Social choice. Welfare and public economics.

(*c*) *Econometrics*

Probability and distribution theory. Estimation and inference. Regression, Monte Carlo. Time series. Likelihood methods, hypothesis testing, asymptotic theory. Dynamic models. Cointegration. Modelling and diagnostic tests. Simultaneous equations, indentification, instrumental variables and related methods. Applications of these methods will include earnings functions and other cross-sections, macro-economic time series models, finance.

All three papers will be set in two parts (A and B). Questions must be selected from both parts. Questions in part A will involve the use of mathematical techniques.

The papers shall be set and administered by the examiners appointed to examine the M.Phil. in Economics. Applications must be made by the Friday of eighth week in Michaelmas Full Term. The examination will be held in the eighth week of Trinity Full Term. The examiners may also examine any candidate viva voce. In exceptional circumstances, the Economics Graduate Studies Committee may give permission for a candidate to defer one of these papers. This paper will then be taken at the same time as the final examination.

Candidates who pass these papers will proceed to the second year of the course and take the Final Examination at the end of the second year. Candidates who fail only one out of the three papers may, by permission of the Economics Graduate Studies Committee, proceed to the second year of the course and resit the one failed paper at the same time as the final examination. Otherwise, candidates who fail the first-year examination will be permitted to resit all three papers at the end of their second year but will not be permitted to enter the final examination at that time. If they then pass the three compulsory papers, they will be permitted to proceed with the course and enter the final examination at the end of their third year. In exceptional cases, the Economics Graduate Studies Committee may permit the deferral of resitting one of the three papers at the end of the second year until the final examination. No candidate will be permitted to sit any of the compulsory papers more than once.

Final Examination

No candidate shall enter the final examination unless he or she has already passed the three compulsory papers in the first-year examinations, save that the Economics Graduate Studies Committee may permit any candidate who has failed one of the compulsory papers to resit that paper at the same time as the final examination.

All candidates must offer two advanced papers and submit a thesis.* Candidates may offer *both* papers from Schedule I, or they may apply to offer *one* paper from those listed in Schedule II, below.

Candidates must deliver two copies of the thesis (clearly marked with the candidate's name, college, and the words 'M.Phil. in Economics' and accompanied by a statement signed by the candidate that it is the candidate's own work except where otherwise indicated) to the Clerk of the Schools, High Street, Oxford OX1 4BG, by noon on Wednesday in the third week of Trinity Full Term in which the final examination is to be taken. Successful candidates will be required to deposit one copy of their thesis in the Economics Library.

The Examiners may also examine any candidate viva voce.

SCHEDULE I

Advanced Papers for the M.Phil. in Economics

Advanced Papers are normally available in the following subject areas:

1. Public Economics
2. International Economics
3. Economics of Industry
4. Advanced Econometrics
5. Advanced Economic Theory
6. Labour Economics
7. Development Economics
8. Financial Economics

Other Advanced Papers may sometimes be available. Some that have been offered in recent years are:

1. The History of Economic Thought from Hume to J. S. Mill
2. Command and Transitional Economies
3. The Economics of OECD Countries
4. Economic Growth in History

A *descriptive list* of Advanced Papers for an academic year, together with their rubrics, will be published before the beginning of the year by the Department of Economics. The rubrics attached to each paper will give general guidance on the topics on which questions may be set; but candidates will not be expected to answer questions from all parts of the field. Not all Advanced Papers on the descriptive list may be available in that year.

The *definitive list* of titles of Advanced Papers for any one year will be circulated to candidates and their supervisors before Friday of the second week of Michaelmas Term of that year.

---

* Theses must be of not more than 30,000 words and must be typewritten. The thesis must be accompanied by a statement that it is the candidate's own work except where otherwise indicated. See the regulation on p. 508 concerning the preparation and dispatch of theses. Candidates are reminded that work submitted for the Degree of M.Phil. may subsequently be incorporated in a thesis submitted for the Degree of D.Phil.

SCHEDULE II

The following Advanced Papers (if available) from the M.Phil. in Economic and Social History:

1. The Economic History of Europe between the Wars
2. Industrial and Business History of Britain since 1870
3. Macroeconomic Behaviour of the British Economy since 1870

Choices under Schedule II have to be approved by the Director of the M.Phil. in Economics not later than Friday of the second week of the second Michaelmas Term of the course.

English Studies [From 1 October 2004: (Medieval Period)]

(*See also the general notice at the commencement of these regulations.*)

The regulations made by the Board of the Faculty of English Language and Literature are as follows:

[Until 1 October 2004:

Each candidate will be admitted to take the examination in a specific year and will be required to offer one of the following courses. Not all courses may be available in any given year.

Any candidate may be examined *viva voce*, at the discretion of the examiners.

Any candidate who wishes to take an examination later than the one to which he has been admitted must apply to the board for permission to do so by not later than Thursday of the first week of that Trinity Term in which he was to have taken the examination. He must at the same time state which examination he wishes to enter for and his application must have the support of his college and of his supervisor.

Successful candidates who have submitted a thesis as part of the examination will be required to deposit one copy of the thesis in the Bodleian Library unless the examiners direct to the contrary.*

Teaching may not be available for every option in every year and candidates are advised to enquire when they submit their applications for admission.

The examiners may award a distinction for excellence in the whole examination.

Written examination

1. Except as provided in (2) below, each candidate will be required to offer the two subjects of Group A and two subjects chosen from Group B of the course for which he has opted. Subjects in Group B marked with an asterisk are compulsory for all candidates. Special conditions governing the choice of subjects in Group B in individual courses are set out below in the detailed prescriptions for these courses.

2. Candidates will be required to offer a thesis of about 20,000 words, on some topic† approved by the board or by a person or persons to whom it may delegate the function of giving such approval, save that candidates in courses (i) and (ii) may be allowed, in exceptional circumstances, to offer a third paper in Group B instead of the thesis. A thesis involving the edition of a text may, if the candidate so wishes, exceed 20,000 words by not more than the length of the text.] Candidates submitting a thesis‡ must deliver two copies to the Clerk of the Schools, High Street, Oxford,

* Candidates will also be required to sign a form stating whether they give permission for their thesis to be consulted.

† The relationships between religion or philosophy or science and literature or between literature and another art, in one of the specified periods, are among the topics which the board would consider suitable.

‡ See the regulation on p. 508 concerning the preparation and dispatch of theses. Candidates are reminded that work submitted for the Degree of M.Phil. may be subsequently incorporated in a thesis submitted for the Degree of D.Phil.

by noon on Monday of the eighth week of the Hilary Full Term in which the examination is to be taken.

3. Each candidate's choice of subjects shall require the approval of a person or persons to whom the board may delegate the function of giving such approval. Approval must be applied for on or before Saturday of the second week of Michaelmas Term preceding the examination.

Candidates who have offered Medieval Latin Language and Literature or The Latin Literature of the British Isles before the Norman Conquest in List B of Course II of the Honour School of English Language and Literature or candidates who have offered Medieval Latin Language and Literature in the Honour School of Classics and Modern Languages will not be permitted to offer the corresponding subject or subjects (8 or 9) in the M.Phil. in English Studies.

4. The method of examination of subjects in Group A will be by essays written by the candidate on themes chosen by himself from a list drawn up by the examiners. He will be required to write *two* essays (of about 4,000–5,000 words each) on each of the subjects of Group A; and if, according to the detailed prescriptions of any subject of Group A, a candidate is required or has opted to study two authors or topics, he must write one essay on each. The essays must be the work of the candidate alone and he must not consult any other person (including his supervisor) in any way concerning either his choice of themes from the list drawn up by the examiners or the method of handling the themes chosen. The list of themes will be communicated by the examiners to the candidate by Saturday of the sixth week of Hilary Full Term. The lists will be addressed to the candidates at their colleges and it is the responsibility of each candidate to collect the list from his college. The finished essays must be delivered by the candidate to the Clerk of the Schools at the Examination Schools by noon on Monday of the third week of Trinity Full Term. The essays must be presented in properly scholarly form, and two typed copies of each must be submitted.* Any candidate may be examined *viva voce* on the subjects of Group A.] In Courses (i) and (ii) the examiners may set a written test of ability to translate from Old or Middle English, as the case may be, into Modern English.

5. The method of the examination of the subjects of Group B will be by essays of 2,500 words each, two essays to be written for each subject. The topics for these essays will be chosen by the student (who may seek the advice of the supervisor or tutor prior to submission of the topic), and must be sent for approval to the Chair of Examiners (who may consult the External Examiners and, where necessary, the General Supervisor of the M.Phil.) by Thursday of fourth week of Trinity Term. Candidates may be required by the Examiners to change or revise the topics initially submitted. The examiners will inform candidates of their final approval of topics on Thursday of fifth week of Trinity Term. Once the topics have been accepted, candidates are forbidden to approach the General Supervisor, their tutor, or any other person, for advice or guidance. The four completed essays, two for each subject, each one clearly headed by the essay title and the name of the Group B subject to which it relates, must be submitted to the Clerk of Schools by noon on Thursday of the seventh week of Trinity Term.

6. Any candidate may be examined *viva voce* about the extended essays and library papers.

7. Candidates are warned that they must avoid duplicating in their answers to one part of the examination material that they have used in another part of the examination.

---

* A clear copy will be acceptable as the second copy.

8. No candidate who has failed any of the above subjects will be awarded the degree in that examination. Candidates failing up to two subjects will be required to resit those two; candidates failing more than two will be required to resubmit the written work specified for each of the above subjects.

Course (i) English Medieval Studies until 1100

Group A

1. Old English Literature. Candidates will be expected to have read widely throughout the period and to show such knowledge of the historical and cultural background as is necessary for a profitable study of Old English Literature.

2. A major topic in Old English Literature. Candidates may offer *one* of the following: (*a*) Old English verse with a study of *either* heroic poetry *or* biblical poetry *or* the school of Cynewulf; (*b*) Alfredian prose *or* the Old English homily.

Group B

Candidates who have read Course II of the Honour School of English Language and Literature will not be permitted to offer subject B.1. Candidates who have not read Course II in the Honour School, and who do not offer subject B.1, will be required to attend a course on the history of the English Language up to 1100 and to pass a qualifying examination to be held at the end of the first Hilary Full Term after their admission. In individual cases the faculty board may at its discretion permit a candidate who has failed the examination to take it again in Trinity Term or at a later date approved by the board. If a second examination is held in Trinity Term the examiners will normally set such a date for this examination as will enable them to report to the Graduate Studies Committee of the board at its meeting on Monday of eighth week of that term.

Candidates who have offered subject B.11 in Course II of the Honour School of English Language and Literature will not be allowed to offer subject 12.

Candidates may, with the permission of the board,* substitute (*a*) for one of the subjects of Group B, a subject chosen from any of those of Course (ii), or (*b*) for two of the subjects of Group B, one of the options not chosen under A.2, or both the subjects in Old Norse Literature of Course (ii).

No candidate may offer more than two of subjects 6–11 inclusive. Candidates who offer any of papers 4, 7, 8, and 9 will be expected to translate and comment on passages from the texts prescribed for the relevant paper(s) under examination conditions (1 hour for each paper).

1. The History of the English Language to 1100. The following texts are recommended as a basis for study: *Sweet's Anglo-Saxon Reader* (revised D. Whitelock), nos. xxxi, xxxii; the language of Alfred and of Ælfric; the glosses to the Lindisfarne Gospels, *St Mark,* chaps. i–viii.

2. Old English Textual Criticism, including a special study of the following: *Cædmon's Hymn*; *The Dream of the Rood,* Wulfstan's *Sermo Lupi ad Anglos, Beowulf.*

3. The Reigns of Ethelred the Unready and Canute.

4. Eddaic and Skaldic Verse. The following texts are prescribed: *Guðrúnarkviður* I-III, Grottasöngr, *Vafþrúðnismál, Baldrs draumar, Ragnarsdrápa* (Bragi), *Haraldskæði* (Þorbjörn hornklofi), *Hákonarmál* (Eyvindr), *Vellekla* (Einarr Skálaglamm), the verses in *Eyrbyggja saga.*

5. The Palaeography of Insular Manuscripts up to 1100. (Candidates selecting this option will be required to transcribe from and comment on specimens written in English and Latin under examination conditions (1 hour).)

---

* Candidates should ask their supervisors to apply to the board on their behalf as soon as possible (the board meets in the first week of Michaelmas Term).

6. The Norsemen in England. The study of contemporary texts in the original languages will be expected. Attention is particularly directed to *The Old English Chronicle* 800–955 (MS A), 979–1042 (MS C), *The Battle of Maldon, Encomium Emmæ, Historia de Sancto Cuthberto, Hofuðlausn* (Egill), *Víkingarvísur* (Sigvatr), *Kúntsdrápa* (Sigvatr), *Hofuðlausn* (Óttarr Svarti), *Knútsdrápa* (Óttarr Svarti).

7. Old Saxon, with a study of the *Heliand.*

8. Medieval Latin Language and Literature. The following texts are prescribed: Abelard: *Historia Calamitatum,* ed. J. Monfrin (Paris, 1976); Peter the Venerable: *Selected Letters,* nos. 9, 24, 43, 53, 115, ed. J. Martin, Toronto Medieval Latin Texts (Toronto, 1974); Notker, *Liber Hymnorum,* ed. W. v. den Steinen (Bern/Munich, 1960), *proemium,* pp. 10–18, 84, 88; *Ruodlieb,* vv. 1–252 (ed. Reclam); The Archpoet, *Poems* (ed. Reclam); Walter of Châtillon, *Moralische-satirische Gedichte,* nos. 2, 6, 17, 18, ed. Strecker (Heidelberg, 1929); *Oxford Book of Medieval Latin Verse* (rev. edn.), ed. F. J. E. Raby (Oxford, 1970), nos. 75–80, 83, 92, 103, 119–29, 157–9, 169–73, 175–6, 207–32, 239; Geoffrey of Monmouth: *Historia Regum Britanniae,* Book IX, ed. J. Hammer, Medieval Academy of America (Cambridge, Mass., 1951).

9. The Latin Literature of the British Isles: from the Origins to the Norman Conquest. The following texts are prescribed: Gildas, *de Excidio* pref., chaps. 1–10, ed. M. Winterbottom, Arthurian Period Sources 7 (London/Chichester, 1978); Aldhelm, *de Virginitate,* prose, chaps. 1–5; verse, ll. 1–105, 2861–904, ed. R. Ehwald, *MGH, Auctores Antiquissimi,* xv (Berlin, 1919); Bede, *Vita S. Cuthberti* prose, pref., chaps. 1–5, ed. B. Colgrave, *Two 'Lives' of Saint Cuthbert* (repr. New York, 1969), metrical *Life pref.,* chaps. 1–5, ed. W. Jaager, *Palaestra,* 198; Alcuin, *Two Alcuin Letter-Books,* 1, nos. 1–14, ed. C. Chase, Toronto Medieval Latin Texts (Toronto, 1975); *Oxford Book of Medieval Latin Verse,* no. 80, rev. edn. F. J. E. Raby (Oxford, 1970); *Versus de . . . Sanctis Euboricensis Ecclesiae,* ll. 1–130, 1596–1657, ed. E. Dümmler, *MGH, Poetae,* 1 (Berlin, 1881); Asser, *Vita Alfredi,* chaps. 1–15, ed. Stevenson, rev. D. Whitelock (Oxford, 1959); Æthelweard, *Chronicle,* Book IV, ed. A. Campbell (London, 1962); Ælfric, *Life of St Ethelwold,* ed. M. Winterbottom, *Three Lives of English Saints,* Toronto Medieval Latin Texts (Toronto, 1972); Columbanus, *Epistle,* 1, ed. G. Walker, Scriptores Latini Hiberniae II (Dublin, 1970); *Hisperica Famina* vv. 571–612, ed. M. Herren (Toronto, 1974).

10. Old English Metre and Poetic Diction.

11. The History of the English Church, *either* to the death of Bede, *or* from the death of Alfred to the Norman Conquest.

12. The Archaeology of Early Anglo-Saxon England. (This paper will be identical with the paper of the same title of the M.St. in European Archaeology and will be examined by written paper as specified in paragraph 4(*a*) of the regulations for the M.St. in European Archaeology.

13. Early Middle English Literature. Candidates are expected to have read widely in English literature of the period *c.*1100–*c.*1350.

Course (ii) English Medieval Studies from 1100 to 1500

Group A

1. English Literature 1100–1500. Candidates will be expected to have read widely throughout the period and to show such knowledge of the historical and cultural background as is necessary for a profitable study of the English literature of the period.

2. Langland *or* Gower *or* Malory.

Group B

Candidates who have read Course II of the Honour School of English Language and Literature will not be able to offer subject B.5. Candidates who have offered

Medieval Latin Language and Literature or The Latin Literature of the British Isles: from the Origins to the Norman Conquest in List C of Course II of the Honour School of English Language and Literature or candidates who have offered Medieval Latin Language and Literature in the Honour School of Classics and Modern Languages will not be permitted to offer the corresponding subject or subjects (11 or 12) in the M.Phil. in English Studies. Candidates who have not read Course II in the Honour School, and who do not offer subject B.5, will be required to attend a course on the history of the English language up to 1400 and to pass a qualifying examination to be held at the end of the first Hilary Full Term after their admission. In individual cases the faculty board may at its discretion permit a candidate who has failed the examination to take it again in Trinity Term or at a later date approved by the board. If a second examination is held in Trinity Term the examiners will normally set such a date for this examination as will enable them to report to the Graduate Studies Committee of the board at its meeting on Monday of eighth week of that term.

Candidates may, with the permission of the board,* substitute for one of the subjects of Group B a subject chosen from any of those of Course (i) *or* Prose fiction with special reference to Sidney's *Arcadia* from A.2(b) of Course (iv).

No candidate may offer more than two of subjects 9–15 inclusive.

Candidates who offer any of papers 6, 7, 9, 10, 11, 12, 13, or 14 will be expected to translate and comment on passages from the texts or author prescribed for the relevant paper(s) under examination conditions (1 hour for each paper).

1. Chaucer. Candidates will be required to show knowledge of the content and literary criticism of Chaucer's works, and may be required to show knowledge of the canon and of textual criticism.

2. Devotional literature of the fourteenth and fifteenth centuries.

3. The medieval drama.

4. Early Middle English Literature. Candidates are expected to have read widely in English literature of the period *c.*1100–*c.*1350.

5. The History of the English Language from 1100 to 1500. The following texts are recommended as a basis for study: *The Peterborough Chronicle, 1070–1154*; *Ancrene Wisse* (Corpus MS); *Cursor Mundi* (Cotton MS); *London English 1384–1425*, eds. Chambers and Daunt; *Paston Letters,* ed. N. Davis (Clarendon Medieval and Tudor Series, Oxford, 1958).

6. Anglo-Norman Literature. The following texts are prescribed: Benedeit, *Voyage of St Brendan*; Gaimar, *Estorie des Engleis*; *La Seinte Resureccion* (ANTS); *Les Fragments du Tristan de Thomas* (ed. B. H. Wind); M. Paris, *Life of St Edward the Confessor* (ANTS); *The Romance of Horn* (ANTS).

7. Old Norse Literature, 1. The following texts are prescribed: *Njáls saga, Egils saga, Óláfs saga helga* (*Heimskringla*), *Kormaks saga, Skáldskaparmál, Haustlöng.*

8. The Palaeography of Manuscripts written in England from 1100 to 1500. (Candidates will be required to transcribe from and comment on specimens written in English under examination conditions (1 hour).)

9. Dante, *La Divina Commedia.*

10. Old French Literature: *either* Chrétien de Troyes *or Le Roman de la Rose.*

11. Medieval Latin Language and Literature. The following texts are prescribed: Abelard: *Historia Calamitatum,* ed. J. Monfrin (Paris, 1967); Peter the Venerable: *Selected Letters,* nos. 9, 24, 43, 53, 115, ed. J. Martin, Toronto Medieval Latin Texts (Toronto, 1974); Notker, *Liber Hymnorum,* ed. W. v. den Steinen (Bern/Munich,

---

* Candidates should ask their supervisors to apply to the board on their behalf as soon as possible (the board meets in the first week of Michaelmas Term).

1960), *proemium,* pp. 10–18, 84, 88; *Ruodlieb,* vv. 1–252 (ed. Reclam); The Archpoet, *Poems* (ed. Reclam); Walter of Châtillon, *Moralische-satirische Gedichte,* nos. 2, 6, 17, 18, ed. Strecker (Heidelberg, 1929); *Oxford Book of Medieval Latin Verse* (rev. edn.), ed. F. J. E. Raby (Oxford, 1970), nos. 75–80, 83, 92, 103, 119–29, 157–9, 169–73, 175–6, 207–32, 239; Geoffrey of Monmouth: *Historia Regum Britanniae,* Book IX, ed. J. Hammer, Medieval Academy of America (Cambridge, Mass., 1951).

12. The Latin Literature of the British Isles: from the Origins to the Norman Conquest. The following texts are prescribed: Gildas, *de Excidio* pref., chaps. 1–10, ed. M. Winterbottom, Arthurian Period Sources 7 (London/Chichester, 1978); Aldhelm, *de Virginitate,* prose, chaps. 1–5; verse, ll. 1–105, 2861–904, ed. R. Ehwald, MGH, *Auctores Antiquissimi,* xv (Berlin, 1919); Bede, *Vita S. Cuthberti,* prose, pref., chaps. 1–5, ed. B. Colgrave, *Two 'Lives' of Saint Cuthbert* (repr. New York, 1969), metrical *Life pref.,* chaps. 1–5, ed. W. Jaager, *Palaestra,* 198; Alcuin, *Two Alcuin Letter-Books,* 1, nos. 1–14, ed. C. Chase, Toronto Medieval Latin Texts (Toronto, 1975); *Oxford Book of Medieval Latin Verse,* no. 80, rev. edn. F. J. E. Raby (Oxford, 1970); *Versus de . . . Sanctis Euboricensis Ecclesiae,* ll. 1–130, 1596–1657, ed. E. Dümmler, *MGH, Poetae,* 1 (Berlin, 1881); Asser, *Vita Alfredi,* chaps. 1–15, ed. Stevenson, rev. D. Whitelock (Oxford, 1959); Æthelweard, *Chronicle,* Book IV, ed. A. Campbell (London, 1962); Ælfric, *Life of St Ethelwold,* ed. M. Winterbottom, *Three Lives of English Saints,* Toronto Medieval Latin Texts (Toronto, 1972); Columbanus, *Epistle,* 1, ed. G. Walker, Scriptores Latini Hiberniae II (Dublin, 1970); *Hisperica Famina* vv. 571–612, ed. M. Herren (Toronto, 1975).

13. Medieval Welsh Literature. Candidates may offer *one* of the following:

(*a*) Medieval Welsh tales and romances with special reference to *Pedeir Keinc y Mabinogi* (ed. I. Williams, 1951), *Culhwch ac Olwen* (ed. R. Bromwich and D. S. Evans, 1988), *Owein* (ed. R. L. Thomson, 1975), *Peredur vab Efrawc* (ed. G. W. Goetinck, 1976), *Gereint vab Erbin* in *Llyfr Gwyn Rhydderch* (ed. J. G. Evans and R. M. Jones, 1973, pp. 193–226), *Cyfranc Lludd a Llevelys* (ed. I. Williams, 1922), *Breuddwyd Maxen* (ed. I. Williams, 1920), *Breudwyt Ronabwy* (ed. M. Richards, 1948)

(*b*) Medieval Welsh religious literature with special reference to *Blodeugerdd Barddas o Ganu Crefyddol Cynnar* (ed. M. Haycock, 1994), *The Medieval Welsh Religious Lyric* (ed. C. A. McKenna, 1991), and *Llyvyr Agkyr Llandewivrevi* (ed. J. Morris Jones and J. Rhys).

(*c*) *Gwaiath Dafydd ap Gwilym* (ed. T. Parry) and *Gwaith Iolo Goch* (ed. D. Johnston, 1988).

14. Old Norse Literature, II. The following texts are prescribed: *Grettis saga, Laxdæla saga, Eyrbyggja ssaga, Völsunga saga, Hrólfs saga kraka, Gautreks saga, Sólarljóð, Íslendinga saga* (Sturla).

15. Medieval Philosophy. Candidates must offer topic (i) below and any *one* other topic. Candidates are recommended to study the texts indicated.

(i) Aristotelian philosophy in the thirteenth century: Aquinas, *De Unitate Intellectus,* and *Summa Theologica,* I. i–ii.

Recommended reading: F. van Steenberghen, *Aristotle in the West (The Origins of Latin Aristotelianism*), trans. L. Johnston (Louvain, 1955).

(ii) Dialectic and theology from 1070 to 1150: Anselm, *Proslogion*; Abelard, *Historia Calamitatum, Sic et Non* (Prologue).

(iii) English philosophy in the first half of the fourteenth century: Duns Scotus, *De Primo Principio*; Ockham, *Philosophical Writings,* ed. and trans. P. Boehner (1957), section II (pp. 18–45).

(iv) Philosophy outside the Schools: Boethius, *Consolatio Philosophiae* (Books I, IV, V), its tradition, translation, imitations, commentaries.

16. The Literature of Dissent. Among the areas covered will be: texts that deal with political, social, theological and ecclesiastical dissent in the period *c.*1100–*c.*1500, including discussions of issues concerning the position of the poor, women, the uneducated. Materials beyond the accepted range of literary texts, and from works in Latin and French as well as in English, may be included.

Course (iii) SHAKESPEARE AND THE DRAMA TO 1642

Group A

1. Texts and contexts: relationships between literature and society. Among the areas covered may be:

authorship and the book-trade; censorship and patronage; the Court; economics; education and the universities; the family and marriage; gender and sexuality; music; philosophy; political history and theory; the professions; religion and the Church; science and superstition; social history, theory and structures; theatre design; theatrical companies and staging; travel; visual arts.

At least one essay must deal with the theatre.

2. Shakespeare:

(i) Shakespeare's earlier plays.

The plays to be studied will be: the English history plays (except *Henry VIII*); the comedies (except *Measure for Measure* and *All's Well that Ends Well*); *Titus Andronicus*; *Romeo and Juliet.*

(ii) Shakespeare's later plays.

The plays to be studied will be: the tragedies (except *Titus Andronicus* and *Romeo and Juliet*); the Roman plays; the romances; *Measure for Measure*; *All's Well that Ends Well*; *Troilus and Cressida; Henry VIII.*

Group B

1. Drama, 1500–93.
2. Tragedy, 1595–1642.
3. Comedy, Tragicomedy, and Romance, 1595–1642.
4. Textual Criticism and Scholarship of Shakespeare.
5. Criticism of Shakespeare.
6. The Masque.
7. One or more of the following options from other M.Phil. courses:

Course (ii), Paper B.3: Medieval Drama.

Course (iv), B.1–4; 1. Spenser; 2. Jonson; 3. Donne; 4. Milton.

Course (iv), A.2 (*a*): Prose Fiction.

Course (iv) ENGLISH LITERATURE, 1500–1660

Group A

1. Texts and contexts: relationships between literature and society. Among the areas covered may be:

authorship and the book-trade; censorship and patronage; the Court; economics; education and the universities; the family and marriage; gender and sexuality; music; philosophy; political history and theory; the professions; religion and the Church; science and superstition; social history, theory and structures; theatre design; theatrical companies and staging; travel; visual arts.

2. *Either* (*a*) *one* of the following:

Non-fictional prose. The paper will include themes on the following topics and authors:

More and his circle; Elyot; Ascham; Harrison; travel-writing; the pamphleteers; Hooker; Bacon; character-writing; Burton; biography; Browne; Taylor.

Historical and political writing. The paper will include themes on the following topics:

Historical prose, verse, and drama; political satire; 'advice to princes'; political theory; diaries; letters on matters of state; political biography; antiquarian and chivalric discourse.

Prose Fiction. The paper will include themes on the following authors:
Lyly; Sidney; Greene; Lodge; Nashe; Deloney; Wroth.

or (b) two of the following:

Love Poetry.
Religious and Devotional Verse.
Secular Narrative Verse.
The Sonnet.

or (c) one of the following subjects from Course (iii):

B.1. Drama, 1500–93.
B.2. Tragedy, 1595–1642.
B.3. Comedy, Tragicomedy, and Romance, 1595–1642.

Group B

*1. Spenser, *2. Jonson, *3. Donne, *4. Milton.
5. Language, Rhetoric, and Style, 1500–1660.
6. The History and Theory of Literary Criticism in England, 1500–1660.
7. The History of the English Language, 1500–1660.
8. Comparative Literature, including Classical, Italian, French, and Spanish writing; English versions of the Bible; Tudor and Stuart translations. Candidates must propose for approval by or on behalf of the Board the field of study in which the paper is to be set.
9. *Either* Subject A.2(*a*) of Course (iii): Shakespeare's Earlier Plays *or* Subject A.2(*b*) of Course (iii): Shakespeare's Later Plays.

Course (v) English Literature, 1660–1800

Group A

1. Poetry 1660–1800.
2. The Novel 1660–1800.

(Candidates must not answer under A.1 or A.2 on the author chosen for special study under B.1.)

Group B

1. **One* author chosen from Dryden, Swift, Pope, Defoe, Fielding, Richardson, Johnson.
2. The History and Theory of Literary Criticism 1660–1800.
3. Comedy 1660–1800.
4. Literature and Society in the Reign of Charles II.
5. The Literature of the Scriblerus Club.
6. Women Writers 1660–1800.
7. Historiography 1660–1800.
8. Biography and Autobiography 1660–1800.
9. Political Writing 1660–1800.
10. Religious and Philosophical Writing 1660–1800.

Course (vi) English Romantic Studies

Group A

1. Romantic Literature in its Social, Intellectual, and Political Context.
2. Wordsworth and Coleridge.

---

* One of these four papers must be chosen.

Group B

†1. The work of *two* of the following: Byron, Shelley, Keats.

2. Blake, with special reference to *The Marriage of Heaven and Hell, Songs of Innocence and Songs of Experience, The Book of Urizen, Milton.*

3. The Poetry and Prose of Scott.

(Candidates offering B.3 may not answer on Scott under B.4, the Novel in the Romantic Period.)

4. The Novel in the Romantic Period.

5. Romantic Literary Theory and Literary Criticism.

6. Non-fictional Romantic Prose, with special reference to *Confessions of an English Opium-Eater, Suspiria de Profundis, Essays of Elia, The Spirit of the Age.*

7. Romantic Drama and Dramatic Criticism.

8. The Romantic Visual Arts in Britain.

9. German Romanticism and its Relations with English Romantic Literature.

10. The Antecedents of English Romantic Literature, with special reference to Milton and the eighteenth-century blank-verse tradition, OR the Later Influence and Reputation of any one *or* two Major English Romantic Writers. (Candidates wishing to offer the second alternative must obtain approval, by or on behalf of the board, for the one *or* two major English Romantic Writers of their choice.)

Course (vii) English Literature, 1830–1900

Group A

1. The Victorian Novel.
2. Victorian Poetry.

Group B

3. Dickens *or* Eliot *or* Hardy *or* James *or* Tennyson *or* Elizabeth Barrett Browning *or* Robert Browning *or* Matthew Arnold (as a poet).
4. The Discourse of Criticism.
5. Gender and Writing.
6. The Aesthetic Movement from De Quincey to Wilde.
7. The Urban Experience.
8. The English Abroad.
9. Literature and Religion.
10. The Victorian Theatre.
11. One of the options specified for course (vi), English Romantic Studies or for course (viii), English Literature 1880–The Present Day.

The Group B options may not all be available every year.

Course (viii) English Literature, 1880–The Present Day

Group A

1. The relationship between society and literature.

The paper will include themes on not less than twelve of the following topics: aestheticism; the symbolist movement; realism; political and social movements; Irish politics and literature; imperialism; anthropology and myth; feminism; war; psychoanalysis; the influence of other media; the relationship between the arts; modernism; literary magazines and other modes of literary production; the influence of major thinkers; religion; science.

2. *One* novelist chosen from James, Conrad, Joyce, Lawrence, Woolf.

---

† This subject is compulsory.

Group B

*1. *One* poet chosen from Hardy, Yeats, Eliot, Auden and Pound.

2. English Literature of the period 1880–1910 *or* the period 1910–30, *or* the period 1930–45, *or* the period 1945–70, *or* the period 1970–the present day.

3. The History and Theory of Literary Criticism, 1880–the present day.

Candidates will be expected to demonstrate that they have read texts they select for this subject in the original languages.

4. Biography and/or Political Writing, 1880–the present day.

5. English and/or American Drama, 1880–the present day.

6. American Poetry. Candidates wishing to offer this subject must propose and obtain approval by or on behalf of the board of *two* American poets for study.

7. American Fiction. Candidates wishing to offer this subject must propose and obtain approval by or on behalf of the board of *two* American novelists for study.

8. The History of Ideas, 1880–the present day. Candidates wishing to offer this subject must propose and obtain approval by or on behalf of the board of a field of study.

9. Comparative Literature. Candidates wishing to offer this subject must propose and obtain approval by or on behalf of the board of a field of study related to their other work.]

[From 1 October 2004: Every candidate must follow for at least six terms a course of study in English.

In the first year candidates must follow the courses and submit the essays and dissertations prescribed for the M.St. in English. Candidates must have achieved a pass mark in the first-year assessments before they are allowed to proceed to the second year.

In the second year candidates must offer three of the following subjects, or two subjects and a dissertation of 20,000 words on a topic related to their course of study. The dissertation may incorporate work submitted for the first-year dissertation.

Syllabus

1. The Palaeography of Manuscripts written in England from 1100–1500. (Candidates will be required to transcribe from and comment on specimens written in English under examination conditions (1 hour).)

2. Special author: Cynewulf, Alfred, Ælfric, Wulfstan, Gower, Langland, Chaucer, Dante, or Malory.

3. Old English metre and poetic diction.

4. Early Middle English Literature. Candidates are expected to have read widely in English literature of the period *c.*1100–*c.*1350.

5. Devotional literature of the fourteenth and fifteenth centuries.

6. The medieval drama.

7. Old Norse Literature, I. The following texts are prescribed: *Njáls saga*, *Egils saga*, *Óláfs saga helga (Heimskringla)*, *Kormaks saga*, *Skáldskaparmál*, *Haustlöng*.

8. Old Norse Literature, II. The following texts are prescribed: *Grettis saga*, *Laxdœla saga*, *Eyrbyggja saga*, *Völsunga saga*, *Hrólfs saga kraka*, *Gautreks saga*, *Sólarljóð*; *Íslendinga saga* (Sturla).

9. Eddaic and Skaldic Verse. The following texts are prescribed: *Guðrúnarkviða I-III*, *Grottasöngr*, *Vafþrúðnismál*, *Baldrs draumar*; *Ragnarsdrápa* (Bragi), *Haraldskvæði* (þorbjörn hornklofi), *Hákonarmál* (Eyvindr), *Vellekla* (Einarr skálaglamm), the verses in *Eyrbyggja saga*.

* This subject is compulsory.

10. The Latin Literature of the British Isles: from the Origins to the Norman Conquest. The following texts are prescribed: Gildas, *de Excidio* pref., chaps. 1–10, ed. M. Winterbottom, Arthurian Period Sources 7 (London/Chichester, 1978); 45 Aldhelm, *de Virginitate*, prose, chaps. 1–5; verse, 11. 1–105, 2861–904, ed. R. Ehwald, MGH, *Auctores Antiquissimi*, xv (Berlin, 1919); Bede, *Vita S. Cuthberti*, prose, pref., chaps. 1–5, ed. B. Colgrave, *Two 'Lives' of Saint Cuthbert* (repr. New York, 1969), metrical *Life pref.*, chaps. 1–5, ed. W. Jaager, *Palaestra*, 198; Alcuin, *Two Alcuin Letter-Books*, I, nos. 1–14, ed. C. Chase, Toronto Medieval Latin Texts (Toronto, 1975); Oxford Book of Medieval Latin Verse, no. 80, rev. edn. F. J. E. Raby (Oxford, 1970); *Versus de ... Sanctis Euboricensis Ecclesiae*, 11. 1–130, 1596–1657, ed. E. Dümmler, *MGH*, *Poetae*, I (Berlin, 1881); Asser, *Vita Alfredi*, chaps. 1–15, ed. Stevenson, rev. D. Whitelock (Oxford, 1959); Æthelweard, *Chronicle*, Book IV, ed. A. Campbell (London, 1962); Ælfric, *Life of St Æthelwold*, ed. M. Winterbottom, *Three Lives of English Saints*, Toronto Medieval Latin Texts (Toronto, 1972); Columbanus, *Epistle*, I, ed. G. Walker, Scriptores Latini Hiberniae II (Dublin, 1970); *Hisperica Famina* vv. 571–612, ed. M. Herren (Toronto, 1975).

11. Medieval Latin Language and Literature. The following texts are prescribed: Abelard: *Historia Calamitatum*, ed. J. Monfrin (Paris, 1967); Peter the Venerable: *Selected Letters*, nos. 9, 24, 43, 53, 115, ed. J. Martin, Toronto Medieval Latin Texts (Toronto, 1974); Notker, *Liber Hymnorum*, ed. W. v. den Steinen (Bern/Munich, 1960), *proemium*, pp. 10–18, 84, 88; *Ruodlieb*, vv. 1–252 (ed. Reclam); The Archpoet, *Poems* (ed. Reclam); Walter of Châtillon, *Moralische-satirische Gedichte*, nos. 2, 6, 17, 18, ed. Strecker (Heidelberg, 1929); *Oxford Book of Medieval Latin Verse* (rev. edn.), ed. F. J. E. Raby (Oxford, 1970), nos. 75–80, 83, 92, 103, 119–29, 157–9, 169–73, 175–6, 207–32, 239; Geoffrey of Monmouth: *Historia Regum Britanniae*, Book IX, ed. I. Hammer, Medieval Academy of America (Cambridge, Mass., 1951).

12. Medieval Welsh literature. Candidates may offer one of the following:

(*a*) Medieval Welsh tales and romances with special reference to *Pedeir Keinc y Mabinogi* (ed. I. Williams, 1951), *Culhwch ac Olwen* (ed. R. Bromwich and D. S. Evans, 1988). *Owein* (ed. R. L. Thomson, 1975), *Peredur vab Efrawc* (ed. G. W. Goetinck, 1976), *Gereint vab Erbin in Llyfr Gwyn Rhydderch* (ed. J. G. Evans and R. M. Jones, 1973, pp. 193–226), *Cyfranc Lluda Llevelys* (ed. I. Williams, 1922), *Breuddwyd Maxen* (ed. I. Williams, 1920), *Breudwyt Ronabwy* (ed. M. Richards, 1948).

(*b*) Medieval Welsh religious literature with special reference to *Blodeugerdd Barddas o Ganu Crefyddol Cynnar* (ed. M. Haycock, 1994), *The Medieval Welsh Religious Lyric* (ed. C. A. McKenna, 1991), and *Llyvyr Agkyr Llandewivrevi* (ed. J. Morris Jones and J. Rhys).

(*c*) *Gwaiath Dafydd ap Gwilym* (ed. T. Parry) and *Gwaith Iolo Goch* (ed. D. Johnston, 1988).

13. Anglo-Norman Literature. The following texts are prescribed: Benedeit, *Voyage of St Brendan*; Gaimar, *Estorie des Engleis*; *La Seinte Resureccion* (ANTS); *Les Fragments du Tristan de Thomas* (ed. B. H. Wind); M. Paris, *Life of St Edward the Confessor* (ANTS); *The Romance of Horn* (ANTS).

14. Old French Literature: *either* Chrétien de Troyes *or Le Roman de la Rose*.

15. Medieval Philosophy. Candidates must offer topic (i) below and any one other topic. Candidates are recommended to study the texts indicated.

(i) Aristotelian philosophy in the thirteenth century: Aquinas, *De Unitate Intellectus*, and *Summa Theologica*, I. i–ii.

Recommended reading: F. van Steenberghen, *Aristotle in the West (The Origins of Latin Aristotelianism)*, trans. L. Johnston (Louvain, 1955).

(ii) Dialectic and theology from 1070 to 1150: Anselm, *Proslogion*; Abelard, *Historia Calamitatum*, *Sic et Non* (Prologue).

(iii) English philosophy in the first half of the fourteenth century: Duns Scotus, *De primo Principio*; Ockham, *Philosophical Writings*, ed. and trans. P. Boehner (1957), section II (pp. 18–45).

(iv) Philosophy outside the Schools: Boethius, *Consolatio Philosophiae* (Books I, IV, V), its tradition, translation, imitations, commentaries.

16. The Archaeology of Anglo-Saxon England. (This paper will be identical with the paper of the same title of the M.St. in European Archaeology and will be examined by written paper as specified in paragraph 4(*a*) of the regulations for the M.St. in European Archaeology.)

17. The History of the English Church, either to the death of Bede, or from the death of Alfred to the Norman Conquest.

18. The Reigns of Ethelred the Unready and Canute.

19. The Norsemen in England. The study of contemporary texts in the original languages will be expected. Attention is particularly directed to *The Old English Chronicle* 800–955 (MS A), 979–1042 (MS C), *The Battle of Maldon*, *Encomium Emmae*, *Historia de Sancto Cuthberto*, *Höfuðlausn* (Egill), *Vikingarvísur* (Sigvatr), *Knútsdrápa* (Sigvatr), *Höfuðlausn* (Ottarr svarti), *Knútsdrápa* (Ottarr svarti).

Examination

The method of examination will be by library paper. Candidates must offer three papers (or two if they are submitting a dissertation) and answer two questions per paper. One list of questions for each option they have selected will be delivered to candidates' colleges on the Thursday of the Fourth Week of Trinity Term. Candidates must submit a completed library paper for each option to the Schools by noon on Thursday of the seventh week of Trinity Term, except that candidates who are taking a third option may submit one paper by noon on Thursday of eighth week. For subjects 2–6 and 9–10 and 16 there will also be a one-hour translation test in eighth week.

Candidates offering a dissertation must seek approval of the topic from the board or by a person or persons to whom it may delegate the function of giving such approval. (A dissertation involving the edition of a text may, if the candidate so wishes, exceed 20,000 words by not more than the length of the text.) Candidates submitting a dissertation must deliver two copies to the Clerk of the Schools, High Street, Oxford, by noon on Thursday of the first week of the Trinity Full Term in which the examination is to be taken.

Each candidate's choice of subjects shall require the approval of a person or persons to whom the board may delegate the function of giving such approval. Approval must be applied for on or before Saturday of the second week of Michaelmas Term preceding the examination.

Candidates who have offered Medieval Latin Language and Literature or The Latin Literature of the British Isles before the Norman Conquest in List B of Course II of the Honour School of English Language and Literature or candidates who have offered Medieval Latin Language and Literature in the Honour School of Classics and Modern Languages will not be permitted to offer the corresponding subject or subjects (10 and 11) in the M.Phil. in English Studies.

Any candidate may be examined viva voce about the extended essays, library papers, and dissertation.

Candidates are warned that they must avoid duplicating in their answers to one part of the examination material that they have used in another part of the examination.

No candidate who has failed any of the above subjects will be awarded the degree in that examination. Candidates who fail any one of the three papers (or any one of the two papers and the dissertation) may re-submit that element by noon on the last Monday of the Long Vacation; candidates who fail more than one element of the examination (including one element plus the translation paper where applicable) must re-submit those elements (and, where applicable, take the translation paper) according to the timetable for the examination in the following year. A candidate may only resubmit or retake a paper on one occasion.]

European Archaeology

Within the Division of Life and Environmental Sciences, the course shall be administered by the Committee for the School of Archaeology. The regulations made are as follows:

1. Candidates for admission must apply to the Committee for the School of Archaeology. They will be required to produce evidence of their appropriate qualifications for the proposed course which may include their suitable proficiency in relevant ancient or modern languages.

2. Candidates must follow for six terms a course of instruction in European Archaeology.

3. The registration of candidates will lapse from the Register of M.Phil. students on the last day of Trinity Full Term in the academic year after that in which their name is first entered in it, unless the committee decides otherwise.

4. All candidates are required:

(*a*) to satisfy the examiners in a Qualifying Examination identical with that for the degree of Master of Studies in European Archaeology and governed by regulations 4–8 for that degree, in the Trinity Full Term of the academic year in which their name is first entered on the Register of M.Phil. students except that under regulation 4(*b*) of that degree a 10,000 word dissertation may not normally be offered in place of one of the subject options (examined by two pre-set essays or by three-hour written paper). Candidates whose work in the Qualifying Examination is judged by the examiners to be of the standard required for the degree of M.St. in European Archaeology, but not of the standard required to proceed to the second year of the M.Phil. in European Archaeology, may be offered the option of resitting the Qualifying Examination under Ch. VI, Sect. VI, § 2, cl. 4, or of being granted permission to supplicate for the degree of Master of Studies in European Archaeology;

(*b*) to deliver to the Clerk of the Schools, High Street, Oxford, not later than noon on the Friday of the sixth week of Trinity Full Term in the academic year after that in which their name is first entered on the Register for M.Phil. Students, a thesis* of not more than 25,000 words (excluding bibliography and any descriptive catalogue or other factual matter, but including notes and

* See the regulation following Ch. VI, Sect. VI, § 4, concerning the preparation and dispatch of theses. Candidates are reminded (i) that two copies are required but that one of these may be a reproduction or carbon copy of the other, provided that any maps, diagrams, or other illustrations in the second copy are adequately reproduced, (ii) that the copy of the thesis deposited in the Ashmolean or the Balfour Library shall be the one containing the original illustrations, and (iii) that work submitted for the Degree of M.Phil. may be subsequently incorporated in a thesis submitted for the Degree of D.Phil.

appendices) on the subject approved in accordance with regulations 7 and 10 below;

(*c*) to present themselves for written examination in accordance with regulation 5 below in the Trinity Full Term of the academic year after that in which their name is first entered on the Register for M.Phil. Students;

(*d*) to present themselves for an oral examination as required by the examiners.

5. The written examination shall comprise one subject chosen from Schedules A–B for the Master of Studies in European Archaeology. [Candidates who offered a subject from Schedule B in the qualifying examination may not normally offer another subject from Schedule B.] The subject may be examined, at the candidate's choice, either by two pre-set essays of 5,000 words each, or by a written paper.

6. The choice of subjects for thesis and examination must be approved by the candidate's supervisor and by the committee, having regard to the candidate's previous experience and to the availability of teaching. The subject for the thesis will normally be related to the subject chosen under regulation 5 above.

7. Candidates will be expected to show sufficient general knowledge of Ancient History and Geography for a proper understanding of their subjects.

8. The subject for examination and the chosen method of examination must be submitted for approval by the committee in time for its meeting in eighth week of the Trinity Full Term of the academic year in which the candidate's name is first entered on the Register for M.Phil. students. Notice of the subject must be given to the Registrar not later than Friday of the eighth week of the Michaelmas Full Term preceding the examination.

9. Candidates intending to offer pairs of pre-set essays in place of the written examination (as specified in 5 above) will select essay topics from a list offered by their supervisors. The proposed essay titles, countersigned by the supervisor, must be submitted for approval to the Chairman of Examiners by noon on Friday of the seventh week of the Hilary Full Term preceding the examinations. Candidates must submit two copies of their essays by not later than noon on the Friday of the sixth week of Trinity Full Term, to the Examination School. Essays must be typed or printed.

10. The proposed thesis title must be submitted for approval by the committee in time for its meeting in the eighth week of the Trinity Full Term of the year in which the candidate's name is first entered on the Register for M.Phil. Students.

11. Candidates will normally be expected to undertake a programme of relevant practical work (e.g. excavation, travel, or museum study), to be approved by their supervisors beforehand.

12. Candidates are advised that adequate reading knowledge of an appropriate language or languages (other than English) may be necessary to reach the standard required by the examiners.

13. Candidates will be required to deposit one copy of the thesis with the Clerk of the Schools. Successful candidates will be required to deposit one copy of the thesis in the Ashmolean Library or the Balfour Library, as directed by the examiners. Such candidates will be required to complete a form stating whether they give permission for their thesis to be consulted.

14. Candidates whose work in the Final Examination is judged by the examiners not to be of the standard required for the degree of M.Phil. in European Archaeology, but whose work in the Qualifying Examination nevertheless reached the standard required for the degree of M.St. in European Archaeology, may be offered the option of resitting the M.Phil. Final Examination under Ch. VI, Sect. VI, § 2, cl. 4, or of

being granted permission to supplicate for the degree of Master of Studies in European Archaeology.

15. The examiners may award a distinction for excellence in the whole examination.

European Literature*

(*See also the general notice at the commencement of these regulations.*)

The regulations made by the Board of the Faculty of Medieval and Modern Languages are as follows:

1. All candidates shall be required

(*a*) To offer either *one* or *two* literatures:

(i) A candidate who offers *one* literature shall select it from the following: French, German, Italian, Spanish (including Latin-American), Portuguese (including Brazilian), Russian, Czech, Slovak, Byzantine and Modern Greek, Celtic, and Medieval Latin.

(ii) A candidate who offers *two* literatures shall select them from the following: French, German, Italian, Spanish (including Latin-American), Portuguese (including Brazilian), Russian, Czech, Slovak, Byzantine and Modern Greek, Celtic and English. Candidates may, as one of their literatures, offer Classical Latin or Classical Greek, provided that the other literature selected is not English; and they may, as one of their literatures, offer Medieval Latin, provided that the other literature selected is not Classical Latin or Classical Greek or English.

Any candidate may, with the approval of the Modern Languages Board, offer the literature of any other language falling under the direction of that Board.

Candidates may show knowledge where relevant of literatures other than those specially selected. Candidates offering English must show knowledge of English literature in the narrower sense, but may also if they wish show knowledge of American literature.

(*b*) To present themselves for viva voce examination at the time appointed by the examiners.

(*c*) To offer A, B and C as defined in 2 below.

2. The examination shall consist of the following:

(A) *either*

(i) Methods of Criticism and the Theory of Literature. All candidates must attend such lectures, seminars, and classes as their supervisor shall determine. All candidates must present one seminar paper during their course, and submit a written essay based on some aspect of the work done for the seminar. This essay, which shall be of no more than 5,000 words, inclusive of a bibliography of works consulted, must be submitted to and assessed by, one assessor (who shall not normally be the candidate's supervisor), and the mark awarded to the essay must be submitted to the examiners. The essay, which shall be written in English, must be typed and must be delivered to the assessor by the end of the ninth week of Hilary Term of the candidate's first year as a student for the examination.

(ii) Methods of Criticism and History of Ideas in Germany from the Eighteenth to the Twentieth Centuries. All candidates must attend such lectures, seminars, and classes as their supervisor shall determine. All candidates must present one seminar paper during their course, and submit a written essay based on

---

* European Literature is taken to extend to literatures outside the continent of Europe but written in a language of European origin, in either North or South America.

some aspect of the work done for the seminar. This essay, which shall be of no more than 5,000 words, inclusive of a bibliography of works consulted, must be submitted to, and assessed by, one assessor (who shall not normally be the candidate's supervisor), and the mark awarded to the essay must be submitted to the examiners. The essay, which may be written in English or German, must be typed and must be delivered to the assessor by the end of the ninth week of Hilary Term of the candidate's first year as a student for the examination.

Or

(iii) Methods of Scholarship. Each candidate shall be required to offer *either* (1) the history of the book, *or* (2) palaeography with textual criticism. Candidates will be examined on three essays on topics agreed by them with their supervisor relating *either* to the history of the book (for (1)) *or* to palaeography with textual criticism (for (2)). The essays shall be submitted to the supervisor by the end of the ninth week of the second term as a student for the examination, and shall be marked, signed, and dated by the supervisor. The essays shall be examined by the examiners who shall, in assessing the marks they award, take account of the stage at which each essay was completed. For (2), candidates will in addition be required to undertake a practical transcription test, made without reference to dictionaries or handbooks, on a short manuscript text selected by the supervisor, who will also mark, sign, and date the candidate's work.

The test should take place by the end of the fourth week of the Trinity Term in which the examination is to be taken. The mark should be sent by the supervisor to the Chairman of Examiners.

The work submitted under (i) must be written in English; the work submitted under (ii) may be written in English or German; the work submitted under (iii) may be written in English or, subject to the approval of the Faculty Board, in a language appropriate to the literature concerned.

Approval must be sought for the choice of options in (A) by the end of the fourth week of the Michaelmas Term of the candidate's first year as a student for the examination.

(B) A thesis, which may be written in English or, with the approval of the Faculty Board, in the language appropriate to the literature concerned, of approximately 20,000 words and not more than 25,000 words on a subject approved by the board or by a person or persons to whom the board may delegate this function. The subject of the thesis shall be related *either* to the fields of study represented by (A) (i) or (ii), *or* to one or both of the candidate's Special Subjects (C). When seeking approval for the subject of the thesis, every candidate shall submit with the proposed title a written statement of not more than 500 words explaining the scope of the topic and the manner in which it is proposed to treat it.

Candidates shall seek approval (by application to the Modern Languages Graduate Office, 41 Wellington Square, Oxford) for the proposed subject of their thesis by the end of the fourth week of Trinity Term in their first year.

The thesis must be presented in proper scholarly form. Two copies, typed in double-spacing on one side only of quarto or A4 paper, each copy bound or held firmly in a stiff cover, must be delivered to the Clerk of the Schools, Examination Schools, High Street, Oxford by noon on Thursday of the sixth week of the Trinity Term in which the examination is to be taken.* †Successful

* See the regulation concerning the preparation and dispatch of theses. Candidates are reminded that work submitted for the Degree of M.Phil. may subsequently be incorporated in a thesis submitted for the Degree of D.Phil.

† Such candidates will also be required to sign a form stating whether they give permission for their theses to be consulted.

candidates will be required to deposit one copy of their thesis in the Bodleian Library.

(C) Candidates shall offer two Special Subjects. These may either be chosen from the Special Subjects proposed by members of the Modern Language Faculty and listed in the 'Graduate Studies in Modern Languages' prospectus, or be Special Subjects of their own devising, provided that each subject has the written support of the candidate's supervisor and is approved by or on behalf of the Modern Languages Board. A proposal for a Special Subject of the candidate's own devising shall be accompanied by a statement (of approximately 100 words) of the character and scope of the Subject proposed. Approval of all Special Subjects must be sought, by application to the Modern Languages Graduate Office, 41 Wellington Square, by the end of the fourth week of the Trinity Term of the candidate's first year as a student for the examination. Approval of Special Subjects proposed will be dependent on the availability of teaching and examining resources at the relevant times.

Candidates will be examined on a portfolio of work (which may be written in English, or, with the approval of the Faculty Board, in the language appropriate to the literature concerned) on topics they have agreed with their supervisor within each Special Subject. The portfolio shall be submitted to the supervisor by Friday of the first week of Hilary Term of the candidate's second year as a student for the examination. The essay or essays shall be marked, signed and dated by the supervisor for that Special Subject. It is expected that essays will normally be submitted to the examiners in unrevised form. However, in cases where an essay submitted for examination represents a revised version of an earlier essay, the date and supervisor's mark should refer to the revised version, and the supervisor's comments should indicate the nature and extent of the revisions which have been made and the reasons for submitting a revised version.

The essay or essays contained within the portfolio for each Special Subject should be of approximately 9,000 words in total, though where the subject or approach requires greater length, candidates shall not be penalized for exceeding this guideline.

The essays shall be examined by the examiners who shall, in deciding the marks they award, take account of the stage at which each essay was completed.

Candidates may be given an opportunity (where relevant) to show knowledge of related developments in the arts.

Candidates shall seek approval (by application to the Modern Languages Graduate Office, 41 Wellington Square, Oxford) for the proposed subject of their thesis by the end of the fourth week of the second term after that in which their names have been placed on the Register of M.Phil. Students, i.e. normally by the end of the fourth week of Trinity Term in their first year.

The thesis (*two copies*) must be typewritten and must be delivered to the Clerk of the Schools, Examination Schools, High Street, Oxford, by noon on Thursday of the sixth week of the Trinity Full Term in which the examination is to be taken.*

Successful candidates will be required to deposit one copy of their theses in the Bodleian Library.

Each candidate's choice of papers shall be subject to the approval of the Board of the Faculty of Medieval and Modern Languages or of a person or persons to whom the board may delegate the function of giving such approval. Approval shall be given only if the choice of papers proposed, and any titles of Special Subjects of

* Such candidates will also be required to sign a form stating whether they give permission for their theses to be consulted.

the candidate's own devising, have the written support of the candidate's supervisor. Candidates shall seek approval (by application to the Modern Languages Graduate Office, 41 Wellington Square, Oxford) by the end of the fourth week of the second term after that in which their names have been placed on the Register of M.Phil. students, i.e. normally by the end of the fourth week of Trinity Term in their first year.

A proposal for a Special Subject or Special Subjects of the candidate's own devising shall be accompanied by a *brief* statement of the candidate's view of the character and scope of the Special Subject or Special Subjects proposed.

Approval of Special Subjects proposed will be dependent on the availability of teaching and examining resources at the relevant times.

3. Candidates shall be required at the time of admission to satisfy the board that they possess the appropriate linguistic knowledge, if necessary by a written test.

4. If it is the opinion of the examiners that the work done by a candidate while not of sufficient merit to qualify for the degree of M.Phil. is nevertheless of sufficient merit to qualify for the Degree of Master of Studies in European Literature, the candidate shall be given the option of resitting the M.Phil. examination under Ch. VI, Sect. VI, §2, cl. 4 or of being granted permission to supplicate for the Degree of Master of Studies.

5. In the case of resubmission, candidates shall be required to resubmit all the material by noon on Thursday of the sixth week of the first Trinity Term following their first examination. Candidates may resubmit on one occasion only.

6. The examiners may award a Distinction for excellence in the whole examination.

General Linguistics and Comparative Philology

(*See also the general notice at the commencement of these regulations.*)

The regulations made by the Committee for Comparative Philology are as follows:

1. Candidates shall normally have a degree in a subject which has given them at least some experience of linguistic or philological work. Those intending to offer options chosen from C or D below should normally have, and may be required to demonstrate, some knowledge of the chosen (group of) language(s) and those intending to offer options chosen from C will normally be expected to be able to read secondary literature in French and German.

2. Each candidate is required:

(*a*) to present himself for written examination as defined in regulation 2 below;

(*b*) to deliver to the Clerk of the Schools, High Street, Oxford, not later than noon on the Friday of the first week of the Trinity Term in the academic year in which he is examined, two copies of a thesis of not more than 25,000 words (excluding references, text material, and appendices but including footnotes) on the subject approved in accordance with regulation 5 below;

(*c*) to present himself or herself for an oral examination if and when required by the examiners.

3. The examination shall consist of four parts:

(*a*) One general paper as indicated in A.

(*b*) Three papers which must be chosen from those listed in B or must be those listed in C or those listed in D.

A. Linguistic Theory.

B. (i) Phonetics and Phonology.

(ii) Syntax.

(iii) Semantics.

(iv) Historical and comparative linguistics.
(v) Theory of translation.
(vi) History and structure of a language.
(vii) Experimental Phonetics.
(viii) Sociolinguistics.
(ix) Computational Linguistics.
(x) Any other subject which, from time to time, the committee at its own discretion may consider suitable.

C. (i) The comparative grammar of two Indo-European languages or language groups.
(ii) The historical grammar of the languages or language groups selected.
(iii) Translation from, and linguistic comment upon, texts in the languages selected.

D. (i) The history of one or two languages.
(ii) The structure of the language or languages selected.
(iii) *Either* (*a*) Translation from, and/or linguistic comment upon, texts in the language or languages selected,
Or (*b*) Any paper from B above except B (vi).

4. Option B(ii) shall consist of:
(*a*) an exercise, set during Week 8 of Michaelmas Term of the second year, on a topic directly related to material covered during lectures given during that term. Candidates will be required to submit a written answer to the Chairman of Examiners, c/o Clerk of the Schools, Examination Schools, High Street, Oxford, by not later than noon on Friday of Week 1 of the following Hilary Term.
(*b*) An essay of not more than 5,000 words on some problem in syntactic theory to be selected in consultation with the supervisor and approved by the Chairman of Examiners for report to the Committee for Comparative Philology and General Linguistics not later than Monday of Week 1 of Hilary Term in the year of the examination.

The essay (in two typewritten copies) must be sent in a parcel bearing the words 'Essay for the Syntax option in the M.Phil. in General Linguistics and Comparative Philology' to the Chairman of Examiners for the Degree of M.Phil. in General Linguistics, c/o Clerk of the Schools, Examination Schools, High Street, Oxford, not later than noon on Friday of Week 8 of Hilary Term in the second year. The essays shall be accompanied by a certificate signed by the candidate indicating that it is the candidate's own work, except where otherwise specified. This certification must be submitted separately in a sealed envelope addressed to the Chairman of Examiners for the M.Phil. in General Linguistics and Comparative Philology.

5. Of the two languages or language groups selected by the candidates who wish to offer the papers mentioned in C above, one must be studied in greater depth than the other.

Combinations previously offered under the auspices of the Committee for Comparative Philology are:

(*a*) Greek with the elements of Sanskrit Philology.
(*b*) Italic with the elements of Old Irish Philology.
(*c*) Germanic with the elements of Greek Philology.
(*d*) Greek with the elements of Anatolian Philology.
(*e*) Romance with the elements of Italic Philology.
(*f*) Italic with the elements of Greek Philology.
(*g*) Sanskrit with the elements of Greek Philology.

(*h*) Greek with the elements of Slavonic Philology.

(*i*) Celtic with the elements of Italic Philology.

Other combinations will be allowed subject to the approval of the committee and the availability of teaching.

6. The language or languages selected by the candidates who wish to offer the papers mentioned in D above may be ancient (e.g. Ancient Greek, Latin, Sanskrit, Akkadian, etc.) or modern (e.g. French, Italian, German, English, Turkish, etc.). Only languages for which teaching is available at the time may be offered.

7. The choice of the subjects for the thesis and examination will be subject to the approval of the candidate's supervisor and the committee, having regard to the candidate's previous experience and to the availability of teaching. Not all options may be offered every year. The subjects which a candidate wishes to offer for examination must be submitted to the committee for approval not later than Monday of the first week in Michaelmas Term in the academic year in which the candidate is to be examined.

The subject of the thesis must be submitted for approval by the committee not later than Monday of the first week in Michaelmas Term in the academic year in which the candidate is to be examined.

8. The examiners may require a successful candidate to deposit one of the submitted copies of his thesis in the Bodleian Library. Such a candidate will be required to complete a form stating whether he gives permission for his thesis to be consulted.

Candidates are reminded that work submitted for the degree of M.Phil. may subsequently be incorporated in a thesis submitted for the degree of D.Phil.

9. If it is the opinion of the examiners that the work done by a candidate is not of sufficient merit to qualify him for the degree of M.Phil. but is nevertheless of sufficient merit to qualify him for the Degree of Master of Studies in General Linguistics and Comparative Philology, the candidate shall be given the option of resitting the M.Phil. examination under Ch. VI, Sect. VI, §2, cl. 4 or of being granted permission to supplicate for the Degree of Master of Studies.

10. The examiners may award a Distinction for excellence in the whole examination.

Greek and/or Latin Languages and Literature

(*See also the general notice at the commencement of these regulations.*)

The regulations made by the Board of the Faculty of Classics are as follows:

1. *Qualifications.* Candidates must satisfy the board that they possess the necessary qualifications in Greek and/or Latin to profit by the course.

2. *Course.* Every candidate must follow for at least six terms a course of instruction in Greek and/or Latin Languages and Literature. Candidates will, when they enter for the examination, be required to produce from their society a certificate that they are following such a course.

3. *Options.* See the schedule below. Candidates are required to offer a thesis (C) and any *two* options chosen from A and B.

4. *Approval of Options.* The choice of options will be subject to the approval of the candidate's supervisor and of the Graduate Studies Committee in Classics, having regard to the candidate's previous experience, the range covered by the proposed options, and the availability of teaching and examining resources.

Not all options may be available in any given year.

Candidates must submit their provisional choice of *options* to the Administrator, Classics Centre, 67 St Giles', Oxford OX1 3LU not later than Tuesday of first week in the Hilary Full Term next after the beginning of their course; the proposed *thesis title* not later than Tuesday of first week in the Trinity Full Term next following; and the proposed titles of any *pre-submitted essays* (*see* §§ 5 and 6) as soon as practicable, but in any case no later than Tuesday of first week in the Hilary Full Term of the second year of the course (except that the titles of essays to be examined at the end of the first year of study in accordance with cl. 7 below should be submitted no later than the Tuesday of first week in the Hilary Full Term of the *first* year of the course).

5. *Examination.* Each option in section A will be examined by (i) a written paper (three hours) of passages for translation and comment, in which the passages for comment will be set only from the books listed under α in each case, while passages for translation will be set from the books listed under both α and β in each case, and (ii) by three presubmitted essays (see §6 below) which between them display knowledge of more than a narrow range of the topic. For the examinations to be set in the options under Section B, see the detailed schedule.

6. *Presubmitted essays.* Essays should each be of between 5,000 and 7,500 words (these limits to exclude the bibliography, any text that is being edited or annotated, any translation of that text, and any descriptive catalogue or similar factual matter, but to include quotations, notes and appendices). A note of the word-count must be included.

Supervisors or others are permitted to give bibliographical help with, and to discuss a first draft of, such essays.

The essays (two typewritten or printed copies) must be delivered in a parcel bearing the words 'Essays presubmitted for the M.Phil. in Greek and/or Latin Languages and Literature' to the Clerk of the Schools, Examination Schools, High Street, Oxford OX1 4BG, to arrive by noon on Thursday of sixth week in the appropriate Trinity Full Term.

7. One of the two options taken from A and B must be completed by the end of the first year of study. If it is an option to be examined by presubmitted essays, these must be delivered as in §6 above, but to arrive by noon on the Thursday of sixth week in the Trinity Full Term of the first year of study for the M.Phil.

8. *Oral Examination.* Candidates are required to present themselves for oral examination if summoned by the examiners.

9. *Distinction.* The examiners may award a distinction for excellence in the whole examination.

10. A candidate who fails to satisfy the examiners may enter for the examination on one (but not more than one) subsequent occasion (as provided by Ch. VI, Sect. VI, § 2, paragraph 4). If it is the opinion of the examiners that the work done by a candidate, while not of sufficient merit to qualify for the degree of M.Phil., is nevertheless of sufficient merit to qualify for the degree of Master of Studies in Greek and/or Latin Languages and Literature, the candidate shall be given the option of resitting the M.Phil. or of being granted leave to supplicate for the degree of Master of Studies.

SCHEDULE

Section A

1.	Aeschylus	α	*Seven against Thebes, Agamemnon, Choephori, Eumenides.*
		β	*Persae, Supplices.*
2.	Euripides	α	*Medea, Electra, Heracles, Ion, Orestes.*
		β	*Alcestis, Hippolytus, Hecuba, Trojan Women, Helen.*
3.	Plato	α	*Phaedrus, Gorgias.*
		β	*Ion, Republic X, Gorgias, Helen.*

4.	Hellenistic poetry	α	Theocritus 1, 3, 7, 10, 13, 15, 16, 28; Callimachus, *Hymns* 1, 5, 6; frr. 1, 67–75, 110, 178, 191, 194, 260 (this last fr. to be read in Callimachus, *Hecale* (ed. A. S. Hollis) frr. 69–74); epigrams 2, 4, 8, 13, 16, 19, 21, 25, 27, 28, 29, 30, 41, 43, 46, 50 Pf.; Herodas 4; Apollonius, *Argonautica* III; Asclepiades 1, 2, 3, 10, 11, 12, 16, 18, 25, 26, 28, 32 Page.
		β	Apollonius, *Argonautica* IV. 1–481; Moschus, *Europa*; Herodas 2, 6; Callimachus, *Hymn* 2.
5.	Greek Comedy	α	Aristophanes, *Wasps, Birds, Ecclesiazusae*; Menander, *Dyscolus, Samia.*
		β	Aristophanes, *Clouds, Thesmophoriazusae, Wealth*; Menander, the remaining works included in *Menander, Plays and Fragments*, translated by N. Miller (Penguin Classics).
6.	Lucretius	α	Books I, III, and V.
		β	Books II, IV, and VI.
7.	Cicero the orator	α	*Pro Sexto Roscio Amerino, Pro Archia, Pro Milone, Pro Marcello, Philippics* I, II.
		β	Auctor ad Herennium I, II. 1–12, 47–50, IV. 11–16; Cicero, *De Imperio Cn. Pompei, Pro C. Rabirio perduellionis reo, Pro Caelio, De Oratore* II. 71–216, 290–349.
8.	Horace	α	*Epodes, Odes* II, IV, *Carmen Saeculare, Epistles* I, II.
		β	*Satires* I, *Odes* I.
9.	The Ancient Novel	α	Apuleius, *Metamorphoses* I, IV.28–VI.24, VIII–XI; Petronius, *Satyrica* 26.7–78 (*Cena Trimalchionis*).
		β	Apuleius, *Metamorphoses* II, III, IV.1–27, VI.25–32; VII; [Lucian], *Onos*; Petronius, *Satyrica* 1–26.6, 79–117; Longus, *Daphnis and Chloe*; Heliodorus, *Aethiopica*; Chariton, *Callirhoe.*

10. Any other text or combination of texts approved by the Graduate Studies Committee in Classics.

In 1–9 passages for translation and comment will be set from the editions listed in the regulations for the Honour School of Literae Humaniores. The editions to be used for any option approved under 10 will be specified by the Graduate Studies Committee in Classics.

Section B

1. *The transmission of Greek texts, and the elements of palaeography and textual criticism*, with closer study of Sophocles, *Ajax* 1–1184. Candidates will be required (i) to presubmit two essays on some aspect of the transmission of Greek texts or textual criticism, (ii) to transcribe a passage from a medieval manuscript (1 hour), and (iii) to answer questions on passages from the prescribed play (3 hours). (Candidates will be expected to show such knowledge of Greek metre as is necessary to the proper handling of the text.)

2. *The transmission of Latin texts, and the elements of palaeography and textual criticism,* with closer study of Ovid, *Heroides* 3, 5, 8, 9, 16, 17. Candidates will be required (i) to presubmit two essays on some aspect of the transmission of Latin texts or textual criticism, (ii) to transcribe a passage from a medieval manuscript (1 hour), and (iii) to answer questions on passages from the prescribed poems (3 hours).

(Candidates will be expected to show such knowledge of Latin metre as is necessary to the proper handling of the text.)

3. *Greek and Latin Papyrology, with special reference to literary papyri.* Candidates will be required (i) to submit two essays that between them display more than a narrow range of the topic, and (ii) to undertake a practical test, in their own time, in deciphering and commenting on original papyri. (The examiners, in consultation with the supervisor and/or the teacher of the course, will assign each candidate a papyrus or small group of papyri not later than Saturday of sixth week in the Hilary Full Term preceding the candidate's final term; he or she must prepare an edition of it, in proper scholarly form, and deliver two typed copies of this edition to the Clerk of the Schools not later than noon on Thursday of sixth week in the Trinity Full Term in which the examination will be taken. The copies should be accompanied by a statement signed by the candidate to the effect that they are solely his or her own work. This statement must be placed in a sealed envelope bearing the candidate's examination number and presented together with the copies.)

4. *Comparative Philology, with special reference to the history of the Greek and/or Latin language.* Two papers will be set. Paper (i), Essays, will cover (*a*) basic questions about the comparative and/or historical grammar of Greek and/or Latin, and (*b*) questions about the history of the Greek and/or Latin language. Paper (ii), texts for translation and linguistic commentary, will include a compulsory question with passages from *either* Greek dialect inscriptions *or* Latin archaic inscriptions; other passages will be set from Greek and/or Latin literary texts; there will be an opportunity to show knowledge of Linear B and/or Oscan and Umbrian.

5. *Theory and methodology of classical literary studies.* Candidates will be expected to be familiar with the major theoretical and methodological issues that arise in the study of ancient literature, and with the major positions in contemporary critical theory and their relationship to classical studies. They will be required to show knowledge of a range of issues in these areas. Examination will be by means of six presubmitted essays; a dissertation of between 10,000 and 20,000 words may be substituted for three of these essays. (The dissertation word limits exclude the bibliography, any text that is being edited or annotated, any translation of that text, and any descriptive catalogue or similar factual matter, but include quotations, notes and appendices. A note of the word-count must be included.)

6. *Intermediate Greek.* There will be one three-hour paper. Candidates will be expected to be familiar with *An Anthology of Greek Prose*, ed. D. A. Russell (OUP 1991), nos. 17, 18, 23, 24, 33, 40, 44, 66, 78, from which a selection of passages will be set for translation.

Candidates will also be expected to translate from two of the following texts: (i) Herodotus I. 1–94 [ed. Hude, OCT]; (ii) Plutarch, *Life of Antony* 1–9, 23–36, 71–87 [ed. Pelling, CUP]; (iii) Euripides, *Bacchae* [ed. Diggle, OCT]. Alternative texts for translation under this head may be offered by agreement with the Graduate Studies Committee.

7. *Intermediate Latin.* There will be one three-hour paper. Candidates will be expected to be familiar with *An Anthology of Latin Prose*, ed. D. A. Russell (OUP 1990), nos. 7, 12, 22, 23, 34, 52, 63, from which a selection of passages will be set for translation.

Candidates will also be expected to translate from two of the following texts: (i) Cicero, *Pro Caelio* [ed. OCT]; (ii) Pliny, *Letters* I. 6, 9, 13, 19; VII. 21, 24, 26, 29; VIII. 16, 17; IX. 6, 12, 15, 27, 33, 39; X. 31, 32, 96, 97 [ed. M. B. Fisher and M. R. Griffin, CUP 1973]; (iii) Ovid, *Metamorphoses* 8 [ed. A. S. Hollis, OUP 1970]. Alternative texts for translation under this head may be offered by agreement with the Graduate Studies Committee.

8. Any other subject approved by the Graduate Studies Committee in Classics, which will determine the method of examination.

Section C

A thesis of up to 25,000 words, on a subject to be proposed by the candidate in consultation with the supervisor, and approved by the Graduate Studies Committee in Classics. (The thesis word limit excludes the bibliography, any text that is being edited or annotated, any translation of that text, and any descriptive catalogue or similar factual matter, but includes quotations, notes and appendices. A note of the word-count must be included.) Supervisors or others are permitted to give bibliographical help and to discuss drafts.

The thesis (two typewritten or printed copies) must be delivered in a parcel bearing the words 'Thesis for the M.Phil. in Greek and/or Latin Languages and Literature' to reach the Clerk of the Schools, Examination Schools, High Street, Oxford OX1 4BG, by noon on Thursday of sixth week in the Trinity Full Term in which the examination is to be taken.

The examiners may invite a successful candidate to agree that one copy of his or her thesis be deposited in the Bodleian Library.

Greek and/or Roman History

(See also the general notice at the beginning of these regulations.)

1. Every candidate must follow, for at least six terms, a course of instruction in Greek and/or Roman History. Candidates will, when they enter for the examination, be required to produce from their society a certificate that they are following such a course.

2. Candidates may satisfy the Examiners in not more than three options in the Trinity Term of the first year of their course.

3. (*a*) In the case of options in languages, Schedule A below, candidates will be examined by written examination. Dictionaries may be brought by candidates for their use, except for options A (i) and A (ii).

(*b*) For options in topics and techniques, Schedules B and C below, candidates will be required to pre-submit two essays of not more than 5,000 words in length, which between them display knowledge of more than a narrow range of the topic covered by the course. (The essay word limit excludes the bibliography, any text that is being edited or annotated, any translation of that text, and any descriptive catalogue or similar factual matter, but includes quotations, notes and appendices.)

Supervisors or others are permitted to give bibliographical help with and to discuss drafts of essays. Such essays (two typewritten or printed copies) must be sent in a parcel bearing the words 'Essays presubmitted for the M.Phil. in Greek and/or Roman History' to the Clerk of the Schools, High Street, Oxford, OX1 4BG by noon on the Thursday of the sixth week of the Trinity Term in which the examination is to be taken.

4. Every candidate shall be examined viva voce unless individually dispensed by the examiners.

5. If it is the opinion of the examiners that the work done by a candidate, while not of sufficient merit to qualify for the degree of M.Phil., is nevertheless of sufficient merit to qualify for the degree of Master of Studies in Greek and/or Roman History, the candidate shall be given the option of resitting the M.Phil. (as provided by Ch. VI, Sect. VI, § 2, paragraph 4) or of being granted leave to supplicate for the degree of Master of Studies.

6. *Syllabus*

Candidates must offer four options from A, B, and C below, together with a dissertation as described in D below. Up to two options may be chosen from A, provided that not more than one option is a modern language. *Not all options may be available in any given year.*

A

(i) Intermediate Greek, as prescribed for the Master of Studies in Greek and/or Roman History. Paper A (ii)
(ii) Intermediate Latin, as prescribed for the Master of Studies in Greek and/or Roman History, Paper A (iv).
(iii) French
(iv) German
(v) Italian
(vi) any other language which the candidate has satisfied the Graduate Studies Committee in Ancient History is relevant to their other papers including any dissertation.

B

(i) Greek Numismatics
(ii) Roman Numismatics
(iii) Greek Epigraphy
(iv) The Epigraphy of the Roman World
(v) Documentary Papyrology
(vi) Any of the following papers on the B list of the M.St. in Greek and/or Latin Language and Literature: (i)–(iv); (vii)
(vii) Any of the papers from Schedule B of the M.St. in Classical Archaeology
(viii) Any other subject approved by the Graduate Studies Committee in Ancient History.

C

(i) The Greeks and the Mediterranean world, 900–500 BC. Candidates will be expected to show knowledge of the material evidence from the Greek world and the areas of contact between Greek and other Mediterranean peoples
(ii) Herodotus and Greek History 650–479 BC
(iii) Greek Archaeology 500–323 BC. Candidates will be expected to show knowledge of the architecture, sculpture, vase-painting, and other applied arts of the period, with an ability to apply the evidence of excavation, epigraphy, and coinage where appropriate
(iv) Thucydides and Greek History, 479–403 BC
(v) Greek History from the end of the Peloponnesian War to the death of Philip of Macedon
(vi) Athenian Democracy in the Classical Age. Candidates will be expected to show knowledge of the social, administrative, and constitutional developments in Athens from 462 to 321 BC but will only be required to show such knowledge of external affairs as is necessary for an understanding of the working of Athenian democracy
(vii) Alexander the Great
(viii) Hellenistic History 323–200 BC
(ix) Rome and the Greek East from the end of the First Punic War to the end of the Third Punic war
(x) The Archaeology and Art of Roman Italy in the Late Republic and Early Empire. Candidates will be expected to show knowledge of the material culture of Italy in the period *c.*200 BC–AD 200, of problems of method and

chronology and an ability to apply numismatic and written evidence where appropriate

(xi) Rome in the late Republic, 146 BC–44 BC

(xii) Cicero

(xiii) The establishment of the Principate from the Dictatorship of Caesar to the death of Tiberius

(xiv) Cities and Settlement in the Roman Empire. Candidates will be expected to show knowledge of the cities of the Roman Empire, from Augustus to the Tetrarchy, and of the changing forms and patterns of urban and other settlement

(xv) The early Principate, AD 14 to AD 70

(xvi) Civic life of the Roman Empire from the Flavian to the Severan Period. Candidates will be expected to show knowledge of the economic, social, and cultural history of the cities of the Roman Empire in the second century AD, and to show adequate knowledge of the general history of the period

(xvii) The Roman Empire 31 BC–AD 284

(xviii) The Roman Empire AD 284–410

(xix) Religion, Culture and Society, from Julian the Apostate to St Augustine, AD 350–395

(xx) Greek Historians and Historiography

(xxi) Roman Historians and Historiography

(xxii) The History of Sexuality in archaic and classical Greece

(xxiii) Greek Religion

(xxiv) Roman Religion. In addition to Roman religion in the narrow sense, religious phenomena of the Graeco Roman World in the Roman period (including relevant aspects of Judaism and Christianity) may be studied under this heading.

(xxv) Roman Egypt

(xxvi) Roman Gaul

(xxvii) The Church in the Roman Empire from the beginnings to AD 312

(xxviii) Roman Private Law

(xxix) The Economy of the Roman Empire

(xxx) The Ecology, Agriculture, and Settlement History of the central Mediterranean area 1000 BC–AD 600

(xxxi) The City of Rome. This option is run in collaboration with the British School at Rome, and involves attendance at the residential course organized by the School annually in Rome; only those accepted by the School may take the option. Applications for places should be made through the Graduate Studies Committee by the end of Michaelmas Term.

(xxxii) Athens and Attica. This option is run in collaboration with the British School at Athens, and involves attendance at the residential course organized by the School in even numbered years at Athens; only those accepted by the School may take the option. Application for places should be made through the Graduate Studies Committee by the end of Michaelmas Term.

(xxxiii) Any other subject approved by the Graduate Studies Committee in Ancient History.

D

A dissertation of not more than 25,000 words on a subject to be approved by the Graduate Studies Committee in Ancient History. (The dissertation word limit excludes the bibliography, any text that is being edited or annotated, any translation of that text, and any descriptive catalogue or similar factual matter, but includes quotations, notes and appendices.)

The dissertation (two typewritten or printed copies) must be sent in a parcel bearing the words 'Dissertation for the M.Phil. in Greek and/or Roman History' to The Chairman of the Examiners, c/o The Clerk of the Schools, Examination Schools, High Street, Oxford, to arrive no later than the Thursday of the sixth week of the Trinity Full Term in which the examination is to be taken.

7. All options, including the dissertation, require the approval of the candidate's supervisor and the Graduate Studies Committee in Ancient History, having regard to the candidate's previous experience, the range covered by the chosen options, and the availability of teaching and examining resources. The options must be submitted for approval not later than the Friday of the fifth week of Michaelmas Term in the candidate's first academic year. Candidates will not normally be allowed to be examined in languages of which they are native speakers or which they have previously studied in taught courses for more than two years.

History of Science, Medicine, and Technology

(*See also the general notice at the commencement of these regulations.*)

The regulations of the Board of the Faculty of Modern History are as follows:

(1) Every candidate must follow for at least six terms a course of instruction in History of Science, Medicine, and Technology, and must upon entering for the examination produce from his or her society a certificate to that effect.

(2) The examination will consist of the following parts:

Qualifying test

Every candidate must pass a qualifying test. The test shall consist of the satisfactory completion of two courses on

1. Methods and themes in economic and social history: an introduction to research.

2. *Either* Methods and themes in the history of medicine (if the candidate's dissertation project lies in the field of history of medicine) *or* Methods and themes in the history of science and technology (if the candidate's dissertation project lies in the field of history of science and technology).

A paper from another established course within the University may be substituted for one of the standard courses where this would provide a more appropriate training for the candidate's dissertation focus. Such a choice will need formal approval from both the Course Director and the Chairman of the Graduate Studies Committee of the Board of the Faculty of Modern History.

The organizers of each course shall not later than the Friday of the sixth week of the Trinity Term preceding the examination submit to the examiners a list of candidates who have satisfactorily completed a qualifying course. No candidate who has failed the qualifying test of two courses will be permitted to supplicate for the degree. Candidates who fail a qualifying course once will be permitted to take it again, not later than one year after the initial attempt.

Final Examination

The examination shall consist of four papers and a dissertation.

I. Three advanced papers at least two of which must be selected from Schedule I below ('Advanced Papers for the M.Phil. and M.Sc. in History of Science, Medicine, and Technology'), and not more than one from any other M.Phil., the choice of which must be approved by the chairman of the Graduate Studies Committee of the Modern History Board not later than Monday of the fourth week of the second Michaelmas Term of the course.

Candidates must take at least two of their advanced papers as three-hour written examinations. For each of their remaining advanced papers candidates must choose to be assessed either by written examination or by two 5,000-word essays. Essays may only be submitted in lieu of written papers for subjects in Schedule I or for papers from other M.Phil.s where similar provision exists in the regulations for those examinations. The essays must be the work of the candidates alone and they must not consult any other person including their supervisors in any way concerning the method of handling the themes chosen. The themes chosen by the candidate must be submitted for approval by the chairman of examiners, c/o the Clerk of the Schools, High Street, Oxford, not later than the Monday of the fifth week of Hilary Term. Candidates will be informed within two weeks, by means of a letter directed to their colleges, whether the topics they have submitted have been approved. The finished essays must be delivered by the candidate to the Clerk of the Schools, Examination Schools, High Street, Oxford, by noon on Monday the third week of Trinity Full Term. The essays must be presented in proper scholarly form, and two typed copies of each must be submitted. Candidates may be examined viva voce on the subjects on which they submit essays. Candidates who have not delivered essays as prescribed by the due date on any of their subjects must sit the written examination in those subjects.

II. *Either* (i) one paper in a discipline or skill or sources or methods selected from Schedule II below.

or (ii) A fourth advanced paper selected from Schedule I or from any additional list of papers for the M.Phil. and M.Sc. in History of Science, Medicine, and Technology approved by the Graduate Studies Committee of the Board of the Faculty of Modern History and published in the definitive list of Advanced Papers as set out in Schedule I.

III. A dissertation of not more than 30,000 words, including appendices but excluding bibliography on a topic approved by the candidate's supervisor. The dissertation must be delivered not later than noon on the Monday of the first week of the Trinity Full Term in which the examination is to be taken to the Clerk of the Schools, High Street, Oxford. Dissertations submitted must not exceed the permitted length. If they do the examiners will reduce the marks awarded. The presentation and footnotes should comply with the requirements specified in the Regulations of the Educational Policy and Standards Committee for the degree of M.Litt. and D.Phil. and follow the *Conventions for the presentation of dissertations and theses* of the Board of the Faculty of Modern History.

Each dissertation must include a short abstract which concisely summarizes its scope and principal arguments, in about 300 words.

Candidates must submit by the specified date two copies of their dissertations. These must be securely and firmly bound in either hard or soft covers. One copy of an M.Phil. dissertation which is approved by the examiners must be deposited in the Bodleian Library. This finalized copy should incorporate any corrections or amendments which the examiners may have requested. It must be in a permanently fixed binding, drilled and sewn, in a stiff board case in library buckram, in a dark colour, and lettered on the spine with the candidate's name and initials, the degree, and the year of submission.

3. Candidates may, if they so wish, be examined in up to two of their four papers (or submit essays in lieu of these papers as provided for above) at the end of their first year.

4. The examiners will permit the use of any hand-held pocket calculator subject to the conditions set out below under the heading 'Use of calculators in examinations' in the *Special Regulations concerning Examinations*.

5. Each candidate must attend an oral examination when required to do so by the examiners.

6. The examiners may award a distinction for excellence in the whole examination.

7. If it is the opinion of the examiners that the work done by a candidate, while not of sufficient merit to qualify for the degree of M.Phil., is nevertheless of sufficient merit to qualify for the degree of Master of Science in History of Science, Medicine, and Technology, the candidate shall be given the option of resitting the M.Phil. (as provided by Ch. VI, Sect. vi, § 2, para. 4) or of being granted leave to supplicate for the degree of Master of Science.

8. A candidate who fails the examination will be permitted to retake it on one further occasion only, not later than one year after the initial attempt.

Such a candidate whose dissertation has been of a satisfactory standard may resubmit the same piece of work, while a candidate who has reached a satisfactory standard on the written papers will not be required to retake that part of the examination.

Schedule I

Advanced Papers for the M.Phil. and M.Sc. in History of Science, Medicine, and Technology

A broad range of the course resources are shared with the corresponding courses in Economic and Social History, and Advanced Papers are therefore available in the subject areas listed here.

1. Economic and business history
2. History of science and technology
3. Social history
4. Historical demography
5. History of medicine

A descriptive list of Advanced Papers will be published by the Board of the Faculty of Modern History in September for the academic year ahead (not all options may be available in every year). The definitive list of the titles of Advanced Papers for any one year will be circulated to candidates and their supervisors and posted on the Faculty notice board not later than Friday of Third Week of Michaelmas Term.

Schedule II

The paper in a relevant discipline or skill may be:

1. One of the papers from the M.Phil. in Economics.

2. One of the papers from the M.Phil. in Sociology or in Comparative Social Policy.

3. One of the papers from the M.Phil. in Russian and East European Studies.

4. One suitable paper from another Master's degree under the auspices of the Faculty of Modern History approved from time to time by the Graduate Studies Committee of the Board of Modern History.

5. One suitable paper from another Master's degree on the recommendation of the candidate's supervisor and endorsed by the Course Director.

Choices under Schedule II have to be approved by the Chairman of the Graduate Studies Committee of the Board of the Faculty of Modern History not later than Monday of the fourth week of the second Michaelmas Term of the course. Candidates wishing to take a paper under 1, 2, 3, or 5 will also need the approval of the appropriate course convener and the Graduate Studies Committee of the relevant faculty board or inter-faculty committee who need to be satisfied that each candidate has an adequate background in the subject. Not all options may be available in any one year.

International Relations

(*See also the general notice at the commencement of these regulations.*)

The regulations made by the Social Sciences Board are as follows:

Qualifying Test

Every candidate must pass a qualifying test before the end of the third term from commencement of the course unless given exemption by the International Relations Graduate Studies Committee. The qualifying test shall be set and administered by the examiners appointed to examine for the M.Phil. in International Relations. This test shall consist of three parts, as follows:

1. A formally assessed essay of between 4,000 and 6,000 words on research design as it bears on some aspect of international relations. The Research Design Essay will normally be related to the subject of the student's proposed M.Phil. thesis. The date of submission, the scope and the format are as stated in the *Notes of Guidance* for Graduate Students in International Relations as published annually by the Department of Politics and International Relations.

2. A single, three-hour examination paper covering material from the core papers as taught in the first two terms. Details of the scope and coverage are given in the *Notes of Guidance* for Graduate Students in International Relations. The examination shall take place on the Thursday of noughth week of Trinity Term, the exact time to be set by the examiners.

3. The examiners must also be satisfied that candidates have satisfactorily completed their designated course of research training, and candidates must submit to the examiners all course work completed as a part of their research methods training. The coursework requirements, including administrative arrangements and dates of submission, are set out in the *Notes of Guidance* for Graduate Students in International Relations. Candidates should note that the *Notes of Guidance* will set dates for the submission (and, where necessary resubmission) of work for individual research modules.

Entries for the qualifying test must be made on the appropriate form, obtainable from the University Offices, by Friday of the fourth week of the Hilary Full Term following the candidate's admission. Candidates who fail the examination part of the qualifying test may retake it in the eighth week of the same Trinity Term. Candidates who fail the research design essay or the course work submitted for the research modules may resubmit their work on the last Friday of the week falling two weeks before Week One of the following Michaelmas Term.

Final Examination

No candidate shall enter the final examination unless he or she has already passed the qualifying test or has been granted exemption by the Graduate Studies Committee as stated above. In the final examination every candidate must offer:

1. A thesis of not more than 30,000 words, excluding bibliography, to be delivered to the Clerk of the Schools, High Street, Oxford, by noon on Monday in the first week of the Trinity Full Term in which the examination is to be taken. Two hard-bound copies of the thesis must be accompanied by a statement that it is the candidate's own work except where otherwise indicated. Successful candidates will be required to deposit one copy of their thesis in the Bodleian Library.

2. *The Development of the International System since 1900.* The history of the relations between states in peace and war, and the development of the international system since 1900. It will include such topics as: the pre-1914 system; the balance of power and the causes of the First World War; the effects of the peace settlement and the rise of liberal and realist approaches to international relations; collective security and the League of Nations system; political and economic co-operation in the

interwar period; the USA, Soviet Union, Middle East, and Far East in the inter-war years; the impact of domestic politics and ideology on foreign policy; the causes of the Second World War; the relationship between politics and strategy in the Second World War; post-war reconstruction and the origins of the Cold War; the evolution of the Cold War; decolonization and self-determination; regional conflicts; integration in Western Europe; détente and the end of the Cold War; the evolution of international economic institutions; the evolution of security institutions; and international relations in the post Cold War world.

3. *Contemporary Debates in International Relations Theory*: Ideas about, and explanations of, international relations, concentrating mainly (but not exclusively) on the major theoretical approaches in the academic study of international relations since 1945. The key theories and approaches to be examined include: realism and neo-realism; theories about war, security, and the use of force in international relations; classical liberalism, globalization, and transformation in world politics; theories about inter-state co-operation and transnationalism; the concept of international society; constructivism and the impact of law and norms in international relations; neo-Marxist and critical theory approaches to international relations; normative theory and international ethics.

4. Two subjects chosen from the following. (Teaching in some options may not be available every year. Students will be advised during the first year of the course of the teaching arrangements for the optional subjects).

(*a*) *The International History of West Europe since 1945.* The Cold War in Europe; West European politics, the Atlantic Alliance and European unity; Germany, France, and Britain in European international history; European détente; causes and consequences of the end of the Cold War in Europe.

(*b*) *The Politics of the United Nations and its Agencies.* Examines the evolving role of the United Nations in world politics. After a theoretical and historical introduction, the option examines the role and significance of the United Nations system in five functional areas: development, human rights, security, humanitarian action, and forced migration.

(*c*) *The USSR and Russia in International Relations since 1945.* The evolution of Soviet foreign policy under Stalin and Khrushchev; the rise and fall of détente; the USSR and the Third World; ideology and Soviet foreign policy; the role of the military and military factors; the emergence of Russian foreign policy; the making of Russian foreign policy and the role of domestic factors; NATO enlargement and relations with Europe; policy in the 'near abroad', including Ukraine, Central Asia and the Caucasus.

(*d*) *Strategic studies.* The development of strategic thought and practice, and the place of strategic factors in international relations, since the early nineteenth century, with main emphasis on the period since the First World War. The course, which is varied from year to year in accordance with the research interests of the graduate students participating, encompasses the following: security concerns as motives of state behaviour; the phenomenon of civil war and international response to it; the military implications of technological changes, including in weapons, delivery systems, information management and communications; strategic doctrine and practice in specific states, including the major powers, and in different regions of the world; the emergence of doctrines of deterrence, limited war, and peacekeeping; the roles of alliances and international organizations (including the United Nations) in the authorization and management of force; aspects of international law relating to armed conflict; the attempts to develop alternatives to reliance on national armaments; negotiations about, and measures of, arms limitation and disarmament; the role of guerrilla warfare and non-violent forms of pressure in international relations; political assumptions of strategic thought.

(*e*) *The United States in International Relations since 1945.* This course examines the foreign policy of the United States since the end of the Second World War. Special emphasis is placed on the forces and factors that have shaped US foreign policy such as political culture, coalitions, the bureaucracy, and cognitive schemas and on the theories used by political scientists to explain the sources and the making of US foreign policy.

(*f*) *The International Relations of the Middle East.* This course covers the international politics of the Middle East and of the Persian Gulf with an emphasis on the period since 1945. There are three main elements: the foreign policies of the Arab states and the relations between them; the Arab–Israeli conflict; and external involvement in the affairs of the region. The course also examines a number of issue areas such as the impact of economic power, the role of Islam, secular ideologies, security, and the causes and consequences of war.

(*g*) *International Political Economy.* The interrelationship between the world economy and the international political system, including the principal theories regarding international political economy. The course seeks to integrate readings and discussions on theory and methodology and analysis of contemporary issues in IPE. Topics will include: the reconstruction of the international economy after 1945; the role of the US in the post-war period and theories of hegemonic stability; the politics of international trade and the evolution of the GATT/WTO system; the development of regional economic arrangements and the relationship between regionalism, multilateralism and globalization in the world economy; the political economy of the European Single Market; the European Monetary Union; current issues in transatlantic economic relations.

(*h*) *The Function of Law in the International Community.* This course examines the basic aspects of the international legal system, including the sources of international law, the relationship between national law and international law, jurisdiction, state responsibility, and human rights. A central focus is the role of law in international politics, that is, in the day to day relations between states and international organizations, and between states and individuals. The study of the theoretical and analytical aspects of international law, through the literature, is complemented by a practical focus on current issues, including the use of force, international humanitarian law, dispute management, economic conflict, and the role generally of international organizations, particularly the United Nations. Details of the international law documents that will be available to candidates in the examination room will be given in the Notes of Guidance to Graduate Students in International Relations and in the examiners' Advice to Candidates.

(*i*) *The International Relations of East Asia.* The Yalta settlement in 1945 and its contributions to establishing a durable security order in the region; the origins and impact of the Cold War in the region, in particular through an examination of the Korean War, the transformation of the American occupation of Japan, and the onset of the Sino–American hostility; the fracturing of the Cold War system examined via the sub-regional organization, ASEAN, the onset of the Sino–Soviet and Sino–Vietnamese conflicts, the Sino–American rapprochement; the features of the post Cold War era, including an examination of newly-established institutions such as the ASEAN regional Forum (ARF) and Asia Pacific Economic Cooperation Forum (APEC). The course also examines a number of issues, such as the international causes and consequences of the economic rise of the regional states of democratization, and the impact of nuclear weapons. The course content varies to some degree from year to year in accordance with the research interests of those taking this option.

(*j*) *Classical Theories of International Relations.* This option provides an advanced understanding of the history and thought on International Relations in the period of the classical European state system, with particular emphasis on the period

1750–1939. Topics will include: theories of the state and the development of the concept of sovereignty; nationalism and national self-determination; international institutions (including international law, international organizations, the balance of power, and diplomacy); war and the use of force (including the evolution of strategic thought, doctrines of intervention, and ideas arising from the rise of the peace movement); liberal, marxist and mercantilist approaches to international political economy; imperialism and the expansion of international society; revolution and its impact on international relations; theories of progress and of historical change. The works bearing on these subjects by, *inter alia*: Rousseau, Herder, Mill, Mazzini, Hegel, Vattel, Hume, Kant, Burke, Castlereagh, von Gentz, Oppenheim, Clausewitz, Smith, Cobden, Bentham, List, Marx, Lenin, Angell, Wilson, Nietzsche, Carr, Zimmern. Candidates will also be expected to demonstrate knowledge of the principal methodological approaches to the history of political thought.

(*k*) *The International Relations of the Developing World.* The paper analyses the international relations of developing countries from 1945 to the present day. The focus is on the characteristics of developing states and their interaction with the political, economic, and military arrangements in the international system. The paper will address topics including: decolonization and the emergence of the Third World; the nature of the state and problems of state building in developing countries; the political and economic forces which have shaped international arrangements for trade and finance since 1944; political and economic constraints on growth in the world economy; the international financial institutions and their political impact; the new politics of global investment; intervention, conflict and their consequences; security and the politics of alliance formation; regionalism and 'regimes'.

(*l*) *The International Relations of Latin America.* The history of US–Latin American relations, including the regional significance of the Cold War, impact of the end of the Cold War, and the making of US policy towards the region. Relations between the major European states and the European Union and the sub-continent. Foreign and security policies of the principal Latin American states, including interstate alliances, rivalries within the region and the international aspects of internal conflicts. Latin American perspectives on non-interventionism, international law, dispute settlements, the international human rights and regional and international organizations. Regional and sub-regional co-operation and integration schemes, including the Andean Community, Mercosur, NAFTA, and the proposed Free Trade Area of the Americas. The political economy of the multi-national corporation, and international flows of capital, of labour (including undocumented migrants remittances), and narcotics. Theories of dependency and underdevelopment; liberalism; realism and foreign policy making. Interactions between domestic and international policy, including the international dimensions of democratization.

(*m*) *International Normative Theory.* An analysis of the role of norms and ethics in international affairs. Topics include: state sovereignty, national self-determination, global society and cultural diversity, just war, humanitarian intervention, human rights, international justice, transnational environmental responsibility, and the interrelationships of common morality, international law, and political effectiveness in the cases of specific norms. Candidates will be expected to demonstrate knowledge of the principal contemporary approaches to the study of ethics and norms in International Relations.

(*n*) *The Balkan Crises of the 1990s.* An examination of the nature of the communist state of Yugoslavia; Yugoslavia's international position, including the concept of non-alignment, and economic aspects of its external relations: the exile communities, the Yugoslav Gastarbeiter, and the role of Yugoslavia's foreign debt. The impact of the collapse of communism in the Balkans and the reappearance of regional rivalries, e.g. in Macedonia, will be studied, but the main focus will be the internationalization of the growing conflicts in the former Yugoslavia. An examination of the Bosnian and Kosovan conflicts and the differing responses on the part of international organizations, most notably the UN and EU. An examination both of state policy by major powers (especially the USA, Germany, the UK, and Russia), and of the role of individual diplomatists. An examination of the Balkan crises as ones in which traditional international notions of balance of power, individual diplomatic initiative, and national self-interest combined with newer concepts of institutional power-brokering and multi-national action in Europe's most febrile region.

(*o*) *Special Topic in International Relations*. To be decided annually by the International Relations Graduate Studies Committee and where available, to be notified to candidates by the end of Hilary Term of their first year.

5. Candidates must present themselves for viva voce examination when requested by the examiners. The examiners shall not fail any candidate without inviting him or her to attend such an examination.

The examiners may award a distinction for excellence in the whole examination.

Judaism and Christianity in the Graeco-Roman World

(*See also the general notice at the commencement of these regulations.*)

The regulations made by the Boards of the Faculties of Oriental Studies and Theology are as follows:

Candidates will be admitted to take the examination as defined below in a specific year. In exceptional circumstances candidates may be allowed to take an examination later than one to which they were admitted. Permission for this must be sought from the faculty board not later than Monday of the week before the first week of the Trinity Term in which the examination was to have been taken. The application must have the support of the candidate's college and be accompanied by a statement from the supervisor.

I. All candidates shall be required:

(*a*) To satisfy the boards that they possess the necessary knowledge of Hebrew and Greek to profit by the course.

(*b*) To present themselves for a written examination and to offer a thesis, as specified below.

(*c*) To present themselves for viva voce examination unless individually dispensed by the examiners. (No candidate will be failed without a viva.)

II. Candidates shall offer five papers and a thesis, not to exceed 20,000 words.* The thesis must fall primarily into either A or B below. Two papers must fall into the area of the thesis and three into the other area, and A(1) and B(1) must be included, unless the boards shall otherwise determine.

A. Judaism

(1) Jewish literature, history, and institutions from 200 BC to AD 200.

---

* See the regulation on p. 508 concerning the preparation and dispatch of theses.

The thesis must be on a subject approved by the faculty boards (or by a person or persons to whom they may delegate the power of giving such approval). Candidates are advised in their own interests to submit titles for approval as early as possible.

When submitted, the thesis must be accompanied by a signed statement by the candidate that the thesis is his own work except where otherwise indicated; successful candidates may be required to deposit one copy of the thesis in the Bodleian and in that case would also be required to sign a form stating whether they give permission for the thesis to be consulted.

Candidates are reminded that work submitted for the Degree of M.Phil. may subsequently be incorporated in a thesis submitted for the Degree of D.Phil.

(2) Jewish historiography (with prescribed texts).
(3) Jewish Bible interpretation (with prescribed texts).
(4) Jewish eschatology (with prescribed texts).
(5) Jewish wisdom literature (with prescribed texts).

B. Christianity
(1) Christian literature, history, and institutions to AD 180.
(2) The Gospels and the historical Jesus (with prescribed texts).
(3) Acts and the Pauline corpus (with prescribed texts).
(4) The Apostolic Fathers (with prescribed texts).
(5) The Apologists (with prescribed texts).

Note: Texts will be announced by the boards in the seventh week of Michaelmas Full Term in the first year of the course.

III. The Examiners may award a Distinction for excellence in the whole examination.

Latin American Studies

(*See also the general notice at the commencement of these regulations.*)

For the purposes of this examination, 'Latin America' will be interpreted as covering mainland America from the northern border of Mexico, South to Cape Horn, with the addition of Cuba, Haiti, the Dominican Republic, and Puerto Rico.

The regulations are as follows:

1. Candidates must follow for three terms a course of instruction in the M.Sc. in Latin American Studies with the exception of the extended essay. Examinations at the end of the first year will serve to qualify for entry onto the second year of the course.

2. During the first year, candidates will develop a thesis topic, which will be the subject of fieldwork in the long vacation between the first and second year.

3. In the second year, candidates for the M.Phil. will:

(*a*) offer a thesis* of not more than 30,000 words, including footnotes and appendices, on a topic taken from their major discipline. A page of tables may be taken as the equivalent of 150 words. The title should be submitted for approval of the Latin American Centre committee not later than noon on the Friday of week nought of Trinity Term in the first year of the course. Two typewritten copies of the thesis must be delivered to the Examination Schools and addressed to the Chairman of Examiners for the M.Phil. in Latin American Studies, c/o Clerk of the Schools, Examination Schools, High Street, Oxford, by noon on the fifth Monday of Trinity Full Term in the calendar year in which the examination is to be taken. Successful candidates will be required to deposit one copy of their thesis in the Bodleian Library, and will be required to sign a form stating whether they will permit their thesis to be consulted.

(*b*) take a further examination in one additional paper from an option in another discipline, or by agreement with the relevant department, take a methodology or other paper from an appropriate M.Phil. in the relevant discipline.

4. *Viva Voce examination*

Candidates must present themselves for viva voce examination when required to do so by the examiners.

---

* See the regulation on p. 508 concerning the preparation and dispatch of theses. Candidates are reminded that work submitted for the Degree of M.Phil. may subsequently be incorporated in a thesis submitted for the Degree of D.Phil.

5. *Language qualification*

Candidates will be tested in the language or languages relevant to the subjects they propose to offer under (1), (2) and (3) above by the end of their first term, and will be required to satisfy the Area and Development Studies Committee by the end of their first year that their knowledge of these is adequate. A further test will be set in the third term for candidates who have not reached the required standard at the first attempt.

A candidate who fails the examination will be permitted to re-take it on one further occasion only, not later than one year after the attempt. Such a candidate whose dissertation has been of a satisfactory standard may re-submit the same piece of work, while a candidate who has reached a satisfactory standard on the written papers will not be required to re-take that part of the examination.

The examiners may award a distinction for excellence in the whole examination.

Law

(See the regulations for the Bachelor of Civil Law and Magister Juris)

Material Anthropology and Museum Ethnography

(*See also the general notice at the commencement of these regulations.*)

Within the Division of Life and Environmental Sciences, the course shall be administered by the School of Anthropology. The regulations made by the divisional board are as follows:

The examinations shall consist of the following.

1. *Qualifying Examination*

Every candidate will be required to satisfy the examiners in an examination for which if he or she is successful, he or she will receive the Diploma in Material Anthropology and Museum Ethnography in the academic year in which the candidate's name is first entered on the register of M.Phil. students or, with the approval of the divisional board, in a subsequent year. If he or she passes the examination at the appropriate level, he or she will be allowed to proceed to the M.Phil. If he or she is successful in the M.Phil. Final Examination, the M.Phil. will subsume his or her Diploma.

2. *Final Examination*

This shall be taken in the Trinity Term of the academic year following that in which the candidate's name is first entered on the register of M.Phil. students or, with the approval of the divisional board, in a subsequent year.

Each candidate shall be required

(i) to present himself or herself for written examination in accordance with I below;

(ii) to submit a thesis in accordance with II below;

(iii) to present himself or herself for oral examination as required by the examiners.

I. The written papers shall consist of the following:

A. A paper in the theoretical field of material anthropology and museum ethnography

B. A paper consisting of two Parts: Part I relating to research methods in material anthropology and museum ethnography and Part II to a paper in the area and/or topic of the candidate's thesis.

II. *Thesis*

Each candidate shall be required to submit a thesis of not more than 30,000 words (excluding references and appendices) on a subject approved by the supervisor. The thesis may be based on the analysis of objects in the collections of the Pitt Rivers

Museum or a topic from one of the subject areas covered during the qualifying year. The candidate shall send to the Secretary of Faculties, with the written approval of his supervisor, the proposed title of the thesis for consideration by the Board of the Faculty of Anthropology and Geography, by noon on Monday of the first week of Michaelmas Term in the academic year following that in which his or her name was entered on the register of M.Phil. students. The thesis (two copies) must be typewritten and delivered to the Clerk of the Schools, High Street, Oxford, not later than Monday of the second week of Trinity Term in the academic year in which the Final Examination is taken.

The examiners shall require a successful candidate to deposit a copy of his or her thesis in the Balfour Library. If the thesis is superseded by a D.Phil. thesis by the same student partly using the same material, the Board of the Faculty of Anthropology and Geography may authorize the withdrawal of the M.Phil. thesis from the Balfour Library. Such candidates will be required to sign a form stating whether they give permission for their thesis to be consulted.

The examiners may award a distinction for excellence in the whole examination.

If it is the opinion of the examiners that the work which has been required of a candidate is not of sufficient merit to qualify him or her for the Degree of M.Phil., the candidate shall be given the option of resitting the M.Phil. examination under Ch. VI, Sect. VI, §2, cl. 4 or of being granted permission to supplicate for the Diploma.

Mathematics for Industry

(*See also the general notice at the commencement of these regulations.*)

The regulations made by the Divisional Board of Mathematical and Physical Sciences are as follows:

1. The examination will consist of:

(i) a written examination consisting of four papers on the syllabus described in Schedule 1, two of which will normally be taken in the first year and two in the second, provided that the faculty board may give approval to a candidate to take all four papers on one occasion;

(ii) a thesis on a topic selected by the candidate in consultation with his supervisor and approved by the M.Phil. Supervisory Committee (Mathematics for Industry), c/o The Mathematical Institute, 24–9 St. Giles', Oxford, OX1 3LB, to which applications for approval should be sent not later than Friday of the fourth week of the Hilary Full Term of the second year;

(iii) an oral examination on the thesis, on the six special topics chosen from Schedule 2, and, unless the candidate shall have been individually dispensed by the examiners, on topics in Schedule 1.

2. Candidates must normally enter for the whole examination by Friday of the fourth week of the Hilary Full Term of their first year and will be required to state the papers on which they wish to be examined in that year.

3. For the special topics in Schedule 2, and on the classwork associated with Schedule 1, the examiners will take into account the result of an assessment organized by the M.Phil. Supervisory Committee (Mathematics for Industry). The committee shall be responsible for notifying the candidate of the arrangements for the assessment, and for forwarding the results of all candidates to the Chairman of the M.Phil. examiners before the oral examination. The assessment will be made by giving the candidate questions to answer over a period of twenty-four hours or a mini-project to develop over a period of a week, and candidates will be required to sign a statement that the work offered for assessment is theirs alone. The questions or

mini-projects will be set within six weeks of the end of the relevant lecture course and will be suggested by the course lecturers.

4. Three typewritten copies of the thesis must be delivered not later than noon on September 15 in the year in which the examination is completed to the Chairman of the M.Phil. Examiners (Mathematics for Industry), c/o The Clerk of the Schools, Examination Schools, High Street, Oxford, together with a list of six special topics from Schedule 2 on which the candidate wishes to be orally examined.

5. In the written examination the examiners will permit the use of any hand-held pocket calculators subject to the conditions set out under the heading 'Use of calculators in examinations' in the *Special Regulations concerning Examinations.*

6. The examiners may award a distinction for excellence in the whole examination.

SCHEDULE 1

A. Linear and non-linear ordinary differential equations; phase plane and asymptotic methods. First-order partial differential equations, hyperbolic systems, and weak solutions. Use of Fourier and Laplace transforms, Green and Riemann functions, and complex variable theory in the solution of linear partial differential equations. Mathematical modelling of problems in applied science using differential equations.

B. Numerical linear algebra: solution of large sets of linear equations and eigenvalue problems by iterative methods. Ordinary differential equations: multistep and Runge-Kutta methods, matrix and shooting methods; stiffness. Partial differential equations: difference methods for parabolic, hyperbolic, and elliptic equations; stability, convergence, and error analysis; simple finite element methods. Optimization and approximation: unconstrained and constrained minimization, quasi-Newton and gradient methods; best approximation of functions, splines, error bounds.

C. Statistics; hypothesis testing, point and interval estimation, large sample theory of maximum likelihood estimation and likelihood ratio tests. Linear models; regression and analysis of variance. Autoregressive moving average models of time series; analysis in the time and frequency domain.

D. Combinatorial optimization, linear and dynamic programming; sequencing and scheduling, network algorithms and computational complexity. Stochastic modelling of processes with a discrete state space. Methods of simulation; queueing theory. Inventories, reliability and decision analysis.

SCHEDULE 2

Mathematical modelling of industrial and other scientific problems.

Further topics in applied analysis, statistics, and applied probability.

Numerical solution of integral equations and boundary value problems; finite element methods; computational fluid dynamics.

Communication theory, complexity and cryptography.

Medical Anthropology

(*See also the general notice at the commencement of these regulations.*)

Within the Division of Life and Environmental Sciences, the course shall be administered by the School of Anthropology. The regulations made by the divisional board are as follows:

1. The Division of Life and Environmental Sciences shall elect for the supervision of the course a Standing Committee, which shall have power to arrange lectures and other instruction. The course director shall be responsible to the Standing Committee.

The examination shall consist of the following:

1. *Qualifying Examination*

Every candidate will be required to satisfy the examiners in an examination for which, if he or she passes at the appropriate level, he or she will be allowed to proceed to the second year of the M.Phil. Candidates must follow a course of instruction in Medical Anthropology for at least three terms, and will, when entering for the examinations, be required to produce a certificate from their supervisor to this effect. Every candidate for the M.Phil. qualifying examination will be required to satisfy the examiners in four written papers to be taken in the Trinity Term of the academic year in which the candidate's name is first entered on the Register of M.Phil. Students or, with the approval of the Divisional Board, in a subsequent year. The following four papers will have to be taken:

I *Medical Anthropology A: Concepts of disease, illness, health and medicine in global perspective.*

The scope of this paper includes the following topics: epidemiology, global distribution of disease patterns, co-existence of alternative therapeutic or healing systems, phenomenology of the body, and cross-cultural concepts of health, pain, illness, disease causation, diagnosis and cure. Topics analysed from conjoined biological and socio-cultural perspectives include human growth and personhood, adaptability, nutrition, health and social inequality, reproduction and fertility, disease identification and epidemiology. Issues associated with informed consent; preparation of research proposals.

II *Medical Anthropology B: Theory and practice of bio-medicine and of other medical systems.*

The scope of this paper includes the impact of different medical systems on the health of populations, issues of public health and policy on a comparative and global basis, including specific campaigns (e.g. that of eliminating smallpox in South Asia and attempts to characterize and treat AIDS). It draws on ethnographies of particular societies to illustrate and test theoretical claims in medical anthropology, covering different ways in which people manage fertility, reproduction, death and disease, patient–healer relations, the explanatory roles of divination, herbalism, alternative therapies, drama therapy, religion, shamanism, sorcery and culturally defined concepts of risk, vulnerability, fate and evil.

III *Medical Anthropology C: Critical medical anthropology.*

The scope of this paper includes a critique of the assumptions and methods of this sub-field of anthropology and of its links with other fields and disciplines, including the place of material culture in medicine. It also includes critique of the Cartesian mind-body dichotomy and methodological problems specially affecting medical anthropology; fieldwork and data collection methods; quantitative and qualitative techniques; cultural property and indigenous rights; ethnical issues.

IV *Medical Anthropology D: Ecological and bio-medical anthropology.*

The scope of this paper includes consideration of the concept of well-being as being broader than conventional concepts of health and comprising ecological, biological, and socio-cultural perspectives; relationships between bio-diversity, ecological change and changing patterns of disease, diagnosis and cure; the role of economic transformation in health and environmental issues; changing relationships between diet, nutrition, infection, human growth and chronic disease; pharmacology and genomics in research and practice; health and ethics.

2. *Final Examination*

Candidates must follow a course of instruction in Medical Anthropology for at least three terms, and will, when entering for the final examination, be required to produce a certificate from their supervisor to this effect.

The final examination shall be taken in the Trinity Term of the academic year following that in which the candidate's name is first entered on the Register of M.Phil. Students or, with the approval of the Divisional Board, in a subsequent year.

Each candidate shall be required:

(1) to submit evidence of practical work, a written essay and a research proposal in accordance with I below;

(2) to submit a thesis in accordance with II below;

(3) to present himself or herself for oral examination as required by the examiners. The oral examination may be on the candidate's written assignments, or dissertation, or both.

I. *Methods of fieldwork and social research*

(*a*) The satisfactory completion of a course of practical work in (i) participant observation, in-depth interviewing, archival research, and qualitative data analysis; (ii) basic principles of statistical inference, and statistical models for the analysis of quantitative social science data, and (iii) methods of data collection, including questionnaire design, interviewing, and coding.

Candidates shall submit to the School of Anthropology Graduate Studies Committee by noon on Monday of sixth week of the third term of the second year of the course reports of the practical work completed, accompanied by a statement that they are the candidate's own work except where otherwise indicated. The Medical Anthropology Course Director, or a deputy, shall draw to the attention of the examiners the names of any candidates who have failed to complete to a satisfactory level of quality the course of practical work, and the examiners may require candidates to retake the course or a specified part thereof. The reports of practical work shall be available for inspection by the examiners.

(*b*) Candidates will be required to produce an essay of up to 2,500 words evaluating the research design, methods of data collection and analysis, and any ethical or philosophical issues that arise in a specified research paper in Medical Anthropology. The Medical Anthropology Course Director shall publish a list of research papers not later than noon on Monday of the first week of the third term; candidates will be required to select one from this list of papers as the subject of their essay.

Candidates shall submit their essay to the Clerk of Schools by 12 noon on Monday of the sixth week of the third term of the second year of the course, accompanied by a statement that it is the candidate's own work except where otherwise indicated.

(*c*) Candidates will be required to produce a detailed plan of research on the topic of their thesis. This plan of research should contain statements on (1) the research question(s) and the relevance of the question(s) to a field of anthropological or ethnographic knowledge, (2) the research methods to be used, (3) a schedule of research work.

Candidates shall submit their essay to the Clerk of Schools by 12 noon on Monday of the sixth week of the third term of the second year of the course, accompanied by a statement that it is the candidate's own work except where otherwise indicated.

II. *Thesis*

Each candidate shall be required to submit a thesis of not more than 30,000 words (excluding references and appendices) on a subject approved by the supervisor. He or she shall send to the Secretary of Faculties, with the written approval of his or her supervisor, the proposed title of the thesis for consideration by the School of Anthropology, by noon on the Monday of first week of Michaelmas Term in the academic year following that in which his or her name was entered on the Register of M.Phil. Students. The thesis (two copies) must be typewritten and delivered to the Clerk of the Schools, High Street, Oxford, not later than noon on Monday of the fourth week of Trinity Term in the academic year in which the Final Examination is taken.

The Examiners shall require a successful candidate to deposit a copy of his or her thesis in the Tylor Library. If the thesis is superseded by a D.Phil. thesis by the same student partly using the same material, the Divisional Board of Life and Environmental Sciences may authorize the withdrawal of the M.Phil. thesis from the Tylor Library. Such candidates will be required to sign a form stating whether they give permission for their thesis to be consulted.

The examiners may award a distinction for excellence in the whole examination. If it is the opinion of the examiners that the work which has been required of a candidate is not of sufficient merit to qualify him or her for the Degree of M.Phil. the candidate shall be given the option of resitting the M.Phil. examination under Ch. Vi, sect. VI, § 2, cl. 4.

Modern European History

(*See also the general notice at the commencement of these regulations.*)

The regulations of the Board of the Faculty of Modern History are as follows:

1. Candidates will be required to have a working (i.e. good reading) knowledge of at least one of the European Languages (apart from English) relevant to the subject matter of their dissertation. Unless exempted by the Course Director, candidates will be tested in the language or languages they propose to offer at the start of Trinity Term of their first year. If they have not satisfied examiners in the Language Test by 1 August of their first year, candidates may not proceed to the second year of their course.

2. Every candidate must follow for at least six terms a course of instruction in Modern European History and must upon entering for the examination produce from his/her society a certificate to this effect.

3. *Syllabus*

The examination shall comprise:

I. for each of two Optional Subjects (*a*) two extended essays of up to 5,000 words, including footnotes; (*b*) the marked assessment by the seminar convenor of one seminar presentation accompanied by the candidate's written notes (of no more than 3,000 words) for the presentation;

II. two examination papers on historical methodology;

III. a dissertation of up to 30,000 words.

I. *Extended essays*

Two extended essays each from two of the following Optional Subjects:

1 Religion and politics in early modern Europe
2 Women, religion, and modernity
3 The Enlightenment 1720–99
4 Social unrest, emancipation, and nationalism: the European Revolutions of 1847–52
5 Varieties of Modernism in Britain and Europe 1870–1920
6 The clash of the Titans and the loss of European supremacy between 1914 and 1920
7 Europe's mid-century crisis 1930–1950.

It is expected that additional Optional Subjects will be approved from time to time by the Graduate Studies Committee of the Board of the Faculty of Modern History. A descriptive list of Optional Subjects will be published by the Board of the Faculty of Modern History in September for the academic year ahead. The definitive list of Optional Subjects for any one year will be circulated to candidates and their supervisors and posted on the Faculty notice board not later than Friday of Third Week of Michaelmas Term of the academic year in which the paper is to be taken.

Candidates should make written application for the approval of their Optional Subjects and essay topics, to reach the Course Director, M.Phil. in Modern European History, c/o Graduate Office, Modern History Faculty, Broad Street, Oxford OX1 3DB, not later than Friday of the Fourth Week of Hilary Term of their first term. Two type-written copies of the extended essays must be sent to the Chairman of the Examiners for the M.Phil. in Modern European History, c/o Clerk of the Schools, Examination Schools, High Street, Oxford, by noon on Friday of Noughth Week of Trinity Term in the candidate's first year. The written notes of the seminar presentations are to be handed in to the seminar convenor immediately after each presentation.

Teaching may not be available for all the Optional Subjects each year, and restrictions may be imposed on the combination of Optional Subjects that may be taken in a particular year.

II. *Historical Methodology Papers*

Two three hour written examination papers on historical methodology: 'Source criticism', to be examined in Trinity Term of the candidate's first year; and 'Historical controversies', to be examined in Trinity term of the candidate's second year.

III. *Dissertation*

A dissertation of not more than 30,000 words, including footnotes and appendices but excluding bibliography, on a topic approved by the candidate's supervisor and the Course Director of the M.Phil. in Modern European History. Candidates should make written application for the approval of the topic of their dissertation to reach the Course Director, M.Phil. in Modern European History, by noon on Monday of Week 7 of the Trinity Term of their first year. The dissertation must be delivered not later than noon on the Monday of the seventh week of the Trinity Full Term in the candidate's second year to the Clerk of the Schools, High Street, Oxford. Dissertations submitted must not exceed the permitted length. If they do the examiners will reduce the marks awarded. The presentation and footnotes should comply with the requirements specified in the Regulations of the Educational Policy and Standards Committee for the degrees of M.Litt. and D.Phil. and follow the *Conventions for the presentation of dissertations and theses* of the Faculty of Modern History.

Each dissertation must include a short abstract which concisely summarizes its scope and principal arguments, in about 300 words.

Candidates must submit by the specified date two copies of their dissertation. These must be securely and firmly bound in either hard or soft covers. One copy of an M.Phil. dissertation which is approved by the examiners must be deposited in the Bodleian Library. This final copy should incorporate any corrections or amendments which the examiners may have requested. It must be hard bound, in a dark colour, and lettered on the spine with the candidate's name and initials, the degree, and the year of submission.

4. A candidate who is unable to continue with the two-year course at the end of the first year may, with the support of his or her college and supervisor, apply to the Director of Graduate Studies in Modern History for permission to transfer to the status of a student for the M.St. in Modern History and to enter that examination in the current year. A candidate whose application for transfer is approved may offer the essays based on her or his first Optional Subject as the period paper and the three-hour examination paper on historical methodology: 'Source Criticism' in place of the required examination paper for the M.St. in Modern History. A candidate may choose for his or her dissertation either a topic from the second Optional Subject or a revised version of the initially intended dissertation topic. Approval of the essay and dissertation titles must be sought in advance from the Chairman of

Examiners for the M.St. in Modern History (c/o Graduate Office, Modern History Faculty, Board Street, Oxford OX1 3BD).

5. Candidates must present themselves for an oral examination if required to do so by the examiners.

6. The examiners may award a distinction to candidates who have performed with special merit in all parts of the examination.

7. A candidate who fails the examination will be permitted to re-take the examination on one further occasion only, not later than one year after the initial attempt. A candidate whose dissertation has been of satisfactory standard will not be required to re-submit the dissertation. A candidate who has reached a satisfactory standard on the written examination papers will not be required to re-take those papers. A candidate who has reached a satisfactory standard on both the extended essays and seminar papers will not be required to re-take these.

Music

(*See also the general notice at the commencement of these regulations.*)

The regulations made by the Board of the Faculty of Music are as follows:

Musicology and Performance

Each candidate will be required:

(1) To follow for the first three terms, undertaking such coursework as may be required, the M.Phil. seminar 'Issues in the performance of music', two seminars freely chosen out of the three core seminars of the M.St. (Historiography, Aesthetics, and Criticism of Music), and such special topics seminars of the M.St. course as are recommended by the supervisor in conjunction with the Director of Graduate Studies;

(2) To pursue the study of a chosen first-study instrument (including voice);

(3) To take a four-part examination at the end of the first year, achieving an appropriate level of attainment as a condition of entering the second year of the course. The examination will comprise:

- (*a*) a three-hour paper on 'Issues in the performance of Music' and on two of the three core seminars of the M.St. (as specified in (1) above);
- (*b*) one course-related essay of no more than 5,000 words (to be submitted not later than Friday of the eighth week of the Trinity Term in which the examination is held);
- (*c*) an extended piece of written work (up to 10,000 words or their equivalent), comprising an introduction to or significant portion of the thesis* or editorial exercise which will form a major component of the final-year submission (see (4) below); this project will be related to some aspect of musicology or performance of music, its title and subject-matter having been approved by the Faculty Board at its first Trinity Term meeting of the candidate's first year; it should be submitted not later then the second Monday in July;
- (*d*) a recital of not more than thirty minutes duration, the programme of which will have been approved by the Director of Graduate Studies.

(4) To present not later than noon on the Friday of the first week of the Trinity Term of the second year, two copies of *either* a thesis* of not more than 30,000 words on a subject related to Musicology or performance of music and

---

* See the regulation on p. 508 concerning the preparation and dispatch of theses. Candidates are reminded that work submitted for the Degree of M.Phil. may subsequently be incorporated in a thesis submitted for the Degree of D.Phil.

approved by the board (see 2(*c*) above) *or* a substantial editorial exercise, including prefatory matter, approved by the board. Successful candidates will be required to deposit one copy of the thesis or edition in the Music Faculty Library.*

(5) To give a recital of not more than sixty minutes duration, vocal or instrumental, the programme of which shall be chosen by the examiners from two possible programmes submitted by the candidate and approved by the board (these will not include works offered in the first-year recital, 3(*d*) above).

The examiners may award a distinction for excellence in the whole examination. The board's approval for proposed subjects of theses should be sought by writing to the Director of Graduate Studies, Music Faculty Board, University Offices, Wellington Square, at the latest by the Friday of the fourth week of the Trinity Term in the academic year preceding that in which the examination is to take place. Candidates offering a recital should submit their programmes to the same address at the latest by Friday of the first week of Hilary Term in the year in which the examination is to take place. They will be informed of the examiners' choice of programme by the Friday of eighth week in the same term.

Oriental Studies

(*See also the general notice at the commencement of these regulations.*)

The regulations made by the Board of the Faculty of Oriental Studies are as follows:

1. Every candidate must present himself for a written examination in one of the following subjects.

(i) Cuneiform Studies.
(ii) Egyptology (including Graeco-Roman and Christian Egypt).
(iii) Medieval Arabic Thought.
(iv) Modern Middle Eastern Studies.
(v) Classical Indian Religion.
(vi) Modern Jewish Studies.
(vii) Jewish Studies in the Graeco-Roman Period.
(viii) Islamic Art and Archaeology.
(ix) Ottoman Turkish Studies.
(x) Classical and Medieval Islamic History.
(xi) Modern Chinese Studies.
(xii) Modern Chinese Art and Literature.
(xiii) Tibetan and Himalayan Studies.

2. Candidates for subject (i) must satisfy the person appointed by the board to interview them that they possess a working knowledge of French and German; candidates for (ii) must satisfy the Oriental Studies Board by the time of their qualifying examination that they possess a working knowledge of French and German, and candidates who wish to offer Greek papyrology must possess a fluent knowledge of Greek; and for subject (vi) candidates must satisfy the person appointed by the board to interview them that they possess a working knowledge of one of the following languages: French, German, Russian, Polish, Yiddish, Arabic. For subject (ix) and the Turkish option in subject (x) candidates must satisfy the person appointed by the board to interview them that they possess a sound reading knowledge of Modern Turkish or Arabic or Persian. For subject (xi), Modern

---

* Candidates will also be required to sign a form stating that they give permission for the thesis to be consulted.

Chinese Studies, candidates will normally have a first degree in a discipline relevant to their elective subject. For subject (xii) Modern Chinese Art and Literature, candidates shall normally have a first degree in art or literature. A candidate who fails any part or parts of the Qualifying Examination may retake such part or parts during the Long Vacation prior to the second year of the course, except in the cases of the M.Phil. in Classical Indian Religion and the M.Phil. in Modern Middle Eastern Studies. A candidate who fails any part or parts of the Qualifying Examination may retake such part or parts during the Long Vacation prior to the second year of the course, except in the cases of the M.Phil. in Classical Indian Religion and the M.Phil. in Modern Middle Eastern Studies. A candidate who fails any part or parts of the Qualifying Examination for these two courses may retake such part or parts during Trinity Term of the first year of study.

3. Subject to such regulations as the board may hereinafter make, every candidate must offer a thesis* on a subject approved by the board (or by a person or persons to whom it may delegate the power of giving such approval), and as far as possible falling within the scope of the subject offered by the candidate in the examination. The thesis should be presented not later than noon on the Friday of the second week of the Trinity Term in which the examination is taken except in (ii) below, in which the thesis should be presented not later than noon on the Friday of the fourth week of the Trinity Term in which the examination is taken.

Successful candidates will be required to deposit one copy of the thesis in the Bodleian.

4. Every candidate will be examined viva voce in the subjects of the school unless he shall have been individually excused by the examiners.

[From 1 October 2004:

5. The examiners may award a distinction for excellence in the whole examination.]

Subjects

(i) *Cuneiform Studies*

Candidates offering this subject will be required

(A) To pass a qualifying examination:

Each candidate will be required, unless exempted by the Oriental Studies Board, to pass a qualifying examination in Sumerian and Akkadian not later than the end of the third term after that in which his or her name has been placed on the register.

(B) to offer the following papers:

1. The Sumerian language, including the following set books:
   (i) The Lament for Sumer and Urim: lines 1–114 and 360–519.
   (ii) Sumerian legal records.

2, 3. Akkadian set books, (*a*) for candidates who have obtained honours in the Honour School of Oriental Studies, (*b*) for all other candidates:

2. Akkadian set books I.
   (i) (*a*): The Middle Assyrian Laws.
   (*b*): The Laws of Hammurabi: prologue, epilogue, and selected laws.
   (ii) (*a* and *b*). Mari Letters and Administrative Documents.

---

* See the regulation on p. 508 concerning the preparation and dispatch of theses. Candidates are reminded that work submitted for the Degree of M.Phil. may subsequently be incorporated in a thesis submitted for the Degree of D.Phil.

3. Akkadian set books II.
   (iii) (*a* and *b*). The Epic of Gilgamesh: tablets 1, 2, 6 and 11.
   (iv) (*a* and *b*). The Babylonian Theodicy.
   (v) (*a*): Babylonian historical texts.
   (*b*): The Prism of Sennacherib: ii 37–iii 49 and v 17–vi 85 (3rd and 8th campaigns and building inscription).

A list of the texts and editions to be used in papers 1–3 is available from the Oriental Institute. Instead of one or two of numbers 1 (i), 1 (ii), 2 (i), 2 (ii), 3 (iii), 3 (iv), and 3 (v), candidates may propose their own list(s) of texts. No more than one substitution may be made in any single paper. The choice of texts must be approved by the Board in each case.

4. Unseen translation of passages from Akkadian texts. Passages may be set from royal inscriptions of the Old Akkadian period and from texts of all categories from all other phases of the Akkadian language (both Babylonian and Assyrian) but excluding peripheral dialects (i.e. Nuzi, Elam, Boğazköy, Kültepe, Ugarit, Alalaḫ, and Amarna-Canaanite).

The use of *A Concise Dictionary of Akkadian* and R. Labat, *Manuel d'épigraphie akkadienne*, will be permitted for paper 4.

5. General questions on ancient Mesopotamian history, religion, law, art, science, and economics.

(C) to present a thesis of not more than 20,000 words.*

(ii) *Egyptology*

This course covers topics relating to dynastic, Graeco-Roman, and Christian Egypt.

A. *Qualifying Examination*

Each candidate will be required, unless exempted by the Oriental Studies Board, to pass a qualifying examination in Egyptian and/or Coptic not later than the end of the third term after he or she is admitted. Candidates offering options relating to the Graeco-Roman period may be required to pass a qualifying examination in Greek.

B. *Final Examination*

1. A candidate who has a first degree in Egyptology or equivalent qualification must offer Section I, *three* papers from Section II, and a thesis of not more than 30,000 words on a subject to be approved by the board.

2. All other candidates must offer Section I, *two* papers from Section II, Section III, and a thesis of not more than 20,000 words on a subject to be approved by the board.

3. All applications for approval of options and thesis title must reach the Secretary, Board of the Faculty of Oriental Studies, Oriental Institute, on or before Monday in the sixth week of Trinity Full Term in the academic year preceding that in which the examination is to be taken. For options under Section II applicants must include a detailed definition of the topics offered and a list of primary sources, to be countersigned by their supervisors.

4. For the Final Examination the following papers will be set:

I. (i) A general paper on Egyptology.
Questions will be set on method, theory, bibliography, and the history of

---

* See regulations for theses on p. 508.

Egyptology. Candidates will be expected to answer some questions outside the areas of their fields of specialization.

(ii) Unprepared translation from Egyptian texts.

Passages may be set for translation from texts of all periods from the end of the Old Kingdom to the Conquest of Alexander. Texts of other periods may be set with the permission of the board.

II. *Two* (for candidates under 2 above) or *three* (for candidates under 1 above) papers in a special field selected from the list below, of which one will be on an appropriate category of primary source material.

Since all fields may not be available in every year, candidates must confirm with the Graduate Studies Committee of the Oriental Studies Board that the field they intend to offer is available by the end of the second term after they are admitted. Some related fields (e.g. demotic with Greek papyrology) may be combined with the permission of the board.

One paper in the special field will be set as a take-home examination. The answer or answers for this examination should be typed and presented in proper scholarly form. Candidates will be informed as to which paper is to be examined as a take-home on Friday of Eighth Week of the Hilary Term preceding the Final examination; conventions for the setting of the paper will be released at the same time. The question paper for the take-home examination will be distributed to candidates in the Oriental Institute at 10 a.m. on Monday of First Week in Full Term in the term in which the final examination is to be offered. The completed examination must be handed in to the Clerk of the Examination Schools no later than 12 noon on Monday of Second Week. The completed paper should not exceed 5,000 words in length.

The following fields will normally be available:

Archaeology
Art and iconography
Christian Egypt
Demotic
Egyptian grammar
Graeco-Roman hieroglyphic texts
Greek papyrology
Hieratic texts
Egyptian literary *or* religious texts
Periods of history, from the early dynastic to the Byzantine.

III. Prescribed texts in Middle and Late Egyptian (two papers). The list of texts to be offered must be submitted for approval by the board with other applications for approval under 3 above.

(iii) *Medieval Arabic Thought*

A. *Qualifying Examination*

Each candidate will be required, unless exempted by the Oriental Studies Board, to pass a qualifying examination in Arabic not later than the end of the third term after that in which his name has been placed on the register. The examination shall be of such a nature as to satisfy the board that the candidate is capable of using Arabic philosophical texts.

B. *Final Examination*

Every candidate must offer *one* paper chosen from papers 1–3 in the following list, *two* papers chosen from papers 4–6, and paper 7.

In papers 1, 2, 3, and 7 all candidates will be required to translate and comment upon Arabic passages. Optional questions containing Arabic passages for translation and comment will be set in the other papers.

A. Greek into Arabic

1. The translation movements of the ninth and tenth centuries. Questions will be set on the history of translation into Arabic, individual translators and their styles, and the development of terminology. Some of these questions will have special reference to the Greek and Arabic versions of a text of the candidate's choice.

2. The Arabic tradition of *either* Plato *or* Aristotle *or* Ptolemy *or* Galen *or* Neo-Platonism. Questions will be set on the transmission to the Arabs and the place in Arabic thought of the cardinal doctrines of the author or school of thought chosen.

3. The ancient legacy in the Arabic sources. Each candidate will be expected to show knowledge of the relevant parts of *one* of the following works as a source for Greek thought and its transmission to the Arabs:

(i) Abū Sulaymān al-Sijistānī, *Ṣiwān al-ḥikma.*
(ii) Ibn al-Nadīm, *Al-Fihrist.*
(iii) Ibn al-Qifṭī, *Taʾrīkh al-ḥukamāʾ*.
(iv) Ibn Abī Uṣaybiʿa, *ʿUyūn al-anbāʾ fī ṭabaqāt al-aṭibbāʾ*.
(v) al-Ashʿarī, *Maqālāt al-islāmiyyīn.*
(vi) Ibn Ḥazm, *Al-Fiṣal fī l-milal.*
(vii) Al-Shahrastānī, *Al-Milal wa-l-niḥal.*

B. History of Medieval Arabic Thought

4. The history of Arabic thought during *one* of the following periods:

(i) The sixth to eighth centuries AD, with special reference to Egypt, Syria, and Iraq.
(ii) The ninth century AD, with special reference to Iraq.
(iii) The tenth century AD, with special reference to Baghdad.
(iv) The twelfth century AD, with special reference to Muslim Spain.

5. The origins and development in Islam of *one* of the following subjects:

(i) Epistemology.
(ii) Metaphysics.
(iii) Theology.
(iv) Cosmology.
(v) Anthropology.
(vi) Moral and political thought.

6. The life and thought of *one* of the following authors:

(i) Ghazālī.
(ii) Ibn Sīnā.
(iii) Bīrūnī.

7. An Arabic text of the candidate's choice. Candidates will be expected to offer a text relevant to one of the subjects listed in paper 5.

C. *Thesis*

Each candidate must offer a thesis of not more than 30,000 words.* A candidate who has not been exempted from taking the qualifying examination will be expected to offer as the subject of his thesis an annotated translation of an Arabic text.

Candidates must obtain the approval of the Board of the Faculty of Oriental Studies for:

(i) the text to be offered in paper 1;
(ii) the text to be offered in paper 7;
(iii) the subject of the thesis;

---

* See regulations for theses on p. 508.

(iv) any option in papers 2 to 6 other than those contained in the regulations.

Such approval shall be obtained as early as possible after the candidate's name has been placed on the Register of B.Phil. and M.Phil. Students, and not later than the second meeting of the Board in the Michaelmas Term preceding the term in which the candidate proposes to take the final examination.

(iv) *Modern Middle Eastern Studies*

A. *Qualifying Examination*

Every candidate must pass a qualifying examination not later than the end of the second term from the commencement of the course. A candidate with an intermediate level of proficiency (the equivalent of 2–3 years of study) in Arabic or Turkish may offer respectively Advanced Arabic or Advanced Turkish. A candidate with native fluency or who has satisfied the examiners in the Second Public Examination in Arabic or Persian or Turkish or Hebrew, or has passed a similar examination in another university, must offer a different language for examination. The examination will consist of two papers:

(i) A language examination in Arabic or Advanced Arabic or Hebrew or Persian or Turkish or Advanced Turkish, (subject to the availability of teaching), based on grammar knowledge and reading comprehension. The use of a dictionary will be permitted in this paper.

(ii) A general methodological paper on the Middle East in the twentieth century.

Entries must be made on the appropriate form, obtainable from the University Offices, by Friday in the second week of Hilary Full Term following the candidate's admission. Candidates who fail the Qualifying Examination may at the discretion of the board be allowed to retake it in the first week after the following Full Trinity Term.

B. *Final Examination*

It is strongly recommended that candidates for the Final Examination should, in the course of the Long Vacation preceding the year in which they propose to take the examination, attend a recognized language course in an appropriate Middle Eastern country.

1. All candidates must offer

(*a*) one language paper in Arabic or Hebrew or Persian or Turkish, subject to the availability of teaching, based on knowledge of grammar, translation from the Oriental language to English, and reading comprehension, for which the use of a dictionary will be permitted; or, for candidates who offered Advanced Arabic or Advanced Turkish for the Qualifying Examination, one language paper in Arabic or Turkish respectively based on prose composition, translation from the Oriental language to English, and reading comprehension, for which the use of a dictionary will be permitted;

(*b*) a thesis of not more than 30,000 words on a subject to be approved by the board;

(*c*) three papers from (1)–(10), provided that instead of one of these papers, a candidate may offer a paper on a subject not included in the list below, with the approval of the board.

(1) History of the Middle East, 1860–1958.
(2) Politics of the Middle East.
(3) Economic history of the Middle East, 1800–1945.
(4) Economics of the Middle East.
(5) Geography of the Middle East.
(6) Social anthropology of the Middle East.
(7) Islam in the Middle East in the twentieth century.
(8) International Relations of the Middle East.

(9) Iranian history, 1921–79.
(10) History of Turkey, 1908–80.
(11) Arabic popular culture, 1900 to the present day.

Teaching for some options may not be available in every year. Applicants for admission will be advised whether teaching will be available in the options of their choice.

2. All applications for approval must reach the Secretary, Board of the Faculty of Oriental Studies, Oriental Institute, on or before the Monday in the second week of the Michaelmas Full Term preceding the examination.

(v) *Classical Indian Religion*

A. *Qualifying Examination*

Candidates must pass a qualifying examination in Sanskrit not later than the end of the second term of the academic year in which the candidate's name is first entered on the register of M.Phil. students unless exempted by the Board of the Faculty of Oriental Studies.

B. *Final Examination*

Candidates will be required to offer the following four papers, but a candidate may submit a thesis of not more than 20,000 words on a subject approved by the board instead of Paper (iv).

(i) (*a*) Unprepared translation from epic and commentarial Sanskrit.

(*b*) Translation from the set books in two of the following sections:

1. (i) *Bṛhadāraṇyaka Upaniṣad* I. 2, 4, 5; II. 3, 4; IV. 1–4; (ii) *Yājñavalkyasmṛti, Ācārādhyāya* 10–166, 198–216, 217–70, *Prāyaścittādhyāya* 1–44; (iii) Kumārila. *Ślokavārtika, saṃbandhākṣepaparihāra* 42c–114b; (iv) Śaṅkara, *Upadeśasāhasrī, padyabandha: caitanyaprakaraṇa and dṛśiprakaraṇa.*
2. (i) Rāmānuja. *Gītābhāṣya, Upodghāta*; on XVIII. 12–17, 64–6; (ii) *Bhāgavatapurāṇa* X. 29, 31, 32, 33 vv. 20–40.
3. (i) *Kiraṇāgama, Vidyāpāda, patalas* 1–7; (ii) *Mataṅgapārameśvarāgama, Kriyāpāda* 1. 2c–3b with commentary of Bhaṭṭa Rāmakaṇṭha; (iii) Abhinavagupta, *Tantrāloka* 15, 1c–16; 15, 146–79b; (iv) *Tantrasāra, āhnika* 1; *āhnika* 13, p. 149^2 to p. 154^1.
4. (i) Vasubandhu, *Abhidharmakośabhāṣya*, pp. 803^5–805^6, 1218^4–1234^2; (ii) Candrakīrti, *Prasannapadā* on *Mūlamadhyamakakārikā* 17. 2–10; (iii) *Sādhanamālā* 251; (iv) *Hevajrasekaprakriyā*.

(ii) History of Indian Religions I: Vedic religion, *Upaniṣads,* early Buddhism, Jainism and materialism.

(iii) History of Indian Religions II: Hinduism from the epics and the *sūtra* literature to Caitanya; Mahāyāna Buddhism.

In Papers (ii) and (iii) candidates will be expected to show background knowledge of relevant social and political history. Emphasis will be laid on the study of primary sources, which may, however, be read in translation.

(iv) Approaches to the study of Indian religion:

Candidates will be asked to give a critical appreciation of the contributions of different disciplines (theology, anthropology, philology etc.) and to discuss the application of various theoretical approaches (e.g. evolutionism, diffusionism, dialectical materialism, phenomenology, structuralism) to the subject.

(vi) *Modern Jewish Studies*

A *Qualifying Examination*

Candidates must pass a qualifying examination in Hebrew not later than the end of the second term of the academic year in which the candidate's name is first entered on the Register of M.Phil. students unless exempted by the Board of the Faculty of Oriental Studies. The examination will consist of a language examination in Hebrew based on grammar knowledge and reading comprehension. The use of a dictionary will be permitted in this paper.

B *Final Examination*

Candidates will present themselves for a written examination. The examination shall be taken in the Trinity Term of the academic year following that in which the candidate's name is first entered on the Register of M.Phil. students. The examination shall consist of four papers from the following list. Candidates proposing to offer a paper not included in the list below must obtain the permission of the Board of the Faculty of Oriental Studies. All applications for approval must be sent to the Secretary of the Board on or before the Monday in the second week of the Michaelmas Full Term preceding the examination.

1. The Jewish experience in Europe, from *c.*1700 to the present day, *or* The Jewish experience in the United Kingdom or the United States.
2. Introduction to modern Jewish sociology.
3. Economic developments, migrations, and demographic trends in the modern Jewish world.
4. Religious movements in Judaism from *c.*1700 to the present day.
5. Modern Jewish thought.
6. Hebrew literature and society (with prescribed texts):
   (*a*) Hebrew literary centres prior to 1948 *or* (*b*) Hebrew literature in Israel from 1948.
7. Modern Jewish politics.
8. The State of Israel: (*a*) The history of the State of Israel *or* (*b*) Israeli society and culture.
9. The origins of Jewish nationalism.
10. Jewish-Muslim relations in the modern period *or* Jewish–Christian relations in the modern period.
11. Jewish literature in the nineteenth and twentieth centuries.
12. Modern Yiddish literature.

Teaching for some options may not be available in every year. Applicants for admission will be advised whether teaching will be available in the options of their choice.

Prescribed texts will be announced by the Board in the seventh week of Michaelmas Full Term in the first year of the course.

C *Thesis*

A candidate shall submit a thesis of not more than 30,000 words on a topic selected in consultation with his or her supervisor and approved by the faculty Board. Applications for such approval should be submitted not later than the second meeting of the Board in the Michaelmas Term preceding the term in which the candidate proposes to take the final examination, in the academic year following that in which the candidate's name was entered in the Register of M.Phil. students. Three typewritten copies of the thesis must be delivered to the Clerk of the Schools not later than noon on Friday of the first week of the Trinity Full Term in which the examination is to be taken.

(vii) *Jewish Studies in the Graeco-Roman Period*

A. *Qualifying Examination*

Candidates must pass a qualifying examination in Jewish Studies not later than the end of the third term after that in which the candidate's name is first entered on the register of M.Phil. students unless exempted by the Board of the Faculty of Oriental Studies.

B. *Final Examination*

Every candidate shall submit a thesis of not more than 30,000 words* and present himself for a written examination. The written examination shall consist of Paper 1 and three further papers to be chosen from Papers 2 to 8.

(1) Jewish literature, history, and institutions from 200 BC to AD 425.
(2) Jewish historiography with prescribed texts.
(3) Jewish law with prescribed texts.
(4) Jewish Bible interpretation with prescribed texts.
(5) Jewish eschatology with prescribed texts.
(6) Jewish liturgy with prescribed texts.
(7) Jewish wisdom literature with prescribed texts.
(8) Jewish papyrology and epigraphy with prescribed texts.

Notes. 1. Candidates must satisfy the Board of the Faculty of Oriental Studies before admission to the course that they possess the necessary qualifications in the Hebrew language to profit by the course. Those wishing to take options 2 or 8 must show evidence of their knowledge of Greek.

2. Papers 2–8 will contain passages for translation and comment as well as general questions relating to the prescribed texts.

3. Texts will be announced by the board in the seventh week of Michaelmas Full Term in the first year of the course.

(viii) *Islamic Art and Archaeology*

1. *Qualifying Examination*

Every candidate will be required to satisfy the examiners in an examination, to be known as the Qualifying Examination for the M.Phil. in Islamic Art and Archaeology not later than the end of the third term after that in which the candidate's name is first entered on the Register of M.Phil. Students unless exempted by the Board of the Faculty of Oriental Studies. The examination will include (i) a portfolio, containing reports on the practical work completed during the year (according to the schedule given in the Course Handbook) and signed by their supervisor. (ii) an essay of approximately 5,000 words on a subject of bibliographical and/or historiographical interest relevant to the subject proposed for the thesis, to be approved by the Board of the Faculty of Oriental Studies not later than its second meeting in Michaelmas Term; (iii) and a language examination in Arabic or Persian or Turkish, the content of which shall be of such a nature as to satisfy the board that the candidate is capable of using Arabic or Persian or Turkish texts for the study of the history of Islamic art and archaeology.

The portfolio and essay in (i) and (ii) above must be submitted in a parcel to the Clerk of the Schools, High Street, Oxford, at least fourteen days before the first day of the examination. The portfolio and essay must bear the candidate's examination number but not the candidate's name, which must be concealed. The parcel must bear the words 'QUALIFYING EXAMINATION FOR THE M.PHIL. IN ISLAMIC ART AND ARCHAEOLOGY' in block capitals in the bottom left-hand corner. The parcel must contain a certificate signed by the candidate declaring that the work is the candidate's own, and placed in a sealed envelope bearing the candidate's examination number and addressed to the Chairman of Examiners.

2. *Final Examination*

This shall be taken in the Trinity Term of the academic year following that in which the candidate's name is first entered on the Register of M.Phil. Students, or, with the approval of the faculty board, in a subsequent year.

---

* See regulations for theses on p. 508.

1. A candidate who has satisfied the examiners in the Second Public Examination in Arabic or Persian or Turkish, or has passed a similar examination in another university, must offer Papers I–III for the M.St. in Islamic Art and Archaeology, together with a thesis* of not more than 30,000 words on a subject to be approved by the board.

2. All other candidates must offer

(*a*) Arabic or Persian or Turkish unprepared translation. The use of dictionaries will be permitted.

(*b*) Arabic or Persian or Turkish prepared texts (copies available from the Faculty Office, Oriental Institute).

(*c*) Papers I–III for the M.St. in Islamic Art and Archaeology.

(*d*) A thesis* of not more than 30,000 words on a subject to be approved by the board.

3. Applications for approval of the thesis subject must reach the Secretary, Board of the Faculty of Oriental Studies, Oriental Institute, on or before Monday in the sixth week of Trinity Full Term in the academic year preceding that in which the examination is to be taken.

Successful candidates will be required to deposit one copy of the thesis in the Eastern Art Library. Such candidates will be required to complete a form stating whether they give permission for their thesis to be consulted.

If it is the opinion of the examiners that the work which has been required of a candidate is not of sufficient merit to qualify him or her for the Degree of M.Phil., the candidate shall be given the option of resitting the M.Phil. examination under Ch. VI, Sect. VI, § 2, cl. 4 or of being granted permission to supplicate for the Degree of Master of Studies.

(ix) *Ottoman Turkish Studies*

A. *Qualifying Examination*

Every candidate will be required, unless exempted by the Oriental Studies Board, to pass a qualifying examination in Ottoman Turkish not later than the end of the third term after that in which his or her name has been placed on the register.

B. *Final Examination*

Every candidate will be required to offer the following four papers and a thesis* of not more than 30,000 words on a subject to be approved by the Board of the Faculty of Oriental Studies not later than at its second meeting in the Michaelmas Full Term preceding the examination.

(1) Essay questions on Ottoman history and institutions, 1453–1699.

(2) Ottoman historical texts:
Peçevi, *Tarih* (Istanbul, AH 1283), vol. ii, pp. 36–95.
Naima, *Tarih* (Istanbul, AH 1281–3), vol. i, pp. 66–108.

(3) Ottoman texts in modern transcription and post-1928 Ottomanizing texts:
Mehmed Neşrî, *Kitâb-i cihan-nümâ* (Ankara, 1949), vol. i, pp. 311–55.
Y. K. Karaosmanoğlu, *Bir Serencam* (Istanbul, 1943), pp. 5–46.
Gazi Mustafa Kemal, *Nutuk* (Istanbul, 1934), vol. ii, pp. 181–6; vol. iii, pp. 308–19.
Köprülüzade M. Fuat, *Türk dili ve edebiyatı hakkında araştırmalar* (Istanbul, 1934), pp. 1–44.
İ. H. Uzunçarşılı, *Osmanlı devletinin merkez ve bahriye teşkilâtı* (Ankara, 1948), pp. 58–78.

---

* See regulation on p. 508 concerning the preparation and dispatch of theses. Candidates are reminded that work submitted for the Degree of M.Phil. may be subsequently incorporated in a thesis submitted for the Degree of D.Phil.

(4) Ottoman documents:
Ottoman Documents, ed. Repp (copies are available from the Oriental Institute).

Teaching for the course may not be available in every year: applicants for admission will only be accepted if teaching is available.

(x) *Classical and Medieval Islamic History*

A. *Qualifying Examination*

Each candidate will be required, unless exempted by the Oriental Studies Board, to pass a qualifying examination in Arabic or Persian or Turkish not later than the end of the third term after that in which his name has been placed on the register. The content of the examination shall be of such nature as to satisfy the board that the candidate is capable of using Arabic or Persian or Turkish historical texts. The use of a dictionary will be permitted in the examination.

B. *Final Examination*

1. A candidate who has satisfied the examiners in the Second Public Examination in Arabic or Persian or Turkish, or has passed a similar examination in another university, must offer four papers chosen from papers (4) to (12) in the list below, together with a thesis* of not more than 30,000 words on a subject to be approved by the board, provided that he may offer a paper on a subject not included in the list below, with the approval of the board.

2. All other candidates must offer

(*a*) papers (1) to (3); and

(*b*) three papers chosen from (4) to (12), provided that (i) instead of one of these papers, a candidate may offer a thesis* of not more than 30,000 words, on a subject approved by the board; and (ii) instead of one of these papers, a candidate may offer a paper on a subject not included in the list below, with the approval of the board.

3. In the list below the choice from papers (4) to (12) is subject to the availability of teaching. All candidates must obtain the approval of the board for the papers which they wish to offer. All applications for approval must reach the Secretary, Board of the Faculty of Oriental Studies, Oriental Institute, as early as possible after the candidate's name has been placed on the register, and not later than the Monday in the second week of Michaelmas Full Term preceding the examination:

(1) Arabic or Persian or Turkish unprepared translation. The use of dictionaries will be permitted.
(2) Arabic or Persian or Turkish prepared texts I (copies available from the Oriental Institute).
(3) Arabic or Persian or Turkish prepared texts II (copies available from the Oriental Institute).
(4) Islamic history 600–1000.
(5) The Seljuqs.
(6) Mamluk Egypt.
(7) The rise of the Ottomans to 1566.
(8) The Safavids.
(9) Moghul India.
(10) Arabic or Persian or Turkish literature in any one of the periods covered by papers (4) to (9).
(11) A paper chosen from the M.Phil. in Medieval Arabic Thought.

---

* See the regulation on p. 508 concerning the preparation and dispatch of theses. Candidates are reminded that work submitted for the Degree of M.Phil. may be subsequently incorporated in a thesis submitted for the Degree of D.Phil.

(12) The geography of the Middle East.

(xi) *Modern Chinese Studies*

Candidates are required to spend a period of at least four months on an approved course of language study in East Asia

I. *Qualifying Examination*

Candidates are required to spend a period of at least four months on an approved course of language study in East Asia, unless exempted by the Oriental Studies Faculty Board. Every candidate must pass a qualifying examination before the end of the third term from the candidate's admission to the M.Phil. degree programme. The examination shall take place not later than the end of the second term from the candidate's admission to the programme. Full details of the Qualifying Examination will be provided in the examination conventions, which will be made available to the candidates in the eighth week of the first term of the candidate's admission. Candidates must make their entries for the Qualifying Examination on the appropriate form by Friday in the eighth week of the first term of the candidate's admission. Candidates who fail either or both parts of the Qualifying Examination may be allowed to retake that part or parts at the end of the Long Vacation of the first year of the course.

The Qualifying Examination shall consist of two parts, as follows:

(1) *General paper on Modern China*

This is a single, three-hour examination paper on topics on Modern China, which all candidates will study in a course of lectures, classes, and tutorials during the first and second terms of the first year. Details of this two-term course shall be provided in the M.Phil. handbook and the course syllabus available from the Course Director.

(2) *Chinese language paper*

All candidates must offer a Chinese language paper, which includes an oral test. An outline of the oral test and written paper will be provided in the M.Phil. handbook and will be provided in detail in the examination conventions.

II. *Final Examination*

No candidate shall enter the Final Examination unless he or she has already passed the two parts of the first-year Qualifying Examination. The examination shall take place not later than the end of the third term of the second year from the candidate's admission to the M.Phil. degree programme. Full details of the examination will be provided in the examination conventions that will be made available to the candidates in the second term of the second year of the course. Candidates must make their entries for the Final Examination by filling out the appropriate examination entry form by Friday of the first week of the second term of the second year from the candidate's admission to the course. A candidate who fails this examination will be permitted to re-take it on one further occasion only, not later than one year after the initial attempt.

Such a candidate whose dissertation has been of a satisfactory standard may re-submit the same piece of work, while a candidate who has reached a satisfactory standard on the written papers will not be required to re-take that part of the examination.

The Final Examination shall consist of four parts, as follows:

(1) *Thesis*

The thesis will not be more than 30,000 words on a subject approved by the Oriental Studies Faculty Board, to be delivered to the Clerk of the Schools, High Street, Oxford, by Noon of Monday of the Second Week of Trinity Term of the second year from the candidate's admission to the programme. The thesis must be accompanied by a statement that it is the candidate's own work except where otherwise indicated. Successful candidates will be required to deposit one copy of the thesis in the Bodleian Library, and to sign a form stating whether they give permission for it to be consulted.

(2) *Paper on Modern China: Frameworks, methodologies, research tools*
This is a single, three-hour examination paper on approaches and methods of research on modern China. In preparation for this paper, a course of weekly seminar classes and tutorials will be provided in the first and the second term of the second year. Details of this course shall be provided in the M.Phil. handbook and in the course syllabus available from the Course Director.

(3) *Elective paper*
Candidates must elect one examination paper offered as part of another Master's (M.Phil. M.Sc., or M.St.) degree programme in the University. A list of papers approved for this purpose by the Oriental Studies Faculty Board will be available from the Course Director. Students are free to elect any one of these papers in consultation with their supervisor, and must do so by filling out the examination entry form. The examiners may, at their discretion, either require candidates to sit the standard examination paper for this elective paper, or else set a paper specifically for students on the M.Phil. in Modern Chinese Studies.

(4) *Two Chinese language papers (one oral, one written)*
The Oral examination will consist of two parts: a comprehension group test and an individual test. Full details of the oral examination will be provided in the course handbook and the examination conventions. The written language paper will be of a duration of three hours and will comprise a translation into Chinese, comprehension exercise, and translation into English.

The papers under (2) and (4) above will be taken in the Eighth Week of the third term of the final year. The examiners may examine any candidate viva voce.

(xii) *Modern Chinese Art and Literature*

I. *Qualifying Examination*

Candidates are required to spend a period of at least four months on an approved course of language study in East Asia unless exempted by the Oriental Studies Faculty Board. Every candidate must pass a qualifying examination before the end of the third term from the candidate's admission to the M.Phil. degree programme. The examination shall take place not later than the end of the second term from the candidate's admission to the programme. Full details of the Qualifying Examination will be provided in the examination conventions, which will be made available to the candidates in the eighth week of the first term of the candidate's admission. Candidates must make their entries for the Qualifying Examination on the appropriate form by Friday in the eighth week of the first term of the candidate's admission. Candidates who fail either or both parts of the Qualifying Examination may be allowed to retake that part or parts at the end of the Long Vacation of the first year of the course.

The Qualifying Examination shall consist of two parts, as follows:

(1) *General paper on Modern China*

This is a single, three-hour examination paper on topics on Modern China, which all candidates study in a course of lectures, classes, and tutorials during the first and second terms of the first year. Details of this two-term course shall be provided in the M.Phil. handbook and the course syllabus available from the Course Director.

(2) *Chinese language paper*

All candidates must offer a Chinese language paper, which includes an oral test. An outline of the oral test and written paper will be provided in the M.Phil. handbook and will be provided in detail in the examination conventions.

II. *Final Examination*

No candidate shall enter the Final Examination unless he or she has already passed the two parts of the first-year Qualifying Examination. The examination shall take place not later than the end of the third term of the second year from the candidate's admission to the M.Phil. degree programme. Full details of the examination will be provided in the examination conventions that will be made available to the candidates in the second term of the second year of the course. Candidates must make their entries for the Final Examination by filling out the appropriate examination entry form by Friday of the first week of the second term of the second year from the candidate's admission to the course. A candidate who fails this examination will be permitted to re-take it on one further occasion only, not later than one year after the initial attempt.

Such a candidate whose dissertation has been of a satisfactory standard may re-submit the same piece of work, while a candidate who has reached a satisfactory standard on the written papers will not be required to re-take that part of the examination.

The Final Examination shall consist of four parts, as follows:

(1) *Thesis*

The thesis will be not more than 30,000 words on a subject approved by the Oriental Studies Faculty Board, to be delivered to the Clerk of the Schools, High Street, Oxford, by Noon of Monday of the Second Week of Trinity Term of the second year from the candidate's admission to the course. The thesis must be accompanied by a statement that it is the candidate's own work except where otherwise indicated. Successful candidates will be required to deposit one copy of the thesis in the Bodleian Library, and to sign a form stating whether they give permission for it to be consulted.

(2)–(3) *Two written papers on Modern Chinese Art and Literature*

Candidates will be introduced to the development of modern Chinese painting and fiction throughout the twentieth century. They will learn about the major artists and writers; the modes of production; influences from abroad; the effect of politics, especially extreme Leftist policies such as the Cultural Revolution; trends and fashions; and the fragmentation of contemporary arts and literature. Topics include the following:

(i) *Art and Literature 1900–49*

Chinese painting 1900–49: addressing the past
Chinese painting 1900–49: approaching the foreign
May 4th and republican Fiction
Leftist ideology and practice in fiction

(ii) *Art and Literature 1949–2000*

Painting 1949–79: from the Yan'an Forum to the Cultural Revolution
The Avant-garde in Art, 1979–
Taiwan fiction
Fiction and the State 1949–79
Post-reform fiction: unity to fragmentation.

(4) *Two Chinese language papers (one oral, one written)*

The Oral examination will consist of two parts: a comprehension group test and an individual test. Full details of the oral examination will be provided in the course handbook and the examination conventions. The written language paper will be of a duration of three hours and will comprise a translation into Chinese, comprehension exercise, and translation into English.

The papers under (2), (3), and (4) above will be taken in the Eighth Week of the third term of the final year. The examiners may examine any candidate viva voce.

(xiii) *Tibetan and Himalayan Studies*

I. *Qualifying Examination*

Candidates must pass a qualifying examination in Tibetan language at the end of the Hilary Term of their first year. This will consist of a written and an oral examination.

II. *Final Examination*

1. All candidates will be required to offer the following three papers, to offer a thesis of not more than 20,000 words, and to present themselves for an oral examination.

(i) Unseen translation both from and into Tibetan.

(ii) Translation from two set texts, which will include a modern Tibetan novel and a classical work. The texts will be announced by the board in the seventh week of Michaelmas Full Term of the first year of the course.

(iii) History and civilization of Tibet and the Himalayas. Topics covered will include the history, politics, religion, and anthropology of the region.

2. Candidates will be orally examined on their knowledge of spoken Tibetan. Details of the oral examination will be provided in outline in the course handbook and in detail in the examination conventions.

3. *Thesis*

Candidates must submit a thesis of not more than 20,000 words on a topic selected by the candidate in consultation with his or her supervisor and approved by the faculty board. Applications for approval should be submitted not later than the Friday of the seventh week of the Michaelmas Term preceding that in which the candidate is to be examined.*

Philosophical Theology

(*See also the general notice at the commencement of these regulations.*)

The regulations made by the Board of the Faculty of Theology are as follows:

Candidates will be admitted to take the examination as defined below in a specific year. In exceptional circumstances candidates may be allowed to take an examination later than one to which they were admitted. Permission for this must be sought from the faculty board not later than Monday of the week before the first week of the Trinity Term in which the examination was to have been taken. The application must have the support of the candidate's college and be accompanied by a statement from the supervisor.

Candidates shall be required:

(*a*) To present themselves for a written examination in each of the papers prescribed below, from one of which they may normally expect to be exempted by the faculty board depending on their previous qualifications;

(*b*) to present a thesis* of not more than 30,000 words on a topic in philosophical theology to be approved by the faculty board (the thesis must be accompanied by a signed statement by the candidate that the thesis is his or her own work except where otherwise indicated; successful candidates may be required to deposit one copy of the thesis in the Bodleian and to sign a form stating whether they give permission for the thesis to be consulted);

(*c*) to present themselves for a viva voce examination unless individually dispensed by the examiners (no candidate will be failed without a viva).

1. *Philosophy of Religion*

with syllabus for examination the same as that for essays for the B.Phil. in Philosophy.

---

* See regulation for theses on p. 508.

2. *Either Moral Philosophy*
or Metaphysics and Theory of Knowledge
or Philosophical Logic and Philosophy of Language
or Philosophy of Science
or Philosophy of Mind and of Action

with syllabus for examination the same as that for essays for the B.Phil. in Philosophy.

3. *History of Philosophical Theology*

The paper will contain questions on philosophical influences on theology during the patristic period, the early medieval period, and the period 1760–1860. Candidates are required to show knowledge of two of the three periods, and, within each of those two periods, of some of the principal relevant writings, viz. for the patristic period of works of Origen and Augustine, for the early medieval period of works of Anselm and Aquinas, and for the period 1760–1860 of works of Kant, Kierkegaard, and Schleiermacher. Study of texts in the original languages will not be required.

4. Either *The Development of Christian Doctrine to AD 451*
or *Theology in Western Europe from Gabriel Biel to Calvin*

as specified for the M.Phil. in Theology (paper 1 of Section A and paper 1 of Section C of the Christian Doctrine option).

The Examiners may award a Distinction for excellence in the whole examination.

If it is the opinion of the examiners that the work done by a candidate is not of sufficient merit to qualify him or her for the Degree of M.Phil. but is nevertheless of sufficient merit to qualify him or her for the Degree of Master of Studies in Philosophical Theology, the candidate shall be given the option of resitting the M.Phil. examination under Ch. VI, Sect. VI, §2, cl. 4 or of being granted permission to supplicate for the Degree of Master of Studies.

Politics (Comparative Government, Political Theory, European Politics and Society)

(*See also the general notice at the commencement of these regulations.*)

The regulations made by the Social Sciences Board are as follows:

Qualifying Test

Every candidate must pass a qualifying test before the end of the third term from commencement of the course unless given exemption by the Politics Graduate Studies Committee. The qualifying test shall be set and administered by the examiners appointed to examine for the M.Phil. degrees in Politics. This test shall consist of three parts, as follows:

1. A formally assessed essay of between 4,000 and 6,000 words on research design as it bears on some aspect of politics. The essay will normally be related to the subject of the student's proposed M.Phil. thesis. The date of submission and the format are as stated in the Notes of Guidance for Graduate Students in Politics as published annually by the Department of Politics and International Relations.

2. A single three-hour examination paper. The examination paper will be divided into three sections: A. Comparative Government, B. Political Theory, and C. European Integration. Candidates for the M.Phil. examinations in Comparative Government and in Political Theory must answer at least one question from sections A and B and may not answer questions in section C. Candidates for the M.Phil. in European Politics and Society must answer at least one question from each of sections A and C, and may not answer questions

from section B. The examination shall take place on the Thursday of noughth week of Trinity Term, the exact time to be decided by the examiners.

3. The examiners must be satisfied that candidates have satisfactorily completed their designated course of research training. The course work requirements, including administrative arrangements and dates of submission, are set out in the Notes of Guidance for Graduate Students in Politics.

4. Candidates in European Politics and Society will be required to have a working (i.e. good reading) knowledge of two of the following languages of the European Union, viz. English, and one of French, German, Italian, and Spanish. Unless exempted by the Politics Graduate Studies Committee, candidates will be tested in the language or languages they propose to offer by the end of their third term.

Candidates who fail the examination part of the qualifying test may retake it in the seventh week of the same Trinity Term. Candidates whose research design fails to satisfy may resubmit on the Friday of the week falling two weeks before week one of the following Michaelmas Full Term. Arrangements for the resubmission of other coursework are set out in the Notes of Guidance for Graduate Studies in Politics.

Final examination

No candidate shall enter the final examination unless he has already passed the qualifying test or has been granted exemption by the Graduate Studies Committee as stated above. In the final examination every candidate must offer:

(1) A thesis* of not more than 30,000 words, excluding bibliography, two copies to be delivered to the Clerk of the Schools, High Street, Oxford by noon on Monday in the first week of the Trinity Full Term in which the examination is to be taken. The thesis must be accompanied by a statement that it is the candidate's own work except where otherwise indicated. Successful candidates will be required to deposit one copy of their thesis in the Bodleian Library.

(2) Four subject papers.

Candidates sitting for the M.Phil. (Comparative Politics) are required to take the core paper (*a*) and must select three papers from the following list: b, c, e–u, subject to the following constraints. That is, candidates may offer no more than two of papers e, f, g, and h; and no more than two of k, l, m, n, o, p, q. Candidates who take (*b*) may also take one paper from v–z, aa–ac.

Candidates sitting for the M.Phil. (Political Theory) are required to take the core paper (*b*) and any other three papers from the following list: a, t–z, aa–ac.

Candidates sitting for the M.Phil. (European Politics and Society) are required to take core papers (*c*) and (*d*), and any other two papers from the list b, e–ai.

Candidates may, with the special permission of the Graduate Studies Committee in politics, offer subjects outside this list. Applications must be made by the last Friday of the Trinity Term preceding that in which the examination is to be taken, and must be supported by the student's supervisor. Supervisors should ensure that applications are submitted as early as possible so that if approval is not given, the candidate has sufficient time to choose an alternative. Candidates for the M.Phil. (Comparative Politics) may propose to submit the coursework for research training as designated in the M.Phil. (Political Theory) as one of their four papers. Candidates for the M.Phil. (Political Theory) may propose to

* See the regulations on p. 508 concerning the preparation and dispatch of theses. Candidates are reminded that if after completing the M.Phil. they are accepted by the Politics Graduate Studies Committee for registration for the D.Phil., work submitted for the Degree of M.Phil. may subsequently be incorporated in a thesis submitted for the Degree of D.Phil.

do this with respect to the designated coursework for the M.Phil. (Comparative Government).

Teaching in some options may not be available each year: students are normally advised at the beginning of the course of the teaching arrangements for these options.

(*a*) Comparative Government (this paper cannot be taken with (*d*)).

The theory and practice of government in modern states.

(*b*) Political Theory

A critical examination of political concepts and theories, including social concepts and theories with political relevance.

(*c*) European Integration

Theory and practice of integration in Europe. Political, historical, economic, social, and legal aspects of integration.

(*d*) Comparative European Government and Politics (this paper cannot be taken with (*a*))

The constitutions and formal structures of government of Western European states, including the United Kingdom; political parties; electoral behaviour; interest representation; the policy process.

(*e*) The History and Politics of South Asia

The political history, political sociology, political institutions, and political economy of South Asia (India, Pakistan, Sri Lanka, and Bangladesh) since 1947; the state, political institutions, party politics, and 'movement' politics; conditions for democracy; the politics of gender, class, caste, religion, and ethnicity; the evolution of political ideologies; social organization, culture and indentities as they bear on politics; the politics of 'development'.

(*f*) The History and Politics of West Africa

The political history, political sociology, political institutions and political economy of West Africa since 1939: nationalism and transfers of power; forms of government, civilian and military; parties and elections; conditions for democracy; class, ethnicity, religion, and gender; business, labour, and peasantries; agricultural policies and economic reforms; West African regional politics and institutions and the influence of external agencies. Candidates will be required to show knowledge of Nigeria and of at least one Francophone country.

(*g*) The History and Politics of East/Central Africa

The political history, political sociology, political institutions, and political economy of East Africa since 1939: nationalism and transfers of power; forms of government, civilian and military; parties and elections; conditions for democracy; class, ethnicity, religion, and gender; business, labour, and peasantries; agricultural policies and economic reforms; East African regional politics and institutions and the influence of external agencies. East/Central Africa is taken to include Zimbabwe, Zambia, Malawi, Mozambique, Angola, Congo (Kinshasa), Rwanda, Burundi, Uganda, Tanzania, Kenya.

(*h*) The History and Politics of South Africa

The political history, political sociology, political institutions, and political economy of South Africa since 1902: the formation of the South African state; liberalism; Afrikaner and African nationalisms; segregation, apartheid, and capitalism; the transformation of the agrarian economy; parties and elections; class, race, ethnicity, and gender; business and labour; the politics of Botswana, Lesotho, Swaziland, and Namibia;

Southern African regional politics and institutions and the influence of external agencies.

(*i*) The History and Politics of Central and Eastern Europe since 1945.

The history and politics of Poland, Czechoslovakia, Hungary, Romania, and Bulgaria since 1945, and of the German Democratic Republic (1949–90). The relations between these states, and the influence of Soviet and Western (especially German) policies upon them. Candidates will be expected to show detailed knowledge of at least *two* countries. A knowledge of an East European language and/or German is highly desirable.

(*j*) Sociology of politics

As specified for the M.Phil. in Sociology.

(*k–q*) *The Politics and Government of major States.*

(*k*) The Politics and Government of the UK;
(*l*) The Politics and Government of the USA;
(*m*) The Politics and Government of France;
(*n*) The Politics and Government of Russia;
(*o*) The Politics and Government of Germany;
(*p*) The Politics and Government of Italy;
(*q*) The Politics and Government of China.

Candidates will be expected to show a thorough knowledge of the recent political development of the country chosen, of its political structure, and of the manner in which its system of government operates. They must be able to read the available literature in a language of the country selected, except in the case of Russia and China.

(*r*) The Politics of Democracy in Latin America

Definitions of democracy in Latin America; the conditions for stable democratic regimes; the breakdown of democratic regimes; transitions from authoritarian regimes; parties and electoral systems; political participation; political ideologies; the role of constitutions in theory and practice; public administration; policy making in democratic systems; civil-military relations; the international context of democracy.

(*s*) Executive Government

Candidates will explore generic and comparative themes in executive government and bureaucracy using a range of analytical perspectives. Candidates are expected to be familiar with the politics of bureaucracy in at least one country and to show awareness of the basic literature in the comparative study of bureaucracy.

(*t*) Theory of Voting

The properties of majority rule. The Condorcet and Borda rules. The main modern results on majority rule (including the median voter theorem, Arrow's, May's, Sen's, and Gibbard's Theorems). The relationship between majority rule and proportional representation, and between proportional representation and apportionment. Normative consequences of the formal results on voting.

(*u*) Democratization: Theory and Practice

Theory. Democratic theory and democratization; theories of regime change; the establishment, stabilization, and breakdown of democratic regimes; interactionist, structuralist, and discourse-based interpretations; economic and sociological correlates; issues of comparative methodology; definitions, concepts, and cultural relativism; constitutions, institutional design, and party organization; democratization and international politics.

Practice. Candidates will be expected to show knowledge of the main analytical issues arising from contemporary democratization experiences in at least *two* of the following clusters of countries:

China (including Hong Kong, Singapore, and Taiwan)
East-Central Europe (post-communist countries excluding the former USSR)
Middle America (i.e. Mexico, Central America, and the Caribbean)
South America
South Asia
Southern Africa (Angola, Botswana, Mozambique, Namibia, South Africa)
Southern Europe (Greece, Italy, Portugal, Spain, Turkey)
Sub-Saharan Africa (other than Southern Africa)
Ex-USSR states

Note: Candidates taking options to study the politics of any of these areas, in addition to this paper, will be required to show knowledge of at least one other region.

(*v*) Plato and Aristotle

Candidates will be expected to show knowledge of the major writings on ethics and politics in the work of Plato and Aristotle. Questions may also be asked on the ethical and political thought of the Pre-Socratics.

(*w*) Political Theories from Machiavelli to Burke

The authors to be studied will include: Machiavelli, Hobbes, Locke, Hume, Montesquieu, Rousseau, and Burke.

(*x*) Political Theories of Hegel and Marx.

In addition to a knowledge of the original text, candidates will be expected to show some knowledge of later developments in Hegelian and Marxist ideas, and to be able to discuss the theories of Hegel and Marx in the context of contemporary political thought. Candidates are required to show knowledge of the work of both of these authors.

(*y*) European Nationalist Doctrines

Ideas of nationality, its criteria and claims, from the late eighteenth to the early twentieth century; cultural, political and ethnic versions of the nation; the idea of the nation state; liberal nationalism and the nationalism of the anti-democratic and anti-parliamentary right; modern theories of nationalism. The paper will include the study of some of the relevant writings of some of the following authors: J.-J. Rousseau, Abbe Sieyes, Edmund Burke, J. G. Herder, J. G. Fichte, S. T. Coleridge, Joseph de Maistre, G. W. F. Hegel, Thomas Carlyle, J. G. Mazzini, J. A. de Gobineau, J. Michelet, E. Renan, E. A. Freeman, H. von Treitschke, H. S. Chamberlain, M. Barres, F. Meinecke, C. Schmitt.

(*z*) The History of Liberal Thought in the nineteenth and twentieth centuries

The development of liberal thought in the nineteenth and twentieth centuries, including the study of key thinkers and significant liberal traditions. The paper will include the study of some of the following authors and topics: Bentham and the philosophical radicals, J. S. Mill, the new liberalism, German liberalism (Weber and national liberalism), French solidarism and republicanism, American liberalism (Croly and Dewey), social democracy, Berlin and pluralism, Hayek, and the Rawlsians.

(*aa*) Issues in Contemporary Continental European Social and Political Thought

A critical examination of the issues in contemporary European social and political thought: politics and power, state and society, the political subject, ideology and language—as specified by the bibliography issued by the sub-faculty of Politics.

(*ab*) Ideologies and Political Traditions in Modern Europe

The conceptual and historial analysis of the principal political ideologies of Europe from the late nineteenth century: theories of ideologies and political traditions; conservatism, liberalism; socialism, communism; anarchism; nationalism; fascism; republicanism.

(*ac*) Contemporary Political Philosophy

Recent developments in political philosophy. Candidates will be expected to show knowledge of the work of selected authors working within the analytical tradition of political philosophy, as well as critical ability in dealing with political concepts and theories.

(*ad*) European Social Policy

As specified for the combined M.Sc. and M.Phil. in Comparative Social Research.

(*ae*) European Community Law

As specified for the M.Juris in European and Comparative Law.

(*af*) The Economics of European Integration

Major common policies and the EU budget. Theory and practice of economic integration; trade, customs unions, non-tariff barriers; monetary integration, the European Monetary System, monetary union; external economic relations of the EU; trade policy, relations with US and Japan, trade relations with Less Developed Countries; economic integration of central and Eastern Europe.

(*ag*) The International History of West Europe since 1945

The Cold War in Europe; West European international politics, the Atlantic Alliance and European unity; Germany, France, and Britain in European international history; European détente; causes and consequences of the end of the Cold War in Europe.

Candidates may also opt to take one or more of the following papers as specified for the M.Phil. in International Relations:

(*ah*) Economic Aspects of World Politics

(*ai*) Strategic Studies

(3) The examiners may also examine any candidate viva voce; they shall not fail any candidate without inviting him or her to attend such an examination.

The examiners may award a distinction for excellence in the whole examination.

Russian and East European Studies

Candidates admitted in Michaelmas Term 1996 must take the examination according to the 1996 regulations

(*See also the general notice at the commencement of these regulations.*)

The regulations made by the Area and Development Studies Committee are as follows:

First year examinations

There will be three compulsory papers to be taken at the end of the first year of the course.

(*a*) A formally assessed essay of between 4,000 and 6,000 words on methodology to be submitted to the Clerk of the Schools by the Friday of first week of the Trinity Term in the academic year in which candidates begin the course. It must be typed or printed on one side of the paper only, and include appropriate bibliographical references. It must state clearly, on both the envelope and the front sheet of the essay, the candidate's name, college and degree course.

(*b*) An examination paper on *Twentieth Century Russian and Soviet History: themes and comparisons.*

(*c*) An examination paper on *Political and Economic Transitions in the Former Soviet Union and Eastern Europe.*

The papers shall be set and administered by the examiners appointed to examine the M.Phil. in Russian and East European Studies. Applications must be made by the Friday of eighth week in Michaelmas Full Term in the academic year in which candidates begin the course. The examination will be held in the eighth week of Trinity Full Term.

Candidates who pass these papers will proceed to the second year of the course and take the final examination at the end of the second year. Candidates who fail one or both of the examination papers may, by permission of the Area and Development Studies Committee, proceed to the second year of the course and resit the failed papers during the final examination. Candidates who fail the methodology essay may, at the discretion of the Area and Development Studies Committee, be allowed to revise and resubmit that work no later than the Friday of sixth week of the Trinity Term in the academic year in which they begin the course.

Candidates will also be required to demonstrate competence in Russian or, in the case of candidates who select at least one special subject and a thesis topic concerned with Eastern Europe, in a relevant East European langauge (see below).

Final examination

No candidate shall enter the final examination unless he or she has already passed the three compulsory papers in the first-year examination, save that the Area and Development Studies Committee may permit any candidate who has failed one or both of the compulsory examination papers to resit the papers at the same time as the final examination. In the final examination, every candidate must offer:

(*a*) a thesis of not more than 30,000 words on a subject approved by the committee, to be delivered to the Clerk of the Schools, High Street, Oxford, by Friday in the first week of Full Term in which the final examination is taken. The thesis must be accompanied by a statement that the thesis is the candidate's own work except where otherwise indicated. Successful candidates will be required to deposit one copy of the thesis in the Bodleian.*

(*b*) two subjects chosen from the following list. The subjects which candidates wish to offer for examination must be submitted to the committee for approval by the Monday of sixth week in the Michaelmas Term in which they begin the course.

---

* Such candidates will also be required to sign a form stating whether they give permission for their thesis to be consulted.

Note: as not all special subjects may be available in every year, candidates should apply to the Management Committee for Russian and East European Studies for permission to offer them before undertaking any work on them.

Group A: Economics

1. The Economic History of Russia and the Soviet Union, 1900–91.
2. The Economic History of Eastern Europe, 1945–89.
3. Transitions from Command to Market Economies in the Former Soviet Union and Eastern Europe.
4. The Politics and Economics of Soviet and Post-Soviet Ukraine.

Group B: History

1. The History of Poland and Hungary, 1506–1795.
2. The Habsburg Monarchy, 1790–1918.
3. Russian Social and Political Thought, 1825–1917.
4. The History of Russia, 1861–1917.
5. The Russian Revolution and Civil War.
6. The History of Eastern Europe, 1918–45.
7. The History since 1918 of Individual East European Countries: *either* Bulgaria *or* Hungary *or* Poland *or* Romania *or* Yugoslavia *or* Czechoslovakia.

Group C: Politics

1. Soviet and Post-Soviet Russian Politics.
2. Soviet and Post-Soviet Russian Foreign Policy.
3. Soviet and Post-Soviet Russian Defence Policy.
4. Eastern Europe under Communist Rule, 1944–90.
5. The Balkan Crises of the 1990s.

Group D: Literature

1. Russian Literature before Pushkin.
2. Pushkin and Romanticism.
3. The Rise of the Russian Novel.
4. Russian Drama in the 19th and 20th Centuries.
5. The Russian Experience of Modernity, 1905–1945.
6. The GULag and the Russian Literary Process.
7. Post-Soviet Russian Literature.
8. Czech and Slovak Literature since 1945.
9. Polish Literature since 1945.

Group E: Society, Culture and Social Policy

1. Soviet and Post-Soviet Regional Development.
2. Health and Welfare in the Soviet Union and Russia.
3. Gender and Representation in Russian Culture from 1800.
4. Eurasianism and Russian Cultural Identity.

Candidates must also present themselves for *viva voce* examination when required to do so by the examiners.

The examiners may award a distinction for excellence in the whole examination.

Language Requirement

Before admission to the examination all candidates will be required to produce evidence of a satisfactory knowledge of Russian or, in the case of candidates who select at least one special subject and a thesis topic concerned with Eastern Europe, of a relevant East European language.

As teaching is not available in all East European languages, candidates should apply to the Area and Development Studies Committee for permission to offer an East European language before undertaking any work on it.

All candidates with a good previous knowledge of Russian or an East European language will be required to pass, on the Monday of Seventh Week in the Michaelmas Term in which they begin the course, a qualifying test in Russian or a relevant East European language. The two-hour test will be administered by an examiner appointed by the committee, and will consist of one unseen written paper.

Candidates who fail the qualifying test in the Michaelmas Term in which they begin the course, will be recommended to attend language classes approved by the committee until they resubmit themselves for the test in the First Week of the Trinity Term of their initial year. The committee will remove from the Register of Bachelor and Master of Philosophy Students the name of any candidate who fails the test a second time.

Those candidates with little or no previous knowledge of Russian will be required to pass the written qualifying test in Russian in the First Week of the Michaelmas Term of their second year. Such candidates will be required to attend language classes approved by the committee during the first year of the course. Attendance at a special language course in the vacation preceding matriculation is recommended. Candidates who fail the qualifying test in the First Week of the Michaelmas Term of their second year will be required to resubmit themselves for the test in the Seventh Week of that Michaelmas Term. The committee will remove from the Register of Bachelor and Master of Philosophy Students the name of any candidate who fails the test a second time.

Slavonic Studies

(*See also the general notice at the commencement of these regulations.*)

The regulations made by the Board of the Faculty of Medieval and Modern Languages are as follows:

1. Candidates will be required to satisfy the examiners in a Qualifying Examination identical with that for the M.St. in Slavonic Studies, in the academic year in which their names are first entered on the Register of M.Phil. Students, before proceeding to the final examination for the M.Phil. in the following year. Holders of the M.St. in Slavonic Studies are exempt from this Qualifying Examination.

2. In the final examination for the M.Phil. each candidate will be required to take two subjects from the Schedules listed for the M.St., excluding Schedule 2 v. Candidates must take at least one subject from Schedule 2 i–iv, if they have not already done so for the M.St. or for the Qualifying Examination. Candidates may not repeat subjects which they have taken for the M.St. or for the Qualifying Examination, nor take subjects from Schedules from which they have already taken two subjects for the M.St. or for the Qualifying Examination.

3. Each candidate will be required to present a thesis of approximately 20,000 words and not more than 25,000 words on a subject which must be approved by the commiteee not later than its first meeting in the Michaelmas Term of the year in which the candidate takes the final examination for the M.Phil. Two copies of the thesis must be delivered to the Clerk of the Schools at least thirty days before the first examination. Work submitted in the thesis for the Degree of M.Phil. may subsequently be incorporated in a thesis submitted for the Degree of D.Phil.

4. Candidates must present themselves for oral examination unless dispensed by the examiners.

5. Candidates will be expected to be able to read secondary literature in at least one European language other than English and the Slavonic languages, and may be required to demonstrate this ability. Candidates will also be expected to attend a course of lectures on bibliographical, library, and archival resources in the field of Slavonic Studies.

6. If it is the opinion of the examiners that the work done by a candidate is not of sufficient merit to qualify him for the Degree of M.Phil. but that nevertheless his or her work in the Qualifying Examination was of sufficient merit to qualify him or her for the Degree of M.St. in Slavonic Studies, the candidate shall be given the option of resitting the M.Phil. examination under Ch. VI, Sect. VI, §2, cl. 4 or of being granted permission to supplicate for the Degree of Master of Studies.

7. The examiners may award a distinction for excellence in the whole examination.

Social Anthropology

(*See also the general notice at the commencement of these regulations.*)

The regulations made by the Divisional Board of Life and Environmental Sciences are as follows:

The examination shall consist of the following:

1. *Qualifying Examination*

Every candidate will be required to satisfy the examiners in an examination for which if he or she is successful, he or she will receive the Diploma in Social Anthropology in the academic year in which the candidate's name is first entered on the register of M.Phil. Students or, with the approval of the faculty board, in a subsequent year. If he or she passes the examination at the appropriate level, he or she will be allowed to proceed to the M.Phil. If he or she is successful in the M.Phil. Final Examination, the M.Phil. will subsume his or her Diploma.

2. *Final Examination*

This shall be taken in the Trinity Term of the academic year following that in which the candidate's name is first entered on the Register of M.Phil. Students or, with the approval of the faculty board, in a subsequent year.

Each candidate shall be required:

(1) to present himself or herself for written examination in accordance with I below;

(2) to submit a thesis in accordance with II below;

(3) to present himself or herself for oral examination as required by the examiners.

I. The written papers shall consist of the following:

A. A paper in the field of theory in social and cultural anthropology.

B. A paper consisting of two Parts: Part I relating to methods in social and cultural anthropology and Part II to the area and/or topic of the candidate's thesis.

II. *Thesis**

Each candidate shall be required to submit a thesis of not more than 30,000 words (excluding references and appendices) on a subject approved by the

* See the regulation on p. 508 concerning the preparation and dispatch of theses. Candidates are reminded (i) that two copies are required but that one of these may be a reproduction or carbon copy of the other, provided that any maps, diagrams,

supervisor. He or she shall send to the Secretary of Faculties, with the written approval of his supervisor, the proposed title of the thesis for consideration by the Divisional Board of Life and Environmental Sciences, by noon on the Monday of first week of the Michaelmas Term in the academic year following that in which his or her name was entered on the Register of M.Phil. Students. The thesis (two copies) must be typewritten and delivered to the Clerk of the Schools, High Street, Oxford, not later than noon on Monday of the second week of the Trinity Term in the academic year in which the Final Examination is taken.

The examiners shall require a successful candidate to deposit a copy of his or her thesis in the Tylor Library. If the thesis is superseded by a D.Phil. thesis by the same student partly using the same material, the Divisional Board of Life and Environmental Sciences may authorize the withdrawal of the M.Phil. thesis from the Tylor Library. Such candidates will be required to sign a form stating whether they give permission for their thesis to be consulted.

The examiners may award a distinction for excellence in the whole examination.

If it is the opinion of the examiners that the work which has been required of a candidate is not of sufficient merit to qualify him or her for the Degree of M.Phil. the candidate shall be given the option of resitting the M.Phil. examination under Ch. VI, sect. VI, §2, cl. 4 or of being granted permission to supplicate for the Diploma.

Sociology

(*See also the general notice at the commencement of these regulations.*)

The regulations made by the Board of the Faculty of Social Studies are as follows:

Qualifying test

Every candidate must pass a qualifying test at the end of the third term from the beginning of the course in the *two* compulsory papers, *Methods of Social Research* and *Sociological analysis*, and *one Optional Paper* from the list of optional papers, specified by the Department of Sociology. This list will be published annually by Friday of the third week of Michaelmas Full Term in the Department of Sociology. Candidates may after special permission of the Director of Graduate Studies for Sociology offer subjects outside this list. This may include subjects from the list published in conjuction with the M.Phil. or M.Sc. in Comparative Social Policy with the permission of the Director of Graduate Studies for Social Policy. This may also include papers offered in any other relevant master's degree in the University subject to the permission of the relevant Graduate Studies Committee as appropriate. The examiners may examine candidates viva voce. Candidates who fail the qualifying test may, in exceptional circumstances, at the discretion of the Sociology and Social Policy Graduate Studies Committee, be allowed to retake the test before the beginning of the first week of the next academic year. The Sociology and Social Policy Graduate Studies Committee can decide that the retake shall consist of the whole test or parts thereof.

Final Examination

Every candidate must offer:

or other illustrations in the second copy are adequately reproduced, (ii) that if a copy of the thesis is deposited in the Tylor Library it shall be the one containing the original illustrations, and (iii) that work submitted for the Degree of M.Phil. may be subsequently incorporated in a thesis submitted for the Degree of D.Phil.

1. One further optional paper from the list of optional papers specified by the Department of Sociology. Candidates may after special permission of the Director of Graduate Studies for Sociology offer subjects outside this list.

2. A thesis* of not more than 30,000 words to be delivered to the Clerk of the Schools, High St, Oxford, by noon on Friday of the sixth week of the Trinity Full Term in which the examination is to be taken. Successful candidates will be required to deposit a copy of their thesis in the Department of Sociology.

The examiners may examine any candidate viva voce.

The examiners may award a Distinction for excellence in the whole examination on the basis of the material submitted to them in both the qualifying and the final examination.

Compulsory Papers

Methods of Social Research

(*a*) The satisfactory completion of a course of practical work in (i) basic principles of statistical inference, and statistical models for the analysis of quantitative social science data, and (ii) methods of data collection, including questionnaire design, interviewing and coding.

Candidates shall submit to the Sociology and Social Policy Graduate Studies Committee by noon on Friday of the sixth week of the third term of the course reports of the practical work completed, accompanied by a statement that they are the candidate's own work except where otherwise indicated. The Director of Graduate Studies, or a deputy, shall draw to the attention of the examiners the names of any candidates who have failed to complete to a satisfactory level of quality the course of practical work, and the examiners may require candidates to retake the course or a specified part thereof. The reports of practical work shall be available for inspection by the examiners.

(*b*) Candidates will be required to produce an essay of up to 2,500 words evaluating the research design, methods of data collection and analysis, and any ethical or philosophical issues that arise in a specified research paper. The Director of Graduate Studies shall publish a list of research papers not later than noon on Monday of the first week of the second term; candidates will be required to select one from this list of papers as the subject for their essay.

Candidates shall submit their essay to the Clerk of the Schools by 12 noon on Monday of the first week of the third term of the course, accompanied by a statement that it is the candidate's own work except where otherwise indicated.

Sociological Analysis. The object and objective of sociological analysis in relation to other social sciences. The nature of different sociological explanations, their possibilities and methodological implications. The relevance of rationality and of its limits with regard to both individual agents and institutions. The interrelationships between description and explanation, theory and empirical data, macro- and micro-levels of analysis as they emerge from areas of major sociological enquiry.

Theology

(*See also the general notice at the commencement of these regulations.*)

The regulations made by the Board of the Faculty of Theology are as follows:

Candidates will be admitted to take the examination as defined below in a specific year. In exceptional circumstances candidates may be allowed to take an examination later than one to which they were admitted. Permission for this must be sought from the faculty board not later than Monday of the week

* See the regulations on p. 508 concerning the preparation and dispatch of theses.

before the first week of the Trinity Term in which the examination was to have been taken. The application must have the support of the candidate's college and be accompanied by a statement from the supervisor.

1. Every candidate shall be required:

(*a*) to present himself or herself for a written examination in one of the subjects prescribed below;

(*b*) to present a thesis* of not more than 20,000 words in the case of subjects (*a*) and (*b*) or of not more than 30,000 words in the case of subjects (*c*), (*d*), and (*e*). The subject of the thesis must be approved by the faculty board. The candidate should submit to the meeting of the board's Graduate Studies Committee in the first week of Michaelmas Term in his or her second year: the proposed title, a short statement of how the subject will be treated, and the signature of the supervisor indicating his approval. The completed thesis must be accompanied by a signed statement by the candidate that it is his or her own work except where otherwise indicated. Successful candidates may be required to deposit one copy of the thesis in the Bodleian†;

(*c*) to present himself or herself for a viva voce examination unless individually dispensed by the examiners.

A candidate who fails the examination will be permitted to retake it on one further occasion only, not later than one year after the initial attempt. Such a candidate whose thesis has been of satisfactory standard will not be required to submit the same piece of work, while a candidate who has reached a satisfactory standard on the written papers will not be required to retake that part of the examination.

Candidates who have successfully completed the examination for the M.St. in Theology may apply to the Theology Board's Graduate Studies Committee for permission to proceed in a further three terms to the examination for the M.Phil. in Theology.

2. The subjects for examination are:

(*a*) Old Testament
(*b*) New Testament
(*c*) Christian Doctrine
(*d*) Ecclesiastical History
(*e*) Christian Ethics.

3. Candidates intending to offer a 10,000–15,000 word essay should make written application for approval for the essay topic to the Graduate Studies Office, University Offices, Wellington Square, Oxford not later than Monday of fifth week in Hilary Term preceding the examination. All applications should be accompanied by a recommendation from the supervisor. The essay must be typewritten and must be sent to the Chairman of Examiners for the Degree of M.Phil. in Theology, c/o the Clerk to the Schools, Examination Schools, High Street, Oxford, at least fourteen days before the first day of the examination. The essay must be accompanied by a signed statement by the candidate that the essay is his or her own work except where otherwise indicated.

---

* See the regulation on p. 508 concerning the preparation and dispatch of theses. Candidates are reminded that work submitted for the Degree of M.Phil. may be subsequently incorporated in a thesis submitted for the Degree of D.Phil.

† Candidates will also be required to sign a form stating whether they give permission for the thesis to be consulted.

Candidates intending also to offer three short essays in place of an examination paper must give notice of their intention not later then the Monday of fifth week in Hilary Term preceding the examination. They must submit *two copies* of their essays at least fourteen days before the first day of the examination.

Old Testament

Candidates will be required to offer papers (i), (ii), and (iii), and *either* paper (iv) *or* paper (v).

Any one of papers (i), (ii), and (v) may be replaced by a long essay (10,000–15,000 words). In addition any two of papers (i), (ii), and (v) may each be replaced by three short essays of not more than 5,000 words each.

(i) *The Literature of the Old Testament and the Apocrypha in its Historical Setting. Either* (A) a general paper comprising the following two sections: (1) passages for comment from the Old Testament and Apocrypha in English; (2) literary and historical questions; Archaeology and Old Testament study; the canon, text, and versions of the Old Testament. Candidates will be required to answer Section 1 and at least two and not more than three questions from Section 2. *Or* (B) a paper on an area for special study approved by the Board of the Faculty of Theology within the scope of the subject. The choice of area must be submitted for approval by the board at its first meeting in the Trinity Term *preceding* the academic year in which the candidate is to be examined.

(ii) *Old Testament Theology.* This paper includes questions on such topics as the nature and method of Old Testament theology; the theological ideas of the Old Testament (e.g. ideas of God, creation, election, covenant, sacrifice, atonement, life after death, etc.); Israelite religion and the religions of the Ancient Near East; the relation between the Old Testament and the New Testament. Candidates will be required to answer three and not more than four questions.

(iii) *Prescribed Hebrew Texts.* This paper includes passages for translation with textual and exegetical comments from each of the following: 2 Samuel 9–20; Isaiah 40–55; Amos; Ecclesiastes. Candidates will be required to attempt four passages.

(iv) *Either* (A) unseen passages for translation from the Hebrew text of the Old Testament; *or* (B) the Aramaic portions of the Old Testament (Daniel 2.4–7.28; Ezra 4.8–6.18; 7.12–26); *or* (C) the Septuagint (Genesis 2–4; Isaiah 42, 52–3; Psalms 2, 21 (MT22), 109 (MT 110); Proverbs 1, 8, 9). Candidates will be expected to translate and comment on four passages, one from each of the groups of texts, and to answer one question of a general nature on the Septuagint, with reference to the set texts.

(v) *The History and Principles of Biblical Study.* This paper includes questions on such topics as method in biblical study, the history of the interpretation of the Bible, both Jewish and Christian, the use and interpretation of the Bible today.

New Testament

Candidates will be required to offer papers (i) and (ii), and any two out of papers (iii), (iv), and (v).

Any one of papers (iii), (iv), and (v) may be replaced by a long essay (10,000–15,000 words), and additionally, any one of these papers may be replaced by three short essays of not more than 5,000 words each.

(i) Religion and Literature of the New Testament: the Four Gospels and Acts in Greek.

Candidates will be required to translate and to comment on matters of literary, historical, and theological importance from a selection of these set texts.

(ii) Religion and Literature of the New Testament: the Epistles and Apocalypse in Greek.

Candidates will be required to translate and to comment on matters of literary, historical, and theological importance from a selection of these set texts.

(iii) New Testament Theology: General Paper.

(iv) Varieties of Judaism: 200 BE–CE 200.

Candidates should be prepared to show knowledge of the following texts (in English):

I Enoch, chs. 6–20, 46–51, 89–94 (tr. M. A. Knibb, in H. F. D. Sparks, *The Apocryphal Old Testament,* OUP, 1984).

Qumran Community Rule, Damascus Rule, Commentary on Habbakuk, Messianic Rule, Midrash on the Last Days (tr. G. Vermes, in *The Dead Sea Scrolls in English,* Pelican Books, 2nd edn., 1975).

Josephus, Jewish War II (Loeb, 1956); Antiquities XVIII (Loeb, 1965); Against Apion II (Loeb, 1956).

IV Ezra (ed. B. M. Metzger, in J. H. Charlesworth, ed., *The Old Testament Pseudepigrapha,* 2 vols., Darton, Longman and Todd, 1983, 1985).

Shemoneh 'Esreh (The Authorized Daily Prayer Book).

Mishnah Tractates Sanhedrin, Aboth, Mikwaoth (tr. H. Danby, *The Mishnah,* OUP, 1933).

Targum Neofiti Genesis 1–4, 22 (ed. A. Díez Macho, *Neophyti 1,* Consejo Superior de Investigaciones Científicas, Madrid–Barcelona, 1968).

The Wisdom of Solomon (RSV).

Philo, Migration of Abraham (Loeb, 1958); On Rewards and Punishments; On the Virtues (Loeb, 1960).

Joseph and Aseneth (ed. C. Burchard, in Charlesworth, op. cit.).

Sibylline Oracles III (ed. J. J. Collins, in Charlesworth, op. cit.).

Candidates may offer any or all of the following texts in the original languages:

Qumran Community Rule 1–4, in E. Lohse, ed., *Die Texte aus Qumran, Hebräisch und Deutsch* (2nd edn., Darmstadt, Wissenschaftliche Buchgesellschaft, 1971).

Qumran Commentary on Habakkuk (ed. E. Lohse, op. cit.).

Philo, *Life of Moses* I, 1–44 (Loeb, 1958).

Josephus, *Antiquities* XVIII, 1–28, 63–4, 109–19 (Loeb, 1965).

Joseph and Aseneth, in M. Philonenko, ed. *Joseph et Aséneth* (E. J. Brill, 1968).

(v) The History and Principles of Biblical Study (= Paper (v) for the Old Testament).

Christian Doctrine

Candidates will be required to offer one of the following sections:

Section A: History of Doctrine: Patristic Theology

Section B: History of Doctrine: Scholastic Theology

Section C: History of Doctrine: Reformation Theology

Section D: Issues in Theology with special reference to Patristic Theology

Section E: Issues in Theology with special reference to Scholastic Theology

Section F: Issues in Theology with special reference to Reformation Theology

Section G: Issues in Theology with special reference to Theology from Kant to the present day.

In Sections A–C candidates will not be required to translate passages from the set texts but will be required to comment on passages given in the original languages.

M.St. **candidates are** *not* **required to study texts marked with an asterisk.**

Section A—History of Doctrine: Patristic Theology

Candidates will be required to offer *either* papers 1, 2(*a*), and 2(*b*) or (*c*), *or* papers 1, 3(*a*), and 3(*b*) or (*c*).

1. The Development of Christian Doctrine to AD 451.

2(*a*). Hellenistic Philosophy and Christian Theology: General Paper.

2(*b*). Prescribed texts to be studied in Greek:

Ps.-Aristotle, *De Mundo* (Loeb)
*Plutarch, *De E apud Delphos* (Loeb)
Albinus, *Epitome* VIII–XI (Budé)
Plotinus, *Enneads* 1.6, V.1 (Loeb or *Oxford Classical Texts*).
Origen, *Contra Celsum* VII (*Sources Chrétiennes* (S.C.))
Gregory of Nyssa, *Quod non sint Tres Dii* (Migne, P. G., Vol. 45)
*——— *De Hominis Opificio* (Migne, P. G., Vol. 44)
Dionysius the Areopagite, *De Mystica Theologia* (Migne, P. G., Vol. 3).

2(*c*). Prescribed texts to be studied in Latin:

*Augustine, *Contra Academicos* (Corpus Christianorum Series Latina (C.C.S.L., Vol. XXIX)
——— *Confessions* X–XII (C.C.S.L., Vol. XXVII)
——— *De Civitate Dei* VIII–X (C.C.S.L., Vol. XLVII)
——— *De Trinitate* XII, XIII (C.C.S.L., Vols. L and LA)

3(*a*). Christology in the Patristic Period: General Paper.

3(*b*). Prescribed texts to be studied in Greek:

*Origen, *Dialogue with Herakleides* 1, 1–8.17 (S.C., Vol. 67)
Athanasius, *De Incarnatione* (S.C., Vol. 199)
*Athanasius, *Epistle to Epictetus* (Migne, P. G., Vol. 26)
Gregory of Nazianzus, *Theological Orations* 4 (S.C., Vol. 250)
Theodore of Mopsuestia, *De Incarnatione* VII (ed. H. B. Swete, *Theodore of Mopsuestia's Commentaries on the Pauline Epistles* (Vol. II, pp. 293–7))
Cyril of Alexandria, 2nd and 3rd letters to Nestorius; 2nd Letter to Succensus (*Oxford Early Christian Texts*); Letter to John of Antioch (ed. T. H. Bindley, *The Oecumenical Documents of the Faith*)
The Chalcedonian Definition of the Faith (ed. T. H. Bindley, op. cit.).

3(*c*). Prescribed texts to be studied in Latin:

Tertullian, *Adversus Praxean* (ed. E. Evans)
*——— *De Carne Christi* (ed. E. Evans)
Hilary, *De Trinitate* X (C.C.S.L., Vol. LXIIA)
Augustine, *De Trinitate* IV (C.C.S.L., Vol. L)
——— *Epistle* 137 (*Corpus Scriptorum Ecclesiasticorum Latinorum,* Vol. XXXXIIII)
——— *Sermons* 186, 187 (Migne, P. L., Vol. 38)
Leo 1, *Tome* (ed. T. H. Bindley, *Oecumenical Documents*)
——— *Sermon* 8 (XXVIII) (S.C., Vol. 22)

Section B—History of Doctrine: Scholastic Theology

1. Doctrine and Methods. To be studied in relation to such works as:

Anselm, *Proslogion*
———*Cur Deus Homo*
Abelard, *Sic et Non*
The Gloss on Romans
Bernard, *De Gratia et libero arbitrio*
Hugh of St Victor, *De sacramentis christianae fidei*

Peter Lombard, *IV Libri Sententiarum,* Bk. IV
Bonaventure, *De reductione artium ad theologiam*
——— *Breviloquium*
Albert, *In librum Dionysii de mystica theologia*
Bacon, *Compendium studii theologiae*
Scotus, *Prologue to the Ordinatio.*

2. The Thought of Aquinas: General Paper.

3. Prescribed texts to be studied in Latin.

Summa Theologiae: Prima Pars, qq. 1–2, 12–13, 43;
Prima Secundae, Prologue, qq. 6–10*, 18–21, 106–14;
Secunda Secundae, qq. 23–7;
Tertia Pars, Prologue*, qq. 7–8*, 46–9, 60–5, 75–6.

Section C—History of Doctrine: *Reformation Theology*

1. Theology in Western Europe from Gabriel Biel to Calvin.

2. Protestant and Tridentine Teaching on the Doctrines of Grace, Freewill and Predestination: General Paper.

3. Prescribed texts to be studied as follows (the Latin texts in the original language):

*Luther, *Lectures on Romans,* chapter 8 (1515–16) (Weimar Ausgabe (W.A.) LVI) (Scholia)
*——— *Disputation against Scholastic Theology* (1517) (W.A. I 221–8).
*——— *The Heidelberg Disputation* (1518) (W.A. I 350–65).
——— *On the Bondage of the Will* (1525) (W.A. XVIII 661–699)
Calvin, *Institutes* (1559), II 1–2; III 11–14, 21, 24.
Council of Trent, *Sessio* V (1546), *Decretum super peccato originali.*
——— *Sessio* VI (1547), *Decretum et canones de justificatione.*

Section D—Issues in Theology with special reference to Patristic Theology

Candidates will be required to offer papers 1 and 2 and *either* 3 and 4 *or* 5 and 6.

1. A paper on *Current Issues in Theology.* Candidates will be expected to discuss problems of theological method, and to show a critical understanding of the main themes in systematic theology, taking account of the impact on Christian theology of contemporary philosophy, critical historical studies, the natural and social sciences, and non-Christian religions and ideologies.

2. The Development of Christian Doctrine to AD 451 (as prescribed for paper 1 of Section A).

3. Hellenistic Philosophy and Christian Theology (as prescribed for paper 2(*a*) of Section A).

4. Prescribed texts to be studied in English:

Ps.-Aristotle, *De Mundo* (Loeb)
*Plutarch, *De E apud Delphos* (Loeb)
Plotinus, *Enneads* I.6, V.1 (Loeb)
Origen, *Contra Celsum* VII (tr. H. Chadwick, *CUP*)
Gregory of Nyssa, *Quod non sint Tres Dii (Library of Christian Classics* (LCC), Vol. III)
*——— *De Hominis Opificio* 1–16 (*Nicene and Post-Nicene Fathers*) (NPNF)
Dionysius the Areopagite, *De Mystica Theologia**

---

* Copies of a translation of this work are available in the Theology Faculty Library.

Augustine, *Contra Academicos (Ancient Christian Writers)*
——*The City of God* VIII–X (tr. H. Bettenson, *Penguin Books*).

5. Christology in the Patristic Period: General Paper (as prescribed for paper 3(*a*) of Section A).

6. Prescribed texts to be studied in English:

Tertullian, *Adversus Praxean* (tr. E. Evans)
*——*De Carne Christi* (tr. E. Evans)
Athanasius, *De Incarnatione* (tr. A. Robertson in NPNF or LCC, Vol. III)
——*Contra Arianos* 3, 26–58 (NPNF)
*——*Epistle to Epictetus* (NPNF)
Gregory of Nazianzus, *Theological Orations* 4 (LCC, Vol. III)
Theodore of Mopsuestia, *De Incarnatione* VII (ed. M. Wiles and M. Santer, *Documents in Early Christian Thought*)
Cyril of Alexandria, 2nd and 3rd Letters to Nestorius: Letter to John of Antioch; 2nd Letter to Succensus (*Oxford Early Christian Texts*)
The Chalcedonian Definition of the Faith (LCC, Vol. III)
Leo I, *Tome* (LCC, Vol. III)
——*Sermon* 28 (ed. Wiles and Santer: *Documents*).

Section E—Issues in Theology with special reference to Scholastic Theology

1. Current Issues in Theology (as specified for paper 1 of Section D).

2. Doctrine and Methods. A general study of the origins and history of scholastic theology, dealing with the influence of Anselm and Abelard; the rise of the cathedral schools and the universities, and the development of the disputation technique—in relation to such people as the Victorines and Peter Lombard; and the principal representatives of developed scholasticism, such as Bonaventure, Albert the Great, Aquinus, and Scotus. (The texts indicated for Section B, paper 1, give a good idea of the ground to be covered.)

3. The Thought of Aquinas: General Paper (as specified for paper 2 of Section B).

4. Prescribed texts to be studied in English:

Summa Theologiae

Prima Pars
qq. 1 Theology
2–11 The God of 'Classical Theism'
12–13 Knowing and Naming God, Analogy Theory
27–32 The Doctrine of the Trinity
43 The Mission of the Divine Persons

Prima Secundae
qq. 6–10 Human Action
18–21 Principles of Morality
90–94 Law and Politics
106–114 Grace and Justification

Secunda Secundae
qq. 1–2 Faith
23–27 Charity as Friendship

Tertia Pars
qq. 1 The Purpose of the Incarnation
7–15 Christ's Holiness and Knowledge
46–49 The Passion of Christ
60–65 The Sacraments

75–78 The Eucharistic Presence.
in the Blackfriars edition vols. 1, 2, 3, 6, 7, 48, 49, 54, 56, 58.

Section F—Issues in Theology with special reference to Reformation Theology

1. Current Issues in Theology (as specified for paper 1 of Section D).

2. Theology in Western Europe from Gabriel Biel to Calvin (as specified for paper 1 of Section C).

3. Protestant and Tridentine teaching on the Doctrines of Grace, Freewill and Predestination: General Paper (as specified for paper 2 of Section C).

4. Prescribed texts to be studied in English:

*Luther, *Lectures on Romans,* chapters 7 and 8 (1515–16) (*Library of Christian Classics,* Vol. XV)
*——— *Disputation against Scholastic Theology* (1517) (LCC, Vol. XVI)
*——— *The Heidelberg Disputation* (1518) (LCC, Vol. XVI)
——— *On the Bondage of Will* (1525), Parts I–III (LCC, Vol. XVII)
Calvin, *Institutes* (1559) II 1–2; III 11–14, 21, 24 (LCC, Vol. XX, pp. 241–89, 725–88; Vol. XXI, pp. 920–32, 964–87).
Council of Trent, Session V (1546) *Decree concerning original sin*
Council of Trent, Session VI (1547) *Decree and canons concerning justification* (H. J. Schroeder, *Canons and decrees of the Council of Trent: original text with English Translation* (1941, pp. 21–3, 29–46)).

Section G—Issues in Theology with special reference to Theology from Kant to the present day

1. Current Issues in Theology (as specified for paper 1 of Section D).

2. Doctrines and Methods from Kant to Troeltsch, to be studied against the history of ideas in the period. Candidates should be prepared to show knowledge of the following:

I. Kant, *Religion within the boundaries of mere reason* in A. W. Wood, G. di Giovanni, eds., *Religion and Rational Theology* (Cambridge: Cambridge University Press, 1996)
S. T. Coleridge, *Aids to Reflection*, ed. J. Beer (London: Princeton University Press, 1993)
G. W. F. Hegel, *Lectures on the Philosophy of Religion*, ed. P. C. Hodgson (Berkeley: University of California Press, 1985), vol. III, pp. 310–47
F. D. E. Schleiermacher, *The Christian Faith* (Edinburgh: T&T Clark, 1928), pp. 1–128
F. C. Baur, 'Introduction to Lectures on the History of Christian Dogma' in P. C. Hodgson, ed., *Ferdinand Christian Baur on The Writing on Church History* (New York: Oxford University Press 1962), pp. 259–366
S. Kierkegaard, *Philosophical Fragments* (Princeton: Princeton University Press, 1962)
E. Troeltsch, 'Historical and Dogmatic Method in Theology' in *Religion in History* (Minneapolis: Fortress Press, 1991), pp. 11–32
A. von Harnack, *What is Christianity?* (London: Williams and Norgate, 1901).

3. The Doctrine of Revelation. To be studied in relation to such works as:

*J. Baillie, *Our Knowledge of God*
K. Barth, *Church Dogmatics* **I**, 2, Chs. II and III; **II**, 1, Ch. V
E. Brunner, *Revelation and Reason*
*A. Dulles, *Revelation Theology*
*H. H. Farmer, *Revelation and Religion*
H. L. Mansel, *The Limits of Religious Thought Examined*
F. D. Maurice, *What is Revelation?*

*G. Moran, *Theology of Revelation*
H. R. Niebuhr, *The Meaning of Revelation*
*ed. J. M. Robinson, *Theology as History*
P. Tillich, *Systematic Theology,* Vol. I
Vatican I, *Dogmatic Constitution, 'Dei Filius' on Catholic Faith* Chs. II, III, IV and Canons (ed. K. Rahner, *The Teaching of the Catholic Church,* pp. 31–40)
Vatican II, *Constitution on Divine Revelation.*

ECCLESIASTICAL HISTORY

Candidates admitted in Michaelmas Term 1996 may take the examination according to the 1996 regulations.

Candidates will be required to offer three papers:

(i) A general paper on the nature and practice of ecclesiastical history. Candidates will be expected to answer questions on the various understandings of history which have been advanced within Christianity at different periods. They will also be expected to show knowledge of the variety of approaches to historical method which have emerged as a result of the modern professionalization of teaching and research in history. They will be expected to be familiar with short extracts from Christian historians (listed below), chosen as illuminating the outlook and purpose of the writers. Knowledge of these passages will be taken as a basis for candidates commenting on the work of those historians.

Acts, Ch. 1.
Eusebius, *Ecclesiastical History* (the preface and VIII. 13.8 and 9);
Bede's *History of the English Church and People* (the preface) and 'The Six Ages of the World' (the first part of chapter xlvi of *De Tempore Ratione*);
Orderic Vitalis, *The Ecclesiastical History* (the prologue);
Joachim of Fiore, *The Seven Seals* and 'The Three Status' from *The Exposition of the Apocalypse*;
J. Calvin, *Preface to Chrysostom's Homilies* in W. Ian P. Hazlett. 'Calvin's Latin Preface to his proposed French edition of Chrysostom's Homilies: Translation and Commentary', in *Humanism and Reform: the Church in Europe, England and Scotland, 1400–1643,* ed. J. Kirk (Studies in Church History, Subsidia 8), 1991, pp. 129–150);
J. Foxe, ed. J. Pratt, *Acts and Monuments* (8 vols., 4th edn., 1877) [and cognate editions from Cattley and Townsend or Pratt], I, pp. 3–15.;
G. Burnet, *History of the Reformation* (6 vols., 1865 edn.), I, pp. 1–19;
F.-C. Baur, *The Epochs of Church Historiography* (the preface and introduction) and 'The Place of the History of Dogma in the Realm and the Theological Sciences' from *Introduction to Lectures on the History of Christian Dogma*;
Lord Acton's letter to the contributors to the *Cambridge Modern History*;
H. Butterfield, *Christianity and History* (Fontana 1957, pp. 29–39).

(ii) A general paper on one of the following:
- (*a*) The Early Church AD 303–461
- (*b*) The Western Church AD 1050–1280.
- (*c*) The Reformation AD 1500–1660
- (*d*) European Christianity AD 1800–1950

(iii) One of the following special subjects:
1. The Council of Chalcedon
2. General Councils of the Western Church from Lateran III (1189) to Basel–Florence (1431–45).
3. English Protestant Identities 1558–1660
4. Religion and the English Enlightenment 1660–1762

5. Ritualism and Revivalism in England 1860–90
6. The Churches and Social Problems in Britain 1875–1924
7. Apologetics and Theology in Britain 1908–39

With the Board's permission three essays of not more than 5,000 words may be submitted in place of paper (ii).

The special subject papers are to be studied through the following texts:

1. *The Council of Chalcedon*

Passages for comment will be set from amongst the following texts. Candidates may choose to answer only on English-language passages, but will not normally be allowed to proceed to a D.Phil. unless at least one passage in Greek or Latin is satisfactorily attempted.

Original Languages

Cyril of Alexandria, *Second and Third Letters to Nestorius,* ed. and trans. L. R. Wickham, 1983.

Decrees of Ephesus (431) and Chalcedon (451) in N. Tanner (ed.), *Decrees of Ecumenical Councils*, Vol. I (Sheed and Ward, 1990).

Epistula Leonis ad Flavianum, in C. A. Heurtley (ed.), *De Fide et Symbolo*, 1991, pp. 205–16.

English

Cyril of Alexandria, *Second and Third Letters to Nestorius*, ed. and trans. L. R. Wickham, 1983.

Acts of Ephesus and Chalcedon in H. R. Percival, *The Seven Ecumenical Councils* (Library of Nicene and Post-Nicene Fathers XIV, Edinburgh 1899, repr. Grand Rapids: Eerdmans 1991), pp. 196–288. Note: this includes *all* documents and canons.

The *Formula of Reunion* (433) and the *Tome of Leo*, in E. R. Hardy, *Christology of the Later Fathers*, 1954, pp. 255–70.

2. *General Councils of the Western Church from Lateran III (1189) to Basel–Florence (1431–45)*

In English, although candidates will be given the opportunity to show knowledge of the texts in Latin.

The decrees of the Councils are to be found in *Decrees of Ecumenical Councils*, ed. N. Tanner, (Sheed and Ward, 1990), vol. i, pp. 211–25 (Lateran III), 230–71 (Lateran IV), 278–301 (Lyons I), 309–31 (Lyons II), 336–401 (Vienne), 405–51 (Constance), 455–591 (Basel–Florence).

3. *English Protestant Identities 1558–1660*

L. Andrews, Sermons *Nativity 10, Nativity 15, Ressurrection 15, Whitsun 11, Gunpowder 6, Of the worshipping of imaginations,* in *Works,* eds. J. P. Wilson and J. Bliss, 9 vols., 1841–54, vols. I. pp. 153–74, 249–64; III, pp. 23–28, 301–22; IV, pp. 296–317; V, pp. 54–70

R. Baxter, *The Autobiography of Richard Baxter*, ed. N. H. Keeble, 1974, pp. 3–141

G. Bray, (ed.), *Documents of the English Reformation*, 1994, pp. 284–311, 318–63, 397–452, 481–543

R. Browne, 'A Treatise of reformation without tarrying' and 'A true and short declaration' in *The Writings of Robert Harrison and Robert Browne*, eds. A. Peel and L. H. Carlson, 1953

G. Fox, *A Journal or historical account of the life, travels, sufferings . . . of . . . George Fox*, ed. J. L. Nickalls, 1952, pp. 1–391

R. Hooker, *Laws of Ecclesiastical Polity*, Bks. IV, chs. 1–6; V, chs. 67–68; VII, chs. 10–18, in *Works of Hooker*, ed. W. Speed Hill, 7 vols., 1977–93, vols. I, pp. 272–92; II, pp. 330–59; III, pp. 202–63

J. Jewel, *An apology of the Church of England*, in *Works of John Jewel*. . ., ed. J. Ayre, 4 vols., 1845–50, III, pp. 52–112

W. L. Lumpkin (ed.), *Baptist Confessions of faith,* 1959, pp. 79–235

W. Perkins, *A golden chaine*, abbr. in *The Works of William Perkins*, ed. I. Breward, 1970, pp. 169–261

L. J. Trinterud (ed.), *Elizabethan Puritanism*, 1971, pp. 40–383

The Works of . . . John Whitgift . . ., ed. J. Ayre, 3 vols., 1851–3, vols. I, pp. 1–12, 171–87; III, pp. 468–551

J. Williams, *the Holy Table: Name and Thing*, 1637, repr. in facsimile in B. Williams (ed.), *The Work of Archbishop John Williams*, 1988

4. *Religion and the English Enlightenment 1660–1762*

Anon., *An exact relation of the wonderful cure of Mary Maillard*, 1730

The Conway Letters, ed. M. Nicholson, revised S. Hutton, 1992

D. Hume, *Of Superstition and Enthusiasm*, 1741

———, *Of Miracles*, 1748

———, *The Natural History of Religion*, 1757

J. Locke, *The Reasonableness of Christianity*, 1695

T. Sprat, *The History of the Royal Society*, 1667

E. Stillingfleet, *Origines Sacrae*, 1662

J. Toland, *Christianity not mysterious*, 1696

———, *Nazarenus*, 1718

Selected Letters of Horace Walpole, ed. W. S. Lewis, 1973

W. Whiston, *Mr Whiston's Memoirs*, 1749

M. Wortley Montague, *Embassy Letters* 1716–18.

5. *Ritualism and Revivalism in England 1860–1890*

R. W. Enracht, *Catholic Worship*, 1871

J. W. Burgon, *Romanising within the Church of England*, 1873

W. E. Gladstone, *The Church of England and Ritualism.* 1875

J. C. Ryle, *What do we Owe to the Reformation?,* 1877

E. W. Benson, The 'Lincoln' Judgement, 1890

William Booth, *In Darkest England and the Way Out*, 1890

W. R. Moody, *Life of Dwight L. Moody*, 1900

S. Spurgeon and W. J. Harrald (eds.), C. H. Spurgeon's 'Autobiography', 4 vols., 1897–1900

G. Edwards, *From Crow-Scaring to Westminster*, 1922

6. *The Churches and Social Problems in Britain* 1875–1924

Andrew Mearns, *The Bitter Cry of Outcast London*, 1883

B. G. Westcott, *Social Aspects of Christianity*, 1887

H. P. Hughes, *Social Christianity*, 1889

William Booth, *In Darkest England and the Way Out*, 1890

S. D. Headlam, *Christian Socialism*, 1892

S. E. Keeble, *Industrial Day-dreams*, 1886

C. S. Devas, *The Pope and the People*

William Cunningham, *Christianity and Social Questions*, 1910

R. H. Tawney, *The Acquisitive Society*, 1921

Proceedings of a Conference on Christian Politics, Economics, and Citizenship, 1924

7. *Apologetics and Theology in Britain 1908–1939*

G. K. Chesterton, *Orthodoxy*, 1908
P. T. Forsyth, *The Justification of God*, 1917
Charles Gore, *The Reconstruction of Belief*, 1921
William Temple, *Christus Veritas*, 1924
H. Christopher Dawson, *Progress and Religion*, 1929
Evelyn Underhill, *Worship*, 1936
Doctrine in the Church of England, 1938
T. S. Eliot, *The Idea of a Christian Society*, 1939.

Christian Ethics

All candidates shall offer paper (i) Christian Moral Concepts: General Paper.

Candidates shall offer two of the following papers, in one of the following combinations: (ii) and any other paper; (iii)(*a*) and (*b*); (iv)(*a*) and (*b*).

(i) *Christian Moral Concepts: General Paper.* Candidates will be expected to discuss conceptual and methodological questions arising in contemporary Christian moral thought in its major traditions. They will be expected to discuss questions raised for these ideas by other streams of contemporary Western thought, especially moral philosophy and the human sciences, including the authority and interpretation of Scriptural moral teaching.

(ii) *Historical Traditions of Christian Ethics.* Candidates will be expected to show an understanding of the principal moral concepts in the Scriptures and the major historical traditions of Christian thought, in relation to such works as:

Clement of Alexandria, *Stromateis* VII (*Library of Christian Classics,* 'Alexandrian Christianity')
Augustine, *On Christian Doctrine* I (tr. D. W. Robertson)
——— *On the Nature of the Good* (NPNF, series 1, vol. 4)
——— *The Lord's Sermon on the Mount* (NPNF, series 1, vol. 6)
Aquinas, *Summa Theologiae* 2–1, qq. 1–5, 18–21, 49–70
Luther, 'Two Kinds of Righteousness', 'The Freedom of a Christian' (*Works,* vol. 31)
Joseph Butler, *Sermons*
Jonathan Edwards, *Two Dissertations: Concerning the End for which God Created the World and the Nature of True Virtue*
Kierkegaard, *The Concept of Dread*
——*Fear and Trembling*

(iii)(*a*) *Sexuality and Marriage: Christian traditions of discussion.* To be studied in relation to such works as:

Clement of Alexandria, *Stromateis III (Library of Christian Classics,* 'Alexandrian Christianity')
Gregory of Nyssa, *On Virginity (Nicene and Post-Nicene Fathers* (NPNF), series 2, vol. 5)
Augustine, *On the Good of Marriage (Library of the Fathers* (LF), vol. 22; NPNF series 1, vol. 5)
———*City of God* XIV (NPNF, series 1, vol. 2)
Aquinas, *Summa Theologiae* Supplement qq. 41–48
Luther, 'That parents should neither compel nor hinder the marriage of their children'
———'The Estate of Marriage' (both in *Works,* vol. 45)
John Milton, 'The Doctrine and Discipline of Divorce'
———'Tetrachordon' (both in *Prose Works*)
Kirkegaard, *Either/Or*

(iii)(*b*) *Sexuality and Marriage: contemporary moral problems.* Candidates will be expected to discuss contemporary problems in the ethics of marriage and sexuality with an understanding of the bearing of theological thought on them and an awareness of the questions arising for Christian ethics from scientific and philosophical discussions. Topics may include: monogamy, divorce, sacramentality of marriage, vocations of singleness, homosexuality, the social relations of men and women, parenthood, family structure, eroticism, pornography, sexuality and the law, pastoral care of the sexually handicapped.

(iv)(*a*) *Christian Political Thought: traditions of discussion.* To be studied in relation to such works as:

Eusebius of Caesarea, *Oration in Praise of Constantine* (NPNF, series 2, vol. 1)
Augustine, *City of God* XIX
——Letter 189 (NPNF, series 1, vol. 1)
Aquinas, *On Kingship* (ed. I. T. Eschmann)
——*Summa Theologiae* 12–1, qq. 90–108; 2–2, qq. 40–42
Marsilius of Padua, *Defensor Pacis* I (tr. A. Gewirth)
Luther, 'Temporal Authority', 'Whether soldiers too can be saved' (*Works,* vols. 45, 46)
Richard Hooker, *Laws of Ecclesiastical Polity* VIII
Hugo Grotius, *On the Law of War and Peace*
John Locke, *Two Treatises of Civil Government*

(iv)(*b*) *Christian Political Thought: contemporary questions.* Candidates will be expected to discuss contemporary questions in political thought with a knowledge of Christian contributions to them and an understanding of the bearing of theological ideas upon them, as well as an awareness of challenges to Christian thought from other contemporary sources. Topics may include: power and authority, justice and rights, economic justice, nationhood and international order, 'just war' and 'just revolution', deterrence, punishment, policing, democracy, religion and politics, secularism and pluralism.

The Examiners may award a Distinction for excellence in the whole examination.

If it is the opinion of the examiners that the work done by a candidate is not of sufficient merit to qualify him for the Degree of M.Phil. but is nevertheless of sufficient merit to qualify him for the Degree of Master of Studies in Theology, the candidate shall be given the option of resitting the M.Phil. examination under Ch. VI, Sect. VI, §2, cl. 4 or of being granted permission to supplicate for the Degree of Master of Studies.

World Archaeology

Within the Division of Life and Environmental Sciences, the course shall be administered by the Committee for the School of Archaeology. The regulations made are as follows:

1. Candidates for admission must apply to the Committee for the School of Archaeology. They will be required to produce evidence of their appropriate qualifications for the proposed course including their suitable proficiency in relevant ancient or modern languages.

2. Candidates must follow for six terms a course of instruction in World Archaeology.

3. The registration of candidates will lapse from the Register of M.Phil. students on the last day of the Trinity Full Term in the academic year after that in which their name is first entered in it, unless the committee decides otherwise.

4. All candidates are required:

(*a*) to satisfy the examiners in a Qualifying Examination identical with that for the degree of Master of Studies in World Archaeology and governed by regulations 4–8 for that degree, in the Trinity Full Term of the academic year in which their name is first entered on the Register of M.Phil. students except that under regulation 4(*b*) of that degree a 10,000 word dissertation may not normally be offered in place of one of the subject options (examined by two pre-set essays or by three-hour written paper). Candidates whose work in the Qualifying Examination is judged by the examiners to be of the standard required for the degree of M.St. in World Archaeology, but not of the standard required to proceed to the second year of the M.Phil. in World Archaeology, may be offered the option of resitting the Qualifying Examination under Ch. VI, Sect. VI, § 2, cl. 4, or of being granted permission to supplicate for the degree of Master of Studies in World Archaeology;

(*b*) to deliver to the Clerk of the Schools, High Street, Oxford, not later than noon on the Friday of the sixth week of Trinity Full Term in the academic year after that in which their name is first entered on the Register for M.Phil. Students, a thesis* of not more than 25,000 words (excluding bibliography and any descriptive catalogue or other factual matter, but including notes and appendices) on the subject approved in accordance with regulations 7 and 10 below;

(*c*) to present themselves for written examination in accordance with regulation 5 below in the Trinity Full Term of the academic year after that in which their name is first entered on the Register for M.Phil. Students;

(*d*) to present themselves for an oral examination as required by the examiners.

5. The written examination shall comprise one subject chosen from schedules A–B for the Master of Studies in World Archaeology. [Candidates who offered a subject from Schedule B in the qualifying examination may not normally offer another subject from Schedule B.] The subject may be examined, at the candidate's choice, either by two pre-set essays of 5,000 words each, or by a written paper.

6. The choice of subjects for thesis and examination must be approved by the candidate's supervisor and by the committee, having regard to the candidate's previous experience and to the availability of teaching. The subject for the thesis will normally be related to the subject chosen under regulation 5 above.

7. Candidates will be expected to show sufficient general knowledge of Ancient History and Geography for a proper understanding of their subjects.

8. The subject for examination and the chosen method of examination must be submitted for approval by the committee in time for its meeting in eighth week of the Trinity Full Term of the academic year in which the candidate's name is first entered on the Register for M.Phil. students. Notice of the subject must be given to the Registrar no later than Friday of the eighth week of the Michaelmas Full Term preceding the examination.

9. Candidates intending to offer pairs of pre-set essays in place of the written examination (as specified in 5 above) will select essay topics from a list offered by their supervisors. The proposed essay titles, countersigned by the supervisor, must be submitted for approval to the Chairman of Examiners by noon on Friday of the seventh week of the Hilary Full Term preceding the examinations. Candidates must

---

* See the regulation following Ch. VI, Sect. VI, § 4, concerning the preparation and dispatch of theses. Candidates are reminded (i) that two copies are required but that one of these may be a reproduction or carbon copy of the other, provided that any maps, diagrams, or other illustrations in the second copy are adequately reproduced, (ii) that the copy of the thesis deposited in the Ashmolean or the Balfour Library shall be the one containing the original illustrations, and (iii) that work submitted for the Degree of M.Phil. may be subsequently incorporated in a thesis submitted for the Degree of D.Phil.

submit two copies of their essays by not later than noon on Friday of the sixth week of Trinity Full Term, to the Examination Schools. Essays must be typed or printed.

10. The proposed thesis title must be submitted for approval by the committee in time for its meeting in the eighth week of the Trinity Full Term of the year in which the candidate's name is first entered on the Register for M.Phil. Students.

11. Candidates will normally be expected to undertake a programme of relevant practical work (e.g. excavation, travel, or museum study), to be approved by their supervisors beforehand.

12. Candidates are advised that adequate reading knowledge of an appropriate language or languages (other than English) may be necessary to reach the standard required by the examiners.

13. Candidates will be required to deposit one copy of the thesis with the Clerk of the Schools. Successful candidates will be required to deposit one copy of the thesis in the Ashmolean Library or the Balfour Library, as directed by the examiners. Such candidates will be required to complete a form stating whether they give permission for their thesis to be consulted.

14. Candidates whose work in the Final Examination is judged by the Examiners not to be of the standard required for the degree of M.Phil. in World Archaeology but whose work in the Qualifying Examination nevertheless reached the standard required for the degree of M.St. in World Archaeology, may be offered the option of resitting the M.Phil. Examination under Ch. VI, Sect. VI, § 2, cl. 4, or of being granted permission to supplicate for the degree of Master of Studies in World Archaeology.

15. The examiners may award a distinction for excellence in the whole examination.

7

REGULATIONS FOR THE DEGREE OF MASTER OF STUDIES

Ch. VI, Sect. XXXI]

General Regulations

§1. Degree of Master of Studies

1. Any person who has

(*a*) been admitted as a student for the Degree of Master of Studies under the provisions of this section,

(*b*) satisfied the examiners in one of the examinations prescribed in this section, and

(*c*) kept three terms of statutory residence as a matriculated member of the University after admission as a Student for the Degree of Master of Studies,

may supplicate for the Degree of Master of Studies.

2. For the purpose of this section the words 'board' or 'faculty board' shall include any committee or other body authorized to admit candidates for the Degree of Master of Studies.

§2. Examinations for the Degree of Master of Studies

1. The examinations for the degree and the bodies responsible for the supervision of each examination shall be as listed below.

(Examination)	(Board)
Archaeological Science	Life and Environmental Sciences
Byzantine Studies	Classics and Modern History
Celtic Studies	Modern Languages
Chinese Studies	Oriental Studies
Classical Archaeology	Life and Environmental Sciences
Classical Armenian Studies	Oriental Studies
Classical Hebrew Studies	Oriental Studies
English Local History	Continuing Education
European Archaeology	Life and Environmental Sciences
European Literature	Modern Languages
Forced Migration	Area and Development Studies Committee

General Linguistics and Comparative Philology	Committee for Comparative Philology and General Linguistics
Greek and/or Latin Languages and Literature	Classics
Greek and/or Roman History	Classics
Historical Research	Modern History
Historical Research (Medieval History)	Modern History
History of Art and Visual Culture	Modern History
International Human Rights Law	Committee on Continuing Education
Islamic Art and Archaeology (Research Methods and Techniques)	Oriental Studies
Islamic Art and Archaeology	Oriental Studies
Japanese Studies	Oriental Studies
Jewish Studies	Oriental Studies
Jewish Studies in the Graeco-Roman Period	Oriental Studies
Korean Studies	Oriental Studies
Legal Research	Law
Modern History	Modern History
Modern Jewish Studies	Oriental Studies
Modern Middle Eastern Studies	Oriental Studies
Music	Music
Oriental Studies	Oriental Studies
Philosophical Theology	Theology
Philosophy	Philosophy
Professional Archaeology	Life and Environmental Sciences
Psychodynamic Practice	Continuing Education
Research Methods in English	English Language and Literature
Science and Religion	Theology
Slavonic Studies	Modern Languages
Study of Religion	Theology
Syriac Studies	Oriental Studies
Theology	Theology
Theology (Research)	Theology
Women's Studies	Modern Languages
World Archaeology	Life and Environmental Sciences
Yiddish Studies	Modern Languages

2. The subjects of each examination shall be determined, subject to the approval of the Educational Policy and Standards Committee,

by regulation of the boardconcerned, which shall have power to arrange lectures and courses of instruction for the examination.

3. No full-time student shall be admitted as a candidate for examination for the degree until he shall have spent at least three terms at work in Oxford after his admission as a student for the degree; time spent outside Oxford during term as part of an academic programme approved by Council shall count towards residence for the purpose of this clause.

4. Part-time students for the degree shall in each case be required to pursue their course of study for twice the number of terms required of an equivalent full-time student. Part-time students will not be required to keep statutory residence but must attend for such instruction and undertake such supervised fieldwork as the faculty board or committee concerned shall require. The Director of Graduate Studies of the faculty board concerned, or the director of the department concerned, as the case may be, shall keep a register of attendance of part-time students. No student shall be granted leave to supplicate unless the register shows satisfactory attendance by him or her.

5. A candidate who has failed to satisfy the examiners in any one of the examinations may enter again for that examination on one, but not more than one, subsequent occasion.

6. A board shall have power to authorize by regulation the award by the examiners of distinctions to candidates in an examination under its supervision.

§3. Admission of Candidates

1. Any person may be admitted by the board concerned as a candidate for an examination for the Degree of Master of Studies provided the following conditions have been satisfied:

(*a*) The application must be supported by the candidates' college.

(*b*) A candidate must either (i) have passed all the examinations required for the Degree of Bachelor of Arts and have obtained first or good second class honours in the Second Public Examination, or have obtained such honours in a degree examination of another university, such university having been approved by Council for the purpose of senior status, or (ii) in the opinion of the board, be otherwise adequately qualified to undertake the course.

2. An application for admission of a candidate who has passed the examinations required for the Degree of Bachelor of Arts shall be sent to the Secretary of Faculties by the head or tutor of his or

her college, and shall be accompanied by a statement of the subject which he or she proposes to study and evidence of his or her fitness to undertake a course of study therein.

3. An application for admission by a graduate of another university shall be sent to the Secretary of Faculties by the head or tutor of the college to which he or she belongs or to which he or she has applied for admission, and shall be accompanied by all the necessary certificates from his or her previous university and by a statement of the subject which he or she proposes to study and evidence of his or her fitness to undertake a course of study therein.

4. An application for admission by any other candidate shall be sent to the Secretary of Faculties by the head or tutor of the college to which he or she belongs or to which he or she has applied for admission, and shall be accompanied by evidence of his or her previous education and by a statement of the subject which he or she proposes to study and evidence of his or her fitness to undertake a course of study therein.

5. The Secretary of Faculties shall bring any application submitted under cll. 2, 3, or 4 before the appropriate board for its approval. Such approval shall not be granted unless the board is satisfied that the candidate is well fitted to enter on the course of study proposed by him or her.

6. A board shall have power to appoint a standing committee of its own members to consider the applications of candidates and to report to the board.

7. It shall be the duty of the Secretary of Faculties to notify a candidate of the decision of a board as soon as may be.

8. A member of the University who holds the status of Probationer Research Student or the status of student for another higher degree or postgraduate diploma within the University may, with the approval of the board which admitted him or her, transfer to the status of Student for the Degree of Master of Studies, in which case the date of his or her admission as a Probationer Research Student or to the status of student for a higher degree or post-graduate diploma shall then be reckoned, unless the board shall determine otherwise, as the date of his or her admission as a Student for the Degree of Master of Studies.

9. A candidate for the B.Phil. in Philosophy may, with the approval of the Board of the Faculty of Philosophy, transfer to the status of a Student for the Degree of Master of Studies in Philosophy. The application must be submitted not later than Thursday of the

fourth week of the Trinity Term in which he or she wishes to take the examination for the Degree of Master of Studies. The date of the candidate's admission as a B.Phil. Student shall then be reckoned as the date of his or her admission as a Student for the Degree of Master of Studies.

10. A student holding the status of Probationer Research Student may, with the approval of the board which admitted him or her, be admitted as a candidate for an examination for the Degree of Master of Studies. Time spent as a student holding the status of Probationer Research Student shall count as time spent working for the Degree of Master of Studies.

11. A Student for the Degree of Master of Studies who is not a graduate of the University may wear the same gown as that worn by Students for the Degree of Doctor of Philosophy.

12. A Student for the Degree of Master of Studies shall cease to hold such status if

(i) he or she shall have been refused permission to supplicate for the Degree of Master of Studies, or
(ii) the board concerned shall, in accordance with provisions set down by regulation by the Educational Policy and Standards Committee, and after consultation with the student's society and supervisor, have deprived the student of such status;
(iii) he or she shall have been transferred under the relevant provisions to another status;
(iv) he or she shall not have entered for the relevant examination within six terms for a full-time student and twelve terms for a part-time student.

§4. Supervision of Students

1. Every candidate on admission as a Student for the Degree of Master of Studies shall be placed by the board which admitted him under the supervision of a graduate member of the University or other competent person selected by the board, and the board shall have power for sufficient reason to change the supervisor of any student.

2. It shall be the duty of a supervisor of a student to direct and superintend the work of the student for any part of the student's course in which supervision is required and to undertake such duties as shall be from time to time be set out in the relevant Notes of Guidance issued by the Educational Policy and Standards Committee.

3. The supervisor shall send a report on the progress of the student to the board at the end of each term and at any other time when the board so requests, or he or she deems it expedient. The supervisor shall communicate the contents of the report to the student on each occasion that a report is made, so that the student is aware of the supervisor's assessment of his or her work during the period in question. In addition, he or she shall inform the board at once if he is of the opinion that the student is unlikely to reach the standard required for the Degree of Master of Studies.

The Secretary of Faculties shall send a copy of each report by the supervisor to the student's society.

§5. Duties of the Secretary of Faculties

It shall be the duty of the Secretary of Faculties

(*a*) to keep a record of the names of those candidates who have been admitted as students for each examination for the Degree of Master of Studies and, where they have been examined, of the results of the examination;

(*b*) to publish at the end of the year the names of those persons in that year, to whom permission to supplicate for the Degree of Master of Studies has been granted, together with a statement of the course which each has pursued.

SPECIAL REGULATIONS

Except where otherwise indicated, all material submitted for examination (dissertations, extended essays, etc) shall be accompanied by a certificate signed by the candidate indicating that it is the candidate's own work, except where otherwise specified. This certificate must be submitted separately in a sealed envelope addressed to the chairman of examiners of the degree course in question.

Archaeological Science

1. Within the Division of Life and Environmental Sciences, the course shall be administered by the Committee for the School of Archaeology. The regulations made are as follows:

2. Candidates for admission must apply to the Committee for the School of Archaeology.

3. Candidates must follow a course of instruction in Archaeological Science for at least three terms and for a substantial part of the first two subsequent vacations, as determined by the course timetable, and will, when they enter their names for the examination, be required to produce a certificate from their supervisors to this effect.

4. The registration of candidates will lapse at the end of Trinity Term in the academic year of their admission, unless it shall have been extended by the committee.

5. The written examination, which will be taken in the second week of Trinity Term, will consist of three papers on the syllabus described in the Schedule.

6. Each candidate will be required to submit a report of approximately 5,000 words, on a practical project selected in consultation with the supervisor and

approved by a person designated for this purpose by the Committee for the School of Archaeology.

7. Three typewritten copies of the report on the practical project must be sent, not later than noon on the Friday of ninth week of the Trinity Term in the year in which the examination is taken, to the M.St. Examiners (Archaeological Science), c/o Clerk of the Schools, High Street, Oxford.

8. The examiners may require to see the records of practical work carried out during the first two terms of the course.

9. Candidates must present themselves for an oral examination as required by the examiners. This may be on the candidate's written papers, or practical work, or both.

10. The examiners may award a distinction for excellence in the whole examination.

SCHEDULE

(i) *Principles and practice of scientific dating*

The principles of scientific dating methods including radiocarbon, luminescence, uranium series, and dendro-chronology. The practical aspects of these methods and the problems encountered in their application. The statistical analysis of chronological information in the study of archaeological sites and cultures.

(ii) *Bio-archaeology*

Scientific methods for the study of biological remains from archaeological sites; introduction to the analysis of plant and faunal remains including indicators of disease and artefactual analysis; theoretical and practical aspects of quantitative methods for diet reconstructon by isotopic analysis; introduction to ancient DNA studies; residue analysis.

(iii) *Materials analysis and the study of technological change*

Introduction to the history of technology; theoretical and practical aspects of materials analysis methods—SEM, microprobe, TIMS, ICP, ICP-MS, XRF, XRD, PIXE, FTIR, and NAA; application to analysis to different material types—stone, ceramics, vitreous materials, and metals; provenance of raw materials; case studies of application to archaeological problems.

Byzantine Studies

1. Candidates must satisfy the Committee for Byzantine Studies and the appropriate faculty boards that they possess the necessary qualifications in Greek (ancient or modern) and/or Latin to profit by the course.

2. Every candidate must follow for at least three terms a course of instruction in Byzantine Studies. Candidates will, when they enter for the examination, be required to produce from their society a certificate that they are following such a course.

3. Each candidate will be required to present himself/herself for an oral examination unless exempted by the examiners.

4. *Syllabus.* The written examination shall consist of four papers: I, II, III and IV below.

Each candidate may, with the agreement of his/her supervisor, submit in lieu of any *one* of papers II, III, or IV *either* two extended essays, each not more than 5,000 words in length, *or* a dissertation of not more than 10,000 words; the topics for both essays and dissertation are to be approved by the Committee for Byzantine Studies. Essays and dissertations (*two copies*) must be typewritten or word-processed and delivered to the Clerk of the Schools, High Street, at least fourteen days before the first day of the examination.

I. All Candidates will be required to demonstrate a basic knowledge of Byzantine Greek, Classical Armenian, Syriac, Classical Arabic, Church Slavonic, or Medieval Latin.

II, III, and IV. Candidates will be required to offer three options which they must take from three different sections in the Schedule A–H below, *except* that candidates may take two options from *either* Section E *or* Section F.

A. General Byzantine History

Candidates will be required to offer a paper which focuses on *either* early Byzantine history (to 717) *or* later Byzantine history (to 1453). Candidates will be given a wide choice of questions on the history of Byzantium and its neighbours.

B. Auxiliary Disciplines

Candidates will be required to offer a paper on either Byzantine Papyrology or any two of the following:

(1) Greek Palaeography.
(2) Byzantine Epigraphy.
(3) Byzantine Numismatics.
(4) Byzantine Sigillography.

C. History Special Subjects

(1) *The Eastern Roman Empire in the reign of Justinian, 527–65.*

(i) Procopius, *History of the Wars,* trans. H. B. Dewing (Loeb Classics, 1914–28): Bks. i. ii; Bk. iii, 9–20; Bk. v. 5–11, 14; Bk. vi, 11–13, 16–30; Bk. vii, 14, 38, 40; Bk. viii, 1–17, 25.
(ii) Procopius, *Buildings,* trans. H. B. Dewing (Loeb Classics, 1940).
(iii) Procopius, *Secret History,* trans. H. B. Dewing (Loeb Classics, 1935).
(iv) *The History of Menander the Guardsman,* trans. R. C. Blockley (Liverpool, 1985), fragments 1–6, pp. 41–91.
(v) *The Chronicle of John Malalas,* trans. E. Jeffreys, M. Jeffreys, and R. Scott (Melbourne, 1986), Bk. xviii, pp. 245–307.
(vi) Justinian, *Novellae,* 7–8, 13, 15, 17, 32–4, 38, 43, 45, 80, 85–6, 106, 110, 120, 128, 130, 136, 146, 161, trans. S. P. Scott, *The Civil Law* (Cincinnati, 1932), vols. xvi–xvii.
(vii) *The Syriac Chronicle known as that of Zachariah of Mitylene,* trans. F. J. Hamilton and E. W. Brooks (London, 1899), ix, 15–16, 19–26.
(viii) John of Ephesus, *Lives of the Eastern Saints,* trans. E. W. Brooks, *Patrologia Orientalis,* xviii, pp. 513–26 (John of Tella), 526–40 (John of Hephaestopolis), 690–7 (James Baradai): xix, pp. 153–8 (James Baradai and Theodore).

(2) *Byzantium in the Age of Constantine Porphyrogenitus, 913–959.*

(i) *The Book of the Eparch,* trans. E. H. Freshfield in *Roman Law in the Later Roman Empire* (Cambridge, 1938).
(ii) Philotheus, *Cletorologium,* trans. N. Oikonomides in *Les Listes de préséance byzantines des IX et X siècles* (Paris, 1972), pp. 100/1–24/12.
(iii) Nicholas I, Patriarch of Constantinople, *Letters,* 5, 8, 9, 16, 25, 27, trans. R. J. H. Jenkins and L. G. Westerink (Washington DC, 1973).
(iv) Constantine Porphyrogenitus, *De Administrando Imperio,* chapters 1–13, 29–46, trans. R. J. H. Jenkins (Washington DC, 1967).
(v) Constantine Porphyrogenitus, *De Cerimoniis,* ed. J. J. Reiske (Bonn, 1829), Bk. ii, chapters 44 (pp. 660/13–664/2), 45 (pp. 664/3–669/14), 47–8 (pp. 680/1–692/2) (in translation).
(vi) Georgius Monachus Continuatus, *Vitae Imperatorum Recentiorum,* ed. I. Bekker (Bonn, 1838), pp. 874/5–924 (in translation).
(vii) Theophanes Continuatus, *Chronographia,* Bk. vi; *De Constantino Porphyrogenneto,* ed. I. Bekker (Bonn, 1838), pp. 426/3–430/21, 436/1–469/4 (in translation).

(viii) Georgius Cedrenus, *Historiarum Compendium,* ed. I. Bekker, vol. ii (Bonn, 1839), pp. 320/17–338/13 (in translation).

(ix) Cosmas, *Le Traité contre les Bogomiles,* trans. A. Vaillant (Paris, 1945), Part I, pp. 53–92.

(x) *The Russian Primary Chronicle,* trans. S. H. Cross and O. P. Sherbowitz-Wetzor (Cambridge, Mass., 1953), ad. an. 904–55, pp. 64–84.

(xi) Yahya ibn Said, Ibn al-Atir, Kamal al-Din, trans. M. Canard in A. A. Vasiliev, *Byzance et les Arabes,* vol. ii (2) (Brussels, 1950), pp. 91–8, 145–62, 180–4.

(xii) Ibn Miskawaih, trans. D. S. Margoliouth in H. F. Amedroz and D. S. Margliouth, *The Eclipse of the Abbasid Caliphate,* iv (Oxford, 1921), pp. 163–213 (AH 313–16).

(xiii) *Vie de saint Luc le Stylite* (879–979), trans. F. Vanderstuyf, in *Patrologia Orientalis,* vol. xi (1915), chapters 10–32 (pp. 199–225), 43–7 (pp. 237–43).

(xiv) Nicephorus Phocas, *Skirmishing,* trans. G. T. Dennis, *Three Byzantine Military Treatises* (Washington DC, 1985), preface, chapters 1–9, 19–20 (pp. 147–73, 215–23).

(xv) Nicholas I, Patriarch of Constantinople, *Miscellaneous Writings,* trans. L. G. Westerink (Washington DC, 1981), no. 200 B.

(xvi) J. Zepos and P. Zepos, *Jus Graecoromanum,* i (Athens, 1931), Collatio Tertia, *Novellae* 5, 6, 8, pp. 205–17, 222–26 (in translation).

D. Theology and Church History

The Iconoclast Controversy and the Missions to the Slavs, 717–886.

(i) Theophanes, *Chronicle,* Annus mundi 6209 to the end, trans. H. Turtledove (Philadelphia, 1982), pp. 85–182.

(ii) Extracts from the Acts of the Council of Constantinople (754) and the Council of Nicaea (787) as given in D. J. Sahas, *Icon and Logos: Sources in Eighth-Century Iconoclasm* (Toronto, 1986), pp. 47–185.

(iii) Germanus of Constantinople, *On the Divine Liturgy,* trans. P. Meyendorff (Crestwood, 1984).

(iv) John of Damascus, *On the Divine Images,* trans. D. Anderson (Crestwood, 1980).

(v) Theodore the Studite, *On the Holy Icons,* trans. C. P. Roth (Crestwood, 1981).

(vi) Photius, *Homilies,* 3, 4, 10, 17, trans. C. Mango (Cambridge, Mass., 1958).

(vii) *Epanagoge,* extracts as given in E. Barker, *Social and Political Thought in Byzantium* (Oxford, 1957), pp. 89–96.

(viii) The Life of Peter of Atroa, trans. V. Laurent (*Subsidia Hagiographica* 29: Brussels, 1956).

(ix) The Lives of Constantine/Cyril and Methodius, trans. F. Dvornik, *Les Legénddes de Constantin et de Méthode vues de Byzance* (Prague, 1933), pp. 349–93.

E. Art and Archaeology

(1) *City, country, and economy in the Byzantine Empire, AD 284–700.*
Constantinople; a selection of major provincial cities; the development of the Holy Land; land tenure and farming; manufacture and trade.

(2) *City, country, and economy in the Byzantine Empire, AD 630–1453.*
Urban decline from 600; urban revival in the Middle Byzantine period; land tenure and farming; manufacture and trade; the role of the monastery.

(3) *Byzantine art and architecture, AD 284–700.*
Church buildings; the cult of martyrs; Christian iconography; secular buildings; secular and pagan iconography; mosaics and wallpaintings; illuminated MSS; luxury objects; objects of daily use.

(4) *Byzantine art and architecture, AD 630–1453.*
Architectural development; architectural decoration; impact of Iconoclasm on art; mosaics and wallpainting; illuminated MSS; luxury objects; objects of daily use (metal, ceramic, glass); influence of Byzantine art on other cultures.

(5) *Byzantium: the transition from Antiquity to the Middle Ages, AD* 500–1100.
Study of material evidence illuminating the transformation of Byzantium from an antique to a medieval society. Coverage extends from its period of greatest territorial expansion through to its economic and political recovery after the 'Dark Age'. Subjects include changes in urban life, in land tenure and use, in the role of the monastery, in church architecture, in manufacture and trade, and the Byzantine impact on foreign prestige monuments.

(6) *Byzantine Constantinople.*
Utilitarian infrastructure, ceremonial architecture, cult building, and general topography will be studied, combining surviving structures, excavated sites, and key written texts. The social and economic character of the city will be assessed during periods of initial expansion, recession, economic recovery until its conquest by the Fourth Crusade and the final centuries before its fall to the Ottoman Turks.

F. LITERATURE

(1) *Byzantine hagiography.*
Texts: Life of Anthony; Theodoret of Cyrrhus, selections; Theodore of Sykeon; Miracles of Demetrios; Andreas Salos; Luke the Stylite.

(2) *Byzantine historiography.*
Texts; selections from Zosimus; Procopius; Theophanes; Psellos; Choniates; Anna Comnena; Sphrantzes.

(3) *Byzantine vernacular literature* (in Greek).
Texts: selections from Malalas, *Chronicle*; John Moschos, *Pratum Spirituale*; Leontios of Neapolis, Symeon the Fool; Prodromic Poems; one example of Chivalry Romance; Digenis Akrites.

(4) *Byzantine scholarship.*
Selected texts will be prescribed.

G. EASTERN AREAS AND NEIGHBOURS

(1) *Armenian History, c.450–800.*
Selected texts will be prescribed.

(2) *Armenian History, c.800–1100*
Selected texts will be prescribed.

(3) *Armenian Literature.*
Selected texts will be prescribed.

(4) *Syria before and after the Arab conquest, c.450–860.*
Selected texts will be prescribed.

(5) *Syriac literature.*
Selected texts will be prescribed.

(6) *Byzantium and Islam, c.630–900*
Selected texts will be prescribed.

(7) *Byzantium and Islam, c.800–1100*
Selected texts will be prescribed.

(8) *The formation of Islamic Art.*

(9) *Early Arabic thought and its classical heritage.*
Selected text will be prescribed.

H. Byzantium and its Northern Neighbours

(1) 370–800.
Selected texts will be prescribed.

(2) 800–1204.
Selected texts will be prescribed.

5. *Teaching in all the options may not be available each year, and applicants for admission will be advised whether teaching will be available in the options of their choice.*

6. The examiners may award a distinction for excellence in the whole examination.

Celtic Studies

1. All candidates shall be required at the time of admission to satisfy the Board of the Faculty of Medieval and Modern Languages (if necessary, by written test) that they possess the appropriate qualifications for the proposed course, including suitable proficiency in relevant languages. Normally the course will be restricted to candidates who have taken a first degree in a relevant subject area.

2. All candidates must follow a course of instruction in Celtic Studies at Oxford for a period of three terms, unless the Board of the Faculty of Medieval and Modern Languages in exceptional circumstances shall permit an extension of time, and they shall, when they enter their names for the examination, be required to produce from their society a certificate stating that they are following the course of instruction for the period prescribed.

3. Candidates shall be required:

(*a*) to offer themselves for written examination as defined below.

(*b*) to offer themselves for viva voce examination at the time appointed by the examiners.

4. The subjects and papers of the examination shall be as follows:

(*a*) *Either*

(1) Two papers, one on each of two subjects selected from the following:

(i) Historical and comparative Celtic linguistics.

(ii) Irish literature up to the Cromwellian wars (4(*b*) for the M.Phil. in Celtic Studies).

(iii) Welsh literature up to the Reformation (4(*c*) for the M.Phil. in Celtic Studies).

Or

(2) Two papers as follows:

(i) One paper on a subject selected from those described in section (*a*) (1) above.

(ii) One paper on a Special Subject to be chosen from the list given in section 4(*d*) of the regulations for the M.Phil. in Celtic Studies. Candidates are allowed to offer a Special Subject of their own devising provided that it is similar in character and scope to those listed for the M.Phil. in Celtic Studies and that it is approved under the arrangements set out in section 7 of the regulations for that M.Phil. (Candidates shall, however, seek approval for their choice of Special Subject, whether it involves a title of their devising or not, by application to the Modern Languages Graduate Office, 41 Wellington Square, Oxford, by the end of the fourth week of their first term as a student for the examination).

(*b*) A dissertation of approximately 8,000 words and not more than 10,000 words on a topic approved by the Board of the Faculty of Medieval and Modern Languages or by a person or persons to whom the board may delegate the function of giving such approval. Candidates shall seek approval (by application to the Modern Languages Graduate Office, 41 Wellington Square, Oxford) for the proposed topic of their dissertation by the end of the fourth week of their second term as a student for the examination.

The dissertation must be the work of the candidate alone and aid from others must be limited to prior discussion as to the subject and advice on presentation. It must be presented in proper scholarly form. Two copies, typed in double-spacing on one side only of quarto or A4 paper, each copy bound or held firmly in a stiff cover, must be delivered to the Chairman of the Examiners for the Degree of M.St. in Celtic Studies, c/o Clerk of the Schools, High Street, Oxford, not later than Monday of the fourth week of the Trinity Full Term in which the examination is to be taken.

5. Other arrangements for the above papers and subjects shall be as specified for the M.Phil. in Celtic Studies.

6. The examiners may award a distinction for excellence in the whole examination.

Chinese Studies

1. Candidates must either have taken a degree in Chinese in the Honour School of Oriental Studies at Oxford or a comparable degree from another university, or must satisfy the board that they possess the necessary qualifications in the Chinese language to profit by the course.

2. Every candidate must follow for at least three terms a course of instruction in Chinese Studies. Candidates will, when they enter for the examination, be required to produce from their society a certificate that they are doing so.

3. *Syllabus*

I. Prescribed texts, with special reference to a subject approved by the board.

Texts will be announced by the board in the seventh week of Michaelmas Full Term preceding the examination.

II. *either* Classical Chinese unprepared translation
or Japanese.

Candidates may choose Japanese only if the board is satisfied that they possess a good knowledge of Classical Chinese. Candidates who have taken Chinese in the Honour School of Oriental Studies at Oxford are required to take Japanese.

III. Bibliography and techniques of sinology, with special reference to the subject chosen in Paper I.

Exercises will be set at the conclusion of the two papers (I and II) taken in the Examination Schools. Each candidate will be assigned one or more exercises set on a topic directly relating to the course of instruction he has followed, and will be required to submit a written answer to the chairman of examiners by a date which the chairman will announce, but which shall, in any case, be not sooner than two days and not later than seven days from the date of the examination.

IV. A dissertation of not more than 15,000 words on a topic approved by the board at its second meeting in Michaelmas Term. The dissertation must be sent to the chairman of examiners, c/o Clerk of the Schools, Examination Schools, High Street, Oxford, not later than noon on Friday of the fifth week of Trinity Full Term.

Every candidate will be examined viva voce unless he shall have been individually excused by the examiners.

The examiners may award a distinction for excellence in the whole examination.

Classical Archaeology

1. Within the Division of Life and Environmental Sciences, the course shall be administered by the Committee for the School of Archaeology. The regulations made are as follows:

2. Candidates for admission must apply to the Committee for the School of Archaeology. They will be required to produce evidence of their appropriate qualifications for the proposed course, including their suitable proficiency in relevant ancient or modern languages.

3. Candidates must follow for three terms a course of instruction in Classical Archaeology.

4. The registration of candidates will lapse on the last day of the Trinity Term in the academic year of their admission, unless it shall have been extended by the committee.

5. The written examination shall comprise three subjects:

(*a*) one subject on a period selected from Schedule A below, to be examined by written paper;

(*b*) two subjects selected from Schedules A–C. [Not more than one subject may normally be taken from Schedule C.] Each of these subjects may be examined, at the candidate's choice, either by two pre-set essays (each of 5,000 words) or by written paper.

In lieu of one of the subjects in (*b*) above, M.St. (but not normally M.Phil.) candidates may offer, with the permission of the committee, a dissertation of not more than 10,000 words (excluding bibliography and descriptive catalogue or similar factual matter, but including notes and appendices).

The topic of the dissertation should be connected with one of the subjects chosen by the candidate under 4(*a*) and (*b*) above and must be approved by the candidate's supervisor. If the candidate has elected to be examined by pre-set essays in another part of the examination, the topic of the dissertation must be clearly distinct from the pre-set essay titles. The dissertation must be the work of the candidate alone, and aid from others must be limited to prior discussion of the subject, bibliographic advice, help with access to study material and advice on presentation. The dissertation must be a new piece of work, substantially different from any dissertation previously submitted by the candidate for a degree of this or another university. When the dissertation is submitted, it must be accompanied by a statement, signed by the candidate, confirming that these conditions have been met. The proposed title of the dissertation, countersigned by the supervisor, must be submitted for approval by the committee by noon on the Monday of the seventh week of the Michaelmas Full Term preceding the examination. Two copies typed or printed (the second may be a photocopy) in double spacing on one side only of A4 paper and bound simply or filed securely, must be delivered in a parcel bearing the words 'Dissertation for the M.St. in Classical Archaeology' to the Clerk of the Schools, High Street, Oxford, not later than noon on the Monday of the fifth week of Trinity Full Term and should bear the candidate's examination number but not his or her name. Candidates will be required to deposit one copy of the dissertation with the Clerk of the Schools.

Schedule A: Periods

Aegean to 1100
Dark Age, 1200–700
Archaic, 800–480
Classical, 500–300
Hellenistic, 330–30
Late Republican, 200–30 BC
Early Imperial, 30 BC–AD 120
Middle Imperial, AD 70–250
Late Roman and Early Byzantine, 280–700
Byzantine, 600–1453

Schedule B: Subjects

Archaeology of the early Greek polis
Greek architecture
Greek sculpture
Greek vase-painting

Greek burial customs
Anatomy and the figure in Greek art
History of collecting classical antiquities
Greek coinage
Myth in Greek and Roman art
Greek and Roman wallpainting
Classical and Hellenistic portraits
Art and cities of Roman Asia
Historical narrative in Hellenistic and Roman art
Roman portraits
Roman sculpture
Roman architecture
Roman coinage
Topography of ancient Rome
Archaeology of the Roman Economy
Pompeii and Ostia
Roman North Africa
Cities and settlement in the Roman Empire
Landscape archaeology in the Greek and Roman world
Town, country and economy in the Late Roman Empire (4th–7th centuries)
Town, country and economy in the Byzantine Empire (7th–15th centuries)
Late Roman and Byzantine architecture
Late Roman and Byzantine mosaics and painting
Late Roman and Byzantine minor arts
Problems and methods in ancient art-history
Theory and method in Greek and Roman archaeology

Schedule C: Other subjects

Any subject offered in the M.St. in Byzantine Studies, Greek and/or Latin Languages and Literature, European Archaeology, Greek and Roman History, History of Art, Near Eastern Archaeology, Women's Studies, World Archaeology.

Candidates may apply for other subjects to be approved by the committee, which shall define their scope and inform both the candidate and the examiners of this definition in writing.

Not all subjects may be available in any one year.

6. Candidates will be expected to show a general knowledge of Ancient History and Geography, so far as they are concerned with their periods and subjects.

7. Candidates must present themselves for an oral examination as required by the examiners.

8. The period and subjects to be offered by candidates and their chosen method of examination, duly approved by their supervisors, must be submitted for approval to the committee in time for its meeting in eighth week of the Michaelmas Full Term preceding the examination. Notice of options to be offered by candidates must be given to the Registrar not later than Friday of the eighth week of that same term.

9. Candidates intending to offer pairs of pre-set essays in place of one or two written examinations (as specified in 4 above) will select essay topics from a list offered by their supervisor. The proposed essay titles, countersigned by the supervisor, must be submitted for approval of the Chairman of Examiners by noon on Friday of the seventh week of the term in which the instruction for that subject is given. Candidates must deliver to the Examination Schools two copies of their essays not later than noon on Monday of the second week of the term following that in which the instruction for that subject was given. Essays must be typed or printed and

should bear the candidate's examination number but not his or her name. Any illustrations must be included in both copies.

10. The examiners may award a distinction for excellence in the whole examination.

Classical Armenian Studies

1. Candidates must satisfy the board that they possess the necessary qualifications to profit by the course.

2. Every candidate must follow for at least three terms a course of instruction in Classical Armenian Studies. Candidates will, when they enter for the examination, be required to produce from their society a certificate that they are doing so.

3. *Syllabus*

There will be four papers:

I. Essay questions on the language, literature, history, and culture of Ancient and Medieval Armenia.

II–IV. Passages for translation and commentary, and essay questions on prescribed texts in Classical and, where relevant, post-Classical Armenian, with special reference to three of the following subjects (passages for unprepared translation from and into Classical Armenian will be set):

(1) Biblical texts.
(2) Homiletic and polemical literature.
(3) Hagiographic texts.
(4) Historical literature of the 5th–9th centuries.
(5) Historical literature of the 10th–14th centuries.
(6) Religious and secular verse.
or any other subject approved by the board.

Texts will be announced by the board in the third week of Michaelmas Full Term preceding the examination.

Every candidate will be examined viva voce unless he shall have been individually excused by the examiners.

The examiners may award a distinction for excellence in the whole examination.

Teaching for the course may not be available in every year. Applicants for admission will be advised of this.

Classical Hebrew Studies

1. Candidates must satisfy the Board of the Faculty of Oriental Studies before admission to the course that they possess the appropriate qualifications in Classical Hebrew to profit by the course.

2. Every candidate must follow for at least three terms a course of study in Classical Hebrew Studies. Candidates will, when they enter for the examination, be required to produce from their society a certificate that they are doing so.

3. *Syllabus*

There will be four papers:

I. Essay questions on the history and literature of Israel and Judah in the Biblical period.

II. Prepared and unprepared Biblical texts.

III–IV. Two of the following:

(1) Classical Hebrew Language;
(2) The principles and practice of textual criticism;
(3) North-west Semitic epigraphy;

(4) Aramaic;
(5) Dead Sea Scrolls;

or any other subject approved by the board.

Texts will be announced by the board in the third week of the Michaelmas Full Term preceding the examination.

Every candidate will be examined viva voce unless he or she shall have been individually excused by the examiners.

The examiners may award a distinction for excellence in the whole examination.

Teaching for some options may not be available in every year. Applicants for admission will be advised of this.

English

Every candidate must follow for at least three terms a course of study in English.

Syllabus

The following subjects are prescribed:

A. Literature, Contexts, and Approaches
B. Bibliography, Palaeography, and Theories of Text
C. Special Options

The Faculty Board shall prescribe from year to year the particular courses which will be offered for each of these subjects. Courses under A will be taught over Michaelmas and Hilary Terms. Courses on bibliography and palaeography will be taught mainly in Michaelmas Term and courses on Theories of Text in Hilary Term. There will be two lists of Special Options, one for Michaelmas Term and one for Hilary Term.

Candidates must take A and four other subjects: two in Michaelmas Term (of which one at least must be a Special Option) and two in Hilary Term (of which one at least must be a Special Option). They must also offer a dissertation. Courses under A will be divided according to chronological period and candidates must take the course appropriate to their period of specialization.

Candidates will be required to attend the lectures and classes prescribed by the Faculty Board for the courses they have chosen, and undertake such written work, exercises or presentations for those courses as the course tutors shall prescribe.

Essays

In Michaelmas Term candidates will be required to submit an essay of 5,000–7,000 words on a topic related to one of the special options taken under C in that term; the essay must be delivered to the Clerk of the Schools, High Street, not later than noon on Thursday of the tenth week of Michaelmas Term. In Hilary Term candidates will be required to submit two essays of 5,000–7,000 words each, of which one must be on a topic related to one of the special options taken under C in that term and the other on a topic related either to an option taken under B (in either term) or to a second special option taken under C in that term. The two essays must be delivered to the Clerk of the Schools, High Street, not later than noon on Thursday of the tenth week of Hilary Term. Candidates must gain approval of the topic of their essays by writing to the Chairman of the M.St. Examiners, care of the English Faculty Office, by Friday of the sixth week of Michaelmas Term (for the first essay) and of Hilary Term (for the second and third essays).

[*Note*: additionally, candidates offering the course in the palaeography of manuscripts up to 1500 under B will be required to take a test in manuscript transcription, and the assessment will be in the form of a description of a manuscript, of about 2,500 words, instead of an essay. Candidates offering bibliography in the period 1550 to the present day under B will be required also to attend a course in manuscript reading and transcription and pass a test in transcription.]

Not later than noon on Monday on the sixth week of Trinity Term, candidates must deliver to the Clerk of the Schools two copies of a dissertation (about 10,000 words) on a subject related to their course of study. The dissertation must be presented in proper scholarly form. Candidates must gain approval of the topic of their dissertation by writing to the Chairman of the M.St. Examiners, care of the English Faculty Office, by Friday of the sixth week of Hilary Term, providing a provisional essay title and an outline of the topic of not more than 200 words.

Candidates who fail any part of the examination may resubmit that part by noon on the last Monday of the following Long Vacation.

The examiners may award a distinction for excellence in the whole examination.

European Archaeology

1. Within the Division of Life and Environmental Sciences, the course shall be administered by the Committee for the School of Archaeology. The regulations made are as follows:

2. Candidates for admission must apply to the Committee for the School of Archaeology. They will be required to produce evidence of their appropriate qualifications for the proposed course, which may include their suitable proficiency in relevant ancient or modern languages.

3. Candidates must follow for three terms a course of instruction in European Archaeology.

4. The registration of candidates will lapse on the last day of the Trinity Full Term in the academic year of their admission, unless it shall have been extended by the committee.

5. The written examination shall comprise three subjects;

(*a*) one subject selected from Schedules A–B to be examined by written paper;

(*b*) two further subjects selected from Schedules A–B. [Not more than one subject of the three selected may normally be taken from Schedule B.] Each of these subjects may be examined, at the candidate's choice, either by two pre-set essays (each of 5,000 words) or by written paper.

In lieu of one of the subjects in (*b*) above, M.St. (but not normally M.Phil.) candidates may offer, with the permission of the committee, a dissertation of not more than 10,000 words (excluding bibliography and descriptive catalogue or similar factual matter, but including notes and appendices).

The topic of the dissertation should be connected with one of the subjects chosen by the candidate under 4(*a*) and (*b*) above and must be approved by the candidate's supervisor. If the candidate has elected to be examined by pre-set essays in another part of the examination, the topic of the dissertation must be clearly distinct from the pre-set essay titles. The dissertation must be the work of the candidate alone, and aid from others must be limited to prior discussion of the subject, bibliographic advice, help with access to study material and advice on presentation. The dissertation must be a new piece of work, substantially different from any dissertation previously submitted by the candidate for a degree of this or another university. When the dissertation is submitted, it must be accompanied by a statement, signed by the candidate, confirming that these conditions have been met. The proposed title of the dissertation, countersigned by the supervisor, must be submitted for approval by the committee by noon on the Monday of the seventh week of the Hilary Full Term preceding the examination. Two copies typed or printed (the second may be a photocopy) in double spacing on one side only of A4 paper and bound simply or filed securely, must be deliverd in a parcel bearing the words 'Dissertation for the M.St. in European Archaeology' to the Clerk of Schools, High Street, Oxford, not later than noon on the Friday of the sixth week of Trinity Full Term. Candidates will be required to deposit one copy of the dissertation with the Clerk of the Schools.

Schedule A: Main subjects

Palaeolithic and Mesolithic Europe
Neolithic and Bronze Age Europe
Aegean Archaeology to 1100 BC
The Greeks and the Mediterranean World *c*.950–500 BC
The transformation of the Celtic World 500 BC–AD 100.
Cities and settlements in the Roman Empire
The Archaeology of Roman Italy
Western Europe in the early Middle Ages: 400–900 AD
Late Roman and early Byzantine Archaeology AD 284–700
Byzantium: the transition from Antiquity to the Middle Ages AD 500–1100
Themes in Archaeological Science
The Archaeology of Early Anglo-Saxon England.
The Archaeology of Late Saxon England.
Archaeological Sources for the Middle Ages.

Schedule B: Related Subjects

Any subject offered in the M.St. in World Archaeology or Classical Archaeology.

Candidates may apply for other subjects to be approved by the committee, which shall define their scope and inform both the candidate and the examiners of this definition in writing. Not all course options may be available in any given year.

6. Candidates will be expected to show a general knowledge of Ancient History and Geography, so far as they are concerned with their subjects.

7. Candidates must present themselves for an oral examination as required by the examiners.

8. The subjects to be offered by the candidates and their chosen method of examination, duly approved by their supervisors, must be submitted for approval to the committee in time for its meeting in eighth week of the Michaelmas Full Term preceding the examination. Notice of options to be offered by candidates must be given to the Registrar not later than Friday of the eighth week of that same term.

9. Candidates intending to offer pairs of pre-set essays in place of one or two written examinations (as prescribed in 4 above) will select essays topics from a list offered by their supervisor. The proposed essay titles, countersigned by the supervisor, must be submitted for approval to the Chairman of Examiners by noon on Friday of the seventh week of the Hilary Full Term preceding the examinations. Candidates must submit two copies of their essays by not later than noon on Friday of sixth week of Trinity Full Term, to the Examination schools. Essays must be typed or printed.

10. The examiners may award a distinction for excellence in the whole examination.

European Literature

1. Every candidate must follow a course of instruction in European Literature at Oxford for a period of three terms, unless the Board of the Faculty of Medieval and Modern Languages in exceptional circumstances shall permit an extension of time, and he shall, when he enters his name for the examination, be required to produce from his society a certificate stating that he is following the course of instruction for the period prescribed.

2. Candidates shall be required:

(*a*) To offer *one* literature to be selected from the following: French, German, Italian, Spanish (including Latin American), Portuguese (including Brazilian), Russian, Czech, Slovak, Byzantine and Modern Greek, Celtic, and Medieval Latin.

Candidates may, with the approval of the Board of the Faculty of Medieval and Modern Languages, offer the literature of any other language falling under the direction of that board.

Candidates may show knowledge where relevant of literatures other than the one selected.

(*b*) To present themselves for viva voce examination unless dispensed by the examiners.

(*c*) To offer A, B, and C, as defined in 3 below.

3. The examination shall consist of the following:

(A) *either*

(i) Methods of Criticism and the Theory of Literature [2(A)(i) for the M.Phil. in European Literature]

or

(ii) Methods of Criticism and History of Ideas in Germany from the Eighteenth to the Twentieth Centuries. [2(A)(ii) for the M.Phil. in European Literature]

or

(iii) Methods of Scholarship. [2(A)(iii) for the M.Phil. in European Literature]

or

(iv) A methodological essay of approximately 5,000 words on a topic or issue related to the candidate's Special Subject or disseration, to be submitted in two typed copies to the Modern Languages Graduate Office (41 Wellington Square) by the fourth week of Trinity Term.

The work submitted under (i) must be written in English; the work submitted under (ii) may be written in English or German; the work submitted under (iii) or (iv) may be written in English or, subject to the approval of the Faculty Board, in a language appropriate to the literature concerned.

Candidates must seek approval for their choice of option in (A) by the end of the fourth week of Michaelmas Term.

(B) A dissertation of between 8,000 and 10,000 words and written in English, or, with the approval of the Faculty Board, in the language appropriate to the literature concerned, on a topic connected with that offered in (A)(i) or (A)(ii) above or (C) below, but distinct from those covered by the essays submitted under (A) or (C), and approved by the Modern Languages Board. Candidates shall seek approval (by application to the Modern Languages Graduate Office, 41, Wellington Square, Oxford) for the proposed topic of their dissertation by the end of the fourth week of Hilary Term.

The dissertation must be presented in proper scholarly form. Two copies, typed in double-spacing on one side only of quarto or A4 paper, each copy bound or held firmly in a stiff cover, must be delivered to the Clerk of the Schools, Examination Schools, High Street, Oxford, by noon on Thursday of the sixth week of Trinity Term.

(C) One Special Subject. The regulations will be as in 2(C) for the M.Phil. in European Literature, except that candidates shall offer one Special Subject instead of two and shall not be permitted to revise the content of the essay(s) submitted in the portfolio. Candidates must, however, seek approval of their special Subjects by the end of the fourth week of Michaelmas Term. The portfolio of work shall be submitted to the supervisor by Friday of the first week of Hilary Term.

Unless indicated to the contrary above, other arrangements for the above papers and subjects shall be as specified for the M.Phil. in European Literature.

In the case of resubmission, candidates shall be required to resubmit all the material by noon on Thursday of the sixth week of the first Trinity Term following their first examination. Candidates may resubmit on one occasion only.

4. The examiners may award a Distinction for excellence in the whole examination.

General Linguistics and Comparative Philology

1. Candidates shall normally have a degree in a subject which has given them at least some experience of linguistic or philological work. Those intending to offer options chosen from C or D below should normally have, and may be required to demonstrate, some knowledge of the chosen (group of) language(s) and those intending to offer options chosen from C will normally be expected to be able to read secondary literature in French and German.

2. The names of all candidates for the M.St. must be registered with the secretary of the Committee for Comparative Philology.

3. Every candidate shall pursue a course of study in General Linguistics and Comparative Philology for at least one academic year under the supervision of the committee. Such study shall be pursued at Oxford.

4. Any person may be admitted to a course of study approved by the committee, provided that he has *either* (*a*) passed the examinations required for the degree of Bachelor of Arts, *or* (*b*) taken a degree at some other university, such degree and such university having been approved by Council, and provided further that he has satisfied the committee that he is qualified to pursue the study of General Linguistics and Comparative Philology.

5. The committee shall have power in exceptional circumstances to admit a person not qualified under the provisions of clause 3 above, who has nevertheless satisfied the committee that he is qualified to pursue the study of General Linguistics and Comparative Philology.

6. The examination shall consist of three parts:

(*a*) one general paper as indicated in A;

(*b*) two papers both of which must be chosen from those listed in B, or those listed in C (except that, at the discretion of the committee, candidates may submit a paper from list B in place of one of those from list C), or those listed in D.

In lieu of one of the papers in list B or C or D candidates may offer with the permission of the committee a thesis of no more than 15,000 words (excluding references and appendices) to be written on a subject within the field of the M.St.

The thesis (in two typewritten copies) must be sent in a parcel bearing the words 'Thesis for the M.St. in General Linguistics and Comparative Philology' to the Clerk of the Schools, Examination Schools, High Street, Oxford, not later than noon on the Friday of the first week of the Trinity Term in the academic year in which the examination takes place.

A. Linguistic Theory.

B. (i) Phonetics and Phonology.
(ii) Syntax.
(iii) Semantics.
(iv) Historical and comparative linguistics.
(v) Theory of translation.
(vi) History and structure of a language.
(vii) Experimental Phonetics.
(viii) Sociolinguistics.
(ix) Computational Linguistics.
(x) Any other subject which, from time to time, the committee at its own discretion may consider suitable.

C. (i) The comparative grammar of two Indo-European languages or language-groups.

(ii) The historical grammar of the two languages or language-groups selected.
(iii) Translation from, and linguistic comment upon, texts in the languages selected.

D. (i) The history of one or two languages.
(ii) The structure of the language or languages selected.
(iii) *Either* (*a*) Translation from, and/or linguistic comment upon, texts in the language or languages selected,
Or (*b*) Any paper from B above except B (vi).

7. Option B(ii) shall consist of:

(*a*) an exercise, set during Week 8 of Michaelmas Term, on a topic directly related to material covered during lectures given during that term. Candidates will be required to submit a written answer to the Chairman of Examiners, c/o the Clerk of the Schools, Examination Schools, High Street, Oxford, by not later than noon on Friday of Week 1 of the following Hilary Term.

(*b*) An essay of not more than 5,000 words on some problem in syntactic theory to be selected in consultation with the supervisor and approved by the Chairman of Examiners for report to the Committee for Comparative Philology and General Linguistics not later than Monday of Week 1 of Hilary Term in the year of the examination.

The essay (in two typewritten copies) must be sent in a parcel bearing the words 'Essay for the Syntax option in the M.St. in General Linguistics and Comparative Philology' to the Chairman of Examiners for the Degree of M.St. in General Linguistics, c/o the Clerk of the Schools, Examination Schools, High Street, Oxford, not later than noon on Friday of Week 1 of Trinity Term in the year of the examination. The essays shall be accompanied by a certificate signed by the candidate indicating that it is the candidate's own work, except where otherwise specified. This certification must be submitted separately in a sealed envelope addressed to the Chairman of Examiners for the M.St. in General Linguistics and Comparative Philology.

8. Of the two languages or language-groups selected by the candidates who wish to offer the papers listed in C above, one must be studied in greater depth than the other.

Combinations previously offered under the auspices of the Committee for Comparative Philology are:

(*a*) Greek with the elements of Sanskrit Philology.
(*b*) Italic with the elements of Old Irish Philology.
(*c*) Germanic with the elements of Greek Philology.
(*d*) Greek with the elements of Anatolian Philology.
(*e*) Romance with the elements of Italic Philology.
(*f*) Italic with the elements of Greek Philology.
(*g*) Sanskrit with the elements of Greek Philology.
(*h*) Greek with the elements of Slavonic Philology.
(*i*) Celtic with the elements of Italic Philology.

Other combinations are allowed subject to the approval of the committee and the availability of teaching.

9. The language or languages selected by candidates who wish to offer the papers mentioned in D above may be ancient (e.g. Ancient Greek, Latin, Sanskrit, Akkadian, etc.) or modern (e.g. French, Italian, German, English, Turkish, etc.). Only languages for which teaching is available at the time can be offered.

10. The choice of the subjects for examination will be subject to the approval of the candidate's supervisor and the committee, having regard to the candidate's

previous experience and the availability of teaching. Not all options may be offered every year. The subjects which a candidate wishes to offer for examination must be submitted to the committee for approval not later than Tuesday of the sixth week of the Michaelmas Term in the academic year in which the candidate is to be examined.

11. If a thesis is offered, the subject must be submitted for approval by the committee not later than Tuesday of the sixth week of the Michaelmas Term in the academic year in which the candidate is to be examined.

12. Each candidate is required to present himself for an oral examination if and when required by the examiners.

13. The examiners may award a Distinction for excellence in the whole examination.

Greek and/or Latin Languages and Literature

1. Candidates must satisfy the board that they possess the necessary qualifications in Greek and/or Latin to profit by the course.

2. Every candidate must follow for at least three terms a course of instruction in Greek and/or Latin Languages and Literature. Candidates will, when they enter for the examination, be required to produce from their society a certificate that they are following such a course.

3. *Syllabus*

Candidates must normally offer *either* two options from A, B, and C below, together with a dissertation as described in D below, *or* three options taken from A, B, and C (in which case at least one option must be taken from B and at least one from C).

A

EITHER (i) Classical Greek: *either*

(*a*) *Elementary Greek*. There will be one three-hour paper, consisting of passages of Greek which will test knowledge of Attic grammar and competence in translation from Greek into English.

or

(*b*) *Intermediate Greek*. There will be one three-hour paper. Candidates will be expected to be familiar with *An Anthology of Greek Prose* ed. D. A. Russell (Oxford University Press 1991), Nos. 17, 18, 23, 24, 33, 40, 44, 66, 78, from which a selection of passages will be set for translation.

Candidates will also be expected to translate from two of the following texts: (i) Herodotus I. 1–94 [ed. Hude, OCT]; (ii) Plutarch, *Life of Antony* 1–9, 23–36, 71–87 [ed. Pelling, Cambridge University Press 1988]; (iii) Euripides, *Bacchae* [ed. Diggle, OCT]. Alternative texts for translation under this head may be offered by agreement with the Graduate Studies Committee.

OR (ii) Latin: *either*

(*a*) *Elementary Latin*. There will be one three-hour paper, consisting of passages of Latin prose which will test knowledge of classical Latin grammar and competence in translation from Latin into English.

or

(*b*) *Intermediate Latin*. There will be one three-hour paper. Candidates will be expected to be familiar with *An Anthology of Latin Prose* ed. D. A. Russell (OUP 1990), nos. 7, 12, 22, 23, 34, 52, and 63, from which a selection of passages will be set for translation.

Candidates will also be expected to translate from TWO of the following texts:

(i) Cicero, *Pro Caelio* [ed. OCT].
(ii) Pliny, *Letters* I.6, 9, 13, 19; VII.21, 24, 26, 29; VIII.16, 17; IX.6, 12, 15, 27, 33, 39; X.31, 32, 96, 97 (ed. M. B. Fisher and M. R. Griffin, CUP 1973)
(iii) Ovid, *Metamorphoses* 8 (ed. A. S. Hollis, OUP 1970)

Alternative texts for translation under this head may be offered by agreement with the Graduate Studies Committee.

B

(i) *Methods and Techniques of Scholarship*. Candidates are required to offer *two* of the following topics:

(*a*) Greek Literary Papyrology;
(*b*) Greek Palaeography;
(*c*) Latin Palaeography;
(*d*) Greek Metre;
(*e*) Latin Metre.

Each of these options will be examined in one paper of 1½ hours except for Greek Literary Papyrology, which will be examined by a practical test taken in the candidate's own time (as prescribed for Greek and Latin Papyrology in the M.Phil. for Greek and/or Latin Languages and Literature). Option B(i)(*a*) may not be combined with option B(x) below.

(ii) *Greek Textual Criticism* (Sophocles, *Ajax* 1–1184).
(iii) *Latin Textual Criticism* (Honour School of Literae Humaniores, option III.10).
(iv) *Historical Linguistics and Comparative Philology.*

Each of options (ii)–(iv) will be examined in one paper of three hours.

(v) Any option available in the M.St. in Classical Archaeology, Schedule B.

Option (v) will be examined *either* by two presubmitted essays *or* by one written paper of three hours.

(vi) Any option available in the M.St. in Greek and/or Roman History, Lists B and C.
(vii) *Constructions of Roman Women.*
(viii) *Literary Theory for Classical Studies.*

Each of options (vi–viii) will be examined by two presubmitted essays.

(ix) *Computing and Classical Literary Studies.* This option will be examined by means of a project.
(x) *Greek and Latin Literary Papyrology.* This option will be examined by one presubmitted essay and by a practical test taken in the candidate's own time (as prescribed for Greek and Latin Papyrology in the M.Phil. for Greek and/or Latin Languages and Literature). This option may not be combined with option B(i)(*a*) above.
(xi) Any other subject approved by the Graduate Studies Committee in Classics, which will determine the method of examination.

C

Each of the following options will be examined by (*a*) one paper of translation (1½ hours) and (*b*) two pre-submitted essays. The texts listed are those which should be studied in preparation for the pre-submitted essays. Passages will be set for translation only from those texts in section (α). Passages for translation will be set from the editions listed in the regulations for the Honour School of Literae Humaniores, whenever applicable. For any option approved under (xxi) the edition will be specified by the Graduate Studies Committee in Classics.

(i) *Early Greek Hexameter Poetry*:

α *Odyssey* V, I–XIII, 92;
Hesiod *Works and Days* (including the bracketed portions);

β *Odyssey* I–IV, XIII 92–end;
Theogony;
Fragments of the Epic Cycle (in H. G. Evelyn-White, *Hesiod, The Homeric Hymns and Homerica* (Loeb), pp. 480–533).

(ii) *Greek Lyric and Elegiac Poetry*:

α D. A. Campbell, *Greek Lyric Poetry* (Macmillan, repr. Bristol Classical Press) pp. 1–97 (omitting Archilochus 112, 118, Semonides 29, Ibycus 282a);
M. L. West, *Delectus ex Iambis et Elegis Graecis* (Oxford Classical Text) Archilochus 23, 188–92, 196, and 196A;

β M. Davies, *Poetarum Melicorum Graecorum Fragmenta* (Oxford), Stesichorus pp. 154–75 (*Geryoneis*), fr. 193, 209, 217, 222(*b*), Ibycus S151;
M. L. West, *Iambi et Elegi Graeci*, 2nd edition, vol. 2 (Oxford 1992) Simonides Fr. eleg. 11 and 19–20.

(iii) *Pindar and Bacchylides*:

α Pindar, *Olympians* 2, 3, 6, 12, 14; *Pythians* 3, 4, 5, 6, 10; *Nemeans* 1, 5, 7, 9, 10;

β Bacchylides 3, 5, 17, 18;
Pindar *Isthmians* 1, 2, 5;
Pindar frr. 40 (*Paean 6*), 109, 114, 116, 127 Bowra.

(iv) *Aeschylus*:

α *Agamemnon, Eumenides*;

β *Seven against Thebes, Choephori.*

(v) *Euripides*:

α *Medea, Ion*;

β *Electra, Heracles, Orestes, Hippolytus.*

(vi) *Thucydides and Rhetoric*:

α Thucydides I. 20–3, 31–44, 66–88, 139–46; II. 34–65; III. 1–85; V. 86–116;

β Herodotus VII. 8–19;
Gorgias, *Helen*;
Antiphon, *Tetralogies.*

(vii) *Plato*:

α *Phaedrus;*

β *Gorgias.*

(viii) *Greek Comedy* (*Old and New*):

α Aristophanes, *Wasps*;
Menander, *Dyscolus*;

β Aristophanes, *Birds, Ecclesiazusae*;
Menander, *Samia.*

(ix) *Hellenistic Poetry*:

α Theocritus, 1, 3, 7, 10, 13, 15, 16, 28;
Callimachus, *Hymns* 1, 5, 6; frr. 1, 67–75; 110, 178, 191, 194, 260 (this last fr. to be read in Callimachus, *Hecale* (ed. A. S. Hollis) frr. 69–74); epigrams 2, 4, 8, 13, 16, 19, 21, 25, 27, 28, 29, 30, 41, 43, 46, 50 Pf.;

β Herodas 4;
Apollonius, *Argonautica* III.

(x) *Virgil*;

α *Aeneid*, IX–XII;

β *Aeneid*, I–VIII.

(xi) *Latin Didactic Poetry*:
α Lucretius VI;
Virgil, *Georgics*;
β Lucretius IV;
Ovid, *Ars Amatoria*.

(xii) *Latin Satire*:
α Horace, *Satires* I;
Juvenal 1, 3–6, 14;
β Horace, *Satires* II:
Persius, *Prologus*, 1, 5, 6;
Juvenal 8–11.

(xiii) *Latin Historiography*:
α Sallust, *Jugurtha*;
Tacitus, *Histories* I;
B Livy, *Preface*, I, XXI.

(xiv) *Cicero the Orator*:
α *Pro Archia*;
Pro Milone;
Philippics I, II;
β *Pro Sexto Roscio Amerino*;
Pro Marcello.

(xv) *Horace*:
α *Odes* II, IV;
Carmen Saeculare;
Epistles I;
β *Epodes*;
Epistles II.

(xvi) *Ovid*:
α *Metamorphoses* I–III;
Tristia I;
β *Heroides* 18–21;
Fasti IV;
Metamorphoses IV and VIII–XV.

(xvii) *Seneca and Lucan*:
α Seneca, *Phaedra*;
Lucan I, VII;
β Seneca, *Thyestes*;
Lucan VIII, IX.

(xviii) *Greek New Comedy and Roman Comedy*:
α Menander, *Dyscolus*;
Plautus, *Pseudolus*;
Terence, *Eunuchus*;
β Menander, *Samia*.
Plautus, *Bacchides*.
This subject may not be combined with (viii) (*Greek Comedy* (*Old and New*)).

(xix) *Ancient Literary Criticism*:
(*a*) Aristotle, *Poetics*
(*b*) Longinus, *On the Sublime* 1–17, 33–44
(*c*) Horace, *Satires* 1–4 and 10, *Epistles* II. 1, and *Ars Poetica*
(*d*) Tacitus, *Dialogus*
Translation will be of any **two** of these four sets of texts.

(xx) *The Ancient Novel*

α Apuleius, *Metamorphoses* I, IV 28–VI 24, XI;
Longus, *Daphnis and Chloe*;

β Apuleius, *Metamorphoses* IV 1–27, VI 25–32, IX;
Heliodorus, *Aethiopica* X.

(xxi) Any other text or combination of texts approved by the Graduate Studies Committee in Classics.

D

A dissertation (if offered) should be of not more than 10,000 words on a subject to be proposed by the candidate in consultation with the overall supervisor or the supervisor for the dissertation, and approved by the Graduate Studies Committee in Classics. (The dissertation word limit excludes the bibliography, any text that is being edited or annotated, any translation of that text, and any descriptive catalogue or similar factual matter, but includes quotations, notes, and appendices. A note of the word-count must be included.) Supervisors or others are permitted to give bibliographical help and to discuss drafts.

4. The choice of options and/or dissertation will be subject to the approval of the candidate's supervisor and the Graduate Studies Committee in Classics, having regard to the candidate's previous experience, the range covered by the candidate's choices, and the availability of teaching and examining resources. The options which the candidate wishes to offer must be submitted to the Administrator, Classics Centre, 65–7 St Giles', Oxford OX1 3LU, for approval not later than the Wednesday of the first week of Michaelmas Full Term. The candidate should also indicate by this date whether or not he or she wishes to offer a dissertation; the title of the dissertation need not be given until the Friday of the first week of Hilary Term (see under 8(i) below).

Not all options may be available in any given year.

5. In those options for which candidates are examined by presubmitted essays, two essays should be submitted, each of not more than 5,000 words in length, which between them display knowledge of more than a narrow range of the topic. (The essay word limit excludes the bibliography, any text that is being edited or annotated, any translation of that text, and any descriptive catalogue or similar factual matter, but includes quotations, notes, and appendices. A note of the word-count must be included.) Supervisors or others are permitted to give bibliographical help with, and to discuss a first draft of, such essays. Supervisors are also required to certify that, in their tutorial and class work, students have covered a wider range of topics within the overall subject.

6. Candidates are required to present themselves for oral examination if summoned by the examiners.

7. The examiners may award a distinction for excellence in the whole examination.

8. *Submission of proposed titles for essays and dissertations:*

(1) All those submitting options examined by presubmitted essays must submit the proposed titles of two of those essays through their supervisors to the Administrator, Classics Centre, 65–7 St Giles', Oxford OX1 3LU, not later than Friday of first week of Hilary Full Term. The proposed dissertation title, for those offering that option, should also be submitted by Friday of the first week of Hilary Full Term.

(2) Those offering more than two presubmitted essays should offer their proposed titles for the remaining essays by Friday of the first week of Trinity Full Term.

(3) The final confirmation of the title of the dissertation, if different from that submitted under (1) above, should be submitted not later than Friday of the first week of Trinity Full Term.

9. *Delivery of final copies of essays and dissertations:*

(1) Two typewritten or printed copies of each presubmitted essay should be sent in a parcel bearing the words 'Essays presubmitted for the M.St. in Greek and/or Latin Languages and Literature' to the Clerk of the Schools, Examination Schools, High Street, Oxford OX1 4BG. At least two of the essays must be sent as above to arrive not later than noon on the Thursday of the fifth week of Hilary Full Term; any others must be sent as above to arrive not later than noon on the Thursday of the sixth week of Trinity Full Term.

(2) Two typewritten or printed copies of dissertations should be delivered in a parcel bearing the words 'Dissertation for the M.St. in Greek and/or Latin Languages and Literature' to the Clerk of the Schools, Examination Schools, High Street, Oxford OX1 4BG, to arrive not later than noon on the Thursday of the sixth week of Trinity Full Term in which the examination is to be taken.

Greek and/or Roman History

1. Every candidate must follow, for at least three terms, a course of instruction in Greek and/or Roman History. Candidates will, when they enter for the examination, be required to produce from their society a certificate that they are following such a course.

2. (*a*) In the case of options in languages, Schedule A below, candidates will be examined by written examination. Dictionaries may be brought by candidates for their use except for options A (i)–(iv).

(*b*) For options in topics and techniques, Schedules B and C below, candidates will be required to pre-submit two essays of not more than 5,000 words in length, which between them display knowledge of more than a narrow range of the topic covered by the course. (The essay word limit excludes the bibliography, any text that is being edited or annotated, any translation of that text, and any descriptive catalogue or similar factual matter, but includes quotations, notes, and appendices.)

Supervisors or others are permitted to give bibliographical help with and to discuss drafts of essays. Such essays (two typewritten or printed copies) must be sent in a parcel bearing the words 'Essays presubmitted for the M.St. in Greek and/or Roman History' to the Clerk of the Schools, High Street, Oxford, OX1 4BG, to reach him by noon on the Thursday of the sixth week of the Trinity Term in which the examination is to be taken.

3. Every candidate shall be examined *viva voce* unless individually dispensed by the examiners.

4. *Syllabus*

Candidates must offer *either* two options from A, B, and C below, together with a dissertation as described in D below, *or* three options from A, B, and C. In either case not more than one paper shall normally be taken from A (*not all options may be available in any given year*).

A

(i) *Elementary Greek.* There will be one three-hour paper, consisting of passages of Greek which will test knowledge of Attic grammar and competence in translation from Greek into English.

(ii) *Intermediate Greek.* There will be one three-hour paper. Candidates will be expected to be familiar with *An Anthology of Greek Prose,* ed. D. A. Russell (Oxford University Press 1991), Nos. 17, 18, 23, 24, 33, 40, 44, 66, 78, from which a selection of passages will be set for translation. Candidates will also be expected to translate from (i) Herodotus I. 1–94 (ed. Hude, OCT) and (ii) Plutarch, *Life of Antony* 1–9, 23–36, 71–87 (ed. Pelling, Cambridge

University Press 1988). Alternative texts for translation under this head may be offered by agreement with the Graduate Studies Committee.

(iii) *Elementary Latin.* There will be one three-hour paper, consisting of passages of Latin prose which will test knowledge of classical Latin grammar and competence in translation from Latin into English.

(iv) *Intermediate Latin.* There will be one three-hour paper. Candidates will be expected to be familiar with *An Anthology of Latin Prose* ed. D. A. Russell (Oxford University Press 1990), nos. 7, 12, 22, 23, 34, 52, 63, from which a selection of passages will be set for translation. Candidates will also be expected to translate from (i) Cicero, *Pro Caelio* [ed. Clark OCT] and (ii) Pliny, *Letters*, 1.6, 9, 13, 19; VII.21, 24, 26, 29, VIII.16, 17; IX.6, 12, 15, 27, 33, 39; X.31, 32, 96, 97 (ed. M. B. Fisher and M. R. Griffin, Cambridge University Press 1973). Alternative texts for translation under this head may be offered by agreement with the Graduate Studies Committee.

(v) French

(vi) German

(vii) Italian

(viii) Any other language which the candidate has satisfied the Graduate Studies Committee in Ancient History is relevant to their other papers including any dissertation.

B

(i) Greek Numismatics.

(ii) Roman Numismatics.

(iii) Greek Epigraphy.

(iv) The epigraphy of the Roman World.

(v) Documentary papyrology.

(vi) any of the following papers on the B list of the M.St. in Greek and/or Latin Language and Literature: (i)–(iv); (vii).

(vii) any of the papers from Schedule B of the M.St. in Classical Archaeology.

(viii) any other subject approved by the Graduate Studies Committee in Ancient History.

C

(i) The Greeks and the Mediterranean world, 900–500 BC. Candidates will be expected to show knowledge of the material evidence from the Greek world and the areas of contact between Greek and other Mediterranean peoples.

(ii) Herodotus and Greek History 650–479 BC.

(iii) Greek Archaeology 500–323 BC. Candidates will be expected to show knowledge of the architecture, sculpture, vase-painting and other applied arts of the period, with an ability to apply the evidence of excavation and coinage where appropriate.

(iv) Thucydides and Greek History, 479–403 BC.

(v) Greek History from the end of the Peloponnesian War to the death of Philip of Macedon.

(vi) Athenian Democracy in the Classical Age. Candidates will be expected to show knowledge of the social, administrative and constitutional developments in Athens from 462 to 321 BC, but will only be required to show such knowledge of external affairs as is necessary for an understanding of the working of Athenian democracy.

(vii) Alexander the Great.
(viii) Hellenistic History 323–200 BC.
(ix) Rome and the Greek East 240–146 BC.
(x) The Archaeology and Art of Roman Italy in the Late Republic and Early Empire. Candidates will be expected to show knowledge of the material culture of Italy in the period *c*.200 BC–AD 200, of problems of method and chronology, and an ability to apply numismatic and written evidence where appropriate.
(xi) Rome in the late Republic, 146 BC–44 BC.
(xii) Cicero.
(xiii) The establishment of the Principate from the Dictatorship of Caesar to the death of Tiberius.
(xiv) Cities and Settlement in the Roman Empire. Candidates will be expected to show knowledge of the cities of the Roman Empire, from Augustus to the Tetrarchy, and of the changing forms and patterns of urban and other settlement.
(xv) The early Principate, AD 14 to AD 70.
(xvi) Civic life of the Roman Empire from the Flavian to the Severan Period Candidates will be expected to show knowledge of the economic, social and cultural history of the cities of the Roman Empire in the second century AD, and to show an adequate knowledge of the general history of the period.
(xvii) The Roman Empire 31 BC to AD 284.
(xviii) The Roman Empire AD 284–410.
(xix) Religion, Culture, and Society, from Julian the Apostate to Saint Augustine, AD 350–395.
(xx) Greek Historians and Historiography.
(xxi) Roman Historians and Historiography.
(xxii) The History of Sexuality in archaic and classical Greece.
(xxiii) Greek Religion. (xxiv) Roman Religion. In addition to Roman religion in the narrow sense, religious phenomena of the Graeco-Roman world in the Roman Period (including relevant aspects of Judaism and Christianity) may be studied under this heading.
(xxv) Roman Egypt. (xxvi) Roman Gaul.
(xxvii) The Church in the Roman Empire from the beginnings to AD 312.
(xxviii) Roman Private Law.
(xxix) The Economy of the Roman Empire.
(xxx) The Ecology, Agriculture, and Settlement History of the central. Mediterranean area 100 BC–AD 600.
(xxxi) The City of Rome. This option is run in collaboration with the British School at Rome, and involves attendance at the residential course organized by the School annually in Rome; only those accepted by the School may take the option. Applications for places should be made through the Graduate Studies Committee by the end of Michaelmas Term.
(xxxii) Athens and Attica. This option is run in collaboration with the British School in Athens, and involves attendance at the residential course organized by the School in alternate years at Athens (beginning in 1998); only those accepted by the School may take the option. Applications for places should be made through the Graduate Studies Committee by the end of Michaelmas Term.
(xxxiii) Any other subject approved by the Graduate Studies Committee in Ancient History.

D

A dissertation of not more than 10,000 words on a subject to be approved by the Graduate Studies Committee in Ancient History. (The dissertation word limit excludes the bibliography, any text that is being edited or annotated, any translation of that text, and any descriptive catalogue or similar factual matter, but includes quotations, notes, and appendices.)

The dissertation (two typewritten or printed copies) must be sent in a parcel bearing the words 'Dissertation for the M.St. in Greek and/or Roman History' to The Chairman of the Examiners, c/o The Clerk of the Schools, Examinations Schools, High Street, Oxford, to arrive no later than noon on the Thursday of the sixth week of the Trinity Full Term in which the examination is to be taken.

6. All options, including the dissertation, require the approval of the candidate's supervisor and the Graduate Studies Committee in Ancient History, having regard to the candidate's previous experience, the range covered by the chosen options and the availability of teaching and examining resources. The options must be submitted for approval not later than the Friday of the fifth week of the Michaelmas Term in the academic year in which the candidate intends to be examined. Candidates will not normally be allowed to be examined in languages of which they are native speakers or which they have previously studied in taught courses for more than two years.

Historical Research

The regulations of the Board of the Faculty of Modern History are as follows:

1. Every candidate for the M.St. must follow for at least three terms a course of instruction in Historical Research, and must, upon entering the examination, produce from his or her society a certificate to that effect.

2. *Syllabus*

(*a*) Every candidate must attend such lectures, seminars, and classes as his or her supervisor shall determine.

(*b*) Every candidate must present one seminar paper of up to 2,500 words during the course related to his or her intended research. A written version of the paper must be submitted at the end of the seminar at which it is delivered; it must be assessed by one or two assessors (such assessors should not normally include the candidate's supervisor) and the mark submitted to the examiners. The assessors will notify the candidate within a week if the presentation has not reached the required standard, in which case an additional period will be allowed for revision and resubmission of the paper. The work done for the seminar paper may form the basis of *either* the extended essay required under 2(c) below, *or* the dissertation required under 2(d) below.

(*c*) Every candidate must, after consultation with his or her supervisor,
either (i) submit an extended essay of up to 5,000 words in one of the following subjects relevant to the general area of the candidate's intended research:
either material covered in a specified training course
or a skill involved in the pursuit of research (to be demonstrated on historical material relevant to the candidate's research topic)
or historiography and/or bibliography in the broad area in which the candidate's thesis topic lies. The essay should test a candidate's work in a class or seminar attended over a period of at least one term. Notice of the subject of the essay must reach the Chairman of the Examiners for the M.St. in Historical Research by the Friday of fourth week of Hilary Term. Two typewritten copies of the essay must be sent to the Chairman of the

Examiners, c/o Clerk of the Schools, Examination Schools, High Street, Oxford, not later than noon on Monday of third week of Trinity Term **or (ii)** offer an examination paper in a language or skill relevant to the candidate's research topic, on the recommendation of the candidate's supervisor and the period interviewer, and approved by the Director of Graduate Studies not later than Friday of fourth week of Michaelmas Term. Such permission will only be granted for languages or skills which the candidate has not acquired in advance of the course. The candidate should normally be told the format and timing of the examination by the second Monday of Hilary Full Term. The examination has to take place by Friday of seventh week of Trinity Term at the latest.

(*d*) Every candidate must submit a dissertation of not more than 10,000 words. This should be either a section of the candidate's proposed thesis or an essay on a relevant topic, and it should be accompanied by a brief statement, limited to 500 words, of the subject of the thesis and the manner in which the candidate proposes to treat it.

Two typewritten copies of the dissertation must be sent to the Chairman of Examiners, c/o Clerk of the Schools, Examination Schools, High Street, Oxford, not later than noon on Friday of fifth week of Trinity Term.

3. Candidates must present themselves for an oral examination. In this examination the dissertation referred to in 2(*d*) will be discussed, and the candidate's general command of his/her field will be tested.

4. The examiners may award a distinction to candidates who have performed with special merit in the examination.

5. The Examiners may give permission that a candidate who fails one element of the examination may re-sit that part at the end of the following long vacation. Such re-submission constitutes the one re-entry into the examination permitted by the decree for the degree of Master of Studies. A candidate who fails more than one element and desires to re-sit must re-take the entire examination at the end of the next academic year.

Historical Research (Medieval History)

The regulations of the Board of the Faculty of Modern History are as follows:

1. Candidates for the M.St. in Historical Research (Medieval History) must follow for at least three terms a course of instruction and directed research and must, upon entering the examination, produce from their society a certificate to that effect.

2. Candidates will be required to choose an area or topic of historical study within the field of medieval history, which will be subject to the approval of the Graduate Studies Committee of the Board of Modern History. Candidates will be required to direct their study to this chosen area or topic during Michaelmas and/or Hilary Terms. Candidates must submit to the Chairman of the Examiners of the M.St. in Historical Research (Medieval History) by Friday of first week of Trinity Term two typewritten copies of a piece of written work (between 3,500 and 5,000 words) normally based on an aspect of historiography or methodology relevant to this area or topic of historical study.

3. Candidates must attend such skills seminars and associated courses as the supervisor shall determine. On the recommendation of the candidate's supervisor and the period interviewer, if approved by the Director of Graduate Studies not later than Friday of fourth week of Michaelmas Term, such skills may include formal training in a language relevant for the candidate's original research. The candidate should normally be told the format and timing of the language examination by the second Monday of Hilary Term, and the examination has to take place before the end of ninth week of Trinity Term. Unless given leave to take a language examination, candidates must submit to the Chairman of the Examiners of the M.St. in Historical

Research (Medieval History) by Friday of first week of Trinity Term two typewritten copies of an extended essay (between 5,000 and 7,000 words) based on one of the skills or associated courses.

4. Candidates will be required to attend a weekly seminar on the interpretation of historical evidence for the medieval period.

5. The examiners may make the marks awarded to the candidates for the written work and extended essay known to the Director of Graduate Studies where necessary for the purpose of grant applications. However, the pass list shall be issued only following the completion of the whole examination, including submission of the dissertation, in September or October.

6. Candidates must choose a dissertation subject, after due consultation with their supervisor, within the area or topic of historical study referred to in clause 2. above.

7. Candidates are required to submit two typewritten copies of a dissertation, which shall not normally exceed 15,000 words, to the Chairman of the Examiners by 31 August of the academic year in which they are registered for the degree.

8. Candidates are required to present themselves for an oral examination if and when required by the examiners.

9. The examiners may award a distinction to candidates who have performed with special merit in the examination.

10. The Examiners may give permission that candidates who fail one of the essays outlined in clause 5 above may hand in a revised version of the work to the Chairman of Examiners by 31 August of the academic year in which they are registered for the degree for re-assessment within the same examination process. Such revision would *not* constitute a re-entry into the examination. After the final examination in the autumn, the Examiners may give permission that candidates who fail the examination on the basis of the dissertation element, or whose revised essay is still found unsatisfactory, may re-submit the unsatisfactory piece of work at the end of the following Michaelmas Term. Such re-submission would constitute the one re-entry into the examination permitted by the decree for the degree of Master of Studies. Candidates who fail more than one element of the examination and desire to re-sit must re-take the entire examination at the end of the next academic year.

History of Art and Visual Culture

(See also the general notice at the commencement of these regulations.)

The regulations of the Board of the Faculty of Modern History are as follows:

1. Every candidate must follow for at least three terms a course of instruction in the History of Art, and must, upon entering for the examination, produce from his or her society a certificate to this effect.

2. *Syllabus*

The course shall comprise: I, one compulsory paper; II, one optional paper chosen by the candidate; and III, a dissertation.

I. The compulsory paper entitled 'An introduction to historiography and methods of art history' is taken in Michaelmas Term and will comprise one extended essay of between 4,000 and 5,000 words and a written examination in Trinity Term.

II. Optional papers covering topics and issues of art history and visual culture from the later Middle Ages to the present, as approved from time to time by the Committee of the History of Art, are taken in Hilary Term. A definitive list of the optional papers available in any one year will be posted on the notice boards of the Department of the History of Art and of the Faculty of Modern History by Friday of Fourth Week of Michaelmas Term at the latest. Optional papers will be examined by two extended essays of between 4,000 and 5,000 words.

III. A dissertation of not more than 15,000 words on a topic in the history of art, to be approved by the candidate's supervisor and the Professor of the History of

Art prior to the submission of essay and dissertation titles to the Chairman of Examiners for the degree.

3. Candidates shall make written application for the approval of the titles of their extended essays in their optional paper, and also notify the examiners of the title of their dissertation, by Friday of Fourth Week of Hilary Term. Communications with the examiners should be addressed to the Chairman of Examiners for the M.St. in History of Art and Visual Culture, c/o The Clerk of the Schools, Examination Schools, High Street, Oxford, OX1 4BG.

4. Two typewritten or printed copies of the extended essay for the compulsory paper must be sent to the Chairman of the Examiners at the address above by noon on Friday of Week One of Hilary Term. Two typewritten or printed copies of each extended essay for the optional paper must be sent to the Chairman of the Examiners at the same address by noon on Friday of Week Nine of Hilary Term. Two typewritten or printed copies of the dissertation must be sent to the Chairman of Examiners at the same address by noon on Friday of Week Seven of Trinity Term. The dissertation must include a short abstract which concisely summarizes its scope and principal arguments, in about 300 words. Both the essays and the dissertations must be (individually) securely and firmly bound in either hard or soft covers; and the presentation and footnotes should comply with the requirements specified in the Regulations of the Educational Policy and Standards Committee for the degrees of M.Litt. and D.Phil. and follow the *Conventions for the presentation of dissertations and theses* of the Board of the Faculty of Modern History.

5. Candidates must present themselves for an oral examination if required to do so by the examiners.

6. The examiners may award a distinction for excellence in the whole examination.

7. A candidate who fails the examination will be permitted to re-take the examination on one further occasion only, not later than one year after the initial attempt. Such a candidate whose dissertation has been of satisfactory standard will not be required to re-submit the dissertation, while a candidate who has reached a satisfactory standard on *both* the extended essays and the written examination paper will not be required to re-take those parts of the examination.

International Human Rights Law

1. Candidates must follow a course of instruction in International Human Rights Law. The course will be taken on a part-time basis over a period of six terms.

2. Every candidate will be required to satisfy the examiners in the following:

(*a*) attendance at classes, individual tutorials, group seminars, and other teaching sessions as required;

(*b*) four written papers, each of three hours' duration, as set out below:

- (i) Fundamentals of Human Rights Law
- (ii) Human Rights Advocacy I
- (iii) Human Rights Advocacy II
- (iv) an elective paper, to be chosen from the schedule below;

(*c*) a pre-course portfolio consisting of six essays, each of 2,000 words in length, covering key concepts and issues of the course;

(*d*) a written portfolio consisting of three essays or exercises, each of 1,500 words in length, covering the period of supervised private study;

(*e*) a research skills portfolio of five short exercises, covering skills required in the production of a dissertation, and a statement of 1,000 words in length which identifies the dissertation topic, hypothesis and methodology and provides an outline of the dissertation and schedule for completion;

(*f*) submission of a dissertation of no more than 15,000 words on a topic selected by the student in consultation with the tutor and agreed by the Board of Studies, to be forwarded to the examiners c/o Registry, Department for

Continuing Education, Wellington Square, Oxford, OX1 2JA, for receipt by such date as the examiners shall determine and shall notify the candidates and tutors.

3. Candidates may be required to attend a viva voce examination at the end of the course of study at the discretion of the examiners.

4. The examiners may award a distinction for excellence in the whole examination.

5. Candidates who fail to satisfy the examiners in the written examinations under 2(*b*), the written portfolios under 2(*c*)–(*e*), or the dissertation under 2(*f*) may be permitted to resubmit work in respect of the part or parts of the examination which they have failed for examination on not more than one occasion which shall normally be within one year of the original failure.

Schedule

(i) Rights of Minorities, Groups and Indigenous Peoples
(ii) International Human Rights and Refugee Law
(iii) International Human Rights of Women
(iv) Human Rights and the International Criminal Process.

Islamic Art and Archaeology

1. Candidates must satisfy the Board of the Faculty of Oriental Studies before admission to the course that they possess the necessary qualifications in Arabic or Persian or Ottoman Turkish to profit by the course.

2. Every candidate must follow for at least three terms a course of instruction in Islamic Art and Archaeology. Candidates will, when they enter for the examination, be required to produce from their society a certificate that they are following such a course.

3. The examiners may award a distinction for excellence in the whole examination.

4. *Syllabus.*

(*a*) *Attendance.* Every candidate must attend such lectures, seminars, and classes as his or her supervisor shall determine, and must, upon entering the examination, provide evidence of his or her attendance to the examiners.

(*b*) *Written Examination.* Every candidate must take three written papers, as follows:

I. **From Late Antiquity to Islam**

Aspects of the art and archaeology of the Near East during the transition from Late Antiquity to the formation of Islam, 550–900.

II. **The Breakdown of the Caliphate**

Aspects of the art and archaeology of the Islamic world, 900–1250.

III. **The Great Empires**

Aspects of the art and archaeology of the Islamic world, 1250–1700.

(*c*) *Portfolio.* Candidates must submit a portfolio, containing reports on the practical work completed during their course (according to the schedule given in the Course Handbook) and signed by their supervisor, to the Clerk of the Schools, High Street, Oxford, not later than noon on the Monday of first week of Trinity Term of the year in which they sit the examination. The portfolio must bear the candidate's examination number (but not the candidate's name, which must be concealed), must contain a signed declaration that the work is the candidate's own, and must be contained in a parcel bearing the words 'PORTFOLIO FOR THE M.ST. IN ISLAMIC ART AND ARCHAEOLOGY' in block capitals in the bottom left-hand corner.

(*d*) *Thesis.* Every candidate must submit a thesis of approximately 15,000 words on a subject in Islamic Art and Archaeology to be approved by the Board of the Faculty of Oriental Studies not later than its second meeting in Michaelmas Term. Candidates must submit two bound, typewritten or printed copies of the thesis to the Clerk of the Schools, High Street, Oxford, on or before the first Monday in September in the year in which they sit the examination. The thesis must bear the candidate's examination number (but not the candidate's name, which must be concealed), must contain a signed declaration that the work is the candidate's own, and must be contained in a parcel bearing the words 'THESIS FOR THE M.ST. IN ISLAMIC ART AND ARCHAEOLOGY' in block capitals in the bottom left-hand corner.

(*e*) *Oral Examination.* Every candidate will be examined viva voce unless exempted by the examiners.

Islamic Art and Archaeology (Research Methods and Techniques)

1. Candidates must satisfy the Board of the Faculty of Oriental Studies before admission to the course that they possess the necessary qualifications in Arabic or Persian or Ottoman Turkish to profit by the course.

2. Every candidate must follow for at least three terms a course of instruction in Islamic Art and Archaeology. Candidates will, when they enter for the examination, be required to produce from their society a certificate that they are following such a course.

3. The examiners may award a distinction for excellence in the whole examination.

4. *Syllabus*

(*a*) *Attendance.* Every candidate must attend such lectures, seminars, and classes as his or her supervisor shall determine, and must, upon entering the examination, provide evidence of his or her attendance to the examiners.

(*b*) *Portfolio.* Candidates must submit a portfolio, containing reports on the practical work completed during their course (according to the schedule given in the Course Handbook) and signed by their supervisor, to the Clerk of the Schools, High Street, Oxford, not later than noon on the Monday of first week of Trinity Term of the year in which they sit the examination. The portfolio must bear the candidate's examination number (but not the candidate's name, which must be concealed), must contain a signed declaration that the work is the candidate's own, and must be contained in a parcel bearing the words 'PORTFOLIO FOR THE M.ST. IN ISLAMIC ART AND ARCHAEOLOGY (RESEARCH METHODS AND TECHNIQUES)' in block capitals in the bottom left-hand corner.

(*c*) *Essays on Research Methods and Techniques.* Candidates will be required to submit an essay of approximately 5,000 words on each of two subjects in Islamic Art and Archaeology chosen from the following list with the approval of the Board of the Faculty of Oriental Studies not later than its second meeting in Michaelmas Term.

1. Archaeology
2. Architecture
3. Ceramics
4. Metalwork
5. Numismatics
6. Painting
7. Textiles
8. Another subject to be approved by the Board of the Faculty of Oriental Studies.

Candidates must submit two copies of the two essays in (*c*) above to the Clerk of the Schools, High Street, Oxford, not later than noon on the Monday of first week of Trinity Term of the year in which they sit the examination. The essays must be typewritten or printed, must bear the candidate's examination number (but not the candidate's name, which must be concealed), must contain a signed declaration that the work is the candidate's own, and must be contained in a parcel bearing the words 'ESSAYS FOR THE M.ST. IN ISLAMIC ART AND ARCHAEOLOGY (RESEARCH METHODS AND TECHNIQUES)' in block capitals in the bottom left-hand corner.

(*d*) *Thesis.* Every candidate must submit a thesis of approximately 15,000 words upon a chosen subject to be approved by the Board of the Faculty of Oriental Studies not later than its second meeting in Michaelmas Term, which may be an essay on a topic relevant to the subject for the proposed D.Phil. or M.Litt. thesis, or a discussion of the historical and archaeological/art historical background of the subject on which the student proposes to work, or what might become a short section of the thesis.

Candidates must submit two typewritten or printed copies of the thesis to the Clerk of the Schools, High Street, Oxford, on or before the first Monday in September in the year in which they sit the examination. The thesis must bear the candidate's examination number (but not the candidate's name, which must be concealed), must contain a signed declaration that the work is the candidate's own, and must be contained in a parcel bearing the words 'THESIS FOR THE M.ST. IN ISLAMIC ART AND ARCHAEOLOGY (RESEARCH METHODS AND TECHNIQUES)' in block capitals in the bottom left-hand corner.

(*e*) *Written Examination.* Candidates will be required to sit one paper chosen from Papers I–III of the M.St. in Islamic Art and Archaeology.

(*f*) *Oral Examination.* Every candidate will be examined viva voce unless exempted by the examiners.

Japanese Studies

1. Candidates must *either* have taken Japanese in the Oxford Honour School of Oriental Studies *or* have taken a comparable degree from another university, *or* must satisfy the Board of the Faculty of Oriental Studies that they possess the necessary qualifications in the Japanese language to profit by the course.

2. Every candidate must follow for at least three terms a course of instruction in Japanese Studies. Candidates will, when they enter for the examination, be required to produce from their society a certificate that they are so doing.

3. *Syllabus*

There will be three written examination papers and a dissertation, as specified below.

I. Prescribed texts, with special reference to a subject approved by the board. Texts will be announced by the board in the seventh week of Michaelmas Full Term preceding the examination.

II. *Either* Classical Japanese translation
or Classical or Modern Chinese
or Korean.

The choice of language will be subject to approval by the faculty board.

III. Bibliography and research methods with special reference to the subject chosen in Paper I.

The examination will take the form of the exercises to be set at the conclusion of the two papers (I and II). Each candidate will be assigned one or more exercises set on a topic directly relating to the course of instruction he or she has followed, and will be required to submit a written answer to the Chairman of Examiners, c/o Clerk of Schools, Examination Schools, High Street, Oxford, by a date which the Chairman will announce, but which shall, in any case, be not sooner than two days and not later than seven days from the date on which Paper II is taken.

IV. A dissertation of not more than 15,000 words on a topic approved by the board by Friday of the seventh week of Michaelmas Full Term. The dissertation must be sent to the Chairman of Examiners, c/o Clerk of the Schools, Examination Schools, High Street, Oxford, not later than noon on Friday of the fifth week of Trinity Full Term.

4. Every candidate will be examined viva voce unless he or she shall have been individually excused by the examiners.

5. The examiners may award a distinction for excellence in the whole examination.

Jewish Studies

1. Every candidate must follow for at least three terms a course of instruction in Jewish Studies. Candidates will, when they enter for the examination, be required to produce from their society a certificate that they are doing so.

2. *Syllabus*

I. Three terms of *either* Biblical Hebrew, *or* Modern Hebrew, *or* Yiddish. Written examination will take place at the end of Trinity Term.

II. *Six* options from the following list, *three* to be taken in Michaelmas Term, *three* in Hilary Term.

Three options will be examined by essay. Three options will be examined by written examination. Candidates may choose which options are examined by essay and which by written examination. The three essays, of not more than 4,000 words each on subjects set by the examiners, are to be submitted to the Clerk of the Schools, High Street, Oxford by 12 noon on the Friday of Noughth Week of Trinity Term. Candidates will be notified of the essay topics by the Chairman of Examiners at 12 noon on the Friday of 8th Week of Hilary Term.

1. Dead Sea Scrolls
2. Introduction to Judaism
3. Introduction to Maimonides
4. Introduction to Talmud
5. Israeli Government and Politics
6. Jewish and Christian Bible Translation and Interpretation in Antiquity
7. Jewish History 200 BCE to 70 CE
8. Judaism and Islam: Medieval Intellectual Traditions
9. Modern European Jewish History
10. Questions of Jewish Identity in Yiddish Literature
11. Speech and Silence: Methods of Response in Modern Hebrew Literature
12. Survey of Medieval Jewish History
13. The Emergence of Modern Religious Movements in Judaism
14. The History of the Arab–Israeli Conflict
15. The Rise of Formative Judaism and Christianity
16. Witnessing the Holocaust
17. Such other options as may be approved by the Oriental Studies Board.

Teaching for some options may not be available every year.

III. Each candidate shall be required to present a dissertation of not more than 10,000 words, on a subject approved by the Committee for Graduate Studies of the Oriental Studies Board, to the Clerk of the Schools by 12 noon on Friday of the sixth week of Trinity Full Term in the year in which he or she completes the course.

3. Candidates may be called for a viva voce examinatiion.

4. The examiners may award a distinction to candidates for excellence in the whole examination.

Jewish Studies in the Graeco-Roman Period

1. Candidates must satisfy the Board of the Faculty of Oriental Studies before admission to the course that they possess the necessary qualification in the Hebrew

language to profit by the course. Those wishing to take options (*e*) or (*f*) must show evidence of their knowledge of Greek.

2. Every candidate must follow for at least three terms a course of study in Jewish Studies in the Graeco-Roman Period. Candidates will, when they enter for the examination, be required to produce from their society a certificate that they are doing so.

3. *Syllabus*

There will be four papers:

I. Essay questions on Jewish history and institutions from 200 BC to AD 135.

II–IV. Prescribed texts. Passages for translation and comment and essay questions (a passage, or passages, for unprepared translation may also be set) on three of the following:

(*a*) Dead Sea scrolls
(*b*) Mishnah
(*c*) Midrash
(*d*) Targum
(*e*) Septuagint
(*f*) Hellenistic Jewish literature
or any other subject approved by the board.

Texts will be announced by the board in the third week of Michaelmas Full Term preceding the examination.

Every candidate will be examined viva voce unless he shall have been individually excused by the examiners.

The examiners may award a distinction for excellence in the whole examination.

Teaching for some options may not be available in every year. Applicants for admission will be advised of this.

Korean Studies

1. Candidates must have a knowledge of Korean at least up to the standard of a first degree.

2. Every candidate must follow for at least three terms a course of instruction in Korean Studies. Candidates will, when they enter for the examination, be required to produce from their society a certificate that they are doing so.

3. *Syllabus*

I. Prescribed texts, to be announced by the board in the Oriental Institute in the seventh week of Michaelmas Full Term preceding the examination.

II. *either* Modern Korean unprepared translation
or Classical Chinese
or Modern Japanese

Candidates who already possess a sufficient knowledge of Modern Korean will be required to choose Classical Chinese or Modern Japanese.

III. Bibliography and techniques of Koreanology.

The examination will take the form of exercises to be set at the conclusion of the two papers (I and II) taken in the Examination Schools. Each candidate will be assigned one or more exercises set on a topic directly relating to the course of instruction he or she has followed, and will be required to submit a written answer to the chairman of examiners by a date which the chairman will announce at the conclusion of the written papers, but which shall, in any case, be not sooner than two days and not later than seven days from the date of the examination.

IV. A dissertation of not more than 15,000 words on a topic approved by the board at its second meeting in Michaelmas Term. The dissertation must be sent to the Chairman of Examiners, c/o Clerk of the Schools, Examination Schools, High Street, Oxford, not later than noon on Friday of the fifth week of Trinity Full Term.

4. Every candidate will be examined viva voce unless he or she shall have been individually excused by the examiners.

5. The examiners may award a distinction for excellence in the whole examination.

Legal Research

1. Candidates for admission to the course will be required to produce evidence of their appropriate qualifications for the course.

2. Candidates must follow a course of instruction in Legal Research Method approved by the Law Board, and must satisfy the examiners that they have completed to the required standard such tests or exercises in Legal Research Methods as may be prescribed by the Law Board as part of such a course of instruction. Where the Law Board judges that it has sufficient evidence of a candidate's proficiency in legal research method, it may in exceptional circumstances dispense a candidate from this requirement.

3. Every candidate on admission as a student shall be placed by the board of the Law Faculty under the supervision of a graduate member of the University or other competent person selected by the board, and the board shall have power for sufficient reasons to change the supervisor of any student.

4. Examination for the Degree shall be by thesis, and by oral examination. The thesis must not exceed 30,000 words and should not normally be less than 25,000 words in length (the limit to include all notes but to exclude all tables and bibliography, and the candidate to state the number of words in the thesis to the nearest hundred words). The examiners must satisfy themselves that the thesis affords evidence of serious study by the candidate and of ability to discuss a difficult problem critically; that the candidate possesses a good general knowledge of the field of learning within which the subject of the thesis falls; that the thesis is presented in a lucid and scholarly manner, and that the candidate has made a worthwhile contribution to knowledge or understanding in the field of learning within which the subject of the thesis falls to the extent that could reasonably be expected within the time normally spent as a student for the Degree.

5. At any time not earlier than the third nor later than the fifth term after the term of admission, a candidate may apply to the Board for examination. Such application shall be made to the Secretary of Faculties and shall be accompanied by

(1) a statement as to what part, if any, of his or her thesis has already been accepted, or is being currently submitted, for any degree in this University or elsewhere;

(2) a statement that the thesis is the candidate's own work, except where otherwise indicated;

(3) two copies or, if leave has been obtained from the Board of the Faculty of Law, one copy of his or her thesis either at the same time as his or her application or at such later time as the Educational Policy and Standards Committee shall by regulation permit. The thesis must be securely and firmly bound in either hard or soft covers. Loose-leaf binding is not acceptable.

6. On receipt of any such application the Secretary of Faculties shall submit it to the Board. The Board shall thereupon appoint two examiners whose duties shall be:

(1) to consider the thesis sent in by the student under the provisions of the preceding clause, provided that they shall exclude from consideration in making their report any part of the thesis which has already been accepted, or is being concurrently submitted, for any degree in this University or elsewhere, and shall have the power to require the candidate to produce for their inspection the complete thesis so accepted or concurrently submitted.

(2) to examine the candidate orally on the subject of his or her thesis and on subjects relevant to his or her field of study, and, if they wish on such matters as will enable them to discharge their duties under sub-paragraph (3) or (4);

(3) to report to the Board whether on the basis of the thesis submitted, the oral examination, and, where applicable, the report referred to in paragraph (7), the candidate:

(i) should be awarded the Degree;

(ii) should be awarded the Degree with Distinction; or

(iii) should be given the opportunity to re-submit for the Degree within a further three terms.

The Educational Policy and Standards Committee shall have power, on the application of a faculty board in a special case, to authorise the appointment of a third examiner (or an assessor), upon such conditions and to perform such functions as the committee shall approve; any fee paid to such an additional examiner or assessor shall be met from the funds at the disposal of the committee.

The Educational Policy and Standards Committee shall have power to make regulations concerning the notice to be given of the oral examination and of the time and place at which it may be held.

7. On receipt of the report of the examiners, it shall be the duty of the board to decide whether the candidate is qualified to supplicate for the Degree of Master of Studies, with or without the award of a Distinction, and, if not, to indicate that the candidate should be given the opportunity to apply for re-examination.

The board may not permit the candidate to supplicate for the degree unless and until the Director of the Course in Legal Research Method, failing whom the Director of Graduate Studies (Research), has certified that the candidate has satisfied or been exempted from the requirements of that course.

8. If the board has adopted a recommendation that the candidate be given the opportunity to resubmit, and the candidate indicates the wish to take up that opportunity, the candidate shall retain the status and obligations of a Student for the Degree of Master of Studies and shall be permitted to apply to be re-examined within the period specified in para.6 (5) (iii) above. Upon receiving such an application, the Board may reappoint the previous examiners, or may appoint different examiners instead of any or all of the previous examiners, as it shall judge appropriate.

9. The board may exempt any candidate who has re-submitted for the Degree from oral examination provided that the examiners are satisfied, without examining the candidate orally, that they can recommend to the board that the candidate has reached the standard required for the Degree.

Modern History

The regulations of the Board of the Faculty of Modern History are as follows:

1. Candidates must satisfy the board that they have sufficient reading knowledge of the relevant languages to follow the course.

2. Every candidate must follow for at least three terms a course of instruction in Modern History and must upon entering for the examination produce from his or her society a certificate to that effect.

3. *Syllabus*

The examination shall comprise: I, two extended essays of up to 5,000 words and the seminar presentation; II, an examination paper; and III, a dissertation of up to 15,000 words.

Teaching may not be available for all periods and subjects every year, and candidates are advised to enquire when they submit their applications for admission.

I. *Extended essays and Seminar Presentation*

Either (*a*) two essays and one seminar presentation in any one of the periods in British or European History in the list (i)–(x) below:

Medieval history

(i) British history, 300–1100;

(ii) British history, 1000–1500;

(iii) European history, 300–1100;

(iv) European history, 1000–1500;

Early modern history

(v) British history, 1450–1750;

(vi) European history; 1450–1750;

Modern history

(vii) British history, 1750–1918;

(viii) British history, 1914 to the present;

(ix) European history, 1750–1918;

(x) European history, 1914 to the present;

In periods (v) to (x) candidates may elect, with the support of their supervisor, to take an appropriate Optional Subject from the M.Phil. in Modern European History.

On application by the candidate's supervisor the Course Convenor jointly with the Director of Graduate Studies shall have power to approve relevant taught papers from other Masters' courses within the Faculty. A complete list of the available taught papers in Masters' courses within the Faculty of Modern History will be posted on the Faculty notice board not later than Friday of Third week of Michaelmas Term.

or (*b*) two essays and one seminar presentation in any one of the periods in the History of the British Commonwealth and Empire and South Asian History from the list (i)–(iii) below:

British Commonwealth History

(i) since *c.*1840;

South Asian History

(ii) India and the World Economy, 1700–1860;

(iii) Aspects of social change in South Asia, *c.*1860 to the present

or (*c*) two essays and one seminar presentation in the History of the United States of America from the 18th century to the present:

Topics in the History of the United States of America from the 18th century to the present.

II. *An examination paper in the area of study elected under I above:*

Medieval history, 300–1500

Issues and approaches in medieval history

Political and social thought: Scholasticism and Humanism (see note (*a*))

Early modern history, 1450–1750

Methods in early modern history

Source criticism

Historical controversies

Modern history, 1750 to the present

Modern political and social theory

Source criticism

Historical controversies

Concepts and methods of imperial history (see note (*a*))

Quantitative methods and computer applications for historians (see note (*a*))

British Commonwealth History

Concepts and methods of imperial history

South Asian History
Concepts and methods in South Asian History
United States History
Methods and evidence in the History of the United States of America
Note (*a*): These options are only available on application by the candidate's supervisor, and the choice must be approved by the Course Convenor jointly with the Director of Graduate Studies.

III. *Dissertation*
A dissertation of not more than 15,000 words on a topic falling within the scope of the period chosen by the candidate for the extended essays under I above.

4. Candidates should make written application for the approval of the essay and dissertation topics, to reach the Chairman of the Examiners for the M.St. in Modern History, c/o The Graduate Office, Modern History Faculty, Broad Street, Oxford, not later than Friday of the Fourth Week of Hilary Term. All applications should be accompanied by a recommendation from the supervisor.

5. Two typewritten copies of the extended essays must be sent to the Chairman of the Examiners at the address above, by noon on Friday of Noughth Week of Trinity Term at the latest.

6. Two typewritten copies of the dissertation must be sent to the Chairman of the Examiners at the address above, by noon on Friday of Sixth Week of Trinity Term at the latest.

7. Candidates must present themselves for an oral examination if required to do so by the examiners.

8. The examiners may award a distinction to candidates who have performed with special merit in all parts of the examination.

9. A candidate who fails the examination will be permitted to retake it on one further occasion only, not later than one year after the initial attempt. Such a candidate whose dissertation has been of satisfactory standard may re-submit the same piece of work, while a candidate who has reached a satisfactory standard on both the extended essays and the written examination paper will not be required to retake those parts of the examination.

Modern Jewish Studies

1. Candidates must satisfy the board that they possess the necessary qualification in the Hebrew language to profit by the course. Those wishing to take option (9) must show evidence of their knowledge of Yiddish.

2. Every candidate must follow for at least three terms a course of instruction in Modern Jewish Studies. Candidates will, when they enter for the examination, be required to produce from their society a certificate that they are doing so.

3. *Syllabus*
There will be four papers. Candidates will be examined by written examination except that in lieu of a written examination in one subject a candidate may elect to submit an essay of not more than 8,000 words on the subject of his or her choice. Such a subject must be approved by the Committee for Graduate Studies of the Oriental Studies Board not later than at its last meeting in Hilary Term of the year in which the candidate takes the M.St. examination. Two typed copies of the essay must be delivered to the Clerk of the Schools on Friday of the Fifth Week of the Trinity Term in which the examination is written.

I. Passages for translation and comment and essay questions on prescribed texts in Hebrew. Texts will be announced by the Board of the Oriental Institute in the seventh week of Michaelmas Full Term preceding the examination.

II–IV. Three papers from the following list:

(1) Hebrew literature 1888–1948.

(2) The literature of the State of Israel.

(3) Jewish literature of the nineteenth and twentieth centuries.

(4) Major trends in Jewish religion and thought since 1789.

(5) The Jewish experience in Europe 1789–1945.

(6) The rise of Jewish nationalism.

(7) The history of the State of Israel.

(8) Introduction to modern Jewish sociology.

(9) Yiddish literature and culture.

(10) Muslim–Jewish relations in the modern world.

(11) Modern Jewish politics.

or any other subject approved by the Board.

Texts will be announced by the Board in the third week of Michaelmas Full Term preceding the examination.

Every candidate will be examined viva voce unless he shall have been individually excused by the examiners.

The examiners may award a distinction for excellence in the whole examination.

Teaching for some options may not be available in every year. Applicants for admission will be advised of this.

Modern Middle Eastern Studies

Only candidates with native fluency or who have satisfied the examiners in the Second Public Examination in Arabic or Hebrew or Persian or Turkish, or have passed a similar examination in another university, will be eligible to sit the Final Examination for the M.St. in Modern Middle Eastern Studies.

1. Candidates shall be required to attend for at least three terms such lecture courses and participate in such seminars as their supervisor shall specify, and to submit to the Clerk of the Schools not later than the end of the eighth week of the third term, or by such other time as the Graduate Studies Committee of the Board of the Faculty of Oriental Studies shall specify, a certificate (on a form available from the Oriental Studies Faculty) signed by the member of the academic staff responsible for the course or seminars concerned, confirming their attendance and participation.

Final Examination

2. All candidates must offer

(*a*) Two typed copies of a single piece of written work (presented in proper scholarly form) of no more than 10,000 words in length. The topic of the work must be approved by the Board of the Faculty of Oriental Studies at its first meeting in the Hilary Term preceding the examination. Candidates shall submit their written work to the Clerk of the Schools, High Street, Oxford, not later than the end of the sixth week of Trinity Term.

(*b*) two papers from (1)–(11), provided that instead of one of these papers, a candidate may offer a paper on a subject not included in the list below, with the approval of the board, such approval to be given by Friday of fourth week of the Hilary Term.

(1) History of the Middle East, 1860–1958.

(2) Politics of the Middle East.

(3) Economic history of the Middle East, 1800–1945.

(4) Economics of the Middle East.

(5) Geography of the Middle East.

(6) Social anthropology of the Middle East.

(7) Islam in the Middle East in the twentieth century.
(8) International Relations of the Middle East.
(9) Iranian history, 1797–1921.
(10) Iranian history, 1921–1979.
(11) History of Turkey, 1908–80.

Teaching for some options may not be available in every year. Applicants for admission will be advised whether teaching will be available in the options of their choice.

The subjects which candidates wish to offer for examination must be submitted for approval by the Oriental Studies Faculty Board at its first meeting in the Hilary Full Term preceding the examinations.

3. Candidates will be required to attend for oral examination on a date to be specified by the examiners or the assessors.

4. Entries for the examination must be made on the proper form, which may be obtained from the Head Clerk, University Offices, Wellington Square, and submitted on or before the eighth week of the Michaelmas Full Term following the candidate's admission.

5. The examiners may award a distinction for excellence in the whole examination.

Music (Musicology)

1. Every candidate for the M.St. must follow for at least three terms a course of instruction in musicology, and must, upon entering for the examination, produce from his or her society a certificate to that effect. Candidates must also satisfy the Board that they have, or will acquire, sufficient reading knowledge of the languages relevant to the course.

2. Syllabus

(*a*) Every candidate must attend such lectures, seminars, and classes as his or her supervisor, in consultation with the Director of Graduate Studies, shall determine, and must undertake such course work as may be required.

(*b*) Every candidate must take a three-hour written paper in Aesthetics, Criticism and Historiography of Music.

(*c*) Every candidate must submit an essay of not more than 10,000 words, together with a substantial, annotated bibliography. In the case of those wishing to continue their research for the degree of M.Litt. or D.Phil., the essay can be either a section of the candidate's proposed thesis, or an essay on a related topic.

(*d*) Every candidate must submit a portfolio of course-work consisting of at least four essays arising from the courses mentioned in 2(*a*), to be submitted not later than Friday of the eighth week of Trinity Term. Two typewritten copies of the essay required under 2(*c*) above must be submitted not later than the second Monday in July. All material must be sent to the Chairman of Examiners for the M.St. in Music (Musicology), c/o Clerk of the Schools, Examination Schools, High Street, Oxford.

The topic for the essay required under 2(*c*) above must be submitted for approval by the Director of Graduate Studies, Faculty of Music, by Monday of the third week of Hilary Term.

3. Candidates may be summoned for a viva voce examination, at which any aspect of the candidate's submissions and course work might be subject to discussion. The list of candidates required to present themselves for a viva voce examination will be published at a time to be announced by the examiners.

4. The examiners may award a distinction to candidates who have performed with special merit.

5. A candidate who fails the examination will be permitted to retake it on one further occasion only, not later than one year after the initial attempt. Such a candidate whose work has been of satisfactory standard on the course work related essays will not be required to resubmit the same pieces of work, while a candidate who has reached a satisfactory standard on the written examination paper will not be required to retake that part of the examination.

Oriental Studies

Admission is subject to the discretion of the Board of the Faculty of Oriental Studies. The faculty board will not permit students to be admitted to the course if an M.St. in a particular subject under the aegis of the board is considered more appropriate.

Requirements

1. Candidates shall be required to attend for at least three terms such lecture courses and participate in such seminars as their supervisor shall specify, and to submit to the Clerk of the Schools not later than the end of the eighth week of Trinity Term, or by such other time as the Graduate Studies Committee of the Board of the Faculty of Oriental Studies shall specify, a certificate (on a form available from the Oriental Studies Faculty) signed by the member of the academic staff responsible for the course or seminars concerned, confirming their attendance and participation.

2. The examination is in three parts. For the first part candidates may choose between two options, mode A or B.

MODE A

(i) Candidates shall submit to the Clerk of the Schools, High Street, Oxford, two typed copies of a piece of written work of not less than 5,000 and not more than 7,000 words in length. The piece of written work must be presented in proper scholarly form. Candidates shall specify how it relates to their proposed subject of research. The written work may be any one of the following:

(*a*) what might become part of a thesis for the M.Litt. or D.Phil.;
(*b*) an essay on the theoretical issues raised by the subject which the candidate is proposing for the thesis;
(*c*) an essay on a topic relevant to that subject;
(*d*) a discussion of the historical and literary background or of the source-material which is relevant to the proposed subject.

(ii) Candidates shall be required *either* to offer themselves for two papers on subjects approved by the board *or* to submit to the Clerk of the Schools two typed copies of a second piece of written work (also presented in proper scholarly form) of not less than 5,000 and not more than 7,000 words in length relevant to the proposed thesis for the M.Litt. or the D.Phil., subject to the approval of the faculty board.

MODE B

Candidates shall submit to the Clerk of the Schools two typed copies of a single piece of written work (presented in proper scholarly form) of approximately 12,000 words in length, being what might be a substantial draft chapter or chapters of a proposed thesis for the M.Litt. or the D.Phil.

3. For the second part of the examination each candidate will be required to write a prescribed essay on methods and research materials, relating to the area of study chosen for (2) above.

The topic will be set at the conclusion of the course, at a date which the chairman of examiners will announce. Each candidate will be required to submit the essay in proper scholarly form to the chairman of examiners not more than seven days after the assignment of the topic.

4. The board's decision on the candidate's choice of options as in 2 above shall be made after consultation with the supervisor no later than the Friday of the fourth week of Hilary Term.

5. The written work (other than the papers offered under mode A (ii) above and the essay under 3 above) must be submitted to the Clerk of the Schools not later than the end of the sixth week of the Trinity Term or by such other time as the Graduate Studies Committee of the Board of the Faculty of Oriental Studies shall specify. Examination papers offered under Mode A (ii) above, if offered, shall normally be sat in the eighth week of Trinity Term.

6. For the third part of the examination candidates will be required to attend for oral examination on a date to be specified by the examiners or the assessors (which will not be later than two weeks after that by which all written work has to be submitted).

7. Entries for the examination must be made on the proper form, which may be obtained from the Head Clerk, University Offices, Wellington Street, and submitted by Friday of the fifth week of the Hilary Term following the candidate's admission.

8. Candidates who fail any part of the examination may be required to resubmit such piece or pieces of written work as the examiners may determine and/or may be required to attend for a further oral examination on any such resubmitted work or on any written examination paper in accordance with arrangements to be made by the examiners. The decision of the examiners after any such resubmission and/or further oral examination will be final.

9. The examiners may award a distinction for excellence in the whole examination.

Philosophical Theology

Candidates shall be required:

(*a*) to present themselves for a written examination in each of the papers prescribed below, from one of which they may normally expect to be exempted by the faculty board depending on their previous qualifications;

(*b*) to present an essay of not more than 15,000 words on a topic in philosophical theology to be approved by the faculty board;

(*c*) to present themselves for a viva voce examination unless individually dispensed by the examiners (no candidate will be failed without a viva).

A candidate who fails the examination will be permitted to retake it on one further occasion only, not later than one year after the initial attempt. Such a candidate whose 15,000 word essay has been of satisfactory standard may resubmit the same piece of work, while a candidate who has reached a satisfactory standard on the written papers will not be required to retake that part of the examination.

Candidates should make a written application for approval of the essay topic to arrive at the Graduate Studies Office not later than Monday of fifth week in Hilary Term. In cases where there is some doubt about the acceptability of the proposal candidates are advised to submit their applications earlier if possible. All applications should be accompanied by a recommendation from the supervisor. The essay (two copies) must be typewritten and sent to the Chairman of the Examiners for the

M.St. in Philosophical Theology, c/o the Clerk of the Schools, Examination Schools, High Street, Oxford, EITHER at least fourteen days before the first day of the examination, OR at least twenty-eight days before the first day of Michaelmas Full Term following the examination. Candidates must notify examiners of their intention to submit early or late when seeking approval of their essay topic.

The examiners may award a distinction to candidates who have performed with special merit in the whole examination.

1. *Philosophy of Religion*

As specified for Part B of the B.Phil. in Philosophy.

2. *History of Philosophical Theology.*

The paper will contain questions on philosophical influences on theology during the patristic period, the early medieval period, and the period 1760–1860. Candidates are required to show knowledge of two of the three periods and, within each of those two periods, of some of the principal relevant writings, viz. for the patristic period of works of Origen and Augustine, for the early medieval period of works of Anselm and Aquinas, and for the period 1760–1860 of works of Kant, Kierkegaard, and Schleiermacher. Study of texts in the original languages will not be required.

3. Either *The Development of Christian Doctrine to AD 451*
or *Theology in Western Europe from Gabriel Biel to Calvin*

as specified for the M.Phil. in Theology (paper 1 of Section A and paper 1 of Section C of the Christian Doctrine option).

Philosophy

1. Every candidate must follow for at least three terms a course of instruction in Philosophy. Candidates will, when they enter for the examination, be required to produce from their society a certificate that they are following such a course.

2. The subjects available shall be the same as for the B.Phil. in Philosophy. Candidates may, if special permission is given by the Graduate Studies Committee in Philosophy, offer subjects not included in this list. Such Permission should be sought from the Committee, through the Director of Graduate Studies, at the time of application for admission to the course or as soon as possible afterwards, and in any case not later than the 1 October preceding the examination. Candidates must satisfy the examiners in two subects, and the choice of subjects must be notified on the entry form for the examination, to be submitted by Friday of the eighth week of the Michaelmas Full Term preceding the examination.

3. Candidates will be examined by submitting two essays on each subject they offer. Topics for essays will be prescribed by the examiners on every subject offered by any candidate and will be published on the notice board of the Examination Schools, High Street, Oxford, OX1 4BG, on the morning of the last Wednesday of Hilary Full Term in the year in which the examination is to be taken. The examiners shall (i) offer a choice of topics in each subject, (ii) set, for each subject, an upper limit, which shall in no case exceed 10,000 words, to the total extent of the two essays together. Two copies of each essay submitted must be delivered to the Clerk of the Schools at the above address by noon on the Friday of the second week of Trinity Full Term in the year in which the examination is to be taken. Essays must be typed or printed. Candidates who on any of their subjects have not delivered essays as prescribed by the due date shall, unless they show exceptional cause to the examiners, be deemed to have withdrawn from the examination.

Candidates are not permitted to seek or accept any help, even bibliographical, from supervisors or anybody else, with the preparation of essays.

4. Every candidate will be examined viva voce unless individually dispensed by the examiners.

The examiners may award a distinction for excellence in the whole examination.

Professional Archaeology

1. Candidates must normally have completed the Postgraduate Diploma in Professional Archaeology (or the Postgraduate Diploma in Field Archaeology). Candidates who have not completed the necessary preliminary diplomas must satisfy the admitting body that they have achieved a comparable standard.

2. Every candidate must follow for at least three terms a part-time course of instruction in Professional Archaeology and must upon entering for the examination produce from his or her society a certificate to that effect.

3. The examination will consist of the following parts:

(i) attendance at a course on research methods:

(ii) a dissertation of not more than 15,000 words on a topic selected by the student in consultation with his or her tutor and approved by the examiners. The dissertation must be delivered not later than noon on the third Friday in September of the year of the course to the Chairman of Examiners for the Degree of M.St. in Professional Archaeology, c/o Registry, 1 Wellington Square, Oxford. The dissertation must be accompanied by a statement that it is the candidate's own work;

(iii) a viva voce examination.

4. The examiners may award a distinction for excellence in the whole examination.

5. A candidate whose dissertation fails to satisfy the examiners may be permitted to resubmit the dissertation on one further occasion, not later than one year after the initial attempt.

6. Any candidate who is successful in the examination for the M.St. in Professional Archaeology will subsume his or her postgraduate diploma.

Psychodynamic Practice

1. Applicants will normally be expected to have satisfactorily completed the Postgraduate Diploma in Psychodynamic Practice. Applications for exemption from this requirement will be considered by the relevant board of studies.

2. *Course*

The course will consist of research methodology lectures, group research seminars and group clinical seminars, individual tutorials, and continuing personal therapy and supervised practice. The course will be taken on a part-time basis for a period of one year's duration.

3. Every candidate will be required to satisfy the examiners in the following:

(*a*) attendance at weekly classes, group seminars, individual tutorials, and personal therapy and placement sessions;

(*b*) submission of a dissertation of no more than 15,000 words on a topic selected by the student in consultation with the research tutor and course director and agreed by the external examiner. The dissertation must be forwarded to the examiners c/o Registry, Department for Continuing Education, Wellington Square, Oxford, OX1 2JA, for receipt not later than noon on the last Friday of September in the year in which the course is studied. Material already submitted for the Postgraduate Diploma in Psychodynamic Practice may not be included;

(*c*) participation in a minimum of 12 placement supervisions and at least 100 hours of client/patient contact, and submission of an end-of-year report by a candidate's placement supervisor;

(*d*) participation in a minimum of 40 hours of personal therapy;

(*e*) submission of termly reports from both research and clinical tutors;

(*f*) a viva voce examination at the end of the course of study.

4. The examiners may award a distinction for excellence in the whole examination.

5. A candidate whose dissertation fails to satisfy the examiner may be permitted to resubmit on one further occasion only not later than one year after the initial failure. Approval for deferral must be obtained from the relevant board of studies.

6. If any candidate who is successful in the examination for the Degree of Master of Studies in Psychodynamic Practice has previously successfully completed the Posgraduate Diploma in Psychodynamic Practice, the Master of Studies will subsume his or her diploma.

Science and Religion

1. Each candidate will be required to follow a course of instruction for three terms and present himself or herself for examination in each of the three subjects prescribed below.

For papers I and II an essay of 5,000–7,000 words or three essays of 2,000–3,000 words each on titles proposed by the candidate and approved by the Faculty Board may be submitted for the written examination. Candidates intending to offer essays in place of an examination should make a written application for approval of the topic(s), to arrive at the Graduate Studies Office, University Offices, Wellington Square, Oxford, not later than Monday of fifth week in Hilary Term. The essays (two copies) must be typewritten and sent to the Chairman of Examiners for the M.St. in Science and Religion, c/o the Clerk of Schools, Examination Schools, High Street, Oxford, not later than fourteen days before the first day of the examination.

2. Each candidate will be required to present himself or herself for a viva voce examination unless individually exempted by the examiners.

3. A dissertation of not more than 15,000 words on a topic proposed by the candidate and approved by the Faculty Board may be submitted to meet the requirement for paper III. Candidates who wish to proceed to the M.Litt. or D.Phil. are advised that they should take this option, proposing a topic which they intend to make the subject of their thesis.

Candidates intending to take this option should make a written application for approval of the dissertation topic, to arrive at the Graduate Studies Office, University Offices, Wellington Square, Oxford, not later than Monday of fifth week in Hilary Term. All applications should be accompanied by a recommendation from the supervisor. The dissertation (two copies) must be typewritten and sent to the Chairman of Examiners for the M.St. in Science and Religion, c/o the Clerk of Schools, Examination Schools, High Street, Oxford, at least twenty-eight days before the first day of Michaelmas Term following the examination. The dissertation must be accompanied by a signed statement that it is the candidate's own work, except where otherwise indicated.

4. The examiners may award a distinction to candidates who have performed with special merit in the whole examination.

Schedule of Papers

I (*a*) *Current Issues in Theology*

Candidates will be expected to discuss problems of theological method and to show a critical understanding of the main themes in systematic theology, taking account of the impact on Christian theology of contemporary philosophy, critical historical studies, the natural and social sciences, and non-Christian religions and ideologies. Further details of this paper are given under the regulations for the degree of M.Phil. in Theology (Christian Doctrine, Section D—Issues in Theology with special reference to Patristic Theology).

By permission of the Faculty Board paper (*b*) may be taken as an alternative.

(*b*) *The Nature of Religion*

The aim of this paper is to examine the main classical and contemporary approaches to the study of religions, the problems involved in the comparative study of religions, and the relation between religious belief, theology, and the study of religions. Further details of this paper are given under the regulations for the degree of Master of Studies in the Study of Religion, of which it is a component.

II *The Nature of Science*

The aim of this paper is to examine issues in the history of philosophy of science that illuminate the nature of science and the grounds on which scientific knowledge is routinely differentiated from other bodies of knowledge.

By studying crucial episodes in the history of science and cultural issues in the philosophy of science, students should develop a sound grasp of the foundations of scientific knowledge, the nature of scientific methods, and the changing world-views with which the sciences have been associated.

III *Science and Religion*

The focus of this paper will be on the relation between science and religion as they have been constructed in both past and present. Competing models of integration and separation will be evaluated with reference to specific case-studies, including major figures of the 'scientific revolution' such as Galileo and Newton and such later thinkers as Farady, Darwin, and Einstein.

Slavonic Studies

1. Candidates must have taken *either* Russian (as sole language *or* as one of two languages) *or* Czech (with Slovak) in the Oxford Honour School of Modern Languages, *or* have taken a comparable degree in a Slavonic language from another university, *or* must satisfy the committee that they possess the necessary qualifications in a Slavonic language to profit by the course.

2. Candidates must follow for at least three terms a course of instruction in Slavonic Studies.

3. Each candidate will be required to take one language from Schedule 1 and three subjects from Schedules 2–10. Candidates may take no more than two subjects from any one Schedule.

4. Candidates will be examined by written examination, except that in lieu of written examination in one subject a candidate may elect under Schedule 2.v to submit an essay of approximately 8,000 words and not more than 10,000 words on a subject of the candidate's choice. Such a subject must be approved by the committee not later than its last meeting in the Hilary Term of the year in which the candidate takes the M.St. examination. Two typed copies of the essay must be delivered to the Clerk of the Schools at least a fortnight before the first examination. Work submitted in the form of an essay for the Degree of M.St. may subsequently be incorporated in a thesis submitted for the Degre of M.Phil., or may be used as the basis for the piece of written work required for admission to the status of student for the Degrees of M.Litt. or D.Phil.

5. Candidates must present themselves for oral examination unless dispensed by the examiners.

6. The examiners may award a distinction for excellence in the whole examination.

Schedule 1.

Unseen translation from any one of the following languages (this must not be a language previously studied by the candidate to degree standard):

i. Belorussian
ii. Bulgarian
iii. Croatian
iv. Czech
v. Macedonian
vi. Polish
vii. Russian
viii. Serbian
ix. Slovak
x. Slovene
xi Sorbian
xii. Ukrainian

Schedule 2.

i. Cyrillic Palaeography
ii. Textual Criticism
iii. Methods of Metrical Analysis
iv. Methods of Criticism and the Theory of Literature (from the M.St. course in European Literature)
v. A subject of the candidate's choice, approved by the committee.

Schedule 3.

i. Comparative Slavonic Philology
ii. Old Church Slavonic
iii. History of Church Slavonic

Schedule 4.

The History of:

i. Belorussian *or* Ukrainian
ii. Bulgarian *or* Macedonian
iii. Croatian
iv. Czech *and* Slovak
v. Polish
vi. Russian
vii. Serbian
viii. Slovene
ix. Sorbian

Schedule 5.

The Structure and Present State of:

i. Belorussian
ii. Bulgarian
iii. Croatian
iv. Czech
v. Macedonian
vi. Polish
vii. Russian
viii. Serbian
ix. Slovak
x. Slovene
xi. Sorbian
xii. Ukrainian.

Schedule 6.

i. Russian Literature before Pushkin.

ii. Pushkin and Romanticism.
iii. Gender and Representation in Russian Culture from 1800.
iv. The Rise of the Russian Novel.
v. Russian Drama in the 19th and 20th Centuries.
vi. The Russian Experience of Modernity, 1905–1945.
vii. The GULag and the Russian Literary Process.
viii. Post-Soviet Russian Literature.

Schedule 7.

i. Czech Literature since 1774.
ii. Polish Literature, 1798–1883.
iii. Slovak Literature since 1783.

Schedule 8.

i. Russian Social and Political Thought, 1825–1917.
ii. The History of Russia, 1861–1917.
iii. The Russian Revolution and the Civil War.

Schedule 9.

i. Byzantine Civilization and its Expansion, 913–1204.
ii. The History of the Balkans, 1774–1918.
iii. The History since 1918 of *either* Bulgaria, *or* Yugoslavia and its successor states (M.Phil. in Russian and East European Studies B.7).

Schedule 10.

i. Bohemia from the Hussite Wars to the Battle of the White Mountain (1415–1620).
ii. The History of Poland and Hungary, 1506–1795 (M.Phil. in Russian and East European Studies B.1).
iii. The Habsburg Monarchy, 1790–1918 (M.Phil. in Russian and East European Studies B.2).
iv. The History since 1918 of *either* Poland, *or* Czechoslovakia and its successor states (M.Phil. in Russian and East European Studies B.7).

Teaching for some options may not be available in every year. Applicants for admission will be advised whether teaching will be available in the options of their choice.

Study of Religion

1. Each candidate will be required to follow a course of instruction for three terms and present himself or herself for examination in three subjects as set out in the syllabus.

2. Candidates intending to offer a 10,000–15,000 word essay should make a written application for approval for the essay topic (and, where required in the regulations, for permission to substitute the essay for paper) to arrive at the Graduate Studies Office not later than the Monday of fifth week in Hilary Term. In cases where there is some doubt about the acceptability of the proposal candidates are asked to submit their applications earlier if possible. All applications should be accompanied by a recommendation from the supervisor. The essay must be typewritten and sent to the Chairman of Examiners for the Degree in M.St. in the Study of Religion, c/o the Clerk to the Schools, Examination Schools, High Street, Oxford, *either* at least fourteen days before the first day of the examination *or* at least twenty eight days before the first day of Michaelmas Full Term following the examination. Candidates intending also to offer three short essays in place of an examination paper must give notice of their intention not later than Monday of fifth week in Hilary Term. They must submit their essays at least fourteen days before the day of the examination.

3. Each candidate will be required to present himself or herself for an oral examination unless individually dispensed by the examiners.

4. The oral examination shall be held at two points in the year: within three weeks after the written examination for those candidates who submit 10,000–15,000 word essays before the examination or who do not submit such essays, and in the last week of September or the first week in October for those who submit such essays at the end of the Long Vacation. Candidates must notify examiners of their intention to submit early or late when seeking approval of their essay topic. [The examiners may make the marks awarded to candidates known to the Director of Graduate Studies where they need to be known for the purpose of grant applications, but the pass list shall be issued following the completion of the whole examination in September or October.]

5. The examiners may award a distinction to candidates who have performed with special merit in the whole examination.

6. A candidate who fails the examination will be permitted to retake it on one further occasion only, not later than one year after the initial attempt. Such a candidate whose 10,000–15,000 word essay has been of satisfactory standard may resubmit the same piece of work, while a candidate who had reached a satisfactory standard on the written papers will not be required to retake that part of the examination.

Syllabus

Candidates shall offer three papers:

1. The Nature of Religion

2 and 3. Two papers selected from papers on the major texts and doctrines of (a) Buddhism, (b) Christianity, (c) Islam, (d) Judaism, or (e) any other paper that may from time to time be approved by the Board of the Faculty of Theology.

Candidates who have degree qualifications which include a study of a particular religious tradition may *not* offer that tradition as one of their papers.

An essay of 10,000–15,000 words may be offered in place of one paper. Three essays of not more than 5,000 words may be submitted in place of a further paper.

The Nature of Religion

The aim of this paper is to examine the main classical and contemporary approaches to the study of religions, the problems involved in comparative study of religions, and the relation between religious belief, theology and the study of religions.

1. Students should know the work of key figures in the study of religions, the main attempts to define religion and the problems of defining religion. The works of J. G. Frazer ('The Golden Bough'), Edward Tylor, Rudolf Otto, Evans-Pritchard, and Cantwell Smith are important in this respect.

2. They should be aware of the differing approaches to the study of religion in phenomenology, anthropology, sociology, psychology, philosophy, and theology. By the use of examples, the strengths and limits of each approach should be investigated.

3. They should be aware of the major exaplanations that have been offered of religious belief, particularly by Durkheim, Freud, Feuerbach, and Jung, and of the problems in giving such general explanations.

4. They should be aware of some major authors who have attempted comparative studies in religion, and the problems of such comparative studies. They should be aware of some of the issues involved in claims for religious truth and rationality, and attitudes to religious conflict and diversity. Relevant authors for study would be John Bowker, Ninian Smart, John Hick, Paul Knitter, and Max Müller.

They should have sufficient data to take an informed view of the place of religion in the modern world.

The subject is to be studied by the use of texts from amongst the following:

Friedrich Schleiermacher, *Speeches on Religion* (CUP, 1988).

Rudolf Otto, *The Idea of the Holy* (Penguin, 1959).

Eric Sharpe, *Understanding Religion* (Duckworth, 1983).

Ninian Smart, *The Phenomenon of Religion* (Macmillan, 1973).
Ian Markham, *A Reader in World Religions* (Macmillan, 1995).
John Hinnells, *New Dictionary of Religions* (Penguin, 1995).
Emile Durkhiem, *Elementary Forms of Religious Life* (Allen and Unwin, 1967)
Max Weber, *The Sociology of Religion* (Boston, Beacon Press, 1956).
E. E. Evans-Pritchard, *Theories of Primitive Religion* (Clarendon Press, 1965).
Sigmund Freud, *The Future of an Illusion,* and *Totem and Taboo* (in 'Complete Works', Hogarth Press, 1927 and 1913, respectively).
Sir James Frazer, *The Golden Bough* (Abridged, Macmillan 1922).
William James, *The Varieties of Religious Experience* (Collins, 1960).
J. Waardenburg, *Classical Approaches to the Study of Religion* (Mouton, 1973).
Frank Whaling, *Contemporary Approaches to the Study of Religion* (Mouton, 1984).
G. Van der Leeuw, *Religion in Essence and Manifestation* (Harper & Row, 1967).
John Hick, *An Interpretation of Religion* (Macmillan, 1989).
Paul Knitter, *No Other Name?* (SCM, 1985).
John Bowker, *The Sense of God.* (SCM, 1987).
Wilfred Cantwell Smith, *The Meaning and End of Religion* (Harper & Row, 1962).

(*a*) *Buddhism*

The earliest Buddhist doctrine and practice will be studied against the background of the early Upanishads and other religious movements in north-east India round the 5th century BCE. Practice includes both meditation and monastic life. The primary source is the Pali Canon supplemented by the commentarial literature of the Theravadin tradition.

(*b*) *Christianity*

The major themes of Christian theology will be considered in their historical context and with special reference to their use by twentieth-century theologians.

Texts:

(a) Augustine, *The City of God,* selected passages (Penguin, 1972).
Anselm, *Cur Deus Homo?* (St Anselm: 'Basic Writings': Open Court, 1962).
Aquinas, *Summa Theologiae,* selected passages (Blackfriars, 1964–).
Calvin, *Institutes of the Christian Religion,* selected passages (Eerdmans, 1989).
Schleiermacher, *The Christian Faith* (T. and T. Clark, 1989).
Rahner, *Foundations of Christian Belief* (Darton, Longman and Todd, 1978).
Barth, *Church Dogmatics* 2, 1 (T. and T. Clark, 1937).

(b) *Deuteronomy* and the *Gospel of Matthew,* either in the original or in translation.

(*c*) *Islam*

The paper will consist of a broad introduction to Islamic history and religion from the Prophet Muhammad to the modern period, with particular emphasis on the formative period (7th to the 11th century, CE).

Candidates will cover the following topics in lectures and tutorials:

1. Muhammad and the Arabian milieu
2. Qur'an
3. Hadith
4. Law
5. Theology
6. Sects
7. Sufism
8. Islam and other monotheisms
9. Modern Islam

(*d*) *Judaism*

Jewish religion and thought since 70 CE with reference both to its historical development and to Judaism in the modern world.

Selections from the texts below will be assigned by the course tutor not later than the beginning of Michaelmas Term:

MISHNA: tractate *Berakhot*

MEKHILTA: on the Ten Commandments

Twersky, I. (ed.) *A Maimonides Reader.* (New York: Berhrman House, 1972).

Other recommended books

Urbach, E. E. tr. I. Abrahams. *The Sages.* (Cambridge Ma. and London: Harvard University Press. 1987.)

Saadia Gaon. *The Book of Beliefs and Opinions,* tr. Samuel Rosenblatt. (New Haven: Yale University Press and London: Oxford University Press, 1948.)

Scholem, Gershom G., *Major Trends in Jewish Mysticism.* (New York: Schocken Books, 1954.)

Jacobs, Louis. *Principles of the Jewish Faith: An Analytical Study.* (London: Vallentine, Mitchell, 1964.)

Rubenstein, Richard, *After Auschwitz: history, theology and contemporary Judaism.* 2nd ed. (Baltimore and London: Johns Hopkins University Press, 1992.)

Syriac Studies

1. Candidates must satisfy the Board of the Faculty of Oriental Studies before admission to the course that they possess the necessary qualification in the Syriac language to profit by the course.

2. Every candidate must follow for at least three terms a course of study in Syriac Studies. Candidates will, when they enter for the examination, be required to produce from their society a certificate that they are doing so.

3. *Syllabus*

There will be four papers:

I. Essay questions on the history, literature, and culture of the Syriac Churches.

II–IV. Passages for translation and comment, and essay questions on prescribed texts in Syriac, with special reference to three of the following subjects (a passage, or passages, for unprepared translation may also be set):

(1) Biblical versions;
(2) Exegetical literature;
(3) Early poetry;
(4) Liturgy;
(5) Historical literature;
(6) Secular literature;
(7) Monastic literature;
(8) Hagiography;
(9) Translations of Greek patristic texts;
or any other subject approved by the board.

Texts will be announced by the board in the third week of Michaelmas Full Term preceding the examination.

Every candidate will be examined viva voce unless he or she shall have been individually excused by the examiners.

The examiners may award a distinction for excellence in the whole examination.

Teaching for the course may not be available in every year. Applicants for admission will be advised of this.

Theology

1. Each candidate will be required to follow a course of instruction for three terms and present himself or herself for examination in one of the following subjects specified for the M.Phil. in Theology: Old Testament, New Testament, Christian Doctrine (one of the options A–G), Ecclesiastical History, Christian Ethics, Biblical Interpretation. (The selection of papers within these subjects available to M.St. candidates is indicated below. Reading lists and lists of prescribed texts will be found under the regulations for the M.Phil. (unless otherwise stated in the regulations for a particular subject) *M.St. candidates are not required to study texts marked with an asterisk.* For ease of reference the numbering of papers as given in the M.Phil. regulations is also provided below.)

2. Candidates intending to offer a 10,000–15,000 word essay should make a written application for approval for the essay topic (and, where required in the regulations, for permission to substitute the essay for a paper) to arrive at the Graduate Studies Office not later than Monday of fifth week in Hilary Term. In cases where there is some doubt about the acceptability of the proposal candidates are asked to submit their applications earlier if possible. All applications should be accompanied by a recommendation from the supervisor. The essay must be typewritten and must be sent to the Chairman of Examiners for the Degree of M.St. in Theology, c/o the Clerk to the Schools, Examination Schools, High Street, Oxford, EITHER at least fourteen days before the first day of the examination OR at least twenty-eight days before the first day of Michaelmas Full Term following the examination. The essay must be accompanied by a signed statement by the candidate that the essay is his or her own work except where otherwise indicated.

Candidates mut notify examiners of their intention to submit early or late when seeking approval of their essay topic.

Candidates intending also to offer three short essays in place of an examination paper must give notice of their intention not later than the Monday of fifth week in Hilary Term. They must submit *two copies* of their essays at least fourteen days before the day of the examination.

3. Each candidate will be required to present himself or herself for an oral examination.

4. The Oral examination shall be held at two points in the year: within three weeks after the written examination; and in the last week of September or the first week of October for candidates who submit such essays (see paragraph 2, above at the end of the Long Vacation. Candidates must notify examiners of their intention to submit early or late when seeking approval of their essay topic.

5. The examiners may award a distinction to candidates who have performed with special merit in the whole examination.

6. A candidate who fails the examination will be permitted to retake it on one further occasion only, not later than one year after the initial attempt. Such a candidate whose 10,000–15,000 word essay and/or three essays of not more than 5,000 words have been of satisfactory standard is not required to submit the same pieces of work, while a candidate who has reached a satisfactory standard on the written papers will not be required to re-take the written papers.

OLD TESTAMENT

All candidates shall offer paper (iii) Prescribed Hebrew texts.

Candidates shall also offer two papers chosen from the following list, *or* one paper chosen from the following list and an essay of 10,000–15,000 words on a research topic approved by the Board, *or* three essays of not more than 5,000 words each falling within the scope of one of papers (i), (ii), or (v) in the following list and one essay of 10,000–15,000 words on a research topic approved by the Board.

Paper (i) (*a*) The Literature of the Old Testament and Apocrypha in its Historical Setting.

Paper (i) (*b*) A paper on an area for special study approved by the Board within the scope of paper (i) (*a*).

Paper (ii) Old Testament theology.

Paper (iv) (*b*) The Aramaic portions of the Old Testament, *or* Paper (iv) (*c*) The Septuagint (Genesis 2–4; Isaiah 42, 52–3; Psalms 2, 21 (MT22), 109 (MT 110); Proverbs 1, 8, 9). Candidates will be expected to translate and comment on four passages, one from each of the groups of texts, and to answer one question of a general nature on the Septuagint, with reference to the set texts.

Paper (v) The History and Principles of Biblical Study.

Texts to be studied may differ from those for the M.Phil. The texts will be published by the board in the Theology Centre by the end of the third week of Michaelmas Full Term preceding the examination.

Candidates who wish to proceed to the M.Litt. or D.Phil. are advised that they should offer a 10,000–15,000 word essay on the topic they intend to make the subject of their thesis.

New Testament

Candidates shall offer three papers:

1. *Either* Paper (i) Religion and Literature of the New Testament: the Four Gospels and Acts in Greek.

or Paper (ii) Religion and Literature of the New Testament: the Epistles and Apocalypse in Greek.

2. and 3. Two papers chosen from the following:

Paper (iii) New Testament Theology: General Paper.

Paper (iv) Varieties of Judaism: BCE 200–CE 200.*

Paper (v) The History and Principles of Biblical Study (=paper (v) for the Old Testament).

Whichever of papers (i) and (ii) has not been chosen under 1.

With the Board's permission, candidates may submit *either* an essay of 10,000–15,000 words on a research topic approved by the Board in place of one of the papers under 2. and 3., *or* three essays of not more than 5,000 words in place of one of the papers under 2. and 3. *or* an essay of 10,000–15,000 words on a research topic approved by the Board in place of one of the papers under 2. and 3. together with three essays of not more than 5,000 words in place of the other of the papers under 2. and 3.

Candidates who wish to proceed to the M.Litt. or D.Phil. are advised that they should offer a 10,000–15,000 word essay on the topic they intend to make the subject of their thesis.

The board shall have power to direct particular candidates to offer such papers as it shall determine.

Christian Doctrine

Section A—History of Doctrine: Patristic Theology

(i) Candidates shall offer three of the following papers, subject to (ii)–(iv) below.

(ii) All candidates must offer paper 1 unless exempted by the Theology Board. Applications for exemption must be submitted on the entry form for the examination, and will be considered by the Theology Board at its first meting in Hilary Term.

---

* The set texts for this paper are those for the M.Phil. in Theology. Candidates who wish to proceed to the M.Phil. or D.Phil. may, with the approval of the board, offer an alternative selection of texts.

(iii) All candidates must offer paper 4.

(iv) An essay of 10,000–15,000 words may be offered in place of one of papers 1, 2, 3, or 5, or in addition to the candidate's three written papers.

1. Paper 1 The Development of Christian Doctrine to AD 451.
2. Paper 2(a) Hellenistic Philosophy and Christian Theology: General Paper.
3. Paper 3(a) Christology in the Patristic Period: General Paper.
4. Translation, commentary and essays on *either* [Basil of Caesarea], *Epistle* 38 (in *St Basil: the Letters,* Loeb edition vol. 1, tr. R. J. Deferrari, London 1926) *or* Boethius, *De Trinitate* (in *Boethius: Tracts* etc., Loeb edition, tr. J. F. Stewart and E. K. Rand, London).
5. Byzantine Theology.

Candidates may offer one of the following:

Either

Paper 5 (*a*) *AD 451–682*

Candidates will be expected to show familiarity with the history of the Byzantine Church in this era, the doctrines of its principal theologians and the following texts:

Ps.-Dionysius the Areopagite, *The Divine Names* (tr. C. Luibheid, in *Ps.Dionysius The Complete Works,* Paulist Press: Classics of Western Spirituality, New York, 1987).

John Climacus: *The Ladder of Divine Ascent* (tr. C. Luibheid and N. Russell, Paulist Press: Classics of Western Spirituality, New York, 1982).

St Isaac of Nineveh, *The Ascetical Life* (tr. M. Hansbury, St Valdimir's Seminary Press, New York, 1989).

Maximus the Confessor: *Four Centuries on Love* (tr. G. Berthold, Paulist Press: Classics of Western Spirituality, New York, 1985).

The Trial of Maximus the Confessor (tr. Berthold, *op. cit.*)

Acts of the Fifth Ecumenical Council (Constaninople II) in *the Seven Ecumenical Councils*, T. & T. Clark: Library of the Nicene and Post-Nicene Fathers, XIV.

Acts of the Sixth Ecumenical Council (Constaninople III), in *ibid.*

Or

Paper 5 (*b*) *AD 726–1453*

Candidates will be expected to show knowledge of the history of the Byzantine Church in this era, the doctrines of its principal theologians and the following texts:

St Germanus of Constantinople: *On the Divine Liturgy* (tr. P. Meyendorff, St Vladimir's Seminary Press, New York, 1984).

St John Damascene, *On the Orthodox Faith,* Books I and III (tr. J. Salmon, T. & T. Clark: Library of the Nicene and Post-Nicene Fathers IX).

St Theodore the Studite: *On the Holy Icons* (tr. C. P. Roth, St Vladimir's Seminary Press, New York, 1981).

St Symeon the New Theologian: *Discourses* 1, VII–IX, XI–XV (tr. C. J. de-Catanzaro, Paulist Press: Classics of Western Spirituality New York, 1980).

St Gregory Palamas: *The Triads* (tr. N. Grendle, Paulist Press; Classics of Western Spirituality, New York, 1983).

N. Cabasilas, *The Life in Christ* (tr. C. J. deCatanzaro, St Vladimir's Seminary Press, New York, 1974).

Acts of the Seventh Ecumenical Council (Nicea II), in *The Seven Ecumenical Councils,* T. & T. Clark, Library of the Nicene and Post-Nicene Fathers XIV.

Section B—History of Doctrine: *Scholastic Theology*

Candidates shall offer three papers:

1. Paper 1 Doctrine and Methods.
2. Paper 2 The Thought of Aquinas: General Paper.
3. Paper 3 Prescribed texts to be studied in Latin.

An essay may be submitted in place of paper 2.

Section C—History of Doctrine: Reformation Theology

Candidates shall offer three papers:

1. Paper 1 Theology in Western Europe from Gabriel Biel to Calvin.
2. Paper 2 Protestant and Tridentine Teaching on the Doctrines of Grace, Freewill, and Predestination: General Paper.
3. Paper 3 Prescribed texts (Latin texts to be studied in the original language).

An essay may be submitted in place of paper 2.

Section D—Issues in Theology with special reference to Patristic Theology

Candidates shall offer four papers:

1. Paper 1 Current Issues in Theology.
2. Paper 2 The Development of Christian Doctrine to AD 451 (=paper 1 of Section A).
3. and 4.

Either Paper 3 Hellenistic Philosophy and Christian Theology General Paper (= paper 2(*a*) of Section A).
Paper 4 Prescribed texts to be studied in English.

or Paper 5 Christology in the Patristic Period: General Paper (=paper 3(*a*) of Section A).
Paper 6 Prescribed texts to be studied in English.

An essay may be submitted in place of paper 1.

Section E—Issues in Theology with special reference to Scholastic Theology

Candidates shall offer four papers:

1. Paper 1 Current Issues in Theology.
2. Paper 2 Doctrine and Methods.
3. Paper 3 The Thought of Aquinas: General Paper.
4. Paper 4 Prescribed texts to be studied in English.

An essay may be submitted in place of paper 1.

Section F—Issues in Theology with special reference to Reformation Theology

Candidates shall offer four papers:

1. Paper 1 Current Issues in Theology.
2. Paper 2 Theology in Western Europe from Gabriel Biel to Calvin.
3. Paper 3 Protestant and Tridentine Teaching on the Doctrines of Grace, Freewill, and Predestination: General Paper.
4. Paper 4 Prescribed texts to be studied in English.

An essay may be submitted in place of paper 1.

Section G—Issues in Theology with special reference to Theology from Kant to the present day

Candidates shall offer three papers:

1. Paper 1 Current Issues in Theology.
2. Paper 2 Doctrines and Methods from Kant to Troeltsch.
3. Paper 3 The Doctrine of Revelation.

An essay may be submitted in place of paper 1 or paper 3.

Ecclesiastical History

Candidates shall offer:

(i) A general paper on the nature and practice of Ecclesiastical History;

(ii) A general paper on one of the following periods:

- (*a*) The Early Church, AD 303–461.
- (*b*) The Western Church, AD 1050–1280.
- (*c*) The Reformation, AD 1500–1660.
- (*d*) European Christianity, AD 1800–1950.

(iii) An essay of 10,000–15,000 words on some topic related to one of the periods specified in (ii).

With the Board's permission, three essays of not more than 5,000 words may be submitted in place of paper (ii).

Christian Ethics

All candidates shall offer paper (i) Christian Moral Concepts: General Paper.

Candidates shall offer two of the following papers, in one of the following combinations: (ii) and any other paper; (iii)(*a*) and (*b*); (iv)(*a*) and (*b*).

(ii) Historical Traditions of Christian Ethics.
(iii)(*a*) Sexuality and marriage: Christian traditions of discussion.
(iii)(*b*) Sexuality and marriage: contemporary moral problems.
(iv)(*a*) Christian political thought: traditions of discussion.
(iv)(*b*) Christian political thought: contemporary questions.

Candidates may offer an essay of 10,000–15,000 words, demonstrating capacity in research and scholarly argument, in place of any paper except paper (i). The subject of the essay may be drawn from any part of the syllabus covered in the regulations, but substantial material from the essay may not be reused in answering questions on any paper.

Biblical Interpretation

Candidates shall offer three papers:

1. *The History and Principles of Biblical Study* (as set for Paper (v) Old Testament).

2. Either *Old Testament Theology* (as set for Paper (ii) Old Testament) or *New Testament Theology* (as set for Paper (iii) New Testament).

3. *The History of Biblical Interpretation.*

One of the following periods shall be selected to be studied in such texts as listed:

A AD 100–604

The Epistle of Barnabas.
Justin Martyr—*Dialogue with Trypho.* ANF I.
Melito of Sardis—*Paschal Homily* ed. S. G. Hall, OUP.
Irenaeus—*Against the Heretics*, Books III–V. ANF I.
Tertullian—*On The Resurrection*
Against Marcion Book IV, ed. E. Evans, OUP.
Origen—*On First Principles Book IV*, ed. G. W. Butterworth.
Commentaries on John and Matthew. ANF IX.
Homilies on Genesis and Exodus, tr. R. E. Heine, Fathers of the Church 71.
Commentary on John, tr. R. E. Heine, FC 80.
Tyconius—*The Book of Rules I–III* in K. Froehlich, *Biblical Interpretation in the Early Church.* Fortress 1984.
Chrysostom—*Homilies on Genesis* 1–17 tr. R. Hill, FC 74.
Homilies on St Paul's Epistles: Romans, LF. 1877.
Homilies on Matthew 1–8, LF, 1876.
St John tr. T. A. Goggin FC 33 and 41.
Cyril of Alexandria—*Commentary on John* 1–8, LF, 1874.
Jerome—*Homilies* tr. M. L. Ewald, FC, 48 and 57.
Augustine—*On Christian Doctrine*, ed. D. W. Robertson, LLA 1958.
Confessions Bks. 10–13, ed. H. Chadwick, OUP 1991.
On the Spirit and The Letter, LCC VIII.
Homilies on John XIV, ed. H. F. Stewart, CUP, 1900.

Classics of Western Spirituality, 1984.
Tractates on John, tr. J. W. Rettig, FC 78 and 79.

B AD 1050–1650

Hugh St Victor—*Didascalion*, ed. J. Taylor, 1990.
Bernard of Clairvaux—*On the Song of Songs*. CF 4, 7, 31, 40.
William of St Thierry—*Exposition on the Song of Songs*, CF 6.
Anselm to Ockham—Selections, ed. E. R. Fairweather, LCC 10 1956.
Joachim of Fiore—*Selected writings*. In *Apocalyptic Spirituality*, CWS 19, ed. B. McGinn.
Eckhart—*The Essential Sermons, Commentaries, Treatises and Defence*, ed. E. Colledge and B. McGinn, CWS 1981.
Erasmus—*Paraphrases on Romans and Galatians*. Toronto 1984.
On the Freedom of the Will (1524) LCC 17.
Luther—*Lectures on Romans* (1515/6) LCC 15.
Commentary on Galatians (1535) ed. P. S. Watson.
Lectures on Genesis 1–14, American ed. 1–2.
Lectures on the Psalms AE., X–XI.
Thomas Müntzer—*Sermon before the Princes, The Testimony of Luke and the Exposé of False Faith*. (Collected Works, tr. P. Matheson).
Calvin—*Commentary on Romans*, ed. R. Mackenzie.
Commentary on St John, ed. T. H. L. Parker.
Melanchthon—*Loci Communes* (1521) ed. W. Pauck, LCC 19.
Bucer—*On the Kingdom of Christ* (1557) ed. W. Pauck, LCC 19.
Cranmer—*Defence of the true and catholic doctrine of the sacrament* (1550) ed. G. E. Duffield, 1964.
W. Tyndale—*Work* (1525/34) ed. G. E. Duffield, 1964.
L. de Léon—*The Names of Christ*, ed. M. Duran and W. Kluback, London 1984.

C AD 1640–1930

G. Winstanley—Fire in the Bush (In Winstanley, *The Law of Freedom and other Writings*, ed. C. Hill).
J. Locke—*The Reasonableness of Christianity* (1695), London, 1824, 1946.
A Paraphrase and Notes on the Epistles of St Paul (1707), Oxford 1987.
A. Collins—*A Discourse of the Grounds and Reasons of the Christian Religion*, London 1737.
R. Lowth—*Lectures on the Sacred Poetry of the Hebrews* (1753) London 1829.
H. S. Reimarus—*Fragments*, London 1971.
F. D. E. Schleiermacher—*The Life of Jesus* (1864) ed. J. C. Verheyden, London 1975.
D. F. Strauss—*The Life of Jesus Critically Examined* (1835), ed. P. Hodgson, London 1973.
H. Ewald—*History of Israel* (1843–55) London 1867–86.
F. C. Baur—*Paul* (1845), 2 V Edinburgh 1875.
Church History Vol. 1, London, 1878.
B. Jowett—*On the Interpretation of Scripture, Essays and Reviews*, London 1860.
J. W. Colenso—*The Pentateuch and The Books of Joshua I*, 1864.
E. Renan—*Life of Jesus*, London 1864.
J. Wellhausen—*Prolegomena to the History of Israel* (1878), Edinburgh 1885.
J. B. Lightfoot—*Essay on the work entitled Supernatural Religion*, London 1889.
W. R. Smith—*The Religion of the Semites*, London 1889.
A. Harnack—*What is Christianity?* (1900) London 1901.
H. Gunkel—*The History of Religion: Understanding of the New Testament. The Monist*, Chicago 1903.

A. Schweitzer—*The Quest of the Historical Jesus* (1906) London 1910.
Paul and his Interpreters (1911) London 1912.
W. Bousset—*Kyrios Christos* (1921²) Philadelphia 1970.
K. Barth—*The Epistle to the Romans* (1921²) London 1933.

With the Board's permission an essay of 10,000–15,000 words on a research topic approved by the Board may be submitted in place of any one of the above papers.

With the Board's permission, three essays of not more than 5,000 words each may be submitted in place of a further paper.

Candidates who wish to proceed to the M.Litt. or D.Phil. are advised that they should offer a 10,000–15,000 word essay on the topic they intend to make the subject of their thesis.

Theology (Research)

1. Each candidate must hold PRS status in the University and follow for at least three terms a course of instruction and directed research and will be required to produce from their society a certificate that they are following such a course.

2. Candidates will be expected to attend such lectures and seminars as their supervisor shall recommend.

3. The examiners may award a distinction for excellence in the whole examination.

4. *Qualifying Examination*

Candidates may be required to pass a qualifying examination in a language unless dispensed by the Examiners on the sole ground that further proof of linguistic competence is unnecessary. Normal expectations for this requirement are indicated separately for each field of study below, but the Board of the Faculty of Theology may make a further requirement in the case of any candidate if it deems that competence in a language is indispensible for the study of primary sources, provided that no candidate may be required to pass two qualifying examinations. The Chairman of Examiners may not give dispensation to a candidate in cases where the Faculty Board has already imposed a specific requirement on that candidate. Examinations shall be set at such times as may be determined by the Board of the Faculty of Theology, but will normally be set on one occasion during Michaelmas and Trinity Terms, and on two occasions during Hilary Term. Candidates may apply to the Chairman of Examiners for dispensation from the Qualifying Examinations, or for another Qualifying Examination than that normally expected in the field of study not later than the end of Michaelmas Term. The written support of a candidate's supervisor is required.

5. Proposals for titles of dissertations, major papers, and essays must be submitted to the Chairman of Examiners by Friday of week 8 of Hilary Term. Candidates are advised to allow time for communication with the Examiners to take place before the Board's permission is granted, and are advised to submit their proposals as early as possible. All proposals should be accompanied by a brief indication of how the subject will be treated. Proposals for titles of dissertations should also be accompanied by a brief account of the primary and secondary sources to be used.

6. All major papers and essays must be submitted to the Chairman of Examiners not later than noon on Friday of week 9 of Trinity Term. All communications with the examiners should be addressed to the Chairman of Examiners for the M.St. in Theology (Research), c/o the Clerk to the Schools, Examination Schools, High Street, Oxford.

7. *Syllabus*

(*a*) Dissertation. Every candidate must submit a dissertation of 12,000–15,000 words upon a chosen subject from one of the six fields of study listed below. The title, which will have been proposed by the candidate and approved by the Board of the Faculty of Theology, should not overlap any of those offered for other essays within the same field.

Two copies of the dissertation, which must be typewritten or printed, must be sent in a parcel bearing the words 'Dissertation for the M.St. in Theology (Research)' to The Chairman of Examiners, c/o Clerk to the Schools, Examination Schools, High Street, Oxford, at least twenty-eight days before the first day of Michaelmas Full Term following the examination.

Every candidate must attend a viva voce examination which may concern the matter treated in the dissertation and any related question of academic context, method, or background.

(*b*) Every candidate will be required to satisfy the examiners in the dissertation and on one field of study from those detailed in the schedule of papers below:

Schedule of Papers

I Old Testament

(*a*) Three essays of between 2,000 and 3,000 words each on titles proposed by the candidate and approved by the Board of the Faculty of Theology.

(*b*) EITHER an essay of 5,000–7,000 words on a subject proposed by the candidate and approved by the Faculty Board, OR, with the permission of the Faculty Board, an examination in Old Testament exegesis.

(*c*) A qualifying examination in Hebrew will normally be required.

II New Testament

(*a*) Three essays of between 2,000 and 3,000 words each on titles proposed by the candidate and approved by the Board of the Faculty of Theology.

(*b*) EITHER An examination in New Testament Exegesis.

Candidates will be expected to translate and comment on passages from the New Testament in Greek and to answer questions on a wide range of subjects concerned with the theology, ethics, and history of the New Testament.

OR, with the permission of the Faculty Board, an essay of 5,000–7,000 words on a subject proposed by the candidate and approved by the Faculty Board.

(*c*) A qualifying examination in Greek will normally be required.

III Ecclesiastical History

(*a*) An examination paper on The Nature and Practice of Ecclesiastical History, as prescribed for the M.Phil. in Theology, and to be sat at the same time.

(*b*) Three essays of not more than 5,000 words each, on titles proposed by the candidate and approved by the Board of the Faculty of Theology.

The titles of the essays should all fall within *one* of the following periods:

1. The Early Church AD 303–476
2. The Western Church AD 476–1050
3. The Western Church AD 1050–1400
4. English Church History AD 1066–1272
5. European Christianity AD 1400–1800
6. European Christianity AD 1800–1950

One of the essays may concern a specific discipline or skill related to the period (for example; palaeography, archival surveys). With the permission of the Chairman of Examiners and on the written recommendation of the candidate's supervisor, when the candidate is required to display a specific skill, such as palaeography, an appropriate examination may be taken as a substitute for one of the essays.

(*c*) A qualifying examination in Greek will normally be required for those submitting titles in period 1, and a qualifying examination in Latin for those submitting titles in period 2, 3, or 4.

IV Christian Doctrine

(*a*) *Either* (1): An examination paper on set texts in Latin or Greek:

EITHER as prescribed for the M.St. in Theology (Christian Doctrine, section A paper 4). A candidate proposing a dissertation on a topic in patristic theology is required to take this alternative.

OR as prescribed for the M.St. in Theology (Christian Doctrine, section B paper 3). A candidate proposing a dissertation on a topic in medieval theology is required to take this alternative.

OR as prescribed for the M.St. in Theology (Christian Doctrine, section C paper 3). A candidate proposing a dissertation on a topic in Reformation theology is required to take this alternative.

OR (2): An examination on Doctrines and Methods from Kant to the Present Day, as prescribed for the M.St. in Theology (Christian Doctrine, section G paper 2).

(*b*) One major paper of not exceeding 7,500 words:

OR: Two essays of not exceeding 5,000 words;

on a title or titles proposed by the candidate and approved by the Board of the Faculty of Theology. In submitting titles the candidate should explain how they form a coherent preparation for their doctoral studies, either in terms of historical period, or in terms of theme, or both.

(*c*) A qualifying examination will normally be required in a major research language to be proposed by the candidate.

V Christian Ethics

(*a*), (*b*) Two major papers of not exceeding 7,500 words each:

OR: one major paper of not exceeding 7,500 words *and* three essays of between 2,000 and 3,000 words each:

OR: six essays of between 2,000 and 3,000 words each.

The titles to be proposed by the candidate and approved by the Board of the Faculty of Theology.

In submitting titles for the dissertation, for major papers and for essays, candidates are required to explain in which pieces of work they intend to display competence in each of the following skills:

(i) exploring an ethical question, substantive or conceptual, *in relation to contemporary discussion.*

(ii) the *interpretation of a Biblical text* of moral significance.

(iii) the *discussion of a non-Biblical text* of moral significance *from some period of history prior to 1900.*

More than one of these competencies may be demonstrated in the dissertation or in a single major paper, but not in a single essay.

(*c*) A qualifying examination will normally be required in a major research language to be proposed by the candidate.

VI Science and Religion

(*a*) A written examination in each of the three subjects as prescribed for the M.St. in Science and Religion. An essay of 5,000 to 7,000 words, or three essays of 2,000 to 3,000 words may be substituted for each of the three papers specified.

(*b*) A dissertation as prescribed above, on a subject *from the field of science and religion.*

The titles of the essays and dissertation to be proposed by the candidate and approved by the Board of the Faculty of Theology.

In submitting titles for the dissertation and for essays, candidates are required to explain in which pieces of work they intend to display competence in each of the following skills:

(i) exploring a historical debate in which scientific and religious issues are involved.
(ii) exploring a philosophical debate with a bearing on the discussion of *science and religion*.
(iii) analysing a contemporary issue on the interface between science and religion.

Women's Studies

1. Every candidate must follow, for at least three terms, a course of instruction in Women's Studies. Candidates will when they enter for the examination, be required to produce from their society a certificate that they are following such a course.
2. Candidates are required to present themselves for viva voce examination if summoned by the examiners.
3. The examiners may award a distinction for excellence in the whole examination.
4. Syllabus

Candidates must offer A below, one option from B, and a dissertation (C).

A. Theory and Method

B. Options:

(i) Women, Language and Power in Early-Modern England
(ii) Women Writers of English Literature 1660–1789
(iii) Romantic Feminism: Women Writers and their Reception
(iv) Gender and Writing in Victorian England
(v) Women and Modernism
(vi) African American Women Writers
(vii) Language and Gender
(viii) Literature and Sexual Orientation
(ix) Sexuality and Sex Work: Literature and Film
(x) From Books to Bodies: Women and Religion in Western Europe 500–1500
(xi) Witchcraft in Early-Modern England, Scotland and New England
(xii) Polite Society in Eighteenth-Century Britain
(xiii) Women's Intellectual History *c.*1850–1950
(xiv) History, Society, and the Modern Body
(xv) Feminist Biography and Autobiography
(xvi) Women and Politics
(xvii) Gender and Development
(xviii) Feminism and the Social Sciences
(xix) Feminist Ethics
(xx) Gender and Representation in Russian Culture from 1800
(xxi) German Women's Writing 1450–1750 in its Social Context
(xxii) Contemporary Women's Writing in German
(xxiii) Women's Emancipation and its Adversaries in German and Austrian Modernism
(xxiv) Medieval German Women Writers in German and/or Latin
(xxv) Nineteenth-Century French Women's Writing
(xxvi) Simone de Beauvoir as Theorist and Writer
(xxvii) Contemporary Francophone Women's Writing
(xxviii) Greek Women Writers in the Twentieth Century
(xxix) Italian Women Writers 1950–1990
(xxx) Brazilian and Portuguese Women Writers in the Twentieth Century
(xxxi) Women in Old Icelandic Literature
(xxxii) The History of Sexuality in Archaic and Classical Greece
(xxxiii) Constructions of Roman Women
(xxxiv) Women in Late Antiquity and Byzantium

(xxxv) Any other option approved by the Joint Standing Committee for the M.St. in Women's Studies.

Not all options may be available in any given year. Information on the availability of options is obtainable from 1 October of the year in question from the joint Standing Committee for the M.St. in Women's Studies (by application to the Modern Languages Graduate Studies Office, 41 Wellington Square).

C. A dissertation of up to 15,000 words (and not less than 13,000), excluding footnotes and bibliography, on a subject proposed by the candidate in consultation with the dissertation supervisor. A letter detailing the title and subject of the dissertation, accompanied by a letter of recommendation from the dissertation supervisor, must be submitted for approval to the Chair of Examiners (c/o Modern Languages Graduate Studies Office) not later than Friday of 4th week of Hilary Term. Any subsequent significant change of title and/or subject should be discussed with and approved by the dissertation supervisor, and the candidate should write (with a supporting letter from the supervisor) to the Chair of Examiners by no later than Friday of Noughth week of Trinity Term. The subject matter of the dissertation may be related to that of either or both of the two pieces of written work submitted for the Theory and Methods and Option courses, but material deployed in such pieces of work may not be repeated in the dissertation.

5. In the case of A and B candidates will be examined by the submission of written work. One essay submitted under A should be of 6,000 words, excluding footnotes and bibliography. The essay submitted under B should be of up to 10,000 words (and not less than 9,000 words), excluding footnotes and bibliography. The titles and topics of the written work proposed, accompanied by a letter of recommendation from the general supervisor and option tutor respectively, must be submitted for approval to the Chair of Examiners (c/o Modern Languages Graduate Studies Office) not later than Friday of 4th week of Hilary Term. Any subsequent significant change of title and/or subject should be discussed with and approved by the supervisor or option tutor, and the candidate should write (with a supporting letter from the supervisor or tutor) to the Chair of Examiners by no later than Friday of Noughth week of Trinity Term.

The two pieces of written work under A and B (two typewritten or printed copies of each piece, bearing on the front the candidate's examination number but neither his or her name nor the name of his or her college) must be delivered in a parcel bearing the words 'Written work submitted for the M.St. in Women's Studies' to the Clerk of the Schools, Examination Schools, High Street, Oxford not later than noon on Friday of 1st week of Trinity Term.

Supervisors or others are permitted to give bibliographical help with and to discuss drafts of written work submitted. The written work must be accompanied, under a separate cover, by a signed statement by the candidate that it is his or her own work except where otherwise indicated.

In the case of C, the dissertation (two typewritten or printed copies, bearing on the front the candidate's examination number but neither his or her name nor the name of his or her college) must be delivered in a parcel bearing the words 'Dissertation submitted for the M.St. in Women's Studies' to the Clerk of the Schools, Examination Schools, High Street, Oxford, not later than noon on Friday of 8th week of Trinity Term. Students must also submit two copies of a brief abstract (no more than 500 words) outlining the rationale and approach of the thesis. Candidates must themselves retain one typewritten or printed copy of their work. Supervisors or others are permitted to give bibliographical help with and to discuss drafts of dissertations. The dissertation must be accompanied, under a separate cover, by a signed statement by the candidate that it is his or her work except where otherwise indicated.

6. A candidate who fails to submit any of the three written elements (that is, the two pieces of written work and the dissertation) by the dates specified above shall be deemed to have withdrawn from the examination.

7. If the two pieces of written work, submitted for A and B, and/or the dissertation, submitted for C, fail the examination, the candidate shall not be granted leave to supplicate for the degree of M.St. Such a candidate is permitted to resubmit the elements of the examination that have failed to satisfy the examiners, on one further occasion only. The two pieces of written work (A and B) shall be resubmitted by noon on the Friday of the first week of the Trinity Term following their first examination, and the dissertation (C) shall be resubmitted by not later than noon on the Friday of the eighth week of the Trinity Term following their first examination.

World Archaeology

1. Within the Division of Life and Environmental Sciences, the course shall be administered by the Committee for the School of Archaeology. The regulations made are as follows:

2. Candidates for admission must apply to the Committee for the School of Archaeology. They will be required to produce evidence of their appropriate qualifications for the proposed course, which may include their suitable proficiency in relevant ancient or modern languages.

3. Candidates must follow for three terms a course of instruction in World Archaeology.

4. The registration of candidates will lapse on the last day of the Trinity Full Term in the academic year of their admission, unless it shall have been extended by the committee.

5. The written examination shall comprise three subjects:

(*a*) one subject selected from Schedules A–B below to be examined by written paper;

(*b*) two further subjects selected from Schedules A–B [Not more than one subject of the three selected may normally be taken from Schedule B.] Each of these subjects may be examined at the candidate's choice either by two pre-set essays (each of 5,000 words) or by written paper.

In lieu of one of the subjects in (*b*) above, M.St. (but not normally M.Phil.) candidates may offer, with the permission of the committee, a dissertation of not more than 10,000 words (excluding bibliography and descriptive catalogue or similar factual matter, but including notes and appendices).

The topic of the dissertation should be connected with one of the subjects chosen by the candidate under 4(*a*) and (*b*) above and must be approved by the candidate's supervisor. If the candidate has elected to be examined by pre-set essays in another part of the examination, the topic of the dissertation must be clearly distinct from the pre-set essay titles. The dissertation must be the work of the candidate alone, and aid from others must be limited to prior discussion of the subject, bibliographic advice, help with access to study material and advice on presentation. The dissertation must be a new piece of work, substantially different from any dissertation previously submitted by the candidate for a degree of this or another university. When the dissertation is submitted, it must be accompanied by a statement, signed by the candidate, confirming that these conditions have been met. The proposed title of the dissertation, countersigned by the supervisor, must be submitted for approval by the committee by noon on the Monday of the seventh week of the Michaelmas Full Term preceding the examination. Two copies typed or printed (the second may be a photocopy) in double spacing on one side only of A4 paper and bound simply or filed securely, must be delivered in a parcel bearing the words 'Dissertation for the M.St. in World Archaeology' to the Clerk of the Schools, High Street, Oxford, not later than noon on the Friday of the sixth week of Trinity Full Term. Candidates will be required to deposit one copy of the dissertation with the Clerk of the Schools.

Schedule A: Main subjects

Palaeolithic Archaeology
The Archaeology of colonialism: prehistoric and recent
Hunter-gatherers past and present in a world perspective
African hunter-gatherers
African farming and states
Regional studies in Australian and Pacific prehistory
Chinese Archaeology
The formation of the Islamic World
Archaeological method and theory

Schedule B: Related subjects

Any subject offered in the M.St. in European Archaeology or Classical Archaeology.

Candidates may apply for other subjects to be approved by the committee, which shall define their scope and inform both the candidate and the examiners of this definition in writing. Not all course options may be available in any given year.

6. Candidates will be expected to show a general knowledge of Ancient History and Geography, so far as they are concerned with their subjects.

7. Candidates must present themselves for an oral examination as required by the examiners.

8. The subjects to be offered by the candidates and their chosen method of examination, duly approved by their supervisors, must be submitted for approval to the committee in time for its meeting in eighth week of the Michaelmas Full Term preceding the examination. Notice of options to be offered by candidates must be given to the Registrar not later than Friday of the eighth week of that same term.

9. Candidates intending to offer pairs of pre-set essays in place of one or two written examinations (as specified in 4 above) will select essay topics from a list offered by their supervisor. The proposed essay titles, countersigned by the supervisor, must be submitted for approval to the Chairman of Examiners by noon on Friday of the seventh week of the Hilary Full Term preceding the examinations. Candidates must submit two copies of their essays by not later than noon on Friday of the sixth week of Trinity Full Term to the Examination Schools. Essays must be typed or printed.

10. The examiners may award a distinction for excellence in the whole examination.

Yiddish Studies

1. All candidates shall be required at the time of admission to satisfy the board (if necessary, by written and oral tests) that they possess the appropriate qualifications for the proposed course, including suitable proficiency in written and spoken Yiddish. Normally the course will be restricted to candidates who have taken a first degree in a relevant subject area.

2. All candidates must follow a course of instruction in Yiddish Studies at Oxford for a period of three terms, unless the Board of the Faculty of Medieval and Modern Languages in exceptional circumstances shall permit an extension of time and they shall, when they enter their names for the examination, be required to produce from their society a certificate stating that they are following the course of instruction for the period prescribed.

3. Candidates shall be required:

(*a*) to offer themselves for written examination as defined below:

(*b*) to offer themselves for viva voce examination if required to do so by the examiners.

4. *Syllabus*

Candidates must offer both components of A below, one option from B, and a dissertation (C).

A.

(i) Modern Yiddish Literature (1864–1939).

(ii) History of the Yiddish Language.

B.

(i) Old Yiddish Literature (survey).

(ii) Old Yiddish Literature: Secular and Religious Trends.

(iii) Old Yiddish: Between Folklore and Literature.

(iv) Nineteenth-Century Yiddish Literature.

(v) Modern Yiddish Poetry.

(vi) Yiddish Drama and Theatre.

(vii) Twentieth-Century Centres of Yiddish Literature and Culture.

(viii) Sociology of Yiddish.

(ix) History of Yiddish Studies.

(x) Yiddish Stylistics.

(xi) Yiddish Bibliography and Booklore.

(xii) Any other option approved by the board.

Candidates shall seek approval (by application to the Modern Languages Graduate Office, 37 Wellington Square, Oxford) of their proposed option by the end of the fourth week of their first term.

Teaching for some options listed under B may not be available in every year. Applicants for admission will be advised of this.

C.

A dissertation of approximately 8,000 words and not more than 10,000 words on a subject proposed by the candidate in consultation with the supervisor and approved by the Board of the Faculty of Medieval and Modern Languages. Candidates shall seek approval (by application to the Modern Languages Graduate Office, 41 Wellington Square, Oxford) for the proposed topic of their dissertation by the end of the fourth week of their second term.

The dissertation must be presented in proper scholarly form. Two copies, typed in double-spacing on one side only of A4 paper, each bound or held firmly in a stiff cover bearing on the front the candidate's examination number but neither his or her name nor the name of his or her college, must be delivered in a parcel bearing the words 'Dissertation submitted for the M.St. in Yiddish Studies' to the Clerk of the Schools, High Street, Oxford, not later than noon on the Friday of the seventh week of Trinity Term. Candidates must themselves retain one copy of the dissertation.

Supervisors or others are permitted to give bibliographical help during the preparation of the dissertation and to discuss drafts.

5. The examiners may award a distinction for excellence in the whole examination.

NOTES

8

REGULATIONS FOR THE DEGREE OF MASTER OF SCIENCE BY COURSEWORK*

Ch. VI, Sect. VII]

General Regulations

§1. Degree of Master of Science by Coursework

1. Any person who has been admitted to the status of student for the degree of Master of Science by Coursework, who has satisfied the conditions prescribed by this section, and has satisfied the examiners as required, may supplicate for the Degree of Master of Science by Coursework.

2. The Educational Policy and Standards Committee shall have power to make and vary such regulations as may be necessary for carrying out the duties laid upon it and upon the Secretary of Faculties by this section.

3. For the purposes of this section, the words 'board', 'faculty board', or 'board of the faculty' shall include any committee authorized to admit candidates for the Degree of Master of Science by Coursework.

4. A Student for the Degree of Master of Science by Coursework who is not a graduate of the University may wear the same gown as that worn by Students for the Degree of Doctor of Philosophy.

§2. Status of Student for the Degree of Master of Science by Coursework

1. Any person who, in the opinion of the board concerned, is well qualified and well fitted to undertake the course of study for which application is made, may be admitted to the status of Student for the Degree of Master of Science by Coursework.

2. It shall be the duty of the Secretary of Faculties to keep a Register of those admitted to the status of Student for the Degree of Master of Science by Coursework.

---

* This regulation should be read in conjunction with the associated regulations made by the individual faculty or divisional boards, to be found on pp. 837–82.

§3. Admission of Candidates for the Degree of Master of Science by Coursework

1. A candidate seeking admission as a Student for the Degree of Master of Science by Coursework shall apply to the board under whose aegis the proposed course of study falls. Candidates for admission shall be required to provide such information as the board may determine from time to time by regulation. Applicants shall in addition be required to undertake such other tests and meet such conditions as, subject to the approval of the Educational Policy and Standards Committee, a board may determine by regulation.

2. Applications shall be made through the Secretary of Faculties, and it shall be the duty of the Secretary of Faculties to submit each application to the board concerned and to inform the candidate of the outcome, as soon as may be.

3. No person shall be admitted as a Student for the Degree of Master of Science by Coursework under these provisions unless he or she is also a member of a college, and unless the application for admission as a Student for the Degree of Master of Science by Coursework has the approval of that college. The Secretary of Faculties shall forward the application to the candidate's college or to the college to which the candidate wishes to apply for membership, as appropriate; and admission by the faculty board shall be conditional upon admission by an approved society.

4. A student registered for any other higher degree or diploma in the University may apply for transfer to the status of Student for the Degree of Master of Science by Coursework. The board concerned shall have power to make such transfer, provided that it is satisfied that the student is well qualified and well fitted to undertake the course of study for which application is made, and that the application has the support of the candidate's society. A candidate who transfers status in this way shall be reckoned as having held the status of Student for the Degree of Master of Science by Coursework from the time of admission to his or her previous status, unless the board shall determine otherwise.

5. A student holding the status of Probationer Research Student may, with the approval of the board which admitted him or her, be admitted as a candidate for an examination for the Degree of Master of Science by Coursework. Time spent as a student holding the status of Probationer Research Student shall count as time spent working for the Degree of Master of Science.

§4. Supervision of Students for the Degree of Master of Science by Coursework

1. Every candidate on admission as a Student for the Degree of Master of Science by Coursework shall be placed by the board

concerned under the supervision of a member of the University or other competent person selected by the board, and the board shall have power for sufficient reason to change the supervisor of any student or to arrange for joint supervision by more than one supervisor, if it deems it necessary.

2. It shall be the duty of the supervisor of a student entered upon a course of study to direct and superintend the work of the student, to meet the student regularly, and to undertake such duties as shall be from time to time be set out in the relevant Notes of Guidance issued by the Educational Policy and Standards Committee.

3. The supervisor shall submit a report on the progress of a student to the board three times a year, and at any other time when the board so requests or the supervisor deems it expedient. The supervisor shall communicate the contents of the report to the student on each occasion that a report is made, so that the student is aware of the supervisor's assessment of his or her work during the period in question. In addition, the supervisor shall inform the board at once if he or she is of the opinion the student is unlikely to reach the standard required for the Degree of Master of Science by Coursework.

4. It shall be the duty of every Student for the Degree of Master of Science by Coursework to undertake such guided work and to attend such seminars and lectures as his or her supervisor requests; to attend such meetings with his or her supervisor as the supervisor reasonably arranges; and to fulfil any other requirements of the Educational Policy and Standards Committee as set out in relevant Notes of Guidance issued by the Educational Policy and Standards Committee.

§5. Residence and other Requirements for Students for the Degree of Master of Science by Coursework

1. No full-time Student for the Degree of Master of Science by Coursework shall be granted leave to supplicate unless, after admission, he or she has kept statutory residence and pursued his or her course of study at Oxford for at least three terms.

2. A full-time student working towards the examination in Applied Social Studies or Social Research shall not be given leave to supplicate unless, after admission as a graduate student, he or she has kept statutory residence and pursued his or her course of study at Oxford for at least six terms, save that the board may dispense from statutory residence any candidate for the examination in Applied Social Studies who is required as part of the course to

undertake fieldwork away from Oxford, for the time such fieldwork necessarily occupies, up to a maximum of two terms.

3. No full-time Student for the Degree of Master of Science by Coursework shall retain that status for more than six terms in all, except that any candidate for the Examination in Applied Social Studies and Social Research or Educational Studies may retain that status for nine terms in all.

4. Part-time students for the Degree of Master of Science by Coursework shall in each case be required to pursue their course of study for twice the number of terms required of an equivalent full-time student. Part-time students shall not be required to keep statutory residence but must attend for such instruction and undertake such supervised fieldwork as the faculty concerned shall require. The Director of Graduate Studies of the board concerned, or director of the department concerned, as the case may be, shall keep a register of attendance of part-time students. No student shall be granted leave to supplicate unless the register shows satisfactory attendance by him or her.

5. Part-time students may hold the status of Student for the Degree of Master of Science by Coursework for up to twice the number of terms for which equivalent full-time students may hold that status.

6. A Student for the Degree of Master of Science by Coursework shall cease to hold that status if:

(i) he or she shall have been refused permission to supplicate for the Degree of Master of Science by Coursework;

(ii) the board concerned shall, in accordance with provisions set down by regulation by the Educational Policy and Standards Committee, and after consultation with the student's society and supervisor, have deprived the student of such status;

(iii) he or she shall have been transferred under the relevant provisions to another status;

(iv) he or she shall not have entered for the relevant examination within the time specified under this subsection.

§6. Examination of Students

1. The examinations for the Degree of Master of Science by Coursework shall be under the supervision of the boards authorized to admit candidates for the Degree of Master of Science by Coursework. The examinations for the degree and the bodies responsible for the supervision of each examination are listed below.

Examination	*Board*
Advanced Cognitive Therapy Studies	Continuing Education
Applied and Computational Mathematics	Mathematical and Physical Sciences
Applied Linguistics and Second Language Acquisition	Social Sciences
Applied Landscape Archaeology	Continuing Education
Applied Social Studies	Social Sciences
Applied Statistics	Mathematical and Physical Sciences
Archaeological Science	Life and Environmental Sciences
Biodiversity, Conservation, and Management	Life and Environmental Sciences
Bioinformatics	Continuing Education/ Mathematical and Physical Sciences
Biology (Integrative Bioscience)	Life and Environmental Sciences
Comparative Social Policy	Social Sciences
Computer Science	Mathematical and Physical Sciences
Criminology and Criminal Justice	Law
Diagnostic Imaging	Medical Sciences
Economic and Social History	Modern History
Economics for Development	Social Sciences
Educational Research Methodology	Social Sciences
Educational Studies	Social Sciences
Environmental Change and Management	Life and Environmental Sciences
Environmental Geomorphology	Life and Environmental Sciences
Evidence-based Health Care	Medical Sciences/ Continuing Education
Evidence-based Social Work	Social Sciences
Forced Migration	Area and Development Studies Committee
Forestry: Science, Policy, and Management	Life and Environmental Sciences

Geometry, Mathemetical Physics, and Analysis	Mathematical and Physical Sciences
History of Science: Instruments, Museums, Science, Technology	Modern History
History of Science, Medicine, and Technology	Modern History
Human Biology	Life and Environmental Sciences
Industrial Relations and Human Resource Management	Management
Latin American Studies	Area and Development Studies
Management Research	Management
Material Anthropology and Museum Ethnography	Life and Environmental Sciences
Mathematical Finance	Mathematical and Physical Sciences/Continuing Education
Mathematical Modelling and Scientific Computation	Mathematical and Physical Sciences
Mathematics and Foundations of Computer Science	Mathematical and Physical Sciences
Medical Anthropology	Life and Environmental Sciences
Natural, Society, and Environmental Policy	Life and Environmental Sciences
Neuroscience	Medical Sciences
Pharmacology	Medical Sciences
Politics and International Relations Research	Social Sciences
Professional Development in Education	Social Sciences
Public Policy in Latin America	Area and Developmental Studies Committee
Research in Psychology	Medical Sciences
Russian and East European Studies	Area and Development Studies
Science and Medicine of Athletic Performance	Medical Sciences
Social Anthropology	Life and Environmental Sciences
Sociology	Social Scienes

Software Engineering	Mathematical and Physical Sciences/Continuing Education
Theoretical Chemistry	Mathematical and Physical Sciences
Visual Anthropology	Life and Environmental Sciences

The subjects of each examination shall be determined by regulation by the board concerned, which shall have power to arrange lectures and courses of instruction for the examination. The examination shall consist of:

(i) a written dissertation on a subject approved by the board or by a person or persons to whom the board may delegate the function of giving such approval;

(ii) a written examination;

(iii) an oral examination;

provided that a board shall have power by regulation to exclude any one of parts (i), (ii), or (iii) from the examination for a particular course of study and to authorize the examiners to dispense individual candidates from the oral examination. This provision notwithstanding, the examiners may, if they deem it expedient, set a candidate a further written examination after examining the candidate orally.

2. No candidate shall be permitted to take an examination under the preceding clause unless he or she has been admitted as a candidate for the examination in question by the body responsible for the course and has satisfied any other conditions prescribed in the regulations for that course.

3. Unless otherwise provided in this subsection, the number and distribution of examiners shall be as set out in Sect. II. A, §1, cl. 8 of this chapter. A board shall have power to prescribe that examiners be appointed for candidates individually in such manner as shall be appropriate for the particular course of study.

4. A candidate who has failed to satisfy the examiners in the examination may enter again for the examination on one, but not more than one, subsequent occasion.

5. A board may prescribe by regulation that students undertaking a particular course of study shall take the examination in a specific term as a condition of admission, and a student wishing to take an examination later than the one to which he or she has been admitted must apply to the board for permission to do so.

SPECIAL REGULATIONS

Except where otherwise indicated, all material submitted for examination (dissertations, extended essays, etc) shall be accompanied by a certificate signed by the candidate indicating that it is the candidate's own work, except where otherwise specified. This certificate must be submitted separately in a sealed envelope addressed to the chairman of examiners of the degree course in question.

Advanced Cognitive Therapy Studies

Regulations

1. The course will consist of lectures, tutorials, seminars, and classes on the principle and practice of advanced cognitive therapy studies, together with clinical practice and practice in supervision of cognitive therapy trainees. The course will be taken on a part-time basis over a period of not less than six terms and not more than nine terms.

2. Every candidate will be required to satisfy the examiners in the following:

(*a*) attendance at the appropriate classroom-based courses including small group case supervisions;

(*b*) supervised treatment of patients with cognitive therapy;

(*c*) skill in supervising cognitive therapy trainees;

(*d*) four audio- or videotape presentations of therapy sessions;

(*e*) four extended written case studies, each of no more than 4,000 words covering a range of different problem areas and including two straightforward and two complex cases;

(*f*) two written assignments, each of no more than 4,000 words, one covering the principles of supervision, and one covering the design, delivery and evaluation of a training event;

(*g*) a presentation of a brief cognitive therapy training event;

(*h*) a dissertation of no more than 15,000 words on a topic approved by the examiners.

The presentation under (*d*) and (*g*), the assessed work under (*e*) and (*f*), and the dissertation under (*h*), shall be forwarded to the examiners for consideration by such dates as the examiners shall determine and shall notify the candidates and tutors.

3. Candidates will be expected to attend a viva voce examination at the end of the course of studies unless individually dispensed by the examiners.

4. The examiners may award a distinction to candidates for the M.Sc.

5. Candidates who fail to satisfy the examiners in the audio- or videotape presentations under 2(*d*) and 2(*g*), the assessed work under 2(*e*) and 2(*f*), or the dissertation under 2(*h*), may be permitted to resubmit work in respect of the part or parts of the examination which they have failed for examination on not more than one occasion which shall normally be within one year of the original failure.

Applied and Computational Mathematics

1. The Divisional Board of Mathematical and Physical Sciences shall elect for the supervision of the course an organizing committee which shall have power to approve lectures and other instruction, and approve the research topics chosen by candidates. There will also be a course organizer who will be responsible for setting up the programme and carrying out decisions of the committee.

2. The organizing committee shall appoint for each candidate a supervisor.

3. Each candidate shall follow a course of study in Applied and Computational Mathematics for at least three terms and for a substantial part of the three subsequent

vacations, as determined by the course timetable, and will be required to produce a certificate from their academic advisor to this effect.

4. Candidates will be examined in the following ways:

(i) they will be assessed on four courses chosen from a list approved each year by the organizing committee in the areas of applied mathematics and numerical analysis as specified in the Schedule. The assessment of each course will take the form either of a written examination or a short project or continuous assessment of classwork as laid down by the organizing committee;

(ii) they will be required to attend modelling and practical numerical analysis classes and to submit projects on both courses for assessment by the class tutor;

(iii) each candidate will be required to submit to the examiners two copies of a typewritten or printed dissertation on a research project chosen for study, and approved by the standing committee;

(iv) each candidate will be required to give a public oral presentation on a subject of his or her choice related to the content of his or her dissertation on a date to be determined by the standing committee.

5. Each candidate will be examined viva voce.

6. Before being given leave to supplicate, candidates must have demonstrated understanding of and competence in the topics covered by the professional development programme to the satisfaction of the course organizer, who shall submit a certificate to the examiners to this effect. The organizing committee will each year approve the programme.

7. The dissertation must be sent to the Chairman of Examiners, M.Sc. in Applied and Computational Mathematics, c/o Clerk of the Schools, Examination Schools, High Street, Oxford by the first Friday in September.

8. The viva voce examinations will be conducted in September in the year in which the candidate is examined on dates to be determined by the examiners.

9. The examiners may award a distinction for excellence in the whole examination.

10. The examiners shall retain one copy of each dissertation of each successful candidate for deposit in the most appropriate departmental library.

SCHEDULE

The theory of ordinary and partial differential equations transform methods, applications of complex variable theory, distributions, asymptotic methods. Further topics in applied analysis. Application of mathematics to problems in physical sciences, finance, biology and medicine.

The numerical solution of ordinary and partial differential equations and integral equations. Finite element methods, topics in numerical linear algebra, mathematical methods for optimization and approximation.

Applied Landscape Archaeology

1. Every candidate must follow for at least six terms a part-time course of instruction in Applied Landscape Archaeology and must upon entering for examination produce from his or her society a certificate to that effect.

2. The examination will consist of the following parts:

A Core Topics

Every candidate must submit two written assignments of no more than 2,500 words in length for each of the two core topic courses on:

(1) Method and Theory in Landscape Archaeology;

(2) Managing Twenty-first Century Landscapes.

One core topic will be taken in each year of the course.

B Advanced Papers

Every candidate must follow four of the six Advanced Paper courses listed in the Schedule below, and submit one written assignment of no more than 5,000 words in length for each paper. Candidates will take two Advanced Papers per year of the M.Sc.

C Dissertation

A dissertation of not more than 15,000 words, including appendices but excluding bibliography, on a topic approved by the candidate's supervisor. The dissertation must be delivered not later than noon on the last Monday in September of the second year of the course to the Chairman of Examiners for the Degree of M.Sc. in Applied Landscape Archaeology, c/o Clerk of the Schools, High Street, Oxford.

3. Candidates must attend one compulsory field training week (or in exceptional circumstances equivalent day or weekend schools) during their registration on the course.

4. Each candidate must attend a viva voce examination when required to do so by the examiners.

5. The examiners may award a distinction for excellence in the whole examination.

6. A candidate who fails a core topic or advanced paper, or whose dissertation fails to satisfy the examiners, may be permitted to retake the paper, or resubmit the dissertation, on one further occasion only, not later than one year after the initial attempt.

SCHEDULE

Advanced Papers are available in the following areas:

1. Archaeological prospection
2. Reading the historic landscape
3. Ceramics in the landscape
4. Digital landscapes
5. Placement work
6. Geoarchaeology

Not all advanced papers will be available in any one year and the definitive list of advanced papers available in any one year will be circulated to candidates and their supervisors during the second week of Michaelmas Term.

Applied Linguistics and Second Language Acquisition

1. Candidates may only be admitted to the course if they have successfully obtained an honours degree which contained a substantial element of second language learning and/or linguistics.

2. Every candidate will be required to complete all eight Modules of the course unless he/she can make a case for prior accreditation (by virtue of having successfully completed the Diploma in Educational Studies, Modern Foreign Languages) in which case they will be required to complete six modules.

3. Every candidate will be required to satisfy the examiners in the following:

(i) Satisfatory attendance at the appropriate classroom-based courses;

(ii) Satisfactory performance in each of the end of Module Assignments.

Two word-processed or printed copies of each of four module assignments must be delivered to the M.Sc. Examiners, c/o Department of Educational Studies, 15 Norham Gardens, Oxford OX2 6PY, no later than 5 p.m. on the Friday of Week 1 of Hilary Full Term, and two word-processed or printed copies of each of four further module assignments must be delivered to the M.Sc. Examiners, c/o Department of Educational Studies, 15 Norham Gardens, Oxford OX2 6PY, no later than 5 p.m. on the Friday of Week 1 of Trinity Full Term. Part-time students must submit assignments for two module assignments on each of these occasions over a period of two years.

4. A dissertation of between 15,000 and 20,000 words (including appendices, endnotes and a reference section) on a subject selected by the candidate in consultation with the supervisor, which must be closely related to one or more of the themes of the course. The subject selected by the candidate must be approved by the supervisor on behalf of the Tutor for Higher Degrees and Academic Board of the Department. Candidates must give notice to the M.Sc. examiners, c/o Department of Education Studies, 15 Norham Gardens, Oxford, OX2 6PY concerning the subject of their dissertation by the first day of the fifth week of Hilary Term of the course (for full-time candidates) and of the second year of the course (for part-time candidates).

5. Three word processed or printed copies of the dissertation must be delivered to the M.Sc. examiners, c/o Department of Educational Studies, 15 Norham Gardens, Oxford, OX2 6PY, no later than 30 September of the year in which the final Module examination has been taken. One copy should be hard bound and two soft bound, and should be anonymous except for the candidate number. Candidates wishing to submit dissertations later than this date must obtain the approval of the Academic Board by the last day of the preceding Trinity Full Term. Such approval will only be granted in exceptional circumstances. The hard bound copy of the dissertation of each candidate who is successful at examination shall be retained by the Department for deposit in the departmental library.

6. The examiners may award a distinction for excellence in the whole examination.

7. The M.Sc. in Applied Linguistics and Second Language Acquisition, if successfully completed, subsumes a candidate's previously completed diploma course in Modern Foreign Languages Teaching and Learning.

8. Each candidate may:

(i) re-sit *a maximum of two* of the eight (or six where the diploma has been completed) end of Module assignments. These must, unless in exceptional circumstances, be re-submitted within one month of the date of notification of the outcome.

9. If more than two of the eight module assignments are failed, or if either or both of any resubmitted module assignments are failed, the candidate may retake the entire examination for the eight modules one further time on the next occasion they are examined (usually the following year).

10. The candidate *may* also be examined orally. The oral examination may only be on the candidate's dissertation.

Schedule

Module A First Language Acquisition and Bilingualism
Module B Theories, Progression, and Methods
Module C Individual and Group Differences
Module D Input and Interaction
Module E Accessing Meaning
Module F Producing and Communicating Meaning
Module G Vocabulary Acquisition
Module H Error, Analysis, Interlanguage, and Testing
Optional Double Module: Teaching English as a Foreign Language Certificate.

Applied Social Studies (This course will cease at 30 September 2004 and last admissions are with effect from 1 October 2002)

1. Candidates must follow, for at least six terms, or in the case of a part-time candidate at least twelve terms, a course of instruction in Applied Social Studies

and will, when entering for the examinations, be required to produce a certificate from their society to this effect.

2. The examination will be in three parts as follows:

Part A: Qualifying Tests

(*a*) Law test.

(*b*) Applied Social Studies I, in social sciences (social policy, psychology, and sociology).

The Examiners may call borderline candidates for viva voce examination.

Candidates will not be allowed to proceed to the final examinations unless they have passed the qualifying tests in law and social sciences. Candidates will have the opportunity of resitting these examinations in the second week before Michaelmas Term in their second year.

Part B: Examination of Practice

Candidates will be required to complete to the satisfaction of the examiners two periods of supervised social work practice. Competence in social work practice will be examined by means of the reports submitted by practice teachers which must include a written account by the candidate of the work undertaken and an analysis of not more than 3,000 words by the candidate of a specific piece of practice undertaken during each period of supervised practice, demonstrating the student's understanding and knowledge of relevant theory as applied to social work practice.

In each period of supervised practice candidates must demonstrate the range of skills necessary to provide an effective social work service to clients and an understanding of discrimination and disadvantage and how they may be addressed. Candidates will be required to show competence in the following areas of social work practice: sustaining professional relationships with clients and others; assessment of needs and strengths of individuals, families, groups, and communities; collation and evaluation of relevant information; planning appropriate action; initiating and undertaking appropriate intervention; evaluation of the aims and outcomes of social work. In addition, in the second period of supervised practice, students are required to demonstrate an ability to transfer knowledge and skills to new situations.

In Part B, any candidate may be called to viva voce examination of practice competence. No candidate shall be deemed to have failed to satisfy the examiners in Part B without having the opportunity of attending such an examination. The examiners may also seek further information from the candidate's practice teacher about any candidate to assist their deliberations. In the case of a marginal candidate the practice teacher will be expected to be in attendance at the examiners' meeting.

Candidates will not be allowed to proceed to the final period of supervised practice until they have demonstrated competence in the initial period of supervised practice to the satisfaction of the examiners and have passed the qualifying tests in law and social sciences. Candidates who fail to satisfy the examiners in relation to the initial period of supervised practice but have passed the qualifying tests in law and social sciences may be permitted by the examiners to repeat the initial period of supervised practice and will in that case be required to submit themselves for a further qualifying examination of practice before being allowed to proceed to the final period of supervised practice.

Candidates who fail to satisfy the examiners in relation to the final period of supervised practice may be permitted by the examiners to repeat this final period of supervised practice and will in that case be required to submit themselves for a further examination of practice.

Part C: Final examination

(*a*) Two papers as follows: Applied Social Studies II; Applied Social Studies III.

(*b*) A thesis of not more than 12,000 words, including appendices but excluding bibliography. Candidates will be expected to demonstrate in the thesis an appreciation of the uses of critical enquiry in social work.

Two copies of the thesis must be delivered to the Clerk of the Schools, High Street, Oxford, by noon on Friday in the sixth week of the Trinity Term in which the examination is taken, in a parcel bearing in the bottom right-hand corner in block capitals the words 'THESIS FOR THE M.Sc. IN APPLIED SOCIAL STUDIES'. Successful candidates will be required to deposit a copy of their thesis in the library of the Department of Social Policy and Social Work.

The examiners may call borderline candidates for viva voce on their papers or thesis, or both.

Syllabus of Papers

Law Test

The English legal system. The nature and sources of law, adjudication, judicial discretion. The relationship between English law and European Community Law. The legal basis for social work intervention. Citizens' rights and obligations.

Candidates will be required to show a knowledge of such parts of the law as are relevant to social work, and in particular aspects of the law relating to:

(*a*) sex discrimination, race discrimination, and disability discrimination;

(*b*) social security;

(*c*) the criminal justice process in respect of police powers, prosecuting, sentencing; enforcement of sentences and penalties and executive release decisions, prison rules;

(*d*) children and families;

(*e*) community care;

(*f*) mental health.

Applied Social Studies I

British social institutions and social structure. The distribution of life chances in relation to education, social mobility, and employment opportunities. The significance of class, race, age, and gender. The character, methods, and limitations of empirical sociological enquiry. The meaning of community, theories of deviance, and the nature of bureaucracies and the professions.

Demand and need for public welfare. Definition and measurement of poverty. Models of welfare. The aims, function, and structure of British social services. The place of state, voluntary effort, kinship, communities, and markets in supply and distribution of welfare and the outcome for different social groups.

Aspects of developmental, social, and personal psychology. Early experiences and their effects, socialization. Social interaction, group processes, and inter-group relations. The formation and change of social attitudes. Human motivation. The structure and organization of human personality.

Applied Social Studies II

The application of sociology, psychology, social policy, criminology, law, and social work theory to personal and social issues. The evaluation of policies and practices designed to address them. Candidates will be required to demonstrate detailed knowledge of specific social work services to meet particular needs.

A list of topics to be included will be published by the examiners not later than the Friday of the sixth week of Michaelmas Term in the academic year in which the examination is taken.

Applied Social Studies III

Social work principles, values, theory, and research. The place of social work within the public services. Ideological, legal, and organizational influences on social work practice in an ethnically diverse society. Institutional and individual forms of discrimination. The structure of, and organizational processes within, social work agencies. Evaluation of the effectiveness of different methods of social work.

Applied Statistics

1. The Divisional Board of Mathematical and Physical Sciences shall elect for the supervision of the course a standing committee which shall have power to arrange lectures and other instruction.

2. Candidates shall follow for at least three terms a course of instruction in Statistics, and will, when entering their name for the examination, be required to produce from their society a certificate that they are doing so.

3. The examination will consist of:

(i) a written examination consisting of two papers on the syllabus described in the schedule;

(ii) a dissertation on a subject selected in consultation with the supervisor and approved by the chairman of the committee.

4. Candidates must submit to the chairman of the committee by the end of Hilary Term in the year in which they enter the examination, the title and a brief statement of the form and scope of their dissertation, together with the name of a person who has agreed to act as their supervisor during the preparation of the dissertation.

5. Two typewritten or printed copies of the dissertation must be sent not later than noon on 15 September in the year in which the written examination is taken, to the M.Sc. examiners (Applied Statistics), c/o the Clerk of the Schools, Examination Schools, High Street, Oxford. The examiners may retain one copy of the dissertation of each candidate who passes the examination for deposit in an appropriate departmental library.

6. Each candidate will be expected to have displayed evidence of the ability to apply statistical methods to real data.

The examiners will take into account the results of an assessment of ability to apply statistical methods to real data organized by the supervisory committee. The supervisory committee will be responsible for notifying the candidates of the arrangements for the assessment, and for forwarding the assessed material to the chairman of the examiners before the end of the Trinity Term in the year in which the assessment is made.

7. In the written examination the examiners will permit the use of any hand-held pocket calculators subject to the conditions set out under the heading 'Use of calculators in examinations' in the *Special Regulations concerning Examinations*.

Candidates may use language dictionaries in the written examination, but should notify the Chairman of the Examiners of their intention to do so not later than two weeks before the examination.

8. The examiners may also examine any candidate viva voce.

9. The examiners may award a distinction for excellence in the whole examination.

10. If it is the opinion of the examiners that the work done by the candidate is not of sufficient merit to qualify for the Degree of M.Sc., but is nevertheless of sufficient merit to qualify for the Diploma in Applied Statistics, the candidate shall be given the option of resitting the M.Sc. examination under Ch. VI, Sect. VII, 4, cl. 5, or of being issued with a diploma in the form prescribed in Ch. VI, Sect. II, Schedule E.

SCHEDULE

Paper 1: Principles of statistical analysis

Statistical distribution theory; statistical inference; statistical methods.

Paper 2: Further statistical methodology

Topics in statistical methodology chosen from a list approved by the standing committee and published in the *University Gazette* before the end of the Trinity Term in the academic year before which the written examination is to be taken.

Archaeological Science

1. Within the Division of Life and Environmental Sciences, the course shall be administered by the Committee for the School of Archaeology. The regulations made are as follows:

2. Candidates for admission must apply to the Committee for the School of Archaeology.

3. Candidates must follow a course of instruction in Archaeological Science for at least three terms and for a substantial part of the three subsequent vacations, as determined by the course timetable, and will, when they enter their names for the examination, be required to produce a certificate from their supervisors to this effect.

4. The written examination, which will be taken in the second week of Trinity term, will consist of three papers on the syllabus described in the Schedule.

5. Each candidate will be required to submit a dissertation of approximately 15,000 to 20,000 words, on a research area selected in consultation with the supervisor and approved by a person designated for this purpose by the Committee for the School of Archaeology.

6. Three typewritten copies of the dissertaton must be sent, not later than noon on 30 September in the year in which the examination is taken, to the M.Sc. Examiners (Archaeological Science), c/o Clerk of the Schools, High Street, Oxford. The examiners will retain one copy of the dissertation of each candidate for the departmental library.

7. The examiners may require to see the records of practical work carried out during the course.

8. Candidates must present themselves for an oral examination as required by the examiners. This may be on the candidate's written paper, or dissertation, or both.

9. The examiners may award a distinction for excellence in the whole examination.

SCHEDULE

(i) *Principles and practice of scientific dating*

The principles of scientific dating methods including radiocarbon, luminescence, uranium series and dendro-chronology. The practical aspects of these methods and the problems encountered in their application. The statistical analysis of chronological information in the study of archaeological sites and cultures.

(ii) *Bio-archaeology*

Scientific methods for the study of biological remains from archaeological sites; introduction to the analysis of plant and faunal remains including indicators of disease and artefactual analysis; theoretical and practical aspects of quantitative methods for diet reconstruction by isotopic analysis; introduction to ancient DNA studies; residue analysis.

(iii) *Materials analysis and the study of technological change*

Introduction to the history of technology; theoretical and practical aspects of materials analysis methods—SEM, microprobe, TIMS, ICP, ICP-MS, XRF, XRD, PIXE, FTIR and NAA; application of analysis to different material types—stone, ceramics, vitreous materials and metals; provenance of raw materials; case studies of application to archaeological problems.

Biodiversity, Conservation, and Management

1. The Life and Environmental Sciences Divisional Board shall elect for the supervision of the course a standing committee. The Course Director will be responsible to the standing committee.

2. Candidates must follow a course of instruction in Biodiversity, Conservation, and Management for at least three terms, and will, when entering for the examination, be required to produce a certificate from the Course Director to this effect.

3. The examination will consist of:

(i) a written examination of three three-hour papers based on eight core courses as described in the schedule;

(ii) two assessed essays based on option courses;

(iii) a dissertation on a subject selected in consultation with the supervisor and Course Director and approved by the standing committee.

4. Candidates must submit to the Course Director by the end of eighth week of Hilary Term in the year in which they enter the examination, the title and a brief statement of the form and scope of their dissertation, together with the name of a person who has agreed to act as their supervisor during preparation of the dissertation.

5. The dissertation shall be of a maximum length of 15,000 words excluding appendices and references.

6. Two double-spaced, bound typewritten or printed copies of the dissertation must be sent, not later than noon on the first Friday in September in the year in which the written examination is taken, to the M.Sc. examiners (Biodiversity, Conservation, and Management), c/o the Clerk of the Schools, Examination Schools, High Street, Oxford OX1 4BG. The examiners may retain one copy of the dissertation of each candidate who passes the examination for deposit in an appropriate library. Both copies must bear the candidate's examination number but not his/her name.

The dissertation shall be accompanied by a statement certifying that the dissertation is the candidate's own work except where otherwise indicated.

7. In the written examination, the examiners will permit the use of hand-held pocket calculators subject to the conditions set out under the heading 'Use of calculators in examinations' in the *Special Regulations concerning Examinations*.

8. The examiners may also examine any candidate viva voce on the candidate's written papers, dissertation, or both.

9. To complete the course successfully the candidate must satisfy the examiners in each of the three specified elements (core courses, options and dissertation). A candidate who has failed to satisfy the examiners in any of the three elements may enter again for the examination in those elements on one, but not more than one, subsequent occasion.

10. Arrangements for reassessment shall be as follows:

(i) *Core courses*. Candidates who fail any of the core-course examinations may resit the examination in the Trinity Term of the following academic year.

(ii) *Options*. Candidates who fail any of the assessed essays may resubmit that essay or essays to the Clerk of the Schools by noon on Friday four weeks after week nine of the term in which the essay or essays were first submitted.

(iii) *Dissertation*. Candidates who fail the dissertation may resubmit the dissertation by the required date in Trinity Term of the following academic year.

11. The examiners may award a distinction for excellence in the whole examination.

SCHEDULE

(*a*) *Core courses*

(i) *Biodiversity: its definition, meaning, and significance*. This course will cover the origin and evolution of the term Biodiversity. It will provide an advanced understanding of the definitions, measurement and terminologies used in biodiversity discourse and discuss the different perceptions and uses of this term in society.

(ii) *Developing a critical understanding of the science of biodiversity*. This course will critically examine the data and analytical techniques used to legitimise biodiversity as a scientific and policy imperative. It will discuss the validity of perceived 'truths' and how these have shaped contemporary biodiversity research, policy, and practice. It will examine the wide range of methods needed to integrate qualitative/quantitative data and to link different components measured by different stakeholders.

(iii) *Practical techniques for biodiversity assessment and monitoring.* This course will provide an advanced introduction to the techniques of collecting and analysing biodiversity data. It will cover subject areas such as research design, ecological field techniques, rapid biodiversity assessment techniques, laboratory and statistical techniques, remote sensing, and GIS.

(iv) *Conservation conventions, legislation and the role of statutory agencies.* This course will study the genealogy of conservation and environmental law and its relationship to international conventions. It will focus on how these statutes relate to and structure the operations of Governments, NGO and corporate bodies. It will also cover the processes of conservation policy-making, implementation of national and local biodiversity action plans, and the stakeholder consultation processes that must accompany them.

(v) *Strategic conservation planning.* This course will provide an advanced introduction into spatial and species-based approaches for conservation planning. It will focus on a critical examination of high profile global schemes, in particular those promoted by international NGOs, and discuss cutting edge approaches employing landscape, social values and climatic frameworks.

(vi) *Biodiversity, communities, and local economic development.* This course will study current debates on the relationship between biodiversity and people in developing countries. In particular it will consider issues surrounding integrated conservation development projects, the protectionist versus community-based conservation debate, and the role of traditional approaches to biodiversity conservation.

(vii) *Conservation, ethics, values, and society.* This course will explore the emergence of the aesthetic, ethical, economic and prudence-based values that underpin conservation. It will analyse the development of conservation as a social movement and the challenges it faces in an increasingly globalised world.

(viii) *Professional skills for conservationists.* This course will provide an advanced introduction into the essential skills required by the modern conservation practitioner. Subjects covered will include understanding organizational management, consultancy methodology, negotiation, fund raising, conservation project management, leadership and communication skills, and developing a critical understanding of political and economic structures and how they relate to conservation.

(*b*) *Option courses*

Candidates will be expected to show advanced knowledge of two of the option courses on offer in any one year. The topics on offer and details will be approved by the standing committee and published in the *Gazette* before the end of Trinity Term of the academic year preceding that in which the written papers are to be taken.

Bioinformatics

1. The Board of the Division of Mathematical and Physical Sciences, in consultation with the Continuing Education Board, shall elect for the supervision of the course a standing committee that shall have the power to arrange lectures and other instruction.

2. Every candidate must follow for at least 9 and at most 12 terms a part-time course of instruction in the theory and practice of bioinformatics. Candidates must take 9 modules as set out in the Schedule.

3. Every candidate will be required to satisfy the examiners in the following:

(*a*) attendance at nine modules chosen from those in the Schedule for the M.Sc. in

Bioinformatics, comprising a programme of study approved by the Programme Director;

(*b*) nine written assignments, one on each of the modules specified in the Schedule below;

(*c*) a dissertation of not more than 50 pages of A4 in length (excluding tables, appendices, footnotes and bibliography), on a subject selected by the candidate in consultation with the supervisor and approved by the chairman of the Standing Committee.

The assessed work set out in clause 3(*b*), and the dissertation under (*c*), shall be forwarded to the examiners c/o Registry, Department of Continuing Education, 1 Wellington Square, Oxford OX1 2JA, for consideration by such date as the examiners shall determine and of which they shall notify candidates.

4. Candidates may be required to attend a viva voce examination at the end of the course of studies at the discretion of the examiners.

5. The examiners may award a distinction to candidates for the M.Sc.

6. Candidates who fail to satisfy the examiners in any part of the examination may be permitted to resubmit work in respect of the part or parts of the examination which they have failed for examination on not more than one occasion which shall normally be within one year of the original failure.

7. The Standing Committee shall have the discretion to permit any candidate to be exempted from submitting up to one of the total of nine written assignments required under 3(*b*) above, provided that the standing committee is satisfied that such a candidate has undertaken equivalent study, of an appropriate standard, normally at another institution of higher education.

Schedule

Section A: Mandatory Modules

Students must take the following modules:

1 The power of bioinformatics in modern research, introduction to the software

2 The experimental-bioinformatics interface—current challenges and emerging solutions

Section B: Foundation Modules

Students must take three modules from the following list:

1 Biology, principles: basic molecular biology

2 Biology, experimental techniques in

3 Introduction to statistics and maths for bioinformatics

4 Bioinformatics applications of computing, an introduction to techniques

5 Algorithm design and complexity

Section C: Advanced Modules

Students must take four modules from the following list:

1 Functional and comparative genomics

2 Sequence assembly and annotation

3 Molecular evolution

4 Microarray bioinformatics

5 Database management systems

6 Symbolic machine learning

7 Statistical data mining

8 Statistical genetics

9 Population genetics

The Standing Committee shall approve the content of at least three advanced modules to be given each year, the titles of which shall be published annually in Hilary Term in the *University Gazette*.

Biology (Integrative Bio-Science)

1. The Life and Environmental Sciences Divisional Board shall elect for the supervision of the course an organizing committee which shall have power to arrange lectures and other instruction. The organizing committee shall appoint for each candidate an academic committee consisting of the supervisors of the candidate's two research projects and one member of the organizing committee, who will serve as the candidate's academic supervisor.

2. Each candidate must follow a course of study in Biology for at least three terms and for a substantial part of the three subsequent vacations, as determined by the course timetable, and will, when entering for examination, be required to produce a certificate from the academic supervisor to this effect. There will be no written examination.

3. Candidates shall be examined in all of the following ways:

(i) each candidate will be required to submit to the examiners two copies of a typewritten or printed essay of approximately 3,000 words (excluding bibliography, tables, figures and appendices) on each of four topics specified or agreed by the course organizers, one essay relating to the Techniques in Molecular Biology course and the other three essays relating to three of the Research in the Biosciences courses chosen for further study, as set out in the schedule. Candidates shall not deal with substantially the same material in their essays submitted for different topics;

(ii) each candidate will be required to submit to the examiners one practical notebook for each of the six subject areas taught set out in (a) and (b) of the schedule;

(iii) each candidate will be required to submit to the examiners two copies of a typewritten or printed dissertation of not more than 10,000 words (excluding bibliography, tables, figures and appendices) on each of the two research projects chosen for study, as set out in the schedule;

(iv) each candidate will be required to give two public oral presentations on subjects of his or her choice related to the content of the course, on dates to be determined by the examiners.

4. Each candidate will be examined viva voce.

5. Before being given leave to supplicate, candidates must have demonstrated understanding of and competence in the topics covered by the Core Research Skills teaching and the Professional Development Programme as set out in the schedule, to the satisfaction of the organizing committee.

6. The required written submissions must be sent to the Chairman of Examiners, M.Sc. in Biology, c/o The Clerk of the Schools, Examination Schools, High Street, Oxford, OX1 4BG; they must be submitted by dates to be specified by the Organizing Committee and which will be published in the University *Gazette* not later than the start of Michaelmas Term of the academic year in which the examination is taken. Each submission must be accompanied by a certificate signed by the candidate indicating that it is the candidate's own work, except where specifically acknowledged.

7. The viva voce examinations will be conducted in September in the year in which the candidate is examined on dates to be determined by the examiners.

8. The examiners may award a distinction for excellence in the whole examination.

9. The examiners shall retain one copy of each extended essay and both copies of each dissertation of each successful candidate, the essays and one copy of each dissertation for deposit in the Zoology Department Library and the other dissertation to be given to the project supervisor.

SCHEDULE

The syllabus for study will include five principal components:

(a) Research in the Biosciences

This will consist of five taught courses of lectures with associated practicals, demonstrations and seminars, detailing research approaches, methodologies and results in specific subject areas of bioscience. The subject areas will be approved annually by the organizing committee. Details of those courses offered in each academic year will be published in the *Gazette* before the end of the preceding Trinity Term. Candidates will be expected to submit practical notebooks for all the courses, and to show advanced knowledge of three of these subjects by submitting essays relating to them as specified in Regulation 3.

(b) Core Research Skills: Techniques in Molecular Biology

This will consist of a taught course of lectures with associated practicals, demonstrations and seminars, detailing research approaches and methodologies in molecular biology. Candidates will be expected to submit a practical notebook for this course, and to show advanced knowledge of this subject by submitting an essay relating to it, as specified in Regulation 3.

(c) Core Research Skills: The Acquisition, Handling and Analysis of Bioscience Information.

Integrated lectures and classes providing training in transferable core research skills in the following areas:

(i) Safety and good research practice
(ii) Research Techniques
(iii) Statistics
(iv) Computing and information technology
(v) Libraries and databases
(vi) Writing grant applications.

(d) Professional Development Programme for Bioscientists

To provide transferable personal skills for a career in scientific research, this programme will consist of taught classes with interactive discussions and practical assignments in the following areas:

(i) Creativity, teamwork, and leadership
(ii) Time management and learning skills
(iii) Presentation skills, verbal and written
(iv) Career planning, assessing personal skills and values, CVs and interview techniques
(v) Exploitation of science: getting ideas to the market-place, patents, intellectual property rights
(vi) The relationship between academic and industrial research
(vii) Government science policy and research funding.
(viii) Ethical and Social Issues in Science.

(e) Research Projects

Each candidate will undertake two research projects in dissimilar areas of bioscience, each involving original laboratory, museum, or field research under the supervision of a research supervisor, on subjects selected in consultation with the candidate's academic committee selected by the organizing committee.

Comparative Social Policy

Every candidate must follow, for at least three terms, a course of instruction in Comparative Social Policy.

The examination will be in four parts.

A. A compulsory paper in *Methods of Social Research*. As specified for the M.Phil. in Sociology.

B. A compulsory paper in *Comparative Social Policy/Welfare States*. As specified for the M.Phil. in Comparative Social Policy.

C. One optional paper. This may be from the list of optional papers as specified for the M.Phil. in Comparative Social Policy. Teaching in some options may not be available every year. Candidates may, after special permission of the Sociology and Social Policy Graduate Studies Committee, offer subjects outside this list. This may include papers offered in other relevant master's degrees in the University, subject to permission by the relevant Graduate Studies Committee as appropriate.

D. A thesis of not more than 10,000 words on a topic within the subject of the course, to be specified jointly by supervisor and student. Two typewritten copies of the thesis must be delivered to the Clerk of the Schools, Examination Schools, High Street, Oxford, by noon of the weekday on or nearest to 15 August of the year in which the examination is to be taken. Successful candidates will be required to deposit a copy of their thesis in the library of the Department of Social Policy and Social Work.

The examiners may examine any candidate viva voce.

The examiners may award a Distinction for excellence in the whole examination on the basis of the material submitted to them.

Computer Science

1. The Divisional Board of Mathematical and Physical Sciences, in consultation with the Sub-faculty of Computation, shall elect for the supervision of the course an organizing committee which shall have power to arrange lectures and other instruction.

The committee shall elect a chairman from its own members; the chairman shall have power to approve applications on behalf of the committee. The committee shall be responsible for appointment of a supervisor for each student.

2. Candidates must follow a course of instruction in Computer Science for at least three terms and a substantial part of the three subsequent vacations, as determined by the course timetable, and will be required to produce a certificate from their supervisors to that effect.

3. The examination shall be in three parts, as follows:

(i) Candidates shall submit a written assignment on each of seven and no more than eight topics chosen from a list of topics approved by the organizing committee and published in the *University Gazette* by not later than the Friday of eighth week of the Trinity Term in the academic year preceding the examination. The list of courses shall be divided into two sections: Schedule A and Schedule B. Candidates shall be required to select at least four topics from Schedule B.

(ii) Candidates shall submit a dissertation of not more than 30,000 words, plus not more than 30 pages of diagrams, tables, listing etc., on a subject selected by the candidate in consultation with the supervisor and approved by the director of the course.

(iii) There shall be an examination viva voce, unless the candidate shall have been individually dispensed by the examiners, on the dissertation and on any of the topics for which he or she submitted a written assignment, to take place on the first Friday in October.

4. Every candidate must submit to the director of the course no later than the first Monday in Trinity Full Term in the year of the examination the title and a brief statement of the form and scope of his or her dissertation, together with an essay of not more than 3,000 words, describing the background of the project, its objectives and its plan of work. The submission must be approved by the person who has agreed to act as supervisor during the preparation of the dissertation.

Candidates will be expected to demonstrate in their dissertation an appreciation of the role of methods studied in the course as contributing to the design and development of computing systems.

5. Two typewritten or printed copies of the dissertation must be delivered not later than noon on the first Friday in September in the year of the examination to the M.Sc. Examiners (Computer Science), c/o the Clerk of the Schools, Examination Schools, High Street, Oxford.

One copy of the thesis of each successful candidate will normally be presented to the Computing Laboratory Library.

6. Before the end of the third week of Michaelmas Term, each candidate in consultation with their supervisor must submit for approval by the director of the course a list of topics which will be taken in that term, and similarly a list of the remaining topics being taken must be submitted for approval before the end of the third week of Hilary Term. A total of seven topics must be selected with at least four from Schedule B; candidates shall be allowed to choose a maximum of eight topics. The choice must exclude any topics which substantially overlap the topics of the candidate's undergraduate degree or other recent academic study.

7. For each topic, the lecturer on the course of instruction shall prescribe a schedule of practical work, tutorial exercises and a written assignment, and shall make available to the Chairman of Examiners evidence showing the extent to which each candidate has pursued an adequate course of practical and class work.

8. With the permission of the organizing committee, a candidate may offer up to two alternative topics to replace any of the topics listed in Schedule B. An application for such replacement must be made to the director of the course by the end of the first week of the term in which the lecture course on the topic is given; it must be approved by the student's supervisor and by the lecturer on the course, who thereby undertakes to accept appointment as assessor for the topic.

9. Not later than noon on a date to be determined by the examiners, who are responsible for making sure candidates are aware of that date and that the date is announced at the head of the assignment sheet, the completed assignment for that project and all associated practicals must be delivered to the M.Sc. Examiners (Computer Science), c/o The Clerk of the Schools, Examination Schools, High Street, Oxford.

No candidate shall attend classes or receive any form of individual tuition in the subject of an assignment between the time when the assignment is made available to the candidate and the time fixed for the delivery of the assignment to the examiners.

10. A list of those candidates who have satisfied the examiners in a particular topic shall be posted in the vestibule of the Computing Laboratory within three working weeks of the final date for submission of assignments.

11. Any candidate who has not satisfied the examiners in four topics by the beginning of the Trinity Term shall be deemed to have failed the degree course.

To satisfy the examiners a candidate must attain a minimum standard in seven of the assignments under clause 3(i) and pass five of them (including at least three from Schedule B or assignments on alternative topics approved under clause 8), pursue an adequate course of practical work, and attain an adequate level of achievement in all three parts of the examination.

12. The examiners may award a distinction for excellence in the whole examination.

13. A candidate who fails the examination will be permitted to retake it on one further occasion only, not later than one year after the initial attempt. Such a candidate whose dissertation has been of satisfactory standard may resubmit the same piece of work, while a candidate who has reached a satisfactory standard on

the written assignments will not be required to retake that part of the examination.

A candidate who has passed in exactly four of the assignments under clause 3(i) will be required to reattend the course and obtain a pass in one further topic, selected from Schedule B.

Criminology and Criminal Justice

1. Every candidate must follow, for at least three terms, a course of instruction in Criminology and Criminal Justice.

2. There shall be a board of studies for the course, to be chaired by the Director of the Centre for Criminological Research and comprising the director of studies and such other members of the Centre for Criminological Research and the Faculty of Law as provide teaching for the course, plus one student representative.

3. The course will consist of three elements: core course in Analytical Criminology and Criminal Justice, options, and thesis. The core course will run throughout the first two terms (Michaelmas and Hilary). Options will run for six weeks in each term (Michaelmas, Hilary and Trinity). Candidates will be required to choose two options in each of the first two terms and one for the final term. The dissertation will be 12,000–15,000 words long on a topic to be agreed by the board of studies.

4. The options are listed in Schedule A below.

5. Not all options will necessarily be taught or examined in any one year. Details of those which are available will be published in the M.Sc. in Criminology and Criminal Justice Course Book produced by the Centre for Criminological Research for the year of the examination, subject to any amendment posted on the designated notice board in the Centre for Criminological Research by Monday of week minus 1 of the Michaelmas Term before the examination is held.

6. In addition to the options set out in Schedule A, candidates may offer any other option that may be approved from time to time by regulation published in the *Gazette* by the end of the Monday of week minus 1 of the Michaelmas Term before the examination is held.

7. The course shall be assessed as follows:

(i) *Core Course*: There shall be a three-hour examination for the core course to be taken in week one of Trinity Term.

(ii) *Options*: Options other than 'Design and Evaluation of Research' shall be examined by means of an assessed essay of no less than 3,500 and no more than 5,000 words, for which time will be set aside during the last two weeks of each term. A title, or choice of titles (as determined by the course leader for the option), shall be posted on the designated noticeboard at the Centre for Criminological Research by noon on the Friday of week six of the relevant term. Candidates shall be required to submit the essay to the Clerk of the Schools, Examination Schools, High Street, Oxford not later than three weeks after this date, by noon.

For 'Design and Evaluation of Research', there shall be a special ongoing assessment exercise, the nature of which will be explained to students at the beginning of the option; precise details of the assessment will be posted on the designated noticeboard at the Centre for Criminological Research by noon on the Friday of week four of the relevant term.

(iii) *Dissertation*: Two typewritten copies of the dissertation shall be submitted to the Clerk of the Schools by noon on Friday of week nine of Trinity Term. One bound copy of the dissertation of each candidate who passes the examination shall be deposited in the library at the Centre for Criminological Research.

8. The degree of M.Sc. shall be awarded to any candidate who achieves a mark of at least 60 per cent for (*a*) the assessed essays, (*b*) the core course paper, and (*c*) the dissertation. For this purpose, the individual marks of the five assessed essays will be aggregated and an average mark awarded for the assessed essays as a whole. The examiners may award a distinction to any candidate who achieves marks of at least 70 per cent on at least half of the papers: in this calculation, both the core course and the dissertation shall count as two papers and each option shall count as one.

9. Arrangements for reassessment shall be as follows:

(i) *Core Course*: Candidates who fail the core-course examination may resit the examination in the Trinity Term of the following academic year. Such candidates who have completed successfully either or both of (*a*) the options (i.e. have obtained an aggregate mark of 60 per cent or more) and (*b*) the dissertation may carry forward the marks gained for those part or parts of the course.

(ii) *Options:* Candidates who have failed to obtain an aggregate mark of 60 per cent for their assessed essays in Michaelmas, Hilary, and Trinity Terms may resubmit those essays in which they have received a mark of 59 per cent or less to the Clerk of the Schools, Examination Schools, High Street, Oxford according to the standard timetable for submitting essays in the following academic year. Such candidates who have completed successfully (*a*) the core course examination, (*b*) the dissertation, and (*c*) any essay for which they have received a mark of 60 per cent or more, may carry forward the marks gained for those part or parts of the course.

(iii) *Dissertation*: Candidates who fail the dissertation may resubmit the dissertation by the required date in the Trinity Term of the following academic year. Such candidates who have completed successfully either or both of (*a*) the core course and (*b*) the options may carry forward the marks gained for those part or parts of the course.

Schedule A

1. Policing
2. Sentencing
3. Dilemmas of Custody
4. The Design and Evaluation of Research
5. Community Penalties
6. Human Rights and Criminal Justice
7. International Perspectives in Restorative Justice
8. Comparative Criminal Justice
9. International Perspectives on the Death Penalty
10. Psychology and Psychiatry in the Criminal Justice System.

Diagnostic Imaging

1. The Medical Sciences Board shall elect for the supervision of the course an organizing committee which shall have power to arrange lectures and other instruction.

2. Every candidate must follow for at least three terms, or, in the case of part-time students, for at least six terms, a course of instruction in Diagnostic Imaging.

3. Candidates will be required to present themselves for written and oral examination and to submit two written assignments and a dissertation in prescribed form on an approved topic.

4. Candidates will be required either,

Option A (Basic Radiological Science)

to take three papers of three hours each:

Paper 1 X-Rays, Radiological Procedures, and Radiography.

Paper 2 Nuclear Medicine and Ultrasonography.

Paper 3 Computed Tomography and Magnetic Resonance Imaging.

or

Option B (Interventional Neuroradiology)

to take three papers of three hours each:

Paper 1 Pathology, Physiology, and Anatomy relevant to Interventional Neuroradiology.

Paper 2 Diagnosis in Interventional Neuroradiology.

Paper 3 Interventional Neuroradiological Techniques.

Examination questions will reflect aspects of the subject as described in the schedule.

5. For Option A, candidates will normally hold a first degree or equivalent qualification in the physical, biological or medical science. For Option B, candidates must be registered with the General Medical Council, hold an appropriate contract with the National Health Service, and have had appropriate previous experience in Diagnostic Radiology and/or Neurosurgery.

6. Each candidate will be required to submit, for assessment of their progress, a written assignment of no more than 4,000 words by the end of each of their first two terms, or, in the case of part-time students, by the end of their second and fourth terms. The assignments will be on separate topics agreed with the candidate's supervisor and approved by the organizing committee. The assignments must be word-processed and will subsequently be submitted to the examiners as part of the candidate's whole examination.

7. Each candidate will be required to submit a dissertation of no more than 15,000 words on a subject selected in consultation with the candidate's supervisor and approved by the organizing committee. The dissertation may vary from an account of original research work to a survey of the literature. Dissertations which reproduce substantially work submitted in the other written assignments will not be admissible.

8. Three word-processed and appropriately bound copies of a dissertation must be delivered to the relevant Option Director by a date prescribed by the examiners, together with the two written assignments described above. The examiners shall retain two copies of the dissertation of each candidate who passes the examination, for deposit in the departmental library.

9. An oral examination will be held and this may include questions on the candidate's dissertation, assignments, or written papers.

10. The examiners may award a distinction for excellence in the whole examination.

Schedule for Option A (Basic Radiological Science)

Paper 1: X-Rays, Radiological Procedures, and Radiography

Atomic and nuclear physics, ionizing radiation and interactions with matter, biological effects of ionizing radiation. Production of X-rays, formation of radiographic images, design of equipment for generating X-rays. Measurement of quantity and quality of ionizing radiations. Image receptors: photographic film, intensifying screens, fluoroscopy, image intensification and television systems. Computed imaging and digital systems.

Radiological contrast media: pharmacology, indications, contraindications and complications.

Technique of radiological contrast media examinations in the demonstration of gastrointestinal, hepatobiliary and urogenital tracts. Angiography and cardiovascular examination. Recognition of anatomy displayed by these techniques, especially pertaining to the gastrointestinal, genitourinary, cardiovascular, and musculoskeletal systems. Advantages and disadvantages of these techniques in practice. Radiological protection; instrumentation, national and international legislation.

General principles of interventional radiology: guided drainage, biopsy, and interventional angiography.

Positioning and care of the patient in radiography, standard radiographic projections. General principles of microradiography, macroradiography and soft-tissue radiography. High voltage techniques and influence of exposure factors. General principles and methods of application of tomography. Film quality control and faults.

Paper 2: Nuclear Medicine and Ultrasonography

Radioactivity and radioactive sources. Radiation detectors and scintigraphic equipment. Measurement of radio-activity, Gamma-ray spectroscopy, Radioisotope generators and radio-pharmaceuticals.

Imaging devices; system performance and analysis. Static and dynamic imaging. Emission tomography. Protection of the patient in nuclear medicine.

Biological distribution of radionuclides. Recognition of anatomy and function demonstrated by scintigraphy.

Production, nature propagation and detection of ultrasound. Imaging methods and date display. Doppler effect and flow-sensitive imaging. Safety of ultrasound.

Tissue characterisation by ultrasonography. Recognition of normal anatomy displayed by ultrasonography, especially the contents of the abdomen and pelvis and musculoskeletal system. Applications in the chest and face and neck. Ultrasound contrast agents. Interventional uses of ultrasonography. Clinical applications of ultrasonography. Advantages and disadvantages of ultrasonography.

Paper 3: Computed Tomography and Magnetic Resonance Imaging

Design of computed tomographic equipment; production of X-rays, detection, data collection, image reconstruction and display, helical and multislice technology. Characteristics of CT images: matrix, pixels, voxels. Dynamic imaging. Radiation dosimetry in CT and patient protection.

Contrast media and other drugs used in computed tomography. Patient positioning and care. Advantages and disadvantages of computed tomography.

Physical principles of magnetic resonance. Equipment design, magnets, and coils. Image production and array processing. Characteristics of magnetic resonance images: matrix, pixels, voxels, image contrast considerations. Effects of flow and flow-related imaging. Dynamic imaging.

Hazard of magnetic fields and patient protection.

General principles of magnetic resonance spectroscopy and functional magnetic imaging.

Normal anatomy displayed by computed, tomography and magnetic resonance imaging, especially pertaining to the head and neck, trunk and limbs. Clinical applications of both techniques, including relationship to other techniques. Advantages and disadvantages of both techniques in practice. Interventional uses of both techniques.

Schedule for Option B (Interventional Neuroradiology)

Paper 1: Pathology, Physiology, and Anatomy relevant to Interventional Radiology

Pathology of lesions amenable to interventional neuroradiological techniques. The natural history of such conditions and the indications for interventional measures.

Anatomy of the central nervous system with special reference to vascular anatomy including common variations to the normal pattern. The embryology and phylogeny of the blood supply of the head and spine. Vascular physiology with special reference to the cerebral and spinal circulations. Normal and potential sites of collateral circulation. Endovascular routes to lesion of the head and spine.

Paper 2: Diagnosis in Interventional Neuroradiology

The clinical and radiological diagnosis of conditions amenable to interventional neuroradiological techniques including recognition of common symptoms and signs associated with such conditions.

Radiological techniques for localization and evaluation of cerebral and spinal lesion, including angiography, myelography, CT and MR scanning, doppler ultrasound (transcranial and intra-operative), and the use of radio-pharmaceuticals. Electrophysiological and cerebral blood flow measurement techniques as well as neurological and cardiovascular monitoring pertinent to interventional neuroradiological procedures.

Paper 3: Interventional Neuroradiological Techniques

Interventional techniques for biopsy, embolization, thrombolysis, and angioplasty. Delivery systems: their construction and applications. Embolization materials including balloons, coils, particulate and liquid embolic agents and their advantages and disadvantages for different applications. Pre- and post-procedural precautions, including informed consent, and the recognition and management of complications.

The official name, constitution pharmacology, modes of administration, clinical agents used in interventional neuroradiological techniques. Sedation and the provision of analgesia during procedures. In particular, the use of anticoagulation, fibrinolytic, and anticonvulsant agents.

Economic and Social History

(See also the general notice at the commencement of these regulations.)

The regulations of the Board of the Faculty of Modern History are as follows:

1. Every candidate must follow for at least three terms a course of instruction in Economic and Social History and must upon entering for the examination produce from his or her society a certificate to that effect.

2. The examination will consist of the following parts:

Qualifying test

Every candidate must pass a qualifying test. The test shall consist of the satisfactory completion of two courses on

(1) Methodological introduction to research in the social sciences and history.

(2) *Either* Quantitative methods and computer applications for historians

or A paper from another established course within the University where this would provide a more appropriate training for the candidate's dissertation focus. Such a choice will need formal approval from both the Course Director and the Chairman of the Graduate Studies Committee of the Board of the Faculty of Modern History.

The organizers of each course shall not later than the Friday of the sixth week of the Trinity Term preceding the examination submit to the examiners a list of candidates who have satisfactorily completed a qualifying course. No candidate who has failed the qualifying test of two courses will be permitted to supplicate for the degree. Candidates who fail a qualifying course once will be permitted to take it again, not later than one year after the initial attempt.

Final examinations

The examination shall consist of two papers and a dissertation.

Candidates must take at least one of their papers as a three-hour written examination. For the remaining paper candidates must choose to be assessed either by written examination or by two 5,000 word essays. Essays may be only submitted in lieu of written papers for subjects in Schedule I below ('Advanced Papers for M.Phil. and M.Sc. in Economic and Social History') or for other papers permitted in Schedule II below where similar provision exists in the regulations for those examinations. The essays must be the work of the candidates alone and they must not consult any other person including their supervisors in any way concerning the method of handling the themes chosen. The themes chosen by the candidate must be submitted for approval by the chairman of examiners, c/o the Clerk of the Schools, High Street, Oxford, not later than the Monday of the fifth week of Hilary Term. Candidates will be informed within two weeks, by means of a letter directed to their colleges, whether the topics they have submitted have been approved. The finished essays must be delivered by the candidate to the Clerk of the Examination Schools, High Street, Oxford, by noon on Monday of the third week of Trinity Full Term. The essays must be presented in proper scholarly form, and two typed copies of each must be submitted. Candidates may be examined viva voce on the subjects on which they submit essays. Candidates who have not delivered essays as prescribed by the due date on any of their subjects must sit the written examination in those subjects.

I. One advanced paper selected from Schedule I below.

II. *Either* (i) one paper in a relevant discipline or skill or sources or methods selected from Schedule II below;

or (ii) a second advanced paper selected from Schedule I or from any additional list of papers for the M.Phil. and M.Sc. in Economic and Social History approved by the Graduate Studies Committee of the Board of the Faculty of Modern History and published in the definitive list of Advanced Papers as set out in Schedule I.

III. A dissertation of not more than 15,000 words, including appendices but excluding bibliography, on a topic approved by the candidate's supervisor. The dissertation must be delivered not later than noon on the last Monday in September of the year in which the examination is taken to the Clerk of the Schools, Examination Schools, High Street, Oxford. Dissertations submitted must not exceed the permitted length. If they do the examiners will reduce the marks awarded. The presentation and footnotes should comply with the requirements specified in the Regulations of the Educational Policy and Standards Committee for the degrees of M.Litt. and D.Phil. and follow the *Conventions for the presentation of dissertations and theses* of the Board of the Faculty of Modern History.

Each dissertation must include a short abstract which concisely summarizes its scope and principal arguments, in about 300 words.

Candidates must submit by the specified date two copies of their dissertations. These must be securely and firmly bound in either hard or soft covers.

3. The examiners will permit the use of any hand-held pocket calculator subject to the conditions set out below under the heading 'Use of calculators in examinations' in the *Special Regulations concerning Examinations*.

4. Each candidate must attend an oral examination when required to do so by the examiners.

5. The examiners may award a distinction for excellence in the whole examination.

6. A candidate who fails the examination will be permitted to re-take it on one further occasion only, not later than one year after the initial attempt.

Such a candidate whose dissertation has been of satisfactory standard may re-submit the same piece of work, while a candidate who has reached a satisfactory standard on the written papers will not be required to re-take that part of the examination.

SCHEDULE I

Advanced Papers for the M.Phil. and M.Sc. in Economic and Social History

A broad range of the course resources are shared with the corresponding courses in History of Science, Medicine, and Technology, and Advanced Papers are therefore available in the subject areas listed here.

1. Economic and business history
2. History of science and technology
3. Social history
4. Historical demography
5. History of medicine

A descriptive list of Advanced Papers will be published by the Board of the Faculty of Modern History in September for the academic year ahead (not all options may be available in every year). The definitive list of the titles of Advanced Papers for any one year will be circulated to candidates and their supervisors and posted on the Faculty notice board not later than Friday of Third Week of Michaelmas Term.

SCHEDULE II

The paper in a relevant discipline or skill may be:

1. One of the papers from the M.Phil. in Sociology or in Comparative Social Policy.

2. One suitable paper from another Master's degree under the auspices of the Faculty of Modern History approved from time to time by the Graduate Studies Committee of the Board of the Faculty of Modern History.

3. One suitable paper in a related skill or discipline other than those specified in paragraphs 1 to 2 above on the recommendation of the candidate's supervisor and endorsed by the Course Director.

Choices under Schedule II have to be approved by the chairman of the Graduate Studies Committee of the Board of the Faculty of Modern History not later than Monday of the fourth week of Michaelmas Term. Candidates wishing to take a paper under 1 or 3 will also need the approval of the appropriate course convenor and the Graduate Studies Committee of the relevant faculty board or inter-faculty committee who need to be satisfied that each candidate has an adequate background in the subject. Not all options may be available in any one year.

Economics for Development

1. Every candidate for the M.Sc. must follow a course of instruction in Economics for Development for at least three terms. Candidates will, when entering for the examination, be required to produce a certificate from their society to this effect.

2. The examination will consist of:

(*a*) the following written papers, the syllabuses for which are given in the schedule:

(i) Economic Theory
(ii) Development Economics
(iii) Quantitative Methods

(*b*) an extended essay.

3. The extended essay shall be on a subject selected by the student in consultation with the supervisor, and approved by the faculty board's standing committee for the M.Sc. by the end of the first week of the Trinity Full Term in which the examination is taken. The essay shall not exceed 10,000 words. Two typewritten copies must be

delivered to the Clerk of the Schools, Examination Schools, High Street, Oxford, by noon on Friday of the eighth week of the Trinity Full Term in which the examination is taken.

4. The candidate may also be examined orally.

5. Part-time candidates will be examined on two papers at the end of their first year and on one paper at the end of their second year.

6. In the written examination the examiners will permit the use of any hand-held pocket calculators subject to the conditions set out under the heading 'Use of calculators in examinations' in the *Special Regulations concerning Examinations*.

Schedule

(i) *Economic Theory*

Questions will be set on those aspects of economic theory likely to be helpful in the study of economic development.

Candidates are expected to reach a postgraduate level in modern micro- and macroeconomic theory, and also be able to explain how this theory should be modified to take account of the structural and institutional characteristics of developing countries. The topics covered will normally include the following (with candidates required to answer at least one question each in micro and macro economics). *Microeconomics*: producer and consumer theory with applications to development: household models; general equilibrium, welfare theorems; welfare analysis and policy evaluation; imperfect competition with applications to public service delivery; investment and savings with applications to human capital; economics of information with applications to sharecropping; and open economy models. *Macroeconomics*: open economy macroeconomics; dynamic macroeconomic models; investment, savings and money; fiscal issues and debt; exchange rates; international macroeconomic transmission; and economic growth.

(ii) *Development Economics*

Questions will be set on development topics from a series of taught modules. The modules offered may vary from year to year, but will normally include such topics as: human development, poverty and inequality; human capital and economics of education; industry and technology; rural development; macroeconomic management; liberalization and reform; international issues; and poverty, risk and development.

(iii) *Quantitative Methods*

Candidates will be expected to answer questions on the theory and practice of quantitative methods used in development economics.

Candidates are expected to reach a postgraduate level in modern econometric methods, particularly in their application to the analysis of data on developing economies. Specific topics to be covered will normally include the following: probability theory, sampling theory and statistical inference. Econometric methodology. Estimation methods (Least Squares, Maximum Likelihood, Generalized Method of Moments). Semi-parametric and non-parametric estimation. Econometric methods for analysis of cross-section, time-series and panel data. Econometric analysis of dynamic models, simultaneous equation systems, limited dependent variable models.

Educational Research Methodology

1. Candidates must follow for three terms (or six terms part-time) a course of instruction in Educational Research Methodology as prescribed in Schedule A and will, when entering for the examination, be required to produce a certificate from a supervisor appointed for the purpose by the Academic Board of the Department for Educational Studies to this effect.

2. The examination will be in two parts as follows:
Part I: Written examination (as prescribed in cl. 3 below).
Part II: A dissertation (as prescribed in cll. 4 and 5 below).

Candidates may also be required to attend an oral examination.

Candidates shall be deemed to have passed the examination if they have satisfied the examiners in both Part I and Part II provided that candidates must pass Part I before submitting a dissertation for Part II. At the close of the examination in Part I the examiners shall publish a list of candidates who have satisfied them in that part of the examination.

3. The written papers of the examination are set out in schedule B.

4. Candidates will be required to submit a dissertation of 12,500 to 15,000 words, the title to be selected in consultation with the supervisor, relevant to the subject of the course, and approved by the Academic Board not later than the first day of Trinity Term in the year in which they complete the written examination.

5. Three typewritten/wordprocessed copies of the dissertation must be delivered to the M.Sc. Examiners, c/o Department of Educational Studies, 15 Norham Gardens, Oxford, OX2 6PY, not later than noon 30 September in the year in which the written examination is completed, except as provided below. One copy should be hard bound and two soft bound, which should be anonymous except for the candidate number. Candidates wishing to submit dissertations later than 30 September in the year in which the written examination is to be completed must obtain the approval of the Academic Board of the Department for Educational Studies by the last day of the preceding Trinity Term, but no dissertation may be submitted later than 30 September in the year following, unless the committee exceptionally approves a later date for submission. The hard bound copy of the dissertation of each candidate who passes the examination shall be retained by the department for deposit in the departmental library.

6. The oral examination may be on the candidate's written papers, dissertation, or both.

Schedule A

(i) *Philosophy of Educational Research*

(*a*) Nature of an 'educational practice'; connected concepts of 'teaching' and 'learning'; implications of these conceptual issues for the pursuit of educational research.

(*b*) Criticism of educational research examined, with special reference to an understanding of educational practice.

(*c*) Philosophical and conceptual analysis; the links between educational research and epistemology, philosophy of mind, ethics, and the philosophy of the social sciences.

(*d*) Explanation and evidence; causes, intentions, motives, historicism, social rules, and norms.

(*e*) Truth and verification; positivism, interpretivism; quantitative and qualitative; critical theory; action research.

(*f*) Ethical dimension of research.

(ii) *Statistical methods in educational research*

(*a*) Types of quantification and measurement, and their use in educational practice and research.

(*b*) Types of data and pitfalls of confusion—discrete, continuous, time series, panel data.

(*c*) Descriptive statistics: measures of central tendency, dispersion, association, and correlation.

(*d*) The normal distribution and its significance in educational and psychological research and measurement.

(*e*) Sampling: sampling frames, simple and stratified random samples; estimation of statistics and confidence intervals; sampling error and bias in the interpretation of research results.

(*f*) Statistical inference (concepts of hypothesis testing, size and power, use of Z, t, chi-squared, F and χ^2).

(*g*) Purpose of statistical modelling; introduction to linear models, including linear regression, logistic regression, logistic models for contingency tables.

(iii) *General Academic and Employment Skills*

(*a*) Organization of the research process; identification of library resources and how to use them; bibliographic sources and methods; the use of annals, theses, journals, and conference proceedings; maintaining a personal research bibliography including the use of bibliographic packages such as EndNote.

(*b*) Basic computing skills including the use of word processors, spreadsheets, databases, and graphical presentation.

(*c*) Evaluating research, including refereeing and book reviews.

(*d*) Ethical and legal issues; privacy and confidentiality; the attribution of ideas and intellectual property rights, including copyright; ownership of data; the Data Protection Act; informed consent; the role of ethical committees; constraints on researchers involved in contract and consultancy work; the political context of research, including the uses made of published work; BERA, AERA, and BPS codes of practice.

(*e*) Exploitation of research and intellectual property rights.

(*f*) Writing and presentation skills; publishing research; writing for, and presenting to, different audiences.

(*g*) Research management and team-working skills; setting appropriate time scales; writing research proposals; costing research proposals.

(*h*) Career development; searching for employment opportunities; networking and negotiation; critical evaluation of personal and career development needs; (long and short-term career planning).

(iv) *Strategies for Education Research*

(*a*) Types of education research questions in relation to diverse purposes of educational research; a brief history of educational research; the politics of educational research.

(*b*) Formulating research problems and questions, and hypotheses; issues in the framing of research questions.

(*c*) Assumptions, rationales and purposes, disciplines and political, ethical, and technical problems of experimental, survey, action research, ethnographic and case study research strategies, life history research; strategies for educational evaluation studies; philosophical, historical, and comparative research in education.

(*d*) Relation of research strategies to philosphical traditions, socio-political positions and economic constraints; understanding the significance of alternative epistemological positions for theory construction, research design and the selection of appropriate analytical techniques.

(*e*) Generalizability, validity, reliability, and replicability of research.

(*f*) Critique of research papers.

(*g*) Gaining access and ethical approval for research.

(*h*) Current controversies in Educational Research.

(v) *Methods of data collection and analysis*

(*a*) Data collection versus data generation/construction.

(*b*) Techniques of questioning: questionnaires; attitude scales; repertory grids; attainment tests; structured and semi-structured interviews; ethnographic interviews; focus groups; telephone and e-mail interviews; the use of the internet for data collection.

(*c*) Techniques of observation (e.g. structured classroom observation; participant observation).

(*d*) Assessment strategies, e.g. tests, task and rating scales.

(*e*) Types of primary and secondary documentary evidence including historical archives.

(*f*) Procedures for interpretation of qualitative data in non-quantitative terms; semiological techniques for the analysis of educational texts, official documents and writings through the formalized study of textual code systems and discursive structures; discourse, and narrative analysis.

(*h*) Secondary data analysis and the use of data from large scale surveys, longitudinal and cross-sectional studies.

(*i*) Use of computers for analysis of quantitative and qualitative data including graphs, charts, and flow diagrams.

(*j*) Data management.

(vi) *Optional subjects of which one must be offered*

Options are intended to provide students with the opportunity to both broaden their knowledge of educational research methods and to consolidate their learning in relation to topics covered in the core course.

(*a*) *Researching teaching and learning*: different approaches to researching, teaching and learning, e.g. ethnography, ethnomethodological approaches, survey research, experiments, quasi-experiments, case study, phenomenology and phenomenography.

(*b*) *Measurement and assessment*: the construction and use of tests, questionnaires, and tasks; the construction of scales; factor analysis and assessment of validity and reliability of scales.

(*c*) *School improvement and school effectiveness*: a brief history of the two research traditions; measuring effectiveness—raw data, regression methods and multilevel modelling; action research and improving classroom practice.

(*d*) *Educational policy analysis*: different approaches to policy analysis and their differing purposes; case studies of educational policy development; implementation and evaluation of educational policy.

(*e*) *Qualitative data analysis*: ethnomethodological and phenomenological approaches; discourse analysis and semiotics; theory generation using inductive approaches.

Schedule B

(i) Philosophy of the Social Sciences and Educational Research.
(ii) Strategies for Educational Research.
(iii) Methods of Data Collection and Analysis (incorporating Statistical Methods in Social Science).

Educational Studies

SYLLABUS B: *Full-time*

1. The subjects of the examination shall be as follows:

(*a*) Comparative and International Education.

(*b*) Teacher Education and Development.

Candidates will be required to undertake a course of instruction in one of the subjects (*a*) or (*b*).

2. Candidates must follow for three terms, a course of instruction in either (*a*) or (*b*) and will, when entering for the examination, be required to produce a certificate from a supervisor appointed for the purpose by the Academic Board to this effect.

3. The examination will be in two parts as follows:

Part I. Written examination (as prescribed in cll. 4 and 5 below).

Part II. A dissertation (as prescribed in cll. 6 and 7 below).

Candidates may also be required to attend an oral examination.

Candidates shall be deemed to have passed the examination if they have satisfied the examiners in both Part I and Part II provided that candidates must pass Part I before submitting a dissertation for Part II. At the close of the examination in Part I, the examiners shall publish a list of candidates who have satisfied them in that part of the examination.

4. The written papers of the examination are set out in the Schedule below.

Candidates in the subject Comparative and International Education will be required to offer papers (i), (ii) and (iii).

Candidates in the subject Teacher Education and Development will be required to offer three papers, consisting of either three papers chosen out of papers (iv)–(vii), or two papers chosen out of papers (viii)–(xi), and one further paper from papers (i)–(iii).

5. Candidates will be required to submit a dissertation of 15,000 to 20,000 words, the title to be selected in consultation with the supervisor, relevant to the subject of the course, and approved by the committee not later than the first day of Trinity Term in the year in which they complete the written examination.

6. Three typewritten/wordprocessed copies of the dissertation must be delivered to the M.Sc. Examiners, c/o Department of Educational Studies, 15 Norham Gardens, Oxford, OX2 6PY, not later than noon on 30 September in the year in which the written examination is completed, except as provided below. One copy should be hard bound and two soft bound, which should be anonymous except for the candidate number. Candidates wishing to submit dissertations later than 30 September in the year in which the written examination is to be completed must obtain the approval of the Academic Board by the last day of the preceding Trinity Term, but no dissertation may be submitted later than 30 September in the year following, unless the board exceptionally approves a later date for submission. The hard bound copy of the dissertation of each candidate who passes the examination shall be retained by the department for deposit in the departmental library.

7. The oral examination may be on the candidate's written papers, dissertation, or both.

Schedule

(i) *Comparative Education* (*Systematic Studies and Research*)

(*a*)

Historical development of Comparative Education.
Schools of Comparative Education.
Historical Origins of education systems.
Selected issues in comparative context; centralisation, access and entitlement, gender, the education of minorities, special needs.
Case studies: UK, USA, Japan, Germany, France, Nigeria, India
Levels of enrolment and attainment in comparative context

(*b*)

Problems of comparing and contrasting
Methods of data collection
The IEA studies

Single country and cross-national studies
Ethnocentrism
Misuse of comparative data

(ii) *Education in Europe (East and West)*

Education systems in Western and Eastern Europe
EU education and training policy
Primary, secondary, and higher education models
Vocational education policy
Curricula and examinations
Teacher education
Student mobility
Processes of educational change in Eastern Europe

(iii) *Education in Developing Countries*

Development theories and the educational dimension
Colonialism and education—legacies and links
Education and national development
International aid and education development
Education for all—the post-Jomtien era
Urbanisation, migration, and education
Gender, development, and education
Selected issues, trends and cases from Africa, Asia, Latin America and the tropical island zones.

(iv) *Classroom Teaching and Learning*

How do children learn? Philosophical, psychological, and sociological perspectives on the processes of children's learning. Classrooms as contexts for learning.

Learning different kinds of knowledge. Concepts, subject-specific skills, generic skills, values; problems of learning in specific areas of different subjects; students' alternative understandings, misconceptions, and errors.

How do teachers teach? Different theoretical and research perspectives on classroom teaching processes; the nature of classroom and subject-specific discourse; teachers' craft knowledge and students' learning strategies; class teaching for individual learning; the assessment of learning.

(v) *Teacher Education and Development*

Pre-Service Teacher Education. Student teachers' professional learning; problems of initial teacher education; distinctive contributions of schools and universities; skills and strategies of mentoring; managing school-based teacher education; reflective practice and initial teacher education.

In-Service Teacher Education. (i) Induction into teaching: socialization into schools; problems of beginning teachers; findings from research on induction; developing strategies to support beginning teachers. (ii) Teachers' continuing professional development: critical reflective practice; working with colleagues; teachers' investigation of their own classrooms; development and sharing of knowledge about teaching and learning; effects of mentoring on mentors' teaching development.

(vi) *The Nature of School Subjects*

Philosophies and ideologies of the subject. The attempt to provide epistemological justification for subject structuring of the school curriculum. Constructions of individual subjects in the context of schooling; the influence of academic, professional, political, and institutional factors. Impact of subject ideologies on classroom practice.

Pedagogical strategies for subject teaching. Pedagogical reasoning; the nature and development of subject teachers expertise in making subject knowledge accessible.

(vii) *Strategies and Skills for Classroom Research*

Strategies: Types of research questions about classroom learning and teaching. Strategies appropriate to the questions: surveys; experiments; ethnography; case study; action research.

Data gathering and analysis: Observing teachers' and students' classroom activities; systematic and participant observation. Talking with teachers and students. Diaries and written records. Classroom artefacts. Quantitative and qualitative analysis of data.

Issues in classroom research: Impact of the researcher; research and theory; research or evaluation; demonstrating validity; research and teaching.

English Local History

1. Every candidate must follow for at least six terms a part-time course of instruction in English Local History and must upon entering for the examination produce from his or her society a certificate to that effect.

2. The examination will consist of the following parts:

Qualifying Test

Every candidate must pass a qualifying test. The test shall consist of the satisfactory completion of two courses on:

(1) Concepts and methods: an introduction to research in local history;

(2) Skills for local history.

The organizers of each course shall, not later than the end of the Michaelmas Term preceding the examination, submit to the examiners a list of candidates who have satisfactorily completed a qualifying course. No candidate who has failed the qualifying test of two courses will be permitted to supplicate for the degree. Candidates who fail a qualifying course once will be permitted to take it again, not later than one year after the initial attempt.

Final examinations

The examination shall consist of two advanced papers and a dissertation. One of the advanced papers may be taken during the third term of study.

I. *Either*

(1) two advanced papers from Schedule A below,

or

(2) one advanced paper from Schedule A below and a second paper from Schedule B, which consists of papers also offered as part of the M.Sc. in Economic and Social History. Other papers may be added subject to the approval of the Chairman of the Graduate Studies Committee of the History Faculty Board and of the Board of Studies of the Committee for Continuing Education Board.

II. A dissertation of not more than 15,000 words, including appendices but excluding bibliography, on a topic approved by the candidate's supervisor. The dissertation must be delivered not later than noon on the last Monday in September of the second year of the course to the Chairman of Examiners for the Degree of M.Sc. in English Local History, c/o Clerk of the Schools, High Street, Oxford.

SCHEDULE A

(1) The formation of the English countryside: settlement, church, and society in rural England, 900–1200.

(2) Manorial economy and society in the later middle ages.

(3) Kinship, culture, and community: provincial élites in early modern England.
(4) English architecture, 1500–1640.
(5) Enclosure and rural change, 1750–1850.
(6) Religion and community in England, 1830–1914.
(7) The social history of English architecture, 1870–1940.
(8) The English suburb, 1800–1939.

SCHEDULE B

Advanced Papers are available in the following areas:
(1) Economic and business history.
(2) History of science and technology.
(3) Social history.
(4) Historical demography.
(5) History of medicine.

A list of Advanced Papers will be published by the Board of Studies for the M.St. in English Local History in September for the academic year ahead (not all options may be available in every year). The definitive list of the titles of Advanced Papers for any one year will be circulated to candidates and their supervisors not later than Friday of the third week of Michaelmas Term. Teaching for the Advanced Papers will take place in Hilary Term.

In any given year some of these courses may not be available. Applicants for admission will be advised of this.

3. The examiners will permit the use of any hand-held pocket calculator subject to the conditions set out under the heading 'Use of calculators in examinations' in the *Special Regulations concerning Examinations.*

4. Each candidate must attend an oral examination when required to do so by the examiners.

5. The examiners may award a distinction for excellence in the whole examination.

6. A candidate who fails an advanced paper, or whose dissertation fails to satisfy the examiners, may be permitted to retake the paper, or resubmit the dissertation, on one further occasion only, not later than one year after the initial attempt.

Environmental Change and Management

1. The Life and Environmental Sciences Divisional Board shall elect for the supervision of the course a standing committee. The Course Director will be responsible to the standing committee.

2. Candidates must follow a course of instruction in Environmental Change and Management for at least three terms, and will, when entering for the examination be required to produce a certificate from the Course Director to this effect.

3. The examination will consist of:
   (i) a written examination of three papers on the syllabus described in the schedule:
   (ii) a dissertation on a subject selected in consultation with the supervisor and Course Director and approved by the standing committee.
   (iii) two assessed essays based on Option courses.

4. Candidates must submit to the Course Director by the end of the Hilary Term in the year in which they enter the examination, the title and a brief statement of the form and scope of their dissertation, together with the name of a person who has agreed to act as their supervisor during preparation of the dissertation.

5. The dissertation shall be of maximum length 15,000 words excluding appendices and references.

6. Two typewritten or printed copies of the dissertation must be sent, not later than noon on the first Friday in September in the year in which the written examination is taken, to the M.Sc. examiners (Environmental Change and Management), c/o the Clerk of the Schools, Examination Schools, High Street, Oxford OX1 4BG. The examiners may retain one copy of the dissertation of each candidate who passes the examination for deposit in an appropriate department library.

7. In the written examination the examiners will permit the use of any hand-held pocket calculators subject to the conditions set out under the heading 'Use of calculators in examinations' in the *Special Regulations concerning Examinations*.

8. The examiners may also examine any candidate viva voce on the candidate's written papers, dissertation, or both.

9. To complete the course successfully the candidate must achieve, on average, a pass mark over the three elements and a pass mark must be obtained in the dissertation and in the written examination. In the event of a failed dissertation, the candidate will be allowed to resubmit a dissertation in the following year.

10. The examiners may award a distinction for excellence in the whole examination.

SCHEDULE

(i) *Issues and driving forces.* Candidates will be expected to have a knowledge of the critical issues in current and future environmental change as applied to terrestrial, aquatic, and atmospheric systems. Forces driving change including resource scarcity, population, land use, and climatic factors. Strategies appropriate for the management of changing environments.

(ii) *Methods and techniques for environmental management.* Candidates will be expected to have a knowledge of methods for environmental management. These include: basic computing and modelling, experimental design, data acquisition and handling; remote sensing and GIS; methods of ecological and economic analysis.

(iii) *Managing the environment.* Candidates will be expected to have a knowledge of law, policy, ethics, and economics as they apply to issues of environmental change.

(iv) *Options.* Candidates will be expected to show advanced knowledge of two of the option courses on offer in any one year. The topics on offer and details will be approved by the standing committee and published in the *Gazette* before the end of Trinity Term of the academic year preceding that in which the written papers are to be taken.

Environmental Geomorphology

1. The Life and Environmental Sciences Divisional Board shall elect for the supervision of the course a standing committee. The Course Director and Deputy Director will be responsible to the standing committee.

2. Candidates must follow a course of instruction in Environmental Geomorphology for at least three terms, and will, when entering for the examination, be required to produce a certificate from the Course Director to this effect.

3. The examination will consist of:

(i) a written examination of one paper on the Scientific Nature and Theory of Geomorphology as described in the schedule;

(ii) a dissertation on a subject selected in consultation with the supervisor and Course Director and approved by the standing committee;

(iii) two assessed essays based on Option-courses in Thematic Geomorphology;

(iv) a practical notebook.

4. Candidates must submit to the Course Director by the end of fourth week of Hilary Term in the year in which they enter the examination, the title and a brief statement of the form and scope of their dissertation, together with the name of a person who has agreed to act as their supervisor during preparation of the dissertation.

5. The dissertation shall be of a maximum length of 15,000 words excludiung appendices and references.

6. Two double-spaced, bound typewritten or printed copies of the dissertation must be sent, not later than noon on the 1 September in the year in which the written examination is taken, to the M.Sc. examiners (Environmental Geomorphology), c/o the Clerk of the Schools, Examination Schools, High Street, Oxford OX1 4BG. The examiners may retain one copy of the dissertation of each candidate who passes the examination for deposit in an appropriate library. Both copies must bear the candidate's examination number but not his/her name.

7. One copy of the practical notebook must be sent, not later than 12 noon on Friday of the first week of Trinity Term in the year in which the written examination is taken, to the M.Sc. examiners (Environmental Geomorphology), c/o the Clerk of the Schools, Examination Schools, High Street, Oxford OX1 4BG. The notebook must bear the candidate's examination number but not the candidate's name, which must be concealed.

8. In the written examination the examiners will permit the use of hand-held pocket calculators subject to the conditions set out under the heading 'Use of calculators in examinations' in the *Special Regulations concerning Examinations.*

9. The examiners may also examine any candidate viva voce on the candidate's written papers, practical notebook, dissertation, or all three.

10. The examiners may award a distinction for excellence in the whole examination.

SCHEDULE

(i) *Scientific Theory and Nature of Geomorphology.* Candidates will be expected to have a knowledge of the main theories in geomorphology, and of the nature of landforms and the processes that mould them.

(ii) *Methods for Geomorphological Research.* Candidates will be expected to have a knowledge of methods for geomorphological research. These include basic computing, and modelling, experimental design, data acquisition and handling; remote sensing and GIS; field survey; laboratory and field techniques.

(iii) *Options in Thematic Geomorphology.* Candidates will be expected to show advanced knowledge of two of the option courses on offer in any one year. The topics on offer and details will be approved by the standing committee and published in the *Gazette* before the end of Trinity Term of the academic year preceding that in which the written papers are to be taken.

Evidence-based Health Care

1. The Divisional Board of Medical Sciences, in consultation with the Continuing Education Board, shall elect for the supervision of the course a standing committee which shall have the power to arrange lectures and other instruction.

2. Except as provided for under (6) below, every candidate must follow for at least six and at most twelve terms a part-time course of instruction in the theory and practice of evidence-based health care.

3. Every candidate will be required to satisfy the examiners in the following:

(*a*) attendance at the appropriate classroom-based courses;

(*b*) the following portfolios of written work, each of which shall not exceed 4,000 words in length:

  (i) a critical appraisal and analysis based on a minimum of three comprehensive literature searches closely related to the rest of the candidate's course work;

  (ii) evidence of ability to introduce the principles and practice of evidence-based health care in the candidate's work-based setting;

(iii) an account of the implementation and monitoring by the candidate of an aspect of health care change;

(*c*) an overall appraisal and analysis, which shall not exceed 4,000 words, of the work undertaken during modules (i)–(iii) of Schedule A (less any exemption);

(*d*) two written assignments, one spanning modules (v) and (vi) and a second covering module (vii) of Schedule A, each assignment not exceeding 4,000 words;

(*e*) a portfolio of statistical exercises, based on material covered in modules (v) and (vi) of the Schedule A;

(*f*) two written assignments, one on each of two modules chosen from those listed in Schedule B, each assignment not exceeding 4,000 words;

(*g*) a dissertation of not more than 25,000 words (including appendices and footnotes but excluding bibliography), on a subject selected by the candidate in consultation with the supervisor and approved by the Chairman of the Standing Committee;

The portfolio under (*b*), the overall appraisal and analysis under (*c*), the written assignments under (*d*) and (*f*) and the statistical exercises under (*e*), will be forwarded to the examiners c/o Registry, Department for Continuing Education, Wellington Square, Oxford OX1 2JA, for consideration by such date as the examiners shall determine and shall notify candidates.

4. Three typewritten or printed copies of the dissertation must be sent not later than 30 September in the year in which the examination is taken to the M.Sc. Examiners (Evidence-based Health Care), c/o Registry, Department for Continuing Education, Wellington Square, Oxford OX1 2JA. The dissertation must be accompanied by a statement that it is the candidate's own work except where otherwise indicated.

5. Candidates may, at the discretion of the examiners, be required to attend a viva voce examination.

6. The examiners may award a distinction for excellence in the whole examination.

7. Any candidate who has successfully completed the Postgraduate Diploma in Evidence-based Health Care may on admission to the M.Sc. be exempted from the requirement to submit, for the examination for this degree, the written assignments under 3(*b*) and (*d*) above or the statistical exercises under (*e*). Any such candidate may be allowed to count not more than three terms completed in the study of the Postgraduate Diploma in Evidence-based Health Care towards the minimum period of study for the M.Sc., but the actual number of terms, if greater than three, completed in the study of postgraduate diploma shall be counted towards the maximum period of study for the M.Sc. The M.Sc. in Evidence-based Health Care, if successfully completed, will subsume a candidate's previously completed postgraduate diploma.

8. The standing committee shall have the discretion to permit any candidate to be exempted from submitting up to two of the written assignments under 3(*b*), (*d*) or (*f*), or the statistical exercises under (*e*) above, not more than one of which shall be from each of 3(*d*) and (*f*), provided that the standing committee is satisfied that such a candidate has undertaken equivalent study, of an appropriate standard, normally at another institution of higher education.

9. Each candidate may, with the approval of the chairman of the standing committee, resubmit one written assignment and one only undertaken whilst registered for the M.Sc. if the course leader(s) deem that assignment unsatisfactory. This shall normally be within one year of the initial failure.

Schedule A

(i) The Practice of Evidence-based Health Care.
(ii) Planning for Evidence-based Health Care.

(iii) Implementing and Monitoring Change in Health Care.
(iv) A reflective dossier.
(v) Architecture of Applied Health Research Part 1.
(vi) Architecture of Applied Health Research Part 2.
(vii) Research Protocol Development.

Schedule B

(i) Advanced Issues in Clinical Trials.
(ii) Special Topics in Clinical Trials.
(iii) Advanced Issues in Overviews.
(iv) Special Topics in Overviews.
(v) Advanced Library Sciences.
(vi) Advanced Statistical Analysis.
(vii) Health Status Measurement.
(viii) Community Health Assessment.
(ix) Economic Appraisal of Health and Health Care.
(x) Sociological Analysis of Health and Health Care.
(xi) Health Screening Methodology.
(xii) Qualitative Methods in Health and Health Care.
(xiii) International Comparative Health Care.
(xiv) Practice Skills Development.

In June and December each year a list of Schedule B modules will be published in the University Gazette. *Each such list, which will have been approved by the Standing Committee for the M.Sc., and which will have been a selection from the full set above, will contain those Schedule B modules which will be available during the following nine months.*

Evidence-Based Social Work

1. Candidates may only be admitted to the course if they have successfully obtained an honours degree to First Class or good Upper Second Class standard.

2. Candidates must follow for at least three terms a course of instruction in Evidence-Based Social Work, and will, when entering for the examination, be required to produce a certificate from their supervisor to that effect.

3. Every candidate will be required to satisfy the examiners in the following:

(i) A compulsory core paper, Evidence-based interventions;
(ii) A compulsory Research Methods paper, for which students will be examined on the basis of a methods work book and an essay of up to 2,500 words;
(iii) One Option paper;
(iv) A thesis of not more than 10,000 words, describing the evaluation of a project on a topic decided jointly with, and approved by, the supervisor on behalf of the Department.

4. Two printed or word-processed copies of the Research Methods essay must be delivered to the M.Sc. Examiners (Evidence-Based Social Work), c/o the Clerk of the Schools, Examination Schools, High Street, Oxford OX1 4BG, no later than 12 noon on Friday of Sixth Week of the Trinity Term in which the examination has been taken.

5. Two printed or word-processed copies of the thesis must be delivered to the M.Sc. examiners (Evidence-based Social work), c/o the Clerk of the Schools, Examination Schools, High Street, Oxford OX1 4BG, no later than noon on Monday of the second week in September of the year in which the examination has been taken.

6. A candidate who fails the examination may enter for one subsequent examination only, provided this is within six terms of his or her initial registration. A

candidate who has attained a satisfactory mark in any one of the four components of the examination in 3 above will not be required to retake the component(s) concerned.

7. Each candidate must attend an oral examination when required to do so by the examiners.

8. The examiners may award a distinction for excellence in the whole examination.

Schedule

(i) *Evidence-Based Intervention* (core course): Candidates will be expected to have a knowledge of major theories underlying evidence-based interventions. The course will introduce students to a comparative perspective and use exemplary intervention research studies to illustrate important theoretical, ethical, methodological, and practice issues.

(ii) *Research Methods* (core course): Candidates will be expected to have a knowledge of major quantitative and qualitative techniques, and research designs for understanding social problems and evaluating interventions. There will be a particular emphasis on the appraisal and design of randomized controlled trials for evaluating social interventions.

(iii) *Option course*: This will enable students to link evidence-based solutions to a range of social problems in their country of origin. Not every option will be offered in any one year, and applicants for admission will be advised of this. Areas from which options may be offered include: promoting the welfare of children and families; multicultural mental health interventions; substance misuse and offending; interventions in relation to HIV and AIDS; community work; refugees and asylum seekers; day care for young children and their families.

Forced Migration

1. Candidates will be expected to attend such lectures and seminars as their supervisor/course director shall recommend.

2. Candidates will, when they enter for their examination, be required to produce a certificate from their society that they are following a course of study in the field which they have pursued in Oxford for at least three terms.

3. Candidates must present themselves for an oral examination unless exempted by the examiners.

4. The examiners may award a distinction for excellence in the whole examination. Every candidate will be required to satisfy the examiners in two papers and two essay papers as follows:

Paper I: International Legal and Normative Framework

The international legal and normative framework in relation to refugees and displaced persons. International and domestic application of individual and group rights to displaced persons and refugees. Implications of displaced populations for international order and for the security and stability of states. Activities and involvement of the relevant international organs, governments, and inter-governmental and non-governmental organizations regarding forced migration. The creation and dissolution of states. Concepts of intervention and their justifications. The evolutions of humanitarian responses to forced migration. The organizational culture of assistance.

Paper II: Causes and Consequences of Forced Migration

Theories of the causes of forced migration and humanitarian crises. Historical dimensions and social dynamics of forced migration. Coercion and conflict. Poverty and vulnerability. The impact of forced migrants on host populations and governments. Coping mechanisms, survival strategies, and psychological adaptation of affected populations. Nationalism, ethnicity, and group identity. Integration in rural and urban settings. The impact of resettlement programmes on the livelihood and economic autonomy of affected populations. Repatriation and social reconstruction.

Multidisciplinary Thesis

Each student will be required to write a thesis of not less than 10,000 and not more than 15,000 words on a topic relevant to forced migration. The purpose of this thesis is to ensure that the students have engaged in a multidisciplinary analysis of a single issue in forced migration to gain an awareness of the complex inter-relations in the field.

The topic of the thesis will require approval by the chairman of examiners. This thesis must be the work of the candidate alone and aid from others must be limited to prior discussion as to the subject and advice on presentation. The thesis must be presented in proper scholarly form, in two copies typed, in double-spacing on one side only of quarto or A4 paper, each copy bound or held firmly in a stiff cover, and must be delivered to the Clerk of the Schools, Examination Schools, High Street, Oxford, no later than Friday noon of week six in Trinity Term.

Research Methods Group Essay

Each student must display an understanding of research methods relevant to forced migration. This will be in the form of a group essay of approximately, but no more than 5,000 words, based on directed field research conducted during a four-week period in Hilary Term. The essay will present findings and engage with topics which include: epistemology of social science; social science paradigms; ethics and values; quantitative, qualitative, and participatory methods of date collection; the presentation of statistical information; research design; sampling theory; hypothesis testing; questionnaire design; participant observation; participatory learning and action; and evaluative research.

The essay must be presented in a proper scholarly form and delivered to the Clerk of Schools, Examination Schools, High Street, Oxford, no later than Friday noon in week eight of Hilary Term.

A candidate who fails the examination will be permitted to retake it on one further occasion only, not later than one year after the initial attempt. A candidate who has reached a satisfactory standard on any of the three components of the examination: (i) the thesis; (ii) the two written papers; (iii) the research methods group essay, will not be required to retake that part of the examination. Candidates may also be required to attend an oral examination, which may be on one or more of the candidate's written examinations, thesis or group essay. Any candidate who fails a group assignment may be considered for a pass on the basis of an oral examination.

Forestry: Science, Policy, and Management

1. *Course*

The Divisional Board of Life and Environmental Sciences shall elect for the supervision of the course an Education Committee which shall have power to arrange lectures and other instruction and to advise the faculty board on matters concerning its responsibility for the syllabus and examination.

On successful completion of the course candidates should be familiar with the social, economic, and environmental contexts of forestry, the relationship between forestry and other forms of land use, and with the science and practice of forestry.

Every candidate shall follow a course of study for at least three terms, and in addition for three periods, the first of one week immediately preceding the Michaelmas Full Term, the second of up to two weeks between Hilary and Trinity Terms, and the third of three weeks immediately following the end of Trinity Full Term, provided that the Director of the Oxford Forestry Institute or the deputy may exempt any candidate from the first or second additional period, but not both.

Candidates shall, when entering for the examination, be required to produce a certificate from their society to the effect that the course in Forestry: Science, Policy and Management outlined above has been followed.

2. *Syllabus*

The syllabus for study shall provide general coverage of Forestry: Science, Policy and Management and, where appropriate, scope for specialization in particular aspects.

The subjects which shall be followed in the syllabus of study shall be:

(i) *The Contexts, Development, and Application of Forestry*

(*a*) The social, political, and economic contexts of forestry
(*b*) The physical and biological environments
(*c*) The objectives of forestry
(*d*) Resource and land use options
(*e*) The development, expression, and implementation of forest policies including rural development
(*f*) Planning, management, and evaluation of forestry activities

(ii) *The Science and Practice of Forestry*

(*a*) Ecology and silviculture
(*b*) Inventory and monitoring
(*c*) Crop and product protection
(*d*) Conservation and use of genetic resources
(*e*) Harvesting, marketing, and utilization
(*f*) Applied soil science

(iii) *Special Option*

Every candidate will be required to study an applied science, which must be approved by the Director of the Oxford Forestry Institute or the deputy and the Chairman of Examiners. Normally four combinations of topics will be offered, containing elements of most of the following: anatomy and properties of wood, and wood deterioration; forest botany and systematics; forest entomology and pathology; forest genetics and tree breeding; forest inventory and prediction, including bio-diversity assessment and ecological surveys; soils.

A list of the topics being offered in any year will be published in the course handbook which is given to candiates at the start of Michaelmas Term. Candidates must inform the Director of the Institute (or the deputy) which of the options they wish to follow, by no later than Friday of the fifth week of Michaelmas Term.

(iv) *Essay*

In the essay, which may be presented in the form of a scientific paper, candidates will be required to show a knowledge of more than one of the fields of forestry on a subject approved by the Director of the Oxford Forestry Institute or the deputy, and Chairman of Examiners. Normally a choice of six topics will be set by the examiners, and a seventh possibility will be a subject of a candidate's choice that has been approved by the Chairman of Examiners. Candidates are warned that they should avoid repetition in papers covering subjects 2(i)–(iii) or material used in their essay and that substantial repetition may be penalised. The subject of the essay must be approved by 5 p.m. on the Friday of the fourth week of Michaelmas Term. No essay shall be less than 3,000 words nor exceed 5,000 words, the limit to include all notes and appendices, but references shall not be included in the word count.

(v) *Practical Management Exercise*

Candidates will be required to present a written practical management exercise, of not more than 7,000 words (excluding tables and appendices), for an area specified by the Director of the Oxford Forestry Institute or the deputy.

(vi) *Dissertation*

Candidates will be required to present a dissertation of not more than 20,000 words (excluding tables and appendices), on a subject approved by the Director of the Oxford Forestry Institute or the deputy and the Chairman of Examiners. The subject of the dissertation must be approved by 5 pm on the Friday of the first week of Trinity Term.

The essay, practical management exercise, and dissertation must be the candidate's own work. Tutors may, however, discuss with the candidates the proposed fields of study and the sources available; they may also read and comment on a first draft.

3. *Examination*

Candidates shall be examined by three written papers, one on each of the subjects 2(i)–(iii).

Two typewritten copies of each of the essay, the practical management exercise and dissertation must be sent to the Chairman of the Examiners, M.Sc. in Forestry, c/o Clerk of the Schools, Examination Schools, High Street, Oxford. The essay must be submitted not later than noon on the Friday of the noughth week of Hilary Full Term, the management exercise not later than noon on the Friday of the noughth week of Trinity Term, and the dissertation not later than noon on 7 September, in the calendar year in which the written examination is taken, or if this is a weekend, the Monday immediately following 7 September. The copies of the essay, the practical management exercise and the dissertation shall each be accompanied by a certificate signed by the candidate indicating that the work submitted is the candidate's own work except where specifically acknowledged, and that it has not been submitted wholly or substantially for another degree of this University, or for a degree of any other institution. The examiners will retain one copy of each, and those of outstanding quality will be deposited in the departmental library.

Part of the formal assessment of the dissertation by the examiners will be a presentation of the work, in a form to be determined by the examiners.

Candidates may also be called for a viva voce examination before the end of September on a date fixed by the examiners.

In the written examination, the examiners will not provide calculators, but will permit the use of hand-held calculators subject to the conditions set out under the heading 'Use of calculators in examinations' in the *Special Regulations concerning Examinations*.

The examiners may award a distinction for excellence in the whole examination.

History of Science: Instruments, Museums, Science, Technology

(*See also the general notice at the commencement of these regulations*)

The regulations of the Board of the Faculty of Modern History are as follows:

1. Candidates must follow for three terms a course of instruction arranged by the Museum of the History of Science and as prescribed in Schedule A and will, when entering for the examination, be required to produce a certificate from their supervisor to this effect.

2. The examination will be in two parts as follows.

Part I: Written examination as prescribed in Schedule B below. Candidates will be required to sit all three papers.

Part II: A dissertation of not more than 15,000 words, including footnotes and appendices, but excluding bibliography, on a topic approved by the candidate's supervisor and by the Professor of the History of Science (or its chairman on behalf of the committee). Dissertation titles must be approved before the first day of Trinity Term in the year in which the examination is taken. The dissertation must be delivered not later than noon on the last Monday in September of the year in which the examination is taken to the Clerk of the Schools, Examination Schools, High

Street, Oxford. Where approval has been given by the committee, the dissertation work may include a practical museum project or a computer project. In such cases the record of the work will be presented in an appropriate form and a reduced word limit for the written submission will be set by the committee on the recommendation of the candidate's supervisor.

3. Each candidate must attend an oral examination unless excused by the examiners.

4. The examiners may award a distinction for excellence in the whole examination.

5. A candidate who fails the examination will be permitted to retake it on one further occasion only, not later than one year after the initial attempt. Such a candidate whose dissertation has been of satisfactory standard may resubmit the same piece of work, while a candidate who has reached a satisfactory standard on the written papers will not be required to retake that part of the examination.

Schedule A

(i) Introduction to the histories of science, technology and instrumentation: historiographies of science, technology, and instrumentation; instruments as an historical resource; the histories of collections, museums, and museologies with particular reference to science.

(ii) Mathematical instruments to 1600: ancient and medieval astronomical instruments, including the armillary sphere, astrolabe, torquetum, quadrant, etc; the mathematical arts in the Renaissance and the rapid development of instrumentation from the later fifteenth century; the expanded domain of mathematical practice in astronomy, navigation, surveying, drawing, calculations, etc.

(iii) Instruments of the seventeenth century; the new categories of optical and natural philosophical instruments and their conceptual and methodological implications; the telescope, including its application to measuring instruments, the microscope, the thermometer, the air-pump, the barometer and magnetic instruments; the role of instrumentation for experiment and mechanical philosophy.

(iv) Instrumentation, 1700–1850: the rise of fashionable natural philosophy in England, France, and the Netherlands; the growth of new instrument markets and new traditions of making and marketing; electricity, optics, and experimental practice; the evolution of the microscope and telescope and their changing roles in amateur and professional practices; the development of mathematical instruments through agencies of the state, such as national observatories, longitude commissions, and national surveys; the rise to dominance of London mathematical instrument makers and the subsequent challenges from makers in Paris and in centres in Germany.

(v) Scientific instruments in the modern age: laboratory and industrial studies with particular reference to physics; photography, spectroscopy, and astrophysics; electrical measuring instruments, electrical technology, telegraphy, and radio; instruments in the biological and human sciences; the changing relationship between the scientist and the instrument maker.

(vi) Science collections today: the documentation and management of science historical collections and their use in education and museum display.

Schedule B

(i) Science, technology, and instrumentation to 1700.

(ii) Science, technology, and instrumentation, 1700–1850.

(iii) Science, technology, and instrumentation since 1850.

History of Science, Medicine, and Technology

(See also the general notice at the commencement of these regulations.)

The regulations of the Board of the Faculty of Modern History are as follows:

1. Every candidate must follow for at least three terms a course of instruction in History of Science, Medicine, and Technology, and must upon entering for the examination produce from his or her society a certificate to that effect.

2. The examination will consist of the following parts:

Qualifying test

Every candidate must pass a qualifying test. The test shall consist of the satisfactory completion of two courses on

(1) Methods and themes in economic and social history: an introduction to research.

(2) *Either* Methods and themes in the history of medicine (if the candidate's dissertation project lies in the field of history of medicine) *or* Methods and themes in the history of science and technology (if the candidate's dissertation project lies in the field of history of science and technology).

A paper from another established course within the University may be substituted for one of the standard courses where this would provide a more appropriate training for the candidate's dissertation focus. Such a choice will need formal approval from both the Course Director and the Chairman of the Graduate Studies Committee of the Board of the Faculty of Modern History.

The organizers of each course shall not later than the Friday of the sixth week of the Trinity Term preceding the examination submit to the examiners a list of candidates who have satisfactorily completed a qualifying course. No candidate who has failed the qualifying test of two courses will be permitted to supplicate for the degree. Candidates who fail a qualifying course once will be permitted to take it again, not later than one year after the initial attempt.

Final examinations

The examination shall consist of two papers and a dissertation.

Candidates must take at least one of their papers as a three-hour written examination. For the remaining paper candidates must choose to be assessed either by written examination or by two 5,000-word essays. Essays may only be submitted in lieu of written papers for subjects in Schedule I below ('Advanced Papers for M.Phil. and M.Sc. in History of Science, Medicine, and Technology') or for other papers permitted in Schedule II below where similar provision exists in the regulations for those examinations. The essays must be the work of the candidates alone and they must not consult any other person including their supervisors in any way concerning the method of handling the themes chosen. The themes chosen by the candidate must be submitted for approval by the chairman of examiners, c/o the Clerk of the Schools, High Street, Oxford, not later than the Monday of the fifth week of Hilary Term. Candidates will be informed within two weeks, by means of a letter directed to their colleges, whether the topics they have submitted have been approved. The finished essays must be delivered by the candidate to the Clerk of the Examination Schools, High Street, Oxford, by noon on Monday of the third week of Trinity Full Term. The essays must be presented in proper scholarly form, and two typed copies of each must be submitted. Candidates may be examined viva voce on the subjects on which they submit essays. Candidates who have not delivered essays as prescribed by the due date on any of their subjects must sit the written examination in those subjects.

I. One advanced paper selected from Schedule I below.

II. *Either* (i) one paper in a relevant discipline or skill or sources or methods selected from Schedule II below;

or (ii) a second advanced paper selected from Schedule I or from any additional list of papers for the M.Phil. and M.Sc. in History of Science, Medicine, and

Technology approved by the Graduate Studies Committee of the Board of the Faculty of Modern History and published in the definitive list of Advanced Papers as set out in Schedule I.

III. A dissertation of not more than 15,000 words, including appendices but excluding bibliography, on a topic approved by the candidate's supervisor. The dissertation must be delivered not later than noon on the last Monday in September of the year in which the examination is taken to the Clerk of the Schools, Examination Schools, High Street, Oxford. Dissertations submitted must not exceed the permitted length. If they do the examiners will reduce the marks awarded. The presentation and footnotes should comply with the requirements specified in the Regulations of the Educational Policy and Standards Committee for the degrees of M.Litt. and D.Phil. and follow the *Conventions for the presentation of dissertations and theses* of the Board of the Faculty of Modern History.

Each dissertation must include a short abstract which concisely summarizes its scope and principal arguments, in about 300 words.

Candidates must submit by the specified date two copies of their dissertations. These must be securely and firmly bound in either hard or soft covers.

3. The examiners will permit the use of any hand-held pocket calculator subject to the conditions set out below under the heading 'Use of calculators in examinations' in the *Special Regulations concerning Examinations.*

4. Each candidate must attend an oral examination when required to do so by the examiners.

5. The examiners may award a distinction for excellence in the whole examination.

6. A candidate who fails the examination will be permitted to retake it on one further occasion only, not later than one year after the initial attempt.

Such a candidate whose dissertation has been of satisfactory standard may resubmit the same piece of work, while a candidate who has reached a satisfactory standard on the written papers will not be required to retake that part of the examination.

Schedule I

Advanced Papers for the M.Phil. and M.Sc. in History of Science, Medicine, and Technology

A broad range of the course resources are shared with the corresponding courses in Economic and Social History, and Advanced Papers are therefore available in the subject areas listed here.

1. Economic and business history
2. History of science and technology
3. Social history
4. Historical demography
5. History of medicine

A descriptive list of Advanced Papers will be published by the Board of the Faculty of Modern History in September for the academic year ahead (not all options may be available in every year). The definitive list of the titles of Advanced Papers for any one year will be circulated to candidates and their supervisors and posted on the Faculty notice board not later than Friday of Third Week of Michaelmas Term.

Schedule II

The paper in a relevant discipline or skill may be:

1. One of the papers from the M.Phil. in Sociology or in Comparative Social Policy.

2. One suitable paper from another Master's degree under the auspices of the Faculty of Modern History approved from time to time by the Graduate Studies Committee of the Board of the Faculty of Modern History.

3. One suitable paper in a related skill or discipline other than those specified in paragraphs 1 to 2 above on the recommendation of the candidate's supervisor and endorsed by the Course Director.

Choices under Schedule II have to be approved by the Chairman of the Graduate Studies Committee of the Board of the Faculty of Modern History not later than Monday of the fourth week of Michaelmas Term. Candidates wishing to take a paper under 1 or 3 will also need the approval of the appropriate course convenor and the Graduate Studies Committee of the relevant faculty board or inter-faculty committee who need to be satisfied that each candidate has an adequate background in the subject. Not all options may be available in any one year.

Human Biology

1. The Life and Environmental Sciences Divisional Board shall elect for the supervision of the course a Standing Committee, which shall have power to arrange lectures and other instruction. The course director will be responsible to this organizing committee.

2. Candidates must follow a course of instruction in Human Biology, including training in research, for at least three terms, and will, when entering for the examination, be required to produce a certificate from their supervisor to this effect.

3. Candidates will be required to present themselves for written and oral examinations and to submit three copies of a dissertation in a prescribed form on an approved topic as defined below.

4. The written examination will consist of four papers, one on each of the subjects listed under sections (i), (ii) and (iii) of the Schedule below.

5. Each candidate will be required to submit a dissertation of approximately 15,000 to 20,000 words, on a subject selected in consultation with the supervisor and approved by the Professsor of Biological Anthropology. Approval of the dissertation topic must occur not later than the fourth week of Hilary Term of the year in which the candidate is admitted to the course of study.

6. Three typewritten copies of the dissertation must be sent, not later than noon on 30 September in the year in which the examination is taken, to the M.Sc. Examiners (Human Biology), c/o Department of Biological Anthropology, 58 Banbury Road, Oxford, OX2 6QS. The examiners shall retain one copy of the dissertation of each candidate who passes the examination for deposit in the departmental library.

7. The oral examination will focus principally on the candidate's dissertation.

8. The examiners will require to see the records of practical class work carried out by the candidate during the course.

9. Candidates will be expected to acquire a knowledge of modern statistical methods and quantitative techniques relevant to Human Biology.

10. The examiners may award a distinction for excellence in the whole examination.

11. If it is the opinion of the examiners that the work done by a candidate is not of sufficient merit to qualify for the Degree of M.Sc. but is nevertheless of sufficient merit to qualify for the Diploma in Human Biology, the candidate shall be given the option of resitting the M.Sc. examination or being issued with a diploma in the form prescribed in Ch. VI, Sect. II, SCHEDULE E.

Schedule

(i) *Human Genetics and Individual Variability*

(*a*) Molecular genetics and genome organization

(*b*) Reproduction, growth and development: a genetic perspective
(*c*) Mendelian and chromosomal disease
(*d*) Human biochemical genetics
(*e*) Genetics of complex traits

(ii) *Population variability: genetic and environmental determinants*
(*a*) Principles of population genetics
(*b*) Human diversity at the molecular level
(*c*) Demographic components of human variability
(*d*) Environmental determinants of phenotypic variability in populations
(*e*) Genetic epidemiology of disease in human populations

(iii) *Evolution of humans and other primates*
(*a*) Living primates: a survey
(*b*) Primate behaviour
(*c*) Evolution of non-human primates
(*d*) Hominid evolution: palaeontological and molecular data
(*e*) Bio-cultural perspective on human evolution

(iv) *Special option*

Every candidate will be required to study a special option. The special options will be approved by the Organizing Committee and published in the University Gazette before the end of the Trinity Term of the academic year preceding that in which the examination is taken. The details of how the syllabus is to be covered, and the associated lectures may vary from year to year. The arrangements for lectures and a detailed description of the special options will be included in a document approved by the Organizing Committee in Trinity Term, and circulated to all candidates for this M.Sc. course before the beginning of Michaelmas Term.

Industrial Relations and Human Resource Management

1. Candidates must follow a course of instruction for at least three terms, including two terms in Industrial Relations and Human Resource Management, and will, when they enter their names for the examination, be required to produce a certificate from their supervisors to this effect.

2. The examination will consist of the following papers. Candidates must complete
(i) Core Course in Management Research as prescribed in the schedule;
(ii) Two specialist papers from the list of courses which may be offered. The list of subjects and the syllabuses from which the papers may be selected shall be approved by the M.Sc. Course Director and published in the *Gazette* not later than the end of the Trinity Full Term of the academic year preceding the year of the examination.
(iii) Research methodology, as prescribed in the schedule. There will be three components to the final Research Methodology mark, which will consist of a combination of tests and assignments, to be produced during Michaelmas and Hilary Terms. The Research Methodology teachers will set the assessment exercises associated with each component of the Methodology courses. Students will be informed at the beginning of each course whether the method of assessment will be a test, or a written assignment.

Assignments must be presented not later than the time and date stipulated for each exercise; the M.Sc. Course Director will publish these by the first Monday of each term in which the assignments must be taken. The required number of copies must be delivered to the Examination Schools and addressed to the Chairman of Examiners for the M.Sc. in Industrial Relations and Human Resource Management, c/o Clerk of the Schools, High Street, Oxford, accompanied by a statement that it is the candidate's own work.

(iv) Dissertation. Candidates are required to submit a dissertation in a field of Industrial Relations and Human Resource Management. The dissertation should demonstrate an ability to identify, formulate, implement and present a research project. Two typewritten copies of the dissertation, not exceeding 15,000 words in length, must be delivered to the Examination Schools and addressed to the Chair of Examiners for the M.Sc. in Industrial Relations and Human Resource Management, c/o Clerk of the Schools, Examination Schools, High Street, Oxford, by noon on the first Monday of August in the calendar year in which the examination is taken.

3. (i) Candidates who fail any part of the Research Methodology assessment may resubmit, or resit, the failed assessment only once by noon on Friday of Week 8 of the following term. Candidates who fail one of the written parts of the examination other than the dissertation may enter again for that part in the following academic year. Otherwise, candidates who fail more than one part of the examination will be permitted to resit all the papers during the following academic year.

(ii) A candidate who has failed to satisfy the examiners in the dissertation may resubmit it on one, but not more than one, subsequent occasion, which shall be no later than the 1st of August of the following year.

4. Candidates may be required to attend an oral examination on any of the four parts of the examination.

5. The examiners may award a distinction for excellence in the whole examination.

Schedule

(*a*) *Core Course in Management Research*

This course consists of three modules:

(*i*) *Module 1: Advances in Organization Analysis*

Organization behaviour and theory. Vertical integration. Long-term contracts and gift exchange. Logic of collective action. Trust as social capital. Inter-organizational networks and new forms of organization. Virtual organizations and markets. Sociological perspectives on organization, esp. the construction and negotiation of organizational boundaries and relations between procedures and consumers.

(*ii*) Module 2: Economics of Organization

Rationality in economics. Bargaining theory. Labour contracts. The size of the firm. The firm and its financiers. Reputation-based trade. Monitoring and banking. Managers, firms and stock-holders.

(*iii*) *Module 3: Comparative Management*

Theories of comparative management, including cultural, institutional, sociological and economic analyses. Concepts of varieties of capitalism and national economic distinctiveness. Path dependence and system embeddedness. Managerial styles. Comparative systems, strategic choices, and performance outcomes. Trends of convergence, divervence, and mediation of economic forces. Corporate and economic adjustment paths. National and international economic regulation. Multi-level comparative analysis. Comparative methodology. Contemporary topics in comparative and international management.

(*b*) *Research Methodology*

The nature of research in management studies and its relation to other social sciences, epistemology, strategies for literature review, research design, qualitative methods, interviewing, questionnaire design and ethnography, data sources and data collection, statistical methods, statistical and econometric modelling, analysis and interpretation of qualitative and quantitative data, presentation of research results.

Latin American Studies

Each candidate will be required to follow a course of instruction for three terms and to present himself or herself for examination in the compulsory general paper and two additional papers in the chosen discipline at the end of Trinity Term in the year of registration. Students whose first langauge is not Spanish or Portuguese will be required to demonstrate a reading knowledge of one of those languages by the end of Michaelmas Term. Native speakers and holders of a recognized higher qualification in Spanish or Portuguese would be exempt from this requirement. In addition, each candidate will be required to submit an extended essay, not exceeding 10,000 words, which will be equal to one written paper. The title of the extended essay must be approved by the Latin American Centre committee not later than noon on the Saturday of eighth week of the Michaelmas Full Term preceding the written examination. Two typewritten copies of the extended essay must be delivered to the Clerk of the Examination Schools, addressed to the Chair of Examiners for the M.Sc. in Latin American Studies, c/o Clerk of the Schools, Examination Schools, High Street, Oxford, by noon on the fifth Monday of Trinity Full Term in the calendar year in which the examination is taken.

2. Candidates who fail one of the three papers without compensating strengths on the other papers and the extended essay will be allowed to retake the examination in the following Trinity Term. Candidates who fail more than one paper will be deemed to have failed the examination. Candidates who fail the extended essay will be allowed to resubmit in the following Trinity Term.

3. Candidates may be required to attend an oral examination on any of the four parts of the examination.

4. The examiners may award a distinction for excellence in the whole examination.

Schedule of Papers

1(*a*) General paper: Latin America since *c.*1900

Introductory lectures/classes on the Politics, Economics, and History of Latin America will be given in Michaelmas and Hilary Terms. Students will write essays for individual tutors in all three disciplines for this common paper.

(*b*) Two optional subjects from the following disciplines:

History

(*a*) Latin America from Independence to the First World War (compulsory paper)

(*b*) A choice of one optional paper from:

Social Revolutions in Latin America

The History of a Country or Group of Countries. Candidates may choose from the following list:

(i) Brazil
(ii) Mexico
(iii) Chile and Argentina
(iv) Peru and Bolivia
(v) Colombia, Venezuela, and Ecuador

The Military in Latin America since 1930 (a joint paper with Politics)

Politics

(*a*) *The Politics of Democracy in Latin America* (compulsory paper)

(*b*) A choice of one optional paper from:

(i) *Social Policies in Latin America*
(ii) *The Military in Latin America since 1930* (jointly with History)
(iii) *The Politics of a Major Country or Countries* (see History listing)
(iv) *The International Relations of Latin America*

Economics

(*a*) *Introduction to the Latin American Economies* (compulsory paper)

(*b*) A choice of one optional paper from:

(i) *Further issues in Latin American Development*

(ii) *The Economic Development of a single country*

(iii) *Human Development in Latin America*

Management Research

1. Candidates must follow for three terms a course of instruction in Management Research and will, when entering for the examination be required to produce a certificate from a supervisor for the M.Sc. in Management Research appointed for the purpose to this effect.

2. The examination will consist of the following papers, the rubrics for which are set out in the schedule:

(i) Core Course in Management Research, as prescribed in the schedule.

(ii) Two specialist papers from the list of courses which may be offered. The list of subjects and the syllabuses from which the papers may be selected shall be approved by the M.Sc. Course Director and published in the *Gazette* not later than the end of the Trinity Term of the academic year preceding the year of the examination. Students may replace one of the specialist papers with any other appropriate course offered in the University, with the agreement of the Course Director and the body responsible for the course concerned.

(iii) Research Methodology, as prescribed in the schedule. There will be three components to the final Research Methodology mark, which will consist of a combination of tests and assignments, to be produced during Michaelmas and Hilary terms. The Research Methodology teachers will set the assessment exercises associated with each component of the Methodology courses. Students will be informed at the beginning of each course whether the method of assessment will be a test, or a written assignment.

Assignments must be presented not later than the time and date stipulated for each exercise; the M.Sc. Course Director shall publish these by the first Monday of each term in which the assignments must be taken. The required number of copies must be delivered to the Examination Schools and addressed to the Chairman of Examiners for the M.Sc. in Management Research, c/o Clerk of the Schools, High Street, Oxford, accompanied by a statement that it is the candidate's own work.

(iv) Dissertation. Candidates are required to submit a dissertation in a field of management research. The dissertation should demonstrate an ability to identify, formulate, implement and present a research project. Two typewritten copies of the dissertation, not exceeding 15,000 words in length, must be delivered to the Examination Schools and addressed to the Chairman of Examiners for the M.Sc. in Management Research, c/o Clerk of the Schools, Examination Schools, High Street, Oxford, by noon on the first Monday of August in the calendar year in which the examination is taken.

3. (i) Candidates who fail any part of the Research Methodology assessment may resubmit or resit the failed assessment only once by noon on Friday of Week 8 of the following term. Candidates who fail one of the written parts of the examination other than the dissertation may enter again for that part in September of the same year. Otherwise, candidates who fail more than one part of the examination will be permitted to resit all the papers during the following academic year.

(ii) A candidate who has failed to satisfy the examiners in the dissertation may resubmit it on one, but not more than one, subsequent occasion, which shall be no later than the 1st of August of the following year.

4. Candidates may be required to attend an oral examination on any of the four parts of the examination.

5. The examiners may award a distinction for excellence for the whole examination.

Schedule

(*a*) *Core Course in Management Research*

This course consists of three modules:

(*i*) *Module 1: Advances in Organization Analysis*

Organization behaviour and theory. Vertical integration. Long-term contracts and gift exchange. Logic of collective action. Trust as social capital. Inter-organizational networks and new forms of organization. Virtual organizations and markets. Sociological perspectives on organization, esp. the construction and negotiation of organizational boundaries and relations between producers and consumers.

(*ii*) *Module 2: Economics of Organization*

Rationality in economics. Bargaining theory. Labour contracts. The size of the firm. The firm and its financiers. Reputation-based trade. Monitoring and banking. Managers, firms and stock-holders.

(*iii*) *Module 3: Comparative Management*

Theories of comparative management, including cultural, institutional, sociological and economic analyses. Concepts of varieties of capitalism and national economic distinctiveness. Path dependence and system embeddedness. Managerial styles. Comparative systems, strategic choices, and performance outcomes. Trends of convergence, divergence, and mediation of economic forces. Corporate and economic adjustment paths. National and international economic regulation. Multi-level comparative analyses. Comparative methodology. Contemporary topics in comparative and international management.

(*b*) Research Methodology

The nature of research in management studies and its relation to other social sciences, epistemology, strategies for literature review, research design, qualitative methods, interviewing, questionnaire design and ethnography, data sources and date collection, statistical methods, statistical and econometric modelling, analysis and interpretation of qualitative and quantitative date, presentation of research results.

Material Anthropology and Museum Ethnography

1. The Life and Environmental Sciences Divisional Board shall elect for the supervision of the course a Standing Committee, which shall have power to arrange lectures and other instruction. The course director will be responsible to this organizing committee.

2. Candidates must follow a course of instruction in Social and Cultural Anthropology for at least three terms, and will, when entering for the examinations, be required to produce a certificate from their supervisor to this effect.

3. Candidates will be required to present themselves for written and oral examinations and to submit three copies of a dissertation in prescribed form on an approved topic as defined below.

4. The written examination will consist of four papers on the syllabus described in the Schedule.

5. Each candidate will be required to submit a dissertation of approximately 10,000 words, on a subject selected in consultation with the supervisor and approved by the Chairman of Examiners. The proposed title of the dissertation, together with a paragraph describing its scope and the supervisor's written endorsement, must be

submitted to the Chairman of Examiners by Monday of the first week of Trinity Term.

6. Three typewritten copies of the dissertation must be delivered not later than noon on the second Monday in September in the year in which the examination is taken, to the Chairman of Examiners, M.Sc. in Material Anthropology and Museum Ethnography/Social Anthropology, c/o Clerk to the Schools, Examination Schools, High Street, Oxford.

The examiners shall retain one copy of the dissertation of each candidate who passes the examination for deposit in the departmental library.

7. The oral examination may be on the candidate's written papers, or dissertation, or both.

8. The examiners may award a distinction for excellence in the whole examination.

9. If it is the opinion of the examiners that the work done by a candidate is not of sufficient merit to qualify for the Degree of M.Sc. but is nevertheless of sufficient merit to qualify for the Diploma in Material Anthropology and Museum Ethnography, the candidate shall be given the option of resitting the M.Sc. examination or being issued with a diploma in the form prescribed in Ch. VI, Sect. II, Schedule E.

Schedule

Every candidate will be required to satisfy the examiners in four papers as follows:

I *Social and Cultural Anthropology A: History and Development* (paper and syllabus shared with the M.Sc. in Social Anthropology).

The scope of this paper includes the following topics: history and development of the subject, and the relation between academic research, museums, and the imperial context of anthropology's past; relations to other subjects, including archaeology and history. Key authors and debates in the development of anthropology, with particular reference to: kinship, marriage, gender, and sexuality; space, place, and culture; environment and cultural landscapes in transition; land and property rights; production and consumption; transactions and modes of exchange; the division of labour and the comparative anthropology of work; technology and social change; the colonial process and its legacy; nationalism, ethnicity, migration, and transnationalism; urbanism.

II *Social and Cultural Anthropology B: Theory and Methods* (paper and syllabus shared with the M.Sc. in Social Anthropology.

The scope of this paper includes the following topics: concepts of the individual, society and the person of anthropological perspective; issues of the body, theories of practice, phenomenology; theories of power, order and law; aspects of disorder and violence in society; systems of knowledge and belief; ritual and myth; symbolism and symbolic classification; moral systems and the world religions; oral literature and historical memory; linguistics and artistic modes of communication; aesthetic anthropology; methodological approaches to the study of arts, performance and material culture; museums, written texts and representation. Fieldwork and data collection methods; quantitative and qualitative techniques; cultural property and indigenous rights; applications of film and sound recording; preparing research proposals; ethical problems.

III and IV *Optional Papers*

Candidates must choose two optional papers. Titles of available options will be made known at the beginning of each academic year. They will be divided into three lists, as follows:

List A: The Social Anthropology of a Selected Region.
List B: Topics in Material Anthropology.
List C: Anthropology and Practical Issues.

Candidates for the degree of M.Sc. in Material Anthropology and Museum Ethnography must select at least one of their options from List B.

Mathematical Finance

1. The Board of the Division of Mathematical and Physical Sciences, in consultation with the Board of Studies of the Continuing Education Board, shall elect for the supervision of the course a standing committee which shall have the power to arrange lectures and other instruction.

2. Subject to the provision in 7 below, every candidate must follow for at least six and at most twelve terms a part-time course of instruction in the theory and practice of Mathematical Finance. The subjects of the course will consist of the modules listed in the Schedule.

3. Every candidate will be required to satisfy the examiners in the following:

(*a*) attendance at the appropriate classroom-based courses;

(*b*) submission of five module assignments, one for each of modules 1 to 5;

(*c*) three written 'special topic' assignments, each of no more than 10 pages of A4 in length (excluding tables, appendices, footnotes, and bibliography), on the candidate's choice of advanced modules from those currently listed in the schedule.

(*d*) a three-hour written examination, covering material relevant to modules 1 to 5;

(*e*) a dissertation of not more than fifty pages of A4 in length (excluding tables, appendices, footnotes, and bibliography), on a subject selected by the candidate in consultation with the supervisor and approved by the chairman of the standing committee. The assessed work set out in clauses (*b*) and (*c*), and the dissertation under (*d*), shall be forwarded to the examiners c/o Registry, Department of Continuing Education, 1 Wellington Square, Oxford OX1 2JA, for consideration by such date as the examiners shall determine and of which they shall notify candidates.

4. Candidates may be required to attend a viva voce examination at the end of the course of studies at the discretion of the examiners.

5. The examiners may award a distinction for excellence in the whole examination.

6. Candidates who fail to satisfy the examiners in the module assignments under (*b*), the written 'special topic' assignments under (*c*), the written examination under (*d*), or the dissertation under (*e*) may be permitted to resubmit work in respect of the part or parts of the examination which they have failed for examination on not more than one occasion which shall normally be within one year of the original failure.

7. The standing committee shall have the discretion to permit any assignments submitted as part of the course for the Postgraduate Diploma in Mathematical Finance to be submitted for the examination for the M.Sc. No more than three terms of study undertaken for the Postgraduate Diploma may be counted towards the minimum period of study for the M.Sc.; the entire period of study undertaken for the Postgraduate Diploma shall be counted towards the maximum period of study for the M.Sc.

8. If any candidate who is successful in the examination for the M.Sc. in Mathematical Finance has previously successfully completed the Postgraduate Diploma, and for that examination has incorporated the assignments submitted for the

Postgraduate Diploma into the M.Sc., then the subsequent award will subsume his or her previous award.

Schedule

Section A: Core Modules

Modules 1 to 5 shall be given each year.

1. Foundation: a review of technical requisites
2. Introduction to Finance: the basic building blocks of finance practice and theory
3. Asset allocation: models for investment decisions
4. Equity, Currency, and Commodity Derivatives
5. Interest Rates and Products: models for the fixed income markets

Section B: Advanced Modules

The Standing Committee shall approve the content of at least three advanced modules to be given each year which shall be published annually in the *Gazette* in or before week eight of Hilary Term.

Mathematical Modelling and Scientific Computing

1. Candidates must follow for at least three terms a course of instruction in Mathematical Modelling and Scientific Computing and will, when entering for the examination, be required to produce a certificate from their supervisors to this effect.

2. The examination will consist of:

(i) a written examination consisting of two papers from the syllabus described in Schedule 1;

(ii) a short dissertation on a topic selected by the candidate in consultation with the supervisor and approved by the board of examiners. Between twenty-five and fifty typed pages is the preferred length, and the dissertation is not expected to contain original work;

(iii) an oral examination on the dissertation, and, unless the candidate shall have been individually dispensed by the examiners, on topics in Schedule 1, and on the special topics chosen from Schedule 2.

3. When entering for the examination a candidate will be required to state the topic proposed for his dissertation. Such notice must be given to the Registrar not later than Friday of the fourth week of Hilary Full Term preceding the examination.

4. For the special topics in Schedule 2, and on the classwork associated with topics in Schedule 1, the examiners will take into account the result of an assessment organized by the M.Sc. Supervisory Committee (Mathematical Modelling and Scientific Computing). The committee shall be responsible for notifying the candidate of the arrangements for the assessment, and for forwarding the results of all candidates to the chairman of the M.Sc. examiners before the oral examination. The assessment will be made by giving the candidate questions to answer over a period of 24 hours or a mini-project to develop over a period of a week and candidates will be required to sign a statement that the work offered for assessment is theirs alone. The questions or mini-project will be set within six weeks of the end of the relevant lecture course and will be suggested by the course lecturers.

5. Two typewritten copies of the dissertation must be delivered not later than noon on a date to be specified by the examiners which will be a Friday in mid-September in the year in which the written examination is taken, to the M.Sc. Examiners (Mathematical Modelling and Scientific Computing), c/o the Clerk of the Schools, Examination Schools, High Street, Oxford, together with a list of four special topics from Schedule 2 on which the candidate wishes to be orally examined.

6. In the written examination the examiners will permit the use of any hand-held pocket calculators subject to the conditions set out under the heading 'Use of

calculators in examinations' in the *Special Regulations concerning Examinations*.

7. The examiners may award a distinction for excellence in the whole examination.

SCHEDULE I

A. The theory of linear and non-linear ordinary differential equations. Transform methods, applications of complex variable theory, asymptotic methods. Partial differential equations and their applications to scientific and industrial problems. Mathematical modelling.

B. The numerical solution of ordinary differential equations, including eigenvalue problems. The numerical solution of partial differential equations of elliptic, hyperbolic, and parabolic type; finite element methods. Topics in numerical linear algebra including methods for large sparse matrices.

SCHEDULE 2

Mathematical modelling of industrial and other scientific problems, further topics in applied analysis.

Numerical methods in optimization, approximation, and linear algebra.

Numerical solution of integral equations, and differential equations.

[*Note*. The details of how the syllabus is to be covered, and the associated lectures, may vary from year to year. The arrangements for lectures and a detailed description of the special topics in Schedule 2 will be included in a document approved by a faculty board at its second meeting in Trinity Term, and circulated to all candidates for this M.Sc. course before the beginning of Michaelmas Term.]

Mathematics and Foundations of Computer Science

1. The Divisional Board of Mathematical and Physical Sciences shall elect for the supervision of the course a standing committee which shall have power to arrange lectures and other instruction.

2. Candidates shall follow for at least three terms a course of instruction in Mathematics and Foundations of Computer Science.

3. The examination shall be in three parts, as follows:

(*a*) Candidates shall successfully complete a written assignment on each of five courses chosen from a list of courses approved by the standing committee and published in the *University Gazette* by not later than the Friday of eighth week of the Trinity Term preceding the examination. The list of courses shall be divided into two sections: Section A (Mathematical Foundations) and Section B (Applicable Theories). Each section shall be divided into schedule I (basic) and schedule II (advanced). Candidates shall be required to satisfy the examiners in at least two courses taken from section B and in at least two courses taken from schedule II.

(*b*) Candidates shall submit a short dissertation on a topic selected by the candidate in consultation with the supervisor and approved by the standing committee. The dissertation must bear regard to course material from Sections A or B. Between thirty-five and sixty-five typed pages is the preferred length;

(*c*) There shall be an oral examination on the dissertation and its background material, and the candidate shall normally be expected to give a short presentation on the dissertation.

4. Candidates must submit to the chairman of the standing committee by the end of the second week of Trinity Term in the year in which they enter the examination, the title and a brief statement of the form and scope of their dissertation, together with the name of a person who has agreed to act as their supervisor during the preparation of the dissertation.

5. Two typewritten copies of the dissertation must be delivered not later than noon on 1 September in the year in which the examination is taken, to the M.Sc. Examiners (Mathematics and Foundations of Computer Science), c/o the Clerk of the Schools, Examination Schools, High Street, Oxford. The dissertation must be accompanied by a certificate from the candidate's society to the effect that he or she has followed for three terms a course of instruction in Mathematics and Foundations of Computer Science. The examiners may retain one copy of the dissertation of each candidate who passes the examination for deposit in an appropriate departmental library.

6. Candidates shall notify the Registrar of their intention to offer a written assignment for a lecture course not later than the Friday of the third week of each term. No candidate may offer more than four courses in one term. There will be a written assignment for each course. The topics in the assignment will be suggested by the relevant lecturer not later than the Monday of eighth week of the term during which the course is given. These topics will be sufficient to offer options appropriate to the course. The choice of topics will vary from year to year. Completed assignments must be delivered not later than noon on the Monday of the eleventh week of the term during which the course in offered, to the M.Sc. Examiners (Mathematics and Foundations of Computer Science), c/o the Clerk of the Schools, Examination Schools, High Street, Oxford, together with a signed statement that the work offered for assessment is the candidate's own.

7. A candidate who does not submit a written assignment on a course for which he or she has entered, by noon on the Monday of the eleventh week of the relevant term, shall be deemed to have failed the course in question.

8. A list of those candidates who have satisfied the examiners in particular courses in the relevant term shall be posted in the Mathematical Institute by the Friday preceding the following Full Term.

9. If a candidate is deemed to have failed a particular course, he or she shall not be permitted to re-enter for examination in that course.

Any candidate who has not satisfied the examiners in four courses by the beginning of the Trinity Term shall be deemed to have failed the degree course.

10. A candidate who has failed to satisfy the examiners in the examination may enter again for the examination on one, but not more than one, subsequent occasion, not later than one year after the initial attempt. No written assignment shall be submitted to the examiners on more than one occasion.

11. The examiners may award a distinction for excellence in the whole examination.

Medical Anthropology

1. The Life and Environmental Sciences Divisional Board shall elect for the supervision of the course a Standing Committee, which shall have power to arrange lectures and other instruction. The course director will be responsible to this organizing committee.

2. Candidates must follow a course of instruction in Medical Anthropology for at least three terms, and will, when entering for the examination, be required to produce a certificate from their supervisor to this effect.

3. Candidates will be required to present themselves for written and, where invited, oral examinations, and to submit three copies of a dissertation in prescribed form on an approved topic as defined below.

4. The written examination will consist of four papers on the syllabus described in the Schedule.

5. Each candidate will be required to submit a dissertation of approximately 10,000 words, on a subject selected in consultation with the supervisor and approved by the Chairman of Examiners. The proposed title of the dissertation together with a paragraph describing its scope and the supervisor's written endorsement, must be submitted to the Chairman of Examiners by Monday of the first week of Trinity Term.

6. Three typewritten copies of the dissertation must be delivered not later than noon on the second Monday in September in the year in which the examination is taken, to the Chairman of the Examiners, M.Sc. in Medical Anthropology, c/o Clerk of the Schools, Examination Schools, High Street, Oxford.

The examiners shall retain one copy of the dissertation of each candidate who passes the examination for deposit in the departmental library.

7. An oral examination, if held, may be on the candidate's written papers, or dissertation, or both.

8. The examiners may award a distinction for excellence in the whole examination.

Schedule

Every candidate will be required to satisfy the examiners in four papers as follows:

1. *Concepts of disease, illness, health, and medicine in global perspective*

The scope of this paper includes the following topics: epidemiology, global distribution of disease patterns, co-existence of alternative therapeutic or healing systems, phenomenology of the body, and cross-cultural concepts of health, pain, illness, disease causation, diagnosis, and cure. Topics analysed from conjoined biological and socio-cultural perspectives include human growth and personhood, adaptability, nutrition, health and social inequality, reproduction and fertility, disease identification, and epidemiology. Issues associated with informed consent; preparation of research proposals.

2. *Theory and practice of bio-medicine and of other medical systems*

The scope of this paper includes the impact of different medical systems on the health of populations, issues of public health and policy on a comparative and global basis, including specific campaigns (e.g. that eliminating small-pox in South Asia and attempts to characterize and treat AIDS). It draws on ethnographies of particular societies to illustrate and test theoretical claims in medical anthropology, covering different ways in which people manage fertility, reproduction, death and disease, patient-healer relations, the explanatory roles of divination, herbalism, alternative therapies, dramatherapy, religion, shamanism, sorcery, and culturally defined concepts of risk, vulnerability, fate, and evil.

3. *Critical medical anthropology*

The scope of this paper includes a critique of the assumptions and methods of this sub-field of anthropology and of its links with other fields and disciplines, including the place of material culture in medicine. Critique of the Cartesian mind-body dichotomy and methodological problems specially affecting medical anthropology; field-work and data collection methods; quantitative and qualitative techniques; cultural property and indigenous rights; preparing research proposals; ethical issues.

4. *Ecological and bio-medical anthropology*

The scope of this paper includes consideration of the concept of well-being as being broader than conventional concepts of health and comprising ecological, biological, and socio-cultural perspectives; relationships between biodiversity, ecological change, and changing patterns of disease, diagnosis, and cure; the role of economic transformation in health and environmental issues; changing relationships between diet, nutrition, infection, human growth, and chronic disease; pharmacology and genomics in research and practice; health and ethics.

Nature, Society, and Environmental Policy

1. The Life and Environmental Sciences Divisional Board shall elect for the supervision of the course a standing committee. The Course Director and Deputy Director will be responsible to the standing committee.

2. Candidates must follow a course of instruction in Human Geography for at least three terms, and will, when entering for the examination, be required to produce a certificate from the Course Director to this effect.

3. The examination will consist of:
 (i) a written examination of two three-hour papers, one based on Research Skills and the other based on a choice between Nature and Society, and Global Transitions, as described in the schedule;
 (ii) two assessed essays based upon option courses;
 (iii) either a dissertation on a subject selected in consultation with the supervisor and Course Director and approved by the Standing Committee:
 (iv) or two additional assessed essays drawn from option courses due no later than the Friday of ninth-week of Trinity Term.

4. Candidates who select (iii) must submit to the Course Director by the end of eighth week of Hilary Term in the year in which they enter the examination, the title and a brief statement of the form and scope of their dissertation, together with the name of a person who has agreed to act as their supervisor during preparation of the dissertation.

It may be (*a*) a theoretical argument related to themes in contemporary human geography, or (*b*) a piece of empirically based research, or (*c*) an extended treatment of an issue which is intended to be the basis for future research for the degree of M.Litt. or D.Phil. In that case (*c*), it may be part of a proposal and/or application for further degree study.

5. The dissertation shall be of a maximum length of 15,000 words excluding appendices and bibliography.

6. Two double-spaced, bound typewritten or printed copies of the dissertation must be sent, not later than noon on the 1 September in the year in which the written examination is taken, to the M.Sc. examiners (Nature, Society, and Environmental Policy), c/o the Clerk of the Schools, Examination Schools, High Street, Oxford OX1 4BG. The examiners may retain one copy of the dissertation of such candidate who passes the examination for deposit in an appropriate library. Both copies must bear the candidate's examination number but not his/her name.

The dissertation shall be accompanied by an abstract not exceeding 150 words and a statement certifying that the dissertation is the candidate's own work except where otherwise indicated.

7. In the written examination the examiners will permit the use of hand-held pocket calculators subject to the conditions set out under the heading 'Use of calculators in examinations' in the *Special Regulations concerning Examinations*.

8. The examiners may also examine any candidate viva voce on the candidate's written papers, dissertation, or both.

9. The examiners may award a distinction for excellence in the whole examination.

SCHEDULE

 (i) *Research Skills.* Candidates will be expected to have a knowledge of research methods in human, environmental, and geographical research. These will include qualitative and quantitative methods relevant to contemporary research themes.

(ii) *Nature and Society.* Candidates will be expected to have a knowledge of relevant debates and issues related to human interaaction with, and construction of, nature as well as the appropriate environmental policy responses.

(iii) *Global Transitions.* Candidates will be expected to have knowledge of relevant debates and issues concerning globalization, the changing economic geography of the landscape as well as the appropriate environmental policy responses.

Neuroscience

1. The Divisional Board of Medical Sciences shall elect for the supervision of the course an organizing committee which shall have power to arrange lectures and other instruction.

2. The organizing committee shall appoint for each candidate an academic advisor.

3. Each candidate shall follow a course of study in Neuroscience for at least three terms and for a substantial part of the three subsequent vacations, as determined by the course timetable, and will, when entering for the examination, be required to produce a certificate from their academic advisor to this effect.

4. Candidates shall be examined in all of the following ways:

(i) each candidate must pass a qualifying examination at the end of the first term from the beginning of the course. The test shall consist of the satisfactory completion of the Neuroscience Introductory Course and one three-hour written paper on the topics covered in that course, as set out in the Schedule; the organizing committee shall not later than the end of the Hilary Term preceding the examination submit to the examiners a list of candidates who have satisfactorily completed the qualifying examination. Candidates who fail the qualifying examination once shall be permitted to take it again in the first week of Hilary Term of the year of the final examination;

(ii) each candidate will be required to submit to the examiners *either* two copies of a typewritten or printed essay of not more than 3,000 words on a topic approved by the organizing committee in each of the five modules chosen for study, as set out in the Schedule, *or* in the case of the modules specified by the organizing committee one practical notebook in each module chosen for study; candidates must submit their titles for approval by deadlines determined by the organizing committee and posted in the *Gazette* no later than the end of the preceding term;

(iii) each candidate will be required to submit to the examiners three copies of a typewritten or printed dissertation of not more than 10,000 words (excluding bibliography and appendices) on each of the two research projects chosen for study, as set out in the Schedule;

(iv) each candidate will be required to give a public oral presentation on each of his or her research projects, on dates to be determined by the organizing committee.

5. Each candidate will be examined viva voce.

6. Before being given leave to supplicate, candidates must have demonstrated understanding of and competence in the topics covered by the professional development programme as set out in the Schedule, to the satisfaction of the programme organizers, who shall submit a ceritificate to the examiners to this effect.

7. The required written submissions must be sent to the Chairman of Examiners, M.Sc. in Neuroscience, c/o Clerk of the Schools, Examination Schools, High Street, Oxford, on the following dates:

The dissertations on the first and second research projects must be submitted by dates to be specified by the organizing committee and which will be published in the *University Gazette* not later than the start of Michaelmas Term of the academic year in which the examination is taken. The essays or the practical notebooks for each module must be submitted by deadlines determined by the organizing committee and posted in the *Gazette* no later than the end of the preceding term. Each submission must be accompanied by a certificate indicating that it is the candidate's own work.

8. The viva voce examinations will be conducted in September in the year in which the candidate is examined on dates to be determined by the examiners.

9. The examiners may award a distinction for excellence in the whole examination.

10. The examiners shall retain one copy of each dissertation of each successful candidate for deposit in the most appropriate departmental library.

Schedule

The syllabus for study will include four principal components:

(*a*) **Professional Development Programme for Neuroscientists**

Candidates will be required to follow the same Professional Development Programme as that prescribed in the regulations for the M.Sc. in Biology (Integrative Bioscience).

(*b*) **Introduction to Neuroscience**

Five module introduction to neuroscience, each consisting of lectures and practicals and a concluding seminar. Candidates who have already received training in neuroscience may, at the discretion of the organizing committee, be exempted from attendance at one or more of the introductory modules. Such candidates will be required to pass the qualifying examination which will cover the topics covered in the Introduction to Neuroscience. They will be required to follow an alternative course of instruction approved by the organizing committee.

Module I: Introduction to the brain

Module II: Neuroanatomy

Module III: Neuronal Cell and Molecular Biology

Module IV: Synapses and transduction

Module V: Systems overview.

Candidates will also be required to take courses on experimental design, computing, and statistics, approved by the organizing committee.

(*c*) **Specialist neuroscience courses**

This will consist of five taught courses consisting of lectures, seminars, practicals, and demonstrations, chosen from a list of courses in neuroscience to be approved annually by the organizing committee. These will be grouped under three headings: molecular, cellular, and systems, and candidates will be required to choose at least one course under each of the three headings. Details of the courses available in each academic year will be published in the *Gazette* in the preceding Trinity Term.

(*d*) **Laboratory research projects**

Two research projects based on the candidate's laboratory placements, each under the supervision of a research supervisor, on subjects selected in consultation with the organizing committee. The research projects shall be in separate areas of neuroscience.

Pharmacology

1. The Divisional Board of Medical Sciences shall appoint for the supervision of the course an organizing committee, which shall have the power to arrange lectures and other instruction.

2. The organizing committee shall appoint for each candidate an academic advisor (*mentor*).

3. Each candidate shall:

(*a*) follow a course of study in Pharmacology for at least three terms and for a substantial part of the three subsequent vacations, as determined by the course timetable;

(*b*) attend practical classes which will be compulsory (a record of attendance will be kept);

(*c*) when they submit their dissertations in September, produce a certificate from their academic advisor to the effect that they have fulfilled the requirements of (*a*) and (*b*).

4. Candidates shall be examined in all of the following ways:

(i) each candidate must pass a qualifying exam at the end of the Michaelmas Term. The test shall consist of one three-hour written paper on the topics covered by the Pharmacology Introductory Course, as set out in the Schedule. The organizing committee shall not later than the end of the Hilary Term preceding the final examination submit to the examiners a list of candidates who have satisfactorily completed the qualifying examination. Candidates who fail the qualifying examination once shall be permitted to take it again in the first week of the Hilary Term of the year of the final examination.

(ii) each candidate must pass a three-hour data handling and experimental design examination at the beginning of the Hilary Term and a further examination at the beginning of Trinity Term examining material taught in the previous term. In each case candidates must pass the examination in order to proceed with the course, and those who fail shall be permitted to sit the examination on one further occasion only.

(iii) each candidate will be required to submit to the examiners two copies of a typewritten or printed essay of not more than 3,000 words on a topic approved by the organizing committee and one practical notebook in which all practical class experiments are recorded.

(iv) each candidate will be required to submit to the examiners three copies of a typewritten or printed dissertation of not more than 10,000 words (excluding bibliography and appendices) on the research project selected for study as set out in the Schedule;

(v) each candidate will be expected to give a public oral presentation on his or her research project, on dates to be determined by the organizing committee.

5. Each candidate shall be examined viva voce.

6. Before being given leave to supplicate, candidates must have demonstrated understanding of and competence in the topics covered by the professional development programme as set out in the Schedule, to the satisfaction of the programme organizers, who shall submit a certificate to the examiners to this effect.

7. The required written submissions must be sent to the chairman of examiners, M.Sc. in Pharmacology, c/o Clerk of the Schools, Examination Schools, High Street, Oxford on the following dates:

(*a*) The dissertation on the research project must be submitted by dates to be specified by the organizing committee and which will be published in the *University Gazette* not later than the start of Michaelmas Term of the academic year in which the examination is taken.

(*b*) The essay and the practical notebook must be submitted by deadlines determined by the organizing committee and posted in the *Gazette* no later than the end of the term preceding submission. Each submission must be accompanied by a certificate indicating that it is the candidate's own work.

8. The viva voce examination will normally be conducted in September in the year in which the candidate is examined on dates to be determined by the examiners.

9. The examiners may award a distinction for excellence in part of or in the whole examination.

10. The examiners shall retain one copy of each dissertation of each successful candidate for deposit in the Radcliffe Science library.

Schedule

The syllabus for study will include four principal components:

(*a*) **Professional Development Programme for Pharmacology**

Candidates will be required to follow the same Professional Development Programme as that prescribed in the regulations for the M.Sc. in Biology (Integrative Bioscience) and the M.Sc. in Neuroscience.

(*b*) **Introduction to Pharmacology**

Three module introduction to pharmacology, each consisting of lectures and practical classes. Candidates who have already received training in some of the topic areas covered may, at the discretion of the organizing committee, be exempted from attendance at one or more of the introductory lecture series. Such candidates will be required to pass the qualifying examination, which will cover the topics covered in the Introduction to Pharmacology.

Module I: Cells
Module II: Tissue and Organism Pharmacology
Module III: Neuropharmacology

Candidates will also be required to take courses on experimental design, data interpretation, computing and statistics, approved by the organizing committee. Candidates will be required to obtain a Home Office licence and will follow the course of study required for modules 1 to 4 of this.

(*c*) **Advanced pharmacology courses**

This will consist of five taught courses consisting of lectures, seminars, practical classes and tutorials approved annually by the organizing committee. Details of the courses available in each academic year will be published in the *Gazette* in the preceding Trinity Term.

(*d*) **Laboratory research project**

The research project based on the candidates' laboratory placement, under the supervision of a research supervisor, on a subject selected in consultation with the organizing committee.

Political Theory Research

1. A candidate for the M.Sc. in Political Theory Research shall follow for three terms a course of instruction in Political Theory Research and will, when entering for the examination, be required to produce a certificate from his or her society to this effect. Notice of the subjects in which the candidate is to be examined must be submitted to the Department of Politics and International Relations as required by the Department's timetable.

2. Candidates must attend, and satisfactorily complete the designated coursework for assessment according to the Department's timetable, the following courses of lectures and classes from the Department's Research Methods Programme:

An approved course from the M.Phil. in Politics (Political Theory) as directed by the Politics Graduate Studies Committee

Ethics

Philosophy of the Social Sciences

either Formal Analysis for Politics Research *or* Research Methods for Political Theory

Research Design

At least two short courses from the Department's Research Methods Programme.

Candidates who fail an assessed piece of work must successfully resubmit the coursework by the end of the sixth week of Trinity Term.

3. Candidates are required to sit a written examination paper. The examination paper shall consist of the Qualifying Test as for the M.Phil. in Politics (Political Theory). Candidates who fail the Qualifying Test Examination may retake the examination at a date stipulated in the Regulations for the relevant M.Phil.

4. Two copies of a Research Design paper of 4,000 to 6,000 words must be submitted. The Research Design paper must be printed on one side of A4 sheets. It must be handed in to the Clerk of the Schools, Examination Schools, High Street, Oxford, by noon on the Friday of noughth week of Trinity Term. Papers must be clearly marked on the front page with the candidate's examination number and the words 'M.Sc. in Political Theory Research'. Candidates who fail may, at the discretion of the Examiners, be allowed to resubmit by the end of sixth week of Trinity Term.

5. Two copies of a thesis of not more than 10,000 words must be submitted. The thesis must be typed or printed on one side of A4 sheets. It must be handed to the Clerk of the Schools, Examination Schools, High Street, Oxford, by noon on the Friday of seventh week of Trinity Term. The thesis must be clearly marked with the candidate's examination number and the words 'M.Sc. in Political Theory Research'.

6. The examiners may also examine any candidate viva voce; they shall not fail any candidate without inviting him or her to attend such an examination. The examiners may award a distinction for excellence in the whole examination.

Politics and International Relations Research

1. A candidate for the M.Sc. in Politics and International Relations Research shall follow for three terms a course of instruction in Politics and International Relations Research and will, when entering for the examination, be required to produce a certificate from his or her society to this effect. Notice of the subjects in which the candidate is to be examined must be submitted to the Department of Politics and International Relations as required by the Department's timetable.

2. Candidates must attend and satisfactorily complete the Introduction Programme and the designated coursework for assessment according to the Department's timetable, the following courses of lectures and classes from the Department's Research Methods Training Programme:

An approved core course from the M.Phil. in Politics, the M.Phil. in European Politics and Society, the M.Phil. in Russian and East European Studies, the M.Phil. in Development Studies, the M.Phil. in Latin American Studies, the M.Phil. in Chinese Studies, the M.Phil. in International Relations, or the M.Phil. in Modern Middle Eastern Studies as directed by the Politics Graduate Studies Committee and the International Relations Graduate Studies Committee

Basic Statistical Analysis

Philosophy of the Social Sciences

Formal Analysis for Politics Research

Research Design

At least two short courses from the Department's Research Methods programme

Candidates who fail an assessed piece of work must successfully resubmit the coursework by the end of the sixth week of Trinity Term.

3. Where necessitated by a candidate's choice of subject the Politics Graduate Studies Committee and the International Relations Graduate Studies Committee

may require a candidate to pass a test of proficiency in a language other than English, as set out for the M.Phil. in Latin American Studies, the M.Phil. in Russian and East European Studies, the M.Phil. in European Politics and Society, or another M.Phil. approved by the Politics Graduate Studies Committee and the International Relations Graduate Studies Committee.

4. Candidates are required to sit a written examination paper. The examination paper shall consist of the Qualifiying Test as for the M.Phil. in Politics, the M.Phil. in Russian and East European Studies, the M.Phil. in Chinese Studies, the M.Phil. in International Relations (Contemporary Debates in International Relations Theory), the M.Phil. in Development Studies, the M.Phil. in Latin American Studies, the M.Phil. in Modern Middle Eastern Studies, or another M.Phil. approved by the Politics Graduate Studies Committee and the International Relations Graduate Studies Committee. Candidates may be directed by the Politics Graduate Studies Committee and the International Relations Graduate Studies Committee in consultation with the examiners to answer questions from any one section of a question paper. Candidates who fail the Qualifying Test Examination may, at the discretion of the Examiners, be allowed to resit the examination at a date stipulated in the Regulations for the relevant M.Phil.

5. Two copies of a Research Design paper of 4,000 to 6,000 words must be submitted. The Research Design paper must be printed on one side of A4 sheets. It must be handed in to the Clerk of the Schools, Examination Schools, High Street, Oxford, by noon on the Friday of noughth week of Trinity Term. Papers must be clearly marked on the front page with the candidate's examination number and the words 'M.Sc. in Politics and International Relations Research'. Candidates who fail may, at the discretion of the Examiners, be allowed to resubmit by the end of sixth week of Trinity Term.

6. Two copies of a thesis of not more than 10,000 words must be submitted. The thesis must be typed or printed on one side of A4 sheets. It must be handed to the Clerk of the Schools, Examination Schools, High Street, Oxford, by noon on the Friday of seventh week of Trinity Term. The thesis must be clearly marked with the candidate's examination number and the words 'M.Sc. in Politics and International Relations Research'.

7. The examiners may also examine any candidate viva voce; they shall not fail any candidate without entitling him or her to attend such an examination. The examiners may award a distinction for excellence in the whole examination.

Professional Development in Education

1. Candidates may only be admitted to the course if they have successfully completed the course leading to a Post-graduate Diploma in Educational Studies from Oxford University.

2. Every candidate must follow for at least three and at most nine terms a part-time course of instruction in Professional Development in Education.

3. Every candidate will be required to satisfy the examiners in the following:

Satisfactory attendance at the appropriate classroom-based courses.

Two written assignments, one on each of the two modules, chosen from those listed in the schedule. Each assignment should not exceed 4,000 words. All assignments must be typed or printed. Assignment 1 should be submitted no later than 5 p.m. on the Friday of week 1 of Hilary Full Term and Assignment 2 no later than 5 p.m. on the Friday of week 1 of Trinity Full Term.

A dissertation of not more than 25,000 words (including appendices, endnotes, and a bibliography), on a subject selected by the candidate and supervisor, which must be closely related to the candidate's programme of study for the PGDES. The subject selected by the candidate and supervisor must be approved on behalf of the Academic Board of the Department for Educational Studies by the Tutor for Higher Degrees.

4. Three typewritten/wordprocessed or printed copies of the dissertation must be delivered to the M.Sc. Examiners, c/o Department of Educational Studies, 15 Norham Gardens, Oxford OX2 6PY, no later than noon on 30 September of the year in which the written assignments are presented. One copy should be hard bound and two soft bound, which should be anonymous except for the candidate number. Candidates wishing to submit dissertations later than 30 September of the year in which the written assignments are presented must obtain the approval of the Academic Board by the last day of the preceding Trinity Full Term; such approval will only be granted in exceptional circumstances. The hard bound copy of the dissertation of each candidate who passes the examination shall be retained by the department for deposit in the departmental library.

5. The examiners may award a distinction for excellence in the whole examination.

6. The M.Sc. in Professional Development in Education, if successfully completed, subsumes a candidate's previously completed diploma course.

7. Each candidate may, with the approval of the Academic Board, resubmit one written assignment (and one only) undertaken whilst registered for the M.Sc. if the original assignment is deemed unsatisfactory. This will normally be resubmitted by noon on the last Friday in September of the year in which the written assignments are presented.

8. Each candidate may, with the approval of the Academic Board, resubmit their dissertation undertaken whilst registered for the M.Sc. if the original dissertation is deemed unsatisfactory. This shall normally be within one year of the initial failure.

9. The candidate may also be examined orally. The oral examination may be on the candidate's dissertation, on the written assignments, or both.

Schedule

The Effective School

Topics will include:

A study of the development of the Effective Schools literature.
The links of this literature with the Schools' Improvement Movement.
The value of the findings of this literature to practitioners.
Criticisms of this literature.

Classroom Teaching and Learning

Topics will include:

How do children learn? Philosophical, psychological, and sociological perspectives on the processes of children's learning. Classrooms as contexts for learning.
Learning different kinds of knowledge. Concepts, subject-specific skills, generic skills, values; problems of learning in specific areas of different subjects; students' alternative understandings, misconceptions, and errors.
How do teachers teach? Different theoretical and research perspectives on classroom teaching processes; the nature of classroom and subject-specific discourse; teachers' craft knowledge and students' learning strategies; class teaching for individual learning; the assessment of learning.

Educational Leadership and Management

Topics will include:

A theoretical understanding of the nature of organisations—structure, climate, functions—and its application in educational establishments.
The organization, management, and development of schools and colleges as professionally staffed establishments.

An introduction to theories and practice of leadership and management in educational establishments.

The development of effective teams as professional and management groups.

A consideration of appropriate issues in collective and individual accountability including processes of professional review and development at personal, group, and institutional level.

Theoretical and practical applications of theories of innovation and organizational renewal.

Consideration of issues, experience, developments, and the implications of site-based prescriptions in the management of 'effective' schools.

Professional Learning and Development

Topics will include:

Pre-service Teacher Education: Student teachers' professional learning; problems of initial teacher education; distinctive contributions of schools and universities; skills and strategies of mentoring; managing school-based teacher education; reflective practice and initial teacher education.

In-service Teacher Education: (i) Induction into teaching: socialization into schools; strategies to support beginning teachers; findings from research in induction; developing strategies to support beginning teachers. (ii) Teachers' continuing professional development: critical reflective practice; working with colleagues; teachers' investigations of their own classrooms; development and sharing of knowledge about teaching and learning; effects of mentoring on mentors' teaching development.

Strategies and Skills for School and Classroom Research

Topics will include:

Strategies: Types of research questions about schools and classrooms.

Strategies appropriate to the questions: surveys; experiments; ethnographies; case study; action research.

Data gathering and analysis: Observation; systematic and participant observation. Talking with teachers and students. Diaries and written records. Classroom and school artefacts. School statistics. Quantitative and qualitative analysis of data.

Issues in classroom and school research: Impact of the researcher; research and theory; research or evaluation; demonstrating validity; demonstrating reliability.

Public Policy in Latin America

1. Candidates shall follow for at least three terms a course of instruction in Public Policy in Latin America and will, when entering for the examination, be required to produce a certificate from their supervisors to this effect.

2. Each candidate will be examined on one of the subject areas set out below. The examination will consist of the following:

(*a*) one written paper;

(*b*) a dissertation of not more than 15,000 words;

(*c*) an oral examination.

3. Not later than the Monday of the fifth week of the Michaelmas Term in which they are admitted, candidates shall submit for approval by the Inter-faculty Area and Developmental Studies Committee, the subject area in which they propose to work and the title of their proposed dissertations.

4. Two typewritten or printed copies of the dissertation must be sent to the examiners (M.Sc. in Public Policy in Latin America), c/o Clerk of the Schools, Examination Schools, High Street, Oxford, not later than 12 noon on Friday of the seventh week of the followingTrinity Term.

5. The oral examination will normally be held in the ninth week of Trinity Term.

Schedule

(i) *Latin American Economic Policies*

Monetary and fiscal policy; incomes policy and income distribution; external financing and forms of planning, including sectoral planning. Candidates will be expected to cover the historical, institutional, and political aspects of policies, as well as the strictly economic dimension.

(ii) *Development Options*

Development strategies and constraints on development. Export-led growth, export diversification, and industrialization studies in relation to the use, ownership, and control of factors of production. Land tenure, land use, and agrarian reform. Urbanization and regional development problems and policies. Latin American economic integration.

(iii) *Problems of Government*

The structure and functioning of government, including local government. The role of bureaucracy. The budgetary process. Pressure groups, the organization of interests and policy-making. Welfare policies. Policy-making and implementation in education, housing, and transport.

(iv) *Latin America in the International Arena*

Latin American relations with the OECD nations, the Soviet Bloc, and the rest of the 'Third World'. Latin America and North–South economic issues. The scope for independent foreign policy. The politics of trade, finance, and investment. Border disputes and other rivalries within the region. Regional organizations. Latin America in international organizations.

Research in Psychology

1. The Medical Sciences Board shall, in consultation with the School of Social Sciences and Law at Oxford Brookes University, elect for the supervision of the course a course committee which shall have the power to arrange lectures and other instruction.

2. The course committee shall appoint an academic advisor for each candidate.

3. Each candidate shall follow a course of study in Research in Psychology for at least three terms and for a substantial part of the three subsequent vacations, as determined by the course timetable, and shall, when entering for the examination, be required to produce a certificate from their academic advisor to this effect.

4. The syllabus shall include six principal course components as listed in the schedule below, and candidates shall be examined in accordance with the schedule below. Candidates must achieve a pass in each of the components in order to pass the examination overall. Candidates who do not achieve a pass mark, but who achieve at least 30 per cent, may resubmit assessments on one further occasion only. When the failed assessment is an assessed seminar, the form taken by additional assessment is at the discretion of the Course Tutor. Candidates may not proceed to the Research Project unless they have gained a pass in each of the other course components. The marks for each assessed piece of work within each course component shall be made available to the examiners.

5. Candidates may be required to attend an oral examination at the discretion of the examiners and this may include questions on the candidate's dissertation, assignments, or written papers.

6. The examiners may award a distinction for excellence in the whole examination.

Schedule

(*a*) **Research Methods: Design and Analysis**

The lectures and seminars shall cover: techniques for data collection, discussions of the advantages and disadvantages of different research designs, methods of quantitative and qualitative data analysis, methods of communicating quantitative data, critical assessment of research evidence, introduction to issues connected with the philosophy of science and the nature of explanation, critiques of psychological theory. Each candidate shall be required to submit an essay of no more than 3,000 words on a topic chosen from a list published by the course committee at the beginning of the term in which the essay must be submitted. Deadlines for submission shall be notified to students at the same time. In addition candidates shall sit a class test, and shall be required to make a seminar presentation during the course. Seminar topics must be approved by the course tutor. Each of these elements shall be marked and shall contribute to the overall result for this course component.

(*b*) **Methods in Cognitive Neuropsychology**

A systematic review of the neurological foundations of cognitive neuropsychology and the major methodologies upon which it draws. Functional neuroanatomy. Major neurological disorders. Neuropsychological assessment: the neurological examination, single case studies, brain imaging techniques. Experimental methods. Designing quantitative research studies including meta-analysis. Clinical applications.

Each candidate shall be required to submit an essay of no more than 4,000 words on a topic chosen from a list published by the course committee at the beginning of the term in which the essay must be submitted. Deadlines for submission shall be notified to students at the same time.

(*c*) **Statistical Theory and Methods**

A course comprising: classes on descriptive and inferential statistics, an introduction to multinomial and multivariate analysis, a short practical course in the analysis of data, a series of seminars on the philosophy of science including measurement theory, modelling, and current controversies.

Each candidate shall be required to submit a portfolio of SPSS data analyses carried out during the course. Deadlines for submission shall be notified to students by the course committee at the beginning of the term in which the work must be submitted.

(*d*) **Project Design and Assessed Seminar Presentations**

Practical instruction in research and presentation skills. Detailed planning of the research project to be carried out under (*f*).

Each candidate shall be required to present a seminar based on the ideas and design of the student's research project. The seminar materials and the presentation shall be assessed. Candidates shall also submit a 3,000 word literature review relating to their research project. Each of these elements shall be marked and shall contribute to the overall result for this course component.

(*e*) **Computer Modelling of Cognitive Processes**

The course shall consist of an analysis of the main types of computer model and the role that models play in understanding cognition followed by more detailed consideration of specific models drawn from key research domains in psychology.

Each candidate shall be required to submit an essay of no more than 3,000 words on a topic chosen from a list published by the course committee at the beginning of the term in which the essay must be submitted. Deadlines for submission shall be notified to students at the same time. In addition candidates shall be required to make a seminar presentation during the course. Seminar topics must be approved by the course tutor. Each of these elements shall be marked and shall contribute to the overall result for this course component.

(*f*) **Research Project (thesis)**

Each student shall carry out a project under the supervision of a research supervisor on a subject selected in consultation with the academic advisor and approved by the course committee. By the commencement of the course, the course committee shall notify candidates of the last date by which project proposals must have been submitted for their approval. The course committee shall be responsible for the appointment of the research supervisor. The Research Project course component shall consist of data collection, analysis of the data, and writing a thesis on the project.

Candidates shall be required to submit to the examiners not later than noon on the third Monday in September three copies of a typewritten or printed thesis of not more than 10,000 words in length (excluding bibliography and any appendices) on his or her research project. The cover of the copies must bear the candidate's examination number and name of the examination, but not their name or college, and must be sent in a parcel to, 'The Chairman of Examiners: M.Sc. in Research in Psychology, c/o the Clerk of the Schools, Examination Schools, High Street, Oxford'. The thesis must be accompanied by a signed statement by the candidate that the thesis is his or her own work.

Russian and East European Studies

1. Each candidate will be required to follow a course of instruction for three terms and to present himself or herself for examination in the two compulsory papers in week eight of Trinity Term. In addition, there will be a Methodology paper, examined by extended essay on a pass–fail basis. Each candidate will be required to submit two typewritten copies of the extended essay, to be addressed to the Chair of Examiners for the M.Sc. in Russian and East European Studies, c/o Clerk of the Schools, Examination Schools, High Street, Oxford, by noon on the Friday of the ninth week of Hilary Term in the calendar year in which the examination is taken. Two copies of a thesis, not exceeding 15,000 words, will be delivered to the Chair of Examiners for the M.Sc. in Russian and East European Studies, c/o Clerk of the Schools, Examination Schools, High Street, Oxford, by noon on the Friday of the sixth week of Trinity Term in the calendar year in which the examination is taken.

2. The marking conventions will be those of other M.Sc. degrees.

3. Candidates who fail one or more parts of the examination may be required to attend an oral examination. A candidate who fails one or more examination papers, but whose thesis is of a satisfactory standard, will not be required to submit the same piece of work. Candidates who fail more than two of the four parts of the examination will be deemed to have failed the examination, and will be allowed to retake the examination in the following year.

4. Candidates may be required to attend an oral examination on any of the four parts of the examination.

5. The examiners may award a distinction for excellence in the whole examination.

Schedule of Papers

1. Twentieth-Century Russian and Soviet History (compulsory paper Michaelmas Term).

This course covers the history of the Russian Empire, the Soviet Union, and the Russian Federation in the twentieth century. It deals with politics, economics, sociology, nationhood, religion, and culture. While the main periods are examined individually, there is also an emphasis on tracking themes between periods. Thus attention is given to the October Revolution, the origins of the USSR, Stalinism, World War II, postwar attempts at consolidation and reform, including Gorbachev's 'perestroika'. There is also a focus on the one-party state, 'the national question', problems of 'everyday life', and other such themes which affect our understanding of the century as a whole. The general objective is to investigate the connections of everything in recent Russian history with everything else.

2. Political and Economic Transitions in the former Soviet Union and Eastern Europe (compulsory paper Hilary Term).

This course takes a multi- and interdisciplinary approach to the analysis of post-Communist transitions. Eight two-hour seminars review area studies and disciplinary approaches. Contending interpretations and theories are evaluated by assessing their usefulness in understanding and explaining the complex processes involved in transition in a range of post-communist states. Seminars cover perspectives on transition in the political science (3 sessions), economics and social studies (3 sessions), regional studies (1 session), and international relations literature (1 session), and their application to post-communist developments. The course thus provides students with a solid grounding in theories bearing on transition and sufficient empirical knowledge to assess the arguments associated with different approaches.

3. Methodology (examined by extended essay in Trinity Term)

During the first four weeks of Michaelmas Term there will be a new course on REES Area Studies in Disciplinary Perspective, which is derived from 4 of the sessions which were in the old M.Phil. methodology course (Politics, Economics, International Relations, and Literature). Methodological training will continue in weeks five to eight through a course on Social Science and Soviet Economic History, showing how the application of social science techniques can assist in the analysis of selected issues in Soviet economic history.

In Hilary Term, the Methodology course will consist of 8 sessions: Databases, spreadsheets, and statistics; Regional analysis using geographical information systems; Web-based acquisition of bibliographical material and data; Development of presentational skills using Powerpoint and other techniques.

4. Thesis (examined in Trinity Term).

Science and Medicine of Athletic Performance

1. The Medical Sciences Board shall elect for the supervision of the course a standing committee which shall have the power to arrange lectures and other instruction.

2. Every candidate must follow for at least six terms a course of instruction in the Science and Medicine of Athletic Performance. The course of instruction will consist of the modules set out in the schedule and the examiners will require confirmation from the Course Director of satisfactory attendance by each candidate.

3. In the first year of the course, candidates must elect to take at least five of the Level I modules listed in the schedule. One paper will be set for each of the modules which candidates elect to take and candidates must offer and satisfy the examiners in the papers for the modules that they take.

4. The examiners shall make a recommendation, based on the performance of candidates in the first year examinations, as to whether each candidate is likely to attain the level of performance required for the successful completion of the second year of the course. Admission to the second year will be determined by the standing committee in the light of the examiners' recommendations, evidence of adequate arrangements made by each candidate to undertake the Project Module and interview of each candidate by the Course Director. A candidate may appeal to the Medical Sciences Board against the decision of the Standing Committee.

5. In the second year of the course, candidates must take the Project Module and three further modules not studied in the first year including no more than one Level I module. One paper will be set for each of the modules, other than the Project Module, which candidates elect to take and candidates must offer and satisfy the examiners in the papers for the three modules that they take.

6. Candidates must submit and satisfy the examiners in a dissertation based on the Project Module. The length of the dissertation shall be not more than 10,000 words (excluding tables, appendices, footnotes and bibliography) and each candidate shall select the subject of his or her dissertation in consultation with the Course Director. The subject of each dissertation shall also be subject to the approval of the standing committee. The dissertation shall be forwarded to the examiners c/o the Course Director for the M.Sc. in Science and Medicine of Athletic Performance, University Laboratory of Physiology, Parks Road, Oxford by such date as the examiners shall determine and of which they shall notify candidates. The dissertation shall be accompanied by a statement certifying that the dissertation is the candidate's own work except where otherwise indicated.

7. Candidates who fail a module examination may be permitted, at the discretion of the standing committee, to retake the examination on no more than one occasion normally no later than one term after the first examination. Candidates may be permitted to retake no more than one failed module examination in each year of the course. Failure of more than one module examination in one year of the course shall constitute failure of the whole examination for the M.Sc.

8. The registration of a candidate shall lapse on the last day of the Trinity Term in the year after the year of his or her admission unless it shall have been extended by the Medical Sciences Board.

9. Candidates may be called for a viva voce examination. The examiners will give as much notice as possible to candidates of a requirement to attend such an examination.

10. The examiners may award a distinction for excellence in the whole examination.

11. The standing committee shall have the discretion to permit any modules examined for the Postgraduate Diploma in Science and Medicine of Athletic Performance to count towards the examination requirements for the M.Sc. A period of study for the Postgraduate Diploma may be counted towards the minimum period of study required for the M.Sc.

12. If any candidate who is successful in the examination for the M.Sc. in Science and Medicine of Athletic Performance has previously successfully completed the Postgraduate Diploma, and the standing committee has agreed that, for that examination, modules examined for the Postgraduate Diploma should count towards the examination requirements for the M.Sc., then the award of the M.Sc. will subsume the award of the Postgraduate Diploma.

Schedule

Level I Modules

1. Structural and biomechanical basis of physical performance
2. Genetic and biochemical basis of physical performance
3. Muscle energetics, motor control, and training
4. Cardio-respiratory and renal adaptations to physical performance
5. Genes and gender
6. Drugs and performance

Level II Modules

7. Endurance exercise and the unexplained underperformance syndrome
8. Psychology of elite performance
9. Advanced biomechanics, injury, and sport for the disabled
10. Economics, commerce, and finance of sport
11. Project Module.

Social Anthropology

1. The Life and Environmental Sciences Divisional Board shall elect for the supervision of the course a Standing Committee, which shall have power to arrange lectures and other instruction. The course director will be responsible to this organizing committee.

2. Candidates must follow a course of instruction in Social and Cultural Anthropology for at least three terms, and will, when entering for the examinations, be required to produce a certificate from their supervisor to this effect.

3. Candidates will be required to present themselves for written and oral examinations and to submit three copies of a dissertation in prescribed form on an approved topic as defined below.

4. The written examination will consist of four papers on the syllabus described in the Schedule.

5. Each candidate will be required to submit a dissertation of approximately 10,000 words, on a subject selected in consultation with the supervisor and approved by the Chairman of Examiners. The proposed title of the dissertation, together with a paragraph describing its scope and the supervisor's written endorsement, must be submitted to the Chairman of Examiners by Monday of the first week of Trinity Term.

6. Three typewritten copies of the dissertation must be delivered not later than noon on the second Monday in September in the year in which the examination is taken, to the Chairman of the Examiners, M.Sc. in Social Anthropology/Material Anthropology and Museum Ethnography, c/o Clerk to the Schools, Examination Schools, High Street, Oxford.

The examiners shall retain one copy of the dissertation of each candidate who passes the examination for deposit in the departmental library.

7. The oral examination may be on the candidate's written papers, or dissertation, or both.

8. The examiners may award a distinction for excellence in the whole examination.

9. If it is the opinion of the examiners that the work done by a candidate is not of sufficient merit to qualify for the Degree of M.Sc. but is nevertheless of sufficient merit to qualify for the Diploma in Social Anthropology, the candidate shall be given the option of resitting the M.Sc. examination or being issued with a diploma in the form prescribed in Ch. VI, Sect. II Schedule E.

Schedule

Every candidate will be required to satisfy the examiners in four papers as follows:

I *Social and Cultural Anthropology A: History and Development* (paper and syllabus shared with the M.Sc. in Material Anthropology and Museum Ethnography)

The scope of this paper includes the following topics: history and development of the subject, and the relation between academic research, museums, and the imperial context of anthropology's past; relations to other subjects, including archaeology and history. Key authors and debates in the development of anthropology, with particular reference to: kinship. marriage, gender, and sexuality; space, place, and culture; environment and cultural landscapes in transition; land and property rights; production and consumption; transactions and modes of exchange; the division of labour and the comparative anthropology of work; technology and social change; the colonial process and its legacy; nationalism, ethnicity, migration, and transnationalism; urbanism.

II *Social and Cultural Anthropology B: Theory and Methods* (paper and syllabus shared with the M.Sc. in Material Anthropology and Museum Ethnography)

The scope of this paper includes the following topics: concepts of the individual, society and the person in anthropological perspective; issues of the body, theories of practice, phenomenology; theories of power, order and law; aspects of disorder and violence in society; systems of knowledge and belief; ritual and myth; symbolism and symbolic classification; moral systems and the world religions; oral literature and historical memory; linguistic and artistic modes of communication; aesthetic anthropology; methodological approaches to the study of arts, performance, and material culture; museums, written texts and representation. Fieldwork and data collection methods; quantitative and qualitative techniques; cultural property and indigenous rights; applications of film and sound recording; preparing research proposals; ethical problems.

III and IV *Optional Papers*

Candidates must choose two optional papers. Titles of available options will be made known at the beginning of each academic year. They will be divided into three lists, as follows:

List A: The Social Anthropology of a Selected Religion.
List B: Topics in Material Anthropology.
List C: Anthropology and Practical Issues.

Candidates for the degree of M.Sc. in Social Anthropology must select one of their options from List A, and the other from List B or List C.

Sociology

Every candidate must follow, for at least three terms, a course of instruction in Sociology.

The examination will be in four parts:

A. A compulsory paper in *Methods of Social Research*. As specified for the M.Phil. in Sociology.

B. A compulsory paper in *Sociological Analysis*. As specified for the M.Phil. in Sociology.

C. One optional paper. This will be from a list published annually by Friday of the third week of Michaelmas Full Term in the Department of Sociology. Candidates may, after special permission of the Director of Graduate Studies for Sociology offer subjects outside this list. This may include subjects from the list published in conjunction with the M.Phil. or M.Sc. in Comparative Social Policy with the permission of the Director of Graduate Studies for Social Policy. This may also include papers offered in other relevant master's degrees in the University, subject to permission by the relevant Graduate Studies Committee as appropriate.

D. A thesis of not more than 10,000 words on a topic within the subject of the course, to be specified jointly by supervisor and student. Two typewritten copies of the thesis must be delivered to the Clerk of the Schools, Examination Schools, High Street, Oxford, by noon of the weekday on or nearest to 15 August of the year in which the examination is to be taken. Successful candidates will be required to deposit a copy of their thesis in the Department of Sociology.

The examiners may examine any candidate viva voce.

The examiners may award a Distinction for excellence in the whole examination on the basis of the material submitted to them.

Software Engineering

The Divisional Board of Mathematical and Physical Sciences, in consultation with the Sub-faculty of Computation, and the Board of Studies of the Continuing Education Board, shall elect for the supervision of the course a standing committee which shall have the power to arrange lectures and other instruction.

2. The course will consist of lectures, tutorials, seminars, and classes in the theory and practice of Software Engineering. The course may be taken over a period of not less than two years, and not more than four years.

3. Every candidate will be required to satisfy the examiners in the following:

(*a*) attendance at a practical course and nine further courses chosen from those in the Schedule for the M.Sc. in Software Engineering, comprising a programme of study approved by the Programme Director;

(*b*) submission of an assignment based on the practical course;

(*c*) submission of nine written assignments based on the courses chosen in 3(*a*) above;

(*d*) a dissertation of not more than 20,000 words (including appendices and footnotes but not inclding bibliography) on a subject selected by the candidate in consultation with the supervisor and approved by the Programme Director;

(*e*) a viva voce examination, unless individually dispensed by the examiners.

The assignments under (*b*) and (*c*) and two typewritten or printed copies of the dissertation shall be forwarded to the examiners for consideration by such dates as the examiners shall determine and shall notify candidates, supervisors, and tutors. The dissertation must be accompanied by a statement that it is the candidate's work except where otherwise indicated.

4. The examiners may award a distinction for excellence in the whole examination.

5. The standing committee shall have the discretion to permit any assignments submitted as part of the course for the Postgraduate Certificate in Software Engineering, or the Postgraduate Certificate in Object Technology, or the Postgraduate Diploma in Software Engineering to be submitted for the examination for the M.Sc. No more than one calendar year of study undertaken for the Postgraduate Certificate and/or the Postgraduate Diploma may be counted towards the minimum period of study for the M.Sc.; the entire period of study undertaken for the Postgraduate Certificate and/or the Postgraduate Diploma shall be counted towards the maximum period of study for the M.Sc.

6. If any candidate who is successful in the examination for the M.Sc. in Software Engineering has previously successfully completed the Postgraduate Diploma, or Certificate, or the Postgraduate Certificate in Object Technology, and for that examination has incorporated the assignments submitted for the Postgraduate Certificate or Postgraduate Diploma into the M.Sc., then the subsequent award will subsume his or her previous award.

7. The standing committee shall have the discretion to permit any candidate to be exempted from submitting up to two of the total of nine written assignments required under 3(*c*) above, provided that the standing committee is satisfied that such a candidate has undertaken equivalent study, of an appropriate standard, normally at another institution of higher education.

8. Candidates who fail to satisfy the examiners may re-enter the examination on not more than one occasion which shall normally be within one year of the initial failure. No written assignment shall be submitted to the examiners on more than one occasion.

SCHEDULE

(i) Software Engineering Mathematics.

(ii) Specification and Design.

(iii) Functional Programming.
(iv) Concurrency and Distributed Systems.
(v) Software Development Management.
(vi) Software Testing.
(vii) Object orientation.
(viii) Object-oriented Programming.
(ix) Object-oriented Design.
(x) Distributed Objects.
(xi) Design Patterns.
(xii) Advanced Concurrency Tools.
(xiii) Database Design.
(xiv) Web Services.
(xv) Extensible Markup Language.
(xvi) Process Quality and Improvement.
(xvii) Advanced Software Developments.
(xviii) Machine-Assisted Software Engineering.
(xix) Management of Risk and Quality.
(xx) Safety Critical Systems.
(xxi) Security Principles.
(xxii) Requirements Engineering.
(xxiii) Performance Modelling
(xxiv) Any other module as defined by the course director and approved by the standing committee.

In June and December each year a list of modules will be published in the *University Gazette*. Each such list, which will have been approved by the standing committee and which will be a selection from the full set above, will contain those modules which will be available during the following nine months.

Theoretical Chemistry

1. The course shall be under the supervision of the Coulson Professor of Theoretical Chemistry or an appointed deputy, who shall have power to arrange lectures and other instruction.

2. Candidates shall follow for at least three terms a course of instruction in Theoretical Chemistry.

3. The examination shall be in three parts, as follows:

(*a*) Candidates shall successfully complete a written assignment on each of the lecture courses listed below.

(*b*) Candidates shall submit a short dissertation on a topic selected by the candidate in consultation with the supervisor and approved by the Coulson Professor of Theoretical Chemistry or an appointed deputy. Between thirty-five and sixty-five typed pages is the preferred length.

(*c*) There shall be an oral examination on the dissertation and its background material.

4. The Coulson Professor of Theoretical Chemistry or an appointed deputy shall make available to the examiners a certificate showing the extent to which the candidate has an adequate command of (*a*) mathematics and (*b*) computational chemistry. Candidates must submit for approval to the Coulson Professor of Theoretical Chemistry or an appointed deputy by the end of Hilary Term in the year in which they enter the examination the title and brief statement of the form and scope of their dissertation, together with the name of a person who has agreed to act as their supervisor during the preparation of the dissertation. Approval shall normally be given not later than two weeks after submission of a proposal.

5. Two typewritten copies of the dissertation must be delivered, not later than noon on 15 September in the year in which the examination is taken, to the M.Sc. Examiners (Theoretical Chemistry), c/o the Clerk of the Schools, Examination Schools, High Street, Oxford. The dissertation must be accompanied by a statement that it is the candidate's own work except where otherwise indicated, and a certificate from the candidate's society to the effect that he or she has followed for three terms a course of instruction in Theoretical Chemistry. The examiners may retain one copy of the dissertation of each candidate who passes the examination for deposit in an appropriate departmental library.

6. For each lecture course two topics shall be prescribed by the relevant lecturer not later than the Monday of the eighth week of the term during which the lectures are given. Different topics shall be set each year. Completed assignments on one topic for each lecture course must be delivered not later than noon on the Monday on the eleventh week of the term during which the course is offered, to the M.Sc. Examiners (Theoretical Chemistry), c/o the Clerk of the Schools, Examination Schools, High Street, Oxford.

7. A candidate who does not submit a written assignment on a lecture course by noon on the Monday of eleventh week of the relevant term shall be deemed to have failed the lecture course in question.

8. A list of those candidates who have satisfied the examiners in particular lecture courses in the relevant term shall be posted in the Physical and Theoretical Chemistry Laboratory, by the Friday preceding the following Full Term.

9. If a candidate is deemed to have failed a particular lecture course, he or she shall not be permitted to re-enter for examination in that lecture course.

Any candidate who has not satisfied the examiners in four lecture courses by the beginning of the Trinity Term shall be deemed to have failed the degree course.

10. A candidate who has failed to satisfy the examiners in the examination may enter again for the examination on one, but not more than one, subsequent occasion, not later than one year after the initial attempt. No written assignment shall be submitted to the examiners on more than one occasion.

11. The examiners may award a distinction for excellence in the whole examination.

List of lecture courses

Quantum Mechanics
Statistical Mechanics
Molecular Quantum Mechanics
Applied Statistical Mechanics
Many-body quantum and statistical mechanics.

Instruction will also be provided in mathematics and computational chemistry.

The Coulson Professor of Theoretical Chemistry or an appointed deputy shall have power to delete courses and to add other lecture courses to this list, and shall publish details of the full list including such additional courses in the *University Gazette* by not later than the Friday of the eighth week of the Trinity Term in the year preceding the examination.

Visual Anthropology

1. The Life and Environmental Sciences Divisional Board shall elect for the supervision of the course a Standing Committee, which shall have power to arrange lectures and other instruction. The course director will be responsible to this organizing committee.

2. Candidates must follow a course of instruction in Visual Anthropology for at least three terms, and will, when entering for the examination, be required to produce a certificate from their supervisor to this effect.

3. Candidates will be required to submit three copies of five pieces of written work, a portfolio of coursework notes, to present themselves for a written and, where invited, oral examination, and to submit three copies of a dissertation in prescribed form on an approved topic as defined below.

4. The assessed written work will consist of:

(i) two essays of no more than 4,000 words for Paper 1 on the syllabus described in the Schedule; for Paper 1 a list of essay titles will be announced no later than Monday of the fourth week of Michaelmas Term. Three typewritten copies of the essays, together with three copies of any associated non-print materials, must be delivered not later than noon of the Monday of the first week of Hilary Term to the Chairman of the Examiners, M.Sc. in Visual Anthropology, c/o Clerk of the Schools, Examination Schools, High Street, Oxford. Non-print materials shall not constitute more than fifteen minutes of viewing/reading time in the case of video or multimedia submissions.

(ii) two essays of no more than 4,000 words for Paper 2 on the syllabus described in the Schedule, on any subject relevant to the Paper as agreed with the candidate's supervisor. Three typewritten copies of the essays, together with three copies of any associated non-print materials, must be delivered not later than noon of the Monday of the first week of Trinity Term to the Chairman of the Examiners, M.Sc. in Visual Anthropology, c/o Clerk of the Schools, Examination Schools, High Street, Oxford. Non-print materials shall not constitute more than fifteen minutes of viewing/reading time in the case of video or multimedia submissions.

(iii) a research proposal relating to the subject of the candidate's intended doctoral research *or* a general essay on visual anthropological methods of no more than 5,000 words for Paper 3 on the syllabus described in the Schedule. Three typewritten copies of the research proposal or essay, together with three copies of any associated non-print materials, must be delivered not later than noon of the Monday of the sixth week of Trinity Term to the Chairman of the Examiners, M.Sc. in Visual Anthropology, c/o Clerk of the Schools, Examination Schools, High Street, Oxford. Non-print materials shall not constitute more than fifteen minutes of viewing/reading time in the case of video or multimedia submissions.

(iv) a portfolio of notes and written exercises relating to research methods in visual anthropology. The portfolio must be submitted to the Chairman of the Examiners not later than Monday of the seventh week of Trinity Term.

(v) a dissertation of approximately 10,000 words, on a subject selected in consultation with the supervisor and approved by the Chairman of Examiners. The proposed title of the dissertation together with a paragraph describing its scope and the supervisor's written endorsement, must be submitted to the Chairman of Examiners by Monday of the first week of Trinity Term. Three typewritten copies of the dissertation, together with three copies of any associated non-print materials, must be delivered not later than noon of the second Monday in September in the year in which the examination is taken to the Chairman of the Examiners, M.Sc. in Visual Anthropology, c/o Clerk of the Schools, Examination Schools, High Street, Oxford. Non-print materials shall not constitute more than fifteen minutes of viewing/reading time in the case of video or multimedia submissions.

The examiners shall retain one copy of the dissertation, and any associated non-print materials, of each candidate who passes the examination for deposit in the departmental library.

5. The written examination will consist of one three-hour paper for Paper 4 on the syllabus described in the Schedule.

6. An oral examination, if held, may be on the candidate's submitted written work, written examination paper, or dissertation, or all three.

7. The examiners may award a distinction for excellence in the whole examination.

Schedule

Every candidate will be required to satisfy the examiners in four papers as follows:

1. *Visual Anthropology: history and analysis.*

The scope of this paper includes the following topics: history and development of anthropological and ethnological photography, of documentary and ethnographic film, and of visual display in the museum; introduction to film and photographic theory and to anthropological theories of representation; the Colonial archive and Colonial documentary practices; the ethnography of film, photography and other visual representational practices; key concepts including objectivity and subjectivity, point of view, frame, and representation.

2. *Contemporary themes in visual anthropology.*

The scope of this paper includes critical anthropological approaches to the following topics: phenomenological, semiotic and post-structuralist approaches to visual media; film and photographs as material culture; social uses and local practices of visual media use, including indigenous media; professional visual media production; visual media and contemporary arts practices; image ethics; digital media practice; audience response and reception theory; art, peformance and display; detailed study of the work of one or more contemporary ethnographic filmmaker or photographer. [Note: some topics may vary slightly from year to year.]

3. *Research methods in visual anthropology.*

The scope of this paper includes: fieldwork and data collection methods, visual and non-visual, including photo- and film/video-elicitation; qualitative and quantitative techniques; cultural property and indigenous rights; preparing research proposals; ethnical problems; curating photography; elementary still photographic, video and digital multimedia production and presentation techniques.

4. *Option paper.*

Candidates must select one option paper from those taught each year for the M.Sc. in Social Anthropology. Titles of options will be made known at the beginning of each academic year and candidates may select their option from any of Lists A, B, or C.

REGULATIONS FOR THE DEGREE OF MASTER OF THEOLOGY (IN APPLIED THEOLOGY) AND FOR THE POSTGRADUATE DIPLOMA IN APPLIED THEOLOGY

Ch. VI, Sect. XXXV]

(i) **General Regulations**

1. The Board of the Faculty of Theology shall have power to award Postgraduate Diplomas in Applied Theology. Any person who has been admitted under the provisions of this section as a Student for the Postgraduate Diploma in Applied Theology, who has satisfied the conditions prescribed in the relevant regulations made by the faculty board under Section B below, and who has satisfied the examiners for the diploma may be awarded the Postgraduate Diploma in Applied Theology.

2. Any person who has been admitted under the provisions of this section as a Student for the Degree of Master of Theology, who has satisfied the conditions prescribed in the relevant regulations made by the faculty board under Section A below, and who has satisfied the examiners for the degree may supplicate for the Degree of Master of Theology. Alternatively, such persons may be awarded the Postgraduate Diploma in Applied Theology if they have satisfied the conditions prescribed in the relevant regulations made by the faculty board under Section B below and have satisfied the examiners for the diploma.

3. The examinations for the Degree of Master of Theology and for the Postgraduate Diploma in Applied Theology shall be under the supervision of the Board of the Faculty of Theology which shall have power to make regulations governing the examinations.

4. There shall be a committee for the supervision of arrangements for the Degree of Master of Theology and for the Postgraduate Diploma in Applied Theology which shall be called the Master of Theology Studies Committee. This committee shall consist of two representatives of the Board of the Faculty of Theology (at least one of whom shall be a member of the board's Graduate Studies Committee) and one representative of each of the participating

institutions, as listed in the Schedule below. The committee may co-opt up to three additional members. The committee shall have such powers and duties in respect of the Degree of Master of Theology and the Postgraduate Diploma in Applied Theology as may from time to time be prescribed by the Board of the Faculty of Theology.

5. The Board of the Faculty of Theology shall have the power to admit as students for the Degree of Master of Theology and for the Postgraduate Diploma in Applied Theology candidates nominated by the institutions listed in the Schedule below.

6. Each of the institutions listed in the Schedule below shall make a return to the Registrar by the end of the first week of Michaelmas Full Term, showing the names of all persons nominated in that term as Students for the Degree of Master of Theology and for the Postgraduate Diploma in Applied Theology, and the Registrar shall keep a register of such students.

7. The Board of the Faculty of Theology shall have power, on the advice of a student's society or other institution, to remove temporarily or permanently the name of a student from the register.

SCHEDULE

The participating institutions for the Degree of Master of Theology and for the Postgraduate Diploma in Applied Theology are: Blackfriars; Campion Hall; Greyfriars; Harris Manchester College; Mansfield College; Regent's Park College; Ripon College, Cuddesdon; St Benet's Hall; St Stephen's House; and Wycliffe Hall.

(ii) SPECIAL REGULATIONS

A. Regulations for the course of instruction for the Master of Theology (in Applied Theology) at the participating institutions listed in the Schedule.

1. Candidates who must be members of the University shall be graduates in theology, or shall hold an equivalent theological qualification, and shall have satisfied the Master of Theology Studies Committee of their ability to undertake the course.

2. A candidate may complete Part I of the course *either* in ONE year full-time (residential), with a maximum two additional years for Part II (dissertation);
or TWO years part-time (non-residential), with a maximum two additional years for Part II (dissertation).
In both cases there shall be no residence requirements for the period in which the dissertation is written.

3. Part-time candidates shall be required to attend courses of instruction organized by the participating institutions for one day a week during six terms, together with one three-day residential study conference organized by the Master of Theology Studies Committee in each of the first two years of their course.

4. The examination will consist of an extended essay of up to 7,000 words on each of the three compulsory and two optional units (Part I), and a dissertation of not more than 25,000 words on an aspect of applied theology (Part II).

Extended essays must be the candidate's own work, and must be typed or printed on one side of the paper. Essays must include a bibliography and footnotes (only the latter being included in the word count). Candidates may receive tutorial guidance in the preliminary stages of composition; tutors may also read or comment on a first draft, giving the candidate not more than one tutorial session at this further stage. Normal graduate supervision shall be provided for the preparation of the dissertation in Part II. When submitted, the extended essays must be accompanied by a certificate signed by the candidate indicating that it is the candidate's own work. This certificate must be submitted separately in a sealed envelope addressed to the Chairman of the Examiners for the M.Th. in Applied Theology at the address below.

Approval for the specific titles of the extended essays must be obtained from the Chairman of Examiners for the M.Th. in Applied Theology not less than two months before the essays are to be submitted for examination.

Extended essays may be submitted to the Chairman of the Examiners, M.Th. in Applied Theology, c/o the Clerk of the Schools, High Street, Oxford OX1 4BG, by 12 noon on the Friday before 1 May and 1 October in any year, provided that all extended essays must have been submitted by 12 noon on the Friday before 1 October following the third term in which a candidate's name has been on the register if the course is being taken full-time, or the sixth term if part-time. Candidates may delay the submission of their extended essay for Unit 4 until the May following the end of the first year of their course. Participating institutions shall submit with each essay a list of subjects covered in tutorials and/or seminars attended by the candidate during the course of the relevant unit.

5. In Part I, a candidate whose extended essay fails to reach the level which the examiners have determined to be the pass mark (or the required average for passing Part I) may be allowed to resubmit that work once only, within the next two examination periods, provided that no extended essay is submitted later than the submission of the dissertation.

In Part II, if the examiners are satisfied that the dissertation has reached the required level for the M.Th., but minor corrections are needed, they shall require the candidate to make these corrections before they submit their report. If the dissertation fails to reach the required level, the examiners may, but are not obliged to, give a candidate permission to revise and resubmit a dissertation at one further examination period, not later than three terms after the first submission.

6. No full-time student for the Degree of Master of Theology shall retain that status for more than twelve terms in all, and no part-time student for the degree shall retain that status for more than eighteen terms in all.

Part I

All candidates must take the first *three* units and a minimum of any *two* others.

1. *The Christian Doctrine of God in Pastoral Theology*

Candidates will be expected to explore the relation of the Christian doctrine of God to aspects of pastoral practice, examining the mutual influence of theological concepts and pastoral experience. They should be able to draw upon a knowledge of the doctrine of God as it has been developed in scripture, traditional formulations, and modern thought.

2. *The Social Context of Theology*

Candidates will examine the interaction between theology and its social context, considering both the social determinants of theology and theology as a factor in shaping society. Candidates will be expected to show sufficient knowledge of various approaches to the sociology of religion to be able to consider specific issues in applied theology.

3. *An Experiential Project with Theological Reflection*

Candidates will be expected to offer a considered evaluation of a project undertaken in either a church or secular setting in which the candidate shares in the concerns and experiences of those involved. The written work should be based upon contact made over a period of not less than twenty-one days and should contain theological reflection upon the situation using the doctrinal, sociological, and psychological skills acquired by the candidate. Candidates may delay submission of Unit 3 until the May following the end of the first year of their course.

4. *Pastoral Psychology*

Candidates will study the contribution of psychological studies to pastoral understanding and practice; the principles of psychological explication with particular reference to the psychology of religious experience; the importance of the psychological dimension in particular areas of pastoral concern, for instance human development, marriage, sickness, death, and bereavement.

5. *The Use of the Bible*

Candidates will be expected to study the use of the Bible in preaching, worship, and ethics, the phenomenon of diversity in the Bible; the contribution of hermeneutics to the use of the Bible in pastoral ministry; and the quest for a critical standpoint in contextual study of the Bible.

6. *Mission in the Modern World*

Candidates will study the theological foundations of mission in the mission of the triune God, and the relationship of the Church to it, together with factors in the modern world affecting mission such as industrialization, urbanization, a secular society, and new forms of imperialism. In particular candidates will examine the meaning of contextualization and sensitivity to culture.

7. *Ecclesiology in an Ecumenical Context*

Candidates will examine the doctrines of the Church, the ministry and the sacraments in their relationship to the concrete realities of the life of the Church and the nature of its authority. The study will be made in the light of current thought across the Christian traditions.

8. *Spirituality and Worship*

Candidates will examine the place of public and personal prayer and worship in the life of the Church: ways in which worship relates to the whole life of the Church and its mission in the world; rites of the Church related to people and their needs; non-verbal aspects of liturgy and cultural factors that affect our understanding of them and their use; insights into worship and prayer gained from other areas of study, especially from the human sciences; the prayer of individuals, or tradition, as they are expressed today, including current trends and developments.

9. *Inter-Faith Dialogue*

Candidates will be expected to embark on a critical examination of the nature of inter-faith dialogue and its relationship to Christian mission. In addition, candidates may consider the possibility of dialogue of christianity with a non-Christian religious tradition; and may study a particular example of inter-faith dialogue known to the candidate.

10. *Christian Ethics*

Candidates will study Christian ethics either on its own terms or in relation to other contemporary patterns of moral thought. Special regard will be shown to the perspective of Christian moral thinking on particular questions in personal and social ethics.

11. *Historical Theology*

Candidates will examine the ways in which historical materials (relating to the history of Christian life and thought) are used to address questions in the theology and ministry of the present day.

12. *Science and Faith in the Modern World*

Candidates will explore the methodology of science and theology; the development of science since the Enlightenment in the fields of physics, biology, and geology; the paradigm shifts in scientific understanding of creation, which have taken place in the twentieth century; and the contribution of biblical interpretation and natural theology to the doctrine of creation. Using the insights gained from pastoral experience and from an understanding of the doctrine of God candidates will study appropriate apologetic responses of the science–faith debate.

Part II

1. The title of the proposed dissertation, together with a summary, must be submitted for approval by the Master of Theology Studies Committee in the final term of Part I of the course. The committee shall approve a supervisor for the writing of the dissertation.

2. The dissertation (two copies) shall be submitted to the Chairman of the Examiners, M.Th. in Applied Theology, c/o the Clerk of the Schools, High Street, Oxford OX1 4BG, not later than 12 noon on the Friday before 1 October following the ninth term in which a candidate's name has been on the register if the course is being taken full-time, or the twelfth term if part-time.

3. The thesis must be printed or typed on one side of the paper only, with a margin of 3 to 3.5 cms on the left-hand edge of each page, and must be securely and firmly bound in either hard or soft covers. Loose-leaf binding is not acceptable.

4. The completed dissertation must be accompanied by a signed statement by the candidate that it is his or her own work except where otherwise indicated. This statement must be submitted separately in a sealed envelope addressed to the Chairman of Examiners for the M.Th. in Applied Theology at the above address.

5. All candidates are required to present themselves for a viva voce examination unless individually dispensed by the examiners.

6. Certain successful theses, on the recommendation of the examiners, should be deposited in the Theology Faculty Library. The library copy of thesis must be in a permanently fixed binding, drilled and sewn, in a stiff board case in library buckram, in a dark colour, and lettered on the spine with the candidate's name and initials, the degree, and the year of submission.

B. Regulations for the course of instruction for the Post-graduate Diploma in Applied Theology at the participating institutions listed in the Schedule.

1. The entry requirements for the course are as prescribed at A.1. above.

2. A candidate may complete the course either in ONE year full-time (residential) *or* TWO years part-time (non-residential).

3. Part-time candidates shall be required to attend courses of instruction organized by the participating institutions for one day a week during six terms, together with one three-day residential study conference organized by the M.Th. Studies Committee in each of the two years of their course.

4. The examination will consist of an extended essay of up to 7,000 words on each of the three compulsory and two optional units of Part I of the M.Th. course as set out above. The regulations concerning extended essays are as prescribed at A.4. above.

5. No full-time student for the Diploma shall retain that status for more than six terms in all, and no part-time student for that award shall retain that status for more than nine terms in all.

6. Candidates who have successfully completed the Diploma at an appropriate level may subsequently proceed to Part II of the M.Th. on the recommendation of the M.Th. Studies Committee. At the discretion of the Committee, transfer of Diploma candidates to Part II of the M.Th. course may be allowed to those candidates who have reached the required standard in the four papers submitted by the end of their first year.

REGULATIONS FOR THE DEGREE OF MASTER OF BUSINESS ADMINISTRATION

Ch. VI, Sect. XXXIII]

(i) General Regulations

§1. Degree of Master of Business Administration (Full-time and Part-time)

1. Any person who has been admitted to the status of student for the Degree of Master of Business Administration, who has satisfied the conditions prescribed by this section, and who has satisfied the examiners as required, may supplicate for the Degree of Master of Business Administration.

2. The Social Sciences Board with the concurrence of the Educational Policy and Standards Committee shall have power to make and vary such regulations as may be necessary for carrying out the duties laid upon it and upon the Secretary of Faculties by this section.

3. A Student for the Degree of Master of Business Administration who is not a graduate of the Univesity may wear the same gown as that worn by Students for the Degree of Doctor of Philosophy.

§2. Status of Student for the Degree of Master of Business Administration

1. Any person who, in the opinion of the MBA Committee, is well qualified and well fitted to undertake the course of study for which application is made, may be admitted to the status of Student for the Degree of Master of Business Administration. Decision on entry is made by the Head of MBA programmes or the EMBA Director (for part-time students) following an interview.

2. It shall be the duty of the Secretary of Faculties to keep a Register of these admitted to the status of Student for the Degree of Master of Business Administration.

§3. Admission of Candidates

1. A candidate seeking admission as a Student for the Degree of Master of Business Administration shall apply to the MBA Committee. Candidates for admission shall be required to provide

such information as the committee may determine from time to time by regulation. Applicants shall in addition be required to undertake such other tests and meet such conditions as, subject to the approval of the Social Sciences Board, the committee may determine by regulation.

2. No person shall be admitted as a Student for the Degree of Master of Business Administration under these provisions unless he or she is also a member of some college, hall, or other approved society, and unless the application for admission as a Student for the Degree of Master of Business Administration has the approval of that society. The Head of MBA programmes shall forward the application to the candidate's society or to the society to which the candidate wishes to apply for membership, as appropriate; and admission by the committee shall be conditional upon admission by an approved society.

3. A student registered for any other higher degree or diploma in the University may apply for transfer to the status of Student for the Degree of Master of Business Administration. The committee shall have power to make such transfer, provided that it is satisfied that the student is well qualified and well fitted to undertake the course of study for which application is made, and that the application has the support of the candidate's society. A candidate who transfers status in this way shall be reckoned as having held the status of Student for the Degree of Master of Business Administration from the time of admission to his or her previous status, unless the committee shall determine otherwise.

§4. Supervision of Students

1. Every candidate on admission as a Student for the Degree of Master of Business Administration shall be placed by the MBA Committee under the supervision of a member of the University or other competent person selected by the committee, and the committee shall have power for sufficient reason to change the supervisor of any student or to arrange for joint supervision by more than one supervisor, if it deems necessary.

2. It shall be the duty of the supervisor of a student entered upon a course of study to direct and superintend the work of the student, to meet the student regularly, and to undertake such duties as shall be from time to time set out in the Divisional Board's memorandum of guidance for students and supervisors.

3. The supervisor shall submit a report on the progress of a student to the committee three times a year, and at any other time when the committee so requests or the supervisor deems expedient.

The supervisor shall communicate the contents of the report to the student on each occasion that a report is made, so that the student is aware of the supervisor's assessment of his or her work during the period in question. In addition, the supervisor shall inform the committee at once if he or she is of the opinion that the student is unlikely to reach the standard required for the Degree of Master of Business Administration.

4. It shall be the duty of every Student for the Degree of Master of Business Administration to undertake such guided work and to attend such seminars and lectures as his or her supervisor requests; to attend such meetings with his or her supervisor as the supervisor reasonably arranges; and to fulfil any other requirements of the Divisional Board as set out in its memorandum of guidance for students and supervisors.

§5. Residence and other Requirements

1. No full-time Student for the Degree of Master of Business Administration shall be granted leave to supplicate unless, after admission, he or she has kept statutory residence and pursued his or her course of study at Oxford for at least thirty-two weeks.

2. No full-time Student for the Degree of Master of Business Administration shall retain that status for more than six terms in all.

3. Part-time students for the Degree of Master of Business Administration shall in each case be required to pursue their course of study over an elapsed time of 21 months. Part-time students shall not be required to keep statutory residence but must attend for such instruction and undertake such supervised coursework as the MBA committee shall require. The part-time MBA Director shall keep a register of attendance of part-time students. No student shall be granted leave to supplicate unless the register shows satisfactory attendance by him or her.

4. Part-time students may hold the status of Student for the Part-time Degree of Master of Business Administration for a period not exceeding 48 months.

5. A Student for the Degree of Master of Business Administration shall cease to hold that status if:

(*a*) he or she shall have been refused permission to supplicate for the Degree of Master of Business Administration;

(*b*) the MBA Committee shall, in accordance with provisions set down by regulation by the Divisional Board, and after consultation with the student's society and supervisor, have deprived the student of such status;

(*c*) he or she shall have been transferred under the relevant provisions to another status; or

(*d*) he or she shall not have entered for the relevant examination within the time specified under this sub-section.

§6. Examination of Students

1. The examination for the Degree of Master of Business Administration shall be under the supervision of the MBA Committee. The subjects of each examination shall be determined by regulation by the committee, which shall have power to arrange lectures and courses of instruction for the **[Until 1 October 2004:** examination**]** **[From 1 October 2004:** assessment**]**. The **[Until 1 October 2004:** examination**]** **[From 1 October 2004:** assessment**]** shall consist of:

(*a*) course assignments;

(*b*) written examinations;

(*c*) written reports on a business project approved by the committee; and

(*d*) an oral examination;

provided that the committee shall have power by regulation to authorize the examiners to dispense individual candidates from the oral examination. This provision notwithstanding, the examiners may, if they deem expedient, set a candidate a further written examination after examining the candidate orally.

2. No candidate shall be permitted to take an examination under the preceding clause unless he or she has been admitted as a candidate for the examination in question by the committee and has satisfied any other conditions prescribed in the regulations for that course.

3. Unless otherwise provided in this sub-section, the number and distribution of examiners shall be as set out in Sect. II. A, § 1, cl. 9 of this chapter.

4. A candidate who has failed to satisfy the examiners in the examination may enter again on one, but not more than one, subsequent occasion for that part of the examination which he or she failed.

(ii) Special Regulations

A. Full-time students

1. Candidates must follow for at least three terms a course of instruction in Management Studies. Candidates must complete

(*a*) all courses from the schedule of required courses, and satisfy the examiners in the assignment and/or examination associated with each course;

(*b*) **[Until 1 October 2004:** four**]** **[From 1 October 2004:** eight**]** electives, and satisfy the examiners in the assignment and/or examination associated with each course, the list of electives to be published **[Until 1 October 2004:** annually**]** by the MBA Director before the first Monday of **[Until 1 October 2004:** Hilary Term**]** **[From 1 October 2004:** the preceding term**]**;

(*c*) a written report on a new business development project of not more than 8,000 words. Such projects must be undertaken in groups and approved by the MBA Director;

(*d*) a written report on a consulting project of not more than 15,000 words. Such projects must be undertaken in groups and approved by the MBA Director; **[From 1 October 2004:** or, an individual project which would be supervised by one of the SBS faculty or associates. Such projects must be approved by the MBA Director.**]**

(*e*) a case study examination, on which questions may be set relevant to all the required courses held throughout the year (details of which are set out in the course handbook);

(*f*) candidates may be required to attend an oral examination on any of the above.

2. Assignments and written reports on projects must be presented not later than the time and date stipulated for each exercise; these will be published before the first Monday of each term by the MBA Director in which the assignment or project must be undertaken. The required number of copies must be delivered to the Examination Schools, and addressed to the Chairman of Examiners for the MBA, c/o Clerk of the Schools, High Street, Oxford. In cases where such work contains material of a commercially sensitive nature, access to such work may be restricted for a length of time to be decided by the Chairman of Examiners.

3. The examiners may award a distinction for excellence in the whole examination to candidates for the Degree.

4. In exceptional circumstances, a candidate wishing to take an examination later than the one to which he or she has been admitted may do so by application to the Chairman of Examiners.

B. Part-time students

1. Every candidate wishing to take the course on a part-time basis must follow for not less than 21 months a course of instruction in Management Studies. Candidates must complete:

(*a*) all courses from the schedule of required courses, and satisfy the examiners in the assignment and/or examination associated with each course;

(*b*) four electives, and satisfy the examiners in the assignment and/or examination associated with each course, the list of electives to be published not later than the first Monday of First Week of the term preceding the term in which the electives take place;

(*c*) a written report on a new business development project of not more than 8,000 words. Such projects must be approved by the part-time MBA Director;

(*d*) a written report on a business project of not more than 15,000 words. Such projects must be approved by the part-time MBA Director;

(*e*) a case study examination, on which questions may be set relevant to all the required courses held throughout the year (details of which are set out in the course handbook);

(*f*) candidates may be required to attend an oral examination on any of the above.

Schedule

The following courses are required to be taken during Michaelmas and Hilary Terms for full-time students, and during the first year of the course for part-time students. Details can be found in the course handbook.

[Until 1 October 2004:

(*a*) Financial Reporting
(*b*) Finance I
(*c*) Finance II
(*d*) People and Organizations
(*e*) Operations Management
(*f*) Marketing Management
(*g*) Strategic Management
(*h*) Global and Comparative Business
(*i*) Corporate Responsibility
(*j*) Decision Science
(*k*) Financial Management
(*l*) Industrial Organization
(*m*) Macro-Economic and Finance**]**

[From 1 October 2004:

(*a*) Decision Science
(*b*) Managerial Economics
(*c*) Financial Reporting
(*d*) Strategy
(*e*) Finance I
(*f*) Developing Effective Managers
(*g*) Operations Management
(*h*) Marketing
(*i*) Financial Management
(*j*) International Business and Global Governance**]**

REGULATIONS FOR THE DEGREE OF MASTER OF FINE ART

Ch. VI, Sect. XXXVI]

(i) General Regulations

§1. Degree of Master of Fine Art

1. Any person who has been admitted to the status of Student for the Degree of Master of Fine Art, who has satisfied the conditions prescribed by this section, and who has satisfied the examiners as required, may supplicate for the Degree of Master of Fine Art.

2. The Educational Policy and Standards Committee shall have power to make and vary such regulations as may be necessary for carrying out the duties laid upon it and upon the Secretary of Faculties by this section.

3. A Student for the Degree of Master of Fine Art who is not a graduate of the University may wear the same gown as that worn by Students for the Degree of Doctor of Philosphy.

§ 2. Status of Student for the Degree of Master of Fine Art

1. Any person who, in the opinion of the Committee for the Ruskin School of Drawing and Fine Art, is well qualified and well fitted to undertake the course of study for which application is made, may be admitted to the status of Student for the Degree of Master of Fine Art.

2. It shall be the duty of the Secretary of Faculties to keep a Register of those admitted to the status of Student for the Degree of Master of Fine Art.

§ 3. Admission of Candidates

1. A candidate seeking admission as a Student for the Degree of Master of Fine Art shall apply to the Committee for the Ruskin School of Drawing and Fine Art. Candidates for admission shall be required to provide such information as the committee may determine from time to time by regulation. Applicants shall in addition be required to undertake such other tests and meet such conditions as, subject to the approval of the Educational Policy and Standards Committee, the committee may determine by regulation.

2. Applications shall be made through the Secretary of Faculties, and it shall be the duty of the Secretary of Faculties to submit each

application to the committee and to inform the candidate of the outcome, as soon as may be.

3. No person shall be admitted as a Student for the Degree of Master of Fine Art under these provisions unless he or she is also a member of some college, hall, or other approved society, and unless the application for admission as a Student for the Degree of Master of Fine Art has the approval of that society. The Secretary of Faculties shall forward the application to the candidate's society or to the society to which the candidate wishes to apply for membership, as appropriate; and admission by the committee shall be conditional upon admission by an approved society.

4. A student registered for any other higher degree or diploma in the University may apply for transfer to the status of Student for the Degree of Master of Fine Art. The committee shall have power to make such transfer, provided that it is satisfied that the student is well qualified and well fitted to undertake the course of study for which application is made, and that the application has the support of the candidate's society. A candidate who transfers status in this way shall be reckoned as having held the status of Student for the Degree of Master of Fine Art from the time of admission to his or her previous status, unless the committee shall determine otherwise.

§ 4. **Supervision of Students**

1. Every candidate on admission as a Student for the Degree of Master of Fine Art shall be placed by the Committee for the Ruskin School of Drawing and Fine Art under the supervision of a member of the University or other competent person selected by the committee, and the committee shall have power for sufficient reason to change the supervisor of any student or to arrange for joint supervision by more than one supervisor, if it deems necessary.

2. It shall be the duty of the supervisor of a student entered upon a course of study to direct and superintend the work of the student, to meet the student regularly, and to undertake such duties as shall be from time to time set out in the relevant Notes of Guidance issued by the Educational Policy and Standards Committee.

3. The supervisor shall submit a report on the progress of a student to the committee three times a year, and at any other time when the committee so requests or the supervisor deems expedient. The supervisor shall communicate the contents of the report to the student on each occasion that a report is made, so that the student is aware of the supervisor's assessment of his or her work during the period in question. In addition, the supervisor shall inform the

committee at once if he or she is of the opinion that the student is unlikely to reach the standard required for the Degree of Master of Fine Art.

4. It shall be the duty of every Student for the Degree of Master of Fine Art to undertake such guided work and to attend such seminars and lectures as his or her supervisor requests; to attend such meetings with his or her supervisor as the supervisor reasonably arranges; and to fulfil any other requirements of the relevant Notes of Guidance issued by the Educational Policy and Standards Committee.

§ 5. Residence and other Requirements

1. No full-time Student for the Degree of Master of Fine Art shall be granted leave to supplicate unless, after admission, he or she has kept statutory residence and pursued his or her course of study at Oxford for at least forty weeks.

2. No full-time Student for the Degree of Master of Fine Art shall retain that status for more than two years in all.

3. A Student for the Degree of Master of Fine Art shall cease to hold that status if:

(*a*) he or she shall have been refused permission to supplicate for the Degree of Master of Fine Art;

(*b*) the Committee for the Ruskin School of Drawing and Fine Art shall, in accordance with provisions set down by regulation by the General Board, and after consultation with the student's society and supervisor, have deprived the student of such status;

(*c*) he or she shall have been transferred under the relevant provisions to another status; or

(*d*) he or she shall not have entered for the relevant examination within the time specified under this sub-section.

§ 6. Examination of Students

1. The examination for the Degree of Master of Fine Art shall be under the supervision of the Committee for the Ruskin School of Drawing and Fine Art. The subjects of each examination shall be determined by regulation by the committee, which shall have power to arrange lectures and courses of instruction for the examination.

2. No candidate shall be permitted to take an examination under the preceding clause unless he or she has been admitted as a candidate for the examination in question by the committee and has satisfied any other conditions prescribed in the regulations for that course.

3. Unless otherwise provided in this sub-section, the number and distribution of examiners shall be as set out in Sect. II. A, § 1, cl. 9 of this chapter.

4. A candidate who has failed to satisfy the examiners in the examination may enter again on one, but not more than one, subsequent occasion for that part of the examination which he or she failed.

(ii) Special Regulations

1. Applicants will be expected to have completed a good honours degree which should normally be in Fine Art.

2. The examination shall include both practical and written work.

3. Every candidate for the examination must follow for at least two terms a course of study in contemporary art and cultural theory, and must by noon on Friday of the eighth week of the Hilary Term submit to the Chairman of the Examiners in Fine Art, Examination Schools, High Street, Oxford OX1 4BG a certificate to that effect from his or her supervisor.

4. Syllabus

(*a*) Every candidate must submit during the Long Vacation, and not later than noon on the Monday three weeks prior to the start of Michaelmas Full Term, an exhibition of completed projects chosen from one or more of the subjects 1–8.

1. Drawing
2. Digital image handling
3. Sculpture
4. Painting
5. Performance
6. Printmaking
7. Photography
8. Video and film

(*b*) Every candidate must submit full documentation of their studio project. This should be either a carousel of not more than 30 × 35 mm slides or a 10 minute VHS video tape, and it should be accompanied by a brief statement of not more than 500 words.

This submission must be sent to the Chairman of Examiners in Fine Art, Examination Schools, not later than noon on the Monday three weeks prior to the start of Michaelmas Full Term.

(*c*) Every candidate must present one seminar paper of up to 2,500 words during Hilary Term related to his or her studio project. A written version of the paper must be submitted by noon on Friday of the eighth week of the Hilary Term to the Chairman of Examiners in Fine Art, Examination Schools. The work done for the seminar paper may form the basis of the extended essay required under (*d*) below.

(*d*) Every candidate must, after consultation with his or her supervisor, submit an extended essay of at least 4,000 words. This may be an account of the methodology used in the studio project, an exposition of its theoretical framework, or an essay on another topic of direct relevance to the project. Notice of the subject of the essay must reach the Chairman of the Examiners in Fine Art, Examination Schools, by noon on the Friday of the tenth week of Hilary Term. Three typewritten or printed copies of the essay must be sent to the Chairman of the Examiners in Fine Art, Examination Schools, not later than noon on the Friday of the tenth week of Trinity Term.

5. Candidates must present themselves for an oral examination unless individually dispensed from this requirement by the examiners. In this examination the essay referred to in 4(*d*), the submission in 4(*b*) and the candidate's general command of their field will be discussed.

6. A candidate who fails the examination may re-sit at the end of the following Michaelmas Term.

7. The examiners may award a distinction for excellence in the examination.

9

REGULATIONS FOR ADMISSION AS A PROBATIONER RESEARCH STUDENT*

Ch. VI, Sect. XXXII]

(i) General Regulations

§1. Status of Probationer Research Student

1. Any person intending to work for the Degree of Master of Letters or of Master of Science by research or of Doctor of Philosophy must apply in the first instance for admission as a Probationer Research Student, except as provided in Ch. VI, Sect. V, §2, cl. 1 (*b*) and (*c*); Ch. VI, Sect. VII.A, §2, cl. 1 (*b*); and Ch. VI. Sect. VIII, §2, cl. 1 (*b*).

2. The Educational Policy and Standards Committee shall have power to make and vary such regulations as may be necessary for carrying out the duties laid upon it and upon the Secretary of Faculties by this section.

3. For the purposes of this section the words 'board', 'faculty board', 'board of the faculty' or divisional board shall include any body with powers to admit students to the status of Probationer Research Student.

4. A Probationer Research Student who is not a graduate of the University may wear the same gown as that worn by Students for the Degree of Doctor of Philosophy.

§2. Admission of Candidates as Probationer Research Students

1. The board to which a prospective student's branch of study belongs may admit any person as a Probationer Research Student provided that the board is satisfied (1) that the candidate is well fitted and well qualified to conduct work for a research degree, (2)

* This decree should be read in conjunction with the associated regulations made by the individual faculty or divisional boards, to be found on pp. 837–82.

References within this regulation to part-time students relate to a small number of pilot schemes approved by the University for a limited period. There is no general provision for the award of research degrees through part-time study within the University.

that the branch of study proposed by the candidate is one which may profitably be pursued under the superintendence of the board, (3) that supervision will be available, and (4) that the faculty board or department under whose aegis the research is to be conducted has adequate facilities to enable the research to be undertaken.

2. Applications for admission shall be forwarded to the Secretary of Faculties, according to such timetables as the Educational Policy and Standards Committee shall determine. The Secretary of Faculties shall be responsible for transmitting the candidate's application to the faculty board or department concerned, together with a statement of the branch of study which the candidate intends to pursue, and such evidence of his or her fitness to undertake the proposed study as may be required by the board or department.

3. No person shall be admitted as a Probationer Research Student unless he or she is also a member of a college, and unless the application for admission as a Probationer Research Student has the approval of his or her college. The Secretary of Faculties shall forward the application to the candidate's college or to the college to which the candidate wishes to apply for membership, as appropriate; and admission by the board shall be conditional upon admission by an approved society.

4. A student already on the register of graduate students and holding the status of student for another degree, and who wishes to read for the M.Sc. by Research, M.Litt., or D.Phil. may apply for transfer to the status of Probationer Research Student, provided that before admitting the student to that status the board concerned shall be satisfied that he or she fulfils the conditions set out in clause 1 above. Students who transfer in this way shall be reckoned as having been admitted as Probationer Research Students from the time they were admitted to their previous status.

5. It shall be the duty of the Secretary of Faculties to notify candidates of the decision of the board as soon as may be and to inform a candidate whose application has been approved by the board of the term from which his or her admission as a Probationer Research Student is to be reckoned.

6. It shall be the duty of the Secretary of Faculties to keep a Register of those admitted to the status of Probationer Research Student.

7. A board may grant a student suspension from the Register or deprive a student of his or her status; and in such cases it shall at all times follow procedures determined by the Educational Policy and Standards Committee by regulation. A board may also reinstate

a student to the Register, provided that the total number of terms a student has spent as a Probationer Research Student has not exceeded five terms in the case of a full-time student, or ten terms in the case of a part-time student.

§3. Supervision of Probationer Research Students

1. Every candidate, on admission as a Probationer Research Student, shall be placed by the board concerned under the supervision of a member of the University or other competent person selected by the board, and the board shall have power for sufficient reason to change the supervisor of any student or to arrange for joint supervision by more than one supervisor, if it deems it necessary.

2. It shall be the duty of a supervisor to advise a student as to the courses of instruction and classes, if any, which he or she should attend, and generally to direct and superintend the student's work. It shall also be the supervisor's duty to assist a student, when satisfied of his or her competence, in the selection of a subject for his or her thesis.

3. The supervisor shall submit a report on the progress of the student to the board three times each year, and at any other time when the board so requests or the supervisor deems it expedient; and shall undertake such other duties as shall be from time to time set out in the relevant Notes of Guidance issued by the Educational Policy and Standards Committee. The supervisor shall communicate the contents of the report to the student on each occasion that a report is made, so that the student is aware of the supervisor's assessment of his or her work during the period in question. In addition, the supervisor shall inform the board at once if he or she is of the opinion that a student is unlikely to reach the standard required for admission at least to the status of student for the Degree of Master of Letters or of Science.

The Secretary of Faculties shall send a copy of each report by the supervisor to the student's college, and to the Director of Graduate Studies or other nominated person under the board concerned.

4. It shall be the duty of a Probationer Research Student to pursue any course of study preparatory to research recommended by his or her supervisor, and in particular to attend such courses of instruction as the supervisor may advise or the board concerned may require. A board may award a certificate of graduate attainment at the end of the Trinity Term in the year of the student's admission as Probationer Research Student. Subject to the approval of the Educational Policy and Standards Committee, each board shall

have power to determine by regulation what test or condition, if any, it may require before awarding such a certificate.

§4. Residence and other Requirements of Probationer Research Students

1. A full-time Probationer Research Student who has been admitted under the provisions of the preceding sub-section shall normally keep statutory residence and pursue his or her course of study at Oxford during the period in which he or she holds the status of Probationer Research Student. Time spent outside Oxford during term as part of an academic programme approved by Council shall count towards residence for the purpose of this clause.

2. A board may, on application from a candidate, and with the support of his or her college and supervisor, grant dispensation from such residence in exceptional circumstances, on the grounds that it is necessary to the student's work that he or she should be allowed to study at some other place than Oxford.

3. Part-time students holding the status of Probationer Research Student shall in each case be required to pursue their course of study for a minimum of six terms, and a maximum of twelve terms, prior to an application for transfer of status, save that students who have completed the requirements for the Degrees of Master of Studies or Master of Science (by Coursework) by part-time study may, with the permission of the board or other relevant body, apply for transfer of status after three terms. Part-time students shall not be required to keep statutory residence, but must attend for such instruction as the board or other relevant body shall require, subject to the approval of the Committee for Graduate Studies of the General Board. No student may apply to the relevant faculty board or other body for the appointment of examiners unless his or her supervisor has certified that the student has fulfilled the requirements for part-time students laid down by the board or other relevant body.

4. Any student may, with the permission of the board, alter the subject of research approved by the board, provided that the conditions of suitability set out in §2, cl. 1 of this section continue to be met. In such cases the date of the student's admission for all the purposes of this section shall remain unchanged, unless the board shall determine otherwise.

5. A full-time student may hold the status of Probationer Research Student for up to six terms, and a part-time student for up to twelve terms, including the term in which he or she was admitted.

6. A Probationer Research Student shall cease to hold such status if:

(i) he or she shall not have gained admission to another status within six terms of admission as a full-time student to the status of Probationer Research Student, or within twelve terms for a part-time student;

(ii) the board concerned shall, in accordance with provisions set down in §2, cl. 7, and after consultation with the student's college and supervisor, have deprived the student of such status.

NOTES

10

REGULATIONS FOR THE DEGREE OF MASTER OF LETTERS*

Ch. VI, Sect. V]

(i) General Regulations

§1. Degree of Master of Letters

1. Any person who has been admitted to the status of Student for the Degree of Master of Letters and who has satisfied the conditions prescribed by this decree may supplicate for the Degree of Master of Letters.

2. The Educational Policy and Standards Committee shall have power to make and vary such regulations as may be necessary for carrying out the duties laid upon it and upon the Secretary of Faculties by this section.

3. For the purposes of this section the words 'board', 'faculty board', 'board of the faculty', 'divisional board' shall include any body with powers to admit students to read for the Degree of Master of Letters.

4. A Student for the Degree of Master of Letters who is not a graduate of the University may wear the same gown as that worn by Students for the Degree of Doctor of Philosophy.

§2. Status of Student for the Degree of Master of Letters

1. The following may be admitted to the status of Student for the Degree of Master of Letters:

---

* This regulation should be read in conjunction with the associated regulations made by the Educational Policy and Standards Committee and individual boards, to be found on pp. 825–35. Those provisions of this regulation which govern admission to, and transfer from, one status to another shall apply only to research students first registered from Michaelmas Term 1991 or later. Students first registered for a research degree before that term shall continue to be subject to the relevant sections of the 1990 *Examination Decrees* in this respect.

References within this regulation to part-time students relate to a small number of pilot schemes approved by the University for a limited period. There is no general provision for the award of research degrees through part-time study within the University.

(i) a member of the University who, having held the status of Probationer Research Student under the provisions of Ch. VI, Sect. XXXII has successfully completed the relevant qualifying test or tests and fulfilled the other requirements for transfer to M.Litt. status prescribed in §3 of this section;

(ii) a member of the University who, having held the status of student for another higher degree within the University, has successfully completed the relevant qualifying test or tests and fulfilled the other requirements for transfer to M.Litt. status prescribed in §3 of this section;

(iii) a member of the University who has successfully completed the examination for the Degree of Bachelor or Master of Philosophy or Master of Science by Coursework or of Bachelor of Civil Law and who has fulfilled the conditions laid down in §3 of this section for applicants in that category.

2. It shall be the duty of the Secretary of Faculties to keep a register of those admitted to the status of Student for the Degree of Master of Letters.

3. A board may grant a student suspension from the Register or deprive a student of his or her status; and in such cases it shall at all times follow the procedures determined by the Educational Policy and Standards Committee by regulation. A board may also reinstate a student to the Register, provided that the number of terms a student has spent with the status of Student for the Degree of Master of Letters shall not have exceeded fifteen in all in the case of a full-time student, or eighteen terms in the case of a part-time student.

§3. Admission of Candidates to the Status of Student for the Degree of Master of Letters

1. Candidates qualified under §2 of this section may apply for admission as a Student for the Degree of Master of Letters to the board concerned through the Secretary of Faculties. Such applications shall be accompanied by:

(i) a statement from the supervisor that he or she approves the proposed subject for a thesis and considers the candidate well qualified to undertake research in that subject;

(ii) a statement of support for the application from the candidate's college;

(iii) a statement of the subject of the thesis and of the manner in which the candidate proposes to treat it.

2. Candidates qualified under §2, cl. 1 (i) and (ii) of this section shall in addition be required to submit written work, the precise

manner and form of which shall be determined by regulation by each board. This shall be considered by two assessors appointed by the board, neither of whom shall normally be the candidate's supervisor, and who shall examine the candidate orally. Upon completion of their examination of the candidate's application, the assessors shall make a recommendation as to whether it should be granted. In each case the assessors shall make a reasoned written report to the board in support of their recommendation.

3. The board shall consider the candidate's application together with the material supplied in accordance with clauses 1 and 2 above. No application shall be granted unless the board is satisfied that the candidate is capable of carrying out research, that the subject of the thesis and the manner of its treatment proposed by the candidate are acceptable, that the subject is one which may profitably be pursued under the superintendence of the board, and that the board or department concerned is satisfied that it has adequate facilities to enable the research to be undertaken.

4. Subject to the approval of the Educational Policy and Standards Committee, each board may determine by regulation what other test or condition, if any, it requires before admitting a candidate to M.Litt. status. Each board shall be empowered, without further authority, to require from the supervisor any further confidential report on an applicant's suitability to pursue research towards the Degree of Master of Letters.

5. It shall be the duty of the Secretary of Faculties to submit any application made under these provisions to the board concerned, and to notify the candidate of the outcome as soon as may be.

6. A student qualified under §2, cl. 1 (i) or (ii) of this section whose application for transfer to M.Litt. status is successful shall be reckoned as having been admitted to the status of student for the Degree of Master of Letters with effect from the date of admission to his or her previous status, unless the board determines otherwise.

7. A student qualified under §2, cl. 1 (iii) of this section whose application for admission to M.Litt. status is successful shall be admitted as a Student for the Degree of Master of Letters from the beginning of the term in which admission takes place.

§4. Supervision of Students for the Degree of Master of Letters

1. Every candidate on admission as a Student for the Degree of Master of Letters shall be placed by the board concerned under the supervision of a member of the University or other competent

person selected by the board, and the board shall have power for sufficient reason to change the supervisor of any student or to arrange for joint supervision by more than one supervisor, if it deems it necessary.

2. It shall be the duty of a supervisor to direct and superintend the work of the student, to meet the student regularly, and to undertake such duties as shall be from time to time be set out in the relevant Notes for Guidance issued by the Educational Policy and Standards Committee.

3. The supervisor shall submit a report on the progress of the student to the board three times a year, and at any other time when the board so requests or he or she deems it expedient. The supervisor shall communicate the contents of the report to the student on each occasion that a report is made, so that the student is aware of the supervisor's assessment of his or her work during the period in question. In addition, the supervisor shall inform the board at once if he or she is of the opinion that the student is unlikely to reach the standard required for the Degree of Master of Letters.

The Secretary of the Faculties shall send a copy of each report by the supervisor to the student's college, and to the Director or other nominated person under the faculty board concerned.

4. It shall be the duty of every Student for the Degree of Master of Letters to undertake such guided work as his or her supervisor requests; to attend such meetings with his or her supervisor as the latter reasonably arranges; and to fulfil any other requirements of the General Board set out from time to time in the relevant Notes of Guidance issued by the Educational Policy and Standards Committee.

§5. Residence and other Requirements for Students for the Degree of Master of Letters

1. Except as provided in clause 3 of this sub-section, a Student for the Degree of Master of Letters who has been admitted for full-time study under the provisions of §3 of this section shall be required to be on the Register for at least six terms, and during this period shall keep statutory residence and pursue his or her course of study at Oxford. Time spent outside Oxford during term as part of an academic programme approved by Council shall count towards residence for the purpose of this clause.

2. The board concerned may dispense a student on application through his or her college and with the support of the supervisor from not more than three terms of such residence and study in

Oxford, provided that such dispensation shall be granted only on grounds that it is necessary to the student's work that he or she should be allowed to study at some other place than Oxford.

3. A student who has successfully completed the examination for the Degree of Master or Bachelor of Philosophy or of Master of Studies or of Master of Science by Coursework, or a student under the supervision of the Board of the Faculty of Law admitted under the provisions of §2, cl. 1 (iii) of this section, shall keep statutory residence and pursue his or her course of study at Oxford for not less than three terms after such admission.

4. Any student who, after admission under §3 of this section, has kept statutory residence and studied at Oxford for a period of forty-two days, not necessarily consecutive, but falling within the same academic year, may apply to the board concerned for leave to reckon such period as one term towards the total required under clause 1 of this sub-section. The board shall have power to grant such leave provided that:

(i) no day so reckoned which falls within any term shall also be reckoned for the purpose of keeping that term;
(ii) no student who has kept the Michaelmas, or the Hilary, or the Trinity Term shall be allowed to reckon in this manner any day that falls within the eight weeks beginning on the first day of Full Term in Michaelmas, or Hilary, or Trinity Term, as the case may be;
(iii) no student shall be allowed to reckon in this manner more than one such period in the same academic year;
(iv) no student shall be allowed to reckon more than three terms in the same academic year.

For the purposes of this clause, the academic year shall begin on the first day of Michaelmas Term and end on the day preceding the first day of Michaelmas Term in the following calendar year.

Applications for leave to reckon any period as a term under the provisions of this clause shall be made to the board, through the Secretary of Faculties, by the student's college.

5. Part-time students holding the status of student for the Degree of Master of Letters shall in each case be required to pursue their course of study for a minimum of twelve terms, subject to the provisions of § 3, cl. 6. Part-time students shall not be required to keep statutory residence, but must attend for such instruction as the board or other relevant body shall require, subject to the approval of the Educational Policy and Standards Committee. No student may apply to the relevant faculty board or other body for

the appointment of examiners unless his or her supervisor has certified that the student has fulfilled the requirements for part-time students laid down by the board or other relevant body.

6. Any student may, with the permission of the board, alter the subject of research approved by the board, provided that the conditions of suitability set out in §2 above continue to be met. In such cases the date of the student's admission for all the purposes of this section shall remain unchanged, unless the board shall determine otherwise.

7. If a full-time Student for the Degree of Master of Letters has held that status for nine terms, or a part-time student for fifteen terms, but has been prevented by exceptional circumstances from completing his or her thesis, the board shall have power to grant an extension of time for a period or periods not exceeding six terms in all for a full-time student, or three terms in all for a part-time student, to be determined by the board. Applications for such extension of time shall be made through the Secretary of Faculties not later than the term in which the student is due to apply for permission to supplicate, and must be accompanied by statements of support from the student's society and supervisor.

8. A Student for the Degree of Master of Letters shall cease to hold such status if:

(i) he or she shall have been refused permission to supplicate for the Degree of Master of Letters;

(ii) the board concerned shall in accordance with §2 cl. 3 of this section, and with the provisions set down by regulation by the Educational Policy and Standards Committee, and after consultation with the student's college and supervisor, have deprived the student of such status;

(iii) he or she shall have been transferred under the relevant provisions to another status;

(iv) he or she shall have failed to complete his or her thesis within nine terms for a full-time student, or fifteen terms for a part-time student or within such further extension of time as may have been granted by the board concerned.

§6. Examination of Students for the Degree of Master of Letters

1. A Student for the Degree of Master of Letters who has fulfilled the applicable residence and other requirements set out in §5, and whose status has not expired, may apply for the appointment of examiners and for leave to supplicate for the Degree of Master of Letters.

2. Such applications should be made to the board concerned through the Secretary of Faculties. They shall include:

(i) a certificate from the student's college that the application has the approval of that college;

(ii) a certificate from the supervisor that the candidate has pursued his or her course of study in Oxford in accordance with the provisions of §5 of this section;

(iii) a statement by the candidate of what part, if any, of the thesis has already been accepted, or is being concurrently submitted, for any degree or diploma or certificate or other qualification in this University or elsewhere;

(iv) a statement by the candidate that the thesis is his or her own work, except where otherwise indicated.

3. The supervisor shall consult with the candidate concerning possible examiners, and forward to the board the names of suggested examiners with details of any special considerations which the candidate wishes to make known about any potential examiners.

4. The student shall also submit for examination, at such time as the Educational Policy and Standards Committee shall by regulation require:

(i) two printed or typewritten copies of a thesis;

(ii) two printed or typewritten copies of an abstract of the thesis, which shall not normally exceed 300 words.

5. On receipt of an application for the appointment of examiners the board concerned shall appoint two examiners, neither of whom shall be the candidate's supervisor, and whose duties shall be:

(i) to consider the thesis and the abstract of it submitted by the student under the provisions of the preceding clause, provided that they shall exclude from consideration in making their report any part of the thesis which has already been accepted, or is being concurrently submitted, for any degree or other qualification in this University or elsewhere (except for the Degree of Bachelor of Civil Law of this University) and shall have the power to require the candidate to produce for their inspection the complete thesis so accepted or concurrently submitted;

(ii) to examine the student orally, and also, if they think fit, by a written examination, in the subject of the thesis and in other relevant subjects;

(iii) to report to the board through the Secretary of Faculties;

(iv) to return to the student the copies of the thesis and of the abstract thereof submitted for examination.

The Educational Policy and Standards Committee shall have power to make regulations concerning the notice to be given of the oral examination and of the time and place at which it may be held. The examination may be attended by any member of the University in academic dress, while non-members may attend only with the consent of the examiners. In the case of theses submitted to the Divisional Boards of the Life and Environmental Sciences, Mathematical and Physical Sciences, and Medical Sciences, the Proctors after consultation with the relevant faculty board may decide (either at their own discretion or at the request of the candidate or the supervisor or department) to forbid the attendance of any person or all persons (other than the examiners and the candidate) or to impose any condition on attendance if and to the extent that such action is in their view necessary to protect the interests of the University or the candidate or both, and the examiners shall be informed accordingly and shall include this information in the notice of examination. The student, or his or her college, may within fourteen days of the date of the Proctors' decision appeal in writing to the Chairman of the Educational Policy and Standards Committee (who may nominate another member of the committee, other than one of the Proctors, to adjudicate the appeal).

6. Having completed the examination the examiners may make one of the following recommendations in their report to the board:

(i) that the candidate should be granted leave to supplicate for the Degree of Master of Letters. In this case the examiners must include in their report statements that:

1. the candidate possesses a good general knowledge of the field of learning within which the subject of the thesis falls;
2. that the candidate has shown competence in investigating the chosen topic;
3. that the candidate has made a worthwhile contribution to knowledge or understanding in the field of learning within which the subject of the thesis falls;
4. that the thesis is presented in a lucid and scholarly manner;
5. that it merits of the award of the Degree of Master of Letters.

Examiners shall bear in mind that their judgement of the extent of the candidate's contribution to knowledge or understanding of the relevant field of learning shall take into account what may reasonably be expected of a capable and diligent student after two years of full-time study in the case of a full-time student, or twelve terms in the case of a part-time student.

If the examiners are satisfied that the candidate's thesis is of sufficient merit for the degree but consider, nevertheless, that before the thesis is deposited the candidate should make minor corrections (which are not sufficiently substantial to justify reference back for re-examination), they must require the candidate to correct the thesis to their satisfaction before they submit their report. If the candidate has not completed these corrections within three calendar months of the date of the oral examination, his or her name shall be removed by the Secretary of Faculties from the Register of Students for the Degree of Master of Letters, provided that the board may, on good cause shown by the candidate, grant an extension of time of three further calendar months in which the candidate may fulfil this requirement before the removal of his or her name from the Register. No subsequent extension shall be granted, but it shall be open to a candidate who has failed to fulfil this requirement within those three or six months in total, as the case may be, to apply to the board for reinstatement as a Student for the Degree of Master of Letters, with the support of his or her society and supervisor, upon submission to the Secretary of Faculties of a copy of his or her thesis incorporating the required corrections, and upon payment of such reinstatement fee as may from time to time be prescribed by Council by decree. Permission to supplicate shall not be granted until this fee has been paid;

(ii) that the board should refer the thesis back to the student in order that he or she may revise it for re-examination. If the examiners so recommend they shall annex to their report to the board a statement (for transmission to the student) setting out the respects in which the thesis falls below the standard required for the degree. If the board adopts this recommendation the student shall retain the status and obligations of a Student for the Degree of Master of Letters, and may apply again for the appointment of examiners, in accordance with the procedure laid down in this subsection, not later than the fourth term after that in which the board gave permission so to reapply. If such permission shall have been given by a board during a vacation, it shall be deemed to have been given in the term preceding that vacation;

(iii) that the board should refuse the candidate's application for leave to supplicate.

7. In each case the examiners must embody in their report, in support of their recommendation, an account of the scope, character, and quality of the candidate's work.

8. On receipt of the examiners' report the board shall reach a decision on whether to accept the examiners' recommendation, provided that no candidate shall be given leave to supplicate unless the examiners have made the statements required in clause 6 (i) above.

9. A candidate who has been granted leave to supplicate by a board shall be required to submit to the Secretary of Faculties a copy of his or her thesis, incorporating any amendments or corrections required by the examiners and approved by the board. It shall be the duty of the Secretary of Faculties to deposit this copy of the thesis in the Bodleian or other appropriate university library. Leave to supplicate shall in all cases be conditional upon fulfilment of this requirement.

10. In an exceptional case in which a board is unable to accept the examiners' recommendation, or in which the examiners cannot reach an agreed recommendation, the board shall have power to appoint one or two new examiners as it deems necessary, to conduct such further examination of the candidate as the board may require. The board shall make a report on any such case to the Educational Policy and Standards Committee.

11. The board may exempt a candidate who is being re-examined under the provisions of clause 6 (ii) above from the oral examination, provided that the examiners are able to certify that they are satisfied, without examining the candidate orally, that they can recommend to the board in the terms required by clause 6 (i) above that he or she be given leave to supplicate for the Degree of Master of Letters.

12. It shall be the duty of the Secretary of Faculties to notify the candidate of the board's decision as soon as may be. The Secretary of Faculties shall also be responsible for publishing at the end of each academic year the names of those candidates to whom permission to supplicate has been granted during that year, together with a statement of the subject of the thesis written by each.

13. When, on the conclusion of the investigation of a complaint made by a candidate, the Proctors recommend that a candidate be re-examined, the board shall have power to hold a new examination.

11

REGULATIONS FOR THE DEGREE OF MASTER OF SCIENCE BY RESEARCH*

Ch. VI, Sect. VII. A]

(i) General Regulations

§1. Degree of Master of Science by Research

1. Any person who has been admitted to the status of Student for the Degree of Master of Science by Research and who has satisfied the conditions prescribed by this decree, may supplicate for the Degree of Master of Science.

2. The Educational Policy and Standards Committee shall have power to make and vary such regulations as may be necessary for carrying out the duties laid upon it and upon the Secretary of Faculties by this section.

3. For the purpose of this section the words 'board', 'faculty board', 'board of the faculty' or 'divisional board' shall include any committee with powers to admit candidates for the Degree of Master of Science by Research.

4. A Student for the Degree of Master of Science by Research who is not a graduate of the University may wear the same gown as that worn by Students for the Degree of Doctor of Philosophy.

§2. Status of Student for the Degree of Master of Science by Research

1. The following may be admitted to the status of Student for the Degree of Master of Science by Research:

---

* This regulation should be read in conjunction with the associated regulations made by the Educational Policy and Standards Committee and individual boards, to be found on pp. 825–35. Those provisions of this regulation which govern admission to, and transfer from, one status to another shall apply only to research students first registered from Michaelmas Term 1991 or later. Students first registered for a research degree before that term shall continue to be subject to the relevant sections of the 1990 *Examination Decrees* in this respect.

References within this regulation to part-time students relate to a small number of pilot schemes approved by the University for a limited period. There is no general provision for the award of research degrees through part-time study within the University.

(i) a member of the University who, having held the status of Probationer Research Student under the provisions of Ch. VI, Sect. XXXII, has successfully completed the relevant qualifying test for transfer to M.Sc. status prescribed in §3 of this section;

(ii) a member of the University who, holding the status of student for another higher degree within the University, has successfully completed the relevant qualifying test for transfer to M.Sc. status prescribed in §3 of this section.

2. It shall be the duty of the Secretary of Faculties to keep a Register of those admitted to the status of Student for the Degree of Master of Science by Research.

3. A board may grant a student suspension from the Register or deprive a student of his or her status; and in such cases it shall at all times follow procedures determined by the Educational Policy and Standards Committee by regulation. A board may also reinstate a student to the Register, provided that the number of terms a student has spent as a Student for the Degree of Master of Science shall not have exceeded fifteen in all in the case of a full-time student, or eighteen terms in the case of a part-time student.

§3. Admission of Candidates for the Degree of Master of Science by Research

1. A candidate qualified under §2 of this section may apply for admission as a Student for the Degree of Master of Science by Research to the board under whose aegis the proposed subject of research falls. Such applications should be made through the Secretary of Faculties, and must be accompanied by:

(i) a statement from the supervisor (where appropriate) that he or she approves the proposed subject for a thesis and considers the candidate well fitted to undertake research;

(ii) a statement of the subject of the proposed thesis and details of the manner in which the candidate proposes to treat it;

(iii) a statement of support for the application from the candidate's society.

2. Applicants shall in addition be required to undertake such other tests and meet such other conditions as, subject to the approval of the Educational Policy and Standards Committee, a board may determine by regulation.

3. The board shall consider the candidate's application together with the material supplied in accordance with clauses 1 and 2 above. No application shall be granted unless the board is satisfied that the candidate is capable of carrying out research, that the subject

of the thesis and the manner of its treatment proposed by the candidate are acceptable, that the subject is one which may profitably be pursued under the superintendence of the board, and that the board or department concerned is satisfied that it has adequate facilities to enable the research to be undertaken.

4. It shall be the duty of the Secretary of Faculties to submit any application made under these provisions to the board concerned and to inform a candidate of the outcome as soon as may be.

5. A candidate who is admitted to the status of Student for the Degree of Master of Science by Research shall be reckoned as having held that status from the time of admission to his or her previous status, unless the board shall determine otherwise.

§4. Supervision of Students for the Degree of Master of Science by Research

1. Every candidate on admission as a Student for the Degree of Master of Science by Research shall be placed by the board concerned under the supervision of a member of the University or other competent person selected by the board, and the board shall have power for sufficient reason to change the supervisor of any student or to arrange for joint supervision by more than one supervisor, if it deems it necessary.

2. It shall be the duty of a supervisor to direct and superintend the work of the student, to meet the student regularly, and to undertake such duties as shall be from time to time set out in Notes of Guidance issued by the Educational Policy and Standards Committee. The supervisor shall submit a report on the progress of the student to the board three times a year, and at any other time when the board so requests or the supervisor deems it expedient; and shall carry out such other duties as are set out in Notes of Guidance issued by the Educational Policy and Standards Committee. The supervisor shall communicate the contents of the report to the student on each occasion that a report is made, so that the student is aware of the supervisor's assessment of his or her work during the period in question. In addition, the supervisor shall inform the board at once if he or she is of the opinion the student is unlikely to reach the standard required for the Master of Science by Research.

The Secretary of Faculties shall send a copy of each report by the supervisor to the student's college and to the Director of Graduate Studies or other nominated person under the faculty board concerned.

3. It shall be the duty of every Student for the Degree of Master of Science by Research to undertake such guided work as his or her supervisor requests; to attend such meetings with his or her supervisor as the latter reasonably arranges; and to fulfil any other requirements set out in Notes of Guidance issued by the Educational Policy and Standards Committee.

§5. Residence and other Requirements for Students for the Degree of Master of Science by Research

1. A Student for the Degree of Master of Science by Research shall, after admission for full-time study, keep statutory residence and pursue his or her work at Oxford for at least three terms. Time spent outside Oxford during term as part of an academic programme approved by Council shall count towards residence for the purpose of this clause.

2. Any student who, after admission under §3 of this decree, has kept statutory residence and studied at Oxford for a period of forty-two days, not necessarily consecutive, but falling within the same academic year, may apply to the board concerned for leave to reckon such period as one term towards the total required under the preceding clause. The board shall have power to grant such leave provided that:

(i) no day so reckoned which falls within any term shall also be reckoned for the purpose of keeping that term;
(ii) no student who has kept the Michaelmas, or the Hilary, or the Trinity Term shall be allowed to reckon in this manner any day that falls within the eight weeks beginning on the first day of Full Term in Michaelmas, or Hilary, or Trinity Term, as the case may be;
(iii) no student shall be allowed to reckon in this manner more than one such period in the same academic year;
(iv) no student shall be allowed to reckon more than three terms in the same academic year.

For the purposes of this clause, the academic year shall begin on the first day of Michaelmas Term and end on the day preceding the first day of Michaelmas Term in the following calendar year.

3. Applications for leave to reckon any period as a term under the provisions of the preceding clause shall be made to the board, through the Secretary of Faculties, by the student's society.

4. Part-time students holding the status of Student for Degree of Master of Science by Research shall in each case be required to pursue their course of study for a minimum of twelve terms, subject to the provisions of § 3, cl. 5. Part-time students shall not be required

to keep statutory residence, but must attend for such instruction as the board or other relevant body shall require, subject to the approval of the Committee for Graduate Studies of the General Board. No student may apply to the relevant board or other body for the appointment of examiners unless his or her supervisor has certified that the student has fulfilled the requirements for part-time students laid down by the board or other relevant body.

5. Any student may, with the permission of the board, alter the subject of research approved by the board, provided that the conditions of suitability set out in §2 above continue to be met. In such cases the date of the student's admission for all the purposes of this section shall remain unchanged, unless the board shall determine otherwise.

6. If a full-time Student for the Degree of Master of Science by Research has held that status for nine terms, or a part-time student for fifteen terms but has been prevented by exceptional circumstances from completing his or her thesis, the board shall have power to grant an extension of time for a period or periods not exceeding six terms in all for a full-time student, or three terms in all for a part-time student, to be determined by the board. Applications for such an extension of time shall be made through the Secretary of Faculties not later that the term in which the student is due to apply for permission to supplicate.

7. A Student for the Degree of Master of Science by Research shall cease to hold such status if:

(i) he or she shall have been refused permission to supplicate for the Degree of Master of Science;

(ii) the board concerned shall, in accordance with provisions set down by regulation by the Educational Policy and Standards Committee, and after consultation with the student's society and supervisor, have deprived the student of such status.

(iii) he or she shall have failed to complete his or her thesis within nine terms for a full-time student, or fifteen terms for a part-time student, or within such further extension of time as may have been granted by the board concerned.

§6. Examination of Students for the Degree of Master of Science by Research

1. Candidates who have fulfilled the applicable residence and other requirements set out in §5 of this section, and whose status has not expired, may apply for the appointment of examiners and for leave to supplicate for the Degree of Master of Science by Research.

2. Applications for the appointment of examiners should be made to the board concerned through the Secretary of Faculties. They shall include:

(i) a certificate from the student's society that the application has the approval of that society;

(ii) a certificate from the supervisor that the candidate has pursued his or her course of study in Oxford in accordance with the provisions of §5 of this section;

(iii) a statement by the candidate what part, if any, of the thesis has already been accepted, or is being concurrently submitted for any degree or diploma or certificate or other qualification in this University or elsewhere;

(iv) a statement by the candidate that the thesis is his or her own work, except where otherwise indicated.

3. The supervisor shall consult with the candidate concerning possible examiners, and forward to the board the names of suggested examiners with details of any special considerations which the candidate wishes to make known about any potential examiners.

4. The student shall also submit for examination, at such time as the Educational Policy and Standards Committee shall by regulation require:

(i) two printed or typewritten copies of a thesis;

(ii) two printed or typewritten copies of an abstract of the thesis, which shall not normally exceed 300 words.

5. On receipt of an application for the appointment of examiners the board concerned shall appoint two examiners neither of whom shall be the candidate's supervisor, and whose duties shall be:

(i) to consider the thesis and the abstract of it submitted by the student under the provisions of the preceding clause, provided that they shall exclude from consideration in making their report any part of the thesis which has already been accepted, or is being concurrently submitted, for any degree or other qualification in this University or elsewhere and shall have the power to require the candidate to produce for their inspection the complete thesis so accepted or concurrently submitted;

(ii) to examine the student orally, and also, if they think fit, by a written examination, in the subject of the thesis and in other relevant subjects;

(iii) to report to the board through the Secretary of Faculties;

(iv) to return to the student the copies of the thesis and of the abstract thereof submitted for examination.

The Educational Policy and Standards Committee shall have power to make regulations concerning the notice to be given of the oral examination and of the time and place at which it may be held. The examination may be attended by any member of the University in academic dress, while non-members may attend only with the consent of the examiners. In the case of theses submitted to the Life and Environmental Sciences, Mathematical and Physical Sciences, and Medical Sciences Boards, the Proctors after consultation with the relevant divisional board may decide (either at their own discretion or at the request of the candidate or the supervisor or department) to forbid the attendance of any person or all persons (other than the examiners and the candidate) or to impose any condition on attendance if and to the extent that such action is in their view necessary to protect the interests of the University or the candidate or both, and the examiners shall be informed accordingly and shall include this information in the notice of examination. The student, or his or her college, may within fourteen days of the date of the Proctors' decision appeal in writing to the Chairman of the Educational Policy and Standards Committee (who may nominate another member of the committee, other than one of the Proctors, to adjudicate the appeal).

6. Having completed the examination the examiners may make one of the following recommendations in their report to the board:

(i) that the candidate should be granted leave to supplicate for the Degree of Master of Science by Research. In this case the examiners must include in their report statements that:

1. the candidate possesses a good general knowledge of the field of learning within which the subject of the thesis falls;
2. that the candidate has shown competence in investigating the chosen topic;
3. that the candidate has made a worthwhile contribution to knowledge or understanding in the field of learning within which the subject of the thesis falls;
4. that the thesis is presented in a lucid and scholarly manner;
5. that it merits of the award of the Degree of Master of Science.

Examiners shall bear in mind that their judgement of the extent of the candidate's contribution to knowledge or understanding of the relevant field of learning shall take into account what may reasonably be expected of a capable and diligent student after two years of full-time study in the case of a full-time student, or twelve terms in the case of a part-time student.

If the examiners are satisfied that the candidate's thesis is of sufficient merit for the degree but consider, nevertheless, that before the thesis is deposited the candidate should make minor corrections (which are not sufficiently substantial to justify reference back for re-examination), they must require the candidate to correct the thesis to their satisfaction before they submit their report. If the candidate has not completed these corrections within three calendar months of the date of the oral examination, his or her name shall be removed by the Secretary of Faculties from the Register of Students for the Degree of Master of Science by Research, provided that the board may, on good cause shown by the candidate, grant an extension of time of three further calendar months in which the candidate may fulfil this requirement before the removal of his or her name from the Register. No subsequent extension shall be granted, but it shall be open to a candidate who has failed to fulfil this requirement within those three or six months in total, as the case may be, to apply to the board for reinstatement as a Student for the Degree of Master of Science by Research, with the support of his or her society and supervisor, upon submission to the Secretary of Faculties of a copy of his or her thesis incorporating the required corrections, and upon payment of such reinstatement fee as may from time to time be prescribed by Council by decree. Permission to supplicate shall not be granted until this fee has been paid;

(ii) that the board should refer the thesis back to the student in order that he or she may revise it for re-examination. If the examiners so recommend they shall annexe to their report to the board a statement (for transmission to the student) setting out the respects in which the thesis falls below the standard required for the degree. If the board adopts this recommendation the student shall retain the status and obligations of a Student for the Degree of Master of Science, and may apply again for the appointment of examiners, in accordance with the procedure laid down in this subsection, not later that the fourth term after that in which the board gave permission so to reapply. If such permission shall have been given by a board during a vacation, it shall be deemed to have been given in the term preceding that vacation;

(iii) that the board should refuse the candidate's application for leave to supplicate.

7. In each case the examiners must embody in their report, in support of their recommendation, an account of the scope, character, and quality of the candidate's work.

8. On receipt of the examiners' report the board shall reach a decision on whether to accept the examiners' recommendation, provided that no candidate shall be given leave to supplicate unless the examiners have made the statements required in clause 6 (i) above.

9. A candidate who has been granted leave to supplicate by a board shall be required to submit to the Secretary of Faculties a copy of his or her thesis incorporating any amendments or corrections required by the examiners and approved by the board, with a view to its deposit in the Bodleian or other appropriate university library. Permission to supplicate shall in all cases be conditional upon fulfilment of this requirement.

10. In an exceptional case in which a board is unable to accept the examiners' recommendation, or in which the examiners cannot reach an agreed recommendation, the board shall have power to appoint one or two new examiners as it deems necessary, to conduct such further examination of the candidate as the board may require. The board shall make a report on any such case to the Educational Policy and Standards Committee.

11. The board may exempt a candidate who is being re-examined under the provisions of clause 6 (ii) above from the oral examination, provided that the examiners are able to certify that they are satisfied, without examining the candidate orally, that they can recommend to the board in the terms required by clause 6 (i) above that he or she be given leave to supplicate for the Degree of Master of Science.

12. It shall be the duty of the Secretary of Faculties to notify the candidate of the board's decision as soon as may be. The Secretary of Faculties shall also be responsible for publishing at the end of each academic year the names of those candidates to whom permission to supplicate has been granted during that year, together with a statement of the subject of the thesis written by each.

13. When, on the conclusion of the investigation of a complaint made by a candidate, the Proctors recommend that a candidate be re-examined, the board shall have power to hold a new examination.

NOTES

12

REGULATIONS FOR THE DEGREE OF DOCTOR OF PHILOSOPHY*

A.

Ch. VI, Sect. VIII]

(i) General Regulations

§1. Degree of Doctor of Philosophy

1. Any member of the University who has been admitted to the status of Student for the Degree of Doctor of Philosophy and who has satisfied the conditions prescribed by this decree may supplicate for the Degree of Doctor of Philosophy.

2. The Educational Policy and Standards Committee shall have power to make and vary such regulations as may be necessary for carrying out the duties laid upon it and upon the Secretary of Faculties by this section.

3. For the purposes of this section the words 'board', 'faculty board', 'board of the faculty' or 'divisional board' shall include any body which has power to admit students to read for the Degree of Doctor of Philosophy.

4. Students for the Degree of Doctor of Philosophy who are not graduates of the University may wear a long gown of black stuff, whose shape and ornaments shall be in accordance with a pattern approved by the Vice-Chancellor and Proctors and preserved in the University Offices, Wellington Square.

---

* This regulation should be read in conjunction with the associated regulations made by the Educational Policy and Standards Committee and individual boards, to be found on pp. 825–35. Those provisions of this regulation which govern admission to, and transfer from, one status to another shall apply only to research students first registered from Michaelmas Term 1991 or later. Students first registered for a research degree before that term shall continue to be subject to the relevant sections of the 1990 *Examination Decrees* in this respect.

References within this regulation to part-time students relate to a small number of pilot schemes approved by the University for a limited period. There is no general provision for the award of research degrees through part-time study within the University.

§2. Status of Student for the Degree of Doctor of Philosophy

1. The following may be admitted to the status of Student for the Degree of Doctor of Philosophy:

(i) a member of the University who, having held the status of Probationer Research Student under the provisions of Ch. VI, Sect. XXXII, or having held the status of student for another higher degree within the University, or having completed the requirements for another higher degree within the University, has successfully completed the relevant qualifying test for entry to D.Phil. status prescribed in §3 of this section;

(ii) a member of the University who has been given leave to supplicate for the Degree of Master or Bachelor of Philosophy, or of Master of Science by Research, or of Master of Letters, or of Bachelor of Civil Law, provided that the subject of the thesis offered by the candidate in the examination for that degree shall be in the broad field of research proposed for the D.Phil.

2. It shall be the duty of the Secretary of Faculties to keep a Register of those admitted to the status of Student for the Degree of Doctor of Philosophy.

3. A board may grant a student suspension from the Register or deprive a student of his or her status; and in such cases it shall at all times follow procedures determined by the Educational Policy and Standards Committee by regulation. A board may also reinstate a student to the Register, provided that the number of terms a student has spent with the status of Student for the Degree of Doctor of Philosophy shall not have exceeded twenty-one in all in the case of a full-time student, or twenty-seven terms in the case of a part-time student.

§3. Admission of Candidates to the Status of Student for the Degree Doctor of Philosophy

1. Candidates qualified under §2 of this section may apply for admission as Student for the Degree of Doctor of Philosophy to the board concerned through the Secretary of Faculties. Such applications shall be accompanied by:

(i) a statement from the supervisor that he or she approves the proposed subject for a thesis and considers the candidate well-fitted to undertake advanced research;

(ii) a statement of support for the application from the candidate's society;

(iii) a statement of the subject of the proposed thesis and details of the manner in which the candidate proposes to treat it.

2. Save for those applying under the provisions of § 2, cl. 1 (ii) of this section, applicants shall in addition be required to submit written work to the board, which work shall be assessed by two assessors appointed by the board, neither of whom shall normally be the candidate's supervisor. The precise manner and form of the written work shall be determined by regulation by each board. The process of assessment shall normally include an interview with the applicant; it shall always do so if the assessors are unable to certify that they are satisfied without interviewing the applicant that they can recommend transfer to D.Phil. status. Upon completion of their assessment of the candidate's work, the assessors shall make a recommendation as to whether the application for transfer to D.Phil. status should be granted. In each case the assessors shall make a reasoned written report to the board in support of their recommendation.

3. The board shall consider the candidate's application together with the material supplied in accordance with clauses 1 and 2 above. No application for transfer shall be granted unless the assessors shall have certified and the board is satisfied that the candidate is capable of carrying out advanced research, and that the subject of the thesis and the manner of its treatment proposed by the candidate are acceptable; and unless the board or department under whose aegis the research is to be conducted has adequate facilities to enable the research to be undertaken.

4. Subject to the approval of the Educational Policy and Standards Committee, each board shall have power to determine by regulation what other test or condition, if any, it may require before approving admission to D.Phil. status. Each board shall be empowered, without further authority, to require from the supervisor any further confidential report on an applicant's suitability to pursue research towards the D.Phil.

5. It shall be the duty of the Secretary of Faculties to submit any application made under these provisions to the board concerned, and to inform the candidate of the outcome as soon as may be.

6. An applicant who transfers to the status of Student for the Degree of Doctor of Philosophy shall be reckoned as having held that status from the time he or she was admitted to his or her previous status unless the board shall determine otherwise.

§4. Confirmation of Status as a Student for the Degree of Doctor of Philosophy

1. A candidate who has been admitted to the status of Student for the Degree of Doctor of Philosophy must, not later than the ninth term or normally earlier than the sixth term after that in which he or she was initially admitted to the status of a Probationer Research Student or to the status of a student for another higher degree of the University, or the eighteenth and twelfth terms respectively in the case of a part-time student, apply to the faculty board or committee concerned for confirmation of his or her status as a D.Phil. Student. A board or committee may, for good reason, permit a candidate to defer for a maximum of three terms his or her application for confirmation of status. A student who has been admitted to the status of Student for the Degree of Doctor of Philosophy after successfully completing the requirements for the Degree of Master (or Bachelor) of Philosophy, or having held the status of Student for the M.Litt. or M.Sc. by Research, may be exempted by the board or committee concerned from the requirement for confirmation of status. With the exception of students who have been exempted under this provision, all Students for the Degree of Doctor of Philosophy must have their status confirmed before making an application for the appointment of examiners.

2. Candidates applying for confirmation of their status shall submit their application to the board concerned, through the Secretary of Faculties; and such applications shall be accompanied by:

(i) certification from the supervisor that the candidate's progress has been such as to warrant confirmation of status;

(ii) a statement of support for the application from the candidate's society.

3. Each faculty board shall, subject to the approval of the Educational Policy and Standards Committee, determine by regulation any other conditions which a student must fulfil before his or her status may be confirmed.

4. A Student for the Degree of Doctor of Philosophy shall cease to hold such status unless it has been confirmed within twelve terms of his or her admission to that status in the case of a full-time student, or twenty-four terms in the case of a part-time student, in accordance with the provisions of this section.

5. If, after considering a candidate's application for confirmation of status, a board concludes that the student's progress does not warrant this, the board may approve his or her transfer to the status

of Student for the Degree of Master of Science by Research or of Master of Letters, as appropriate.

§5. Supervision of Students for the Degree of Doctor of Philosophy

1. Every candidate on admission as a Student for the Degree of Doctor of Philosophy shall be placed by the board which approved his or her application under the supervision of a member of the University or other competent person selected by the board, and the board shall have power for sufficient reason to change the supervisor of any student or to arrange for joint supervision by more than one supervisor, if it deems it necessary.

2. It shall be the duty of a supervisor to direct and superintend the work of the student, to meet the student regularly, and to undertake such duties as shall be from time to time set out in Notes of Guidance issued by the Educational Policy and Standards Committee. The supervisor shall submit a report on the progress of the student to the board three times a year as required, and at any other time when the board so requests or the supervisor deems it expedient; and shall carry out such other duties as are set out in Notes of Guidance issued by the Educational Policy and Standards Committee. The supervisor shall communicate the contents of the report to the student on each occasion that a report is made, so that the student is aware of the supervisor's assessment of his or her work during the period in question. In addition, the supervisor shall inform the board at once if he or she is of the opinion the student is unlikely to reach the standard required for the Degree of Doctor of Philosophy.

The Secretary of Faculties shall send a copy of each report by the supervisor to the student's college, and to the Director of Graduate Studies or other nominated person under the board concerned.

3. It shall be the duty of every Student for the Degree of Doctor of Philosophy to undertake such guided work as his or her supervisor requests; to attend such meetings with his or her supervisor as the latter reasonably arranges; and to fulfil any other requirements of the Educational Policy and Standards Committee set out in its memorandum of guidance for students and supervisors.

§6. Residence and other Requirements for Students for the Degree of Doctor of Philosophy

1. Except as provided in clause 2 of this subsection, a Student for the Degree of Doctor of Philosophy shall after admission for full-time study keep statutory residence and pursue his or her course

of study at Oxford for at least six terms, provided that a Student for the Degree of Doctor of Philosophy who is also a Bachelor or Master of Philosophy or Master of Science or Master of Letters or Master of Studies or Bachelor of Civil Law or Magister Juris or Master of Theology (except for those who hold the degree having studied for it at Westminster College) shall keep statutory residence and pursue his or her course of study at Oxford for at least three terms after admission as a Student for the Degree of Doctor of Philosophy. Time spent outside Oxford during term as part of an academic programme approved by Council shall count towards residence for the purpose of this clause.

2. The board concerned may dispense a student for the Degree of Doctor of Philosophy, on application through his or her society and with the support of his or her supervisor, from not more than three terms of residence and study in Oxford either on the ground that it is necessary to the student's work that he or she should be allowed to pursue his or her course of study at some other place than Oxford, or for other good cause.

3. Students exceptionally permitted to undertake their research in a well-found laboratory outside Oxford shall not be required to keep statutory residence, but must attend for such instruction as the board shall require.

4. Any student who, after admission under §3 of this section, has kept statutory residence and studied at Oxford for a period of forty-two days, not necessarily consecutive, but falling within the same academic year, may apply to the board concerned for leave to reckon such period as one term towards the total required under the preceding clause. The board shall have power to grant such leave provided that:

(i) no day so reckoned which falls within any term shall also be reckoned for the purpose of keeping that term;

(ii) no student who has kept the Michaelmas, or the Hilary, or the Trinity Term shall be allowed to reckon in this manner any day that falls within the eight weeks beginning on the first day of Full Term in Michaelmas, or Hilary, or Trinity Term, as the case may be;

(iii) no student shall be allowed to reckon in this manner more than one such period in the same academic year;

(iv) no student shall be allowed to reckon more than three terms in the same academic year.

For the purposes of this clause, the academic year shall begin on the first day of Michaelmas Term and end on the day preceding the first day of Michaelmas Term in the following calendar year.

Applications for leave to reckon any period as a term under the provisions of this clause shall be made to the board, through the Secretary of Faculties, by the student's society.

5. Part-time students holding the status of Student for the Degree of Doctor of Philosophy shall in each case be required to pursue their course of study for a minimum of twelve terms, subject to the provisions of § 3, cl. 6. Part-time students shall not be required to keep statutory residence, but must attend for such instruction as the board or other relevant body shall require, subject to the approval of the Educational Policy and Standards Committee. No student may apply to the relevant faculty board or other body for the appointment of examiners unless his or her supervisor has certified that the student has fulfilled the requirements for part-time students laid down by the faculty board or other relevant body.

6. Any student may, with the permission of the board alter the subject of the research originally approved provided that the conditions of suitability set out in §3 of this section continue to be met. In such cases the date of the student's admission for all the purposes of this section shall remain unchanged, unless the board shall order otherwise.

7. If a full-time Student for the Degree of Doctor of Philosophy has held that status for twelve terms, or a part-time student for twenty-four terms, but has been prevented by exceptional circumstances from completing his or her thesis, the board shall have power to grant an extension of time for a period or periods, not exceeding nine terms in all for a full-time student, or three terms in all for a part-time student, to be determined by the board. Applications for such extension of time shall be made through the Secretary of Faculties not later than the term in which the student is due to apply for permission to supplicate.

8. A Student for the Degree of Doctor of Philosophy shall cease to hold that status if:

(i) he or she shall have been refused permission to supplicate for the Degree of Doctor of Philosophy; or

(ii) the board concerned shall in accordance with §2, cl. 3 of this section, and with the provisions set down by regulation by the Educational Policy and Standards Committee and after consultation with the student's college and supervisor, have deprived the student of such status;

(iii) he or she shall have been transferred under the relevant provisions to another status;

(iv) he or she shall have failed to complete his or her thesis within twelve terms for a full-time student, or twenty-four terms for a part-time student or within such further extension of time as may have been granted by the board concerned.

§7. Examination of Students for the Degree of Doctor of Philosophy

1. A Student for the Degree of Doctor of Philosophy who has fulfilled the applicable residence and other requirements set out in §6 of this section and whose status has not expired, may apply to the board concerned for the appointment of examiners and for leave to supplicate for the Degree of Doctor of Philosophy.

2. Such applications should be made to the board concerned through the Secretary of Faculties. They shall include:

(i) a certificate from the student's college that the application has the approval of that college;
(ii) a certificate from the supervisor that the student has pursued his or her course of study in Oxford in accordance with the provisions of §6 of this section;
(iii) a statement by the candidate of what part, if any, of the thesis has already been accepted, or is concurrently being submitted, for any degree or diploma or certificate or other qualification in this University or elsewhere;
(iv) a statement by the candidate that the thesis is his or her own work, except where otherwise indicated.

3. The supervisor shall consult with the candidate concerning possible examiners, and forward to the board the names of suggested examiners together with details of any special considerations which the candidate wishes to make known about any potential examiners.

4. The candidate shall also submit for examination, at such time and in such format as the General Board of the Faculties shall by regulation permit:

(i) two printed or typewritten copies of a thesis;
(ii) two printed or typewritten copies of an abstract of the thesis, which shall not normally exceed 300 words.

5. On receipt of an application the board concerned shall appoint two examiners, neither of whom shall be the candidate's supervisor, and whose duties shall be:

(i) to consider the thesis and the abstract of it submitted by the student, provided that they shall exclude from consideration in making their report any part of the thesis which has already been accepted, or is being concurrently submitted, for any degree or other qualification in this University or elsewhere otherwise than as part of the requirements of this University for the Degree of Bachelor of Philosophy or of Master of Philosophy or of Bachelor of Civil Law, or as part of the dissertation submitted by a Student for the Degree of Master of Science by Coursework or of Master of Studies, and shall have the power to require the candidate to produce for their inspection the complete thesis so accepted or concurrently submitted;

(ii) to examine the student orally in the subject of his or her thesis;

(iii) to satisfy themselves by examination (oral, written, or both) whether the student possesses a good general knowledge of the particular field of learning within which the subject of the thesis falls;

(iv) to report to the board through the Secretary of Faculties on the scope, character, and quality of the work submitted;

(v) to return to the student the copies of the thesis and the abstracts thereof.

The Educational Policy and Standards Committee shall have power to make regulations concerning the notice to be given of the oral examination, and of the time and place of at which it may be held. The examination may be attended by any member of the University in academic dress, while non-members may attend only with the consent of the examiners. In the case of theses submitted to the Life and Environmental Sciences, Mathematical and Physical Sciences, and Medical Sciences Boards, the Proctors after consultation with the relevant Divisional Board may decide (either at their own discretion or at the request of the candidate or the supervisor or department) to forbid the attendance of any person or all persons (other than the examiners and the candidate) or to impose any condition on attendance if and to the extent that such action is in their view necessary to protect the interests of the University or the candidate or both, and the examiners shall be informed accordingly and shall include this information in the notice of examination. The student, or his or her college, may within fourteen days of the date of the Proctors' decision appeal in writing to the Chairman of the Educational Policy and Standards Committee (who may nominate another member of the committee, other than one of the Proctors, to adjudicate the appeal).

6. Having completed the examination of a candidate for the first time, the examiners may make any one of recommendations (i), (ii) or (iv) below only. Having completed the examination of a candidate

who has revised and re-submitted his or her thesis, the examiners may make any one of recommendations (i)–(vi). The recommendations are:

(i) that the board should grant the candidate leave to supplicate for the Degree of Doctor of Philosophy. In making this recommendation, the examiners must include in their report statements that:

1. the student possesses a good general knowledge of the particular field of learning within which the subject of the thesis falls;
2. the student has made a significant and substantial contribution in the particular field of learning within which the subject of the thesis falls;
3. the thesis is presented in a lucid and scholarly manner;
4. in their opinion the thesis merits the Degree of Doctor of Philosophy;
5. the student has presented a satisfactory abstract of the thesis.

Examiners shall bear in mind that their judgement of the substantial significance of the work should take into account what may reasonably be expected of a capable and diligent student after three or at most four years of full-time study in the case of a full-time student, or eight years in the case of a part-time student.

If the examiners are satisfied that the candidate's thesis is of sufficient merit to qualify for the degree but consider, nevertheless, that before the thesis is deposited the candidate should make minor corrections (which are not sufficiently substantial to justify reference back for re-examination), they must require the candidate to correct the thesis to their satisfaction before they submit their report. If the candidate has not completed these corrections within three calendar months of the date of the oral examination, his or her name shall be removed by the Secretary of Faculties from the Register of Students for the Degree of Doctor of Philosophy, provided that the board may, on good cause shown by the candidate, grant an extension of time of three further calendar months in which the candidate may fulfil this requirement before the removal of his or her name from the Register. No subsequent extension shall be granted, but it shall be open to a candidate who has failed to fulfil this requirement within those three or six months in total, as the case may be, to apply to the board for reinstatement as a Student for the Degree of Doctor of Philosophy, with the support of his or her society and supervisor, upon submission to the Secretary of Faculties of a copy of his or her thesis incorporating the required corrections, and upon payment of such reinstatement fee as may from time to time be prescribed by Council by decree. Permission to supplicate shall not be granted until this fee has been paid;

(ii) that the board should offer the candidate a choice between (*a*) reference of the thesis back to him or her in order that he or she may revise it for re-examination for the Degree of Doctor of Philosophy, and (*b*) leave to supplicate for the Degree of Master of Letters or of Master of Science, as appropriate, on the basis that the thesis has not reached the standard required for the Degree of Doctor of Philosophy but has nevertheless reached that required for the Degree of Master of Letters or of Master of Science. If the board adopts this recommendation, and the student chooses to revise the thesis for re-examination for the Degree of Doctor of Philosophy, the student shall retain the status and obligations of a Student for the Degree of Doctor of Philosophy and shall be permitted to apply again for the appointment of examiners, in accordance with the procedure laid down in this sub-section, not later than the seventh term after that in which the board gave permission so to reapply. If such permission shall have been given by a board during a vacation, it shall be deemed to have been given in the term preceding that vacation;

(iii) that the board should refer the student's thesis back in order that he or she may present it for re-examination for the Degree of Master of Letters or of Master of Science only. If the board adopts the recommendation the student shall be transferred forthwith to the status of Student for the Degree of Master of Letters or Student for the Degree of Master of Science as the case may be, and shall be permitted to apply for permission to supplicate for the Degree of Master of Letters or Master of Science in accordance with the provisions of Ch. VI, Sect. v, §6 or of Ch. VI, Sect. vii. A, §6 as the case may be. If such permission shall have been given by a board during a vacation, it shall be deemed to have been given in the term preceding that vacation. The word limit for a thesis resubmitted under this provision shall be that specified by the D.Phil. regulations under which it was originally submitted;

(iv) that the board should refer the student's thesis back in order that he or she may present it for re-examination either under (ii) above for the Degree of Doctor of Philosophy or, if the student chooses, under (iii) above for the Degree of Master of Letters or of Master of Science only. The board shall adopt such a recommendation only if it is fully satisfied that the thesis as it stands is not of the standard required for the Degree of Doctor of Philosophy, nor for the Degree of Master of Letters or of Master of Science as the case may be, but that the candidate could reach the standard required for the Degree of Doctor of Philosophy. If such permission shall have been given by a board during a vacation, it shall be deemed to have been given in the term preceding that vacation;

(v) that the thesis has not reached the standard required for the Degree of Doctor of Philosophy but has nevertheless reached that required of the Degree of Master of Letters or of Master of Science, and that the candidate may be granted leave to supplicate for one of the latter degrees on the basis of the thesis as it stands;

(vi) that the student's application for leave to supplicate should be refused.

7. If the examiners recommend reference back of the student's application under clause 6 (ii) or (iii) or (iv) above, they shall annex to their report to the board a statement (for transmission to the candidate) setting out the respects in which the thesis falls below the standard required for the degree in question, and what changes are necessary for it to reach that standard, save that examiners of a thesis submitted for the first time may, in exceptional circumstances, and notwithstanding a recommendation under clause 6 (ii) or (iv) above, certify that they are unable to indicate how the thesis might be changed, within the time allowed, in order to reach the required standard for the degree of Doctor of Philosophy.

8. On receipt of the examiners' report the board shall reach a decision on whether to accept the examiners' recommendation, provided that no candidate shall be given leave to supplicate for the Degree of Doctor of Philosophy unless the examiners have made the statements required in clause 6 (i) above.

9. A candidate who has been granted leave to supplicate by a board shall be required to submit to the Secretary of Faculties a copy of his or her thesis, incorporating any amendments or corrections required by the examiners and approved by the board, with a view to deposit in the Bodleian or other appropriate university library. Permission to supplicate shall in all cases be conditional upon fulfilment of this requirement.

10. In an exceptional case in which a board is unable to accept the examiners' recommendation, or in which the examiners cannot

reach an agreed recommendation, the board shall have power to appoint one or two new examiners as it deems necessary, to conduct such further examination of the candidate as the board may require. The board shall make a report on any such case to the Educational Policy and Standards Committee.

11. The board may exempt a candidate who is being re-examined under the provisions of clause 6 (ii)–(v) above from the oral examination, provided that the examiners are able to certify that they are satisfied without examining the candidate orally that they can recommend to the board in the terms required by clause 6 (i) above that he or she be given leave to supplicate for the Degree of Doctor of Philosophy.

12. It shall be the duty of the Secretary of the Faculties to notify the candidate of the board's decision as soon as may be. The Secretary of Faculties shall also be responsible for publishing at the end of each academic year the names of those candidates to whom permission to supplicate has been granted during that year, together with a statement of the subject of the thesis written by each.

13. When, on the conclusion of the investigation of a complaint made by a candidate, the Proctors recommend that a candidate be re-examined, the board shall have power to hold a new examination.

NOTES

*GENERAL REGULATIONS OF THE EDUCATIONAL POLICY AND STANDARDS COMMITTEE GOVERNING THE EXAMINATION OF STUDENTS FOR THE DEGREES OF M.SC. BY RESEARCH, M.LITT., AND D.PHIL., AND CONCERNING THE MAINTENANCE OF THE REGISTER

1. Regulations governing the content and length of theses.

(i) ***Material for transfer or submission***

Material submitted for transfer to, or for the award of, the degrees of M.Litt., M.Sc. by Research, and D.Phil., shall be wholly or substantially the result of work undertaken while the student holds the status of Probationer Research Student or the status of a student for the degree concerned, except that a candidate may make application for a dispensation from this requirement to the Educational Policy and Standards Committee.

(ii) ***Prior publication***

Prior publication of material arising from research undertaken while holding the status of Probationer Research Student or the status of a student for the M.Litt., M.Sc. by Research, or D.Phil., is fully acceptable, but the inclusion of published papers within a thesis may be subject to special regulation by the board concerned. Candidates should note that the acceptance of such material for publication does not of itself constitute proof that the work is of sufficient quality or significance to merit the award of the degree concerned. This remains a judgement of the relevant board on the recommendation of its examiners.

(iii) ***Thesis length***

If a thesis exceeds the permitted length, the board concerned may decline to appoint examiners or to forward the thesis to examiners already appointed, and may return it to the candidate for revision. If the examiners find that a thesis which has been forwarded to them exceeds the permitted length, they should report the fact to the relevant board and await further instructions before proceeding with the examination.

2. Preparation and submission of theses for the Degrees of M.Litt., M.Sc. by Research, and D.Phil.

---

* Those provisions of this regulation which govern admission to, and transfer from, one status to another shall apply only to research students first registered from Michaelmas Term 1991 or later. Students first registered for a research degree before that term shall continue to be subject to the relevant sections of the 1990 *Examination Decrees* in this respect.

(i) ***Text and footnotes***

Candidates should note that the purpose of these regulations is not only to ease the task of the examiners (which is obviously in the candidates' interests), but also to ensure that the copy finally deposited in the Bodleian or other university library is of a standard of legibility which will allow it (subject to applicable copyright rules) to be photocopied or microfilmed if required in future years.

The thesis must be typed or printed on one side of the paper only, with a margin of 1.25 to 1.5 inches (32 to 38 mm) on the left-hand side of each page. Theses in typescript should present the main text in *double spacing* with quotations and footnotes in single spacing. In the case of word-processed or printed theses, where the output resembles that of a typewriter, double spacing should be taken to mean a distance of about 0.33 inch or 8 mm between successive lines of text. Candidates are advised that it is their responsibility to ensure that the print of their thesis is of an adequate definition and standard of legibility.

Footnotes should normally be placed at the bottom of each page. Where they are given at the end of each chapter or at the end of the thesis, two separate unbound copies of footnotes should also be presented, for the convenience of the examiners.

Candidates should carefully note the regulations concerning word limits which individual boards have made. In such cases, candidates should state the approximate number of words in their theses.

Theses must be submitted in English unless for exceptional reasons a board otherwise determines in the term in which the candidate is first admitted as a research student.

The pages of the thesis must be numbered. Each copy should have an abstract included (see below).

(ii) ***Examiners' copies: binding and presentation***

At the time of their examination, candidates must submit two copies of their thesis, which must be securely and firmly bound in either hard or soft covers. Loose-leaf binding is not acceptable. Candidates are responsible for ensuring that examiners' copies are securely bound and should note that theses which do not meet this requirement will not be accepted.

Candidates should pack each copy of the thesis intended for the examiners into a separate but *unsealed* parcel or padded envelope, ready in all respects, except the address, to be posted to the examiners when appointed. Each parcel should bear the candidate's name and society and the words 'M.LITT./M.SC./D.PHIL. (as appropriate) THESIS AND ABSTRACT' in BLOCK CAPITALS in the bottom left-hand corner. A slip giving the address to which the examiners should write in order to contact the candidate about arrangements for the oral examination should be enclosed with each copy of the thesis. Candidates are responsible for ensuring that their examiners have no difficulty in communicating with them. The separate copies thus packed should be submitted to the Graduate Studies Offices, Wellington Square, Oxford. If sent or posted they should be enclosed in one covering parcel.

The theses of candidates who fail to follow this advice are liable to delay in being forwarded to the examiners.

(iii) ***Date of submission of examiners' copies***

Candidates may submit the examiners' copies of their thesis, prepared as described above, at the same time as they apply for the appointment of their examiners. If they intend, however, to submit the examiners' copies at a later date, they will be required to state, at the time of their application for appointment of examiners, the date by which they will submit. This should be as soon as possible after the date of application and may in no case be later than the last day of the vacation immediately following the term in which application for the appointment of examiners has been made.

(iv) ***Library copies: binding and presentation***

Once the board has granted a candidate leave to supplicate, he or she must submit a finalized copy of the thesis, as approved by the examiners, to the Graduate Studies Office for deposit in the relevant university library. This should incorporate any corrections or amendments which the examiners may have requested of the candidate. The examiners must confirm in writing in their report to the board that any corrections required have been made.

The library copy of the thesis must be in a permanently fixed binding, drilled and sewn, in a stiff board case in library buckram, in a dark colour, and lettered on the spine with the candidate's name and initials, the degree, and the year of submission.

Candidates should note that leave to supplicate is conditional upon receipt by the Graduate Studies Office of the library copy of their thesis and that candidates may not proceed to take their degree until they have fulfilled the requirement to submit a library copy of the thesis.

(v) ***Abstracts***

The abstract of the thesis should concisely summarize its scope and principal arguments, in about 300 words. It should be printed or typewritten, on one side only, of A4-sized paper. Each copy of the abstract should be headed with the title of the thesis, the name and college of the candidate, the degree for which it is submitted, and the term and year of submission.

One copy of the abstract prepared at the time of the examination should be bound into each of the examiners' copies of the thesis. Subsequently, when the examination is completed, candidates should also arrange for a copy of the abstract to be bound into the library copy of their thesis, and should submit with the library copy a separate, unbound copy of their abstract which may be despatched to ASLIB and published. The copy of the abstract which is earmarked for dispatch to ASLIB should be presented separately in a form suitable for microfilming, i.e. it should be (1) on one side of a single sheet of A4 paper, (2) a typed, single-spaced top copy, a clear photocopy, or a printed copy (i.e. it should not be a carbon or poor photocopy), and (3) headed up with name, college, year and term of submission and the title of the thesis.

It should be noted that some boards have made regulations requiring the submission of more detailed abstracts in addition to the general requirement of an abstract not normally exceeding 300 words.

3. **Conduct of Oral Examinations for the Degrees of M.Litt., M.Sc. by Research, and D.Phil.**

(i) The oral examination shall be held at Oxford in a suitable university or college building, unless the Proctors give special permission for it to be held at some other place. It shall, except in special circumstances, begin not earlier than 9 a.m. nor later than 5 p.m. and may be held in term or vacation. The student or his or her college, other society, or approved institution, may within fourteen days of the date of the Proctors' decision in respect of the granting of consent, appeal in writing to the Chairman of the Educational Policy and Standards Committee (who may nominate another member of the committee, other than one of the Proctors, to adjudicate the appeal).

(ii) The examination may be attended by any member of the University in academic dress. No person who is not a member of the University may attend it except with the consent of both examiners.

(iii) The place and time of the examination shall be fixed by the examiners, who shall be responsible for informing the candidate of the arrangements made. It shall be the duty of candidates to ensure that any letter addressed to them at their college or any other address which they have given is forwarded to them if necessary. The examiners shall allow reasonable time for receiving an acknowledgement from the candidate of their summons.

(iv) Except as provided in clause (v) below, the day shall be fixed by the examiners to suit their convenience. So that candidates may know what arrangements for absence from Oxford they may safely make, the examiners shall inform candidates within a reasonable time of the date fixed.

(v) Candidates may apply to the board concerned for the oral examination to be held not later than a certain date, provided that this date shall not be earlier than one calendar month after the date on which the thesis has been received at the University Offices or after the date on which the examiners have agreed to act, whichever is the later. If the board is satisfied that there are special circumstances justifying this application, it will ask the examiners to make arrangements to enable the oral examination to be held within the period specified.

In such cases the examiners, when invited to act, will be informed that the candidate has asked that the oral examination should be held not later than a certain date, and acceptance of the invitation to examine will be on the understanding that they would seek to meet this request. If is not practicable to meet the student's request, then the board shall decide how to proceed.

(vi) Notice of the examination shall be given in one of the following ways:

1. it may be published in the *University Gazette** not later than the day before it is due to take place;
2. Not later than two days before the examination the examiners may
   (*a*) inform the Graduate Studies Office in writing; and
   (*b*) post a notice in the Examination Schools; and
   (*c*) if the examination is to be held at a place other than the Examination Schools, post a notice also at the place of the examination.

The notice shall state the name of the candidate, the subject of the thesis, the place, day, and hour of the examination, and the names of the examiners.

If an examination is held without the giving of the notice required by this regulation it shall be invalid, unless the Proctors, on receipt of a written application from the examiners, shall determine otherwise. The student or his or her college, other society, or approved institution, may within fourteen days of the date of the Proctors' decision in respect of the granting of consent, appeal in writing to the Chairman of the Educational Policy and Standards Committee (who may nominate another member of the committee, other than one of the Proctors, to adjudicate the appeal).

(vii) If, owing to illness or other urgent and unforeseen cause, an examiner is unable to attend the examination, it shall be postponed to a later date, provided that, if the Proctors are satisfied that postponement would be a serious hardship to the candidate, they may authorize another member of the board concerned to attend the examination as a substitute, but such substitute shall not be required to sign the report. The Proctors shall determine what payment, if any, the substitute examiner shall receive.

(viii) Candidates are strongly recommended to take a copy of their thesis to the examination.

4. Suspension of Graduate Students from the Register

(i) If, for good cause, a student is temporarily unable to carry out his or her research or coursework, the board concerned may grant him or her a request for a temporary suspension of status, for not less than one and not more than three terms at any one time. Applications for suspension of status should be made to the board

* Notice should reach the editor at the Oxford University Press, Great Clarendon Street, not less than six days before publication.

concerned, c/o the Graduate Studies Office, Wellington Square; and should be accompanied by statements of support from a student's supervisor and society. No student may be granted more than six terms' suspension of status in this way by a board.

(ii) A board may for sufficient reason, and after consultation with the student's supervisor and college, temporarily suspend him or her from the Register on its own initiative.

5. **Removal of Graduate Students from the Register**

1. A board which considers that it may be necessary to consider the removal of a student from the Register on academic grounds shall, except in cases requiring immediate action, follow the procedures for counselling and warnings set out in paras. 4–6.

2. A board shall not be required to follow the procedures for the removal of a graduate student from the Register where a student ceases to hold the status of a student for a degree through failure to meet the requirements laid down in the decrees and regulations governing that degree. In particular where a student fails to achieve transfer within the prescribed time his or her status automatically lapses, and his or her name is removed from the Register.

3. A board shall not be required to follow the procedures for counselling and warnings set out below in cases of particular gravity and/or urgency or where it considers, for whatever reason, that immediate action is required, and in such circumstances a board may immediately notify the Educational Policy and Standards Committee as set out at paragraph 6 below and the matter will proceed as set out in that and subsequent paragraphs. In these circumstances, the board should indicate to the Educational Policy and Standards Committee why the procedures for counselling and warnings are not to be followed in that instance.

4.1. Subject to para. 3 above, wherever practicable, the formal procedures for the removal of a student from the Register should be preceded by private and informal counselling involving the student's supervisor and college, with the object of establishing the cause of any problem and advising appropriate remedial action.

4.2. If informal means are not effective in producing the necessary improvement, the student will be invited to a formal interview. Written notice of a formal interview should be given at least seven days before it takes place. Such notice will include an indication of the nature and purpose of the interview and the problem or problems that the interview is intended to address. The student will have the right to put his or her case and to be accompanied by a friend. The formal interview will be conducted by the head of department or Director of Graduate Studies who on conclusion of the interview and if further action is considered necessary will issue either (*a*) a first formal warning, to be confirmed in writing to the student and to his or her supervisor and society, setting out the reason for which it is given, and specifying a period of time for improvement to be made (which period should in no case be less than one month or more than three months); or (*b*) a final warning as set out in 5 below.

4.3. If the student unreasonably fails to attend the formal interview, a formal warning in writing may be issued without interview, and the student shall be required to acknowledge receipt of the formal warning.

5.1. If the first formal warning issued under 4.2 above is not effective in producing the necessary improvement, the head of department or Director of Graduate Studies shall invite the student to a second formal interview. The procedure will be as for the first formal interview. At the conclusion of the interview the head of department or Director of Graduate Studies shall, if further action is required, issue a final warning, which shall be confirmed in writing to the student and to his or her supervisor and society.

5.2. Where a final warning is issued under 4.2 or 5.1 above the warning itself and the written conformation should make it clear that if the necessary improvement is not achieved within the specified period, the board may initiate action for the removal of the student from the Register of Graduate Students.

6. Where a final written warning is issued to a graduate student, a copy of the written warning shall be sent to the Educational Policy and Standards Committee. Where, following a final written warning, the necessary improvement is not achieved within the specified period and further action is indicated, the Educational Policy and Standards Committee shall be informed by the Secretary of the board concerned. A full report of the action taken by the board in relation to the student shall be made to the Proctors who shall decide whether further action should be taken and, if so, whether under the relevant disciplinary procedures of the University or under the board's power to remove a student from the Register of Graduate Students on academic grounds. The Proctors' ruling (which may include a decision that no further action is to be taken) shall be taken without reference to the Educational Policy and Standards Committee, and shall be final.

7.1. Where the Proctors determine that it is appropriate for the matter to be considered under the board's power to initiate action for the removal of a student from the Register of Graduate Students, the board shall seek the approval of the Chairman of the Educational Policy and Standards Committee to undertake any such action. Where such approval is given, the board shall inform the student and the student's college and supervisor, in writing, with a minimum of seven days' notice, of its intention to consider the removal of the student from the Register, set out its reasons and invite comments. In particular the board shall inform the student of his or her right under paragraph 7.3 to present his or her case.

7.2. A board shall delegate the task of hearing the student's case to a panel comprising at least three of its members and shall set out the terms of reference to be followed by the panel. The board shall not appoint any member who has had a previous connection with the student or his or her work.

7.3. The student may be accompanied by a friend and shall have the right to hear and to challenge any evidence presented to the panel. The student may present his or her case in writing or orally, or both, as the student wishes, and the student's society and supervisor shall have the same rights. (All written evidence shall be circulated to the student, the student's supervisor, and the student's college not less than four days before the panel considers the case.) In conducting a hearing, the panel shall ensure that the student has every opportunity to hear and to challenge the case made out by the board for the removal of the student from the Register including any evidence (written or oral) which the panel will consider in reaching a conclusion. Where the student fails to appear without good cause, the panel may proceed in the student's absence.

8. The panel shall then determine its decision as to whether the student's name shall, or shall not, be removed from the Register of Graduate Students. The decision shall be communicated to the student, college, and supervisor. The student shall also be advised in writing of the reasons for the decision and of his or her rights of appeal. The board shall also inform the Educational Policy and Standards Committee of all cases where the board has decided to deprive a student of his or her status.

9.1. A student or his or her society may appeal in writing against the decision of the faculty board within fourteen days of the date of the letter from the board conveying its decision. The appeal shall be addressed to the Educational Policy and Standards Committee (c/o the Secretary, Educational Policy and Standards Committee, University Offices, Wellington Square, Oxford OX1 2JD), which shall appoint a sub-committee to conduct a hearing of the student's appeal.

9.2. The sub-committee shall include a minimum of three members of the Educational Policy and Standards Committee, which shall appoint one of the chosen members as chairman, with the power to cast an additional vote if necessary. The sub-committee may seek such legal advice as it believes to be necessary for the proper conduct of its duties, and shall have power to require any members of the University to assist it in the hearing.

9.3. The sub-committee shall give the board, the student, the student's college, and the student's supervisor, not less than seven days' notice in writing, of the date and time of the hearing, and shall give them the opportunity to make representations to the sub-committee orally and/or in writing. The student may be accompanied by a friend and shall have the right to hear and to challenge any evidence (written or oral) presented to the sub-committee; the student may present his or her case in writing, or orally, or both, as the student wishes: the board, the student's college, and the student's supervisor shall have the same rights. (All written evidence shall be circulated to the faculty board, the student, the student's supervisor, and the student's college not less than four days before the sub-committee considers the case.)

9.4. At the conclusion of a hearing, the sub-committee shall have power to:

(i) confirm the board's decision to remove the student's name from the Register of Graduate Students:

(ii) uphold the student's appeal and direct that the student's name shall remain on the Register of Graduate Students;

(iii) impose such lesser penalty or requirement in place of the removal of the student's name from the Register of Graduate Students as it deems appropriate.

9.5. In reaching its decision, the sub-committee shall have regard to:

(*a*) whether the board correctly followed the required procedures, and, in the case of procedural irregularity or irregularities, whether any irregularity or irregularities were such as to have materially prejudiced the board's inquiry;

(*b*) whether the board's decision could reasonably have been reached on the evidence before it;

(*c*) any evidence presented to the sub-committee which was not available to the board's panel;

(*d*) any mitigating circumstances offered by or on behalf of the student;

(*e*) any other factors which in the opinion of the sub-committee are relevant to a fair consideration of the student's appeal.

9.6. The sub-committee shall communicate its decision to the student, to the student's society and supervisor, and to the board, in writing, within two months of the conclusion of any hearing. The decision of the sub-committee will be final, subject only to a complaint to the Proctors.

6. **Reinstatement of Graduate Students to the Register**

A student who has lapsed from the Register or has withdrawn or whose name has been removed from the Register by the board concerned may apply for reinstatement to his or her former status on the Register. Such applications shall be addressed by the student to the board concerned, and shall be accompanied by written statements commenting on the application from the candidate's college and former supervisor. The board shall reach a decision on such applications and shall determine the date from which any reinstatement granted under these provisions shall be effective. No reinstatement may be granted under these provisions if the student's name has been on the Register of students of the relevant status for the maximum number of terms allowed under the decree governing that status.

7. **Memorandum of Guidance for Supervisors and Research Students**

ACADEMIC RESPONSIBILITIES

Responsibilities of the supervisor

1. In considering an invitation to supervise a research student, the supervisor must recognise and accept the responsibilities both to the student and to the relevant board or committee implicit in the supervisory relationship.

2. Where practicable, the supervisor should assign the student some directed reading before arrival. This might be of a general background nature so as to put the student in a position to discuss the topic with the supervisor soon after arrival, or it might form the start of a survey of current literature. The supervisor is required to meet the new student not later than the second week of Full Term.

3. The supervisor is responsible for giving early advice about the nature of research and the standard expected, and about the planning of the research programme. The supervisor should ensure that, where the student's research forms part of a funded research programme, sufficient financial support will be available for the duration of the student's period of study; if there is any doubt, he or she should agree with the student an alternative fallback project at an early stage. The supervisor is also responsible for advising the student about literature and sources, attendance at classes, and requisite techniques (including helping to arrange instruction where necessary). The supervisor should discuss with the student the lecture list for his or her subject and related lecture lists. The supervisor should identify with the student any subject-specific skills necessary for the proposed research.

4. Where during his or her first year of research a student wishes, in addition to contact with his or her supervisor(s), to have limited consultation with one or two other academics the supervisor should try to identify (in conjunction with the Director of Graduate Studies for the faculty, sub-faculty or department) such colleagues and to arrange for an approach to them by the student.

5. Where a supervisor operates as a co-supervisor or as a part of a supervisory team, it is important to clarify the responsibilities of each supervisor and to co-ordinate advice and guidance.

6. Where the thesis is likely to involve statistical analysis or tabulation of numerical results, the supervisor should arrange for the student to obtain advice, at an early stage, about the design of any experiment or the collection and storage of data, and about its subsequent analysis.

7. The supervisor should ensure that the student works within a planned framework which marks out the stages which the student should be expected to have completed at various points in his or her period of study. The nature of the framework will of course vary widely from subject to subject, but in all subjects the formulation of the topic, planning and management of time should begin at an early stage. Particular attention should be given to the selection and refinement of the research topic, which in the case of the D.Phil. should be one which a diligent student may reasonably be expected to complete within three (or at most four) years of full-time study.

8. The supervisor should meet with the student regularly. Supervisor and student should agree a formal schedule of meetings on a termly or annual basis. The supervisor should also be accessible to the student at other appropriate times when advice is needed. The supervisor should also request written work as appropriate and in accordance with the plan discussed with the student. Such work should be returned with constructive criticism and in reasonable time.

9. The supervisor should tell the student from time to time how well, in the supervisor's opinion, work is getting on, and try to ensure that the student feels properly directed and able to communicate with the supervisor. It is essential that

when problems arise, corrective action is clearly identified and full guidance and assistance are given to the student.

10. The supervisor is required to report to the board on the student's work three times a year, once at the end of each term. Each report should state the nature and extent of recent contact with the student, and, if there has been none, state why this is so. The report should also make clear whether the student is making satisfactory progress, bearing in mind that a D.Phil. thesis should normally be completed within three (or at least four) years of full-time research. Any student who has not satisfied his or her supervisor on at least one occasion in an academic year that he or she is making progress will be liable to have his or her name removed from the register.

11. The supervisor should aim to ensure that by the end of the first year the topic or goal of the student's research is clearly defined, that the student has the necessary background knowledge, and that the required resources are available. The supervisor must have ascertained by then that the student can write a coherent account of his or her work in good English.

12. The supervisor should try to ensure that unnecessary delays do not occur. These have been known to arise, for example, for reasons such as:

(*a*) insufficient effort at the outset in choosing and formulating the research topic;
(*b*) a slow start because of the time taken to adjust to research work;
(*c*) distractions from the main line of inquiry;
(*d*) superfluous attempts to tie up every loose end; and, mainly in the sciences,
(*e*) inadequate and delayed planning and assembly of apparatus and equipment;
(*f*) insufficient collection or recording of data at an early stage, so that work has to be repeated in the later stages.

13. The supervisor should arrange for students to have the opportunity to discuss their research with other staff and students in the subject area (see also (4) above) and to communicate to others in the wider academic community, both orally and in writing, his or her research findings.

14. Where a student undertakes research as part of a team or group the supervisor should ensure that this is in full awareness of the way in which the student's own contribution fits into the work of the remainder of the group.

15. The supervisor should not be absent on leave unless he or she has ensured that appropriate temporary supervision has been arranged for the student.

Responsibilities of the student

1. The student must accept his or her obligation to act as a responsible member of the University's academic community.

2. The student should take ultimate responsibility for his or her research programme and endeavour to develop an appropriate working pattern, including an agreed and professional relationship with the supervisor(s). The student should discuss with the supervisor the type of guidance and comment which he or she finds most helpful, and agree a schedule of meetings.

3. He or she should make appropriate use of the teaching and learning facilities available within the University.

4. It is the student's responsibility to seek out and follow the regulations relevant to his or her course, including faculty/departmental handbooks/notes of guidance, and to seek clarification from supervisors and elsewhere if this is necessary.

5. The student should not hesitate to take the initiative in raising problems or difficulties, however elementary they may seem. He or she should ensure that any problems regarding the project are drawn to the attention of the supervisor so that appropriate guidance may be offered.

6. The student should seek to maintain progress in accordance with the plan of work agreed with the supervisor, including in particular the presentation of the required written material in sufficient time for comment and discussion before proceeding to the next stage. As groundwork for the thesis, the student should as soon as possible write rough drafts of possible chapters. Students in the sciences should keep a systematic record of all that has been attempted and accomplished. Both the student and the supervisor will want to keep a record of all formal, scheduled meetings. They may well want to agree a record of what has been discussed and decided.

7. The student should recognise that a supervisor may have many competing demands on his or her time. The student should hand in work in good time to the supervisor and give adequate notice of unscheduled meetings. The need for adequate notice also applies to requests for references from the supervisor.

8. The student should be aware that the provision of constructive criticism is central to a satisfactory supervisory relationship, and should always seek a full assessment of the strengths and weaknesses of his or her work.

9. If the student feels that there are good enough grounds for contemplating a change of supervision arrangements, this should first be discussed with the supervisor or, if this seems difficult, with the appropriate head of department, director of graduate studies or their deputies, or the college adviser.

10. Where problems arise, it is essential that a student gives full weight to any guidance and corrective action proposed by the supervisor.

11. The student should provide regular reports on his or her progress to the board in accordance with any requirements of the Educational Policy and Standards Committee. The student must satisfy the supervisor on his or her progress at least once a year and should inform the supervisor at once of any circumstances that might require his or her mode of study to be modified or his or her registration as a graduate student to be extended, suspended or withdrawn.

12. The student should ensure that the standard of his or her English is sufficient for the presentation of a thesis. Students whose first language is not English should take advice on this.

13. The student should make full use of the facilities for career guidance and development, and should consult their supervisor for advice and encouragement where appropriate.

14. The student should ensure that he or she allows adequate time for writing up the thesis, taking the advice of the supervisor. Particular attention should be paid to final proof-reading.

15. It is the student's responsibility to decide when he or she wishes to submit the thesis for examination, after taking due account of the supervisor's opinion, though this is only advisory. It is in the student's interests to ensure that the final version has been made available to the supervisor in good time before the intended date of submission.

Responsibilities of faculties and/or departments

1. Faculties and/or departments should provide information about:
(i) any induction provided on a departmental, faculty or University basis;
(ii) welfare arrangements within the University, e.g. the Counselling Service, Student Hardship and Access funds, the provisions for support offered by the Proctors and the Assessor;
(iii) any general transferable skills from which the student is likely to profit

during the course of his or her research, and the available provision at departmental, faculty and university level.

2. Faculties and/or departments should ensure that there is appropriate monitoring of a student's work and progress and that reports are submitted on a termly basis in accordance with the University's requirements.

3. Faculties and/or departments should endeavour to provide opportunities for a student to:
   (i) defend his or her findings to appropriate research seminars and respond to potentially critical questioning;
   (ii) at an appropriate stage to present his or her findings to national, and if appropriate, international conferences.

4. *Faculties and/or departments should*
   (i) help the student to present work in a clear and professional manner;
   (ii) help the student to develop his or her communication skills, especially for different audiences;
   (iii) provide some guidance in oral examination techniques.

Safety and Health

Supervisors of all students, whether in the arts or the sciences, should consider carefully the safety implications of their students' research. Those supervising students (particularly those in the sciences) are responsible for all aspects of safety under their control, and in particular for the safe conduct of all experiments carried out in the course of their students' research. In the event of an accident, inadequate supervision may render the supervisor liable to prosecution. Supervisors should also ensure that their students are made aware that in the event of injury to other persons as a result of their negligence, the student could be subject to civil claims for damages. Advice on the legal responsibilities for safety may be obtained from the University Safety Officer. For their part, *students* must carry out research with proper regard to good health and safety practices. Supervisors and students should be aware of the need for adequate health insurance and health precautions when travelling abroad. In case of doubt, reference should be made to the University Medical Officer.

NOTES

SPECIAL REGULATIONS OF DIVISIONAL AND FACULTY BOARDS CONCERNING THE STATUS OF PROBATIONER RESEARCH STUDENT AND THE DEGREES OF M.LITT., M.SC. BY RESEARCH, AND D.PHIL.

A. HUMANITIES DIVISION

1. COMMITTEE FOR COMPARATIVE PHILOLOGY AND GENERAL LINGUISTICS

1. *Probationer Research Students*

Candidates for admission will normally be expected to have a first or upper second class degree. They will be required to submit evidence (in the form of essays written in English) of their competence in the broad subject of their intended research and should have a basic knowledge of the language(s) in which the main secondary literature is written.

2. *M.Litt. status*

(i) Candidates for admission must submit a piece of written work, normally of about 5,000 words, in the broad field of their proposed thesis. From time to time the committee may make other requirements of candidates in order to ascertain their ability to engage in research.

(ii) Probationer Research Students applying for transfer to M.Litt. status must inform the committee in writing of their intention eleven days before the beginning of the Trinity Term of their first year, and should at the same time indicate the subject of their proposed thesis and of the written work which they will submit. The written work and other statements required must be submitted by the Wednesday of the Second Week of that Trinity Term. In special circumstances (for example, those who entered Probationer Research Student status after taking an M.St.), it will be possible to follow this procedure one term later.

(iii) M.Phil. students applying for admission to M.Litt. status after taking the M.Phil. should do so by the Trinity Term of their second year at the latest, in accordance with the procedure in (ii) above. Acceptance of applications will in all cases be conditional upon a satisfactory result in the M.Phil. examination.

3. *D.Phil. status*

(i) Candidates for admission must submit a piece of written work, normally of about 5,000 words, in the broad field of their proposed thesis.

(ii) Probationer Research Students applying for transfer to D.Phil. status must inform the committee in writing of their intentions eleven days before the beginning of the Trinity Term of their first year, and should at the same time indicate the subject of their proposed thesis and of the written work which they will submit. The written work and other statements required must be submitted by the Wednesday of the Second Week of that Trinity Term. In special circumstances (for example, those who transferred to Probationer Research Student status from M.St. status), it will be possible to follow this procedure one term later.

(iii) M.Phil. students applying for admission to D.Phil. status after taking the M.Phil. should do so by the Trinity Term of their second year at the latest, in accordance with the procedure in (ii) above. Acceptance of applications will in all cases be conditional upon a satisfactory result in the M.Phil. examination.

4. *Confirmation of D.Phil. status*

(i) Candidates for confirmation of D.Phil. status should submit a detailed plan, and a draft chapter, of their proposed thesis.

(ii) The application shall be examined by an assessor appointed by the committee, not normally the candidate's supervisor, who shall interview the candidate and make a recommendation to the committee. The assessor shall be entitled, if he or she so wishes, to consult with another person (who need not be a member of the University) and who may, but need not, take part in the interview.

5. *Theses*

Theses submitted for the Degree of M.Litt. in Comparative Philology and General Linguistics should not exceed 50,000 words, exclusive of bibliographical references, but including notes, glossary, appendices, etc. unless the candidate has, with the support of his or her supervisor, secured the leave of the committee to exceed this limit.

Theses submitted for the Degree of D.Phil. in Comparative Philology and General Linguistics should not exceed 100,000 words, exclusive of bibliographical references, but including notes, glossary, appendices, etc., unless the candidate has, with the support of his or her supervisor, secured the leave of the committee to exceed this limit.

2. BOARD OF THE FACULTY OF CLASSICS

1. *Admission as Probationer Research Student*

Candidates for admission under this section are required to submit with their application two pieces of written work, each of approximately 2,000 words in length and preferably typed. These must be in English, unless special permission has been given.

Candidates may be required to attend an interview, and will be required to do so in all cases where the faculty board judges this to be practicable.

2. *Admission to M.Litt. status*

Applications from Probationer Research Students for transfer to the status of Student for the Degree of Master of Letters will not normally be considered before the beginning of the candidate's third term as a Probationer Research Student. Transfer will normally take place in the third or fourth term.

The written work to be submitted should be a single essay, preferably typed, on a subject relevant to the candidate's proposed thesis. For candidates in *Languages and Literature* the essay should not be more than 10,000 words in length; for candidates in *Ancient History* it should not be more than 5,000 words in length.

3. *Admission to D.Phil. status*

Applications from Probationer Research Students for transfer to the status of Student for the Degree of Doctor of Philosophy will not normally be considered before the beginning of the candidate's third term as a Probationer Research Student. The board regards the end of the third, or the beginning of the fourth, term as the normal time for this application to be made.

Students who are completing a relevant M.St. course, including those holding the status of Probationer Research Student, and who wish to apply for D.Phil. status on completion of that course, should submit their application, (together with an outline of their proposed research and letter of recommendation from their supervisor) using the appropriate form, by no later than the end of the fifth week of the second term of the M.St. course.

The written work to be submitted should be a single essay, preferably typed, on a subject relevant to the candidate's proposed thesis.

For candidates in *Languages and Literature* the essay should not be more than 10,000 words in length; for candidates in *Ancient History* it should not be more than 5,000 words in length.

4. *Confirmation of D.Phil. status*

Applications from Students for the Degree of Doctor of Philosophy for confirmation of status should be accompanied by a reasoned statement of the nature of the proposed thesis. Candidates in *Ancient History* are required to submit in addition a single essay, preferably typed, of about 5,000 to 10,000 words in length, on a subject relevant to the thesis; candidates in Languages and Literature should be required to submit an essay, of approximately 5,000 words in length. Candidates may also be required to attend an interview.

The board regards the end of the sixth, or the beginning of the seventh, term from the candidate's admission as a Probationer Research Student as the normal time for this application to be made.

5. *Theses*

All candidates when they submit their theses must state the approximate number of words therein both (*a*) including citations and, if they have been granted permission to count citations separately, (*b*) excluding citations. Theses exceeding the limit are liable to be returned unexamined for reduction to the proper length. Candidates who have submitted in their final term may be allowed a maximum period of two terms to effect the necessary reduction.

Theses submitted for the Degree of M.Litt. in *Ancient History and Archaeology* should not exceed 50,000 words, and those submitted for the Degree of D.Phil. should not exceed 100,000 words, excluding the bibliography, any text that is being edited or annotated, and any descriptive catalogue, but including footnotes and appendices. Leave to exceed these limits will only be given in exceptional cases, and upon the presentation of a detailed explanation by the candidate, together with a statement of the excess length required and the written support of the supervisor. Such applications should be made immediately it becomes clear that authorization to exceed the limit will be required, and in any case not later than the Friday of the fifth week of the term before that in which application is made for appointment of examiners. Every candidate submitting a thesis must state the number of words therein.

Theses submitted for the Degree of M.Litt. in *Classical Languages and Literature* should not exceed 60,000 words, and those submitted for the Degree of D.Phil. should not exceed 100,000 words, excluding the length of text being commented on but including citations. Leave to exceed this limit will only be given in exceptional cases and upon the presentation of a detailed explanation by the candidate, together with a statement of the excess length required and the written support of the supervisor, in advance of submission.

Candidates submitting archaeological theses incorporating photographs are required to present original photographs in one copy of the thesis only, provided that the copies in the other two are adequately reproduced.

The copy of the thesis containing the original photographs should be the one deposited in the Bodleian Library.

6. *Written Examination for the D.Phil.*

The board recommends that, when a written examination is held, two papers be set, three hours being allowed for each.

Questions should be set testing candidates' knowledge of matters germane to, but not specifically included in, their treatment of the subject of their thesis, and command of the methods appropriate to the handling of them. Where submitted work is professedly based upon evidence, literary, material, or monumental, candidates should be required in the written examination to satisfy the examiners that they have adequately studied the original sources of such evidence.

The examiners are requested to include in their report to the board a statement of their judgement upon the qualifications shown in these regards by candidates.

3. BOARD OF THE FACULTY OF ENGLISH LANGUAGE AND LITERATURE

General

Candidates for admission to D.Phil. and M.Litt. status, must have been interviewed by one of the persons appointed by the board for this purpose, unless the board determines otherwise.

1. *Transfer to M.Litt. and D.Phil. status*

Research students are normally registered in the first instance for the Degree of Master of Studies in English, and follow the requirements laid down for that degree. Transfer to M.Litt. or D.Phil. status normally takes place at the end of the first year and, in addition to meeting the requirements set out below, is dependent on successful completion of the M.St. course. The board may however permit candidates who have already obtained an equivalent qualification to register as Probationer Research Students for the first year, following such courses as the Board may require. Candidates wishing to transfer to D.Phil. status after completing the M.St. in English will be expected to have taken courses in bibliography, palaeography and theories of text as appropriate to their period of specialization. Those who have not may, in certain circumstances, be allowed to transfer provisionally, on condition of taking those courses in the subsequent year.

2. *Admission to M.Litt. status*

Candidates must give notice of intention to apply for transfer in writing to the Graduate Studies Office by the Friday of the third week of the Trinity Term before they seek entry to M.Litt. status, giving the title of the proposed thesis. By Monday of the seventh week they should submit an application form together with two copies of a detailed outline (not more than 1,000 words) of the proposed subject and of the manner in which it will be treated, including a provisional list of chapters and their proposed coverage; students not taking the M.St. should also submit a piece of written work on the topic of their proposed thesis (of about 10,000 words). The material shall be sent to two assessors who will be asked to report to the Graduate Studies Committee for its meeting in July.

3. *Admission to D.Phil. status*

Candidates must give notice of intention to apply for transfer in writing to the Graduate Studies Office by the Friday of the third week of the Trinity Term before they seek entry to D.Phil. status, giving the title of the proposed thesis. By Monday of the seventh week they should submit an application form together with two copies of a detailed outline (not more than 1,000 words) of the proposed subject and of the manner in which it will be treated, including a provisional list of chapters and their proposed coverage; students not taking the M.St. should also submit a piece of written work on the topic of their proposed thesis (of about 10,000 words). The material shall be sent to two assessors who will be asked to report to the Graduate Studies Committee for its meeting in July.

Any candidate whose application for transfer to M.Litt. or D.Phil. status is refused may reapply on one (only) further occasion.

4. *Admission to D.Phil. status after successful completion of the M.Phil.*

Candidates must give notice of intention to apply for transfer in writing to the Graduate Studies Office by the Friday of the third week of the Trinity Term before they seek entry to D.Phil. status, giving the title of the proposed thesis. By Monday of the seventh week they should submit an application form together with two copies of a detailed outline (not more than 1,000 words) of the proposed subject and of the manner in which it will be treated, including a provisional list of chapters and their proposed coverage. Applicants who have not submitted a dissertation as part of the final-year work for the M.Phil. should also provide a piece of research of not less than 10,000 words. The material shall be sent to two assessors who will be asked to report to the Graduate Studies Committee for its meeting in July. The Graduate Studies Committee may direct the candidate to attend specified classes organized for M.St. Students and to complete the test(s) associated with those classes.

5. *Theses*

Theses submitted to the Board of the Faculty of English Language and Literature for the Degree of M.Litt. should normally be around 40,000 words in length and should in no case exceed 50,000 words, exclusive of the bibliography and of any text that is being edited but including notes, glossary, appendices, etc. Theses submitted for the Degree of D.Phil. should normally be around 80,000 words in length and should in no case exceed 100,000 words, exclusive of the bibliography and of any text being edited, but including notes, glossary, appendices, etc. Leave to exceed these limits will be given only in exceptional cases (e.g. when the subject of the thesis requires extensive quotation from unpublished or inaccessible material, or where substantial and supplementary bibliographical or biographical listings are essential or helpful for an understanding of the arguments of the thesis) and on the recommendation of the supervisor. Applications to exceed the limit of 50,000 words for the M.Litt. or 100,000 words for the D.Phil. must be made in writing to the board's Graduate Studies Committee in advance of the application for appointment of examiners. Each application should include a detailed explanation, a statement of the excess length requested, and a covering letter from the supervisor.

6. *Written Examination for the D.Phil.*

The board recommends that when a written examination is held, it should consist of not more than two papers for each of which three hours should be allowed.

Questions should be set testing candidates' knowledge of matters germane to, or arising out of, their treatment of the subject of their thesis, and command of the methods appropriate to the handling of them. Candidates should be required in the written examination to satisfy the examiners that they have adequately studied the original sources of the evidence upon which the submitted work is based.

The examiners should include in their report to the board a statement of the judgement upon the qualifications shown in these regards by candidates.

4. BOARD OF THE FACULTY OF MEDIEVAL AND MODERN LANGUAGES

1. *Application for admission as a Probationer Research Student*

General

Applicants from the United Kingdom for admission as Probationer Research Students will normally be expected to attend for interview; other applicants required for interview will be notified as appropriate. The interviews will be conducted by or on behalf of a member of the board or its Graduate Studies Committee.

1. *Transfer to M.Litt. and D.Phil. status*

Unless they have successfully completed the M.Phil. in European Literature, research students are normally registered in the first instance for the degree of Master of

Studies in European Literature, and follow the requirements laid down for that degree. Transfer to M.Litt. or D.Phil. status normally takes place at the end of the first year and is dependent on successful completion of the M.St. course though this is in itself not a sufficient condition for transfer.

The board may however (i) permit candidates to register in the first instance for another degree of M.St. or for the degree of M.Phil., or (ii) permit those who have already obtained an equivalent qualification to the degree of M.St. in European Literature to register as Probationer Research Students for the first year, following such courses as the board may require.

2. *Admission to M.Litt. status*

Candidates must give notice of intention to apply for transfer in writing to the Modern Languages Graduate Office, 37 Wellington Square, Oxford, by the end of the fourth week of the third term before they seek entry to M.Litt. status, giving the title of the proposed thesis. By Friday of the eighth week they shall submit an application form together with (i) three copies of a statement (not more than 500 words) of the title of the proposed thesis and of the manner in which the subject will be treated, and of the way in which the proposed treatment relates to existing work relevant to the chosen topic, the statement to include a provisional scheme of the contents of the thesis, and (ii) two typed copies of a piece of written work normally not more than about 10,000 words long (which will usually be the same as the dissertation submitted for the degree of M.St. in European Literature). The material shall be sent to two assessors, neither of whom shall normally be the candidate's supervisor and who, in the case of students for the M.St. in European Literature, shall normally be acting as assessors in that examination also. The assessors shall examine the candidate orally (if appropriate in the course of the examination for that degree).

The assessors will be asked to report to the Graduate Studies Committee for its meeting in July.

3. *Admission to D.Phil. status*

Candidates must give notice of intention to apply for transfer in writing to the Modern Languages Graduate Office, 37 Wellington Square, Oxford, by the end of the fourth week of the third term before they seek entry to D.Phil. status, giving the title of the proposed thesis. By Friday of the eighth week they shall submit an application form together with (i) three copies of a statement (not more than 500 words) of the title of the proposed thesis and of the manner in which the subject will be treated, and of the way in which the proposed treatment relates to existing work relevant to the chosen topic, the statement to include a provisional scheme of the contents of the chosen topic, and (ii) two typed copies of a piece of written work normally not more than about 10,000 words long (which will usually be the same as the dissertation submitted for the degree of M.St. in European Literature).

No application for admission within the terms of §3 of the decree for the Degree of Doctor of Philosophy will normally be considered by the Graduate Studies Committee of the board unless the applicant has previously been interviewed by a member of the Faculty invited to act in this capacity by the committee. The application form must be signed by the person who interviews the candidate.

The material shall be sent to two assessors, neither of whom shall normally be the candidate's supervisor and who, in the case of students for the M.St. in European Literature, shall normally be acting as assessors in that examination also. The assessors shall examine the candidate orally (if appropriate in the course of the examination for that degree).

The assessors will be asked to report to the Graduate Studies Committee for its meeting in July.

The requirements for the submission of a piece of written work at (ii) above and for action by assessors will not apply in the case of candidates who have been given leave to supplicate for the degree of M.Phil. or of M.Litt. whose subject of thesis for that degree is in the broad field of research proposed for the D.Phil.

Any candidate whose application for transfer to M.Litt. or D. Phil. Status is refused may reapply on one (only) further occasion.

4. The board will award a Certificate of Graduate Attainment to a Probationer Research Student whose application for transfer to the status of student for the degree of D.Phil. or M.Litt. is approved by the committee. In exceptional circumstances the committee may recommend the award of the certificate to other Probationer Research Students who are strongly supported by their supervisor.

2. *Application for confirmation of status as a student for the Degree of Doctor of Philosophy*

(*a*) Candidates other than those who have already been given leave to supplicate for the Degree of M.Phil.

(i) Each applicant for confirmation of D.Phil. status must submit two copies of a piece of written work of 15,000 words in length (except where text is accompanied by graphs or statistical material), being a draft of a chapter or chapters of the thesis (excluding the introductory or concluding chapters and any section submitted for the first transfer examination). The student shall show on a provisional list of the contents of the thesis the place he or she plans for the draft chapter(s). This piece of work must be substantially different from that submitted on application for admission to D.Phil. status. Each applicant must also submit, at the time of application, three copies of a statement (of not more than 1,000 words) of the title of the proposed thesis and of the manner in which the subject will be treated, and of work achieved on other parts of the thesis and work remaining to be done.

(ii) Unless permission is given otherwise by the committee, the application for confirmation of D.Phil. status shall be submitted to the Modern Languages Graduate Office, 37 Wellington Square, Oxford, not later than the Friday of the fourth week of the applicant's ninth term from admission to graduate status, and copies of the written work by not later than 30 June. The written work shall be read by two assessors appointed by the Graduate Studies Committee of the board. Neither of the assessors shall normally be the candidate's supervisor. The assessors shall examine the candidate orally.

(iii) The assessors shall report to the committee in writing whether they recommend that the candidate's status as a D.Phil. student should be confirmed. They shall also make a written report, in support of their recommendation, covering the following points: whether the subject of the thesis and the manner of its treatment proposed by the candidate are acceptable; and whether the thesis can reasonably be completed in three or at most four years of full-time study from the date of the candidate's admission as a research student, (Note: students reading for the M.St. in European Literature are considered to be taught-course students). On receipt of the report, the committee shall decide whether to approve the candidate's application. If it reaches the conclusion that the candidate's subject for a thesis is unsatisfactory and/or that the candidate is unlikely to be able to complete the thesis proposed, it may permit resubmission by a date which the committee shall specify. If, after a second application, the committee continues to be unable to give approval, it will *either* admit the candidate to M.Litt. status *or* take appropriate action under the regulations made by the Educational Policy and Standards Committee for the removal of a student from the Register.

(*b*) Candidates who have already been given leave to supplicate for the degree of M.Phil. (Candidates who propose a topic for their D.Phil. which is different from their M.Phil. topic shall be subject to the regulations under (*a*) above).

Applicants must submit to the Modern Languages Graduate Office, 37 Wellington Square, Oxford with their applications three copies of a statement (of not more than 1,000 words) of the title of the proposed thesis and of the manner in which the subject will be treated, and of the way in which the proposed treatment relates to existing work relevant to the chosen topic, and of work achieved on other parts of the thesis and work remaining to be done. The statement should include a provisional scheme of the contents of the thesis, which identifies the place of the M.Phil. thesis in the scheme. Confirmation will be subject to the Graduate Studies Committee of the board being satisfied, on the evidence of the statement and of the examiners of the M.Phil., that the student is capable of carrying out advanced research; that the M.Phil. thesis is in the field of research proposed for the D.Phil.; that the subject can be profitably pursued under the superintendence of the board; and that the thesis can reasonably be expected to be completed in three or at the most four years of full-time study from the date of the candidate's admission as an M.Phil. student. If the committee is not satisfied, it may permit one further application by a date which it shall specify.

7. *Theses*

Theses submitted for the Degree of M.Litt. should not exceed 50,000 words and those submitted for the Degree of D.Phil. should not exceed 80,000 words, excluding the bibliography and any text that is being edited but including notes, glossary, appendices, etc. Leave to exceed these limits will be given only in exceptional cases. Any application for permission to exceed the limit should be submitted with a detailed explanation and statement of the amount of excess length requested, and with a covering letter from the supervisor. Application must be made immediately it seems clear that authorization to exceed the limit will be sought and normally not later than six months before the intended date of submission of the thesis.

Every candidate who is editing a text must also state the length of the text being edited.

In addition to the arrangements for an abstract of the thesis set out in the Educational Policy and Standards Committee's regulations above, three printed or typewritten copies of a fuller abstract of the thesis (which shall not normally exceed 1,500 words for the M.Litt. and 2,500 words for the D.Phil.) prepared by the student is required. A copy of the fuller abstract must be bound into the copy of the thesis which, if the application for leave to supplicate for the degree is successful, will be deposited in the Bodleian Library. The fuller abstract may be bound into the two examiners' copies of the thesis if the candidate so desires.

5. BOARD OF THE FACULTY OF MODERN HISTORY

1. *Admission/First year course work*

In Modern History (which includes medieval history, economic and social history, history of science, and history of art) graduate students are initially admitted *either* as candidates for a taught course *or* as Probationer Research Students. The requirements for all taught courses are laid out in detail under their individual regulations above.

Candidates wishing to conduct research in the field of the *History of Art* may be required by the Faculty Board's Graduate Studies Committee to pass a Qualifying Examination before being admitted to PRS, M.Litt., or D.Phil. status, in which case the course of study for the Examination will be that set for the M.St. in the History of Art and Visual Culture, and will be examined by the examiners for that M.St. at the end of each Trinity Term.

Probationer Research Students: Unless they have elected to enter for examination in the M.St. in Historical Research or the M.St. in Historical Research (Medieval History), or have been otherwise dispensed, Probationer Research Students are required to undertake the work laid down below. Each candidate must normally:

(*a*) attend such lectures, seminars, and classes as his or her supervisor shall determine; and

(*b*) present one seminar paper during the course. Such paper shall normally be assessed by two assessors. Such assessors should not include the candidate's supervisor. The work done for the seminar paper may form the basis of the essay required under (2) below.

(i) Applications for admission/transfer to M.Litt. or D.Phil. status shall be accompanied (or, in the case of candidates for the M.St. in Historical Research and the M.St. in Historical Research (Medieval History), followed at the appropriate date) by:

(1) two copies of a brief statement, limited to 500 words, of the subject of the thesis and the manner in which the candidate proposes to treat it;

(2) two copies of a piece of written work, normally 3,000–5,000 words long (up to 10,000 words in the case of candidates for the M.St. in Historical Research, or up to 15,000 words in the case of candidates for the M.St. in Historical Research (Medieval History)), being *either* (*a*) a section of the proposed thesis, *or* (*b*) an essay on a relevant topic, *or* (except in the case of candidates for the M.St. in Historical Research and the M.St. in Historical Research (Medieval History)) (*c*) an augmented version of the statement required under (1) above; candidates should note that if they adopt alternative (*c*) they must also submit the 500-word statement required by decree;

(3) two copies of a confidential report from the supervisor, which should be sent by the supervisor directly to the Graduate Studies Office.

Successful completion of *either* the work prescribed above *or* of the M.St. in Historical Research *or* the M.St. in Historical Research (Medieval History) is not in itself sufficient qualification for students to advance to M.Litt. or D.Phil. status.

(ii) Candidates for the M.St. in Historical Research *or* the M.St. in Historical Research (Medieval History) who were unsuccessful in the examination, and whose application for transfer to M.Litt. or D.Phil. status was also unsuccessful, will be deemed to have transferred from PRS to M.St. status. They will be permitted to re-enter the M.St. examination and/or to make a further application for transfer on one occasion only.

2. *Readmission after completion of a taught course*

(i) Students who are entered as candidates for the examination in the M.St. in Modern History, M.St. in English Local History, M.Sc. in Economic and Social History, M.Sc. in History of Science: Instruments, Museums, Science, Technology, M.St. in Byzantine Studies, or another relevant Master's course may apply for admission to PRS/M.Litt./D.Phil. status in the term in which they enter the examination for the M.St. in Modern History, M.St. in English Local History, M.Sc. Economic and Social History, or M.St. in Byzantine Studies, etc., normally in their first Hilary Term. Re-admission may be made conditional on such requirements as the Graduate Studies Committee may impose; and admission will normally be to dispensed PRS status. Successful completion of their current degree is not in itself sufficient qualification for students to be re-admitted for a research degree.

(ii) Candidates who have already been given leave to a supplicate for the Degree of M.Phil. in Economic and Social History, or M.Phil. in Byzantine Studies, or M.Phil. in Modern European History, or who are entered as candidates for the examination in these degrees, may apply, usually in their second Hilary Term, for admission to D.Phil. status by submitting two copies of a brief statement, limited to 2,000 words, of the subject of the thesis, the manner in which the candidate proposes to treat it, and the relationship of the M.Phil. dissertation to the proposed D.Phil. thesis. Two copies of a confidential report from the supervisor should be sent directly to the Graduate Studies Office. Successful completion of their current M.Phil. is not in itself sufficient qualification for students to be readmitted for a research degree.

3. *Transfer to M.Litt. or D.Phil. status*

(i) The application shall normally be presented to the Graduate Studies Office not later than Monday of Second Week in the candidate's third term, with statements of support from the candidate's society and supervisor. Dispensed Probationer Research Students will be expected to submit their application not later than Monday of Second Week in their second term. In exceptional cases the Graduate Studies Committee may permit the candidate to postpone submission by up to one term: candidates seeking such postponement should apply to the Director of Graduate Studies well in advance.

(ii) Two copies of a confidential report from the supervisor should be sent by the supervisor directly to the Graduate Studies Office. The Graduate Studies Office shall send both copies of the written work and the confidential report to the candidate's interviewer who will pass on one copy to the second assessor nominated as below.

(iii) The interviewer shall then, together with a second assessor appointed in conjunction with the Director of Graduate Studies, examine the candidate orally. The interviewer shall be entitled after consultation with the Director of Graduate Studies to appoint a deputy to act instead. When the interviewer is also the supervisor, the Director of Graduate Studies shall act as if he or she were the interviewer and shall have power to appoint a deputy and the second assessor.

For candidates for the M.St. in Historical Research and for the M.St. in Historical Research (Medieval History) the viva voce examination will incorporate the Transfer of Status interview. In these cases interviewers and second assessors are appointed by the Examiners.

(iv) The assessors shall report to the Graduate Studies Committee in writing whether the candidate's subject is satisfactory for the degree in question and whether he or she is competent to tackle it.* If they think this is not the case, they may recommend re-submission after a set period of further probation (within the statutory limit of six terms). If they disagree, the Graduate Studies Committee shall decide what should be done. It will be open to candidates to appeal to the Faculty Board against an unfavourable decision.

---

* Assessors are asked to note the important distinction in the criteria for the two degrees. In the case of the M.Litt. candidates are required to have made 'a worthwhile contribution to knowledge or understanding in the field of learning within which the subject of the thesis falls', while for the D.Phil. it is necessary to have made 'a significant and substantial contribution in the particular field of learning within which the subject of the thesis falls'. The phrase 'a significant and substantial contribution', in the case of doctoral theses, is interpreted as work that displays stature, judgement, and persuasiveness in historical exposition and the shaping of conclusions. But examiners are explicitly requested to bear in mind that their judgement of the significance of the work submitted should be based on what may reasonably be expected of a capable and diligent graduate student after three or, at most, four years of full-time study. Similarly, the requirement that candidates for the M.Litt. should make 'a worthwhile contribution to knowledge or understanding' in their chosen field is qualified by the request that examiners should take into account what may be expected after two years of full-time study.

(v) Candidates holding the status of M.Litt. student may apply for transfer to D.Phil. status at any time, within the statutory limit of nine terms. Their Transfer of Status application will be considered according to the procedure laid down for confirmation of D.Phil. status (see below). The interviewer appointed by the Faculty Board shall follow that procedure, except that the interviewer will be asked to state explicitly whether in addition to this procedure a subsequent formal confirmation of D.Phil. status would be desirable, or not.

4. *Confirmation of D.Phil. status*

(i) Application for confirmation of D.Phil. status, with statements of support from the candidate's society and supervisor, shall normally be presented to the Graduate Studies Office not later than Monday of Second Week in the eighth term after admission as Probationer Research Student. In exceptional cases the Graduate Studies Committee may permit the candidate to postpone submission by up to one term: candidates seeking such postponement should apply to the Committee through the Director of Graduate Studies well in advance.

(ii) Application for confirmation of D.Phil. status shall be accompanied by: (1) a statement of up to 500 words of the title of the thesis and of the manner in which the candidate proposes to treat it; (2) a specimen chapter or part of a chapter not longer than 6,000 words; (3) a confidential report from the supervisor which should be sent directly to the Graduate Studies Office. The Graduate Studies Office should send the written work and the confidential report to the interviewer appointed by the Faculty Board.

(iii) The interviewer shall then examine the candidate orally. If the interviewer considers it necessary, a second assessor may be appointed in conjunction with the Director of Graduate Studies. In cases where the interviewer is also the supervisor, the Director of Graduate Studies shall act as if he or she were the interviewer and shall have power to appoint a deputy and, if necessary, a second assessor.

(iv) The interviewer shall report to the Graduate Studies Committee in writing whether the candidate's subject is satisfactory and whether he or she is competent to tackle it. If confirmation is not recommended the interviewer may recommend re-application after a further period (within the statutory limit of nine terms from admission to PRS status) or alternatively transfer to M.Litt. status. It will be open to the candidate to appeal to the Faculty Board against an unfavourable decision.

5. *Theses*

Theses submitted for the Degree of M.Litt. should not exceed 50,000 words and those submitted for the Degree of D.Phil. should not exceed 100,000 words, *including* all notes, appendices, any source material being edited, and all other parts of the thesis whatsoever, *excluding only* the bibliography; any thesis exceeding these limits is liable to be rejected on that ground. Any application for permission to exceed the limit should be submitted with a detailed explanation and statement of the amount of excess length requested, and with a covering letter from the supervisor.

Applications should be made as soon as possible and may not be made later than the last day of the fifth week of the term before that in which application is made for appointment of examiners. The presentation and footnotes should comply with the requirements specified in the Regulations of the General Board for the degrees of M.Litt. and D.Phil. and follow the *Conventions for the presentation of dissertations and theses* of the Faculty of Modern History.

All candidates must submit with their theses two printed or typewritten copies of an abstract of the thesis, which shall not normally exceed 1,500 words for the M.Litt. or 2,500 words for the D.Phil., prepared by the student. This is in addition to the requirement to submit an abstract of not more than 300 words in length required by the General Board's regulations. Copies of both abstracts shall be bound into the copy of the thesis which shall be deposited in the Bodleian Library.

6. BOARD OF THE FACULTY OF MUSIC

1. *Probationer Research Student*

(*a*) Admission

(i) Each candidate for admission as a Probationer Research Student should support the application with:

EITHER

(A) 1. a sample of recent written work (4,000–6,000 words), preferably but not necessarily related to the proposed topic or area of research, such as an undergraduate dissertation (or part of it) or a substantial essay;

2. a proposal for a research topic or area (about 1,000 words), which should include a statement why this work should be carried out at Oxford.

OR

(B) (For those intending to offer compositions as part of the final submission)

1. a sample of written work (2,000–3,000 words);
2. one or two recently completed compositions;
3. a plan of work to be completed in Oxford.

Candidates should expect to attend for interview if required.

(*b*) Course of study

Candidates seeking admission in order to read for the M.Litt. or D.Phil. are normally registered as Probationer Research Students and as such, unless specifically exempted by the board must follow the requirements laid down for the Degree of Master of Studies in Music (Musicology). Such exemption will not normally be granted except to candidates who have already obtained a qualification of equivalent status and breadth elsewhere. Transfer to M.Litt. or D.Phil. status normally takes place at the end of the first year and is dependent on successful completion of the M.St. course (though this in itself is not a sufficient condition of transfer).

Probationer Research Students who have been exempted from the requirements laid down for the Degree of Master of Studies in Music (Musicology) must attend courses as recommended by their supervisors and approved by the Director of Graduate Studies. In most instances these courses of study will be undertaken in the Faculty of Music, but exemptions will be made where more appropriate courses are offered in other faculties.

Students will also undertake foundation work related to their research area or topic under the direction of a supervisor.

A Certificate of Graduate Attainment may be awarded on the basis of satisfactory reports on the work undertaken in the initial year.

(*c*) Transfer to the status of M.Litt. or D.Phil. Student

(i) Probationer research students seeking to transfer to the status of M.Litt. or D.Phil. Student must satisfy the Board of the Faculty of Music that (*a*) they have followed and completed their prescribed courses of study, (*b*) they have undertaken preparatory research work to the satisfaction of their supervisor, (*c*) the proposed research topic is acceptable, and (*d*) they are competent to handle the research topic.

A candidate for transfer to the new status must make a submission in the manner prescribed in the University's *Examination Regulations*.

The faculty board requires that the written work submitted shall be:

EITHER

(A) an essay of about 5,000 words relevant to the topic proposed for the thesis, and a bibliographic essay of the same length reviewing the historical and/or theoretical literature relevant to the thesis topic and its field.

OR

(B) (For those intending to offer compositions as part of the final submission) a portfolio of two significantly contrasted compositions (together lasting between ten and fifteen minutes maximum), a proposed work-schedule for the following year, and a related essay of 5,000–10,000 words.

Two copies of the thesis title, thesis outline, essays and compositions must be submitted. The essay must be typewritten in double spacing, and placed in a temporary form of binding. The submissions must be made through the Secretary of Faculties no later than seven days before the second meeting of the Graduate Studies Committee of the board in the student's third term from admission. Upon the recommendation of the supervisor, the board may permit a student to submit no later than seven days before the second meeting in the fourth term of study.

(ii) On receiving the submissions the board shall appoint two assessors, both of whom shall read the scripts and conduct the oral examination, provided that the board may appoint additional assessors should the need arise.

(iii) Transfer to the new status shall only take place when the board has received satisfactory reports from the assessors, from those who conducted the prescribed courses of study, and from the student's supervisor.

(iv) M.St. students admitted to the status of Probationer Research Students must apply for transfer to M.Litt. or D.Phil. status in their fourth term of graduate study. The submissions required may consist of all or part of the work submitted for the Degree of M.St. provided that it is relevant to the research topic.

(v) Students for the M.Phil. who intend to take the degree may seek admittance to the status of M.Litt. or D.Phil. Student, provided that they satisfy the general regulations of the university, and that they submit a provisional thesis title and outline of the manner in which it is intended to treat the research topic which is acceptable to the board.

2. *M.Litt. Students*

(*a*) Admission

The procedure for the admission of a Probationer Research Student to the status of M.Litt. Student is outlined in section (*c*) of the faculty board's regulations for Probationer Research Students in Music.

(*b*) Supervision

The Graduate Studies Committee of the board will receive a report on each student's progress from his or her supervisor at the end of each term. The committee may request or receive an additional report at the end of the Long Vacation.

3. *D.Phil. Students*

(*a*) Admission

The procedure for the admission of a Probationer Research Student to the status of D.Phil. Student is outlined in section (*c*) of the faculty board's regulations for Probationer Research Students in Music.

(*b*) Supervision

The Graduate Studies Committee of the board will receive a report on each student's progress from his or her supervisor at the end of each term. The committee may request or receive an additional report at the end of the Long Vacation.

(*c*) Confirmation of Status

The status of D.Phil. Student shall normally be confirmed in the sixth term as a research student at Oxford. In addition to the general requirements of the *Decrees*, the Board of the Faculty of Music requires that every student seeking confirmation of status must make a submission consisting of:

EITHER

(A) 1. thesis title, together with an annotated outline of the thesis (both title and outline may be altered or revised forms of those submitted for the examination for admission to D.Phil. status);

2. an essay of about 6,000 words on the current state of the student's research, or a portion of the thesis of comparable length.

OR

(B) 1. an annotated inventory of the proposed contents of the final portfolio of compositions and title of the supporting dissertation;

2. a portfolio of two or more well-contrasted compositions, with a total duration of approximately 25 minutes;

3. an essay relating to the proposed dissertation.

(i) Candidates will be examined orally. Two copies of the thesis title, thesis outline and essay (or thesis extract), or inventory, thesis title, portfolio, and essay must be submitted. The essay (or thesis extract) must be typewritten in double spacing, and placed in a temporary form of binding. The submissions must be made through the Secretary of Faculties no later than seven days before the second meeting of the Graduate Studies Committee in the student's fifth term from admission. Upon the recommendation of the supervisor, the board may permit a student to submit no later than seven days before the second meeting in a subsequent term of study, provided that this falls within the limits set down in the University's *Examination Regulations*.

(ii) On receiving the submissions the board shall appoint two assessors, both of whom shall read the scripts and conduct the examination, provided that the board may appoint additional assessors should the need arise.

(iii) Confirmation of status may only take place when the board has received satisfactory reports from the assessors, and from the student's supervisor.

4. *Final submission*

EITHER

(A) For the Degree of M.Litt. a thesis not exceeding 50,000 words, or for the Degree of D.Phil. a thesis not exceeding 100,000 words, exclusive of any text being edited but including notes, bibliography, glossary, appendices, etc.

OR

(B) For the Degree of M.Litt. a portfolio of compositions of no more than 30 minutes' duration and a supporting dissertation of up to 30,000 words. For the Degree of D.Phil. a portfolio of musical compositions, totalling approximately 45 minutes' duration, and a supporting dissertation of up to 45,000 words.

7. BOARD OF THE FACULTY OF ORIENTAL STUDIES

1. *M.Litt. in Oriental Studies*

The first year of graduate study in the Oriental Faculty will be regarded as a qualifying period, during which the student shall be registered as a Probationer Research Student. This will culminate in a qualifying examination set by two assessors appointed by the board, with a view to assessing a candidate's application for admission to M.Litt. status.

The subjects or fields of study to be covered by the examination will be decided by the Graduate Studies Committee of the Oriental Studies Board by the end of the first term on the recommendation of the supervisor. All students will normally be required to submit a piece of formal written work relevant to the field of their research. Where it is felt necessary, particular subjects (up to a total of two) will in addition be examined orally or by written papers.

The course of study for the qualifying examination in the field of Chinese Studies will be that required for the M.St. in Chinese Studies, and the examination will be set and examined by the examiners for the M.St. at the end of each Trinity Term.

On the basis of the results of the examination the faculty board will decide whether the student should be accepted for admission to M.Litt. status.

Candidates who have successfully completed the M.St. in Oriental Studies may be recommended for admission to M.Litt. status on the basis of the results of the examination, subject to the submission of a satisfactory outline (of not more than 500 words) of the proposed subject of the thesis.

2. *D.Phil. in Oriental Studies*

The first year of graduate study in the Oriental Studies Faculty will be regarded as a qualifying period during which the student shall be registered as a Probationer Research Student. At the end of the first year the student seeking admission to D.Phil. status will be set a qualifying examination by the supervisor which will be considered by two assessors appointed by the board.

The format of the examination, together with the subjects or fields of study to be covered by it, will be decided by the Graduate Studies Committee of the Oriental Studies Board by the end of the first term on the recommendation of the supervisor. All students will normally be required to submit a piece of formal written work relevant to the field of their research of between 5,000 and 10,000 words in length.

The course of study for the qualifying examination in the field of Chinese Studies will be that required for the M.St. in Chinese Studies, and the examination will be set and examined by the examiners for the M.St. at the end of each Trinity Term. On the basis of the results of the examination the faculty board will decide whether the student should be accepted for admission to D.Phil. status.

Candidates who have successfully completed the M.St. in Oriental Studies may be recommended for admission to D.Phil. status on the basis of the results of the examination, subject to the submission of a satisfactory outline (of not more than 500 words) of the proposed subject of the thesis.

Candidates who have successfully completed the M.Phil. in Oriental Studies may be recommended for admission to D.Phil. status on the basis of the results of the examination, subject to the submission of a satisfactory outline (of not more than 500 words) of the proposed subject of the thesis. In exceptional cases, such candidates may be recommended for admission to confirmed D.Phil. status.

The board requires from each applicant for confirmation of D.Phil. status a written statement of the manner in which he or she proposes to treat the subject. The board will approve such applications only if the assessors appointed by the board shall have certified that a piece of work written by the applicant (of 10,000–15,000 words in length) is of the requisite standard to justify the confirmation. Assessment of the application shall include a viva voce examination of the candidate by two persons appointed by the board.

3. *Theses*

Theses submitted for the Degree of M.Litt. should not exceed 50,000 words and those for the Degree of D.Phil. should not exceed 100,000, exclusive of any text that is being edited, and of bibliography, but including notes, glossary, appendices, etc. Leave to exceed this limit will be given only in exceptional cases.

8. BOARD OF THE FACULTY OF PHILOSOPHY

1. *Admission as Probationer Research Student*

Candidates for admission are required to submit with their application one piece of written work of between 4,500 and 5,000 words, on a subject related to the proposed research topic. The piece must be typed and in English, unless by special permission.

2. *Admission to M.Litt. or D.Phil. status*

Applications from Probationer Research Students for transfer to the status of Student for the Degree of Master of Letters or Doctor of Philosophy will not normally be considered before the beginning of the candidate's third term as a Probationer Research Student. The board regards the third term as the normal time for this application to be made and expects applications to be made by the end of the fifth week of the third term.

Applications should be accompanied by a thesis outline of about two pages and a piece of written work of approximately 5,000 words in the area and philosophical style of the proposed thesis. The board will appoint two assessors, who will read the submissions and conduct an interview with the candidate.

3. *Confirmation of D.Phil. status*

Applications from Students for the Degree of Doctor of Philosophy for confirmation of status will not normally be considered before the beginning of the candidate's third term after transfer to D.Phil. status. The board regards the third term after transfer as the normal time for this application to be made and expects applications to be made by the end of the fifth week of third term.

Applications should be accompanied by a thesis outline of about two pages and a piece of written work of approximately 5,000 words, intended as a part of the theseis, in final or near-final draft. The board will appoint one assessor to read the submissions.

4. *Theses*

M.Litt. theses should not exceed 50,000 words, and D.Phil. theses should not exceed 75,000 words, exclusive of bibliographical references, unless the candidate has, with the support of his or her supervisor, secured the leave of the board to exceed this limit.

All candidates when they submit their theses must state the approximate number of words therein both (*a*) including citations and, if they have been granted permission to count citations separately, (*b*) excluding citations. Theses exceeding the limit are liable to be returned unexamined for reduction to the proper length. Candidates who have submitted in their final term may be allowed a maximum period of two terms to effect the necessary reduction.

9. BOARD OF THE FACULTY OF THEOLOGY

1. *Admission to the status of Probationer Research Student*

No application for admission as a Probationer Research Student (whether studying on a full or part-time basis*) will normally be considered by the Graduate Studies Committee of the Board of the Faculty of Theology unless the applicant has previously been interviewed by a member of the committee. But in the case (*a*) of applicants not resident in Britain, or (*b*) applicants transferring from M.Phil. registration, or (*c*) applicants who have been successful in the M.St. examination, the committee has discretion to recommend admission without interview. Unless they have successfully completed the M.Phil. in Theology, research students are normally registered in the first instance for the degree of Master of Studies. Transfer to M.Litt. or D.Phil. status normally takes place at the end of the first year in the case of full-time studies and second year in the case of part-time studies and is dependent on successful completion of the M.St. course (though this is not in itself a sufficient condition of transfer). The board may however permit candidates who

* It should be noted that admission to study on a part-time basis in Theology is reviewed on an annual basis, and is subject to decisions by the University on the availability of doctoral research by means of part-time study.

have already obtained a similar qualification or who are otherwise appropriately qualified to register as Probationer Research Students for the first year.

A student admitted to study on a full-time basis is not permitted to change the basis of his or her study from full-time to part-time at any stage of his or her registration as a graduate student.

In assessing applications from candidates seeking to undertake a research degree through part-time study, the Graduate Studies Committee of the Board of the Faculty of Theology shall have regard to evidence that:

(i) the candidate is suitable to undertake research at doctoral level;

(ii) the candidate's personal and professional circumstances are such that it is both practicable for him or her to fulfil the requirements of the course, and necessary for him or her to study on a part-time basis;

(iii) if appropriate, the candidate has the written support of their present employer for their proposed course of study and its obligations;

(iv) the candidate's proposed topic of research is suitable for part-time study;

(v) the candidate can meet the attendance requirements relating to part-time study.

2. *Attendance requirements (for part-time students)*

Part-time students are required to attend for a minimum of thirty days of university-based work each year, to be arranged with the agreement of their supervisor, for the period that their names remain on the Register of Graduate Students unless individually dispensed by the Graduate Studies Committee on the Board of the Faculty of Theology.

3. *Confirmation of Probationer Research Student status*

A student admitted to Probationer Research Student status on a part-time basis shall, before the end of the sixth term from his or her admission, attend an interview with his or her supervisor, the Director of Graduate Studies (or representative) and one other member of staff in order to confirm (i) the satisfactory completion of his or her research training, and (ii) satisfactory progress in making his or her research plans.

Where the interviewers fail to be satisfied on either (i) or (ii) or both, a further interview shall be held before the end of the ninth term from the candidate's admission. Where the interviewers remain unsatisfied on either (i) or (ii) after the second interview, the Board of the Faculty of Theology may remove the student's name from the Register of Graduate Students.

4. *Transfer from Probationer Research Student status*

(i) Application for transfer from Probationer Research Student status to either M.Litt. or D.Phil. Student status should be submitted not later than Monday of the week before full term in the candidate's fourth term.

(ii) The candidate should submit with the application two typewritten copies of a piece of work normally 3,000 to 5,000 words long, relevant to the proposed thesis and with attention paid, where appropriate, to primary sources, and also a formulation of the subject-matter of the thesis together with a statement in approximately 500 words of how it will be approached.

(iii) The candidate's supervisor may be invited to attend the oral examination to be held as part of the assessment of the student's application.

5. *Confirmation of D.Phil. status*

Candidates applying for confirmation of D.Phil. status will be advised by the faculty board's Graduate Studies Committee whether, in addition to the accompanying certification required by §4 cl. 2 of the D.Phil. decree, they must submit written work and/or be interviewed by an assessor appointed by the board.

6. *Preparation of theses for the Degrees of M.Litt. and D.Phil.*

(i) Theses submitted for the Degree of M.Litt. should not exceed 50,000 words, or 100,000 for the D.Phil., excluding only the bibliography in both cases. The faculty board is prepared to consider an application for a relaxation of this limit in special circumstances.

(ii) In addition to the abstract required for the M.Litt. degree and the D.Phil. degree under the Educational Policy and Standards Committee regulations, the application for leave to supplicate must be accompanied by two printed or typewritten copies of an abstract of the thesis prepared by the candidate of between 1,000 and 1,500 words for an M.Litt., and between 1,500 and 2,500 for a D.Phil. One copy of this abstract should be bound into the copy of the thesis to be deposited in the Bodleian Library.

B. LIFE AND ENVIRONMENTAL SCIENCES

1. ANTHROPOLOGY (SOCIAL AND CULTURAL)

1. *Transfer from M.Phil status to D.Phil status*

A student who has obtained an M.Phil. may only be admitted direct to D.Phil. status on condition that the research topic is a development of the research contained in the M.Phil. thesis or if the student can otherwise demonstrate his or her competence to undertake the proposed research, and that appropriate supervision can be provided.

2. *Transfer from Probationer Research Student status to M.Litt. or D.Phil. status*

This transfer shall normally take place not later than the third term after admission as a research student. The student will be required to show that the research already accomplished shows promise of the ability to produce a satisfactory M.Litt. or D.Phil. thesis on the intended topic. For this purpose, the applicant must submit to the board two copies in typescript of a substantial piece of written work relevant to the proposed thesis, of up to 30,000 words, together with an outline of research plans. These must be submitted to the Graduate Studies Office, Wellington Square. On receiving the application the board shall appoint two assessors. In exceptional cases one assessor, but in the case of joint supervision not both, may be the applicant's supervisor. The assessors shall read the script and interview the candidate before submitting to the board a reasoned written report supporting their recommendation. A student whose first application is unsuccessful may be given one further opportunity to apply for transfer, provided that he or she has not been Probationer Student for than more six terms in all. Whether an application is made for the first or second time, the assessors may recommend that an applicant for D.Phil. status be admitted instead to M.Litt. status.

3. *Confirmation of D.Phil. status by all students, regardless of whether they hold an M.Phil. or not*

Application for confirmation of D.Phil. status shall normally be made not earlier than the fourth term from admission as a research student and not later than the eighth term. The board expects that, in most cases, the transfer application will be made immediately after return from field-work. The student will be required to give evidence confirming that the research already accomplished gives promise of the ability to produce a satisfactory D.Phil. thesis on the intended topic. For this purpose the applicant must submit to the board two copies in typescript as follows: (i) for students in anthropology—a brief summary of the topic of the thesis together with chapter headings and an outline of what each chapter will contain. (ii) for students in archaeology—draft extracts from the proposed thesis of not less than 8,000 words. In all cases the student shall include with the written work an outline of the proposed thesis including an indication of the topics to be covered in individual chapters.

These must be submitted to the Graduate Studies Office, Wellington Square not less than eight days before a stated meeting of the board's Graduate Studies Committee.

On receiving the application the board shall appoint two assessors. In exceptional cases, one assessor may be the applicant's supervisor. The assessors shall read the script and interview the candidate before submitting to the board a reasoned written report supporting their recommendation. A student whose first application is unsuccessful may be given one further opportunity to apply, but if the second application is unsuccessful he or she shall be required to seek transfer to M.Litt. status.

4. *Submission of thesis*

2. BIOLOGICAL ANTHROPOLOGY

1. *Transfer Probationer Research Student status to M.Sc. status*

This transfer shall normally take place not later than the third term after admission as a research student. Applicants will, in addition to satisfying the requirements of Sect. VII. A, §3, cl. 1 be required to undertake such other tests as the faculty, acting through the candidate's head of department, shall determine and specify in the Notes of Guidance issued by the department. A student whose first application is unsuccessful will be permitted to make one further application for transfer.

2. *Transfer from Probationer Research Student status to D.Phil status*

This transfer shall normally take place in the third term after admission as a research student, except that for research students who already hold an M.Sc. degree the transfer will normally take place during the second term after admission. Apart from exceptional circumstances, this transfer will not take place *later* than the fifth term after admission as a research student. For transfer to be approved, the student is required to demonstrate promise of his/her ability to produce a satisfactory D.Phil. thesis on the intended topic. For this purpose, the student will submit three copies of the following two pieces of evidence to the Professor of Biological Anthropology:

(i) Evidence that, over a period of at least two terms, he/she has successfully carried out a programme of research in an area relevant to his/her proposed D.Phil. topic: and

(ii) A written piece of work of approximately 4,000 words, exclusive of bibliography, tables and appendices, that describes the proposed research plan for his/her D.Phil. This research plan shall normally be submitted in the format of a research grant application.

On receiving the application the Professor will consult with the student's supervisor(s) and appoint two assessors, neither of whom will be the student's supervisor(s). Normally, one of the assessors will be appointed from within the department while the second assessor will be appointed from outside the department. After both assessors have read the submitted work the student will be interviewed by a committee consisting of both assessors and the student's supervisor(s), and chaired by the Professor. Following the interview, the two assessors will submit to the Board, a reasoned written report supporting their recommendation. A student whose first application is unsuccessful may be given one further opportunity to apply for transfer. Whether the application is made for the first or second time, the assessors may recommend that an applicant be admitted to M.Sc. status instead of to D.Phil. status.

3. *Confirmation of D.Phil status*

Application for this transfer shall normally be made between the sixth and eighth term following admission to graduate status. Apart from exceptional circumstances, this transfer may not take place later than the ninth term following admission to graduate status. The student will be required to give evidence confirming that the research already accomplished gives promise of the ability to produce a satisfactory D.Phil. thesis on the intended topic and that submission of the D.Phil. thesis is anticipated to occur within the next two terms. For this purpose, the applicant must submit to the Professor of Biological Anthropology three copies of a typed report describing in approximately 3,000 words, exclusive of bibliography, tables and figures, the aims and methods of the proposed thesis and summarizing the results obtained so far. The student shall also append an outline of the proposed thesis including an indication of the topics to be covered in individual chapters. On receiving the application, the Professor will consult with the student's supervisor(s) and appoint two assessors, neither of whom shall be the student's supervisor. Normally, the same two assessors who were appointed to review the student's application for transfer from PRS status, will be appointed to review the application for confirmation of D.Phil. status. After both assessors have read the script the student will be interviewed by a committee consisting of both assessors and the student's supervisor(s), and chaired by the Professor. Following the interview the two assessors will submit to the Board a reasoned written report supporting their recommendation. A student whose first application is unsuccessful may be given one further opportunity to apply for confirmation, but if the second application is unsuccessful he or she shall be required to seek transfer to M.Sc. status.

3. COMMITTEE FOR ARCHAEOLOGY

1. *Transfer from Probationer Research Student status to M.Litt. or D.Phil. status*

This transfer shall normally take place not later than the fourth term after admission as a research student. The student will be required to show that the research already accomplished shows promise of the ability to produce a satisfactory M.Litt. or D.Phil. thesis on the intended topic. For this purpose, the candidate must submit to the committee two copies in typescript of a substantial piece of written work (of between 5,000 and 10,000 words) relevant to the proposed thesis, together with a research proposal. These should normally be submitted to the Graduate Studies Office, Wellington Square, by the Monday of the fifth week in the term in which the application is made. On receiving the application the committee shall appoint two assessors, of whom neither shall normally be the student's supervisor. The assessors shall read the scripts and inverview the candidate before submitting to the Committee for Archaeology reasoned written report supporting their recommendation. A student whose first application is unsuccessful may be given one further opportunity to apply for transfer.

2. *Confirmation of D.Phil. status*

The status of student for the Degree of Doctor of Philosophy shall be confirmed by the committee under the provisions of Sect. VIII, § 4, cl. 1. Candidates who have not first completed an M.Phil. are required to provide a research outline, of approximately 1,000 words, consisting of a table of contents and a summary of how much work has been done on each section of the thesis to date. The committee will appoint two assessors to consider the submitted outlines and reserves the right for the assessors to interview candidates. Candidates who have first completed an M.Phil. are required to apply for confirmation of status by their eleventh term as graduate students, and must submit a draft chapter of the thesis in addition to the research outline specified above. The committee will appoint two assessors who will consider the applications and will normally interview candidates.

3. *Length of D.Phil. theses*

Theses submitted for the Degree of D.Phil. in Archaeology should not normally exceed 80,000 words, excluding bibliography and descriptive catalogue or similar factual matter.

4. BIOCHEMISTRY, PLANT SCIENCES, AND ZOOLOGY

General

All research students will be admitted to the status of Probationer Research Student in the first instance. Individuals may hold this status for a maximum of six terms. Candidates should normally apply to transfer from Probationer Research Student status in the fourth term after admission as a research student. Candidates should discuss with their supervisors whether to apply for transfer to M.Sc. status or to D.Phil. status. and the most appropriate time at which to apply. It is possible to transfer to M.Sc. status initially and thereafter to D.Phil. status if this is appropriate.

1. *Admission of students to the status of Student for the Degree of Master of Science by Research*

Applicants should submit the material specified in Sect. VII. A, §3, cl. l; the board does notnormally require any further test under §3, cl. 2. Candidates may obtain full details from the Director of Graduate Studies of Biological Science, c/o Graduate Studies Office, Wellington Square, Oxford, OX1 2JD.

2. *Admission of students to the status of Student for the Degree of Doctor of Philosophy*

The form of written work to be submitted by candidates for admission as Students for the Degree of Doctor of Philosophy, and the manner of its examination, as required by Sect. VIII, §3, cl. 2, shall be determined by the divisional board acting through the candidate's department or sub-department. Details may be obtained from the Director of Graduate Studies for Biological Sciences, c/o Graduate Studies Office, Wellington Square, Oxford, OX1 2JD.

3. *Confirmation of Status of Student for the Degree of Doctor of Philosophy*

The status of Students for the Degree of Doctor of Philosophy will be confirmed by the board under the provisions of Sect. VIII, §4, cl. 2, when it has received a certificate from the candidate's head of department that he or she is continuing satisfactorily to conduct research. Details may be obtained from the Director of Graduate Studies for Biological Sciences, c/o Graduate Studies Office, Wellington Square, Oxford, OX1 2JD.

4. *Theses*

D.Phil. theses should normally be not more than 50,000 words in length (approximately 170 sides of A4 paper), exclusive of bibliography, appendices, diagrams, and tables. In exceptional circumstances the permission of the board can be sought to exceed this limit, but in no case may a thesis be longer than 75,000 words.

A set of scientific papers prepared as for publication, but not necessarily yet published, that concern a common subject may constitute an acceptable thesis, provided that with the addition of an Introduction, General Discussion, and General Conclusions they constitute a coherent body of work. Such papes should either be incorporated as typescript pages or as offprints bound in to the body of the thesis. Papers written in collaboration should not be included unless the greater part of the work is directly attributed to the candidate himself or herself, and the supervisor so certifies. Joint papers may however be included at appendices in a thesis.

Candidates with some published work may also include this as part of a traditional thesis, normally as an appendix.

Approval to submit a thesis using this format must be sought in advance from the appropriate Director of Graduate Studies for Biological Sciences (c/o Graduate Studies Office, Wellington Square, Oxford, OX1 2JD.

5. GEOGRAPHY

1. *Transfer from Probationer Research Student status to M.Litt., M.Sc., or D.Phil. status*

This transfer shall normally take place not later than the third term after admission as a research student. The student will be required to show that the research already accomplished shows promise of the ability to produce a satisfactory M.Litt., M.Sc., or D.Phil. thesis on the intended topic. For this purpose, the applicant must submit to the Professor of Geography five copies in typescript of a piece of written work relevant to the proposed thesis, of approximately 3,000 words, together with an outline of research plans. On receiving the application the Professor will, on behalf of the board, appoint two assessors (normally two of the Interviewers for Research Students or two of the appointed advisors for that student) neither of whom will normally be the student's supervisor. The assessors shall read the script and interview the candidate before submitting to the board a reasoned written report supporting their recommendation. A student whose first application is unsuccessful may be given one further opportunity to apply for transfer. Whether an application is made for the first or second time, the assessors may recommend that an applicant for D.Phil. status be admitted instead to M.Litt. or M.Sc. status.

2. *Confirmation of D.Phil. status*

Application for confirmation of D.Phil. status shall normally be made not earlier than the fourth term from admission as a research student and not later than the eighth term. The board expects that, in most cases, the transfer application will be made immediately after return from field-work. The student will be required to give evidence confirming that the research already accomplished gives promise of the ability to produce a satisfactory D.Phil. thesis on the intended topic. For this purpose the applicant must submit to the Professor of Geography seven copies in typescript of a report describing in approximately 3,000 words the aims and methods of the projected thesis and summarizing the results obtained so far. The student shall also include with the written work an outline of the proposed thesis including an indication of the topics to be covered in individual chapters. On receiving the application the Professor shall appoint two assessors (normally two of the Interviewers for Research Students or two of the appointed advisors for that student) neither of whom will normally be the student's supervisor. The assessors shall read the script and interview the candidate before submitting to the board a reasoned written report supporting their recommendation. A student whose first application is unsuccessful may be given one further opportunity to apply for confirmation, but if the second application is unsuccessful he or she shall be required to seek transfer to M.Litt. or M.Sc. status.

3. *Submission of theses*

Candidates for the Degrees of M.Sc., M.Litt., and D.Phil. shall submit at least two sets of all maps, diagrams, and other illustrations, one of which may be a reproduction of the original set. The copy of the thesis deposited in the Bodleian shall be one of those with a complete set of maps and illustrations.

Applications for leave to present one set only of maps, diagrams, and other illustrations may be granted in exceptional circumstances, but such concessions shall be granted only very sparingly.

M.Sc. theses should be approximately 40,000 words, inclusive of appendices but exclusive of tables, figures, and references.

M.Litt. theses should not exceed 50,000 words, exclusive of the bibliography, unless for exceptional reasons and on the recommendation of the candidate's supervisor the board otherwise determines.

D.Phil. theses submitted by students in Geography must not exceed 100,000 words, exclusive of the bibliography, but including notes, glossary, appendices, etc., unless for exceptional reasons and on the recommendation of the candidate's supervisor the board otherwise determines.

A D.Phil. thesis may be accepted for examination if comprised of a minimum of four scientific papers submitted for publication if not yet accepted or published. Such a body of work shall be deemed acceptable provided it represented a coherent and focused body of research. It should include an Introduction, a Survey of Literature, and a Conclusion. Current word limits and conditions remain in place.

A D.Phil. thesis submitted under this rubric may include joint publications. In that case, all co-authors must certify in writing to the Director of Graduate Studies of the School that the majority of that work represents the work of the candidate.

Candidates wishing to proceed in this manner must obtain permission from his/her supervisor, the School, and the Divisional Board and must be approved at the time of confirmation of D.Phil. status. Evidence must be submitted at the time permission is sought that the scientific papers have been submitted to identified journals.

If, after a petition is accepted, a candidate wishes to revert to a standard D.Phil. thesis format, the candidate must lodge a petition with his/her supervisor, the School, and Divisional showing good cause for the change.

D.Phil. theses submitted by students in Anthropology (except for Biological Anthropology—see below) must not exceed 100,000 words, including notes (but excluding bibliography, glossary, and appendices containing ethnographic material and archaeological evidence), unless for exceptional reasons and on the recommendation of the candidate's supervisor the board otherwise determines.

D.Phil. theses submitted by students in Biological Anthropology should normally be not more than 40,000 words in length (approximately 140 sides of A4 paper), exclusive of bibliography, appendices, diagrams and tables. In certain circumstances, and particularly where the work for the thesis is non-laboratory based, the permission of the Board can be sought to exceed this limit. One, or more scientific papers may form all, or part, of an acceptable thesis, provided that in combination with a separately written introduction, general discussion and general conclusions, they constitute a continuous theme. Joint papers may only be included in the body of the thesis if the supervisor certifies that the student's contribution represents a major portion of the paper, and further that this inclusion was approved by the Board at the time D.Phil. status was confirmed. Scientific papers, joint or otherwise, may be included as appendices in a thesis without prior approval.

Each candidate may submit at the same time as the thesis two printed or typewritten copies of an abstract of the thesis, more detailed than that required by the Educational Policy and Standards Committee's regulations, but not normally exceeding 1,500 words. A copy of any such abstract must be bound into the copy of the thesis which, if the application is successful, will be deposited in the Bodleian Library (in addition to the copy of the abstract required under the general regulations of the Educational Policy and Standards Committee). A copy of such an abstract may be bound into one or both of the other two copies of the thesis if the candidate so desires.

C. MATHEMATICAL AND PHYSICAL SCIENCES DIVISION

1. MATHEMATICAL SCIENCES

1. *Admission to the status of Probationer Research Student*

Applicants (other than those from overseas) will be notified individually if they are required to attend for interview before a decision is taken on an application for admission.

2. *Admission to the status of Student for the Degree of Master of Science by Research*

A Probationer Research Student may apply for transfer to M.Sc. status at any time within four terms of admission to the status of Probationer Research Student.

Assessment for transfer shall be by oral examination. Two persons appointed by the board shall conduct the examination.

3. *Admission to the status of Student for the Degree of Doctor of Philosophy*

(i) Any person seeking transfer to the status of D.Phil. student must apply to the board, which will approve such application only if two (or, in exceptional cases, three) assessors appointed by the board shall have certified

(*a*) that they have considered the written work submitted by the applicant and are satisfied that it demonstrates a capability of producing research work of the requisite standard and presenting the findings clearly; and

(*b*) that together they have interviewed the candidate and satisfied themselves that the planned programme of research is one that may be profitably undertaken at Oxford and that the candidate has a good knowledge and understanding of the work that is likely to be needed to embark on the programme.

(ii) Before making application to the board for transfer to the status of D.Phil. student, the applicant shall, in consultation with his or her supervisor, prepare a body of written work which shall be submitted as evidence of suitability for transfer.

(iii) Applications shall be in one of two categories:

Category A (open to students who have had no previous experience of research work)

In this category the written work submitted shall consist of a short dissertation on a topic selected in consultation with the supervisor, the preferred length being of between twenty-five and fifty typed pages (or fifteen to thirty printed pages of TEX, depending on fount used).

Most students in Category A will find it desirable to apply in the third term after admission as Probationer Research Student, but application may be made at any time from the second to the fourth term. A form of application for assessment together with a form of application for transfer should be sent to the Secretary of Faculties, University Offices, Wellington Square. The applicant should include with the application a brief description of the proposed subject of research for the D.Phil. degree and a brief statement (courses attended, texts and publications studied etc.) setting out the steps taken to ensure that he or she has the knowledge and understanding likely to be necessary to embark on the planned research work. The applicant should also name a date (not later than four weeks before the start of the Full Term following the date of application (applications made in vacation to be counted as if they had been made in the following term)) by which time he or she undertakes to make available two (or in exceptional cases three) copies of the written work supporting the application.

A student who has applied to the board for transfer to the status of D.Phil. student under Category A and had the application rejected may subsequently re-apply. A candidate failing to secure a Category B transfer to D.Phil. status will be allowed to apply for transfer under Category A.

Category B (open to applicants who have had previous experience of research work; it is expected that this will include many students who have successfully completed a taught master's course)

In this category the written work submitted with the application may consist of either

(*a*) a thesis or dissertation produced in connection with another course of research or study; or

(*b*) work that has been accepted for publication in a learned journal or journals; or

(*c*) other work which is in the opinion of the supervisor of comparable standing.

Students under Category B will make applications immediately after admission to Probationer Research Student status. A form of application for assessment together with a form of application for transfer together with two copies of the written work, should be sent to the Graduate Studies Office, University offices, Wellington Square. In exceptional cases a third copy may be required. The applicant should include with the application a brief description of the proposed subject of research for the D.Phil. degree and a brief statement (courses attended, texts and publications studied, etc.) setting out the steps taken to ensure that he or she has the knowledge and understanding likely to be necessary to embark on the planned research work.

(iv) In both types of application, on receipt of a form of application for assessment the board will appoint two (or in exceptional cases, three) members of the faculty to advise the board on the suitability of the applicant for transfer. Having considered the work submitted they shall arrange to interview the applicant to assess his/her suitability. They shall subsequently report to the board as to whether or not they are satisfied that the conditions described in clause 3(i) above have been met.

(v) On receipt of the report from the board's advisers, and after due consideration of any supervisor's reports that are available the board shall determine

(*a*) that the application be approved; or

(*b*) that the application be rejected, but that the student be allowed to apply for transfer to the status of Student for the Degree of M.Sc. by research; or

(*c*) that the candidate make one further application (under Category A).

4. *Transfer from status of Student for the Degree of Master of Science by Research to status of Student for the Degree of Doctor of Philosophy*

(i) Any person seeking transfer to the status of a D.Phil. student must apply to the board, which will approve such application only if two (or, in exceptional cases, three) persons appointed by the board shall have certified:

(*a*) that they have considered written work submitted by the applicant and are satisfied that it demonstrates a capability of producing research work of the requisite standard and presenting the findings clearly; and

(*b*) that together they have interviewed the candidate and satisfied themselves that the planned programme of research is one that may be profitably undertaken at Oxford and that he or she has a good knowledge and understanding of the work that is likely to be needed to embark on the programme.

(ii) Before making application to the board for transfer to the status of D.Phil. student, the applicant shall in consultation with his/her supervisor prepare a body of written work which shall be submitted as evidence of suitability for transfer.

(iii) Application for transfer from M.Sc. status to D.Phil. student status shall consist of a short dissertation on a topic selected in consultation with the supervisor, the preferred length being of between twenty-five and fifty typed pages (or fifteen to thirty printed pages of TEX, depending on fount used), or a part-written thesis.

Application may be made at any time up to the ninth term after admission. A form of application for assessment together with a form of application for transfer should be sent to the Secretary of Faculties, University Offices, Wellington Square. The applicant should include with the application a brief description of the proposed subject of research for the D.Phil. degree and a brief statement (courses attended, texts and publications studied etc.) setting out the steps taken to ensure that he or she has the mathematical knowledge and understanding likely to be necessary to embark on the planned research work. The applicant should also name a date (not later than four weeks before the start of the Full Term following the date of application (applications made in vacation to be counted as if they had been made in the following term)) by which time he or she undertakes to make available two (or in exceptional cases three) copies of the written work in support of the application.

A student who has applied to the board for transfer to the status of D.Phil. student as above and had the application rejected may not subsequently reapply except with the express permission of the board. Such permission will only be given if the board is satisfied that there are exceptional and extenuating circumstances for so doing.

(iv) On receipt of a form of application for assessment the board will appoint two (or in exceptional cases, three) members of the faculty, neither of whom shall normally be the applicant's supervisor, to advise the board on the suitability of the applicant for transfer. Having considered the work submitted they shall arrange to interview the applicant to assess suitability. They shall subsequently report to the board as to whether or not they are satisfied that the conditions described in clause (i) above have been met.

(v) On receipt of the report from the board's assessors, and after due consideration of any supervisor's reports that are available the board shall determine that the application be approved; or that the application be rejected.

5. *Confirmation of D.Phil. status*

Confirmation of D.Phil. Student status, which will normally take place by the end of the eighth term after that in which the candidate was admitted as a Probationer Research Student, will take the form of an oral examination with two assessors appointed by the board, based on the candidate's own written report of progress.

The assessors shall recommend to the board either that D.Phil. status be confirmed or that reapplication be made after a further period (within the statutory limit). If D.Phil. status is not confirmed, the second application shall normally be made by the end of the tenth term after that in which the candidate was admitted as a Probationer Research Student. Two assessors appointed by the board shall require evidence of progress such as written work and shall indicate to the student precisely what is required. A second oral examination may be held.

If, by the end of the eleventh term after that in which the candidate was admitted as a Probationer Research Student, after considering his or her application(s) for confirmation of status, the board concludes that the student's progress does not warrant this, it shall approve his or her transfer to M.Sc. Student Status.

6. *Thesis*

The text of theses submitted for the Degree of D.Phil. shall not exceed 200 pages, A4 size, double-spaced in normal-size type, but there is no limit on references, numerical tables, diagrams, computer output, etc. The normal length of a thesis, however, is nearer 100 pages (exclusive of the material defined above).

Where some part of the thesis is not solely the work of the candidate or has been carried out in collaboration with one or more persons, the candidate shall submit a clear statement of the extent of his or her own contribution.

2. PHYSICAL SCIENCES

1. *Master of Science by Research*

Applicants for admission as students for the Degree of Master of Science by Research shall in addition to the requirements of Sect. VII. A, §3, cl. 1, be required to undertake such other tests as the sub-faculty concerned, acting through the candidate's head of department or sub-department shall determine. The Notes of Guidance provided by the department or sub-department will give details of these requirements.

2. *Doctor of Philosophy*

The form of written work to be submitted by candidates for admission as Students for the Degree of Doctor of Philosophy, and the manner of its examination, as required by Sect. VIII, §3, cl. 2, shall be determined by the sub-faculty concerned, acting through the candidate's head of department or sub-department. The notes of guidance provided by the department or sub-department will give details of these requirements. All candidates will be examined orally.

3. *Confirmation of status of students for the Degree of Doctor of Philosophy*

The status of Students for the Degree of Doctor of Philosophy will be confirmed by the board under the provisions of Sect. VIII, §4, cl. 1, when it has received a certificate from the candidate's head of department or sub-department that he or she is continuing satisfactorily to conduct research. The candidate and the supervisor will be required to provide a clear indication of the proposed time-table for submission of the thesis.

4. Applicants who are admitted to undertake research under the supervision of the Mathematical and Physical Sciences Divisional Board may, exceptionally, be permitted by the Divisional Board to undertake their research in a well-found laboratory outside the University. Such candidates shall be dispensed from the residence requirements, but shall be required to attend the University for such instruction as the division and department concerned shall require. Before admitting a candidate on this basis, the department concerned shall be required to satisfy itself and the divisional board that appropriate arrangements are in place for approving all aspects of the student's academic work, including the following:

(i) the availability of the equipment and facilities necessary for the project in the agency concerned;
(ii) the existence of a wider collaboration between the department and the agency in which the student is based;
(iii) the subject of their doctoral studies;
(iv) satisfactory induction procedures;
(v) satisfactory health and safety arrangements;
(vi) satisfactory supervision arrangements, to include specification of a minimum number of contact hours between student and supervisor, which shall include not less than two face-to-face meetings between student and supervisor, for a total of at least 8 hours, each term;
(vii) satisfactory arrangements for monitoring the student's progress within the department;
(viii) provision for the student to attend the University for such instruction as the division and department shall require.

Dispensation from these rules shall be sought from the Head of the Mathematical and Physical Sciences Division through the departmental Director of Graduate Studies.

5. *Theses*

(a) Longer abstracts: Geology, Chemistry, and Engineering

Candidates for the Degrees of M.Sc. and D.Phil. in Geology must submit with their theses, in addition to the abstracts of them required of all candidates of up to 300 words, three copies of a longer abstract of not more than 1,500 words for the M.Sc. and 2,500 for the D.Phil., one copy of which shall be bound into the copy of the thesis which, if the application for leave to supplicate for the degree is successful, will be deposited in the Bodleian Library.

Candidates for the Degrees of M.Sc. and D.Phil. in *Chemistry* or *Engineering* may if they wish submit with their theses, in addition to the abstract of them required of all candidates, a longer abstract of not more than 1,500 words for the M.Sc. and 2,500 for the D.Phil. Should such an abstract be submitted, a copy of it must be bound into the copy of the thesis which, if the application for leave to supplicate for the degree is successful, will be deposited in the Bodleian Library. The fuller abstract may be bound into the other two copies of the thesis if candidates so desire.

(b) Word limits

Theses submitted by candidates in *Metallurgy* or *Materials Science* shall not exceed 25,000 words for the M.Sc. and 40,000 words for the D.Phil., A4 size, double-spaced, but there is no limit on references, diagrams, tables, photographs, computer programmes, etc.

Theses submitted by candidates for the Degree of D.Phil. in *Physics* (except *Theoretical Physics*) must not exceed 250 pages, A4 size, double spaced in normal-size type (elite), the total to *include* all references, diagrams, tables, etc.

The text of theses submitted for the degree of D.Phil. in *Theoretical Physics* must not exceed 150 pages as defined above.

Theses submitted by candidates for the Degree of M.Sc. in Physics must not exceed 150 pages as defined above.

Theses submitted by candidates in *Engineering Science* must not exceed 250 pages for the Degree of D.Phil. or 200 pages for the Degree of M.Sc. They should be double spaced on A4 paper, in normal size type (Times New Roman, 12 point), the total to *include* all references, diagrams, tables, appendices, etc.

The text of theses submitted for the Degree of D.Phil. in *Geology and Mineralogy* must not exceed 250 pages as defined above, but there is no limit on diagrams, tables, etc.

In special circumstances the Graduate Studies Committee of the appropriate sub-faculty may, on application made *before* the thesis is submitted, grant leave to exceed the limit by a stated amount. Applications to exceed these limits must explain why the candidate believes the nature of the thesis is such that an exception should be made, and must be supported by the supervisor.

Appointment of examiners

In applying for appointment of examiners, candidates should note that a supervisor is disqualified from appointment, and that the divisional board will not normally appoint as examiner individuals previously closely associated with the work of the candidate, representatives of any organization sponsoring the candidate's research, representatives of any organization at which a candidate dispensed from residence under the provisions of section XVII, cl. 4 above, is based, or former colleagues of the candidate. Dispensation from this rule should be sought from the Head of Division through the departmental Director of Graduate Studies.

D. MEDICAL SCIENCES DIVISION

1. CLINICAL MEDICINE

1. *Admission of students to the status of Student for the Degree of Master of Science by Research*

Students seeking admission to status of degree of Master of Science (by Research) should submit the material specified in Sect. VII.A, §3, cl. 1, normally within three or four terms from admission as a research student. In addition, under the terms of Sect. VII.A, §3, cl. 2, the Applications Committee of the Clinical Medicine Board requires the student to submit a report of not more than 1,500 words, specifying the title of the thesis, and giving an outline of the proposed research. Further details may be found in the *Notes of Guidance for Graduate Students* issued by the Applications Committee.

2. *Admission of students to the status of Student for the Degree of Doctor of Philosophy*

Students seeking admission to the status of degree of Doctor of Philosophy shall submit the material specified in Sect. VIII, §3, cl. 1, normally within four terms from admission as a research student. The written work required under Sect. VII, §3, cl. 2

shall be a report of not less than 1,000 words specifying the title of the thesis and outlining the progress to date of the research and plans for future study.

The student's report shall be considered by two assessors appointed by the Applications Committee of the Clinical Medicine Board, neither of whom shall normally be the student's supervisor. The process of assessment shall normally include an interview by the assessors of the student or a presentation at a suitable seminar by the student. In either case, the assessors shall submit a report in writing to the Applications Committee, making a recommendation as to whether the application for transfer to D.Phil. status should be granted. Further details may be found in the *Notes of Guidance for Graduate Students* issued by the Applications Committee.

3. *Confirmation of status as a Student for the Degree of Doctor of Philosophy*

Students for the degree of Doctor of Philosophy seeking confirmation of their status in accordance with the provisions of Sect. VIII, §4, cl. 2 shall submit the title of the thesis, a brief summary of the thesis, and an account in not more than 500 words stating how much of the thesis is complete and how much remains to be done (with an estimate of the completion date). If confirmation of status is not approved on this evidence, the Applications Committee of the Clinical Medicine Board will appoint assessors to consider the case. The assessors shall interview the candidate and report in writing to the Applications Committee.

Candidates shall normally apply for confirmation of status not later than the end of the ninth term from their admission as a research student.

A set of scientific papers that conern a common subject may exceptionally constitute an acceptable thesis, but only if with the addition of an introduction, general discussion, and general conclusions they constitute a continuous theme. Joint papers may not be included unless the supervisor certifies the extent of the candidate's own contribution. Joint papers may be included as appendices in a thesis. Approval to submit a thesis using this format should be sought from the faculty board (via the Chairman, Applications Committee of the General Board, c/o Graduate Studies Office, Wellington Square, Oxford, OX1 2JD) as soon as possible after admission and not later than the date at which the appointment of examiners is requested.

D.Phil. theses should normally be not more than 50,000 words in length (approximately 170 sides of A4 paper) exclusive of bibliography, appendices, diagrams, and tables. In exceptional circumstances the permission of the board may be sought to exceed this limit.*

2. PHYSIOLOGICAL SCIENCES

General

All research students are admitted to the status of Probationer Research Student in the first instance. Individuals may hold this status for up to six terms. At some appropriate time before the end of the sixth term from admission it will be necessary to decide whether to apply for transfer to M.Sc. status or to D.Phil. status. This is a question which should be considered carefully by the student in consultation with his or her supervisor. It is possible to transfer to M.Sc. status initially and thereafter to D.Phil. status if this seems appropriate.

1. *Admission of students to the status of Student for the Degree of Master of Science by Research*

Applicants should submit the material specified in Ch. VI, Sect. VII. A, §3, cl. 1; the board does not normally require any further test under §3, cl. 2. Candidates may

---

* The provisions relating to the work limit shall apply only to candidates admitted to the status of Probationer Research Student with effect from Michaelmas Term 1992 or later.

obtain full details from the Director of Graduate Studies for Physiological Sciences, c/o Graduate Studies Office, Wellington Square, Oxford, OX1 2JD.

2. *Admission of students to the status of Student for the Degree of Doctor of Philosophy*

The form of written work to be submitted by candidates for admission as Student for the Degree of Doctor of Philosophy, and the manner of its examination, as required by Sect. VIII, §3, cl. 2, shall be determined by the faculty board from time to time. Details may be obtained from the Director of Graduate Studies for Physiological Sciences, c/o Graduate Studies Office, Wellington Square, Oxford, OX1 2JD.

3. *Confirmation of status of Student for the Degree of Doctor of Philosophy*

The status of Student for the Degree of Doctor of Philosophy will be confirmed by the board under the provisions of Sect. VIII, §4, and the manner of its examination shall be determined by the faculty board from time to time. Details may be obtained from the Director of Graduate Studies for Physiological Sciences, c/o Graduate Studies Office, Wellington Square, Oxford, OX1 2JD.

4. *Theses*

Theses submitted for the Degree of D.Phil. should normally contain not more than 50,000 words, exclusive of the list of references, numerical appendices, diagrams, and tables. A set of scientific papers which concern a common subject may exceptionally constitute an acceptable thesis, but only if with the addition of an introduction, general discussion, and general conclusions they constitute a continuous theme. Joint papers may not be included unless the supervisor certifies the extent of the candidate's own contribution. Joint papers may be included as appendices in a thesis. Approval to submit a thesis using this format should be sought from the faculty board (via the Director of Graduate Studies for Physiological Sciences, c/o Graduate Studies Office, Wellington Square, Oxford, OX1 2JD) as soon as possible after admission and not later than the date at which the appointment of examiners is requested.

3. PSYCHOLOGICAL STUDIES

General

All research students will be admitted to the status of Probationer Research Student in the first instance. Individuals may hold this status for a maximum of six terms. Candidates should normally apply to transfer from Probationer Research Student status by Friday of Week 6 of the fifth term after admission as a research student. Candidates should discuss with their supervisors whether to apply for transfer to M.Sc. status or D.Phil. status, and the most appropriate time at which to apply. It is possible to transfer to M.Sc. status initially and thereafter to D.Phil. status if this is appropriate.

1. *Admission of Students to the status of Student for the Degree of Master of Science by Research*

Students seeking admission to the status of Student for the Degree of Master of Science by Research should submit the material specified in Sect. VII. A, § 3, cl. 1. In addition, under the terms of Sect. VII. A § 3, cl. 2, the board requires a report to be made on the work done as a Probationer Research Student. The candidate's supervisor shall also be asked to comment in writing on the report. Details of the required length and contents of the report may be obtained from the Director of Graduate Studies.

The candidate's report and the supervisor's comments shall be considered by two assessors appointed by the board, neither of whom shall normally be the candidate's supervisor. The process of assessment shall normally include an interview with the applicant; it shall always do so if the assessors are unable to certify that they are satisfied without interviewing the applicant that they can recommend transfer to M.Sc. status. Upon completion of their assessment of the candidate's work, the assessors shall make a recommendation as to whether the application for transfer to M.Sc. status should be granted. In each case the assessors shall make a reasoned written report to the board in support of their recommendation.

2. *Admission of Students to the status of Student for the Degree of Doctor of Philosophy*

Students seeking admission to the status of Student for the Degree of Doctor of Philosophy shall submit the material required in Sect. VIII, § 3, cl. 1. The written work required under the terms of Sect. VIII, § 3, cl. 2 shall be in the form of a report on the work done as a Probationer Research Student. The supervisor shall also be asked to comment in writing on the report. Details of the required length and contents of the report may be obtained from the Director of Graduate Studies.

3. *Confirmation of Status of Student for the Degree of Doctor of Philosophy*

Students for the degree of Doctor of Philosophy seeking confirmation of their status in accordance with the provisions of Sect. VIII, § 4, cl. 2 shall submit the title of the thesis, a brief summary, and an account in not more than 500 words stating how much of the thesis is complete and how much remains to be done (with an estimate of the completion date). The supervisor shall also be asked to make a report. If confirmation of status is not approved on this evidence, the Psychological Studies Faculty Board's Graduate Studies Committee shall have power to appoint two assessors to consider the case. The assessors shall interview the candidate and report in writing to the Graduate Studies Committee of the board.

Candidates shall normally apply for confirmation of status in the eighth term from their admission as a research student.

4. *Theses*

Theses for the Degree of M.Sc. should not contain more than 50,000 words. Theses for the Degree of D.Phil. should not contain more than 100,000 words inclusive of appendices, excluding only the list of references and bibliography, and it is advisable that they should be shorter. Theses exceeding these limits are liable to be rejected on that ground. If a report on experimental work is included it must be adequate for the examiners to be able to assess it as an experiment.

A set of scientific papers that concern a common subject may exceptionally constitute an acceptable D.Phil. thesis, but only if with the addition of an introduction, general discussion, and general conclusions they constitute a continuous theme. Joint papers may not be included unless the supervisor certifies the extent of the candidate's own contribution. Joint papers may be included as appendices in a thesis. Approval to submit a thesis using this format should be sought from the faculty board (via the Chairman, Psychological Studies Graduate Studies Committee, c/o Graduate Studies Office, Wellington Square, Oxford OX1 2JD) as soon as possible after admission and not later than the date of transfer to D.Phil. status.

Candidates shall submit, in addition to the abstract of the thesis required by the General Board's regulations, two printed or typewritten copies of a more detailed abstract of the thesis which shall not normally exceed 1,500 words for the M.Sc. and M.Litt. and 2,500 for the D.Phil. A copy of this fuller abstract must be bound into the copy of the thesis which, if the application for leave to supplicate is successful, will be deposited in the Bodleian Library.

E. SOCIAL SCIENCES DIVISION

1. DEPARTMENT OF EDUCATIONAL STUDIES

1. *Admission*

All students (whether studying on a full or part-time basis) are normally admitted as Probationer Research Students. A student admitted to study on full-time basis is not permitted to change the basis of his or her study from full-time to part-time at any stage of his or her registration as a graduate student.

In assessing applications from candidates seeking to undertake a research degree through part-time study, the committee shall have regard to evidence that:

(i) the candidate has a minimum of three years' experience as a professional educator and is currently employed in an established post within an educational institution;

(ii) the candidate can meet the attendance requirements relating to part-time study;

(iii) the candidate has the written support of their present employer for their proposed course of study and its obligations;

(iv) the candidate's proposed topic of research is related to their present or intended professional work.

Probationer Research Students will be required to complete the requirements of the educational research training programme approved by the committee, unless specifically exempted from all or part of it.

Attendance requirements (for part-time students)

Part-time research students are required to attend for a minimum of thirty days of university-based work each year, to be arranged with the agreement of their supervisor, for the period that their names remain on the Register of Graduate Students unless individually dispensed by the Committee for Educational Studies.

Confirmation of Probationer Research Student status

A student admitted to Probationer Research Student status on a part-time basis shall, before the end of the sixth term from his or her admission, attend an interview with his or her supervisor, the Tutor for Research Students (or representative) and one other member of staff in order to confirm (i) the satisfactory completion of his or her research training, and (ii) satisfactory progress in making his or her research plans. Where the interviewers fail to be satisfied on either (i) or (ii) or both, a further interview shall be held before the end of the ninth term from the candidate's admission. Where the interviewers remain unsatisfied on either (i) or (ii) after the second interview, the Committee for Educational Studies may remove the student's name from the Register of Graduate Students.

2. *Transfer to M.Sc. status*

During the term following that in which they have registered as Probationer Research Students, those wishing to transfer to M.Sc. status must submit a paper on their research to a specially constituted panel of two assessors appointed by the committee. The panel will interview candidates and make a recommendation to the committee in an agreed written report. For the interview candidates must submit:

(*a*) an outline description of the research (one side of A4 paper);

(*b*) a detailed research proposal of no more than 6,000 words. This should:

(i) draw upon relevant literature in order to discuss the background to the research, theoretical perspectives, and possible outcomes to the research;

(ii) state key research questions;

(iii) discuss the overall methodological approach, and specific strategies, to be employed in answering these research questions, paying particular attention to practical and ethical issues relevant to the research;

(*c*) a tentative timetable for the research;

(*d*) a list of references.

3. *Transfer to M.Litt. status*

During their third term as Probationer Research Students, those wishing to transfer to M.Litt. status must present a paper on their research to a specially constituted panel of two assessors appointed by the board. The panel will interview candidates and make a recommendation to the board in an agreed written report. For the interview candidates must submit:

(*a*) an outline description of the research (one side of A4 paper);

(*b*) a detailed research proposal of no more than 6,000 words. This should:

(i) draw upon relevant literature in order to discuss the background to the research, theoretical perspectives, and possible outcomes to the research;

(ii) state key research questions;

(iii) discuss the overall methodological approach, and specific strategies, to be employed in answering these research questions, paying particular attention to practical and ethical issues relevant to the research;

(*c*) a tentative timetable for the research;

(*d*) a list of references.

The assessors will make a recommendation in an agreed written report. Candidates seeking to transfer to M.Litt. status will be expected during the interview to show evidence of research-training through successful completion of the requirements of the department's educational research methods course, unless specifically exempted from all or part of it. Students failing to transfer to M.Litt. status in their third term may make another presentation in their fourth term.

4. *Transfer to D.Phil. status*

Those wishing to transfer to D.Phil. status, whether from M.Sc., M.Litt. or direct from Probationer Research Student status, must present a paper on their research to a specially constituted panel of two assessors appointed by the board. The panel will interview candidates and make a recommendation to the board in an agreed written report. For the interview candidates must submit:

(*e*) an outline description of the research (one side of A4 paper);

(*f*) a detailed research proposal of no more than 6,000 words. This should:

(i) draw upon relevant literature in order to discuss the background to the research, theoretical perspectives, and possible outcomes to the research;

(ii) state key research questions;

(iii) discuss the overall methodological approach, and specific strategies, to be employed in answering these research questions, paying particular attention to practical and ethical issues relevant to the research;

(*g*) a tentative timetable for the research;

(*h*) a list of references.

5. *Confirmation of status*

Confirmation of status must be completed within nine terms of registering for the first time at the Department of Educational Studies as *either* an M.Sc. Educational Research Methodology student *or* Probationer Research Student. It is intended to be a comprehensive monitoring of progress towards the final thesis.

Students' applications for Confirmation of Status will be examined by two assessors, on the basis of submission of written material and interview with the supervisor present. The written material to be submitted will consist of:

(i) an abstract of the thesis (one side of A4 paper);

(ii) an outline structure of the thesis, consisting of chapter headings, and a brief statement of the intended content;

(iii) an outline timetable detailing what work has already been carried out, and what activities are planned for the remaining stages;

(iv) normally two completed chapters from the thesis in progress (e.g. literature review; methodology; data analysis procedures; findings).

If confirmation is not granted on this occasion, students will be allowed a further term to reapply.

Candidates seeking to transfer to D.Phil. status will be expected during the interview to show evidence of research training through successful completion of the requirements of the department's educational research method course, unless specifically exempted from all or part of it.

Theses submitted for the Degree of M.Sc. by research should not contain more than 50,000 words, and while it is advisable that they should be considerably shorter, they should not contain fewer than 25,000 words.

6. *Thesis*

A thesis for the Degree of M.Litt. which exceeds 50,000 words, or a thesis for the Degree of D.Phil. which exceeds 100,000 words, in each case excluding the bibliography, is liable to be rejected by the board unless the candidate has, with the support of his or her supervisor, secured the leave of the committee to exceed this limit.

2. ECONOMICS, SOCIAL POLICY AND SOCIAL WORK, SOCIOLOGY, AND AREA AND DEVELOPMENT STUDIES

1. *Transfer to M.Litt. (or M.Sc. by Research) or D.Phil. status*

Students in these subject areas will normally be expected to transfer out of Probationer Research status in their third or fourth term after admission. Applications should be submitted to the sub-faculty Graduate Studies Committee and will comprise the following:

(*a*) a transfer of status form, obtainable from the Graduate Studies Office, signed by the candidate's supervisor and an appropriate college officer. The candidate should indicate clearly on the form the status to which he or she wishes to transfer; and

(*b*) a provisional thesis title and a short outline statement of the proposed research topic, which should include sources and methods to be used; and

(*c*) a piece of written work relevant to the thesis of between 5,000 and 7,000 words.

The Graduate Studies Committee will appoint two assessors, one of whom will normally be a member of the committee, except in cases where neither of the two most appropriate assessors are members of the committee, who will read the work, examine the candidate orally, and submit a written report to the committee.

The committee will then decide whether transfer to the status applied for will be approved. In the case of applications to transfer to D.Phil. status where the committee is not satisfied that the candidate should be allowed to make the transfer it may approve admission to M.Litt. status, (or exceptionally to M.Sc. by Research Status) or approve an extension of time in order to allow the candidate to resubmit at a later date (but before the end of the sixth term after admission to Probationer Research status). The committee may request additional written work or other evidence, or appoint an additional assessor, whenever it is considered necessary.

Individual Graduate Studies Committees may require additional tests or forms of assessment to be completed. Candidates are advised to consult the Notes of Guidance for Graduate Students issued by each Graduate Studies Committee.

Any candidate who is admitted to M.Litt. status (or M.Sc. by Research Status) may subsequently apply for transfer to D.Phil. status before the end of the sixth term after admission to Probationer Research status. The committee will expect to see evidence of substantial developments in the progress of the research since the transfer to M.Litt status (or M.Sc. by Research Status) before this further transfer is approved.

Additional regulations for the Department of Economics

Probationer Research Students in Economics are required to take a qualifying examination, unless exempted from all or part of the examination by the appropriate Graduate Studies Committee, on the grounds of an appropriate previous graduate degree or substantial professional experience since graduation. The examination consists of two papers in the M.Phil. examination, taken at the times set for that examination in Trinity Term. If a student does not pass the examination on the first occasion, or has been given permission, for exceptional reasons, to take the examination later, the examination may be taken on the Monday of the seventh week of the following Michaelmas Term. Arrangements for the Michaelmas examination will be made by the Director of Graduate Studies.

Additional regulations for Development Studies

Probationer Research Students in Development Studies who have been admitted to this status but who have not received appropriate postgraduate training in a relevant aspect of development studies or of research techniques for the social sciences may, with the formal approval of the Director of Graduate Studies, the Course Director of the course concerned, and the Graduate Studies Committee of Area and Development Studies, be required to attend and pass successfully any course listed for the M.Phil. in Development Studies or appropriate course from another postgraduate degree at Oxford University.

This condition shall be conveyed to the student when the offer of a place is made and in such cases transfer to D.Phil. status shall not normally be permitted until this condition has been fulfilled.

2. *Confirmation of D.Phil. status*

Students who have been admitted to D.Phil. status must, not later than the ninth term or normally earlier than the sixth term after that in which he or she was initially admitted to the status of a Probationer Research Student or to the status of a student for another higher degree of the University to D.Phil. status, apply for confirmation of that status. Students would normally be expected to apply for confirmation of D.Phil. status before the end of their ninth term after admission to Probationer Research status.

Requirements for confirmation of status are:

(*a*) completion of the appropriate form, obtainable from the Graduate Studies Office, signed by the supervisor and an appropriate college officer.

(*b*) a comprehensive outline of the treatment of the thesis topic including details of progress made and an indication of the anticipated timetable for submission.

(*c*) two draft chapters intended to form part of the final thesis.

The application must be submitted to the relevant Graduate Studies Committee, who will appoint an assessor or assessors as appropriate. A written report on the application will be made to the committee before confirmation of D.Phil. status is approved.

If the committee does not consider that the candidate's progress warrants confirmation of status it may either (*a*) recommend resubmission of the application at a later date within the normal timetable (not later than six terms after admission to D.Phil. status) or (*b*) approve an extension of D.Phil. status in order to allow time for resubmission of the application or (*c*) approve transfer to M.Litt. status, or (*d*) reject the application.

Individual departments or the Area and Development Studies Committee may require candidates to complete other tests or assessments before confirmation is approved. Candidates are advised to consult the Notes of Guidance for Graduate Students issued by each Graduate Studies Committee.

Additional regulations for the sub-faculty of Economics

Those applying for confirmation of D.Phil. status in Economics shall present the preliminary results of their research at a departmental seminar or workshop as part of the confirmation process, under arrangements to be approved by the Director of Graduate Studies.

3. *Theses*

M.Sc. by Research

Where, exceptionally, transfer has been allowed to M.Sc. by Research status, candidates are required to submit either a thesis or two written papers not exceeding in total 25,000 words in length.

Theses for the Degree of M.Litt. which exceed 50,000 words, theses or written papers for the M.Sc. by Research which exceed in total 25,000 words, and those for the Degree of D.Phil. which exceed 100,000, excluding the bibliography, are liable to be rejected unless candidates have, with the support of their supervisors, secured the leave of the appropriate Academic Studies Committee to exceed this limit. These figures are strictly *maxima*. It is not intended the board's intention that they should be construed as norms, and candidates are advised that many successful theses have been significantly shorter.

3. BOARD OF THE FACULTY OF LAW

[For candidates admitted before Michaelmas Term 1997

1. *Transfer from Probationer Research Student to M.Litt. Status*

(i) All candidates are normally admitted in the first instance as Probationer Research Students, unless they have successfully completed the BCL.

(ii) A Probationer Student must satisfy the following requirements before being admitted to the status of an M.Litt. student. He or she must submit in typescript two copies of (*a*) a piece of written work relevant to the subject which he or she proposes for a thesis, which must be either a short section of the thesis or a short essay on a topic relevant to the subject (approximately 6,000 words): and (*b*), as a distinct requirement, a description or synopsis in up to 2,000 words of the candidate's proposals for the development of the research project into an M.Litt. thesis. The written work and the description or synopsis will be considered by two assessors appointed by the board. There will be an oral examination, and the assessors must satisfy themselves that the candidate's subject for a thesis is satisfactory and that he or she is competent to handle it. They may recommend that the candidate (*a*) pass; (*b*) fail; or (*c*) be permitted to resubmit.

The piece of written work is normally to be submitted, through the Secretary of Faculties, eight days before the third stated meeting of the board's Graduate Studies Committee in the Probationer Student's third term. The Graduate Studies Committee of the board, after consulting the student's supervisor, may for good cause give leave for submission to be deferred to a date not later than the end of the student's sixth term. The committee, may, on the recommendation of the assessors, permit a candidate to resubmit and undergo further oral examination; a candidate granted such permission must submit his or her revised written work before the committee's third stated meeting in his or her sixth term.

A student admitted to read for the M.St. in Legal Research who wishes to transfer to the status of M.Litt. Student must first comply with this regulation not later than the end of the sixth term from admission in the case of full-time students or the ninth term from admission in the case of part-time students. A student applying so to transfer may submit, as written work for the Qualifying Test, work prepared for submission or actually submitted in satisfaction of the requirements for the M.St. in Legal Research.

A student admitted to read for the Diploma in Law who wishes to transfer to the status of M.Litt. student must first comply with this regulation not later than the end of his or her sixth term as a Student for the Diploma in Law.

The board may appoint additional assessors should need arise.

2. *Transfer from Probationer Research Student to D.Phil. Status*

(i) All candidates are normally admitted, in the first instance as Probationer Research Students unless they have successfully completed the BCL.

(ii) The application for transfer from Probationer Research Student to D.Phil. status shall normally be presented to the Graduate Studies Committee of the Law Board towards the end of the candidate's third term. He or she must submit in typescript two copies of (*a*) a piece of written work relevant to the subject which he or she proposes for a thesis, which must be either a short section of a thesis, or a short essay on a topic relevant to the subject (approximately 10,000 words): and (*b*), as a distinct requirement, a description or synopsis in up to 2,000 words of the candidate's proposals for the development of the research project into a D.Phil. thesis. The written work and the description or synopsis will be considered by two assessors appointed by the board. There will be an oral examination and the assessors must satisfy themselves that the candidate's subject for a thesis is satisfactory and that he or she is competent to handle it at the D.Phil. level. They may recommend that the candidate (*a*) pass; (*b*) fail; (*c*) be permitted to resubmit; or (*d*) be admitted to the status of M.Litt. student.

The piece of written work is normally to be submitted, through the Secretary of Faculties, eight days before the third stated meeting of the board's Graduate Studies Committee in the Probationer Student's third term. The Graduate Studies Committee of the Law Board, after consulting the student's supervisor, may for good cause give leave for submission to be deferred to a date not later than the end of the student's sixth term. The committee, may, on the recommendation of the assessors, permit a candidate to resubmit and undergo further oral examination; a candidate granted such permission must submit his or her revised written work before the committee's third stated meeting in his or her sixth term.

A student admitted to read for the M.St. in Legal Research who wishes to transfer to the status of D.Phil. Student must first comply with this regulation not later than the end of the sixth term from admission in the case of full-time students or the ninth term from admission in the case of part-time students. A student applying so to transfer may submit, as written work for the Qualifying Test, work prepared for submission or actually submitted in satisfaction of the requirements for the M.St. in Legal Research.

A student admitted to read for the Diploma in Law who wishes to transfer to the status of D.Phil. student must first comply with this regulation not later than the end of his or her sixth term as a student for the Diploma in Law.

The board may appoint additional assessors should need arise. The assessors shall not normally be appointed until the Secretary of Faculties has received the written work. Both assessors shall read the written work and conduct the oral examination.

3. *Transfer from M.Litt. status to D.Phil. status*

The same procedure is to be followed as that required of Probationer Research Students.

4. *Confirmation of D.Phil. Status*

Candidates must apply for confirmation of D.Phil. status on the basis laid down in the *Regulations* governing the D.Phil. degree. In deciding whether to confirm D.Phil. status, the Graduate Studies Committee of the Law Board will require from the candidate's supervisor a report on how much of the thesis has been completed, with a prognosis of the likelihood of completion, and a recommendation as to whether or not the status should be confirmed.

5. *Theses*

All theses in Law must have a table of contents; and also a table of cases and/or statutes where the thesis deals mainly with case and/or statute law. M.Litt. theses must not exceed 50,000 words and should not normally be less than 40,000 words and D.Phil. theses must not exceed 100,000 words and should not normally be less than 75,000 words, the limit to include all notes but to exclude any tables of cases, and statutes and any bibliography.]

[For candidates admitted after Michaelmas Term 1997

1. *The First Research Year*

(i) All those admitted to a research degree in the Faculty of Law must in the first year of their research complete the course work elements of the M.St. in Legal Research and may not transfer to a new status or proceed to any examination unless they have obtained from the co-ordinator a certificate that they have satisfactorily done so.

(ii) Candidates admitted in the first instance as Probationer Research Students may, with the consent of the Faculty Board, transfer to the status of a student for the M.St. in Legal Research.

2. *Transfer to the D.Phil. or M.Litt.*

(i) Candidates wishing to transfer to the status of student for the degree of D.Phil. or M.Litt. must, subject to sub-paragraphs (ii) and (iii) below, undertake both parts of the Qualifying Test (paragraph 3 below).

(ii) Candidates who at the time of their transfer will have successfully completed the two-year programme based on the BCL or M.Jur. (including the submission of a thesis lying in the field of research which they wish to pursue) are exempt from Part B of the Qualifying Test.

(iii) Candidates who at the time of their transfer will have successfully completed the M.St. in Legal Research shall submit, in lieu of Part B of the Qualifying Test, their successful M.St. thesis. (The attention of candidates who have obtained leave to supplicate for the degree of M.St. in Legal Research is drawn to the fact that transfer to the M.Litt. is in practice excluded by *Examination Regulations* Ch. VI, Sect. v, § 6, 5 (i) which, differently from Ch. VI, Sect. VIII, § 7, 5 (i) relating to examining the D.Phil., provides that M.Litt. examiners must exclude from consideration *inter alia* any material submitted for an M.St.)

(iv) Students who have previously been registered for the M.St. in Legal Research or for the M.Phil. in Law, and have been granted leave to supplicate for either of these degrees, but have been referred on their application to transfer to D.Phil. status, may hold the status of Probationer Research Student, provided that the Faculty Board is satisfied that the student fulfils the conditions set out in Ch. VI, Sect. XXXII, s. 2, cl. 1. Probationer Research Student status in this instance may not be held for more than six terms beyond the date at which they first held the status of a student for the M.St. in Legal Research or for the M.Phil. in Law.

3. *The Qualifying Test*

(i) Part A of the Qualifying Test requires that the candidate shall submit to the Graduate Studies Office two typescript or printed copies of a statement of the subject of the proposed thesis and details of the manner in which the candidate proposes to treat it. This statement shall not exceed 2,000 words.

(ii) Part B of the Qualifying Test requires that the candidate shall submit to the Graduate Studies Office two typescript or printed copies of a substantial piece of written work which may or may not be intended to form part of the proposed thesis but must be relevant to its subject. For transfer to the D.Phil., this Part B submission must not exceed 10,000 words, for the M.Litt., 6,000 words. In each case the candidate must state the number of words used.

(iii) Supervisors of candidates offering Part B are required to discuss with the candidate the names of possible assessors, and to provide the Board with the names of three suitable persons who have indicated who have indicated their willingness to act as assessors if called upon to do so. This notification may be made before the submission of the material, but must be made, at the latest, on the day the material is submitted.

(iv) Subject to sub-paragraph (v) below, candidates admitted as Probationer Research Students to the doctoral or M.Litt. programmes, must submit all materials for the Qualifying Test by the end of the fourth week of Full Term in the third term after the candidate's admission.

(v) Subject to the general time-limit in sub-paragraph (vi) below, the Graduate Studies Committee, having consulted with the supervisor, may, for good cause, allow the Qualifying Test to be deferred.

Applications for deferral must be made through the Graduate Studies Office in time to allow the Graduate Studies Committee to consider the matter in the second week of the candidate's third term.

(vi) In no case may the materials for the Qualifying Test be submitted or resubmitted after the end of the sixth term from the admission of the student to the doctoral or M.Litt. programmes.

4. *Assessing the Qualifying Test*

(i) The Director of Graduate Studies shall appoint two assessors and shall report their appointments to the Board.

(ii) The assessors shall interview the candidate.

(iii) The assessors shall report in writing as to (*a*) the suitability of the candidate's subject for the kind of thesis in question and (*b*) the competence of the candidate to handle it at the required level; and, in accordance with their report, the assessors shall make a recommendation.

(iv) On the first submission for the Qualifying Test, the assessors may recommend (*a*) that the candidate be granted the transfer which has been applied for, or (*b*) that the candidate be permitted to resubmit either for Part A or Part B, or for both parts of the Qualifying Test; or (*c*), in the case of an application to transfer to the D.Phil. from a status other than that of the M.Litt. but subject to paragraph 2 (iii) above, that the candidate be permitted to advance only to the M.Litt.

(v) Unless, for good cause shown, the Director of Graduate Studies, after consultation with the supervisor, agrees to an extension of time, the assessors must lodge their report and recommendation with the Graduate Studies Office within one calendar month of the date on which the materials are sent out to them.

(vi) The Graduate Studies Office shall pass the report and recommendation to the Director of Graduate Studies, who has the authority of the Board to inform the candidate without further delay of the nature of the recommendation and to inform the supervisor of the contents of the report.

(vii) Where the assessors have recommended resubmission or transfer to the M.Litt., the candidate may resubmit at any time before the end of the sixth term from admission. On resubmission, the assessors may recommend (*a*) that the candidate be granted the transfer requested; (*b*) that the candidate be refused permission to transfer or (*c*) in the case of an application to transfer to the D.Phil. from a status other than that of the M.Litt. but subject to paragraph 2 (iii) above, that the candidate be permitted to advance only to the M.Litt. In the case of a Probationer Research Student the recommendation that the candidate be refused permission to transfer has the effect of permitting the candidate to request a retrospective registration for the M.St. in Legal Research under Ch. VI, Sect. XXXI, s. 3, 10 of the *Examination Regulations*.

(viii) The Director of Graduate Studies shall place the report of the assessors before the meeting of the Graduate Studies Committee next following its receipt by the Graduate Studies Office.

(ix) Any resubmission must be made through the Graduate Studies Office within the time limit specified in paragraph 3 (v) and (vi) above.

5. *Confirmation of D.Phil status*

With the exception of those who are exempt from the requirement of confirmation by reason of having attained the status of D.Phil. student after having obtained the degree of M. Phil., all candidates for the D.Phil. must apply for confirmation of that status by the end of the sixth term from their admission to research graduate status or, at the latest, by the end of the second week of the seventh term. The Graduate Studies Committee of the Law Board requires to see, in addition to the completed application form supplied by the Graduate Studies Office, (*a*) a provisional contents page for the thesis, and (*b*) a short statement of the content of each chapter. These statements must not exceed 200 words on each chapter and must indicate whether or not the chapter has been completed either in draft or in final form. The Committee may grant the application or refer it back for resubmission. No further resubmission is permitted after the end of the candidate's ninth term.

6. *Theses*

All theses in law must have a table of contents and also a table of cases and/or statutes where the thesis deals mainly with case and/or statute law. M.Litt. theses must not exceed 50,000 words and should not normally be less than 40,000 words, and D.Phil. theses must not exceed 100,000 words and should not normally be less than 75,000 words, the limit to include all notes but to exclude any tables of cases, and statutes and any bibliography.

7. *Teaching by Postgraduates*

(i) A postgraduate in the Faculty of Law shall be entitled to enter his or her name in the Faculty Board's teaching register at any time but shall not enter into any teaching obligation unless the register also shows that he or she has received permission to teach from the Faculty Board.

(ii) In granting this permission the Faculty Board shall specify the maximum number of hours that the postgraduate may oblige himself or herself to devote to teaching and preparation for teaching.

(iii) The Faculty Board shall not grant any postgraduate permission to teach unless the teaching register also shows that he or she has received such instruction in teaching as the board shall from time to time require.

(iv) In the absence of exceptional circumstances, the Faculty Board shall not grant any postgraduate permission to teach unless he or she has or will have completed at least one year of research before the teaching obligation commences.

(v) Any postgraduate who undertakes a teaching obligation shall be bound to enter details of that obligation in the teaching register.

(vi) The Faculty Board shall have power to delegate to one or more officers of the board its power to give permission to teach, provided that, in making any such delegation, it also specifies the criteria to which that officer or those officers must have regard.

4. DEPARTMENT OF POLITICS AND INTERNATIONAL RELATIONS

Probationer Research Students, unless or until they have entered upon another course, or have been otherwise dispensed from some or all of the following requirements by the relevant Graduate Studies Committee, are required to undertake the work set out below during the first year.

1. A first-year student shall:

(i) attend such lectures, seminars, and classes as his or her supervisor and/or the relevant Graduate Studies Committee shall determine;

(ii) attend and satisfactorily complete such courses from the Department's Programme as directed by their Graduate Studies Committee.

2. Applications for transfer from PRS status to D.Phil. or M.Litt. status must be delivered to the Graduate Studies Office, University Offices, Wellington Square. Applicants in their sixth and final term of Probationer Status must submit their completed application not later than 5 p.m. on the Friday of fifth week of that term. In addition to satisfying the above requirements (i) and (ii), the transfer of status application must include;

(i) an outline of the proposed research topic as specified in the relevant Notes of Guidance for Graduate Students; and

(ii) a piece of typed or printed written work relevant to the thesis (e.g. a draft chapter) of between 5,000 and 7,000 words.

The relevant Graduate Studies Committee will appoint two assessors, one of whom will normally be a member of the committee, except in cases where neither of the two most appropriate assessors are members of the committee, who will read the work, examine the candidate orally, and submit a written report to the committee.

The committee will then decide whether transfer to the status applied for will be approved. In the case of applications to transfer to D.Phil. status where the committee is not satisfied that the candidate should be allowed to make the transfer, it may approve an extension of time in order to allow the candidate to resubmit at a later date (but before the end of the sixth term after admission to Probationer Research status), or it may approve a transfer to M.Litt. status.

3. Candidates whose applications for transfer of status are not successful may, with the approval of the relevant Graduate Studies Committee, submit revised proposals within their first six terms of Probationer status.

4. Though not in itself sufficient qualification for students wishing to advance to M.Litt. or D.Phil. status, the successful completion of the M.Sc. in Politics and International Relations Research may serve in place of 1. (i) and (ii) above, and material submitted as part of the requirements for the M.Sc. may also be used in the transfer application. Probationer Students registered for the M.Sc. in Politics and International Relations Research should normally apply for transfer of status by the end of the Trinity Full Term of their first year of study.

5. SAID BUSINESS SCHOOL

1. *Transfer to M.Litt. or D.Phil. status*

Candidates seeking admission in order to read for the M.Litt. or D.Phil. are normally registered as Probationer Research Students and as such, unless specifically exempted by the committee, must follow the requirements laid down for the degree of Master of Science in Management Research. Transfer to M.Litt. or D.Phil. status normally is dependent on successful completion of the M.Sc. course, though this is not in itself a sufficient condition of transfer. Applications should be submitted to the Graduate Studies Committee and, for students who have completed the M.Sc. in Management Research, will comprise the following:

(*a*) a transfer of status form, obtainable from the school, signed by the candidate's supervisor and an appropriate college officer. The candidate should indicate clearly on the form the status to which he or she wishes to transfer.

(*b*) a good pass in the M.Sc. in Management Research.

(*c*) a thesis proposal of no more than 5,000 words setting out the structure of the thesis and the way in which the student will tackle the thesis, including research propositions, literative review methods of collecting and analysing data, and presentation of results.

Students who have successfully completed and obtained a good pass in the M.Sc. in Industrial Relations and Human Resource Management (or any other Masters course deemed by the committee to be an acceptable prerequisite for research in Management Studies) will be expected to complete steps (*a*) and (*c*) and, in addition, will have to demonstrate sufficient competence in research methodology. They may be required to take the research methodology course of the M.Sc. in Management Research in their first or second year.

The Graduate Studies Committee will appoint two assessors, one of whom will normally be a member of the committee, except in cases where neither of the two most appropriate assessors are members of the committee, who will read the work, examine the candidate orally, and submit a written report to the committee including the results of the written examination.

The committee will then decide whether transfer or re-admission to the status applied for will be approved. In the case of applications to transfer to D.Phil. status where the committee is not satisfied that the candidate should be allowed to make the transfer it may approve admission to M.Litt. status, or approve an extension of time in order to allow the candidate to resubmit at a later date (but before the end of the sixth term after admission to Probationer Research status). The committee may request additional written work or other evidence, or appoint an additional assessor, whenever it is considered necessary.

The student's thesis committee will meet regularly with the student to review progress and will report annually to the committee.

2. *Confirmation of D.Phil. status*

Students who have been admitted to D.Phil. status must, not later than six terms after admission to D.Phil. status, apply for confirmation of that status. The committee for the school would normally expect students to apply for confirmation of D.Phil. status before the end of their ninth term after admission to Probationer Research status.

Requirements for the status are:

(*a*) completion of the appropriate form, obtainable from the Doctorate Co-ordinator in the Course Administration Office of the school signed by the supervisor and an appropriate college office.

(*b*) a comprehensive outline of the treatment of the thesis topic including details of progress made and an indication, where possible, of the anticipated timetable for submission.

Either at least two draft chapters intended to form part of the final thesis *or* one draft chapter which includes material particularly central to the thesis.

The application must be submitted to the Graduate Studies Committee, who will appoint an assessor or assessors as appropriate. A written report on the application will be made to the committee before confirmation on D.Phil. status is approved.

If the committee does not consider that the candidate's progress warrants confirmation of status it may either (*a*) recommend resubmission of the application at a later date within the normal timetable (not later than six terms after admission to D.Phil. status) or (*b*) approve an extension of D.Phil. status in order to allow time for resubmission of the application or (*c*) approve transfer to M.Litt. status, or (*d*) reject the application.

3. *Thesis*

Theses for the Degree of M.Litt. which exceed 50,000 words, and those for the Degree of D.Phil. which exceed 100,000, excluding the bibliography, are liable to be rejected unless candidates have, with the support of their supervisors, secured the leave of the board to exceed this limit. These figures are strictly maxima. It is not the committee's intention that they should be construed as norms, and candidates are advised that many successful theses have been significantly shorter.

F. CONTINUING EDUCATION BOARD

1. For the purposes of this section the word 'board' shall include any body that has been authorized by the Continuing Education Board with power to act on its behalf to admit students to read for the Degree of Doctor of Philosophy; and to assess students with PRS or D.Phil. status.

2. *Admission*

(*a*) Students are admitted to study on part-time basis only.

(*b*) Students are admitted *either*

(i) as Probationer Research Students, *or*

(ii) as a D.Phil. student. Students may, at the discretion of the Continuing Education Board, be admitted to D.Phil. status under the provisions of Sect. VIII, § 2, cl. 1(i). Students who have successfully completed the M.Sc. in Applied Landscape Archaeology, the M.Sc. or M.St. in English Local History, the M.St. in Professional Archaeology, or any other relevant Oxford Masters degree deemed an acceptable prerequisite by the board, may be admitted under these provisions.

(*c*) In assessing applications from candidates seeking to undertake a research degree through part-time study, the board shall have regard to evidence that:

(i) the candidates can meet the attendance requirements relating to part-time study;

(ii) the candidates are well-fitted to undertake research at doctoral level;

(iii) the candidate's personal and professional circumstances are such that it is both practicable for them to fulfil the requirements of the course, and necessary for them to study on a part-time basis;

(iv) if appropriate, the candidates have the written support of their present employer for their proposed course of study and its obligations;

(v) the proposed field of research can be appropriately supervised under the auspices of the Continuing Education Board.

3. *Attendance requirements*

Students are required to attend for a minimum of thirty days of university-based work each year, to be arranged with the agreement of their supervisor, for the period that their names remain on the Register of Graduate Studies unless individually dispensed by the Continuing Education Board.

4. *Probationer Research Student*

A research student in Archaeology or English Local History admitted to Probationer Research Student status shall normally be required to:

(i) attend such lectures, seminars, and classes as his or her supervisor shall determine, and provide evidence of his or her attendance; and

(ii) present one seminar paper which shall be assessed by one or two assessors. Such assessors should not normally include the candidate's supervisor; and

(iii) submit an essay of between 3,000 and 5,000 words, being either a section of the candidate's proposed thesis or an essay on a relevant topic, and a brief statement limited to 500 words, of the subject of the thesis and the manner in which the candidate proposes to treat it.

5. *Admission/transfer to D.Phil. status*

(*a*) Applicants must demonstrate that they are capable of producing research work of the requisite standard and presenting the findings clearly; and that their planned programme of research is one that may be profitably undertaken at Oxford; and that they have a good knowledge and understanding of the work that is likely to be needed to embark on the programme.

(*b*) Students who have successfully completed the M.Sc. in Applied Landscape

Archaeology, the M.St. or M.Sc. in English Local History, the M.St. in Professional Archaeology, or any other relevant Oxford Masters degree deemed an acceptable prerequisite by the board, shall normally apply for admission to D.Phil. status up to the twelfth term after their initial admission as a graduate student.

(*c*) Students who hold the status of Probationary Research Student, shall normally apply for admission to D.Phil. status after a minimum of six terms and no longer than twelve terms.

(*d*) Admission to D.Phil. status may be made conditional on such requirements as the board may impose.

(*e*) Applicants should specify the date by which they undertake to make available two (or in exceptional cases, three) copies of the written work in support of the application. Applicants should do so not later than four weeks before the start of the full term in which they wish to be assessed. Application for transfer should be sent to the Registry, Department for Continuing Education, 1 Wellington Square.

(*f*) Applications for transfer to D.Phil. status shall be accompanied by:

(i) for research students in Archaeology and English Local History

(1) two copies of a brief statement, limited to 500 words, of the subject of the thesis and the manner in which the candidate proposes to treat it;

(2) two copies of a piece of written work, normally 3,000 to 5,000 words long, being *either* (*a*) a section of the proposed thesis, *or* (*b*) an essay on a relevant topic, *or* (*c*) an augmented version of the statement under (1) above;

(3) two copies of a confidential report from the supervisor, which should be sent by the supervisor direct to the Registry of the Department for Continuing Education.

The Registry shall send one copy of the written work and the confidential report each to the assessors appointed by the board.

Candidates should note that if they adopt alternative 2(*c*) above they must also submit the 500 word statement required by general regulation.

(ii) for research students in Software Engineering

(1) a short dissertation on a topic selected in consultation with the supervisor, or a part-written thesis, the preferred length being of between 25 and 50 typed pages.

(2) The applicant should include with the application a brief description of the proposed subject of research for the D.Phil. degree and a brief statement setting out the steps taken to ensure that he or she has the knowledge and understanding likely to be necessary to embark on the planned research work.

(3) two copies of a confidential report from the supervisor, which should be sent by the supervisor direct to the Registry of the Department for Continuing Education.

The Registry shall send one copy of the written work and the confidential report to each of the assessors appointed by the board.

(*g*) Candidates should also note that while as precise a definition of the subject should be given as is possible at this stage of their work, they are not bound to follow the statement precisely, but may reformulate their plan in the light of further study. If reformulation goes so far as to require alteration of the title of the thesis as approved, however, they should seek permission of the relevant board to alter it.

(*h*) Candidates shall be assessed by two assessors appointed by the board, neither of whom will normally be the student's supervisor. The assessors shall certify that they have considered the written work submitted by the applicant and interviewed the applicant. The assessors should also provide a written report of the application to the board for approval of their recommendation. In cases where the assessors decide that the application is not of the required standard to transfer to D.Phil. status their written report should outline the areas in which the application is judged to fall short of the required standard.

(*i*) A student who is unsuccessful may be given one further opportunity to apply for transfer (within the limit of twelve terms).

6. *Confirmation of D.Phil status*

(*a*) Assessors are appointed by the board to assess whether a candidate's work on their thesis is developing satisfactorily and that they may be considered ready to be examined within three further terms. D.Phil. status must be confirmed before a candidate may submit their thesis for examination for the degree of D.Phil.

(*b*) Application for confirmation of D.Phil. status, with statements of support from the candidate's society and supervisor, shall normally be presented to the Registry of the Department for Continuing Education not earlier than four weeks before the end of the twelfth term, and at the latest by four weeks before the end of the eighteenth term, after admission to the status of Probationer Research Student or to status of student for another higher degree of the University.

(*c*) Application for confirmation of D.Phil. status shall normally be accompanied by:

(i) for research students in Archaeology and English Local History

(1) a statement of the title of the thesis and of the manner in which the candidate proposes to treat it. This should include a proposed chapter structure;

(2) a specimen chapter or part of a chapter not longer than 10,000 words in the case of Archaeology or 6,000 words in the case of English Local History;

(3) a confidential report from the supervisor which should be sent directly to the Registry of the Department for Continuing Education.

The Registry should send the written work and the confidential report to the interviewer appointed by the board.

(ii) for Software Engineering students

(1) the candidate's own written report of progress, stating how much of the thesis is complete and how much remains to be done (with an estimate of the completion date);

(2) a statement of the title of the thesis and a specimen chapter;

(3) a confidential report from the supervisor which should be sent directly to the Registry of the Department for Continuing Education.

The Registry should send the written work and the confidential report to the interviewer appointed by the board.

(*d*) Candidates shall be assessed by two assessors appointed by the board, neither of whom will normally be the student's supervisor. The assessment shall include an oral examination. The assessors shall also provide a written report of the application to the board for approval of their recommendation. In cases where the assessors decide that the application is not of the required standard to warrant confirmation of D.Phil. status, their written report should outline the areas in which the application is judged to fall short of the required standard.

(*e*) A student who is unsuccessful may be given one further opportunity to apply for confirmation (within the statutory limit).

7. *Theses*

Theses submitted for the degree of D.Phil. in *Archaeology* should not normally exceed 80,000 words, *excluding* bibliography and descriptive catalogue or similar factual matter.

Theses submitted for the degree of D.Phil. in *English Local History* shall not exceed 100,000 words. This shall *include* all notes, appendices, any source material being edited, and all other parts of the thesis whatsoever *excluding only* the bibliography.

Theses submitted for the degree of D.Phil. in *Software Engineering* shall not normally exceed 200 pages, A4 size, in normal sized type.

Any thesis exceeding these limits is liable to be rejected on that ground. It is recognized that in special circumstances it will be necessary for leave to be granted to exceed this limit by a stated amount. In particular it is recognized that the inclusion of essential edited source material, whether as an appendix or as a main part of the thesis, presents special problems in regard to length; and the board will be prepared to consider applications for edited material to be excluded from the word limit otherwise placed on the thesis. Leave to exceed these limits for other reasons will be given only in most special cases and on the recommendation of the supervisor. Any application for permission to exceed the limit should be submitted with a detailed explanation and statement of the amount of excess length requested, and with a covering letter from the supervisor. Applications should be made as soon as possible and may not be later than the last day of the fifth week of the term before that in which applications made for appointment of examiners.

Theses submitted for the degree of D.Phil. in *Archaeology* and *English Local History* must be accompanied with two printed or typewritten copies of an abstract of the thesis, which shall not normally exceed 2,500 words for the D.Phil., prepared by the student. One copy of the abstract shall be bound into the copy of the thesis which shall be deposited in the Bodleian Library. (This is in addition to the requirement to submit an abstract of not more than 300 words in length required by the Educational Policy and Standards Committee's Regulations.)

13

REGULATIONS FOR THE DEGREES OF DOCTOR OF LETTERS AND DOCTOR OF SCIENCE

Ch. VI, Sect. IX]

General Regulations

1. Any person belonging to one of the following classes may become a candidate for the Degree of Doctor of Letters or of Doctor of Science under the conditions set forth in this Section:*

(*a*) Masters of Arts or Masters of Biochemistry or Chemistry or Earth Sciences or Engineering or Mathematics or Physics (including Masters of Arts or Masters of Engineering of the University of Cambridge, and Masters of Arts of the University of Dublin, who have been incorporated in this University) who have entered upon the thirtieth term from their matriculation (at this University or, if earlier, at Cambridge or Dublin as the case may be);

(*b*) Undergraduates or Bachelors of Arts of the University of Cambridge or Dublin who have been incorporated and have incepted in the Faculty of Arts in this University and have entered upon the thirtieth term from their matriculation at Cambridge or Dublin;

(*c*) Persons on whom the Degree of Master of Arts has been conferred by decree or special resolution, other than a degree *honoris causa,* and who have entered upon the ninth term from their admission to that degree;

(*d*) Doctors of Philosophy, Masters of Science or of Letters, and Bachelors of Letters or of Science who have entered upon the twenty-first term from their matriculation.

2. Any such person may apply for permission to supplicate for the Degree of Doctor of Letters or of Doctor of Science, submitting, with the application, evidence of his fitness. This evidence must consist of published papers or books, and one year at least must

---

* If papers or books published in the calendar year preceding that in which application is made are submitted, the applicant should specify the exact date of publication.

elapse between the publication of any such paper or book and its submission as evidence in support of an application.* The candidate, in his application, shall state whether any part of the work submitted has previously been accepted for a degree.

3. *The application shall be made through the Secretary of Faculties to the board to which the subject of the papers or books in question belongs, and at least two copies of each of such papers or books shall, where possible, be sent with it. The application must further be accompanied by the fee prescribed in Ch. VIII, Sect. I, §2 (see Appendix I) and by a certificate, signed by some officer of, or some person deputed by, the college to which the candidate belongs, showing that his application has the approval of the college. A candidate who submits papers or books which have been produced in collaboration shall state in respect of each item the extent of his own contribution.

Applications for permission to supplicate for the Degree of Doctor of Letters shall be made to one of the following bodies only:

Board of the Faculty of:

Classics;
English Language and Literature;
Law;
Management.
Medieval and Modern Languages and Literature;
Modern History;
Music;
Oriental Studies;
Philosophy;
Theology.

Divisional Board:

Life and Environmental Sciences;
Social Sciences.

Applications for permission to supplicate for the Degree of Doctor of Science shall be made to one of the following boards only:

Divisional Board:

Life and Environmental Sciences;
Mathematical and Physical Sciences;
Medical Sciences.

Committee for:

Archaeology.

---

* All applications must be on the agenda of the meeting of the board at which they are to be considered. They should therefore reach the Secretary of Faculties not less than eight days before the board's meeting.

4. The board shall appoint judges to consider the evidence submitted by any candidate, and to report thereon to the board. In making their report the judges shall state whether the evidence submitted constitutes an original contribution to the advancement of knowledge of such substance and distinction as to give the candidate an authoritative status in some branch or branches of learning.

5. If the board approves the evidence as of sufficient merit for the degree, it shall give leave to the candidate to supplicate for the degree, and shall notify its decision in the *University Gazette.* One copy of each of the papers and books submitted as evidence shall remain in the possession of the University for deposit in Bodley's Library, provided that no book or paper of which the Library already possesses a copy shall be so deposited except with the consent of the candidate and of the Librarian, unless the copy submitted by the candidate shall be of a different issue or shall contain alterations or additions.

6. The boards shall have power to make, and to vary from time to time, such regulations for carrying out the provisions of this Section as they may deem expedient, provided that all such regulations and any variations in them shall be submitted to the Educational Policy and Standards Committee for approval.

NOTES

REGULATIONS FOR DEGREES IN CIVIL LAW AND FOR THE DEGREES OF MAGISTER JURIS AND MASTER OF PHILOSOPHY IN LAW

[*Ch. VI, Sect. X*]

(i) General Regulations

§1. Admission of Candidates for the Degrees of Bachelor of Civil Law, Magister Juris, and Master of Philosophy in Law

1. Any person may be admitted by the Board of the Faculty of Law as a candidate for the Degrees of Bachelor of Civil Law, Magister Juris, or Master of Philosophy in Law provided that the following conditions have been satisfied:

(*a*) The application must be supported by a college.

(*b*) A candidate must either (i) have passed all the examinations required for the Degree of Bachelor of Arts and have obtained honours in the Second Public Examination, or have obtained honours in a degree examination of another university, such university having been approved by Council for the purpose of the status of Senior Student, or (ii) in the opinion of the Board of the Faculty of Law, be otherwise adequately qualified to undertake the course.

(*c*) A candidate must satisfy relevant provisions prescribed in the regulations made by the board, and any conditions the board may impose.

2. Any student for these degrees who is not a graduate of the University may wear the same gown as that worn by Students for the Degree of Doctor of Philosophy.

§2. Degrees of Bachelor of Civil Law and Magister Juris

Any person who has been admitted under the provisions of §1 above may supplicate for the Degree of Bachelor of Civil Law or the Degree of Magister Juris provided:

(i) that he or she has satisfied the examiners in the examinations prescribed in this section; and

(ii) that he or she has kept three terms of statutory residence as a matriculated member of the University after admission as a Student for the Degree of Bachelor of Civil Law or Magister Juris, whichever is the earlier.

§3. Degree of Master of Philosophy in Law

Any person who has been admitted under the provisions of §1 above may supplicate for the Degree of Master of Philosophy in Law provided:

(i) that he or she has satisfied the examiners in the examinations prescribed in this section; and

(ii) that he or she has kept six terms of statutory residence as a matriculated member of the University after admission as a Student for the Degree of Bachelor of Civil Law or Magister Juris, whichever is the earlier.

§4. Examinations for the Degrees of Bachelor of Civil Law, Magister Juris, and Master of Philosophy in Law

1. The examinations for the Degrees of Bachelor of Civil Law, Magister Juris, and Master of Philosophy in Law shall comprise such subjects as the Board of the Faculty of Law shall from time to time by regulation determine.

2. The examinations shall be under the supervision of the board.

§5. Supervision of Students

Every candidate who elects to offer a thesis or dissertation shall seek approval from the Board of the Faculty of Law as prescribed in the regulations made by the board. Subject to such approval, supervision shall be provided as prescribed in Ch. VI, Sect. XXXI, §4, provided that references to the Degree of Master of Studies shall be deemed to refer to the Degrees of Bachelor of Civil Law, Magister Juris, or Master of Philosophy in Law as the case may be.

§6. Admission of Bachelors of Civil Law and Holders of the Degree of Magister Juris or the Degree of Master of Philosophy in Law to the Degree of Doctor of Civil Law

1. Any person who has been admitted to the Degree of Bachelor of Civil Law or to the Degree of Magister Juris or Master of Philosophy in Law, and who has completed fifteen terms from the date of such admission, may apply to the Board of the Faculty of Law for leave to supplicate for the Degree of Doctor of Civil Law. The application shall be made through the Secretary of Faculties, and shall be accompanied by

(1) evidence that the candidate's application has the approval of his or her college;

(2) the fee prescribed in Ch. VIII, Sect. I, §2 (see Appendix I);

(3) evidence of the candidate's fitness for the degree. This evidence must consist of three copies of a published book or of published

books or papers, treating in a scientific manner of one or more legal subjects and consisting of an original contribution to the advancement of knowledge of such substance and distinction as to give the candidate authoritative status in some branch or branches of legal learning. A candidate who submits papers or books which have been produced in collaboration shall state in respect of each item the extent of the candidate's own contribution.

2. On receipt of the application the Board of the Faculty of Law, having determined that the evidence submitted is of the appropriate kind, shall appoint not fewer than two judges, who shall report to the board on the sufficiency of the evidence.

3. If the board, after consideration of the reports of the judges, shall approve the evidence as sufficient for the degree, it shall give leave to the candidate to supplicate for the degree, and shall notify its decision in the *University Gazette*. One copy of the evidence shall remain in the possession of the University for deposit in Bodley's Library, provided that no book or paper of which the Library already possesses a copy shall be so deposited except with the consent of the candidate and of the Librarian, unless the copy submitted by the candidate shall be of a different issue or shall contain alterations or additions.

§7. Admission to the Degrees of Bachelor of Civil Law and Doctor of Civil Law by Accumulation

1. Any person belonging to one of the following classes may apply to the Board of the Faculty of Law for permission to supplicate for the Degrees of Bachelor of Civil Law and Doctor of Civil Law at the same time under the conditions set forth in this sub-section:

(*a*) Masters of Arts, except those on whom the degree has been conferred by decree or special resolution, who have entered upon the sixty-sixth term from their matriculation at this University, or, if they have been incorporated in this University, the sixty-sixth term from their matriculation at the University of Cambridge or of Dublin;

(*b*) persons on whom the Degree of Master of Arts has been conferred by decree or special resolution, other than a degree *honoris causa*, and who have entered upon the forty-fifth term from their admission to that degree;

(*c*) Doctors of Philosophy, or Masters of Letters or of Science or of Studies, who have entered upon the sixty-sixth term from their matriculation at this University.

2. The application of any such person shall be made to the board, and dealt with by the board, in the manner prescribed in §6 above.

3. If the board approves the evidence as sufficient for the Degree of Doctor of Civil Law, it shall give leave to the candidate to supplicate for the Degrees of Bachelor of Civil Law and Doctor of Civil Law at the same time, although the candidate shall not have passed the examination for the former degree.

Special Regulations

Degrees of Bachelor of Civil Law and Magister Juris

1. *Admission criteria*

BCL The Law Board will normally admit to the BCL only candidates whose previous legal training is primarily in the common law.

M.Jur. The Law Board will normally admit to the M.Jur. only candidates whose previous legal training is not primarily in the common law.

2. *Residence*

Candidates for the BCL and M.Jur. must keep three terms statutory residence.

3. *Courses and subjects*

The subjects of the examination are listed in Schedule A below. The details of the courses are set out in the Law Faculty Student Handbook. Each course carries a credit rating which is stated in the Law Faculty Student Handbook for the year of the examination, subject to any amendment posted in the Law Faculty Office by the Monday of week minus 1 of the Michaelmas Term before the examination is held.

Candidates for the BCL and M.Jur. must offer papers carrying a total credit value of at least twelve, and not more than fourteen, units, by taking a minimum of three, and a maximum of five, papers. A dissertation, which is valued at three credits, counts as one paper.

Not all subjects will necessarily be taught or examined in any one year. Details of those which are available will be published in the Law Faculty Student Handbook for the year of the examination, subject to any amendment posted in the Law Faculty Office by Monday of week minus 1 of the Michaelmas Term before the examination is held.

In addition to the subjects in Schedule A, candidates may offer any other subject that may be approved from time to time by regulation published in the *Gazette* by the end of the Monday of week minus 1 of the Michaelmas Term before the examination is held.

No candidate for the BCL or M.Jur. may:

(*a*) offer more than one subject from List III;

(*b*) offer a subject with the same title and/or the same syllabus as one which he or she has previously offered in the Final Honour School of Jurisprudence or Diploma in Legal Studies;

(*c*) offer both Comparative Law of Contract and Comparative Law: Delict (French);

(*d*) offer two subjects having the same syllabus.

BCL Subject to compliance with the requirements on credit rating and other regulations above, candidates for the BCL may offer:

(*a*) any subject in List I or List II which is offered in the year in question;

(*b*) a dissertation under the provisions in Schedule B below.

M.Jur. Subject to compliance with the requirement on credit rating and other regulations above, candidates for the M.Jur. may offer:

(*a*) any subject in List II or List III which is offered in the year in question;

(*b*) any subject in List I which is offered in the year in question and for which they obtain the permission of the Law Board's Director of Graduate Studies (Taught Courses), given on the recommendation of the student's college tutor and a teacher of the subject concerned;
(*c*) a dissertation under the provisions in Schedule B below.

4. *Examinations*

In examinations (except in the case of dissertations and of Jurisprudence and Political Theory) *BCL* candidates will be required to answer 3 or 4 questions, as specified by the examiners, in each paper; *M.Jur.* candidates will not be required to answer more than 3 questions in each paper.

Candidates offering Jurisprudence and Political Theory will be examined under the provisions of Schedule C.

The examiners may award a distinction for excellence in the examination.

Candidates who fail or withdraw from the examination may with the permission of the faculty board and subject to such conditions as it imposes offer themselves for re-examination. Candidates offering themselves for re-examination must retake all of the papers, except that:

(*a*) if all of the written papers are passed and the dissertation failed then only the dissertation need be resubmitted;
(*b*) if the dissertation is passed and one or more of the written papers failed then only the written papers need be re-taken;

provided that nothing in this clause shall prejudice the powers of the Educational Policy and Standards Committee and Proctors to permit partial resits in exceptional circumstances.

If a candidate, having failed or withdrawn from an examination, successfully applies to sit the examination at a later date, and one or more of the subjects studied by that candidate are not available when the candidate comes to be examined, papers shall nevetheless be set for that candidate in those subjects. These papers may not be taken by other candidates.

Candidates who offer two or more of the subjects listed in Schedule D, or who offer one of more of those subjects and a dissertation on a topic recognised by the Graduate Studies Committee in Law as being within the field of European and Comparative Law, shall be awarded the title 'BCL [or M.Jur.] in European and Comparative Law'.

5. *Statutes and Other Source Material*

Details of the statutes and other source material which will be available to candidates in the examination room for certain papers will be given in a notice circulated to candidates by the examiners.

6. *Notice of options*

The date for notification of the options to be offered by candidates is the fourth week of the Michaelmas Full Term preceding the examination.

7. *Examiners*

The examiners appointed to examine subjects in List III shall be those appointed to examine the same subjects in the Honour School of Jurisprudence and shall examine those papers in the examination for the Honour School of Jurisprudence.

Degree of M.Phil. in Law

1. *Admission criteria*

The Law Board will normally admit to the M.Phil. in Law only candidates whose thesis topic and supervisorial arrangements have been approved by the Graduate Studies Committee for Law.

Candidates may signify an intent to take the M.Phil. in Law when they initially apply to do the BCL or M.Jur., or they can do so after they have been admitted for the BCL or M.Jur. In either case they must fill in the appropriate form which can be obtained from the Graduate Studies Office, by the end of the Hilary Term of the year before which they intend to do the M.Phil.

2. *Residence*

Candidates for the M.Phil. in Law must keep 6 terms statutory residence, which may include periods spent in residence while studying for the BCL or M.Jur.

3. *Courses and examination*

Candidates for the M.Phil. in Law shall satisfactorily complete Part 1 and Part 2. Part 1 and Part 2 shall be taken in that order and shall normally be taken in successive years. A candidate wishing to take Part 2 but not to proceed directly from Part 1 to Part 2 in successive years must seek permission from the Graduate Studies Committee for Law. Part 1 shall consist of the BCL or M.Jur. as the case may be.

In Part 2, candidates for the M.Phil. in Law shall follow a course of instruction in Legal Research Method, satisfy the examiners that they have completed to the required standard such tests or exercises in Legal Research Method as may be prescribed as part of such a course of instruction, and be examined by thesis which must not exceed 30,000 words and should not normally be less than 25,000 words, and by oral examination, under the provisions of cll. 1 to 9 of the regulations for the M.St. in Legal Research, provided that:

(*a*) references to the Degree of Master of Studies shall be deemed to refer to Part 2 of the M.Phil. in Law;

(*b*) in cl. 5, the date of application for examination shall be during the Trinity Full Term after the candidate began Part 2 of the M.Phil. in Law. A candidate who wishes to apply for examination at a later date must seek the approval of the Graduate Studies Committee for Law by the end of week four of the same Trinity Full Term.

The thesis may cover the same area of Law as a dissertation offered in the BCL or M.Jur., but the text of the dissertation must not be incorporated into the thesis.

Successful candidates whose Part 1 studies meet the requirements for the Degree of BCL (or M.Jur.) in European and Comparative Law shall be awarded the Degree of M.Phil. in European and Comparative Law.

SCHEDULE A

List I

Corporate Finance Law;
Corporate Insolvency Law;
Crime, Justice and the Penal System;
Evidence;
Legal History: Legislative Reform of the Early Common Law;
The Law of Personal Taxation;
Philosophical Foundations of the Common Law;
Restitution.

List II

Comparative Human Rights;
Comparative Law: Delict (French);
Comparative Public Law;
Competition Law;
Conflict of Laws;

Corporate and Business Taxation;
European Business Regulation;
European Employment and Equality Law;
Global Comparative Financial Law;
Globalization and Labour Rights;
Intellectual Property Rights;
International Dispute Settlement;
International Economic Law;
International Environmental Law;
International Human Rights and the Law of War;
International Law of the Sea;
Jurisprudence and Political Theory;
Philosophical Foundations of Property Rights;
Principles of Civil Procedure;
Problems in Contract and Tort (German and English Law compared);
Regulation;
Roman Law (Delict);
Transnational Commercial Law.

List III

Administrative Law;
Company Law;
Comparative Law of Contract;
Constitutional Law;
Contract;
Criminal Justice and Penology;
Criminal Law;
Ethics;
European Community Law;
Family Law;
History of English Law;
International Trade;
Jurisprudence;
Labour Law;
Land Law;
Principles of Commercial Law;
Public International Law;
[**From 1 October 2004:** Taxation Law]
Tort;
Trusts.

SCHEDULE B

Dissertations

Candidates for the BCL and M.Jur. may offer a dissertation, which must be written in English and must not exceed 12,500 words and should not normally be less than 10,000 words (including notes, but excluding tables of cases or other legal sources) on a subject to be proposed by the candidate in consultation with the supervisor, and approved by the Graduate Studies Committee in Law. In deciding whether to give approval, the committee shall take into account the suitability of the subject matter and availability of appropriate supervision. Candidates should submit the proposed title of the dissertation and a synopsis of its scope in not more than 150 words not later than the end of week 3 of Michaelmas Full Term to the board's Director of Graduate Studies (Taught Courses) who shall, when the topic and supervisor have been confirmed by or on behalf of the board's Committee for Graduate Studies, communicate that information to the Chairman of the Examiners for the BCL and M.Jur.

Supervisors or others are permitted to give bibliographical help and to discuss drafts.

A dissertation carries a credit value of three units. The examiners must judge the extent to which the dissertation affords evidence of significant analytical ability on the part of the candidate. Tables must be incorporated within the dissertation. Notes should appear at the bottom of the page or at the end of the dissertation.

The dissertation (two typewritten or printed copies) must be delivered in a parcel bearing the words 'Dissertation for the BCL' (*or* 'M.Jur.') (as the case may be) to the Clerk of the Schools, Examination Schools, High Street, Oxford OX1 4BG, to arrive not later than noon on the Friday of the fifth week of the Trinity Full Term in which the examination is to be taken. The dissertation must bear the candidate's examination number, but not his or her name and must be accompanied by (i) a signed statement by the candidate that, except as otherwise indicated, the dissertation is his or her own work, and (ii) a statement specifying which part or parts of the dissertation form part of work which has been, or will be, submitted in accordance with the requirements of a course (other than the present) undertaken at this University or any other institution. The examiners shall exclude from consideration any material which is not the candidate's own work or which forms part of work which has been, or will be, submitted in accordance with requirements of a course (other than the present) undertaken at this University or any other institution and shall have power to require the candidate to produce for their inspection the complete work submitted or to be submitted.

SCHEDULE C

Candidates offering Jurisprudence and Political Theory will be examined in that subject by the submission of three essays. Topics for essays will be prescribed by the examiners and published on the notice board of the Examination Schools, High Street, Oxford OX1 4BG, on the morning of the Friday of the eighth week of the Hilary Term preceding the examination. The examiners shall offer a choice of six topics from which candidates shall be required to select three. The total length of the three essays submitted shall be not less than 5,000 words, nor more than 8,000. Two copies of each essay submitted must be delivered to the Chairman of the BCL/M.Jur. Examiners, Examination Schools, High Street, Oxford OX1 4BG, by noon on the Friday preceding the beginning of the Trinity Full Term in which the examination is to be taken. The essays must bear the candidate's examination number, but not his or her name. Every candidate shall sign a certificate to the effect that the essays are his or her own work, and that no help was received, even bibliographical, with their preparation, and the candidate's tutor or tutors in Jurisprudence and Political Theory, or if not available, a Law tutor in the candidate's own college shall countersign the certificate confirming that, to the best of his or her knowledge and belief, these statements are true. Candidates shall further state the total number of words used in their essays. This certificate shall be presented together with the essays.

SCHEDULE D

Subjects in European and Comparative Law:

(From List II) Comparative Human Rights; Comparative Law: Delict; Comparative Public Law; Competition Law; Conflict of Laws; European Business Regulation;

European Employment and Equality Law; Global Comparative Financial Law; Globalization and Labour Rights; Intellectual Property Rights; International Economic Law; Problems in Contract and Tort; Roman Law (Delict) and Damage to Property; Transnational Commercial Law.

(From List III) Comparative Law of Contract; European Community Law.

NOTES

15, 16

DEGREES IN MEDICINE AND SURGERY

Ch. VI, Sect. XI]

A

XI. TIMES AND EXERCISES REQUIRED FOR DEGREES IN MEDICINE

§1. Qualifications of Candidates for the Degree of Bachelor of Medicine

1. Any person who has been admitted to the Degree of Bachelor of Arts with Honours may supplicate for the Degree of Bachelor of Medicine, provided that he shall have passed the examinations hereinafter prescribed.

2. Any person who has been admitted to the Second Examination for the Degree of Bachelor of Medicine by the Medical Sciences Board under the provisions of §3, cl. 16 of this section may supplicate for the Degree of Bachelor of Medicine without having been admitted to the Degree of Bachelor of Arts with Honours, provided that he shall have passed the Second Examination and shall have kept statutable residence for six terms.

3. A Student for the Preliminary Examination in Medicine or for the Degree of Bachelor of Medicine who has been admitted under the provisions of §3, cl. 16 of this section and who is not a graduate of the University may wear the same gown as that worn by Students for the Degree of Doctor of Philosophy.

§2. Subjects and Method of the Examination for the Preliminary Examination in Medicine

1. A candidate may be admitted to the Preliminary Examination in Medicine provided that his or her name is on the Register of Clinical Students and he or she has been admitted to the Degree of Bachelor of Arts with Honours or has obtained a degree of another university deemed adequate for the purpose by the Medical Sciences

Board, and that he or she has satisfied such additional qualifications as the Medical Sciences Board may from time to time prescribe in its regulations.

2. The Preliminary Examination in Medicine shall consist of two parts. Part I may be offered not earlier than three terms, and Part II not earlier than six terms, from the date of entry onto the Register of Clinical Students.

3. The examination shall comprise such subjects and papers as the Medical Science Board shall from time to time by regulation determine.

4. The examiners may award a distinction to candidates of special merit in either Part I or Part II of the examination, provided that all the subjects in that Part have been offered and passed at one examination.

5. The examination shall be under the supervision of the Medical Sciences Board.

§3. Subjects and Method of the Examination for the Degree of Bachelor of Medicine

1. There shall be two examinations for the Degree of Bachelor of Medicine. Both examinations shall be under the supervision of the Medical Sciences Board. The Board shall have power to require candidates for admission to any part of the First or Second Examination to produce certificates of attendance at courses of practical instruction, and such other certificates as the board may from time to time determine, and to define the form of such certificates. It shall be the duty of the Registrar to see that these conditions are observed.

First Examination

2. The subjects of the First Examination shall be:

Part I

1. Organization of the Body
2. Physiology and Pharmacology
3. Biochemistry and Medical Genetics
4. Medical Sociology

Part II

5. Integrative Systems of the Body
6. The Nervous System
7. General Pathology and Microbiology
8. Psychology for Medicine

3. The syllabus of each subject shall be as prescribed from time to time by the Medical Sciences Board by regulation.

4. A candidate may enter his or her name for Part I of the examination not earlier than the third term and for Part II not earlier than the fifth term from having started the course for the First Examination.

5. Subjects 1, 2, 3, 5, 6, and 7 shall each be examined in two Parts, A and B. In each of these subjects, a candidate must offer both Parts A and B at one examination, provided that a candidate who has failed at his or her first attempt to satisfy the examiners in one Part only of a subject may offer that Part alone at a subsequent examination. In each of these subjects, a candidate must pass both Parts, or have accumulated passes in both Parts, in order to pass in that subject. when a candidate who at the first attempt passed only one Part of a subject subsequently passes the remaining Part of that subject, the examiners shall publish his or her name as having passed in that subject.

6. A candidate must offer all four subjects in Part I at one examination, provided that a candidate who has failed at his or her first attempt in any subject or subjects may offer subject 4 or any Part or Parts of subjects 1, 2, or 3 at a subsequent examination (in accordance with clause 5 above), and provided that the Medical Sciences Board may dispense candidates who have already passed a First Public Examination in any subject from the requirements to offer all four subjects at one examination. In Part I, the examiner may publish the name of a candidate as having passed one, two, three, or four subjects, and the examiners may in addition publish the name of a candidate as having passed one Part only of any of the subjects 1, 2, or 3. In Part II, a candidate may offer one, two, three, or four subjects at one examination. In Part II, the examiners may publish the name of a candidate as having passed one, two, three, or four subjects. The examiners may in addition publish the name of a candidate as having passed one Part only of any of the subjects 5, 6, or 7.

7. A candidate shall be deemed to have passed the First Examination if he or she has satisfied the examiners in all the subjects of Parts I and II as specified in clause 2 above.

8. A candidate who has passed Part I of the First Examination shall be deemed to have passed the First Public Examination.

9. No candidate shall be admitted to the examination for Part II of the First Examination without first having passed all the subjects of Part I, save in exceptional circumstances at the discretion

of the Director of Pre-clinical Studies following application from the candidate's society. No candidate may offer any subject or Part of a subject in Part I of the First Examination on more than two occasions, and in Part II of the First Examination on more than three occasions, save in exceptional circumstances at the discretion of the Director of Pre-clinical Studies following application from the candidate's society.

10. The examiners may award a distinction to candidates of special merit in either Part I or Part iI of the examination, provided that all examinations for all four subjects specified for that Part in clause 2 above have been offered in their entirety and passed at one examination which shall be the candidate's first attempt.

11. The examiners may award a Pass with Merit to candidates of special merit in any of the individual subjects 1, 2, 3, 5, 6, or 7, provided that all four subjects of Part I or of Part II of the examination have been offered in their entirety at one examination. The award of Pass with Merit shall be based on performance in Part B of a subject and shall be confined to candidates who have passed Part A of that subject at the same sitting which shall be the candidate's first attempt.

*12. No candidate other than a Senior Student qualified under (*b*) of this clause shall be admitted to the First Examination unless his or her name has been entered on the Register of University Medical Students and he or she has previously passed

(i) either the Qualifying Examination in Chemistry and Physics for medical students provided for in clause 13 below or examinations in chemistry and physics approved by the Medical Sciences Board; and

(ii) either the Qualifying Examination in Zoology for medical students provided for in clause 14 below, or an examination in Biology approved by the Medical Sciences Board.

(*b*) A Senior Student may be admitted to the First Examination if his or her name has been entered on the Register of Medical Students and he or she has previously passed an examination approved by the Medical Sciences Board.

13. There shall be a Qualifying Examination in Chemistry and Physics for medical students, which shall be governed by the following provisions:

---

* Details of examinations approved and the combination of subjects required for the purposes of Ch. VI, Sect. XI. § 3, cl. 12 may be obtained from the Director of Pre-clinical Studies, the Old Observatory, University Laboratory of Physiology, Parks Road.

(*a*) The examination shall be under the supervision of the Medical Sciences Board.
(*b*) The syllabus and number of papers shall be prescribed from time to time by regulations of the Medical Sciences Board.
(*c*) Subject to the provisions of Ch. VI, Sect. II. D, any person may be admitted to the examination whether he or she is a member of the University or not.

14. There shall be a Qualifying Examination in Zoology for medical students, which shall be governed by the following provisions:
(*a*) The examination shall be under the joint supervision of the Medical Sciences and Life and Environmental Sciences Board.
(*b*) The syllabus and number of papers shall be prescribed from time to time by regulations of the Medical Sciences and Life and Environmental Sciences Boards.
(*c*) Subject to the provisions of Ch. VI, Sect. II. D, any person may be admitted to the examination whether he or she is a member of the University or not.

Second Examination

15. The subject of the Second BM Examination shall be clinical medicine in all its aspects.

*16. Candidates may be admitted to the Second Examination if they are on the Register of Clinical Students and satisfy one of the following conditions:
(*a*) they have passed in all the subjects of the Preliminary Examination in Medicine; or
(*b*) they have passed in all the subjects of the First Examination and the Qualifying Examination in the Principles of Clinical Anatomy and have either been admitted to the Degree of Bachelor of Arts with Honours or obtained a bachelor's degree at another university; or
(*c*) they have both
   (i) successfully completed at a university in the United Kingdom a GMC-approved course of study in medical sciences that has included the subjects of the First Examination and the Principles of Clinical Anatomy, and is deemed by the Medical Sciences Board to qualify the candidate for admission; and

---

* Applications for admission to the Second BM Examination under the provisions of this clause should be addressed to the Medical School Offices, John Radcliffe Hospital, Oxford OX3 9DU.

(ii) obtained a bachelor's degree in science or arts at a university, such degree having been approved by that board.

17. The Second Examination shall cover three years, the subjects for each year being prescribed by regulation of the Medical Sciences Board. Each of Years 1 and 2 shall involve a form of assessment prescribed by regulation of the board and notified to candidates by it. No candidate shall commence Year 2 or 3 until he or she has satisfactorily completed Year 1 or 2 respectively (except that a candidate shall be permitted to commence Year 2 if he or she passed all the subjects in the Preliminary Examination in Medicine), unless the Director of Clinical Studies, at his or her discretion and in exceptional circumstances, decides that the candidate may proceed to the next year of study on condition that he or she should undertake remedial work and if necessary be reassessed at a later date. **[From 1 October 2004:** Year 3 shall involve written and clinical examinations and may involve oral examinations. No candidate shall be examined on the Year 3 Vocational Studies Course until he or she has passed the assessments for Years 1 and 2 and the Year 3 General Clinical Skills Course.**]**

18. Candidates who have passed all subjects in the Preliminary Examination in Medicine shall be exempted from the Year 1 assessments of the Second Examination.

19. Breach of the Code of Conduct for Medical Students, as approved and from time to time amended by Council's General Purposes Committee on the recommendation of the Medical Sciences Board, may be deemed to be a ground for removal of a student's name from the Register of Clinical Students according to procedures which shall always be subject to approval by Council's General Purposes Committee on the recommendation of the Medical Sciences Board.

20. The provisions of Ch. VI, Sect. 11. D, concerning the times of holding examinations and the entry of names, and the special regulation concerning dress shall not, unless otherwise prescribed by regulation of the board, apply to Years 1 and 2, except in the case of a formal examination set by the examiners of these stages, as prescribed by regulation of the board.

§4. Qualifying Examination in the Principles of Clinical Anatomy

There shall be a Qualifying Examination in the Principles of Clinical Anatomy for medical students who have passed the First Examination for the Degree of Bachelor of Medicine and who are seeking admission to a course in clinical medicine in Oxford or elsewhere. The examination shall be governed by the following provisions.

(*a*) The examination shall be under the supervision of the Medical Sciences Board.

(*b*) No candidate shall be admitted to this Qualifying Examination unless his or her name has been entered on the Register of University Medical Students and he or she has previously passed the First Examination for the Degree of Bachelor of Medicine.

(*c*) The syllabus and obligations required for candidates, and the method of examination, shall be as prescribed from time to time by regulations of the Medical Sciences Board.

§5. Status of Student for the Degree of Doctor of Medicine*

1. Any person may be admitted to the status of Student for the Degree of Doctor of Medicine if

either

(1) he or she has been admitted to the Degree of Bachelor of Medicine and has entered upon the thirty-sixth term from his or her matriculation, or, in the case of a person who has incorporated as a Bachelor of Medicine, the thirty-sixth term from the date of his or her matriculation at the University of Cambridge, or, in the case of a person who has been admitted to the Second Examination for the Degree of Bachelor of Medicine under the provisions of §3, cl. 16 of this section, the twenty-seventh term from his or her matriculation; *Or*

(2) he or she holds the Degree of Master of Arts of the University (other than a degree by decree or resolution or an honorary degree), has previously been entered in the Register of University Medical Students and has passed the First Examination for the Degree of Bachelor of Medicine of this University, holds a degree qualifying him or her to be placed on the

---

* Students whose proposed outlines for submission (or resubmission) of a dissertation have been approved before 1 April 2002 will be examined under the provisions governing the Degree of Doctor of Medicine as they stood before that date (*Examination Decrees*, 2001, pp. 899–902). Students who were first examined before 1 April 2002 but who will be seeking permission to resubmit after that date will also be re-examined under the old provisions. Judges who examine a student who is required to submit under the old provisions may however, should the thesis not meet the requirements for the award of the degree on initial submission, offer the candidate the option of revising his or her thesis for re-examination (on payment of the appropriate fee) in accordance with clause 9 (2) of subsection 9 below under the legislation as it stood on 1 April 2002.

Medical Register, and has entered upon the thirty-sixth term from his or her matriculation.

2. It shall be the duty of the Secretary of Faculties and Academic Registrar to keep a Register of those admitted to the status of Student for the Degree of Doctor of Medicine.

3. On application for admission to the status of Student for the Degree of Doctor of Medicine, the applicant shall state whether he or she will wish to submit as his or her dissertation a series of papers or books, as permitted under §9, cl. 2 of this section.

§6. Registration for the Degree of Doctor of Medicine

1. Except in the case of submission of published work as a dissertation for the degree, no student shall submit a dissertation until at least the beginning of the sixth term after the Medical Sciences Board has granted his or her admission.

2. A student must carry out the bulk of the research for the dissertation during the period in which he or she is registered.

3. If the dissertation, including published work submitted as a dissertation, has not been submitted for examination before the fifteenth term after admission has been granted, a student shall be required to seek readmission.

§7. Advisers of Students for the Degree of Doctor of Medicine

1. (1) Except in the case of students submitting published work as a dissertation for the degree, every student on admission as a Student for the Degree of Doctor of Medicine shall be allocated to an Adviser in Oxford appointed by the Medical Sciences Board in the student's area of research.

(2) In the case of students working outside Oxford, each student shall be required to seek additional advice from a senior member of the academic or clinical staff at the institution at which the research is to be pursued; and the student shall notify the Medical Sciences Board of the name of that person and provide a written statement signed by that person confirming that he or she is willing to undertake the role of an additional Adviser.

2. (1) It shall be the duty of the Adviser to offer support and assistance to the student in the manner prescribed in the *Memorandum of Guidance for Advisers and Students for the Degree of Doctor of Medicine* as published from time to time by the Medical Sciences Board.

(2) The Adviser shall submit reports on the progress of the student's work at the beginning of each Michaelmas and Trinity Term, and the reports of Advisers outside Oxford shall, in the case of the relevant students, also be received by the Adviser in Oxford.

(3) It shall be the responsibility of the Adviser at the host institution (whether that is Oxford or elsewhere) to inform the Medical Sciences Board if he or she is of the opinion that the student is unlikely to reach the standard required for the Degree of Doctor of Medicine.

3. (1) Except when approval has been given for submission of published work as a dissertation for the degree, it shall be the duty of every Student for the Degree of Doctor of Medicine to seek the advice of the Adviser (or, in the case of students working outside Oxford, both Advisers) at an early stage of the proposed research and to seek comments on his or her dissertation before its submission.

(2) During the course of the research the student shall maintain contact with the Adviser or Advisers in the manner prescribed in the *Memorandum of Guidance for Advisers and Students for the Degree of Doctor of Medicine*.

§8. Confirmation of status as a Student for the Degree of Doctor of Medicine

1. (1) Except in the case of submission of published work as a dissertation, a student registered for the Degree of Doctor of Medicine must, not later than the sixth term and not earlier than the third term after that in which he or she was admitted to the status of Student for the Degree of Doctor of Medicine, apply to the Medical Sciences Board for confirmation of that status.

(2) Except in the case of students submitting published work as a dissertation, all Students for the Degree of Doctor of Medicine shall have their status confirmed before they may make an application for the appointment of examiners.

2. Students applying for confirmation of status shall submit their application to the Medical Sciences Board through the Secretary of Faculties and Academic Registrar; and each application shall be accompanied by:

(1) a report on the work undertaken since registration;

(2) a statement from the Adviser at the place where the work is being undertaken commenting on whether the student's

progress provides firm evidence that the work when completed is likely to reach the standard required for the Degree of Doctor of Medicine.

3. (1) If, after considering a student's application for confirmation of status, the Medical Sciences Board concludes that the student's progress does not warrant confirmation, the board may permit the submission of a further application not later than the third term after the original application.

(2) If the second application is unsuccessful, the student's name shall be removed from the Register of Students for the Degree of Doctor of Medicine.

4. Except in the case of submission of published work as a dissertation for the degree, a Student for the Degree of Doctor of Medicine shall cease to hold that status unless it has been confirmed within nine terms of his or her admission to that status.

§9. Examination of Students for the Degree of Doctor of Medicine

1. A Student for the Degree of Doctor of Medicine who has, where applicable, fulfilled the requirements set out in §§6 and 8 of this section, and whose status has not expired, may apply to the Medical Sciences Board for the appointment of examiners and for leave to supplicate for the Degree of Doctor of Medicine.

2. (1) A Student for the Degree of Doctor of Medicine may *either*

(*a*) submit a dissertation upon a subject which, together with the proposed manner of treating it, has previously been approved by the Medical Sciences Board;

or

(*b*) in exceptional circumstances, submit as his or her dissertation a series of papers or books published at least twelve months before the proposed date of submission, if the previous approval of the Medical Sciences Board has been given after considering the seniority of the student (who shall be required to have held a career-grade post for a period of at least fifteen years prior to submission), and the opinions of any referees who may be consulted.

(2) Submission of published works as a dissertation shall be permitted only when there is evidence of outstanding quality in the scientific papers or other works intended for

submission; it shall also be a requirement that the published works be accompanied by a general introduction and a general conclusion and that they form a continuous theme.

3. Applications for the appointment of examiners and for leave to supplicate shall be made to the Medical Sciences Board through the Graduate Studies Office and shall include:

(1) a statement by the candidate that the thesis is his or her own work, except where otherwise indicated;

(2) a statement by the candidate of what part, if any, of the thesis has already been accepted, or is concurrently being submitted, for any degree or diploma or certificate or other qualification in this University or elsewhere;

(3) a statement, where applicable, from the Adviser at the place where the research was undertaken certifying that the candidate has sought his or her advice as appropriate;

(4) a statement from the candidate's college in support of the application;

(5) two printed or typewritten copies of an abstract of the thesis, which shall not normally exceed 300 words in length.

4. Where the Medical Sciences Board has given approval for submission of published work as a dissertation, two printed or typewritten copies of the thesis may be submitted by the student immediately after approval, in a format which is in accordance with the instructions obtainable from the Medical Sciences Board through the Graduate Studies Office.

5. In all other cases, students shall submit an application in accordance with clause 2 above up to four months in advance of submitting two printed or typwritten copies of the thesis in a format which is in accordance with the instructions obtainable from the Medical Sciences Board through the Graduate Studies Office.

6. If a student has not submitted his or her thesis for examination within twelve months from submission of the application under the provisions of clause 2 above, then the application shall lapse.

7. (1) On receipt of an application the Medical Sciences Board shall appoint two examiners, neither of whom shall be the student's Adviser, and one of whom shall be external to the University.

(2) The duties of the examiners shall be:

(*a*) to consider the thesis and the abstract of it submitted by the candidate, except that they shall exclude from consideration in making their report any part of the thesis that either has already been accepted, or is concurrently being submitted, for any degree or diploma or certificate or other qualification in this University or elsewhere, or does not represent the candidate's own work;

(*b*) to examine the candidate orally in the subject of his or her thesis, unless, in exceptional circumstances in the case of submission of published work as a dissertation, the board agrees, on the recommendation of the examiners, to dispense with this requirement;

(*c*) to report to the Medical Sciences Board through the Secretary of Faculties and Academic Registrar on the scope, character, and quality of the work submitted, in the manner prescribed in clause 9 below;

(*d*) to return to the candidate the copies of the thesis and abstract.

8. (1) The Medical Sciences Board shall have power to make regulations concerning the notice to be given of the oral examination, and of the time and place at which it may be held.

(2) The examination may be attended by any member of the University in academic dress, while non-members may attend only with the consent of the examiners.

(3) The Vice-Chancellor and Proctors after consultation with the board may decide (either at their own discretion or at the request of the student or the supervisor or department) to forbid the attendance of any person or all persons (other than the examiners and the candidate) or to impose any condition on attendance if and to the extent that such action is in their view necessary to protect the interests of the University or the candidate or both, and the examiners shall be informed accordingly and shall include this information in the notice of examination.

9. Having completed the examination, the examiners may make one of the following recommendations in their report to the Medical Sciences Board, or they may alternatively proceed in accordance with the provisions of clause 10 below:

(1) that the board grant the student leave to supplicate for the Degree of Doctor of Medicine, if making this recommendation, the examiners shall include in their report statements that:

(*a*) the student possesses a comprehensive knowledge of the particular field of learning in which the thesis falls;

(*b*) the thesis embodies original observations on either clinical or experimental material;

(*c*) the work done by the student and embodied in the thesis has resulted in an original and substantial contribution to medical science;

(*d*) the thesis is presented in a lucid and scholarly manner;

(*e*) the student has presented a satisfactory abstract of the thesis;

(*f*) in their opinion the thesis merits the award of the Degree of Doctor of Medicine;

(2) that the board offer the student the option of reference of the thesis back to him or her in order that he or she may revise it for re-examination for the Degree of Doctor of Medicine on not more than one occasion, on the basis that the thesis has not reached the standard required for the Degree of Doctor of Medicine; if making this recommendation, the examiners shall annex to their report to the board a statement, for transmission to the student, setting out the respects in which the thesis falls below the standard required for the degree and what changes are necessary for it to reach that required standard, and setting a deadline (subject to the agreement of the board) for resubmission;

(3) that, in the case of a student whose thesis has already been referred back on one occasion, the student's application for leave to supplicate be refused; if making this recommendation, the examiners shall annex to their report a statement, for transmission to the student, setting out the respects in which the thesis falls below the standard required for the degree.

10. (1) If the examiners are satisfied that the student's thesis is of sufficient merit to qualify for the degree but consider, nevertheless, that before the thesis is deposited the student should make minor corrections (which are not sufficiently substantial to justify reference back for re-examination), they shall require the student to correct the thesis to their satisfaction before they submit their report.

(2) If the student has not completed these corrections within three calendar months of the date of the oral examination, his or her name shall be removed by the Secretary of the Faculties and Academic Registrar from the Register of Students for the Degree of Doctor of Medicine, except that the board may, on good cause shown by the student,

grant an extention of time of three further calendar months in which the student may fulfil this requirement before the removal of his or her name from the Register.

(3) No subsequent extension shall be granted, but it shall be open to a student who has failed to fulfil this requirement within those three or six months in total, as the case may be, to apply to the board for reinstatement as a Student for the Degree of Doctor of Medicine, with the support of his or her college and Adviser(s), upon submission to the Secretary of Faculties and Academic Registrar of a copy of his or her thesis incorporating the required corrections, and upon payment of such reinstatement fee as may from time to time be prescribed by Council by decree; leave to supplicate shall not be granted until this fee has been paid.

11. The Medical Sciences Board may exempt a candidate who is being re-examined under the provision of clause 9(2) above from a further oral examination, if the examiners are able to certify that they are satisfied without examining the candidate orally that they can recommend to the board in the terms required by clause 9(1) above that he or she be given leave to supplicate for the Degree of Doctor of Medicine.

12. In an exceptional case in which the Medical Sciences Board is unable to accept the examiners' recommendation, or in which the examiners cannot reach an agreed recommendation, the board shall have power to appoint one or two new examiners, as it deems necessary, to conduct such further examination of the candidate as the board may require.

13. (1) A student who has been granted leave to supplicate by the board shall be required to submit to the Secretary of Faculties and Academic Registrar a copy of his or her thesis, incorporating any amendments or corrections required by the examiners and approved by the board, with a view to deposit in the Bodleian or other appropriate university library.

(2) Leave to supplicate shall in all cases be conditional upon fulfilment of this requirement.

14. (1) It shall be the duty of the Secretary of Faculties and Academic Registrar to notify the student of the board's decision as soon as may be.

(2) The Secretary of Faculties and Academic Registrar shall also be responsible for publishing at the end of each

academic year (except in so far as it may be necessary not to publish any name in order to comply with the provisions of the Data Protection Act 1998) the names of those students to whom permission to supplicate has been granted during that year, together with a statement of the subject of the thesis written by each.

15. When, on the conclusion of an investigation of a complaint made by a student, the Proctors recommend that a student be re-examined, the board shall have power to hold a new examination.

§10. Qualifying Examination in Medical Sociology

There shall be a Qualifying Examination in Medical Sociology for medical students seeking admission to the Second Examination for the Degree of Bachelor of Medicine and to clinical schools of the Universities of Cambridge and London for their clinical course. The examination shall be governed by the following provisions:

(i) The examination shall be under the supervision of the Medical Sciences Board.

(ii) The syllabus and number of papers shall be as prescribed from time to time by regulations of the Medical Sciences Board.

(iii) Subject to the provisions of Sect. II. D, cl. 6 of this chapter, any person may be admitted to the examination whether he be a member of the University or not.

XII. DEGREES IN SURGERY

Ch. VI, Sect. XII]

§1. Degree of Bachelor of Surgery

Every person admitted to the Degree of Bachelor of Medicine shall *ipso facto* be admitted also to the Degree of Bachelor of Surgery.

§2. Degree of Master of Surgery

1. Any person may supplicate for the Degree of Master of Surgery provided that

(*a*) *either*

(i) he has been admitted to the Degree of Bachelor of Surgery and has entered upon the thirtieth term from his matriculation, or in the case of a person who has incorporated as a Bachelor of Surgery, the thirtieth term from the date of matriculation at the University of Cambridge, or in the case of a person who has been admitted to the Second Examination for the Degree of Bachelor of Medicine under the provisions of Ch. VI, Sect. XI, §3, cl. 6, the twenty-first term from his matriculation;

or

(ii) he holds the Degree of Master of Arts of the University (other than a degree by decree or special resolution or a degree *honoris causa*), has previously been entered in the Register of University Medical Students and has passed the First Examination for the Degree of Bachelor of Medicine of this University, holds a medical degree of another British university qualifying him to practise medicine, and has entered upon the thirtieth term from his matriculation;

(*b*) he has passed both parts of the examination hereinafter prescribed.

2. The examination shall be conducted in two parts. The subject of Part I shall be the principles and practice of surgery. Candidates may, under regulations made by the Medical Sciences Board, be permitted to show knowledge of special branches of surgery. Part II shall consist of a thesis, and may include a viva voce examination to test the candidate's general competence in his own field.

3. The examination shall be under the supervision of the Medical Sciences Board. The examination in Part I shall take place at such times as the Medical Sciences Board shall determine, provided that the board shall give not less than three months' notice of the time and place of the examination.

4. No candidate shall be admitted to Part I of the examination earlier than the seventh term from the date of passing the Second Examination for the Degree of Bachelor of Medicine or an equivalent final medical examination from a university approved by Council.*

5. Candidates for Part I of the examination shall pay the fee prescribed in Ch. VIII, Sect. I, §2 (see Appendix I) and shall produce a certificate, countersigned by the Nuffield Professor of Surgery or his deputy showing that they have engaged to his satisfaction for at least five years in the practice of surgery.

6. No candidate shall be admitted to Part II of the examination

(*a*) unless he has passed Part I of the examination;

(*b*) earlier than the sixteenth term from the date of passing the Second Examination for the Degree of Bachelor of Medicine or an equivalent final medical examination from a university approved by Council.*

---

* i.e. a university approved for the purpose of Senior Status or a university especially approved for the purpose of this clause.

7. A candidate for Part II of the examination shall submit as evidence of his fitness to supplicate for the degree a thesis upon a subject previously approved by the Medical Sciences Board, or with the previous approval of that board a book or papers which have already been published under his own name. A candidate may submit joint publications provided that a substantial portion of the work submitted has been written solely by him. He shall make his application to the Medical Sciences Board through the Secretary of Faculties, and shall at the same time submit

(*a*) evidence that the subject of his thesis or published work has been approved by the Medical Sciences Board;

(*b*) four printed or typewritten copies of an abstract, of around 400 to 450 words and not exceeding 600 words, summarizing the scope of the thesis or other evidence, the techniques used, and the principal findings;

(*c*) a certificate from the proper officer of his society that his application has the approval of that society;

(*d*) the fee prescribed in Ch. VIII, Sect. 1, §2 (see Appendix I);

(*e*) such number of copies of his evidence in such form as the board may by regulation direct.

The thesis or other evidence shall be accompanied by a certificate signed by the candidate indicating that it is the candidate's own work except where otherwise indicated. If the thesis or published work has not been submitted for examination before the sixteenth term after approval has been given under this clause, the candidate is required to seek reapproval of his submission.

8. On receipt of any such application, the Secretary of Faculties shall submit it to the Medical Sciences Board. The board shall thereupon appoint two examiners whose duties shall be:

(1) to consider the evidence sent in by the candidate under the provisions of the preceding clause; provided that they shall exclude from consideration in making their report any part of the evidence that *either*

  (*a*) has already been accepted, or is being concurrently submitted for any degree in this or any other University, and shall have the power to require the candidate to produce for their inspection the complete thesis so accepted or concurrently submitted; *or*

  (*b*) does not represent the candidate's own work;

(2) if they think fit to examine the candidate orally;

(3) to report to the board through the Secretary of Faculties;

(4) to return to the Secretary of Faculties, with their report, the copy or copies of the evidence submitted by the candidate.

9. On receipt of the report of the examiners, it shall be the duty of the board to decide whether to permit the candidate to supplicate for the Degree of Master of Surgery, but permission shall in no case be given unless the examiners have reported that the work as embodied in his evidence and tested by his examination has resulted in an original contribution to knowledge deserving publication (whether or not already published) based on clinical and/or experimental observations, and that it is in their opinion of sufficient merit to entitle the candidate to supplicate for the Degree of Master of Surgery.

10. If the board approves the evidence as of sufficient merit for the degree, the board shall notify its decision in the *University Gazette* and one copy of the thesis or of each of the papers and books submitted as evidence shall remain in the possession of the University for deposit in Bodley's Library.

B

1. (a) Qualifying Examination in Chemistry and Physics for medical students

1. One three-hour paper will be set.

2. Candidates will be required to show an elementary knowledge of the following topics with special reference to their application in the study of Biochemistry and Physiology:

Physical Chemistry. Ionic, covalent, and hydrogen bonds; partial ionic character of bonds; bond energy; resonance; atomic and molecular orbitals and their application to stereochemistry of carbon compounds and metal complexes; Van der Waals forces; dipole moments and dipole interactions; conformational differences, and geometrical and optical isomerism shown by simple organic molecules.

First and second laws of thermodynamics and their application to physical and chemical changes; Raoult's Law; ideal and non-ideal behaviour of gases and solutions; Donnan equilibrium.

Kinetics of first and second order reactions. Simple treatment of collision and transition state theories. Catalysis and elementary enzyme kinetics.

Electrode potentials; concentration and redox cells. Measurements of e.m.f. and its applications. Factors affecting conductivities of solutions of electrolytes.

Acid, bases and buffers; electrolyte behaviour of amino acids and proteins.

Spectrophotometry: principles and application.

Organic Chemistry. Relation between physical properties and chemical constitution. Mutual influence of functional groups. Mechanisms of ester hydrolysis, substitution and addition reactions. Steric effects in organic reactions. Topics to be illustrated by reference to simple aliphatic compounds, containing one or two of the following functional groups:

$$\text{halogen}, >C{=}C<, >C{=}O, \text{—}CN, \text{—}NH, \text{—}OH, \text{—}SH, \text{—}COOH$$

and its derivatives; simple organic derivatives of phosphoric acid, including anhydrites and mixed anhydrides.

Aromaticity as illustrated by benzene and its simple derivatives, purines and pyrimidines.

Glucose: properties and evidence for structure (including ring structure, but not proof of configuration). Simple glycosides, glycogen.

Structure and properties of simple lipids.

Principle of amino acid sequence determination.

1. (b) Qualifying Examination in Zoology for medical students

1. One three-hour paper will be set.

2. The syllabus for the examination is as follows:

The nature of living organisms; differences between viruses, bacteria, plants, and animals. Metabolism. The organization of cells. Organs and tissues. Co-ordination; evolution of nervous system and sense organs. Outline of vertebrate embryology. Man's place in the animal kingdom; parasitism. Principles of classification.

The nature and mode of action of the gene. Cells, chromosomes, mitosis, and meiosis. Mendelian inheritance, sex determination, linkage and crossover, and mutation. Introduction to population genetics. Genetic variability in populations and its maintenance. Inheritance of quantitative characteristics. Evolution and its ecological implications. Nature and origin of species.

3. Candidates preparing for the examination before coming into residence should note that they will be required to show an *elementary* knowledge of the following:

The nature of living organisms. The differences between viruses, bacteria, plants, and animals.

The general nature of metabolism, including the relationship between photosynthesis and respiration, and the way in which the sun's energy is used by living organisms.

The structure of animal cells, cytoplasm and nucleus, somatic and germ cells.

The microscopic structure of the main tissues of animals, together with sufficient knowledge of the function of these tissues to make their structure intelligible.

A survey in broad outline of the animal kingdom and Man's place in it with, more particularly, an elementary knowledge of protozoa, platyhelminthes, annelids, insects, molluscs, and the seven living classes of the vertebrates. The evolution of the ear and the heart and arterial arches of vertebrates, as illustrating the evolution of organ systems.

The nature and results of the parasitic way of life, particularly as illustrated by *Taenia* when compared with free-living platyhelminthes.

The elements of embryology. Cleavage, the formation of the germ layers and the extra-embryonic membranes in *Gallus.* Cleavage, germ-layer formation, morphogenetic movements, the origin of the alimentary canal, the heart, the nervous system and the brain in *Rana.*

The nature of the gene. The chromosomes, meiosis, mitosis, gametogenesis and fertilization. The Mendelian laws. The genetical consequences of the cytological events visible in the cell. Means of producing genetic variability and stability. Mutation, linkage, and crossing-over (omitting numerical treatment). Sex determination, sex linkage. The interaction between heredity and the environment.

Asexual and sexual reproduction and their evolutionary consequences.

The types of evidence for evolution. The mechanism of evolution and its ecological background.

The principles employed in classifying animals. The concepts of homology and analogy.

Candidates are required, by the Friday of the week prior to the commencement of the examination, to submit to the Head Clerk, University Offices, Wellington Square, Oxford, a certificate signed by a graduate teacher of Biology confirming that they have dissected a representative mammal and a representative amphibian in sufficient detail to demonstrate the gross anatomical features of the principal systems of the body.

2. First Examination for the Degree of BM

A Core Syllabus and a Composite Syllabus (Core plus Extension) for both Parts I and II will be published annually at the start of Michaelmas Term by the Medical Sciences Board. Guidelines for the scope of these syllabuses are given below, but it shall be the syllabuses and not these guidelines that define the material to be examined. The syllabuses will make appropriate reference to related issues of clinical significance. In each subject, candidates will be expected to have a general understanding of the subjects specified in the syllabus, including methods of study and quantitative analysis of experimental results.

In subjects 1, 2, 3, 5, 6, and 7 two papers will be set. In each Paper A, one one-and-a-quarter-hour paper will be set in a format to examine breadth of knowledge and understanding of the Core Syllabus; and in each Paper B, one two-hour paper will be set to examine deeper knowledge and understanding of a choice of topics included in or closely relating to the Composite Syllabus.

Part I

1. *Organization of the body*

Principles of the organization and development of the human body at a gross and microscopic level, emphasizing the relationship between structure and function. Principles of the endocrine system. Human reproduction. Cell biology and the differentiation of tissues, cell growth and multiplication, abnormal growth and neoplasia.

2. *Physiology and Pharmacology*

The basic physiology and pharmacology of the human body excluding the brain and major sense organs, emphasizing the application of basic physico-chemical principles to the understanding of the function of cells and organs of the body. The relationship of the structure of specific organs to their function. The principles of drug action on the body. The principles of pharmacokinetics.

3. *Biochemistry and Medical Genetics*

Principles of mammalian biochemistry, including the structure and function of macromolecules, the major metabolic pathways and their regulation. Aspects of genetics emphasizing eukaryotic systems: genes, the principles of their expression, and the effects of mutation. The principles of medical genetics.

4. *Medical Sociology for Medical Students*

One one-and-a-half-hour paper will be set on the syllabus specified in the Core Syllabus for Part I.

Part II

5. *Integrative Systems of the Body*

The integrative physiological and pharmacological control of systems and processes of the body, including the neuroendocrine system, and their action in normal and abnormal conditions.

6. *The Nervous System*

The central nervous system: principles of its structure at gross and microscopic levels, normal and abnormal function and development. The vascular system of the central nervous system; cerebrospinal fluid. Neuropharmacology and general anaesthesia. Sensory systems and the control of motor activity. Aspects of neuropsychology.

7. *General Pathology and Microbiology*

The basic molecular and cellular mechanisms underlying disease processes including microbial pathogenicity, non-specific and specific defence mechanisms, and healing. Antimicrobial chemotherapy. Cardiovascular pathology. Immunopathology. Emphasis will be placed on general principles rather than on specific diseases. Aspects of epidemiology and public health.

8. *Psychology for Medicine*

One one-and-a-half-hour paper will be set on the syllabus specified in the Core Syllabus for Part II.

General Regulations of the First Examination

Candidates shall submit notebooks, initialled as satisfactory by the demonstrators, or other certified evidence of satisfactory practical work in the courses associated with each subject of the First Examination with the exception of Medical Sociology and Psychology for Medicine. The practical course for Subject 2 includes the course in elementary statistics defined in the Composite Syllabus for Part I. Each notebook shall be accompanied by a certificate signed by the candidate indicating that the notebook submitted is the candidate's own work. The notebooks or evidence shall be available to the examiners at a time prescribed by the examiners prior to the written examination and shall be taken into consideration by them. Candidates whose notebooks or other evidence are unsatisfactory may be required by the examiners to submit to further examination. Failure to submit an initialled notebook or certified evidence shall result in the candidate being failed in the relevant subject of the examination, unless the candidate has an adequate attendance record at the relevant practical classes and provided the examiners are satisfied, after taking account of the candidate's examination script and any further examination as they shall deem necessary, that the candidate has a satisfactory knowledge and understanding of the practical course.

The Director of Pre-Clinical Studies or his or her deputy is required to make available to the examiners evidence (in the form of a list of names, signed by Director or his or her deputy) to certify that each candidate has a satisfactory attendance record for each practical course defined in the preceding paragraph. Evidence of satisfactory practical work and of attendance at a practical course is normally admissible by the examiners for a period extending no longer than to the end of the academic year following the year in which the course was pursued.

The Director of Pre-Clinical Studies or his or her deputy is required to make available to the examiners evidence (in the form of a list of names, signed by Director or his or her deputy) to certify that each candidate has participated satisfactorily in the *Patient and Doctor Course*.

Candidates may be required to undergo oral examination.

3. Preliminary Examination in Medicine

The examination shall be divided in two parts as follows:

Part I

There will be three sections to the examination, respectively dealing with core knowledge, clinical skills, and supplementary material (used to assess critical-appraisal skills). Candidates must pass all three sections in order to pass the examination; but candidates who fail in any section or sections of the examination at the first attempt need resit only those sections that they have failed.

1. *Core Knowledge*

Candidates will be required to demonstrate their knowledge and understanding of the basic principles of basic medical science as defined in the core syllabus, which will be published from time to time by the Medical Sciences Board. Two papers will assess factual knowledge and problem-solving skills based on the core material; one paper will contain simple tests of core knowledge (such as short answer questions), and the other will be problem-based. These papers will be marked pass–fail only. The marks from these papers will not contribute to the overall mark in the examination, nor to the award of a Distinction.

2. *Clinical Skills*

Candidates will be required to demonstrate, in a practical examination at the bedside or in a skills centre, or in other practical assessment, basic skills in taking a clinical history, performing a simple clinical examination and applying such practical skills as may be defined in the core syllabus published by the Medical Sciences Board. The assessment will include an appraisal of the candidate's communication skills with patients, orally and in writing, and of his or her professional attitude. In addition, candidates will normally be required to produce a certificate, signed by the relevant clinical supervisor, of satisfactory performance in a longitudinal case study undertaken during the course, before they are admitted to the examination. Arrangements for certification will be circulated to students by the course tutor during the first week of the term in which the examination takes place.

3. *Supplementary Material*

Candidates will be required to demonstrate their breadth or reading beyond the core syllabus, their ability to appraise and criticize experimental evidence, and their ability to interpret and draw conclusions from numerical data. Assessment of these features will be by three written papers (of which candidates must offer all three) and an extended essay. The three papers are: Paper 1 ('Systems of the Body') will require essays on subjects connected with the major organ systems, demonstrating their ability to integrate material from more than one system and from both basic science and clinical practice; Paper 2 ('Medicine, The Individual and Society') will require essays on aspects of psychology, behaviour, public health medicine, sociology and epidemiology (including statistics); Paper 3 ('Critical Appraisal') will contain experimental, epidemiological or clinical data for interpretation but may also include descriptions of experimental methods and require candidates to offer criticism of the experimental method. Candidates will be required to submit one extended essay (maximum 4000 words), on a subject of their choice to be approved beforehand by the course's Education Committee. Submission must be made by the beginning of Trinity Term. The essay should illustrate an aspect of medical science or clinical practice, and should demonstrate breadth of reading, critical appraisal of evidence, and originality of thought. Candidates may be also required to present their project in a lecture or poster. Examiners may award Distinction for outstanding performance in these papers by candidates sitting the examination for the first time.

4. *Timing of the Examination*

The examination will be set at the end of the extended Trinity Term and at the end of the long vacation.

5. *Resits*

Candidates may resit the examination not more than once except by dispensation from the Medical Sciences Board.

6. *Oral examination*

Candidates may be required, at the discretion of the examiners, to undergo an oral examination which may include a further clinical examination.

Part II

The Examination will consist of the following components.

1. Essential clinical skills (defined in the curriculum) to be assessed in-course, signed up and with a certificate required as a qualification for entry to the examination. These skills may be resampled during the end-of-year clinical assessment (to ensure currency).

2. Laboratory medicine to be assessed in-course, at the end of the Laboratory Medicine block, signed up and with a certificate required as a qualification for entry to the examination. This knowledge may also be resampled in a different form (problems integrated with clinical material) during the end-of-year (Part II) examination.

3. Core knowledge (defined in the syllabus) to be assessed by two core papers: short-answer questions and problem-based questions, one paper for each type of question. This material will include clinical diagnostic information and both basic and applied science.

4. A clinical long case, followed by a viva; these are to assess clinical history and examination skills, and knowledge of basic differential diagnosis and simple first-line investigations.

5. An OSCE or similar problem-based clinical assessment.

6. Two essay papers and one data interpretation paper to assess the 'extension' science and clinical knowledge, i.e., critical appraisal skills and reading beyond the core.

7. Two projects or clinical essays, to be completed during the year and handed in before the examination.

The Examiners may award Distinctions to candidates who are sitting the examination for the first time, on the basis of excellent performance in both the clinical and basic-science aspects of the assessment (except that the performance in the core knowledge papers should not contribute to the award of distinctions).

Candidates may resit the examination not more than once except by dispensation from the Medical Sciences Board.

Candidates may be required, at the discretion of the examiners, to undergo an oral examination which may include a further clinical examination.

4. *Second examination for the Degree of BM

1. *Syllabus and Examination*

The Second Examination shall be divided as follows:

YEAR 1

In year one, students are required to satisfy the examiners in:

(*a*) The Foundation Course (being an introduction to clinical methods, history taking and physical examination);

(*b*) The Laboratory Medicine Course (concerning the application to human disease of the principles of Laboratory Medicine, including Histopathology, Microbiology, Clinical Biochemistry, Immunology and Haematology);

(*c*) Surgery;

(*d*) Medicine;

(*e*) Special Study approved by the Medical Sciences Board.

Each candidate will be assessed according to the methods of assessment approved by the Medical Sciences Board and notified to candidates before the commencement of each course of instruction.

Candidates must satisfy the relevant head of department or his/her deputy, or in the case of (*d*) to (*g*) below the Director of Clinical Studies, that they have attended a course of instruction, and attained the necessary skills and knowledge in:

(*a*) Clinical Pharmacology;

(*b*) Primary Health Care;

(*c*) Radiology;
(*d*) Medicine and surgery at a district general hospital;
(*e*) Communication skills;
(*f*) Evidence-based medicine and Informatics;
(*g*) Medical ethics and law.

No candidate shall commence year 2 until he or she has satisfactorily completed year 1, unless the Director of Clinical Studies at his or her discretion should, in exceptional circumstances, decide that the candidate may proceed to year 2 on condition that he or she should undertake remedial work and if necessary be reassessed at a later date.

Year 2

In year two, students are required to satisfy the examiners in:

(*a*) Trauma and Orthopaedics, Accident and Emergency and Muscular Skeletal Medicine;
(*b*) Neurology (including neurosurgery);
(*c*) Obstetrics and Gynaecology (including Genito-urinary medicine);
(*d*) Paediatrics;
(*e*) Primary Health Care;
(*f*) Psychiatry;
(*g*) Public Health Medicine.

Each candidate will be assessed according to the methods of assessment approved by the Medical Sciences Board and notified to candidates before the commencement of each course of instruction.

Candidates must satisfy the relevant head of department or his/her deputy, that they have attended a course of instruction in, and attained the necessary skills and knowledge in:

(*a*) Clinical Geratology;
(*b*) Ophthalmology;
(*c*) Otolaryngology;
(*d*) Palliative Care.

No candidate shall commence year 3 until he or she has satisfactorily completed year 2, unless the Director of Clinical Studies at his or her discretion should, in exceptional circumstances, decide that the candidate may proceed to year 3 on condition that he or she should undertake remedial work and if necessary be reassessed at a later date.

Year 3

[**Until 1 October 2004:** In year 3 students are required to satisfy the examiners in:

(*a*) Medicine (including clinical pharmacology and radiology); and
(*b*) Surgery (including radiology).

Candidates must satisfy the relevant head of department or his/her deputy, or in the case of (*b*) and (*d*) below the Director of Clinical Studies, that they have attended a course of instruction in, and attained the necessary skills and knowledge in:

(*a*) An attachment to a District General Hospital including shadowing of a Pre-registration House Officer;
(*b*) An elective atttachment;
(*c*) Dermatology; and
(*d*) Special study and clinical options approved by the Medical Sciences Board.

Candidates must satisfy the Director of Clinical Studies that they have attained the necessary skills and knowledge in Evidence-based medicine.

No candidate shall be examined in year 3 until he or she has satisfactorily completed years 1, 2, and 3. The examination in Year 3 shall consist of:

(i) a three-hour paper in Medicine and Surgery containing short-answer questions, of which some questions may relate to the specialties studied but not formally examined in years 2 and 3 (namely Clinical Geratology, Dermatology, Ophthalmology, Otolaryngology and Palliative Care);

(ii) an essay of not more than 3,000 words on a subject approved by the Director of Clinical Studies. Such approval must be sought by no later than the date set by the Director of Clinical Studies, this normally being during the first week of the academic year in the year which candidate takes the examination (or not later than four weeks before the set date of the written paper in a subsequent examination in the case of any candidate who fails the year 3 examination in Trinity Term and is required to submit a further essay when the examination is retaken). Essays shall be submitted to the Board of Examiners, c/o Medical School Office, John Radcliffe Hospital, Headington, no later than the date set each year by the Director of Clinical Studies, this will normally be the last Friday before the first elective period. A candidate who fails to submit an essay by the due date will fail the whole examination in year 3. A certificate, signed by the candidate in respect of each essay, indicating that it is the candidate's own work and that it has not been submitted for any degree, diploma, or prize or for publication, prior to the commencement of the candidate's third year of clinical studies, must be submitted separately in a sealed envelope addressed to the chairman of the examiners. Candidates who submit an unsatisfactory essay may be required to resubmit the essay before proceeding to the written paper and clinical examination. A candidate who fails the year 3 examination shall not be required to submit a further essay when the examination is retaken provided that a satisfactory standard has been reached in the essay on the occasion of the first attempt at the examination;

(iii) a clinical examination in both medicine and surgery.

Candidates may be required, at the discretion of the examiners, to undergo an oral examination which may include a further clinical examination. **[From 1 October 2004:**

In Year 3 students are required to satisfy examiners in General Clinical Studies and Vocational Skills. Each candidate will be assessed according to the method approved by the Medical Sciences Board and notified to candidates before the commencement of each course of instruction. Students who fail an assessment will have to forfeit part or all of the elective for a period of intensive clinical training.

1. General Clinical Studies

Students are required to satisfy the examiners in:

(*a*) Medicine and Surgery encompassing communication skills, medical ethics and law, radiology, and clinical pharmacology; and

(*b*) Specialties studied but not previously formally examined (namely Clinical Geratology, Dermatology, Ophthalmology, Otolaryngology, and Palliative Care).

Candidates must satisfy the relevant head of Department or his/her deupty, or in the case of (*d*) and (*e*) below the Director of Clinical Studies, that they have attended a course of instruction in:

(*a*) Medicine;

(*b*) Surgery;

(*c*) Dermatology;

(*d*) Clinical practice in a District General Hospital; and

(*e*) Special Study and Clinical Options approved by the Medical Sciences Board.

2. Vocational Skills

Students are required to satisfy the examiners after completing:

(*a*) Special Study and Clinical Options approved by the Medical Sciences Board:

(*b*) A Course to prepare students for work as a pre-registration house officer;

(*c*) An Elective (students who fail an assessment may be required to complete remedial clinical work. These students will forfeit some or all of the elective and instead will be required to produce a satisfactory report at the end of an additional clinical attachment);

(*d*) A Course on Advanced Life Support;

(*e*) A pre-registration House Officer 'shadowing' attachment generally in the hospital in which the graduate expects to work; and

(*f*) An essay of not more than 3,000 words on a subject approved by the Director of Clinical Studies. Such approval must be sought by no later than the date set by the Director of Clinical Studies, this normally being during the first week of the academic year in which the candidate takes the examination. Essays shall be submitted to the Board of Examiners, c/o Medical School Office, John Radcliffe Hospital, Headington, no later than the date set each year by the Director of Clinical Studies. A candidate who fails to submit an essay by the due date will fail the examination. A certificate, signed by the candidate in respect of each essay, indicating that it is the candidate's own work and that it has not been submitted for any degree, diploma, or prize or for publication, prior to the commencement of the candidate's third year of clinical studies, must be submitted separately in a sealed envelope addressed to the chairman of the examiners.]

2. *Assessment*

[Until 1 October 2004: YEARS 1 AND 2

Proposals for the assessment of candidates in years 1 and 2 of the examination shall be drawn up by each specialty group and submitted for approval to the Medical Sciences Board, at such times as the Board shall determine. The form or forms of assessment are chosen from among the following:

1. clinical examination;
2. competency check sheets or logbooks;
3. examination and comment (written or viva voce) on specimens;
4. objective structured clinical examinations;
5. poster presentations;
6. short written tests which may consist in whole or in part of multiple choice questions;
7. submission of case histories and commentaries;
8. viva voce examination; and
9. other tests individually approved by the board.

In clinical subjects, all assessments shall include a separate test of clinical competence. In addition, reports on candidates' attendance and general aptitude shown during the course on instruction shall be made by those responsible for the courses and taken into consideration in association with the performance of candidates in the assessment. A candidate shall be warned (in writing with a copy to the Director of Clinical Studies) by those responsible for the course in question at a reasonable time before the assessment takes place, if his or her attendance and general aptitude are such as seems likely to jeopardize his or her chances of passing the assessment.

The first assessment of candidates shall be carried out during or at the conclusion of each section of the course by the staff, as appointed by the head of the relevant department. A candidate who fails to reach a satisfactory standard in any part of the assessment may offer himself or herself for reassessment on one further occasion. If a candidate fails to reach a satisfactory standard at the second attempt in any part of the assessment, then the candidate shall be deemed to have failed the complete assessment, and the head of department concerned shall require the candidate to be reassessed in the relevant parts of the assessment after completing the necessary coursework; this assessment shall be carried out and adjudged by the staff appointed by the relevant head of department and in the presence of an external examiner. In the event that a candidate's performance is judged to be unsatisfactory at this attempt then his or her name shall be removed from the Register of Clinical Students subject to appeal to the Medical Sciences Board.

It shall be the responsibility of the staff concerned, under the supervision of the divisional board, to give the candidates and the relevant examiners reasonable notice of the dates on which the assessment will be made, to decide on the outcome of each assessment, and to keep departmental records of each assessment. A candidate should not normally be assessed exclusively by staff members who have been responsible for his or her instruction.

YEAR 3

The methods of assessment in year 3 shall be approved by the Medical Sciences Board. A candidate who is unsuccessful in year 3 may be permitted to offer himself or herself in that examination on two further occasions. Failure to satisfy the examiners at the third attempt shall lead, subject to appeal to the Medical Sciences Board, to the removal of that student's name from the register of clinical students.]

[From 1 October 2004:

YEARS 1, 2, AND 3

Proposals for the assessment of candidates in years 1, 2, and 3 of the examination shall be drawn up by each specialty group, or in the case of year 3 by the Board's Clinical Education Committee and submitted for approval to the Medical Sciences Board, at such times as the Board shall determine. The form or forms of assessment are chosen from among the following:

(*a*) clinical examination including long and short cases;
(*b*) competency check sheets, logbooks, or portfolios;
(*c*) examination and comment (written or viva voce) on specimens;
(*d*) objective structured clinical examinations;
(*e*) poster presentations;
(*f*) case presentations;
(*g*) written tests, which may consist in whole or in part of for example multiple choice questions, short-answer questions, extended matching questions or essays;
(*h*) case histories and commentaries;
(*i*) prepared essays;
(*j*) viva voce examination; and
(*k*) other tests individually approved by the Board.

In clinical subjects, all assessments shall include a test of clinical competence. In addition, reports on candidates' attendance and general aptitude shown during the course of instruction shall be made by those responsible for the courses and taken into consideration in assocation with the performance of candidates in the assessment.

A candidate shall be warned (in writing with a copy to the Director of Clinical Studies) by those responsible for the course in question before the assessment takes place, if his or her attendance and general aptitude are such as seems likely to jeopardize his or her chances of passing the assessment.

The first assessment of candidates shall be carried out during or at the conclusion of each component of the course by the staff, as appointed by the head of the relevant department, or, in the case of year 3, by the examiners and/or assessors.

A candidate who fails to reach a satisfactory standard in any part of the assessment may offer himself or herself for reassessment on one further occasion. In the case of examinations in year 3, this reassessment will be in the presence of an external examiner. If a candidate fails to reach a satisfactory standard at the second attempt in any part of the assessment, then the candidate shall be deemed to have failed the complete assessment. The head of department concerned, or his deputy, or, in the case of year 3, the examiners, shall require the candidate to be reassessed after completing the necessary coursework; this assessment shall be carried out and adjudged by the staff appointed by the relevant head of department, or, in the case year 3, by the examiners, and in the presence of an external examiner. In the event that a candidate's performance is judged to be unsatisfactory at this third attempt then his or her name shall be removed from the Register of Clinical Students subject to appeal to the Medical Sciences Board.

It shall be the responsibility of the staff concerned, under the supervision of the divisional board, to give the candidates and the relevant examiners reasonable notice of the dates on which the assessment will be made, to decide on the outcome of each assessment, and to keep departmental records of each assessment. A candidate should not normally be assessed exclusively by staff members who have been responsible for his or her instruction.]

3. *The duties of the examiners*

YEARS 1 AND 2

In the first assessment of candidates in year 1 each relevant pair of examiners shall be required to attend, and if they so wish participate, on at least one occasion each year.

In the first assessment of candidates in year 2 each relevant pair of examiners shall be required to attend, and if they so wish participate, on at least two occasions in each year.

In the reassessment of any candidate who has been deemed to have failed the whole assessment in years 1 and 2, the external examiner shall be present and may participate if he or she wishes.

Year 3 examiners assist with the assessment of the year 1 special study attachment.

YEAR 3

[Until 1 October 2004: In the examination of a candidate in year 3, the chairman of the year 3 examiners and the relevant subject examiners shall arrange and conduct the examination (provided that the chairman and one relevant subject examiner in each subject shall conduct the examination when fewer than ten candidates present themselves).

In considering whether a candidate shall have passed year 3, the year 3 examiners may:

(*a*) have regard to his/her assessments in years 1 and 2 as well as to his/her performance throughout year 3 and;

(*b*) fail a candidate who does not satisfy them in the clinical part of the examination in year 3 even if he or she has satisfied them in other parts in the stage.

[From 1 October 2004:

Assessment of General Clinical Studies

In the examination of a candidate, the chairman of the year 3 examiners and the relevant subject examiners shall arrange and conduct the examination (provided that the chairman and one relevant subject examiner in each subject shall conduct the examination when fewer than ten candidates present themselves).

In considering whether a candidate shall have passed the assessment, the examiners may fail a candidate who does not satisfy them in one part of the assessment, even if he or she has satisfied them in other parts at that stage.

Assessment of Vocational Skills

In the examination of a candidate, the chairman of the year 3 examiners and the relevant subject examiners shall arrange and conduct the examination (provided that the chairman and one relevant subject examiner in each subject shall conduct the examination when fewer than ten candidates present themselves).

In considering whether a candidate shall have passed the examination, the examiners will consider course material and reports that provide evidence of the candidate's performance.

In considering whether a candidate shall have passed the assessment, the examiners may fail a candidate who does not satisfy them in one part of the assessment, even if he or she has satisfied them in other parts at that stage.]

5. Qualifying Examination in the Principles of Clinical Anatomy

The syllabus shall be published annually in Trinity Term by the Medical Sciences Board. Candidates shall be required to submit notebooks, initialled as satisfactory by the demonstrators, or other certified evidence of satisfactory practical work associated with the course. The examination will consist of in-course assessment of a form approved by the Medical Sciences Board. All of these constituent assessments must be passed for a candidate to pass the examination. Any candidate who fails an assessment may be reassessed during the course or at some duly advertised time during the Long Vacation by such means as may be deemed appropriate by the examiners.

The Director of Pre-Clinical Studies or his or her deputy is required to make available to the examiners evidence in the form of a list of names, signed by the Director or his or her deputy) to certify that each candidate has a satisfactory attendance record at the course in the Principles of Clinical Anatomy. Any candidate whose record of attendance is deemed unsatisfactory by the examiners shall be liable to additional examination by such means as may be deemed appropriate by the examiners, or he or she may be failed at the discretion of the examiners.

Candidates may be required to undergo oral examination.

6. Regulations for the Examinations for the Degrees of M.Ch. and DM

[For First Examination in 2004]

DM

1. *Admission*

Students qualified under Ch. VI, Sect. XI, §5 may apply for admission as a Student for the Degree of Doctor of Medicine to the Medical Sciences Board through the Secretary of Faculties and Academic Registrar. Such application shall be accompanied by:

(i) a completed application form (obtainable from the Graduate Studies Office);

(ii) a statement of not more than 1,500 words outlining the proposed scope of the research to be undertaken and provisional thesis title;

and, in the case of students wishing to submit published work, the following additional information:

(iii) a list of the works to be submitted, details of their publication, and a statement on whether any part of the work to be submitted has previously been accepted for a degree. A student who submits work that has been produced in collaboration shall state in respect of each item the extent of his or her own contribution. This statement must be certified by each of the senior and primary authors (where he or she is not the student) in the case of each piece of collaborative work submitted.

A set of published works may constitute an acceptable dissertation but only if with the addition of a general introduction and general conclusion they form a continuous theme.

2. *Confirmation of Status*

Students who have been admitted to DM status, and intend to submit a dissertation for a thesis, must, not later than six terms and not earlier than three terms after admission to DM status, apply for confirmation of that status.

The requirements for confirmation of status are:

(i) completion by the student of the appropriate form (obtainable from the Graduate Studies Office);

(ii) submission by the student of a report of no more than 2,500 words on the work undertaken since registration, including a comprehensive outline of the research topic, details of progress made, and the anticipated timetable for submission of the thesis;

(iii) completion of the appropriate form (obtainable from the Graduate Studies Office) by the Adviser at the place where the work is being undertaken.

The application shall be directed to the Graduate Studies Committee of the Medical Sciences Board, which shall appoint two assessors competent in the student's area of research (who may include the Adviser in Oxford in the case of students working outside Oxford). The assessors shall submit to the board's Graduate Studies Committee a report (using a form obtainable from the Graduate Studies Office) after considering the student's report and, if necessary, interviewing the student. Before a decision is reached on whether or not confirmation of status should be approved the Graduate Studies Committee shall take into account the comments made on the application by the Adviser at the place of work and that Adviser's biannual reports.

If the Graduate Studies Committee does not consider that the student's progress warrants confirmation of status it may either: (*a*) permit the resubmission of the application on one further occasion not later than the third term after the original application; or (*b*) reject the application.

A copy of the assessors' report, amended as necessary by the Graduate Studies Committee, will normally be made available to the student.

3. *Theses*

The requirements for the submission of a thesis are as follows:

(i) The completion by the student of the appropriate form (obtainable from the Graduate Studies Office). The form may be submitted immediately in the case of students submitting published work as a dissertation and up to four months in advance of submitting the thesis in the case of other students.

(ii) The submission of two printed or typewritten copies of the thesis and two printed or typewritten copies of an abstract, formatted and supplied according to the instructions obtainable from the Medical Sciences Board through the Graduate Studies Office.

4. *Oral Examination*

(i) The place, day, and hour of examination shall be fixed by the examiners, who shall be responsible for informing the student by post, and it shall be the duty of the student to ensure that any letter addressed to him or her is forwarded to him or her if away. The examiners shall allow reasonable time for receiving an acknowledgement from the student of their summons. The day shall be fixed by the examiners to suit their own convenience but they are asked, in order that the student may know what arrangements he or she may safely make, to give the student early information of the date fixed, even though it may be some considerable time ahead.

(ii) Notice of the examination shall be given by the examiners to the Graduate Studies Office.

(iii) If, owing to illness or other urgent or unforeseen cause, an examiner is unable to attend the examination, it shall be postponed to a later date, except that, if the Proctors are satisfied that postponement will be a serious hardship to the student, the Proctors may authorize another person to attend the examination as a substitute. The substitute shall not be required to sign the report, but he or she shall receive such remuneration as the Vice-Chancellor and Proctors shall determine.

M.Ch. Part I

1. A candidate for Part I is required to apply by letter to the Registrar at the University Offices, Wellington Square, Oxford, enclosing the examination fee prescribed in Ch. VIII, Sect. I, §2 (see Appendix I) together with a certificate from the proper officer of his society that his entry is made with the approval of that society. He should at the same time send to the Nuffield Professor of Surgery or his deputy

(*a*) the certificate of his hospital appointments required by Ch. VI, Sect. XII, §2, cl. 5, with the request that it should be countersigned and forwarded to the Registrar; and

(*b*) a statement of any special branches of surgery in which he has had experience and in which he wishes to offer himself for examination.

For candidates who under (*b*) above indicate their wish to be examined in special branches of surgery, questions in those branches may be set in one section of the written paper and in the practical and viva voce examination.

2. The examination will consist of:

(i) A written paper in two sections, each section containing four questions, two of which must be answered. The time allowed for each section will be two hours.

(ii) An essay on one of four subjects set by the examiners.

(iii) A practical and viva voce examination including

(*a*) clinical cases;

(*b*) operative surgery and anatomy;

(*c*) pathology, radiodiagnosis, and other diagnostic methods.

M.Ch. Part II

1. Dissertations, theses, or published work for the M.Ch. must be submitted *in English* unless for exceptional reasons the Clinical Medicine Board or the Physiological Sciences Board otherwise determines at the time of approving the subject of a dissertation or thesis, or granting leave to submit published work, as the case may be.

2. Candidates are required to send three copies of any dissertation, thesis, book, or papers submitted. Dissertations or theses must be either printed or typewritten and should not normally exceed 50,000 words (excluding appendices and case reports). Only in exceptional circumstances and with the approval of the Medical Sciences Board is it permitted to exceed this limit.

3. Candidates are required to submit at the same time as their application four printed or typewritten copies of an abstract, of around 400 to 450 words and not exceeding 600 words, summarizing the scope of the dissertation, thesis, or published work, the techniques used, and the principal findings. One copy of the abstract will be used for the appointment of judges or examiners. One copy must be bound into the copy of the dissertation or thesis which, if the applicant is successful, will be deposited in the Bodleian Library. The abstract may also be bound into the other two copies of the dissertation, thesis, or published work if the candidate so desires. Each copy of the abstract shall be headed with the title of the dissertation, thesis,

or published work, the name and college of the candidate, the degree for which it is submitted, and the term of submission.

4. Unless the board has excused the candidate from this requirement, the dissertation or thesis must be typed on one side of the paper only with a margin of 3 to 3.5 cms on the left-hand edge of each paper. The dissertation, thesis, or published work must have a stabbed binding with covers of stout manila or stiff cardboard and a canvas back, or must be stitched and bound in a stiff case. (It should be noted that the dissertation, thesis, or published work must be bound and that a loose-leaf binder of the screw-in type is not acceptable.)

Candidates are advised to pack each copy of the dissertation, thesis, or published work into a separate parcel, ready in all respects, except the address, to be posted to the judges or examiners when appointed. Each parcel should bear the candidate's name and college and the words 'M.Ch. THESIS' as appropriate in BLOCK CAPITALS in the bottom left-hand corner. The separate copies thus packed should be sent to the Secretary of Faculties, University Offices, Wellington Square, Oxford, in one covering parcel.

5. Oral Examination for the M.Ch.

(1) The examination may be attended by any member of the University in academic dress. No person who is not a member of the University may attend it except with the consent of both judges or examiners.

(2) The place, day, and hour of the examination shall be fixed by the judges or examiners, who shall be responsible for informing the candidate thereof by post prepaid, and it shall be the duty of the candidate to ensure that any letter addressed to him is forwarded to him if away. The judges or examiners shall allow reasonable time for receiving an acknowledgement from the candidate of their summons. The day shall be fixed by the judges or examiners to suit their own convenience, but they are asked, in order that the candidate may know what arrangements he may safely make, to give the candidate early information of the date fixed, even though it may be some considerable time ahead.

(3) Notice of the examination shall be given by the judges or examiners to the Secretary of Faculties.

(4) If, owing to illness or other urgent and unforeseen cause, a judge or examiner is unable to attend the examination, it shall be postponed to a later date, provided that, if the Vice-Chancellor is satisfied that postponement will be a serious hardship to the candidate, he may authorize another person to attend the examination as a substitute. Such substitute shall not be required to sign the report, but he shall receive such remuneration as the Vice-Chancellor and Proctors shall determine.

17

REGULATIONS FOR DEGREES IN DIVINITY

Ch. VI, Sect. XIII]

General Regulations

§1. Qualifications of Candidates for the Degree of Bachelor of Divinity

1. Any Master of Arts who has incepted in this University or has been incorporated in this University, or any person upon whom the Degree of Master of Arts has been conferred by decree or special resolution may supplicate for the Degree of Bachelor of Divinity, provided that

(1) he shall have either obtained a First or Second Class in the Honour School of Theology or Philosophy and Theology or passed or have been exempted from the Qualifying Examination hereinafter prescribed; and

(2) he shall have obtained from the Board of the Faculty of Theology a certificate that he has presented published work and/or a thesis of a high standard of merit such as entitles him to supplicate for the degree.

2. The Board of the Faculty of Theology shall have power to exempt a candidate for the Degree of Bachelor of Divinity from the requirement that he pass the Qualifying Examination.

§2. Qualifying Examination

1. The Qualifying Examination shall be in Christian Theology as specified in the regulations below.

2. The examination shall be under the supervision of the Board of the Faculty of Theology.

3. No candidate shall be admitted to examination unless either he is a Master of Arts, or has passed all the examinations required for the Degree of Bachelor of Arts not less than five terms before that in which the examination is held.

4. Candidates holding the Diploma in Theology who satisfied the examiners for the diploma in the same papers as are specified for the Qualifying Examination may, with the approval of the board, be deemed to have passed the Qualifying Examination. Candidates holding the Diploma in Theology who satisfied the examiners for the diploma in three or two of the papers specified for the Qualifying Examination may, with the approval of the board, be deemed to have satisfied the examiners for the Qualifying Examination in those papers, in which case they shall be required, in order to pass the examination, to satisfy the examiners at one examination, in only one other paper or two other papers respectively.

5. Every candidate shall be examined in writing and, unless individually excused by the examiners, viva voce.

§3. Work Submitted and Certificate

1. Every candidate who proposes to present a thesis must notify the Board of the Faculty of Theology, indicating the area of Christian Theology in which he intends to write the thesis. The board shall then assign an Adviser, who shall interview the candidate and advise him on a precise topic. The candidate shall then submit a title and statement of area and method for the board's approval, which must be obtained before the candidate can proceed, and which will not normally be given unless the board is satisfied that the candidate has the linguistic competence appropriate to the subject proposed. The candidate shall be instructed to consult the Adviser further at a point prior to submission of the thesis.

2. A candidate who submits papers or books which have been produced in collaboration shall state in respect of each item the extent of his own contribution.

3. Every candidate must send to the Secretary of Faculties

(1) three copies of the published work or typewritten thesis,*† unless the board, on application from the candidate, shall for special reasons order otherwise;

---

* Published work submitted should not exceed 100,000 words (excluding only the bibliography); a thesis should not exceed 75,000 words (excluding only the bibliography, which in the case of a thesis is compulsory). Unless the board has excused the candidate from this requirement, the thesis must be typed on one side of the paper only, with a margin of 3 to 3.5 cm on the left-hand edge of each page. The thesis must have a stabbed binding with covers of stout manila or stiff cardboard and a canvas back, or must be stitched and bound in a stiff case. (It should be noted that the thesis must be bound and that a loose-leaf binder of the screw-in type is not acceptable.)

Candidates are advised to pack each copy of the thesis intended for the examiners into a separate parcel, ready in all respects, except the address, to be posted to the examiners when appointed. Each parcel should bear the candidate's name and college

(2) a statement of what part, if any, of his work submitted has already been accepted, or is being concurrently submitted, for any degree in this or any other University;

(3) the fee prescribed in Ch. VIII, Sect. 1, §2 (see Appendix I);

(4) evidence that his application has the approval of his society.

4. The work submitted shall be examined by at least two examiners appointed by the board. The examiners shall also publicly examine the candidate in the subject of his submission and in matters relevant thereto.

The examiners shall report‡ to the board through the Secretary of Faculties, and it shall be the duty of the board to decide whether leave to supplicate for the degree shall be granted to the candidate, but such leave shall in no case be granted unless the examiners shall have reported that the work submitted by the candidate and as tested by his public examination is of a high standard of merit such as entitles him to supplicate for the degree, provided further that they shall have excluded from consideration in making their report any part of the work which has already been accepted, or is being concurrently submitted, for any degree in this or any other University, and shall have the power to require the candidate to produce for their inspection the whole of the work so accepted or concurrently submitted.

5. A candidate who has failed to obtain leave to supplicate may apply to the board through the Secretary of Faculties for leave to submit his work again in a revised form. If the board approves the application the candidate shall be permitted to submit his work to the board again after a period, not being less than four months, to

---

and the words 'BD THESIS' in BLOCK CAPITALS in the bottom left-hand corner, and a slip giving the address to which the examiners should write should be enclosed with each copy of the thesis. Candidates are responsible for ensuring that their examiners have no difficulty in communicating with them. The separate copies thus packed, together with the library copy, should be sent to the Secretary of Faculties in one covering parcel.

† The following instruction is issued to candidates by the Board of the Faculty of Theology:

References should be precise; and, where these are to such works as writings of fathers and schoolmen, the title of the treatise and, when these exist, the number of the book, chapter, and section should be given, not only the volume or page or column of particular editions.

‡ If the examiners are satisfied that the candidate's thesis, as it stands, is of sufficient merit to qualify him for the degree but consider, nevertheless, that before the thesis is deposited the candidate should make minor corrections (which are not sufficiently substantial to justify reference back for re-examination), they may require the candidate to correct the thesis to their satisfaction before they submit their report.

be determined by the board, and the provisions of clauses 3 and 4 of this Section shall apply to him.

6. A candidate to whom leave to supplicate has been granted by the board may supplicate for the Degree of Bachelor of Divinity, provided that he has delivered to the Secretary of Faculties a copy of his thesis for deposit in the Bodleian Library.

§4. Degree of Doctor of Divinity

1. Any person belonging to one of the following classes may become a candidate for the Degree of Doctor of Divinity under the conditions set forth in this section:

(*a*) Masters of Arts who have incepted in this University and have entered upon the thirtieth term from their matriculation;

(*b*) Masters of Arts of the University of Cambridge or Dublin who have been incorporated in this University and have entered upon the thirtieth term from their matriculation at Cambridge or Dublin;

(*c*) Undergraduates or Bachelors of Arts of the University of Cambridge or Dublin who have been incorporated and have incepted in the Faculty of Arts in this University and have entered upon the thirtieth term from their matriculation at Cambridge or Dublin;

(*d*) Persons on whom the Degree of Master of Arts has been conferred by decree or special resolution, other than a degree *honoris causa*, and who have entered upon the ninth term from their admission to that degree;

(*e*) Doctors of Philosophy, Masters of Letters or of Science, and Bachelors of Letters or of Science who have entered upon the twenty-first term from their matriculation.

2. A candidate for the Degree of Doctor of Divinity shall apply to the board through the Secretary of Faculties and shall submit with his application work dealing with some subject or subjects of Christian Theology and containing an original contribution to the study thereof. At least three printed copies of all the work submitted shall be provided by the candidate. This evidence must consist of published papers or books and one year at least must elapse between the publication of any such paper or book and its submission as evidence in support of an application.* The evidence may include published work previously submitted successfully by the candidate for the Degree of Bachelor of Divinity.

---

* If papers or books published in the calendar year preceding that in which application is made are submitted, the applicant should specify the exact date of publication.

A candidate who submits work which has been produced in collaboration shall state in respect of each item the extent of his own contribution.

3. The application shall also be accompanied by the fee prescribed in Ch. VIII, Sect. I, §2 (see Appendix I) and by a certificate signed by some officer of, or some person deputed by, the society to which the candidate belongs, and showing that his application has the approval of such society.

4. The work submitted by the candidate shall be examined by at least two judges appointed by the board. They shall report to the board through the Secretary of Faculties, and it shall be the duty of the board to consider their report, and to decide whether the evidence submitted constitutes an original contribution to the advancement of theological knowledge of such substance and distinction as to give the candidate an authoritative status in this branch of learning.

5. If the board, after consideration of the reports of the judges, shall approve the evidence as sufficient for the degree, it shall give leave to the candidate to supplicate for the degree, and shall notify its decision in the *University Gazette.* One copy of each of the papers and books submitted as evidence shall remain in the possession of the University for deposit in Bodley's Library, provided that no book or paper of which the library already possesses a copy shall be so deposited except with the consent of the candidate and of the librarian, unless the copy submitted by the candidate shall be of a different issue or shall contain alterations or additions.

(ii) Special Regulations for the Degree of Bachelor of Divinity

I. *Qualifying Examination*

1. The examination shall be held once a year at the end of Trinity Term.

2. Candidates will be required to take the following subjects in the examination for the Postgraduate Diploma in Theology*

(1) The Four Gospels.

(2) The New Testament Epistles with special reference to St Paul.

(For papers (1) and (2) the prescribed portions of the texts must be offered in Greek.)

(3) *Either* (i) Old Testament: The Pentateuch and the Historical Books
or (ii) Old Testament: Prophets, Psalms, and Wisdom.

(4) The Christian Doctrines of God, of Human Nature and Salvation.

3. The names must be sent to the Registrar, on a form to be obtained previously from the University Offices, Wellington Square. An examination fee as prescribed

* See p. 946.

in Ch. VIII, Sect. I, §2 (see Appendix I) in respect of each candidate must be forwarded at the same time. (Late entries may be made under the provisions of Ch. VI, Sect. II, D, cl. 7.)

4. In order to pass the examination a candidate must satisfy the examiners in all four papers.

A candidate who, at any one examination, has satisfied the examiners in three out of four papers may offer the remaining paper at a later examination.

II. *Oral Examination*

The place, day, and hour of the examination shall be fixed by the examiners, who shall be responsible for informing the candidate thereof by post prepaid, and it shall be the duty of the candidate to ensure that any letter addressed to him at his college, as well as at any other address which he may have given, is forwarded to him if away. The examiners shall allow reasonable time for receiving an acknowledgement from the candidate of their summons.

18

EXAMINATIONS FOR DIPLOMAS AND CERTIFICATES

DIPLOMA IN APPLIED STATISTICS

Ch. VI, Sect. XIV]

General Regulations

1. The Divisional Board of Mathematical and Physical Sciences shall have power to grant Diplomas in Applied Statistics to candidates who have satisfied the conditions prescribed in this section.

2. The examination for the Diploma in Applied Statistics shall be under the supervision of the Divisional Board of Mathematical and Physical Sciences.

3. The Divisional Board of Mathematical and Physical Sciences shall have power to arrange lectures and courses of instruction for the Diploma in Applied Statistics.

4. Subject to the provisions of this section, any member of the University may be admitted to the course and to the examination who has obtained the leave of the Divisional Board of Mathematical and Physical Sciences, provided that

(*a*) he or she has passed all the examinations required for the Degree of Bachelor of Arts and has obtained First or good Second Class Honours in the Second Public Examination, or has obtained such honours in a degree examination of another university, such university having been approved by Council for the purposes of Senior Status, or

(*b*) he or she is, in the opinion of the board, otherwise adequately qualified to undertake the course.

5. Applications for leave under the preceding clauses shall be sent to the Secretary of Faculties through the head or tutor of the society to which the applicant belongs or desires to belong. The board shall have power to determine the character and length of a course of study to be followed by the applicant before he may be admitted to the examination.

6. On admitting an applicant as a candidate for the diploma, the board shall appoint a supervisor who shall direct and superintend the work of the candidate. The supervisor shall send a report on the progress of the candidate to the board at the end of each term (except the term in which the student enters for the examination) and at any other time when the board so requests or he believes it expedient. In particular he shall inform the board at once if he is of the opinion that a student is unlikely to reach the standard required for the diploma. The Secretary of Faculties shall send a copy of each report by the supervisor to the student's society.

7. After admission as a Diploma Student, a candidate must have kept statutory residence and pursued a course of study at Oxford for at least three terms before taking the examination, provided that a candidate for the Degree of Master of Science (Applied Statistics) may, with the approval of the Divisional Board of Mathematical and Physical Sciences, transfer to the status of a Student for the Diploma in Applied Statistics not later than the last date for the receipt of entries for the examination, in which case the date of his admission as a Student for the Degree of Master of Science shall be reckoned as the date of his admission as a diploma student; time spent outside Oxford during term as part of an academic programme approved by Council shall count towards residence for the purpose of this clause.

8. A Student reading for the diploma who is not a graduate of the University may wear the same gown as that worn by Students for the Degree of Doctor of Philosophy.

9. The examiners may award a distinction to a candidate for the diploma.

(ii) SPECIAL REGULATIONS

1. The Divisional Board of Mathematical and Physical Sciences shall elect for the supervision of the course a standing committee which shall have power to arrange lectures and other instruction.

2. Candidates shall follow for at least three terms a course of instruction in Statistics, and will, when entering their name for the examination, be required to produce from their society a certificate that they are doing so.

3. The examination will consist of a written examination consisting of two papers on the syllabus described in the schedule.

4. Each candidate will be expected to have displayed evidence of the ability to apply statistical methods to real data.

The examiners will take into account the results of an assessment of ability to apply statistical methods to real data organized by the standing committee. The committee will be responsible for notifying the candidates of the arrangements for the assessment, and for forwarding the assessed material to the chairman of the examiners before the end of the Trinity Term in the year in which the assessment is made.

SCHEDULE

Paper 1: Principles of statistical analysis

Statistical distribution theory; statistical inference; statistical methods.

Paper 2: Further statistical methodology

Topics in statistical methodology chosen from a list approved by the standing committee and published in the *University Gazette* before the end of the Trinity Term in the academic year before which the written examination is to be taken.

DIPLOMA IN MATERIAL ANTHROPOLOGY AND MUSEUM ETHNOGRAPHY

(i) **General Regulations**

1. There shall be held an examination for the purpose of granting Diplomas in Material Anthropology and Museum Ethnography.

2. Subject to the provisions of this section any member of the University may be admitted as a candidate for the diploma examination who has obtained leave from the Divisional Board of Life and Environmental Sciences:
Provided that:

(*a*) he or she has passed all the examinations required for the degree of Bachelor of Arts and has obtained First or good Second Class Honours in the Second Public Examation, or has obtained such honours in a degree examination of another university, such university having been approved by Council for the purpose of Senior Status; or

(*b*) he or she is, in the opinion of the board, otherwise adequately qualified to undertake the course.

Applications for leave under this clause shall be sent to the Secretary of Faculties through the head or tutor of the society to which the applicant belongs or desires to belong. The board shall have power to determine the character and length of a course of study to be followed by the applicant before he or she may take the examination.

On admitting an applicant as a candidate for the diploma examination the board shall appoint a supervisor who shall direct and superintend the work of the candidate. The Supervisor shall send a report on the progress of the candidate to the board at the end of each term and at any other time when the board so requests or the Supervisor believes it expedient. In particular the Supervisor shall inform the board at once if he or she is of the opinion that a student is unlikely to reach the standard required for the diploma. The Secretary of Faculties shall send a copy of each report by the Supervisor to the student's society.

3. The examination shall be under the supervision of the Divisional Board of Life and Environmental Sciences and that board shall fix the date on which names for the examination shall be entered.

4. After admission as a Diploma Student, a candidate must have kept statutory residence and pursued a course of study at Oxford for at least three terms before taking the examination, provided (*a*) that time spent outside Oxford during term as part of an academic programme approved by Council shall count towards residence for the purpose of this clause and (*b*) that a candidate for the Degree of Master of Science in Material Anthropology and Museum Ethnography may, with the approval of the Divisional Board of Life and Environmental Sciences, transfer to the status of a Student for the Diploma in Material Anthropology and Museum Ethnography not later than the last date for the receipt of entries for the examination, in which case the date of his or her admission as a Student for the Degree of Master of Science shall be reckoned as the date of his or her admission as a Diploma Student.

5. A student reading for the diploma who is not a graduate of the University may wear the same gown as that worn by Students for the Degree of Doctor of Philosophy.

The attention of candidates is directed to Ch. VI, Sect. I. C, *§ 3, cl. 6.*

(ii) SPECIAL REGULATIONS

1. Candidates for admission must apply to the Divisional Board of Life and Environmental Sciences through the Admissions Secretary for Social and Cultural Anthropology.

2. Every candidate for examination must, before admission to the examination, have satisfied the Admissions Secretary for Social and Cultural Anthropology that he or she has been following a course of study in the subject for at least three terms in Oxford, unless the faculty board shall otherwise determine.

3. The registration of a candidate shall lapse on the last day of the Trinity Term in the year of his or her admission unless it shall have been extended by the divisional board.

4. Names for the examination must be entered with the Head Clerk, University Offices, Wellington Square, Oxford, not later than 12 noon on Friday in the fourth week of Hilary Term. (Late entries may be made under the provision of Ch. VI. Sect. II. D, cl 7.)

5. The examination shall include written work and each candidate must attend an oral examination when requested to do so by the examiners.

6. The examiners may award a distinction for excellence in the whole examination.

Syllabus

I Social and Cultural Anthropology A: History and Development (paper and syllabus shared with the Diploma in Social Anthropology)

The scope of this paper includes the following topics: history and development of the subject, and the relation between academic research, museums, and the imperial context of anthropology's past; relations to other subjects, including archaeology and history. Key authors and debates in the development of anthropology, with particular reference to: kinship, marriage, gender and sexuality; space, place, and culture; environment and cultural landscapes in transition; land and property rights; production and consumption; transactions and modes of exchange; the division of labour and the comparative anthropology of work; technology and social change; the colonial process and its legacy; nationalism, ethnicity, migration, and transnationalism; urbanism.

II *Social and Cultural Anthropology B: Theory and Methods* (paper and syllabus shared with the Diploma in Social Anthropology)

The scope of this paper includes the following topics: concepts of the individual, society and the person in anthropological perspective; issues of the body, theories of practice, phenomenology; theories of power, order and law; aspects of disorder and violence in society; systems of knowledge and belief; ritual and myth; symbolism and symbolic classification; moral systems and the world religions; oral literature and historical memory; linguistics and artistic modes of communication; aesthetic anthropology; methodological approaches to the study of arts, performance, and material culture; museums, written texts, and representation. Fieldwork and data collection methods; quantitative and qualitative techniques; cultural property and indigenous rights; applications of film and sound recording; preparing research proposals; ethical problems.

III and IV *Optional Papers*

Candidates must choose two optional papers. Titles of available options will be made known at the beginning of each academic year. They will be divided into three lists, as follows:

List A: The Social Anthropology of a Selected Region.
List B: Topics in Material Anthropology.
List C: Anthropology and Practical Issues.

Candidates for the degree of Diploma in Material Anthropology and Museum Ethnography must select at least one of their options from List B.

DIPLOMA IN HUMAN BIOLOGY

Ch. VI, Sect. XVIII]

(i) **General Regulations**

1. There shall be held an examination for the purpose of granting Diplomas in Human Biology.

2. Subject to the provisions of this section any member of the University may be admitted as a candidate for the diploma examination who has obtained leave from the Divisional Board of Life and Environmental Sciences:

Provided that

(*a*) he has passed all the examinations required for the Degree of Bachelor of Arts and has obtained First or good Second Class Honours in the Second Public Examination, or has obtained such honours in a degree examination of another university, such university having been approved by Council for the purpose of Senior Status; or

(*b*) he is, in the opinion of the board, otherwise adequately qualified to undertake the course.

Applications for leave under this clause shall be sent to the Secretary of Faculties through the head or tutor of the society to which the applicant belongs or desires to belong. The board shall have power to determine the character and length of a course of study to be followed by the applicant before he may take the examination.

On admitting an applicant as a candidate for the diploma examination the board shall appoint a supervisor who shall direct and superintend the work of the candidate. The supervisor shall send a report on the progress of the candidate to the board at the end of each term (except the term in which the student enters for the examination) and at any other time when the board so requests or he believes it expedient. In particular he shall inform the board at once if he is of the opinion that a student is unlikely to reach the standard required for the diploma. The Secretary of Faculties shall send a copy of each report by the supervisor to the student's society.

3. The examination shall be under the supervision of the Divisional Board of Life and Environmental Sciences and that board shall fix the date on which names for the examination shall be entered.

4. After admission as a Diploma Student, a candidate must have kept statutory residence and pursued a course of study at Oxford

for at least three terms before taking the examination, provided (*a*) that time spent outside Oxford during term as part of an academic programme approved by Council shall count towards residence for the purpose of this clause (*b*) that a candidate for the Degree of Master of Science in Human Biology may, with the approval of the Divisional Board of Life and Environmental Sciences, transfer to the status of a Student for the Diploma in Human Biology not later than the last date for the receipt of entries for the examination, in which case the date of his admission as a Student for the Degree of Master of Science shall be reckoned as the date of his admission as a Diploma Student.

5. The examiners may award a distinction to a candidate for the diploma.

6. A student reading for the diploma who is not a graduate of the University may wear the same gown as that worn by Students for the Degree of Doctor of Philosophy.

The attention of candidates is directed to Ch. VI, Sect. I. C, §3, clause 6.

(ii) Special Regulations

1. Every candidate for examination must, before admission to the examination, have satisfied the Admissions Secretary for Human Biology that he is following a course of study in the subject for at least three terms in Oxford, unless the board shall otherwise determine.

2. The registration of a candidate shall lapse on the last day of the Trinity Term in the year of his admission unless it shall have been extended by the divisional board.

3. The examination shall include written work and an oral examination.

Syllabus

(i) *Human Genetics and Individual Variability*
- (*a*) Molecular genetics and genome organization
- (*b*) Reproduction, growth and development: a genetic perspective
- (*c*) Mendelian and chromosomal disease
- (*d*) Human biochemical genetics
- (*e*) Genetics of complex traits

(ii) *Population variability: gentic and environmental determinants*
- (*a*) Principles of population genetics
- (*b*) Human diversity at the molecular level
- (*c*) Demographic components of human variability
- (*d*) Environmental determinants of phenotypic variability in populations
- (*e*) Genetic epidemiology of disease in human populations

(iii) *Evolution of humans and other primates*
- (*a*) Living primates: a survey
- (*b*) Primate behaviour

(*c*) Evolution of non-human primates
(*d*) Hominid evolution: palaeontological and molecular data
(*e*) Bio-cultural perspective on human evolution

(iv) *Special option*

Every candidate will be required to study a special option. The special options will be approved by the Graduate Studies Committee of the Divisional Board of Life and Environmental Sciences and published in the *University Gazette* before the end of the Trinity Term of the academic year preceding that in which the examination is taken. The details of how the syllabus is to be covered, and the associated lectures may vary from year to year. The arrangements for lectures and a detailed description of the special options will be included in a document approved by the Graduate Studies Committee of the Board in Trinity Term, and circulated to all candidates for this course before the beginning of Michaelmas Term.

(v) *Essay*

(*b*) To submit a report of practical work during his course of study. Reports must be sent to the Chairman of Examiners for the Diploma in Human Biology, c/o the Clerk of the Schools, High Street, Oxford, OX1 4BG, not later than fourteen days before the first day of the examination.

(iii) ADMISSION

Candidates for admission as students for the diploma must apply to the Divisional Board of Life and Environmental Sciences through the Admissions Secretary not later than Tuesday in the first week of Michaelmas Term.

(iv) DATE OF THE EXAMINATION

The examination will begin on Thursday in the seventh week of Trinity Full Term.

Names must be entered with the Clerk of the Schools, High Street, Oxford, OX1 4BG not later than 12 noon on Friday in the fourth week of Hilary Full Term. (Late entries may be made under the provisions of Ch. VI, Sect. II. D. cl. 7.)

DIPLOMA IN LEGAL STUDIES

Ch. VI, Sect. XX]

(i) **General Regulations**

1. The Board of the Faculty of Law shall have power to grant Diplomas in Legal Studies to members of the University who have kept residence and pursued a course of study at Oxford for not less than three terms; time spent outside Oxford during term as part of an academic programme approved by Council shall count towards residence for the purpose of this clause.

2. The examination for the Diploma in Legal Studies shall be under the supervision of the Board of the Faculty of Law.

3. The examiners for the diploma shall be such of the Public Examiners in the Honour School of Jurisprudence as shall be required.

4. A Diploma Student must keep statutory residence and pursue a course of study at Oxford for three terms, and may not take the examination for the Diploma earlier or later than in the second term after that with effect from which he or she was admitted as a Diploma student.

5. The examiners may award a distinction to a candidate for the Diploma in Legal Studies.

(ii) Special Regulations

1. The Diploma will normally only be granted to candidates who on admission had no significant previous education in the common law.

2. The examination for the diploma shall be in each Trinity Term.

3. The examination shall consist of any three standard subjects, specified for the Honour School of Jurisprudence selected by the candidate.

4. Candidates in examinations will not be required to answer more than three questions.

5. Candidates may be required to attend a viva voce examination.

DIPLOMA IN SOCIAL ANTHROPOLOGY

(i) General Regulations

1. There shall be held an examination for the purpose of granting Diplomas in Social Anthropology.

2. Subject to the provisions of this section any member of the University may be admitted as a candidate for the diploma examination who has obtained leave from the Divisional Board of Life and Environmental Sciences:

Provided that

(*a*) he or she has passed all the examinations required for the degree of Bachelor of Arts and has obtained First or good Second Class Honours in the Second Public Examination, or has obtained such honours in a degree examination of another university, such university having been approved by Council for the purpose of Senior Status; or

(*b*) he or she is, in the opinion of the board, otherwise adequately qualified to undertake the course.

Applications for leave under this clause shall be sent to the Secretary of Faculties through the head or tutor of the society to which the applicant belongs or desires to belong. The board shall have power to determine the character and length of a course of study to be followed by the applicant before he or she may take the examination.

On admitting an applicant as a candidate for the diploma examination the board shall appoint a supervisor who shall direct and superintend the work of the candidate. The Supervisor shall send a report on the progress of the candidate to the board at the end of each term and at any other time when the board so requests or the Supervisor believes it expedient. In particular the Supervisor shall inform the board at once if he or she is of the opinion that a student is unlikely to reach the standard required for the diploma. The Secretary of Faculties shall send a copy of each report by the Supervisor to the student's society.

3. The examination shall be under the supervision of the Divisional Board of Life and Environmental Sciences and that board shall fix the date on which names for the examination shall be entered.

4. After admission as a Diploma Student, a candidate must have kept statutory residence and pursued a course of study at Oxford for at least three terms before taking the examination, provided (*a*) that time spent outside Oxford during term as part of an academic programme approved by Council shall count towards residence for the purpose of this clause and (*b*) that a candidate for the Degree of Master of Science in Social Anthropology may, with the approval of the Divisional Board of Life and Environmental Sciences, transfer to the status of a Student for the Diploma in Social Anthropology not later than the last date for the receipt of entries for the examination, in which case the date of his or her admission as a Student for the Degree of Master of Science shall be reckoned as the date of his or her admission as a Diploma Student.

5. A student reading for the diploma who is not a graduate of the University may wear the same gown as that worn by Students for the Degree of Doctor of Philosophy.

The attention of candidates is directed to Ch. VI, Sect. I. C, § 3, cl. 6.

(ii) Special Regulations

1. Candidates for admission must apply to the Divisional Board of Life and Environmental Sciences through the Admissions Secretary for Social and Cultural Anthropology.

2. Every candidate for examination must, before admission to the examination, have satisfied the Admissions Secretary for Social and Cultural Anthropology that he or she has been following a course of study in the subject for at least three terms in Oxford, unless the divisional board shall otherwise determine.

3. The registration of a candidate shall lapse on the last day of the Trinity Term in the year of his or her admission unless it shall have been extended by the divisional board.

4. Names for the examination must be entered with the Head Clerk, University Offices, Wellington Square, Oxford, not later than 12 noon on Friday in the fourth week of Hilary Term. (Late entries may be made under the provisions of Ch. VI. Sect. II. D, cl. 7.)

5. The examination shall include written work and each candidate must attend an oral examination when requested to do so by the examiners.

6. The examiners may award a distinction for excellence in the whole examination.

Syllabus

I *Social and Cultural Anthropology A: History and Development* (paper and syllabus shared with the Diploma in Material Anthropology and Museum Ethnography)

The scope of this paper includes the following topics: history and development of the subject, and the relation between academic research, museums, and the imperial context of anthropology's past; relations to other subjects, including archaeology and history. Key authors and debates in the development of anthropology, with particular reference to: kinship, marriage, gender, and sexuality; space, place, and culture; environment and cultural landscapes in transition; land and property rights; production and consumption; transactions and modes of exchange; the division of labour and the comparative anthropology of work; technology and social change; the colonial process and its legacy; nationalism, ethnicity, migration, and trans-nationalism; urbanism.

II *Social and Cultural Anthropology B: Theory and Methods* (paper and syllabus shared with the Diploma in Material Anthropology and Museum Ethnography)

The scope of this paper includes the following topics: concepts of the individual, society and the person in anthropological perspective; issues of the body, theories of practice, phenomenology; theories of power, order and law; aspects of disorder and violence in society; systems of knowledge and belief; ritual and myth; symbolism and symbolic classification; moral systems and the world religions; oral literature and historical memory; linguistic and artistic modes of communication; aesthetic anthropology; methodological approaches to the study of arts, performance, and material culture; museums, written texts and representation. Fieldwork and data collection methods; quantitative and qualitative techniques; cultural property and indigenous rights; applications of film and sound recording; preparing research proposals; ethical problems.

III and IV *Optional Papers*

Candidates must choose two optional papers. Titles of available options will be made known at the beginning of each academic year. They will be divided into three lists, as follows:

List A: The Social Anthropology of a Selected Religion.
List B: Topics in Material Anthropology.
List C: Anthropology and Practical Issues.

Candidates for the Diploma in Social Anthropology must select one of their options from List A, and the other from List B or List C.

POSTGRADUATE DIPLOMA IN THEOLOGY

Ch. VI, Sect. XXII]

(i) **General Regulations**

1. It shall be lawful for the Board of the Faculty of Theology to grant Postgraduate Diplomas in Theology to candidates who have satisfied the conditions prescribed in this Section.

2. The examination shall be under the supervision of the Board of the Faculty of Theology.

3. Subject to the provisions of this Section, any member of the University who has obtained the leave of the Board of the Faculty of Theology and has kept statutory residence for at least three terms may be admitted to the examination for the Postgraduate Diploma in Theology provided that:

(*a*) he or she has passed all the examinations required for the Degree of Bachelor of Arts and has obtained First or good Second Class Honours in the Second Public Examination, or has attained such honours in a degree examination of another university, such university having been approved by Council for the purposes of Senior Status; *or*

(*b*) he or she is, in the opinion of the board, otherwise adequately qualified to undertake the course.

Time spent outside Oxford during term as part of an academic programme approved by Council shall count towards residence for the purpose of this clause.

4. Applications for leave under cl. 3 shall be sent to the Secretary of Faculties, through the Head or tutor of the society to which the applicant belongs or desires to belong. The board shall have power to determine the character and length of a course of study in Theology to be followed by the applicant before he or she may be admitted to the examination.

5. The examiners may award a distinction in any subject in the examination.

6. A student reading for the diploma who is not a graduate of the University shall wear the same gown as that worn by Students for the Degree of Doctor of Philosophy.

(ii) SPECIAL REGULATIONS

All candidates will be required to offer not less than *three* papers (and not more than *five*), of which at least one must normally be either (1) or (2) and another must be either (3), (4) or (5).

(1) *The Four Gospels.* Candidates will be expected to answer questions on the literature and the religion of the gospels, with portions of the text in *either* Greek *or* English.

The prescribed portions of the Greek text* are:

Matthew 3–17 with synoptic parallels (text of Huck-Lietzmann, *Synopsis of the first Three Gospels*).

The prescribed portions of the English text† are:

Matthew 5–7; Mark; John.

(2) *The New Testament Epistles with special reference to St Paul.* Candidates will be expected to answer questions on the theology of these epistles, with portions of the text in *either* Greek *or* English.

The prescribed portions of the Greek text* are:

Romans 1–8.

The prescribed portions of the English text† are:

Romans; 1 Corinthians (edition of text as for paper 1).

(3) *Old Testament*: The Pentateuch and Historical Books. Candidates must demonstrate in essay questions knowledge of the broad range of the syllabus and also of the issues of method involved. They must also show a detailed knowledge of the texts in *either* Hebrew *or* English.

The prescribed portions of the Hebrew text‡ are: Genesis 1–4 and 6–8.

The prescribed portions of the English text† are: *either* Genesis 1–11 *or* Exodus 1–15; and *either* 2 Samuel 1–12 *or* 2 Kings 18–25.

(4) *Old Testament*: Prophets, Psalms, and Wisdom. Candidates must demonstrate in essay questions knowledge of the broad range of the syllabus and also of the issues of method involved. They must also show a detailed knowledge of texts in *either* Hebrew *or* English.

The prescribed portions of the Hebrew texts† are: Isaiah 1, 2, 6, and 7.

The prescribed portions of the English text‡ are: *either* Isaiah 1–12 *or* Zechariah 1–14; and *either* Psalms 73–89 *or* Proverbs 1–12.

(5) *The Christian Doctrines of God, of Human Nature and Salvation.* Candidates will be expected to show knowledge of these especially in relation to the thought of the present day, and to show a sufficient knowledge of both classical Christian doctrine and philosophy of religion to make possible an adequate understanding of modern doctrine.

(6) *Christian Life and Thought in Europe 1789–1914.* As specified for paper (10)A in the Honour School of Theology.

(7) *Christian Moral Reasoning.* As specified for paper 13 in the Honour School of Theology.

(8) *World Religions.* Candidates will be expected to make a study of one of the following religions:

(*a*) Islam;
(*b*) Buddhism;
(*c*) Hinduism.

The syllabuses will be as prescribed for papers (17) *Islam* I, (19) *Buddhism* I, and (21) *Hinduism* I in the Honour School of Theology.

---

* The Greek text used will be the text of the United Bible Societies, 4th edn.

† The English text used will be the New Revised Standard version.

‡ The Hebrew text used will be the *Biblia Hebraica Stuttgartensia* (Stuttgart, 1977)

(9) *Philosophy of Religion.* The subject will include an examination of claims about the existence of God, and God's relation to the world: their meaning, the possibility of their truth, and the kind of justification which can or needs to be provided for them, and the philosophical problems raised by the existence of different religions. One or two questions may also be set on central claims peculiar to Christianity, such as the doctrines of the Trinity, Incarnation, and Atonement.

Every candidate is required to follow for at least three terms a course of instruction in Theology, and he or she will, when he or she enters his or her name for the examination, be required to produce from his or her society a certificate that he or she is following a course of instruction in Theology for at least three terms.

*From candidates who wish to be admitted to the examination under cl. 3 (*b*) of the Decree, the Board of the Faculty of Theology will require evidence that they have followed, or have arranged to follow, for three terms a course of instruction in Theology in Oxford to the satisfaction of the board. Application for the board's approval of the course of instruction should be sent to the Secretary of Faculties, through the Head or a tutor of the candidate's society or prospective society, at the same time as the application for permission to be admitted to the examination.

Before admission to the examination every candidate must have kept at least three terms by residence as a matriculated member of the University. Terms kept prior to admission as a student for the diploma may be reckoned for this purpose.

The Nomination of Examiners shall be made as early as may be in Michaelmas Term.

Except as may be determined by the board from time to time the examination for the diploma will begin at 9.30 a.m. on the Tuesday in the eleventh week from the beginning of Trinity Full Term.

POSTGRADUATE CERTIFICATE IN EDUCATION

Ch. VI, Sect. XXIII]

(i) **General Regulations**

1. The Academic Board of the Department of Educational Studies shall have power to grant Certificates in Education to candidates who have satisfied the conditions prescribed in this section or those prescribed in Ch. X, Sect. XII.

2. The examination for the Certificate in Education shall be under the supervision of the Academic Board which shall have power to make regulations governing the examination and arrange lectures and courses of instruction for the Certificate.

3. Subject to the provisions of this section, any member of the University may be admitted to the course and to the examination

---

* Candidates are advised to obtain the approval of the board for their course of instruction not later than the Michaelmas Term preceding the examination.

who has obtained the leave of the Academic Board, provided that

(*a*) he has passed all the examinations required for the Degree of Bachelor of Arts and has obtained Honours in the Second Public Examination, or has obtained Honours in a degree examination of another university, such university having been approved by Council for the purposes of Senior Status; or

(*b*) he is, in the opinion of the Academic Board, otherwise adequately qualified to undertake the course.

4. Application for leave under the preceding clause shall be sent to the Secretary of the Board through the Head or tutor of the society to which the applicant belongs or desires to belong.

5. After admission as a certificate student, a candidate must have kept statutory residence and pursued a course of study in Oxford for at least three terms before taking the examination.

6. A student reading for the Certificate, who is not a graduate of the University, may wear the same gown as that worn by Students for the Degree of Doctor of Philosophy.

(ii) Special Regulations

1. *Course*

(*a*) The course will consist of lectures, tutorials, seminars, and classes in the theory and practice of education, together with a period of practical experience in a school or other educational establishment.

(*b*) The subjects of the course of study are as follows:

Curriculum Studies, with particular reference to the teaching of a school subject: practical skills, communication, classroom management, the planning and design of teaching programmes, the place of the subject in the school curriculum, curriculum design and evaluation.

Educational Theory: the nature and purpose of education, the growth and learning of children, the measurement of progress; the roles and authority of teachers; the development of the educational system, and the structure and functions of schools.

Practical Experience. Each candidate shall complete at least fifteen weeks, or their equivalent, on teaching practice in a school or other educational establishment nominated for this purpose by the Department of Educational Studies. This requirement may be varied in particular cases by the Academic Board and with the consent of the Examiners.

2. Every candidate will be required to satisfy the examiners in the following:

(*a*) a dissertation of 5,000 to 10,000 words on a topic in educational theory, history, or practice. The title of the dissertation must be submitted for approval to the chairman of the Certificate in Education examiners, Department of Educational Studies, not later than Friday in the second week of Trinity Full Term;

(*b*) an assessment by a person appointed by the Department of Educational Studies to act as supervisor of the candidates' work in the teaching of a school subject. The assessment will be based upon at least three exercises to be submitted to the supervisor by such dates as he shall determine. The exercises shall be on the theory and practice of the teaching of a school subject and shall be presented in such form as shall be determined by the supervisor;

(*c*) an assessment by a person appointed for this purpose by the Department of Educational Studies on the candidate's practical competence as a teacher;

(*d*) an assessment by a person or persons appointed for this purpose by the Department of Educational Studies of the quality of the candidate's study of educational theory as demonstrated in tutorials and seminars.

The dissertation under (*a*) and assessment reports under (*b*), (*c*), and (*d*) shall be forwarded to the examiners for consideration by such date as the examiners shall determine.

Candidates may also be called for viva voce examination.

Candidates who fail the examination may apply to the Academic Board to be re-examined on not more than one occasion which normally shall be within two years of their initial failure.

Candidates who fail to satisfy the examiners in 2(*c*) above shall not be granted permission to re-enter for the examination.

POSTGRADUATE DIPLOMA IN SCIENCE AND MEDICINE OF ATHLETIC PERFORMANCE

General Regulations

1. The Medical Sciences Board shall have power to grant Postgraduate Diplomas in Science and Medicine of Athletic Performance to members of the University who have kept residence and pursued a course of study at Oxford for not less than three terms, on condition that time spent outside Oxford during term as part of an academic programme approved by Council shall count towards residence for the purpose of this clause.

2. The examination for the diploma shall be under the supervision of the Medical Sciences Board.

Special Regulations

1. Every candidate for examination must, before admission to the examination, have satisfied the Course Director for Science and Medicine of Athletic Performance that he or she has been following a course of study in the subject, including at least four of the modules listed in the schedule, for not less than three terms in Oxford.

2. One paper will be set for each of the modules listed in the schedule and candidates must offer and satisfy the examiners in the papers for the modules that they take. Candidates who fail one paper may be permitted, at the discretion of the standing committee, to retake that module examination on no more than one occasion normally no later than one term after the first examination. Failure of more than one paper shall constitute failure of the whole examination.

3. The registration of a candidate shall lapse on the last day of the Trinity Term in the year of his or her admission unless it shall have been extended by the Medical Sciences Board.

4. Names for the examination must be entered with the Clerk of the Schools, High Street, Oxford, not later than 12 noon on Friday in the fourth week of Hilary Term. (Late entries may be made under the provision of Ch. VI. Sect. II D, cl 7.).

5. Candidates may be called for a viva voce examination. The examiners will give as much notice as possible to candidates of a requirement to attend such an examination.

6. The examiners may award a distinction for excellence in the whole examination.

SCHEDULE

1. Structural and biomechanical basis of physical prformance
2. Genetic and biochemical basis of physical performance
3. Muscle energetics, motor control, and training
4. Cardio-respiratory and renal adaptations to physical performance
5. Genes and gender
6. Drugs and performance.

NOTES

19

EXAMINATIONS OPEN TO NON-MEMBERS OF THE UNIVERSITY OF STUDENTS FOR DIPLOMAS AND CERTIFICATES

Ch. X, Sect. V]

1. A Register shall be kept by the Registrar of the University of all students who are studying with a view to obtaining a diploma or certificate granted under the provisions of this Decree and who are not members of the University. The Register shall be entitled the Register of Diploma Students.

2. For the purpose of this Register, each of the bodies empowered to grant diplomas or certificates shall make to the Registrar each term, not later than the end of the second week of Full Term, a return of the names and addresses of all students who have been admitted by such body in that term and who are studying with a view to a diploma or certificate and who are not members of the University.

3. No student shall have his or her name entered, replaced, or retained on the Register unless *either* (1) he or she is more than twenty-five years of age and has satisfied the Vice-Chancellor and Proctors that he or she is of good character, *or* (2) he or she is a graduate of a university approved by Council under Ch. V, Sect. IV, *or* (3) he or she has been admitted as a student for a Diploma or Certificate by the Continuing Education Board, *or* (5) he or she is a member of a society or institution in Oxford established for the purpose of higher study and approved for the purpose of this decree by Council,* *or* (6) he or she is a member of the Public Service, naval, military, or civil, engaged on a course of higher study or research.

4. Before the name of any person is entered or replaced on the Register, he or she shall pay to the Registrar of the University, through the body returning his or her name in pursuance of clause

* The following bodies have been approved under this clause: Ruskin College, Plater College, Templeton College, Ripon College Cuddesdon, St Stephen's House, Wycliffe Hall, and the Oxford Centre for Hebrew and Jewish Studies.

2 above, a fee as prescribed in Ch. VIII, Sect. 1, §2 (see Appendix I). The Registrar shall pay all fees so received to the University Chest. This clause shall not apply to students admitted as candidates for the Special Diploma in Educational Studies, for Postgraduate Diplomas or Postgraduate Certificates awarded by the Continuing Education Board, for the Diploma in Jewish Studies or for the Diploma in Management Studies.

5. The name of any diploma student may be removed, either temporarily or permanently, from the Register either by the Proctors or by the body by which his or her name was returned. No name which has been removed shall be replaced on the Register except with the consent of the authority which removed it. Nothwithstanding the earlier provisions of this clause, the student may within fourteen days of the date of the Proctors' decision appeal in writing to the Chairman of the Educational Policy and Standards Committee (who may nominate another member of the committee, other than one of the Proctors, to adjudicate the appeal). If the Proctors' decision is not upheld, the Educational Policy and Standards Committee may replace the student's name on the Register.

6. No one whose name is not on the Register, except a member of the University, shall be entitled to attend any lecture or course of instruction given under arrangements made by a body which grants any such diploma or certificate as aforesaid.

7. No one except a member of the University shall be permitted to be a candidate in the examination, or any part of the examination, for any such diploma or certificate unless his or her name (1) is on the Register in the term in which such examination or part of an examination is held, or, if the examination is held in vacation, in the term immediately preceding such examination, (2) has been on the Register during at least one previous term or such longer period as may be prescribed by the body under whose authority the examination is held, provided that such body may dispense from this second requirement any candidate who before registration has attended only lectures or courses of instruction given in vacation under arrangements made by such body, or who is a member of the Public Service, naval, military, or civil, engaged on a course of higher study or research.

8. The bodies empowered to grant diplomas or certificates shall cause lists of candidates in the examinations or any parts of examinations for any such diplomas or certificates to be distributed in the usual manner at least three days before the day fixed for the beginning of any such examination.

REGULATIONS FOR THE POSTGRADUATE DIPLOMAS IN EDUCATIONAL STUDIES AND IN LEARNING AND TEACHING IN HIGHER EDUCATION

Ch. X, Sect. II]

(i) General Regulations

1. The Academic Board of the Department of Educational Studies shall have power to grant Postgraduate Diplomas in Educational Studies and Postgraduate Diplomas in Learning and Teaching in Higher Education to candidates who have satisfied the conditions prescribed in this section and any further conditions which the committee may prescribe by regulation.

2. The examinations for the diplomas shall be under the supervision of the Academic Board which shall have power subject to the approval of the Educational Policy Standards Committee to make regulations governing the examinations.

3. Candidates, whether members of the University or not, may be admitted as students for the diplomas under such conditions as the committee shall prescribe, provided that

(i) before admission to a course of study approved by the committee, candidates have satisfied the committee that they have received a good general education, that they have had appropriate educational experience acceptable to the committee, and are well qualified to enter the proposed course of study;

(ii) any person so admitted who is not a member of the University, shall be required to pay to the Curators of the University Chest through the committee the composition fee payable under the provisions of Ch. VIII, Sect. I, §5, cl. I, notwithstanding that he or she is not a member of the University.

4. The Academic Board shall make a return to the Registrar by the end of the sixth week of Michaelmas Term, showing the names of all persons admitted in that term as students for the diplomas, and the Registrar shall add the names of non-members of the University to the Register of Diploma Students.

5. Any person who has been accepted as a candidate for the diplomas and who has satisfactorily pursued a course, whose character and length have been approved by the committee, may be admitted to the examinations.

6. A candidate must apply to the committee for admission to the examinations at such time as the committee shall, by regulation, prescribe. His or her application must be accompanied by:

(*a*) a certificate from the Secretary of the Committee that he or she is satisfactorily pursuing a course of study approved by the committee;

(*b*) such other information as the committee may, by regulation, require.

7. The examiners may award a distinction to a candidate for the diplomas.

(ii) SPECIAL REGULATIONS

1. Candidates for the Postgraduate Diploma in Educational Studies shall be qualified teachers in the United Kingdom, or recognized by the Academic Board as being of equivalent status overseas. They shall normally have had not less than three years' educational experience acceptable to the committee. The committee may in exceptional cases admit to the examination candidates with other qualifications.

2. Candidates for the Postgraduate Diploma in Learning and Teaching in Higher Education shall be engaged as teachers in higher education.

3. Each candidate for the Postgraduate Diploma in Educational Studies will follow a course of study approved by a Standing Committee of the Academic Board. This Standing Committee will include the Professor in Educational Studies, the Reader in Educational Studies, the Tutor for Advanced Courses, and three further members appointed by the Academic Board. The duties of the Standing Committee are to supervise arrangements for teaching and to approve courses of study for the Postgraduate Diploma. Each candidate shall be required to follow *one* of the following options:

(*a*) A full-time course involving a programme of study of three terms in duration which will consist of: an introduction to research methods; an individual programme of study leading to the submission of the dissertation; and a common programme of studies as determined from time to time by the Standing Committee embracing topics from amongst the following areas of study upon which he will be required to submit essays; the development of the educational system of England and Wales; the nature and control of the curriculum; the organization, administration, and management of schools; contemporary work in sociology and psychology in relation to the practice of pedagogy in schools; assessment in education; teacher education; comparative education.

(*b*) A course involving a programme of study of three terms in duration in which each candidate will spend at least 40 per cent of the days of these terms in university-based study, and the remainder of these terms working in his own school or local education authority and engaged in a research and development project. Each programme of study will consist of an introduction to research methods, a research and development project concerned with a signficant aspect of educational practice, which will lead to the submission of the dissertation, and a programme of studies which shall be equivalent in weight to the common programme of studies indicated in 2(*a*) above, which shall incorporate part of that common programme and which shall be related to the research and development project being undertaken by the candidate. The whole programme for each candidate shall be approved by the Standing Committee, which shall satisfy itself that the programme is suitable in its standards and scope for the Postgraduate Diploma in Educational Studies and is practically viable for the candidate for whom it is proposed. Application for approval of programmes is to be received not later than six weeks before the beginning of the term in which the course starts. The Standing Committee, having considered a proposed programme, will inform the candidate of its decision not later than two weeks before the beginning of that term.

(*c*) A course extending over a minimum period of two years and a maximum period not normally exceeding three years from the beginning of the term in which the candidate is admitted for the Postgraduate Diploma course, with no requirements for full-day attendance, but otherwise involving the same requirements as those prescribed in 2(*b*) above.

3. Each student for the Postgraduate Diploma in Educational Studies will be assigned by the Professor in Educational Studies to a supervisor, who will be responsible for directing the student's course of study, including the dissertation. The title of the dissertation is to be submitted to the examiners for approval. The examiners shall notify candidates of the date by which the title must be submitted for approval.

4. All candidates for admission as students for the Postgraduate Diploma in Educational Studies and Postgraduate Diploma in Learning and Teaching in Higher Education must apply to the department not later than two weeks before the start of the term in which the Postgraduate Diploma Courses start.

5. Each candidate for the Postgraduate Diploma in Learning and Teaching in Higher Education will follow a course of study approved by a Standing Committee of the Academic Board. This Standing Committee shall include the Professor in Educational Studies, the Tutor for Advanced Courses, the Course Director for the Postgraduate Diploma in Learning and Teaching in Higher Education, and three further members appointed by the Academic Board. The duties of the Standing Committee are to supervise arrangements for teaching and to approve courses of study for the Postgraduate Diploma in Learning and Teaching in Higher Education.

6. Every candidate for admission to the examination must apply to the Academic Board for entry to the examination by the first day of Hilary Full Term in the academic year in which he wishes to take the examination. Candidates for the Postgraduate Diploma in Educational Studies must, at the same time, state the subject on which he proposes to submit the dissertation.

7. Candidates for the Postgraduate Diploma in Educational Studies must offer a dissertation of between 15,000 and 20,000 words. Two typewritten copies of the dissertation must be delivered to the Postgraduate Diploma Examiners, Department of Educational Studies, 15 Norham Gardens, Oxford, OX2 6PY, not later than noon on 30 September after the completion of the course of studies. Candidates wishing to submit dissertations later than 30 September must obtain the approval of the Academic Board by the last day of the preceding Trinity Term, but no dissertation may be submitted later than noon on 30 September in the year following, unless the Academic Board approves a later date for submission. One bound copy of the dissertation of each candidate who passes the examination shall be retained by the department for deposit in the departmental Library.

8. Candidates for the Postgraduate Diploma in Educational Studies may also be required to attend an oral examination.

9. The examiners for the Postgraduate Diploma in Educational Studies shall also consider, as part of the examination, reports on the candidate's work submitted by his supervisor. Reports shall be submitted at the end of each Full Term except that, in the term in which the candidate takes the examination, a report shall be submitted by the end of the seventh week of Full Term.

Candidates for the Postgraduate Diploma in Learning and Teaching in Higher Education must submit a portfolio of written work of between 12,000 and 15,000 words in total. Portfolios may be submitted at any time up to noon of the Monday of the first week of Full Term following the sixth term of comencement of the course. No portfolio may be submitted later than this unless the Academic Board approves a later date for submission. Two type-written copies of the portfolio should be submitted to the examiners at the Department of Educational Studies, 15 Norham Gardens, Oxford OX2 6PY, together with a statement that the candidate has participated in no fewer than six of the full day seminars in the Diploma programme.

10. Candidates for either the Postgraduate Diploma in Educational Studies or the Postgraduate Diploma in Learning and Teaching in Higher Education who fail the examination may be re-examined on not more than one occasion which normally shall be within one year of their initial failure.

POSTGRADUATE CERTIFICATES (CONTINUING EDUCATION)

Ch. X, Sect. XIV]

General Regulations

1. The Continuing Education Board shall have power to grant Postgraduate Certificates to candidates who have satisfied the conditions prescribed in this section and any further conditions which the board may prescribe by regulation.

2. The examination for each Postgraduate Certificate shall, in consultation with representatives of collaborating departments or faculties, be under the supervision of the Continuing Education Board which shall have power, subject to the approval of the Educational Policy and Standards Committee, to make regulations governing the examination.

3. Candidates, whether members of the University or not, may be admitted as students for a Postgraduate Certificate under such conditions as the board shall prescribe, provided that before admission to a course of study approved by the board, candidates shall have satisfied the board that they have had appropriate educational and professional experience acceptable to the board, and are well-equipped to enter the proposed course of study.

4. Any person who has been accepted as a candidate for a Postgraduate Certificate, and who has satisfactorily pursued a

course, the character and length of which have been approved by the board, may be admitted to the examination.

Special Regulations

Architectural History

1. *Course*

(*a*) The course will consist of lectures and classes on architectural history and on site evaluation and survey. The course may be taken on a part-time basis over a period which shall normally be of one year's duration and shall not exceed two years.

(*b*) The course will consist of three taught units, two of which will be on architectural history and one of which will be on site evaluation and survey, which will be offered in three ten-week terms.

2. Every candidate will be required to satisfy the examiners in the following:

(*a*) attendance at the classroom-based courses;

(*b*) submission of the following portfolio of written work:

(i) three essays or projects linked to unit one each of which shall not exceed 1,500 words in length;

(ii) two essays linked to unit two, each of which shall not exceed 2,000 words in length;

(iii) a workbook linked to unit three;

(iv) a dissertation which shall not exceed 8,000 words in length on a topic agreed by the Board of Studies.

The assignments under (i)–(iii) and the dissertation under (iv) will be forwarded to the examiners c/o the Registry, Department for Continuing Education, Wellington Square, Oxford OX1 2JA by such dates as the examiners shall determine and shall notify to candidates.

3. Candidates may be required to attend a *viva voce* examination at the end of the course of studies at the discretion of the examiners.

4. The examiners may award a distinction to candidates for the certificate.

5. Candidates who fail to satisfy the examiners in the assignments under 2.(i)–(iii), or the dissertation under 2.(iv), or both, may be permitted to resubmit work in respect of part or parts of the examination which they have failed for examination on not more than one occasion which shall normally be within one year of the initial failure.

Clinical Supervision in Organizational Settings

1. *Course*

(*a*) The course will consist of lectures, tutorials, seminars, and course review sessions on clinical supervision in organizational settings. The course will be taken on a part-time basis over a period which shall be of one year's duration;

(*b*) the course will consist of three study terms, each of ten weeks, covering respectively: (i) The Supervisory Relationship; (ii) Group and Organizational Structures and Dynamics; (iii) Key Issues in Contemporary Public Sector Practice.

2. Every candidate will be required to satisfy the examiners in the following:

(*a*) attendance of at least 75% at lectures and seminars, and all tutorials;

(*b*) portfolio of supervisory practice of no more than 5,000 words;

(*c*) clinical paper of no more than 5,000 words, demonstrating integration of the three strands of the course: theory, clinical practice and self-reflection and learning;

(*d*) a theoretical essay of no more than 5,000 words on a key concept of clinical supervision;
(*e*) termly reports from a candidate' clinical seminar tutor;
(*f*) annual report from the candidate's individual tutor.

The assignments under (*b*)–(*d*) will be forwarded to the examiners c/o Registry, Department for Continuing Education, Wellington Square, Oxford OX1 2JA, for consideration by the examiners by such date as the examiners shall determine and shall notify candidates before the start of the academic year in which the assignment is due.

3. Candidates who fail to satisfy the examiners in 2(*b*)–(*d*) above may be permitted to resubmit work in the part or parts of the examination which they have failed for examination on not more than one occasion which shall normally be within one year of the original failure. Approval for deferral must be obtained from the relevant board of studies.

4. If there are reservations over the readiness of a course member to provide clinical supervision safely, a further period of supervision of clinical supervisory practice may be authorised by the Board of Examiners.

5. The examiners may award a distinction to candidates for the certificate.

Evidence-based Health Care

1. *Course*

(*a*) The course will consist of lectures, tutorials, seminars, and classes, on the principles and practice of evidence-based health care. The course may be taken on a part-time basis over a period which shall normally be of one year's, and shall not exceed two years' duration.
(*b*) The course will consist of three modules respectively entitled 'The Practice of Evidence-based Health Care', 'Planning for Change in Evidence-based Health Care' and 'Implementing and Monitoring Change in Health Care', each of which will provide a focus for six weeks of project work in the student's own health care settings.

2. Every candidate will be required to satisfy the examiners in the following:

(*a*) attendance at the classroom-based courses:
(*b*) the following portfolios of written work, each of which shall not exceed 4,000 words in length:
 (i) a critical appraisal and analysis based on a minimum of three comprehensive literature searches closely related to the rest of the candidate's course work;
 (ii) evidence of ability to inculcate in others the principles and practice of evidence-based health care in the candidate's work-based setting;
 (iii) an account of the implementation and monitoring by the candidate of an aspect of health care change;
(*c*) an overall appraisal and analysis, which shall not exceed 4,000 words, of the work undertaken during the three modules (less any exemption).

The portfolios under (*b*), and the overall appraisal and analysis under (*c*), will be forwarded to the examiners c/o Registry, Department for Continuing Education, Wellington Square, Oxford OX1 2JA for consideration by such date as the examiners shall determine and shall notify candidates.

3. Candidates may be required to attend a viva voce examination at the end of the course of studies at the discretion of the examiners.

4. The examiners may award a distinction to candidates for the certificate.

5. The Standing Committee for the M.Sc. in Evidence-based Health Care shall have the discretion to permit any candidate to be exempted from submitting one and one only of the written assignments under 2(*b*), provided the standing committee

is satisfied that such a candidate has undertaken equivalent study, of an appropriate standard, normally at another institution of higher education.

A candidate who fails to satisfy the examiners in the assignments under 2(*b*)–2(*c*) above may be permitted to resubmit work in respect of the part or parts of the examination in which he or she has failed to satisfy the examiners on one further occasion only, normally not later than one year after the initial failure.

Object Technology

1. The Divisional Board of Mathematical and Physical Sciences, in consultation with the Sub-faculty of Computation, and the Board of Studies of the Continuing Education Board, shall elect for the supervision of the course a standing committee which shall have the power to arrange lectures and other instruction.

2. The course will consist of lectures, tutorials, seminars, and classes in the theory and practice of Object Technology. The course may be taken over a period of not less than one year, and not more than two years.

3. Every candidate will be required to satisfy the examiners in the following:

(*a*) attendance at a minimum of four short courses;

(*b*) submission of at least four written assignments, based on modules chosen from those in the Schedule for the Postgraduate Certificate in Object Technology, comprising a programme of study approved by the Programme Director.

The assignments under (*b*) shall be forwarded to the examiners for consideration by such dates as the examiners shall determine and shall notify candidates and tutors.

4. Candidates will be expected to attend a viva voce examination at the end of the course of studies unless dispensed by the examiners.

5. The examiners may award a distinction for excellence in the whole examination.

6. The standing committee for the M.Sc. in Software Engineering shall have the discretion to permit any candidate to be exempted from submitting up to one of the total of four written assignments required under 3 (*b*) above, provided the standing committee is satisfied that such a candidate has undertaken sufficient study, of an appropriate standard, normally at another institution of higher education.

7. Candidates who fail to satisfy the examiners in the assignments under 3 (*b*) may be permitted to resubmit work in respect of part or parts of the examination which they have failed for examination on not more than one occasion which shall normally be within one year of the original failure. No written assignment shall be submitted to the examiners on more than one occasion.

Schedule

(i) Design patterns
(ii) Distributed objects
(iii) Object orientation
(iv) Object-oriented design
(v) Object-oriented programming
(vi) One other module from the schedule of courses for the M.Sc. in Software Engineering.

The standing committee for the M.Sc. in Software Engineering shall have the power to add other courses or delete courses from this list. In June and December each year a list of modules shall be published in the University *Gazette*. Each such list, which will have been approved by the standing committee and which will be a selection from the full set above, will contain those modules which will be available during the following nine months.

Psychodynamic Counselling

1. *Course*

(*a*) The course will consist of lectures, tutorials, seminars, classes, and workshops on psychodynamic theory, philosophy, and techniques. Self exploration will be undertaken in small experiential groups. The course will be taken on a part-time basis over a period which shall be of one year's duration.

(*b*) The course will consist of three study terms, each of ten weeks, covering respectively: (i) The Psychodynamic Approach–Definition: (ii) Process and Skills in Early Sessions: (iii) Practicalities, Technique, and Ethical Implications.

2. Every candidate will be required to satisfy the examiners in the following:

(*a*) attendance at weekly classes, a weekend school, individual tutorials, and review and revision days;

(*b*) two written assignments, each of no more than 3,000 words and each on one key psychodynamic concept;

(*c*) one written assignment, of no more than 4,000 words, to provide a critique of interpersonal processes and techniques in action;

(*d*) an assignment on an area of special interest, of no more than 5,000 words;

(*e*) termly reports from a candidate's course tutor.

The assignments under (*b*)–(*d*) will be forwarded to the examiners c/o Registry, Department for Continuing Education, Wellington Square, Oxford OX1 2JA, for consideration by the examiners by such date as the examiners shall determine and shall notify candidates before the start of the academic year in which the assignment is due.

3. Candidates may be required to attend a viva voce examination at the end of the course of studies.

4. Candidates who fail to satisfy the examiners in 2(*b*)–(*d*) above may be permitted to resubmit work in the part or parts of the examination which they have failed for examination on not more than one occasion which shall normally be within one year of the original failure. Approval for deferral must be obtained from the relevant board of studies.

5. The examiners may award a distinction to candidates for the certificate.

Software Engineering

1. *Course*

The Divisional Board of Mathematical and Physical Sciences, in consultation with the Sub-faculty of Computation, and the Board of Studies of the Continuing Education Board, shall elect for the supervision of the course a standing committee which shall have the power to arrange lectures and other instruction.

2. The course will consist of lectures, tutorials, seminars, and classes in the theory and practice of Software Engineering. The course may be taken over a period of not less than one year, and not more than two years.

3. Every candidate will be required to satisfy the examiners in the following:

(*a*) attendance at a minimum of four short courses;

(*b*) submission of four written assignments, based on courses chosen from those in the Schedule for the M.Sc. in Software Engineering, comprising a programme of study approved by the Programme Director;

(*c*) a viva voce examination, unless individually dispensed by the examiners.

The assignments under (*b*) shall be forwarded to the examiners for consideration by such dates as the examiners shall determine and shall notify candidates and tutors.

4. The examiners may award a distinction for excellence in the whole examination.

5. The standing committee for the M.Sc. in Software Engineering shall have the discretion to permit any candidate to be exempted from submitting one of the total of four assignments required, provided that the standing committee is satisfied that such a candidate has undertaken equivalent study, of an appropriate standard, normally at another institution of higher education.

6. Candidates who fail to satisfy the examiners may re-enter the examination on not more than one occasion which shall normally be within one year of the initial failure. No written assignment shall be submitted to the examiners on more than one occasion.

POSTGRADUATE DIPLOMAS (CONTINUING EDUCATION)

General Regulations

Ch. X, Sect. XV]

1. The Continuing Education Board shall have power to grant Postgraduate Diplomas to candidates who have satisfied the conditions prescribed in this section and any further conditions which the board may prescribe by regulation.

2. The examination for each Postgraduate Diploma shall be under the supervision of the Continuing Education Board which shall have power, subject to the approval of the Educational Policy and Standards Committee, to make regulations governing the examination.

3. Candidates, whether members of the University or not, may be admitted as students for a Postgraduate Diploma under such conditions as the board shall prescribe, provided that before admission to a course of study approved by the board, candidates shall have satisfied the board that they have had appropriate educational experience acceptable to the board, and are well-equipped to enter the proposed course of study.

4. Any person who has been accepted as a candidate for a Postgraduate Diploma, and who has satisfactorily pursued a course, the character and length of which have been approved by the board, may be admitted to the examination.

Special Regulations

Advanced Cognitive Therapy Studies

Regulations

1. The course will consist of lectures, tutorials, seminars, and classes on the principle and practice of advanced cognitive therapy studies, together with clinical practice and practice in supervision of cognitive therapy trainees. The course will be

taken on a part-time basis over a period of not less than four terms and not more than seven terms.

2. Every candidate will be required to satisfy the examiners in the following:

(*a*) attendance at the appropriate classroom-based courses including small group case supervision and supervision of supervision practice;

(*b*) supervised treatment of patients with cognitive therapy;

(*c*) skill in supervising cognitive therapy trainees;

(*d*) four audio- or videotape presentations of therapy sessions;

(*e*) four extended written case studies, each of no more than 4,000 words covering a range of different problem areas and including two straightforward and two complex cases;

(*f*) two written assignments, each of no more than 4,000 words, one covering the principles of supervision, and one covering the design, delivery and evaluation of a training event;

(*g*) a presentation of a brief cognitive therapy training event.

The presentations under (*d*) and (*g*), and the assessed work under (*e*) and (*f*), shall be forwarded to the examiners for consideration by such date as the examiners shall determine and shall notify the candidates and tutors.

3. Candidates will be expected to attend a viva voce examination at the end of the course of studies unless individually dispensed by the examiners.

4. The examiners may award a distinction to candidates for the Diploma.

5. Candidates who fail to satisfy the examiners in the audio- or videotape presentations under 2(*c*), the two case presentations under 2(*d*), the two essays under 2(*e*), or the dissertation under 2(*d*) and 2(*g*), or the assessed work under 2(*e*) and 2(*f*), may be permitted to resubmit work in respect of the part or parts of the examination which they have failed for examination on not more than one occasion which shall normally be within one year of the original failure.

Cognitive Therapy

1. The course will consist of lectures, tutorials, seminars, and classes on the principle and practice of cognitive therapy, together with clinical practice in cognitive therapy. The course will be taken on a part-time basis over a period of not less than one year and not more than two years.

2. Every candidate will be required to satisfy the examiners in the following:

(*a*) attendance at the appropriate classroom-based courses including small group case supervisions;

(*b*) supervised treatment of at least three patients by cognitive therapy;

(*c*) six audio- or videotape presentations of therapy sessions;

(*d*) two written case presentations, each of no more than 3,000 words;

(*e*) two essays, each of no more than 4,000 words, on topics provided by course tutors and approved by the examiners;

(*f*) a dissertation of no more than 10,000 words on a topic approved by the examiners.

The six audio- or videotape presentations under (*c*), the two case presentations under (*d*), the two essays under (*e*), and the dissertation under (*f*) shall be forwarded to the examiners for consideration by such date as the examiners shall determine and shall notify candidates and tutors.

3. Candidates will be expected to attend a viva voce examination at the end of the course of studies unless individually dispensed by the examiners.

4. The examiners may award a distinction to candidates for the Diploma.

5. Candidates who fail to satisfy the examiners in the audio- or videotape presentations under 2(*c*), the two case presentations under 2(*d*), the two essays under

2(*e*), or the dissertation under 2(*f*) may be permitted to resubmit work in respect of the part or parts of the examination which they have failed for examination on not more than one occasion which shall normally be within one year of the original failure.

Evidence-based Health Care

1. *Course*

(*a*) The course will consist of lectures, tutorials, seminars, and classes, on the principles and practice of evidence-based health care. The course may be taken on a part-time basis over a period which shall normally be of two years', and shall not exceed three years', duration.

(*b*) The course will consist of the six modules listed in the Schedule.

2. Every candidate will be required to satisfy the examiners in the following:

(*a*) attendance at the appropriate classroom-based courses;

(*b*) the following portfolios of written work, each of which shall not exceed 4,000 words in length:

(i) a critical appraisal and analysis based on a minimum of three comprehensive literature searches closely related to the candidate's course work;

(ii) evidence of ability to inculcate in others the principles and practice of evidence-based health care in the candidate's work-based setting;

(iii) an account of the implementation and monitoring by the candidate of an aspect of health care change;

(*c*) an overall appraisal and analysis, which shall not exceed 4,000 words, of the work undertaken during modules (i)–(iii) in the Schedule;

(*d*) Two written assignments, one on each of modules (iv) and (vi) of the Schedule less any exemption, each assignment not exceeding 4,000 words.

(*e*) A portfolio of statistical exercises, based on material covered in modules (iv) and (v) of the Schedule.

The portfolios under (*b*), the overall appraisal and analysis under (*c*), the written assignment under (*d*) and the statistical exercises under (*e*), will be forwarded to the examiners c/o Registry, Department for Continuing Education, Wellington Square, Oxford OX1 2JA, for consideration by such date as the examiners shall determine and shall notify candidates.

3. Candidates may be required to attend a viva voce examination at the end of the course of studies at the discretion of the examiners.

4. The examiners may award a distinction to candidates for the Diploma.

5. Any candidate who has successfully completed the Postgraduate Certificate in Evidence-based Health Care may on admission to the Postgraduate Diploma be exempted from the requirement to submit, for the examination for the postgraduate diploma, the written assignments under 2(*b*) above. The Postgraduate Diploma in Evidence-based Health Care, if successfully completed, will subsume a candidate's previously completed certificate.

6. The Standing Committee for the M.Sc. in Evidence-based Health Care shall have the discretion to permit any candidate to be exempted from submitting up to two of the written assignments under 2(*b*)–(*d*) above, (not more than one of which shall be from 2(*d*)) or the statistical exercises under 2(*e*), provided that the standing committee is satisfied that such a candidate has undertaken equivalent study, of an appropriate standard, normally at another institution of higher education.

7. A candidate who fails to satisfy the examiners in the assignments under 2(*b*)–(*e*) above may be permitted to re-submit work in respect of the part or parts of the examination in which he or she has failed to satisfy the examiners on one further occasion only, normally not later than one year after the initial failure.

Schedule

(i) The Practice of Evidence-based Health Care.
(ii) Planning for Change in Evidence-based Health Care.
(iii) Implementing and Monitoring Change in Health Care.
(iv) Architecture of Applied Health Research Part 1.
(v) Architecture of Applied Health Research Part 2.
(vi) Research Protocol Development.

Mathematical Finance

[For candidates who enrolled in January 2002 and subsequently, and available to candidates who enrolled in January 1999, January 2000, or January 2001]

1. The Board of the Division of Mathematical and Physical Sciences, in consultation with the Board of Studies of the Continuing Education Board, shall elect for the supervision of the course a standing committee which shall have the power to arrange lectures and other instruction.

2. The course will be taken on a part-time basis, and every candidate must follow for at least four terms a course of instruction in the theory and practice of Mathematical Finance. The subjects of the course will consist of the modules listed in the Schedule below. Candidates must take the five core modules and one module taken from the list of advanced modules.

3. Every candidate will be required to satisfy the examiners in the following:
(*a*) attendance at the appropriate classroom-based courses;
(*b*) submission of five module assignments, one for each of modules 1 to 5;
(*c*) one written 'special topic' assignment, of no more than 10 pages of A4 in length (excluding tables, appendices, footnotes, and bibliography), on the candidate's choice of advanced module from those currently listed in the schedule;
(*d*) a project report of no more than 25 pages of A4 in length (excluding tables, appendices, footnotes, and bibliography), on a topic agreed by the chairman of the Standing Committee for the Diploma in Mathematical Finance;
(*e*) a three-hour written examination, covering material relevant to modules 1 to 5.

The assignments under (*b*) and (*c*) and the project report under (*d*) shall be forwarded to the examiners c/o Registry, Department of Continuing Education, 1 Wellington Square, Oxford OX1 2JA, for consideration by such date as the examiners shall determine and shall notify candidates.

4. Candidates may be required to attend a viva voce examination at the end of the course of studies at the discretion of the examiners.

5. The examiners may award a distinction to candidates for the Diploma.

6. Candidates who fail to satisfy the examiners in the assignments under (*b*) or the project report under (*c*) may be permitted to resubmit work in respect of the part or parts of the examination which they have failed for examination on not more than one occasion which shall normally be within one year of the original failure.

Schedule

Section A: Core modules

Modules 1 to 5 shall be given each year.

1. Mathematical and Technical Prerequisites.

2. Introduction to Finance and Markets.

3. Equity and FX Options and Applications.

4. Interest Rates and Products.

5. Advanced Black-Scholes Theory (Equity and FX).

Section B: Advanced Modules

The Standing Committee shall approve the contest of at least three advanced modules to be given each year which shall be published annually in the *Gazette* in or before week eight of Hilary Term.

Professional Archaeology

1. *Course*

(*a*) The course will consist of lectures, tutorials, seminars, and classes in the theory and practice of professional archaeology. The course may be taken full-time in one year or on a part-time basis over a period not exceeding three years. Full-time students will be seconded to approved professional archaeological agencies for four periods of three months. Part-time students must normally be employed within approved relevant organizations to register for the Diploma, and their place of work should perform the same function as the placements.

(*b*) The subjects of the course of study will cover topics relevant to professional archaeology, details of which will be published annually.

2. Every candidate will be required to satisfy the examiners in the following:

(*a*) Submission of a portfolio of placement work (or in the case of part-time students, in-house project work);

(*b*) Submission of five written assignments not exceeding 2,500 words in length;

(*c*) Participation in a minimum of five tutorials;

(*d*) Presentation of a project at an induction course;

(*e*) Nine critical reports, not exceeding 2,000 words in length on each of the modules specified in the schedule below (with the exception of the induction course);

(*f*) Submission of assessments by tutors on written assignments under (*b*) and by placement officers on practical work under (*a*).

The portfolio under (*a*), the five assignments under (*b*), the critical reports under (*e*) and assessments under (*f*) shall be forwarded to the examiners, c/o the Registry, Department for Continuing Education, Wellington Square, Oxford OX1 2JA, for consideration, by such date as the examiners shall determine and shall notify candidates, tutors, and project directors.

3. Candidates will be expected to attend a viva voce examination at the end of the course of studies unless dispensed by the examiners.

4. The examiners may award a distinction to candidates for the Diploma.

5. Candidates who fail to satisfy the examiners in the portfolio under 2(*a*), the five written assignments under 2(*b*), and the critical reports under 2(*e*) may be permitted to resubmit work in respect of the part or parts of the examination which they have failed for examination on not more than one occasion which shall normally be within one year of the original failure.

Schedule

I. Core Modules

Candidates are required to attend the following modules:

(i) Induction course

(ii) Introduction to Professional Archaeology

(iii) Survey Week
(iv) Health and Safety course

II. Optional modules

Candidates are required to attend six optional module courses, each of either one or two days, chosen from a list published annually at the start of the academic year.

Psychodynamic Practice

1. *Course*

(*a*) The course will consist of lectures, tutorials, seminars, classes, and supervised practice on the theory and practice of Psychodynamic Practice. Candidates will be required to undertake personal therapy. The course will be taken on a part-time basis over a period which shall be of two years' duration.

(*b*) The course places equal emphasis on theory, practice, and the candidate's personal and professional development. In the first year candidates will study the Historical and Theoretical Perspective, the Psychiatric Perspective, the Contemporary Perspective, and the Developmental Perspective, and be introduced to core clinical models. The organizational perspective will be taught to complement candidates' clinical placements. Candidates will study long term counselling and psychotherapy. The second year will include the study of time limited counselling and psychotherapy and the application of the core theoretical model to varied contexts and clinical populations.

2. Every candidate will be required to satisfy the examiners in the following:

(*a*) attendance at weekly classes, sensitivity group sessions, individual tutorials, a weekend school, and review sessions and revision days;

(*b*) five written assignments as follows:

(i) an initial case study of no more than 3,000 words.
(ii) a second case study, of no more than 3,000 words.
(iii) two elaborated extracts from a candidate's placement log, each of no more than 3,000 words.
(iv) an essay, of no more than 3,000 words, based on theoretical material covered in the course.

(*c*) a dissertation of no more than 10,000 words (including appendices and footnotes but excluding bibliography). The subject of the dissertation must be submitted for approval by the external examiner following consultation with the course director by noon of Friday of fourth week of Hilary Full Term in the second year of the course.

(*d*) participation in a minimum of 25 placement supervisions and at least 200 hours of client/patient contact, and submission of yearly statements from a candidate's placement supervisor;

(*e*) participation in a minimum of 80 hours of personal therapy and submission of a statement from a candidate's personal therapist that there is no obstacle to the candidate continuing to work with patients/clients;

(*f*) Submission of termly reports from the candidate's course tutor and clinical seminar leader;

(*g*) confirmation from the sensitivity group conductor that there are no ethical reasons why the candidate should be discouraged from commencing professional work.

The assignments under (*b*) and three typewritten or printed copies of the dissertation under (*c*) will be forwarded to the examiners c/o Registry, Department for Continuing Education, Wellington Square, Oxford OX1 2JD for consideration by such date as the examiners shall determine and shall notify candidates before the start of the academic year in which the assignment is due.

3. Candidates may be required to attend a viva voce examination at the end of the course of studies.

4. Candidates who fail to satisfy the examiners in any of the assignments in 2(*b*) or the dissertation may be permitted to resubmit work in the part or parts of the examination which they have failed for examination on not more than one occasion which shall normally be within one year of the original failure. Approval for deferral must be obtained from the relevant board of studies. Candidates who fail to obtain a satisfactory report of their placement at the end of the first year will be given additional support. Candidates who fail to obtain a satisfactory report at the end of the second year may be permitted by the examiners to continue in the placement until the required standard is reached, for a period of no more than one year after the end of the second year.

5. The examiners may award a distinction to candidates for the diploma.

Software Engineering

1. *Course*

The Divisional Board of Mathematical and Physical Sciences, in consultation with the Sub-faculty of Computation, and the Board of Studies of the Continuing Education Board, shall elect for the supervision of the course a standing committee which shall have the power to arrange lectures and other instruction.

2. The course will consist of lectures, tutorials, seminars, and classes in the theory and practice of Software Engineering. The course may be taken over a period of not less than one year, and not more than three years.

3. Every candidate will be required to satisfy the examiners in the following:

(*a*) attendance at a practical course and seven further courses chosen from those in the Schedule for the M.Sc. in Software Engineering, comprising a programme of study approved by the Programme Director;

(*b*) submission of an assignment based on the practical course.

(*c*) submission of seven written assignments based on the courses chosen in 3(*a*) above. These shall be forwarded to the examiners for consideration by such dates as the examiners shall determine and shall notify to candidates and tutors;

(*d*) a viva voce examination, unless individually dispensed by the examiners.

The assignments under (*b*) and (*c*) shall be forwarded to the examiners for consideration by such dates as the examiners shall determine and shall notify candidates and tutors.

4. The examiners may award a distinction for excellence in the whole examination.

5. The Standing Committee for the M.Sc. in Software Engineering shall have the discretion to permit any candidate for the postgraduate diploma to be exempted from submitting up to two of the total of seven assignments required under 3 (*b*) above, provided that the standing committee is satisfied that such a candidate has undertaken equivalent study, of an appropriate standard, normally at another institution of higher education.

6. The standing committee shall have the discretion to permit any assignments submitted as part of the course for the Postgraduate Certificate in Software Engineering, or the Postgraduate Certificate in Object Technology, to be submitted for the examination for the Diploma. The corresponding period of study undertaken for the Postgraduate Certificate shall be counted towards the maximum period of study for the Diploma.

7. If any candidate who is successful in the examination for the Postgraduate Diploma in Software Engineering has previously successfully completed the Postgraduate Certificate in Software Engineering, or the Postgraduate Certificate in Object Technology, and for that examination has incorporated the assignments submitted for the Postgraduate Certificate into the Postgraduate Diploma, then the Postgraduate Diploma will subsume his or her Certificate.

8. Candidates who fail to satisfy the examiners may re-enter the examination on not more than one occasion which shall normally be within one year of the initial failure. No written assignment shall be submitted to the examiners on more than one occasion.

UNDERGRADUATE ADVANCED DIPLOMAS (CONTINUING EDUCATION)

Ch. X, Sect. XVI]

(i) General Regulations

1. The Continuing Education Board shall have power to grant Advanced Diplomas (two-year part-time), Advanced Diplomas (one-year full-time), and Advanced Diplomas (one-year part-time) to candidates who have satisfied the conditions prescribed in this section and any further conditions which the board may prescribe by regulation.

2. The examination for each Advanced Diploma (Continuing Education) shall be under the supervision of the Continuing Education Board, which shall have power, subject to the approval of the Educational Policy and Standards Committee, to make regulations governing the examination.

3. Candidates, whether members of the University or not, may be admitted as students for an Advanced Diploma (Continuing Education) under such conditions as the board shall prescribe, provided that before admission to a course of study approved by the board, candidates shall have satisfied the board that they have appropriate educational experience acceptable to the committee and are well-equipped to enter the proposed course of study.

4. Any person who has been accepted as a candidate for an Advanced Diploma (Continuing Education), and who has satisfactorily pursued a course, the character and length of which have been approved by the board, may be admitted to the examination.

Special Regulations

(i) ADVANCED DIPLOMAS (TWO YEAR PART-TIME)

Advanced Diploma in Archaeological Practice

1. *Course*

(*a*) The course will consist of lectures, classes, seminars, and tutorials in Archaeological Practice. The course, which is available on a part-time basis only, will normally be taken over a period of two, and no more than five years.

(*b*) The subjects of the course of study will include topics relevant to landscape archaeology, material culture, or environmental and scientific archaeology.

2. Every candidate will be required to satisfy the examiners in the following:

(*a*) Attendance at the taught courses and at one week's prescribed practical fieldwork;

(*b*) Assignments based on the taught courses and practical fieldwork;

(*c*) One long assignment of up to 5,000 words (including appendices);

(*d*) A dissertation of up to 10,000 words (including appendices) on a topic agreed by the Board of Studies.

Assignments under 2(*b*)–2(*c*) and the dissertation under 2(*d*) will be forwarded to the examiners for consideration by such dates as the examiners shall determine and shall notify candidates.

3. Candidates may be required to attend a viva voce examination at the end of the course of studies.

4. The examiners may award a distinction to candidates for the Advanced Diploma.

5. Candidates who fail to satisfy the examiners in the assignments under 2(*b*)–2(*c*), or the dissertation under 2(*d*), or both, may be permitted to re-submit work in respect of the part or parts of the examination which they have failed for examination on not more than one occasion which shall normally be within one year of the initial failure.

Advanced Diploma in Environmental Conservation

1. *Course*

(*a*) The course will consist of lectures, classes, seminars, and tutorials in Environmental Conservation. The course, which is available on a part-time basis only, will normally be taken over a period of two, and no more than five, years.

(*b*) The subjects of the course of study will be taught in two one-year modules, entitled:

1 Environmental Change and Issues

2 Conservation Management

One module will be offered each year.

2. Every candidate will be required to satisfy the examiners in the following:

(*a*) Attendance at the taught courses and at practical fieldwork sessions;

(*b*) Eight assignments of between 2,000 and 2,500 words in length, based on the taught courses;

(*c*) Two field notebooks based on the practical fieldwork;

(*d*) One long assignment of up to 5,000 words (including appendices);

(*e*) A dissertation of up to 10,000 words (including appendices) on a topic agreed by the Board of Studies.

Assignments under 2(*b*)–2(*d*) and the dissertation under (*e*) will be forwarded to the examiners for consideration by such dates as the examiners shall determine and shall notify candidates.

3. Candidates may be required to attend a viva voce examination at the end of the course of studies.

4. The examiners may award a distinction to candidates for the Advanced Diploma.

5. Candidates who fail to satisfy the examiners in the assignments under 2(*b*)–2(*d*), or the dissertation under 2(*e*), or both, may be permitted to re-submit work in respect of the part or parts of the examination which they have failed for examination on

not more than one occasion which shall normally be within one year of the initial failure.

Advanced Diploma in the History of Art

1. *Course*

(*a*) The course will consist of lectures, classes, seminars, and tutorials in the History of Art. The course, which is available on a part-time basis only, will normally be taken over a period of two, and no more than five, years.

(*b*) The subjects of the course will be taught in two one-year modules, entitled:

1 Art and Architecture from 1900 to 1945

2 Art and Architecture since 1945

One module will be offered each year. Students must complete Module 1 before proceeding to Module 2.

2. Every candidate will be required to satisfy the examiners in the following:

(*a*) Attendance at the taught courses and at study visits;

(*b*) Ten assignments, each of 2,000 words in length, based on the taught courses;

(*c*) One long assignment of up to 5,000 words (including appendices);

(*d*) A dissertation of up to 10,000 words (including appendices) on a topic agreed by the Board of Studies.

Assignments under 2(*b*)–2(*c*) and the dissertation under 2(*d*) will be forwarded to the examiners for consideration by such dates as the examiners shall determine and shall notify candidates.

3. Candidates may be required to attend a viva voce examination at the end of the course of studies.

4. The examiners may award a distinction to candidates for the Advanced Diploma.

5. Candidates who fail to satisfy the examiners in the assignments under 2(*b*)–2(*c*), or the dissertation under 2(*d*), or both, may be permitted to re-submit work in respect of the part or parts of the examination which they have failed for examination on not more than one occasion which shall normally be within one year of the initial failure.

(ii) ADVANCED DIPLOMAS (ONE YEAR FULL-TIME)

Advanced Diploma in British Studies (Language and Society)

1. *Course*

(*a*) The course will consist of lectures, tutorials, and classes in the culture of Britain, with accompanying study in English language. Every candidate must take the course under the supervision of the Continuing Education Board for at least one year. Such study shall be pursued at Oxford.

(*b*) The course will consist of four core subjects as follows:

(i) Pre-sessional course

(ii) English language

(iii) British Studies

(iv) Extended essay option.

2. Candidates will normally be expected to pass an examination at the end of the pre-sessional course before being permitted to proceed to the remainder of the course.

3. In addition, every candidate will be required to satisfy the examiners in the following:

(*a*) A written portfolio of exercises based on the contents of the English language course, which will be of no more than 10,000 words in total;

(*b*) Six assignments based on the theoretical courses in British Studies, each of a maximum of 2,000 words, which will in total be not more than 10,000 words;

(*c*) An extended essay normally of between 4,000 and 5,000 words in length (the limit to include notes) on a topic related to one of the core subjects of study.

Assignments under 3(*a*)–3(*c*) will be forwarded to the examiners for consideration by such dates as the examiners shall determine and shall notify candidates.

4. Candidates may also be called for viva voce examination.

5. The examiners may award a distinction to candidates for the Advanced Diploma.

6. Candidates who fail to satisfy the examiners in any part of the examination may be permitted to re-submit work in respect of the part or parts of the examination which they have failed for examination on not more than one occasion which shall normally be within one year of the initial failure.

(iii) ADVANCED DIPLOMAS (ONE YEAR PART-TIME)

Biblical and Theological Studies (offered at Regent's Park College)

1. *Course*

(*a*) The course will consist of lectures, tutorials, seminars, and classes, on the subject of Biblical & Theological Studies. Candidates will be required also to undertake supervised pastoral practice and preaching. Candidates will be expected to have completed the Undergraduate Diploma in Biblical and Theological Studies offered by the College (formerly the Undergraduate Certificate in Biblical and Theological Studies) or an equivalent course of study approved by the Board of Studies.

(*b*) The course may be taken on a part-time basis only over a period of at least one year and no more than two years. Candidates shall follow six subjects from the Schedule below.

2. Every candidate will be required to satisfy the examiners in the following:

(*a*) Attendance at the thoeretical courses; students must attend a minimum of 75% of the equivalent of 30 two-hour sessions;

(*b*) Three coursework assignments, each of which shall not exceed 3,000 words or equivalent in length, based on the theoretical courses;

(*c*) A dissertation of no more than 10,000 words, on a topic of theological interest to the candidate, the title of which shall be approved by the Course Director;

(*d*) A satisfactory report of the period of supervised pastoral practice and preaching from a candidate's supervisor appointed for this purpose by the Course Director.

Assignments under (*b*) and (*c*) will be forwarded to the examiners for consideration by such dates as the examiners shall determine and shall notify candidates.

3. Candidates may be expected to attend a viva voce examination at the end of the course.

4. The examiners may award a distinction to candidates for the Advanced Diploma.

5. Candidates who fail to satisfy the examiners in the assignments under 2(*b*)–(*c*) may be permitted to resubmit work in respect of part or parts of the examination which they have failed on not more than one occasion which shall normally be within one year of the initial failure.

Schedule

Candidates must complete one group of the three subject groups shown below. Only one subject group is available each year. The definitive list of subjects for one year will be circulated to candidates not later than Friday of the third week of Michaelmas Term of that year. Candidates may not offer for the Advanced Diploma any subject group undertaken as part of the Undergraduate Diploma in Biblical and Theological Studies.

Subject Group A

1. Pastoral theology
2. The Atonement

3. The Reformation
4. 'Romans'
5. Covenant in the Old Testament
6. Ethics

Subject Group B

1. The Sacraments
2. The Church and the Kingdom
3. The Early Church
4. The Psalms
5. Social Context of Theology
6. The Corinthian Letters

Subject Group C

1. Old Testament Prophets
2. Mission
3. Luke and Acts
4. Philosophy
5. Modern Church History
6. God and Revelation

Computing

Course

(*a*) The course will consist of lectures, tutorials, seminars, and classes, on the development of applications on a personal computer. The course, which is available on a part-time basis only, may be taken over a period of at least one, and at most two, years.

(*b*) The subject of the course of study will include Information Engineering and Systems Development (development of skills in information engineering with particular reference to the representation, structuring, and manipulation of data; approaches to systems development techniques; implications of evolving personal computer software tools and hardware; needs analysis, specifications, implementation, and issues of usability and reliability), and Practical Development Skills (use and manipulation of objects; the use of Visual Basic as a macro language to interface to database and spreadsheet engines; analysis of case studies).

2. Every candidate will be required to satisfy the examiners in the following:

(*a*) Attendance at the theoretical courses;

(*b*) Assignments based on the theoretical courses;

(*c*) A dissertation of up to 10,000 words (including appendices) on a topic agreed by the Board of Studies.

Assignments under (*b*) and the dissertation under (*c*) will be forwarded to the examiners for consideration by such dates as the examiners shall determine and shall notify candidates.

3. The examiners may award a distinction to candidates for the Advanced Diploma.

4. Candidates who fail to satisfy the examiners in the assignments under 2(*b*), or the dissertation under 2(*c*), or both, may be permitted to re-submit work in respect of the part or parts of the examination which they have failed for examination on not more than one occasion which shall normally be within one year of the initial failure.

Local History

1. *Course*

The course will comprise two modules:

A. Concepts and Methods for Local History

B. Databases for Historians.

The course, which is available on a part-time, distance learning basis only, will normally be taken over a period of one year, and may not be taken over a period of more than two years.

2. Every candidate will be required to satisfy the examiners in the following:

(*a*) active participation in all parts of the course to the satisfaction of the Course Director;

(*b*) active participation in (electronic) group discussions under the guidance, and to the satisfaction, of the student's academic tutor;

(*c*) four assignments of 2,500 words each, based on the work covered in the Concepts and Methods module (A, above);

(*d*) two assignments of 2,500 words, based on the work covered in the Databases module (B, above);

(*e*) one assignment of 5,000 words, which will be a Local History project involving the use of a database of historical data;

Assignments under 2(*c*)–(*e*) above will be forwarded to the examiners for consideration by such dates as the examiners shall determine and shall notify candidates.

3. Candidates will be required to pass all assignments in both modules to be awarded the Advanced Diploma (one-year). Candidates who fail to satisfy the examiners in the assignments under 2(*c*)–(*e*) may be permitted to resubmit work which they have failed for examination on not more than one occasion which shall normally be within one year of the date on which the assignment was first due to be submitted.

4. Candidates may be required to attend a viva voce examination in person at the end of the course of studies.

5. The examiners may award a Distinction to candidates for the Advanced Diploma.

British Studies (Language and Society)

1. *Course*

(*a*) The course will consist of lectures, tutorials, and classes in the culture of Britain, with accompanying study in English language. Every candidate must take the course under the supervision of the board for at least one year. Such study shall be pursued at Oxford.

(*b*) The course will consist of four core subjects as follows:

(i) Pre-sessional course
(ii) English language
(iii) British Studies
(iv) Extended essay option

2. Candidates will normally be expected to pass an examination at the end of the pre-sessional course before being permitted to proceed to the remainder of the course.

3. In addition, every candidate will be required to satisfy the examiners in the following:

(*a*) A written portfolio of exercises based on the contents of the English language course, which will be of no more than 10,000 words in total;

(*b*) Six assignments based on the theoretical courses in British Studies, each of a maximum of 2,000 words, which will in total be not more than 10,000 words;

(*c*) An extended essay normally of between 4,000 and 5,000 words in length (the limit to include notes) on a topic related to one of the core subjects of study.

Assignments under 3(*a*)–(*c*) will be forwarded to the examiners for consideration by such dates as the examiners shall determine and shall notify candidates.

4. Candidates may also be called for viva voce examination.

5. The examiners may award a distinction to candidates for the Advanced Diploma.

6. Candidates who fail to satisfy the examiners in any part of the examination may be permitted to re-submit work in respect of the part or parts of the examination which they have failed for examination on not more than one occasion which shall normally be within one year of the initial failure.

POSTGRADUATE DIPLOMA IN LEGAL PRACTICE

Ch. X, Sect. XX]

(i) General Regulations

1. The University of Oxford, jointly with Oxford Brookes University, shall have power to grant Postgraduate Diplomas in Legal Practice to candidates recommended by the Legal Practice Course (LPC) Examination Committee, constituted as prescribed in clause 4 below.

2. The course will be open to all persons who under the Law Society's regulations are qualified to enter the Legal Practice Course. Candidates may be admitted under such conditions as the Oxford Institute of Legal Practice (OILP), a joint venture between the University of Oxford and Oxford Brookes University, shall prescribe. Candidates will not, by virtue of their admission to the course, become members of the University.

3. Any person who has been accepted as a candidate for the Postgraduate Diploma in Legal Practice and who has satisfactorily pursued a course the character and length of which have been approved by the Board of Studies of OILP may be admitted to the examination.

4. The LPC Examination Committee shall comprise:

(*a*) the Director of OILP (convenor);

(*b*) the Course Manager of the LPC;

(*c*) all full-time academic staff of OILP;

(*d*) all other staff responsible for units of the LPC;

(*e*) at least three external examiners approved by the Law Society on the recommendation of the Legal Practice Course Committee;

(*f*) one person nominated by the University of Oxford;

(*g*) one person nominated by Oxford Brookes University;

(*h*) the Chief Training Officer of the Law Society or that officer's nominee.

The Chairman of the Examination Committee shall be the Director of OILP or the Director's nominee.

5. The Examination Committee shall:

(*a*) consider each candidate's performance in the examinations, assessed coursework, and skills assessments and make recommendations to the University of Oxford and Oxford Brookes University for the award of the Postgraduate Diploma in Legal Practice, and the two institutions shall have no power to alter such recommendations;

(*b*) consider whether, under the assessment regulations, the performance of any candidate justifies a recommendation for the award of the Postgraduate Diploma with Commendation or Distinction.

6. In the case of a referred or deferred examination or referred or deferred skills assessment, a recommendation for the award of the Postgraduate Diploma in Legal Practice may be made by the Chairman of the Examination Committee after approval of the recommendation by the external examiners. A decision either to fail a candidate or to permit a candidate, who has failed a referred or deferred examination or referred or deferred skills assessment, to repeat the entire diet of assessments may be made by the Chairman of the Examination Committee after approval of the recommendation by the external examiners.

7. No recommendations under clause 5 (*a*) or (*b*) above may be made by the Examination Committee unless a majority of the external examiners approves the recommendation.

(ii) SPECIAL REGULATIONS

1. Candidates will be examined in the following compulsory subjects: Litigation and Advocacy; Conveyancing and Wills; Business Law and Practice; Probate and Administration.

2. Candidates will be examined in two options from the following: Commercial Law; Corporate Finance; Commercial Property; Family Law; Housing Law; Planning and Environmental Law.

3. Examination under cll. 1 and 2 will be by written examination (accounting for 75 per cent of the mark) and coursework (accounting for 25 per cent of the mark).

4. The pass mark in the compulsory subjects and the options shall be 50 per cent. A minimum mark of 50 per cent should normally be obtained in both the examination element and each element of the coursework assessment. However a mark of not less than 45 per cent in one element may be compensated by the mark obtained in the other element, provided the overall mark scored in this subject is 50 per cent or more.

5. The coursework element of each compulsory subject shall consist of two pieces of coursework. The coursework element of each option shall consist of one piece of coursework.

6. Candidates will be assessed on their competence in the following pervasives: Introduction to Revenue Law; Professional Conduct; European Community Law; Financial Services Act.

7. Assessment of the pervasives shall be by means of two assessed exercises in each pervasive. Assessment of the pervasives shall be on a competent/non-competent basis.

8. Candidates will be assessed on their competence in the following skills: Writing and Drafting; Negotiation and Advocacy; Interviewing and Advising; Legal Research.

9. Each skill shall be assessed by means of two practical exercises in that skill. The assessment of each exercise shall be on a competent/non competent basis. If the exercise is oral in form, then the assessment shall be undertaken by two members of staff. The oral exercise will be videotaped, and the tape made available to the external examiners.

10. The Legal Practice Course Committee may, exceptionally, exempt a candidate from taking some or all of the skills assessments or may vary the candidate's assessment programme. Medical evidence of a disability which might prevent or distort a skills assessment must be presented to the Legal Practice Course Committee. The agreement of the external examiners must be obtained for an exemption or variation from any skills assessment.

11. In order to be awarded the Postgraduate Diploma in Legal Practice a candidate will normally be required to pass each of the four compulsory subjects, and to pass two of the optional subjects and be judged competent in each skill and in each pervasive subject.

12. A candidate who has satisfied the conditions in cl. 11 above and has achieved an average of 60 per cent or greater over the compulsory subjects and options and a mark of at least 60 per cent in four subjects or more may be recommended for the award of Postgraduate Diploma in Legal Practice with Commendation.

13. A candidate who has satisfied the conditions in cl. 11 above and has achieved an average of 70 per cent or greater over the compulsory subjects and options and a mark of at least 70 per cent in four subjects or more may be recommended for the award of Postgraduate Diploma in Legal Practice with Distinction.

14. A candidate who fails to be judged competent in one skills assessment exercise shall be given one further opportunity to pass another similar exercise in the same skill.

15. The Examination Committee may, exceptionally, on medical grounds condone a finding that a candidate is not competent in one legal skill provided that the candidate is competent in all other skills assessments.

16. A candidate who fails to submit coursework by the required date for submission or who fails to attend or submit any skills assessment other than for reason of illness or some other cause considered reasonable by the Legal Practice Course Committee shall be deemed to have failed that component of the assessment.

17. The Legal Practice Course Committee shall have power to refer a candidate who fails to achieve a mark of 45 per cent or more in one coursework assessment only. The Legal Practice Course Committee shall require resubmission of a similar coursework on such terms as it shall determine. Under such circumstances, the Postgraduate Diploma cannot be awarded the Commendation or Distinction.

18. The Examination Committee may allow a candidate's overall performance to compensate for failure in one compulsory subject or one option, provided that the failure is within the range of 45–49 per cent of the total marks available for that subject and provided that the candidate has achieved a minimum of 55 per cent of the total marks available in at least one other subject.

19. A candidate who fails at the first attempt to satisfy the Examination Committee in one subject or one skill may be allowed to repeat the assessment component on one further occasion. The referral will normally be in the September following but must be within two years of the meeting of the Examination Committee at which the decision was made.

20. The Examination Committee has discretion to determine the form, conditions, and time of the referral. If a component is assessed by more than one form of assessment and one form has been passed, then the form that has been passed will not be retaken. The maximum mark attainable for a referred subject is 50 per cent. Under such circumstances, the Postgraduate Diploma cannot be awarded with Commendation or Distinction.

21. A candidate who fails at the first attempt to satisfy the Examination Committee in more than one subject or skill may be permitted to repeat the entire diet of assessments (including skills assessments) on one further occasion within two years. Under such circumstances, the Postgraduate Diploma cannot be awarded with Commendation or Distinction.

POSTGRADUATE DIPLOMA IN MANAGEMENT STUDIES

Ch. X, Sect. XXI]

(i) **General Regulations**

1. The Executive Committee of the Saïd Business School shall have power to grant Postgraduate Diplomas in Management Studies to candidates who have satisfied the conditions prescribed in this section and any further conditions which the committee may prescribe by regulation.

2. The examination for the Postgraduate Diploma shall be under the supervision of the Executive Committee of the Saïd Business School which shall have power, subject to the approval of the Divisional Board, to make regulations governing the examination.

3. Candidates, whether members of the University or not, may be admitted as students for the Postgraduate Diploma under such conditions as the committee shall prescribe, provided that before admission to a course of study approved by the committee, candidates shall have satisfied the committee that they have had appropriate educational experience acceptable to the committee, have relevant industrial or commercial experience and are well-equipped to enter the proposed course of study.

4. Any person who has been accepted as a candidate for the Postgraduate Diploma, and who has satisfactorily pursued the course prescribed by the committee, may be admitted to the examination.

(ii) Special Regulations

1. Students of the diploma may hold that status for no more than nine terms.

2. The standing committee shall appoint an academic supervisor to supervise the work of the candidate. The supervisor shall send a report of the work of the candidate to the board at the end of each period of study. The supervisor will inform the board if it is thought that the student is unlikely to reach the standard required by the diploma.

3. Each student will follow a course of study comprising four core courses and a business project. The four core courses are:

Managing the organization. Functional and cross-functional management, finance and accounts, information management, operations management, and human resources.

Managing strategically. Corporate strategy, securing competitive advantage, strategic approaches to leadership, investment, product development, and human resources.

Managing change. Managing personnel and organizational change, reward strategies for change, leading change and change through teamwork, change in manufacturing and services.

A fourth core course from a range of options to be notified to candidates at the start of the course.

Each candidate must submit a business project to be undertaken as part of a group assignment on a subject to be approved by their supervisor. Candidates must submit, no later than Friday of the Sixth Week of the Michaelmas Term in the year after their Part I examination, a report of no more than 6,000 words to their supervisor.

4. The examination will be in three parts:

(*a*) Part I

The examination shall be held after the first two core courses. It shall consist of one written paper covering elements of the first two core courses.

(*b*) Part II

No candidate shall enter the Part II examination unless he or she has already passed Part I. The Part II examination shall consist of one written paper covering elements of the third and fourth core courses.

(*c*) Each candidate will be required to propose, research, and submit a dissertation not exceeding 10,000 words on a topic agreed by the examiners. The dissertation must be submitted to the Chairman of Examiners, c/o the Postgraduate Secretary, Saïd Business School, by Friday of the first week of July in the year in which it is intended to finish the course.

5. The examiners shall also consider, as part of the examination, a report on the candidate's business project submitted by his or her supervisor.

6. The examiners, of whom two shall be appointed, shall have a duty to examine the student in accordance with any regulations prescribed by regulation and to submit a written report to the Graduate Studies Committee of the Saïd Business School which shall decide whether the diploma should be awarded.

7. Candidates may also be required to attend a viva voce examination.

8. The examiners may award a distinction to candidates for the diploma.

9. Candidates who fail an examination may be re-examined on not more than one occasion which normally shall be within one year of their initial failure.

CERTIFICATE IN MANAGEMENT STUDIES

Ch. X, Sect. III]

(i) General Regulations

1. The Executive Committee of the Saïd Business School shall have power to grant Certificates in Management Studies to

candidates who have satisfied the conditions prescribed in this section and any further conditions which the board may prescribe by regulation.

2. The examination for the Certificate in Management Studies shall be under the supervision of the Executive Committee of the Saïd Business School.

3. Any person who has been admitted to a course of study approved for this purpose by the Executive Committee of the Saïd Business School and accepted as a candidate for the certificate by the committee and who has satisfactorily pursued the course, may be admitted to the examination by the committee.

4. Every person who has been accepted as a candidate for the certificate shall be placed by the committee under the supervision of a member of the University or other competent person selected by the committee. It shall be the duty of the supervisor to direct and superintend the work of the candidate and to submit a report to the examiners on the candidate's work.

5. Examination for the certificate shall be by either dissertation or written examination, and (if the examiners think fit) oral examination, under such conditions as the board may by regulation prescribe.

6. A candidate must apply to the committee through the Secretary of Faculties for admission to the examination at such time as the committee may by regulation prescribe. He or she shall at the same time indicate whether he or she wishes to be examined by dissertation or written examination and, if the former, shall submit, for the approval of the committee, the subject on which he or she proposes to submit a dissertation. Applications must be accompanied by

(*a*) the fee prescribed in Ch. VIII, Sect. I, §2 (see Appendix I);
(*b*) a certificate from the candidate's college or confirmation from the Saïd Business School that the candidate has satisfactorily pursued a course of study approved by the committee;
(*c*) such other information as the committee may by regulation require.

7. On receipt of an application, the Secretary of Faculties shall submit it to the committee and the committee shall thereupon appoint two examiners whose duties shall be

(*a*) to examine the student in accordance with such rules as the board may by regulation prescribe;
(*b*) to submit a written report on the examination to the committee through the Secretary of Faculties.

8. On receipt of the examiners' report it shall be the duty of the committee to decide whether the certificates shall be issued or not.

(ii) Special Regulations

1. *Admission*

All candidates for admission as students for the Certificate in Management Studies must apply to the Secretary of Faculties. Applications may be made throughout the academic year. A registration fee as prescribed in Ch. VIII, Sect. I, § 2 (see Appendix I) is payable by non-members of the University under Ch. X, Sect. vii, cl. 4 and must accompany the application for admission. The Secretary of Faculties shall submit all such applications to the Executive Committee of the Saïd Business School.

2. *Entry for the Examination*

Every candidate for admission to the examination must apply to the Executive Committee of the Saïd Business School through the Secretary of Faculties for entry to the examination. Entry may be made at any time during the academic year but should be between two months before the start and two months after the end of the complete course of study which has been approved by the Executive Committee of the Saïd Business School. Candidates must indicate whether they wish to submit a dissertation or complete the written examination. If a candidate elects to submit a dissertation he or she must indicate, at the time of application, the subject chosen.

Every candidate for the certificate shall pursue a course of study approved by the Executive Committee of the Saïd Business School.

3. *The Examination*

(i) The examination will consist of:

(*a*) *Either* a dissertation of no more than 20,000 words on a subject falling within any field of Management Studies to be agreed by the committee.

Two printed copies of the dissertation must be submitted to the Chairman of Examiners c/o the Postgraduate Secretary at the Saïd Business School within six months of an application being approved by the Graduate Studies Committee, or the candidate's application will lapse. The dissertation must be accompanied by a statement that it is the candidate's own work.

Or, (i) a written examination paper of three hours duration. Questions will be set on the fundamental concepts and techniques of management, including any one or more of the following: accounting and financial management, organizational behaviour and human resource management, marketing and strategic management, or any other area which the Executive Committee of the Saïd Business School may from time to time agree related to the course of study.

The written examination must be conducted within six months of an application being approved by the Graduate Studies Committee, or the candidate's application will lapse. All written examinations will be conducted on University premises, and due notice shall be given to each candidate of the time and place for the examination.

(ii) a written assignment of no more than 5,000 words on a subject to be agreed with the candidate's supervisor.

(*b*) A report by the supervisor on the candidate's work.

(*c*) A viva voce examination which may be required at the discretion of the examiners.

(ii) Candidates who fail to satisfy the examiners in any part or parts of the examination may resubmit their dissertation or resit the written examination on not more than one occasion which normally shall be within six months of the initial failure.

CERTIFICATE IN THEOLOGY CERTIFICATE FOR THEOLOGY GRADUATES

Ch. X, Sect. IV]

(i) General Regulations

1. The Board of the Faculty of Theology shall have power to grant the following certificates to candidates who have satisfied the conditions prescribed in this section and any further conditions which the board may prescribe by regulation:

Certificate in Theology;
Certificate for Theology Graduates.

2. The examinations for the above mentioned certificates shall be under the supervision of the Board of the Faculty of Theology.

3. Candidates, both members of the University and others, who have been admitted, under such conditions as the Board of the Faculty of Theology shall prescribe, to courses at Campion Hall, Greyfriars, Mansfield College, Regent's Park College, St. Benet's Hall, Blackfriars, Ripon College Cuddesdon, St. Stephen's House, Wycliffe Hall, and Harris Manchester College may be admitted by the board to the examinations for the above mentioned certificates, provided that they have paid to the Curators of the University Chest, through their colleges or other institutions the fee or fees prescribed in Ch. VIII, Sect. 1, §2 (see Appendix I).

4. The supervision of the arrangements for the above mentioned certificates shall be the responsibility of the Supervisory Committee for the Degree of Bachelor of Theology and the Theology Certificates. The committee shall have such powers and duties in respect of the above mentioned certificates as may from time to time be prescribed by the Board of the Faculty of Theology.

5. Part-time students for the above mentioned certificates shall in each case be required to pursue their course of study for twice the number of terms required of an equivalent full-time student.

6. On completion of their course, candidates who have been awarded the Certificate in Theology may, with the approval of the Board of the Faculty of Theology, offer the remaining papers necessary to meet the requirements for the award of the Bachelor of Theology.

(ii) Special Regulations

A. THE CERTIFICATE IN THEOLOGY

A. 1. *Admission requirements*

Candidates will normally be expected to have five GCSE passes, one of which must be in English Language and two of which must be at Advanced Level. Exemptions from this requirement for mature student candidates or those otherwise qualified may be made at the discretion of the Supervisory Committee.

A. 2. *Course requirements*

The length of the course is two years. A minimum of eight papers must be taken from the syllabus as outlined for the Bachelor of Theology. In Part 1 candidates must take all four papers. In Part 2 they must take one paper each from sections B, C, and D. The Supervisory Committee may dispense a candidate from individual compulsory papers on the basis of previous academic work, but not from the total number of papers required.

B. THE CERTIFICATE FOR THEOLOGY GRADUATES

B. 1. *Admission requirements*

Candidates for the Certificate for Theology Graduates must have obtained an Honours or Joint Honours Degree in Theology. Candidates for the one-year course must have obtained at least second class honours. Candidates for the one-year course who have not taken the Honour School of Theology in Oxford must apply to the Supervisory Committee.

B. 2. *Course requirements*

One-year candidates must take at least four papers. Two-year candidates must take at least eight papers. There are no compulsory papers. All papers will be examined at the same level. Each paper will be examined by an essay of 10,000 words, except that:

(*a*) candidates may integrate two papers in a single essay of 15,000–17,000 words (which will still count as two papers);

(*b*) one-year candidates may substitute a written examination in one paper, and two-year candidates in up to three papers, except for paper D.1;

(*c*) candidates may take papers additional to the minimum requirement by written examination, except for paper D.1.

C. REGULATIONS OF GENERAL APPLICATION

C. 1. *Registration and fees*

Not later than the end of the second week of Michaelmas Term, colleges shall forward to the Registrar the names of non-members of the University who wish to be registered as candidates for either of the two certificates, together with the registration fee prescribed in Ch. VIII, Sect. 1, §2 (see Appendix I) in accordance with Ch. X, Sect. VII, cll. 2 and 4. No registration fee is payable for matriculated members of the University, but colleges shall, by the stated time, notify the Registrar of all such students commencing certificate courses.

C. 2. *Examination*

Further provisions governing the examination for the Certificates in Theology are given in the regulations for the Bachelor of Theology.

POSTGRADATE DIPLOMA IN DIPLOMATIC STUDIES

Ch. X, Sect. XXII]

(i) General Regulations

1. The Area and Development Studies Committee shall have the power to grant Postgraduate Diplomas in Diplomatic Studies to candidates who have satisfied the conditions prescribed in this section and any further conditions which the committee may prescribe by regulation.

2. The examination for the Postgraduate Diploma shall be under the supervision of the Area and Development Studies Committee which shall have the power, subject to the approval of the Divisional Board, to make regulations governing the examination.

3. Candidates, whether members of the University or not, may be admitted as students for the Postgraduate Diploma under such conditions as the committee shall prescribe, provided that before admission to a course of study approved by the committee, candidates shall have satisfied the criteria laid down by the admitting body.

4. Any person who has been accepted as a candidate for the Postgraduate Diploma, and who has satisfactorily pursued the course prescribed by the committee, may be admitted to the examination by the committee.

5. Every person who has been accepted as a candidate for the diploma shall be placed by the committee under the supervision of a member of the University or other competent person selected by the committee. It shall be the duty of the supervisor to direct and superintend the work of the candidate and to submit a report to the examiners on the candidate's work.

(ii) Special Regulations

1. Students for the diploma may hold that status for no more than six terms.

2. Candidates are only eligible to be admitted to the Diploma in Diplomatic Studies if they have achieved a 2.1 standard. Admission to the Diploma will take place at the end of the first term in the year of study, on the basis of a transfer proposal and the first term's assessed written work, as approved by the admissions committee for the programme. The candidate must have achieved a 2.1 standard in the first term of study.

3. Each student will follow a course of study comprising four core courses. The four core courses are:

International Politics. Key concepts in international relations leading to central issues in world politics, with particular emphasis on change in the international system and the evolving role of diplomacy in consequence.

Economics. Basics of international trade theory and macroeconomics, focusing on such applied and political economy topics as trade liberalization, globalization, and international resource transfers.

International Law. Principles of international law and the processes of legal reasoning, and their application to current world problems ranging from the nature of international law to the use of force and conflict settlement.

Diplomatic Practice. Overview of different regions of the world, major international organizations, and current world problems as they affect diplomats. Review of practical aspects of diplomacy and their application to discussion of practical action by means of which governments can address these problems.

In addition, candidates will be required to submit a dissertation of between 10,000 and 12,000 words.

4. *Examinations.* Candidates will be required to take papers in *International Politics, International Law*, and *Economics*, there will be two parts to the examination. Each paper will have two parts. Candidates for the Postgraduate Diploma are required to answer at least two questions from Part B.

5. *Syllabus*

I. Four core modules: *International Politics*, *Economics*, *International Law*, and *Diplomatic Practice*.

II. Each candidate will be required to present a dissertation of not more than 12,000 words, on a subject approved by the Area and Development Studies Graduate Studies Committee, to the Director of Studies, by 12 noon on Friday of sixth week of Trinity Term in the year in which he or she completes the course. All material submitted for the dissertation shall be accompanied by a certificate signed by the candidate indicating that it is the candidate's own work.

6. The examiners may award a distinction to candidates for the Diploma.

7. A candidate whose overall average mark falls below 60 shall be eligible to resit the failed elements on one occasion during the following academic year. Compensation in one paper is allowed.

8. Candidates who fail to satisfy the examiners in the written examinations in all four of the core elements of the Certificate course, or who fail to submit a dissertation of the necessary standard will be eligible to resit on one occasion.

CERTIFICATE IN DIPLOMATIC STUDIES

Ch. X, Sect. V]

(i) **General Regulations**

1. The Area and Development Studies Committee shall have power to grant Certificates in Diplomatic Studies to candidates who have satisfied the conditions prescribed in this section and any further conditions which the committee may prescribe by regulation.

2. The examination for the Certificate in Diplomatic Studies shall be under the supervision of the Area and Development Studies Committee.

3. Any person who has been admitted to a course of study approved for this purpose by the Area and Development Studies

Committee and accepted as a candidate for the certificate and who has satisfactorily pursued the course, may be admitted to the examination.

(ii) Special Regulations

1. Students for the certificate may hold that status for no more than six terms.

2. Each student will follow a course of study comprising four core courses. The four core courses are:

International Politics.
Economics.
International Law.
Diplomatic Practice.

3. *Examinations.* The examination for the Certificate shall be under the supervision of the Area and Development Studies Committee, with the concurrence of the Social Sciences Board. The Area and Development Studies Committee shall have power to make regulations governing the examinations and arrange lectures and courses of instruction of candidates for the certificate.

All candidates will be required to satisfy the examiners in four separate three-hour written examinations covering each of the core areas listed in the preceding paragraph demonstrating that they have mastered the substance of the subjects listed and (where appropriate), that they are able to apply them in their continuing professional careers in the international field.

4. The examiners may award a distinction to candidates for the certificate.

5. A candidate whose overall average mark falls below 50 shall be eligible to resit the failed elements during the following academic year.

6. Candidates who fail to satisfy the examiners in the written examinations in all four of the core elements of the Certificate course, will not be eligible to qualify for the Certificate.

DEGREES & OTHER QUALIFICATIONS OPEN TO MEMBERS OF THE FORMER WESTMINSTER COLLEGE

Students admitted prior to 1 April 2000 by the former Westminster College for degrees and other qualifications validated by the University shall be subject to the provisions of the decrees and regulations governing the relevant course as set out in *Examination Decrees*, 1999, pp. 996–1009, save in so far as these may be amended by agreement between the University and Oxford Brookes University after consultation with the students concerned.

FOUNDATION CERTIFICATE IN ENGLISH LANGUAGE AND LITERATURE

Ch. X, Sect. XVII]

(i) **General Regulations**

1. The Continuing Education Board shall have power to grant Foundation Certificates in English Language and Literature to candidates who have satisfied the conditions prescribed in this section and any further conditions which the committee may prescribe by regulation.

2. The examination for the certificate shall be under the supervision of the Board of Studies of the Continuing Education Board.

3. The Director of the Department for Continuing Education shall keep a register of attendance of students for the certificate. No student shall be granted leave to take the examination unless the register shows satisfactory attendance by him or her.

4. Candidates, whether members of the University or not, may be admitted as students for the certificate under such conditions as the Continuing Education Board shall prescribe provided that, before admission to the course, candidates have satisfied the committee that they are well qualified to enter the proposed course of study.

5. Examination for the certificate shall be by written examination, by coursework essays, and (if the examiners think fit) by oral examination, under such conditions as the Continuing Education Board may by regulation prescribe.

6. The examiners may award a distinction to a candidate for the certificate.

(ii) Special Regulations

1. Not later than the end of the second week of Michaelmas Term, the Department for Continuing Education shall forward to the Registrar the names of non-members of the University who wish to be registered as candidates for the Foundation Certificate in English Language and Literature, together with the registration fee prescribed in Ch. VIII, Sect. I, §2 (see Appendix I) in accordance with Ch. X, Sect. VII, cll. 2 and 4.

2. Every candidate for the certificate must follow for at least six terms, and at most nine terms, a part-time course of instruction in English Language and Literature.

3. The examination will consist of

I. Six papers, of which there will be two on each of the topics set out below. Each paper will be of two hours, with an additional fifteen minutes allowed as reading time in respect of each of the two papers in (*c*) below. One of the two papers on each of these topics shall be taken during the third term of study.

(*a*) Renaissance Literature and Shakespeare
(*b*) Victorian and Modern Literature
(*c*) Criticism: History, Theory, and Practice.

II. Eleven coursework essays, of a format and length approved by the Board of Studies of the Continuing Education Board, and to be submitted at such times as the Board of Studies may lay down. Essays must be the candidate's own work and every candidate must submit a statement to that effect.

III. An oral examination (if the examiners think fit in a particular case).

4. A candidate who fails an examination paper may be permitted to retake that paper on not more than one occasion which normally shall be within one year of the initial failure.

FOUNDATION CERTIFICATE IN MODERN HISTORY

Ch. X, Sect. XXII]

(i) **General Regulations**

1. The Continuing Education Board shall have power to grant Foundation Certificates in Modern History to candidates who have satisfied the conditions prescribed in this section and any further conditions which the committee may prescribe by regulation.

2. The examination for the certificate shall be under the supervision of the Board of Studies of the Continuing Education Board.

3. The Director of the Department for Continuing Education shall keep a register of attendance of students for the certificate. No student shall be granted leave to take the examination unless the register shows satisfactory attendance by him or her.

4. Candidates, whether members of the University or not, may be admitted as students for the certificate under such conditions as the Continuing Education Board shall prescribe provided that, before admission to the course, candidates have satisfied the committee that they are well qualified to enter the proposed course of study.

5. Examination for the certificate shall be by written examination, by coursework essays, and (if the examiners think fit) by oral examination, under such conditions as the Continuing Education Board may by regulation prescribe.

6. The examiners may award a distinction to a candidate for the certificate.

(ii) Special Regulations

1. Not later than the end of the second week of Michaelmas Term, the Department for Continuing Education shall forward to the Registrar the names of non-members of the University who wish to be registered as

candidates for the Foundation Certificate in Modern History, together with the registration fee prescribed in Ch. VIII, Sect. I, § 2 (see Appendix I) in accordance with Ch. X, Sect. VII, cll. 2 and 4.

2. Every candidate for the certificate must follow for at least six terms, and at most nine terms, a part-time course of instruction in Modern History. This will comprise:

(i) Four papers as set out below, each of three hours' duration.
  (*a*) Two papers on British History, 1485–1603 and 1900–1979.
  (*b*) One paper on European History, 1815–1914.
  (*c*) One optional paper (source-based) to be chosen from a list to be published annually by the board of studies before the end of the last week of Trinity Term.

(ii) Ten coursework essays, of a format and length approved by the board of studies of the Continuing Education Board, and to be submitted at such times as the board of studies may lay down. Essays must be the candidate's own work and every candidate must submit a statement to that effect.

(iii) One extended essay of 3,000–4,000 words on a candidate's optional subject. The extended essay must be submitted at such time as the board of studies may lay down, and must be the candidate's own work and every candidate must submit a statement to that effect.

(iv) An oral examination (if the examiners think fit in a particular case).

3. A candidate who fails an examination paper may be permitted to retake that paper on not more than one occasion which normally shall be within one year of the initial failure.

DEGREE OF DOCTOR OF CLINICAL PSYCHOLOGY

Ch. X, Sect. XXIII]

(i) General Regulations

1. The Medical Sciences Board shall have power to admit as Students for the Degree of Doctor of Clinical Psychology candidates nominated by the Directorate of the Oxford Doctoral Course in Clinical Psychology.

2. The Director of the Oxford Doctoral Course shall make a return to the Registrar by the end of the first week of Michaelmas Full Term, showing the names of all persons nominated in that term as Students for the Degree of Doctor of Clinical Psychology, and the Registrar shall keep a register of such students.

3. The Medical Sciences Board shall have power, on the advice of the Director of the Oxford Doctoral Course, to remove temporarily or permanently the name of a student from the register. This power shall include cases where students have been found under the procedures of the course and the Oxfordshire Mental Healthcare Trust guilty of gross

misconduct or in breach of the British Psychological Society's Code of Conduct.

4. Students shall be admitted to the doctoral programme for a probationary period. The external examiner shall conduct a formal mid-course review during the second half of the second year of the course (i.e. between eighteen and twenty-four months after the commencement of the course). Candidates shall be required to complete successfully all elements of the work required before they are permitted to progress onto the second part of the course.

5. Subject to the provisions of clauses 3 and 4 above, students for the Degree of Doctor of Clinical Psychology may hold that status for a maximum of five years.

6. An appeal against a decision of the Board of Examiners for the Doctorate in Clinical Psychology may be made only through the University's procedures and those laid down in the course handbook. No procedures arising from a candidate's status as employee or former employee of the Oxfordshire Mental Healthcare Trust may affect a decision of the examiners.

7. The Proctors shall be responsible for overseeing the proper conduct of the examinations for the Degree in Clinical Psychology. The Proctors shall have power to investigate any complaint or appeal concerning the conduct of the examination and to impose upon any candidate for the examination any penalty equivalent to that which they would be empowered to impose upon a member of the University in similar circumstances.

8. Should any Students for the Degree of Doctor of Clinical Psychology have access to university services and facilities, they will be required to observe the appropriate statutes, decrees, regulations, and/or rules governing the use of such services and facilities. The Proctors shall have power to investigate any alleged breaches of those statutes, decrees, regulations, and/or rules and to deal with the matter and impose any penalty equivalent to that which they would have been empowered to impose upon a member of the University in similar circumstances.

(ii) Special Regulations

1. Candidates shall follow a course of training in Clinical Psychology for a period of at least three years. The training shall consist of Clinical, Academic, and Research elements, and candidates will be required to demonstrate their competence in all three elements. The precise periods of training, and the amount of time to be spent on each element, will be notified to candidates by the Course Director prior to the commencement of the course.

2. Candidates shall be examined in all of the following ways:

(*a*) Clinical Activity

Each candidate shall undertake five or six supervised clinical placements providing experience in five of the following areas:

(i) Adult; (ii) Child; (iii) Learning Disabilities; (iv) Older Adults; (v) Elective (to be chosen by the candidate in consultation with the course tutors, subject to the availability of appropriate supervision. Candidates may choose to undertake one (twelve month) or two (six month) elective placements).

Candidates shall submit to the Board of Examiners a report on five of the above clinical placements. The report shall consist of not more than 4,000 words including tables and diagrams but excluding references and appendices. Candidates shall also submit to the Clinical Tutor a notebook (Log Book) for each placement. The candidate's supervisor shall complete, in consultation with the Clinical Tutor, an Evaluation of Clinical Competence (ECC). The Reports and ECC Forms shall be assessed as part of the examination. The notebooks shall be available to the examiners.

(*b*) Academic Activity

Candidates shall be required to follow a programme of study, as prescribed by the Director of the Course, in each of the following areas:

(i) Adult mental health; (ii) Children; (iii) Learning disabilities; (iv) Older adults; (v) Specialist teaching.

Candidates are required to submit an extended essay in each of the five areas. The essay shall not exceed 5,000 words including tables and diagrams but excluding references, and shall be on a subject approved in advance by the examiners.

(*c*) Research Activity

Candidates shall offer the following:

(i) Two small scale Research Projects of approximately 4,500 words in length including tables and diagrams but excluding references and appendices. Each project shall be carried out within a clinical placement within the first two years of training and shall be of direct relevance to the work of the clinical placement. This shall normally be on any two of the first three placements.

(ii) A research dissertation of between 15,000 and 25,000 words, including tables, diagrams, references, and appendices. The Research Dissertation shall consist of a research report of a significant and substantial investigation with human participants and shall be of clinical relevance. The subject of the Research Dissertation must be approved in advance by the examiners. All candidates will be examined on the Dissertation viva voce.

3. Candidates shall be required to satisfy the examiners in each of the assessment units described in clause 2 above.

4. Guidelines on the preparation and submission of all written work will be updated annually as required and will be included in the 'Assessment Procedures and Regulations Handbook'.

5. Deadlines for the submission of all assessed work (i.e. essay titles, essays, small-scale research projects, reports of clinical activity, dissertation proposals and dissertations) will be published annually by the Directorate in the 'Annual Course Syllabus Book' at the start of the academic year. They will also be lodged with the Proctors, and posted in the Course Office.

6. All material submitted for examination must be sent to the Chairman of Examiners of the Doctorate in Clinical Psychology, c/o the Administrator, Isis Education Centre, Warneford Hospital, Headington, Oxford. It shall be accompanied by a certificate signed by the candidate indicating that it is the candidate's own work, except where otherwisee specified. In the case of the report of clinical activity, small-scale research project, and dissertation, this must be supported by a signed statement from the candidate's supervisor indicating that the material submitted is the candidate's own work. These certificates must be submitted separately in a sealed envelope addressed to the chairman of examiners for the Doctorate in Clinical Psychology.

20

RECOGNIZED STUDENTS

Ch. X, Sect. XII]

1. There shall be a Register of Recognized Students who are not members of the University.

2. The board of a faculty or divisional board may place the name of any applicant on the Register of Recognized Students:

Provided that the applicant

(*a*) is not a member of the University,

(*b*) possesses the qualifications required from candidates for admission to the status of Senior Student except that persons not so qualified may in exceptional cases be admitted,

(*c*) is placed under an academic adviser appointed by the board. It shall be the duty of the academic adviser to advise on the work of the student but not to give systematic instruction. He or she shall submit a report on the progress of the student to the board at the end of each term.

3. Application for admission as a Recognized Student shall be made to the Secretary of Faculties for submission to the appropriate faculty board and shall be accompanied by

(*a*) evidence of the degrees previously obtained by the applicant,

(*b*) a statement of the proposed subject of study,

(*c*) a certificate from a professor or head of a department of the University of Oxford supporting the application.

4. If an applicant for admission as a Recognized Student shall propose a subject of study which is outside the scope of the board of any faculty or divisional board but which may in the opinion of the Educational Policy and Standing Committee be profitably studied at Oxford, that committee may, on the recommendation of a delegacy or committee constituted under the provisions of Ch. III or X, deal with his or her case as if it were the board of a faculty.

5. For each term for which his or her name is on the Register, every Recognized Student shall pay to the Curators of the University Chest, within fourteen days from the beginning of Full Term (or from the date of the decision to place his or her name on the

Register, in the case of a decision taken during Full Term and applying to that term), a fee at the annual rate specified in Ch. VIII, Sect. 1, §6, cl. 14 (i) (*d*).

6. A Recognized Student shall cease to hold that status

(*a*) if he or she shall have failed to pay the fees required under clause 5,

(*b*) if his name shall have been removed from the Register by the faculty or divisional board concerned.

7. Every Recognized Student shall be entitled

(i) to use the University Libraries subject to the provision of the statutes governing particular Libraries,

(ii) to attend lectures advertised in the lists of boards of faculties and other bodies:

Provided that attendance

(*a*) at lectures described as seminars or classes or informal instruction shall be subject to the permission of the holder,

(*b*) at lectures given in any college building shall be subject to the right of the college concerned to refuse admission.

(iii) to work in any university department or institution subject to the agreement of the head of that department or institution.

8. No Recognized Student shall have his or her name on the Register of Recognized Students for more than three terms.

9. A faculty or divisional board shall have power to remove from the Register the name of any Recognized Student which it has placed on the Register.

21

VISITING STUDENTS

Ch. X, Sect. XIII]

1. There shall be a Register of Visiting Students who are members of a college or other society but who are not members of the University. Council may determine from time to time conditions for admission to the Register and the maximum numbers of the members of each college or other society who may be admitted as Visiting Students in any one year.

2. Application for admission as a Visiting Student shall be made to the Registrar through the candidate's society within fourteen days after the society has admitted the candidate. The application shall provide such particulars as Council shall from time to time specify, and shall include an undertaking by the candidate, in terms approved from time to time by Council, (i) as to conduct and (ii) as to payment when due of the fees payable to the University while holding the status of Visiting Student.

3. For each term in which his or her name is on the Register, every Visiting Student shall pay:

(*a*) to his or her college or other society for transmission to the Curators of the Chest, within fourteen days from the beginning of Full Term (or, in the term of admission, within fourteen days from the day on which his or her name was entered on the Register), a fee at the annual rate specified in Ch. VIII, Sect. 1, §6, cl. 15 (i) (*d*); and

(*b*) to the Curators of the University Chest, within fourteen days of the same being demanded, such fee or fees as shall be prescribed in accordance with cl. 6 below.

4. A Visiting Student shall cease to hold that status (i) after three terms, or (ii) forthwith if:

(*a*) he or she shall have failed to pay the fees required under cl. 3;

(*b*) he or she ceases to be a member of a college or other society;

(*c*) he or she is matriculated, or his or her name is placed on the Register of Diploma Students or the Register of Recognized Students; or

(*d*) in accordance with the prescribed procedure, he or she is found to have committed a breach of his undertaking as to conduct and it is held that his status is to cease as a consequence.

5. Every Visiting Student shall be entitled:

(*a*) to use the university libraries subject to the provisions of the statutes or decrees governing particular libraries, and to the general regulations and rules of the libraries concerned.

(*b*) to attend lectures advertised in the lists of boards of faculties and other bodies, provided that:

(i) attendance at lectures described as seminars or classes or informal instruction shall be subject to the permission of the holder, and

(ii) attendance at lectures given in any college building shall be subject to the right of the college concerned to refuse admission.

6. A Visiting Student may be permitted to work, and receive teaching or supervision, in any university laboratory, subject to

prior arrangement agreed between his or her society and the head of department, and subject to the payment of such fee or fees as may be prescribed, and to such conditions as may be determined, by the head of department in accordance with arrangements approved from time to time by Council.

7. No Visiting Student shall be eligible to be a candidate for any examination, or scholarship, prize, or other award of the University.

22

GENERAL RULES RESPECTING UNIVERSITY EXAMINATIONS

Ch. VI, Sect. II. A]

A. *APPOINTMENT OF EXAMINERS*

§1. Number of Examiners, and their Assignment to the Various Parts of the Examinations

1. The number of Moderators, Public Examiners, and other examiners in university examinations shall, unless there is provision to the contrary in any decree or regulation, be such as is required to provide that each candidate for the examination concerned shall be examined by at least two examiners.

2. It shall be the duty of the chairman of the examiners for each Honour School to designate such of their number as may be required for the examination for the Pass School of the same name. In the case of examinations which consist of two parts, it shall be the duty of the chairman of the examiners for Part I of the examination so to designate.

3. The Second Examination for the Degree of Bachelor of Medicine shall be conducted by examiners appointed in each subject as follows:

Two in Pathology
Two in Paediatrics
Two in Public Health
Two in Primary Health
Two in Neurology

Two in Trauma and Orthopaedics, Accident and Emergency, and Musculo-Skeletal Medicine
Two in Obstetrics and Gynaecology
Two in Psychiatry
Two in Medicine
Two in Surgery.

In the examination in year 3 the Director of Clinical Studies shall be an examiner *ex officio*.

There shall also be the following assessors and additional examiners who shall assist at the discretion of the chairman of the year 3 examiners;

(i) to examine the **[Until 1 October 2004:** essays**] [From 1 October 2004:** vocational skills course**]** in year 3: the examiners in year 3 shall appoint, to serve for one examination only, such number of assessors as are required according to the number of candidates and the **[Until 1 October 2004:** subject-matter of the essays**] [From 1 October 2004:** course-material**]** submitted;

(ii) to examine **[Fom 1 October 2004:** The General Clinical Studies Examination**]** in year 3: for each multiple of five (or fraction thereof) by which the number of candidates at any examination is expected to exceed ten, two additional examiners, of whom one shall be a physician and one a surgeon.

4. The examiners, other than the relevant examiners for each subject, in the Second Examination for the Degree of Bachelor of Medicine, appointed under the provisions of the preceding clause, shall not have the duty of signing pass lists, but may be required at the discretion of the chairman of the year 3 examiners to assist in the marking of scripts in the written examination in year 3.

5. For the First Examination for the Degree of Bachelor of Medicine two examiners shall be appointed in each of the main subjects (Anatomy, Biochemistry, Medical Sociology, Pathology, Pharmacology, and Physiology) covered by the papers in that examination. One of the examiners for the Biochemistry paper shall also act as examiner for the Biochemistry and Cell Biology paper in the Preliminary Examination in Physiological Sciences.

There shall also be two additional Moderators (who shall be external examiners) who shall be appointed in two of the above subject groups as may be decided from time to time by the Medical Sciences Board, or by a nominating committee acting on its behalf, subject to the approval of the Vice-Chancellor and Proctors.

As many of the above examiners as shall be appropriate shall also serve as examiners for the Qualifying Examinations in Chemistry and Physics for medical students.

6. The number of examiners in the Qualifying Examination in Zoology for medical students shall be three, of whom the Director of Pre-Clinical Studies or a deputy, nominated by him or her and approved by the Medical Sciences Board, shall be chairman *ex officio* and the others shall be nominated one by the Medical Sciences Board and one by the Divisional Board of Life and Environmental Sciences, or by a nominating committee acting on behalf of the faculty board concerned, subject in each case to the approval of the Vice-Chancellor and Proctors.

7. Two examiners, at least one of whom is clinically qualified, shall be appointed for the Qualifying Examination in the Principles of Clinical Anatomy. The method of appointment and term of office of these examiners shall be as for examiners for the First Examination for the Degree of Bachelor of Medicine. They may be assisted in the conduct of in-course assessments by the appointment of assessors.

8. If an *ex officio* examiner is for any reason unable to act he shall nominate a deputy who shall be a member of Congregation to act for him subject to the approval of the Vice-Chancellor and Proctors.

9. Notwithstanding any provisions to the contrary elsewhere in this sub-section, for each degree, certificate, or diploma for which courses at Westminster Institute of Education, Oxford Brookes University are validated, there shall be such Examination Boards, with such membership and terms of reference, as Oxford Brookes University shall from time to time determine. That university shall deposit annually with the Proctors the procedures for election, the membership, the terms of reference, and the procedures of each Examination Board.

10. Notwithstanding any provisions to the contrary elsewhere in this sub-section, for the Diploma in Jewish Studies, there shall be such an Examination Board, with such membership and terms of reference, as the Oxford Centre for Hebrew and Jewish Studies shall from time to time determine. The centre shall deposit annually with the Proctors the procedures for election and the membership, terms of reference, and procedures of this Examination Board, provided always that there shall be at least one external examiner.

11. Notwithstanding any provisions to the contrary elsewhere in this sub-section, for the Degree of Doctor of Clinical Psychology there shall be a Board of Examiners with such constitution and terms of reference as the Directorate of the Oxford Doctoral Course in Clinical Psychology shall determine. The Course Director shall

deposit annually with the Proctors the procedures for nominating examiners, and the terms of reference and conventions of the Board of Examiners.

§2. Concerning the Nomination of Examiners

1. The Moderators, the Public Examiners, and the other examiners in university examinations shall, unless there is provision to the contrary in any decree or regulation, be nominated by the divisional board, faculty board or other university body having supervision over the examination concerned, subject in the case of each nomination to the approval of the Vice-Chancellor and Proctors; provided

(*a*) that responsibility for making nominations in respect of any examination which is under the joint supervision of more than one board or other body shall be delegated to a nominating committee appointed jointly for this purpose by the boards or other bodies concerned;

(*b*) that the board or other body responsible for making nominations in respect of any other examination under its supervision may delegate such responsibility to a nominating committee appointed by it for this purpose;

(*c*) that no nominating committee shall consist of fewer than four members;

(*d*) that the Proctors and the Registrar shall be informed annually of the composition of each nominating committee;

(*e*) that the members of any nominating committee set up under provisos (*a*) and (*b*) above shall hold their places for three years, and one-third of the members (or, in the event that the total number of members is not exactly divisible by three, the proportion nearest to one-third to allow a regular annual rotation of vacancies) shall retire every year; in the case of a casual vacancy, the person elected shall serve for the remainder of the period for which the vacating member was elected; no vacating member who has completed a full period of three years shall be re-eligible until the expiry of two years from the end of that period; and a vacating member who has not completed a full term may be re-elected immediately for a full term;

(*f*) that where it is necessary to nominate, for one examination only, a Moderator or examiner to fill a vacancy caused by death, or resignation, or removal for misconduct, or to act as substitute when leave of absence has been granted on account of sickness or other urgent cause, the nomination may be made by the Vice-Chancellor and Proctors;

(*g*) that nominations for examiners for the Degree of Doctor of Clinical Psychology shall be made by a committee comprising two persons elected by the Directorate of the Oxford Doctoral Course in Clinical Psychology and two persons elected by the Medical Sciences Board, and such nominations shall be required to be made in writing by at least three of the members of the nominating committee and shall thereafter be subject to the approval of the Vice-Chancellor and Proctors;

(*h*) that nominations for examiners for courses validated at Westminster Institute of Education, Oxford Brookes University or at the Oxford Centre for Hebrew and Jewish Studies shall be made by a committee comprising not fewer than six persons elected by the Board of the Faculty of Theology or the Academic Committee of the Department of Educational Studies as appropriate for the examination concerned (in the case of courses validated at Westminster Institute of Education, Oxford Brookes University) or by the Board of the Faculty of Oriental Studies (in the case of courses validated at the Oxford Centre for Hebrew and Jewish Studies) and not fewer than three persons elected by Westminster Institute of Education, Oxford Brookes University or by the Oxford Centre for Hebrew and Jewish Studies (as the case may be), and such nominations shall be required to be made in writing by at least four of the members of the nominating committee and shall thereafter be subject to the approval of the Vice-Chancellor and Proctors.

2. The quorum at any meeting of a nominating committee set up under clause 1 (*a*) or (*b*) above shall be two-thirds of the total number of members of that committee (or, in the event that the total number of members is not exactly divisible by three, the integer next above the fractional number representing two-thirds of the total).

3. Every nomination shall be made by a majority of votes. When the votes are equal, the chairman of the divisional board, faculty board or other body, or of a nominating committee acting on its behalf, shall have an additional, casting vote, provided that he or she shall notify the Vice-Chancellor and Proctors in writing, when the nomination concerned is forwarded to them for their approval, that the nomination has been made by such a casting vote.

4. By the Monday before the beginning of each Full Term the board or other university body having supervision over the

examination concerned, or the nominating committee acting on its behalf (as the case may be), shall be sent notice of the vacancies in examinerships to be filled in that term.

5. The board or other body, or the nominating committee acting on its behalf (as the case may be), shall submit to the Registrar by 5 p.m. on the first Tuesday of Full Term recommendations for new examiners, signed by not fewer than two of the members; provided

(*a*) that recommendations for new examiners for the Degree of Bachelor of Philosophy and Master of Philosophy in subjects other than Classical Archaeology, European Archaeology, and World Archaeology shall be so submitted by 5 p.m. on Friday in the sixth week of Full Term;

(*b*) that if notice of a vacancy in an examinership is received after the Monday before the Full Term in which it is to be filled, the date by which nominations in writing in accordance with the preceding provisions of this clause must be received, and the date for any meeting of the board or other body, or of the nominating committee acting on its behalf (as the case may be), which may be necessary, shall be fixed by the Vice-Chancellor.

The chairman of the board or other body, or the member senior in service on the nominating committee acting on its behalf (as the case may be), shall be responsible for the submission of recommendations duly signed.

6. If by the appointed time the requisite nominations shall not have been submitted in accordance with the provisions of clause 5 above, or if any nominees are ineligible, or if the Vice-Chancellor and Proctors wish to challenge a nomination or propose an alternative, a meeting of the relevant board or other body, or of the nominating committee acting on its behalf (as the case may be), shall be held at a stated time to be fixed by the Vice-Chancellor.

7. On the nomination of a board or other body, or of a nominating committee acting on its behalf, any person who is appointed as an examiner to act as an external arbiter of standards or to provide academic expertise not otherwise obtainable from within the University may be designated as an external examiner by the Vice-Chancellor and Proctors.

This designation will not be applied to those holding posts in the University, colleges, permanent private halls, theological colleges, or other Oxford institutions associated with the University in the examination of candidates.

Unless they are appointed to examine in separate subjects or in separate parts of an examination divided into Part I and Part II, no two persons who are, or have been during the preceding two years, on the teaching staff of the same college or university or other institution shall be nominated to serve at the same time as external examiners in the same examination.

Those designated as external examiners shall be entitled to a retaining fee the maximum yearly level of which shall be determined from time to time by the Planning and Resources Allocation Committee.

§3. Qualifications of Examiners

If an examiner is a member of the University, he shall be of the standing required for the Degree of Master of Arts and shall hold a degree of the University other than the BA or B.Mus., provided that the Vice-Chancellor and Proctors may dispense from this requirement on good cause shown.

§4. Examiners from the same College

Unless they are appointed to examine in separate subjects or in the separate parts of an examination divided into Part I and Part II, no two persons who are, or have been during the two years preceding, on the teaching staff of the same college shall be nominated to serve at the same time

(1) as Moderators in the same part of the examination,

(2) as Public Examiners in the same school:

Provided that (i) when nine or more examiners are nominated to serve in one of the following honour schools, two but not more than two of them altogether in the same honour school may be persons who are, or have been during the two years preceding, on the teaching staff of the same college:

Honour School of English Language and Literature,
Honour School of Jurisprudence,
Honour School of Modern History,
Part I and Part II of the subject Chemistry in the Honour School of Natural Science;

(ii) when seven examiners are nominated in the Honour School of Geography, two but not more than two of them altogether in the same examination may be persons who are, or have been during the two years preceding, on the teaching staff of the same college.

Council shall have power to dispense from this provision on good cause shown.

§5. Time of making Nominations

Examiners may be nominated at any time:

Provided that

(i) Nominations to the office of Moderator, Public Examiner, or Examiner for the Degrees of Bachelor of Music, Bachelor of Philosophy, Master of Philosophy, Master of Science, Bachelor of Civil Law, Magister Juris, for the Second Examination for the Degree of Bachelor of Medicine, and for the Qualifying Examination in Zoology for medical students, shall take place as early as may be in term in accordance with the Schedule below.

(ii) The nomination of Additional Moderators or Public Examiners in any subject shall take place as early as may be after a candidate has given notice of his intention to offer that subject.

(iii) All nominations shall be published in the *University Gazette* as soon as possible after the nominee has accepted.

§6. Entry of Examiners upon Office

Every examiner shall enter upon office on the first day of the full term after that in which he shall have been nominated, with the exception of additional Moderators or Public Examiners, who shall enter upon office as soon as they have been nominated. The Vice-Chancellor and Proctors may dispense from this requirement on good cause shown.

§7. Term of Office of Examiners and of Reappointment to Office

1. Examiners for the Degree of Bachelor of Music, for the First Examination for the Degree of Bachelor of Medicine and for the Qualifying Examination in Zoology and Medical Sociology for medical students, shall hold office for two years. Examiners for the Degrees of Bachelor of Civil Law and Magister Juris shall hold office for two years, except for external examiners who shall hold office for up to three years. Examiners for the Second Examination for the Degree of Bachelor of Medicine shall hold office for three years.

2. Examiners for the Degree of Bachelor of Philosophy and for the Degree of Master of Philosophy shall hold office for three years, except that in the examinations in Greek and/or Latin Languages and Literature, Oriental Studies, European Literature, Celtic Studies, Research Methods in Modern Languages, Slavonic Studies, Ancient History, Latin American Studies, Theology, Philosophical Theology, Eastern Christian Studies, Judaism and Christianity in the Graeco-Roman World, General Linguistics and Comparative Philology,

Material Anthropology and Museum Ethnography, Medical Anthropology, Social Anthropology, and Development Economics they shall hold office for one examination, and in the examinations in Classical Archaeology, European Archaeology, Music, Russian and East European Studies, and World Archaeology they shall hold office for one examination at a time, provided that at least one examiner shall have held office on the occasion of the previous examination.

3. Examiners for the Degree of Master of Surgery shall hold office for four years.

4. Examiners for the Degree of Master of Science shall hold office as follows:

in Advanced Cognitive Therapy Studies for three examinations;
in Development Economics for three examinations;
in Applied Social Studies for three examinations;
in Evidence-Based Social Work for three examinations;
in Comparative Social Research for three examinations;
in Management (Industrial Relations) for three examinations;
in Management Research for one examination;
in Applied Statistics for two examinations;
in Forestry: Science, Policy, and Management for three examinations;
in Bioinformatics for three examinations;
in Mathematical Finance for three examinations;
in Mathematical Modelling and Scientific Computing for three examinations;
in Applied and Computational Mathematics for three examinations;
in Geometry, Mathematical Physics, and Analysis for three examinations; in Mathematics and Foundations of Computer Science, for one examination;
in Computer Science and Software Engineering for three examinations;
in Applied Linguistics and Second Language Acquisition for three examinations;
in Educational Studies, Educational Research Methodology, and Professional Development in Education for three examinations (at least two examiners to retire each year);
in Human Biology for three examinations;
in Public Policy in Latin America for one examination;
in Diagnostic Imaging for three examinations;
in Sociology for three examinations;
in Biology for three examinations;

in Environmental Change and Management and in Environmental Geomophology for three examinations;
in Biodiversity, Conservation, and Management for three examinations;
in Nature, Society, and Environmental Policy for three examinations;
in Neuroscience for three examinations;
in Theoretical Chemistry for one examination;
in Evidence-based Health Care for three examinations;
in Politics and International Relations Research for three examinations;
in Material Anthropology and Museum Ethnography, Medical Anthropology, Social Anthropology, and Visual Anthropology for one examination;
in Science and Medicine of Athletic Performance for three years;
in Applied Landscape Archaeology for three examinations;
in Archaeological Science for one examination at a time, provided that at least one examiner shall have held office on the occasion of the previous examination;
in Forced Migration for three examinations
in Criminology and Criminal Jusice for two examinations;
in Latin American Studies for three examinations;
in Russian and East European Studies for three examinations.

5. Examiners in the Qualifying Examination for the Degree of Bachelor of Divinity and for any diploma shall hold office for three examinations, provided that examiners in the examination for the Diploma in Applied Statistics shall hold office for two examinations.

6. Examiners for the Certificates in Theology and the Degrees of Bachelor of Theology (except at Westminster Institute of Education, Oxford Brookes University) and Master of Theology (except at Westminster Institute of Education, Oxford Brookes University) shall hold office for three years save that the two examiners from the Faculty of Theology appointed to monitor standards across the whole range of papers shall be appointed for one year and shall be eligible for reappointment annually for up to two further years.

7. Examiners for the Postgraduate Diploma in Management Studies shall hold office for three years.

8. Examiners for the Postgraduate and Foundation Certificates granted by the Committee on Continuing Education shall serve for three years.

9. Examiners for the Postgraduate Diploma in Diplomatic Studies and the Certificate in Diplomatic Studies shall serve for three years.

10. Moderators shall hold office as follows:

in Law Moderations for two years;

in Moderations in Oriental Studies (Chinese) for one year, to act if required;

in Moderations in Oriental Studies (Japanese) for one year, to act if required;

in Honour Moderations in Classics for two years;

in the Preliminary Examinations in Chemistry, in Earth Sciences, in Engineering Science, in Metallurgy and Science in Materials, and in Physics for two years;

in Honour Moderations in Mathematics for three years;

in Computation in Honour Moderations in Mathematics and Computer Science for three years;

in Philosophy in Honour Moderations in Mathematics and Philosophy for three years;

in Philosophy in Moderations in Physics and Philosophy for three years;

in Moderations in English Language and Literature for two years;

in Honour Moderations in Classics and English for two years;

in Honour Moderations in Geography for two years;

in the Preliminary Examination in Geography for one year;

in Ancient History in Honour Moderations and the Preliminary Examination in Ancient and Modern History for three years;

in Honour Moderations and the Preliminary Examination in Music for two years;

in Modern History in Honour Moderations and the Preliminary Examinations in Modern History, Modern History and English and Ancient and Modern History for two years;

in the Preliminary Examination for Modern Languages for two years;

in the Preliminary Examination in Oriental Studies for one year, to act if required;

in the Preliminary Examination in Classics during three examinations;

in the Preliminary Examination for Theology for two years;

in the Preliminary Examination for Philosophy, Politics, and Economics for two years;

in the Preliminary Examination in Psychology, Philosophy, and Physiology for two years;

in Biological Sciences in Honour Moderations and the Preliminary Examination for two years;

in the Preliminary Examination in Molecular and Cellular Biochemistry for two years;

in the Preliminary Examination in Human Sciences for two years;

in Honour Moderations and the Preliminary Examination in Modern History and Economics for two years;
in Philosophy in the Preliminary Examination in Philosophy and Modern Languages for three years;
in the Preliminary Examination in Mathematics for three years;
in the Preliminary Examination in Mathematics and Computer Science for three years;
in the Preliminary Examination in Mathematics and Philosophy for three years;
in the Preliminary Examination in Physics and Philosophy for three years;
in the Preliminary Examination in English and Modern Languages for one year;
in the Preliminary Examination in European and Middle Eastern Languages for one year;
in the Preliminary Examination in Classics and English for two years;
in the Preliminary Examination in English Language and Literature for one year;
in the Preliminary Examination in Physiological Sciences for two years.
in Honour Moderations in Archaeology and Anthropology for two years;
in the Preliminary Examination in Archaeology and Anthropology for two years;
in Honour Moderations and the Preliminary Examination in Classical Archaeology and Ancient History for three years.

11. Public Examiners shall hold office during three examinations: except that

(1) in the Honour School of Modern Languages examiners shall hold office for two examinations;

(2) in the Honour School of Natural Science examiners in Molecular and Cellular Biochemistry shall hold office for two years and shall examine in Part I in the first year of office and in Part II in the second year;

(3) in the Honour School of Natural Science internal and external examiners in Chemistry shall hold office for four years, provided that each examiner shall examine in Part I only in the first and third years and in Part II only in the second and fourth years of office;

(4) in the Honour School of Natural Science examiners in Physiological Sciences, shall hold office for three years, and the other examiners shall hold office for two years;

(5) in the Honour School of Natural Science (Metallurgy and Science of Materials) and in the Honour School of Materials, Economics, and Management the internal examiners shall normally hold office for two years; the external examiners may be invited to act for four years rather than two, thus examining two cycles of Parts I and II;

(6) in the Honour School of Physics the examiners shall hold office for three years;

(7) in the Honour School of Engineering Science the examiners shall hold office for three years;

(8) in the Honour School of Engineering, Economics, and Management, and in the Honour School of Engineering and Materials examiners shall hold office for three years, provided that in his first year of office an examiner in Metallurgy or Economics shall examine in Part I only, and in the third year of office in Part II only;

(9) in the Honour School of Oriental Studies and in the Honour School of Human Sciences examiners shall hold office for one examination;

(10) in the Honour School of English Language and Literature examiners shall hold office for two examinations, except that external examiners may hold office for a third examination;

(11) in the Honour School of Modern History examiners who have completed one period of three years may be nominated to hold office for one, two, or three, years;

(12) in the Honour School of English and Modern Languages examiners shall hold office for one year;

(13) in the Honour School of European and Middle Eastern Languages examiners shall hold office for one year;

(14) in the Honour School of Classics and English, examiners in English shall hold office for one year;

(15) in the Honour School of Modern History and English examiners in English shall hold office for one year;

(16) in the Qualifying Examination in Statistics for candidates offering Psychology in the Honour School of Psychology, Philosophy, and Physiology, examiners shall hold office for two years;

[Until 1 October 2005: (17) in the Honour Schools of Mathematics **[Until 1 October 2004:** and Mathematical Sciences**]** examiners appointed in 2002 or earlier shall hold office for four years, provided that in his or her first and third years each examiner shall examine in Part I of the Honour School of Mathematics **[Until 1 October 2004:** and in the Honour School of Mathematical Sciences**]** only and in his or her second and fourth years of office shall examine in Part II of the Honour School of Mathematics only; examiners appointed in 2003 or later shall normally hold office for three years.]

(18) in the Honour School of Jurisprudence examiners shall hold office for two examinations, except that external examiners may hold office for a third examination.

12. Examiners for the Preliminary Examination in Fine Art and for the Final Examination in Fine Art shall in each case hold office for three years.

13. Examiners for the Degree of Master of Studies shall hold office for one examination, provided that in the examinations in Classical Archaeology, European Archaeology, and World Archaeology at least one examiner shall have held office on the occasion of the previous examination.

14. Examiners for the Degree of Master of Business Administration (full-time and part-time) shall hold office for two years.

15. No examiner who has held office for the full period shall hold office again in the same examination until the expiration of one year from the termination of his former service:

Provided that

(i) an examiner in the Honour School of Oriental Studies or in the Honour School of Human Sciences or in the examinations in Greek and Latin Languages and Literature, Oriental Studies, European Literature, Celtic Studies, Ancient History, Russian and East European Studies, Latin American Studies, Classical Archaeology, European Archaeology, World Archaeology, Archaeological Science, Music, Theology, Eastern Christian Studies, and General Linguistics and Comparative Philology for the degree of Master of Philosophy, or in the examinations for the Degree of Master of Studies, or in the examinations in Engineering Science and in Archaeological Science for the Degree of Master of Science, or in the examination in Modern History, or in the examination in Greek and/or Roman History for the Degree of Master of Studies, or in the examinations mentioned in the proviso to clause 6 of this subsection, may hold office for three successive years, but thereafter shall not hold office again until the expiration of one year from the termination of his former service;

(ii) an examiner for the Second Examination for the Degree of Bachelor of Medicine shall be re-eligible for a further three years, but shall not thereafter hold office again until the expiration of one year from the termination of his former service;

(iii) An additional examiner in Year 3 of the Second Examination for the Degree of Bachelor of Medicine may hold office for three successive years, but shall not thereafter hold office again until the expiration of five years in the case of an external examiner, and two years in the case of an internal examiner, from the termination of his or her former service.

(iv) a Moderator for the Preliminary Examination and Moderations in Oriental Studies may hold office until he has acted in four successive examinations, but thereafter shall not hold office again until the expiration of one year from the termination of his former service;

(v) a Moderator in a language other than French, German, Italian, Spanish, Russian, or Latin in the Preliminary Examination for Modern Languages may hold office until he has acted in four successive examinations, but thereafter shall not hold office again until the expiration of one year from the termination of his former service;

16. Examiners who have not held office for the full period may be renominated either for a full period or for such period as together with the period of office they have just completed, will constitute a full period.

17. If it shall be necessary for the due regulation of the succession among the examiners in any examination that an examiner or examiners shall retire before the end of the normal period of service, then the junior shall retire.

18. The Vice-Chancellor and Proctors may dispense from any of the requirements of this subsection on good cause shown.

§8. Casual Vacancies

1. An examiner may on account of sickness or other urgent cause obtain from the Vice-Chancellor and Proctors leave of absence for a period of time not extending over more than one examination; and a person statutably qualified to examine in such examination shall be appointed to act as his substitute during that period. If such leave of absence is granted before the first day of the Full Term in which, or following which, the said examination is to begin, the appointment shall be made by the appropriate divisional board, faculty board or other body, or nominating committee acting on its behalf (as the case may be), in the manner hereinbefore provided;

if on or after that day, the appointment shall be made by the Vice-Chancellor and Proctors.

2. If any examiner die, or resign his place, or be removed from the same by the Vice-Chancellor or by the two Proctors, his place shall be filled by the appointment of a statutably qualified examiner. The appointment shall be made in the manner prescribed in clause 1 above. If the appointment be made by the Vice-Chancellor and Proctors, the examiner shall hold office for one examination only; if made otherwise, he shall hold office for the residue of the period of office of the person whom he succeeds.

3. A person appointed under the provisions of this subsection shall enter upon office forthwith.

4. In any case arising under clause 1 or clause 2 of this subsection, the Vice-Chancellor and Proctors shall determine what remuneration, if any, shall be paid to each of the persons concerned.

§9. Removal of Examiners for Misconduct

If any examiner shall in the conduct of the examination for which he is appointed so act as in the judgement of the Vice-Chancellor or of the two Proctors to appear unmindful of the obligations of his office and the credit of the University, he shall be removed from his office by the Vice-Chancellor or by the two Proctors, as the case may be.

SCHEDULE: NOMINATIONS OF MODERATORS AND EXAMINERS

1. In Michaelmas Term:

Moderators

Moderations in Oriental Studies (Chinese).
Moderations in Oriental Studies (Japanese).
Preliminary Examination in Oriental Studies.

Public Examiners

Honour School of Oriental Studies.

Other Examinations

(*a*) Degree of Master of Philosophy except in Sociology.
(*b*) Degree of Master of Studies in Classical Archaeology, European Archaeology, and World Archaeology.
(*c*) Degree of Master of Science (by coursework) in Archaeological Science.
(*d*) Qualifying Examination in Zoology for medical students.

2. In Hilary Term:

Public Examiners

Honour School of Human Sciences and Honour School of Natural Science (Biological Sciences).

Other Examinations

(*a*) Degree of Master of Science (by coursework) in Archaeological Science and in Public Policy in Latin America.
(*b*) Further examiners for the Degrees of Master of Philosophy and Master of Studies in Classical Archaeology, European Archaeology, and World Archaeology.

3. In Trinity Term:

Moderators

(*a*) All Honour Moderations.
(*b*) Moderations in English Language and Literature, Law Moderations and Moderations in Physics and Philosophy.
(*c*) All Preliminary Examinations except Oriental Studies.

Public Examiners

(*a*) All Honour Schools except Human Sciences, Natural Science (Biological Sciences), and Oriental Studies.
(*b*) Qualifying Examination in Statistics for candidates offering Psychology in the Honour School of Psychology, Philosophy, and Physiology.

Other Examinations

(*a*) Degree of Bachelor of Fine Art.
(*b*) Degree of Bachelor of Music.
(*c*) Degree of Master of Science (by course of special study in subjects other than Archaeological Science and Public Policy in Latin America).
(*d*) Degree of Bachelor of Civil Law and Degree of Magister Juris.
(*e*) First Examination for the Degree of Bachelor of Medicine.
(*f*) Years 1, 2, and 3 of the Second Examination for the Degree of Bachelor of Medicine.
(*g*) Part I of the Examination for the Degree of Master of Surgery.
(*h*) Degree of Bachelor of Philosophy.
(*i*) Degree of Master of Philosophy in Sociology.

B. *APPOINTMENT OF ASSESSORS TO EXAMINERS*

Ch. VI, Sect. II. B]

1. In Trinity Term of each year the Divisional Board of Mathematical and Physical Sciences, or the appropriate nominating

committee acting on its behalf (as the case may be), shall appoint (i) assessors for the Supplementary Subjects in the Final Honour School of Natural Science to act if required in the following year with the examiners in the Final Honour School of Natural Science; and (ii) assessors for projects in the Final Honour School of Engineering Science, Parts I and II, to act if required in the following year with the Public Examiners in the Final Honour School of Engineering Science.

2. In Trinity Term of each year

(i) the Divisional Board of Medical Sciences, or the appropriate nominating committee acting on its behalf (as the case may be), shall appoint an assessor for paper (3) of the Preliminary Examination for Psychology, Philosophy, and Physiology to act, if required, in the following year with the moderators in that examination; and

(ii) the Divisional Board of Medical Sciences, or the appropriate nominating committee acting on its behalf (as the case may be), shall appoint, as an assessor for paper (4) of the Preliminary Examination for Psychology, Philosophy, and Physiology, the examiner appointed in that year for the Qualifying Examination in Statistics for candidates offering Psychology in the Honour School of Psychology, Philosophy, and Physiology, if he has not already been appointed as a Moderator in the Preliminary Examination for Psychology, Philosophy, and Physiology, to act, if required, in the following two years with the moderators in that examination.

3. So far as is not provided for in the preceding clauses, the examiners (under which term shall be included Moderators) in any examination may appoint other persons to act with them in particular parts of the examination as assessors:

Provided that

(i) The same person shall not act as examiner and assessor in the same examination.

(ii) All such appointments shall be subject to the approval of the Vice-Chancellor and Proctors which shall be sought by the Chairman of the Examiners.

(iii) The examiners for the M.Sc. in Applied Social Studies shall appoint at least one assessor, who shall be a practising social worker, to act with them for Part B of the examination.

(iv) A person appointed to act as an assessor in any examination may also act as an assessor for any papers set in any other examination which are the same as those in the examination in which that person was originally appointed to act.

4. The Proctors shall inform the Clerk of the Examination Schools of names of all persons appointed as assessors.

5. The persons acting as assessors shall make a report to the examiners on the parts of the examination submitted to them, but shall have no right of voting on the place of any candidate in a Class List, nor on the question of his having satisfied the examiners, or having been adjudged worthy of distinction.

The Board of Examiners shall have power, subject to the provisions of Ch. VI, Sect. II. C, §1, cl. 16, to invite an assessor to take part in the viva voce examinations.

6. The provisions of Ch. VI, Sect. II. A, §3, §8, §9, and Sect. II. C, §1, cl. 16, respecting examiners shall apply to assessors appointed under the provisions of this Section.

Provided that the provisions of Ch. VI, Sect. II. A, §3 shall not apply to an assessor appointed to act in an oral examination in the Honour Schools of Modern Languages, Modern History and Modern Languages, Philosophy and Modern Languages, Classics and Modern Languages, English and Modern Languages, or European and Middle Eastern Languages if he holds a post of lector in the language concerned in either the University or in one of the colleges.

7. The remuneration of assessors shall be according to a scale drawn up by Council.

8. Council shall have power to make and vary such regulations as may be necessary for carrying out the provisions of this Section.

Regulation of the General Board

Duties of assessors not ordinarily resident in Oxford

Assessors who are not ordinarily resident in Oxford shall be required, as part of their duties, to set at least one paper in the examination for which they are appointed to act.

C. *CONDUCT OF EXAMINATIONS*

Ch. VI, Sect. II. C]

§1. Duties of Examiners

Appointment and Duties of Chairman

1. So soon as the majority of examiners for any examination is complete, those examiners shall be empowered to appoint one of their body to act as chairman:

Provided always that

(i) the examiners in the Final Honour School of Natural Science shall appoint a chairman for each subject in the examination;

(ii) the examiners in the Diploma in Law shall not be required to appoint a chairman.

2. Every such appointment shall be notified forthwith to the Vice-Chancellor, c/o The Clerk of the Schools, who will arrange that notice of these appointments is published in the *University Gazette.* Except with the permission of the Vice-Chancellor, no person who is not a resident member of Congregation shall be eligible for appointment as chairman.

3. It shall be the duty of the Senior Resident Examiner or, if none of the examiners in an examination be resident, of the Registrar to take such steps as may be necessary for the due observance of the provisions of this subsection. Until such time as a chairman has been appointed, the Senior Resident Examiner shall be responsible for fulfilling the duties of chairman.

4. The chairman shall be responsible for conducting the business of the Board of the Examiners. He shall convene at least one meeting of the examiners before the examination and by this and other means shall ensure that all arrangements for the proper conduct of the examination have been made and understood:

Provided that no examiner who is not resident in Oxford shall be required to attend such a meeting.

Notice to be given of Examinations

5. The Chairman of Examiners in each examination shall, subject to the provisions of Section II. D, cl. 1 of this decree, on the advice of the Clerk of the Schools, and subject to the agreement of the Vice-Chancellor and Proctors, fix and give public notice of the time and place for the beginning of each examination, and shall afterwards give such notice as he or she shall deem necessary of the further attendance required of candidates.

6. The examiners shall determine the order in which the candidates shall be examined viva voce in those examinations in which a viva voce examination is held.

Submission of Papers to Examiners

7. The papers proposed for the examination in writing of candidates in any examination shall be previously submitted to all the examiners conducting that examination, provided that

(i) in the Preliminary Examination in Natural Science, and in the Final Honour School of Natural Science it shall be sufficient that the papers in each subject shall be submitted to all the examiners acting together in the conduct of the examination in that subject (which in the case of Chemistry and Materials Science in the Honour School of Natural Science shall mean not only the examiners acting in Part I but also the examiners acting in Part II of the examination);

(ii) in the Honour School of Oriental Studies it shall be sufficient that the paper in each main subject and, where appropriate, additional language, shall be submitted to the chairman of the examiners and the examiners acting together in the conduct of the examination in that main subject and additional language.

Supervision and Invigilation of Examinations

8. One examiner at least shall be present to check every examination paper before the start of the examination in case of query:

Provided that:

(i) no examiner who is not resident in Oxford shall be required to attend;

(ii) the chairman may appoint an assessor to attend in place of an examiner;

(iii) in the Second Examination for the Degree of Bachelor of Medicine during the whole time of the practical examination at least one examiner or assessor or Master of Arts of the University appointed for the purpose by the Vice-Chancellor and Proctors on the recommendation of the chairman of examiners shall be present in the building in which the practical examination is being held;

(iv) in the examination for the Degree of Master of Surgery at least two examiners shall be present during the whole time of the written examination.

9. Unless the Proctors otherwise determine, one invigilator shall be required for the first fifty candidates and for each additional fifty candidates or fraction of that number.

10. The Assistant Registrar and Clerk of the Schools shall draw up for the approval of the Proctors a list of Masters of Arts of the University or any other persons whom he or she deems suitable to invigilate examinations. The Assistant Registrar and Clerk of the Schools shall, in consultation with the chairman, deploy persons from the approved list to invigilate each examination.

11. Persons other than examiners appointed to supervise or to invigilate under the provisions of clauses 10 and 11 shall be paid in

accordance with a scale drawn up by the Educational Policy and Standards Committee of Council.

The Number of Examiners who shall act together

12. The number of Moderators or Public Examiners who shall act together in the conduct of any examination shall never be less than three:

Provided that: (*a*) two examiners shall always act together in those parts of the First Public Examination in which the number of Moderators appointed under Ch. VI, Sect. II. A, Schedule A and those parts of the Second Public Examination for which the number of Public Examiners appointed under Ch. VI, Sect. II. A, Schedule B is two only; (*b*) in the Preliminary Examination in Oriental Studies the number of Moderators who shall act together shall never be less than two; (*c*) in an oral examination in the Honour Schools of Classics and Modern Languages, English and Modern Languages, European and Middle Eastern Languages, Modern History and Modern Languages, Modern Languages, and Philosophy and Modern Languages, and two examiners or one examiner and one assessor may act together.

Viva voce Examination

13. Only one candidate at a time shall be examined viva voce in any one examination, but in cases approved by the Vice-Chancellor and Proctors, the examiners in any examination may be permitted to divide themselves into groups which may conduct a viva voce examination simultaneously.

14. No examiner, other than an examiner in the Second Examination for the Degree of Bachelor of Medicine, or in the Honour School of Oriental Studies, shall examine viva voce any candidate who belongs to any college or hall or society in which he is tutor or in which he has been tutor during the two years preceding, or who has been instructed by him (otherwise than at a lecture or class open to all members of the University) within the two years preceding:

Provided that the Vice-Chancellor and Proctors may relieve any Board of Examiners of the restriction imposed by this clause if it would cause difficulty in the conduct of the examination.

15. Subject to the provisions of clause 16 all the examiners in the examination for the Degree of Bachelor of Music, and all the examiners in the subject in which a viva voce examination is being held in each examination for the Degree of Bachelor of Medicine shall be present at the viva voce examination:

Provided that in the Second Examination for the Degree of Bachelor of Medicine it shall be the duty of the chairman of the examiners to arrange that one of the other examiners shall assist in conducting the viva voce examination in a subject in which there is only one examiner.

Oral examinations in Modern Languages

16. The examiners in modern languages in each of the following honour schools shall conduct, during the academic year in which they act, any oral examinations which may be required by regulation of the faculty board or boards concerned. The examiners who shall act in each oral examination shall be as designated by the chairman of the examiners in the Honour School of Modern Languages. The examiners in each of the honour schools shall indicate in the class list issued by them any language or languages offered by a candidate in the colloquial use of which they have adjudged him worthy of distinction.

Classics and Modern Languages
English and Modern Languages
European and Middle Eastern Languages.
Modern History and Modern Languages
Modern Languages
Philosophy and Modern Languages.

Approval of Conventions

17. The conventions to be used by the examiners in any examination shall be approved annually by the faculty board or other body responsible for the course and the examination, subject to the right of a board of examiners to make minor adjustments to the conventions during any particular examination, without reference to the responsible body, if there are exceptional circumstances which so require. In the event of a dispute between the examiners and the responsible body, the matter shall be referred to the Proctors who shall act as arbiters to resolve the dispute.

Nothing in this provision shall affect the authority of the examiners in the making of academic judgements on the performance of each candidate.

Adjudication on the Merits of a Candidate

18. No examiner shall take part in adjudicating on the merits of any candidate who shall not have given careful attention to the examination of such candidate. And no examiner in adjudicating on the merits of any candidate shall take account of any circumstance, not forming part of, or directly resulting from, the

examination itself, except as provided under §4, cl. 1, of this section.

19. If in voting upon the place to be assigned to a candidate in any Class List the examiners shall be equally divided, the chairman of the examiners in that examination shall have a second or casting vote:

Provided that if the candidate in question shall be of the same college or hall or society as the chairman of the examiners or of any college or hall or society in which he is tutor or in which he has been tutor during the two years preceding, or shall have been privately taught by him during the two years preceding, then the casting vote shall be with the senior of the examiners who is not disqualified in like manner.

20. Candidates whose performance is not sufficient for the award of Honours but is deemed equivalent to the performance required for the award of a Pass Degree under the Pass Degree Regulations for the relevant Honour School shall be awarded a Pass Degree. If the examiners for any Pass Degree are divided in opinion as to the work of a candidate, the case of that candidate shall be decided by the votes of the majority; and if in voting the examiners shall be equally divided, the senior examiner who votes shall have a second or casting vote.

**Class Lists*

21. So soon as the examiners in any Honours examination have examined and fully considered the work of all the candidates they shall distribute the names of such candidates as shall be judged by them to have shown sufficient merit into three classes (of which the second class shall be divided into two divisions) according to the merit of each candidate and shall draw up a list accordingly with the names in each class arranged alphabetically in the form set out in the appropriate Schedule annexed to this Section:

Provided that:

(i) The second class in Honour Moderations (except in the case of Honour Moderations in Classics) and in the examinations for the Degree of Bachelor of Civil Law and the Degree of Magister Juris shall not be divided.

(ii) The examiners in Parts IA and IB of the examination in Chemistry or in Part I of the examination in Molecular and Cellular Biochemistry or in Materials Science and Science of

* Under Decree (1) of 28 February 2002 (*Gazette*, Vol. 132, p. 834), such changes may be made to the provisions of the regulations governing the preparation and publication of class and pass lists as are necessary to comply with the provisions of the Data Protection Act 1998.

Materials in the Honour School of Natural Science or in Part I of the examination in the Honour Schools of Engineering, Economics, and Management, or Metallurgy, Economics, and Management shall draw up, in the form set out in Schedule B, an alphabetical list of the candidates who have shown sufficient merit to obtain Honours and the respective chairmen of the examiners shall deposit the candidates' exercises with the Clerk of the Schools for the use of the examiners in Part II at the next succeeding examination.

(iii) If a candidate in Honour Moderations or in any Final Honour School or in the Final Examination for the Degree of Bachelor of Fine Art has not been judged by the examiners to be worthy of Honours but:

(*a*) has satisfied the Moderators in any Honour Moderations, the Moderators shall give notice thereof at the close of the examination in the manner provided in Schedule B,

(*b*) has satisfied the examiners in an Honour School or in the Final Examination for the Degree of Bachelor of Fine Art, the examiners shall give notice thereof at the close of the examination in the manner provided in Schedule B and such candidate shall be entitled to supplicate for the Degree of Bachelor of Arts or the Degree of Bachelor of Fine Art respectively, provided that he shall not thereby be disqualified from offering himself at any future examination in the same manner as he might have done if he had not satisfied the examiners as aforesaid.

(iv) If a candidate in any Honour School of the First or Second Public Examination or in the Final Examination for the Degree of Bachelor of Fine Art is disqualified by standing from obtaining Honours in that school or examination, but has in the judgement of the examiners shown sufficient merit to entitle him, but for such disqualification, to a place in the Class List, the examiners shall give notice thereof at the close of the examination for candidates in any Honour School of the First or Second Public Examination or in the Final Examination for the Degree of Bachelor of Fine Art in the manner provided in Schedule B in the case of those candidates not seeking Honours, and such a candidate in a Final Honour School shall be entitled to supplicate for the Degree of Bachelor of Arts or in the Bachelor of Fine Art Final Examination for the Degree of Bachelor of Fine Art in the same manner as if he had obtained Honours in the examination aforesaid.

(v) The chairman of the examiners in each honours examination shall draw up a list of the names and colleges of candidates who have failed the examination. If no candidate has failed the examination, the chairman of the examiners shall draw up a statement to this effect.

(vi) If a candidate whose name appears in the Class List for the Honour School of Jurisprudence has successfully completed Course 2 in accordance with the regulations of the Board of the Faculty of Law, there shall be added, in brackets after his or her name, the word (French) or symbol (Fr) (or the adjective or symbol appropriate to such other national law as the candidate has studied), or, if the candidate has not studied the national law of another European country, the word (European) or symbol (Eur). At the foot of the list shall appear an indication that (French) or (Fr) (or other adjective or symbol) denotes English Law with French (or appropriate adjective) Law.

**Lists for Pass Examinations and for Diplomas and Certificates*

22. (*a*) The Moderators or examiners in any Pass or Preliminary or Qualifying Examination or in any examination for a course of special study for the Degree of Master of Science or in any examination for the degree of Master of Studies or for a diploma or certificate except the Diploma in Law or the Certificate in Management Studies shall as soon as may be draw up, or in the case of the First and Second Public Examination cause the Clerk of the Schools to draw up, alphabetical lists of the names of all candidates who have satisfied them or have been adjudged by them worthy of distinction in the form set out in the appropriate Schedule annexed to this Section:

Provided that:

(i) the examiners shall not adjudge a candidate worthy of distinction unless authorized to do so under the section of the decree governing the particular examination;

(ii) in an examination where a candidate is not required to pass in all subjects at one and the same examination the examiners shall at the same time append to the names of those candidates who have not completed the requirements of the examination a list of the subjects in which they have passed.

---

* Under Decree (1) of 28 February 2002 (*Gazette*, Vol. 132, p. 834), such changes may be made to the provisions of the regulations governing the preparation and publication of class and pass lists as are necessary to comply with the provisions of the Data Protection Act 1998.

(*b*) The chairman of the moderators or examiners shall draw up a list of the names and colleges of candidates who have failed the examination. If no candidate has failed the examination, the chairman of the examiners shall draw up a statement to this effect.

*List of Approved Musical Exercises for the Degree of Bachelor of Music**

23. At the close of the examination of the Musical Exercises for the Degree of Bachelor of Music submitted to them in any term, the examiners shall make and sign lists of the candidates whose exercises have been approved by them in the form set out in Schedule C.

*Publication of Examination Lists**

24. Subject to the provisions of clause 27 of this sub-section, each list drawn up under the provisions of clauses 22, 23, or 24 shall be certified by the signature of all the examiners who have acted together in the conduct of the examination, or who have drawn up the list, as the case may be, except that, (i) in the case of Years 1 and 2 of the Second Examination for the Degree of Bachelor of Medicine, the lists shall be certified by the signature of the Director of Clinical Studies only or (ii) provided that lists in respect of each main subject and additional language in the Honour School of Oriental Studies shall be signed by the chairman of the examiners and the examiners who have acted together in the conduct of the examination in each main subject and additional language or (iii) in the case of the Preliminary Examination in Physical Sciences the list as agreed by all the examiners shall be certified by the signatures of the chairman of examiners and the five sub-chairmen for the main subject groups.

25. The examiners shall all sign four copies of the lists drawn up under the provisions of clauses 22, 23, or 24 and shall cause one of the copies to be fixed to a notice board at the Examination Schools, and three to be sent to the Registrar, except that the chairman of the examiners shall draw up and sign two copies only of the lists and statements required under the provisions of clauses 22 (v) and 23 (*b*) and shall send both copies to the Registrar.

26. All the lists drawn up under the provisions of clauses 25 and 26 shall be fair copies and shall show no name to have been added

* Under Decree (1) of 28 February 2002 (*Gazette*, Vol. 132, p. 834), such changes may be made to the provisions of the regulations governing the preparation and publication of class and pass lists as are necessary to comply with the provisions of the Data Protection Act 1998.

or erased or transferred from one position to another. Examiners shall have no power to alter such lists after publication:

Provided that they may issue a supplementary list or lists with the consent given in writing of the Vice-Chancellor and Proctors and provided that any supplementary list correcting an accidental error or omission in the original list may, subject to the consent of the Vice-Chancellor and Proctors, be certified by the signature of the chairman of examiners only.

27. The names shall be entered on the lists in the same way as they appear on the lists of candidates issued by the Registrar.

28. Notwithstanding any provisions of clauses 1–18 above to the contrary, the duties of examiners for examinations for courses validated at Westminster College shall be as determined by Westminster College from time to time and lodged annually with the Proctors.

29. Notwithstanding any of the provisions of this section to the contrary, the duties of examiners for examinations for the Oxford Doctoral Course in Clinical Psychology shall be determined by the Chair of the Board of Examiners, who shall be elected by the Board of Examiners.

§2. Custody of Records

The lists sent to the Registrar under the provisions of §1, cl. 26 shall, after the close of the examination, remain in the custody of the Registrar; and any question thereafter arising, with respect to the result of any examination, shall be determined by reference to such lists.

§3. Issue of Diplomas and Certificates

When a candidate for a diploma or certificate has satisfied the examiners or has obtained a Distinction in the subjects of the examination, a diploma or certificate, as the case may be, shall be issued to the candidate in the form set out in Schedule E:

Provided that the words 'at Oxford' may be omitted in the following diplomas and certificates issued to a member of the University who has kept by residence all the terms required for the Degree of Bachelor of Arts:

Diploma in Human Biology.

§4. Illness or other Urgent Causes affecting Candidates for Examinations

1. If it shall come to the notice of a candidate's college or other society or approved institution that that candidate's performance

in any part of any examination is likely to be, or has been, affected by factors of which the examiners have no knowledge, that college, society, or approved institution shall, through its Senior Tutor or other proper officer, inform the Proctors of these factors. The Proctors shall pass this information to the chairman of examiners if, in their opinion, it is likely to assist the examiners in the performance of their duties.* The student, or his or her society, may within fourteen days of the date of the Proctors' decision appeal in writing to the Chairman of the Educational policy and Standards Committee (who may nominate another member of the committee, other than one of the Proctors, to adjudicate the appeal). If the examination is one in which Honours may be awarded the examiners may adopt one of the following courses, taking account of the information passed to them:

(*a*) if they consider the candidate has submitted enough work to allow them to determine his or her proper class, they may award the candidate the class his or her performance merits;

(*b*) if they are unable to adopt course (*a*) but consider, on the evidence of the work submitted, that but for the illness or other urgent cause affecting the candidate's performance, he or she would have obtained classified Honours, they may deem the candidate to have obtained Honours and publish his or her name accordingly at the foot of the Class List under the words 'declared to have deserved Honours';

(*c*) if they are unable to adopt course (*a*) or course (*b*) but are nevertheless satisfied with the work submitted, they may include the candidate's name on the Pass List to show that the candidate has satisfied the examiners;

(*d*) if they are unable to adopt course (*a*), (*b*), or (*c*) they shall fail the candidate.

Where the examiners have adopted course (*b*), (*c*), or (*d*) above it shall be open to the candidate to apply if necessary to Council for consideration of his or her standing for Honours at a future examination.

2. A candidate in any examination† may, through his or her society, apply to the Proctors to certify that the candidate will be

---

* In some cases a medical certificate submitted under clause 2 may not contain all the particulars about the candidate's disability which it would be useful for the examiners to know. In such cases it should not be supposed that submission under clause 1 is superfluous because a submission has already been made for the candidate in question under clause 2. See §1, cl. 18 of this section.

† See also the special regulations below concerning the use of wordprocessors in examinations and dictation of papers; visually-impaired candidates; religious festivals and holidays; and dyslexic candidates.

or has been prevented by illness or other urgent cause from presenting himself or herself at the appointed time or place for any part of an examination (a candidate is deemed to have presented himself or herself for a written paper if he or she was present in the place deisgnated for the examination and had the opportunity to see the question paper there). Each application for consideration by the Proctors must be submitted in writing by the Senior Tutor or other proper officer of the candidate's society. Sufficient evidence must be sent in support of the application. Where illness is pleaded, a medical certificate from a qualified medical practitioner must be sent, and this certificate must specify, with dates, the bearing of the illness on the candidate's attendance at the examination. Where it is proposed that a candidate is to be examined in a place or at a time other than that appointed for the examination, written permission must be obtained from the Proctors for the candidate to be examined in that place or at that time, together with their approval of the name of a Master of Arts of the University, or any other person who in their opinion seems suitable, who is prepared to invigilate. The Proctors may authorize the examiners either (*a*) to examine the candidate at another place or time under such arrangements as the Proctors deem appropriate, or (*b*) provided that the work that the candidate has submitted is of sufficient merit, to act as if he or she had completed that part of the examination. If the application is granted, it shall be the duty of the Proctors to send a written authorization promptly to the chairman of examiners of the relevant examination and to inform the candidate's society and the Clerk of the Schools.

Where the Proctors have given permission for an examination to be held in a place or at a time other than that appointed for the examination, the invigilator or another person approved by the Proctors should attend the Schools at least fifteen minutes before the examination begins, to receive the examination paper and any necessary writing materials from the Clerk of the Schools, and should bring a letter addressed to the chairman of the examiners concerned containing the name of the candidate, the subject in which the candidate is being examined, and the authorization of the Proctors (if a copy of this has not already been sent to the Clerk of the Schools). The invigilator should sign the list kept by the Clerk of the Schools of examination papers which are issued in this way, and should verify that the details recorded on the list are correct. The candidate's work must be handed as soon as possible after the time appointed for the collection of papers to the Clerk of the Schools, who will make the appropriate entry in his or her register. The Clerk will obtain a receipt when forwarding work done outside the Schools.

A candidate, through his or her society, may within fourteen days of the date of the Proctors' decision whether or not to grant his or her application appeal against that decision in writing to the Chairman of the Educational Policy and Standards Committee (who may nominate another member of the committee, other than one of the Proctors, to adjudicate the appeal).

If after receiving the Proctors' authorization the examiners agree to act as if the candidate had completed the part of the examination concerned, and the examination is one in which Honours may be awarded, the examiners may (subject always to the approval of the Proctor) adopt one of the following courses:

(*a*) if they consider the candidate has submitted enough work to allow them to determine his or her proper class, they may award the candidate the class his or her performance merits;

(*b*) if they are unable to adopt course (*a*) but consider, on the basis of the work submitted, that but for the candidate's absence he or she would have obtained classified Honours, they may deem the candidate to have obtained Honours and publish his or her name accordingly at the foot of the Class List under the words 'declared to have deserved Honours';

(*c*) if they are unable to adopt course (*a*) or course (*b*) but are nevertheless satisfied with the work submitted, they may include the candidate's name on the Pass List to show that the candidate has satisfied the examiners;

(*d*) if they are unable to adopt course (*a*), (*b*), or (*c*) they shall fail the candidate.

Where the examiners have adopted course (*b*), (*c*), or (*d*) above it shall be open to the candidate to apply to Council for consideration of his standing for Honours at a future examination.

3. Subject to the provisions above a candidate who fails to appear at the time and place appointed for any part of his or her examination shall be deemed to have withdrawn from the examination.

§5. Interpretation of Certain Terms

Examiners and Examinations

1. (*a*) In Ch. VI, Sections II. A, B, C, and D, unless the context otherwise require, the word 'Examiners' shall be taken to include Moderators, Public Examiners, examiners for the Degrees of Bachelor of Fine Art, Bachelor of Music, Bachelor of Philosophy, Bachelor of Civil Law, Magister Juris, Bachelor of Medicine, Master of

Surgery, Master of Science, Master of Philosophy, Master of Studies, Bachelor of Divinity (Qualifying Examination only), Bachelor of Theology, Bachelor of Education, Master of Theology, Master of Education, Doctor of Clinical Psychology, and examiners for any diploma or certificate.

(*b*) The word 'Examination' shall be taken to include any exercise in which examiners specified above act together as an examining body.

Membership of a College

2. For the purpose of this Section of the statute a person shall be deemed to be a member of that college only through which he pays his dues or has compounded for the payment of his dues to the University, but in case he is a tutor or fellow of another college, then of that college or those colleges only of which he is tutor or fellow.

Seniority

3. In the interpretation of all provisions by which the examiners in any examination are distinguished as Junior or Senior respectively, seniority shall be estimated according to the provisions of Ch. I, Sect. VIII.

Tenure of Office

4. Every examiner shall be deemed to hold office until the beginning of the period of office of his successor.

Full Term

5. For the purpose of this statute Council shall before the end of Trinity Term in each year appoint the day on which Full Term shall begin in each term of the academic year next but one following.

SCHEDULE A

English Moderations, Law Moderations, Moderations in Oriental Studies (Chinese), Moderations in Oriental Studies (Japanese), Moderations in Physics and Philosophy, and Preliminary Examinations (including the Preliminary Examination in Fine Art)

(i) Candidates who have satisfied the Moderators

Names of candidates who in [here insert term and year] *have satisfied* [*have been adjudged worthy of distinction by* (if the award of a distinction is permitted by the relevant decree)] *the Moderators in* [here insert title of examination].

A. B.—College
C. D.—Hall
E. F.—Society

G. H.
I. J. *Moderators*
K. L.

(ii) Candidates who have passed part of a Preliminary Examination

Names of candidates who in [here insert term and year] *have satisfied the Moderators in the* [here insert title of examination] *in* [here insert subject or subjects and, in the case of the Preliminary Examination for Modern Languages, the language passed].

A. B.—College
C. D.—Hall
E. F.—Society

G. H.
I. J. *Moderators*
K. L.

(iii) Candidates who, having previously passed part of a Preliminary Examination, have now satisfied the Moderators in the remainder of the examination

Names of candidates who, having previously passed part of [here insert title of examination], *have in* [here insert term and year] *satisfied the Moderators in the remainder of the examination.*

A. B.—College
C. D.—Hall
E. F.—Society

G. H.
I. J. *Moderators*
K. L.

(iv) Candidates who have satisfied the examiners in the Preliminary Examination in Fine Art

Names of candidates who in [here insert term and year] *have satisfied the examiners in the Preliminary Examination in Fine Art.*

A. B.—College
C. D.—Hall
E. F.—Society

G. H.
I. J. *Examiners*
K. L.

[In the Preliminary Examination in Classics an indication of the course taken shall be affixed to the name of each candidate.]

SCHEDULE B

Honour Moderations, Final Honour Schools, and Examinations for the Degree of Bachelor of Fine Art, Master of Biochemistry, Master of Chemistry, Master of Earth Sciences, Master of Engineering, Master of Mathematics, Master of Physics, Bachelor of Theology, and Bachelor of Education

Names of candidates who in [here insert term and year] *were adjudged worthy of Honours by* [here insert proper designation of examiners] *in* [here insert title of examination].

THE NAMES IN EACH CLASS ARE ARRANGED IN ALPHABETICAL ORDER

Class I

A. B.—College
C. D.—Hall
E. F.—Society

Class II

[*In honour schools, in the Final Examination for the Degree of Bachelor of Fine Art, and in Honour Moderations in Classics, Class II shall be divided into Division* 1 *and Division* 2]

A. B. – College
C. D. – Hall
E. F. – Society

Class III

[*Except in examination where it is not permissible to award Class III.*]

A. B.—College
C. D.—Hall
E. F.—Society

[In Honour Moderations in Classics and in the Honour School of Literae Humaniores an indication of the course taken shall be affixed to the name of each candidate.]

Candidates disqualified for Honours by Standing

Names of candidates who, although not placed in the Class List because they have exceeded the statutory number of terms from matriculation, have in [here insert term and year] *satisfied the Moderators* [or *examiners*] *in* [here insert title of examination]

A. B.—College
C. D.—Hall
E. F.—Society

G. H.
I. J. *Moderators or*
K. L. *Examiners.*

Names of candidates who, although disqualified from obtaining Honours because they had exceeded the statutory number of terms from matriculation, have in [here insert term and year] *satisfied the Examiners in Part I of the Honour School of* [here insert title of examination].

A. B.—College
C. D.—Hall
E. F.—Society

G. H.
I. J. *Examiners.*
K. L.

Candidates who fail to obtain Honours

Names of candidates who in [here insert term and year] *were awarded a Pass in the First Public Examination by the Moderators in Honour Moderations in* [here insert title of examination].

A. B.—College
C. D.—Hall
E. F.—Society

G. H.
I. J. *Moderators.*
K. L.

Names of candidates who in [here insert term and year] *were awarded by the examiners a Pass in the Final Examination for the Degree of Bachelor of Fine Art,* [*or the Degree of Bachelor of Theology, or the Degree of Bachelor of Education*]

A. B.—College
C. D.—Hall
E. F.—Society

G. H.
I. J. *Examiners.*
K. L.

Candidates who have obtained Honours in Parts IA with IB of the Examination in Chemistry or in Part I of the Examination in Molecular and Cellular Biochemistry or in Metallurgy and Science of Materials in the Final Honour School of Natural Science

Names of candidates who in [here insert term and year] *having been examined in Part I of the examination in Chemistry* [*or in Molecular and Cellular Biochemistry or in Metallurgy and Science of Materials*] *in the Final Honour School of Natural Science, were adjudged worthy of Honours.*

A. B.—College
C. D.—Hall
E. F.—Society

G. H.
I. J. *Moderators or*
K. L. *Examiners.*

Candidates who have obtained Honours in Part I of the Examination in the Honour School of Engineering Science, or in Engineering and Computing Science, or in Engineering and Materials.

Names of candidates who in [here insert term and year] *having been examined in Part I of the examination in the Honour School of*

Engineering Science [or *in the Honour School of Engineering and Computing Science,* or *in the Honour School of Engineering and Materials*], *were adjudged worthy of Honours.*

A. B.—College
C. D.—Hall
E. F.—Society

G. H.
I. J. *Examiners*
K. L.

Candidates who have obtained Honours in Part I of the Examination in the Honour School of Engineering, Economics, and Management or the Honour School of Materials, Economics, and Management

Names of candidates who in [here insert term and year] *having been examined in Part I of the examination in the Honour School of Engineering, Economics, and Management* [*or in the Honour School of Metallurgy, Economics, and Management*], *were adjudged worthy of Honours.*

A. B.—College
C. D.—Hall
E. F.—Society

G. H.
I. J. *Examiners.*
K. L.

Candidates who have obtained Honours in Parts A with B of the Examination in the Honour School of Mathematics (four-year course), or the Honour School of Mathematics and Philosophy, or the Honour School of Mathematics and Statistics (four-year course)

Names of candidates who in [here insert term and year] *having been examined in Parts A and B of the examination in the Honour School of Mathematics* [*or the Honour School of Mathematics and Philosophy, or the Honour School of Mathematics and Statistics*], *were adjudged worthy of Honours.*

A. B.—College
C. D.—Hall
E. F.—Society

G. H.
I. J. *Examiners.*
K. L.

Candidates in [subject] **in the Honour School of Natural Science who have passed the examination in a Supplementary Subject in that Honour School**

Names of candidates who in [here insert term and year] *have satisfied* [*have been adjudged worthy of distinction by*] *the examiners in* [here insert title of Supplementary Subject].

A. B.—College
C. D.—Hall
E. F.—Society *G. H.—Chairman.*

Candidates in Pass Schools, and in the Qualifying Examination in Statistics for candidates offering Psychology in the Honour School of Psychology, Philosophy, and Physiology, in the Qualifying Examination in Zoology for medical students, and in the Qualifying Examination in Principles of Clinical Anatomy

Names of candidates who in [here insert term and year] *have satisfied the examiners in* [here insert title of examination].

A. B.—College
C. D.—Hall
E. F.—Society *G. H.*
I. J. *Examiners.*
K. L.

Candidates in Part IA of Chemistry in the Final Honour School of Natural Science

Names of candidates who may proceed to Part IB in [here insert term and year].

A. B.—College
C. D.—Hall
E. F.—Society *G. H.*
I. J. *Examiners*
K. L.

Candidates in Part A of the Examination in the Honour School of Computer Science, or the Honour School of Mathematics, or the Honour School of Mathematics and Computer Science, or the Honour School of Mathematics and Statistics

Names of candidates who were awarded a Pass in Part A of the examination in the Honour School of Computer Science [or the Honour School of Mathematics, or the Honour School of Mathematics and Computer Science, or the Honour School of Mathematics and Statistics] *and may proceed to Part B in* [here insert term and year].

A. B.—College
C. D.—Hall
E. F.—Society *G. H.*
I. J. *Examiners.*
K. L.

SCHEDULE C

Examinations for the Degrees in Music and Medicine, for the Degree of Doctor of Clinical Psychology, for the Degrees of Master of Letters, Master of Science, Master of Studies, Master of Philosophy, and for the Degree of Bachelor of Philosophy, Master of Theology, Master of Education, and Bachelor of Divinity

(*a*) Qualifying Examination for the Degree of Bachelor of Divinity

Names of candidates who in [here insert term and year] *have satisfied the examiners in the Qualifying Examination for the Degree of Bachelor of Divinity.*

A. B.—College
C. D.—Hall
E. F.—Society

G. H.
I. J. *Examiners.*
K. L.

(*b*) Examination for the Degree of Bachelor of Music

(i) *Names of candidates who in* [here insert term and year] *have satisfied the examiners in the Examination for the Degree of Bachelor of Music.*

A. B.—College
C. D.—Hall
E. F.—Society

G. H.
I. J. *Examiners.*
K. L.

(ii) *Names of candidates whose Exercises for the Degree of Bachelor of Music have been approved by the examiners in* [here insert term and year].

A. B.—College
C. D.—Hall
E. F.—Society

G. H.
I. J. *Examiners.*
K. L.

(*c*) Qualifying Examination in Classical Archaeology, European Archaeology, and World Archaeology for the Degree of Master of Philosophy

Names of candidates who in [here insert term and year] *have satisfied the examiners in the Qualifying Examination in Classical Archaeology, European Archaeology, and World Archaeology for the Degree of Master of Philosophy.*

A. B.—College
C. D.—Hall
E. F.—Society

G. H.
I. J. *Examiners.*
K. L.

(*d*) Qualifying Examination in Social Anthropology for the Degree of Master of Philosophy

Names of candidates who in [here insert term and year] *have satisfied the examiners in the Qualifying Examination in Social Anthropology for the Degree of Master of Philosophy.*

A. B.—College
C. D.—Hall
E. F.—Society

G. H.
I. J. *Examiners.*
K. L.

(*e*) Qualifying Examination in Persian or Arabic for the Degree of Master of Philosophy

Names of candidates who in [here insert term and year] *have satisfied the examiners in the Qualifying Examination in Persian or Arabic for the Degree of Master of Philosophy.*

A. B.—College
C. D.—Hall
E. F.—Society

G. H.
I. J. *Examiners.*
K. L.

(*f*) Examination for the Degrees of Bachelor and Master of Philosophy

(i) *Names of candidates who in* [here insert term and year] *have satisfied the examiners in* [here insert subject] *in the examination for the Degree of Bachelor* [*or Master*] *of Philosophy* [here insert where applicable *and have thereby completed all the examination requirements for the Degree*].

A. B.—College
C. D.—Hall
E. F.—Society

G. H.
I. J. *Examiners.*
K. L.

(ii) *Names of candidates who in* [here insert term and year] *have satisfied the examiners that they are worthy of the award of the Degree of Master of Studies in* [here insert subject].

A. B.—College
C. D.—Hall
E. F.—Society

G. H.
I. J. *Examiners.*
K. L.

(*g*) Examination for the Degree of Master of Science

Names of candidates who in [here insert term and year] *have satisfied the examiners in* [here insert subject] *in the examination for the Degree of Master of Science* [here insert where applicable *and have thereby completed all the examination requirements for the Degree*].

A. B.—College
C. D.—Hall
E. F.—Society

G. H.
I. J. *Examiners.*
K. L.

(*h*) Examinations for the Degrees of Bachelor of Medicine and Bachelor of Surgery

(i) Candidates passing subjects in the First Examination

For candidates passing all subjects in Part I or Part II:

Names of candidates for the Degrees of Bachelor of Medicine and Bachelor of Surgery who in [here insert term and year] *have satisfied the Examiners in* [here enter Part of examination] *of the First Examination for the Degree of Bachelor of Medicine in all four subjects.*

D indicates the name of a candidate who was adjudged by the Examiners to be worthy of a Distinction.

M1, M2, M3 [in Part I or] *M5, M6, M7* [in Part II] *indicate the name of a candidate who was adjudged by the Examiners to be worthy of a Merit in the subjects so specified.*

A. B.—College
C. D.—Hall
D *E. F.—Society* *M1, M2, M3*

G. H.
I. J. *Examiners*
K. L.

***Or*, for candidates passing certain specified subjects only (either at first sitting, or by accumulation having passed Part A or Part B of a subject at a previous attempt):**

Names of candidates for the Degrees of Bachelor of Medicine and Bachelor of Surgery who in [here insert term and year] *have satisfied the Examiners in* [here enter Part of examination] *of the First Examination for the Degree of Bachelor of Medicine in* [here insert the number of subjects (viz. one, two, or three)] *subjects.*

1, 2, 3, 4 [in Part I or] *5, 6, 7, 8* [in Part II] *indicate the subjects passed by each candidate.*

M1, M2, M3 [in Part I or] ***M5, M6, M7*** [in Part II] *indicate the name of a candidate who was adjudged by the Examiners to be worthy of a Merit in the subjects so specified.*

A. B.—College ***1, 2***
C. D.—Hall ***2, 3***
E. F.—Society ***M1, M2***

G. H.
I. J. *Examiners*
K. L.

***Or*, for candidates passing either Part A or Part B only of specified subjects:**

Names of candidates for the Degrees of Bachelor of Medicine and Bachelor of Surgery who in [here insert term and year] *have satisfied the Examiners in* [here enter Part of examination] *of the First Examination for the Degree of Bachelor of Medicine in either Part A only or Part B only of specified subjects.*

1A**, or **1B, 2A** or **2B, 3A** or **3B [in Part I or] ***5A** or **5B, 6A** or **6B, 7A** or **7B*** [in Part II] *indicate the part-subjects passed by each candidate.*

A. B.—College ***1A***
C. D.—Hall ***2B, 3B***
E. F.—Society ***3B***

G. H.
I. J. *Examiners*
K. L.

(ii) **Candidates passing subjects in the Preliminary Examination in Medicine**

Names of candidates who in [here insert term and year] *have satisfied* [or *have been adjudged worthy of a Distinction by*] *the Examiners in* [here enter Part of examination] *of the Preliminary Examination in Medicine.*

A. B.—College
C. D.—Hall
E. F.—Society

G. H.
I. J. *Examiners*
K. L.

(ii) **Candidates passing subjects in the First Examination**

Names of candidates for the Degrees of Bachelor of Medicine and Bachelor of Surgery who in [here insert term and year] *have satisfied the Examiners in the First Examination for the Degree of Bachelor of Medicine in* [here insert subject or subjects].

A. B.—College
C. D.—Hall
E. F.—Society

G. H.
I. J. *Moderators.*
K. L.

(iii) Candidates passing years 1 and 2 of the Second Examination

Names of candidates in the Second Examination for the Degrees of Bachelor of Medicine and Bachelor of Surgery who in [here state term and year] *have achieved a satisfactory standard in* [here insert year or years].

A. B.—College
C. D.—Hall
E. F.—Society *G. H.—Director of Clinical Studies.*

(iv) Candidates passing [Until 1 October 2004: subjects in] [From 1 October 2004: General Clinical Studies of year 3 of] the Second Examination

Names of candidates in the Second Examination for the Degree of Bachelor of Medicine and Bachelor of Surgery who in [here insert term and year] *have satisfied the examiners in* **[From 1 October 2004:** *General Clinical Studies of* **]** *year 3.*

A. B.—College
C. D.—Hall
E. F.—Society

G. H.
I. J. Examiners.
K. L.

[From 1 October 2004:
(iv) Candidates passing the Vocational Skills Course of Year 3 of the Second BM Examination

Names of candidates in the Second BM Examination for the Degrees of Bachelor of Medicine and Bachelor of Surgery who in [here insert term and year] *have satisfied the examiners in the Vocational Skills Course of Year 3.*

A. B.—College
C. D.—Hall
E. F.—Society

G. H.
I. J. *Examiners*
K. L.

Candidates passing in Part I of the Examination for the Degree of Master of Surgery

Names of candidates for the Degree of Master of Surgery who in [here insert term and year] *have satisfied the examiners in Part I of the examination.*

A. B.—College
C. D.—Hall
E. F.—Society

G. H.
I. J. *Examiners.*
K. L.

(*i*) Examinations for the Degree of Master of Studies

(i) *Names of candidates who in* [here insert term and year] *have satisfied* [*or have been adjudged worthy of distinction by*] *the examiners in* [here insert subject] *for the Degree of Master of Studies* [here insert where applicable *and have thereby completed all the examination requirements for the Degree*].

(ii) *Names of candidates who in* [here insert term and year] *have satisfied the examiners that they are worthy of the award of a Diploma in* [here insert subject].

A. B.—College
C. D.—Hall
E. F.—Society

G. H.
I. J. *Examiners.*
K. L.

(*j*) Examinations for the Degrees of Master of Theology and Master of Education

Names of candidates who in [here insert term and year] *have satisfied the examiners in the examinations for the Degree of Master of Theology* [or *Master of Education*] [here insert where applicable *and have thereby completed all the examination requirements for the Degree*].

A. B.—College
C. D.—Hall
E. F.—Society

G. H.
I. J. *Examiners.*
K. L.

(*k*) Examinations for the Degree of Master of Business Administration (full-time and part-time)

Names of candidates who in [here insert term and year] *have satisfied the examiners in the examinations for the Degree of Master of Business Administration* [here insert where applicable *and have thereby completed all the examination requirements for the Degree*].

A. B.—College
C. D.—Hall
E. F.—Society

G. H.
I. J. *Examiners.*
K. L.

(*l*) Examination for the Degrees of Bachelor of Civil Law and Magister Juris

Names of candidates who in [here insert term and year] *have satisfied* [or *have been adjudged worthy of distinction by the examiners in* [here insert title of examination].

A. B.—College
C. D.—Hall
E. F.—Society

G. H.
I. J. *Examiners.*
K. L.

[Candidates who acquire four or more credits by offering two or more of the subjects listed in Schedule E of Part 14, or by offering one of those subjects and a dissertation on a topic recognized by the Graduate Studies Committee in Law as being within the fields of European and Comparative Law, shall be awarded the title 'Bachelor of Civil Law [*or* Magister Juris, *or* Master of Philosophy] in European and Comparative Law'].

(*m*) Examination for the Degree of Doctor of Clinical Psychology

Names of candidates who in [here insert term and year] *have satisfied the examiners for the Degree of Doctor of Clinical Psychology* [here insert where applicable *and have thereby completed all the examination requirements for the Degree*].

A. B.—Harris Manchester College

C. D.
E. F. *Examiners.*
G. H.

SCHEDULE D

(*a*) Examination for Diplomas and Certificates

Names of candidates who in [here insert term and year] *have satisfied* [*or have been adjudged worthy of distinction by*] *the examiners for the Postgraduate Diploma* [*or Certificate*] *in* [here insert title of diploma or certificate].

A. B.—College
C. D.—Hall
E. F.—Society

G. H.
I. J. *Examiners.*
K. L.

(*b*) Examination for Postgraduate Certificates (Continuing Education)

Names of candidates who in [here insert term and year] *have satisfied* [or *have been adjudged worthy of distinction by*] *the examiners for the Postgraduate Certificate in* [here insert title of certificate].

A. B.—College
C. D.—Hall
E. F.—Society

G. H.
I. J. *Examiners.*
K. L.

(*c*) Examination for Postgraduate Diplomas (Continuing Education)

Names of candidates who in [here insert term and year] *have satisfied* [or *have been adjudged worthy of a distinction by*] *the examiners for the Postgraduate Diploma in* [here insert title of diploma].

A. B.—College
C. D.—Hall
E. F.—Society

G. H.
I. J. *Examiners.*
K. L.

(*d*) Examination for Foundation Certificates (Continuing Education)

Names of candidates who in [here insert term and year] *have satisfied* [or *have been adjudged worthy of distinction by*] *the examiners for the Foundation Certificate in* [here insert title of certificate] [here insert where applicable *and have thereby completed all the examination requirements for the certificate*].

A. B.—College
C. D.—Hall
E. F.—Society

G. H.
I. J. *Examiners.*
K. L.

SCHEDULE E

Forms in which Diplomas and Certificates are to be issued

(i) Diploma in Applied Statistics, and Postgraduate Diploma in Theology

This is to certify that A. B. of on [*such a date*] satisfied [*or* was adjudged worthy of distinction by] the examiners appointed by the University to examine in the subjects prescribed for the Postgraduate Diploma in Theology, [*or* for the Diploma in Applied Statistics].

Signed on behalf of the Board of the Faculty of Theology [*or* of Medieval and Modern Languages, *or* of the Social Sciences, *or* Mathematical and Physical Sciences Divisional Board].

C. D.–Chairman.
E. F.–Secretary.

The subjects in which a candidate for the Postgraduate Diploma in Theology has satisfied the examiners shall be stated in the diploma.

(ii) Diploma in Human Biology

This is to certify that A. B. of having pursued at Oxford an approved course of study, on [*such a date*] satisfied [*or* was adjudged worthy of distinction by] the examiners appointed by the University to examine in the subjects prescribed for the Diploma in Human Biology.

Signed on behalf of the Divisional Board of Life and Environmental Sciences.

C. D.–Chairman.
E. F.–Secretary.

(iii) Postgraduate Certificate in Education†

This is to certify that A. B. has pursued an approved course of study and professional training under the supervision of the Social Sciences Divisional Board and in ..... Term 19 satisfied the examiners appointed by the University to examine in the subjects prescribed for the Postgraduate Certificate in Education.

C. D.–Registrar or Deputy.
E. F.–Director of the Department of Educational Studies.
[Here insert date.]

† The form of the certificate for the Postgraduate Certificate in Education and for other diplomas and certificates awarded to students on courses validated by the University at the Westminster Institute of Education, Oxford Brookes University, shall be as agreed from time to time between the two universities.

(iv) Certificate in Management Studies

This is to certify that A. B. has pursued at Templeton College a course of study in Management Studies and has satisfied the Board of the Faculty of Management in the following subject: [here insert subject].

C. D.–Chairman.
E. F.–Secretary.

(v) Postgraduate Diploma in Educational Studies

This is to certify that A. B. has pursued an approved course of study under the supervision of the Social Sciences Divisional Board and in Trinity Term 19 satisfied [*or* was adjudged worthy of distinction by] the examiners appointed by the University to examine in the subjects prescribed for the Postgraduate Diploma in Educational Studies.

C. D.–Registrar or Deputy.
E. F.–Director of the Department of Educational Studies.

(vi) Postgraduate Certificates (Continuing Education)

This is to certify that A. B. has pursued an approved course of study under the supervision of the Continuing Education Board and in [*such a a term and year*] satisfied [*or* was adjudged worthy of distinction by] the examiners appointed by the University to examine in the subjects prescribed for the Postgraduate Certificate in [*here insert title of certificate*].

Signed on behalf of the Board of Studies of the Continuing Education Board.

C. D.–Chairman.
E. F.–Secretary.

(vii) Postgraduate Diplomas (Continuing Education)

This is to certify that A. B. has pursued an approved course of study under the supervision of the Continuing Education Board and in [*such a term and year*] satisfied [*or* was adjudged worthy of distinction by] the examiners appointed by the University to examine in the subjects prescribed for the Postgraduate Diploma in [here insert title of diploma].

Signed on behalf of the Board of Studies of the Continuing Education Board.

C. D.–Chairman.
E. F.–Secretary.

(viii) Certificates in Theology

This is to certify that A. B. having pursued an approved course of study and having satisfied the examiners appointed by the University in the [*number*[subjects certified overleaf by the candidate's institution was awarded the Three-year Certificate in Theology [*or* the Two-Year Certificate in Theology *or* the Certificate for Theology Graduates] [with distinction *or* with merit] on [*date*].

Signed on behalf of the Board of the Faculty of Theology.

C. D.–Chairman.
E. F.–Secretary.

(ix) Diploma in Legal Studies

This is to certify that A. B. of has pursued at Oxford an approved course of legal studies and on [*such a date*] satisfied [*or* was adjudged worthy of distinction by] the examiners appointed by the Univesity to examine in the subjects prescribed for the Diploma in Legal Studies.

Signed on behalf of the Board of the Faculty of Law.

C. D.–Chairman.
E. F.–Secretary.

(x) Foundation Certificate in English Language and Literature

This is to certify that A. B. has pursued an approved course of study, and in [*such a term and year*] satisfied [*or* was adjudged worthy of distinction by] the examiners appointed by the University to examine in the subjects prescribed for the Foundation Certificate in English Language and Literature.

Signed on behalf of the Board of Studies of the Continuing Education Board.

C. D.—Chairman.
E. F.—Secretary.

(xi) Diplomas (Continuing Education)

This is to certify that A. B. has pursued an approved course of study under the supervision of the Continuing Education Board and in [*such a term and year*] satisfied [*or* was adjudged worthy of a distinction by] the examiners appointed by the University to examine in the subjects prescribed for the Diploma in [here insert title of diploma].

Signed on behalf of the Board of Studies of the Continuing Education Board.

C. D.—Chairman.
E. F.—Secretary

(xii) Diploma in Jewish Studies

This is to certify that A. B. has pursued an approved course of study at the Oxford Centre for Hebrew and Jewish Studies validated by the University and under the supervision of the Board of the Faculty of Oriental Studies and on [*such a date*] satisfied the examiners appointed by the University to examine in the subjects prescribed for the Diploma in Jewish Studies.

C. D.—Registrar or Deputy.
E. F.—President of the Oxford Centre for Hebrew and Jewish Studies.
G. H.—Chairman of the Board of the Faculty of Oriental Studies.

(xiii) Foundation Certificate in Social and Political Science

This is to certify that A. B. has pursued an approved course of study, and in [*such a term and year*] satisfied [*or* was adjudged worthy of distinction by] the examiners appointed by the University to examine in the subjects prescribed for the Foundation Certificate in Social and Political Science.

Signed on behalf of the Board of Studies of the Continuing Education Board.

C. D.—Chairman.
E. F.—Secretary

(xiv) Postgraduate Diploma in Legal Practice

This is to certify that A. B. has pursued an approved course of study under the supervision of the Board of Studies of the Oxford Institute of Legal Practice and in [*such a year*] satisfied [*or* was adjudged worthy of a commendation by *or* was adjudged worthy of a distinction by] the University of Oxford and Oxford Brookes University on the recommendation of the Examination Committee of the Oxford Institute of Legal Practice in the subjects prescribed for the Postgraduate Diploma in Legal Practice.

C. D.—Registrar or Deputy, University of Oxford.
E. F.—Academic Secretary or Deputy, Oxford Brookes University.

(xv) Postgraduate Diploma in Management Studies

This is to certify that A. B. has pursued an approved course of study under the supervision of the Board of the Faculty of Management and in [*such a term and year*] satisfied [*or* was adjudged worthy of distinction by] the examiners appointed by the University to examine in the subjects prescribed for the Postgraduate Diploma in Management Studies.

C.D.—Registrar or Deputy
E.F.—Peter Moores Dean of the Saïd Business School.

(xvi) Foundation Certificate in Modern History

This is to certify that A. B. has pursued an approved course of study, and in [*such a term and year*] satisfied [*or* was adjudged worthy of distinction by] the examiners appointed by the University to examine in the subjects prescribed for the Foundation Certificate in Modern History.

Signed on behalf of the Board of Studies of the Committee on Continuing Education.

C.D.—Chairman.
E.F.—Secretary.

(xvii) Postgraduate Diploma in Diplomatic Studies

This is to certify that A. B. has pursued an approved course of study, and in [*such a term and year*] satisfied [*or* was adjudged worthy of distinction by] the examiners appointed by the University to examine in the subjects prescribed for the Postgraduate Diploma in Diplomatic Studies.

Signed on behalf of the Board of Examiners of the Area and Development Studies Committee.

C.D.—Chairman.
E.F.—Secretary.

(xviii) Certificate in Diplomatic Studies

This is to certify that A. B. has pursued an approved course of study, and in [*such a term and year*] satisfied [*or* was adjudged worthy of distinction by] the examiners appointed by the University to examine in the subjects prescribed for the Certificate in Diplomatic Studies.

Signed on behalf of the Board of Examiners of the Area and Development Studies Committee.

C.D.—Chairman.
E.F.—Secretary.

CONDUCT AT EXAMINATIONS*

Regulations of the Proctors

N.B. At the time of going to press, these regulations were under review. Readers are advised to check (in the *University Gazette*

* For the avoidance of doubt, the Proctors wish to make clear that any examination described in any decree or regulation as a qualifying examination is covered by these regulations.

from 20 June 2002 onwards, or in the 2002–3 edition of the *Proctors' and Assessors' Memorandum of Essential Information for Students*) for amendments to these regulations.

(i) The name of any candidate who withdraws from an examination should be notified through his society to the Head Clerk, University Offices, Wellington Square, who will notify the Chairman of Examiners and the Clerk of the Schools.

(ii) A candidate who desires to withdraw from an examination at any time after the start of the first paper, must inform an Examiner or Invigilator and the Clerk of the Schools at once and his College as soon as possible.

(iii) A candidate may not withdraw from an examination after the written part of the examination is complete. The point of completion shall be deemed to be the conclusion of the last paper for which the candidate has entered, or the time by which a dissertation or other written material is due to be submitted, whichever is the later. However, a candidate who fails to appear for a viva voce examination subsequent to the completion of the written examination will be deemed to have failed the entire examination unless he or she can, through his or her college, satisfy the Proctors that his or her absence was due to illness or other urgent and reasonable cause. A candidate or his college, other society, or approved institution may within fourteen days of the date of the Proctors' decision appeal in writing to the Chairman of the Educational Policy and Standards Committee (who may nominate another member of the Committee, other than one of the Proctors, to adjudicate such appeal).

(iv) No candidate shall present for an examination any part, or the substance of any part, of another person's work, as if it were the candidate's own work.

(v) A candidate who fails to appear for any part of an examination other than a viva voce as specified in cl. (iii) above, will be deemed to have withdrawn from the entire examination unless he or she can, through his or her college, satisfy the Vice-Chancellor and Proctors that his or her absence was due to illness or other urgent and reasonable cause. A candidate or his college, other society or approved institution may within fourteen days of the date of the Proctors' decision appeal in writing to the Chairman of the Educational Policy and Standards Committee (who may nominate another member of the Committee, other than one of the Proctors, to adjudicate such appeal).

(vi) Candidates must present themselves for examination in full academic dress, i.e. *subfusc* clothing, cap and gown. Graduates also wear hoods.

(vii) Candidates who arrive more than half an hour late for any paper are liable to disqualification.

(viii) Candidates may not leave examination rooms until half an hour after the papers have been set.

(ix) A candidate on a taught course may communicate with Examiners only through the Senior Tutor or equivalent officer of his or her College. In the event of any such candidate wishing to pursue a complaint about the conduct of a University examination, the complaint must be notified to the Senior Tutor or equivalent officer as soon as possible and not later than six months after the publication of the results of the examination concerned. The Senior Tutor or equivalent officer shall forward the complaint and any subsequent correspondence promptly to the Proctors and may (but is not required to) comment to the Proctors on the complaint. The Senior Tutor or equivalent officer may also, with the six-month limit specified above, make a complaint to the Proctors on behalf of a taught-course candidate. A candidate for a research degree may communicate a complaint regarding the conduct of the examination of his or her thesis direct to the Proctors: such a complaint must be made to the Proctors (but under no circumstances made direct to the Examiners) as soon as possible and not later than twelve months after the formal notification of the result of the examination concerned by the Graduate Studies Office. A Supervisor may also, within this twelve-month limit, make a complaint to the Proctors on behalf of a research-degree candidate. In investigating complaints about the conduct of University examinations, the Proctors have no remit to question the academic judgement of Examiners.

(x) Candidates may not use any paper in examinations except that provided for them.

(xi) No candidate shall make use of unfair means in any University examination.

(xii) Candidates may not take unnecessary articles into examination rooms. Candidates who bring unnecessary articles to a building in which examinations are being held must not take them beyond the areas designated for the deposit of bags and other personal belongings.

(xiii) No candidate shall take into, or attempt to take into, a University examination any material relevant to the examination, and no candidate shall use, or attempt to use, such material in an examination, unless a valid permission has previously been given.

(xiv) Except for the drawing of diagrams, no candidate shall use pencil for the writing of an examination unless prior permission has been obtained from the Proctors.

(xv) Smoking is forbidden in both the Examination Schools and any other room where an examination is being held.

(xvi) Candidates must leave the Examination Schools and any other place where an examination is being held as directed.

(xvii) Parties or celebrations may not be held in or near the Examination Schools, the Schools Quadrangle, or any other building which is being used for examinations.

(xviii) No member of the University shall knowingly assist a candidate to breach, or attempt to breach, a Special Regulation concerning examinations, and no candidate shall solicit assistance from any other person which might lead to a knowing breach of such a Regulation.

(xix) A candidate whose native language is not English and who wishes to take into any examination a bilingual dictionary (covering English and the candidate's native language) must obtain permission from the Proctors in advance through the Senior Tutor or equivalent officer of his or her college. Where regulations or examiners' instructions forbid the use of dictionaries, permission shall not be given.

TYPING OF ILLEGIBLE SCRIPTS IN UNIVERSITY EXAMINATIONS

Regulations of the Proctors

If a chairman of examiners shall consider that a script or scripts of a candidate in an examination are illegible, he shall thereupon inform the Proctors and the Senior Tutor or other proper officer of that candidate's college or other society or approved institution, provided that, if there shall be a dispute as to the illegibility of a script or scripts, the question shall be referred to the Proctors, whose ruling on the question shall be conclusive. The Senior Tutor or other proper officer shall then arrange for the candidate to dictate his illegible script(s) to a typist under the invigilation of a Master of Arts of the University or of Cambridge University or any other person who in the opinion of the Proctors seems suitable; the typist and invigilator having been approved beforehand by the Proctors. The dictation and typing shall be undertaken in a place to be approved by the Proctors, but *subfusc* need not be worn; the candidate shall dictate his script to the typist in the presence of the invigilator and shall ensure that the typescript is in every respect identical in form and content to the original script. No carbon copies may be taken. The use of a tape-recorder is not permitted. The cost of typing and invigilation shall not be a charge on university funds.

The examiners shall read the typescript page by page with the original script beside it and shall immediately report any discrepancy to the Proctors.

USE OF WORD-PROCESSORS IN EXAMINATIONS AND THE DICTATION OF PAPERS

Regulations of the Proctors

The use of word-processors or the dictation of papers will not be permitted in Public Examinations except as provided in regulations or where the Proctors give special permission on grounds of medical need or other urgent cause.

Where a candidate, on grounds of medical need or other urgent cause, seeks permission to use a word-processor or dictate his or her papers, the Senior Tutor or other proper officer of that candidate's college or other society or approved institution should send a medical certificate or statement from a chartered psychologist that the candidate is suffering from a condition that makes it essential for him or her to use a word-processor or to dictate his or her answers, and the name and date of the examination which the candidate wishes to take, to the Proctors and obtain from them

(1) leave in writing for the candidate to use a typewriter or dictate his papers;

(2) approval of the name of a Master of Arts of the University, or any other person who in the opinion of the Vice-Chancellor and Proctors seems suitable, who is prepared to invigilate;

(3) approval of the name of the amanuensis, where an amanuensis is required, who may also act as invigilator if approved by the Vice-Chancellor and Proctors;

(4) approval of the room to be provided for the examination of the candidate.

In the event that leave is given for the use of a word-processor, whether for the candidate's own use or for use by an amanuensis during the dictation of papers, the Proctors shall specify in each case such detailed arrangements as they deem appropriate for the preparation and use of any equipment and computer software during the examination and for the conduct of the examination. It shall be the duty of the Proctors to send this authorization promptly to the chairman of the examiners of the relevant examination, with copies to the Senior Tutor or other proper officer of the candidate's college, other society or approved institution and to the Clerk of the Schools.

The invigilator should attend at the Schools to receive the paper at least a quarter of an hour before the examination begins, bringing a letter addressed to the chairman containing the name of the candidate, the subject in which he is being examined, and the authorization by the Proctors (if this has not already been sent).

A single copy of the candidate's word-processing script should be printed for submission to the examiners. No additional copies may be made of work submitted for examination. The use of a tape-recorder is not permitted.

The candidate's work should be handed as soon as possible after the time appointed for the collection of the papers to the Clerk of the Schools who will make the appropriate entry in his or her register. The Clerk will obtain a receipt when forwarding work done outside the Schools.

The cost of the arrangement in any particular case shall not be a charge on the University Chest unless the Proctors authorize the candidate to use word-processing facilities under the control of the Clerk of the Schools for the benefit of candidates with special needs.

In the event that the Proctors decline to give permission for a candidate to use a word-processor or to dictate his or her papers, the candidate concerned or his or her college, other society or approved institution may within fourteen days of the date of the Proctors' decision appeal in writing to the Chairman of the Educational Policy and Standards Committee (who may nominate another member of the Committee, other than one of the Proctors, to adjudicate such appeal).

VISUALLY-IMPAIRED CANDIDATES IN EXAMINATIONS

Regulations of the Proctors

Where any college or other society or approved institution has a visually-impaired candidate for examination, the Senior Tutor or other proper officer should inform both the chairman of that examination and the Clerk of the Schools by letter, not later than three months before the date of the examination, of the candidate's name and state whether brailled or other alternative format papers will be required, and if so what subjects will be taken by the candidate.*

* Attention is drawn to the fact that the Royal National Institute for the Blind is no longer able to undertake the transcription of candidates' *scripts* from braille.

The Senior Tutor or other proper officer should secure an invigilator, and if necessary an amanuensis, and obtain the approval of the Proctors by application to the Junior Proctor. The invigilator must be a Master of Arts of the University or any other person who in the opinion of the Proctors seems suitable, and the same person may act as invigilator and amanuensis.* The Senior Tutor should also make application, if required, to the Junior Proctor on behalf of the candidate for the granting of extra time in the examination and any other special arrangements (such as the use of a typewriter or word-processor) relating to the conduct of the examination.

The Senior Tutor or other proper officer should further arrange for the provision of a room for the examination of the candidate and obtain the sanction of the Proctors, application for which may be made through the Junior Proctor. (NB. It is always difficult, and in Trinity Term impracticable, to provide rooms for visually-impaired candidates in the Examination Schools.)

When brailled or other alternative format papers are required, the Chairman should submit a copy of the necessary manuscripts to the Clerk of the Schools at least *eight* weeks before the date of the examination. The account for producing such papers will be sent to the Clerk of the Schools for transmission to the Curators of the University Chest.

A candidate (or his or her college or other society, or approved institution) who is dissatisfied with any aspect of the Proctor's decision in respect of an application for special examination arrangements relating to his or her visual impairment, may within fourteen days of the date of the Proctors' decision appeal in writing to the Chairman of the Educational Policy and Standards Committee (who may nominate another member of the Committee, other than one of the Proctors, to adjudicate such appeal).

RELIGIOUS FESTIVALS AND HOLIDAYS COINCIDING WITH EXAMINATIONS

Regulations of the Proctors

Where any college or other society or approved institution has a candidate who is forbidden, for reasons of faith, from taking papers on religious festivals or other special days (not being Sundays), the Senior Tutor or other proper officer should inform the Junior Proctor by letter of the name of the candidate and

* For the procedure for collecting examination scripts see footnote to Ch. VI, Sect II. C, §4, cl. 4.

particulars of his or her faith at the same time as the candidate's examination entry is submitted.

If the papers have not been set in such a way that the candidate is permitted to take all of them on the days prescribed, the chairman of the examiners of the relevant examination shall inform the Senior Tutor or other proper officer and also appoint a time earlier or for preference later than the prescribed time at which the candidate must take each paper that he or she is forbidden to take at the prescribed time.

The Senior Tutor or other proper officer shall then secure from among the Masters of Arts of the University of Oxford or the University of Cambridge or any other person who in the opinion of the Proctors seem suitable an invigilator or invigilators for whose appointment he or she shall obtain the approval of the Proctors. The Senior Tutor or other proper officer shall further arrange for the internment under invigilation of the candidate for the whole of each period from the beginning of the time prescribed for any paper which he or she is forbidden to take at the prescribed time until the end of the time appointed for him or her to take that paper or as the case may be from the beginning of the appointed time until the end of the prescribed time. If the prescribed time for any paper being a time at which the candidate is not forbidden to take papers falls within any such period, then the Senior Tutor or other proper officer shall arrange for the candidate to take that paper at the prescribed time in incarceration under invigilation. When these arrangements are completed the Senior Tutor or other proper officer shall submit them for approval to the Proctors, who if satisfied will inform the chairman of examiners and the Clerk of the Schools accordingly.

If in the opinion of the Chairman of Examiners any paper (as, for example, a practical paper in a scientific subject), which according to the provisions of the preceding paragraph the candidate should take in incarceration under invigilation, is unsuitable to be taken under such conditions, then the chairman shall submit for approval to the Proctors other conditions under which the candidate must take at an appointed time either that paper or some alternative equivalent to it, and the Senior Tutor or other proper officer shall thereafter make such arrangements to that end as the Proctors may direct.

The cost of the arrangement in any particular case shall not be a charge on the University Chest.

DYSLEXIC CANDIDATES IN EXAMINATIONS

Regulations of the Proctors

A candidate who is dyslexic may apply to the Proctors, through the Senior Tutor or other proper officer of his or her college, other society or approved institution (a) for special examination arrangements relating to the dyslexia, and (b) for the condition to be taken into account by the Examiners as a special factor that may affect his or her performance in examinations. Such application should be made as soon as possible after matriculation and in any event not later than the date of entry of the candidate's name for the first examination for which special arrangements are sought. The application must be supported by a statement from a chartered psychologist approved by the Proctors. Such statement is to be based on a review of an assessment of the candidate carried out by a suitably-qualified person and on such further assessment of the candidate as the chartered psychologist considers necessary in order to form a judgement. The Proctors will issue guidance periodically on the nature of the assessments which will be considered appropriate.

Candidates who are reported to be dyslexic by one of the approved chartered psychologists will normally be allowed extra time in examinations. The Proctors will also have regard to any recommendation from such chartered psychologist for other special arrangements (e.g. use of a word-processor). The special arrangements approved by the Proctors will normally apply to all University Examinations to be taken by the candidate during his or her course of study; it shall be the responsibility of the candidate to apply as described above for any subsequent change to these arrangements.

In each case, the Proctors will give authority for appropriate statements explaining the effects of dyslexia to be supplied to the chairman of examiners of the relevant examination and placed on the examination scripts of the dyslexic candidate, in order to assist the examiners in adjudicating the merits of the candidate's work.

A candidate or his or her college, other society or approved institution who is dissatisfied with any aspect of the Proctors' decision in respect of his or her application for special examination arrangements relating to dyslexia, may within fourteen days of the date of the Proctors' decision appeal in writing to the Chairman of the Educational Policy and Standards Committee (who may nominate another member of the Committee, other than one of the Proctors, to adjudicate such appeal).

USE OF CALCULATORS IN EXAMINATIONS

Regulations made by the Boards of Life and Environmental Sciences, Mathematical and Physical Sciences, Modern History, Classics, Medical Sciences, and Social Sciences, the Committee on Continuing Education, and Standing Committees for Joint Honour Schools involving Engineering Science or Metallurgy, and Human Sciences

Except where otherwise provided, the following conditions will apply in any examination, except those at Westminster College, in which candidates are permitted to use hand-held pocket calculators.

(1) No calculator for which a mains supply is essential will be allowed: it is the responsibility of the candidate to ensure that the power supply of the calculator is adequately charged.

(2) Any calculator deemed by the Proctors or the examiners to cause a disturbance will not be allowed.

(3) Output from a calculator shall be by visible display only.

(4) Candidates are required to clear any user-entered data or programmes from the memories of their calculators immediately before starting each examination.

(5) No storage media external to the calculator are permitted.

(6) Input to the calculator during the examination shall be by its own keys or switches only.

(7) The examiners may inspect any calculator during the course of the examination.

USE OF COMPUTERS IN EXAMINATIONS

Regulations made by the General Board

Except where otherwise provided, the following conditions will apply in any examination in which candidates are permitted to use computers.

(1) No material such as cassettes, discs, or any other device on which machine readable files can be stored may be taken into the examination room.

(2) No password or user name other than any specified on the examination paper shall be used.

(3) The examination paper shall contain a list of files, if any, which it is permitted to access. None of these files shall be deleted, written to, or tampered with in any way. No other file shall be accessed (except any files created by candidates during the course of the examination).

(4) Any files which candidates are permitted to access during the examination shall be previously submitted for approval to all examiners conducting that examination.

(5) If it is permitted to access remotely held files which are held in a file store containing other files, the permitted files shall be accessed by user names and passwords which are used solely for the purposes of the examination. Such names and passwords shall not be revealed to the candidates until the start of the examination and shall be specified on the examination paper.

(6) In the event of any computer failure not involving the loss of any files in use in the examination and lasting less than one half hour, or not more than two separate failures, together lasting less than one half hour, the examination shall be extended by the amount of time lost.

(7) In the event of any computer failure not covered by (6), the examination in question shall cease forthwith. An entirely new paper shall be set at a time and place which shall have been previously announced in the timetable for the examination: but it shall be open to any candidate who shall have submitted work during or at the end of the sitting of the original paper to elect to be assessed upon that work and not to sit the new paper.

(8) In the event of any examination being aborted on a second occasion the examiners shall determine the outcome of that examination by an alternative method after consultation with the Proctors.

D. *TIMES FOR HOLDING EXAMINATIONS AND THE ENTRY OF NAMES*

Ch. VI, Sect. II. D]

Times for holding Examinations

1. The Vice-Chancellor and Proctors shall, after consultation with the Educational Policy and Standards Committee and the Clerk of the Schools, fix the days on which university examinations shall begin and shall give public notice of such days.

Entry of Names

2. The Registrar shall receive the names of candidates for all examinations except the examinations enumerated in the Schedule annexed to this clause. For those examinations names shall be received in the manner prescribed by the Regulations governing the respective examinations.

SCHEDULE

Certificate in Management Studies.
,, Education.
Postgraduate Diploma in Educational Studies.
Second Examination for the Degree of Bachelor of Medicine.

3. The Registrar shall fix the days for entering names after consultation with the Educational Policy and Standards Committee, and he shall give public notice of the place and hour at which he will receive names.

4. Candidates shall state on their forms of entry the options they intend to offer, if the regulations of the examination for which they are entering permit the offer of options.

5. The form in which candidates shall draw up their lists of books and subjects shall be determined by the Registrar, who may also require candidates to give such information as is necessary to ensure that the provisions for admission to the several examinations are observed:

Provided that every candidate

(i) for the examination for the Diploma in Theology *or* for the Diploma in Applied Statistics *or* for the Diploma in Legal

Studies shall also produce a certificate from his society of having followed a course of instruction in Theology *or* Statistics *or* in Legal Studies, as the case may be, for at least three terms;

(ii) for any of the examinations set out in the Schedule annexed to this clause shall also forward a certificate from the society to which he belongs, showing that his entry is made with the approval of such society;

(iii) For the First or Second Examination for the Degree of Bachelor of Medicine shall also forward such certificates of instruction as are required by the provisions of Section XI of this statute;

(iv) for Part I of the examination for the Degree of Master of Surgery shall also forward a certificate as required under Section XII, §3, cl. 5 of this statute.

SCHEDULE

Examinations for the Degree of Bachelor of Civil Law and the Degree of Magister Juris.

First and Second Examination for the Degree of Bachelor of Medicine.

Part I of the examination for the Degree of Master of Surgery.

Qualifying Examination for the Degree of Bachelor of Divinity.

Examinations for the Degrees of Bachelor and Master of Philosophy.

Examinations for the Degree of Master of Science by Coursework.

Examination for the Diploma in:

Applied Statistics.

Theology.

Examinations for the Degree of Master of Studies.

Examinations for the Degree of Master of Business Administration (full-time and part-time).

6. The name of every candidate may be given in by himself on the day appointed by the Registrar, or transmitted through his tutor to the Registrar, in either case on a form to be supplied by the Registrar:

Provided that the names of candidates who are not already members of the University, except in the case of those examinations for diplomas and certificates which are open to non-members of the University, shall be sent to the Registrar by the Head or a tutor of a society, on a form to be supplied by the Registrar, together with a declaration that such candidate in his opinion bona fide desires admission to his society.

Late Entries

7. Where a candidate whose name has not been entered for an examination by the date fixed by the Registrar under the provisions of clause 3 of this section wishes his or her name to be entered after that date, the procedure shall be as follows:

(*a*) the candidate shall apply in writing through the Senior Tutor or other proper officer of his or her college or other society or approved institution to both the Registrar and the chairman of examiners for the candidate's name to be so entered;

(*b*) the Registrar shall, in consultation with the chairman of examiners, determine whether the candidate proposes to offer a book or subject or part of the examination which has not already been offered by some other candidate whose name has been entered under the provisions of clause 3 of this section and whether any other change in the conduct of the examination, as already arranged, would be involved;

(*c*) if no change in the conduct of the examination as referred to in sub-clause (*b*) would be involved, the Registrar shall, subject to the payment by the candidate of a late-entry fee, grant permission for the candidate to be admitted to the examination;

(*d*) if some such change would be involved, the Registrar shall ask the chairman of examiners whether he or she is, nevertheless, willing to consent to the candidate being admitted to the examination, and, if the chairman consents, the Registrar shall, subject to the payment by the candidate of a late-entry fee, grant permission for the candidate to be admitted to the examination;

(*e*) if the chairman of examiners refuses to give the consent referred to in sub-clause (*d*), the Registrar shall refer the matter to the Vice-Chancellor and Proctors for decision, and, if they give permission, this shall be subject to the payment by the candidate of a late-entry fee.

The late-entry fee payable under sub-clauses (*c*), (*d*), and (*e*) shall be such sum as the Proctors shall from time to time determine, and different sums may be specified in respect of permission given under different sub-clauses.

8. Notwithstanding the provisions of the preceding clause, the Divisional Board of Social Sciences may make provision for late entry, as appropriate, in the regulations for the Certificate in Management Studies, the Certificate in Education, and the Special Diploma in Educational Studies. Candidates permitted to enter late

for these examinations shall pay such sum as the Proctors shall from time to time determine.

9. Where a candidate for any written examination in which a thesis (or other exercise) may be, or is required to be, submitted as part of that examination wishes to be permitted to present such thesis (or other exercise) later than the date prescribed by statute, decree, or regulation, the procedure shall be as follows:

(*a*) the candidate shall apply in writing through the Senior Tutor or other proper officer of his or her college or other society or approved institution to the Proctors for such permission;

(*b*) the Proctors shall consult the chairman of examiners about any such application and shall then decide whether or not to grant permission;

(*c*) it shall be a condition of any permission granted under sub-clause (*b*) that the candidate shall pay a late-presentation fee, the amount of which shall be determined by the Proctors according to the facts of the particular case. If permission is granted, the examiners shall accept and mark such a thesis (or other exercise) as if it has been submitted by the date prescribed by statute, decree, or regulation.

Thereafter, the examiners may reduce the mark if and only if

(1) they have been given leave to do so by the Proctors and

(2) they are satisfied that such action is warranted by the evidence forwarded to them by the Proctors. In accordance with the provisions of regulation (v) of the Proctors' Regulations concerning Conduct at Examinations, if a candidate fails to submit a thesis (or other written exercise) without prior permission, the Proctors may after making due enquiries into the circumstances permit the candidate to remain in the examination and to submit the work late under arrangements similar to those set out in sub-clauses (*a*)–(*c*) above. A candidate or his or her society may within fourteen days of the date of the Proctors' decision appeal in writing to the Chairman of the Educational Policy and Standards Committee (who may nominate another member of the committee, other than one of the Proctors, to adjudicate the appeal).

Submission of Theses or other Exercises

10. Where a candidate for any written examination (other than for the D.Phil., M.Litt., or M.Sc. by Research) in which a thesis (or other exercise) may be, or is required to be, submitted as part of that examination presents a thesis (or other exercise) which exceeds the word limit prescribed by the relevant statute, decree,

or regulation, the examiners, if they agree to proceed with the examination of the work, may reduce the mark by up to one class (or its equivalent). Where a candidate submits such a thesis (or other exercise), the title or subject matter of which differs from that which was approved by the faculty board concerned, the examiners may similarly reduce the mark by up to one class (or its equivalent).

Late Alteration of Options

11. Where a candidate whose name has been entered for an examination the regulations for which permit the offering of options wishes to alter his or her choice of options, the procedure shall be as follows:

(*a*) the candidate shall apply in writing through the Senior Tutor or other proper officer of his or her college or other society or approved institution to both the Registrar and the chairman of examiners for the alteration to be made;

(*b*) the Registrar shall, in consultation with the chairman of examiners, determine whether the candidate proposes to offer a book or subject or part of the examination which has not already been offered by some other candidate whose name has been entered under the provisions of clause 3 of this section and whether any other change in the conduct of the examination, as already arranged, would be involved:

(*c*) if no change in the conduct of the examination as referred to in sub-clause (*b*) would be involved, the Registrar shall, subject to the payment by the candidate of a late-alteration fee, grant permission for the alteration to be made;

(*d*) if some such change would be involved, the Registrar shall ask the chairman of examiners whether he or she is, nevertheless, willing to consent to the alteration, and, if the chairman consents, the Registrar shall, subject to the payment by the candidate of a late-alteration fee, grant permission for the alteration to be made;

(*e*) if the chairman of examiners refuses to give the consent referred to in sub-clause (*d*), the Registrar shall refer the matter to the Proctors for decision, and, if they give permission, this shall be subject to the payment by the candidate of a late-alteration fee. A candidate or his or her society may within fourteen days of the date of the Proctors' decision appeal in writing to the Chairman of the Educational Policy and Standards Committee (who may nominate another member of the committee, other than one of the Proctors, to adjudicate the appeal).

The late-alteration fee payable under sub-clauses (*c*), (*d*), and (*e*) shall be such sum as the Vice-Chancellor and Proctors shall from time to time determine, and different sums may be specified in respect of permission given under different sub-clauses.

12. The Proctors shall be empowered to waive the payment of a fee under clauses 7–9 and 11 above in such circumstances as they see fit.

Publication of Names of Candidates

13. The Registrar shall arrange the names of candidates for each examination in alphabetical order and shall sign the lists, which shall be headed in accordance with the form set out in the Annexed Schedule;

Provided that

(i) this clause shall not apply to entries for the examinations specified in the Schedule annexed to clause 2 of this Section;

(ii) the names of candidates entered late in accordance with the provisions of clause 7 of this Section shall be placed on supplemental lists.

14. If through change of name, migration, or otherwise, the identity of a candidate offering himself for any examination shall not be prima facie evident, the Registrar may require such further evidence of identity as he may deem necessary.

Transmission of Names of Candidates and Lists of Books and Subjects to the Examiners

15. The Registrar, when he has received the names of candidates for any examination, shall send the lists of books and subjects offered by the candidates to the chairman of the examiners in the examination for which they present themselves.

16. The Registrar, before sending the lists to the chairman of the examiners, shall examine them and shall refer back to any candidate for amendment any list which is not in accordance with the relevant Decrees or Regulations.

Examinations for courses at Westminster College validated by the University

17. Notwithstanding any provisions of the above clauses to the contrary, the entry of names, late entries, late alteration of names of candidates, and transmission of names of candidates and lists of books and subjects to the examiners for examination for courses at Westminster College validated by the University shall be governed by regulations laid down from time to time by Westminster College and lodged annually with the Proctors.

Examination for the Degree of Doctor of Clinical Psychology validated by the University

18. Notwithstanding any provision of the above clauses to the contrary, the entry of names, late entries, late alteration of names and candidates, and transmission of names of candidates and lists of books and subjects to the examiners for the examination for the Degree of Doctor of Clinical Psychology shall be governed by regulations laid down from time to time by the Directorate of the Oxford Doctoral Course in Clinical Psychology and lodged annually with the Proctors.

APPENDIX I

REGULATIONS ON FINANCIAL MATTERS

Section I. Fees and Dues payable to the University

§1. *Fees payable at Matriculation*

The matriculation fee shall be £161, provided that no fee shall be payable by any person who is certified by his or her college as being liable to pay in the term of his or her matriculation a composition fee under the provisions of §6 of this Section or by any person on whom a degree is to be conferred by special resolution, or by a clinical student who has already paid an admission fee of £10 under the provisions of §8, cl. 1 of this Section, or by any other person who is permitted by regulation to be matriculated without the payment of a matriculation fee.

§2. *Fees payable by candidates on registration, entry for an examination, application for leave to supplicate, or resubmission of a thesis for certain degrees*

	£
(*a*) On entering or replacing the name of a non-member of the University on the Register of Diploma and Certificate Students	80.00
(*b*) On admission to the Status of Student for the Degree of DM and for each subsequent year that the name of the student remains on the register of students for the degree	250.00
(*c*) On entering for certain examinations:	
Foundation Certificates in English Language and Literature and in Modern History	41.00
Certificates in Theology	46·00
Certificate in Management Studies	80·00
Qualifying Examination for the degree of BD	58·00
Degree of B.Mus	168·00
Degrees of B.Phil., M.Phil., M.Th., M.Sc. (by Coursework), and M.St. on re-entering the examination*	278·00
Diplomas in Applied Statistics, and in Human Biology on re-entering the examination*	148·00
Degree of M.Ch., Part I	88·00
(*d*) On applying for leave to supplicate	

* The fee is payable only if required by §6, cl. 3, below.

for the degree of BD	152·00
for the degree of M.Ch., Part II	334·00
for the degree of DM	350·00
for the degrees of DD, DCL, D.Litt, D.Sc., and D.Mus.	537·00
(*e*) On resubmission of a thesis for the degree of M.Litt., M.Th., M.Sc., or D.Phil., or on reinstatement on the Register of Students for the degree of M.Litt., M.Sc. (by Research), or DPhil., or before a revised or new dissertation is examined for the degree of M.Sc. in Educational Studies or Educational Research Methodology	100·00
(*f*) On resubmission for the degree of DM	350.00

§3. *Fee payable by candidates on registration for courses validated by the University*

For the Degree of Doctor of Clinical Psychology	1,000.00

§4. *Fees payable in respect of degrees*

1. Every person shall pay £10 on supplicating for admission to the degree of MA, provided that

(i) no fee shall be payable by any person on whom a degree has been conferred by special resolution or who incorporates in virtue of having obtained an educational position in the University;

(ii) no fee shall be payable by a Master of Surgery on supplicating for admission to the Degree of Master of Arts.

2. The following fees shall be paid by every person

	£
(*a*) accumulating the Degrees of Bachelor and Doctor of Civil Law	15·00
(*b*) whose name shall have been given in to the Registrar after the hour prescribed	17·00

§5. *In respect of certificates and personal data*

1. Every person shall pay the fee prescribed below in each case for certificates issued, on request, by the Head Clerk, University Offices, Wellington Square, Oxford OX1 2JD:

	£
(*a*) for the first certificate attesting admission to any degree, which shall include a statement of the class obtained in the case of the BCL or BFA or the B.Th. or Magister Juris, and a statement of the class obtained in the honour school in the case of the BA or the M.Biochem. or the M.Chem. or the M.Earth Sc. or the M.Eng. or the M.Math. or the M.Phys.	no charge
(*b*) for each of the second and subsequent certificates attesting admission to any degree	5·00
(*c*) for each certificate attesting matriculation or the passing of any examination	5·00
(*d*) for each complete record of a graduate of the University	17·00

(In all cases postage within the European Community is included, but postage elsewhere is payable in addition to categories (*b*)–(*d*).)

2. Every person making a request to be supplied with personal data under Section 7 of the Data Protection Act 1998 shall pay the fee determined from time to time by Council.*

---

* Such requests should be addressed to the Data Protection Officer, University Offices, Wellington Square, Oxford, OX1 2JD, from whom details of the current fee can be obtained. The fee is subject to a maximum prescribed from time to time by the Home Secretary under the Act.

§6. *Composition fees payable by members of the University*

1. Every member of the University shall pay a composition fee as specified in cl. 15 below for each academic year in which he is working in Oxford:

(i) For the Degree of BA or the Degree of M.Biochem. or the Degree of M.Chem. or the Degree of M.Earth Sc. or the Degree of M.Eng. or the Degree of M.Math. or the Degree of M.Phys. (Those working for an honour school requiring the study of one or more languages for an academic year outside Oxford or for Law with Law Studies in Europe, or for an honour school requiring a period of study shorter than a year outside Oxford, or for Part II in Chemistry or Metallurgy and Science of Materials or Molecular and Cellular Biochemistry in the Honour School of Natural Science, or for Part II in the Honour Schools of Engineering Science or Engineering and Computing Science or Engineering, Economics, and Management or Engineering and Materials or Materials, Economics, and Management, shall be deemed for all the purposes of this clause to be working in Oxford for the degree of BA or the Degree of M.Biochem. or the Degree of M.Chem. or the Degree of M.Eng., whether or not their work is being undertaken in Oxford);

(ii) for the Degree of BFA;

(iii) for the degree of B.Th.;

(iv) for the Degree of BCL or Magister Juris;

(v) for a second Honour school;

(vi) for the First Examination for the Degree of BM;

(vii) for the Diploma in Theology;

(viii) for the Diploma in Legal Studies;

(ix) on the Foreign Service Programme;

(x) for the Diploma in European Studies;

(xi) for the Postgraduate Diploma in Educational Studies; or

(xii) for the Certificate in Education (those working for the certificate shall be deemed for all the purposes of this clause to be working in Oxford, whether or not their work is being undertaken in Oxford).

The fee shall be paid as follows:

(*a*) in the case of those whose fees are paid under the terms of the Education (Mandatory Awards) Regulations (or under corresponding arrangements approved by the Scottish Education Department, the Northern Ireland Ministry of Education, or the Education Departments in the Channel Islands or Isle of Man) the fees shall be paid in accordance with the arrangements laid down in those regulations;

(*b*) in the case of those working for an undergraduate degree and liable to payment in full or part of the University composition fee as specified in clause 15 below, the fee shall be collected in accordance with the provisions of clause 14 below;

(*c*) in all other cases the fee shall be paid at the end of Michaelmas Term by all those who have been working in Oxford in that term. Those who begin working in Oxford in Hilary or Trinity Term shall pay the fee at the end of that term. On application by the society of the member of the University concerned, and subject to the approval of Council's Educational Policy and Standards Committee some part of the fee may be remitted.

On application by their society, and subject to the approval of Council's Educational Policy and Standards Committee, some part of the fee for an academic year may subsequently be returned to those who do not work in Oxford for the whole of that year.*

---

* The general rule agreed by Council is that, for each complete term not spent working in Oxford, one third of the annual fee shall be returned.

2. Every member of the University shall pay a composition fee at the appropriate annual rate specified in cl. 15 below for each term from and including the term in which he or she begins to work for the Second Examination for the Degree of Bachelor of Medicine up to and including the term in which he or she completes all the stages of the examination, or ceases to work for the examination.

3. (*a*) Subject to the provisions of cll. 4 and 5 below, every member of the University shall pay a composition fee at the appropriate annual rate specified in cl. 15 below for each term in which he or she is registered as a Probationer Research Student or is working for one of the qualifications listed below, from and including the term in which he or she is first so registered or begins working for such qualification, up to and including the term in which he or she takes the examination* or (in the case of a degree or diploma by thesis only) submits his or her thesis:†

(i) the Degree of B.Phil.;
(ii) the Degree of M.Sc.;
(iii) the Degree of M.St.;
(iv) the Degree of MBA;
(v) the Degree of M.Litt.;
(vi) the Degree of M.Phil.;
(vii) the Degree of M.Th. (except at Westminster Institute of Education, Oxford Brookes University);
(viii) the Degree of D.Phil.;
(ix) any diploma or certificate other than:
- (*a*) the Diploma in Theology;
- (*b*) the Diploma in Legal Studies;
- (*c*) the Diploma in European Studies;
- (*d*) the Postgraduate Diploma in Educational Studies;
- (*e*) the Certificate in Education;
- (*f*) the Certificate in Management Studies;
- (*g*) the Certificate in Theology; or
- (*h*) certificates issued by the Board of Studies in Education under the provisions of Ch. X, Sect. III.

Candidates who continue to work for one of the qualifications listed above after failing an examination shall pay a composition fee for each term in which they receive tuition or supervision; but if they receive no further tuition or supervision, they shall pay no further composition fees but shall pay the fee prescribed in §2 above when they re-enter. Candidates whose thesis submitted for the degree of M.Litt., M.Sc., or D.Phil., or the Diploma in Law, has been referred back shall pay no further composition fees, but shall pay the fee prescribed in §2 above when they apply for re-examination; and candidates whose dissertation for the degree of M.Sc. in Educational Studies did not satisfy the examiners shall pay the fee prescribed in §2 above before a revised or new dissertation for Part II of the examination is examined. For the purposes of this clause 'term' shall include any period of forty-two days' residence reckoned as a term of residence under the Regulations for Residence in the University provided that not more than three composition fees shall be payable in the same academical year.

---

* Where the examination comprises a written examination *followed* by the submission of a dissertation, the relevant term is that in which the written examination is taken, save that the relevant term for a student for the Degree of M.Th. is that in which his or her dissertation is submitted (subject to the provisions of cl. 5 of this sub-section).

† A thesis submitted other than during Full Term shall be deemed for this purpose to have been submitted during the preceding term.

(*b*) Subject to the provisions of cll. 4 and 5 below, every member of the University who, after withdrawal or lapse of status, is reinstated as a student working for one of the qualifications listed in sub-cl. (*a*) above, shall on reinstatement pay a composition fee for each term from and including that in which his or her status terminated up to and including that in which reinstatement takes effect, and such fee or fees shall be paid at the rate (or respective rates) which would have been applicable if he or she had remained liable for fees under sub-cl. (*a*) above, provided that not more than one fee shall be required to be paid under this clause in respect of any one term.

(*c*) In the event that any fee, or the relevant instalment towards the fee, remains unpaid after the due date of payment, the student shall be subject to the provisions in clause 14 (*b*)–(*e*) below.

4. The number of composition fees payable under cl. 3 above by those working for the degree of D.Phil. shall not exceed nine provided that:

(*a*) candidates for the D.Phil. may count towards this figure up to six composition fees paid while working for any one of the degrees of M.St., M.Sc. by Coursework, M.Phil., M.Th., M.Juris., B.Phil., or BCL;

(*b*) candidates for the D.Phil. who have held the status of Probationer Research Student, or of Student for the Degree of M.Sc. by Research or M.Litt. or for the Diploma in Law, before transferring* to work for the degree of D.Phil. shall be deemed for the purpose of this sub-section to have been working for the D.Phil. from the term in which they began working for the course from which they have transferred, and may count towards their D.Phil. fee liability any fees paid while holding their previous status, subject to the payment on transfer of any consequent additional fees for which they are liable.

5. The number of composition fees payable under cl. 3 above by those working for any qualification other than the degree of D.Phil. shall not exceed six in respect of each qualification, save that those receiving tuition or supervision after failing an examination shall continue to pay composition fees for each term in which they receive tuition or supervision, and those who are part-time Students for the Degree of Master of Science in Applied Social Studies or Educational Studies or Professional Development in Education shall pay not more than twelve composition fees, those who are students for the Degree of Master of Science in Software Engineering shall pay not more and not fewer than six composition fees (at the half rate) irrespective of the period for which they are registered for that degree, and those who are Students for the Degree of Master of Theology shall not pay more than six fees (at the half rate) while working for Part II of that degree.

6. Every member of the University who, not holding an academic appointment in the University or the colleges, has been matriculated in order to study in the University otherwise than for a degree, diploma, or certificate of the University shall pay a composition fee at the appropriate annual rate specified in cl. 15 below for each term in which he or she is studying in the University.

7. Every member of the University shall pay such other fees applicable to him or her as may be prescribed by any statute or regulation.

8. Fee requirements relating to full-time students holding the status of Probationer Research Student or that of a Student for the Degrees of D.Phil., B.Th., M.Litt., or M.Sc. by Research shall also apply to part-time students holding the same status, save that part-time students shall be required to pay half the applicable full-time fee over twice the applicable length of time for full-time students.

---

* A candidate is not deemed to be '*transferring* to work for the Degree of D.Phil.', when he or she is admitted as a D.Phil. Student after satisfying the examiners for the Degree of M.Sc. by Research or M.Litt., or for the Diploma in Law.

9. Notwithstanding the provisions of cl. 15 below, the University shall remit three-fifths of the prescribed composition fees payable by any overseas student who establishes, by information certified to the Secretary of the Chest by an officer of the student's college or society, that at least half of the cost of the student's maintenance (as distinct from university or college fees) in the relevant year has been provided by resident Junior Members of the University (otherwise than from funds of common rooms contributed directly or indirectly by local education authorities or other grant-paying authorities in payment of membership fees); provided that the number of students whose fees are remitted under this clause shall not in any one year exceed thirty-five and that any arrangements required for determining the allocation between colleges or other societies of the benefits available under this clause shall be subject to approval from time to time by Council's Educational Policy and Standards Committee.

10 (*a*). Notwithstanding the provisions of cl. 15 below, the University shall remit:

(i) three-quarters of the prescribed composition fees payable by employees of the University holding established posts offering the possibility of reappointment to the retiring age, and

(ii) one half of the prescribed composition fees payable by any other employees, for as long as they shall be certified to the Secretary of the Chest by the relevant head of department or (in the case of non-departmentally organized employment) chairman of the appropriate faculty board, body of curators or body of delegates, to be respectively:

(1) full-time employees of the University holding established posts offering the possibility of reappointment to the retiring age, or full-time employees of the University holding other posts, or CUF, special, or faculty lecturers, and

(2) undertaking work, for the degree in question, which does not impair the discharge of their duties as employees, and which will equip them for the better performance of their duties in the long term.

(*b*) For the purposes of cll. 4 and 5 of this subsection, each composition fee paid which is the subject of remission under sub-cl. (*a*) (i) above shall count only as one half, and each composition fee paid which is the subject of remission under sub-cl. (*a*) (ii) above shall count as a full fee, in reckoning the number of fees paid.*

11. Council's Educational Policy and Standards Committee shall have power to approve exchange arrangements with other universities under which no fees are payable on either side. Any of the fees prescribed in cl. 15 below, and the matriculation fee prescribed in §1 of this Section, which would otherwise have been payable by any person working in Oxford under those exchange arrangements shall be remitted.

12 (*a*). Where admission as a graduate student is reckoned from a term earlier than that in which the application for admission was approved, on the grounds that:

(i) a term or terms had been spent at another university on a course of study directly relevant to the work subsequently undertaken for the degree of M.Litt., M.Sc., or D.Phil., and

(ii) the earlier study had not led to the award of a qualification of any university, and was under the supervision of a person who has subsequently taken up an appointment at Oxford,

Subject to the approval of Council's Educational Policy and Standards Committee any fees payable under cl. 3 above in respect of such term or terms may be remitted either wholly or in part.

---

* Any employee of the University admitted to read for a degree of the University before 1 January 1991 shall pay fees for that degree under the student–employee provisions which were in force in Michaelmas Term 1990.

(*b*) Subject to the approval of Council's Educational Policy and Standards Committee where a clinical student has already spent at least three terms working full-time for the Degree of M.Sc. by research and has paid at least three composition fees in respect thereof, any further fees payable in respect of the M.Sc. course for terms in which he or she is also working as a clinical student at a university clinical school outside Oxford may be remitted.

13. Not later than the fourteenth day after the last day of every Full Term the Head or Bursar of every society shall send to the Secretary of the Chest a schedule signed by himself or herself containing the names of all members of the society who were liable to pay the composition fees referred to in cll. 1–3 and cl. 6 above, in respect of that term. The Head or Bursar of every society shall also:

(*a*) in respect of composition fees payable under cl. 1 above, send to the Secretary of the Chest within five working days of the end of every month of the academic year (the first month of the academic year being taken as October) the sum collected by the society in that month;

(*b*) in respect of composition fees payable under cll. 2, 3, and 6 above, send to the Secretary of the Chest within fourteen days of the last day of every Full Term the sum of such fees, provided that in the case of such fees payable for Michaelmas Term, if at that date a society shall not have received payment in full by the fee-paying bodies, the society

(i) may transmit by that date either 80 per cent of the amount required to be transmitted, or the total amount of fees received by that date, whichever is the greater, and

(ii) shall transmit the outstanding balance within one month of the stated date.

14. (*a*) The annual university tuition fee shall be paid on or before the seventh day of Michaelmas Full Term (or the term in which the student commences his or her course, as the case may be) unless the Bursar of the student's college certifies in writing that

(i) the college has approved the student's application to pay by instalments, the first such instalment having been paid; and/or

(ii) the student has applied for, and is *prima facie* eligible for, a contribution to his or her fee from his or her local education authority (or equivalent body), and the college is of the opinion that no contribution will be required from the student.

(*b*) In the event that any fee payable by the student, or the relevant instalment towards such a fee, remains unpaid after the due date of payment it shall be the duty of the Bursar of the student's college to notify the student concerned that, in the event that the fees due have not been paid in full within four weeks from the date of such notification, the student shall be liable for suspension from access to the premises and facilities of the University (including the Examination Schools and other places of examination) from the end of such four-week period until such time as outstanding fees have been paid. The Bursar shall also inform the Registrar that he or she has so notified the student concerned; and if the fees due have not been paid in full within the specified four-week period, the Bursar shall inform the Registrar of the position, whereupon, subject to the other provisions of this clause, the University shall have the right forthwith to suspend the student concerned from access to the premises and facilities of the University.

(*c*) A student who wishes to show cause why he or she should not be so suspended shall be entitled to apply before the expiry of the four-week period of notice to a Fees Panel in accordance with the procedures set out below.

(i) Each Fees Panel shall comprise three persons appointed by Council, one of whom shall normally be the Assessor or a former Assessor, and one of whom shall be a college bursar (not being the Bursar of the student's college).

(ii) The student shall make a written submission to the Bursar of his or her college setting out the reasons why the payment of his or her fees should be deferred, and the Bursar shall forward this submission to the panel with an indication whether the college supports or does not support the application.

(iii) The panel shall be empowered

(1) to confirm that the student will be suspended until such time as the fees due are paid in full; or

(2) to defer suspension subject to payment according to a schedule of payments set out by the panel, which may or may not as the panel shall decide contain additional financial penalties for deferment of payment; or

(3) to recommend to Council's Educational Policy and Standards Committee that outstanding fees be remitted.

(*d*) There shall be no appeal against a decision of the Fees Panel. A student may, however, make a further application under the procedures outlined above for relief from suspension or such terms as may have been imposed by a Fees Panel if the Bursar of his or her college supports an application on the basis that the student's financial circumstances have changed for reasons beyond his or her control.

15. (i) For 2003–4 composition fees payable under cl. 1 above shall be of the following amounts, and those payable under cll. 2 and 6 above shall be at the following annual rates:*

(*a*) for members of the University (other than part-time students) entitled, in accordance with the Appendix to this subsection, to be charged fees at the appropriate 'home' rate the fee shall be £1,125;
except that for those working for an honour school requiring the study of one or more languages for an academic year outside Oxford, or for Law with Law Studies in Europe, and where the period of full-time study in Oxford is not more than ten weeks in total in the year, the fee, during that year, shall be £550;

(*b*) for members of the University entitled, in accordance with the Appendix to this subsection, to be charged fees at the appropriate 'home' rate and liable to pay a composition fee under cl. 6 above, the rate specified in (*a*) above;

(*c*) for part-time students working for the Postgraduate Diploma in Educational Studies and entitled, in accordance with the Appendix to this subsection, to be charged fees at the appropriate 'home' rate, £200;

(*d*) for Recognised and Visiting Students, £3,910;

(*e*) for members of the University working on the Foreign Service Course, £10,424;

(*f*) for members of the University working for the Diploma in European Studies, £19,108;

(*g*) for all other members of the University, the appropriate amount or rate specified in the schedule below.

(ii) For 2003–4, composition fees payable under cl. 3 above shall be at the following annual rates, save in the case of the Postgraduate Diploma in Management Studies where the specific fee shall be paid in the first year of the course only:*

(*a*) for members of the University entitled, in accordance with the Appendix to this subsection, to be charged fees at the appropriate 'home' rate, £2,940, or half that rate if part-time students for the Degree of Master of Science in

---

* The fee payable each term will be one-third of the specified figure; in appropriate cases that payable in Michaelmas Term will be rounded up to the nearest pound; that payable in Trinity Term will be rounded down; and that payable in Hilary Term will be rounded either up or down as necessary to produce the correct total.

Applied Social Studies or Diagnostic Imaging or Educational Studies or Professional Development in Education or Software Engineering or for the Degree of Master of Studies or for the Degree of Master of Theology (except at Westminster College).

(*b*) for members of the University working for the Degree of Master of Business Administration (full-time), £21,000; for members of the University working for the Degree of Master of Business Administration (part-time), £32,000; notwithstanding any general provisions to the contrary, £1,000 of this fee shall be payable by the student as a non-refundable deposit at the time of his or her acceptance of the offer by the University of admission to the course, and the balance shall be payable by the student in advance of the start of the course.

(*c*) for members of the University working for the Degree of M.Sc. in Management Research Methodology, or the Degree of M.Sc. in Industrial Relations and Human Resource Management, £10,000.

(*d*) for members of the University working for the Postgraduate Diploma in Management Studies, £750.

(*e*) for members of the University working for the Degree of M.St. in International Human Rights Law, £5,444.

(*f*) for members of the University working for the Degree of M.Sc. in Bioinformatics, £7,000 in the first year, £4,625 in the second year, and £4,625 in the third year.

(*g*) for members of the University working for the Degree of Master of Science in Science and Medicine of Athletic Performance or the Postgraduate Diploma in Science and Medicine of Athletic Performance, a fee equivalent to that payable under Category B in the schedule below.

(*h*) for all other members of the University, the appropriate rate specified in the schedule below, or half that rate if part-time students as aforesaid.

SCHEDULE*

Category A. Composition fees of £7,818 (or £3,910) (in the case of part-time students) (or at that annual rate) shall be paid by:

---

* *Note on overseas fee rates for 2004–5* Subject to the approval of Congregation, Council has agreed the introduction of a new category governing fees for overseas students (intermediate between the present Categories A and B), to be introduced w.e.f. 1 September 2004 (i.e. for the academic year 2004–5). The new fee category will apply to students studying certain courses which have hitherto attracted Category A rates. It will apply only to those students on such courses who begin their studies for the course on or after 1 September 2004, and *not* to those already on course at that date. Details of which courses will attract the new fee category will be available in Michaelmas Term 2003. Council has also approved an increase of 4.5% in fee rates for overseas students for 2004–5, as compared with 2003–4, again subject to approval by Congregation. Any current or prospective student seeking further information about fee rates for overseas students in 2004–5 should apply in the first instance to his or her college or department for clarification.

Fees payable by students resident in the Isle of Man, Jersey, or Guernsey shall pay fees in one of four bands,[1] which for 2003–4 are as follows:

Band A	£18,258
Band B	£8,114
Band C	£6,086
Band D	£4,057

[1] Details of which courses attract which fee rate may be obtained from the University Offices (Planning and Resource Allocation Section), or from college offices.

(i) those working for:

Preliminary Examinations or Moderations or Honour Moderations or Honour Schools, other than those specified under Category B (i) below;
the Diploma in Theology;
the Diploma in Legal Studies;
the Special Diploma in Social Studies;
the Special Diploma in Social Administration;
the Postgraduate Diploma in Educational Studies;
the Certificate in Education;

(ii) those admitted as students by Divisional Boards or committees other than

(*a*) those admitted by the Medical Sciencess Board to work within the departments in the Faculty of Clinical Medicine, and

(*b*) those specified under Category B (ii) below;

(iii) those liable to pay a composition fee under the provisions of §6, cl. 6 above, except those specified under Category B (iii) or Category C below.

Category B. Composition fees of £10,424 (or at that annual rate) shall be paid by:

(i) those working for:

the Preliminary Examination in:
- Biochemistry;
- Biology;
- Chemistry;
- Earth Sciences;
- Engineering Science;
- Mathematics and Computer Science;
- Materials Science;
- Music;
- Physics;
- Physiological Sciences;
- Psychology, Philosophy, and Physiology;

Honour Moderations in:
- Computer Science;
- Mathematics and Computer Science;
- Music;

the Honour School of:
- Computer Science;
- Engineering Science;
- Engineering and Computing Science;
- Engineering and Materials;
- Engineering, Economics, and Management;
- Experimental Psychology;
- Mathematics and Computer Science;
- Mathematics and Statistics;
- Materials, Economics, and Management;
- Music;
- Natural Science;
- Physics;
- Psychology, Philosophy, and Physiology;

the Degree of BFA;
the First Examination for the Degree of BM;

(ii) those admitted as students by the:

Life and Environmental Sciences Board to work within the Departments of Biochemistry, Plant Sciences, or Zoology;

Medical Sciences Board to work within the Departments of Human Anatomy, Pathology, Pharmacology, Physiology, or Experimental Psychology;

Mathematical and Physical Sciences Board to work within the departments in the Faculty of Physical Sciences;

(iii) those liable to pay a composition fee under the provisions of §6, cl. 6 above, and who are studying a subject listed in (i) above or which falls within the scope of the board of any division as specified in (ii) above.

Category C. Composition fees shall be paid at the annual rate of £19,108 by clinical students liable to pay a composition fee under the provisions of §6, cl. 2 above, and by all other students admitted by the Medical Sciences Board to work within departments in the Faculty of Clinical Medicine.

Appendix

*Definition of persons entitled to be charged university composition fees at the appropriate 'home' rate**

1. A person who on the relevant date
   (*a*) is settled in the United Kingdom within the meaning of the Immigration Act 1971, and
   (*b*) meets the residence conditions referred to in paragraph 9.

2. A person who is a refugee, ordinarily resident in the United Kingdom and Islands, who has not ceased to be so ordinarily resident since he or she was recognized as a refugee, or is the spouse or child of such a refugee.

3. (1) A person who
   (*a*) has been informed in writing by a person acting under the authority of the Secretary of State for the Home Department that, although he or she is considered not to qualify for recognition as a refugee, it is thought right to allow him or her to enter or remain in the United Kingdom,
   (*b*) has been granted leave to enter or remain accordingly, and
   (*c*) has been ordinarily resident in the United Kingdom and Islands throughout the period since he or she was granted leave to enter or remain,

   or who is the spouse or child of such a person.

   (2) For the purposes of this paragraph 'child' includes a person adopted in pursuance of adoption proceedings and a step-child.

4. A person who was admitted to his or her course in pursuance of arrangements with an institution outside the United Kingdom for the exchange of students on a fully reciprocal basis.

5. A person who is a national of a member state of the European Community, or who is the child of such a national, who meets the residence conditions referred to in paragraph 9.

6. a person who is an EEA migrant worker who
   (*a*) may not be required to pay higher fees, or who may not be made ineligible for an award under rules of eligibility, by virtue of Article 7 (2) or (3) of Council Regulation (EEC) No. 1612/68 on freedom of movement of workers within the Community, as extended by the EEA Agreement, or, where he or she is a national of the United Kingdom, by virtue of an enforceable Community right to be treated no less favourably than a national of another

---

* Notes of guidance on the interpretation of, in particular, the phrase 'ordinarily resident' have been sent to all colleges and are available at the Graduate Studies Office in the University Offices.

member state in relation to matters which are the subject of Article 7 (2) and (3), and

(*b*) meets the residence conditions referred to in paragraph 9.

7. A person who is the spouse of an EEA migrant worker and who

(*a*) is installed in the United Kingdom with his or her spouse, and

(*b*) meets the residence conditions referred to in paragraph 9.

8. (1) A person who is a child of an EEA migrant worker and who

(*a*) may not be required to pay higher fees, or may not be made ineligible for an award under rules of eligibility, by virtue of Article 12 of the above-mentioned Council Regulation, or, where his or her migrant worker parent is a national of the United Kingdom, by virtue of an enforceable Community right to be treated no less favourably than the child of a national of another member state in relation to matters which are the subject of Article 12, and

(*b*) meets the residence conditions referred to in paragraph 9.

(2) For the purposes of this paragraph 'parent' includes a guardian, any other person having parental responsibility for a child, and any person having care of a child, and 'child' shall be construed accordingly.

9. The residence conditions referred to above are that

(*a*) the person has been ordinarily resident throughout the three-year period preceding the relevant date, in the case of a person mentioned in paragraph 1, in the United Kingdom and Islands, or, in the case of a person mentioned in paragraphs 5 to 8, in the European Economic Area; and

(*b*) his or her residence in the United Kingdom and Islands, or in the European Economic Area, as the case may be, has not during any part of the period referred to in sub-paragraph (*a*) been wholly or mainly for the purpose of receiving full-time education.

10. A reference in this Appendix to the relevant date is a reference to 1 September, 1 January, or 1 April closest to the beginning of the first term of the person's course.

11. In any case where the relevant date is before 1 September 2000 a person who

(*a*) at the relevant date was settled in the United Kingdom within the meaning of the Immigration Act 1971,

(*b*) neither had the right of abode in the United Kingdom nor was settled therein within the meaning of that Act at, or at a time before, the beginning of the three-year period preceding that date, and

(*c*) at any time during that period was ordinarily resident in Hong Kong.

12. A person who is spending a year abroad on an approved course of language study required by the honour school for which he or she is working.

§7. *Fees payable by certain students of Science*

1. If a person who is not a member of the University is admitted to work, and receive instruction or supervision, in any university laboratory or clinical academic department by the head of the department, he or she shall pay to the Secretary of the Chest such fee or fees as shall be prescribed by the head of the department in accordance with arrangements approved from time to time by Council's Educational Policy and Standards Committee.

2. The head of each department shall have discretion to fix a fee or fees for any member of the University who is working in his or her department, unless that member is liable to pay a composition fee under the provisions of §6 of this Section or would be liable but for the provisions of cll. 4 or 5 thereof.

3. The head of each department shall send to the Secretary of the Chest not later than the end of the third week of Full Term, or in the case of students working in the vacation only, as soon as may be, a list of the names of the students attending

lectures or working in his or her department other than those liable to pay a fee covering that term under §6, cll. 1 and 3 of this section.

4. No fee shall be payable under the provisions of this subsection by any person who is paying a fee under the provisions of §8 of this Section, or whose name is on the Register of Recognized Students or the Register of Visiting Students, or by any salaried employee who is receiving instruction or supervision in the department in which he or she is working.

5. For the purposes of this subsection the word 'Term' shall include the vacation following.

§8. *Fees payable by certain Clinical Students*

1. Every person attached to the clinical school under regular instruction for a qualifying medical examination of another university or of a recognized professional institution shall, unless liable to pay a composition fee under the provisions of §6 of this Section, pay to the Regius Professor of Medicine a fee of £10 on admission and a composition fee every three months at the annual rate specified in cl. 15 of the said §6 which would be applicable to him or her if liable for fees under cl. 2 thereof.

2. The Regius Professor of Medicine shall have discretion to fix fees for persons attached to the clinical school who are not under regular instruction but who would otherwise be liable to pay a fee or fees under cl. 1 above.

3. Within fourteen days of the last day of every Full Term the Regius Professor of Medicine shall

(i) send to the Secretary of the Chest a schedule specifying (*a*) the names of all the persons who were liable to pay any of the fees referred to in cll. 1 and 2 above since the preparation of the previous schedule, and (*b*) the particular fees payable by such persons, and

(ii) account to the curators for the fees so specified.

between those at the 'home' and 'overseas' rates, for the remainder of the course then being undertaken.

OTHER FEES PAYABLE

	£
1. *Late entry for examinations*	
(*a*) where a candidate proposes to offer a book or subject or part of the examination which has already been offered by a candidate who entered by the due date and no change in the conduct of the examination is involved	30·00
(*b*) where the provisions of (*a*) are not satisfied but the chairman of examiners is willing to consent	60·00
2. *Late alteration of options*	
(*a*) where a candidate proposes to offer a book or subject or part of the examination which has already been offered by a candidate who entered by the due date and no change in the conduct of the examination is involved	30·00
(*b*) where the provisions of (*a*) are not satisfied but the chairman of examiners is willing to consent	60·00

APPENDIX III

REGULATIONS FOR CANDIDATES SUPPLICATING FOR DEGREES

DEGREE DAYS 2003–5

Ceremonies will be held in the Sheldonian Theatre for the purpose of granting graces and conferring degrees on the days shown below.

All ceremonies will be divided, the first part commencing at 11.30 a.m. and the second part at 2.30 p.m.

MICHAELMAS TERM 2003
Friday, 3 October (College Specific)
Saturday, 4 October
Saturday, 25 October
Saturday, 8 November
Saturday, 29 November

HILARY TERM 2004
Saturday, 24 January (in absence only)
Saturday, 6 March

TRINITY TERM AND LONG VACATION 2004
Saturday, 8 May (College Specific)
Saturday, 22 May
Saturday, 12 June
Saturday, 17 July
Saturday, 31 July

MICHAELMAS TERM 2004
Friday, 1 October (College Specific)
Saturday, 2 October
Saturday, 23 October
Saturday, 6 November
Saturday, 27 November

HILARY TERM 2005
Saturday, 22 January (in absence only)
Saturday, 5 March

TRINITY TERM 2005

The Proctors propose to conduct a review of arrangements for degree ceremonies from Trinity Term 2005 onwards; dates and times of ceremonies will be published at the conclusion of this review.

1. Names of candidates must be entered, through the authorities of a college or hall, with the Head Clerk, University Offices, Wellington Square, Oxford, not later than 12 noon on the Wednesday, ten days before the ceremony.

The doors of the Sheldonian Theatre will normally open to visitors one hour before the commencement of the ceremony.

Tickets will be required by visitors.

2. Candidates are presented for degrees by the appropriate officers, as indicated below. Where presentation is by a professor, the professor should be notified in advance through the candidate's society.

3. Degree days will also be deemed to have been held on 24 January 2004 and 22 January 2005 for the purpose of conferring degrees in absence. Names of candidates should be entered in accordance with the usual provisions for degree ceremonies.

ADDENDUM I

[Until 1 October 2004: for candidates embarking on the Honour School of Natural Science (Physics) in or before October 2001

HONOUR SCHOOL OF NATURAL SCIENCE

A

1. The Honour School of Natural Science shall include Physics (three-year course and four-year course).

2. The examinations in Physics respectively for the three-year course and the four-year course shall consist of two parts (A and B) as prescribed in regulations of the Mathematical and Physical Sciences Board.

3. (*a*) Save as provided in cl. 3 (*c*) below, the name of a candidate offering Physics in either the three-year course or the four-year course shall not be published in a Class List until he or she has completed Parts A and B of the respective examinations.

(*b*) A student who has been admitted to the Status of Senior Student may be admitted to Part A of either the three-year course or the four-year course in the term in which he or she has completed not fewer than five terms of residence.

(*c*) In such cases as shall be approved by the Mathematical and Physical Sciences Board, a Senior Student may be deemed to have satisfied the Examiners in Part A of the four-year course in Physics and may be admitted to Part B of the examination in the term in which the student has completed at least six terms of residence.

(*d*) The Examiners in Physics for the four-year course shall be entitled to award a pass or classified honours to candidates in the Second Public Examination who have reached a standard considered adequate. The Examiners shall give due consideration to the performance in both parts of the examination. A candidate who obtains only a pass or fails to satisfy the Examiners may enter again for Part B of the Examination on one, but not more than one, subsequent occasion.

(*e*) A candidate adjudged worthy of honours in the Second Public Examination for the four-year course in Physics may supplicate for the Degree of Master of Physics provided that he or she has fulfilled all the conditions for admission to a degree of the University as specified in Ch. I, Sect. 1, §1, cl. 1.

4. The examination in General Subject: Physics shall be under the supervision of the Mathematical and Physical Sciences Board.

5. In the Honour School of Natural Science examiners in Physics shall hold office for three years.

B

1. The examination includes the General Subject: Physics.

2. For the General Subject: Physics, candidates are restricted to models of calculators included in a list provided by the Chairman of the Examiners not later than Wednesday of the fourth week of the Michaelmas Full Term preceding the examination.

PHYSICS (THREE-YEAR COURSE)

1. The Examination shall be in two parts.

2. In Part A:

(*a*) A candidate shall be required

(i) to offer five written papers on the fundamental principles of physics, and

(ii) to submit to the examiners such evidence as they may require of the successful completion of practical work normally pursued during the four terms preceding that in which the candidate is admitted to Part A of the Second Public Examination.

The syllabuses for the five written papers will be published in the course handbook by the Sub-faculty of Physics not later than the beginning of Michaelmas Full Term for examination five terms thence.

(*b*) A candidate may also offer

either (i) a three-hour written paper in theoretical physics, *or* (ii) a one and a half-hour written paper in theoretical physics.

The syllabuses for these papers will be published as in cl. 2(*a*).

A candidate offering (i) or (ii) need only submit evidence of the successful completion of practical work normally pursued during one and a half or two terms respectively of the four terms specified in cl. 2(*a*) (ii).

3. In Part B a candidate shall be required to offer

(*a*) a written paper on one subject chosen from a list published by the Sub-faculty of Physics, and

(*b*) *either* (i) an extended essay on a subject approved by the Chairman of the Sub-faculty of Physics or an authorized deputy, *or* (ii) an account of practical work completed in four weeks subsequent to Part A of the examination.

The list of subjects and the syllabuses for the written paper in 3(*a*) will be published by the Sub-faculty of Physics at the start of Michaelmas Full Term of the academic year in which Part B of the examination is taken.

4. With respect to subjects under clause 3(*a*), a candidate may propose to the Chairman of the Sub-faculty of Physics or deputy, not later than the first week of the Trinity Full Term in the academic year preceding that in which the examination is to be taken, another subject paper or papers. Candidates will be advised of the decision by the end of the eighth week of that term.

5. In clauses 2 and 3, practical work may be replaced by project work, if an appropriate supervisor is available. The subject, duration, and replacement value shall be approved by the Chairman of the Sub-faculty of Physics or deputy with the agreement of the Chairman of Physics or deputy.

6. In clause 3, a candidate may, as an alternative to the written paper 3(*a*), take an assessed course of instruction in a foreign language. A candidate proposing to be assessed on competence in a foreign language must have the proposal approved by the Chairman of the Sub-faculty of Physics or deputy and the Director of the Language Centre or deputy.

PHYSICS (FOUR-YEAR COURSE)

1. The Examination shall be in two parts.

2. In Part A of the examination shall be the same as the Part A of the examination for the three-year course in Physics and the same conditions, arrangements, and examination timings shall apply.

3. Part B of the examination shall be taken at a time not less than four terms after Part A. In Part B a candidate shall be required to offer

(i) one written paper that shall be the same as the written paper offered for Part B of the examination for the three-year course and for which the same conditions, arrangements and timings shall apply;

(ii) written papers on each of two major options; and

(iii) an account *either* of advanced practical work, *or* of a project, *or* of other advanced work.

4. The detailed requirements and arrangements for 3 (ii) and 3 (iii) and the list of major options and the syllabuses from which the two written papers in 3 (ii) may be selected shall be approved by the Sub-faculty of Physics with the agreement of the Chairman of Physics or deputy and published in the course handbook not later than the beginning of Michaelmas Full Term of the academic year preceding the year of Part B of the examination. The proposed nature of practical, project or other advanced work and its duration shall be submitted for approval to the Chairman of the Sub-faculty of Physics or deputy with the agreement of the Chairman of Physics or deputy.

5. In clause 3 (i), a candidate may, as an alternative to a written paper, take an assessed course of instruction in a foreign language. A candidate proposing to be assessed on competence in a foreign language must have the proposal approved by the Chairman of the Sub-faculty of Physics or deputy and the Director of the Language Centre or deputy.

PASS SCHOOL OF NATURAL SCIENCE

Pass School of Natural Science (Physics)

Three-year course

1. Candidates shall be required *either*

(*a*) to satisfy the examiners in five papers on the fundamental principles of physics as specified for Part A of the three-year course for the Honour School of Natural Science (Physics) and to pursue an adequate course of practical work for three terms.

or

(*b*) to satisfy the examiners in a choice of four out of the five specified papers on the fundamental principles of physics and to pursue an adequate course of practical work for five terms.

2. The Chairman of Physics or deputy shall make available to the examiners evidence showing the extent to which each candidate has pursued an adequate course of practical work. Candidates shall submit completed their notebooks of practical work to the examiners by a date (which shall be in the second half of Trinity Full Term) to be prescribed by the examiners. For an account of an experiment to be considered by the examiners, it must be signed by a demonstrator. Examiners may require a candidate to take a practical examination.

Four-year course

1. Candidates shall be required to satisfy the examiners as prescribed for Part A of the four-year course for the Honour School of Natural Science (Physics).

2. Also candidates shall *either* satisfy the examiners in one of the three written papers prescribed for Part B of the four-year course for the Honour School of Natural Science (Physics) *or* the Chairman of Physics or deputy shall make available to the examiners evidence showing the extent to which a candidate has pursued an adequate course of advanced practical work subsequent to taking the examination for Part A of the four-year course for the Honour School of Natural Science (Physics).

ADDENDUM II

[Until 1 October 2004: for candidates embarking on the Honour School of Physics and Philosophy in or before October 2001

HONOUR SCHOOL OF PHYSICS AND PHILOSOPHY

A

1. The subject areas of the Honour School of Physics and Philosophy shall be (*a*) Physics and (*b*) Philosophy.

2. All candidates must offer (*a*) and (*b*). The examination shall consist of Part A and Part B. A candidate in the Final Honour School of Physics and Philosophy may be admitted as a candidate for the examination in Physics for Part A no earlier than the eighth term from matriculation, and for the examination in Philosophy for Part A no earlier than the ninth term from matriculation. In the case of both (*a*) Physics and (*b*) Philosophy candidates shall be admitted to part B of the examination no earlier than the twelfth term from matriculation.

3. No candidate shall be admitted to the examination in this school unless that candidate has either passed or been exempted from the First Public Examination.

4. The examination in this school shall be under the joint supervision of the Boards of the Faculties of Literae Humaniores and Mathematical and Physical Sciences, which shall appoint a standing joint committee to make regulations concerning it, subject always to the preceding clauses of this subsection.

5. (i) The examiners for Physics shall be such of the Public Examiners in Physics in the Honour School of Natural Sciences as may be required; those for Philosophy shall be nominated by a committee of which the three elected members shall be appointed by the Board of the Faculty of Literae Humaniores.

(ii) It shall be the duty of the chairman of the Public Examiners in Physics in the Honour School of Natural Science to designate such of their number as may be required for Physics and Philosophy, and when this has been done and the examiners for Philosophy have been nominated, the number of the examiners in Physics and Philosophy shall be deemed to be complete.

B

1. The examination consists of Part A and Part B. Each part will consist of two subject areas, Physics and Philosophy. In Part A candidates will take three papers in Physics and will be examined on three subjects in Philosophy, one of these subjects being open to choice. In Part B, candidates will offer four subjects as specified in the *Schedule* below.

2. The highest honours can be obtained by excellence either in Physics or in Philosophy, provided that adequate knowledge is shown in the other subject area. An honours classification will be awarded only if performance in both Physics and Philosophy is of honours standard in either Part A or Part B.

3. Candidates for Part A must give to the Registrar notice of their choice of the optional Philosophy subject not later than Friday in the eighth week of the Michaelmas Full Term preceding that part of the examination.

Candidates for Part B must give to the Registrar notice of their choice of written papers not later than Friday in the eighth week of the Michaelmas Full Term preceding that part of the examination.

4. For the Physics papers, the Examiners will permit the use of any hand-held calculator subject to the conditions set out under the heading 'Use of calculators in examinations' in the *Special Regulations concerning Examinations* and further elaborated in the Physics Course Handbook.

Schedule

Part A

Physics

Candidates are required to

(i) take a three-hour written paper in theoretical physics,

(ii) take two written papers on the fundamental principles of physics.

(iii) submit to the examiners such evidence as they may require of the successful completion of practical work normally pursued during the four terms preceding that in which the candidate is admitted to Part A of the Second Public Examination.

The syllabuses for the three papers under (i) and (ii) above will be specified as part of the published requirements and arrangements for Part A of the Honour School of Natural Science (Physics: four-year course). The choice of papers under (ii) above shall be approved by the Sub-faculty of Physics and published in the course handbook not later than the beginning of Michaelmas Term for examination five terms thence.

Philosophy

Candidates are required to take three subjects as specified in the provisions for Physics and Philosophy in the Regulations for Philosophy in all Honour Schools including Philosophy.

Part B

Candidates are required to offer Advanced Philosophy of Physics as well as three subjects in Physics and/or Philosophy. These subjects will consist of written papers except under the conditions below.

(i) The list of subjects and syllabuses from which the Physics papers may be selected shall be approved by the Sub-faculty of Physics and published in the course handbook not later than the beginning of Michaelmas Full Term of the academic year preceding the year of Part B of the examination. Those candidates offering at least two subjects in Physics must submit, as one of them, an essay or practical project normally undertaken in the term in which the candidate is admitted to Part B of the Second Public Examination. The proposed nature of the essay or project and its duration shall be submitted for approval to the Chairman of the Sub-faculty of Physics or deputy with, in the case of a project, the agreement of the Chairman of Physics or deputy.

(ii) The syllabus of the Advanced Philosophy of Physics subject, and the list of subjects and syllabuses for those candidates offering one or more further subjects in Philosophy, are as specified in the provisions for Physics and Philosophy in the Regulations for Philosophy in all Honour Schools including Philosophy.

PASS SCHOOL OF PHYSICS AND PHILOSOPHY

(i) DECREE

Pass School of Physics and Philosophy

(Ch. VI, Sect. I, C, § 3)

(ii) REGULATIONS

The examination consists of Part A and Part B. Each part includes examinations on (*a*) Physics and (*b*) Philosophy.

A candidate may be admitted to the examination in Physics for Part A no earlier than the eighth term from matriculation, and to the examination in Philosophy for Part A no earlier than the ninth term from matriculation. In the case of both (*a*) Physics and (*b*) Philosophy candidates shall be admitted to Part B of the examination no earlier than the twelfth term from matriculation.

Candidates must give notice to the Registrar of their choice of the paper in Physics and of the subject in Philosophy in Part B of the examination not later than Friday in the eighth week of the Michaelmas Full Term preceding that part of the examination.

In Part A a candidate must offer two papers in Physics and two subjects in Philosophy. The syllabuses for the two Physics papers shall be approved by the Sub-faculty of Physics and published in the course handbook not later than the beginning of Michaelmas Full Term for examination five terms thence. The subjects in Philosophy are 102 (*Knowledge and Reality*) and 120 (*Intermediate Philosophy of Physics*) as specified in the provisions for Physics and Philosophy in the Regulations for Philosophy in all Honour Schools including Philosophy.

In Part B a candidate must offer one paper in Physics and one subject in Philosophy. The Physics paper will be chosen by the candidate from a list of papers and syllabuses which shall be approved by the Sub-faculty of Physics with the agreement of the Chairman of Physics or deputy and published in the course handbook not later than the beginning of Michaelmas Full Term of the academic year preceding the year of Part B of the examination. The Philosophy subject will be chosen from the subjects specified in the Regulations for Philosophy in all Honour Schools including Philosophy, except subjects 102, 105, 106 and 120; the arrangements for subject 199 are as specified in the provisions for Physics and Philosophy in those Regulations.

In lieu of the written paper in Physics in Part B a candidate may offer an essay or project, provided that the candidate is not offering subject 199 in Philosophy. The proposed nature of the essay or project and its duration shall be submitted for approval to the Chairman of the Sub-faculty of Physics or deputy with, in the case of a project, the agreement of the Chairman of Physics or deputy.

PHILOSOPHY IN ALL HONOUR SCHOOLS INCLUDING PHILOSOPHY

Physics and Philosophy

Part A: candidates are required to take subject 102, subject 120 and one further subject selected from the list of subjects 101–122 above, except that neither subject 105 nor subject 106 nor subject 121 may be taken. In this School, candidates must answer at least one question from the section on Philosophy of Science in subject 102.

Part B: candidates are required to take subject 121. Those candidates offering one or more further Philosophy subjects must choose them from the subjects 101–104, 107–199 above, except that subject 123 may not be taken.

Where subject 199 is taken, the body responsible for approving applications is the Board of the Faculty of Philosophy. Applications for approval of subject should be directed to the Chairman of the Board, c/o The Administrator, Philosophy Centre, 10 Merton Street.

The same Philosophy subject may not be taken in both parts of the final examination.

INDEX

The figures in heavy type indicate the main reference to certain subjects

NOTES

NOTES

NOTES

NOTES

NOTES

Fundamentals of Friction: Macroscopic and Microscopic Processes

edited by

I. L. Singer

Tribology Section – Code 6170,
U.S. Naval Research Laboratory,
Washington, DC, U.S.A.

and

H. M. Pollock

School of Physics and Materials,
University of Lancaster,
Lancaster, U.K.

Kluwer Academic Publishers

Dordrecht / Boston / London

Published in cooperation with NATO Scientific Affairs Division

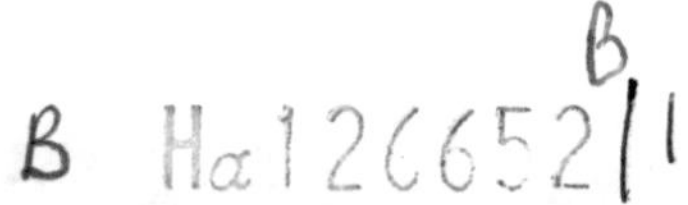

Proceedings of the NATO Advanced Study Institute on
Fundamentals of Friction
Braunlage, Harz, Germany
July 29–August 9, 1991

Library of Congress Cataloging-in-Publication Data

Fundamentals of friction : macroscopic and microscopic processes / edited by I.L. Singer, H.M. Pollock.
p. cm. -- (NATO ASI series. Series E, Applied sciences ; no. 220)
"Published in cooperation with NATO Scientific Affairs Division."
Synthesis of material from lectures, discussions, and workshops from the NATO Advanced Study Institute on the Fundamentals of Friction, held July/August 1991 at Braunlage, Germany.
Includes bibliographical references and index.
ISBN 0-7923-1912-5 (alk. paper)
1. Friction--Congresses. 2. Tribology--Congresses. I. Singer, I. L. (Irwin L.) II. Pollock, H. M. (Hubert M.) III. NATO Advanced Study Institute on the Fundamentals of Friction (1991 : Braunlage, Germany) IV. North Atlantic Treaty Organization. Scientific Affairs Division. V. Series.
TA418.72.F85 1992
620.1'1292--dc20 92-24977

ISBN 0-7923-1912-5

Published by Kluwer Academic Publishers,
P.O. Box 17, 3300 AA Dordrecht, The Netherlands.

Kluwer Academic Publishers incorporates the publishing programrnes of
D. Reidel, Martinus Nijhoff, Dr W. Junk and MTP Press.

Sold and distributed in the U.S.A. and Canada
by Kluwer Academic Publishers,
101 Philip Drive, Norwell, MA 02061, U.S.A.

In all other countries, sold and distributed
by Kluwer Academic Publishers Group,
P.O. Box 322, 3300 AH Dordrecht, The Netherlands.

Printed on acid-free paper

Printed in the Netherlands